Readings in Ethical Theory

THE CENTURY PHILOSOPHY SERIES

Justus Buchler, Editor

second edition

Readings in Ethical Theory

Edited by

Wilfrid Sellars
University of Pittsburgh

John Hospers
*University of Southern
California*

APPLETON-CENTURY-CROFTS
Educational Division
NEW YORK MEREDITH CORPORATION

Library of Congress Card Number: 75-107425

Preface

The enthusiastic response to *Readings in Philosophical Analysis* has reinforced our conviction that there is a genuine need for collections of important papers and other readings in the various areas of philosophy. The present volume is an attempt to satisfy this need in the field of ethical theory. More specifically, our aim has been to provide a balanced and first-hand account of the theoretical controversies that have developed in ethics since the publication in 1903 of Moore's *Principia Ethica*.

With the exception of a very few cases in which it seemed clear from the beginning that an item belonged in our collection, we have pondered our choices seriously and long. In many cases it was extremely difficult for us to make up our minds. More than one "final" list was scrapped when excluded items made their absence felt, and had it not been for the necessity of meeting a deadline, this process might have gone on indefinitely.

> "In Deliberation, the last Appetite . . . immediately adhering to the action . . . is that wee call the WILL. . . ."*

In this sense only did we "will" the following group of selections rather than any one of a number of lists between which, like Buridan's ass, we hesitated.

Though the volume as a whole is organized by topics rather than by publication date, we have followed, *ceteris paribus*, the chronological order of items within each section, thus reproducing the sequence in which controversy developed. However, we have occasionally seen fit to violate chronological order even here, namely when the logical or pedagogical order of ideas was such that an issue could be more clearly grasped by doing so. For example, in Part IV, the essay "Free-will and Psychoanalysis," though chronologically later, has been placed before the three remaining essays of the section, inasmuch as the empirical material it contains gives body to the more abstract treatment of moral freedom in the remaining essays.

Teachers who use this book should by no means feel it incumbent upon them to assign the material in the order in which it is presented in this anthology. As a matter of fact, the order in which the selections are printed is the result of highlighting only a few of the complex interrelationships which exist between them. It is useful primarily as a *point d'appui* for the exploration of the controversies to be found in the literature of ethical theory, but it is not the order in which the selections are necessarily to be read or taught. We can conceive of several equally valid sequences in which the readings might be studied, and have no doubt that colleagues who use the book will think of still others. Since many of the essays deal with a variety of topics, it was by no means obvious in many cases where a given essay belonged, and our grouping has been accompanied by an awareness of the fact that the compartments are not water-tight and many

---

* Thomas Hobbes, *Leviathan*, Part I, Chapter 6, quoted from the Clarendon Press (Oxford) edition, 1909, p. 46.

v

selections bulge their compartments. We hasten to add that we did not begin with the Part headings and look for material appropriate to them; rather the headings varied with the successive lists of essays in the process of mutual accommodation.

Our thanks are due to the many friends and colleagues who have aided and encouraged us in this enterprise, and particularly to Professor William Frankena of the University of Michigan, whose detailed suggestions and comments at all stages have been invaluable, though he must not be held responsible for the contents of the volume. We wish finally to tender our apologies and regrets to those whose essays, sometimes at the last moment, we were obliged to omit; particularly in those cases where permission to reprint had already been secured from both author and publisher. The bibliography at the end of the volume exhibits the richness from which we had to choose, and our publishers have indeed been generous in giving us as much space as they have.

This book should be of particular use in introductory courses in ethics at the senior college level, second courses in ethics, courses in ethical theory, and seminars in moral philosophy and theory of value. It also contains invaluable material for courses and seminars in contemporary philosophy and in philosophical analysis.

We wish to express our deep appreciation to the authors of the articles included in this anthology for their kind permission to reprint, either in full or by way of excerpt, the material here presented. Our gratitude is also extended to the original editors and publishers of these essays for their friendly cooperation.

In the seventeen years since the first edition of this book appeared, the literature of ethical theory has become so extensive as to defy encapsulation in one volume, however lengthy. Nevertheless, the passage of time has dated the first edition sufficiently to make us try. In the revised edition we have not only attempted to update the material and delete those selections which in the light of recent developments seemed less important; we have also attempted to alter somewhat the range of subjects treated. We have, for example, included some representative twentieth-century readings in normative ethics—an area which, except for G. E. Moore's two brief chapters on utilitarianism, was not included in the first edition. And we have, on the other hand, eliminated all readings specifically devoted to the free-will problem, except insofar as it bears directly on the problem of moral responsibility—a policy which seemed advisable in view of the great variety of books and anthologies now available which are devoted exclusively to the problems of free-will and determinism.

W.S.

J.H.

Contents

I
Introductory

The Elements of Ethics

BERTRAND RUSSELL

I. THE SUBJECT-MATTER OF ETHICS[1]

1. The study of Ethics is perhaps most commonly conceived as being concerned with the questions "What sort of actions ought men to perform?" and "What sort of actions ought men to avoid?" It is conceived, that is to say, as dealing with human conduct, and as deciding what is virtuous and what vicious among the kinds of conduct between which, in practice, people are called upon to choose. Owing to this view of the province of ethics, it is sometimes regarded as *the* practical study,

Reprinted from *Philosophical Essays* by Bertrand Russell by permission of George Allen & Unwin Ltd. and Simon & Schuster, Inc.

The author had requested that the following note be printed in conjunction with this selection: " 'The Elements of Ethics' was written under the influence of Moore's *Principia Ethica*. There are some important points in which, not long after publishing it, I came to disagree with the theory that it advocates. I do not now think that 'good' is undefinable, and I think that whatever objectivity the concept may possess is political rather than logical. I was first led to this view by Santayana's criticisms of my work in his *Winds of Doctrine*, but have since found confirmation in many other directions. I am not, however, quite satisfied with any view of ethics that I have been able to arrive at, and that is why I have abstained from writing again on the subject."

[1] What follows is largely based on Mr. G. E. Moore's *Principia Ethica*, to which the reader is referred for fuller discussions. Sections I. and II. of the following essay are reprinted from the *New Quarterly*, February, 1910; section III. from the *New Quarterly*, May, 1910; section IV. from the *Hibbert Journal*, October, 1908; and sections V. and VI. from the *New Quarterly*, September, 1910.

to which all others may be opposed as theoretical; the good and the true are sometimes spoken of as independent kingdoms, the former belonging to ethics, while the latter belongs to the sciences.

This view, however, is doubly defective. In the first place, it overlooks the fact that the object of ethics, by its own account, is to discover true propositions about virtuous and vicious conduct, and that these are just as much a part of truth as true propositions about oxygen or the multiplication table. The aim is, not practice, but propositions about practice; and propositions about practice are not themselves practical, any more than propositions about gases are gaseous. One might as well maintain that botany is vegetable or zoology animal. Thus the study of ethics is not something outside science and co-ordinate with it: it is merely one among sciences.

2. In the second place, the view in question unduly limits the province of ethics. When we are told that actions of certain kinds ought to be performed or avoided, as, for example, that we ought to speak the truth, or that we ought not to steal, we may always legitimately ask for a reason, and this reason will always be concerned, not only with the actions themselves, but also with the goodness or badness of the consequences likely to follow from such actions. We shall be told that truth-speaking generates mutual confidence, cements friendships, facilitates the dispatch of business, and hence increases the wealth of the society which practises

3

it, and so on. If we ask why we should aim at increasing mutual confidence, or cementing friendships, we may be told that obviously these things are good, or that they lead to happiness, and happiness is good. If we still ask why, the plain man will probably feel irritation, and will reply that he does not know. His irritation is due to the conflict of two feelings—the one, that whatever is true must have a reason; the other, that the reason he has already given is so obvious that it is merely contentious to demand a reason for the reason. In the second of these feelings he may be right; in the first, he is certainly wrong. In ordinary life, people only ask *why* when they are unconvinced. If a reason is given which they do not doubt, they are satisfied. Hence, when they do ask *why*, they usually have a logical right to expect an answer, and they come to think that a belief for which no reason can be given is an unreasonable belief. But in this they are mistaken, as they would soon discover if their habit of asking *why* were more persistent.

It is the business of the philosopher to ask for reasons as long as reasons can legitimately be demanded, and to register the propositions which give the most ultimate reasons that are attainable. Since a proposition can only be proved by means of other propositions, it is obvious that not all propositions can be proved, for proofs can only begin by assuming something. And since the consequences have no more certainty than their premises, the things that are proved are no more certain than the things that are accepted merely because they are obvious, and are then made the basis of our proofs. Thus in the case of ethics, we must ask why such and such actions ought to be performed, and continue our backward inquiry for reasons until we reach the kind of proposition of which proof is impossible, because it is so simple or so obvious that nothing more fundamental can be found from which to deduce it.

3. Now when we ask for the reasons in favour of the actions which moralists rec-

ommend, these reasons are, usually, that the consequences of the actions are likely to be *good*, or if not wholly good, at least the best possible under the circumstances. Hence all questions of conduct presuppose the decision as to what things other than conduct are *good* and what *bad*. What is called good conduct is conduct which is a means to other things which are good on their own account; and hence the study of what is good on its own account is necessary before we can decide upon rules of conduct. And the study of what is good or bad on its own account must be included in ethics, which thus ceases to be concerned only with human conduct.

The first step in ethics, therefore, is to be quite clear as to what we mean by good and bad. Only then can we return to conduct, and ask how right conduct is related to the production of goods and the avoidance of evils. In this, as in all philosophical inquiries, after a preliminary analysis of complex data we proceed again to build up complex things from their simpler constituents, starting from ideas which we understand though we cannot define them, and from premises which we know though we cannot prove them. The appearance of dogmatism in this procedure is deceptive, for the premises are such as ordinary reasoning unconsciously assumes, and there is less real dogmatism in believing them after a critical scrutiny than in employing them implicitly without examination.

II. THE MEANING OF GOOD AND BAD

4. Good and Bad, in the sense in which the words are here intended (which is, I believe, their usual sense), are ideas which everybody, or almost everybody, possesses. These ideas are apparently among those which form the simplest constituents of our more complex ideas, and are therefore incapable of being analysed or built up out

of other simpler ideas. When people ask "What do you mean by *Good?*" the answer must consist, not in a verbal definition such as could be given if one were asked "What do you mean by *Pentagon?*" but in such a characterisation as shall call up the appropriate idea to the mind of the questioner. This characterisation may, and probably will, itself contain the idea of *good*, which would be a fault in a definition, but is harmless when our purpose is merely to stimulate the imagination to the production of the idea which is intended. It is in this way that children are taught the names of colours: they are shown (say) a red book, and told that that is red; and for fear they should think *red* means *book*, they are shown also a red flower, a red ball, and so on, and told that these are all red. Thus the idea of redness is conveyed to their minds, although it is quite impossible to analyse redness or to find constituents which compose it.

In the case of *good*, the process is more difficult, both because goodness is not perceived by the senses, like redness, and because there is less agreement as to the things that are good than as to the things that are red. This is perhaps one reason that has led people to think that the notion of *good* could be analysed into some other notion, such as *pleasure* or *object of desire*. A second reason, probably more potent, is the common confusion that makes people think they cannot understand an idea unless they can define it—forgetting that ideas are defined by other ideas, which must be already understood if the definition is to convey any meaning. When people begin to philosophise, they seem to make a point of forgetting everything familiar and ordinary; otherwise their acquaintance with redness or any other colour might show them how an idea can be intelligible where definition, in the sense of analysis, is impossible.

5. To explain what we mean by Good and Bad, we may say that a thing is good when on its own account it ought to exist, and bad when on its own account it ought not to exist. If it seems to be in our power to cause a thing to exist or not to exist, we ought to try to make it exist if it is good, and not exist if it is bad. When a thing is good, it is fitting that we should feel pleasure in its existence; when it is bad, it is fitting that we should feel pain in its existence. But all such characterisations really presuppose the notions of good and bad, and are therefore useful only as means of calling up the right ideas, not as logical definitions.

It might be thought that *good* could be defined as the quality of whatever we ought to try to produce. This would merely put *ought* in the place of *good* as our ultimate undefined notion; but as a matter of fact the good is much wider than what we ought to try to produce. There is no reason to doubt that some of the lost tragedies of Aeschylus were good, but we ought not to try to re-write them, because we should certainly fail. What we ought to do, in fact, is limited by our powers and opportunities, whereas the good is subject to no such limitation. And our knowledge of goods is confined to the things we have experienced or can imagine; but presumably there are many goods of which we human beings have absolutely no knowledge, because they do not come within the very restricted range of our thoughts and feelings. Such goods are still goods, although human conduct can have no reference to them. Thus the notion of good is wider and more fundamental than any notion concerned with conduct; we use the notion of good in explaining what right conduct is, but we do not use the notion of right conduct in explaining what good is.

6. A fairly plausible view is that *good* means the same as *desired*, so that when we say a thing is good we mean that it is desired. Thus anything is good which we either hope to acquire or fear to lose. Yet it is commonly admitted that there are bad desires; and when people speak of bad desires, they seem to mean desires for what is

bad. For example, when one man desires another man's pain, it is obvious that what is desired is not good but bad. But the supporter of the view that *good* means *desired* will say that nothing is good or bad in itself, but is good for one person and perhaps bad for another. This must happen, he will say, in every case of a conflict of desires; if I desire your suffering, then your suffering is good for me, though it is bad for you. But the sense of *good* and *bad* which is needed in ethics is not in this way personal; and it is quite essential, in the study of ethics, to realise that there is an impersonal sense. In this sense, when a thing is good, it ought to exist on its own account, not on account of its consequences, nor yet of who is going to enjoy it. We cannot maintain that for me a thing ought to exist on its own account, while for you it ought not; that would merely mean that one of us is mistaken, since in fact everything either ought to exist or ought not. Thus the fact that one man's desire may be another man's aversion proves that *good*, in the sense relevant to ethics, does not mean the same as *desired*, since everything is in itself either good or not good, and cannot be at once good for me and bad for you. This could only mean that its effects on me were good, and on you bad; but here good and bad are again impersonal.

7. There is another line of argument, more subtle but more instructive, by which we can refute those who say that *good* means *desired*, or who propose any other idea, such as pleasure, as the actual *meaning* of good. This line of argument will not prove that the things that are good are not the same as the things that are desired; but it will prove that, if this were the case, it could not be proved by appealing to the *meaning* of the word "good." So far, it might be thought that such an argument could only have a purely logical importance. But in fact this is not so. Many ethical theories have been based upon the contention that "good" means so-and-so, and people have accepted consequences of this

contention which, if they had relied upon inspection untrammelled by false theory, they would almost certainly have rejected. Whoever believes that "good" means "desired" will try to explain away the cases where it seems as if what is desired is bad; but if he no longer holds this theory, he will be able to allow free play to his unbiassed ethical perceptions, and will thus escape errors into which he would otherwise have fallen.

The argument in question is this: If any one affirms that the good is the desired, we consider what he says, and either assent or dissent; but in any case our assent or dissent is decided by considering what the good and the desired really are. When, on the contrary, some one gives a definition of the meaning of a word, our state of mind is quite different. If we are told "a pentagon is a figure which has five sides," we do not consider what we know about pentagons, and then agree or disagree; we accept this as the meaning of the word, and we know that we are getting information, not about pentagons, but merely about the *word* "pentagon." What we are told is the sort of thing that we expect dictionaries to tell us. But when we are told that the good is the desired, we feel at once that we are being told something of philosophical importance, something which has ethical consequences, something which it is quite beyond the scope of a dictionary to tell us. The reason of this is, that we already know what we mean by the good, and what we mean by the desired; and if these two meanings always applied to the same objects, that would not be a verbal definition, but an important truth. The analogue of such a proposition is not the above definition of a pentagon, but rather: "A pentagon (defined as above) is a figure which has five angles." Whenever a proposed definition sets us thinking whether it is true in fact, and not whether that is how the word is used, there is reason to suspect that we are not dealing with a definition, but with a significant proposition, in which the word professedly defined has a meaning already known to us, either as simple or as defined in some other way. By applying this test, we shall easily convince ourselves that all hitherto suggested definitions of the good are significant, not merely verbal, propositions; and that therefore, though they *may* be true in fact, they do not give the meaning of the word "good."

The importance of this result is that so many ethical theories depend upon the denial of it. Some have contended that "good" means "desired," others that "good" means "pleasure," others again that it means "conformity to Nature" or "obedience to the will of God." The mere fact that so many different and incompatible definitions have been proposed is evidence against any of them being really definitions; there have never been two incompatible definitions of the word "pentagon." None of the above are really definitions; they are all to be understood as substantial affirmations concerning the things that are good. All of them are, in my opinion, mistaken in fact as well as in form, but I shall not here undertake to refute them severally.

8. It is important to realise that when we say a thing is good in itself, and not merely as a means, we attribute to the thing a property which it either has or does not have, quite independently of our opinion on the subject, or of our wishes or other people's. Most men are inclined to agree with Hamlet: "There is nothing good or bad but thinking makes it so." It is supposed that ethical preferences are a mere matter of taste, and that if X thinks A is a good thing, and Y thinks it is a bad thing, all we can say is that A is good for X and bad for Y. This view is rendered plausible by the divergence of opinion as to what is good and bad, and by the difficulty of finding arguments to persuade people who differ from us in such a question. But difficulty in discovering the truth does not prove that there is no truth to be discovered. If X says A is good, and Y says A is bad, one of them must be mistaken, though

it may be impossible to discover which. If this were not the case, there would be no difference of opinion between them. If, in asserting that A is good, X meant merely to assert that A had a certain relation to himself, say of pleasing his taste in some way; and if Y, in saying that A is not good, meant merely to deny that A had a like relation to himself: then there would be no subject of debate between them. It would be absurd, if X said "I am eating a pigeon pie," for Y to answer "that is false: I am eating nothing." But this is no more absurd than a dispute as to what is good, if, when we say A is good, we mean merely to affirm a relation of A to ourselves. When Christians assert that God is good, they do not mean merely that the contemplation of God arouses certain emotions in them: they may admit that this contemplation rouses no such emotion in the devils who believe and tremble, but the absence of such emotions is one of the things that make devils bad. As a matter of fact, we consider some tastes better than others: we do not hold merely that some tastes are ours and other tastes are other people's. We do not even always consider our own tastes the best: we may prefer bridge to poetry, but think it better to prefer poetry to bridge. And when Christians affirm that a world created by a good God must be a good world, they do not mean that it must be to their taste, for often it is by no means to their taste, but they use its goodness to argue that it *ought* to be to their taste. And they do not mean merely that it is to God's taste: for that would have been equally the case if God had not been good. Thus *good* and *bad* are qualities which belong to objects independently of our opinions, just as much as *round* and *square* do; and when two people differ as to whether a thing is good, only one of them can be right, though it may be very hard to know which is right.

9. One very important consequence of the indefinability of *good* must be emphasised, namely, the fact that knowledge as to

what things exist, have existed, or will exist, can throw absolutely no light upon the question as to what things are good. There might, as far as mere logic goes, be some general proposition to the effect "whatever exists, is good," or "whatever exists, is bad," or "what will exist is better (or worse) than what does exist." But no such general proposition can be proved by considering the *meaning* of "good," and no such general proposition can be arrived at empirically from experience, since we do not know the whole of what does exist, nor yet of what has existed or will exist. We cannot therefore arrive at such a general proposition, unless it is itself self-evident, or follows from some self-evident proposition, which must (to warrant the consequence) be of the same general kind. But as a matter of fact, there is, so far as I can discover, no self-evident proposition as to the goodness or badness of all that exists or has existed or will exist. It follows that, from the fact that the existent world is of such and such a nature, nothing can be inferred as to what things are good or bad.

10. The belief that the world is wholly good has, nevertheless, been widely held. It has been held either because, as a part of revealed religion, the world has been supposed created by a good and omnipotent God, or because, on metaphysical grounds, it was thought possible to *prove* that the sum-total of existent things must be good. With the former line of argument we are not here concerned; the latter must be briefly dealt with.

The belief that, without assuming any ethical premiss, we can prove that the world is good, or indeed any other result containing the notion of good, logically involves the belief that the notion of good is complex and capable of definition. If when we say that a thing is good we mean (for example) that it has three other simpler properties, then, by proving that a thing has those three properties we prove that it is good, and thus we get a conclusion involving the notion of *good*, although our

premisses did not involve it. But if *good* is a simple notion, no such inference will be possible; unless our premisses contain the notion of good, our conclusion cannot contain it. The case is analogous to the case of elements and compounds in chemistry. By combining elements or compounds we can get a new compound, but no chemical operation will give an element which was not present in the beginning. So, if good is simple, no propositions not containing this notion can have consequences which do contain it.

As a matter of fact, those who have endeavoured to prove that the world as a whole is good have usually adopted the view that all evil consists wholly in the absence of something, and that nothing positive is evil. This they have usually supported by defining *good* as meaning the same as *real*. Spinoza says:[2] "By reality and perfection I mean the same thing"; and hence it follows, with much less trouble than metaphysicians have usually taken in the proof, that the real is perfect. This is the view in "Abt Vogler": "The evil is null, is nought, is silence implying sound."

Whenever it is said that all evil is limitation, the same doctrine is involved; what is meant is that evil never consists in the existence of something which can be called bad, but only in the non-existence of something. Hence everything that does exist must be good, and the sum-total of existence, since it exists most, must be the best of all. And this view is set forth as resulting from the *meaning* of evil.

The notion that non-existence is what is *meant* by evil is refuted exactly as the previous definitions of good were refuted. And the belief that, as a matter of fact, nothing that exists is evil, is one which no one would advocate except a metaphysician defending a theory. Pain and hatred and envy and cruelty are surely things that exist, and are not merely the absence of their opposites; but the theory should hold that they are indistinguishable from the

[2] *Ethics*, pt. ii. df. vi.

blank unconsciousness of an oyster. Indeed, it would seem that this whole theory has been advanced solely because of the unconscious bias in favour of optimism, and that its opposite is logically just as tenable. We might urge that evil consists in existence, and good in non-existence; that therefore the sum-total of existence is the worst thing there is, and that only non-existence is good. Indeed, Buddhism does seem to maintain some such view. It is plain that this view is false; but logically it is no more absurd than its opposite.

11. We cannot, then, infer any results as to what is good or bad from a study of the things that exist. This conclusion needs chiefly, at the present time, to be applied against evolutionary ethics. The phrase "survival of the fittest" seems to have given rise to the belief that those who survive are the fittest in some ethical sense, and that the course of evolution gives evidence that the later type is better than the earlier. On this basis, a worship of force is easily set up, and the mitigation of struggle by civilisation comes to be deprecated. It is thought that what fights most successfully is most admirable, and that what does not help in fighting is worthless. Such a view is wholly destitute of logical foundation. The course of nature, as we have seen, is irrelevant in deciding as to what is good or bad. A priori, it would be as probable that evolution should go from bad to worse, as that it should go from good to better. What makes the view plausible is the fact that the lower animals existed earlier than the higher, and that among men the civilised races are able to defeat and often exterminate the uncivilised. But here the ethical preference of the higher to the lower animals, and of the exterminators to the exterminated, is not based upon evolution, but exists independently, and unconsciously intrudes into our judgment of the evolutionary process. If evolutionary ethics were sound, we ought to be entirely indifferent as to what the course of evolution may be, since whatever it is is thereby proved to be the best. Yet if it should turn out that the negro or the Chinaman was able to oust the European, we should cease to have any admiration of evolution; for as a matter of fact our preference of the European to the negro is wholly independent of the European's greater prowess with the Maxim gun.

Broadly, the fact that a thing is unavoidable affords no evidence that it is not an evil; and the fact that a thing is impossible affords no evidence that it is not a good. It is doubtless foolish, in practice, to fret over the inevitable; but it is false, in theory, to let the actual world dictate our standard of good and evil. It is evident that among the things that exist some are good, some bad, and that we know too little of the universe to have any right to an opinion as to whether the good or the bad preponderates, or as to whether either is likely in the future to gain on the other. Optimism and pessimism alike are general theories as to the universe which there is no reason whatever for accepting; what we know of the world tends to suggest that the good and the evil are fairly balanced, but it is of course possible that what we do not know is very much better or very much worse than what we do know. Complete suspense of judgment in this matter is therefore the only rational attitude.

III. RIGHT AND WRONG

12. The ideas of right and wrong conduct are, as we have seen, those with which ethics is generally supposed to be most concerned. This view, which is unduly narrow, is fostered by the use of the one word *good*, both for the sort of conduct which is *right*, and for the sort of things which ought to exist on account of their intrinsic value. This double use of the word *good* is very confusing, and tends greatly to obscure the distinction of ends and means. I shall therefore speak of *right* actions, not of

good actions, confining the word *good* to the sense explained in Section II.

The word "right" is very ambiguous, and it is by no means easy to distinguish the various meanings which it has in common parlance. Owing to the variety of these meanings, adherence to any one necessarily involves us in apparent paradoxes when we use it in a context which suggests one of the other meanings. This is the usual result of precision of language; but so long as the paradoxes are merely verbal, they do not give rise to more than verbal objections.

In judging of conduct we find at the outset two widely divergent methods, of which one is advocated by some moralists, the other by others, while both are practised by those who have no ethical theory. One of these methods, which is that advocated by utilitarians, judges the rightness of an act by relation to the goodness or badness of its consequences. The other method, advocated by intuitionists, judges by the approval or disapproval of the moral sense or conscience. I believe that it is necessary to combine both theories in order to get a complete account of right and wrong. There is, I think, one sense in which a man does right when he does what will probably have the best consequences, and another in which he does right when he follows the dictates of his conscience, whatever the probable consequences may be. (There are many other senses which we may give to the word *right*, but these two seem to be the most important.) Let us begin by considering the second of these senses.

13. The question we have to ask ourselves is: What do we mean by the dictates of the moral sense? If these are to afford a *definition* of right conduct, we cannot say that they consist in judging that such and such acts are *right*, for that would make our definition circular. We shall have to say that the moral sense consists in a certain specific *emotion of approval* towards an act, and that an act is to be called right when the agent, at the moment of action,

feels this emotion of approval towards the action which he decides to perform. There is certainly a sense in which a man ought to perform any act which he approves, and to abstain from any act which he disapproves; and it seems also undeniable that there are emotions which may be called approval and disapproval. Thus this theory, whether adequate or not, must be allowed to contain a part of the truth.

It is, however, fairly evident that there are other meanings of right conduct, and that, though there is an emotion of approval, there is also a judgment of approval, which may or may not be true. For we certainly hold that a man who has done an action which his conscience approved may have been mistaken, and that in some sense his conscience ought not to have approved his action. But this would be impossible if nothing were involved except an emotion. To be mistaken implies a judgment; and thus we must admit that there is such a thing as a *judgment* of approval. If this were not the case we could not reason with a man as to what is right; what he approves would be necessarily right for him to do, and there could be no argument against his approval. We do in fact hold that when one man approves of a certain act, while another disapproves, one of them is mistaken, which would not be the case with a mere emotion. If one man likes oysters and another dislikes them, we do not say that either of them is mistaken.

Thus there is a judgment of approval,[3] and this must consist of a judgment that an act is, in a new sense, right. The judgment

---

[3] The judgment of approval does not always coincide with the emotion of approval. For example, when a man has been led by his reason to reject a moral code which he formerly held, it will commonly happen, at least for a time, that his emotion of approval follows the old code, though his judgment has abandoned it. Thus he may have been brought up, like Mohammed's first disciples, to believe it a duty to avenge the murder of relations by murdering the murderer or his relations; and he may continue to *feel* approval of such vengeance after he has ceased to *judge* it approvingly. The *emotion* of approval will not be again in question in what follows.

of approval is not merely the judgment that we feel the emotion of approval, for then another who disapproved would not necessarily hold our judgment of approval to be mistaken. Thus in order to give a meaning to the judgment of approval, it is necessary to admit a sense of *right* other than approved. In this sense, when we approve an act we judge that it is right, and we may be mistaken in so judging. This new sense is *objective*, in the sense that it does not depend upon the opinions and feelings of the agent. Thus a man who obeys the dictates of his conscience is not always acting rightly in the objective sense. When a man does what his conscience approves, he does what he *believes* to be objectively right, but not necessarily what *is* objectively right. We need, therefore, some other criterion than the moral sense for judging what is objectively right.

14. It is in defining objective rightness that the consequences of an action become relevant. Some moralists, it is true, deny the dependence upon consequences; but that is to be attributed, I think, to confusion with the subjective sense. When people argue as to whether such and such an action is right, they always adduce the consequences which it has or may be expected to have. A statesman who has to decide what is the right policy, or a teacher who has to decide what is the right education, will be expected to consider what policy or what education is likely to have the best results. Whenever a question is at all complicated, and cannot be settled by following some simple rule, such as "thou shalt not steal," or "thou shalt not bear false witness," it is at once evident that the decision cannot be made except by consideration of consequences.

But even when the decision can be made by a simple precept, such as not to lie or not to steal, the justification of the precept is found only by consideration of consequences. A code such as the Decalogue, it must be admitted, can hardly be true *without exception* if the goodness or badness of consequences is what determines the rightness or wrongness of actions; for in so complex a world it is unlikely that obedience to the Decalogue will always produce better consequences than disobedience. Yet it is a suspicious circumstance that breaches of those of the Ten Commandments which people still hold it a duty to obey do, as a matter of fact, have bad consequences in the vast majority of instances, and would not be considered wrong in a case in which it was fairly certain that their consequences would be good. This latter fact is concealed by a question-begging addition of moral overtones to words. Thus, e.g., "Thou shalt do no murder" would be an important precept if it were interpreted, as Tolstoy interprets it, to mean "thou shalt not take human life." But it is not so interpreted; on the contrary, some taking of human life is called "justifiable homicide." Thus murder comes to mean "unjustifiable homicide"; and it is a mere tautology to say, "Thou shalt do no unjustifiable homicide." That this should be announced from Sinai would be as fruitless as Hamlet's report of the ghost's message: "There's ne'er a villain, dwelling in all Denmark, but he's an arrant knave." As a matter of fact, people do make a certain classification of homicides, and decide that certain kinds are justifiable and certain others unjustifiable. But there are many doubtful cases: tyrannicide, capital punishment, killing in war, killing in self-defence, killing in defence of others, are some of these. And if a decision is sought, it is sought usually by considering whether the consequences of actions belonging to these classes are on the whole good or bad. Thus the importance of precepts such as the Ten Commandments lies in the fact that they give simple rules, obedience to which will in almost all cases have better consequences than disobedience; and the justification of the rules is not wholly independent of consequences.

15. In common language the received code of moral rules is usually presupposed, and an action is only called *immoral* when

it infringes one of these rules. Whatever does not infringe them is regarded as permissible, so that on most of the occasions of life no one course of action is marked out as alone *right*. If a man adopts a course of action which, though not contrary to the received code, will probably have bad consequences, he is called unwise rather than immoral. Now, according to the distinction we have made between objective and subjective rightness, a man may well act in a way which is objectively wrong without doing what is subjectively wrong, i.e. what his conscience disapproves. An act (roughly speaking, I shall return to this point presently) is *immoral* when a man's conscience disapproves it, but is judged only unwise or injudicious when his conscience approves it, although we judge that it will probably have bad consequences. Now the usual moral code is supposed, in common language, to be admitted by every man's conscience, so that when he infringes it, his action is not merely injudicious, but immoral; on the other hand, where the code is silent, we regard an unfortunate action as objectively but not subjectively wrong, i.e. as injudicious, but not immoral. The acceptance of a moral code has the great advantage that, in so far as its rules are objectively right, it tends to harmonise objective and subjective rightness. Thus it tends to cover all frequent cases, leaving only the rarer ones to the individual judgment of the agent. Hence when new sorts of cases become common, the moral code soon comes to deal with them; thus each profession has its own code concerning cases common in the profession, though not outside it. But the moral code is never itself ultimate; it is based upon an estimate of probable consequences, and is essentially a method of leading men's judgment to approve what is objectively right and disapprove what is objectively wrong. And when once a fairly correct code is accepted, the exceptions to it become very much fewer than they would otherwise be, because one of the consequences of admitting exceptions is to weaken the code, and this consequence is usually bad enough to outweigh the good resulting from admitting such and such an exception. This argument, however, works in the opposite direction with a grossly incorrect code; and it is to be observed that most conventional codes embody some degree of unwarrantable selfishness, individual, professional, or national, and are thus in certain respects worthy of detestation.

16. What is objectively right, then, is in some way dependent on consequences. The most natural supposition to start from would be that the objectively right act, under any circumstances, is the one which will have the best consequences. We will define this as the *most fortunate* act. The most fortunate act, then, is the one which will produce the greatest excess of good over evil, or the least excess of evil over good (for there may be situations in which every possible act will have consequences that are on the whole bad). But we cannot maintain that the most fortunate act is always the one which is objectively right, in the sense that it is what a wise man will hold that he ought to do. For it may happen that the act which will in fact prove the most fortunate is likely, according to all the evidence at our disposal, to be less fortunate than some other. In such a case, it will be, at least in one sense, objectively wrong to go against the evidence, in spite of the actual good result of our doing so. There have certainly been some men who have done so much harm that it would have been fortunate for the world if their nurses had killed them in infancy. But if their nurses had done so their action would not have been objectively right, because the probability was that it would not have the best effects. Hence it would seem we must take account of probability in judging of objective rightness; let us then consider whether we can say that the objectively right act is the one which will *probably* be most fortunate. I shall define this as the *wisest* act.

The *wisest* act, then, is that one which, when account is taken of all available data, gives us the greatest expectation of good on the balance, or the least expectation of evil on the balance. There is, of course, a difficulty as to what are to be considered available data; but broadly we can distinguish, in any given state of knowledge, things capable of being foreseen from things which are unpredictable. I suppose account to be taken of the general body of current knowledge, in fact the sort of consideration which people expect when they ask legal or medical advice. There is no doubt this brings us nearer to what is objectively right than we were when we were considering the actually most fortunate act. For one thing, it justifies the unavoidable limitation to not very distant consequences, which is almost always necessary if a practical decision is to be reached. For the likelihood of error in calculating distant consequences is so great that their contribution to the *probable* good or evil is very small, though their contribution to the *actual* good or evil is likely to be much greater than that of the nearer consequences. And it seems evident that what it is quite impossible to know cannot be relevant in judging as to what conduct is right. If, as is possible, a cataclysm is going to destroy life on this planet this day week, many acts otherwise useful will prove to have been wasted labour, for example, the preparation of next year's Nautical Almanac; but since we have no reason to expect such a cataclysm, the rightness or wrongness of acts is plainly to be estimated without regard to it.

17. One apparent objection at once suggests itself to the definition. Very few acts are of sufficient importance to justify such elaborate and careful consideration as is required for forming an opinion as to whether they are the wisest. Indeed, the least important decisions are often those which it would be hardest to make on purely reasonable grounds. A man who debates on each day which of two ways of taking exercise is likely to prove most beneficial is considered absurd; the question is at once difficult and unimportant, and is therefore not worth spending time over. But although it is true that unimportant decisions ought not to be made with excessive care, there is danger of confusion if this is regarded as an objection to our definition of objective rightness. For the act which, in the case supposed, is objectively wrong is the act of deliberation, not the act decided upon as the result of deliberation. And the deliberation is condemned by our definition, for it is very unlikely that there is no more beneficial way of spending time than in debating trivial points of conduct. Thus, although the wisest act is the one which, after complete investigation, appears likely to give the most fortunate results, yet the complete investigation required to show that it is the wisest act is only itself wise in the case of very important decisions. This is only an elaborate way of saying that a wise man will not waste time on unimportant details. Hence this apparent objection can be answered.

18. One further addition is required for the definition of the objectively right act, namely, that it must be *possible*. Among the acts whose consequences are to be considered we must not include such as are either physically impossible to perform or impossible for the agent to think of. This last condition introduces difficulties connected with Determinism, which are discussed in Section IV. Ignoring these difficulties, we may say that the objectively right act is that one which, of all that are possible, will probably have the best consequences.

19. We must now return to the consideration of subjective rightness, with a view to distinguishing conduct which is merely mistaken from conduct which is immoral or blameworthy. We here require a new sense of *ought*, which it is by no means easy to define. In the objective sense, a man ought to do what is objectively right. But in the subjective sense, which we have now to ex-

amine, he sometimes ought to do what is objectively wrong. For example, we saw that it is often objectively right to give less consideration to an unimportant question of conduct than would be required for forming a truthworthy judgment as to what is objectively right. Now it seems plain that if we have given to such a question the amount and kind of consideration which is objectively right, and we then do what *appears* to us objectively right, our action is, in some sense, subjectively right, although it may be objectively wrong. Our action could certainly not be called a sin, and might even be highly virtuous, in spite of its objective wrongness. It is these notions of what is sinful and what is virtuous that we have now to consider.

20. The first suggestion that naturally occurs is that an act is subjectively right when it is judged by the agent to be objectively right, and subjectively wrong when it is judged to be objectively wrong. I do not mean that it is subjectively right when the agent judges that it is the act which, of all that are possible, will probably have the best results; for the agent may not accept the above account of objective rightness. I mean merely that it is the one towards which he has the judgment of approval. A man may judge an act to be right without judging that its consequences will be probably the best possible; I only contend that, when he *truly* judges it to be right, then its consequences will probably be the best possible. But his judgment as to what is objectively right may err, not only by a wrong estimate of probable consequences, or by failing to think of an act which he might have thought of, but also by a wrong theory as to what constitutes objective rightness. In other words, the definition I gave of objective rightness is not meant as an analysis of the meaning of the word, but as a mark which in fact attaches to all objectively right actions and to no others.

We are to consider then the suggestion that an act is moral when the agent approves it and immoral when he disapproves it; using *moral* to mean *subjectively* right and *immoral* to mean *subjectively wrong*. This suggestion, it is plain, will not stand without much modification. In the first place, we often hold it immoral to approve some things and disapprove others, unless there are special circumstances to excuse such approval or disapproval. In the second place, unreflecting acts, in which there is no judgment either of approval or disapproval, are often moral or immoral. For both these reasons the suggested definition must be regarded as inadequate.

21. The doctrine that an act is never immoral when the agent thinks it right has the drawback (or the advantage) that it excuses almost all the acts which would be commonly condemned. Very few people deliberately do what, at the moment, they believe to be wrong; usually they first argue themselves into a belief that what they wish to do is right. They decide that it is their duty to teach so-and-so a lesson, that their rights have been so grossly infringed that if they take no revenge there will be an encouragement to injustice, that without a moderate indulgence in pleasure a character cannot develop in the best way, and so on and so on. Yet we do not cease to blame them on that account. Of course it may be said that a belief produced by a course of self-deception is not a genuine belief, and that the people who invent such excuses for themselves know all the while that the truth is the other way. Up to a point this is no doubt true, though I doubt if it is always true. There are, however, other cases of mistaken judgment as to what is right, where the judgment is certainly genuine, and yet we blame the agent. These are cases of thoughtlessness, where a man remembers consequences to himself, but forgets consequences to others. In such a case he may judge correctly and honestly on all the data that he remembers, yet if he were a better man he would remember more data. Most of the actions commonly condemned as selfish probably come under this head. Hence we must

admit that an act may be immoral, even if the agent quite genuinely judges that it is right.

Unreflecting acts, again, in which there is no judgment as to right or wrong, are often praised or blamed. Acts of generosity, for example, are more admired when they are impulsive than when they result from reflection. I cannot think of any act which is more blamed when it is impulsive than when it is deliberate; but certainly many impulsive acts are blamed—for example, such as spring from an impulse of malice or cruelty.

22. In all these cases where reflection is absent, and also in the case of inadequate reflection, it may be said that blame does not belong properly to the act, but rather to the character revealed by the act, or, if to some acts, then to those previous deliberate acts by which the character has been produced which has resulted in the present act. The cases of self-deception would then be dismissed on the ground that the self-deceiver never really believes what he wishes to believe. We could then retain our original definition, that a moral act is one which the agent judges to be right, while an immoral one is one which he judges to be wrong. But I do not think this would accord with what most people really mean. I rather think that a moral act should be defined as one which the agent would have judged to be right if he had considered the question candidly and with due care, if, that is to say, he had examined the data before him with a view to discovering what was right, and not with a view to proving such-and-such a course to be right. If an act is unimportant, and at the same time not obviously less right than some obvious alternative, we shall consider it neither moral nor immoral; for in such a case the act does not deserve careful consideration. The amount of care which a decision deserves depends upon its importance and difficulty; in the case of a statesman advocating a new policy, for example, years of deliberation may sometimes be

necessary to excuse him from the charge of levity. But with less important acts, it is usually right to decide even when further reflection might show the present decision to be erroneous. Thus there is a certain amount of reflection appropriate to various acts, while some right acts are best when they spring from impulse (though these are such as reflection would approve). We may therefore say that an act is moral when it is one which the agent would judge to be right after an appropriate amount of candid thought, or, in the case of acts which are best when they are unreflecting, after the amount and kind of thought requisite to form a first opinion. An act is immoral when the agent would judge it to be wrong after an appropriate amount of reflection. It is neither moral nor immoral when it is unimportant and a small amount of reflection would not suffice to show whether it was right or wrong.

23. We may now sum up our discussion of right and wrong. When a man asks himself: "What ought I to do?" he is asking what conduct is *right* in an objective sense. He cannot mean: "What ought a person to do who holds my views as to what a person ought to do?" for his views as to what a person ought to do are what will constitute his answer to the question "What ought I to do?" But the onlooker, who thinks that the man has answered this question wrongly, may nevertheless hold that, in acting upon his answer, the man was acting rightly in a second, subjective, sense. This second sort of right action we call *moral* action. We held that an action is *moral* when the agent would judge it to be *right* after an appropriate amount of candid thought, or after a small amount in the case of acts which are best when they are unreflecting; the appropriate amount of thought being dependent upon the difficulty and the importance of the decision. And we held that an action is *right* when, of all that are possible, it is the one which will probably have the best results. There are many other meanings of *right*, but

these seem to be the meanings required for answering the questions: "What ought I to do?" and "What acts are immoral?"

IV. DETERMINISM AND MORALS

24. The importance to ethics of the free-will question is a subject upon which there has existed almost as much diversity of opinion as on the free-will question itself. It has been urged by advocates of free-will that its denial involves the denial of merit and demerit, and that, with the denial of these, ethics collapses. It has been urged on the other side that, unless we can foresee, at least partially, the consequences of our actions, it is impossible to know what course we ought to take under any given circumstances; and that if other people's actions cannot be in any degree predicted, the foresight required for rational action becomes impossible. I do not propose, in the following discussion, to go into the free-will controversy itself. The grounds in favour of determinism appear to me overwhelming, and I shall content myself with a brief indication of these grounds. The question I am concerned with is not the free-will question itself, but the question how, if at all, morals are affected by assuming determinism.

In considering this question, as in most of the other problems of ethics, the moralist who has not had a philosophical training appears to me to go astray, and become involved in needless complications, through supposing that right and wrong in conduct are the ultimate conceptions of ethics, rather than good and bad, in the *effects* of conduct and in other things. The words *good* and *bad* are used both for the sort of conduct which is *right* or *wrong*, and for the sort of effects to be expected from right and wrong conduct, respectively. We speak of a *good* picture, a *good* dinner, and so on, as well as of a *good* action. But there is a great difference between these two mean-

ings of *good*. Roughly speaking, a *good* action is one of which the probable effects are *good* in the other sense. It is confusing to have two meanings for one word, and we therefore agreed in the previous section to speak of a *right* action rather than a *good* action. In order to decide whether an action is *right*, it is necessary, as we have seen, to consider its probable effects. If the probable effects are, on the whole, better than those of any other action which is possible under the circumstances, then the action is *right*. The things that are good are things which, on their own account, and apart from any consideration of their effects, we ought to wish to see in existence: they are such things as, we may suppose, might make the world appear to the Creator worth creating. I do not wish to deny that right conduct is among the things that are good on their own account; but if it is so, it depends for its intrinsic goodness upon the goodness of those other things which it aims at producing, such as love or happiness. Thus the rightness of conduct is not the fundamental conception upon which ethics is built up. This fundamental conception is intrinsic goodness or badness.

As the outcome of our discussions in the previous section, I shall assume the following definitions. The *objectively right* action, in any circumstances, is that action which, of all that are possible, gives us, when account is taken of all available data, the greatest expectation of probable good effects, or the least expectation of probable bad effects. The *subjectively right* or *moral* action is that one which will be judged by the agent to be objectively right if he devotes to the question an appropriate amount of candid thought, or, in the case of actions that ought to be impulsive, a small amount. The appropriate amount of thought depends upon the importance of the action and the difficulty of the decision. An act is neither moral nor immoral when it is unimportant, and a small amount of reflection would not suffice to show whether it was right or wrong. After these preliminaries, we can pass to the consideration of our main topic.

25. The principle of causality—that every event is determined by previous events, and can (theoretically) be predicted when enough previous events are known—appears to apply just as much to human actions as to other events. It cannot be said that its application to human actions, or to any other phenomena, is wholly beyond doubt; but a doubt extending to the principle of causality must be so fundamental as to involve all science, all everyday knowledge, and everything, or almost everything, that we believe about the actual world. If causality is doubted, morals collapse, since a right action, as we have seen, is one of which the probable effects are the best possible, so that estimates of right and wrong necessarily presuppose that our actions can have effects, and therefore that the law of causality holds. In favour of the view that human actions alone are not the effects of causes, there appears to be no ground whatever except the sense of spontaneity. But the sense of spontaneity only affirms that we can do as we choose, and choose as we please, which no determinist denies; it cannot affirm that our choice is independent of all motives,[4] and indeed introspection tends rather to show the opposite. It is said by the advocates of free-will[5] that determinism destroys morals, since it shows that all our actions are inevitable, and that therefore they deserve neither praise nor blame. Let us consider how far, if at all, this is the case.

26. The part of ethics which is concerned, not with conduct, but with the meaning of good and bad, and the things that are intrinsically good and bad, is plainly quite independent of free-will. Causality belongs to the description of the existing world, and we saw that no inference can be drawn from what exists to what is good. Whether, then, causality holds always, sometimes, or never is a question wholly irrelevant in the consideration of intrinsic goods and evils. But when we come to conduct and the notion of *ought*, we cannot be sure that determinism makes no difference. For we saw that the objectively right action may be defined as that one which, of all that are *possible* under the circumstances, will probably on the whole have the best consequences. The action which is objectively right must therefore be in some sense *possible*. But if determinism is true, there is a sense in which no action is possible except the one actually performed. Hence, if the two senses of possibility are the same, the action actually performed is always objectively right; for it is the only possible action, and therefore there is no other possible action which would have had better results. There is here, I think, a real difficulty. But let us consider the various kinds of possibility which may be meant.

In order that an act may be a *possible* act, it must be physically possible to perform, it must be possible to think of, and it must be possible to choose if we think of it. Physical possibility, to begin with, is obviously necessary. There are circumstances under which I might do a great deal of good by running from Oxford to London in five minutes. But I should not be called unwise, or guilty of an objectively wrong act, for omitting to do so. We may define an act as physically possible when it will occur if I will it. Acts for which this condition fails are not to be taken account of in estimating rightness or wrongness.

27. To judge whether an act is possible to think of is more difficult, but we certainly take account of it in judging what a man ought to do. There is no *physical* impossibility about employing one's spare moments in writing lyric poems better than any yet written, and this would certainly be a more useful employment than most

---

[4] A *motive* means merely a *cause of volition*.

[5] I use *free-will* to mean the doctrine that not all volitions are determined by causes, which is the denial of determinism. Free-will is often used in senses compatible with determinism, but I am not concerned to affirm or deny it in such senses.

people find for their spare moments. But we do not blame people for not writing lyric poems unless, like FitzGerald, they are people that we feel could have written them. And not only we do not blame them, but we feel that their action may be objectively as well as subjectively right if it is the wisest that *they* could have thought of. But what they *could* have thought of is not the same as what they *did* think of. Suppose a man in a fire or a shipwreck becomes so panic-stricken that he never for a moment thinks of the help that is due to other people, we do not on that account hold that he does right in only thinking of himself. Hence in some sense (though it is not quite clear what this sense is), some of the courses of action which a man does not think of are regarded as possible for him to think of, though others are admittedly impossible.

There is thus a sense in which it must be possible to think of an action, if we are to hold that it is objectively wrong not to perform the action. There is also, if determinism is true, a sense in which it is not possible to think of any action except those which we do think of. But it is questionable whether these two senses of possibility are the same. A man who finds that his house is on fire may run out of it in a panic without thinking of warning the other inmates; but we *feel*, rightly or wrongly, that it was possible for him to think of warning them in a sense in which it is not possible for a prosaic person to think of a lyric poem. It may be that we are wrong in feeling this difference, and that what really distinguishes the two cases is dependence upon past decisions. That is to say, we may recognise that no different choice among alternatives thought of at any time would have turned an ordinary man into a good lyric poet; but that most men, by suitably choosing among alternatives actually thought of, can acquire the sort of character which will lead them to remember their neighbours in a fire. And if a man engages in some useful occupation of which a natural effect is to destroy his nerve, we may conceivably hold that this excuses his panic in an emergency. In such a point, it would seem that our judgment may really be dependent on the view we take as to the existence of free-will; for the believer in free-will cannot allow any such excuse.

If we try to state the difference we feel between the case of the lyric poems and the case of the fire, it seems to come to this: that we do not hold an act objectively wrong when it would have required what we recognise as a special aptitude in order to think of a better act, and when we believe that the agent did not possess this aptitude. But this distinction seems to imply that there is not such a thing as a special aptitude for this or that virtue; a view which cannot, I think, be maintained. An aptitude for generosity or for kindness may be as much a natural gift as an aptitude for poetry; and an aptitude for poetry may be as much improved by practice as an aptitude for kindness or generosity. Thus it would seem that there is no sense in which it is possible to think of some actions which in fact we do not think of, but impossible to think of others, except the sense that the ones we regard as possible would have been thought of if a different choice among alternatives actually thought of had been made on some previous occasion. We shall then modify our previous definition of the objectively right action by saying that it is the probably most beneficial among those that occur to the agent at the moment of choice. But we shall hold that, in certain cases, the fact that a more beneficial alternative does not occur to him is evidence of a wrong choice on some previous occasion.

28. But since occasions of choice do often arise, and since there certainly is a sense in which it is possible to choose any one of a number of different actions which we think of, we can still distinguish some actions as right and some as wrong. Our previous definitions of objectively right actions and of moral actions still hold, with the modification that, among physically

possible actions, only those *which we actually think of* are to be regarded as possible. When several alternative actions present themselves, it is certain we can both do which we choose, and choose which we will. In this sense all the alternatives are possible. What determinism maintains is, that our will to choose this or that alternative is the effect of antecedents; but this does not prevent our will from being itself a cause of other effects. And the sense in which different decisions are possible seems sufficient to distinguish some actions as right and some as wrong, some as moral and some as immoral.

Connected with this is another sense in which, when we deliberate, either decision is possible. The fact that we judge one course objectively right may be the cause of our choosing this course: thus, before we have decided as to which course we think right, either is possible in the sense that either will result from our decision as to which we think right. This sense of possibility is important to the moralist, and illustrates the fact that determinism does not make moral deliberation futile.

29. Determinism does not, therefore, destroy the distinction of right and wrong; and we saw before that it does not destroy the distinction of good and bad: we shall still be able to regard some people as better than others, and some actions as more right than others. But it is said that praise and blame and responsibility are destroyed by determinism. When a madman commits what in a sane man we should call a crime, we do not blame him, partly because he probably cannot judge rightly as to consequences, but partly also because we feel that he could not have done otherwise: if all men are really in the position of the madman, it would seem that all ought to escape blame. But I think the question of choice really decides as to praise and blame. The madman, we believe (excluding the case of wrong judgment as to consequences), did not choose between different courses, but was impelled by a blind impulse. The sane man who (say) commits a murder has, on the contrary, either at the time of the murder or at some earlier time, chosen the worst of two or more alternatives that occurred to him; and it is for this we blame him. It is true that the two cases merge into each other, and the madman may be blamed if he has become mad in consequence of vicious self-indulgence. But it is right that the two cases should not be too sharply distinguished, for we know how hard it often is in practice to decide whether people are what is called "responsible for their actions." It is sufficient that there is a distinction, and that it can be applied easily in most cases, though there are marginal cases which present difficulties. We apply praise or blame, then, and we attribute responsibility, where a man, having to exercise choice, has chosen wrongly; and this sense of praise or blame is not destroyed by determinism.

30. Determinism, then, does not in any way interfere with morals. It is worth noticing that free-will, on the contrary, would interfere most seriously, if anybody really believed in it. People never do, as a matter of fact, believe that any one else's actions are not determined by motives, however much they may think *themselves* free. Bradshaw consists entirely of predictions as to the actions of engine-drivers; but no one doubts Bradshaw on the ground that the volitions of engine-drivers are not governed by motives. If we really believed that other people's actions did not have causes, we could never try to influence other people's actions; for such influence can only result if we know, more or less, what causes will produce the actions we desire. If we could never try to influence other people's actions, no man could try to get elected to Parliament, or ask a woman to marry him: argument, exhortation, and command would become mere idle breath. Thus almost all the actions with which morality is concerned would become irrational, rational action would be wholly precluded

from trying to influence people's volitions, and right and wrong would be interfered with in a way in which determinism certainly does not interfere with them. Most morality absolutely depends upon the assumption that volitions have causes, and nothing in morals is destroyed by this assumption.

Most people, it is true, do not hold the free-will doctrine in so extreme a form as that against which we have been arguing. They would hold that most of a man's actions have causes, but that some few, say one per cent, are uncaused spontaneous assertions of will. If this view is taken, unless we can mark off the one per cent of volitions which are uncaused, every inference as to human actions is infected with what we may call one per cent of doubt. This, it must be admitted, would not matter much in practice, because, on other grounds, there will usually be at least one per cent of doubt in predictions as to human actions. But from the standpoint of theory there is a wide difference: the sort of doubt that must be admitted in any case is a sort which is capable of indefinite diminution, while the sort derived from the possible intervention of free-will is absolute and ultimate. In so far, therefore, as the possibility of uncaused volitions comes in, all the consequences above pointed out follow; and in so far as it does not come in, determinism holds. Thus one per cent of free-will has one per cent of the objectionableness of absolute free-will, and has also only one percent of the ethical consequences.

In fact, however, no one really holds that right acts are uncaused. It would be a monstrous paradox to say that a man's decision ought not to be influenced by his belief as to what is his duty; yet, if he allows himself to decide on an act because he believes it to be his duty, his decision has a motive, i.e. a cause, and is not free in the only sense in which the determinist must deny freedom. It would seem, therefore, that the objections to determinism are mainly attributable to misunderstanding of

its purport. Hence, finally, it is not determinism but free-will that has subversive consequences. There is therefore no reason to regret that the grounds in favour of determinism are overwhelmingly strong.

V. EGOISM

31. We have next to consider an objection to the view that objective rightness consists in probably having the best consequences on the whole. The objection I mean is that of egoism: that a man's first duty is to himself, and that to secure his own good is more imperative than to secure other people's. Extensions of this view are, that a man should prefer the interest of his family to that of strangers, of his countrymen to that of foreigners, or of his friends to that of his enemies. All these views have in common the belief that, quite apart from practicability, the ends which one man ought to pursue are different from those which another ought to pursue.

Egoism has several different meanings. It may mean that every man is psychologically bound to pursue his own good exclusively; it may mean that every man will achieve the best result on the whole by pursuing his own good; it may mean that his own good is the only thing a man ought to think good; and it may mean, lastly, that there is no such thing as the general good at all, but only individual goods, and that each man is only concerned with what is good for himself. These meanings all presuppose that we know what is meant by "my good"; but this is not an easy conception to define clearly. I shall therefore begin by considering what it is capable of meaning.

32. "My good" is a phrase capable of many different meanings. It may mean any good that I desire, whether this has any further special relation to me or not. Or, again, it may mean my pleasure, or any state of mind in me which is good. Or it

may include honour and respect from others, or anything which is a good and has some relation to me in virtue of which it can be considered *mine*. The two meanings with which we shall be concerned are: (1) any good I desire, (2) any good having to me some relation other than that I desire it, which it does not have to others, of the kind which makes it *mine*, as my pleasure, my reputation, my learning, my virtue, etc.

The theory that every man is psychologically bound to pursue his own good exclusively is, I think, inconsistent with known facts of human nature, unless "my good" is taken in the sense of "something which I desire," and even then I do not necessarily pursue what I desire most strongly. The important point is, that what I desire has not necessarily any such other relation to me as would make it my good in the second of the above senses. This is the point which must now occupy us.

If "my good" means a good which is mine in some other sense than that I desire it, then I think it can be shown that my good is by no means the only object of my actions. There is a common confusion in people's thoughts on this subject, namely the following: If I desire anything, its attainment will give me more or less pleasure, and its non-attainment will give me more or less pain. Hence it is inferred that I desire it on account of the pleasure it would give me, and not on its own account. But this is to put the cart before the horse. The pleasure we get from things usually depends upon our having had a desire which they satisfy; the pleasures of eating and drinking, for example, depend upon hunger and thirst. Or take, again, the pleasure people get from the victory of their own party in a contest. Other people would derive just the same pleasure from the victory of the opposite party; in each case the pleasure depends for its existence upon the desire, and would not exist if the desire had not existed. Thus we cannot say that people only desire pleasure. They desire all kinds of things, and pleasures come from

desires much oftener than desires from imagined pleasures. Thus the mere fact that a man will derive some pleasure from achieving his object is no reason for saying that his desire is self-centred.

33. Such arguments are necessary for the refutation of those who hold it to be obvious *a priori* that every man must always pursue his own good exclusively. But, as is often the case with refutations of *a priori* theories, there is an air of logic-chopping about a discussion as to whether desire or the pleasure expected from its satisfaction ought to have priority. Let us leave these questions, and consider whether, as a matter of fact, people's actions can be explained on the egoistic hypothesis. The most obvious instances to the contrary are, of course, cases of self-sacrifice—of men to their country, for example, or of parents to children. But these instances are so obvious that the egoistic theory is ready with an answer. It will maintain that, in such cases, the people who make the sacrifice would not be happy if they did not make it, that they desire the applause of men or of their own consciences, that they find in the moment of sacrifice an exaltation which realises their highest self, etc. etc. etc. Let us examine these arguments. It is said that the people in question would not be happy if they did not make the sacrifice. This is often false in fact, but we may let that pass. Why would they not be happy? Either because others would think less well of them, or because they themselves would feel pangs of conscience, or because they genuinely desired the object to be attained by their sacrifice and could not be happy without it. In the last case they have admittedly a desire not centred in self; the supposed effect upon their happiness is due to the desire, and would not otherwise exist, so that the effect upon happiness cannot be brought in to account for the desire. But if people may have desires for things that lie outside their ego, then such desires, like others, may determine action, and it is possible to pursue an object which is not "my"

good in any sense except that I desire and pursue it. Thus, in all cases of self-sacrifice, those who hold the egoistic theory will have to maintain that the outside end secured by the self-sacrifice is not desired. When a soldier sacrifices his life he does not desire the victory of his country, and so on. This is already sufficiently preposterous, and sufficiently contrary to plain fact. But it is not enough. Assuming that this is the case, let us suppose that self-sacrifice is dictated, not by desire for any outside end, but by fear of the disapproval of others. If this were so there would be no self-sacrifice if no one would know of its non-performance. A man who saw another drowning would not try to save him if he was sure that no one would see him not jumping into the water. This also is plainly contrary to fact. It may be said that the desire for approval, as well as the fear of disapproval, ought to be taken into account; and a man can always make sure of approval by judicious boasting. But men have made sacrifices universally disapproved, for example, in maintaining unpopular opinions; and very many have made sacrifices of which an essential part was that they should not be mentioned. Hence the defender of psychological egoism is driven back on the approval of conscience as the motive to an act of self-sacrifice. But it is really impossible to believe that all who deny themselves are so destitute of rational foresight as this theory implies. The pangs of conscience are to most people a very endurable pain, and practice in wrong-doing rapidly diminishes them. And if the act of self-denial involves the loss of life, the rapture of self-approbation, which the virtuous man is supposed to be seeking, must in any case be very brief. I conclude that the psychology of egoism is only produced by the exigencies of a wrong theory, and is not in accordance with the facts of observable human nature.

Thus when we consider human actions and desires apart from preconceived theories, it is obvious that most of them are ob-

jective and have no direct reference to self. If "my good" means an object belonging to me in the sense of being a state of my mind, or a whole of which a state of my mind is a part, or what others think about me, then it is false that I can only desire or pursue my good. The only sense in which it is true is when "my good" is taken to mean "what I desire"; but what I desire need not have any other connection with myself, except that I desire it. Thus there is no truth in the doctrine that men do, as a matter of fact, only desire or pursue objects specially related to themselves in any way except as objects desired or pursued.

34. The next form of egoism to be considered is the doctrine that every man will best serve the general good by pursuing his own. There is a comfortable eighteenth-century flavour about this doctrine—it suggests a good income, a good digestion, and an enviable limitation of sympathy. We may admit at once that in a well-ordered world it would be true, and even that, as society becomes better organized, it becomes progressively truer, since rewards will more and more be attached to useful actions. And in so far as a man's own good is more in his control than other people's, his actions will rightly concern themselves more with it than with other people's. For the same reason he will be more concerned with the good of his family than with that of people with whom he has less to do, and more with the good of his own country than with that of foreign countries. But the scope of such considerations is strictly limited, and every one can easily find in his own experience cases where the general good has been served by what at any rate appears to be a self-sacrifice. If such cases are to be explained away, it is necessary to alter the conception of "my own good" in a way which destroys the significance of the doctrine we are considering. It may be said, for example, that the greatest of goods is a virtuous life. It will then follow that whoever lives a virtuous life secures for himself the greatest of goods. But if the

doctrine means to assert, as it usually does, that self-centred desires, if they are prudent and enlightened, will suffice to produce the most useful conduct, then a refutation may be obtained either from common experience or from any shining example of public merit. The reformer is almost always a man who has strong desires for objects quite unconnected with himself; and indeed this is a characteristic of all who are not petty-minded. I think the doctrine depends for its plausibility, like psychological egoism, upon regarding every object which I desire as *my* good, and supposing that it must be mine in some other sense than that I desire it.

35. The doctrine that my good is the only thing that I ought to think good can only be logically maintained by those who hold that I ought to believe what is false. For if I am right in thinking that my good is the only good, then every one else is mistaken unless he admits that my good, not his, is the only good. But this is an admission which I can scarcely hope that others will be willing to make.

But what is really intended is, as a rule, to deny that there is any such thing as the general good at all. This doctrine cannot be logically refuted, unless by discovering in those who maintain it some opinion which implies the opposite. If a man were to maintain that there is no such thing as colour, for example, we should be unable to disprove his position, provided he was careful to think out its implications. As a matter of fact, however, everybody does hold opinions which imply a general good. Everybody judges that some sorts of communities are better than others; and most people who affirm that when they say a thing is good they mean merely that they desire it, would admit that it is better two people's desires should be satisfied than only one person's. In some such way people fail to carry out the doctrine that there is no such concept as *good*; and if there is such a concept, then what is good is not good for *me* or for *you* but is simply good.

The denial that there is such a thing as good in an impersonal sense is only possible, therefore, to those who are content to have no ethics at all.

36. It is possible to hold that, although there is such a thing as the general good, and although this is not always best served by pursuing my own good, yet it is always right to pursue my own good exclusively. This doctrine is not now often held as regards individuals; but in international politics it is commonly held as regards nations. Many Englishmen and many Germans would admit that it is right for an English statesman to pursue exclusively the good of England, and a German the good of Germany, even if that good is to be attained by greater injury to the other. It is difficult to see what grounds there can be for such a view. If good is to be pursued at all, it can hardly be relevant who is going to enjoy the good. It would be as reasonable for a man on Sundays to think only of his welfare on future Sundays, and on Mondays to think only of Mondays. The doctrine, in fact, seems to have no merit except that it justifies acts otherwise unjustifiable. It is, indeed, so evident that it is better to secure a greater good for A than a lesser good for B, that it is hard to find any still more evident principle by which to prove this. And if A happens to be some one else, and B to be myself, that cannot affect the question, since it is irrelevant to the general maxim who A and B may be.

If no form of egoism is valid, it follows that an act which ought to be performed may involve a self-sacrifice not compensated by any personal good acquired by means of such an act. So unwilling, however, are people to admit self-sacrifice as an ultimate duty that they will often defend theological dogmas on the ground that such dogmas reconcile self-interest with duty. Such reconciliations, it should be observed, are in any case merely external; they do not show that duty *means* the pursuit of one's own interest, but only that the acts which it dictates are those that further one's own interest. Thus when it is pretended that there are *logical* grounds making such reconciliations imperative, we must reply that the *logical* purpose aimed at could only be secured by showing that duty *means* the same as self-interest. It is sometimes said that the two maxims, "You ought to aim at producing the greatest possible good" and "You ought to pursue your own interest," are equally evident; and each is supposed to be true in all possible circumstances and in all possible worlds. But if that were the case, a world where self-interest and the general good might conflict ought not only to be non-existent, but inconceivable; yet so far is it from being inconceivable that many people conceive it to be exemplified in the actual world. Hence the view that honesty is the best policy may be a comfort to the reluctant saint, but cannot be a solution to the perplexed logician. The notion, therefore, that a good God or a future life can be *logically* inferred to remove the apparent conflict of self-interest and the general good is quite unwarrantable. If there were a logical puzzle, it could only be removed by showing that self-interest and the general good *mean* the same thing, not by showing that they coincide in fact. But if the above discussion has been sound, there is no logical puzzle: we ought to pursue the general good, and when this conflicts with self-interest, self-interest ought to give way.

VI. METHODS OF ESTIMATING GOODS AND EVILS

37. In order to complete our account of ethics, it would be natural to give a list of the principal goods and evils of which we have experience. I shall, however, not attempt to give such a list, since I hold that the reader is probably quite as capable as I am of judging what things are good and what bad. All that I propose to do in this section is to examine the view that we can

never know what is good and what bad, and to suggest methods to be employed and fallacies to be avoided in considering intrinsic goodness or badness.

There is a widespread ethical scepticism, which is based upon observation of men's differences in regard to ethical questions. It is said that A thinks one thing good, and B thinks another, and there is no possible way in which either can persuade the other that he is wrong. Hence, it is concluded, the whole thing is really only a matter of taste, and it is a waste of time to ask which is right when two people differ in a judgment of value.

It would be absurd to deny that, as compared with physical science, ethics does suffer from a measure of the defect which such sceptics allege. It must be admitted that ultimately the judgment "this thing is good" or "that thing is bad" must be an immediate judgment, which results merely from considering the thing appraised, and cannot be proved by any argument that would appeal to a man who had passed an opposite immediate judgment. I think it must also be admitted that, even after every possible precaution against error has been taken, people's immediate judgments of value do still differ more or less. But such immediate differences seem to me to be the exception: most of the actual differences are of a kind which argument might lessen, since usually the opinion held is either one of which the opposite is demonstrable or one which is falsely believed to be itself demonstrable. This second alternative embraces all false beliefs held because they flow from a false theory; and such beliefs, though often the direct contraries of what immediate inspection would lead to, are apt to be a complete bar to inspection. This is a very familiar phenomenon. Sydney Smith, believed to be always witty, says "pass the mustard," and the whole table is convulsed with laughter. Much wrong judgment in ethics is of this nature.

38. In regard to the things that are

good or bad, in themselves, and not merely on account of their effects, there are two opposite errors of this sort to be avoided— the one the error of the philosopher, the other that of the moralist. The philosopher, bent on the construction of a system, is inclined to simplify the facts unduly, to give them a symmetry which is fictitious, and to twist them into a form in which they can all be deduced from one or two general principles. The moralist, on the other hand, being primarily concerned with conduct, tends to become absorbed in means, to value the actions men ought to perform more than the ends which such actions serve. This latter error—for in theorising it is an error—is so forced upon us by the exigencies of practice that we may easily come to feel the ultimate ends of life far less important than the proximate and intermediate purposes which we consciously endeavour to realise. And hence most of what they value in this world would have to be omitted by many moralists from any imagined heaven, because there such things as self-denial and effort and courage and pity could find no place. The philosopher's error is less common than the moralist's, because the love of system and of the intellectual satisfaction of a deductive edifice is rarer than the love of virtue. But among writers on ethics the philosopher's error occurs oftener than the other, because such writers are almost always among the few men who have the love of system. Kant has the bad eminence of combining both errors in the highest possible degree, since he holds that there is nothing good except the virtuous will—a view which simplifies the good as much as any philosopher could wish, and mistakes means for ends as completely as any moralist could enjoin.

39. The moralist's fallacy illustrates another important point. The immediate judgments which are required in ethics concern intrinsic goods and evils, not right and wrong conduct. I do not wish to deny that people have immediate judgments of right and wrong, nor yet that in action it is

usually moral to follow such judgments. What I mean is that such judgments are not among those which ethics must accept without proof, provided that (whether by the suggestions of such judgments or otherwise) we have accepted some such general connection of right action with good consequences as was advocated in Section III. For then, if we know what is good and bad, we can discover what is right or wrong; hence in regard to right and wrong it is unnecessary to rely upon immediate inspection—a method which must be allowed some scope, but should be allowed as little as possible.

I think when attention is clearly confined to good and bad, as opposed to right and wrong, the amount of disagreement between different people is seen to be much less than might at first be thought. Right and wrong, since they depend upon consequences, will vary as men's circumstances vary, and will be largely affected, in particular, by men's beliefs about right and wrong, since many acts will in all likelihood have a worse effect if they are generally believed to be wrong than if they are generally believed to be right, while with some acts the opposite is the case. (For example, a man who, in exceptional circumstances, acts contrary to a received and generally true moral rule, is more likely to be right if he will be thought to be wrong, for then his action will have less tendency to weaken the authority of the rule.) Thus differences as regards rules of right action are not a ground for scepticism, provided the different rules are held in different societies. Yet such differences are in practice a very powerful solvent of ethical beliefs.

40. Some differences as to what is good in itself must, however, be acknowledged even when all possible care has been taken to consider the question by itself. For example, retributive punishment, as opposed to deterrent or reformative punishment, was almost universally considered good until a recent time; yet in our own day it is very generally condemned. Hell

can only be justified if retributive punishment is good; and the decay of belief in hell appears to be mainly due to a change of feeling on this point.

But even where there seems to be a difference as to ends, this difference is often due to some theory on one side or on both, and not to immediate inspection. Thus in the case of hell, people may reason, consciously or unconsciously, that revelation shows that God created hell, and that therefore retributive punishment must be good; and this argument doubtless influences many who would otherwise hold retributive punishment to be bad. Where there is such an influence we do not have a genuine difference in an immediate judgment as to intrinsic good or bad; and in fact such differences are, I believe, very rare indeed.

41. A source of apparent differences is that some things which in isolation are bad or indifferent are essential ingredients in what is good as a whole, and some things which are good or indifferent are essential ingredients in what is bad as a whole. In such cases we judge differently according as we are considering a thing in isolation or as an ingredient in some larger whole. To judge whether a thing is in itself good, we have to ask ourselves whether we should value it if it existed otherwise than as an ingredient in some whole which we value. But to judge whether a thing ought to exist, we have to consider whether it is a part of some whole which we value so much that we prefer the existence of the whole with its possibly bad part to the existence of neither. Thus compassion is a good of which some one's misfortune is an essential part, envy is an evil of which some one's good is an essential part. Hence the position of some optimists, that all the evil in the world is necessary to constitute the best possible whole, is not logically absurd, though there is, so far as I know, no evidence in its favour. Similarly the view that all the good is an unavoidable ingredient in the worst possible whole is not logically absurd; but this view, not being agreeable, has found no advocates.

Even where none of the parts of a good whole are bad, or of a bad whole good, it often happens that the value of a complex whole cannot be measured by adding together the values of its parts; the whole is often better or worse than the sum of the values of its parts. In all aesthetic pleasures, for example, it is important that the object admired should really be beautiful: in the admiration of what is ugly there is something ridiculous, or even sometimes repulsive, although, apart from the object, there may be no difference in the value of the emotion *per se*. And yet, apart from the admiration it may produce, a beautiful object, if it is inanimate, appears to be neither good nor bad. Thus in themselves an ugly object and the emotion it excites in a person of bad taste may be respectively just as good as a beautiful object and the emotion it excites in a person of good taste; yet we consider the enjoyment of what is beautiful to be better, as a whole, than an exactly similar enjoyment of what is ugly. If we did not we should be foolish not to encourage bad taste, since ugly objects are much easier to produce than beautiful ones. In like manner, we consider it better to love a good person than a bad one. Titania's love for Bottom may be as lyric as Juliet's for Romeo; yet Titania is laughed at. Thus many goods must be estimated as wholes, not piecemeal; and exactly the same applies to evils. In such cases the wholes may be called *organic unities*.

42. Many theorists who have some simple account of the sole good have also, probably without having recognised them as such, immediate judgments of value inconsistent with their theory, from which it appears that their theory is not really derived from immediate judgments of value. Thus those who have held that virtue is the sole good have generally also held that in heaven it will be *rewarded* by happiness. Yet a reward must be a good; thus they plainly *feel* that happiness also is a good. If

virtue were the sole good it would be logically compelled to be its own reward.

A similar argument can be brought against those who hold that the sole good is pleasure (or happiness, as some prefer to call it). This doctrine is regarded as self-evident by many, both philosophers and plain men. But although the general principle may at first sight seem obvious, many of its applications are highly paradoxical. To live in a fool's paradise is commonly considered a misfortune; yet in a world which allows no paradise of any other kind a fool's paradise is surely the happiest habitation. All hedonists are at great pains to prove that what are called the higher pleasures are really the more pleasurable. But plainly their anxiety to prove this arises from an uneasy instinct that such pleasures are higher, even if they are not more pleasurable. The bias which appears in hedonist arguments on this point is otherwise quite inexplicable. Although they hold that, "quantity of pleasure being equal, pushpin is as good as poetry," they are careful to argue that quantity of pleasure is *not* equal, but is greater in the case of poetry—a proposition which seems highly disputable, and chiefly commended by its edifying nature. Any one would admit that the pleasure of poetry is a greater good than the pleasure of bathing on a hot day; but few people could say honestly that it is as intense. And even states of mind which, as a whole, are painful, may be highly good. Love of the dead may easily be the best thing in a life; yet it cannot but be full of pain. And conversely, we condemn pleasure derived from the love of what is bad; even if we admit that the pleasure in itself is a good, we consider the whole state of mind bad. If two bitter enemies lived in different countries, and each falsely believed that the other was undergoing tortures, each might feel pleasure; yet we should not consider such a state of things good. We should even think it much worse than a state in which each derived pain from the belief that the other was in torture. It may, of course, be said that this is due to the fact that hatred in general causes more pain than pleasure, and hence is condemned broadly on hedonistic grounds, without sufficient regard to possible exceptions. But the possibility of exceptions to the principle that hatred is bad can hardly be seriously maintained, except by a theorist in difficulties.

Thus while we may admit that all pleasure, in itself, is probably more or less good, we must hold that pleasures are not good in proportion to their intensity, and that many states of mind, although pleasure is an element in them, are bad as a whole, and may even be worse than they would be if the pleasure were absent. And this result has been reached by appealing to ethical judgments with which almost every one would agree. I conclude, therefore, from all that has been adduced in this section, that although some ultimate ethical differences must be admitted between different people, by far the greater part of the commonly observed differences are due either to asking the wrong question (as, e.g., by mistaking means for ends), or to the influence of a hasty theory in falsifying immediate judgments. There is reason to hope, therefore, that a very large measure of agreement on ethical questions may be expected to result from clearer thinking; and this is probably the chief benefit to be ultimately derived from the study of ethics.

43. We may now sum up our whole discussion of ethics. The most fundamental notions in ethics, we agreed, are the notions of intrinsic good and evil. These are wholly independent of other notions, and the goodness or badness of a thing cannot be inferred from any of its other qualities, such as its existence or non-existence. Hence what actually occurs has no bearing on what ought to occur, and what ought to occur has no bearing on what does occur. The next pair of notions with which we were concerned were those of objective right and wrong. The objectively right act is the act which a man will hold that he

ought to perform when he is not mistaken. This, we decided, is that one, of all the acts that are possible, which will probably produce the best results. Thus in judging what actions are *right* we need to know what results are *good*. When a man is mistaken as to what is objectively right, he may nevertheless act in a way which is subjectively right; thus we need a new pair of notions, which we called *moral* and *immoral*. A moral act is virtuous and deserves praise; an immoral act is sinful and deserves blame. A moral act, we decided, is one which the agent would have judged right after an appropriate amount of candid reflection,[6] where the appropriate amount of reflection depends upon the difficulty and importance of his decision. We then considered the bearing of determinism on morals, which we found to consist in a limita-

tion of the acts which are *possible* under any circumstances. If determinism is true, there is a sense in which no act is possible except the one which in fact occurs; but there is another sense, which is the one relevant to ethics, in which any act is possible which is contemplated during deliberation (provided it is *physically* possible, i.e. will be performed if we will to perform it). We then discussed various forms of egoism, and decided that all of them are false. Finally, we considered some mistakes which are liable to be made in attempting to form an immediate judgment as to the goodness or badness of a thing, and we decided that, when these mistakes are avoided, people probably differ very little in their judgments of intrinsic value. The making of such judgments we did not undertake; for if the reader agrees, he could make them himself, and if he disagrees without falling into any of the possible confusions, there is no way of altering his opinion.

[6] Or after a small amount in the case of acts which ought to be impulsive.

II

The Analysis of Ethical Concepts

The Indefinability of Good

G. E. MOORE

PRINCIPIA ETHICA: PREFACE

It appears to me that in Ethics, as in all other philosophical studies, the difficulties and disagreements, of which its history is full, are mainly due to a very simple cause: namely to the attempt to answer questions, without first discovering precisely *what* question it is which you desire to answer. I do not know how far this source of error would be done away, if philosophers would *try* to discover what question they were asking, before they set about to answer it; for the work of analysis and distinction is often very difficult: we may often fail to make the necessary discovery, even though we make a definite attempt to do so. But I am inclined to think that in many cases a resolute attempt would be sufficient to ensure success; so that, if only this attempt were made, many of the most glaring difficulties and disagreements in philosophy would disappear. At all events, philosophers seem, in general, not to make the attempt; and, whether in consequence of this omission or not, they are constantly endeavouring to prove that 'Yes' or 'No' will answer questions, to which *neither* answer is correct, owing to the fact that what they have before their minds is not one question, but several, to some of which the true answer is 'No,' to others 'Yes.'

I have tried in this book to distinguish clearly two kinds of question, which moral

Reprinted from *Principia Ethica* by G. E. Moore by permission of Cambridge University Press. Published in 1903.

philosophers have always professed to answer, but which, as I have tried to shew, they have almost always confused both with one another and with other questions. These two questions may be expressed, the first in the form: What kind of things ought to exist for their own sakes? the second in the form: What kind of actions ought we to perform? I have tried to shew exactly what it is that we ask about a thing, when we ask whether it ought to exist for its own sake, is good in itself or has intrinsic value; and exactly what it is that we ask about an action, when we ask whether we ought to do it, whether it is a right action or a duty.

But from a clear insight into the nature of these two questions, there appears to me to follow a second most important result: namely, what is the nature of the evidence, by which alone any ethical proposition can be proved or disproved, confirmed or rendered doubtful. Once we recognise the exact meaning of the two questions, I think it also becomes plain exactly what kind of reasons are relevant as arguments for or against any particular answer to them. It becomes plain that, for answers to the *first* question, no relevant evidence whatever can be adduced: from no other truth, except themselves alone, can it be inferred that they are either true or false. We can guard against error only by taking care, that, when we try to answer a question of this kind, we have before our minds that question only, and not some other or others; but that there is great danger of such errors of confusion I have tried to shew, and also what are the chief precautions by the use of which we may guard against them. As for the *second* question, it becomes equally plain, that any answer to it *is* capable of proof or disproof—that, indeed, so many different considerations are relevant to its truth or falsehood, as to make the attainment of probability very difficult, and the attainment of certainty impossible. Nevertheless the *kind* of evidence, which is both necessary and alone relevant to such proof and disproof, is capable of exact definition. Such evidence must contain propositions of two kinds and of two kinds only: it must consist, in the first place, of truths with regard to the results of the action in question—of *causal* truths—but it must *also* contain ethical truths of our first or self-evident class. Many truths of both kinds are necessary to the proof that any action ought to be done; and any other kind of evidence is wholly irrelevant. It follows that, if any ethical philosopher offers for propositions of the first kind any evidence whatever, or if, for propositions of the second kind, he either fails to adduce both causal and ethical truths, or adduces truths that are neither, his reasoning has not the least tendency to establish his conclusions. But not only are his conclusions totally devoid of weight: we have, moreover, reason to suspect him of the error of confusion; since the offering of irrelevant evidence generally indicates that the philosopher who offers it has had before his mind, not the question which he professes to answer, but some other entirely different one. Ethical discussion, hitherto, has perhaps consisted chiefly in reasoning of this totally irrelevant kind.

One main object of this book may, then, be expressed by slightly changing one of Kant's famous titles. I have endeavoured to write 'Prolegomena to any future Ethics that can possibly pretend to be scientific.' In other words, I have endeavoured to discover what are the fundamental principles of ethical reasoning; and the establishment

of these principles, rather than of any conclusions which may be attained by their use, may be regarded as my main object. I have, however, also attempted, in Chapter VI, to present some conclusions, with regard to the proper answer to the question 'What is good in itself?' which are very different from any which have commonly been advocated by philosophers. I have tried to define the classes within which all great goods and evils fall; and I have maintained that very many different things are good and evil in themselves, and that neither class of things possesses any other property which is both common to all its members and peculiar to them.

In order to express the fact that ethical propositions of my *first* class are incapable of proof or disproof, I have sometimes followed Sidgwick's usage in calling them 'Intuitions.' But I beg it may be noticed that I am not an 'Intuitionist,' in the ordinary sense of the term. Sidgwick himself seems never to have been clearly aware of the immense importance of the difference which distinguishes his Intuitionism from the common doctrine, which has generally been called by that name. The Intuitionist proper is distinguished by maintaining that propositions of my *second* class—propositions which assert that a certain action is *right* or a *duty*—are incapable of proof or disproof by any enquiry into the results of such actions. I, on the contrary, am no less anxious to maintain that propositions of *this* kind are *not* 'Intuitions,' than to maintain that propositions of my *first* class *are* Intuitions.

Again, I would wish it observed that, when I call such propositions 'Intuitions,' I mean *merely* to assert that they are incapable of proof; I imply nothing whatever as to the manner or origin of our cognition of them. Still less do I imply (as most intuitionists have done) that any proposition whatever is true, *because* we cognise it in a particular way or by the exercise of any particular faculty: I hold, on the contrary, that in every way in which it is possible to cognise a true proposition, it is also possible to cognise a false one.

When this book had been already completed, I found, in Brentano's 'Origin of the Knowledge of Right and Wrong,'[1] opinions far more closely resembling my own, than those of any other ethical writer with whom I am acquainted. Brentano appears to agree with me completely (1) in regarding all ethical propositions as defined by the fact that they predicate a single unique objective concept; (2) in dividing such propositions sharply into the same two kinds; (3) in holding that the first kind are incapable of proof; and (4) with regard to the kind of evidence which is necessary and relevant to the proof of the second kind. But he regards the fundamental ethical concept as being, not the simple one which I denote by 'good,' but the complex one which I have taken to define 'beautiful'; and he does not recognise, but even denies by implication, the principle which I have called *the principle of organic unities*. In consequence of these two differences, his conclusions as to what things are good in themselves, also differ very materially from mine. He agrees, however, that there are many different goods, and that the love of good and beautiful objects constitutes an important class among them.

I wish to refer to one oversight, of which I became aware only when it was too late to correct it, and which may, I am afraid, cause unnecessary trouble to some readers. I have omitted to discuss directly the mutual relations of the several different notions, which are all expressed by the word 'end.' The consequences of this omission may perhaps be partially avoided by a

---

[1] 'The Origin of the Knowledge of Right and Wrong.' By Franz Brentano. English Translation by Cecil Hague. Constable, 1902.—I have written a review of this book, which will, I hope, appear in the *International Journal of Ethics* for October, 1903. I may refer to this review for a fuller account of my reasons for disagreeing with Brentano.

reference to my article on 'Teleology' in Baldwin's *Dictionary of Philosophy and Psychology*.

If I were to rewrite my work now, I should make a very different, and I believe that I could make a much better book. But it may be doubted whether, in attempting to satisfy myself, I might not merely render more obscure the ideas which I am most anxious to convey, without a corresponding gain in completeness and accuracy. However that may be, my belief that to publish the book as it stands was probably the best thing I could do, does not prevent me from being painfully aware that it is full of defects.

PRINCIPIA ETHICA: CHAPTER I THE SUBJECT-MATTER OF ETHICS

1. It is very easy to point out some among our every-day judgments, with the truth of which Ethics is undoubtedly concerned. Whenever we say, 'So and so is a good man,' or 'That fellow is a villain'; whenever we ask, 'What ought I to do?' or 'Is it wrong for me to do like this?'; whenever we hazard such remarks as 'Temperance is a virtue and drunkenness a vice'—it is undoubtedly the business of Ethics to discuss such questions and such statements; to argue what is the true answer when we ask what it is right to do, and to give reasons for thinking that our statements about the character of persons or the morality of actions are true or false. In the vast majority of cases, where we make statements involving any of the terms 'virtue,' 'vice,' 'duty,' 'right,' 'ought,' 'good,' 'bad,' we are making ethical judgments; and if we wish to discuss their truth, we shall be discussing a point of Ethics.

So much as this is not disputed; but it falls very far short of defining the province of Ethics. That province may indeed be defined as the whole truth about that which is at the same time common to all such judgments and peculiar to them. But we have still to ask the question: What is it that is thus common and peculiar? And this is a question to which very different answers have been given by ethical philosophers of acknowledged reputation, and none of them, perhaps, completely satisfactory.

2. If we take such examples as those given above, we shall not be far wrong in saying that they are all of them concerned with the question of 'conduct'—with the question, what, in the conduct of us, human beings, is good, and what is bad, what is right, and what is wrong. For when we say that a man is good, we commonly mean that he acts rightly; when we say that drunkenness is a vice, we commonly mean that to get drunk is a wrong or wicked action. And this discussion of human conduct is, in fact, that with which the name 'Ethics' is most intimately associated. It is so associated by derivation; and conduct is undoubtedly by far the commonest and most generally interesting object of ethical judgments.

Accordingly, we find that many ethical philosophers are disposed to accept as an adequate definition of 'Ethics' the statement that it deals with the question what is good or bad in human conduct. They hold that its enquiries are properly confined to 'conduct' or to 'practice'; they hold that the name 'practical philosophy' covers all the matter with which it has to do. Now, without discussing the proper meaning of the word (for verbal questions are properly left to the writers of dictionaries and other persons interested in literature; philosophy, as we shall see, has no concern with them), I may say that I intend to use 'Ethics' to cover more than this—a usage, for which there is, I think, quite sufficient authority. I am using it to cover an enquiry for which, at all events, there is no other word: the general enquiry into what is good.

Ethics is undoubtedly concerned with the question what good conduct is; but, being concerned with this, it obviously does not start at the beginning, unless it is prepared to tell us what is good as well as what is conduct. For 'good conduct' is a complex notion: all conduct is not good; for some is certainly bad and some may be indifferent. And on the other hand, other things, beside conduct, may be good; and if they are so, then, 'good' denotes some property, that is common to them and conduct; and if we examine good conduct alone of all good things, then we shall be in danger of mistaking for this property, some property which is not shared by those other things: and thus we shall have made a mistake about Ethics even in this limited sense; for we shall not know what good conduct really is. This is a mistake which many writers have actually made, from limiting their enquiry to conduct. And hence I shall try to avoid it by considering first what is good in general; hoping, that if we can arrive at any certainty about this, it will be much easier to settle the question of good conduct: for we all know pretty well what 'conduct' is. This, then, is our first question: What is good? and What is bad? and to the discussion of this question (or these questions) I give the name of Ethics, since that science must, at all events, include it.

3. But this is a question which may have many meanings. If, for example, each of us were to say 'I am doing good now' or 'I had a good dinner yesterday,' these statements would each of them be some sort of answer to our question, although perhaps a false one. So, too, when A asks B what school he ought to send his son to, B's answer will certainly be an ethical judgment. And similarly all distribution of praise or blame to any personage or thing that has existed, now exists, or will exist, does give some answer to the question 'What is good?' In all such cases some particular thing is judged to be good or bad: the question 'What?' is answered by 'This.' But this is not the sense in which a

scientific Ethics asks the question. Not one, of all the many million answers of this kind, which must be true, can form a part of an ethical system; although that science must contain reasons and principles sufficient for deciding on the truth of all of them. There are far too many persons, things and events in the world, past, present, or to come, for a discussion of their individual merits to be embraced in any science. Ethics, therefore, does not deal at all with facts of this nature, facts that are unique, individual, absolutely particular; facts with which such studies as history, geography, astronomy, are compelled, in part at least, to deal. And, for this reason, it is not the business of the ethical philosopher to give personal advice or exhortation.

4. But there is another meaning which may be given to the question 'What is good?' 'Books are good' would be an answer to it, though an answer obviously false; for some books are very bad indeed. And ethical judgments of this kind do indeed belong to Ethics; though I shall not deal with many of them. Such is the judgment 'Pleasure is good'—a judgment, of which Ethics should discuss the truth, although it is not nearly as important as that other judgment, with which we shall be much occupied presently—'Pleasure *alone* is good.' It is judgments of this sort, which are made in such books on Ethics as contain a list of 'virtues'—in Aristotle's 'Ethics' for example. But it is judgments of precisely the same kind, which form the substance of what is commonly supposed to be a study different from Ethics, and one much less respectable—the study of Casuistry. We may be told that Casuistry differs from Ethics, in that it is much more detailed and particular, Ethics much more general. But it is most important to notice that Casuistry does not deal with anything that is absolutely particular—particular in the only sense in which a perfectly precise line can be drawn between it and what is general. It is not particular in the sense just

noticed, the sense in which this book is a particular book, and A's friend's advice particular advice. Casuistry may indeed be *more* particular and Ethics *more* general; but that means that they differ only in degree and not in kind. And this is universally true of 'particular' and 'general,' when used in this common, but inaccurate, sense. So far as Ethics allows itself to give lists of virtues or even to name constituents of the Ideal, it is indistinguishable from Casuistry. Both alike deal with what is general, in the sense in which physics and chemistry deal with what is general. Just as chemistry aims at discovering what are the properties of oxygen, *wherever it occurs*, and not only of this or that particular specimen of oxygen; so Casuistry aims at discovering what actions are good, *whenever they occur*. In this respect Ethics and Casuistry alike are to be classed with such sciences as physics, chemistry and physiology, in their absolute distinction from those of which history and geography are instances. And it is to be noted that, owing to their detailed nature, casuistical investigations are actually nearer to physics and to chemistry than are the investigations usually assigned to Ethics. For just as physics cannot rest content with the discovery that light is propagated by waves of ether, but must go on to discover the particular nature of the ether-waves corresponding to each several colour; so Casuistry, not content with the general law that charity is a virtue, must attempt to discover the relative merits of every different form of charity. Casuistry forms, therefore, part of the ideal of ethical science: Ethics cannot be complete without it. The defects of Casuistry are not defects of principle; no objection can be taken to its aim and object. It has failed only because it is far too difficult a subject to be treated adequately in our present state of knowledge. The casuist has been unable to distinguish, in the cases which he treats, those elements upon which their value depends. Hence he often thinks two cases to be alike in respect of value, when in reality they are alike only in some other respect. It is to mistakes of this kind that the pernicious influence of such investigations has been due. For Casuistry is the goal of ethical investigation. It cannot be safely attempted at the beginning of our studies, but only at the end.

5. But our question 'What is good?' may have still another meaning. We may, in the third place, mean to ask, not what thing or things are good, but how 'good' is to be defined. This is an enquiry which belongs only to Ethics, not to Casuistry; and this is the enquiry which will occupy us first.

It is an enquiry to which most special attention should be directed; since this question, how 'good' is to be defined, is the most fundamental question in all Ethics. That which is meant by 'good' is, in fact, except its converse 'bad,' the *only* simple object of thought which is peculiar to Ethics. Its definition is, therefore, the most essential point in the definition of Ethics; and moreover a mistake with regard to it entails a far larger number of erroneous ethical judgments than any other. Unless this first question be fully understood, and its true answer clearly recognised, the rest of Ethics is as good as useless from the point of view of systematic knowledge. True ethical judgments, of the two kinds last dealt with, may indeed be made by those who do not know the answer to this question as well as by those who do; and it goes without saying that the two classes of people may lead equally good lives. But it is extremely unlikely that the *most general* ethical judgments will be equally valid, in the absence of a true answer to this question: I shall presently try to shew that the gravest errors have been largely due to beliefs in a false answer. And, in any case, it is impossilbe that, till the answer to this question be known, any one should know *what is the evidence* for any ethical judgment whatsoever. But the main object of Ethics, as a systematic science, is to give

correct *reasons* for thinking that this or that is good; and, unless this question be answered, such reasons cannot be given. Even, therefore, apart from the fact that a false answer leads to false conclusions, the present enquiry is a most necessary and important part of the science of Ethics.

6. What, then, is good? How is good to be defined? Now, it may be thought that this is a verbal question. A definition does indeed often mean the expressing of one word's meaning in other words. But this is not the sort of definition I am asking for. Such a definition can never be of ultimate importance in any study except lexicography. If I wanted that kind of definition I should have to consider in the first place how people generally used the word 'good'; but my business is not with its proper usage, as established by custom. I should, indeed, be foolish, if I tried to use it for something which it did not usually denote: if, for instance, I were to announce that, whenever I used the word 'good,' I must be understood to be thinking of that object which is usually denoted by the word 'table.' I shall, therefore, use the word in the sense in which I think it is ordinarily used; but at the same time I am not anxious to discuss whether I am right in thinking that it is so used. My business is solely with that object or idea, which I hold, rightly or wrongly, that the word is generally used to stand for. What I want to discover is the nature of that object or idea, and about this I am extremely anxious to arrive at an agreement.

But, if we understand the question in this sense, my answer to it may seem a very disappointing one. If I am asked 'What is good?' my answer is that good is good, and that is the end of the matter. Or if I am asked 'How is good to be defined?' my answer is that it cannot be defined, and that is all I have to say about it. But disappointing as these answers may appear, they are of the very last importance. To readers who are familiar with philosophic terminology, I can express their importance by saying that they amount to this: That propositions about the good are all of them synthetic and never analytic; and that is plainly no trivial matter. And the same thing may be expressed more popularly, by saying that, if I am right, then nobody can foist upon us such an axiom as that 'Pleasure is the only good' or that 'The good is the desired' on the pretence that this is 'the very meaning of the word.'

7. Let us, then, consider this position. My point is that 'good' is a simple notion, just as 'yellow' is a simple notion; that, just as you cannot, by any manner of means, explain to any one who does not already know it, what yellow is, so you cannot explain what good is. Definitions of the kind that I was asking for, definitions which describe the real nature of the object or notion denoted by a word, and which do not merely tell us what the word is used to mean, are only possible when the object or notion in question is something complex. You can give a definition of a horse, because a horse has many different properties and qualities, all of which you can enumerate. But when you have enumerated them all, when you have reduced a horse to his simplest terms, then you can no longer define those terms. They're simply something which you think of or perceive, and to any one who cannot think of or perceive them, you can never, by any definition, make their nature known. It may perhaps be objected to this that we are able to describe to others, objects which they have never seen or thought of. We can, for instance, make a man understand what a chimaera is, although he has never heard of one or seen one. You can tell him that it is an animal with a lioness's head and body, with a goat's head growing from the middle of its back, and with a snake in place of a tail. But here the object which you are describing is a complex object; it is entirely composed of parts, with which we are all perfectly familiar—a snake, a goat, a lioness; and we know, too, the manner in which those parts are to be put together, because

we know what is meant by the middle of a lioness's back, and where her tail is wont to grow. And so it is with all objects, not previously known, which we are able to define: they are all complex; all composed of parts, which may themselves, in the first instance, be capable of similar definition, but which must in the end be reducible to simplest parts, which can no longer be defined. But yellow and good, we say, are not complex: they are notions of that simple kind, out of which definitions are composed and with which the power of further defining ceases.

8. When we say, as Webster says, 'The definition of horse is "a hoofed quadruped of the genus Equus," ' we may, in fact, mean three different things. (1) We may mean merely: 'When I say "horse," you are to understand that I am talking about a hoofed quadruped of the genus Equus.' This might be called the arbitrary verbal definition: and I do not mean that good is indefinable in that sense. (2) We may mean, as Webster ought to mean: 'When most English people say "horse," they mean a hoofed quadruped of the genus Equus.' This may be called the verbal definition proper, and I do not say that good is indefinable in this sense either; for it is certainly possible to discover how people use a word: otherwise, we could never have known that 'good' may be translated by 'gut' in German and by 'bon' in French. But (3) we may, when we define horse, mean something much more important. We may mean that a certain object, which we all of us know, is composed in a certain manner: that it has four legs, a head, a heart, a liver, etc., etc., all of them arranged in definite relations to one another. It is in this sense that I deny good to be definable. I say that it is not composed of any parts, which we can substitute for it in our minds when we are thinking of it. We might think just as clearly and correctly about a horse, if we thought of all its parts and their arrangement instead of thinking of the whole: we could, I say, think how a horse differed

from a donkey just as well, just as truly, in this way, as now we do, only not so easily; but there is nothing whatsoever which we could so substitute for good; and that is what I mean, when I say that good is indefinable.

9. But I am afraid I have still not removed the chief difficulty which may prevent acceptance of the proposition that good is indefinable. I do not mean to say that *the* good, that which is good, is thus indefinable; if I did think so, I should not be writing on Ethics, for my main object is to help towards discovering that definition. It is just because I think there will be less risk of error in our search for a definition of 'the good,' that I am now insisting that *good* is indefinable. I must try to explain the difference between these two. I suppose it may be granted that 'good' is an adjective. Well 'the good,' 'that which is good,' must therefore be the substantive to which the adjective 'good' will apply: it must be the whole of that to which the adjective will apply, and the adjective must *always* truly apply to it. But if it is that to which the adjective will apply, it must be something different from that adjective itself; and the whole of that something different, whatever it is, will be our definition of the good. Now it may be that this something will have other adjectives, beside 'good,' that will apply to it. It may be full of pleasure, for example; it may be intelligent: and if these two adjectives are really part of its definition, then it will certainly be true, that pleasure and intelligence are good. And many people appear to think that, if we say 'Pleasure and intelligence are good,' or if we say 'Only pleasure and intelligence are good,' we are defining 'good.' Well, I cannot deny that propositions of this nature may sometimes be called definitions; I do not know well enough how the word is generally used to decide upon this point. I only wish it to be understood that that is not what I mean when I say there is no possible definition of good, and that I shall not mean this if I use

the word again. I do most fully believe that some true proposition of the form 'Intelligence is good and intelligence alone is good' can be found; if none could be found, our definition of *the* good would be impossible. As it is, I believe *the* good to be definable; and yet I still say that good itself is indefinable.

10. 'Good,' then, if we mean by it that quality which we assert to belong to a thing, when we say that the thing is good, is incapable of any definition, in the most important sense of that word. The most important sense of 'definition' is that in which a definition states what are the parts which invariably compose a certain whole; and in this sense 'good' has no definition because it is simple and has no parts. It is one of those innumerable objects of thought which are themselves incapable of definition, because they are the ultimate terms by reference to which whatever *is* capable of definition must be defined. That there must be an indefinite number of such terms is obvious, on reflection; since we cannot define anything except by an analysis, which, when carried as far as it will go, refers us to something, which is simply different from anything else, and which by that ultimate difference explains the peculiarity of the whole which we are defining: for every whole contains some parts which are common to other wholes also. There is, therefore, no intrinsic difficulty in the contention that 'good' denotes a simple and indefinable quality. There are many other instances of such qualities.

Consider yellow, for example. We may try to define it, by describing its physical equivalent; we may state what kind of light-vibrations must stimulate the normal eye, in order that we perceive it. But a moment's reflection is sufficient to show that those light-vibrations are not themselves what we mean by yellow. *They* are not what we perceive. Indeed we should never have been able to discover their existence, unless we had first been struck by the patent difference of quality between the different colours. The most we can be entitled to say of those vibrations is that they are what corresponds in space to the yellow which we actually perceive.

Yet a mistake of this simple kind has commonly been made about 'good.' It may be true that all things which are good are *also* something else, just as it is true that all things which are yellow produce a certain kind of vibration in the light. And it is a fact, that Ethics aims at discovering what are those other properties belonging to all things which are good. But far too many philosophers have thought that when they named those other properties they were actually defining good; that these properties, in fact, were simply not 'other,' but absolutely and entirely the same with goodness. This view I propose to call the 'naturalistic fallacy' and of it I shall now endeavour to dispose.

11. Let us consider what it is such philosophers say. And first it is to be noticed that they do not agree among themselves. They not only say that they are right as to what good is, but they endeavour to prove that other people who say that it is something else, are wrong. One, for instance, will affirm that good is pleasure, another, perhaps, that good is that which is desired; and each of these will argue eagerly to prove that the other is wrong. But how is that possible? One of them says that good is nothing but the object of desire, and at the same time tries to prove that it is not pleasure. But from his first assertion, that good just means the object of desire, one of two things must follow as regards his proof:

(1) He may be trying to prove that the object of desire is not pleasure. But, if this be all, where is his Ethics? The position he is maintaining is merely a psychological one. Desire is something which occurs in our minds, and pleasure is something else which so occurs; and our would-be ethical philosopher is merely holding that the latter is not the object of the former. But what has that to do with the ques-

tion in dispute? His opponent held the ethical proposition that pleasure was the good, and although he should prove a million times over the psychological proposition that pleasure is not the object of desire, he is no nearer proving his opponent to be wrong. The position is like this. One may says a triangle is a circle: another replies 'A triangle is a straight line, and I will prove to you that I am right: *for*' (this is the only argument) 'a straight line is not a circle.' 'That is quite true,' the other may reply; 'but nevertheless a triangle is a circle, and you have said nothing whatever to prove the contrary. What is proved is that one of us is wrong, for we agree that a triangle cannot be both a straight line and a circle: but which is wrong, there can be no earthly means of proving, since you define triangle as straight line and I define it as circle.'—Well, that is one alternative which any naturalistic Ethics has to face; if good is *defined* as something else, it is then impossible either to prove that any other definition is wrong or even to deny such definition.

(2) The other alternative will scarcely be more welcome. It is that the discussion is after all a verbal one. When A says 'Good means pleasant' and B says 'Good means desired,' they may merely wish to assert that most people have used the word for what is pleasant and for what is desired respectively. And this is quite an interesting subject for discussion: only it is not a whit more an ethical discussion than the last was. Nor do I think that any exponent of naturalistic Ethics would be willing to allow that this was all he meant. They are all so anxious to persuade us that what they call the good is what we really ought to do. 'Do, pray, act so, because the word "good" is generally used to denote actions of this nature': such, on this view, would be the substance of their teaching. And in so far as they tell us how we ought to act, their teaching is truly ethical, as they mean it to be. But how perfectly absurd is the reason they would give for it! 'You are to

do this, because most people use a certain word to denote conduct such as this.' 'You are to say the thing which is not, because most people call it lying.' That is an argument just as good!—My dear sirs, what we want to know from you as ethical teachers, is not how people use a word; it is not even, what kind of actions they approve, which the use of this word 'good' may certainly imply: what we want to know is simply what *is* good. We may indeed agree that what most people do think good, is actually so; we shall at all events be glad to know their opinions: but when we say their opinions about what *is* good, we do mean what we say; we do not care whether they call that thing which they mean 'horse' or 'table' or 'chair,' 'gut' or 'bon' or 'ἀγαθός'; we want to know what it is that they so call. When they say 'Pleasure is good,' we cannot believe that they merely mean 'Pleasure is pleasure' and nothing more than that.

12. Suppose a man says 'I am pleased'; and suppose that is not a lie or a mistake but the truth. Well, if it is true, what does that mean? It means that his mind, a certain definite mind, distinguished by certain definite marks from all others, has at this moment a certain definite feeling called pleasure. 'Pleased' *means* nothing but having pleasure, and though we may be more pleased or less pleased, and even, we may admit for the present, have one or another kind of pleasure; yet in so far as it is pleasure we have, whether there be more or less of it, and whether it be of one kind or another, what we have is one definite thing, absolutely indefinable, some one thing that is the same in all the various degrees and in all the various kinds of it that there may be. We may be able to say how it is related to other things: that, for example, it is in the mind, that it causes desire, that we are conscious of it, etc., etc. We can, I say, describe its relations to other things, but define it we can *not*. And if anybody tried to define pleasure for us as being any other natural object; if anybody were to say,

for instance, that pleasure *means* the sensation of red, and were to proceed to deduce from that that pleasure is a colour, we should be entitled to laugh at him and to distrust his future statements about pleasure. Well, that would be the same fallacy which I have called the naturalistic fallacy. That 'pleased' does not mean 'having the sensation of red,' or anything else whatever, does not prevent us from understanding what it does mean. It is enough for us to know that 'pleased' does mean 'having the sensation of pleasure,' and though pleasure is absolutely indefinable, though pleasure is pleasure and nothing else whatever, yet we feel no difficulty in saying that we are pleased. The reason is, of course, that when I say 'I am pleased,' I do *not* mean that 'I' am the same thing as 'having pleasure.' And similarly no difficulty need be found in my saying that 'pleasure is good' and yet not meaning that 'pleasure' is the same thing as 'good,' that pleasure *means* good, and that good *means* pleasure. If I were to imagine that when I said 'I am pleased,' I meant that I was exactly the same thing as 'pleased,' I should not indeed call that a naturalistic fallacy, although it would be the same fallacy as I have called naturalistic with reference to Ethics. The reason of this is obvious enough. When a man confuses two natural objects with one another, defining the one by the other, if for instance, he confuses himself, who is one natural object, with 'pleased' or with 'pleasure' which are others, then there is no reason to call the fallacy naturalistic. But if he confuses 'good,' which is not in the same sense a natural object, with any natural object whatever, then there is a reason for calling that a naturalistic fallacy; its being made with regard to 'good' marks it as something quite specific, and this specific mistake deserves a name because it is so common. As for the reasons why good is not to be considered a natural object, they may be reserved for discussion in another place. But, for the present, it is sufficient to notice this: Even if it were a natural object, that would not alter the nature of the fallacy nor diminish its importance one whit. All that I have said about it would remain quite equally true: only the name which I have called it would not be so appropriate as I think it is. And I do not care about the name: what I do care about is the fallacy. It does not matter what we call it, provided we recognise it when we meet with it. It is to be met with in almost every book on Ethics; and yet it is not recognised: and that is why it is necessary to multiply illustrations of it, and convenient to give it a name. It is a very simple fallacy indeed. When we say that an orange is yellow, we do not think our statement binds us to hold that 'orange' means nothing else than 'yellow,' or that nothing can be yellow but an orange. Supposing the orange is also sweet! Does that bind us to say that 'sweet' is exactly the same thing as 'yellow,' that 'sweet' must be defined as 'yellow'? And supposing it be recognised that 'yellow' just means 'yellow' and nothing else whatever, does that make it any more difficult to hold that oranges are yellow? Most certainly it does not: on the contrary, it would be absolutely meaningless to say that oranges were yellow, unless yellow did in the end mean just 'yellow' and nothing else whatever—unless it was absolutely indefinable. We should not get any very clear notion about things, which are yellow—we should not get very far with our science, if we were bound to hold that everything which was yellow, *meant* exactly the same thing as yellow. We should find we had to hold that an orange was exactly the same thing as a stool, a piece of paper, a lemon, anything you like. We could prove any number of absurdities; but should we be the nearer to the truth? Why then, should it be different with 'good'? Why, if good is good and indefinable, should I be held to deny that pleasure is good? Is there any difficulty in holding both to be true at once? On the contrary, there is no meaning in saying that pleasure is good, unless good is something

different from pleasure. It is absolutely useless, so far as Ethics is concerned, to prove, as Mr. Spencer tries to do, that increase of pleasure coincides with increase of life, unless good *means* something different from either life or pleasure. He might just as well try to prove that an orange is yellow by shewing that it always is wrapped up in paper.

13. In fact, if it is not the case that 'good' denotes something simple and indefinable, only two alternatives are possible: either it is a complex, a given whole, about the correct analysis of which there may be disagreement; or else it means nothing at all, and there is no such subject as Ethics. In general, however, ethical philosophers have attempted to define good, without recognising what such an attempt must mean. They actually use arguments which involve one or both of the absurdities considered in § 11. We are, therefore, justified in concluding that the attempt to define good is chiefly due to want of clearness as to the possible nature of definition. There are, in fact, only two serious alternatives to be considered, in order to establish the conclusion that 'good' does denote a simple and indefinable notion. It might possibly denote a complex, as 'horse' does; or it might have no meaning at all. Neither of these possibilities has, however, been clearly conceived and seriously maintained, as such, by those who presume to define good; and both may be dismissed by a simple appeal to facts.

(1) The hypothesis that disagreement about the meaning of good is disagreement with regard to the correct analysis of a given whole, may be most plainly seen to be incorrect by consideration of the fact that, whatever definition be offered, it may be always asked, with significance, of the complex so defined, whether it is itself good. To take, for instance, one of the more plausible, because one of the more complicated, of such proposed definitions, it may easily be thought, at first sight, that to be good may mean to be that which we

desire to desire. Thus if we apply this definition to a particular instance and say
'When we think that A is good, we are
thinking that A is one of the things which
we desire to desire,' our proposition may
seem quite plausible. But, if we carry the
investigation further, and ask ourselves 'Is
it good to desire to desire A?' it is apparent,
on a little reflection, that this question is itself as intelligible, as the original question
'Is A good?'—that we are, in fact, now asking for exactly the same information about
the desire to desire A, for which we formerly asked with regard to A itself. But it
is also apparent that the meaning of this
second question cannot be correctly
analysed into 'Is the desire to desire A one
of the things which we desire to desire?':
we have not before our minds anything so
complicated as the question 'Do we desire
to desire to desire to desire A?' Moreover
any one can easily convince himself by
inspection that the predicate of this proposition—'good'—is positively different from
the notion of 'desiring to desire' which enters into its subject: 'That we should desire
to desire A is good' is *not* merely equivalent to 'That A should be good is good.' It
may indeed be true that what we desire to
desire is always also good; perhaps, even
the converse may be true: but it is very
doubtful whether this is the case, and the
mere fact that we understand very well
what is meant by doubting it, shews clearly
that we have two different notions before
our minds.

(2) And the same consideration is sufficient to dismiss the hypothesis that 'good'
has no meaning whatsoever. It is very natural to make the mistake of supposing that
what is universally true is of such a nature that its negation would be self-contradictory: the importance which has been
assigned to analytic propositions in the
history of philosophy shews how easy
such a mistake is. And thus it is very easy
to conclude that what seems to be a
universal ethical principle is in fact an
identical proposition; that, if, for example,

whatever is called 'good' seems to be pleasant, the proposition 'Pleasure is the good'
does not assert a connection between two
different notions, but involves only one,
that of pleasure, which is easily recognised
as a distinct entity. But whoever will attentively consider with himself what is
actually before his mind when he asks the
question 'Is pleasure (or whatever it may
be) after all good?' can easily satisfy himself that he is not merely wondering whether pleasure is pleasant. And if he will **try**
this experiment with each suggested definition in succession, he may become expert
enough to recognise that in every case he
has before his mind a unique object, with
regard to the connection of which with any
other object, a distinct question may be
asked. Every one does in fact understand
the question 'Is this good?' When he thinks
of it, his state of mind is different from
what it would be, were he asked 'Is this
pleasant, or desired, or approved?' It has a
distinct meaning for him, even though he
may not recognise in what respect it is distinct. Whenever he thinks of 'intrinsic
value,' or 'intrinsic worth,' or says that a
thing 'ought to exist,' he has before his
mind the unique object—the unique property of things—which I mean by 'good.'
Everybody is constantly aware of this notion, although he may never become aware
at all that it is different from other notions
of which he is also aware. But, for correct
ethical reasoning, it is extremely important
that he should become aware of this fact;
and, as soon as the nature of the problem is
clearly understood, there should be little
difficulty in advancing so far in analysis.

14. 'Good,' then, is indefinable; and
yet, so far as I know, there is only one ethical writer, Prof. Henry Sidgwick, who has
clearly recognised and stated this fact. We
shall see, indeed, how far many of the most
reputed ethical systems fall short of drawing the conclusions which follow from
such a recognition. At present I will only
quote one instance, which will serve to
illustrate the meaning and importance of

this principle that 'good' is indefinable, or, as Prof. Sidgwick says, an 'unanalysable notion.' It is an instance to which Prof. Sidgwick himself refers in a note on the passage, in which he argues that 'ought' is unanalysable.[2]

'Bentham,' says Sidgwick, 'explains that his fundamental principle "states the greatest happiness of all those whose interest is in question as being the right and proper end of human action"'; and yet 'his language in other passages of the same chapter would seem to imply' that he *means* by the word "right" "conducive to the general happiness." Prof. Sidgwick sees that, if you take these two statements together, you get the absurd result that 'greatest happiness is the end of human action, which is conducive to the general happiness'; and so absurd does it seems to him to call this result, as Bentham calls it, 'the fundamental principle of a moral system,' that he suggests that Bentham cannot have meant it. Yet Prof. Sidgwick himself states elsewhere[3] that Psychological Hedonism is 'not seldom confounded with Egoistic Hedonism'; and that confusion, as we shall see, rests chiefly on that same fallacy, the naturalistic fallacy, which is implied in Bentham's statements. Prof. Sidgwick admits therefore that this fallacy is sometimes committed, absurd as it is; and I am inclined to think that Bentham may really have been one of those who committed it. Mill, as we shall see,[3a] certainly did commit it. In any case, whether Bentham committed it or not, his doctrine, as above quoted, will serve as a very good illustration of this fallacy, and of the importance of the contrary proposition that good is indefinable.

Let us consider this doctrine. Bentham

seems to imply, so Prof. Sidgwick says, that the word 'right' *means* 'conducive to general happiness.' Now this, by itself, need not necessarily involve the naturalistic fallacy. For the word 'right' is very commonly appropriated to actions which lead to the attainment of what is good; which are regarded as *means* to the ideal and not as ends-in-themselves. This use of 'right,' as denoting what is good as a means, whether or not it be also good as an end, is indeed the use to which I shall confine the word. Had Bentham been using 'right' in this sense, it might be perfectly consistent for him to *define* right as 'conducive to the general happiness,' *provided only* (and notice this proviso) he had already proved, or laid down as an axiom, that general happiness was *the* good, or (what is equivalent to this) that general happiness alone was good. For in that case he would have already defined *the* good as general happiness (a position perfectly consistent, as we have seen, with the contention that 'good' is indefinable), and, since right was to be defined as 'conducive to *the* good,' it would actually *mean* 'conducive to general happiness.' But this method of escape from the charge of having committed the naturalistic fallacy has been closed by Bentham himself. For his fundamental principle is, we see, that the greatest happiness of all concerned is the *right* and proper *end* of human action. He applies the word 'right,' therefore, to the end, as such, not only to the means which are conducive to it; and, that being so, right can no longer be defined as 'conducive to the general happiness,' without involving the fallacy in question. For now it is obvious that the definition of right as conducive to general happiness can be used by him in support of the fundamental principle that general happiness is the right end; instead of being itself derived from that principle. If right, by definition, means conducive to general happiness, then it is obvious that general happiness is the right end. It is not necessary now first to prove or assert that

[2] *Methods of Ethics*, Bk. i, Chap. iii, §§ 2–3 [Chap. iii of Sidgwick's book is reprinted in this volume, pp. 77 ff.]

[3] *Methods of Ethics*, Bk. 1, Chap. iv, § 1.

[3a] [See the selection from *Principia Ethica* printed below under the title "Mill and the Hedonistic Principle."]

general happiness is the right end, before right is defined as conducive to general happiness—a perfectly valid procedure; but on the contrary the definition of right as conducive to general happiness proves general happiness to be the right end—a perfectly invalid procedure, since in this case the statement that 'general happiness is the right end of human action' is not an ethical principle at all, but either, as we have seen, a proposition about the meaning of words, or else a proposition about the *nature* of general happiness, not about its rightness or goodness.

Now, I do not wish the importance I assign to this fallacy to be misunderstood. The discovery of it does not at all refute Bentham's contention that greatest happiness is the proper end of human action, if that be understood as an ethical proposition, as he undoubtedly intended it. That principle may be true all the same; we shall consider whether it is so in succeeding chapters. Bentham might have maintained it, as Professor Sidgwick does, even if the fallacy had been pointed out to him. What I am maintaining is that the *reasons* which he actually gives for his ethical proposition are fallacious ones, so far as they consist in a definition of right. What I suggest is that he did not perceive them to be fallacious; that, if he had done so, he would have been led to seek for other reasons in support of his Utilitarianism; and that, had he sought for other reasons, he *might* have found none which he thought to be sufficient. In that case he would have changed his whole system— a most important consequence. It is undoubtedly also possible that he would have thought other reasons to be sufficient, and in that case his ethical system, in its main results, would still have stood. But even in this latter case, his use of the fallacy would be a serious objection to him as an ethical philosopher. For it is the business of Ethics, I must insist, not only to obtain true results, but also to find valid reasons for them. The direct object of Ethics is

knowledge and not practice; and any one who uses the naturalistic fallacy has certainly not fulfilled this first object, however correct his practical principles may be.

My objections to Naturalism are then, in the first place, that it offers no reason at all, far less any valid reason, for any ethical principle whatever; and in this it already fails to satisfy the requirements of Ethics, as a scientific study. But in the second place I contend that, though it gives a reason for no ethical principle, it is a *cause* of the acceptance of false principles—it deludes the mind into accepting ethical principles, which are false; and in this it is contrary to every aim of Ethics. It is easy to see that if we start with a definition of right conduct as conduct conducive to general happiness; then, knowing that right conduct is conduct universally conducive to the good, we very easily arrive at the result that the good is general happiness. If, on the other hand, we once recognise that we must start our Ethics without a definition, we shall be much more apt to look about us, before we adopt any ethical principle whatever; and the more we look about us, the less likely are we to adopt a false one. It may be replied to this: Yes, but we shall look about us just as much, before we settle on our definition, and are therefore just as likely to be right. But I will try to shew that this is not the case. If we start with the conviction that a definition of good can be found, we start with the conviction that good *can mean* nothing else than some one property of things; and our only business will then be to discover what that property is. But if we recognise that, so far as the meaning of good goes, anything whatever may be good, we start with a much more open mind. Moreover, apart from the fact that, when we think we have a definition, we cannot logically defend our ethical principles in any way whatever, we shall also be much less apt to defend them well, even if illogically. For we shall start with the conviction that good must mean so and so, and shall therefore be inclined either to misunderstand our opponent's arguments or to cut them short with the reply, 'This is not an open question: the very meaning of the word decides it; no one can think otherwise except through confusion.'

15. Our first conclusion as to the subject-matter of Ethics is, then, that there is a simple, indefinable, unanalysable object of thought by reference to which it must be defined. By what name we call this unique object is a matter of indifference, so long as we clearly recognise what it is and that it does differ from other objects. The words which are commonly taken as the signs of ethical judgments all do refer to it; and they are expressions of ethical judgments solely because they do so refer. But they may refer to it in two different ways, which it is very important to distinguish, if we are to have a complete definition of the range of ethical judgments. Before I proceeded to argue that there was such an indefinable notion involved in ethical notions, I stated (§ 4) that it was necessary for Ethics to enumerate all true universal judgments asserting that such and such a thing was good, whenever it occurred. But, although all such judgments do refer to that unique notion which I have called 'good,' they do not all refer to it in the same way. They may either assert that this unique property does always attach to the thing in question, or else they may assert only that the thing in question is *a cause or necessary condition* for the existence of other things to which this unique property does attach. The nature of these two species of universal ethical judgments is extremely different; and a great part of the difficulties, which are met with in ordinary ethical speculation, are due to the failure to distinguish them clearly. Their difference has, indeed, received expression in ordinary language by the contrast between the terms 'good as means' and 'good in itself,' 'value as a means' and 'intrinsic value.' But these terms are apt to be applied correctly only in the more obvious instances; and this

seems to be due to the fact that the distinction between the conceptions which they denote has not been made a separate object of investigation. This distinction may be briefly pointed out as follows.

16. Whenever we judge that a thing is 'good as a means,' we are making a judgment with regard to its causal relations: we judge *both* that it will have a particular kind of effect, *and* that that effect will be good in itself. But to find causal judgments that are universally true is notoriously a matter of extreme difficulty. The late date at which most of the physical sciences became exact, and the comparative fewness of the laws which they have succeeded in establishing even now, are sufficient proofs of this difficulty. With regard, then, to what are the most frequent objects of ethical judgments, namely actions, it is obvious that we cannot be satisfied that any of our universal causal judgments are true, even in the sense in which scientific laws are so. We cannot even discover hypothetical laws of the form 'Exactly this action will always, under these conditions, produce exactly that effect.' But for a correct ethical judgment with regard to the effects of certain actions we require more than this in two respects. (1) We require to know that a given action will produce a certain effect, *under whatever circumstances it occurs.* But this is certainly impossible. It is certain that in different circumstances the same action may produce effects which are utterly different in all respects upon which the value of the effect depends. Hence we can never be entitled to more than a *generalisation*—to a proposition of the form 'This result *generally* follows this kind of action'; and even this generalisation will only be true, if the circumstances under which the action occurs are generally the same. This is in fact the case, to a great extent, within any one particular age and state of society. But, when we take other ages into account, in many most important cases the normal circumstances of a given kind of action will

be so different, that the generalisation which is true for one will not be true for another. With regard then to ethical judgments which assert that a certain kind of action is good as a means to a certain kind of effect, none will be *universally* true; and many, though *generally* true at one period, will be generally false at others. But (2) we require to know not only that *one* good effect will be produced, but that, among all subsequent events affected by the action in question, the balance of good will be greater than if any other possible action had been performed. In other words, to judge that an action is generally a means to good is to judge not only that it generally does *some* good, but that it generally does the greatest good of which the circumstances admit. In this respect ethical judgments about the effects of action involve a difficulty and a complication far greater than that involved in the establishment of scientific laws. For the latter we need only consider a single effect; for the former it is essential to consider not only this, but the effects of that effect, and so on as far as our view into the future can reach. It is, indeed, obvious that our view can never reach far enough for us to be certain that any action will produce the best possible effects. We must be content, if the greatest possible balance of good seems to be produced within a limited period. But it is important to notice that the whole series of effects within a period of considerable length is actually taken account of in our common judgments that an action is good as a means; and that hence this additional complication, which makes ethical generalisations so far more difficult to establish than scientific laws, is one which is involved in actual ethical discussions, and is of practical importance. The commonest rules of conduct involve such considerations as the balancing of future bad health against immediate gains; and even if we can never settle with any certainty how we shall secure the greatest possible total of good, we try at least to assure ourselves

that probable future evils will not be greater than the immediate good.

17. There are, then, judgments which state that certain kinds of things have good effects; and such judgments, for the reasons just given, have the important characteristics (1) that they are unlikely to be true, if they state that the kind of thing in question *always* has good effects, and (2) that, even if they only state that it *generally* has good effects, many of them will only be true of certain periods in the world's history. On the other hand there are judgments which state that certain kinds of things are themselves good; and these differ from the last in that, if true at all, they are all of them universally true. It is, therefore, extremely important to distinguish these two kinds of possible judgments. Both may be expressed in the same language: in both cases we commonly say 'Such and such a thing is good.' But in the one case 'good' will mean 'good as means,' i.e. merely that the thing is a means to good—will have good effects: in the other case it will mean 'good as end'—we shall be judging that the thing itself has the property which, in the first case, we asserted only to belong to its effects. It is plain that these are very different assertions to make about a thing; it is plain that either or both of them may be made, both truly and falsely, about all manner of things; and it is certain that unless we are clear as to which of the two we mean to assert, we shall have a very poor chance of deciding rightly whether our assertion is true or false. It is precisely this clearness as to the meaning of the question asked which has hitherto been almost entirely lacking in ethical speculation. Ethics has always been predominantly concerned with the investigation of a limited class of actions. With regard to these we may ask *both* how far they are good in themselves *and* how far they have a general tendency to produce good results. And the arguments brought forward in ethical discussion have always been of both classes—both such as would prove the conduct in ques-

tion to be good in itself and such as would prove it to be good as a means. But that these are the only questions which any ethical discussion can have to settle, and that to settle the one is *not* the same thing as to settle the other—these two fundamental facts have in general escaped the notice of ethical philosophers. Ethical questions are commonly asked in an ambiguous form. It is asked 'What is a man's duty under these circumstances?' or 'Is it right to act in this way?' or 'What ought we to aim at securing?' But all these questions are capable of further analysis; a correct answer to any of them involves both judgments of what is good in itself and causal judgments. This is implied even by those who maintain that we have a direct and immediate judgment of absolute rights and duties. Such a judgment can only mean that the course of action in question is *the* best thing to do; that, by acting so, every good that *can* be secured will have been secured. Now we are not concerned with the question whether such a judgment will ever be true. The question is: What does it imply, if it is true? And the only possible answer is that, whether true or false, it implies both a proposition as to the degree of goodness of the action in question, as compared with other things, and a number of causal propositions. For it cannot be denied that the action will have consequences: and to deny that the consequences matter is to make a judgment of their intrinsic value, as compared with the action itself. In asserting that the action is *the* best thing to do, we assert that it together with its consequences presents a greater sum of intrinsic value than any possible alternative. And this condition may be realised by any of the three cases:—(*a*) If the action itself has greater intrinsic value than any alternative, whereas both its consequences and those of the alternatives are absolutely devoid either of intrinsic merit or intrinsic demerit; or (*b*) if, though its consequences are intrinsically bad, the balance of intrinsic value is greater than would be produced by any alternative; or (*c*) if, its consequences being intrinsically good, the degree of value belonging to them and it conjointly is greater than that of any alternative series. In short, to assert that a certain line of conduct is, at a given time, absolutely right or obligatory, is obviously to assert that more good or less evil will exist in the world, if it be adopted, than if anything else be done instead. But this implies a judgment as to the value both of its own consequences and of those of any possible alternative. And that an action will have such and such consequences involves a number of causal judgments.

Similarly, in answering the question 'What ought we to aim at securing?' causal judgments are again involved, but in a somewhat different way. We are liable to forget, because it is so obvious, that this question can never be answered correctly except by naming something which *can* be secured. Not everything can be secured; and, even if we judge that nothing which cannot be obtained would be of equal value with that which can, the possibility of the latter, as well as its value, is essential to its being a proper end of action. Accordingly neither our judgments as to what actions we ought to perform, nor even our judgments as to the ends which they ought to produce, are pure judgments of intrinsic value. With regard to the former, an action which is absolutely obligatory *may* have no intrinsic value whatsoever; that it is perfectly virtuous may mean merely that it causes the best possible effects. And with regard to the latter, these best possible results which justify our action can, in any case, have only so much of intrinsic value as the laws of nature allow us to secure; and they in their turn *may* have no intrinsic value whatsoever, but may merely be a means to the attainment (in a still further future) of something that has such value. Whenever, therefore, we ask 'What ought we to do?' or 'What ought we to try to get?' we are asking questions which involve a correct answer to two others, completely different in kind from one another. We must know *both* what degree of intrinsic value different things have, *and* how these different things may be obtained. But the vast majority of questions which have actually been discussed in Ethics—*all* practical questions, indeed—involve this double knowledge; and they have been discussed without any clear separation of the two distinct questions involved. A great part of the vast disagreements prevalent in Ethics is to be attributed to this failure in analysis. By the use of conceptions which involve both that of intrinsic value and that of causal relation, as if they involved intrinsic value only, two different errors have been rendered almost universal. Either it is assumed that nothing has intrinsic value which is not possible, or else it is assumed that what is necessary must have intrinsic value. Hence the primary and peculiar business of Ethics, the determination what things have intrinsic value and in what degrees, has received no adequate treatment at all. And on the other hand a *thorough* discussion of means has been also largely neglected, owing to an obscure perception of the truth that it is perfectly irrelevant to the question of intrinsic values. But however this may be, and however strongly any particular reader may be convinced that some one of the mutually contradictory systems which hold the field has given a correct answer either to the question what has intrinsic value, or to the question what we ought to do, or to both, it must at least be admitted that the questions what is best in itself and what will bring about the best possible, are utterly distinct; that both belong to the actual subject-matter of Ethics; and that the more clearly distinct questions are distinguished, the better is our chance of answering both correctly.

18. There remains one point which must not be omitted in a complete description of the kind of questions which Ethics has to answer. The main division of those questions is, as I have said, into two; the question what things are good in them-

selves, and the question to what other things these are related as effects. The first of these, which is the primary ethical question and is presupposed by the other, includes a correct comparison of the various things which have intrinsic value (if there are many such) in respect of the degree of value which they have; and such comparison involves a difficulty of principle which has greatly aided the confusion of intrinsic value with mere 'goodness as a means.' It has been pointed out that one difference between a judgment, which asserts that a thing is good in itself, and a judgment which asserts that it is a means to good, consists in the fact that the first, if true of one instance of the thing in question, is necessarily true of all; whereas a thing which has good effects under some circumstances may have bad ones under others. Now it is certainly true that all judgments of intrinsic value are in this sense universal; but the principle which I have now to enunciate may easily make it appear as if they were not so but resembled the judgment of means in being merely general. There is, as will presently be maintained, a vast number of different things, each of which has intrinsic value; there are also very many which are positively bad; and there is a still larger class of things, which appear to be indifferent. But a thing belonging to any of these three classes may occur as part of a whole, which includes among its other parts other things belonging both to the same and to the other two classes; and these wholes, as such, may also have intrinsic value. The paradox, to which it is necessary to call attention, is that *the value of such a whole bears no regular proportion to the sum of the values of its parts.* It is certain that a good thing may exist in such a relation to another good thing that the value of the whole thus formed is immensely greater than the sum of the values of the two good things. It is certain that a whole formed of a good thing and an indifferent thing may have immensely greater value than that good thing itself possesses. It is certain that two bad things or a bad thing and an indifferent thing may form a whole much worse than the sum of badness of its parts. And it seems as if indifferent things may also be the sole constituents of a whole which has great value either positive or negative. Whether the addition of a bad thing to a good whole may increase the positive value of the whole, or the addition of a bad thing to a bad may produce a whole having positive value, may seem more doubtful; but it is, at least, possible, and this possibility must be taken into account in our ethical investigations. However we may decide particular questions, the principle is clear. *The value of a whole must not be assumed to be the same as the sum of the values of its parts.*

A single instance will suffice to illustrate the kind of relation in question. It seems to be true that to be conscious of a beautiful object is a thing of great intrinsic value; whereas the same object, if no one be conscious of it, has certainly comparatively little value, and is commonly held to have none at all. But the consciousness of a beautiful object is certainly a whole of some sort in which we can distinguish as parts the object on the one hand and the being conscious on the other. Now this latter factor occurs as part of a different whole, whenever we are conscious of anything; and it would seem that some of these wholes have at all events very little value, and may even be indifferent or positively bad. Yet we cannot always attribute the slightness of their value to any positive demerit in the object which differentiates them from the consciousness of beauty; the object itself may approach as near as possible to absolute neutrality. Since, therefore, mere consciousness does not always confer great value upon the whole of which it forms a part, even though its object may have no great demerit, we cannot attribute the great superiority of the consciousness of a beautiful thing over the beautiful thing itself to the mere addition of the value

of consciousness to that of the beautiful thing. Whatever the intrinsic value of consciousness may be, it does not give to the whole of which it forms a part a value proportioned to the sum of its value and that of its object. If this be so, we have here an instance of a whole possessing a different intrinsic value from the sum of that of its parts; and whether it be so or not, what is meant by such a difference is illustrated by this case.

19. There are, then, wholes which possess the property that their value is different from the sum of the values of their parts; and the relations which subsist between such parts and the whole of which they form a part have not hitherto been distinctly recognised or received a separate name. Two points are especially worthy of notice. (1) It is plain that the existence of any such part is a necessary condition for the existence of that good which is constituted by the whole. And exactly the same language will also express the relation between a means and the good thing which is its effect. But yet there is a most important difference between the two cases, constituted by the fact that the part is, whereas the means is not, a part of the good thing for the existence of which its existence is a necessary condition. The necessity by which, if the good in question is to exist, the means to it must exist is merely a natural or causal necessity. If the laws of nature were different, exactly the same good might exist, although what is now a necessary condition of its existence did not exist. The existence of the means has no intrinsic value; and its utter annihilation would leave the value of that which it is now necessary to secure entirely unchanged. But in the case of a part of such a whole as we are now considering, it is otherwise. In this case the good in question cannot conceivably exist, unless the part exist also. The necessity which connects the two is quite independent of natural law. What is asserted to have intrinsic value is the existence of the whole; and the exist-

ence of the whole includes the existence of its part. Suppose the part removed, and what remains is *not* what was asserted to have intrinsic value; but if we suppose a means removed, what remains is just what *was* asserted to have intrinsic value. And yet (2) the existence of the part may *itself* have no more intrinsic value than that of the means. It is this fact which constitutes the paradox of the relation which we are discussing. It had just been said that what has intrinsic value is the existence of the whole, and that this includes the existence of the part; and from this it would seem a natural inference that the existence of the part has intrinsic value. But the inference would be as false as if we were to conclude that, because the number of two stones was two, each of the stones was also two. The part of a valuable whole retains exactly the same value when it is, as when it is not, a part of that whole. If it had value under other circumstances, its value is not any greater, when it is part of a far more valuable whole; and if it had no value by itself, it has none still, however great be that of the whole of which it now forms a part. We are not then justified in asserting that one and the same thing is under some circumstances intrinsically good, and under others not so; as we are justified in asserting of a means that it sometimes does and sometimes does not produce good results. And yet we are justified in asserting that it is far more desirable that a certain thing should exist under some circumstances than under others; namely when other things will exist in such relations to it as to form a more valuable whole. *It* will not have more intrinsic value under these circumstances than under others; *it* will not necessarily even be a means to the existence of things having more intrinsic value: but it will, like a means, be a necessary condition for the existence of that which *has* greater intrinsic value, although, unlike a means, it will itself form a part of this more valuable existent.

20. I have said that the peculiar relation between part and whole which I have just been trying to define is one which has received no separate name. It would, however, be useful that it should have one; and there is a name, which might well be appropriated to it, if only it could be divorced from its present unfortunate usage. Philosophers, especially those who profess to have derived great benefit from the writings of Hegel, have latterly made much use of the terms 'organic whole,' 'organic unity,' 'organic relation.' The reason why these terms might well be appropriated to the use suggested is that the peculiar relation of parts to whole, just defined, is one of the properties which distinguishes the wholes to which they are actually applied with the greatest frequency. And the reason why it is desirable that they should be divorced from their present usage is that, as at present used, they have no distinct sense and, on the contrary, both imply and propagate errors of confusion.

To say that a thing is an 'organic whole' is generally understood to imply that its parts are related to one another and to itself as means to end; it is also understood to imply that they have a property described in some such phrase as that they have 'no meaning or significance apart from the whole'; and finally such a whole is also treated as if it had the property to which I am proposing that the name should be confined. But those who use the term give us, in general, no hint as to how they suppose these three properties to be related to one another. It seems generally to be assumed that they are identical; and always, at least, that they are necessarily connected with one another. That they are not identical I have already tried to shew; to suppose them so is to neglect the very distinctions pointed out in the last paragraph; and the usage might well be discontinued merely because it encourages such neglect. But a still more cogent reason for its discontinuance is that, so far from being necessarily connected, the second is a property which can attach to nothing, being a self-contradictory conception; whereas the first, if we insist on its most important sense, applies to many cases, to which we have no reason to think that the third applies also, and the third certainly applies to many to which the first does not apply.

21. These relations between the three properties just distinguished may be illustrated by reference to a whole of the kind from which the name 'organic' was derived—a whole which is an organism in the scientific sense—namely the human body.

(1) There exists between many parts of our body (though not between all) a relation which has been familiarised by the fable, attributed to Menenius Agrippa, concerning the belly and its members. We can find in it parts such that the continued existence of the one is a necessary condition for the continued existence of the other; while the continued existence of this latter is also a necessary condition for the continued existence of the former. This amounts to no more than saying that in the body we have instances of two things, both enduring for some time, which have a relation of mutual causal dependence on one another —a relation of 'reciprocity.' Frequently no more than this is meant by saying that the parts of the body form an 'organic unity,' or that they are mutually means and ends to one another. And we certainly have here a striking characteristic of living things. But it would be extremely rash to assert that this relation of mutual causal dependence was only exhibited by living things and hence was sufficient to define their peculiarity. And it is obvious that of two things which have this relation of mutual dependence, neither may have intrinsic value, or one may have it and the other lack it. They are not necessarily 'ends' to one another in any sense except that in which 'end' means 'effect.' And moreover it is plain that in this sense the whole cannot be an end to any of its parts. We are apt to talk of 'the whole' in contrast to one of its parts, when in fact we mean only *the rest* of the parts. But strictly the whole must include all its parts and no part can be a cause of the whole, because it cannot be a cause of itself. It is plain, therefore, that this relation

of mutual causal dependence implies nothing with regard to the value of either of the objects which have it; and that, even if both of them happen also to have value, this relation between them is one which cannot hold between part and whole.

But (2) it may also be the case that our body as a whole has a value greater than the sum of values of its parts; and this may be what is meant when it is said that the parts are means to the whole. It is obvious that if we ask the question 'Why *should* the parts be such as they are?' a proper answer may be 'Because the whole they form has so much value.' But it is equally obvious that the relation which we thus assert to exist between part and whole is quite different from that which we assert to exist between part and part when we say 'This part exists, because that one could not exist without it.' In the latter case we assert the two parts to be causally connected; but, in the former, part and whole cannot be causally connected, and the relation which we assert to exist between them may exist even though the parts are not causally connected either. All the parts of a picture do not have that relation of mutual causal dependence, which certain parts of the body have, and yet the existence of those which do not have it may be absolutely essential to the value of the whole. The two relations are quite distinct in kind, and we cannot infer the existence of the one from that of the other. It can, therefore, serve no useful purpose to include them both under the same name; and if we are to say that a whole is organic because its parts are (in this sense) 'means' to the whole, we must *not* say that it is organic because its parts are causally dependent on one another.

22. But finally (3) the sense which has been most prominent in recent uses of the term 'organic whole' is one whereby it asserts the parts of such a whole to have a property which the parts of no whole can possibly have. It is supposed that just as the whole would not be what it is but for the existence of the parts, so the parts would not be what they are but for the ex-

istence of the whole; and this is understood to mean not merely that any particular part could not exist unless the others existed too (which is the case where relation (1) exists between the parts), but actually that the part is no distinct object of thought—that the whole, of which it is a part, is in its turn a part of it. That this supposition is self-contradictory a very little reflection should be sufficient to shew. We may admit, indeed, that when a particular thing is a part of a whole, it does possess a predicate which it would not otherwise possess—namely that it is a part of that whole. But what cannot be admitted is that this predicate alters the nature or enters into the definition of the thing which has it. When we think of the part *itself*, we mean just *that which* we assert, in this case, to *have* the predicate that it is part of the whole; and the mere assertion that *it* is a part of the whole involves that it should itself be distinct from that which we assert of it. Otherwise we contradict ourselves since we assert that, not *it*, but something else—namely it together with that which we assert of it—has the predicate which we assert of it. In short, it is obvious that no part contains analytically the whole to which it belongs, or any other parts of that whole. The relation of part to whole is *not* the same as that of whole to part; and the very definition of the latter is that it does contain analytically that which is said to be its part. And yet this very self-contradictory doctrine is the chief mark which shews the influence of Hegel upon modern philosophy—an influence which pervades almost the whole of orthodox philosophy. This is what is generally implied by the cry against falsification by abstraction: that a whole is always a part of its part! 'If you want to know the truth about a part,' we are told, 'you must consider *not* that part, but something else—namely the whole: *nothing* is true of the part, but only of the whole.' Yet plainly it must be true of the part at least that it is a part of the whole; and it is obvious that when we say it is, we do *not* mean merely that the whole is a

part of itself. This doctrine, therefore, that a part can have 'no meaning or significance apart from its whole' must be utterly rejected. It implies itself that the statement 'This is a part of that whole' has a meaning; and in order that this may have one, both subject and predicate must have a distinct meaning. And it is easy to see how this false doctrine has arisen by confusion with the two relations (1) and (2) which may really be properties of wholes.

(*a*) The *existence* of a part may be connected by a natural or causal necessity with the existence of the other parts of its whole; and further what is a part of a whole and what has ceased to be such a part, although differing intrinsically from one another, may be called by one and the same name. Thus, to take a typical example, if an arm be cut off from the human body, we still call it an arm. Yet an arm, when it is a part of the body, undoubtedly differs from a dead arm: and hence we may easily be led to say 'The arm which is a part of the body would not be what it is, if it were not such a part,' and to think that the contradiction thus expressed is in reality a characteristic of things. But, in fact, the dead arm never was a part of the body; it is only *partially* identical with the living arm. Those parts of it which are identical with parts of the living arm are exactly the same, whether they belong to the body or not; and in them we have an undeniable instance of one and the same thing at one time forming a part, and at another not forming a part of the presumed 'organic whole.' On the other hand those properties which *are* possessed by the living, and *not* by the dead, arm, do not exist in a changed form in the latter: they simply do not exist there *at all*. By a causal necessity their existence depends on their having that relation to the other parts of the body which we express by saying that they form part of it. Yet, most certainly, *if* they ever did not form part of the body, they *would* be exactly what they are when they do. That they differ intrinsically from the properties of the dead arm and that they form part of the body are propositions not analytically related to one another. There is no contradiction in supposing them to retain such intrinsic differences and yet not to form part of the body.

But (*b*) when we are told that a living arm has no *meaning* or *significance* apart from the body to which it belongs, a different fallacy is also suggested. 'To have meaning or significance' is commonly used in the sense of 'to have importance'; and this again means 'to have value either as a means or as an end.' Now it is quite possible that even a living arm, apart from its body, would have no intrinsic value whatever; although the whole of which it is a part has great intrinsic value owing to its presence. Thus we may easily come to say that, *as* a part of the body, it has great value, whereas *by itself* it would have none; and thus that its whole 'meaning' lies in its relation to the body. But in fact the value in question obviously does not belong to *it* at all. To have value merely as a part is equivalent to having no value at all, but merely being a part of that which has it. Owing, however, to neglect of this distinction, the assertion that a part has value, *as a part*, which it would not otherwise have, easily leads to the assumption that it is also different, as a part, from what it would otherwise be; for it is, in fact, true that two things which have a different value must also differ in other respects. Hence the assumption that one and the same thing, because it is a part of a more valuable whole at one time than at another, therefore has more intrinsic value at one time than at another, has encouraged the self-contradictory belief that one and the same thing may be two different things, and that only in one of its forms is it truly what it is.

For these reasons, I shall, where it seems convenient, take the liberty to use the term 'organic' with a special sense. I shall use it to denote the fact that a whole has an intrinsic value different in amount from the sum of the values of its parts. I shall use it to denote this and only this.

The term will not imply any causal relation whatever between the parts of the whole in question. And it will not imply either, that the parts are inconceivable except as parts of that whole, or that, when they form parts of such a whole, they have a value different from that which they would have if they did not. Understood in this special and perfectly definite sense the relation of an organic whole to its parts is one of the most important which Ethics has to recognise. A chief part of that science should be occupied in comparing the relative values of various goods; and the grossest errors will be committed in such comparison if it be assumed that wherever two things form a whole, the value of that whole is merely the sum of the values of those two things. With this question of 'organic wholes,' then, we complete the enumeration of the kind of problems, with which it is the business of Ethics to deal.

23. In this chapter I have endeavoured to enforce the following conclusions. (1) The peculiarity of Ethics is not that it investigates assertions about human conduct, but that it investigates assertions about that property of things which is denoted by the term 'good,' and the converse property denoted by the term 'bad.' It must, in order to establish its conclusions, investigate the truth of *all* such assertions, *except* those which assert the relation of this property only to a single existent (1-4). (2) This property, by reference to which the subject-matter of Ethics must be defined, is itself simple and indefinable (5-14). And (3) all assertions about its relation to other things are of two, and only two, kinds: they either assert in what degree things themselves possess this property, or else they assert causal relations between other things and those which possess it (15-17). Finally, (4) in considering the different degrees in which things themselves possess this property, we have to take account of the fact that a whole may possess it in a degree different from that which is obtained by summing the degrees in which its parts possess it (18-22).

The Naturalistic Fallacy

W. K. FRANKENA

The future historian of "thought and expression" in the twentieth century will no doubt record with some amusement the ingenious trick, which some of the philosophical controversialists of the first quarter of our century had, of labelling their opponents' views "fallacies." He may even list some of these alleged fallacies for a certain sonority which their inventors embodied in their titles: the fallacy of initial predication, the fallacy of simple location, the fallacy of misplaced concreteness, the naturalistic fallacy.

Of these fallacies, real or supposed, perhaps the most famous is the naturalistic fallacy. For the practitioners of a certain kind of ethical theory, which is dominant in England and capably represented in America, and which is variously called objectivism, non-naturalism, or intuitionism, have frequently charged their opponents with committing the naturalistic fallacy. Some of these opponents have strongly repudiated the charge of fallacy, others have at least commented on it in passing, and altogether the notion of a naturalistic fallacy has had a considerable currency in ethical literature. Yet, in spite of its repute, the naturalistic fallacy has never been discussed at any length, and, for this reason, I have elected to make a study of it in this paper. I hope incidentally to clarify certain confusions which have been made in connexion with the naturalistic fallacy, but my main

interest is to free the controversy between the intuitionists and their opponents of the notion of a logical or quasi-logical fallacy, and to indicate where the issue really lies.

The prominence of the concept of a naturalistic fallacy in recent moral philosophy is another testimony to the great influence of the Cambridge philosopher, Mr. G. E. Moore, and his book, *Principia Ethica*. Thus Mr. Taylor speaks of the "vulgar mistake" which Mr. Moore has taught us to call "the naturalistic fallacy,"[1] and Mr. G. S. Jury, as if to illustrate how well we have learned this lesson, says, with reference to naturalistic definitions of value, "All such definitions stand charged with Dr. Moore's 'naturalistic fallacy.' "[2] Now, Mr. Moore coined the notion of the naturalistic fallacy in his polemic against naturalistic and metaphysical systems of ethics. "The naturalistic fallacy is a fallacy," he writes, and it "must not be committed." All naturalistic and metaphysical theories of ethics, however, "are *based* on the naturalistic fallacy, in the sense that the commission of this fallacy has been the main cause of their wide acceptance."[3] The best way to dispose of them, then, is to expose this fallacy. Yet it is not entirely clear just what is the status of the naturalistic fallacy in the polemics of the intuitionists against other theories. Sometimes it is used as a weapon, as when Miss Clarke says that if we call a thing

Reprinted from *Mind*, 48, 1939, by permission of the author and *Mind*.

[1] A. E. Taylor, *The Faith of a Moralist*, vol. I, p. 104 n.
[2] *Value and Ethical Objectivity*, p. 58.
[3] *Principia Ethica*, pp. 38, 64.

good simply because it is liked we are guilty of the naturalistic fallacy.[4] Indeed, it presents this aspect to the reader in many parts of *Principia Ethica* itself. Now, in taking it as a weapon, the intuitionists use the naturalistic fallacy as if it were a logical fallacy on all fours with the fallacy of composition, the revelation of which disposes of naturalistic and metaphysical ethics and leaves intuitionism standing triumphant. That is, it is taken as a fallacy in advance, for use in controversy. But there are signs in *Principia Ethica* which indicate that the naturalistic fallacy has a rather different place in the intuitionist scheme, and should not be used as a weapon at all. In this aspect, the naturalistic fallacy must be proved to be a fallacy. It cannot be used to settle the controversy, but can only be asserted to be a fallacy when the smoke of battle has cleared. Consider the following passages: (*a*) "the naturalistic fallacy consists in the contention that good *means* nothing but some simple or complex notion, that can be defined in terms of natural qualities"; (*b*) "the point that good is indefinable and that to deny this involves a fallacy, is a point capable of strict proof."[5] These passages seem to imply that the fallaciousness of the naturalistic fallacy is just what is at issue in the controversy between the intuitionists and their opponents, and cannot be wielded as a weapon in that controversy. One of the points I wish to make in this paper is that the charge of committing the naturalistic fallacy can be made, if at all, only as a conclusion from the discussion and not as an instrument of deciding it.

The notion of a naturalistic fallacy has been connected with the notion of a bifurcation between the 'ought' and the 'is,' between value and fact, between the normative and the descriptive. Thus Mr. D. C. Williams says that some moralists have thought it appropriate to chastise as the na-

turalistic fallacy the attempt to derive the Ought from the Is.[6] We may begin, then, by considering this bifurcation, emphasis on which, by Sidgwick, Sorley, and others, came largely as a reaction to the procedures of Mill and Spencer. Hume affirms the bifurcation in his *Treatise*: "I cannot forbear adding to these reasonings an observation, which may, perhaps, be found of some importance. In every system of morality which I have hitherto met with, I have always remarked, that the author proceeds for some time in the ordinary way of reasoning, and establishes the being of a God, or makes observations concerning human affairs; when of a sudden I am surprised to find, that instead of the usual copulations of propositions, *is*, and *is not*, I meet with no proposition that is not connected with an *ought*, or an *ought not*. This change is imperceptible; but is, however, of the last consequence. For as this *ought*, or *ought not*, expresses some new relation or affirmation, it is necessary that it should be observed and explained; and at the same time that a reason should be given, for what seems altogether inconceivable, how this new relation can be a deduction from others, which are entirely different from it. But as authors do not commonly use this precaution, I shall presume to recommend it to the readers; and am persuaded, that this small attention would subvert all the vulgar systems of morality, and let us see that the distinction of vice and virtue is not founded merely on the relations of objects, nor is perceived by reason."[7]

Needless to say, the intuitionists *have* found this observation of some importance.[8] They agree with Hume that it subverts all the vulgar systems of morality, though, of course, they deny that it lets us see that the distinction of virtue and vice is

---

[4] M. E. Clarke, "Cognition and Affection in the Experience of Value," *Journal of Philosophy*, 1938.
[5] *Principia Ethica*, pp. 73, 77.

[6] "Ethics as Pure Postulate," *Philosophical Review*, 1933. See also T. Whittaker, *The Theory of Abstract Ethics*, pp. 19 f.
[7] Book III, part ii, section i.
[8] See J. Laird, *A Study in Moral Theory*, pp. 16 f.; Whittaker, *op. cit.*, p. 19.

not founded on the relations of objects, nor is perceived by reason. In fact, they hold that a small attention to it subverts Hume's own system also, since this gives naturalistic definitions of virtue and vice and of good and evil.[9]

Hume's point is that ethical conclusions cannot be drawn validly from premises which are non-ethical. But when the intuitionists affirm the bifurcation of the 'ought' and the 'is,' they mean more than that ethical propositions cannot be deduced from non-ethical ones. For this difficulty in the vulgar systems of morality could be remedied, as we shall see, by the introduction of definitions of ethical notions in non-ethical terms. They mean, further, that such definitions of ethical notions in non-ethical terms are impossible. "The essential point," says Mr. Laird, "is the irreducibility of values to non-values."[10] But they mean still more. Yellow and pleasantness are, according to Mr. Moore, indefinable in non-ethical terms, but they are natural qualities and belong on the 'is' side of the fence. Ethical properties, however, are not, for him, mere indefinable natural qualities, descriptive or expository. They are properties of a different *kind*—non-descriptive or non-natural.[11] The intuitionist bifurcation consists of three statements:—

(1) Ethical propositions are not deducible from non-ethical ones.[12]
(2) Ethical characteristics are not definable in terms of non-ethical ones.
(3) Ethical characteristics are different in kind from non-ethical ones.

Really it consists of but one statement, namely, (3) since (3) entails (2) and (2) entails (1). It does not involve saying that any ethical characteristics are absolutely indefinable. That is another question, although this is not always noticed.

[9] See C. D. Broad, *Five Types of Ethical Theory*, ch. iv.
[10] *A Study in Moral Theory*, p. 94 n.
[11] See his *Philosophical Studies*, pp. 259, 273 f.
[12] See J. Laird, *op. cit.*, p. 318. Also pp. 12 ff.

What, now, has the naturalistic fallacy to do with the bifurcation of the 'ought' and the 'is'? To begin with, the connexion is this: many naturalistic and metaphysical moralists proceed as if ethical conclusions can be deduced from premises all of which are non-ethical, the classical examples being Mill and Spencer. That is, they violate (1). This procedure has lately been referred to as the "factualist fallacy" by Mr. Wheelwright and as the "valuational fallacy" by Mr. Wood.[13] Mr. Moore sometimes seems to identify it with the naturalistic fallacy, but in the main he holds only that it involves, implies, or rests upon this fallacy.[14] We may now consider the charge that the procedure in question is or involves a fallacy.

It may be noticed at once that, even if the deduction of ethical conclusions from non-ethical premises is in no way a fallacy, Mill certainly did commit a fallacy in drawing an analogy between visibility and desirability in his argument for hedonism; and perhaps his committing *this* fallacy, which, as Mr. Broad has said, we all learn about at our mothers' knees, is chiefly responsible for the notion of a naturalistic *fallacy*. But is it a fallacy to deduce ethical conclusions from non-ethical premises? Consider the Epicurean argument for hedonism which Mill so unwisely sought to embellish: pleasure is good, since it is sought by all men. Here an ethical conclusion is being derived from a non-ethical premise. And, indeed, the argument, taken strictly as it stands, *is* fallacious. But it is not fallacious because an *ethical* term occurs in the conclusion which does not occur in the premise. It is fallacious because any argument of the form "A is B, therefore A is C" is invalid, if taken strictly as it stands. For example, it is invalid to argue that

[13] P. E. Wheelwright, *A Critical Introduction to Ethics*, pp. 40–51, 91 f.; L. Wood, "Cognition and Moral Value," *Journal of Philosophy*, 1937, p. 237.
[14] See *Principia Ethica*, pp. 114, 57, 43, 49. Whittaker identifies it with the naturalistic fallacy and regards it as a "logical" fallacy, *op. cit.*, pp. 19 f.

Croesus is rich because he is wealthy. Such arguments are, however, not intended to be taken strictly as they stand. They are enthymemes and contain a suppressed premise. And, when this suppressed premise is made explicit, they are valid and involve no logical fallacy.[15] Thus the Epicurean inference from psychological to ethical hedonism is valid when the suppressed premise is added to the effect that what is sought by all men is good. Then the only question left is whether the premises are true.

It is clear, then, that the naturalistic fallacy is not a logical fallacy, since it may be involved even when the argument is valid. How does the naturalistic fallacy enter such "mixed ethical arguments" [16] as that of the Epicureans? Whether it does or not depends on the nature of the suppressed premise. This may be either an induction, an intuition, a deduction from a "pure ethical argument," a definition, or a proposition which is true by definition. If it is one of the first three, then the naturalistic fallacy does not enter at all. In fact, the argument does not then involve violating (1), since one of its premises will be ethical. But if the premise to be supplied is a definition or a proposition which is true by definition, as it probably was for the Epicureans, then the argument, while still valid, involves the naturalistic fallacy, and will run as follows:—

(a) Pleasure is sought by all men.
(b) What is sought by all men is good (definition).
(c) Therefore, pleasure is good.

Now I am not greatly interested in deciding whether the argument as here set up violates (1). If it does not, then no 'mixed ethical argument' actually commits any factualist or valuational fallacy, except when it is unfairly taken as complete in its enthy-

mematic form. If it does, then a valid argument may involve the deduction of an ethical conclusion from non-ethical premises and the factualist or valuational fallacy is not really a fallacy. The question depends on whether or not (b) and (c) are to be regarded as ethical propositions. Mr. Moore refuses so to regard them, contending that, by hypothesis, (b) is analytic or tautologous, and that (c) is psychological, since it really says only that pleasure is sought by all men.[17] But to say that (b) is analytic and not ethical and that (c) is not ethical but psychological is to prejudge the question whether 'good' can be defined; for the Epicureans would contend precisely that if their definition is correct then (b) is ethical but analytic and (c) ethical though psychological. Thus, unless the question of the definability of goodness is to be begged, (b) and (c) must be regarded as ethical, in which case our argument does not violate (1). However, suppose, if it be not nonsense, that (b) is non-ethical and (c) ethical, then the argument will violate (1), but it will still obey all of the canons of logic, and it is only confusing to talk of a 'valuational logic' whose basic rule is that an evaluative conclusion cannot be deduced from non-evaluative premises.[18]

For the only way in which either the intuitionists or postulationists like Mr. Wood can cast doubt upon the conclusion of the argument of the Epicureans (or upon the conclusion of any parallel argument) is to attack the premises, in particular (b). Now, according to Mr. Moore, it is due to the presence of (b) that the argument involves the naturalistic fallacy. (b) involves the identification of goodness with 'being sought by all men,' and to make this or any other such identification is to commit the naturalistic fallacy. The naturalistic fallacy is not the procedure of violating (1). It is the procedure, implied in many mixed ethi-

---

[15] See *ibid.*, pp. 50, 139; Wheelwright, *loc. cit.*
[16] See C. D. Broad, *The Mind and Its Place in Nature*, pp. 488 f.; Laird, *loc. cit.*

[17] See *op. cit.*, pp. 11 f.; 19, 38, 73, 139.
[18] See L. Wood, *loc. cit.*

cal arguments and explicitly carried out apart from such arguments by many moralists, of defining such characteristics as goodness or of substituting some other characteristic for them. To quote some passages from *Principia Ethica*:—

(*a*) " . . . far too many philosophers have thought that when they named those other properties [belonging to all things which are good] they were actually defining good; that these properties, in fact, were simply not 'other,' but absolutely and entirely the same with goodness. This view I propose to call the 'naturalistic fallacy.' . . ."[19]

(*b*) "I have thus appropriated the name Naturalism to a particular method of approaching Ethics. . . . This method consists in substituting for 'good' some one property of a natural object or of a collection of natural objects. . . ."[20]

(*c*) " . . . the naturalistic fallacy [is] the fallacy which consists in identifying the simple notion which we mean by 'good' with some other notion."[21]

Thus, to identify 'better' and 'more evolved,' 'good' and 'desired,' etc., is to commit the naturalistic fallacy.[22] But just why is such a procedure fallacious or erroneous? And is it a fallacy only when applied to good? We must now study Section 12 of *Principia Ethica*. Here Mr. Moore makes some interesting statements:—

" . . . if anybody tried to define pleasure for us as being any other natural object; if anybody were to say, for instance, that pleasure *means* the sensation of red. . . . Well, that would be the same fallacy which I have called the naturalistic fallacy. . . . I should not indeed call that a naturalistic fallacy, although it is the same fallacy as I have called naturalistic with reference to Ethics. . . . When a man confuses two natural objects with one another, defining

the one by the other . . . then there is no reason to call the fallacy naturalistic. But if he confuses 'good,' which is not . . . a natural object, with any natural object whatever, then there is a reason for calling that a naturalistic fallacy. . . ."[23]

Here Mr. Moore should have added that, when one confuses 'good,' which is not a metaphysical object or quality, with any metaphysical object or quality, as metaphysical moralists do, according to him, then the fallacy should be called the metaphysical fallacy. Instead he calls it a naturalistic fallacy in this case too, though he recognises that the case is different since metaphysical properties are non-natural[24]—a procedure which has misled many readers of *Principia Ethica*. For example, it has led Mr. Broad to speak of "theological naturalism."[25]

To resume: "Even if [goodness] were a natural object, that would not alter the nature of the fallacy nor diminish its importance one whit."[26]

From these passages it is clear that the fallaciousness of the procedure which Mr. Moore calls the naturalistic fallacy is not due to the fact that it is applied to good or to an ethical or non-natural characteristic. When Mr. R. B. Perry defines 'good' as 'being an object of interest' the trouble is not merely that he is defining *good*. Nor is the trouble that he is defining an *ethical* characteristic in terms of *non-ethical* ones. Nor is the trouble that he is regarding a *non-natural* characteristic as a *natural* one. The trouble is more generic than that. For clarity's sake I shall speak of the definist fallacy as the generic fallacy which underlies the naturalistic fallacy. The naturalistic fallacy will then, by the above passages, be a species or form of the definist fallacy, as would the metaphysical fallacy if Mr. Moore had given that a separate name.[27]

---

[19] p. 10.
[20] p. 40.
[21] p. 58, cf. pp. xiii, 73.
[22] *Cf.* pp. 49, 53, 108, 139.

[23] p. 13.
[24] See pp. 38–40, 110–112.
[25] *Five Types of Ethical Theory*, p. 259.
[26] p. 14.
[27] As Whittaker has, *loc. cit.*

That is, the naturalistic fallacy, as illustrated by Mr. Perry's procedure, is a fallacy, not because it is naturalistic or confuses a non-natural quality with a natural one, but solely becase it involves the definist fallacy. We may, then, confine our attention entirely to an understanding and evalution of the definist fallacy.

To judge by the passages I have just quoted, the definist fallacy is the process of confusing or identifying two properties, of defining one property by another, or of substituting one property for another. Furthermore, the fallacy is always simply that two properties are being treated as one, and it is irrelevant, if it be the case, that one of them is natural or nonethical and the other non-natural or ethical. One may commit the definist fallacy without infringing on the bifurcation of the ethical and non-ethical, as when one identifies pleasantness and redness or rightness and goodness. But even when one infringes on that bifurcation in committing the definist fallacy, as when one identifies goodness and pleasantness or goodness and satisfaction, then the *mistake* is still not that the bifurcation is being infringed on, but only that two properties are being treated as one. Hence, on the present interpretation, the definist *fallacy* does not, in any of its forms, consist in violating (3), and has no essential connexion with the bifurcation of the 'ought' and the 'is.'

This formulation of the definist fallacy explains or reflects the motto of *Principia Ethica,* borrowed from Bishop Butler: "Everything is what it is, and not another thing." It follows from this motto that goodness is what it is and not another thing. It follows that views which try to identify it with something else are making a mistake of an elementary sort. For it *is* a mistake to confuse or identify two properties. If the properties really are two, then they simply are not identical. But do those who define ethical notions in non-ethical terms make this mistake? They will reply

to Mr. Moore that they are not identifying two properties; what they are saying is that two words or sets of words stand for or mean one and the same property. Mr. Moore was being, in part, misled by the material mode of speech, as Mr. Carnap calls it, in such sentences as "Goodness is pleasantness," "Knowledge is true belief," etc. When one says instead, "The word 'good' and the word 'pleasant' mean the same thing," etc., it is clear that one is not identifying two things. But Mr. Moore kept himself from seeing this by his disclaimer that he was interested in any statement about the use of words.[28]

The definist fallacy, then, as we have stated it, does not rule out any naturalistic or metaphysical definitions of ethical terms. Goodness is not identifiable with any 'other' characteristic (if it is a characteristic at all). But the question is: *which* characteristics are other than goodness, which names stand for characteristics other than goodness? And it is begging the question of the definability of goodness to say out of hand that Mr. Perry, for instance, is identifying goodness with something else. The point is that goodness is what it is, even if it is definable. That is why Mr. Perry can take as the motto of his naturalistic *Moral Economy* another sentence from Bishop Butler: "Things and actions are what they are, and the consequences of them will be what they will be; why then should we desire to be deceived?" The motto of *Principia Ethica* is a tautology, and should be expanded as follows: Everything is what it is, and not another thing, unless it is another thing, and even then it is what it is.

On the other hand, if Mr. Moore's motto (or the definist fallacy) rules out any definitions, for example of 'good,' then it rules out all definitions of any term whatever. To be effective at all, it must be understood to mean, "Every term means what it means, and not what is meant by any

[28] See *op. cit.,* pp. 6, 8, 12.

other term." Mr. Moore seems implicitly to understand his motto in this way in Section 13, for he proceeds as if 'good' has no meaning, if it has no unique meaning. If the motto be taken this way, it will follow that 'good' is an indefinable term, since no synonyms can be found. But it will also follow that no term is definable. And then the method of analysis is as useless as an English butcher in a world without sheep.

Perhaps we have misinterpreted the definist fallacy. And, indeed, some of the passages which I quoted earlier in this paper seem to imply that the definist fallacy is just the error of defining an indefinable characteristic. On this interpretation, again, the definist fallacy has, in all of its forms, no essential connexion with the bifurcation of the ethical and the non-ethical. Again, one may commit the definist fallacy without violating that bifurcation, as when one defines pleasantness in terms of redness or goodness in terms of rightness (granted Mr. Moore's belief that pleasantness and goodness are indefinable). But even when one infringes on that bifurcation and defines goodness in terms of desire, the *mistake* is not that one is infringing on the bifurcation by violating (3), but only that one is defining an indefinable characteristic. This is possible because the proposition that goodness is indefinable is logically independent of the proposition that goodness is non-natural: as is shown by the fact that a characteristic may be indefinable and yet natural, as yellowness is; or non-natural and yet definable, as rightness is (granted Mr. Moore's views about yellowness and rightness).

Consider the definist fallacy as we have just stated it. It is, of course, an error to define an indefinable quality. But the question, again, is: which qualities are indefinable? It is begging the question in favour of intuitionism to say in advance that the quality goodness is indefinable and that, therefore, all naturalists commit the definist fallacy. One must know that goodness is indefinable before one can argue that the de-

finist fallacy *is* a fallacy. Then, however, the definist fallacy can enter only at the end of the controversy between intuitionism and definism, and cannot be used as a weapon in the controversy.

The definist fallacy may be stated in such a way as to involve the bifurcation between the 'ought' and the 'is.'[29] It would then be committed by anyone who offered a definition of any ethical characteristic in terms of non-ethical ones. The trouble with such a definition, on this interpretation, would be that an *ethical* characteristic is being reduced to a *non-ethical* one, a *non-natural* one to a *natural* one. That is, the definition would be ruled out by the fact that the characteristic being defined is ethical or non-natural and therefore cannot be defined in non-ethical or natural terms. But on this interpretation, too, there is danger of a *petitio* in the intuitionist argumentation. To assume that the ethical characteristic is exclusively ethical is to beg precisely the question which is at issue when the definition is offered. Thus, again, one must know that the characteristic is non-natural and indefinable in natural terms before one can say that the definists are making a mistake.

Mr. Moore, McTaggart, and others formulate the naturalistic fallacy sometimes in a way somewhat different from any of those yet discussed. They say that the definists are confusing a universal synthetic proposition about *the good* with a definition of *goodness*.[30] Mr. Abraham calls this the "fallacy of misconstrued proposition."[31] Here again the difficulty is that, while it is true that it is an error to construe a universal synthetic proposition as a definition, it is a *petitio* for the intuitionists to say that what the definist is taking for a definition is really a universal synthetic proposition.[32]

---

[29] See J. Wisdom, *Mind*, 1931, p. 213, note 1.
[30] See *Principia Ethica*, pp. 10, 16, 38; *The Nature of Existence*, vol. ii, p. 398.
[31] Leo Abraham, "The Logic of Intuitionism," *International Journal of Ethics*, 1933.
[32] As Mr. Abraham points out, *loc. cit.*

At last, however, the issue between the intuitionists and the definists (naturalistic or metaphysical) is becoming clearer. The definists are all holding that certain propositions involving ethical terms are analytic, tautologous, or true by definition, e.g., Mr. Perry so regards the statement, "All objects of desire are good." The intuitionists hold that such statements are synthetic. What underlies this difference of opinion is that the intuitionists claim to have at least a dim awareness of a simple unique quality or relation of goodness or rightness which appears in the region which our ethical terms roughly indicate, whereas the definists claim to have no awareness of any such quality or relation in that region, which is different from all other qualities and relations which belong to the same context but are designated by words other than 'good' and 'right' and their obvious synonyms.[33] The definists are in all honesty claiming to find but one characteristic where the intuitionists claim to find two, as Mr. Perry claims to find only the property of being desired where Mr. Moore claims to find both it and the property of being good. The issue, then, is one of inspection or intuition, and concerns the awareness or discernment of qualities and relations.[34] That is why it cannot be decided by the use of the notion of a fallacy.

If the definists may be taken at their word, then they are not actually confusing two characteristics with each other, nor defining an indefinable characteristic, nor confusing definitions and universal synthetic propositions—in short they are not committing the naturalistic or definist fallacy in any of the interpretations given above. Then the only fallacy which they commit—the real naturalistic or definist fallacy—is the failure to descry the qualities and relations which are central to morality. But this is neither a logical fallacy nor a logical confusion. It is not even, properly speaking, an error. It is rather a kind of blindness, analogous to colour-blindness. Even this moral blindness can be ascribed to the definists only if they are correct in their claim to have no awareness of any unique ethical characteristics and if the intuitionists are correct in affirming the existence of such characteristics, but certainly to call it a 'fallacy,' even in a loose sense, is both unamiable and profitless.

On the other hand, of course, if there are not such characteristics in the objects to which we attach ethical predicates, then the intuitionists, if we may take them at their word, are suffering from a corresponding moral hallucination. Definists might then call this the intuitionistic or moralistic fallacy, except that it is no more a 'fallacy' than is the blindness just described. Anyway, they do not believe the claim of the intuitionists to be aware of unique ethical characteristics, and consequently do not attribute to them this hallucination. Instead, they simply deny that the intuitionists really do find such unique qualities or relations, and then they try to find some plausible way of accounting for the fact that very respectable and trustworthy people think they find them.[35] Thus they charge the intuitionists with verbalism, hypostatisation, and the like. But this half of the story does not concern us now.

What concerns us more is the fact that the intuitionists do not credit the claim of the definists either. They would be much disturbed, if they really thought that their opponents were morally blind, for they do not hold that we must be regenerated by grace before we can have moral insight, and they share the common feeling that morality is something democratic even though not all men are good. Thus they hold that "we are all aware" of certain unique characteristics when we use the terms 'good,' 'right,' etc., only due to a lack

[33] See R. B. Perry, *General Theory of Value*, p. 30; cf. *Journal of Philosophy*, 1931, p. 520.
[34] See H. Osborne, *Foundation of the Philosophy of Value*, pp. 15, 19, 70.

[35] *Cf.* R. B. Perry, *Journal of Philosophy*, 1931, pp. 520 ff.

of analytic clearness of mind, abetted perhaps by a philosophical prejudice, we may not be aware at all that they are different from other characteristics of which we are also aware.[36] Now, I have been arguing that the intuitionists cannot charge the definists with committing any fallacy unless and until they have shown that we are all, the definists included, aware of the disputed unique characteristics. If, however, they were to show this, then, at least at the end of the controversy, they could accuse the definists of the error of confusing two characteristics, or of the error of defining an indefinable one, and these errors might, since the term is somewhat loose in its habits, be called 'fallacies,' though they are not logical fallacies in the sense in which an invalid argument is. The fallacy of misconstrued proposition depends on the error of confusing two characteristics, and hence could also on our present supposition, be ascribed to the definists, but it is not really a *logical* confusion,[37] since it does not actually involve being confused about the difference between a proposition and a definition.

Only it is difficult to see how the intuitionists can prove that the definists are at least vaguely aware of the requisite unique characteristics.[38] The question must surely be left to the inspection or intuition of the definists themselves, aided by whatever suggestions the intuitionists may have to make. If so, we must credit the verdict of their inspection, especially of those among them who have read the writings of the

intuitionists reflectively, and, then, as we have seen, the most they can be charged with is moral blindness.

Besides trying to discover just what is meant by the naturalistic fallacy, I have tried to show that the notion that a logical or quasi-logical fallacy is committed by the definists only confuses the issue between the intuitionists and the definists (and the issue between the latter and the emotists or postulationists), and misrepresents the way in which the issue is to be settled. No logical fallacy need appear anywhere in the procedure of the definists. Even fallacies in any less accurate sense cannot be implemented to decide the case against the definists; at best they can be ascribed to the definists only after the issue has been decided against them on independent grounds. But the only defect which can be attributed to the definists, *if* the intuitionists are right in affirming the existence of unique indefinable ethical characteristics, is a peculiar moral blindness, which is not a fallacy even in the looser sense. The issue in question must be decided by whatever method we may find satisfactory for determining whether or not a word stands for a characteristic at all, and, if it does, whether or not it stands for a unique characteristic. What method is to be employed is, perhaps, in one form or another, the basic problem of contemporary philosophy, but no generally satisfactory solution of the problem has yet been reached. I shall venture to say only this: it does seem to me that the issue is not to be decided against the intuitionists by the application *ab extra* to ethical judgments of any empirical or ontological meaning dictum.[39]

---

[36] *Principia Ethica*, pp. 17, 38, 59, 61.

[37] But see H. Osborne, *op cit.*, pp. 18 f.

[38] For a brief discussion of their arguments, see *ibid.*, p. 67; L. Abraham, *op. cit.* I think they are all inconclusive, but cannot show this here.

[39] See *Principia Ethica*, pp. 124 f., 140.

How to Derive "Ought" from "Is"[1]

JOHN R. SEARLE

I

It is often said that one cannot derive an "ought" from an "is." This thesis, which comes from a famous passage in Hume's *Treatise*, while not as clear as it might be, is at least clear in broad outline: there is a class of statements of fact which is logically distinct from a class of statements of value. No set of statements of fact by themselves entails any statement of value. Put in more contemporary terminology, no set of *descriptive* statements can entail an *evaluative* statement without the addition of at least one evaluative premise. To believe otherwise is to commit what has been called the naturalistic fallacy.

I shall attempt to demonstrate a counterexample to this thesis.[2] It is not of course to be supposed that a single counterexample can refute a philosophical thesis, but in the present instance if we can present a plausible counterexample and can in addition give some account or explanation of how and why it is a counterexample,

and if we can further offer a theory to back up our counterexample—a theory which will generate an indefinite number of counterexamples—we may at the very least cast considerable light on the original thesis; and possibly, if we can do all these things, we may even incline ourselves to the view that the scope of that thesis was more restricted than we had originally supposed. A counterexample must proceed by taking a statement or statements which any proponent of the thesis would grant were purely factual or "descriptive" (they need not actually contain the word "is") and show how they are logically related to a statement which a proponent of the thesis would regard as clearly "evaluative." (In the present instance it will contain an "ought".)[3]

Consider the following series of statements:

(1) Jones uttered the words "I hereby promise to pay you, Smith, five dollars."

(2) Jones promised to pay Smith five dollars.

(3) Jones placed himself under

Reprinted from *The Philosophical Review*, 73, January 1964, by permission of the author and *The Philosophical Review*.

[1] Earlier versions of this paper were read before the Stanford Philosophy Colloquium and the Pacific Division of the American Philosophical Association. I am indebted to many people for helpful comments and criticisms, especially Hans Herzberger, Arnold Kaufmann, Benson Mates, A. I. Melden, and Dagmar Searle.

[2] In its modern version. I shall not be concerned with Hume's treatment of the problem.

[3] If this enterprise succeeds, we shall have bridged the gap between "evaluative" and "descriptive" and consequently have demonstrated a weakness in this very terminology. At present, however, my strategy is to play along with the terminology, pretending that the notions of evaluative and descriptive are fairly clear. At the end of the paper I shall state in what respects I think they embody a muddle.

(undertook) an obligation to pay Smith five dollars.

(4) Jones is under an obligation to pay Smith five dollars.

(5) Jones ought to pay Smith five dollars.

I shall argue concerning this list that the relation between any statement and its successor, while not in every case one of "entailment," is nonetheless not just a contingent relation; and the additional statements necessary to make the relationship one of entailment do not need to involve any evaluative statements, moral principles, or anything of the sort.

Let us begin. How is (1) related to (2)? In certain circumstances, uttering the words in quotation marks in (1) is the act of making a promise. And it is a part of or a consequence of the meaning of the words in (1) that in those circumstances uttering them is promising. "I hereby promise" is a paradigm device in English for performing the act described in (2), promising.

Let us state this fact about English usage in the form of an extra premise:

(1a) Under certain conditions C anyone who utters the words (sentence) "I hereby promise to pay you, Smith, five dollars" promises to pay Smith five dollars.

What sorts of things are involved under the rubric "conditions C"? What is involved will be all those conditions, those states of affairs, which are necessary and sufficient conditions for the utterance of the words (sentence) to constitute the successful performance of the act of promising. The conditions will include such things as that the speaker is in the presence of the hearer Smith, they are both conscious, both speakers of English, speaking seriously. The speaker knows what he is doing, is not under the influence of drugs, not hypnotized or acting in a play, not telling a joke or reporting an event, and so forth. This list will no doubt be somewhat indefinite because the boundaries of the concept of a promise, like the boundaries of most con-

cepts in a natural language, are a bit loose.[4] But one thing is clear; however loose the boundaries may be, and however difficult it may be to decide marginal cases, the conditions under which a man who utters "I hereby promise" can correctly be said to have made a promise are straightforwardly empirical conditions.

So let us add as an extra premise the empirical assumption that these conditions obtain.

(1b) Conditions C obtain.

From (1), (1a), and (1b) we derive (2). The argument is of the form: If C then (if U then P): C for conditions, U for utterance, P for promise. Adding the premises U and C to this hypothetical we derive (2). And as far as I can see, no moral premises are lurking in the logical woodpile. More needs to be said about the relation of (1) to (2), but I reserve that for later.

What is the relation between (2) and (3)? I take it that promising is, by definition, an act of placing oneself under an obligation. No analysis of the concept of promising will be complete which does not include the feature of the promiser placing himself under or undertaking or accepting or recognizing an obligation to the promisee, to perform some future course of action, normally for the benefit of the promisee. One may be tempted to think that promising can be analyzed in terms of creating expectations in one's hearers, or some such, but a little reflection will show that the crucial distinction between statements of intention on the one hand and promises on the other lies in the nature and degree of commitment or obligation undertaken in promising.

I am therefore inclined to say that (2) entails (3) straight off, but I can have no

[4] In addition the concept of a promise is a member of a class of concepts which suffer from looseness of a peculiar kind, viz. defeasibility. Cf H. L. A. Hart, "The Ascription of Responsibility and Rights," *Logic and Language*, First Series, ed. by A. Flew (Oxford, 1951).

objection if anyone wishes to add—for the purpose of formal neatness— the tautological premise:

(2a) All promises are acts of placing oneself under (undertaking) an obligation to do the thing promised.

How is (3) related to (4)? If one has placed oneself under an obligation, then, other things being equal, one is under an obligation. That I take it also is a tautology. Of course it is possible for all sorts of things to happen which will release one from obligations one has undertaken and hence the need for the *ceteris paribus* rider. To get an entailment between (3) and (4) we therefore need a qualifying statement to the effect that:

(3a) Other things are equal.

Formalists, as in the move from (2) to (3), may wish to add the tautological premise:

(3b) All those who place themselves under an obligation are, other things being equal, under an obligation.

The move from (3) to (4) is thus of the same form as the move from (1) to (2): If *E* then (if *PUO* then *UO*): *E* for other things are equal, *PUO* for place under obligation and *UO* for under obligation. Adding the two premises *E* and *PUO* we derive *UO*.

Is (3a), the *ceteris paribus* clause, a concealed evaluative premise? It certainly looks as if it might be, especially in the formulation I have given it, but I think we can show that, though questions about whether other things are equal frequently involve evaluative considerations, it is not logically necessary that they should in every case. I shall postpone discussion of this until after the next step.

What is the relation between (4) and (5)? Analogous to the tautology which explicates the relation of (3) and (4) there is here the tautology that, other things being equal, one ought to do what one is under an obligation to do. And here, just as

in the previous case, we need some premise of the form:

(4a) Other things are equal.

We need the *ceteris paribus* clause to eliminate the possibility that something extraneous to the relation of "obligation" to "ought" might interfere.[5] Here, as in the previous two steps, we eliminate the appearance of enthymeme by pointing out that the apparently suppressed premise is tautological and hence, though formally neat, it is redundant. If, however, we wish to state it formally, this argument is of the same form as the move from (3) to (4): If *E* then (if *UO* then *O*); *E* for other things are equal, *UO* for under obligation, *O* for ought. Adding the premises *E* and *UO* we derive *O*.

Now a word about the phrase "other things being equal" and how it functions in my attempted derivation. This topic and the closely related topic of defeasibility are extremely difficult and I shall not try to do more than justify my claim that the satisfaction of the condition does not necessarily involve anything evaluative. The force of the expression "other things being equal" in the present instance is roughly this. Unless we have some reason (that is, unless we are actually prepared to give some reason) for supposing the obligation is void (step 4) or the agent ought not to keep the promise (step 5), then the obligation holds and he ought to keep the promise. It is not part of the force of the phrase "other things being equal" that in order to satisfy it we need to establish a universal negative proposition to the effect that no reason could ever be given by anyone for

[5] The *ceteris paribus* clause in this step excludes somewhat different sorts of cases from those excluded in the previous step. In general we say, "He undertook an obligation, but nevertheless he is not (now) under an obligation" when the obligation has been *removed*, e.g., if the promisee says, "I release you from your obligation." But we say, "He is under an obligation, but nonetheless ought not to fulfill it" in cases where the obligation is *overriden* by some other considerations, e.g., a prior obligation.

supposing the agent is not under an obligation or ought not to keep the promise. That would be impossible and would render the phrase useless. It is sufficient to satisfy the condition that no reason to the contrary can in fact be given.

If a reason is given for supposing the obligation is void or that the promiser ought not to keep a promise, then characteristically a situation calling for an evaluation arises. Suppose, for example, we consider a promised act wrong, but we grant that the promiser did undertake an obligation. Ought he to keep the promise? There is no established procedure for objectively deciding such cases in advance, and an evaluation (if that is really the right word) is in order. But unless we have some reason to the contrary, the *ceteris paribus* condition is satisfied, no evaluation is necessary, and the question whether he ought to do it is settled by saying "he promised." It is always an open possibility that we may have to make an evaluation in order to derive "he ought" from "he promised," for we may have to evaluate a counterargument. But an evaluation is not logically necessary in every case, for there may as a matter of fact be no counterarguments. I am therefore inclined to think that there is nothing necessarily evaluative about the *ceteris paribus* condition, even though deciding whether it is satisfied will frequently involve evaluations.

But suppose I am wrong about this: would that salvage the belief in an unbridgeable logical gulf between "is" and "ought"? I think not, for we can always rewrite my steps (4) and (5) so that they include the *ceteris paribus* clause as part of the conclusion. Thus from our premises we would then have derived "Other things being equal Jones ought to pay Smith five dollars," and that would still be sufficient to refute the tradition, for we would still have shown a relation of entailment between descriptive and evaluative statements. It was not the fact that extenuating circumstances can void obligations that drove phi-

losophers to the naturalistic fallacy; it was rather a theory of language, as we shall see later on.

We have thus derived (in as strict a sense of "derive" as natural languages will admit of) an "ought" from an "is." And the extra premises which were needed to make the derivation work were in no cause moral or evaluative in nature. They consisted of empirical assumptions, tautologies, and descriptions of word usage. It must be pointed out also that the "ought" is a "categorical" not a "hypothetical" ought. (5) does not say that Jones ought to pay up if he wants such and such. It says he ought to pay up, period. Note also that the steps of the derivation are carried on in the third person. We are not concluding "I ought" from "I said 'I promise,'" but "he ought" from "he said 'I promise.'"

The proof unfolds the connection between the utterance of certain words and the speech act of promising and then in turn unfolds promising into obligation and moves from obligation to "ought." The step from (1) to (2) is radically different from the others and requires special comment. In (1) we construe "I hereby promise . . ." as an English phrase having a certain meaning. It is a consequence of that meaning that the utterance of that phrase under certain conditions is the act of promising. Thus by presenting the quoted expressions in (1) and by describing their use in (1a) we have as it were already invoked the institution of promising. We might have started with an even more groundfloor premise than (1) by saying:

(1b) Jones uttered the phonetic sequence: /ai+hirbai+pramis+təpei+yu+smiθ +faiv+dalərz/

We would then have needed extra empirical premises stating that this phonetic sequence was associated in certain ways with certain meaningful units relative to certain dialects.

The moves from (2) to (5) are relatively easy. We rely on definitional connections between "promise," "obligate," and "ought," and the only problem which arises is that obligations can be overridden or removed in a variety of ways and we need to take account of that fact. We solve our difficulty by adding further premises to the effect that there are no contrary considerations, that other things are equal.

II

In this section I intend to discuss three possible objections to the derivation.

First Objection

Since the first premise is descriptive and the conclusion evaluative, there must be a concealed evaluative premise in the description of the conditions in (1b).

So far, this argument merely begs the question by assuming the logical gulf between descriptive and evaluative which the derivation is designed to challenge. To make the objection stick, the defender of the distinction would have to show how exactly (1b) must contain an evaluative premise and what sort of premise it might be. Uttering certain words in certain conditions just *is* promising and the description of these conditions needs no evaluative element. The essential thing is that in the transition from (1) to (2) we move from the specification of a certain utterance of words to the specification of a certain speech act. The move is achieved because the speech act is a conventional act; and the utterance of the words, according to the conventions, constitutes the performance of just that speech act.

A variant of this first objection is to say: all you have shown is that "promise" is an evaluative, not a descriptive, concept. But this objection again begs the question and in the end will prove disastrous to the original distinction between descriptive and evaluative. For that a man uttered certain words and that these words have the meaning they do are surely objective facts. And if the statement of these two objective facts plus a description of the conditions of the utterance is sufficient to entail the statement (2) which the objector alleges to be an evaluative statement (Jones promised to pay Smith five dollars), then an evaluative conclusion is derived from descriptive premises without even going through steps (3), (4), and (5).

Second Objection

Ultimately the derivation rests on the principle that one ought to keep one's promises and that is a moral principle, hence evaluative.

I don't know whether "one ought to keep one's promises" is a "moral" principle, but whether or not it is, it is also tautological; for it is nothing more than a derivation from the two tautologies:

All promises are (create, are undertakings of, are acceptances of) obligations,

and

One ought to keep (fulfill) one's obligations.

What needs to be explained is why so many philosophers have failed to see the tautological character of this principle. Three things I think have concealed its character from them.

The first is a failure to distinguish external questions about the institution of promising from internal questions asked within the framework of the institution. The questions "Why do we have such an institution as promising?" and "Ought we to have such institutionalized forms of obligation as promising?" are external questions asked about and not within the institution of promising. And the question "Ought one to keep one's promises?" can be confused with or can be taken as (and I think has often been taken as) an external question roughly expressible as "Ought one to accept the institution of promising?"

But taken literally, as an internal question, as a question about promises and not about the institution of promising, the question "Ought one to keep one's promises?" is as empty as the question "Are triangles three-sided?" To recognize something as a promise is to grant that, other things being equal, it ought to be kept.

A second fact which has clouded the issue is this. There are many situations, both real and imaginable, where one ought not to keep a promise, where the obligation to keep a promise is overridden by some further considerations, and it was for this reason that we needed those clumsy *ceteris paribus* clauses in our derivation. But the fact that obligations can be overridden does not show that there were no obligations in the first place. On the contrary. And these original obligations are all that is needed to make the proof work.

Yet a third factor is the following. Many philosophers still fail to realize the full force of saying that "I hereby promise" is a performative expression. In uttering it one performs but does not describe the act of promising. Once promising is seen as a speech act of a kind different from describing, then it is easier to see that one of the features of the act is the undertaking of an obligation. But if one thinks the utterance of "I promise" or "I hereby promise" is a peculiar kind of description—for example, of one's mental state—then the relation between promising and obligation is going to seem very mysterious.

Third Objection

The derivation uses only a factual or inverted-commas sense of the evaluative terms employed. For example, an anthropologist observing the behavior and attitudes of the Anglo-Saxons might well go through these derivations, but nothing evaluative would be included. Thus step (2) is equivalent to "He did what they call promising" and step (5) to "According to

them he ought to pay Smith five dollars." But since all of the steps (2) to (5) are in *oratio obliqua* and hence disguised statements of fact, the fact-value distinction remains unaffected.

This objection fails to damage the derivation, for what it says is only that the steps *can* be reconstrued as in *oratio obliqua*, that we can construe them as a series of external statements, that we can construct a parallel (or at any rate related) proof about reported speech. But what I am arguing is that, taken quite literally, without any *oratio obliqua* additions or interpretations, the derivation is valid. That one can construct a similar argument which would fail to refute the fact-value distinction does not show that this proof fails to refute it. Indeed it is irrelevant.

III

So far I have presented a counterexample to the thesis that one cannot derive an "ought" from an "is" and considered three possible objections to it. Even supposing what I have said so far is true, still one feels a certain uneasiness. One feels there must be some trick involved somewhere. We might state our uneasiness thus: How can my granting a mere fact about a man, such as the fact that he uttered certain words or that he made a promise, commit *me* to the view that *he* ought to do something? I now want briefly to discuss what broader philosophic significance my attempted derivation may have, in such a way as to give us the outlines of an answer to this question.

I shall begin by discussing the grounds for supposing that it cannot be answered at all.

The inclination to accept a rigid distinction between "is" and "ought," between descriptive and evaluative, rests on a certain picture of the way words relate to the world. It is a very attractive picture, so attractive (to me at least) that it is not entirely clear to what extent the mere presentation of counterexamples can challenge it. What is needed is an explanation of how and why this classical empiricist picture fails to deal with such counterexamples. Briefly, the picture is constructed something like this: first we present examples of so-called descriptive statements ("my car goes eighty miles an hour," "Jones is six feet tall," "Smith has brown hair"), and we contrast them with so-called evaluative statements ("my car is a good car," "Jones ought to pay Smith five dollars," "Smith is a nasty man"). Anyone can see that they are different. We articulate the difference by pointing out that for the descriptive statements the question of truth or falsity is objectively decidable, because to know the meaning of the descriptive expressions is to know under what objectively ascertainable conditions the statements which contain them are true or false. But in the case of evaluative statements the situation is quite different. To know the meaning of the evaluative expressions is not by itself sufficient for knowing under what conditions the statements containing them are true or false, because the meaning of the expressions is such that the statements are not capable of objective or factual truth or falsity at all. Any justification a speaker can give of one of his evaluative statements essentially involves some appeal to attitudes he holds, to criteria of assessment he has adopted, or to moral principles by which he has chosen to live and judge other people. Descriptive statements are thus objective, evaluative statements subjective, and the difference is a consequence of the different sorts of terms employed.

The underlying reason for these differences is that evaluative statements perform a completely different job from descriptive statements. Their job is not to describe any features of the world but to express the speaker's emotions, to express his attitudes, to praise or condemn, to laud or insult, to commend, to recom-

mend, to advise, and so forth. Once we see the different jobs the two perform, we see that there must be a logical gulf between them. Evaluative statements must be different from descriptive statements in order to do their job, for if they were objective they could no longer function to evaluate. Put metaphysically, values cannot lie in the world, for if they did they would cease to be values and would just be another part of the world. Put in the formal mode, one cannot define an evaluative word in terms of descriptive words, for if one did, one would no longer be able to use the evaluative word to commend, but only to describe. Put yet another way, any effort to derive an "ought" from an "is" must be a waste of time, for all it could show even if it succeeded would be that the "is" was not a real "is" but only a disguised "ought" or, alternatively, that the "ought" was not a real "ought" but only a disguised "is."

This summary of the traditional empirical view has been very brief, but I hope it conveys something of the power of this picture. In the hands of certain modern authors, especially Hare and Nowell-Smith, the picture attains considerable subtlety and sophistication.

What is wrong with this picture? No doubt many things are wrong with it. In the end I am going to say that one of the things wrong with it is that it fails to give us any coherent account of such notions as commitment, responsibility, and obligation.

In order to work toward this conclusion I can begin by saying that the picture fails to account for the *different types* of "descriptive" statements. Its paradigms of descriptive statements are such utterances as "my car goes eighty miles an hour," "Jones is six feet tall," "Smith has brown hair," and the like. But it is forced by its own rigidity to construe "Jones got married," "Smith made a promise," "Jackson has five dollars," and "Brown hit a home run" as descriptive statements as well. It is so forced, because whether or not someone got married, made a promise, has five dollars, or hit a home run is as much a matter of objective fact as whether he has red hair or brown eyes. Yet the former kind of statement (statements containing "married," "promise," and so forth) seem to be quite different from the simple empirical paradigms of descriptive statements. How are they different? Though both kinds of statements state matters of objective fact, the statements containing words such as "married," "promise," "home run," and "five dollars" state facts whose existence presupposes certain institutions: a man has five dollars, given the institution of money. Take away the institution and all he has is a rectangular bit of paper with green ink on it. A man hits a home run only given the institution of baseball; without the institution he only hits a sphere with a stick. Similarly, a man gets married or makes a promise only within the institutions of marriage and promising. Without them, all he does is utter words or makes gestures. We might characterize such facts as institutional facts, and contrast them with noninstitutional, or brute, facts: that a man has a bit of paper with green ink on it is a brute fact, that he has five dollars is an institutional fact.[6] The classical picture fails to account for the differences between statements of brute fact and statements of institutional fact.

The word "institution" sounds artificial here, so let us ask: what sorts of institutions are these? In order to answer that question I need to distinguish between two different kinds of rules or conventions. Some rules regulate antecedently existing forms of behavior. For example, the rules of polite table behavior regulate eating, but eating exists independently of these rules. Some rules, on the other hand, do not merely regulate but create or define new forms of behavior: the rules of chess, for example, do not merely regulate an antecedently existing activity called playing

chess; they, as it were, create the possibility of or define that activity. The activity of playing chess is constituted by action in accordance with these rules. Chess has no existence apart from these rules. The distinction I am trying to make was foreshadowed by Kant's distinction between regulative and constitutive principles, so let us adopt his terminology and describe our distinction as a distinction between regulative and constitutive rules. Regulative rules regulate activities whose existence is independent of the rules; constitutive rules constitute (and also regulate) forms of activity whose existence is logically dependent on the rules.[7]

Now the institutions that I have been talking about are systems of constitutive rules. The institutions of marriage, money, and promising are like the institutions of baseball or chess in that they are systems of such constitutive rules or conventions. What I have called institutional facts are facts which presuppose such institutions.

Once we recognize the existence of and begin to grasp the nature of such institutional facts, it is but a short step to see that many forms of obligations, commitments, rights, and responsibilities are similarly institutionalized. It is often a matter of fact that one has certain obligations, commitments, rights, and responsibilities, but it is a matter of institutional, not brute, fact. It is one such institutionalized form of obligation, promising, which I invoked above to derive an "ought" from an "is." I started with a brute fact, that a man uttered certain words, and then invoked the institution in such a way as to generate institutional facts by which we arrived at the institutional fact that the man ought to pay another man five dollars. The whole proof rests on an appeal to the constitutive rule that to make a promise is to undertake an obligation.

We are now in a position to see how

<hr>

[6] For a discussion of this distinction see G. E. M. Anscombe, "Brute Facts," *Analysis* (1958).

[7] For a discussion of a related distinction see J. Rawls, "Two Concepts of Rules," *Philosophical Review*, LXIV (1955).

we can generate an indefinite number of such proofs. Consider the following vastly different example. We are in our half of the seventh inning and I have a big lead off second base. The pitcher whirls, fires to the shortstop covering, and I am tagged out a good ten feet down the line. The umpire shouts, "Out!" I, however, being a positivist, hold my ground. The umpire tells me to return to the dugout. I point out to him that you can't derive an "ought" from an "is." No set of descriptive statements describing matters of fact, I say, will entail any evaluative statements to the effect that I should or ought to leave the field. "You just can't get orders or recommendations from facts alone." What is needed is an evaluative major premise. I therefore return to and stay on second base (until I am carried off the field). I think everyone feels my claims here to be preposterous, and preposterous in the sense of logically absurd. Of course you can derive an "ought" from an "is," and though to actually set out the derivation in this case would be vastly more complicated than in the case of promising, it is in principle no different. By undertaking to play baseball I have committed myself to the observation of certain constitutive rules.

We are now also in a position to see that the tautology that one ought to keep one's promises is only one of a class of similar tautologies concerning institutionalized forms of obligation. For example, "one ought not to steal" can be taken as saying that to recognize something as someone else's property neccessarily involves recognizing his right to dispose of it. This is a constitutive rule of the institution of private property.[8] "One ought not to tell lies"

can be taken as saying that to make an assertion necessarily involves undertaking an obligation to speak truthfully. Another constitutive rule. "One ought to pay one's debts" can be construed as saying that to recognize something as a debt is necessarily to recognize an obligation to pay it. It is easy to see how all these principles will generate counterexamples to the thesis that you cannot derive an "ought" from an "is."

My tentative conclusions, then, are as follows:

1. The classical picture fails to account for institutional facts.

2. Institutional facts exist within systems of constitutive rules.

3. Some systems of constitutive rules involve obligations, commitments, and responsibilities.

4. Within those systems we can derive "ought's" from "is's" on the model of the first derivation.

With these conclusions we now return to the question with which I began this section: How can my stating a fact about a man, such as the fact that he made a promise, commit me to a view about what he ought to do? One can begin to answer this question by saying that for me to state such an institutional fact is already to invoke the constitutive rules of the institution. It is those rules that give the word "promise" its meaning. But those rules are such that to commit myself to the view that Jones made a promise involves committing myself to what he ought to do (other things being equal).

If you like, then, we have shown that "promise" is an evaluative word, but since it is also purely descriptive, we have really shown that the whole distinction needs to be re-examined. The alleged distinction be-

---

[8] Proudhon said: "Property is theft." If one tries to take this as an internal remark it makes no sense. It was intended as an external remark attacking and rejecting the institution of private property. It gets its air of paradox and its force by using terms which are internal to the institution in order to attack the institution.

Standing on the deck of some institutions one can tinker with constitutive rules and even throw some other institutions overboard. But could one

throw all institutions overboard (in order perhaps to avoid ever having to derive an "ought" from an "is")? One could not and still engage in those forms of behavior we consider characteristically human. Suppose Proudhon had added (and tried to live by): "Truth is a lie, marriage is infidelity, language is uncommunicative, law is a crime," and so on with every possible institution.

tween descriptive and evaluative statements is really a conflation of at least two distinctions. On the one hand there is a distinction between different kinds of speech acts, one family of speech acts including evaluations, another family including descriptions. This is a distinction between different kinds of illocutionary force.[9] On the other hand there is a distinction between utterances which involve claims objectively decidable as true or false and those which involve claims not objectively decidable, but which are "matters of personal decision" or "matters of opinion." It has been assumed that the former distinc-

[9] See J. L. Austin, *How to Do Things with Words* (Cambridge, Mass., 1962), for an explanation of this notion.

tion is (must be) a special case of the latter, that if something has the illocutionary force of an evaluation, it cannot be entailed by factual premises. Part of the point of my argument is to show that this contention is false, that factual premises can entail evaluative conclusions. If I am right, then the alleged distinction between descriptive and evaluative utterances is useful only as a distinction between two kinds of illocutionary force, describing and evaluating, and it is not even very useful there, since if we are to use these terms strictly, they are only two among hundreds of kinds of illocutionary force; and utterances of sentences of the form (5)—"Jones ought to pay Smith five dollars"—would not characteristically fall in either class.

How Not to Derive "Ought" from "Is"

JAMES THOMSON
JUDITH THOMSON

Two of the steps in Mr. Searle's derivation[1] are from

(3) Jones placed himself under (undertook) an obligation to pay Smith five dollars,

to

(4) Jones is under an obligation to pay Smith five dollars,

and from that to

(5) Jones ought to pay Smith five dollars.

Since Searle says that the two steps are to be understood in the same way, we shall discuss only the latter.

Searle is aware that even if someone is under an obligation to do something, there may yet be overriding reasons why he ought not or need not do it; that is, reasons sufficient to make it false to say that he ought to do it; so that (4) does not by itself entail (5). But he says that (5) does follow from (4) and another premise (4a)—"Other things are equal"—and he argues that this extra premise "need not in-

volve anything evaluative." His line of argument seems to be this. Suppose that Jones is quite definitely under the obligation, and that the question arises for us whether he ought to pay. There may be reason to think that he need not or ought not, but equally there may not; no such reason may be apparent. And unless we are "actually prepared to give some reason" why Jones ought not or need not keep his promise, then "the obligation holds and he ought to keep the promise." So here is one way in which, given (4), the truth of (4a), and thereby of (5), may get settled: the question is settled because no reason against (5) is apparent. But if the truth of (4a) gets settled in this way, then we shall not have had to evaluate any reasons against (5); so (4a) is "not necessarily evaluative."

This argument is put forward as an explanation of the "force" of the phrase "other things are equal." The explanation seems to us incoherent. Searle is vacillating between two interpretations of (4a). The weak interpretation is that other things are equal if we, who are considering Jones's case, see no reason or know of no reason why he ought not or need not pay. But if this is what (4a) comes to, then (4) and (4a) surely do not *entail* (5). That none of

Reprinted from *The Philosophical Review*, 73, October 1964, by permission of the authors and *The Philosophical Review*.

[1] John R. Searle, "How to Derive 'Ought' from 'Is,'" *Philosophical Review*, LXXIII (1964), 43-58.

us sees or knows of a reason just does not entail that there is none.[2]

Searle has said, however, that the reason (4) does not by itself entail (5) is that, given (4), there may all the same be some overriding reason why Jones ought not or need not pay. So one would expect him to say that, given (4), what we require for (5) is that this should not be the case. This suggests another, rather different, interpretation for (4a): that other things are equal only if there is nothing sufficient to make it false that Jones ought to pay. We could call this the strong interpretation of (4a). It seems to us that (4a) must say or by itself entail at least this much if it is, together with (4), to entail (5).

Now although Searle certainly seems to offer the weak interpretation of (4a)—that is, seems to say that the truth of (4a) is settled if no one is actually prepared to offer counterarguments to (5), and thus is settled without the evaluation of any counterarguments—he also says that (4a) is settled when as a matter of fact there *are* no counterarguments. That is not the same thing. He says that to establish (4a) we need not establish a universal negative proposition "to the effect that no reason could ever be given by anyone"; it is sufficient, to establish it, that "no reason to the contrary can in fact be given." But what does this latter mean? It might mean that no one who is considering Jones's case is in fact in a position to give a reason; this would be the weak interpretation again. But it might mean that there just is no such reason to be given. Now plainly it would be an overstrong interpretation of (4a) to say that it is true only if there is no reason at all to think that (5) is false; all you would require is that there be no *conclusive* reason to think (5) false. Therefore we are inclined to think that Searle is not offering this overstrong interpretation. Nev-

ertheless, it could be left open that he is, or that he is here offering only the strong interpretation and just pointing to what is a sufficient, but not necessary, condition of its truth—for if there is no reason at all to think (5) false, then there certainly is no conclusive reason to think (5) false. It does not matter at which of these two interpretations he is hinting here. Either would indeed help his case: it is plausible to say that (5) is entailed by (4) together with "There is no conclusive reason to think it false to say that Jones ought to pay" (or "There is no reason at all to think it false to say that Jones ought to pay"). But in establishing either of these extra premises, we should surely be establishing a universal negative proposition. And are they not evaluative? Are they not anyway as evaluative as (5)?[3]

In short, Searle's reason for saying that (4a) need not be evaluative is that it is true if no one offers any counterarguments; thus we may settle its truth without having to evaluate any counterarguments. But in so far as this fixes the meaning of (4a), it and (4) do not entail (5). Conversely, if (4a) is given a meaning such that it and (4) do entail (5), it is evaluative.

We suppose it obvious that nothing is gained for Searle's position by his device of rewriting (5) as "Other things being equal, Jones ought . . . ." Let us call this (5′). One of two possibilities now applies. Either (a) (5′) is a conditional with the old (4a) as antecedent; but then under the weak interpretation of its antecedent, (5′) is not entailed by (4), and under the strong interpretation of its antecedent, (5′) is ana-

---

[2] Still less is it enough that none of us is "actually prepared to give" a reason. Mrs. Jones may have a reason, and a good one, but may not be, for all kinds of reasons, prepared to give it (in public, out loud).

[3] One of Searle's aims is to show that the terms "evaluative" and "descriptive" "embody a muddle," and that "the whole distinction needs to be reexamined." But (one of?) the means by which he will do this is this: he will "play along with the terminology," and show that there are counterexamples to the thesis that no set of purely descriptive premises can by itself entail an evaluative conclusion. (One might question this strategy, but we shall not stop to do so.) At all events, in this part of his paper, Searle is taking the notion "evaluative" seriously—seriously enough to have been drawn to the weaker interpretation of (4a).

lytic—if the Law of Excluded Middle is—and therefore not evaluative. Or (b) the *ceteris paribus* clause is meant, not as antecedent of a conditional, but as an adverbial clause.[4] But then its sense, and its role in (5'), want some spelling out; since Searle offers nothing in this direction at all, we are inclined to think it is (a) rather than (b) which he has in mind.

The interest in this confusion lies in its diagnosis: we think that Searle has tried to adapt to his own purposes an observation that may well be true, but will not serve them.

We have a ring which looks like gold, weighs what a gold ring of that size would weigh, is hallmarked, was bought from a well-known jeweler. Moreover, there is no reason that we know of to think it is not gold. Then we are (in some sense) *entitled* to take it to be gold, to expose it for sale as such. We are entitled, being aware of these things, to say "I know it is gold." If someone says "But for all you've said, it still may not be gold," we shall want to ask him whether he has any positive ground for suspicion; and if he can only reply that the fact that these things are so does not entail that it is gold, his doubt can be ignored. We are entitled to go on doing and saying what we do unless and until the doubter is actually prepared to give a reason for thinking the ring is not gold.

Again, if Smith has an abscessed tooth,

and is complaining bitterly, and if moreover there is no reason we know of to think he is not in pain, we are (in that same sense) entitled to take him to be in pain. If someone says "But perhaps he isn't really, for these things don't entail pain," that doubt too can be ignored.

It seems to us that it must be this observation—which is more or less familiar, and has been so perhaps since the appearance of Austin's paper on "Other Minds"—which Searle has in mind when he offers the weak interpretation of (4a), "other things are equal." But the observation does not support the point he wishes to make. For the admitted facts about the ring (about Smith)—even where these include that we know of no reason to think the ring is not gold (Smith is not in pain)—do not after all entail that the ring is gold (Smith is in pain). Given that p we may be (in that sense) entitled to take it that (even give others our word that) q—but this will not make it be true to say that p entails q. Indeed, it was the whole point of this observation that in order to be (in this sense) entitled to take it that q we do *not* need to have grounds that entail q.

Searle's confusion, then, arises from his having conflated a question of entailment with a question of entitlement.

As we noted in footnote 3, Searle's aim is not merely to show that "ought" can be derived from "is," but thereby to cast doubt on the is-ought distinction. In Part III of his paper, he says this distinction arose out of a certain theory of language, a theory which (he thinks) allows no place for statements of what he calls "institutional fact." Thus, for example, "He promised" states an institutional fact, and it is a "constitutive rule" of the institution of promising that "to make a promise is to undertake an obligation." And Searle thinks that when we see and properly understand that there are such statements, we shall no longer be puzzled by the question "How can my stating a fact about a man, such as that he made a promise, commit me to a view about what he ought to do?" But in this

---

[4] It is of course an interesting question just what is the force or meaning of a *ceteris paribus* clause. Perhaps one should begin by distinguishing the cases in which it is prefixed to a general observation. ("Other things being equal, a queen is worth more in the end game than two rooks") from cases in which it is prefixed to a particular statement (Searle's "Other things being equal, Jones ought to pay Smith five dollars"). One might comment on the former remark by saying that other things seldom are equal, meaning that the remark is not a very helpful one, but one could not ask, "But *are* other things equal?" One can ask this only with a particular case (application) in mind. It may be that there is the same difficulty about the inference "Other things being equal, an S is a P; x is an S; so, other things being equal, x is a P" as there is about "The probability of an S being a P is N; x is an S; so the probability that x is a P is N."

part of his paper Searle seems quite to have forgotten how he claimed to derive "ought" from "is": for as he had granted, to say

(1) Jones uttered the words "I hereby promise to pay you, Smith, five dollars."

or even to say

(2) Jones promised to pay Smith five dollars.

is not to be logically committed to the view that Jones ought to pay Smith five dollars. So Searle's explanation of why moralists thought that you could not deduce an "ought" from an "is" does not work. It would explain at most a reluctance to pass from (1) or (2) to

(3) Jones placed himself under (undertook) an obligation to pay Smith five dollars.

But many antinaturalists would be relatively uninterested in the difference of sta-

tus between (1) and (3), and most antinaturalists would be completely unperturbed by the relations between them to which Searle points—that is, by the fact that, in certain circumstances, to say certain words is to commit oneself to do this or that. What does interest them is the difference of status between (1) and (5).

Or we could put it this way. Searle has, if you like, brought out that there is not so sharp a distinction in kind between (1) and (3) as might have been thought. But to show a continuity between (1) and (3) is not thereby to have shown a continuity between (1) and (5). There seems to us to be no reason at all for thinking that it was because they thought there was a sharp distinction in kind between (1) and (3) that the antinaturalists supposed there to be a sharp distinction in kind between (1) and (5), and therefore that "ought" is not derivable from "is."

Ethical Judgments

HENRY SIDGWICK

1. In the first chapter I spoke of actions that we judge to be right and what ought to be done as being "reasonable," or "rational," and similarly of ultimate ends as "prescribed by Reason": and I contrasted the motive to action supplied by the recognition of such reasonableness with "non-rational" desires and inclinations. This manner of speaking is employed by writers of different schools, and seems in accordance with the common view and language on the subject. For we commonly think that wrong conduct is essentially irrational, and can be shown to be so by argument; and though we do not conceive that it is by reason alone that men are influenced to act rightly, we still hold that appeals to the reason are an essential part of all moral persuasion, and that part which concerns the moralist or moral philosopher as distinct from the preacher or moral rhetorician. On the other hand it is widely maintained that, as Hume says, "Reason, meaning the judgment of truth and falsehood, can never of itself be any motive to the Will"; and that the motive to action is in all cases some Non-rational Desire, including under this term the impulses of action given by present pleasure and pain. It seems desirable to examine with some care the grounds of this contention before we proceed any further.

Let us begin by defining the issue raised as clearly as possible. Every one, I

Reprinted from *The Methods of Ethics* (Seventh Edition), The Macmillan Co., 1907, pp. 23–38.

suppose, has had experience of what is meant by the conflict of non-rational or irrational desires with reason: most of us e.g. occasionally feel bodily appetite prompting us to indulgences which we judge to be imprudent, and anger prompting us to acts which we disapprove as unjust or unkind. It is when this conflict occurs that the desires are said to be irrational, as impelling us to volitions opposed to our deliberate judgments; sometimes we yield to such seductive impulses, and sometimes not; and it is perhaps when we do *not* yield that the impulsive force of such irrational desires is most definitely felt, as we have to exert in resisting them a voluntary effort somewhat analogous to that involved in any muscular exertion. Often, again,—since we are not always thinking either of our duty or of our interest,—desires of this kind take effect in voluntary actions without our having judged such actions to be either right or wrong, either prudent or imprudent; as e.g. when an ordinary healthy man eats his dinner. In such cases it seems most appropriate to call the desires "non-rational" rather than "irrational." Neither term is intended to imply that the desires spoken of—or at least the more important of them—are not normally accompanied by intellectual processes. It is true that some impulses to action seem to take effect, as we say "blindly" or "instinctively," without any definite consciousness either of the end at which the action is aimed, or of the means by which the end is to be attained: but this, I conceive, is only the case with impulses that do not occupy consciousness for an appreciable time, and ordinarily do not require any but very familiar and habitual actions for the attainment of their proximate ends. In all other cases—that is, in the case of the actions with which we are chiefly concerned in ethical discussion—the result aimed at, and some part at least of the means by which it is to be realised, are more or less distinctly represented in consciousness, previous to the volition that initiates the movements tending to its realisation. Hence the resultant forces of what I call "non-rational" desires, and the volitions to which they prompt, are continually modified by intellectual processes in two distinct ways; first by new perceptions or representations of means conducive to the desired ends, and secondly by new presentations or representations of facts actually existing or in prospect—especially more or less probable consequences of contemplated actions—which rouse new impulses of desire and aversion.

The question, then, is whether the account just given of the influence of the intellect on desire and volition is not exhaustive; and whether the experience which is commonly described as a "conflict of desire with reason" is not more properly conceived as merely a conflict among desires and aversions; the sole function of reason being to bring before the mind ideas of actual or possible facts, which modify in the manner above described the resultant force of our various impulses.

I hold that this is not the case; that the ordinary moral or prudential judgments which, in the case of all or most minds, have some—though often an inadequate—influence on volition, cannot legitimately be interpreted as judgments respecting the present or future existence of human feelings or any facts of the sensible world; the fundamental notion represented by the word "ought" or "right,"[1] which such judgments contain expressly or by implication,

being essentially different from all notions representing facts of physical or psychical experience. The question is one on which appeal must ultimately be made to the reflection of individuals on their practical judgments and reasonings: and in making this appeal it seems most convenient to begin by showing the inadequacy of all attempts to explain the practical judgments or propositions in which this fundamental notion is introduced, without recognising its unique character as above negatively defined. There is an element of truth in such explanations, in so far as they bring into view feelings which undoubtedly accompany moral or prudential judgments, and which ordinarily have more or less effect in determining the will to actions judged to be right; but so far as they profess to be interpretations of what such judgments mean, they appear to me to fail altogether.

In considering this question it is important to take separately the two species of judgments which I have distinguished as "moral" and "prudential." Both kinds might, indeed, be termed "moral" in a wider sense; and, as we saw, it is a strongly supported opinion that all valid moral rules have ultimately a prudential basis. But in ordinary thought we clearly distinguish cognitions or judgments of duty from cognitions or judgments as to what "is right" or "ought to be done" in view of the agent's private interest or happiness: and the depth of the distinction will not, I think, be diminished by the closer examination of these judgments on which we are now to enter.

This very distinction, however, suggests an interpretation of the notion of rightness which denies its peculiar significance in moral judgments. It is urged that "rightness" is properly an attribute of means, not of ends: so that the attribution of it merely implies that the act judged right is the fittest or only fit means to the realisation of some end understood if not expressly stated: and similarly that the

---

[1] The difference between the significations of the two words is discussed later.

affirmation that anything 'ought to be done' is always made with at least tacit reference to some ulterior end. And I grant that this is a legitimate interpretation, in respect of a part of the use of either term in ordinary discourse. But it seems clear (1) that certain kinds of actions—under the names of Justice, Veracity, Good Faith, etc.—are commonly held to be right unconditionally, without regard to ulterior results: and (2) that we similarly regard as "right" the adoption of certain ends—such as the common good of society, or general happiness. In either of these cases the interpretation above suggested seems clearly inadmissible.[2]

We have therefore to find a meaning for "right" or "what ought to be" other than the notion of fitness to some ulterior end. Here we are met by the suggestion that the judgments or propositions which we commonly call moral—in the narrower sense—really affirm no more than the existence of a specific emotion in the mind of the person who utters them; that when I say 'Truth ought to be spoken' or 'Truthspeaking is right,' I mean no more than that the idea of truthspeaking excites in my mind a feeling of approbation or satisfaction. And probably some degree of such emotion, commonly distinguished as 'moral sentiment,' ordinarily accompanies moral judgments on real cases. But it is absurd to say that a mere statement of my approbation of truthspeaking is properly given in the proposition 'Truth ought to be spoken'; otherwise the fact of another man's disapprobation might equally be expressed by

saying 'Truth ought not to be spoken'; and thus we should have two coexistent facts stated in two mutually contradictory propositions. This is so obvious, that we must suppose that those who hold the view which I am combating do not really intend to deny it: but rather to maintain that this subjective fact of my approbation is all that there is any *ground* for stating, or perhaps that it is all that any reasonable person is prepared on reflection to affirm. And no doubt there is a large class of statements, in form objective, which yet we are not commonly prepared to maintain as more than subjective if their validity is questioned. If I say that 'the air is sweet,' or 'the food disagreeable,' it would not be exactly true to say that I mean no more than that I like the one or dislike the other: but if my statement is challenged, I shall probably content myself with affirming the existence of such feelings in my own mind. But there appears to me to be a fundamental difference between this case and that of moral feelings. The peculiar emotion of moral approbation is, in my experience, inseparably bound up with the conviction, implicit or explicit, that the conduct approved is 'really' right—i.e. that it cannot, without error, be disapproved by any other mind. If I give up this conviction because others do not share it, or for any other reason, I may no doubt still retain a sentiment prompting to the conduct in question, or—what is perhaps more common—a sentiment of repugnance to the opposite conduct: but this sentiment will no longer have the special quality of 'moral sentiment' strictly so called. This difference between the two is often overlooked in ethical discussion: but any experience of a change in moral opinion produced by argument may afford an illustration of it. Suppose e.g. that any one habitually influenced by the sentiment of Veracity is convinced that under certain peculiar circumstances in which he finds himself, speaking truth is not right but wrong. He will probably still feel a repugnance against violating the rule

[2] As, for instance, when Bentham explains (*Principles of Morals and Legislation*, chap. i. § i. note) that his fundamental principle "states the greatest happiness of all those whose interest is in question as being the right and proper end of human action," we cannot understand him really to *mean* by the word "right" "conducive to the general happiness," though his language in other passages of the same chapter (§§ ix. and x.) would seem to imply this; for the proposition that it is conducive to general happiness to take general happiness as an end of action, though not **exactly** a tautology, can hardly serve as the fundamental principle of a moral system.

of truthspeaking: but it will be a feeling quite different in kind and degree from that which prompted him to veracity as a department of virtuous action. We might perhaps call the one a 'moral' and the other a 'quasi-moral' sentiment.

The argument just given holds equally against the view that approbation or disapprobation is not the mere liking or aversion of an individual for certain kinds of conduct, but this complicated by a sympathetic representation of similar likings or aversions felt by other human beings. No doubt such sympathy is a normal concomitant of moral emotion, and when the former is absent there is much greater difficulty in maintaining the latter: this, however, is partly because our moral beliefs commonly agree with those of other members of our society, and on this agreement depends to an important extent our confidence in the truth of these beliefs.[3] But if, as in the case just supposed, we are really led by argument to a new moral belief, opposed not only to our own habitual sentiment but also to that of the society in which we live, we have a crucial experiment proving the existence in us of moral sentiments as I have defined them, colliding with the represented sympathies of our fellow-men no less than with our own mere likings and aversions. And even if we imagine the sympathies opposed to our convictions extended until they include those of the whole human race, against whom we imagine ourselves to stand as *Athanasius contra mundum*; still, so long as our conviction of duty is firm, the emotion which we call moral stands out in imagination quite distinct from the complex sympathy opposed to it, however much we extend, complicate and intensify the latter.

2. So far, then, from being prepared to admit that the proposition 'X ought to be done' *merely* expresses the existence of a certain sentiment in myself or others, I find it strictly impossible so to regard my own

[3] See Book iii. chap. xi. § 1.

moral judgments without eliminating from the concomitant sentiment the peculiar quality signified by the term 'moral.' There is, however, another interpretation of 'ought,' in which the likings and aversions that men in general feel for certain kinds of conduct are considered not as sympathetically represented in the emotion of the person judging, and thus constituting the moral element in it, but as causes of pain to the person of whom 'ought' or 'duty' is predicated. On this view, when we say that a man 'ought' to do anything, or that it is his 'duty' to do it, we mean that he is bound under penalties to do it; the particular penalty considered being the pain that will accrue to him directly or indirectly from the dislike of his fellow-creatures.

I think that this interpretation expresses a part of the meaning with which the words 'ought' and 'duty' are used in ordinary thought and discourse. For we commonly use the term 'moral obligation' as equivalent to 'duty' and expressing what is implied in the verb 'ought,' thus suggesting an analogy between this notion and that of legal obligation; and in the case of positive law we cannot refuse to recognise the connexion of 'obligation' and 'punishment': a law cannot be properly said to be actually established in a society if it is habitually violated with impunity. But as a more careful reflection on the relation of Law to Morality, as ordinarily conceived, seems to show that this interpretation of 'ought'—though it cannot be excluded—must be distinguished from the special ethical use of the term. For the ideal distinction taken in common thought between legal and merely moral rules seems to lie in just this connexion of the former but not the latter with punishment: we think that there are some things which a man ought to be compelled to do, or forbear, and others which he ought to do or forbear without compulsion, and that the former alone fall properly within the sphere of law. No doubt we also think that in many cases where the compulsion of law is undesirable, the fear of moral censure and its consequences supplies a normally useful constraint on the will of any individual. But it is evident that what we mean when we say that a man is "morally though not legally bound" to do a thing is not merely that he "will be punished by public opinion if he does not"; for we often join these two statements, clearly distinguishing their import: and further (since public opinion is known to be eminently fallible) there are many things which we judge men 'ought' to do, while perfectly aware that they will incur no serious social penalties for omitting them. In such cases, indeed, it would be commonly said that social disapprobation 'ought' to follow on immoral conduct; and in this very assertion it is clear that the term 'ought' cannot mean that social penalties are to be feared by those who do not disapprove. Again, all or most men in whom the moral consciousness is strongly developed find themselves from time to time in conflict with the commonly received morality of the society to which they belong: and thus—as was before said—have a crucial experience proving that duty does not mean *to them* what other men will disapprove of them for not doing.

At the same time I admit, as indeed I have already suggested in § 3 of chap. i., that we not unfrequently pass judgments resembling moral judgments in form, and not distinguished from them in ordinary thought, in cases where the obligation affirmed is found, on reflection, to depend on the existence of current opinions and sentiments as such. The members of modern civilised societies are under the sway of a code of Public Opinion, enforced by social penalties, which no reflective person obeying it identifies with the moral code, or regards as unconditionally binding: indeed the code is manifestly fluctuating and variable, different at the same time in different classes, professions, social circles, of the same political community. Such a code always supports to a considerable extent the commonly received code of morality: and most reflective persons think it generally reasonable to conform to the dictates of public opinion—to the Code of Honour, we may say, in graver matters, or the rules of Politeness or Good Breeding in lighter matters—wherever these dictates do not positively conflict with morality; such conformity being maintained either on grounds of private interest, or because it is thought conducive to general happiness or wellbeing to keep as much as possible in harmony with one's fellow-men. Hence in the ordinary thought of unreflective persons the duties imposed by social opinion are often undistinguished from moral duties: and indeed this indistinctness is almost inherent in the common meaning of many terms. For instance, if we say that a man has been 'dishonoured' by a cowardly act, it is not quite clear whether we mean that he has incurred contempt, or that he has deserved it, or both: as becomes evident when we take a case in which the Code of Honour comes into conflict with Morality. If e.g. a man were to incur social ostracism anywhere for refusing a duel on religious grounds, some would say that he was 'dishonoured,' though he had acted rightly, others that there could be no real dishonour in a virtuous act. A similar ambiguity seems to lurk in the common notion of 'improper' or 'incorrect' behaviour. Still in all such cases the ambiguity becomes evident on reflection: and when discovered, merely serves to illustrate further the distinction between the notion of 'right conduct,' 'duty,' what we 'ought' or are under 'moral obligation' to do—when these terms are used in a strictly ethical sense—and conduct that is merely conformed to the standard of current opinion.

There is, however, another way of interpreting 'ought' as connoting penalties, which is somewhat less easy to meet by a crucial psychological experiment. The moral imperative may be taken to be a law of God, to the breach of which Divine penalties are annexed; and these, no doubt, in a Christian society, are commonly conceived to be adequate and universally applicable. Still, it can hardly be said that this belief is shared by all the persons whose conduct is influenced by independent moral convictions, occasionally unsupported either by the law or the public opinion of their community. And even in the case of many of those who believe fully in the moral government of the world, the judgment "I ought to do this" cannot be identified with the judgment "God will punish me if I do not"; since the conviction that the former proposition is true is distinctly recognised as an important part of the grounds for believing the latter. Again, when Christians speak—as they commonly do—of the 'justice' (or other moral attributes) of God, as exhibited in punishing sinners and rewarding the righteous, they obviously imply not merely that God *will* thus punish and reward, but that it is 'right'[4] for Him to do so: which, of course, cannot be taken to mean that He is 'bound under penalties.'

3. It seems then that the notion of 'ought' or 'moral obligation' as used in our common moral judgments, does not merely import (1) that there exists in the mind of the person judging a specific emotion (whether complicated or not by sympathetic representation of similar emotions in other minds); nor (2) that certain rules of conduct are supported by penalties which will follow on their violation (whether such penalties result from the general liking or aversion felt for the conduct prescribed or forbidden, or from some other source). What then, it may be asked, does it import? What definition can we give of 'ought,' 'right,' and other terms expressing the same fundamental notion? To this I should answer that the notion which these terms have in common is too elementary to admit of any formal definition. In so saying, I do not mean to imply that it belongs to the "original constitution of the mind"; i.e. that its presence in consciousness is not

the result of a process of development. I do not doubt that the whole fabric of human thought—including the conceptions that present themselves as most simple and elementary—has been developed, through a gradual process of psychical change, out of some lower life in which thought, properly speaking, had no place. But it is not therefore to be inferred, as regards this or any other notion, that it has not really the simplicity which it appears to have when we now reflect upon it. It is sometimes assumed that if we can show how thoughts have grown up—if we can point to the psychical antecedents of which they are the natural consequents—we may conclude that the thoughts in question are really compounds containing their antecedents as latent elements. But I know no justification for this transference of the conceptions of chemistry to psychology;[5] I know no reason for considering psychical antecedents as really constitutive of their psychical consequents, in spite of the apparent dissimilarity between the two. In default of such reasons, a psychologist must accept as elementary what introspection carefully performed declares to be so; and, using this criterion, I find that the notion we have been examining, as it now exists in our thought, cannot be resolved into any more simple notions: it can only be made clearer by determining as precisely as possible its relation to other notions with which it is connected in ordinary thought, especially to those with which it is liable to be confounded.

In performing this process it is impor-

---

[4] 'Ought' is here inapplicable, for a reason presently explained.

[5] In Chemistry we regard the antecedents (elements) as still existing in and constituting the consequent (compound) because the latter is exactly similar to the former in weight, and because we can generally cause this compound to disappear and obtain the elements in its place. But we find nothing at all like this in the growth of mental phenomena; the psychical consequent is in no respect exactly similar to its antecedents, nor can it be resolved into them. I should explain that I am not here arguing the question whether the *validity* of moral judgments is affected by a discovery of their psychical antecedents. This question I reserve for subsequent discussion. See Book iii. chap. i. § 4.

tant to note and distinguish two different implications with which the word "ought" is used; in the narrowest ethical sense what we judge 'ought to be' done, is always thought capable of being brought about by the volition of any individual to whom the judgment applies. I cannot conceive that I 'ought' to do anything which at the same time I judge that I cannot do. In a wider sense, however,—which cannot conveniently be discarded—I sometimes judge that I 'ought' to know what a wiser man would know, or feel as a better man would feel, in my place, though I may know that I could not directly produce in myself such knowledge or feeling by any effort of will. In this case the word merely implies an ideal or pattern which I 'ought'—in the stricter sense—to seek to imitate as far as possible. And this wider sense seems to be that in which the word is normally used in the precepts of Art generally, and in political judgments: when I judge that the laws and constitution of my country 'ought to be' other than they are, I do not of course imply that my own or any other individual's single volition can directly bring about the change.[6] In either case, however, I imply that what ought to be is a possible object of knowledge: i.e. that what I judge ought to be must, unless I am in error, be similarly judged by all rational beings who judge truly of the matter.

In referring such judgments to the 'Reason,' I do not mean here to prejudge the question whether valid moral judgments are normally attained by a process of reasoning from universal principles or axioms, or by direct intuition of the particular duties of individuals. It is not uncommonly held that the moral faculty deals primarily with individual cases as they arise, applying directly to each case the general notion of duty, and deciding intuitively what

ought to be done by this person in these particular circumstances. And I admit that on this view the apprehension of moral truth is more analogous to Sense-perception than to Rational Intuition (as commonly understood):[7] and hence the term Moral Sense might seem more appropriate. But the term Sense suggests a capacity for feelings which may vary from A to B without either being in error, rather than a faculty of cognition:[8] and it appears to me fundamentally important to avoid this suggestion. I have therefore thought it better to use the term Reason with the explanation above given, to denote the faculty of moral cognition:[9] adding, as a further justification of this use, that even when a moral judgment relates primarily to some particular action we commonly regard it as applicable to any other action belonging to a certain definable class: so that the moral truth apprehended is implicitly conceived to be intrinsically universal, though particular in our first apprehension of it.

Further, when I speak of the cognition or judgment that 'X ought to be done'—in the stricter ethical sense of the term ought[10] —as a 'dictate' or 'precept' of reason to the persons to whom it relates, I imply that in rational beings as such this cognition gives an impulse or motive to action: though in human beings, of course, this is

[6] I do not even imply that any combination of individuals could completely realise the state of political relations which I conceive 'ought' to exist. My conception would be futile if it had no relation to practice: but it may merely delineate a pattern to which no more than an approximation is practically possible.

[7] We do not commonly say that particular physical facts are apprehended by the Reason: we consider this faculty to be conversant in its discursive operation with the relation of judgments or propositions: and the intuitive reason (which is here rather in question) we restrict to the apprehension of universal truths, such as the axioms of Logic and Mathematics.

[8] By cognition I always mean what some would rather call "apparent cognition"—that is, I do not mean to affirm the *validity* of the cognition, but only its existence as a psychical fact, and its claim to be valid.

[9] A further justification for this extended use of the term Reason will be suggested in a subsequent chapter of this Book (chap. viii § 3).

[10] This is the sense in which the term will always be used in the present treatise, except where the context makes it quite clear that only the wider meaning—that of the political 'ought'—is applicable.

only one motive among others which are liable to conflict with it, and is not always—perhaps not usually—a predominant motive. In fact, this possible conflict of motives seems to be connoted by the term 'dictate' or 'imperative,' which describes the relation of Reason to mere inclinations or non-rational impulses by comparing it to the relation between the will of a superior and the wills of his subordinates. This conflict seems also to be implied in the terms 'ought,' 'duty,' 'moral obligation,' as used in ordinary moral discourse: and hence these terms cannot be applied to the actions of rational beings to whom we cannot attribute impulses conflicting with reason. We may, however, say of such beings that their actions are 'reasonable,' or (in an absolute sense) 'right.'

4. I am aware that some persons will be disposed to answer all the preceding argument by a simple denial that they can find in their consciousness any such unconditional or categorical imperative as I have been trying to exhibit. If this is really the final result of self-examination in any case, there is no more to be said. I, at least, do not know how to impart the notion of moral obligation to any one who is entirely devoid of it. I think, however, that many of those who give this denial only mean to deny that they have any consciousness of moral obligation to actions without reference to their consequences; and would not really deny that they recognise some universal end or ends—whether it be the general happiness, or well-being otherwise understood—as that at which it is ultimately reasonable to aim, subordinating to its attainment the gratification of any personal desires that may conflict with this aim. But in this view, as I have before said, the unconditional imperative plainly comes in as regards the end, which is—explicitly or implicitly—recognised as an end at which all men 'ought' to aim; and it can hardly be denied that the recognition of an end as ultimately reasonable involves the recognition of an obligation to do such acts as most conduce to the end. The obligation is not indeed "unconditional," but it does not depend on the existence of any non-rational desires or aversions. And nothing that has been said in the preceding section is intended as an argument in favour of Intuitionism, as against Utilitarianism or any other method that treats moral rules as relative to General Good or Well-being. For instance, nothing that I have said is inconsistent with the view that Truthspeaking is only valuable as a means to the preservation of society: only if it be admitted that it *is* valuable on this ground I should say that it is implied that the preservation of society—or some further end to which this preservation, again, is a means—must be valuable *per se*, and therefore something at which a rational being, as such, ought to aim. If it be granted that we need not look beyond the preservation of society, the primary 'dictate of reason' in this case would be 'that society *ought* to be preserved': but reason would also dictate that truth ought to be spoken, so far as truthspeaking is recognised as the indispensable or fittest means to this end: and the notion "ought" as used in either dictate is that which I have been trying to make clear.

So again, even those who hold that moral rules are only obligatory because it is the individual's interest to conform to them—thus regarding them as a particular species of prudential rules—do not thereby get rid of the 'dictate of reason,' so far as they recognise private interest or happiness as an end at which it is ultimately reasonable to aim. The conflict of Practical Reason with irrational desire remains an indubitable fact of our conscious experience, even if practical reason is interpreted to mean merely self-regarding Prudence. It is, indeed, maintained by Kant and others that it cannot properly be said to be a man's duty to promote his own happiness; since "what every one inevitably wills cannot be brought under the notion of duty." But even granting[11] it to be in some sense true that a man's volition is always directed to the attainment of his own happiness, it does not follow that a man always does what he believes will be conducive to his own *greatest* happiness. As Butler urges, it is a matter of common experience that men indulge appetite or passion even when, in their own view, the indulgence is as clearly opposed to what they conceive to be their interest as it is to what they conceive to be their duty. Thus the notion 'ought'—as expressing the relation of rational judgment to non-rational impulses—will find a place in the practical rules of any egoistic system, no less than in the rules of ordinary morality, understood as prescribing duty without reference to the agent's interest.

Here, however, it may be held that Egoism does not properly regard the agent's own greatest happiness as what he "ought" to aim at: but only as the ultimate end for the realisation of which he has, on the whole, a predominant desire; which may be temporarily overcome by particular passions and appetites, but ordinarily regains its predominance when these transient impulses have spent their force. I quite recognise that this is a view widely taken of egoistic action, and I propose to consider it in a subsequent chapter,[12] But even if we discard the belief, that any end of action is unconditionally or "categorically" prescribed by reason, the notion 'ought' as above explained is not thereby eliminated from our practical reasonings: it still remains in the "hypothetical imperative" which prescribes the fittest means to any end that we may have determined to aim at. When e.g. a physician says, "if you wish to be healthy you ought to rise early," this is not the same thing as saying "early rising is an indispensable condition of the attainment of health." This latter proposition expresses the relation of physiological

facts on which the former is founded; but it is not merely this relation of facts that the word 'ought' imports: it also implies the unreasonableness of adopting an end and refusing to adopt the means indispensable to its attainment. It may perhaps be argued that this is not only unreasonable but impossible: since adoption of an end means the preponderance of a desire for it, and if aversion to the indispensable means causes them not to be adopted although recognised as indispensable, the desire for the end is *not* preponderant and it ceases to be adopted. But this view is due, in my opinion, to a defective psychological analysis. According to my observation of consciousness, the adoption of an end as paramount—either absolutely or within certain limits—is quite a distinct psychical phenomenon from desire: it is a kind of volition, though it is, of course, specifically different from a volition initiating a particular immediate action. As a species intermediate between the two, we may place resolutions to act in a certain way at some future time: we continually make such resolutions, and sometimes when the time comes for carrying them out, we do in fact act otherwise under the influence of passion or mere habit, without consciously cancelling our previous resolve. This inconsistency of will our practical reason condemns as irrational, even apart from any judgment of approbation or disapprobation on either volition considered by itself. There is a similar inconsistency between the adoption of an end and a general refusal to take whatever means we may see to be indispensable to its attainment: and if, when the time comes, we do not take such means while yet we do not consciously retract our adoption of the end, it can hardly be denied that we 'ought' in consistency to act otherwise than we do. And such a contradiction as I have described, between a general resolution and a particular volition, is surely a matter of common experience.

---

[11] As will be seen from the next chapter, I do not grant this.

[12] Chap. ix. of *The Methods of Ethics.*

Does Moral Philosophy Rest on a Mistake?

H. A. PRICHARD

Probably to most students of Moral Philosophy there comes a time when they feel a vague sense of dissatisfaction with the whole subject. And the sense of dissatisfaction tends to grow rather than to diminish. It is not so much that the positions, and still more the arguments, of particular thinkers seem unconvincing, though this is true. It is rather that the aim of the subject becomes increasingly obscure. 'What,' it is asked, 'are we really going to learn by Moral Philosophy?' 'What are books on Moral Philosophy really trying to show, and when their aim is clear, why are they so unconvincing and artificial?' And again: 'Why is it so difficult to substitute anything better?' Personally, I have been led by growing dissatisfaction of this kind to wonder whether the reason may not be that the subject, at any rate as usually understood, consists in the attempt to answer an improper question. And in this article I shall venture to contend that the existence of the whole subject, as usually understood, rests on a mistake, and on a mistake parallel to that on which rests, as I think, the subject usually called the Theory of Knowledge.

If we reflect on our own mental history or on the history of the subject, we

Reprinted from *Mind*, 21, 1912, by permission of *Mind*.

feel no doubt about the nature of the demand which originates the subject. Any one who, stimulated by education, has come to feel the force of the various obligations in life, at some time or other comes to feel the irksomeness of carrying them out, and to recognize the sacrifice of interest involved; and, if thoughtful, he inevitably puts to himself the question: 'Is there really a reason why I should act in the ways in which hitherto I have thought I ought to act? May I not have been all the time under an illusion in so thinking? Should not I really be justified in simply trying to have a good time?' Yet, like Glaucon, feeling that somehow he ought after all to act in these ways, he asks for a *proof* that this feeling is justified. In other words, he asks '*Why* should I do these things?', and his and other people's moral philosophizing is an attempt to supply the answer, i.e. to supply by a process of reflection a proof of the truth of what he and they have prior to reflection believed immediately or without proof. This frame of mind seems to present a close parallel to the frame of mind which originates the Theory of Knowledge. Just as the recognition that the doing of our duty often vitally interferes with the satisfaction of our inclinations leads us to wonder whether we really ought to do what we usually call our duty, so the recognition that we and others are liable to mistakes in knowledge generally leads us, as it did Descartes, to wonder whether hitherto we may not have been always mistaken. And just as we try to find a proof, based on the general consideration of action and of human life, that we ought to act in the ways usually called moral, so we, like Descartes, propose by a process of reflection on our thinking to find a test of knowledge, i.e. a principle by applying which we can show that a certain condition of mind was really knowledge, a condition which *ex hypothesi* existed independently of the process of reflection.

Now, how has the moral question been answered? So far as I can see, the answers all fall, and fall from the necessities of the case, into one of two species. *Either* they state that we ought to do so and so, because, as we see when we fully apprehend the facts, doing so will be for our good, i.e. really, as I would rather say, for our advantage, or better still, for our happiness; *or* they state that we ought to do so and so, because something realized either in or by the action is good. In other words, the reason 'why' is stated in terms either of the agent's happiness or of the goodness of something involved in the action.

To see the prevalence of the former species of answer, we have only to consider the history of Moral Philosophy. To take obvious instances, Plato, Butler, Hutcheson, Paley, Mill, each in his own way seeks at bottom to convince the individual that he ought to act in so-called moral ways by showing that to do so will really be for his happiness. Plato is perhaps the most significant instance, because of all philosophers he is the one to whom we are least willing to ascribe a mistake on such matters, and a mistake on his part would be evidence of the deep-rootedness of the tendency to make it. To show that Plato really justifies morality by its profitableness, it is only necessary to point out (1) that the very formulation of the thesis to be met, *viz.* that

justice is ἀλλότριον ἀγαθόν,* implies that any refutation must consist in showing that justice is οἰκεῖον ἀγαθόν, i.e. really, as the context shows, one's own advantage, and (2) that the term λυσιτελεῖν** supplies the key not only to the problem but also to its solution.

The tendency to justify acting on moral rules in this way is natural. For if, as often happens, we put to ourselves the question 'Why should we do so and so?', we are satisfied by being convinced either that the doing so will lead to something which we want (e.g. that taking certain medicine will heal our disease), or that the doing so itself, as we see when we appreciate its nature, is something that we want or should like, e.g. playing golf. The formulation of the question implies a state of unwillingness or indifference towards the action, and we are brought into a condition of willingness by the answer. And this process seems to be precisely what we desire when we ask, e.g., 'Why should we keep our engagements to our own loss?'; for it is just the fact that the keeping of our engagements runs counter to the satisfaction of our desires which produced the question.

The answer is, of course, not an answer, for it fails to convince us that we ought to keep our engagements; even if successful on its own lines, it only makes us *want* to keep them. And Kant was really only pointing out this fact when he distinguished hypothetical and categorical imperatives, even though he obscured the nature of the fact by wrongly describing his so-called 'hypothetical imperatives' as imperatives. But if this answer be no answer, what other can be offered? Only, it seems, an answer which bases the obligation to do something on the *goodness* either of something to which the act leads or of the act itself. Suppose, when wondering whether we really ought to act in the ways usually

* [Someone else's good, i.e., advantage.—Ed.]
** [To profit (someone), i.e., to be to someone's advantage.—Ed.]

called moral, we are told as a means of re-solving our doubt that those acts are right which produce happiness. We at once ask: 'Whose happiness?' If we are told 'Our own happiness,' then, though we shall lose our hesitation to act in these ways, we shall not recover our sense that we ought to do so. But how can this result be avoided? Appar-ently, only by being told one of two things; *either* that anyone's happiness is a thing good in itself, and that *therefore* we ought to do whatever will produce it, *or* that working for happiness is itself good, and that the intrinsic goodness of such an ac-tion is the reason why we ought to do it. The advantage of this appeal to the good-ness of something consists in the fact that it avoids reference to desire, and, instead, re-fers to something impersonal and objective. In this way it seems possible to avoid the resolution of obligation into inclination. But just for this reason it is of the essence of the answer, that to be effective it must neither include nor involve the view that the apprehension of the goodness of any-thing necessarily arouses the desire for it. Otherwise the answer resolves itself into a form of the former answer by substituting desire or inclination for the sense of obliga-tion, and in this way it loses what seems its special advantage.

Now it seems to me that both forms of this answer break down, though each for a different reason.

Consider the first form. It is what may be called Utilitarianism in the generic sense, in which what is good is not limited to pleasure. It takes its stand upon the dis-tinction between something which is not it-self an action, but which can be produced by an action, and the action which will produce it, and contends that if something which is not an action is good, then we *ought* to undertake the action which will, directly or indirectly, originate it.[1]

But this argument, if it is to restore the sense of obligation to act, must presuppose

an intermediate link, *viz.* the further thesis that what is good ought to be.[2] The neces-sity of this link is obvious. An 'ought,' if it is to be derived at all, can only be derived from another 'ought.' Moreover, this link tacitly presupposes another, *viz.* that the apprehension that something good which is not an action ought to be involves just the feeling of imperativeness or obligation which is to be aroused by the thought of the action which will originate it. Otherwise the argument will not lead us to feel the obligation to produce it by the action. And, surely, both this link and its implica-tion are false.[3] The word 'ought' refers to actions and to actions alone. The proper language is never 'So and so ought to be,' but 'I ought to do so and so.' Even if we are sometimes moved to say that the world or something in it is not what it ought to be, what we really mean is that God or some human being has not made some-thing what he ought to have made it. And it is merely stating another side of this fact to urge that we can only feel the impera-tiveness upon us of something which is in our power; for it is actions and actions alone which, directly at least, are in our power.

Perhaps, however, the best way to see the failure of this view is to see its failure to correspond to our actual moral convic-tions. Suppose we ask ourselves whether our sense that we ought to pay our debts or to tell the truth arises from our recognition that in doing so we should be originating something good, e.g. material comfort in *A* or true belief in *B*, i.e. suppose we ask our-selves whether it is this aspect of the action which leads to our recognition that we ought to do it. We at once and without hesitation answer 'No.' Again, if we take as our illustration our sense that we ought to

---

[1] Cf. Dr. Rashdall's *Theory of Good and Evil,* vol. i, p. 138.

[2] Dr. Rashdall, if I understand him rightly, sup-plies this link (cf. ibid., pp. 135—6).

[3] When we speak of anything, e.g. of some emotion or of some quality of a human being, as good, we never dream in our ordinary conscious-ness of going on to say that therefore it ought to be.

act justly as between two parties, we have, if possible, even less hesitation in giving a similar answer; for the balance of resulting good may be, and often is, not on the side of justice.

At best it can only be maintained that there is this element of truth in the Utilitarian view, that unless we recognized that something which an act will originate is good, we should not recognize that we ought to do the action. Unless we thought knowledge a good thing, it may be urged, we should not think that we ought to tell the truth; unless we thought pain a bad thing, we should not think the infliction of it, without special reason, wrong. But this is not to imply that the badness of error is the reason why it is wrong to lie, or the badness of pain the reason why we ought not to inflict it without special cause.[4]

It is, I think, just because this form of the view is so plainly at variance with our moral consciousness that we are driven to adopt the other form of the view, *viz.* that the act is good in itself and that its intrinsic goodness is the reason why it ought to be done. It is this form which has always made the most serious appeal; for the goodness of the act itself seems more closely related to the obligation to do it than that of its mere consequences or results, and therefore, if obligation is to be based on the goodness of something, it would seem that this goodness should be that of the act itself. Moreover, the view gains plausibility from the fact that moral actions are most conspicuously those to which the term 'intrinsically good' is applicable.

Nevertheless this view, though perhaps less superficial, is equally untenable. For it leads to precisely the dilemma which faces everyone who tries to solve the prob-

lem raised by Kant's theory of the good will. To see this, we need only consider the nature of the acts to which we apply the term 'intrinsically good.'

There is, of course, no doubt that we approve and even admire certain actions, and also that we should describe them as good, and as good in themselves. But it is, I think, equally unquestionable that our approval and our use of the term 'good' is always in respect of the motive and refers to actions which have been actually done and of which we think we know the motive. Further, the actions of which we approve and which we should describe as intrinsically good are of two and only two kinds. They are either actions in which the agent did what he did because he thought he ought to do it, or actions of which the motive was a desire prompted by some good emotion, such as gratitude, affection, family feeling, or public spirit, the most prominent of such desires in books on Moral Philosophy being that ascribed to what is vaguely called benevolence. For the sake of simplicity I omit the case of actions done partly from some such desire and partly from the sense of duty; for even if all good actions are done from a combination of these motives, the argument will not be affected. The dilemma is this. If the motive in respect of which we think an action good is the sense of obligation, then so far from the sense that we ought to do it being derived from our apprehension of its goodness, our apprehension of its goodness will presuppose the sense that we ought to do it. In other words, in this case the recognition that the act is good will plainly *presuppose* the recognition that the act is right, whereas the view under consideration is that the recognition of the goodness of the act *gives rise* to the recognition of its rightness. On the other hand, if the motive in respect of which we think an action good is some intrinsically good desire, such as the desire to help a friend, the recognition of the goodness of the act will equally fail to give rise to the sense of obligation to

---

[4] It may be noted that if the badness of pain were the reason why we ought not to inflict pain on another, it would equally be a reason why we ought not to inflict pain on ourselves; yet, though we should allow the wanton infliction of pain on ourselves to be foolish, we should not think of describing it as wrong.

do it. For we cannot feel that we ought to do that the doing of which is *ex hypothesi* prompted solely by the desire to do it.[5]

The fallacy underlying the view is that while to base the rightness of an act upon its intrinsic goodness implies that the goodness in question is that of the motive, in reality the rightness or wrongness of an act has nothing to do with any question of motives at all. For, as any instance will show, the rightness of an action concerns an action not in the fuller sense of the term in which we include the motive in the action, but in the narrower and commoner sense in which we distinguish an action from its motive and mean by an action merely the conscious origination of something, an origination which on different occasions or in different people may be prompted by different motives. The question 'Ought I to pay my bills?' really means simply 'Ought I to bring about my tradesmen's possession of what by my previous acts I explicitly or implicitly promised them?' There is, and can be, no question of whether I ought to pay my debts from a particular motive. No doubt we know that if we pay our bills we shall pay them with a motive, but in considering whether we ought to pay them we inevitably think of the act in abstraction from the motive. Even if we knew what our motive would be if we did the act, we should not be any nearer an answer to the question.

Moreover, if we eventually pay our bills from fear of the county court, we shall still have done *what* we ought, even though we shall not have done it *as* we ought. The attempt to bring in the motive involves a mistake similar to that involved in supposing that we can will to will. To feel that I ought to pay my bills is to be *moved towards* paying them. But what I can be moved towards must always be an action and not an action in which I am moved in a particular way, i.e. an action

from a particular motive; otherwise I should be moved towards being moved, which is impossible. Yet the view under consideration involves this impossibility, for it really resolves the sense that I ought to do so and so, into the sense that I ought to be moved to do it in a particular way.[6]

So far my contentions have been mainly negative, but they form, I think, a useful, if not a necessary, introduction to what I take to be the truth. This I will now endeavour to state, first formulating what, as I think, is the real nature of our apprehension or appreciation of moral obligations, and then applying the result to elucidate the question of the existence of Moral Philosophy.

The sense of obligation to do, or of the rightness of, an action of a particular kind is absolutely underivative or immediate. The rightness of an action consists in its being the origination of something of a certain kind A in a situation of a certain kind, a situation consisting in a certain relation B of the agent to others or to his own nature. To appreciate its rightness two preliminaries may be necessary. We may have to follow out the consequences of the proposed action more fully than we have hitherto done, in order to realize that in the action we should originate A. Thus we may not appreciate the wrongness of telling a certain story until we realize that we should thereby be hurting the feelings of one of our audience. Again, we may have to take into account the relation B involved in the situation, which we had hitherto failed to notice. For instance, we may not appreciate the obligation to give X a present, until we remember that he has done us an act of kindness. But, given that by a process which is, of course, merely a process of general and not of moral thinking we come

---

[5] It is, I think, on this latter horn of the dilemma that Martineau's view falls; cf. *Types of Ethical Theory*, part ii, book i.

[6] It is of course not denied here that an action done from a particular motive may be *good*; it is only denied that the *rightness* of an action depends on its being done with a particular motive.

to recognize that the proposed act is one by which we shall originate A in a relation B, then we appreciate the obligation immediately or directly, the appreciation being an activity of *moral* thinking. We recognize, for instance, that this performance of a service to X, who has done us a service, just in virtue of its being the performance of a service to one who has rendered a service to the would-be agent, ought to be done by us. This apprehension is immediate, in precisely the sense in which a mathematical apprehension is immediate, e.g. the apprehension that this three-sided figure, in virtue of its being three-sided, must have three angles. Both apprehensions are immediate in the sense that in both insight into the nature of the subject directly leads us to recognize its possession of the predicate; and it is only stating this fact from the other side to say that in both cases the fact apprehended is self-evident.

The plausibility of the view that obligations are not self-evident but need proof lies in the fact that an act which is referred to as an obligation may be incompletely stated, what I have called the preliminaries to appreciating the obligation being incomplete. If, e.g., we refer to the act of repaying X by a present merely as giving X a present, it appears, and indeed is, necessary to give a reason. In other words, wherever a moral act is regarded in this incomplete way the question 'Why should I do it?' is perfectly legitimate. This fact suggests, but suggests wrongly, that even if the nature of the act is completely stated, it is still necessary to give a reason, or, in other words, to supply a proof.

The relations involved in obligations of various kinds are, of course, very different. The relation in certain cases is a relation to others due to a past act of theirs or ours. The obligation to repay a benefit involves a relation due to a past act of the benefactor. The obligation to pay a bill involves a relation due to a past act of ours in which we have either said or implied that we would make a certain return for

something which we have asked for and received. On the other hand, the obligation to speak the truth implies no such definite act; it involves a relation consisting in the fact that others are trusting us to speak the truth, a relation the apprehension of which gives rise to the sense that communication of the truth is something owing by us to them. Again, the obligation not to hurt the feelings of another involves no special relation of us to that other, i.e. no relation other than that involved in our both being men, and men in one and the same world. Moreover, it seems that the relation involved in an obligation need not be a relation to another at all. Thus we should admit that there is an obligation to overcome our natural timidity or greediness, and that this involves no relations to others. Still there is a relation involved, *viz.* a relation to our own disposition. It is simply because we can and because others cannot directly modify our disposition that it is our business to improve it, and that it is not theirs, or, at least, not theirs to the same extent.

The negative side of all this is, of course, that we do not come to appreciate an obligation by an *argument*, i.e. by a process of nonmoral thinking, and that, in particular, we do not do so by an argument of which a premiss is the ethical but not moral activity of appreciating the goodness either of the act or of a consequence of the act; i.e. that our sense of the rightness of an act is not a conclusion from our appreciation of the goodness either of it or of anything else.

It will probably be urged that on this view our various obligations form, like Aristotle's categories, an unrelated chaos in which it is impossible to acquiesce. For, according to it, the obligation to repay a benefit, or to pay a debt, or to keep a promise, presupposes a previous act of another; whereas the obligation to speak the truth or not to harm another does not; and, again, the obligation to remove our timidity involves no relations to others at all.

Yet, at any rate, an effective *argumentum ad hominem* is at hand in the fact that the various qualities which we recognize as good are equally unrelated; e.g. courage, humility, and interest in knowledge. If, as is plainly the case, ἀγαθά (goods) differ ἠ ἀγαθά (*qua* goods), why would not obligations equally differ *qua* their obligatoriness? Moreover, if this were not so there could in the end be only one obligation, which is palpably contrary to fact.[7]

Certain observations will help to make the view clearer.

In the first place, it may seem that the view, being—as it is—avowedly put forward in opposition to the view that what is right is derived from what is good, must itself involve the opposite of this, *viz.* the Kantian position that what is good is based upon what is right, i.e. that an act, if it be good, is good because it is right. But this is not so. For, on the view put forward, the rightness of a right action lies solely in the origination in which the act consists, whereas the intrinsic goodness of an action lies solely in its motive; and this implies that a morally good action is morally good not simply because it is a right action but because it is a right action done because it is right, i.e. from a sense of obligation. And this implication, it may be remarked incidentally, seems plainly true.

In the second place, the view involves that when, or rather so far as, we act from a sense of obligation, we have no purpose or end. By a 'purpose' or 'end' we really mean something the existence of which we desire, and desire of the existence of which leads us to act. Usually our purpose is something which the act will originate, as when we turn round in order to look at a picture. But it may be the action itself, i.e. the origination of something, as when we hit a golf-ball into a hole or kill someone out of revenge.[8] Now if by a purpose we mean something the existence of which we desire and desire for which leads us to act, then plainly, so far as we act from a sense of obligation, we have no purpose, consisting either in the action or in anything which it will produce. This is so obvious that it scarcely seems worth pointing out. But I do so for two reasons. (1) If we fail to scrutinize the meaning of the terms 'end' and 'purpose,' we are apt to assume uncritically that all deliberate action, i.e. action proper, must have a purpose; we then become puzzled both when we look for the purpose of an action done from a sense of obligation, and also when we try to apply to such an action the distinction of means and end, the truth all the time being that since there is no end, there is no means either. (2) The attempt to base the sense of obligation on the recognition of the goodness of something is really an attempt to find a purpose in a moral action in the shape of something

---

[7] Two other objections may be anticipated: (1) that obligations cannot be self-evident, since many actions regarded as obligations by some are not so regarded by others, and (2) that if obligations are self-evident, the problem of how we ought to act in the presence of conflicting obligations is insoluble.

To the first I should reply:

(*a*) That the appreciation of an obligation is, of course, only possible for a developed moral being, and that different degrees of development are possible.

(*b*) That the failure to recognize some particular obligations is usually due to the fact that, owing to a lack of thoughtfulness, what I have called the preliminaries to this recognition are incomplete.

(*c*) That the view put forward is consistent with the admission that, owing to a lack of thoughtfulness, even the best men are blind to many of their obligations, and that in the end our obligations are seen to be co-extensive with almost the whole of our life.

To the second objection I should reply that obligation admits of degrees, and that where obligations conflict, the decision of what we ought to do turns not on the question 'Which of the alternative courses of action will originate the greater good?' but on the question 'Which is the greater obligation?'

[8] It is no objection to urge that an action cannot be its own purpose, since the purpose of something cannot be the thing itself. For, speaking strictly, the purpose is not the *action's* purpose but *our* purpose, and there is no contradiction in holding that our purpose in acting may be the action.

good which, as good, we want. And the expectation that the goodness of something underlies an obligation disappears as soon as we cease to look for a purpose.

The thesis, however, that so far as we act from a sense of obligation, we have no purpose must not be misunderstood. It must not be taken either to mean or to imply that so far as we so act we have no *motive*. No doubt in ordinary speech the words 'motive' and 'purpose' are usually treated as correlatives, 'motive' standing for the desire which induces us to act, and 'purpose' standing for the object of this desire. But this is only because, when we are looking for the motive of the action, say, of some crime, we are usually presupposing that the act in question is prompted by a desire and not by the sense of obligation. At bottom, however, we mean by a motive what moves us to act; a sense of obligation does sometimes move us to act; and in our ordinary consciousness we should not hesitate to allow that the action we are considering might have had as its motive a sense of obligation. Desire and the sense of obligation are coordinate forms or species of motive.

In the third place, if the view put forward be right, we must sharply distinguish morality and virtue as independent, though related, species of goodness, neither being an aspect of something of which the other is an aspect, nor again a form or species of the other, nor again something deducible from the other; and we must at the same time allow that it is possible to do the same act either virtuously or morally or in both ways at once. And surely this is true. An act, to be virtuous, must, as Aristotle saw, be done willingly or with pleasure; as such it is just not done from a sense of obligation but from some desire which is intrinsically good, as arising from some intrinsically good emotion. Thus, in an act of generosity the motive is the desire to help another arising from sympathy with that other; in an act which is courageous and

no more, i.e. in an act which is not at the same time an act of public spirit or family affection or the like, we prevent ourselves from being dominated by a feeling of terror, desiring to do so from a sense of shame at being terrified. The goodness of such an act is different from the goodness of an act to which we apply the term moral in the strict and narrow sense, *viz.* an act done from a sense of obligation. Its goodness lies in the intrinsic goodness of the emotion and of the consequent desire under which we act, the goodness of this motive being different from the goodness of the moral motive proper, *viz.* the sense of duty or obligation. Nevertheless, at any rate in certain cases, an act can be done either virtuously or morally or in both ways at once. It is possible to repay a benefit either from desire to repay it, or from the feeling that we ought to do so, or from both motives combined. A doctor may tend his patients either from a desire arising out of interest in his patients or in the exercise of skill, or from a sense of duty, or from a desire and a sense of duty combined. Further, although we recognize that in each case the act possesses an intrinsic goodness, we regard that action as the best in which both motives are combined; in other words, we regard as the really best man the man in whom virtue and morality are united.

It may be objected that the distinction between the two kinds of motive is untenable, on the ground that the *desire* to repay a benefit, for example, is only the manifestation of that which manifests itself as the *sense of obligation* to repay whenever we think of something in the action which is other than the repayment and which we should not like, such as the loss or pain involved. Yet the distinction can, I think, easily be shown to be tenable. For, in the analogous case of revenge, the desire to return the injury and the sense that we ought not to do so, leading, as they do, in opposite directions, are plainly distinct; and the obviousness of the distinction here seems to remove any difficulty in admitting the existence of a parallel distinction between the desire to return a benefit and the sense that we ought to return it.[9]

Further, the view implies that an obligation can no more be based on or derived from a virtue than a virtue can be derived from an obligation, in which latter case a virtue would consist in carrying out an obligation. And the implication is surely true and important. Take the case of courage. It is untrue to urge that, since courage is a virtue, we ought to act courageously. It is and must be untrue, because, as we see in the end, to feel an obligation to act courageously would involve a contradiction. For, as I have urged before, we can only feel an obligation to *act*; we cannot feel an obligation to *act from a certain desire*, in this case the desire to conquer one's feelings of terror arising from the sense of shame which they arouse. Moreover, if the sense of obligation to act in a particular way leads to an action, the action will be an action done from a sense of obligation, and therefore not, if the above analysis of virtue be right, an act of courage.

The mistake of supposing that there can be an obligation to act courageously seems to arise from two causes. In the first place, there is often an obligation to do that which involves the conquering or controlling of our fear in the doing of it, e.g. the obligation to walk along the side of a precipice to fetch a doctor for a member of our family. Here the acting on the obligation is externally, though only externally, the same as an act of courage proper. In

the second place there is an obligation to acquire courage, i.e. to do such things as will enable us afterwards to act courageously, and this may be mistaken for an obligation to act courageously. The same considerations can, of course, be applied, *mutatis mutandis*, to the other virtues.

The fact, if it be a fact, that virtue is no basis for morality will explain what otherwise it is difficult to account for, *viz.* the extreme sense of dissatisfaction produced by a close reading of Aristotle's *Ethics*. Why is the *Ethics* so disappointing? Not, I think, because it really answers two radically different questions as if they were one: (1) 'What is the happy life?,' (2) 'What is the virtuous life?' It is, rather, because Aristotle does not do what we as moral philosophers want him to do, *viz.* to convince us that we really ought to do what in our non-reflective consciousness we have hitherto believed we ought to do, or if not, to tell us what, if any, are the other things which we really ought to do, and to prove to us that he is right. Now, if what I have just been contending is true, a systematic account of the virtuous character cannot possibly satisfy this demand. At best it can only make clear to us the details of one of our obligations, *viz.* the obligation to make ourselves better men; but the achievement of this does not help us to discover what we ought to do in life as a whole, and why; to think that it did would be to think that our only business in life was self-improvement. Hence it is not surprising that Aristotle's account of the good man strikes us as almost wholly of academic value, with little relation to our real demand, which is formulated in Plato's words: οὐ γὰρ περὶ τοῦ ἐπιτυχόντος ὁ λόγος, ἀλλὰ περὶ τοῦ ὅντινα τρόπον χρὴ ζῆν.[9A]

I am not, of course, *criticizing* Aristotle for failing to satisfy this demand, except so far as here and there he leads us to think that he intends to satisfy it. For my main contention is that the demand cannot be

---

[9] This sharp distinction of virtue and morality as co-ordinate and independent forms of goodness will explain a fact which otherwise it is difficult to account for. If we turn from books on Moral Philosophy to any vivid account of human life and action such as we find in Shakespeare, nothing strikes us more than the comparative remoteness of the discussions of Moral Philosophy from the facts of actual life. Is not this largely because, while Moral Philosophy has, quite rightly, concentrated its attention on the fact of obligation, in the case of many of those whom we admire most and whose lives are of the greatest interest, the sense of obligation, though it may be an important, is not a dominating factor in their lives?

[9A] [For no light matter is at stake; the question concerns the very manner in which human life is to be lived (*Republic*, Bk. I, 352D)—Ed.]

satisfied, and cannot be satisfied because it is illegitimate. Thus we are brought to the question: 'Is there really such a thing as Moral Philosophy, and, if there is, in what sense?'

We should first consider the parallel case—as it appears to be—of the Theory of Knowledge. As I urged before, at some time or other in the history of all of us, if we are thoughtful, the frequency of our own and of others' mistakes is bound to lead to the reflection that possibly we and others have *always* been mistaken in consequence of some radical defect of our faculties. In consequence, certain things which previously we should have said without hesitation that we *knew*, as e.g. that $4 \times 7 = 28$, become subject to doubt; we become able only to say that we thought we knew these things. We inevitably go on to look for some general procedure by which we can ascertain that a given condition of mind is really one of knowledge. And this involves the search for a criterion of knowledge, i.e. for a principle by applying which we can settle that a given state of mind is really knowledge. The search for this criterion and the application of it, when found, is what is called the Theory of Knowledge. The search implies that instead of its being the fact that the knowledge that A is B is obtained directly by consideration of the nature of A and B, the knowledge that A is B, in the full or complete sense, can only be obtained by first knowing that A is B, and then knowing that we knew it by applying a criterion, such as Descartes's principle that what we clearly and distinctly conceive is true.

Now it is easy to show that the doubt whether A is B, based on this speculative or general ground, could, if genuine, never be set at rest. For if, in order really to know that A is B, we must first know that we knew it, then really, to know that we knew it, we must first know that we knew that we knew it. But—what is more important—it is also easy to show that this doubt is not a genuine doubt but rests on a confusion the exposure of which removes the

doubt. For when we *say* we doubt whether our previous condition was one of knowledge, what we *mean*, if we mean anything at all, is that we doubt whether our previous *belief* was *true*, a belief which we should express as the *thinking* that A is B. For in order to doubt whether our previous condition was one of knowledge, we have to think of it not as knowledge but as only belief, and our only question can be 'Was this belief true?' But as soon as we see that we are thinking of our previous condition as only one of belief, we see that what we are now doubting is not what we first *said* we were doubting, *viz.* whether a previous condition of knowledge was really knowledge. Hence, to remove the doubt, it is only necessary to appreciate the real nature of our consciousness in apprehending, e.g. that $7 \times 4 = 28$, and thereby see that it was no mere condition of believing but a condition of knowing, and then to notice that in our subsequent doubt what we are really doubting is not whether this consciousness was really knowledge, but whether a consciousness of another kind, *viz.* a belief that $7 \times 4 = 28$, was true. We thereby see that though a doubt based on speculative grounds is possible, it is not a doubt concerning what we believed the doubt concerned, and that a doubt concerning this latter is impossible.

Two results follow. In the first place, if, as is usually the case, we mean by the 'Theory of Knowledge' the knowledge which supplies the answer to the question 'Is what we have hitherto thought knowledge really knowledge?,' there is and can be no such thing, and the supposition that there can is simply due to a confusion. There can be no answer to an illegitimate question, except that the question is illegitimate. Nevertheless the question is one which we continue to put until we realize the inevitable immediacy of knowledge. And it is positive knowledge that knowledge is immediate and neither can be, nor needs to be, improved or vindicated by the further knowledge that it was knowledge. This positive knowledge sets at rest the inevitable doubt, and, so far as by the 'Theory of Knowledge' is meant this knowledge, then even though this knowledge be the knowledge that there is no Theory of Knowledge in the former sense, to that extent the Theory of Knowledge exists.

In the second place, suppose we come genuinely to doubt whether, e.g., $7 \times 4 = 28$ owing to a genuine doubt whether we were right in believing yesterday that $7 \times 4 = 28$, a doubt which can in fact only arise if we have lost our hold of, i.e. no longer remember, the real nature of our consciousness of yesterday, and so think of it as consisting in believing. Plainly, the only remedy is to do the sum again. Or, to put the matter generally, if we do come to doubt whether it is true that A is B, as we once thought, the remedy lies not in any process of reflection but in such a reconsideration of the nature of A and B as leads to the knowledge that A is B.

With these considerations in mind, consider the parallel which, as it seems to me, is presented—though with certain differences—by Moral Philosophy. The sense that we ought to do certain things arises in our unreflective consciousness, being an activity of moral thinking occasioned by the various situations in which we find ourselves. At this stage our attitude to these obligations is one of unquestioning confidence. But inevitably the appreciation of the degree to which the execution of these obligations is contrary to our interest raises the doubt whether after all these obligations are really obligatory, i.e. whether our sense that we ought not to do certain things is not illusion. We then want to have it *proved* to us that we ought to do so, i.e. to be convinced of this by a process which, as an argument, is different in kind from our original and unreflective appreciation of it. This demand is, as I have argued, illegitimate.

Hence, in the first place, if, as is almost universally the case, by Moral Philosophy is meant the knowledge which would satisfy this demand, there is no such knowledge, and all attempts to attain it are doomed to failure because they rest on a mistake, the mistake of supposing the possibility of proving what can only be apprehended directly by an act of moral thinking. Nevertheless the demand, though illegitimate, is inevitable until we have carried the process of reflection far enough to realize the self-evidence of our obligations, i.e. the immediacy of our apprehension of them. This realization of their self-evidence is positive knowledge, and so far, and so far only, as the term Moral Philosophy is confined to this knowledge and to the knowledge of the parallel immediacy of the apprehension of the goodness of the various virtues and of good dispositions generally, is there such a thing as Moral Philosophy. But since this knowledge may allay doubts which often affect the whole conduct of life, it is, though not extensive, important and even vitally important.

In the second place, suppose we come genuinely to doubt whether we ought, for example, to pay our debts, owing to a genuine doubt whether our previous conviction that we ought to do so is true, a doubt which can, in fact, only arise if we fail to remember the real nature of what we now call our past conviction. The only remedy lies in actually getting into a situation which occasions the obligation, or—if our imagination be strong enough—in imagining ourselves in that situation, and then letting our moral capacities of thinking do their work. Or, to put the matter generally, if we do doubt whether there is really an obligation to originate A in a situation B, the remedy lies not in any process of general thinking, but in getting face to face with a particular instance of the situation B, and then directly appreciating the obligation to originate A in that situation.

On the Idea of a Philosophy of Ethics

JAMES BALFOUR

In this Appendix I propose to extend and apply the remarks on the Idea of a Philosophy in general contained in the first chapter of the Essay, to the Philosophy of Ethics in particular. But, in order to do so, it is necessary, in the first place, to correct an error which, in these days when Science and the Knowable are supposed to be co-extensive, is natural though not the less mischievous;—the error I mean by which Ethics is degraded to a mere section or department of Science. At first sight, and from some points of view, the opinion seems plausible enough. That mankind have passed through many ethical phases (for example) is a fact of history, and history belongs to science; that I hold certain moral laws to be binding is a fact of my mental being; and, like all other such facts, is dealt with by Psychology,—also a branch of science. Physiology, Ethnology, and other sciences all have something to say concerning the origin and development of moral ideas in the individual and in the race; it is not unnatural, therefore, that some men of science, impressed by these facts, have claimed, or seemed to claim, Ethics for their own.

To hold such a view would be a most

Reprinted from *A Defense of Philosophic Doubt* by James Balfour by permission of A. P. Watt & Son as literary agents to the Estate of Lord Balfour and on behalf of Hodder & Stoughton Ltd.

unfortunate error; not to hold clearly and definitely its contrary may lead to much confusion; for though, as will appear, scientific laws form necessary steps in the deduction of subordinate ethical laws, and though the two provinces of knowledge cannot with advantage be separated in practice, still the truth remains that scientific judgments and ethical judgments deal with essentially different subject-matters.

Every scientific proposition asserts either the nature of the relation of space or time between phenomena which have existed, do exist, or will exist; or defines the relations of space or time which would exist if certain changes and simplifications were made in the phenomena (as in ideal geometry), or in the law governing the phenomena (as in ideal physics). Roughly speaking, it may be said to state facts or events, real or hypothetical.

An ethical proposition, on the other hand, though, like every other proposition it states a relation, does not state a relation of space or time. 'I ought to speak the truth,' for instance, does not imply that I have spoken, do speak, or shall speak the truth; it asserts no bond of causation between subject and predicate, nor any co-existence nor any sequence. It does not announce an event; and if some people would say that it stated a fact, it is not certainly a fact either of the 'external' or of the 'internal' world.

One cause, perhaps, of the constant confusion between Ethics and Science is the tendency there appears to be to regard the psychology of the individual holding the moral law as the subject-matter of Ethics, rather than the moral law itself; to investigate the position which the belief in such a proposition as "I ought to speak the truth" holds in the history of the race and of the individual, its causes and its accompaniments, rather than its truth or its evidence; to substitute, in short, Psychology or Anthropology for Ethics. The danger of such confusion will partly be shown by the few remarks which, in order to carry out the train of thought begun in the first chapter, I have to make on the Idea of a Philosophy of Ethics: that is, on the "form which any satisfactory system of Ethics must assume, or be able to assume, whatever be its contents."

The obvious truth that all knowledge is either certain in itself, or is derived by legitimate methods from that which is so, has been already, perhaps, more than sufficiently insisted on; and this, which is true of knowledge in general, is of course also true of ethical knowledge in particular. A little consideration will enable us to go on, and state this further fact, which is peculiar to Ethics. "The general propositions which really lie at the root of any ethical system must themselves be ethical, and can never be either scientific or metaphysical." In other words, if a proposition announcing obligation require proof at all, one term of that proof must always be a proposition announcing obligation, which itself requires no proof. This truth must not be confounded with that which I have just dwelt upon, namely, that Science and Ethics have essentially different subject-matters. This might be so, and yet Ethics might be indebted for all its first principles to Science.

A concrete case will perhaps make clearer this axiom of ethical philosophy. A man (let us say) is not satisfied that he ought to speak the truth. He demands a reason, and is told that truth-telling conduces to the welfare of society. He accepts this ground, and apparently, therefore, rests his ethics on what is purely scientific assertion. But this is not in reality the fact. There is a suppressed premiss required to justify his conclusion, which would run somewhat in this way, 'I ought to do that which conduces to the welfare of society.' And this proposition, of course, is ethical. This example is not merely an illustration, it is a typical case. There is no artifice by which an ethical statement can be evolved from a scientific or metaphysical proposition, or any combination of such; and whenever the reverse appears to be the fact, it will always be found that the assertion, which seems to be the basis of the ethical superstructure, is in reality merely the 'minor' of a syllogism, of which the major is the desired ethical principle.

If this principle be as true as it seems to me to be obvious, it at once alters our attitude towards a vast mass of controversy which has encumbered the progress of moral philosophy. So far as the proof of a basis of morals is concerned it makes irrelevant all discussion on the origin of moral ideas, or on the nature of moral sentiments; and it relegates to their proper sphere in Psychology or Anthropology all discussion on such subjects as association of ideas, inherited instincts, and evolution, in so far, at least, as these are supposed to refer to ultimate moral laws. For it is an obvious corollary from our principle, that the origin of an ultimate ethical belief never can supply a reason for believing it; since the origin of this belief, as of any other mental phenomenon, is a matter to be dealt with by Science; and my thesis is, that (negatively speaking) scientific truth alone cannot serve as a foundation for a moral system; or (to put it positively), if we have a moral system at all, there must be contained in it, explicitly or implicitly, at least one ethical proposition, of which no proof can be given or required.

In one sense, therefore, all Ethics is 'a priori.' It is not, and never can be, founded on experience. Whether we be Utilitarians, or Egoists, or Intuitionists, by whatever name we call ourselves, the rational basis of our system must be something other than an experience or a series of experiences; for such always belong to Science.

Limited indeed is the number of English Moralists who have invariably kept this in view. However foreign it may be to their various systems, an enquiry into origin or into the universality of moral ideas always appears to slip in—not in its proper place, as an interesting psychological adjunct, but—as having an important bearing on the authority of their particular principle. And the necessary result, of course, of these efforts to support ultimate principles, is, that they cease to be ultimate, and become not only subordinate, but subordinate to judgments which, if explicitly stated, would very likely appear far less obvious than they.

There is a whole school of Moralists, for example, who find or invent a special faculty, intellectual or sensitive, by which moral truth is arrived at; who would regard it as a serious blow to morality if the process by which ethical beliefs were produced was found to be common to many other regions of thought. Oddly enough, these are the very people whose systems are often called 'a priori.' Now if by this term be meant that the ordinary maxims of morality are (according to these systems) independent of experience, it is appropriate enough; but if it be meant that they are self-evident, it is a singular misnomer. For it is clear that on their systems rigidly interpreted those maxims derive their evidence, not from their own internal authority, but from the fact that they bear a certain special relation to our mental constitution; so that the ethical proposition which really lies at the root of their ethics is something of this sort:—'We ought to obey all laws the validity of which is recognised by a special innate faculty, whether called Conscience or otherwise.' Now, I do not deny that from a philosophical point of view such propositions as these are possible

foundations of morals; but what I desire to point out is that such a phrase (to take a concrete case) as 'I ought to speak the truth because conscience commands it,' may have two widely different meanings, and may belong to two different systems of Ethics, not commonly distinguished. According to the first and most accurate meaning, 'I ought to speak the truth' is an inference, of which the major premiss must be, 'I ought to do what conscience commands,' and being an inference, cannot obviously be an a priori law. According to the second and inaccurate meaning, 'I ought to speak the truth' is in reality received on its own merits, and conscience is very unnecessarily brought in, either to add dignity to the law, or to account for its general acceptance among mankind, or for some other extra-ethical reason. The first of these views is open to no criticism from the point of view of ethical philosophy; so far as form is concerned it is unassailable. But I greatly suspect that most people who nominally found their morality on conscience really hold the second theory; and in that case, as I think, their statement is misleading, if not erroneous.

So far I have only given a negative description of the nature of an ethical proposition. I have said, indeed, that it announces obligation, but this statement is tautological; for if we knew in what obligation consisted there would be no difficulty in stating the meaning of ethical. Beyond this I have only said that an ethical judgment deals with an essentially different subject-matter from either Science or Metaphysics. Is it possible to say more than this? Is it possible to give any description of ethical propositions which shall add to our knowledge of their character? On general grounds it is plain that this can only be done, supposing that what are "commonly" called ethical propositions form part of a large class of judgments which resemble them in being neither scientific nor metaphysical, but differ from them in some other respect. I myself hold this to be the case. I hold not only that the judgments commonly called ethical (but which, in spite of the clumsiness attendant on changing the meaning of a word in the middle of a discussion, I shall henceforward call "moral") have the two negative characteristics above mentioned in common with a larger class of judgments; but that the distinction between the two classes should be ignored by ethical philosophy, since it depends not on 'form' but on 'matter.' All judgments belonging to either of these classes I shall henceforth call ethical. Those commonly called ethical I shall describe as moral; the rest are either non-moral or immoral. Every possible judgment, then is either moral or non-moral or immoral. The terminology thus being defined, let me explain it, and at the same time my view of the subject.

If a man contemplates any action as one which he chooses to perform, he must do so either because he regards the action as one which he chooses for itself, or because he expects to obtain by it some object which he chooses for itself. And similarly, if he contemplates any object as one he chooses to obtain, he must do so either because he regards that object as chosen for itself, or because it may be a means to one that is. In other words, deliberate action is always directed mediately or immediately to something which is chosen for itself alone; which something may either be itself an action, or what I loosely term an object. Including both, then, under the term 'end,' I define an ethical proposition thus:—"An ethical proposition is one which prescribes an action with reference to an end." Nobody will deny that this definition is true of all moral propositions (most people, indeed, will think that it is too obvious to need stating); but they will probably say, and say truly, that it is also true of a great many propositions which are not usually called moral. Now my object is to show that the distinction between what are usually called moral propositions and that larger class which I have defined above, has no philosophic import, has noth-

ing that is to do with the grounds of obligation. And for this purpose, let me analyse more carefully this larger class (which I call ethical) from a philosophic point of view, that is, with reference to the rational foundation and connection of its parts.

(1) Every proposition prescribing an action with reference to an end, belongs either explicitly or implicitly to a system of such propositions. (2) The fundamental proposition of every such system states an end, which the person who receives that system regards as final—as chosen for itself alone. (3) The subordinate propositions of that system are deduced from the fundamental proposition by means of scientific or theological minor premises. (4) When two such systems conflict, their rival claim can only be decided by a judgment or proposition not contained in either of them, which shall assert which of these respective fundamental 'ends' shall have precedence. (Ethics, then, rests on two sorts of judgments, neither of which can be deduced from the other, and of neither of which can any proof be given or required. The first sort declares an end to be final, the second declares which of two final ends is to be preferred, if they are incompatible. This second sort, of course, is not essential to an ethical system, but can only be required when an individual regards more than one end as final.) (5) No other sort of proposition can possibly lie at the root of an ethical system. (This is merely a restatement of the law dwelt on at the beginning of this discussion.)

Now in so far as this is a complete philosophical diagram of every ethical system, it must show the sort of authority on which every ethical proposition—every imperative—must rest. Yet since it is plain that this diagram takes no account of the differences there may be between moral and immoral ethical systems, how (it may be asked) can we account for the widespread delusion, that these differences affect the authority of the former? This question takes us far afield into the regions of Psychology and Anthropology, but the answer to it may perhaps be suggested as follows. The main reason for this error appears to be false analogy, unchecked by any clear apprehension of the nature of the rational or philosophical peculiarities of an ethical system. And in order to illustrate this, and at the same time to place the theory I am defending under as strong a light as possible, it may be as well to examine the exact bearing which "Universality" and the approval of "Conscience" (two of the chief characteristics of moral as opposed to non-moral or immoral systems) have on obligation.

My position, of course, is that they have no bearing—and in order to show this I offer the following analysis to the reader—taking Universality first. A law may be said to be Universal in one of four senses. It may mean (first) that all intelligences regard themselves as bound by it. This meaning we need not further consider, not only because it is a scientific assertion, and therefore, as I have shown, incapable of becoming the foundation of an ethical system, but also because it is a scientific assertion now entirely discredited. It is quite out of fashion to maintain that Morality is the same in every race and every country, and therefore till, in the revolutions of thought, some one is found to re-assert this doctrine, we need not further discuss it.

The second possible meaning is, that by a universal moral law we mean one by which all intelligences "ought" to regard themselves as bound. This also we may dismiss because it amounts to saying that there is a moral law which obliges all intelligences to be bound by other moral laws. If it is, we are committed to an infinite series of moral laws, each commanding us to be bound by the preceding one. If it is not, then there can be a moral law which (in this sense) is not universal.

In the third place, by a universal moral law we may mean one which we think all men ought to obey. That we do

think this of most moral laws, and that we do not think it of the other ethical laws, namely, the non-moral and the immoral ones, is tolerably certain. It remains to enquire whether the difference bears on obligation; and this enquiry, as it seems to me, may be settled by a very simple consideration. All intelligences means Me and all other intelligences. The first of these constituent parts would be bound by a law held by Me whether it were universal (in this sense) or not. The second would not be bound by a law held by Me whether it were universal in this sense or not. In other words, to be bound by a moral law (and this, by the way, brings out very clearly the difference between being ethically bound and legally bound) is exactly the same thing as to regard it as binding on you; it is not to regard it as binding on someone else; and it is not for someone else to regard it as binding on you; it has therefore, and it can have, no connection with Universality in this third sense.

It is, of course, open to anyone to assert that he recognises no imperative which is not universal (in this sense). This may very well be the fact, and I have no wish to deny it. What I deny is, that the connection between the two is other than empirical and accidental, or that it has any place in the philosophy of obligation.

The fourth and last meaning which I am able to attach to the word Universal, when used of a law, is that it signifies that all people of 'well-constituted minds' do, as a matter of fact, regard themselves as bound by a law so qualified. Now, if 'well-constituted' is defined with reference to morality, and means 'holding the one true moral system,' a proposition that all true or right moral laws are universal, is frivolous and merely verbal. If it be defined with reference to something else—if it means for instance, sane, or well-educated, or Christian, or scientific, or anything non-moral, then the same arguments may be used to show that universality in this sense cannot be a ground of obligation, as I used when speaking of the first sense. For a proposition asserting that any considerable body of men, distinguished from the rest of mankind by some non-moral attribute, hold the same moral code, is very likely to be questionable, and being a scientific assertion, is quite certain to be irrelevant.

So much, then, for Universality. As regards Conscience, I have shown before, that to assume a special faculty which is to announce ultimate moral laws can add nothing to their validity, nor will it do so the more if we suppose its authority supported by such sanctions as remorse or self-approval. Conscience regarded in this way is not ethically to be distinguished from any external authority, as, for instance, the Deity, or the laws of the land. Now, it is plain that no external authority can give validity to ultimate moral laws, for the question immediately arises, why should we obey that authority? Only two reasons can be given. The first is, that it is "right in itself" to obey; the second is, that (through a proper use of sanctions) it will be for our happiness to obey. Now, the first of these is a moral law, which obviously does not derive its validity from the external authority, because the external authority is an authority only by means of it. And the same may be said of the second reason, substituting the words 'ethical but non-moral' for the word 'moral.' In neither case, then, is the external authority the ultimate ground of obligation.

The inevitable ambiguity which arises from the sudden extension of the meaning of the word 'ethical' to imperatives which are immoral or non-moral, makes it, perhaps, desirable that I should very concisely restate, from another point of view, the main position I have been attempting to establish.

All imperatives, all propositions prescribing actions, have this in common:— That if they are to have any cogency, or are to be anything but empty sound, the actions they prescribe must be to the individual by whom they are regarded as binding, either

mediately or immediately desirable. They must conduce, directly or indirectly, to something which he regards as of worth for itself alone. The number of things which are thus in themselves desirable or of worth to somebody or other is, of course, very great. Pleasure or happiness in the abstract, other people's pleasure or happiness, money (irrespective of its power of giving pleasure), power, the love of God, revenge, are some of the commonest of them, and every one of these is regarded by some person or other as an end to be attained for its own sake, and not as means to something else. Now, it is evident that to every one of the ultimate propositions prescribing these ends, and for which, as the ends are ends-in-themselves, no further reason can be given, there will belong a system of dependent propositions, the reasons for which are that the actions they prescribe conduce to the ultimate end or end-in-itself.

If, for instance, revenge against a particular individual is for me an end-in-itself, a proposition which prescribes shooting him from behind a hedge may be one of the subordinate or dependent propositions belonging to that particular system. But whereas the indefinite number of such systems is thus characterised by a common form, it is divided by ordinary usage into three classes, the moral, the non-moral, and the immoral, about the denotation of which there is a tolerable agreement. It would be universally admitted, for instance, that a system founded on the happiness of others was a moral system, while one founded on revenge was immoral; and, though there would be more dispute as to the members of the non-moral class, this is not a question on which I need detain the reader. The denotation then of these names being presumably fixed, what is the connotation? or to limit the enquiry, what is the connotation of a moral system? The apparent answers are as numerous as the number of schools of Moralists. But however numerous they may be, they can all be divided into two classes. The first class merely restate the denotation;—in other words, announce the ultimate end-in-itself of the system, and so, properly speaking, give no answer at all. A Utilitarian, for instance, may simply assert that the greatest happiness of the greatest number is for him the ultimate end of action. If he stops there he evidently shows no philosophic reason for distinguishing the system he adopts from the countless others which exist, or have existed. If he attempts to give any further characteristic of his system, he then belongs to the second class, who do indeed explain the connotation of the word 'moral' according to their usage of it, but whose explanations have, and can have, nothing to do with the grounds of action or the theory of obligation. The sanction of conscience, the emotion of approval, the expectation of reward, the feeling of good desert, glow of conscious merit—these are all most undoubtedly marks or characteristics of moral actions: how they came to be so, whether by education, association of ideas, innate tendency, or howsoever it has happened, matters nothing whatever, except to the psychologist; that they are so is certain, but the significance of the fact is habitually misunderstood. Are they simply the *causes* of good action? Then they have nothing to do with Ethics, which is concerned not with the causes but with the grounds or reasons for action, and would remain wholly unchanged if not a single man ever had done or could do right. Are they the *ends* of action? Is the fact that they are obtained by a certain course a valid reason for pursuing that course? In that case they stand to a person holding that opinion in precisely the same relation as money does to the miser, or revenge to the savage. They are the groundwork of an ethical system, and to state them is simply to denote what ethical system it is which is being alluded to. Are they finally, not ends of action, but merely marks by which certain actions may be known to belong to a particular system? In that case, and for that very reason, they can have nothing to do with the grounds or theory of obligation. Therefore, I am justified in asserting that though

under the general name 'ethical' are included not only moral, but also non-moral and immoral systems, the distinctions regarded from the outside between these subdivisions are not essential, and have no philosophic import—which was the thing to be proved.

The second corollary concerns the functions of the Moral Philosopher. It is clear from what precedes, that it is *not* the business of the moral philosopher to account for the origin of moral ideas, or to analyse and explain that growth of sentiment which collects around the time-honoured maxims of current morality. These are topics which belong to Psychology. Neither is he expected to prove the propositions which lie at the root of any system of morals; for these are incapable of proof. Nor, for the same reason, can he justify the judgments which declare which of two final ends is to be preferred in case of conflict, or how much of one is to be preferred to how much of the others. Nor, in reality, has he any but a subordinate part to play in expounding or deducing the derivative rules of morality; and for this reason.

The deduction of any derivative rule is always necessarily in this form: 'the happiness of mankind ought to be promoted' (this, let us say, is the ultimate unprovable foundation of the system): 'monogamy promotes the happiness of mankind' (this is the scientific—in another system it might have been theological—minor premiss): 'therefore monogamy is a system which ought to be supported.' This is the required derivative rule. Now it should be clear that the only difficulty in deducing this conclusion from the first principle of the system lies in the difficulty of demonstrating the minor premiss; in other words, it lies in the difficulty of a certain sociological investigation, which the speculative moralist as such cannot be expected to undertake.

The important duties of the moralist, for he has important duties, arise from the confused state in which the greater part of mankind are with regard to their ethical first principles. The two questions each man has to ask himself are—What do I hold to be the ultimate ends of action? and—If there is more than one such end, how do I estimate them in case of conflict? These two questions, it will be observed, are questions of fact, not of law; and the duty of the moralist is to help his readers to discover the fact, not to force his own view down their throats by attempting a proof of that which is essentially, and by its very nature, incapable of proof. Above all, he must beware of substituting some rude simplification for (what may perhaps be) the complexity of nature, by deducing (as the Utilitarians do) all subordinate rules from one fundamental principle, when, it may be, this principle only approximately contains actual existing ethical facts.

Since these two questions can be answered, not by ratiocination, but only by simple inspection, the art of the moralist will consist in placing before the enquirer various problems in Ethics free from the misleading particulars which surround them in practice. In other words, his method will be casuistical, and not dogmatic.

It may perhaps seem strange that, after commenting at some length on the prevailing confusion between Ethics and Psychology, I should now have to announce that the business of the Ethical Philosopher (at least, so far as first principles are concerned) is as purely psychological as, according to the two preceding paragraphs, I make it out to be; and it may seem, therefore, as if the difference between my view and that of the Philosophers whom I have attempted to criticise is by no means essential or important. This, however, is not the case. My complaint against these philosophers is that they appear to suppose that a psychological law can serve as a rational basis for an ethical system; so that their chief aim often seems to have been the establishment of their own particular views on the origin and nature of our moral sentiments. I, on the

other hand, altogether deny the possibility of such a basis, and maintain that all that a moralist can do with regard to ethical first principles is, not to prove them or deduce them, but to render them explicit if they are implicit, clear if they are obscure. To do this effectually he must, of course, treat of ideas and notions, and his work will, therefore, in some sense be undoubtedly psychological. To make this statement complete, I should add, that (as appears by my next paragraph) there is no absurdity in supposing that a moralist may in the course of his speculations hit on some entirely new first principle which he has not held even obscurely before, but which commends itself to his mind as soon as it is presented to him.

The third corollary I draw is this—that there are only two senses in which we can rationally talk of a moral system being superior to the one we profess. According to the first sense, superior means superior in form, more nearly in accordance with the ideal of an ethical system just sketched out. According to the second sense, in which the superiority attaches to the matter of the system, it can only mean that the system is one of which we are ignorant, but which we should adopt if present to us. The superiority indicated is a hypothetical superiority.

Now it must be observed that the sense in which we speak of other hypothetical systems as being superior to our own, is by no means identical with that in which we speak of our own as being superior to that of other people. Looking back over history, we perceive a change and development of the moral ideas of the race in the direction of the systems which now prevail; and this change we rightly term an improvement. But, if, arguing from the past, we suppose that this improvement will continue through the indefinite future, we are misled by a false analogy. The change may very well continue, the improvement certainly will not. And the reason is clear. What we mean, or ought to mean, by an improvement in the past, is an approach to our own standard, and since any change at all corresponding in magnitude to this in the future must involve a departure from that standard, it must necessarily be a change for the worse.

In other words,—when we speak of another system as being superior (in matter) to our own, we speak of a possible system which we should accept if we knew it. When we speak of our own system being superior to that of some other person, we assert the superiority unconditionally, and quite irrespectively of the possible acceptance of it by that other person, supposing him to be acquainted with it. If then we believe that development will proceed in the future as it has done in the past, we must suppose that a time will come when the moral ideas of the world would be as much out of our reach, supposing them presented to us, as ours would be out of reach of primitive man. This is also true of scientific ideas: but there is this difference between them, that whereas the change in scientific ideas may be an improvement, that in moral ideas must be a degradation. The grounds of this distinction of course are obvious, viz., that the standard of excellence in the case of scientific ideas is, or is supposed to be, conformity to an infinitely complex external world:—a conformity which may increase with every change in the ideas. The standard of excellence, on the other hand, in moral ideas must necessarily be conformity to our actual ideal, and this conformity must diminish with every change in the ideas.

The point would not perhaps have been worth dwelling on, if it was not that the discussion brings into strong relief the nature, so far as form is concerned, of the criterion of right, and also has some bearing on current theories of optimistic evolution, with which I confess it does not seem possible easily to reconcile it.

The Meaning of "Right"

SIR DAVID ROSS

The purpose of this inquiry is to examine the nature, relations, and implications of three conceptions which appear to be fundamental in ethics—those of 'right,' 'good' in general, and 'morally good.' The inquiry will have much in common with the inquiries, of which there have been many in recent years, into the nature of value, and I shall have occasion to discuss some of the more important theories of value; but my object is a more limited one. I offer no discussion, except at most a purely incidental and illustrative one, of certain forms of value, such as economic value and beauty. My interest will throughout be ethical, and value will be discussed only so far as it seems to be relevant to this interest.

I propose to begin with the term 'right.' A considerable ambiguity attaches to any attempt to discuss the meaning of any term. Professor G. E. Moore has well indicated three main objects that such an attempt at definition may have. 'When we say, as Webster says, "The definition of horse is, 'A hoofed quadruped of the genus Equus,'" we may, in fact, mean three different things. (1) We may mean merely: "When I say 'horse,' you are to understand that I am talking about a hoofed quadruped of the genus Equus." This might be called the arbitrary verbal definition.... (2) We may mean, as Webster ought to mean: "When most English people say 'horse,' they mean a hoofed quadruped of

Reprinted from *The Right and the Good* by Sir David Ross by permission of the Clarendon Press, Oxford. Copyright 1930.

the genus Equus." This may be called the verbal definition proper.... But (3) we may, when we define horse, mean something much more important. We may mean that a certain object, which we all of us know, is composed in a certain manner: that it has four legs, a head, a heart, a liver, etc., etc., all of them arranged in definite relations to one another."[1]

We must ask ourselves whether, in discussing the meaning of 'right,' we are attempting any one of these kinds of definition, or something different from them all. I certainly do not wish *merely* to indicate a sense in which I propose to use the term 'right.' I wish to keep in touch with the general usage of the word. While other things may be called 'right' (as in the phrases 'the right road,' 'the right solution'), the word is specially applied to acts, and it is the sense (by general consent a very important one) in which it is so applied that I wish to discuss. But we must be prepared to find that the general usage of the word is not entirely consistent with itself. Most of the words in any language have a certain amount of ambiguity; and there is special danger of ambiguity in the case of a word like 'right,' which does not stand for anything we can point out to one another or apprehend by one of the senses. Even with words that do stand for such things there is this danger. Even if two people find that the things the one calls red are just the things the other calls red, it is by no means certain that they mean the

[1] *Principia Ethica,* 8.

same quality. There is only a general pre-sumption that since the structure of their eyes (if neither is colour-blind) is pretty much the same, the same object acting on the eyes of the two men produces pretty much the same kind of sensation. And in the case of a term like 'right,' there is noth-ing parallel to the highly similar organiza-tion of different people's eyes, to create a presumption that when they call the same act right, they mean to refer to the same quality of it. In point of fact, there is a se-rious difference of view as to the *application* of the term 'right.' Suppose, for instance, that a man pays a particular debt simply from fear of the legal consequences of not doing so, some people would say he had done what was right, and others would deny this: they would say that no moral value attaches to such an act, and that since 'right' is meant to imply moral value, the act cannot be right. They might gen-eralize and say that no act is right unless it is done from a sense of duty, or if they shrank from so rigorous a doctrine, they might at least say that no act is right unless done from *some* good motive, such as either sense of duty or benevolence.

This difference of view may be due to either of two causes. Both parties may be using 'right' in the same sense, the sense of 'morally obligatory,' and differing as to the further character an act must have in order to have this quality. *Or* the first party may be using 'right' in this sense, and the second in the sense of 'morally good.' It is not clear to me which of these two things is usually happening when this difference of view arises. But it seems probable that both things really happen—that some people fail to notice the distinction between 'right' and 'morally good,' and that others, while distinguishing the meaning of these terms, think that only what is morally good is right. A discussion of the first of these positions only is strictly in point here, where we are discussing the *meaning* of 'right.' It seems to me clear that 'right' does not mean the same as 'morally good'; and

we can test this by trying to substitute one for the other. If they meant the same thing we should be able to substitute, for instance, 'he is a right man' for 'he is a mor-ally good man'; nor is our inability to do this merely a matter of English idiom, for if we turn to the sort of moral judgement in which we do use the word 'right,' such as 'this is the right act,' it is clear that by this we mean 'this act is the act *that ought to be done*,' 'this act is *morally obligatory*'; and to substitute either of these phrases for 'morally good' in 'he is a morally good man' would obviously be not merely unidio-matic, but absurd. It should be obvious, then, that 'right' and 'morally good' mean different things. But some one might say that while 'morally good' has a wider appli-cation than 'right,' in that it can be applied to agents as well as to acts, yet when applied to acts they mean the same thing. I should like therefore to convince him that 'right act' cannot mean the same as 'act that ought to be done' and *also* the same as 'morally good act.' If I can convince him of this, I think he will see the propriety of not using 'right act' in the sense of 'morally good act.'

But we ought first to note a minor difference between the meaning of 'right' and the meaning of 'something that ought to be done' or 'that is my duty' or 'that is incumbent on me.' It may sometimes happen that there is a set of two or more acts one or other of which ought to be done by me rather than any act not belong-ing to this set. In such a case any act of this set is right, but none is my duty; my duty is to do 'one or other' of them. Thus 'right' has a somewhat wider possible application than 'something that ought to be done' or any of its equivalents. But we want an adjective to express the same meaning as 'something that ought to be done,' and though we have 'obligatory' at our disposal, that also has its ambiguity, since it sometimes means 'compulsory.' We should have to say 'morally obligatory' to make our meaning quite clear; and to obviate the necessity of using this rather cumbrous expression, I will use 'right' in this sense. I hope that this paragraph will prevent any confusion arising from this slightly inaccurate usage.

Some might deny the correctness of the distinction just drawn. They might say that when there are two or more acts one or other of which, as we say, we ought to do (it not being our duty to do one rather than another), the truth is that these are simply alternative ways of producing a single result, and that our duty is, strictly, not to do 'one or other' of the acts, but to produce the result; this alone is our duty, and this alone is right. This answer does, I think, fairly apply to many cases in which it *is* the production of a certain result that we think obligatory, the means being optional: e.g. to a case in which it is our duty to convey information to some one, but morally immaterial whether we do so orally or in writing. But in principle, at any rate, there may be other cases in which it is our duty to produce one or other of two or more *different* states of affairs, without its being our duty to produce one of them rather than another; in such a case each of these acts will be right, and none will be our duty.

If it can be shown that **nothing that** ought to be done is ever morally good, it will be clear *a fortiori* that 'morally good' does not *mean* the same as 'that ought to be done.' Now it is, I think, quite clear that the only acts that are morally good are those that proceed from a good motive; this is maintained by those whom I am now trying to convince, and I entirely agree. If, then, we can show that action from a good motive is never morally obligatory, we shall have established that what is morally good is never right, and *a fortiori* that 'right' does not mean the same as 'morally good.' That action from a good motive is never morally obligatory follows (1)

from the Kantian principle, which is generally admitted, that 'I ought' implies 'I can.' It is not the case that I can by choice produce a certain motive (whether this be an ordinary desire or the sense of obligation) in myself at a moment's notice, still less that I can at a moment's notice make it effective in stimulating me to act. I can act from a certain motive only if I have the motive; if not, the most I can do is to cultivate it by suitably directing my attenion or by acting in certain appropriate ways so that on some future occasion it *will* be present in me, and I shall be able to act from it. My *present* duty, therefore, cannot be to act here and now from it.

(2) A similar conclusion may be reached by a *reductio ad absurdum*. Those who hold that our duty is to act from a certain motive usually (Kant is the great exemplar) hold that the motive from which we ought to act is the sense of duty. Now if the sense of duty is to be my motive for doing a certain act, it must be the sense that it is my duty to do that act. If, therefore, we say 'it is my duty to do act A from the sense of duty,' this means 'it is my duty to do act A from the sense that it is my duty to do act A.' And here the whole expression is in contradiction with a part of itself. The whole sentence says 'it is my duty to-do-act-A-from-the-sense-that-it-is-my-duty-to-do-act-A.' But the latter part of the sentence implies that what I think is that it is my duty-to-do-act-A simply. And if, as the theory in question requires, we try to amend the latter part of the expression to bring it into accord with the whole expression, we get the result 'it is my duty to do act A from the sense that it is my duty to do act A from the sense that it is my duty to do act A,' where again the last part of the expression is in conflict with the theory, and with the sentence as a whole. It is clear that a further similar amendment, and a further, and in the end an infinite series of amendments would be necessary in the attempt to bring the last part of the expression into

accordance with the theory, and that even then we should not have succeeded in doing so.

Again, suppose that I say to you 'it is your duty to do act A from the sense of duty'; that means 'it is your duty to do act A from the sense that it is your duty to do act A.' Then *I* think that it is your duty to act from a certain motive, but I suggest that *you* should act under the supposition that it is your duty to do a certain thing, irrespective of motive, i.e. under a supposition which I must think false since it contradicts my own.

The only conclusion that can be drawn is that our duty is to do certain things, not to do them from the sense of duty.[2]

The latter of these two arguments ([1] and [2]) cannot be used against those who hold that it is our duty to act from some other motive than the sense of duty; the sense of duty is the only motive that leads to the infinite series in question. But the first of the two arguments seems in itself sufficient against *any* theory which holds that motive of any kind is included in the content of duty. And though the second argument does not refute the view that we ought to act from some other motive, it would be paradoxical to hold that we ought to act from some other motive but never ought to act from a sense of duty, which is the highest motive.[3]

Let us now return to the three senses in which Professor Moore points out that we may understand an attempt to define a certain term.[4] So far, the position we have taken up with regard to 'right' includes something of each of the first two attitudes he distinguishes. In using 'right' as synonymous (but for the minor distinction already pointed out)[5] with 'what is my duty,' and as distinct from 'morally good,' I believe I am conforming to what most men (if not all men) usually mean when they use the word. But I could not maintain that they always use the word in this way. I am, therefore, to some extent adopting the first of the attitudes he distinguishes, and expressing my own intention to use 'right' in this sense only. And this is justified by the great confusion that has been introduced into ethics by the phrase 'a right action' being used sometimes of the initiation of a certain change in the state of affairs irrespective of motive, and at other times of such initiation from some particular motive, such as sense of duty or benevolence. I would further suggest that additional clearness would be gained if we used 'act' of the thing done, the initiation of change, and 'action' of the doing of it, the initiating of change, from a certain motive. We should then talk of a right act but not of a right action, of a morally good action but not of a morally good act. And it may be added that the doing of a right act may be a morally bad action, and that the doing of a wrong act may be a morally good action; for 'right' and 'wrong' refer entirely to the thing done, 'morally good' and 'morally bad' entirely to the motive from which it is done. A firm grasp of this distinction will do much to remove some of the perplexities of our moral thought.

The question remains, what attitude we are to take up towards Professor Moore's third sense of 'definition.' Are we to hold that 'right' can be defined in the sense of being reduced to elements simpler than itself? At first sight it might appear that egoism and utilitarianism are attempts to define 'right'—to define it as 'productive of the greatest possible pleasure to the agent' or as 'productive of the greatest possible pleasure to mankind'; and I think

---

[2] It should be added, however, that one, and an important one, of our duties is to cultivate in ourselves the sense of duty. But then this is the duty of cultivating in ourselves the sense of duty, and not of cultivating in ourselves, from the sense of duty, the sense of duty.

[3] If any one doubts that it is, I beg him to refer to pp. 164–5, where I give reasons in support of the contention. [In *The Right and the Good.*—Ed.]

[4] Cf. p. i.

[5] pp. 3–4.

these theories have often been so under-stood by some of those who accept them. But the leaders of the school are not unanimous in so understanding their theory. Bentham seems to understand it so. He says[6] that 'when thus interpreted' (i.e. as meaning 'comformable to the principle of utility'), 'the words *ought* and *right* . . . and others of that stamp, have a meaning; when otherwise, they have none.' And elsewhere[7] he says 'admitting (what is not true) that the word *right* can have a meaning without reference to utility.' Yet, as Sidgwick points out,[8] 'when Bentham explains (*Principles of Morals and Legislation*, Chap. I, § I, note) that his fundamental principle "states the greatest happiness of all those whose interest is in question as being the right and proper end of human action," we cannot understand him really to *mean* by the word "right" "conducive to the general happiness"; for the proposition that it is conducive to general happiness to take general happiness as an end of action, though not exactly a tautology, can hardly serve as the fundamental principle of a moral system.' Bentham has evidently not made up his mind clearly whether he thinks that 'right' *means* 'productive of the general happiness,' *or* that being productive of the general happiness is what makes right acts right; and would very likely have thought the difference unimportant. Mill does not so far as I know discuss the question whether right is definable. He states his creed in the form 'actions are right in proportion as they tend to promote happiness,'[9] where the claim that is made is not that this is what 'right' means, but that this is the other characteristic in virtue of which actions that are right are right. And Sidgwick says[10] that the meaning of 'right' or 'ought' 'is too elementary to admit of any formal definition,' and

expressly repudiates[11] the view that 'right' means 'productive of any particular sort of result.'

The most deliberate claim that 'right' is definable as 'productive of so and so' is made by Prof. G. E. Moore, who claims in *Principia Ethica* that 'right' means 'productive of the greatest possible good.' Now it has often been pointed out against hedonism, and by no one more clearly than by Professor Moore, that the claim that 'good' just means 'pleasant' cannot seriously be maintained; that while it may or may not be true that the only things that are good are pleasant, the statement that the good is just the pleasant is a synthetic, not an analytic proposition; that the words 'good' and 'pleasant' stand for distinct qualities, even if the things that possess the one are precisely the things that possess the other. If this were not so, it would not be intelligible that the proposition 'the good is just the pleasant' should have been maintained on the one hand, and denied on the other, with so much fervour; for we do not fight for or against analytic propositions; we take them for granted. Must not the same claim be made about the statement being right means being an act productive of the greatest good producible in the circumstances'? Is it not plain on reflection that this is not what we *mean* by right, even if it be a true statement about what *is* right? It seems clear for instance that when an ordinary man says it is right to fulfil promises he is not in the least thinking of the total consequences of such an act, about which he knows and cares little or nothing. 'Ideal utilitarianism'[12] is, it would appear, plausible only when it is understood not as an analysis or definition of the notion of 'right' but as a statement that all acts that are right, and only these, possess the further characteristic of being productive of

---

[6] *Principles of Morals and Legislation*, Ch. I, § 10.
[7] ib. §14. 10.
[8] *Methods of Ethics*, ed. 7, 26 n.
[9] *Utilitarianism*, copyright eds., 9.
[10] *Methods of Ethics*, ed. 7, 32.

[11] ib. 25–6.
[12] I use this as a well-known way of referring to Professor Moore's view. 'Agathistic utilitarianism' would indicate more distinctly the difference between it and hedonistic utilitarianism.

the best possible consequences, and are right because they possess this other characteristic.

If I am not mistaken, Professor Moore has moved to this position, from the position that 'right' is *analysable* into 'productive of the greatest possible good.' In *Principia Ethica* the latter position is adopted: e.g. 'This use of "right," as denoting what is good as a means, whether or not it is also good as an end, is indeed the use to which I shall confine the word.'[13] 'To assert that a certain line of conduct is, at a given time, absolutely right or obligatory, is obviously to assert that more good or less evil will exist in the world, if it be adopted, than if anything else be done instead.'[14] 'To ask what kind of actions one ought to perform, or what kind of conduct is right, is to ask what kind of effects such action and conduct will produce . . . What I wish first to point out is that "right" does and can mean nothing but "cause of a good result," and is thus always identical with "useful" . . . That the assertion "I am morally bound to perform this action" is identical with the assertion "this action will produce the greatest possible amount of good in the Universe" has already been briefly shewn . . . ; but it is important to insist that this fundamental point is demonstrably certain. . . . Our "duty," therefore, can only be defined as that action, which will cause more good to exist in the Universe than any possible alternative. And what is "right" or "morally permissible" only differs from this, as what will *not* cause *less* good than any possible alternative.'[16]

In his later book, *Ethics*, Professor Moore seems to have to adopt the other position, though perhaps not quite unequivocally. On page 8 he names as one of the 'more fundamental questions' of ethics the question 'what, after all, is it that we mean to say of an action when we say that it is right or ought to be done?' Here it is still suggested that 'right' is perhaps analysable or definable. But to this question *Ethics* nowhere distinctly offers an answer, and on page 9 we find, 'Can we discover any single reason, applicable to all right actions equally, which is, in every case, *the* reason why an action is right, when it is right?' This is the question which Professor Moore in fact sets himself to answer. But the *reason* for an action being right is evidently not the same thing as its *rightness*, and Professor Moore seems already to have passed to the view that productivity of maximum good is not the definition of 'right' but another characteristic which underlies and accounts for the rightness of right acts. Again, he describes hedonistic utilitarianism as asking, 'can we discover any characteristic, over and above the mere fact that they *are* right, which belongs to absolutely *all* voluntary actions which are right, and which at the same time does not belong to any except those which are right?'[16] This is the question which he describes hedonism as essentially answering, and since his own view differs from hedonism not in logical form but just by the substitution of 'good' for 'pleasure,' his theory also seems to be essentially an answer to this question, i.e. not to the question what is rightness but to the question what is the universal accompaniment and, as he is careful to add,[17] the necessitating ground of rightness. Again, he describes hedonistic utilitarianism as giving us 'a criterion, or test, or standard by which we could discern with regard to any action whether it is right or wrong.'[18] And similarly, I suppose, he regards his own theory as offering a different criterion of rightness. But obviously a criterion of rightness is not rightness itself. And, most plainly of all, he says, 'It is indeed quite plain, I think, that the meaning of the two words' ('duty' and 'expediency,' the latter being equivalent to 'tendency to produce the maximum good')

---

[13] p. 18.
[14] p. 25.
[15] pp. 146–8. *Cf.* also pp. 167, 169, 180–1.

[16] p. 17 [p. 13 reset edition of *Ethics*].
[17] pp. 44, 54 [p. 29, 35 reset edition of *Ethics*].
[18] p. 43 [p. 28 reset edition of *Ethics*].

'is *not* the same; for, if it were, then it would be a mere tautology to say that it is always our duty to do what will have the best possible consequences.'[19] If we contrast this with *Principia Ethica*, page 169, 'if I ask whether an action is *really* my duty or *really* expedient, the predicate of which I question the applicability to the action in question is precisely the same,' we see how much Professor Moore has changed his position, and changed it in the direction in which, as I have been urging, it must be changed if it is to be made plausible. And if it is clear that 'right' does not mean 'productive of the greatest possible good,' it is *a fortiori* clear that it does not *mean* 'productive of the greatest possible pleasure, for the agent or for mankind,' but that productivity of the greatest possible pleasure for the agent or for mankind is at most the ground of rightness of acts, rightness itself being admitted to be a distinct characteristic, and one which utilitarianism does not claim to define.

But there are theories other than utilitarianism which claim to define 'right.' It would be tedious to try to refute all such theories. With regard to many of them[20] it seems to be enough to ask one's readers whether it is not clear to them on reflection that the proposed definition of 'right' bears in fact no resemblance to what they mean by 'right.' But there is one group of theories to which some reference should be made, *viz.* those that give what may be called a subjective theory of 'right,' that identify the rightness of an act with its tendency to produce either some feeling or some opinion in the mind of some one who contemplates it. This type of theory has been dealt with very thoroughly by Professor Moore,[21] and I should have little or nothing to add to his convincing refutation. But such theories are perhaps even more prevalent with regard to 'good' than to

'right,' and in my fourth chapter I discuss them at some length. I would ask my readers to read the argument there offered, and to reflect whether the refutation I offer[22] of subjective accounts of 'good' does not apply with equal force to subjective accounts of 'right.'

Any one who is satisfied that neither the subjective theories of the meaning of 'right,' nor what is far the most attractive of the attempts to reduce it to simpler objective elements, is correct, will probably be prepared to agree that 'right' is an irreducible notion.

Nor is this result impugned by inquiries into the historical development of our present moral notions from an earlier state of things in which 'what is right' was hardly disentangled from 'what the tribe ordains.' The point is that we can now see clearly that 'right' does not mean 'ordained by any given society.' And it may be doubted whether even primitive men thought that it did. Their thoughts about what in particular was right were to a large extent limited by the customs and sanctions of their race and age. But this is not the same as to say that they thought that 'right' just meant 'what my race and age ordains.' Moral progress has been possible just because there have been men in all ages who have seen the difference and have practised, or at least preached, a morality in some respects higher than that of their race and age. And even the supporters of the lower morality held, we may suspect, that their laws and customs were in accordance with a 'right' other than themselves. 'It is the custom' has been accompanied by 'the custom is right,' or 'the custom is ordained by some one who has the right to command.' And if human consciousness is continuous, by descent, with a lower consciousness which had no notion of right at all, that need not make us doubt that the notion is an ultimate and irreducible one, or that the rightness (*prima facie*)[23] of

---

[19] p. 173 [p. 107 reset edition of *Ethics*].
[20] e.g. the evolutionary theory which identifies 'right' with 'conducive to life.'
[21] *Ethics*, Chs. 3, 4.

[22] pp. 80–104.
[23] For this qualification cf. pp. 19–20.

certain types of act is self-evident; for the nature of the self-evident is not to be evident to every mind however undeveloped, but to be apprehended directly by minds which have reached a certain degree of maturity, and for minds to reach the necessary degree of maturity the development that takes place from generation to generation is as much needed as that which takes place from infancy to adult life.

In this connexion it may be well to refer briefly to a theory which has enjoyed much popularity, particularly in France— the theory of the sociological school of Durkheim and Lévy-Bruhl, which seeks to replace moral philosophy by the 'science des moeurs,' the historical and comparative study of the moral beliefs and practices of mankind. It would be foolish to deny the value of such a study, or the interest of many of the facts it has brought to light with regard to the historical origin of many such beliefs and practices. It has shown with success that many of the most strongly felt repulsions towards certain types of conduct are relics of a bygone system of totems and fetishes, their connexion with which is little suspected by those who feel them. What must be denied is the capacity of any such inquiry to take the place of moral philosophy. The attitude of the sociological school towards the systems of moral belief that they find current in various ages and races is a curiously inconsistent one. On the one hand we are urged to accept an existing code as something analogous to an existing law of nature, something not to be questioned or criticized but to be accepted and conformed to as part of the given scheme of things; and on this side the school is able sincerely to proclaim itself conservative of moral values, and is indeed conservative to the point of advocating the acceptance in full of conventional morality. On the other hand, by showing that any given code is the product partly of bygone superstitions and partly of out-of-date utilities, it is bound to create in the mind of any one

who accepts its teaching (as it presupposes in the mind of the teacher) a sceptical attitude towards any and every given code. In fact the analogy which it draws between a moral code and a natural system like the human body (a favourite comparison) is an entirely fallacious one. By analysing the constituents of the human body you do nothing to diminish the reality of the human body as a given fact, and you learn much which will enable you to deal effectively with its diseases. But beliefs have the characteristics which bodies have not, of being true or false, of resting on knowledge or of being the product of wishes, hopes, and fears; and in so far as you can exhibit them as being the product of purely psychological and nonlogical causes of this sort, while you leave intact the fact that many people hold such opinions you remove their authority and their claim to be carried out in practice.

It is often said, in criticism of views such as those of the sociological school, that the question of the validity of a moral code is quite independent of the question of its origin. This does not seem to me to be true. An inquiry into the origin of a judgement may have the effect of establishing its validity. Take, for instance, the judgement that the angles of a triangle are equal to two right angles. We find that the historical origin of this judgement lies in certain pre-existing judgements which are its premises, plus the exercise of a certain activity of referring. Now if we find that these pre-existing judgements were really instances of knowing, and that the inferring was also really knowing—was the apprehension of a necessary connexion— our inquiry into the origin of the judgement in question will have established its validity. On the other hand, if any one can show that A holds actions of type B to be wrong simply because (for instance) he knows such actions to be forbidden by the society he lives in, he shows that A has no real reason for believing that such actions have the specific quality of wrongness, since between being forbidden by the community and being wrong there is no necessary connexion. He does not, indeed, show the belief to be untrue, but he shows that A has no sufficient reason for holding it true; and in this sense he undermines its validity.

This is, in principle, what the sociological school attempts to do. According to this school, or rather according to its principles if consistently carried out, no one moral code is any truer, any nearer to the apprehension of an objective moral truth, than any other; each is simply the code that is necessitated by the conditions of its time and place, and is that which most completely conduces to the preservation of the society that accepts it. But the human mind will not rest content with such a view. It is not in the least bound to say that there has been constant progress in morality, or in moral belief. But it is competent to see that the moral code of one race or age is in certain respects inferior to that of another. It has in fact an *a priori* insight into certain broad principles of morality, and it can distinguish between a more and a less adequate recognition of these principles. There are not merely so many moral codes which can be described and whose vagaries can be traced to historical causes; there is a system of moral truth, as objective as all truth must be, which, and whose implications, we are interested in discovering; and from the point of view of this, the genuinely ethical problem, the sociological inquiry is simply beside the mark. It does not touch the questions to which we most desire answers.[24]

[24] For a lucid and up to a point appreciative account of the sociological school, and a penetrating criticism of its deficiencies, see ch. 2 of M. D. Parodi's *Le Problème Moral et la Pensée Contemporaine.*

A Suggested Non-Naturalistic Analysis of Good

A. C. EWING

This article is not intended to state what I positively believe to be true, but to make a suggestion which I think it well worth while working out. The suggestion is not altogether unfamiliar, but it has certain implications that seem to have been so far overlooked, or at any rate have never been developed. I do not think that it is the duty of a philosopher to confine himself in his publications to working out theories of the truth of which he is convinced, though no doubt when he is not convinced of the truth of what he is saying he ought to make the tentative character of his statements clear. It is part of a philosopher's work, as it is of a scientist's, to try out tentative hypotheses and examine their advantages and disadvantages, and I am trying this one out in public in the hope that it may suggest to someone else considerations which would confirm or refute the theory more decisively than I can do. Therefore in this article, when I refer to "my theory," I do not mean a theory which I accept, but a theory in which I am interested here, while in a state of indecision as to its acceptance or rejection. I shall mention openly the difficulties I feel most about it, and not merely give one side of the story.

It has been for some time a common amusement among philosophers to attempt an analysis of "good" which reduces it wholly to terms that are not themselves

Reprinted from *Mind*, 48, 1939, by permission of the author and *Mind*.

ethical, and it has often been assumed that the only alternative to this is to hold that "good" is unanalysable. This is not, however, the case. If we are to escape such an analysis we must indeed hold that at least one ethical term is unanalysable, but this one need not be "good," for good is not the only ethical term. "Good" might then be defined in terms of other ethical concepts, or, more probably, partly in psychological, partly in ethical terms. Such a definition, since it is partly ethical, even though also partly psychological, would not be open to the objections brought against "naturalism." No doubt the number of other ethical terms that could be claimed with the least plausibility to be thus fundamental is very limited. There seem to be three only— ought, right, duty—and these are so closely connected that a definition of "good" in terms of one could easily be turned into a definition in terms of either of the others. I wish in the present article to suggest a definition of this kind. It would, if adopted, cut away the ground beneath the feet of both sides in one of the chief controversies of modern ethics, that between those who hold and those who reject "ideal utilitarianism." It would also, I think, take away some of the apparent plausibility of naturalistic views of ethics.

But as a preliminary it is first necessary to say something about right, ought and duty, and distinguish two different usages of these terms. Firstly, the act that I ought to perform may mean that act of those physically in my power in a given situation which it would be preferable for me to choose in the light of the available evidence. "Available evidence" is here used to mean "evidence of which I am either aware or could become aware without more trouble and loss of time than is practicable under the circumstances." Some philosophers have used "ought" in a sense in which it is to be understood without this reservation,[1] but in ordinary speech we should usually admit that a man had done what he ought even if the act turned out unfortunately owing to some unforeseen consequence, provided the consequence was, humanly speaking, unforeseeable, or could not have been anticipated without obtaining expert advice that was not at the man's disposal. A man may fail to do what he ought in this sense for three reasons: (*a*) because he has made a mistake as to certain matters of fact or anticipated consequences, (*b*) because he has made certain wrong value judgments, (*c*) because, while recognising that he ought to do A, he wishes rather to do B and gives way to the temptation. In the first case it would generally be admitted that he was not *morally* to blame except in so far as the mistake was due to neglect to take adequate trouble in order to find out what he ought to do; but this admission would not prevent us from saying that he ought to have acted differently. We say this even where the only reason for performing the act was that it would give the agent pleasure, in which case we do not usually think of the agent as morally to blame if he knowingly neglects to do it, e.g. "you really ought to have seen this film," "you ought to have ordered clear soup—you know you never care much about thick." Turning to (*c*), we certainly should in most cases admit that the agent was morally to blame in some degree if he believed that he ought to perform the act in this sense and yet did not do it, though,

as I have said, we should, rightly or wrongly, not be inclined to think this if the reason in favour of doing it were simply that it ministered to his own pleasure. In every other case I think we should. In case (*b*) i.e. where he acts wrongly through a mistake not about facts but about values, we should also be inclined to think him to blame morally, and not only intellectually, if we thought the error a big one and he was not insane or handicapped by a very bad education.

But that there are at least two different senses of "ought" seems to be shown by the now commonplace paradox of ethics that a man ought always to do what he thinks his duty even if he is wrong in thinking it his duty, i.e. in thinking that he ought to do it. Obviously this statement would be absurd unless "ought" was being used in two different senses. In the one sense "the act I ought to perform" stands for the act which is most fitting or most desirable in view of the situation; in the other sense it stands for an act neglect to perform which would be morally bad. An act that a given person ought to perform in the first sense might clearly not be an act which he ought to perform in the second sense, namely, because he might have made a mistake as to the consequences of the act and therefore would not be morally to blame for omitting to do what he honestly thought harmful. We may even, as the above paradox shows, blame a person morally for not performing an act that we thought very wrong in the first sense, because he believed it to be right and therefore must have neglected to perform it out of bad motives, so that an act which a man ought not to do in the first sense may be an act that he positively ought to do in the second. E.g. I should think it wrong to subscribe to a loan for helping Japan to conquer China, but if a Japanese honestly thought it his duty to do this I should say that he would be morally to blame if he did not do it.

Note that these are not *definitions* of "ought": if so they would be circular, at

---

[1] *e.g.* Moore, *Ethics*, pp. 190 ff. [pp. 117 ff. reset edition].

least the first, for "preferable act to choose" cannot be understood without already presupposing the notion of "ought," and I think "morally good" (or bad) has to be defined in terms of the second sense of "ought." I think at least the first sense of "ought" unanalysable, but we may still make use of phrases which help the reader to distinguish it from the second. It is clear that the second presupposes the first in the sense that in order ever to do what I ought in the second sense I must have at least some belief about what I ought to do in the first sense; but this does not mean that it is analysable in terms of the first sense. I shall suggest later that it may be, but *prima facie* they are quite different. The notion involved in the first sense is that which Prof. Broad calls fittingness.

I have in this connection been using the term *act* in the same way as Sir David Ross to cover only the initiation of a change, and not its initiation from a certain motive, but I should hold against him that we are under an obligation not only to act, but to act from a right motive. In supporting his view he uses the argument that "ought" implies "can" and that, a motive being a desire, we cannot remove or alter it at the time, though we can voluntarily take steps which will tend to its increase or diminution at some future time.[2] To this I should reply that "motive" is not equivalent to "desire" but to desire qua cause of an act, and if I can control my acts at all it must sometimes be possible for me at the moment of acting to prevent a certain desire from causing me to act and so from becoming a motive, though it is impossible for me to remove the desire except by a gradual process. I thus at the moment of acting determine my motive. I cannot determine immediately what the desires are to be which accompany the act, at least in its initial phase, but I can determine which desire (or desires) is to act as motive. So, following Ross's terminology[3]

in using "act" to stand for the initiation of change, and "action" for the initiating of it from a certain motive, I should hold in disagreement with him that we can apply the terms ought, right, duty, not only to acts but to actions.[3a]

In ordinary speech "right" is used in two senses closely corresponding to those of "ought." *The* right act is in fact synonymous with "the act I ought to perform," but right without the prefix *the* is most commonly used as equivalent to "not wrong." It is thus applied to acts which are permissible but not obligatory as well as to those which are obligatory in either of the senses of "ought." It can also be applied to any one of several alternative acts, where it is the case that I ought to do one of them but it does not matter which. "A wrong act" just means an act which ought not to be done, in one or both of the two senses of "ought." "A duty" (I am here referring to absolute, not *prima facie*, duty) is used most commonly to stand for an act which I ought to perform in the second sense. But, since we can talk about making a mistake as to one's duty, it is also used to stand for an act which I ought to perform in the first sense. However, the term is not usually applied to acts primarily directed towards our own pleasure, however innocent and rational the act be, or to relatively trivial acts, or to acts which there is no possible motive for omitting.

We shall now turn to "good." It is quite impossible to deny that the term is highly ambiguous, and we must be prepared to admit that it is sometimes used in a purely naturalistic, psychological sense. When I say "these strawberries are good" I probably do not mean anything more than that I like them or find them pleasant, and perhaps that most people would do so; when I say "this is a good knife" I probably do not mean anything more than that it is likely to be efficient in carrying out any of the purposes, good or bad, for which knives are primarily used in preference to

---

[2] *The Right and the Good*, p. 5.
[3] p. 7.

[3a] [Cf. Ewing's more elaborate discussion of this point, p. 556 this volume.]

other instruments. The question at issue between naturalist and non-naturalist is not whether "good" is *ever* used in a naturalistic sense, but whether it *always* is so used. But the sense of "good" which is usually being discussed when we ask whether "good" is or is not analysable is that usually distinguished from others by the use of the phrases "intrinsically good," "good as an end," "good-in-itself." It is this sense of "good" that Prof. Moore declares indefinable in *Principia Ethica*, and it is round this sense that the controversy has largely turned.

It is not indeed the only sense of good which the non-naturalist will hold incapable of reduction to naturalistic terms; others are (1) productive of what is intrinsically good, (2) good-making[4] as applied to characteristics, while "good" in the primary sense mentioned above is applied only to particular existents, (3) morally good. But of these other senses (1) and (2) are definable in terms of "intrinsically good" as applied to particulars, and (3) is usually held to stand for either a particular species of intrinsic goodness or for intrinsic goodness as qualifying a particular class of objects. It has usually been assumed that, if goodness ever can reasonably be interpreted non-naturalistically, it must be so interpreted in the sense used by Prof. Moore, *intrinsically good*. This indeed would be disputed by Prof. Campbell, who gives a naturalistic definition of good in this sense, but refuses to give a naturalistic definition of "morally good."[5] He would, however, no doubt not regard the latter as indefinable, but define it in terms of ought in my second sense. At any rate, the definition of "good" I am going to propose now is intended as a definition of "good" in the intrinsic sense (1) above.

It is not necessary here to discuss Prof. Moore's arguments for the view that "good" is indefinable. What Moore is at-

tacking is any attempt to define "good" wholly in non-ethical terms, and in this I agree with him, although I should not accept his arguments in *Principia Ethica* as they stand any more than he himself would do now. What I shall suggest is a definition of "good" partly in ethical and partly in psychological terms. Provided ethical terms are introduced at all, even though they do not make up the whole of the definition, this will save it from the charge of being naturalistic.

Now we may note that Moore has himself suggested a synonym for good as applied to an experience, i.e. "worth having for its own sake."[6] This is not necessarily inconsistent with the view that good is indefinable, for there might be various verbal phrases which could be properly used as synonyms in order to help people to see more clearly what was meant by a term without being themselves eligible as definitions of the term. It might be the case that "worth" in "worth having for is own sake" could itself only be defined in terms of good, so that the phrase would be quite useless as a definition of the latter, and yet the phrase might be appropriately used to help some people to become clearer as to what they meant by "good," and especially to distinguish the sense under discussion from other senses of "good." But I think in fact "worth having for its own sake" can be analysed in a way which does not make it a vicious circle to use the phrase as a definition of good; but before I propound the analysis, I should like the reader to consider carefully whether the phrase "an intrinsically good experience" is or is not the exact equivalent of "an experience worth having for its own sake." In this definition, unlike the naturalistic definitions, it seems clear both that the *definiens* and the *definiendum* are co-extensive, and that this is a necessary proposition. It seems clear that there could not be an experience which was intrinsically good that was not worth

---

[4] To borrow Prof. Broad's term.
[5] "Moral and Non-moral Values," *Mind*, vol. xliv, no. 175, pp. 273 ff.

[6] *Proceedings of Arist. Soc.*, Suppl., vol. **xi**, pp. 122 ff.

having for its own sake, or an experience which was worth having for its own sake that was not intrinsically good. This seems to be not merely a contingent fact but a logical necessity. Now it may well be the case that, say, AB entails and is entailed by C, and yet that AB is not a definition of C; consequently it is impossible strictly to prove that anything is a definition of anything else, and in the present case it is open to anybody to maintain that besides the characteristic expressed by the words "worth having for its own sake" there is another indefinable characteristic "good," if he thinks he can discern such a characteristic, which always necessarily accompanies but is different from the characteristic of being "worth having for its own sake." But I am not clear that I can discern any such characteristic, and I should point to the fact that when in ordinary conversation we wish to convey exactly the meaning of the term "intrinsically good" to a person not familiar with it we should most naturally use just the phrase in question. "Worth having for its own sake" seems to be in fact just the phrase which the man in the street would use when he wishes to express what the philosopher calls "intrinsically" as distinct from "instrumentally good."

But, while "worth having for its own sake" is equivalent to "intrinsically good" when applied to an experience, there is an objection to taking it as equivalent to "intrinsically good" without qualification. It is this: though it is often held that experiences are the only things which can be intrinsically good, we must not define "intrinsically good" in a way which would make it a verbal contradiction to say of anything but an experience that it was intrinsically good. To say that the State is good-in-itself or to say that beautiful objects are good in themselves may be wrong, but is not verbally self-contradictory. Now on the definition of "intrinsically good" suggested it would be meaningless, because experiences are the only kind of things that we can be said to "have" in the sense in which the

term "have" is being used here,[7] though there is another sense or senses of "have" in which it is possible to have a State or to have beautiful objects. But this does not prevent the two phrases being exactly equivalent when they are applied to an experience.

What analysis are we to give of "worth having for its own sake"? Surely it means just "such that, in the absence of any positive reason against it, it ought to be chosen for its own sake." Thus we have a definition of "intrinsically good" in terms of "ought," and while the phrase "worth having for its own sake" can, without verbal contradiction, only be applied to experiences, the definition now given can be applied more widely if there are indeed things other than experiences which are intrinsically good in the sense under discussion. But what is the sense of "ought" here? Not the second, because we are not necessarily thinking of moral obligation. If the experience is merely a pleasure of an innocent but not very elevated kind, most people would hold that I should not be *morally* to blame for deliberately neglecting to produce it in myself, and this, whether a right judgment or not, is certainly not verbally inconsistent with saying that the pleasure is intrinsically good. But it does seem clear that when I say that an experience is intrinsically good I am asserting that it is preferable to have it rather than not, that, other things being equal, I ought to choose it in the first sense of "ought."[8] Whether I should be morally to blame or not for declining to produce it when I could produce it without doing corresponding harm, at any rate it would be rational and desirable to choose to produce it, other things being equal.

I do not wish to insist on the word "choose," to which some people may object. It is always difficult to make ordinary terms serve the purposes of philosophical definition, and I can only use it to cover every-

[7] As Moore points out (*ib.*, p. 124).
[8] v. above, p. 3.

thing I want it to cover by using the term in a somewhat strained sense. "Produce" or "promote" would perhaps have been better terms. And I certainly do not wish to analyse the notion of choice here. What I meant by using the term is that "the good" means "what it is fitting to bring into existence for its own sake," or "what ought to be brought into existence, other things being equal"; but the important point I think is that "good" has been defined in terms of what Ross calls a pro-attitude. When something is good it is fitting that we should welcome it, rejoice in it if it exists, desire and seek it if it does not exist. I think that there is something vague and indeterminate about the use of almost all terms in ordinary speech, and therefore we cannot expect to analyse a common-sense proposition in a way which is both quite precise or definite and quite correct. Sometimes we may be thinking rather of the fact that we ought to welcome a thing when we call it good, sometimes rather of the fact that we ought to seek it, etc. But I think we can see quite clearly that the various attitudes I have mentioned have something in common which is opposite to the common element in condemning, shunning, fearing, regretting, etc. The former may well be called pro-attitudes, the latter anti-attitudes. The former are positive and favourable to their object, the latter negative and hostile. What is good is a suitable object of pro-attitudes, what is evil a suitable object of anti-attitudes. What is intrinsically good is a suitable object of a pro-attitude for its own sake.[9]

It might be suggested that I should have defined "good" in terms of desire rather than in terms of choice, i.e. as what ought to be desired for its own sake. I have not done so for the following reasons. (1) It seems to me that to say we ought to choose a thing because it ought to be desired for its own sake is to put the cart before the horse. It is in general only good to

desire something for its own sake because it is worth having when we have got it. (2) If desire means a certain uneasy emotion, it is not the case that we ought to feel it towards whatever is good. The less we feel this emotion towards what we cannot obtain or bring about, however good that object may be, the better on the whole, since it will only make us less happy without doing any good; but if "desire" means something more than this uneasy emotion, it becomes a striving to pursue and bring about the existence of its object, and if so the definition in terms of desire merges into my definition. This is in fact what we mean when we use the term "desirable," a common synonym for "good"; we do not mean that we ought to feel a certain emotion towards what is described as desirable, but that this object is worth attaining.

Now if the analysis I have suggested be adopted, it has an important bearing on one of the chief controversies of recent years in this country on ethics, that between the "Ideal Utilitarians," who differ indeed from hedonistic utilitarians in holding that there are other goods besides pleasure but agree with them that we ought always to aim at producing the greatest amount of good and the least amount of evil, and those like Ross who think that there are independent "*prima facie* duties*," i.e. that there are certain kinds of acts, e.g. promise-keeping, which carry with them an obligation not derivable from the good they produce or the evil they avert.

Now at the ordinary level the controversy between the two sides is very hard to solve. I think we must admit that the obligation, e.g. to keep promises, is not to be explained solely by the consequences of doing so; but this does not prove that we have a *prima facie* duty to keep promises over and above the duty to produce the greatest possible amount of good; for the Utilitarian, if he is not also a hedonist, can always retort that the act of keeping a promise is good-in-itself, or the act of

[9] For a similar theory v. Osborne, *The Philosophy of Value*, pp. 93 ff.

breaking it bad. In that case the obligation would not be explained entirely by the consequences of the act, and yet it would be derivable from the obligation to produce the greatest good, as the Ideal Utilitarian maintains. For in the good produced by an action must be included not only the good lying in its consequences, but any intrinsic good that belongs to the action itself in its own right. The intrinsic good might indeed be outweighed in certain cases by the badness of the consequences, so that the Ideal Utilitarian could not admit the impossibility of cases arising which would make it a duty to break a promise or violate other *prima facie* duties. But neither does Ross. He holds that two *prima facie* duties may clash and that one has then to give way to the other. It might indeed be doubted whether the keeping of a promise is by itself intrinsically good, e.g., there does not seem to be any intrinsic value in my paying a bill as a matter of course, having no temptation to do otherwise; but it seems plain to me that to break a promise is intrinsically bad, and this evil should therefore be avoided even apart from its consequences; and, if the Utilitarian takes this line, it seems impossible to refute his theory at the usual level at which the controversy is conducted.

But if the suggested analysis of good is adopted the position is radically altered at once. For in that case to say that something is intrinsically good just means to say that I ought to choose it other things being equal, i.e. I have a *prima facie* duty to produce it, so that something like Ross's position becomes inevitable. There is no sense any longer in opposing to it Ideal Utilitarianism, for "good" is now no longer another concept from which we infer what we ought to do. An "intrinsic good" just means something which we have a *prima facie* duty to produce if we can, and to give a list of the different kinds of intrinsic goods is just to give a list of our *prima facie* obligations. It might indeed seem that the view suggested made the utilitarian principle

that we ought always to produce the greatest good in our power a tautology, so that utilitarianism must be true; for "the greatest good" would then have to mean, it seems, "that which we ought to choose in preference to any other." But it would be a Pyrrhic victory, for the whole point of the utilitarian principle was that obligation is derivable from good, while the reverse is true if the suggested analysis of good be correct. The utilitarian would be guilty of a vicious circle if he insisted on deducing obligation from "good" and then accepted an analysis which made "good" itself definable in terms of what we ought to do. That it makes the principle that we ought always to produce the greatest good in our power necessarily true, seems to me the chief argument for Ideal Utilitarianism against Ross's view; for it seems hardly credible that it could ever be a duty deliberately to produce less good when we could produce more; but if the analysis I have suggested were adopted this principle would be accepted in a form which did not contradict the contentions of Ross. The antithesis between a view which based the "ought" or "the right" on the "good" and a view which based it on *prima facie* duties would then disappear. There would still be an antithesis between a view according to which what we ought to do depended entirely on consequences and a view according to which it depended partly on the intrinsic nature of the action; but the former view would seem very unreasonable, for surely we must take account of the intrinsic nature of an action before we decide whether we ought to do it.

It may be objected that there seem clearly to be cases where it is at the very least arguable that the act which I ought to do is not the act which, as far as we can tell, is likely to produce the greatest good, e.g. the case of stealing from a rich miser in order to give the money to a poor man who is deserving. It seems a perfectly intelligible and not self-contradictory position to admit on the one hand that I should do more good if I stole the money and gave it to the poor man, and yet that I still ought to refrain from stealing it. But I suggest that the distinction here is really between (a) what I ought to choose in abstraction from the only available means of producing it, (b) what I ought to choose to produce by these means. Thus I ought to choose that A who is poor should have £100 rather than B who is rich, but I ought not to choose that he should have it through my stealing. We think it a greater good that A should have the £100, and other things being equal I ought to bring this about, if I can, in preference to the other state of affairs; but if I can only bring it about by stealing, other things are not equal. It is better that B should have the £100 and not A than that A should have the £100 obtained by stealing.

But now there arises a new complication. There is a sense in which it is sometimes right to speak of an action as intrinsically good. But, when people describe actions as intrinsically good, I do not think they are usually using the term in the same sense as when they use it, e.g., of pleasant experiences. We regard, e.g., a particular action of self-sacrifice as intrinsically good. Do we mean to say that it is fitting that the person who makes the sacrifice should choose it for its own sake quite apart from consequences? Surely not. That would lead to irrational asceticism. To sacrifice himself when it does no good to anyone is not something which a man ought to choose. The self-sacrificing action does not seem to be intrinsically good in the sense in which, e.g., innocent pleasures, aesthetic experience, personal affection, intellectual activity are held to be so. If it were, we ought to spend most of our time torturing ourselves in order to realise the admittedly very high intrinsic value of self-sacrifice. I suggest, however, that intrinsic goodness as applied to actions may still be analysed in terms of "ought" (in the first sense of the term), provided the psychological term of the analysis is different. I suggest that we

usually mean by good actions simply actions that ought to be admired or approved, which is certainly not the usual meaning of "intrinsically good" in the other case. A pleasure, however innocent, is not something to be admired, though it is something to be liked and, other things being equal, pursued.

But we must add, I think, a qualification and say "morally admired." For we may also admire a cleverness which does not display moral qualities, though our admiration even for the cleverness is lessened if it displays immoral ones. Nor must we use "admired" or "approved" here to stand for "judged good," since in that case we should be guilty of a vicious circle. It must, in the analysis given, stand for an emotion or a state of mind tinged with emotional qualities. I do not wish to discuss the psychological question whether moral admiration is a single emotion or a class or a blend of emotion; but it does seem to me that there is something specific about this kind of admiration which distinguishes it from other kinds. And it is quite clear that there are certain actions to which this kind of feeling is the appropriate reaction, as sympathy is to suffering and certain aesthetic experiences to a great drama. There is, however, a curious point to note here in passing: with persons other than the agent himself the appropriate reaction is admiration, but with the agent himself it is not. A man should not admire himself for his moral virtues. In the opposite case moral disapproval is an appropriate emotion for both the agent and others, but moral disapproval of oneself feels very different from moral disapproval of another. For one thing it is, generally at least, an asthenic, while the latter is generally a sthenic emotion. If we are not willing to regard moral admiration as a specific emotion, we can still retain the principle of the definition but say that good actions in the moral sense are actions more or less admirable on account of their volitional quality, i.e. as showing a persistence of the will in face of what would be a great temptation to most people, and a direction of the will to good ends. Clever or beautiful pieces of work would also be fitting objects of admiration, but for a different reason.

There will then be at least two senses of "intrinsically good," but these, though different, will have two very important points in common: (*a*) they will both be analyses of "good" in terms of "ought" together with a psychological concept, (*b*) the latter will be in both cases that of a "pro-attitude," though the pro-attitude will be different. Admiration and choosing (or pursuing) have both in common something important which may be expressed by this term pro-attitude, they are both in a very definite sense favourable to the object towards which they are directed. That "intrinsically good" should be used in two different senses not clearly distinguished, when the senses have so much in common, is not to be wondered at. I had arrived at this distinction before hearing the paper of Sir David Ross at the International Congress of Philosophy[10] in 1937, but when I heard it this paper provided welcome confirmation of the point that there are two such different senses. He there uses the term "worthy object of interest" of objects which are said to be intrinsically good in the one sense, and the term "admirable" of those which are said to be intrinsically good in the other. This agrees substantially with the theory suggested by me except that he does not claim that the term "admirable" gives an *analysis* of what good means in the second sense of good, though he thinks that "worthy object of interest" does in the first.

I am not prepared to say that, when we speak of a moral action as good, we are never using "intrinsically good" in the first as opposed to the second sense, but in the majority of cases I think it is impossible to distinguish "intrinsically good" as thus applied from "morally admirable." I think this

second sense is also our usual sense when we speak of a man's character or life as good, though we should grant that it could also be good in the first sense of the term. A good character or a morally good life is assuredly a worthy object of pursuit, and is so not merely for any hedonistic advantages it may have to oneself and others. But when we appraise particular actions as good I do not think this is what we are usually thinking of. We are rather thinking of their admirable qualities, and in some cases it is quite certain that actions we rightly admire are not actions which ought to be chosen except for the sake of their consequences.

It is irrelevant to object that we cannot say I ought to feel a certain emotion, such as admiration, because I cannot alter my emotions at a moment's notice. Perhaps our second sense of ought is only applicable where the thing which it is said we ought to do could be brought about by an act of will on our part at the time, but we can certainly speak of the emotions a man ought to have in the sense of "the suitable emotions for him to have" (first sense of ought).

I have thus been using "ought" here in its wider sense, and not in the sense in which failure to do what one ought implies moral blameworthiness.[11] But this still leaves us with two unreduced ethical concepts, i.e. "ought" in its two different senses. However, there remains a possible way of defining one sense of "ought" in terms of the other together with a psychological concept. I suggest, namely, that we might analyse "A ought (second sense) to do this" as meaning "(1) A ought (first sense) to do this, and (2) if he does not do this he ought (first sense) to be in that respect an object of the emotion of moral disapproval," or perhaps as meaning simply (2) without (1).

I have not analysed the proposition as asserting that if he does this he will be a

[10] *Travaux du IXe Congrès International de Philosophie*, xi, p. 78 ff.

[11] v. above, p. 3.

suitable object of moral admiration, because there are many acts which it would be wrong not to do but the doing of which does not call for admiration. It would be very wrong of me to cheat people by not paying my debts, yet I certainly under normal circumstances deserve no admiration for paying my debts, though I should be a suitable object of a condemnatory emotion if I did not do so. I am not at all certain that this account adequately brings out the full, specific nature of the ethical ought, but I put it forward as at least worth discussion.

If the analyses suggested be correct, we have succeeded in reducing the different fundamental ethical concepts to one, "ought" in the first sense given. This, I think, is in principle the same as to reduce them to what Prof. Broad calls the concept of *fittingness*.

Besides settling the issue between Ross's view and Ideal Utilitarianism, my theory has the advantage of being the minimum non-naturalistic theory of ethics, i.e. the theory other than naturalism which admits least in the way of non-natural concepts. For it only admits one unanalysable ethical concept; and as against the theories which hold "good" to be the only such unanalysable concept it has also an advantage in that it is even more difficult to deny that there is a relation of fittingness which is not definable in purely psychological terms than to deny that there is a quality of good which is not thus definable. In these days when naturalistic tendencies are so strong, it is more than ever worth while for a non-naturalist to ask—What is the maximum of concessions I can make without destroying my whole view of ethics? and for a naturalist to ask—Have I refuted all forms of non-naturalistic ethics or only some? (I include under the heading "naturalistic," theories which, while not admitting that ethical statements can be analysed wholly in psychological terms, reduce the additional element to a sort of emotional penumbra, or an expletive added for practical effect, e.g. the theory of Duncan-Jones.) It is a curious fact that the controversy between naturalists and their opponents has centred rather round "good" than round "ought," and I think that this was a mistake in tactics on the part of the latter. I do not think that a plausible naturalistic account of "good" can be given, but at least this is somewhat less difficult than to give a plausible naturalistic account of "ought." Once, however, we have accepted a non-naturalistic view of "ought," it is clearly only reasonable to suppose that there are non-naturalistic senses of good, because "good" in some of its uses at any rate can clearly be analysed in terms of "ought."

Now let us turn to the objections to the theory suggested. Most people will probably be left unsatisfied by it because they will feel that a theory like this gives no real explanation why I ought to do one thing rather than another while Utilitarianism at least does that. One must be careful not to state this objection wrongly. We must not express it by saying that the fact that something ought to be produced is not the reason why it is good; for my theory does not hold it to be the reason why it is good but identical with the fact that it is good. But my theory does leave the fact that we ought to do certain things unexplained, while Utilitarianism explains it further by reference to the good. True, the Utilitarian, if asked to explain why certain things are good-in-themselves, cannot do so but just has to say that he sees them to be good; but at any rate he does carry the explanation one stage further back. And it does to many seem somehow more rational to take propositions such as "this is good" as ultimate and self-vindicating than to hold this view about propositions such as "this is what I ought to do." I seem to be left with nothing but a chaos of *prima facie* duties for none of which there is any reason beyond themselves, and thus to abandon the essential purpose of Ethics, which is to make coherent our ethical beliefs. It is true that the advantage of Utilitarianism relatively to my theory is much less than might seem at first sight, because unless he is a hedonist the utilitarian will have to admit an ultimate variety of intrinsic goods, and it might be argued that this is quite as bad as to admit an ultimate variety of *prima facie* duties. There is a good deal in this reply, but I cannot be at all satisfied with the position unless it is possible on principle to bring the *prima facie* duties into some kind of system.

Now there are different kinds of system. If we could deduce all ethical duties from a single principle, e.g. that I ought always to do what I could will everybody else to do, or from one single type of good, e.g. pleasure, we should have a system of a certain kind. Such systems in ethics seem to me impracticable. They either give only a pretence of explanation, because they leave outside any concrete idea of the good, which has to be smuggled in unnoticed if the system is to work; or they conflict with moral judgments which we see to be true. They do not do justice to the complexity of ethics.

But you may have a system of another kind. The systematic character of a body of beliefs may lie, not in the fact that they are all deducible from one and the same principle, but in the fact that, though no single one of the beliefs can occupy the exalted position of being premiss for all the rest, they are all logically related to each other so that you could not alter any one without contradicting others. It is a system of this sort that is envisaged in the coherence theory of truth. Could the propositions of ethics form a system of this kind? Clearly not in the full sense. For one could deny that it was, e.g., a *prima facie* duty not to lie, without contradicting any other of the *prima facie* duties. But there is still, I think, a sense in which they may be said to form a system. Although I could perhaps deny the existence of any one of the *prima facie* duties without contradicting the assertion of any of the others, they might still form a system in the sense that the different *prima facie* duties were so connected that to fulfil any one, on principle and in general harmonised with and for-

warded the fulfilment of others; and this seems to be the case in fact. The utilitarians hold that it is generally a duty to tell the truth, keep promises, be just, make reparation for wrong one has done, treat our parents with love, look after our children in preference to those of other people, etc., but as is well known they all maintain that these are generally duties because they further other goods. The view that this is the only reason for their being duties has been challenged by non-utilitarians, but hardly the view that they do further other goods and on the whole make for the best state of society attainable all round. Now "further other goods" becomes on the view I have suggested "fulfil other *prima facie* duties." But, if the different *prima facie* duties play into each other's hands in this way, that may well serve as a confirmation that we are on the right lines in admitting them, so that we are not wholly dependent on intuition, but have also this test by consistency to use.

But what about the undoubted clashes between different *prima facie* duties that do occur at times? Surely I may be easily placed in a situation in which I have to break one of two promises because the two are incompatible with each other, or to neglect either my *prima facie* duty to a relative or my *prima facie* duty to the State? Is not this sufficient to show that the line of argument suggested is a cul-de-sac, and that the *prima facie* duties cannot possibly be regarded as constituting a system?

It may be retorted, however, that if we investigate these cases of clash we find that so far from refuting they support the view that the *prima facie* duties constitute a system in some sense like the one I suggested. Let us take one of the acutest possible clashes, that arising in the case of war. Suppose one's country has promised to help another country against aggression,[12] and that country is wrongfully attacked by a Power whose form of government we can-

[12] This was written before the crisis of last September, and is not intended to have any political reference.

not help regarding as a tyranny which has deliberately and persistently set aside in theory and practice principles of justice and liberty which we consider quite fundamental to civilisation. What are we to do? If we fight we are certainly violating *prima facie* duties by the killing and other evil practices which war involves. If we do not fight we are breaking our solemn word and letting a higher form of civilisation be overthrown by a lower, and injustice and wrong triumph over right. I do not propose to answer this question here, but *whichever* answer we give it should be clear that we are violating some *prima facie* duties. But this does not disprove, it on the contrary supports the view that the *prima facie* duties constitute a system. For why does this acute clash arise? Only because somebody has done wrong first. In every war at least one party is to blame. But, if the *prima facie* duties do form a system, surely the only thing to expect is that, if you violate one, you or someone else will be brought to a position in which others have to be violated, as, if you make a mistake in a proposition in the arithmetical system, this will lead to more contradictions. The occurrence of clashes as a resultant of violating one *prima facie* duty is thus not a contradiction, but a confirmation, of the view that the *prima facie* duties constitute a system. If they do constitute a system, clashes are just what one ought to expect under these circumstances; and most of the serious clashes which occur in fact are due to previous violations of duty on the part of some person. If I make two inconsistent promises I must break one, but then I have violated my duty already in making them: I may have to choose between lying and confessing to a crime the knowledge of which will bring great pain to those I love; but then I have already done wrong in committing the crime: I live in a social system in which I cannot give satisfactory opportunities to my family without grasping after material gain somewhat more zealously than is desirable; that is because the social system is morally evil in so far as, through being too

competitive, it encourages selfishness and makes money too much the standard of success: one cannot overthrow a particular existing bad political or economic system rapidly without a violent revolution that will involve great misery and injustice; but that clash arises because the people who think they benefit by it are too much concerned for their own interests and too little for the welfare of others to let it be amended peaceably, and perhaps because the people who lose by it are not disciplined enough to avoid revolutionary excesses. We need not therefore, I think, confine ourselves to saying that the *prima facie* duties are known intuitively; we can add that they are confirmed by the fact that to further one on the whole furthers others, and to violate one involves sooner or later violating others. There is thus a sort of coherence test available in ethics after all.

But we must not go too far in this line of reply. All clashes cannot be explained in this way. Natural disasters, as well as wars and bad social systems, may cause clashes, e.g. there is the well-known case of lying in order to save an invalid from hearing bad news, or again a man might through an earthquake be placed in a position in which he had to choose between saving the life of his child and those of two other persons unknown to him.

So the most we can say is that in general and on principle the *prima facie* duties fit together. To fulfil one tends, of its intrinsic nature, to fulfil others, and to violate one tends to the violation of others.

Let us now consider further objections to our theory. The most serious perhaps is this. If "good" means "what ought to be chosen," "A is better than B" will presumably mean "A ought to be chosen in preference to B," and "this act produces the greatest good" will presumably mean "This act ought to be chosen in preference to any other alternative possible at the time." But if so it would seem to be a tautology to say that I ought, apart from ulterior consequences, always to choose my own greater good in preference to somebody else's lesser good, or the greater good of a total stranger in preference to my mother's lesser good; and these propositions, whether true or not, are certainly not tautologies. They have been maintained, e.g. by utilitarians, and they may even be tenable when one has allowed, in estimating the consequences, for the good effects of encouraging an unselfish spirit and family affection even at the cost of some loss of immediate good; but they would be hotly disputed, and to dispute them does not seem to be equivalent to the self-contradiction of asserting that the greater good is not greater. Therefore, since the theory proposed makes what is clearly a synthetic proposition into a tautology, it would seem that the theory must be mistaken. The objection would be still stronger if we had substituted "ought to be desired" for "ought to be chosen" as an analysis of good; for to say that I ought to desire the good of a stranger as much as the equal good of my mother is quite obviously false.

A person who maintains the analysis of "good" that I have suggested might avoid this objection by admitting the logical possibility that something, A, might be better than something else, B, relatively to one agent but not to another. He might still hold that whatever was good at all (in the sense under discussion) was good for all men, i.e. anyone ought to produce it if he could do so without sacrificing anything else worth producing—or producing anything else, e.g. lies, which ought to be avoided; but he would have to say also that, where the agent had to choose between producing one good thing and another good thing, it would not necessarily be the case that each agent ought to produce the same one. This involves the admission of a certain relativity into the conception of good. What is good relatively to me, though perhaps always also good relatively to you, is not necessarily equally good relatively to you. The innocent pleasure of a close relative of mine is relatively to any mind good, but it might still be bet-

ter relatively to me than it is relatively to you, in this sense of good. This relativity contradicts any notion of intrinsic goodness hitherto propounded by people who took an objective view of ethics, as far as I know; but it may be right for all that and, although not easy about it in my own mind, I am not clear that it involves any of the objections brought against the ordinary types of ethical relativism or subjectivism. We must remember also that to say that A is better than B for me and not for you is not, on the analysis of "good" given, to say that it possesses one quality for me in itself and a contradictory quality for you, but simply that I ought to choose A rather than B and you B rather than A.

But there remains another way out. It may be said that what I ought to choose is not my mother's good but the production of my mother's good by myself. (I cannot indeed choose the former in abstraction from the latter.) Now the production of my mother's good by myself is a different thing from the production of my mother's good by a stranger, and therefore it might easily be the case that I ought to choose the production of my mother's good by myself in preference to the production of a stranger's equal good by myself, while the stranger's son ought to choose the production of his parent's good by himself in preference to the production of my parent's good by himself. To speak of the goods of the parents as equal means that, other things being equal, neither has more claim to pursuit than the other; but if I have a special relation involving obligation to one person which I have not to the other, other things are not equal, and it does not follow that because the goods of A and B are equally worth pursuit *per se*, therefore the whole—good of A + the pursuit and attainment of A's good by me—will be of equal value to the whole—good of B + the pursuit and attainment of B's good by me.

Ross denies that the pursuit of one's own pleasure is a *prima facie* duty, but I should not follow him here. I think that one ought, other things being equal, to do what makes for one's own pleasure, and that the contrary supposition is due to a confusion of the two senses of "ought" above mentioned. It is at any rate arguable that I am not morally to blame for neglecting my own pleasure unnecessarily; but even if this be so, it is unsuitable, unfitting, irrational that I should neglect it. I *ought* to do what furthers my own pleasure in my first, if not in my second, sense of "ought." If I were not under a *prima facie* obligation to do so, I should always be under an obligation to sacrifice any amount of my pleasure, however great, for any amount of somebody else's, however small, provided no other goods were at stake. For I certainly have a *prima facie* obligation to further the pleasure of others, and this could not be counteracted except by a contrary *prima facie* obligation to further my own. We need not therefore follow Ross in denying that pleasure is a good in the non-naturalistic sense in which, e.g., knowledge or love is a good, though it may be a lower kind of good.

If the analysis of good suggested were adopted, it would explain how it is that it has seemed likely to many people that "good" could be analysed naturalistically. The most popular naturalistic analyses of good are in terms of either desire or approval. Now in one sense good has been analysed by me as what ought to be chosen or pursued, and, while a case, though I do not think an adequate case, can no doubt be made out for the view that it would have been better to analyse it as what ought to be desired, pursuit is at any rate very closely connected with desire. And in the other sense treated, "good" has been analysed by me as what ought to be admired or approved. Now "ought" is a relational term, and we do not have a distinct perception of relations in the sense in which we have a distinct perception of qualities. We do not have a distinct idea of what it is like to perceive between-ness or of-ness, in the sense in which we have a distinct idea of what it is like to see colour or feel fear. And it

has often been noticed that it has been one of the most common vices of philosophers to overlook the importance of relations. Now, if the view I have suggested is true, the naturalistic analyses take the concrete, more distinctly perceptible part of goodness but omit the relational element, and therefore, although people feel as if they had left something out, they, misled partly by the fact that "good" is an adjective, look for some other *quality* and cannot find it and then become more and more inclined to adopt the naturalistic view. But what they should have looked for is perhaps a relation. And they could hardly deny that there is such a relation as fittingness on which the concept of "ought" is based, the action which I ought to do being the action which fits the situation. It may also be noted that, while there is some uncertainty as to whether we can find any non-natural qualities other than good, it is very difficult even outside ethics to deny that there are non-natural relations, if we mean by "non-natural" what is not given by sense-perception or introspection. (I do not think "non-natural" a happy term as it suggests the miraculous, but I retain it as the one generally used by philosophers in this connection.) Entailment, probability, causality are cases of non-natural relations that seem to me quite impossible to explain away.

The naturalist will thus be right if he holds that "good" is connected very closely with desire, for what we pursue we desire. And he will also be right if he holds that moral good is very closely connected with the emotion of approval. The theory suggested would also explain how it is that our ability to make the right value judgments depends a good deal on our emotional disposition. For it is hardly to be expected that we should learn thoroughly what emotions it is fitting to feel on certain occasions without frequently feeling these emotions on suitable occasions.

It has been urged as a point in favour of naturalistic theories that they agree best with the way in which we learn the use of ethical words as children. For a very young child "bad" or "wrong" probably mean practically "what its nurse or parents disapprove of"; and it seems to learn the application of the words to acts by hearing them spoken, on the occasion of the acts, in tones or with gestures which express the emotion of disapproval, or by connecting the acts with punishments actual or threatened, punishment being in its very nature a mark of disapproval. (No doubt it can, and should be, shown that actions are wrong as far as possible by pointing out bad consequences and by the use of reasoning generally, but that of itself cannot teach the child the meaning of the words good, bad, right, wrong.) Now this is taken as evidence that "bad" or "wrong" means "disapproved," and similarly with "good," *mutatis mutandis*. But clearly if "bad" does not mean just what is disapproved (either by oneself or others) but what ought to be disapproved, this will equally well explain why the expression of approval or disapproval should be the natural and normal way of teaching a child what is meant by good or bad. For if "good," as applied to actions, means that towards which one ought to feel approval and "bad" that towards which one ought to feel disapproval, you must teach the child the meaning of the words by expressing to it the emotions of approval and disapproval on suitable occasions. (In so far as "good" means what we ought to pursue and "bad" what we ought to avoid, ethical education will consist in inducing the child by example and precept to pursue and avoid what it is suitable to pursue or avoid.) However I do not wish to lay much stress on this as an argument for the theory I have suggested, as against the theory that good is indefinable; but since some people are in fact influenced by this kind of argument in favour of a naturalistic theory I should like to point out that whatever weight it has equally supports my theory. But I must repeat that the whole of this article is of a very tentative character.

Hypostatic Ethics

GEORGE SANTAYANA

If Mr. Russell, in his essay on "The Elements of Ethics" had wished to propitiate the unregenerate naturalist, before trying to convert him, he could not have chosen a more skilful procedure; for he begins by telling us that "what is called good conduct is conduct which is a means to other things which are good on their own account; and hence . . . the study of what is good or bad on its own account must be included in ethics." Two consequences are involved in this: first, that ethics is concerned with the economy of all values, and not with "moral" goods only, or with duty; and second, that values may and do inhere in a great variety of things and relations, all of which it is the part of wisdom to respect, and if possible to establish. In this matter, according to our author, the general philosopher is prone to one error and the professed moralist to another. "The philosopher, bent on the construction of a system, is inclined to simplify the facts unduly . . . and to twist them into a form in which they can all be deduced from one or two general principles. The moralist, on the other hand, being primarily concerned with conduct, tends to become absorbed in means, to value the actions men ought to perform more than the ends which such ac-

Reprinted from *Winds of Doctrine* by George Santayana by permission of J. M. Dent & Sons Ltd. Copyright 1915.

tions serve. . . . Hence most of what they value in this world would have to be omitted by many moralists from any imagined heaven, because there such things as self-denial and effort and courage and pity could find no place. . . . Kant has the bad eminence of combining both errors in the highest degree, since he holds that there is nothing good except the virtuous will—a view which simplifies the good as much as any philosopher could wish, and mistakes means for ends as completely as any moralist could enjoin."

Those of us who are what Mr. Russell would call ethical sceptics will be delighted at this way of clearing the ground; it opens before us the prospect of a moral philosophy that should estimate the various values of things known and of things imaginable, showing what combinations of goods are possible in any one rational system, and (if fancy could stretch so far) what different rational systems would be possible in places and times remote enough from one another not to come into physical conflict. Such ethics, since it would express in reflection the dumb but actual interests of men, might have both influence and authority over them; two things which an alien and dogmatic ethics necessarily lacks. The joy of the ethical sceptic in Mr. Russell is destined, however, to be short-lived. Before proceeding to the expression of concrete ideals, he thinks it necessary to ask a preliminary and quite abstract question, to which his essay is chiefly devoted; namely, what is the right definition of the predicate "good," which we hope to apply in the sequel to such a variety of things? And he answers at once: The predicate "good" is indefinable. This answer he shows to be unavoidable, and so evidently unavoidable that we might perhaps have been absolved from asking the question; for, as he says, the so-called definitions of "good"—that it is pleasure, the desired, and so forth—are not definitions of the predicate "good," but designations of the things to which this predicate is applied by different persons. Pleasure, and its rivals, are not synonyms for the abstract quality "good," but names for classes of concrete facts that are supposed to possess that quality. From this correct, if somewhat trifling, observation, however, Mr. Russell, like Mr. Moore before him, evokes a portentous dogma. Not being able to define good, he hypostasises it. "Good and bad," he says, "are qualities which belong to objects independently of our opinions, just as much as round and square do; and when two people differ as to whether a thing is good, only one of them can be right, though it may be very hard to know which is right." "We cannot maintain that for me a thing ought to exist on its own account, while for you it ought not; that would merely mean that one of us is mistaken, since in fact everything either ought to exist, or ought not." Thus we are asked to believe that good attaches to things for no reason or cause, and according to no principles of distribution; that it must be found there by a sort of receptive exploration in each separate case; in other words, that it is an absolute, not a relative thing, a primary and not a secondary quality.

That the quality "good" is indefinable is one assertion, and obvious; but that the presence of this quality is unconditioned is another, and astonishing. My logic, I am well aware, is not very accurate or subtle; and I wish Mr. Russell had not left it to me to discover the connection between these two propositions. Green is an indefinable predicate, and the specific quality of it can be given only in intuition; but it is a quality that things acquire under certain conditions, so much so that the same bit of grass, at the same moment, may have it from one point of view and not from another. Right and left are indefinable; the difference could not be explained without being invoked in the explanation; yet everything that is to the right is not to the right on no condition, but obviously on the condition that some one is looking in a certain direction; and if some one else at the same time is looking in the opposite direction, what is truly to the right will be truly to the left also. If Mr. Russell thinks this is a contradiction, I understand why the universe does not please him. The contradiction would be real, undoubtedly, if we suggested that the idea of good was at any time or in any relation the *idea* of evil, or the *intuition* of right that of left, or the *quality* of green that of yellow; these disembodied essences are fixed by the intent that selects them, and in that ideal realm they can never have any relations except the dialectical ones implied in their nature, and these relations they must always retain. But the contradiction disappears when, instead of considering the qualities in themselves, we consider the things of which those qualities are aspects; for the qualities of things are not compacted by implication, but are conjoined irrationally by nature, as she will; and the same thing may be, and is, at once yellow and green, to the left and to the right, good and evil, many and one, large and small; and whatever verbal paradox there may be in this way of speaking (for from the point of view of nature it is natural enough) had been thoroughly explained and talked out by the time of Plato, who complained that people should still raise a difficulty so trite and exploded.[1] Indeed, while square is always square, and round round, a thing that is round may actually be square also, if we allow it to have a little body, and to be a cylinder.

But perhaps what suggests this hypostasis of good is rather the fact that what others find good, or what we ourselves have found good in moods with which we retain no sympathy, is sometimes pronounced by us to be bad; and far from inferring from this diversity of experience that the present good, like the others, corresponds to a particular attitude or interest of ours, and is dependent upon it, Mr. Russell and Mr. Moore infer instead that the presence of the good must be independent of all interests, attitudes, and opinions. They imagine that the truth of a proposition attributing a certain relative quality to an object contradicts the truth of another

proposition, attributing to the same object an opposite relative quality. Thus if a man here and another man at the antipodes call opposite directions up, "only one of them can be right, though it may be very hard to know which is right."

To protect the belated innocence of this state of mind, Mr. Russell, so far as I can see, has only one argument, and one analogy. The argument is that "if this were not the case, we could not reason with a man as to what is right." "We do in fact hold that when one man approves of a certain act, while another disapproves, one of them is mistaken, which would not be the case with a mere emotion. If one man likes oysters and another dislikes them, we do not say that either of them is mistaken." In other words, we are to maintain our prejudices, however absurd, lest it should become unnecessary to quarrel about them! Truly the debating society has its idols, no less than the cave and the theatre. The analogy that comes to buttress somewhat this singular argument is the analogy between ethical propriety and physical or logical truth. An ethical proposition may be correct or incorrect, in a sense justifying argument, when it touches what is good as a means, that is, when it is not intrinsically ethical, but deals with causes and effects, or with matters of fact or necessity. But to speak of the truth of an ultimate good would be a false collocation of terms; an ultimate good is chosen, found, or aimed at; it is not opined. The ultimate intuitions on which ethics rests are not debatable, for they are not opinions we hazard but preferences we feel; and it can be neither correct nor incorrect to feel them. We may assert these preferences fiercely or with sweet reasonableness, and we may be more or less incapable of sympathising with the different preferences of others; about oysters we may be tolerant, like Mr. Russell, and about character intolerant; but that is already a great advance in enlightenment, since the majority of mankind have regarded as hateful in the highest degree any

---

[1] Plato, *Philebus*, 14, D. The dialectical element in this dialogue is evidently the basis of Mr. Russell's, as of Mr. Moore's, ethics; but they have not adopted the other elements in it, I mean the political and the theological. As to the political element, Plato everywhere conceives the good as the eligible in life, and refers it to human nature and to the pursuit of happiness—that happiness which Mr. Russell, in a rash moment, says is but a name which some people prefer to give to pleasure. Thus in the *Philebus* (11, D) the good looked for is declared to be "some state and disposition of the soul which has the property of making all men happy"; and later (66, D) the conclusion is that insight is better than pleasure "as an element in human life." As to the theological element, Plato, in hypostasising the good, does not hypostasise it as good, but as cause or power, which is, it seems to me, the sole category that justifies hypostasis, and logically involves it; for if things have a ground at all, that ground must exist before them and beyond them. Hence the whole Platonic and Christian scheme, in making the good independent of private will and opinion, by no means makes it independent of the direction of nature in general and of human nature in particular; for all things have been created with an innate predisposition towards the creative good, and are capable of finding happiness in nothing else. Obligation, in this system, remains internal and vital. Plato attributes a single vital direction and a single moral source to the cosmos. This is what determines and narrows the scope of the true good; for the true good is that relevant to nature. Plato would not have been a dogmatic moralist, had he not been a theist.

one who indulged in pork, or beans, or frogs' legs, or who had a weakness for anything called "unnatural"; for it is the things that offend their animal instincts that intense natures have always found to be, intrinsically and *par excellence*, abominations.

I am not sure whether Mr. Russell thinks he has disposed of this view where he discusses the proposition that the good is the desired and refutes it on the ground that "it is commonly admitted that there are bad desires; and when people speak of bad desires, they seem to mean desires for what is bad." Most people undoubtedly call desires bad when they are generically contrary to their own desires, and call objects that disgust them bad, even when other people covet them. This human weakness is not, however, a very high authority for a logician to appeal to, being too like the attitude of the German lady who said that Englishmen called a certain object *bread*, and Frenchmen called it *pain*, but that it really was *Brod*. Scholastic philosophy is inclined to this way of asserting itself; and Mr. Russell, though he candidly admits that there are ultimate differences of opinion about good and evil, would gladly minimise these differences, and thinks he triumphs when he feels that the prejudices of his readers will agree with his own; as if the constitutional unanimity of all human animals, supposing it existed, could tend to show that the good they agreed to recognise was independent of their constitution.

In a somewhat worthier sense, however, we may admit that there are desires for what is bad, since desire and will, in the proper psychological sense of these words, are incidental phases of consciousness, expressing but not constituting those natural relations that make one thing good for another. At the same time the words desire and will are often used, in a mythical or transcendental sense, for those material dispositions and instincts by which vital and moral units are constituted. It is in reference to such constitutional interests that

things are "really" good or bad; interests which may not be fairly represented by an incidental conscious desire. No doubt any desire, however capricious, represents some momentary and partial interest, which lends to its objects a certain real and inalienable value; yet when we consider, as we do in human society, the interests of men, whom reflection and settled purposes have raised more or less to the ideal dignity of individuals, then passing fancies and passions may indeed have bad objects, and be bad themselves, in that they thwart the more comprehensive interests of the soul that entertains them. Food and poison are such only relatively, and in view of particular bodies, and the same material thing may be food and poison at once; the child, and even the doctor, may easily mistake one for the other. For the human system whiskey is truly more intoxicating than coffee, and the contrary opinion would be an error; but what a strange way of vindicating this real, though relative, distinction, to insist that whiskey is more intoxicating in itself, without reference to any animal; that it is pervaded, as it were, by an inherent intoxication, and stands dead drunk in its bottle! Yet just in this way Mr. Russell and Mr. Moore conceive things to be dead good and dead bad. It is such a view, rather than the naturalistic one, that renders reasoning and self-criticism impossible in morals; for wrong desires, and false opinions as to value, are conceivable only because a point of reference or criterion is available to prove them such. If no point of reference and no criterion were admitted to be relevant, nothing but physical stress could give to one assertion of value greater force than to another. The shouting moralist no doubt has his place, but not in philosophy.

That good is not an intrinsic or primary quality, but relative and adventitious, is clearly betrayed by Mr. Russell's own way of arguing, whenever he approaches some concrete ethical question. For instance, to show that the good is not pleasure, he can avowedly do nothing but appeal "to ethical judgments with which almost every one would agree." He repeats, in effect, Plato's argument about the life of the oyster, having pleasure with no knowledge. Imagine such mindless pleasure, as intense and prolonged as you please, and would you choose it? Is it your good? Here the British reader, like the blushing Greek youth, is expected to answer instinctively, No! It is an *argumentum ad hominem* (and there can be no other kind of argument in ethics); but the man who gives the required answer does so not because the answer is self-evident, which it is not, but because he is the required sort of man. He is shocked at the idea of resembling an oyster. Yet changeless pleasure, without the wearisome intermixture of arbitrary images, is just what the mystic, the voluptuary, and perhaps the oyster find to be good. Ideas, in their origin, are probably signals of alarm; and the distress which they marked in the beginning always clings to them in some measure, and causes many a soul, far more profound than that of the young Protarchus or of the British reader, to long for them to cease altogether. Such a radical hedonism is indeed inhuman; it undermines all conventional ambitions, and is not a possible foundation for political or artistic life. But that is all we can say against it. Our humanity cannot annul the incommensurable sorts of good that may be pursued in the world, though it cannot itself pursue them. The impossibility which people labour under of being satisfied with pure pleasure as a goal is due to their want of imagination, or rather to their being dominated by an imagination which is exclusively human.

The author's estrangement from reality reappears in his treatment of egoism, and most of all in his "Free Man's Worship." Egoism, he thinks, is untenable because "if I am right in thinking that my good is the only good, then every one else is mistaken unless he admits that my good, not his, is the only good." "Most people . . . would

admit that it is better two people's desires should be satisfied than only one person's. . . . Then what is good is not good *for me* or *for you*, but is simply good." "It is, indeed, so evident that it is better to secure a greater good for *A* than a lesser good for *B*, that it is hard to find any still more evident principle by which to prove this. And if *A* happens to be some one else, and *B* to be myself, that cannot affect the question, since it is irrelevant to the general question who *A* and *B* may be." [1a] To the question, as the logician states it after transforming men into letters, it is certainly irrelevant; but it is not irrelevant to the case as it arises in nature. If two goods are somehow rightly pronounced to be equally good, no circumstance can render one better than the other. And if the locus in which the good is to arise is somehow pronounced to be indifferent, it will certainly be indifferent whether that good arises in me or in you. But how shall these two pronouncements be made? In practice, values cannot be compared save as represented or enacted in the private imagination of somebody: for we could not conceive that an alien good *was* a good (as Mr. Russell cannot conceive that the life of an ecstatic oyster is a good) unless we could sympathise with it in some way in our own persons; and on the warmth which we felt in so representing the alien good would hang our conviction that it was truly valuable, and had worth in comparison with our own good. The voice of reason, bidding us prefer the greater good, no matter who is to enjoy it, is also nothing but the force of sympathy, bringing a remote existence before us vividly *sub specie boni*. Capacity for such sympathy measures the capacity to recognise duty and therefore, in a moral sense, to have it. Doubtless it is conceivable that all wills should become cooperative, and that nature should be ruled magically by an exact and universal sympa-

---

[1a] These two passages are quoted from "The Elements of Ethics."

thy; but this situation must be actually attained in part, before it can be conceived or judged to be an authoritative ideal. The tigers cannot regard it as such, for it would suppress the tragic good called ferocity, which makes, in their eyes, the chief glory of the universe. Therefore the inertia of nature, the ferocity of beasts, the optimism of mystics, and the selfishness of men and nations must all be accepted as conditions for the peculiar goods, essentially incommensurable, which they can generate severally. It is misplaced vehemence to call them intrinsically detestable, because they do not (as they cannot) generate or recognise the goods we prize.

In the real world, persons are not abstract egos, like A and B, so that to benefit one is clearly as good as to benefit another. Indeed, abstract egos could not be benefited, for they could not be modified at all, even if somehow they could be distinguished. It would be the qualities or objects distributed among them that would carry, wherever they went, each its inalienable cargo of value, like ships sailing from sea to sea. But it is quite vain and artificial to imagine different goods charged with such absolute and comparable weights; and actual egoism is not the thin and refutable thing that Mr. Russell makes of it. What it really holds is that a given man, oneself, and those akin to him, are qualitatively better than other beings; that the things they prize are intrinsically better than the things prized by others; and that therefore there is no injustice in treating these chosen interests as supreme. The injustice, it is felt, would lie rather in not treating things so unequal unequally. This feeling may, in many cases, amuse the impartial observer, or make him indignant; yet it may, in every case, according to Mr. Russell, be absolutely just. The refutation he gives of egoism would not dissuade any fanatic from exterminating all his enemies with a good conscience; it would merely encourage him to assert that what he was ruthlessly establishing was the absolute

good. Doubtless such conscientious tyrants would be wretched themselves, and compelled to make sacrifices which would cost them dear; but that would only extend, as it were, the pernicious egoism of that part of their being which they had allowed to usurp a universal empire. The twang of intolerance and of self-mutilation is not absent from the ethics of Mr. Russell and Mr. Moore, even as it stands; and one trembles to think what it may become in the mouths of their disciples. Intolerance itself is a form of egoism, and to condemn egoism intolerantly is to share it.

I cannot help thinking that a consciousness of the relativity of values, if it became prevalent, would tend to render people more truly social than would a belief that things have intrinsic and unchangeable values, no matter what the attitude of any one of them may be. If we said that goods, including the right distribution of goods, are relative to specific natures, moral warfare would continue, but not with poisoned arrows. Our private sense of justice itself would be acknowledged to have but a relative authority, and while we could not have a higher duty than to follow it, we should seek to meet those whose aims were incompatible with it as we meet things physically inconvenient, without insulting them as if they were morally vile or logically contemptible. Real unselfishness consists in sharing the interests of others. Beyond the pale of actual unanimity the only possible unselfishness is chivalry—a recognition of the inward right and justification of our enemies fighting against us. This chivalry has long been practised in the battle-field without abolishing the causes of war; and it might conceivably be extended to all the conflicts of men with one another, and of the warring elements within each breast. Policy, hypnotisation, and even surgery may be practised without exorcisms or anathemas. When a man has decided on a course of action, it is a vain indulgence in expletives to declare that he is sure that course is absolutely right. His moral dogma expresses its natural origin all the more clearly the more hotly it is proclaimed; and ethical absolutism, being a mental grimace of passion, refutes what it says by what it is. Sweeter and more profound, to my sense, is the philosophy of Homer, whose every line seems to breathe the conviction that what is beautiful or precious has not thereby any right to existence; nothing has such a right; nor is it given us to condemn absolutely any force—god or man—that destroys what is beautiful or precious, for it has doubtless something beautiful or precious of its own to achieve.

The consequences of a hypostasis of the good are no less interesting than its causes. If the good were independent of nature, it might still be conceived as relevant to nature, by being its creator or mover; but Mr. Russell is not a theist after the manner of Socrates; his good is not a power. Nor would representing it to be such long help his case; for an ideal hypostasised into a cause achieves only a mythical independence. The least criticism discloses that it is natural laws, zoological species, and human ideals, that have been projected into the empyrean; and it is no marvel that the good should attract the world where the good, by definition, is whatever the world is aiming at. The hypostasis accomplished by Mr. Russell is more serious, and therefore more paradoxical. If I understand it, it may be expressed as follows: In the realm of eternal essences, before anything exists, there are certain essences that have this remarkable property, that they ought to exist, or at least that, if anything exists, it ought to conform to them. What exists, however, is deaf to this moral emphasis in the eternal; nature exists for no reason; and, indeed, why should she have subordinated her own arbitrariness to a good that is no less arbitrary? This good, however, is somehow good notwithstanding; so that there is an abysmal wrong in its not being obeyed. The world is, in principle, totally depraved; but as the good is not a power, there is no one to redeem the world. The saints are those who, imitating the impotent dogmatism on high, and despising their sinful natural propensities, keep asserting that certain things are in themselves good and others bad, and declaring to be detestable any other saint who dogmatises differently. In this system the Calvinistic God has lost his creative and punitive functions, but continues to decree groundlessly what is good and what evil, and to love the one and hate the other with an infinite love or hatred. Meanwhile the reprobate need not fear hell in the next world, but the elect are sure to find it here.

What shall we say of this strangely unreal and strangely personal religion? Is it a ghost of Calvinism, returned with none of its old force but with its old aspect of rigidity? Perhaps: but then, in losing its force, in abandoning its myths, and threats, and rhetoric, this religion has lost its deceptive sanctimony and hypocrisy; and in retaining its rigidity it has kept what made it noble and pathetic; for it is a clear dramatic expression of that human spirit—in this case a most pure and heroic spirit—which it strives so hard to dethrone. After all, the hypostasis of the good is only an unfortunate incident in a great accomplishment, which is the discernment of the good. I have dwelt chiefly on this incident, because in academic circles it is the abuses incidental to true philosophy that create controversy and form schools. Artificial systems, even when they prevail, after a while fatigue their adherents, without ever having convinced or refuted their opponents, and they fade out of existence not by being refuted in their turn, but simply by a tacit agreement to ignore their claims: so that the true insight they were based on is too often buried under them. The hypostasis of philosophical terms is an abuse incidental to the forthright, unchecked use of the intellect; it substitutes for things the limits and distinctions that divide them. So physics is corrupted by logic; but the logic that corrupts is perhaps correct, and when it is moral dialectic, it is more important than physics itself. Mr. Russell's ethics *is* ethics. When we mortals have once assumed the moral attitude, it is certain that an indefinable value accrues to some things as opposed to others, that these things are many, that combinations of them have values not belonging to their parts, and that these valuable things are far more specific than abstract pleasure, and far more diffused than one's personal life. What a pity if this pure morality, in detaching itself impetuously from the earth, whose bright satellite it might be, should fly into the abyss at a tangent, and leave us as much in the dark as before!

Value as Any Object of Any Interest [1]

R. B. PERRY

I. PRELIMINARY FORMULATION AND ARGUMENT

49. Exposition and Illustration. It is characteristic of living mind to be *for* some things and *against* others. This polarity is not reducible to that between 'yes' and 'no' in the logical or in the purely cognitive sense, because one can say 'yes' with reluctance or be glad to say 'no.' To be 'for' or 'against' is to view with favor or disfavor; it is a bias of the subject toward or away from. It implies, as we shall see more clearly in the sequel, a tendency to create or conserve, or an opposite tendency to prevent or destroy. This quality appears in many forms, such as liking and disliking, desire and aversion, will and refusal, or seeking and avoiding. It is to this all-pervasive characteristic of the motor-affective life, this *state, act, attitude or disposition of favor or disfavor, to* which we propose to give the name of 'interest.' [2]

This, then, we take to be the original source and constant feature of all value. That which is an object of interest is *eo ipso* invested with value. [3] Any object, whatever it be, acquires value when any interest, whatever it be, is taken in it; just as anything whatsoever becomes a target when anyone whosoever aims at it. In other words, Aristotle was fundamentally mistaken when he said, that as a thing's "apparent good" makes it an object of appetite, so its real good makes it the object of "rational desire." [4] By the same token Spinoza was fundamentally correct when he said that

in no case do we strive for, wish for, long for, or desire anything because we deem it to be good, but on the other hand we deem a thing to be good, because we strive for it, wish for it, long for it, or desire it.[5]

The view may otherwise be formulated in the equation: x is valuable = interest is taken in x. Value is thus a specific relation into which things possessing any ontological status whatsoever, whether real or imaginary, may enter with interested subjects.

This is value *simpliciter,*—value in the elementary, primordial and generic sense.

[1] Parts of the present chapter are reprinted from an article entitled "A Behavioristic View of Purpose," published in the *Journal of Philosophy,* Vol. XVIII, 1921.

[2] Cf. § 14. The term 'interest' has been employed for technical purposes by various psychologists, but by none, I think, in the precise sense in which it is employed here. W. Mitchell. in his *Structure and Growth of Mind,* 1907, defines interest as our "feeling towards" an object, or, as how the object "strikes or affects us" (p. 64); whereas I propose to use the term to embrace desire and disposition as well. G. F. Stout, in his *Groundwork of Psychology,* 1903, uses the term for organized and permanent forms of the emotional life, such as sentiments [pp. 221 ff.]. More commonly 'interest' is employed by psychology to mean *attention.*

[3] An object is valuable when *qualified* by an act of interest; relation to interest assuming, in the experience or judgment of value, the rôle of adjective.

[4] *Metaphysica,* XII, Ch. 7, trans. by W. D. Ross, 1072a.

[5] *Ethics,* Part II, Prop. IX, Note, trans. by R. H. M. Elwes, 1901. It is, of course, possible to desire a thing because it is good, where its goodness consists in its being desired by other subjects, or by some other interest of the same subject. But *in the last analysis* good springs from desire and not desire from good.

It follows that any variation of interest or of its object will determine a variety of value; that any derivative of interest or its object will determine value in a derived sense; and that any condition of interest or its object will determine a conditional value. In short, interest being constitutive of value in the basic sense, theory of value will take this as its point of departure and centre of reference; and will classify and systematize values in terms of the different forms which interests and their objects may be found to assume.

This view has rarely found a perfectly clear and consistent expression. It is, however, essentially conveyed in an early work of Mr. George Santayana:

Apart from ourselves, and our human bias, we can see in such a mechanical world no element of value whatever. On removing consciousness, we have removed the possibility of worth. But it is not only in the absence of all consciousness that value would be removed from the world; by a less violent abstraction from the totality of human experience, we might conceive beings of a purely intellectual cast, minds in which the transformations of nature were mirrored without any emotion. . . . No event would be repulsive, no situation terrible. . . . In this case, as completely as if consciousness were absent altogether, all value and excellence would be gone. . . . Values spring from the immediate and inexplicable reaction of vital impulse, and from the irrational part of our nature. . . . The ideal of rationality is itself as arbitrary, as much dependent on the needs of a finite organization, as any other ideal.[6]

A more recent statement, and one more explicitly in accord with the view here proposed, is the following:

Anything is properly said to have value in case, and only in case, it is the object of the affective motor response which we call being *interested* in, positively or negatively. . . . The

being liked, or disliked, of the object is its value. And since the being liked or disliked, is being the object of a motor-affective attitude in a subject, some sort of a subject is always requisite to there being value at all—not necessarily a *judging* subject, but a subject capable of at least motor-affective response. For the cat the cream has value, or better and more simply, the cat values the cream, or the warmth, or having her back scratched, quite regardless of her probable inability to conceive cream or to make judgments concerning warmth.[7]

52. Summary of the Argument. How is the view here proposed to be proved? What is the evidence upon which it rests?

In the first place, we have reached it by a process of systematic elimination. We have first examined and eliminated those views which affirm value to be indefinable, or to be definable independently of interest. If value cannot be successfully identified or defined without reference to interest, then we must incorporate interest into our definition. We have next examined those views which relate value to interest in some qualified and exclusive sense; first, those views which have proposed to qualify and limit the object of interest; second, those views which have proposed to qualify and limit the act or state of interest itself. The result has been to exhibit a variety of values all having the common generic character of being 'object-of-interest.' We have thus been led to define value as the peculiar relation between any interest and its object; or that special character of an object which consists in the fact that interest is taken in it. We are now justified in framing this hypothesis as a last remaining alternative. There is a certain presumption in favor of this remaining alternative not only because of the elimination of the others, but also because these have all betrayed a common tendency. They have not

[6] *The Sense of Beauty*, 1899, pp. 17–19. Cf. also William James: "The essence of good is to satisfy demand" (*Will to Believe*, etc., 1898, p. 201).

[7] D. W. Prall, *A Study in the Theory of Value*, Univ. of California Publications in Philosophy, Vol. 3, No. 2, 1921, pp. 215, 227. The present writer is in essential agreement with the whole of this admirable monograph.

only through their failure left the field clear for our definition of value, but they have *pointed* to that definition and incidentally argued in its support.

A certain positive plausibility is given to this hypothesis by the fact that in order to create values where they did not exist before it seems to be sufficient to introduce an interest. The silence of the desert is without value, until some wanderer finds it lonely and terrifying; the cataract, until some human sensibility finds it sublime, or until it is harnessed to satisfy human needs. Natural substances or the by-products of manufacture are without value until a use is found for them, whereupon their value may increase to any degree of preciousness according to the eagerness with which they are coveted. There is no entity that can be named that does not, in the very naming of it, take on a certain value through the fact that it is selected by the cognitive purpose of some interested mind. As interests grow and expand, multiplying in number and extending their radius through experience and imagination, the store of cosmic values is enriched and diversified.

But it may be contended that such proof is redundant or verbal. It proves only that objects of interest appear whenever interest is taken in objects; or, it proves at most that what is added to a given situation when interests are introduced corresponds closely to what it is customary to *call* value. It does not add to our knowledge by demonstrating the existence of value where it was not suspected, or by resolving doubts as to what is *really* valuable.

This objection again brings to light the difference between the general definition of value and the solution of special questions of value. The doubts and perplexities of everyday life, as well as the limited theoretical problems of the several value-sciences, commonly assume a general definition of value, and turn upon some question of fact. Is this distant island worth annexing and defending? The answer depends upon the existence of mineral deposits or a good harbor, assuming that it is worth annexing if the satisfactions and utilities which it affords outweigh the sacrifices which it costs. Ought I to surrender my position for the sake of my scruples, or compromise temporarily in the hope of converting others to my way of thinking? The answer depends on certain probable trains of consequences following from each of the alternatives, assuming that the one or the other ought to be adopted in accordance with the principle of human happiness, broadly applied. Is recent American verse to be ranked as genuine poetry? The answer depends experimentally on the sort of feeling aroused in certain persons, such as the critic himself, by the prolonged and attentive reading of it, on the assumption that such a judgment of taste is decisive. Is the economic worth or the aesthetic superiority of a work of art dependent on its moral wholesomeness? The answer is assumed to depend on the record of transactions made in the market place, or the reported sentiments of connoisseurs.

Now the general definition of value does not directly answer any such question, because it does not ascertain the specific facts and probabilities upon which they turn. It concerns itself with the *assumption*, and must therefore always appear to deal with the obvious rather than with the questionable. Its proper task is to make these assumptions explicit and consistent. By so doing it will inevitably affect the solution of such special questions, since it will prescribe the terms or the principle of their solution. But it has to do with the use which is to be made of evidence, rather than with the uncovering of new facts.

It follows that there can be no conclusive proof of a general definition of value, short of its success in facilitating the solution of all special questions of value. Such a definition is *an experiment in generalization.* If we adopt the fact of interest as our centre of reference, and view other facts of the surrounding field *in that relation*—if, in short, we take life *interest-wise*, as it can, in fact, be taken—do the data and the perplexities denoted by 'good' and 'evil,' 'right' and 'wrong,' 'better' and 'worse,' or grouped within the special fields of morality, art, religion and kindred institutions, then fall into place and form a comprehensive system? It is evident that the only proof of which such a hypothesis is capable lies in its complete elaboration. In short the argument for the thesis submitted in the present study is cumulative, and cannot properly claim the assent of the reader until the last chapter is written.

II. REPLY TO THE CHARGE OF RELATIVISM

53. Relativism as an Epithet. Although no conclusive proof of the present view is possible until it is completely elaborated, it has been supposed that there is a conclusive disproof which can be urged without further ado. To attribute value to any object of any interest is at once to expose oneself to the charge of *relativism*, whatever the psychological details, and however successful such a definition may prove for the purposes of systematic generalization.

No one can afford to disregard this charge. Relativism is an epithet which implies disparagement, when, as is often the case, it implies nothing more. Even the respectable scientific authority which has pronounced in its favor has not saved the physical theory of relativity from being regarded as somewhat *risqué*,—as evidence of the corruption of the times or of the malicious influence of the Semitic mind. There is no man who would not rather be absolute than relative, even though he has not the faintest conception of the meaning of either term.

This sentiment is peculiarly strong in the field of values, and preeminently in the province of morals. Nothing could be more

scandalous than these lines of Sir Richard Burton:

"There is no good, there is no bad, these be
    the whims of mortal will;
What works me weal that call I good, what
    harms and hurts I hold as ill.
They change with space, they shift with race,
    and in the veriest space of time,
Each vice has worn a virtue's crown, all good
    been banned as sin or crime."[8]

How much nobler and more edifying in tone are such utterances as these of Froude and Carlyle:

"The eternal truths and rights of things exist, fortunately, independent of our thoughts or wishes, fixed as mathematics, inherent in the nature of man and the world. They are no more to be trifled with than gravitation."
"What have men to do with interests? There is a right way and a wrong way. That is all we need think about it."[9]

Yet there can scarcely be more offence in the adjective 'relative' than there is in the substantive 'relation'; and when we investigate the world in which we live, we discover as a rule that what we took to be an absolute does as a matter of fact both stand in relations and comprise relations. In any case we shall be influenced only by such *theoretical* difficulties as may be urged against a relativistic theory of value, and not in the least by practical or sentimental objections.

54. Epistemological Relativism, or Scepticism. There is unquestionably one form of relativism which is theoretically objectionable. He who identifies the act of *cognizing* values with that act of the subject which *constitutes* them, or holds that values are both known and created in one and the same act, does imply the impossibility of knowing anything whatsoever

[8] Quoted by L. Dickinson, *Meaning of Good*, 1907, p. 5.
[9] J. A. Froude, *Inaugural Lecture at St. Andrews*, 1869, p. 41; Letter of Carlyle to Froude, *Longman's Magazine*, 1892, p. 151.

about value, and thus belies any statements that he himself may make about it. This objection holds against certain philosophers who have identified value with interest, and it therefore behooves us to discover whether our own view is similarly objectionable.

Professor G. E. Moore distinguishes two forms in which this vicious relativism may be stated. In the first place, "it may be held that whenever any man asserts an action to be right or wrong, what he is asserting is merely that he *himself* has some particular feeling toward the action in question."[10] In this case the act of knowing or judging value, is construed as simply an expression of the judge's own interest. The following famous passage from Hobbes is a case in point:

But whatsoever is the object of any man's appetite or desire, that is it which he for his part calleth 'good'; and the object of his hate and aversion, 'evil'; and of his contempt 'vile' and 'inconsiderable.' For these words of good, evil, and contemptible, are ever used with relation to the person that useth them: there being nothing simply and absolutely so; nor any common rule of good and evil, to be taken from the nature of the objects themselves.[11]

The *reductio ad absurdum* of such a view lies, as Professor Moore points out, in the fact that it would lead to the mutual irrelevance of all judgments in which the value-predicates are employed. If in affirming an act to be right or wrong, good or evil, a judge were always referring to *his own present feeling* about it, then no two judges could ever agree or disagree with one another, nor could the same judge ever reaffirm or correct his own past opinions.[12] In other words, on questions of value there could not be any such things as judgment

or opinion in the ordinary sense of these terms. This is not only contrary to fact, but it is inevitably contradicted by the very man who makes the assertion.

A second statement of this vicious relativism is the assertion "that when we judge an action to be right or wrong what we are asserting is merely that somebody or other thinks it to be right or wrong." Generalized and simplified, this assertion is to the effect that value consists in being thought to be valuable—"There is nothing either good or bad, but thinking makes it so." Now the fundamental difficulty with this view lies in the fact that one would then have nothing to think about. If a thing is valuable by virtue of being believed to be valuable, then when one believes a thing to be valuable, one believes that it is believed to be valuable, or one believes that it is believed to be valuable, and so on *ad infinitum*.[13]

In short, there can be no judgment about value, or about anything else, unless there is some content or object other than the act of judgment itself,—a judged as well as a judging.

It is this error or confusion which vitiates the work of Westermarck and others who, not content with a history of moral opinion, have attempted to *define* moral values in *terms* of moral opinion.[14] It is the characteristic and besetting error of all anthropological and sociological theories of value which aim to be scientific or 'positive.'[15] What has been judged with unanimity to be good or evil by members of a social group, is a matter of record; and is thus a fact ascertainable by archaeological or historical methods, and with a precision and indubitableness peculiar to these

---

[10] *Ethics*, Home University Library, p. 89 [p. 55 reset edition].

[11] *Leviathan*, Part I, Ch. VI.

[12] Cf. G. E. Moore, *op. cit.*, pp. 100–103 [pp. 62–3 reset edition].

[13] Cf. G. E. Moore, *op. cit.* pp. 122–124 [pp. 76–7 reset edition].

[14] E. Westermarck, *Origin and Development of Moral Ideas*, 1906, Vol I, *passim*. Westermarck's confusion is largely due to the ambiguity of the term 'approval,' and the absence of any clear notion of judgment.

[15] For a general statement of this position, cf. L. Lévy-Bruhl, *La Morale et la Science des Moeurs*, 1910.

methods. But such methodological preferences do not alter the fact that these judgments, if judgments at all, must have been *about* something; and in theory of value it is this *object*, and not the acts of judgment themselves, which is primarily in question. There are also recorded opinions about the stars, and anthropologists may and do investigate these opinions; but one does not therefore propose to substitute a history of astronomical opinions for astronomy.

Let us now inquire whether the view here proposed is guilty of a vicious or sceptical relativism in either or both of these two senses. In the first place, although defining value as relative to interest, we have not defined value as exclusively relative to the present interest of the judge. Thus if Caesar was ambitious when he waged war upon Pompey, the definition implies that power was in fact good, as being coveted by Caesar. But this fact may have been affirmed by Mark Antony, or afterwards denied by Caesar himself in his own defense. Value, therefore, lends itself to judgment in the ordinary sense,—to judgments which are true or false, and which may agree or disagree.

In the second place, having defined value as constituted by interests, such judgments have a content or object other than themselves. They may refer to the interest of the judge, or to any other interest, past or present, common or unique; but the interest that creates the value is always other than the judgment that cognizes it. Theory of value is not a history of opinion about values, but deals with that to which such opinion refers.

55. The Argument from 'Intrinsic' Value. Professor Moore has further weapons in his arsenal which he believes to be fatal not only to the particular forms of epistemological relativism just rejected, but in general to the view that "by calling a thing 'good' or 'bad' we merely mean that some being or beings have a certain mental attitude towards it"; or that "what we mean by calling a thing 'good' is that it is *desired*, or desired in some particular way."[16] Since we have in effect maintained precisely this view, his objections are relevant and must be met.

He appeals, in the first place, to the fact that we may use the word 'good' without consciously meaning 'object of interest.' Judging by what the speaker has in mind, to say that the object is good is not the same as to say that some one is interested in it.[17] This type of argument would prove altogether too much if it proved anything. No definition has ever been formulated that is perfectly in keeping either with verbal usage or conscious meanings. For words may be mere echoes, and conscious meanings careless and obscure. The absurdity of the argument is especially evident in the case of complex entities, such as the exponents of the present view hold value to be. A complex entity is only summarily denoted in common discourse, and analysis will invariably reveal structure which is not present to a mind which employs terms in a stereotyped sense. It would, for example, scarely be urged that circularity is indefinable because one can judge an object to be circular without judging that all points on its perimeter are equi-distant from the centre. In the one case as in the other the nature of the predicate is revealed not in customary usage, but when doubt has arisen as to its applicability. Where the circularity of an object is in question one falls to measuring; and when its goodness is in question one falls to considering its relation to interests.

A much more serious objection is based upon the notion of *intrinsic* value. We judge a thing to be intrinsically good "where we judge, concerning a particular

[16] *Op. cit.*, pp. 157 [p. 97 reset edition], 159 [pp. 98–9 reset edition.]
[17] This argument is applied primarily to the term 'right,' but is equally applicable to the term 'good.' Cf. *ibid.*, pp. 111 [p. 69 reset edition], 163 [p. 101 reset edition].

state of things, that it would be worth while—would be 'a good thing'—that that state of things should exist, *even if nothing else were to exist besides,* either at the same time or afterwards."[18] If a thing derives value from its relation to an interest taken in it, it would seem impossible that anything whatsoever should possess value in itself. But in that case value would seem always to be borrowed, and never owned; value would shine by a reflected glory having no original source.

The question turns upon the fact that any predicate may be judged synthetically or analytically. Suppose that 'good' were to be regarded as a simple quality like yellow. It would then be possible to judge either synthetically, that the primrose was fair and yellow; or, analytically, that the fair, yellow primrose was fair or yellow. Only the fair, yellow primose would be fair and yellow "even if nothing were to exist besides." But the logic of the situation is not in the least altered if a relational predicate is substituted for a simple quality; indeed it is quite possible to regard a quality as a monadic (a single term) relation. Tangential, for example, is a relational predicate; since a line is a tangent only by virtue of the peculiar relation of single-point contact with another line or surface. Let R^t represent this peculiar relation, and A, B, two lines. One can then judge either synthetically, that $(A) R^t (B)$; or, analytically, that $(A) R^t (B)$ is R^t. Similarly, let S represent an interested subject, O an object, and R^i the peculiar relation of interest, taken and received. We can then judge either synthetically, that $(O) R^i(S)$; or, analytically that $(O) R^i (S)$ is R^i. In other words, one can say either that O is desired by S, or that *O-desired-by-S is a case of the general character 'desired.'*

The situation is complicated, but not logically altered, by the fact that either O, or O's-being-desired-by-S^1, may be desired by S^2, and so stand in a second value-relation of the same type. In other words,

as we have already seen, the question of value is peculiarly recurrent.[19] But value is intrinsic when it is independent of such ulterior interests. Similarly, the primrose *as enjoyed* is intrinsically good; the primrose *as sought for the sake of* such ulterior enjoyment, is instrumentally, conditionally, or otherwise extrinsically good. In other words, according to the present view an object unrelated to a subject cannot be good in itself, any more than, in Professor Moore's view,[20] an object can be good in itself without possessing the specific superadded quality 'good'; but an *object-desired-for-itself,* that is, any value of the variable function $(O) R (S)$, can and does possess value in itself.[21]

The special case of the universe as a whole[22] furnishes a further and peculiarly instructive example. It is evident that by definition the universe as a whole cannot stand in relation to any desiring subject outside itself. In what sense, therefore, can it be said to possess value in accord with our definition? In the first place, it might, for certain familiar metaphysical reasons which are not here in question, be conceived as a single all-embracing interest. The total universe would be divided between a universal subject and a universal object, with a relation of will or love (perhaps of self-love) uniting the two. In that case the world in its unity would possess intrinsic value. Or, independently of such metaphysical speculation, the universe may be said to possess value in so far as loved or hated by its own members, taken sever-

---

[18] *Ibid.,* p. 162 [p. 101 reset edition].

[19] Cf. § 17 and 56.

[20] As set forth above, § 15.

[21] Even Professor Moore says (*ibid.,* p. 167 [pp. 103–4 reset edition]): "I think it is true that no whole can be intrinsically good, unless it *contains* some feeling toward *something* as part of itself." According to this view the 'something' and the 'feeling toward,' taken together, are 'good': there being three factors involved. In my view 'good' *means* the 'feeling toward,' or more precisely, 'the being felt toward.'

[22] Cf. G. E. Moore, *ibid.,* p. 58 [p. 37 reset edition].

ally. Or it may be said to *contain* value,[23] in that it embraces interests and their objects. Or it may be said to be an instrument of value, in that it provides the conditions by which interests and their objects may arise and be conserved. There is no cosmic paradox which can be urged against the definition of value in terms of the interest-relation which could not with equal force be urged against any other view of value, including the view that value is an indefinable quality. For if it be urged that the universe so defined as to embrace all interests cannot be synthetically good through any interest taken in it, it can equally well be urged that the universe so defined as to embrace the indefinable quality 'good,' cannot be good through the super-addition of this quality.

We may safely conclude, therefore, that the definition of value herein proposed provides for intrinsic value in such intelligible senses as are provided for in any other theory of value.

56. The Charge of Circularity. In criticising the view that value is a "relational attitude," Professor W. M. Urban argues that it involves "a definition in a circle."

The value of an object consists, it is said, in its satisfaction of desire, or more broadly, fulfilment of interest. But it is always possible to raise further questions which show conclusively that the value concept is already presupposed. Is the interest itself worthy of being satisfied? Is the object worthy of being of interest? In other words, the fact of intrinsic value requires us to find the essence of value in something other than this type of relation.[24]

This expresses the most popular objection to the present view. The fact of desire is not accepted as final in most judgments of value. Objects of desire are held to be bad despite their being desired, and desires themselves are held to be bad whether or no they are satisfied. Vicious appetites, vulgar taste, o'erweening ambition, are the most notorious of evils. Indeed the general terms 'desire' and 'interest' have acquired a specific flavor of moral disrepute. Must we not conclude therefore that value, instead of flowing from interest, is an independent, if not antagonistic, principle by which interests and their objects are judged? Despite the strong appeal which this argument must make to common-sense, we shall find not only that it rests upon a confusion, but that the very facts to which it refers can be understood only by such a definition of value as is here proposed.

Let us consider, first, the relatively simple case in which *all* desire is condemned. The argument as presented by Schopenhauer and by other Occidental and Oriental advocates of the cult of apathy, is based upon the generalization that desire is doomed to defeat. Desire asks what in the very nature of the case it can never obtain. It asks for private advantage or special privilege in a world which is indifferent to such claims; or it perpetually begets new desires out of its own satisfaction, and is thus in a chronic state of bankruptcy. But why, then, condemn it? Pessimism is founded on a conception of evil, which in turn must be assumed to be the converse of good. There would be no reason for condemning the *futility* of desire as evil unless the *success* of desire were supposed to be good. This implication is more clearly evident in the Stoic cult of resignation. Thus Epictetus exhorts his followers to "demand not that events should happen as you wish; but wish them to happen as they do happen and you will go on well." [25] There would be no meaning in such counsel if 'going on well' were not conceived as con-

---

[23] And thus to be better than no universe at all, by the principle of 'inclusiveness.' Cf. Ch. XXII, Sect. III.

[24] "Value and Existence," *Jour. of Philos.*, Vol. XIII, 1916, pp. 452, 453.

[25] *Ench.* VIII, translated in Bakewell's *Source Book in Ancient Philosophy*, 1907, p. 318.

sisting in some sort of accord between events and what men wish.

Let us now consider those cases which arise not from disaccord between interests and their natural environments, but from disaccord between one interest and another. The same object may be liked or desired by one man, and disliked or avoided by another. Our definition requires us to attribute evil to the object as being disliked, *despite* the fact that it is liked. It may, then, be argued that liking cannot make an object good. Or it may be objected that our definition requires us to affirm that the same object is at one and the same time both evil and good, which is contradictory. But *is* it contradictory? The fact is, on the contrary, that a relational definition, such as that here proposed, is the only means of *avoiding* contradiction. It is not denied that the same object may be both liked and disliked; this is the very premise of the objection. If, then, good is *defined* as being liked, and evil as being disliked, it follows that the same object may *in this sense* be without contradiction both good and evil. A term may always possess relational attributes in opposite senses, provided such relations are sustained toward different terms. The same physical object may be both 'to the right of' and 'to the left of,' both 'above' and 'below'; the same man may be both friend and enemy, both agent and patient.

A yet more common case is that in which one interest is condemned because of being contrary to another interest. Such condemnation arises from the fact that interests conflict, so that the affirmation of one implies the negation of the other. This occurs in sheer struggle where both interests are upon the same plane. When two appetites require for their satisfaction the exclusive use of the same object, the desired object is *good* in relation to each appetite; while each appetite is *evil* in relation to the other, as tending to prevent its satisfaction.

But the case which has most deeply affected popular habits of thought, and

which is mainly responsible for the prejudice against the present theory of value, is the case in which an interest or its object is morally condemned. Interests are deemed 'bad,' and not merely in the sense of being hostile to other rival interests of the same rank; they are deemed 'downright' bad, in a sense in which all judges, including the agent himself, are expected to agree.

The explanation of this case lies, however, in the fact that moral judgments are not concerned with value in the generic sense, but with a specific and complex *aspect* of it. They are concerned with organizations of values, whether in the personal or in the social life. They do not deal with interests *per se,* but with the relation of interests to the comprehensive purposes in which they are incorporated. From the moral point of view value *begins* with the bearing of a 'lower' interest upon a 'higher' interest. To quote Mr. Santayana,

It is in reference to such constitutional interests that things are 'really' good or bad; interests which may not be fairly represented by any incidental conscious desire. No doubt any desire, however capricious, represents some momentary and partial interest, which lends to its objects a certain real and inalienable value; yet when we consider, as we do in human society, the interests of men, whom reflection and settled purposes have raised more or less to the ideal dignity of individuals, then passing fancies and passions may indeed have bad objects, and be bad themselves, in that they thwart the more comprehensive interests of the soul that entertains them.[26]

It is in this sense that appetites may be vicious in relation to health, or efficiency; that special inclinations or passions may corrupt character, or hinder a life-purpose; and that personal ambition may imperil the well-being of the nation, or of humanity at large. But while such values may be absolutes for the moral consciousness, it is the avowed purpose of a general theory of value to analyze and relate them. Theory

[26] G. Santayana, *Winds of Doctrine,* 1913, p. 146.

of value takes all value for its province, even values which are too evident or ignoble for the judgments of common-sense. This does not imply any neglect of 'higher' values, but only the method of understanding the special case in terms of the generic type.

57. Realistic Basis of the Present Definition. We have reached the general conclusion that while there *is* an epistemological relativism which is vicious and self-defeating, the relativity of values is not only logically innocuous but logically helpful and illuminating. The genuine logical difficulties that have attended the theory of value have arisen from a persistent unwillingness to accept the palpable fact that values *are* relative in different senses to different subjects. This unwillingness has taken the form of denying that values are relative to interests at all, or the form of affirming their exclusive relation to some one interest, or to some one type or class of interests. The really vicious relativism arises not from the recognition of relations, but from the *insufficient* recognition of relations. The error of the old geocentric astronomy lay not in its affirmation of the relation of sun, moon and stars to the earth, but in the distorted perspective which under-emphasized or ignored other relations. The same defect has subsequently appeared in the Newtonian mechanics. The error of anthropocentrism lies not in affirming the relation of all things to man, but in an exaggeration of that relation. In all of these cases advancing enlightenment has generalized a relation which was previously thought to be unique.

The analogous case in theory of value is the affirmation in behalf of any subject that its interests constitute the only centre or point of reference for all values. The common and disreputable case is egoism where an agent baldly asserts his own private interests. The more insidious case is that which enjoys among philosophers the highly reputable name of 'idealism.'

This form of relativism arises from the general thesis characteristic of all idealism that the cognitive act creates its objects. According to this thesis, when I know reality, I make it; and since there can be only one reality, what I thus make takes exclusive possession of the field. In making reality myself I must reject the work of others save in so far as it coincides with my own. What holds of objects of knowledge generally, holds of values in particular. Value is held to be relative to the subject's *judgment.* Since one is justified in claiming the assent of others to one's judgment, and must regard other and conflicting judgments as false, one may thus claim priority or exclusiveness for that system of values which centres in oneself. This view is viciously relativistic in that it imputes absoluteness to a limited and partial set of relations. The way of escape lies not in the denial of the relativity of value to interest, but in the *generalization* of that relation. Where all interests are viewed as equally constitutive of value, and none is viewed as exclusive or preëminent, then the relativism of values loses those characters of arbitrariness, contradictoriness and asymmetry, which make it morally and logically objectionable.

It has sometimes been supposed that a realistic theory of knowledge, such as is professed in the present study, implies that values shall be conceived as 'objective' in the sense of being independent of *any* relation to a subject. But such an inference is wholly gratuitous. A realistic theory of knowledge is a theory of *knowledge,* to the effect, namely, that *what* is known is independent as regards its existence and essential nature, of the *act* or *state* of knowledge. It is asserted that when the mountain, for example, is perceived by Mahomet, this relation is something superadded to the mountain; in such wise that the mountain can maintain its historic existence and its mountainous nature uninterruptedly, whether in the presence or in the absence of Mahomet's perception. But this thesis does not imply that only mountains or similar inanimate and insensible beings

can exist or be perceived. Mahomet, for example, perceived his daughter Fatima and
her love for Ali; he was doubtless aware of
his own hopes and fears for the future of
Islam. Realism contends only that love,
hope and fear, like mountains, are independent of the acts of perception or judgment whereby they are known. There is
not the slightest ground for imputing to
realism the grotesque notion that there are
no such things as acts or states of mind, or
that such things cannot be known. If a
realist entertained this grotesque notion he
could not affirm anything about the act of
knowledge itself, which is the central topic
of his discourse. Because he seeks to avoid
a philosophical psycho-mania, there is no
reason to accuse him of psycho-phobia.

The view here opposed may properly
be termed a biocentric or psycho-centric
theory of value, in the sense that values are
held to be functions of certain acts of living
mind to which we have given the name of
interest. Interests and their objects, or the
complex facts, objects-of-interest, can be
known like any other facts. But they do not
have to obtain from anybody's knowledge
of them, permission either to exist or to be
what they are. No subject whatsoever,
human or divine, has the power to make
or unmake them by his own simple
affirmation or denial. When value is
defined in terms of these facts it possesses
the same independence. A value acquires
existence when an interest is generated, regardless of any knowledge about it. A
value will cease to exist when its own sus-
taining interest is destroyed or altered; but
it does not cease to exist simply because it
is cognitively excommunicated. He who
knows values, and takes account of them,
profits from that knowledge through his
better adaptation to the environment in
which he lives; and he who ignores them,
does so at his peril.

III. PROBLEMS AND METHODS

58. Assuming that value is a function of
what may broadly be termed 'interest,' it
becomes imperative to examine the fundamental or generic character of this phenomenon. What is that state, or attitude, or
act, or process, which is characteristic of
living things, which is unmistakably present in the motor-affective consciousness of
man, and which shades away through instinct and reflex to the doubtful borderland
of tropism? Both the vocabulary and the
grammatical structure of common speech
provide for the category of interest. There
is something in our world to which they
serve to call attention. What is it?

The fact that we have found it necessary to paraphrase interest as "the motor-
affective life" indicates the complexity of
the topic. If value in the generic sense is
defined in terms of interest in the generic
sense, then it is evident that the varieties of
value must be understood in terms of the
varieties of interest. These varieties, and
the rival claims to which they give rise,
have provoked most of the controversies of
contemporary psychology. Some interests,
called 'instincts,' are held to be innate, and
others acquired. Some, called 'reflexes,' are
held to be blind and automatic; others are
held to be 'intelligent.' The expression, 'motor-affective,' as well as the traditional division of mind into thought, will, and feeling,
suggests a duality between active and passive interests; or a duality between interests directed to an imagined or represented
future, and those directed to an immediate
present. Terms such as 'character' and 'disposition' testify to a type of interest which
is latent or unconscious, and which manifests
itself in its outward or ulterior effects, rather
than in any present subjective state. The
antithesis between 'impulse' and 'volition'
implies that interest is qualified by the
presence, in some degree, of the intellectual process. The difference between desire
and aversion, pleasure and pain, or liking
and disliking, indicates a peculiar polarity
or opposition of interest. Finally, all of
these modal differences imply corresponding standards of measurement, such as 'intensity' of feeling, or 'strength' of desire.

In undertaking to refine and amplify

the meaning of interest, we are confronted at the outset by a choice of methods. There is a *prima facie* discontinuity between the field of mental states disclosed by introspection, and the field of organic phenomena in which the biologist and other physical scientists conduct their investigations; and if an observer commits himself initially to the former, it would seem that he can never escape its limits. We shall therefore look for interest in the open,—upon the plane and in the context of physical nature.

We cannot determine the rôle of introspective data in interest, unless we first take that view of the matter in which both consciousness and its physical context are taken into account. Behavior or conduct, broadly surveyed in all the dimensions that experience affords, can alone give us the proper perspective. Furthermore, we want if possible to discover what it is to *be* interested, not what it is merely to *feel* interested. What is implied in *being* favorably or unfavorably disposed to anything? It may be that it all comes to nothing more than a peculiar quality or arrangement among the data of introspection, but such a conclusion would be equivalent to an abandonment of the widespread notion that interest is a kind of determination of events. The really important claim made in behalf of interest is the claim that things happen *because* of interest. Are acts performed *on account* of ends? Is it proper to *explain* what takes place in human or animal life, or in the course of nature at large, by the categories of teleology? The most exhaustive introspective analysis of the motor-affective consciousness would leave this question unanswered, and to confine ourselves to the data which such analysis affords would be to prejudge it unfavorably.

For the first time since the moralists and theologians divided the soul from the body, man is beginning to find a place in nature without being stripped of his most distinctive characteristics. He has begun to move about on the surface of the planet while still retaining possession of his faculties. This achievement is due primarily to that general psychological tendency which has acquired the name of 'behaviorism,' from one of its particular and recent manifestations.[27]

Behaviorism, in the general sense, is simply a return to the original Aristotelian view that mind and body are related as activity and organ. The activities of mind, so construed, are observable and describable functions of the physical organism, continuous with those of life, and differing from them in pattern and complexity rather than in constituents. The so-called 'states' of mind, or 'contents of consciousness,' on the other hand, are identified with the environment of behavior, being mental only in so far as behavior selects and combines them. The result is to avoid construing either the subjective or the objective aspect of mind in terms of a unique substance or quality.

It has been objected that this is to leave out 'consciousness.' But what is this 'consciousness' which we are under obligation to include—is it a datum or a theory? It was once said that psychology omitted the soul. And so it did, in so far as the term 'soul' was the name for a theory formulated in theology or "rational" psychology. But psychology never deliberately neglected any of the facts or problems lying within the field of the mental life of man; and as a result of omitting the older theory of the soul, it reached a very much better understanding of the actual mode of existence in question. No one would now think of conceiving the soul as a simple, indivisible and incorruptible static entity, or as a naked act of pure reason. In every philosophy the soul is now a process; or a flowing, and more or less complexly organized, experience. When, therefore, we say the soul is lost, what we really mean is that a theory is

[27] Summaries of this tendency, with bibliography, will be found in G. C. Dickinson, *Economic Motives*, 1922, Ch. VII; A. A. Roback, *Behaviorism and Psychology*, 1923. The best critical exposition is to be found in K. S. Lashley: "The Behavioristic Interpretation of Consciousness," *Psych. Rev.*, Vol. XXX, 1923.

more or less obsolete, as a result of its having been successfully ignored. The soul as an existent fact having a nature and an explanation, is not lost, but found.

Now something of this same outcome may with reasonable safety be predicted in the case of 'consciousness.' If a behaviorist be enlightened he will have no intention of omitting any facts, but only of abandoning a theory which he believes has proved unsatisfactory. He does not abandon *consciousness*, but the introspective *theory* of consciousness; and in so far as the new theory is more successful than the old, consciousness as a group of facts, as something that exists and happens, will have been found and not lost.[28]

The limitations of the introspective theory of consciousness have been most flagrant in the region of the will and the affections; in other words, in that department of human nature with which theory of value is primarily concerned. The failure of introspection to give any satisfactory account of feeling, desire, will, and conation scarcely admits of doubt.

The dubious feelings of 'pleasantness' and 'unpleasantness,' which if they *are* a unique species of introspective data ought to be *indubitable*, are held by some to be simple sensations, by others to be fusions of organic sensations, and by others to be acts

or 'attitudes' of liking or disliking. Desire, viewed introspectively, can never be anything but a combination of ideas and feelings. Exponents of the introspective method have seen the difficulty of accounting in these terms for actual dynamic differences: such as that between desiring a thing, and liking to think of it; or that between real desire, and the sham-desire characteristic of play and aesthetic detachment.[29] As to will, Münsterberg's reduction of this to such terms as "the perception of an attained effect whose idea has gone before" [30] perfectly illustrates the extent to which the method of introspection endeavors to make up the whole of will by piecing together its cognitive shreds and patches. It is evident that the distinctive feature of will lies in this "attained effect" (*erreichten Effektes*), which is the one element in the situation which cannot be defined in introspective terms.

Similarly, wherever accounts of *conation* preserve anything distinctive, they appear to incorporate something of the action of the physical organism. The basic antithesis of favor and disfavor, which is said to distinguish active feelings, is an echo of the antithesis between positive and negative bodily reactions. Thus Professor G. F. Stout speaks of a "mental striving," which "tends to realize itself," and of which the physiological correlate is "the tendency of a neural system to recover a relatively stable condition." What, one may fairly ask, is the common meaning of "tendency" on the mental and the physiological sides? Or is the latter, perhaps, the *real* tendency, and

---

[28] Whether this is or is not a "strict" behaviorism, is a matter of no consequence. I am concerned with the possibilities afforded by a program and a method, broadly conceived. It is too early, even if it were profitable, to discuss questions of orthodoxy and heresy. Most of the current criticisms of behaviorism are irrelevant to the position here taken. Thus Mr. C. D. Broad attacks the behaviorist who says "that all mental processes reduce without residue to the fact that the body is behaving in a certain specific way" (*The Mind and its Place in Nature*, 1925, p. 616). I agree that such a behaviorist (*i.e.*, one who denies or ignores the *content* of consciousness) deserves attack. Mr. Broad also defines the behaviorist as a "reductive materialist" (*ibid.*, p. 612); which fits *some* behaviorists, but not that general tendency of which I make bold to claim Mr. Broad himself as an adherent, in so far as he prefers to view mind as an "emergent characteristic" of the material world (*ibid.*, pp. 610, 650).

[29] An instructive example of the futility of attempting to reduce desire to introspective terms is afforded by the controversy within the school of Meinong on the relations of desire and feeling. Cf. Ch. Ehrenfels, *System der Werttheorie*, 1897, Vol. I, pp. 41, 248–251; A. Meinong, *Über Annahmen*, 1902, pp. 293–296; W. M. Urban, *Valuation*, 1909, pp. 35–37; and the writer's "Behavioristic View of Purpose," *Jour. of Philos.*, Vol. XVIII, 1921.

[30] H. Münsterberg, *Willenshandlung*, 1888, p. 88.

the former the feeling of it?[31] Professor William McDougall says that every instance of instinctive behavior involves "a striving *towards or away from*" an object; and that in all instinctive behavior there is "*a persistent striving towards the natural end of the process,*" which is intensified by obstacles.[32] This account seems clearly to have been derived in the first instance from the organism's action on its environment, and irresistibly suggests that the subjective or introspective sense of striving is the consciousness *of* the stresses and strains incidental to this action.[33]

Almost every recent advance in the motor-affective field of the mental life has resulted from the more or less complete abandonment of the introspective method. The most notable general advance, an advance that has now been accepted by the social sciences as well as by popular opinion, is the rejection of the once-classic view that conduct is ruled by the selfish calculation of pleasure and pain. This theory of human motivation has been superseded by explanations in terms of reflex, instinct, imitation, the learning process, habit, or unconscious 'complex.' These and other allied conceptions, characteristic of what is known as "dynamic psychology," have come into vogue as a result of attempts to describe the behavior of animals, children, men, and social groups; or the misbehavior of criminals, or crowds, or the insane. They do not imply the abandonment of introspection, but they do signify the fruitfulness of a new method in which mind is conceived as an organic rather than as a purely subjective entity. The history of psychology, the record both of its past failures and of its recent successes, thus abundantly justifies our provisional adoption of the objective method. In accord with this method we shall begin our study of interest by an examination of certain peculiarities of the biological organism.

---

[31] *Analytical Psychology*, 1896, Vol. II, pp. 82, 83.

[32] *Social Psychology*, 1910, pp. 26, 27. The italics are mine.

[33] I do not deny the common opinion that the animistic view of nature results from a projection into external objects of the experience of conation, but I do affirm that what is so projected is mainly if not wholly the experience of organic action.

The Meaning of 'Good'

SIR DAVID ROSS

It is round the question of the intrinsically good that the chief controversies about the nature of goodness or of value revolve. For most theories of value may be divided into those which treat it as a quality and those which treat it as a relation between that which has value and something else—which is usually but not always said to be some state of a mind, such as that of being pleased by the object or desiring it or approving of it or finding its desire satisfied by it. And it seems clear that any view which treats goodness as a relation between that which is good and something else denies that anything is intrinsically good, since by calling a thing intrinsically good we mean that it would be good even if nothing else existed. One of the advocates of a relational view of value, Professor Perry, seeks to maintain that a relational view does not involve the denial of intrinsic value, which he evidently thinks would be a consequence hostile if not fatal to his view. 'A . . . serious objection' to his theory, he says,[1] 'is based upon the nature of *intrinsic* value. We judge a thing to be intrinsically good "where we judge, concerning a particular state of things, that it would be worth while—would be 'a good thing'—that that state of things should exist, *even if nothing else were to exist besides,* either at the same time or afterwards." ' [2] If a thing derives value from its relation to an

interest taken in it, it would seem impossible that anything whatsoever should possess value in itself. But in that case value would seem always to be borrowed, and never owned; value would shine by a reflected glory having no original source.

'The question,' he continues, 'turns upon the fact that any predicate may be judged synthetically or analytically. Suppose that "good" were to be regarded as a simple quality like yellow. It would then be possible to judge either synthetically, that the primrose was fair or yellow; or, analytically, that the fair, yellow primrose was fair or yellow. Only the fair, yellow primrose would be fair and yellow "even if nothing were to exist besides." But the logic of the situation is not in the least altered if a relational predicate is substituted for a simple quality; indeed it is quite possible to regard a quality as a monadic a (single term) relation. Tangential, for example, is a relational predicate; since a line is a tangent only by virtue of the peculiar relation of single-point contact with another line or surface. Let R^t represent this peculiar relation, and A, B, two lines. One can then judge either synthetically, that (A) R^t (B); or, analytically, that (A) R^t (B) is R^t. Similarly, let S represent an interested subject, O an object, and R^i the peculiar relation of interest taken and received. We can then judge either synthetically, that (O) R^i (S); or, analytically, that (O) R^i (S) is R^i. In other words, one can say either that O is desired by S, or that

Reprinted from *The Right and the Good* by Sir David Ross by permission of the Clarendon Press, Oxford. Copyright 1930.
[1] *A General Theory of Value,* 132.
[2] G. E. Moore, *Ethics,* 162 [p. 101 reset edition].

O-desired-by-*S* is a case of the general character "desired." '

I assume, as it seems necessary to assume in order to make the example relevant, that 'fair' here = 'beautiful,' and that beauty is taken as a species of goodness. Professor Perry is evidently taking 'yellow' to be a simple, non-relational quality, and holding 'good' to be a relational one, *viz.* = 'object of interest to some one' (loosely represented by 'desired-by-*S*'). I am in doubt about the meaning of 'only' in the sentence 'Only the fair, yellow primrose would be fair and yellow "even if nothing were to exist besides." ' (1) 'Only' may mean 'yet.' If so, Professor Perry is admitting that the fair yellow primrose would be yellow, and would be beautiful if beauty were a non-relational quality, even if there were nothing else in the world. And if this be so, that constitutes a vital difference between such attributes, which would attach to their subject even if there were nothing else in the world, and attributes such as 'desired-by-*S*,' which certainly would not attach to *O* unless *S* existed as well. (2) More probably, I think, 'only' means 'alone'; i.e. Professor Perry is saying that in contrast with the fair yellow primrose, the *primrose* would not be fair and yellow if nothing else were to exist, just as *O* would not be desired by *S* if *S* did not exist as well as *O*.

Now it is true that the primrose could not be fair or yellow if nothing but it existed. It could not be fair if its fairness did not exist, nor yellow if its yellowness did not. But it is equally true that the *fair yellow primrose* (which Professor Perry contrasts with the *primrose* in this respect) could not be fair or yellow if its fairness or its yellowness did not exist; and its fairness and its yellowness are quite as different from the fair yellow primrose as they are from the primrose, so that there is no difference between the primrose and the fair yellow primrose in this respect. But if yellowness, or fairness, is a non-rational quality of the primrose, the primrose might be

yellow or fair though nothing but the primrose *and its attribute* of being yellow or fair existed. On the other hand, if goodness is a relational quality (say = object of interest to some one), nothing could be good unless, besides it and its attribute of 'being an object of interest to some one,' something else existed, *viz.* a person to whom it is an object of interest. The essential difference would remain, that non-relational attributes can be possessed by subjects though nothing but the subjects and the attributes exist; while relational attributes can be possessed by subjects only if something besides both the subjects and the attributes exists, *viz.* the things that form the other terms of the relations. Thus if the definition of an intrinsic attribute as one which its subject would possess if nothing other than the subject existed, be amended into the form 'an intrinsic attribute is one which the subject would possess even if nothing but the subject and the attribute existed,' it is evident that non-relational attributes are intrinsic and that relational attributes cannot be so. If 'good,' then, be defined as Professor Perry defines it, nothing can be intrinsically good. And his attempt to get over the difficulty of the apparent necessity (for a relational view of value) of denying that anything has intrinsic value, by means of the distinction between analytic and synthetic judgments, comes to nothing. '*O*-desired-by-*S*' is not a different object which can truly be said to possess intrinsic value when it is denied that any *O* apart from being desired has intrinsic value. '*O*-desired-by-*S* is good' is simply another way of saying 'any *O* has value not in itself but by virtue of the co-existence with it, and in a certain relation to it, of *S*.' And to say this is to deny intrinsic value to anything. And similarly any other view which identifies goodness with or makes it depend upon a relation between that which is good and something else, denies the existence of intrinsic value.

The theories which identify goodness with some relation are bound to think of this either (I) as a relation between that which is good and some or all of its elements, *or* (II) as a relation between some or all of its elements, *or* (III) as a relation between it or some or all of its elements and something else.

Out of the many theories about the nature of goodness, I am unable to think of any which belongs to type (I), and this type need not, perhaps, be examined. There have been theories of type (II), viz. those that identify the good with the harmonious or coherent. With reference to any such view, the question must first be asked whether it is meant (*a*) that goodness just is coherence, or (*b*) that what is good is good because it is coherent. Only the first of these views is strictly relevant here, where we are inquiring what goodness *is*. The second view does not answer this question; it leaves still open the question what is the nature of the attribute goodness which coherent things are said to have because they are coherent. Now the first view seems to be clearly false. It is surely clear that, however close a connexion there may be between coherence and goodness, we never *mean*, when we call a thing good, that it is coherent. If this were what we meant, 'the coherent, and only the coherent, is good' would be a mere tautology, since it would be equivalent to 'the coherent, and only the coherent, is coherent'; but it is evidently not a mere tautology, but a proposition which if true is very important. The theory then, if it is to have any plausibility, must be understood in the second form; and in this form it is no answer to the question we are asking, what is goodness.

It may be well, however, to offer some comments on the theory in its second form, even if this is not strictly relevant to the present stage of our inquiry. In the first place it may be remarked that any such theory seems to start with the presumption that there is some single attribute, other than goodness, that makes all good things

good, and that the only question is what this attribute is. Now I agree that goodness is a consequential attribute; that anything that is good must be good either by virtue of its whole nature apart from its goodness, or by virtue of something in its nature other than goodness. This seems to me a very important fact about goodness, and one that marks it off from most other attributes. [3] But I cannot agree that the presumption is that there is any *one* characteristic by virtue of which all the things that are good are good. If conscientiousness and benevolence, for instance, are both good, it is just as likely, initially, that conscientiousness is good because it is conscientiousness, and benevolence good because it is benevolence. Still, this must not be assumed to be the case, any more than the opposite view must be assumed. We must be prepared to consider on its merits any suggested general ground of goodness. But when I ask myself whether conscientiousness, or benevolence, for instance, can be held to be good by virtue of the coherence of its elements, I have to ask what the supposed elements are, and in what respect they are supposed to cohere, and to these questions I find no clear answer given by those who hold the theory. It would be more plausible (though not, I think true) to say that the goodness of conscientious or benevolent action depends on its coherence with something outside it, e.g. with the whole system of purposes of the agent, or of the society he lives in. But such a theory would belong not to type (II), which we are examining, but to type (III). Or again, suppose that one judges a particular pleasure to be good, is it not clear that even if most and possibly all pleasures are complex, it is not on account of its being a complex united by the relation of coherence, but on account of its having the felt character of pleasantness, that it is judged to be good?

When we turn to type (III), we find

[3] Cf. pp. 121-2.

that the relation which is identified with goodness (or else held to be what makes good things good) is sometimes held to be necessarily a relation to a mind, while sometimes this limitation is not imposed. I take as a typical view of the latter kind one of which I owe my knowledge to an article by Professor Urban.[4] Professor Sheldon, as reported by Professor Urban, holds that value is 'fulfilment of any tendency whatever.' The essential objection to this theory seems to me to be this. Empty 'tendency' of any reference to the aims of conscious beings (which it is the special point of this theory to do), and what meaning is left for 'fulfilment of any tendency'? What is left is the notion of a thing's being under the influence of a certain force, and of its actually passing into the state it would pass into if acted on by that force alone. And who will say that this purely physical circumstance is either identical or even coextensive with value?

To this Professor Sheldon (as reported by Professor Urban) answers: 'Good is no doubt a different notion from fulfilment, and therefore appears to contain something not authorized in the content of the latter notion. But that is because good or value is the relation between the fulfilment (or furthering) and the tendency, a relation uniquely and sufficiently determined by the two.'[5] To this it seems to me enough to reply that this relation can exist, as much as anywhere else, in the case of bodies acted on by physical forces, where no one would dream of applying the notion of good or value. If we *must* have a relational theory of value, there seems to be much more plausibility in the 'psychological' than in the 'ontological' form of the theory.

The 'psychological' theories as a rule take the form of holding that a thing's being good means either (A) that some person or persons have some feeling towards it, or (B) that some person or persons think it to be good; and such views, or rather those of the first type, have some initial attractiveness. (A) Our judgments that certain things are good are in fact constantly accompanied by feelings towards them—feelings of pleasure, and of regret for their absence; and this fact is apt to lead to one or other of two views, or more often perhaps to a mixture of the two. One view is that by being objects of some such feeling (let us say, adopting Professor Perry's comprehensive phrase, by being 'objects of interest') things acquire a further character, that of value. The other is that to have value is just to be an object of interest, and nothing more. I am rather in doubt how to classify the view put forward in *A General Theory of Value* by Professor Perry himself. Passages could be found in his book to support the interpretation of him as holding the first view; e.g. those in which value is described as *dependent* on interest. But on the whole it seems pretty clear that it is the second view he wishes to maintain. 'The view,' he says,[6] 'may otherwise be formulated in the equation: x is valuable $=$ interest is taken in x'; and immediately after, 'Value is thus a specific relation into which things possessing any ontological status whatsoever, whether real or imaginary, may enter with interested subjects'—i.e. the relation of being objects of interest to them. Again,[7] 'Thus the question' (the question to which he provides an answer) 'is the question, In what consists' (not, On what depends) 'value in the generic sense?'

If the *first* interpretation be the true one, there remain difficult questions to which he provides no answer. If value is something not consisting in, but depending on, being an object of interest, what is value itself, and what is the nature of the relation vaguely described as dependence? Is the relation a causal one, or a logical

[4] *Journal of Philosophy*, 1916, 454.
[5] *Ib.*

[6] *A General Theory of Value*, 116.
[7] *Ib.* 118.

one, and if neither of these, what is it? To these no answer is suggested. But these questions need not be pressed, for I fancy that Professor Perry would accept the *second* interpretation as the true account of his view.

On this second interpretation, the theory is that 'good' and 'object of interest' are just different ways of expressing exactly the same notion. But it is clear that this is not true. It is surely clear that when we call something good we are thinking of it as possessing in itself a certain attribute and are not thinking of it as necessarily having an interest taken in it. If when we attend to something we are impelled to describe it as good, it is surely not impossible to think that, though of course we can only discover its goodness by attending to it, it had its goodness before we attended to it and would have had it if we had not attended to it. And again it is evidently possible to think that some of the things in which an interest has been taken have nevertheless been bad. But if 'good' and 'object of interest' meant exactly the same, it would be impossible to think either of these two things which it clearly is possible to think. The view, therefore, that 'good' and 'object of interest' stand for the same notion must be given up. What the relational theory must maintain, if it is to be plausible, must be something different; it must be that whereas most people think that certain things have a characteristic, goodness, distinct from that of being objects of interest, nothing has any such characteristic. And then the question arises, what could have led mankind to form this quite superfluous notion to which nothing in reality corresponds? It is not as if the notion of goodness were a complex notion formed, like such notions as that of 'centaur,' by a play of fancy in which characteristics found separate in reality are imagined to coexist; for there are no characteristics of which 'good' can be said to be a compound. We may, however, not merely ask how the notion could have come into

being if it were not the apprehension of a reality.[8] We may claim that we are directly aware that conscientious action, for example, has a value of its own, not identical with or even dependent upon our or any one else's taking an interest in it. Our reason informs us of this as surely as it informs us of anything, and to distrust reason here is in principle to distrust its power of ever knowing reality.

Another fatal objection to any theory which identifies good with being an object of interest, or of any particular type of feeling, becomes apparent when we ask by whom the interest or the feeling is supposed to be felt. Some answers escape some objections and others escape others, but each possible answer is exposed to at least one fatal objection of its own. This ground has been very fully covered by Professor Moore in an examination of the corresponding theories about 'right,'[9] and both in the case of 'right' and in the case of 'good' his line of argument seems to me unanswerable. Theories of this type are divisible into those which identify goodness with the presence of some feeling (1) in at least one person, no matter who he is, (2) in the person who judges an object to be good, (3) in a majority of persons of some class or other—say persons belonging to a particular stage in the history of civilization, (4) in a majority of mankind, or (5) in all mankind. To (1) there seem to be four objections. (*a*) It surely can hardly be denied that, whatever feeling we select as the feeling involved—whether for instance this be taken to be pleasure, or approval—a man may doubt whether a certain thing is good, even when he does not doubt that some one or other has had such a feeling towards it. (*b*) If what I mean when I call something good is that some one or other has a certain feeling towards it, and if what any other person means when he calls it bad is

---

[8] Cf. Cook Wilson's argument against the possibility of a fictitious 'simple idea,' *Statement and Inference*, ii. 511–21.

[9] *Ethics*, chs. 3 and 4.

that some one or other has an opposite feeling towards it, we should not be at variance, because both propositions might be true. Yet if anything is clear, it is that we do suppose ourselves to be making incompatible statements about the object. (*c*) If something, without changing its nature, at some moment aroused for the first time the feeling in question in some mind, we should clearly judge not that the object had then first become good, but that its goodness had then first been apprehended. And (*d*) it might be enough to ask whether any one finds it even possible to think that goodness could be brought into being by the feeling of *some one or other*, no matter how vicious or stupid or ignorant he might be. It seems clear that by goodness we mean something at any rate more objective than that.

To the theory in form (2) the primary objection is identical with objection (*b*) above. If all I meant by saying that an object is good were that it arouses a certain feeling in me, and all you meant by saying that it is not good, or is bad, were that it does not arouse that feeling, or arouses an opposite feeling, in you, we should not be at variance, for we might both be right. And objection (*c*) applies with just as much force to this theory as to the previous one.

To the theory in form (3) it may be objected (*a*) that it will follow that two people who claim to be representing the feelings of majorities of different sets of persons will never be at variance if they pronounce the same thing respectively good and bad. Yet it is clear that even when two men belong to different sets of persons, the feelings of a majority of which they would on this view be claiming to represent, they believe themselves to be making incompatible statements when they call something respectively good and bad. Clearly therefore what they claim to be expressing is not the feelings of different majorities. But further (*b*) it is surely plain that there are cases in which a man thinks something

good, without thinking that there is a majority of any class of men who have a certain feeling towards it. Even if we think that a majority of persons at our own stage of civilization, for instance, would have feelings like ours if they attended to the object, we may feel sure that they have not attended to it and therefore have not the feeling in question towards it.

The theory in form (4) is not open to the *first* objection made to the previous theory. For any one who thought that a majority of mankind had a certain feeling towards an object *would* be at variance with any one who thought that they had not this feeling, or had an opposite feeling. But objection (*b*) to theory (3) applies with redoubled force to theory (4).

And finally, to theory (5) it applies with even greater force.

(*B*) The second and remaining type of what I may call purely subjective theories of good is that which holds that for me to think an object good is to think that (1) some one or other, or (2) I, or (3) a majority of some set of men, or (4) a majority of mankind, or (5) all mankind, *think* it good. It is unnecessary and would be tedious to examine these theories as fully as we have examined those of type (*A*). It is enough to point out that corresponding objections are equally fatal to them, and to add a new objection fatal to all theories of type (*B*).

The objections to A_1	apply equally to B_1
" " " A_2	" " " B_2
" " " A_3	" " " B_3
" " " A_4	" " " B_4
" " " A_5	" " " B_5

But apart from these objections to special forms of theory (*B*), the whole theory has one absurdity common to all its forms. It is perfectly evident that the meaning of 'X is good' cannot be identical with the meaning of 'some one (or I, or a majority of some class of men, &c.) thinks that X is good,' since it *is* identical with the meaning of only one element in the latter phrase. Or, to put the same objection otherwise, to say that S thinks X good leaves it an open question whether X *is* good. For opinion has the characteristic, which feeling has not, of being either true or false. If S thinks falsely that X is good, then X is not good; and if S thinks truly that X is good, then X's being good is neither identical with nor dependent on S's thinking it good. In fact, while theory (A) deserves the most serious consideration, and it is excessively hard to be sure whether one is right in rejecting it or may not have been guilty of some logical confusion, theory (B) may be rejected out of hand. Professor Perry, as one might expect, repudiates it with vigour.

I turn to a reconsideration of theory (A) in the light of Professer Perry's discussion. He divides all possible theories of value into four types, according to the view they take of the relation of value to interest, interest being identified 'with the motive-affective life; that is to say, with instinct, desire, feeling; these, and all their family of states, acts, and attitudes.' [10] 'There are four possible relations of value to interest. In the first place, value may be, in its essential nature, quite irrelevant to interest. . . . In the second place, value may be held to be the character of an object which qualifies it to be an end; in other words, that which implies, evokes or regulates interest . . . In the third place, value may be assigned to the objects of certain duly qualified interests, such as the final, harmonious, absolute, or imperative interest. Finally, there is the simpler and more comprehensive view, that value in the generic sense attaches promiscuously to all objects of all interest.' [11]

I am not specially concerned with the two intermediate views, and agree with many of Professor Perry's criticisms of them. I am mainly interested in the first,

which I believe to be true,[12] and in the fourth, which he believes to be true. He takes as a typical expression of the first view Professor Moore's remark 'my point is that "good" is a simple notion, just as "yellow" is a simple notion; that, just as you cannot, by any manner of means, explain to any one who does not already know it, what yellow is, so you cannot explain what good is'; and he treats this view as being best 'understood as an extension of that pan-objectivism which, having concluded that the so-called "secondary qualities," such as colour, have as good a title to extra-mental existence as the so-called primary qualities, such as figure, sees no reason why the so-called "tertiary" qualities, such as good, should not be assigned the same status.' [13]

There may be in some minds a connexion between a realistic view of the secondary qualities and an objective view of goodness, but it should be pointed out that there is no necessary connexion between the two views. For my own part, reflection on the facts of perception and of its illusions forces me to think that there is no such thing as objective colour, for example; I am driven to suppose that colour-sensation is a mental state which is not perception of colour. But colour-sensation[14] is an indubitable fact, and I can with a certain modification accept Professor Moore's comparison. I can say that goodness is a quality which can no more be defined in terms of anything other than itself, than can the quality of the sensation which we describe as being one of 'seeing yellow.' Whatever we may think about the objectivity of colour, there can, I imagine, be no doubt of the indefinability of the character of our sensation. Thus the adoption of

---

[12] I think, of course, that a thing may arouse interest, and will rouse it in a well-constituted mind, *because of* its goodness. What I wish to deny is that its goodness either is or depends on its arousing interest.

[13] *A General Theory of Value*, 29.

[14] i.e. the experience which we habitually, whether rightly or (as I suggest) wrongly, describe as that of seeing colour.

---

[10] *A General Theory of Value*, 27.

[11] *Ib.*

this comparison is in no way bound up with an objective view of secondary qualities. Nor, again, do I think of goodness as 'extra-mental'; for while I do not think it is essentially *for* minds, I think it is essentially a quality *of* states of mind.

Professor Perry's first criticism of the objective view of good is that 'one who upholds this view of good must be prepared to point to a distinct *quale* which appears in that region which our value terms roughly indicate, and which is different from the object's shape and size, from the interrelation of its parts, from its relation to other objects, or to a subject; and from all the other factors which belong to the same context, but are designated by words other than "good." The present writer, for one, finds no such residuum.' [15] The existence of such a residuum is just the point at issue. So far we have only the word of those who agree with Professor Moore that they do discern in certain things a unique quality which can only be expressed by the term 'goodness' or some synonym of 'goodness,' and the word of those who agree with Professor Perry that they do not; and so long as the question is considered on these lines, all that we can do is to invite others to contemplate, for instance, conscientious action, and try for themselves whether they do or do not discern such a quality in it. But Professor Perry is, of course, not content with his *ipse dixit*. He argues that if goodness were an indefinable quality like yellowness its presence, when it is present, should be equally self-evident; and he points to the hesitancy of Professor Moore's report as to what things are good, as showing that the presence of goodness is *not* equally self-evident with that of yellowness. Here he seems to be stressing too much the analogy which Professor Moore has alleged to exist between goodness and yellowness. The analogy exists only in respect to the indefinability of both. It is not argued that in other respects the two quali-

ties are on all fours. In particular, the one is apprehended (if apprehended at all) [16] by sense-perception, the other by intelligence; and there is no reason to anticipate that what is discerned by the intelligence should be as easily discerned as what is discerned by sense-perception. But Professor Perry exaggerates the difference between the ease of discernment in the two cases. There is, he says, 'no serious difference of opinion as to the distribution of terms connoting empirical qualities. "Things wear them in public, and any passer-by may note them." '[17] But does not yellow merge into green, and into orange, and are there not border-line cases in which it is extremely difficult to say whether what we have before us is yellow or green, or whether it is yellow or orange? And if there are things about whose goodness there is room for difference of opinion, are there not other things, such as conscientious action, whose goodness is matter of general agreement?

But I should not like to rest the case for the indefinability of goodness merely on this *argumentum ad hominem*. It seems to me more important to point out that the question whether the presence of a given quality in some particular thing is easily discerned has nothing to do with the question whether the quality is indefinable. If two people differ, for instance, as to whether a particular action is good, their differing implies, no less than their agreeing would have done, that they mean by 'goodness' a definite quality; and their mere differing does not imply that that quality is *not* indefinable any more than their agreement would imply that it *is*. The questions of its definability and of its discernibility are different and not logically connected.

But if I attempt to vindicate Professor

---

[15] *A General Theory of Value*, 30.

[16] This caution seems necessary in view of the doubt I have expressed on p. 86 as to whether colour is something apprehended at all. The sentence in the text *without* the parenthesis would state the defence which I believe Professor Moore would make of his view.

[17] *A General Theory of Value*, 30.

Moore's comparison of goodness with yellowness as being like it an indefinable quality, I do not wish (any more than I imagine he would) to be thought to suppose that it is a quality in other respects like yellowness. The most salient difference is that it is a quality which anything that has it can have only in virtue of having some other characteristic; as e.g. a conscientious act is good in virtue of being conscientious. This I express later by describing it as a consequential and not a fundamental quality.[18]

Professor Perry turns next to mention Professor Laird's presentment of the objective view. Professor Laird, he says, 'appeals to the fact that there is an immediate objectivity in the appreciation of beauty, or in the admiration of conduct. These are not mere subjective states *caused* by an object; they *present* the object, clothed in its quality of charm or moral worth.'[19] Professor Perry points out that there are many adjectives which we apply to objects, and which therefore *prima facie* might appear to stand for qualities of objects apart from any relation to persons, but which on examination turn out to refer simply to the existence of some such relation,—adjectives like 'coveted,' 'boresome,' 'tiresome,' 'hopeful'; and that on the other hand adjectives like 'red' resist all attempts to localize them in the subject and insist on being localized in the object. But it is surely unfair to argue from words like 'coveted,' 'boresome,' 'tiresome,' 'hopeful,' which by their very formation point to a relation between a subject and an object, and the word 'good,' which equally clearly points to nothing of the kind but to a quality resident in the object itself, independent of any subject's reaction to the object. As regards 'beautiful' I am, as I shall point out later,[20] inclined to agree that the fact that lies at the back of our predications of it *is* simply the power something has of producing a cer-

tain kind of emotion in us; and the frequent use of such words as 'charming,' 'delightful,' almost as synonyms of 'beautiful' may be held to lend this view some support. But it is surely a strange reversal of the natural order of thought to say that our admiring an action either is, or is what necessitates, its being good. We think of its goodness as what we admire in it, and as something it would have even if no one admired it, something that it has in itself. We could suppose, for instance, an action of self-denial which neither the doer nor any one else had ever admired. If now some one were to become aware of it and admire it, he would surely pronounce that it had been good even when no one had been admiring it.

Professor Perry makes the further objection that the 'objective' theory derives all its plausibility from its exponents' being preoccupied with 'the aesthetic and contemplative values,' and that it precludes them from giving a comprehensive account of all values. 'The most serious defect of this type of theory is its failure to provide any systematic principle whatsoever. There are as many indefinable values as there are feeling attitudes, and since these are to be regarded as objective qualities rather than as modes of feeling, there is nothing to unite them, not even the principle of feeling. If "good" is a unique quality, then so are "pleasant," "bad," and "ought." There is no way of subsuming pleasant under good, or of defining the opposition of good and bad, or of subsuming both good and ought under a more general category such as value. If, on the other hand, value is defined in terms of interest, then the variability of interest seems to account for both the unity and the diversity of values.'[21] His assumption, then, is that there must be some single sense of 'valuable' in which the word is always used, and his contention is that a subjective theory alone will serve to assign such a single meaning and to show

[18] Cf. pp. 121–2.
[19] *A General Theory of Value*, 31.
[20] pp. 127–30.

[21] *A General Theory of Value*, 34.

the relations between the various specific kinds of value. And under the heading of 'valuable' he includes both things which would not naturally be described as being valuable at all, and things which we can surely recognize to have value only in fundamentally different senses. Does any one really think that obligatoriness is a special form of being valuable? [22] Is it not a hasty assumption to assume that it is an instance of the same kind of thing of which moral goodness or beauty is another instance? And is it not clear that what we call economic values [23] are merely instrumental values, different in kind from the goodness of virtue or of pleasure? The assumption that there must be 'a general theory of value' applicable to value in all the senses of that word seems to me to be unjustified.

At the same time, I am inclined to agree with Professor Perry in one of his contentions, though not in what he (if I understand him aright) seeks to deduce from it. He is seeking to find a single thread of identity which unites all our *applications* of the word good, and to infer from this that the word 'good' has the single *meaning* which he assigns to it. Now when I consider the variety of meanings of 'good' indicated in the preceding chapter—the predicative and the attributive use, the meanings 'successful in his endeavour' and the 'useful,' the instrumental and the intrinsic sense—though I cannot agree that what we mean in all or any of these cases by 'X is good' is 'X is an object of interest to some one,' I am inclined to think that the only thread that connects our *application* of the word in all these senses—i.e. the only common fact that is present whenever we use the term 'good'—is that in each case the *judger* has some feeling of approval or interest towards what he calls good. But this in no way proves that we are always using 'good' in the same *sense*. The *senses* 'intrinsically good' and 'useful' appear to

me entirely different, though whether we use the word good in one or the other we have in both cases a feeling of approval or interest towards what we call good. What common thread there is, is one that connects not the various meanings of good, but our use of it in these various meanings. The attempt to find a common thread in our *application* of the term is not what I am chiefly interested in. What I am interested in, and what I cannot but think to be the more important question for philosophy, is whether there is not a sense of good in which it can be applied to things not as meaning that they are successful or useful members of a class, and not as meaning that they are instrumental to a good beyond themselves, but as meaning that they are good in themselves. And it is surely plain that when we state, for instance, that courage is good, this is what we mean—even if some one may maintain that we are mistaken in making this statement. I have tried to do some justice, briefly, to the other senses, in the preceding chapter, and from that point onwards I have been interested solely in this other and more fundamental sense of 'good.' And of this I feel pretty clear, that though our applications of it are always accompanied by an interest in what we thus call good, the existence of that interest is not what we assert when we so describe things.

Professor Perry turns next to consider in detail Professor Moore's argument for the indefinability of 'good.' He quotes the remark 'it would be absolutely meaningless to say that oranges were yellow, unless yellow did in the end mean just "yellow" and nothing else whatever—unless it were absolutely indefinable.' [24] And to this, taken alone, his objection is well founded. 'It is *not* meaningless,' he points out, 'to say that "the conception of substance is prehistoric," or that "the painting is postimpressionistic," or that "the argument is circular"; and yet in these cases the as-

---

[22] *Ib.*
[23] *Ib.*

[24] G. E. Moore, *Principia Ethica*, 14.

signed predicates are definable.' [25] The statement 'oranges are yellow' certainly is meaningless unless 'yellow' has in this statement a single self-identical meaning. In a sense 'yellow' must mean yellow and nothing else whatever. But this does not show it to be indefinable. For if we could correctly define 'yellow' as say, 'x which is y,' we should not be saying that 'yellow' means anything other than 'yellow,' for 'x which is y' would be just what yellow is. But it might be said in support of the view that 'good' is obviously indefinable, there is a great difference between 'good' and such attributes as 'pre-historic,' 'post-impressionistic,' 'circular.' If a term is definable, i.e. stands for a certain complex,[26] we can use the term intelligently and intelligibly only if we have the definition to some extent before our minds; and we have in fact at least rough definitions of such terms in our minds when we use them. On the other hand, the fact that we use the term 'good' intelligently and intelligibly without having any definition of it in our minds shows that it is indefinable.

Professor Moore uses an argument of somewhat the same type when he argues, against any attempt to define 'good,' that given any set of concepts not containing good, it is always possible to inquire whether a thing answering to this set of concepts is good.[27] Suppose some one claims that 'being-desired-by-anybody is being good,' this claim is met by the fact that even if we know that war is desired by some people, we may still doubt whether it is good.

Both of these arguments amount, I think, to saying that if 'good' stood for any

complex (as on any relational theory it does), we ought, if we use the word intelligently, to have in our minds the notion of a definite relation between definite things. It seems to me clear that we have no such notion in our minds when we use the word in ordinary discourse.

But I cannot be sure that this entirely settles the question. For there seem to be cases in which we seek for the definition of a term and finally accept one as correct. The fact that we accept some definition as correct shows that the term did somehow stand for a complex of elements; yet the fact that we are for some time in doubt whether the term is analysable, and if so, what the correct analysis is, shows that this complex of elements was not distinctly present to our mind before, or during, the search for a definition. It appears as if we cannot avoid recognizing that there is such a thing as using a term which implicitly refers to a certain complex, while yet the complex is not explicitly present to our minds. And in principle this might, it seems, be true of 'good.' The absence of an explicit reference to a complex in our ordinary use of the term should therefore not be taken as necessarily implying that the term is indefinable, nor, in particular, as excluding the possibility of its standing for a relation. The method should, I think, rather be that of attending to any proposed definition that seems at all plausible. If it is the correct definition, what should happen is that after a certain amount of attention to it we should be able to say, 'yes, that is what I meant by "good" all along, though I was not clearly conscious till now that it was what I meant.' If on the other hand the result is that we feel clear that 'that was not what I meant by good,' the proposed definition must be rejected. If, after we have examined all the definitions that possess any initial plausibility, we have found this negative result in every case, we may feel fairly confident that 'good' is indefinable. And there is no initial presumption that it is definable. For it seems clear that

---

[25] A General Theory of Value, 35.

[26] I should explain that I mean by a complex here a complex of elements co-ordinate in respect of universality, in distinction from another class of terms which might be called complex, and which are indefinable, viz. those that involve elements not co-ordinate in respect of universality, as 'red' involves both colour and redness. Cf. Cook Wilson, Statement and Inference, ii. 502–4.

[27] Principia Ethica, 15.

there could be no complex entities unless there were some simple ones; and, in a universe so various as the universe is, there is no reason to suppose that the simple entities are few in number.

In the process of criticizing proposed definitions of a term, there are two moments. Perhaps the most obvious ground for rejection of a definition is that we are able to point to things of which the term is predicable but the definition not, or *vice versa*. And any one will be able without difficulty to think of definitions of 'good' that have been proposed, which come to grief on one or other of these two objections. But even when the denotations of the term and of the definition coincide (or when we cannot be sure that they do not), we can often see that a proposed definition does not express what we *mean* by the term to be defined. It would be on this ground, for example, that we should reject a definition of 'equilateral triangle' as 'triangle with all its angles equal.' And it is on this ground that most of the proposed definitions of 'good' can be rejected—many of the metaphysical definitions, such as those which identify goodness with comprehensiveness or with reality; and many of the psychological definitions, such as those which identify it with being productive of pleasure or with being an object of desire. The point is not that the proposed definition is not seen at first sight to be true, or that it needs inquiry, but that it does not survive inquiry.

Professor Perry's own criticism of Professor Moore takes the following form. Suppose that 'good' be defined as 'desired by some one.' This definition is disproved, says Professor Moore, by the fact that even if war is desired by some one, it is still possible to inquire whether war is good. Professor Perry seems to admit this as fatal to the proposed definition, for he proposes to substitute for it what he evidently thinks of as a different definition, 'good in some sense=desired by some one.' And he endeavours to turn the edge of Professor

Moore's objection by saying that the correctness of *this* definition is quite compatible with our still being able to inquire (as we evidently can) whether war, if it is good in this sense, is also good in some other sense e.g. desired by all men, or obligatory, or beautiful. [28]

This seems to me strangely to miss the point. No one would, I suppose, dream of objecting to the equating of 'good in some sense' with 'desired by some one' on the ground that war though desired by some persons is not desired by every one, or not beautiful, or not obligatory. The objections are (1) that, even though desired by some persons, war is not in any sense good (though there may be elements in it that are good), and (2) that, even if it were in some sense good, what would be *meant* by calling it good is most certainly not that it is desired by some one.

Professor Perry further tries to base an argument for the relativity of good to the interests of individuals, on the fact 'that the question may be submitted once again to each individual judge.' 'If when a given object *a* is already acknowledged to be good the question of its goodness is nevertheless put to a subject *M*, the question is assumed to refer to the special sense of good which is relative to *M*.' [29] This would surely be a nonsensical procedure. If the goodness of *a* is already 'acknowledged,' i.e. admitted by both the persons involved, there is *no* sense in the one asking the other whether the object is good; and anything that the other may say such as 'I desire it' or 'I don't desire it' has *no* relevance to the question whether it is good, which has already *ex hypothesi* been settled in the affirmative.

The advocates of the view he is criticizing are, Professor Perry points out, anxious to secure for 'good' a meaning which shall 'provide judgments of value with a common object which will determine their truth or falsity.' And for this purpose, he insists, 'an interest is as good an object as any

[28] *A General Theory of Value*, 36–7.
[29] *Ib.* 37.

other. The fact that M takes an interest in a, consists in a relation of a to M; but this fact itself is not relative to M's judgment about it, or to the judgment of any other subject.' [30] There is, in fact, a great difference between a view which makes the goodness of an object depend on a subject's judgement that it is good, and one which makes it depend on his interest in it. The former view is one that will not stand a moment's examination; the latter is one that does provide judgements of value with some reality to judge about, and that therefore requires serious consideration. But while it provides for our judgements of value an object independent of our judgements, it fails to do justice to what is also implied in our judgements of value, that when one person says an object is good and another says it is not, they are contradicting one another. For if M only meant 'I take an interest in a' and N only meant 'I do not,' they would *not* be contradicting each other.

Professor Perry sometimes, for brevity, uses as equivalent to 'good' 'enjoyed by a subject,' and sometimes 'desired by a subject.' Neither of these phrases does full justice to his theory. His theory is that to be good is to be an object of *interest*, and interest is thought of as covering both desire and enjoyment; i.e. the goodness of some things consists in their being enjoyed, that of others in their being desired, and that of others, perhaps, in their being both enjoyed and desired (though this, as we shall see, is impossible). Now so long as we say (as he is apt to say) that 'the goodness of the primrose consists in its being desired,' [31] the theory seems at first sight attractive enough. But obviously it is only a rough and ready description of my desire to say I desire a primrose. What I desire is to be seeing it or smelling it or possessing it. As soon as we describe definitely what it is that we desire, we see that it is something which does not yet

exist. There are no doubt cases in which we desire to go on doing what we are doing, or being in the same sort of state that we are in. But even if I desire, for instance, to go on looking at a primrose, what I desire is not the looking which is taking place at present, but the looking which I wish to take place in the immediate future. The object of desire is always something non-existent. If it be said that it exists as a possibility, we must reply that that is an inexact way of saying that the possibility of it exists, which means that though it does not exist, the nature of some or all of the things that do exist is not incompatible with its coming into existence.

It is plain that in so far as goodness were either identical with or dependent upon being desired, nothing could both exist and be good. Now I suppose that we are all convinced both that some things that exist now are good and that things of certain kinds, which may come into existence in the future, will be good if and when they exist; and I suppose that apart from these convictions we should have little or no interest in the topic of 'good,' and ethics in particular would go by the board. Yet in so far as the theory identifies the good with the desired, it denies both these convictions. But it might be replied that the goodness of existent things consists in their being enjoyed, and the goodness of non-existent things in their being desired. I must take leave, however, to doubt whether we can say of a non-existent thing that it *is* good. However much one were convinced that conscientiousness, for example, is good, and that A might *become* conscientious, no one would say 'A's conscientiousness is good' if he were convinced that A is not in fact conscientious. But, our opponent might reply, we can say of *kinds* of thing that they are good even if we are not convinced that any instances of these kinds exist. We might say 'perfectly conscientious action is good,' even if (as Kant suggests) we are not convinced that there has ever been such an action. But that is only a short-hand way of saying that without

[30] *Ib.* 38.
[31] Cf. *A General Theory of Value*, 133.

being sure that such an action ever has existed, we can be sure that *if* any existed it would be good. Hypothetical goodness presupposes hypothetical existence just as actual goodness presupposes actual existence. And if so, being good can never be identical with being desired, or even compatible with it.

The relation in which the primrose stands to desire is not that of being desired but that of exciting desire. This is a relation in which existing things *can* stand to desire, and the theory might be transmuted into the form, 'the good is that which excites desire.' But the excitants of desire fall into two classes. There are things our experience of which is such as to make us desire to remain in our existing relation to them, or to get into some closer relation to them, and to others like them; and there are things our experience of which is such as to make us desire to get away from them. Things of the second class are just as decidedly excitants of some desires as things of the first class are of others. And obviously one main sub-class (if not the whole) of the second class consists of things that cause pain. Thus if 'good' meant 'excitant of desire' we should be led to the conclusion that things that cause pain are, as such, an important class of goods. This conclusion would evidently not be accepted, and therefore the theory would have to be modified into the form 'the good is that which excites the desire to maintain our relations with it, or to get into closer relations with it, and with others of its kind'—what we may, for short, call 'positive desire.'

Now, on the face of it, some of the things that excite positive desire[32] do so because they are judged to be good. *Prima facie* one would say that if the consciousness of a good disposition in oneself or the contemplation of it in another leads me to wish to maintain and develop that sort of disposition, it is not because I feel it to be

pleasant but because I judge it to be good. But this alternative is not open to Professor Perry, for, in basing our taking an interest in the thing on our thinking it good, it would involve the giving up of his main thesis, that a thing's being good either is or is based upon our taking an interest in it. All that is left for him therefore is to identify what is good with that which by virtue of the pleasure it causes excites desire for a closer relation with it and with other things like it. What is good, then, for him is that which excites pleasure and thereby excites such a desire. And though he includes both these elements in his formula, the fact of exciting pleasure is evidently the root fact of which the other is a mere consequence.

Not only, however, is pleasantness the fundamental and tendency to excite desire only a consequential element in goodness, according to the theory in the form in which it seems necessary to restate it, but it is far more plausible to put forward pleasantness, than to put forward this tendency, as the essence of goodness. If we say 'that which produces so-and-so is, as doing so, good,' we are evidently implying that what is produced is intrinsically good, and what produces it instrumentally good. And it is plausible enough to say 'pleasure is intrinsically good, and what produces it instrumentally good'; there is a pretty general agreement that pleasure, whether it is the good or not, is at least good. But there is no general agreement that desire, or even positive desire, is good. If we take the moral standpoint we must say that some desires are good and others bad, and that when desires are good they are good not because they are desires but because they are the sort of desires they are. And if we take the hedonistic standpoint, we must say that desires are good or bad (which will mean 'pleasant or unpleasant') not in virtue of being desires but mainly (I suppose) in virtue of their being supposed to be likely or unlikely to be fulfilled. Desire (even positive desire) thus not being a thing necessarily good in itself, there is no reason why, in general, things that excite

[32] Desire, of course, not for them to exist but for us to be in some new relation to them or to continue to be in the same relation to them.

desire (or positive desire) should be good. So long as we thought of things as objects of desire, it was perhaps not unplausible to say that objects of desire are good even when the desire is not; but if we recast the theory in the form in which we have found it necessary to recast it, and say the good is that which excites positive desire, i.e. which is to it as cause to effect, there is no reason (obvious or alleged) why, positive desires not being always good, their excitants should nevertheless always be so.

The most favourable way, then, of presenting the theory we are examining is to exclude from it the reference to desire and to reduce it to the form 'what is good is that which produces pleasure.'[33] But no one would in fact say that everything which produces pleasure is good unless he thought pleasure itself good;[34] and the theory emerges in the final form 'pleasure, and pleasure alone, is good by its own nature; and what produces pleasure, and only what produces pleasure, is good because it produces something good.' The heart of the theory, then, in spite of all it has said by way of attack on ordinary notions of intrinsic good, is that there is one thing, and one thing only, that is intrinsically good, viz. pleasure. The theory when reduced to its simple terms seems to be our old friend, hedonism. After all the able refutations of hedonism that have been published in recent years, it seems to me unnecessary to tread once more on this rather hackneyed ground, and I suppose that Professor Perry would agree that hedonism is untenable, and claim that his own theory is tenable

only in virtue of elements that distinguish it from hedonism. But these elements are, if I am not mistaken, among the least tenable elements in his theory.

There is, however, one more point of view from which the theory may be examined. Professor Perry describes 'the most popular' objection to it as being that 'the fact of desire is not accepted as final in most judgments of value. Objects of desire are held to be bad in spite of their being desired, and desires themselves are held to be bad whether or no they are satisfied.'[35] I need not consider (a) one form of this objection with which I have no sympathy—the view of Schopenhauer and others that all desire is bad; that is an extravagance of quietism for which there is little to be said. (b) The first real difficulty to which the theory is exposed is that named next by Professor Perry, viz. the fact that 'the same object may be liked or desired by one man, and disliked or avoided by another.'[36] This fact, taken with the identification of 'good' with 'object of interest,' leads to the conclusion that the same thing may be both good and bad. On the face of it, this result is paradoxical, and all but self-contradictory; but he claims that 'a relational definition, such as that here proposed, is the only means of avoiding contradiction.'[37] The claim is an odd one: by identifying good with object of interest we get into the paradox of calling the same thing good and bad (a paradox which an absolute theory at least escapes, whatever be its other merits or demerits); and then we triumphantly get out of the difficulty by saying, 'Oh, but good only means good for one person, and bad only means bad for another person, so that there is no paradox.'

Is it not clear that when we assert the goodness of anything we do assert something which we believe to be incompatible with the same thing's being bad? We may describe a thing as 'both good and bad,'

[33] This is ambiguous, since it may mean '"good" means "productive of pleasure,"' or 'what is good is good because it produces pleasure'; i.e. the ambiguity involved in the theory from the start (cf. pp. 80–1) still remains.

[34] And inferred from this that what produces it is good. But it is surely plain that it does not follow from a thing's being good that what produces it is good, in the same sense of 'good.' It must be admitted that we often call 'good' things that are merely useful, but then 'good' is being used improperly. Where I use the phrase 'instrumentally good,' I use it to indicate this common but loose sense of 'good.'

[35] A General Theory of Value, 134.
[36] Ib. 135.
[37] Ib. 136.

but such language is not strict. (i) We may mean that the thing contains some elements that are good and some that are bad, but then *that* is the right way of putting the matter, and 'the thing is both good and bad' is only a loose way of putting it. It is implied in our thought on the subject both that if we push our analysis far enough we shall find some elements that are simply good and others that are simply bad, *and* that the whole is not both good and bad but is either on the whole good or on the whole bad. (ii) It may be suggested that, without thinking of a thing as consisting of good and bad elements, we may judge it to be good from one point of view and bad from another—that a state of mind, say, may be morally good and intellectually bad. But this turns out to be reducible to the former case, in which analysis reveals a good and a bad element. If we take a temporal section of the history of a mind, however short be the section there will be elements in it of knowledge and opinion which have a certain value, and actions or dispositions to act which have a certain value (positive or negative). The whole state of mind, then, cannot be judged from the moral point of view, nor from the intellectual, but some elements in it from the one and some from the other. And each such element will have a goodness that is incompatible with its being bad, or a badness that is incompatible with its being good; and the whole state of mind will have a degree of goodness or *else* a degree of badness, which can be assessed only from a point of view in which we transcend both the moral and the intellectual point of view.

(c) 'The case which has most deeply affected popular habits of thought, and which is mainly responsible for the prejudice against the present theory of value,' says Professor Perry, 'is the case in which an interest or its object is morally condemned.'[38] It is certainly an obvious objection to the theory that all objects of interest are good, that in point of fact we

do judge to be bad many things in which nevertheless some one or other takes or has taken an interest. Professor Perry's answer to this objection is to urge that in such a case we are performing a *moral* judgement, and that 'moral judgments are not concerned with value in the generic sense, but with a specific and complex *aspect* of it. . . . They do not deal with interests *per se*, but with the relation of interests to the complex purposes in which they are incorporated.'[39]

In answer to this it is important to point out that the term 'moral judgement' contains a serious ambiguity. There are three types of judgement which have by various writers been termed moral judgements. These are (i) the judgements in which an act is pronounced to be right or wrong; (ii) the judgements in which an action or disposition is judged to be morally good, or bad, or indifferent, i.e. to have (or fail to have) the kind of goodness or badness that only dispositions and actions can have; (iii) the judgements in which something is said to be good or bad or indifferent *sans phrase*. The first two may be said to be departmental judgements, in the sense that each of them is applicable only to one class of objects, the first to acts considered apart from their motives, the second to dispositions and actions considered in respect of their motives. Judgements of the third class are not in any way departmental; they may be made about anything in the whole world. It can be said of some things—I suggest, as at any rate an adumbration of the things of which it can be said, virtue, knowledge and well-grounded opinion, and pleasure[40]—that they are good; of others—vice, badly grounded opinion, and pain—that they are bad; and of other things that they are indifferent, i.e. considered in themselves, though many of them may be instrumental to good or to evil. In making such judge-

---

[38] *Ib.* 136.

[39] *Ib.* 136–37.

[40] To avoid making any statement too complicated, I omit a further kind of good which will be mentioned later, cf. p. 138.

ments we are not adopting a *narrowly* ethical standpoint; we are saying for instance that wisdom and pleasure are good, though they are not morally good. We are taking the most commanding point of view that can be taken with regard to the value of the things in the universe. Yet this is a point of view which a moral philosopher should, in part of his inquiry, adopt, since ethics is the study of that which we ought to do, and of what is involved in its being what we ought to do, and since what we ought to do depends to a large extent (though, as I have urged, not entirely) on the goodness or the badness of the things we can in our acts bring into being.

It would, however, be a mistake to spend time in arguing the question whether the theory of good in general belongs to ethics or to metaphysics. The other two types of judgement belong exclusively to ethics. Goodness in general runs out beyond the strict scope of ethics, if ethics be the philosophical study of good conduct; for some of the things that are good are neither conduct nor dispositions to conduct. But the study of the meaning of good in general, and of the types of thing that are good, is either a part of ethics, or a part of metaphysics to which the study of purely ethical problems inevitably leads us: which it is, depends on how we define ethics and metaphysics. Neither ethics nor metaphysics is a study to which definite limits have hitherto been set, or one, probably, to which they can profitably be set. The only way, perhaps, in which we could prescribe a quite rigid programme for metaphysics would be by saying that it is the study of the characteristics possessed in common by everything that is; and from this point of view the theory of goodness would have to be pronounced not to be part of metaphysics. But whether we widen our notion of metaphysics to make it include the theory of all very widely distributed characteristics (among which goodness and badness are included), or treat the study of value as a part of ethics, or recognize an intermediate science of axiology

(or theory of value) less wide than metaphysics and wider than ethics, is a question the discussion of which does not lead us any distance at all towards understanding the facts.

We must return, however, to the objection Professor Perry is at the moment considering, and to his answer to it. The objection is that many of the things in which people find pleasure and which they desire are nevertheless bad. His answer is that they are not bad in general but only bad from the ethical standpoint. And our answer to that is that while there is what may be called a narrowly ethical standpoint from which we judge such and such an action to be vicious or morally bad, there is also a more commanding standpoint from which we view the agent's total state of mind at the time and judge that in spite of any elements of pleasure-value it may contain it is on the whole a bad thing, a thing for whose occurrence the world is the worse. This is not the narrowly ethical standpoint, for it is the same standpoint from which we judge that the occurrence of a pain is, considered apart from its accompaniments, a bad thing, though a pain is not morally bad. Now if from this, which is the most commanding standpoint, we say that many states of mind in which their owners have taken interest and found pleasure are nevertheless bad, 'good' cannot be identical with 'object of interest.'

My general conclusion is that Professor Perry's arguments have not succeeded either in refuting the view that goodness is an intrinsic quality of certain things, or in defending from attack the view that it is identical with being an object of interest to some mind.[41]

[41] I may refer here to the weighty final chapter of Meinong's last treatment of the problem of value, in his *Zur Grundlegung der allgemeinen Werttheorie*. It is remarkable that though he approaches the problem from the side of the subjective act of valuation, and of the analysis of this, he concludes that there are 'unpersonal goods,' in the sense that there are goods which are not essentially for a subject at all, though they are in a subject (cf. p. 147 of his work). This is exactly the position I wish to establish.

Moral and Non-Moral Values: A Study in the First Principles of Axiology

C. A. CAMPBELL

1

It would, I suppose, be pretty generally agreed that the fundamental cleavage within value-philosophy at the present day is between those who hold that **goodness** (or value) is a simple unanalysable—and hence indefinable—*quality* which certain things possess, and those who hold that it consists in a *relation* of some kind between the things of which value is predicated and some mind or minds. As labels will be convenient for views of which we shall have much to say in the sequel, let us call these two schools of thought the 'Objectivist' and the 'Subjectivist' respectively.

Of these schools, the Objectivist is, of course, by far the more recent—dating virtually from the publication of *Principia Ethica* some thirty years ago. And I do not think it unfair to suggest that its considerable authority has been due much less to its own positive merits than to certain apparently irremediable defects in the Subjectivist theories which seem to offer the only plausible alternatives. Its authority can hardly be accounted for by the logical arguments which appeared to Dr. Moore in 1903 to prove irresistibly that goodness could only be a simple quality: for these arguments have not, as a rule, been found

satisfactory even by those who are most sympathetic with the general trend of the theory, and they are not now, one learns,[1] acceptable to Dr. Moore himself. Nor is the doctrine qualified to attract adherents by any power of affording an intelligent comprehension of the vast and varied panorama of value-judgments disclosed to us by the student of comparative cultures: for this is just what any view of value which denies the relevance of subjective interests is singularly incompetent to do. Indeed, the advantage of Subjectivism with respect to this important requirement of a sound value-theory is at once so great and so evident that only the presence of very grave counter-balancing disabilities seems able to explain the preference accorded in so many quarters to the claims of the Objectivist type of theory.

It must be admitted, however, that very grave difficulties do beset the path of the Subjectivist. Two, I think, are outstanding, and are constantly being adduced by critics as manifestly fatal to the pretensions of Subjectivism. Let me state them very briefly.

(1) If what we mean when we predicate goodness of X is that X is liked (or desired, approved, etc.) by some mind or minds, then goodness must be something of

Reprinted from *Mind*, 44, 1935, by permission of the author and *Mind*.

[1] *Proceedings of the Aristotelian Society*, Supplementary Vol. XI., p. 127.

a highly contingent character. It must, apparently, be something that comes into being and passes away not only (as is natural enough) through changes in the nature of X, but also on account merely of changes in certain conscious states. And it is very difficult to believe that this is what we do, in fact, mean, at least in our more considered and unqualified value-judgments. When we assert that knowledge is good, or that beauty is good, surely we do not mean that knowledge and beauty own this character only if and when certain conscious states are directed towards them? Is it not evident that we regard the goodness of each of these 'goods' as possessed of the same kind of permanence as the nature of the thing itself, and not as something which fluctuates with the fluctuation of any person's or group of persons', feelings towards the thing?

(2) Among conventionally accepted good things there is one whose goodness we feel it quite peculiarly repugnant to identify with any relation to subjective interests. I refer to moral virtue. In the case of other good things—such as knowledge—we at least do not feel that there is anything inherently absurd in enquiring whether the goodness we attribute to the thing may not be derivable from its being an object of interest to some subject or subjects (or from its being a means to the attainment of some such object of interest). However difficult it may be to devise a formula which avoids the difficulty alluded to under (1), we at least recognise nothing crassly incongruous in undertaking the attempt. But the case of moral virtue appears to fall into quite a different category. When a man in defiance of strong temptations rises to what he recognises to be his duty, it seems merely inept to suggest that his dutiful act derives the value which we all regard it as possessing from any subjective feelings that are entertained towards it by any one. We seem to see quite clearly that we need pay no attention to the presence or absence of any subjective feelings

whatsoever in order to know that the act has value. Whether or not the act may have some *further* value in virtue of a relation to subjective feelings, we may here be content to leave as an open question. But it can only be by confusion that we fail to distinguish the 'supplementary' value which the act may possess on *this* account from the value which it possesses simply and solely in virtue of its being the kind of act that it is, i.e., an act of duty.

Now I do not believe, for reasons which I shall later explain, that the former of these difficulties is really insuperable. But I confess that the latter difficulty does seem to me fatal to any purely Subjectivist theory of value. It is, I think, quite hopeless to seek to identify the value we attribute to moral virtue with any relation to anything that can legitimately be called a subjective interest. Indeed, the simple appeal to reflect upon our own value-responses to moral virtue seems to me to be by far the most effective weapon in the whole armoury of the critics of Subjectivism, and it has probably been responsible for making more converts to the general Objectivist stand-point than all other arguments put together. It is very noticeable—and, as I shall attempt to show, highly significant—how frequently it recurs at critical junctures in the pages of Dr. W. D. Ross's recent important work. [2] I cite here only a single typical passage, from the chapter on 'the Nature of Goodness.' 'We may claim,' writes Dr. Ross, 'that we are directly aware that conscientious action, for example, has a value of its own, not identical with or even dependent upon our or any one else's taking an interest in it. Our reason informs us of this as surely as it informs us of anything, and to distrust reason here is in principle to distrust its power of ever knowing reality.' [3] It is a claim, I think, whose cogency will strike home to almost every reader. But note how immeasurably it would be weakened in its effect if, instead

[2] *The Right and the Good.*
[3] *Ibid. p.* 82.

of the *moral* value of 'conscientiousness,' we were to insert some non-moral value—even one of the so-called 'intrinsic' values like 'knowledge.' It is possible that, if we were to substitute 'knowledge,' we should still feel an *inclination* to assert that this good 'has a value of its own, not identical with or even dependent upon our or any one else's taking an interest in it.' But I doubt if there is one of us who would go so far as to contend that 'our reason informs us of this as surely as it informs us of anything, and to distrust reason here is in principle to distrust its power of ever knowing reality.' The strength of the case against Subjectivism depends, I think, far more than is generally recognised upon the special instance of the value we apprehend in moral virtue.

Still, a single argument, if it be sound, is enough to establish any position: and I am willing to admit, on the strength of the argument we have been considering, **that** an adequate theory of value is not possible on purely Subjectivist lines. But before we acquiesce in a thorough-going **and general** rejection of Subjectivism, there is one alternative which, as it seems to me, we ought to explore with a great deal of care. Is it absolutely necessary, I want to ask, that we should extend to the meaning of value or goodness generally those characteristics which we find ourselves forced to apply to it in the case of moral virtue? Is it quite certain that we mean the same thing by 'good' when we judge that moral virtue is good as we do when we judge that knowledge is good—or indeed as we do in any other of those instances (the crucial ones, of course, for the determination of the ultimate nature of value) in which we predicate goodness in an apparently 'absolute' sense? If this is *not* so, then it may remain possible to give a Subjectivist account of value in respect of non-moral values, even while we recognise that such an account is definitely false in respect of moral values: a consummation which would deliver us from the embarrassment, which presses so

sorely upon the Objectivist school, of holding a theory of value which leaves in outer darkness by far the larger proportion of the value-judgments of mankind.

I hope that the reader will not dismiss this alternative too hastily as savouring of mere convenient eclecticism. It has, I believe, a much more solid base. Indeed it is, in my opinion (which I shall endeavour to substantiate in this paper), the one view capable of introducing coherence into the general theory of value. I believe that the chief source of the confusion which envelops current value philosophy lies precisely in the failure to recognise that there is an absolutely vital distinction of kind between our value-reaction to the value of moral virtue and our value-reaction to any other value whatsoever.

To explain my thesis in more formal terms, what I am going to argue is that a subjectivist definition of value is valid, *save only* in the single case of the value which inheres in moral virtue. How exactly we are to understand the meaning of value in the latter connection, and what is the nature of the identity or analogy between it and value in the former connection which leads us to employ the same term 'value,' or 'goodness,' in respect of both, are questions which must engage our attention at some later stage. But our chief preoccupation will be with the meaning of value in the former connection; and our chief problem in the effort to vindicate a subjectivist interpretation of 'non-moral' values will be to devise a formula in terms of subjective feelings which will escape, along with other difficulties, the major difficulty alluded to at the outset of this paper.

2

It is perhaps desirable, before we settle to the task of constructing a subjectivist formula for non-moral values, to say something more of a general character in support of the uniqueness of the value which we attribute to moral virtue. Let us begin by trying to give to the difference in kind which we allege, at least the status of an initial probability: for the reader who is already persuaded that this alleged difference at least *may* have a foundation in fact, is likely to explore with considerably greater sympathy the hypothesis that a subjectivist interpretation is valid for non-moral values.

One piece of evidence in support of the validity of the distinction has already been referred to, and I shall develop it only briefly. I quoted [4] a passage from Dr. Ross which purported to show that the value which we accord to conscientious action cannot be given a subjectivist interpretation, and I invited the reader to observe the effect upon the argument of substituting for conscientious action some non-moral value. If we carefully examine our value-reactions in the two cases, it seems to me that the difference between them is very marked, and highly important. We feel, so Dr. Ross contends, completely certain that conscientious action has value irrespective of any subjective interest in it—a value to which subjective liking and disliking are merely irrelevant. I think that very few persons, if any, would maintain that a value like beauty (or, as I should prefer to express it, aesthetic experience) evokes a corresponding assurance. The habit of mind, engendered by a long tradition, which tempts us to take it as established verity that Truth, Beauty and Goodness are a sort of holy trinity of 'intrinsic' values may, and only too probably will, predispose us to believe in objectivity in this value-realm also. But we surely cannot pretend that we here enjoy anything even approximating to *certitude*. We should not stake the very validity of our reason upon the objectivity of this value. The difference in our attitudes is very easy to understand

if the distinction I am contending for is *bene fundatum*. It is not easy to explain on any other hypothesis.

Further evidence may be derived from considering a problem which has evidently very much exercised the author of *The Right and the Good*—the problem of the commensurability of values. If we suppose that the goodness, possessed by moral virtue on the one hand, and by non-moral good on the other hand, is goodness in the same sense of goodness, then presumably it should be possible, since goodness admits of a more and less, to measure the goodness of virtue against the goodness of the other goods in at least a rough and ready, approximate fashion. Yet in actual truth it seems impossible to dissent from Dr. Ross's own considered judgment that the goodness of virtue is really incommensurable with the goodness of any of the other 'intrinsic goods.' Critical examination of our own value-responses strongly suggests that we decline to accept any amount, however large, of a good like knowledge as exceeding in value the very smallest amount of moral virtue. 'When I ask myself,' says Dr. Ross, 'whether any increase in knowledge, however great, is worth having at the cost of a wilful failure to do my duty or of a deterioration of character, I can only answer in the negative.' [5] And this is surely a correct answer. For my own part, I should say that the very question has about it an unreal, artificial flavour. It is the kind of question which no one could seriously put to himself save in a mood of half-conscious sophistry, or else—as here—under the influence of a philosophical motive which demands the explicit examination of even the most remotely possible alternatives. I am not myself aware of any philosopher, with the possible exception of Dr. Moore—who in theory assigns to moral virtue a very modest degree of value—likely to return an affirmative

---

[4] p. 275.

[5] *The Right and the Good*, p. 152.

answer to the question, and it seems fair to take the negative answer as possessing a pretty high measure of certainty.

Now if the goodness of virtue is really felt to be incommensurable with the goodness of other good things, can we still hold that we are meaning by 'goodness' the same thing in both cases? Dr. Ross tries to evade the difficulty, which his own candour has so clearly exposed, by suggesting that 'virtue belongs to a higher order of value, beginning at a point higher on the scale of value than that which (the others) ever reach.'[6] But I feel very doubtful whether this supposed relationship will bear examination. If it is really the *same scale* to which they belong—and this condition seems to be necessary if they are to be defended as 'good' in the same sense—two difficulties emerge. In the first place, since it does not seem possible to set any assignable limit to the amount imaginable of goods like knowledge and pleasure, must we not say that at *some* point the goodness possessed by these goods equals the goodness possessed by the minimal amount of virtue? And, in the second place, ought we not to feel that with increasing amounts of knowledge and pleasure we are continuously *getting nearer to* the degree of goodness which the minimal amount of virtue possesses? I think that if the values do indeed belong, as Dr. Ross says they do, to the *same scale of value*, an affirmative answer to both of these questions is logically entailed. Yet it seems to me in the last degree doubtful whether an affirmative answer can be supported by the actual responses of our value-consciousness, and I imagine that Dr. Ross's own recognition of the peculiar claims of moral value must make him extremely reluctant to accept that answer himself.

Now the difficulties, it should be noticed, which beset the attempt to measure the value of virtue against the value of other goods, are precisely what one would expect if the thesis that I am to defend in this paper is a sound one. If virtue is a value not just of a *higher order* but in a *different category*, if it is, in fact, the one thing which has a value independent of all relation to subjective interests, then little wonder that we are aware of an inherent impropriety in seeking to apply a common yard-stick to it and other goods.

3

It is rather more than time, however, that we passed on to our main task. Our real problem still awaits us, *viz.*, to justify the contention that all value-judgments other than those referring to moral virtue involve an essential reference to human liking.[7] Let me say a word or two, first of all, about the method I propose to adopt.

Naturally, I shall not attempt to deal explicitly with every variety of value-judgment. Our main concern must be with those judgments which are especially appealed to by the Objectivists as furnishing indubitable instances of the apprehension of a value which is not reducible to subjectivist terms. There is, indeed, no list common to all the Objectivists; but the claims of knowledge and aesthetic experience (Truth and Beauty, in popular parlance) have received such wide-spread acknowledgment that it is certain that no Subjectivist theory has any hope of acceptance which cannot make clear the disguised relationship to human liking which obtains in their case. If we can find a formula in terms of human liking which can be regarded as representing fairly what is really

---

[6] *The Right and the Good*, p. 150. In the context the statement relates only to the non-moral value of 'pleasure,' but the sequel makes it clear that Dr. Ross intends his view to apply to other non-moral values also.

[7] I shall explain shortly why, in my judgment, 'liking' is to be preferred in this connection to 'interest' or 'desire,' or any other term that Subjectivist axiologists have proposed.

meant by goodness or value in the value-judgments directed upon these crucial instances, it will probably be agreed that we have surmounted by far the greatest obstacle to the vindication of our general thesis.

Now the formula which I shall venture to put forward is, as might be expected from the nature of the case, of a somewhat intricate character. The one thing abundantly certain is that no simple formula—such as 'liked by the person judging,' or 'liked by the majority of the community'—has the faintest chance of withstanding criticism. But, because of its complexity, our formula, if stated baldly at this juncture, would convey very little meaning indeed. I propose, therefore, to lead up to it gradually by undertaking a systematic examination of the nature and growth of our value-consciousness in so far forth as the value-consciousness *is* rooted in human liking.

For the sake of clearness, let me outline very briefly in advance the main stages through which we shall pass on the way to our goal.

I shall start from what appears to me to be the most rudimentary expression of 'subjective value-consciousness'—if I may so entitle the value-consciousness that is rooted in human liking—*viz.*, that which is ingredient in simple private liking and which manifests itself in the concept 'good-for-self.' I shall then endeavour to show how, by an entirely natural development, incited by the growing recognition of certain distinctions which force themselves upon an intelligent subject of experience, that value-consciousness comes eventually to identify with 'good for self' only objects of its liking *which are qualified in a highly specific way.* I next turn to consider the reaction of our value-consciousness to the recognition (in practice, of course, present from the start) that other persons also have likes and dislikes, and that there are also likes and dislikes which may be said to be inherent in our common human nature as such. This leads us to see that our value-consciousness (still operating on the basis solely of human likes and dislikes) will naturally take a vital interest not only in the concept 'good for self,' but also in the concept 'good for man,' and that what it means by 'good for man' is an object of liking to human nature qualified in a specific way parallel to that which we found to be involved in the developed concept 'good for self.' We then observe that the formula to which we have been led in considering the true meaning of 'good for man' is one which, if applied to the matter of experience, must issue in a list of goods which bears a remarkable resemblance to that which is currently supposed to represent goods that are intrinsic and objective, goods without any relational qualification. This discovery suggests the possibility that the concept which controls our recognition of the so-called intrinsic goods is really the concept 'good for man.' An explanation will, of course, require to be given of how it is that the relational qualification—good *for man*—if it controls our thoughts, does not appear in our speech. If we really mean 'good for man,' why do we say just 'good'? This difficulty, however, proves to be superficial. Further difficulties are also considered and rejected, and the final conclusion come to that our real meaning when we seem to be asserting intrinsic goodness of such goods as knowledge, aesthetic emotion, etc., is that they are specifically qualified objects of liking to human nature.

4

We start, then, from the experience of simple private liking. That which we like, we 'put a value upon,' as the common phrase has it. It is, to be sure, only a value-*for-self*, not a value *in itself*. For the value which we attach to the thing merely in so far forth as it is an object of our liking is certainly not regarded by us as a value 'in the nature of things,' nor even as a value for anyone besides the person liking. But it certainly *is* regarded as a *value*. It is possible to dispute the relevance of the term 'value' here, only if we quite arbitrarily, and indeed perversely, decide that the term 'value' is to be used as the equivalent of the term 'objective value.' There seems no excuse whatever for such a usage, which can hardly be so much as intelligibly formulated to oneself without drawing a distinction in thought between objective and subjective value; a distinction which, if admitted, at once makes nonsense of the proposed identification of 'value' with 'objective value.'

I take it, then, to be indisputable that there is a fundamental manifestation of value-consciousness which is the consciousness of 'value-for-self.' But before we go any further, a word must be said about the choice of 'liking' as the basis of that consciousness. That the interruption may be as brief as possible, I shall do little more than tabulate the chief grounds (as I see them) for preferring 'liking' to certain other terms that have from time to time been suggested in a subjectivist interest.

If we compare 'liking' first of all with 'desire,' the advantage of the former term is two-fold.

(1) We often ascribe value to an object (or state, activity, etc.) understood to be already in existence, and which we therefore—since desire is always for something conceived as not yet existing—cannot be said to desire. Perhaps it will be said that desire *is* present in such cases, in that we desire the continuance in existence of the object. But clearly that desire is posterior to the consciousness of the value of the object. It is because we value the object, 'like' its existence, that we desire the continuance of its existence. 'Liking' is to be preferred, then, in that, unlike 'desire,' it applies indifferently to the existent and the non-existent, just as valuing does.

(2) Desire, as ordinarily understood, is always an *actual* state of mind, whereas

there are certainly value-*dispositions*. It is awkward, if not impossible, to say that a person desires an object if he does not have a present conscious attitude towards it. Yet he may certainly be said to value an object under these conditions. We may legitimately say that X values exercise, even if we know that while we say it X is in bed asleep. In this respect too, then, 'liking' shows its superiority to 'desire.' For 'likes and dislikes' signify conative dispositions quite as much as they do present mental states.

The claims of 'pleasure' to be the basis of value-consciousness have some *prima facie* strength. But a fatal objection is that we can certainly feel pleasure without being conscious of an object which we are pleased with, or at, whereas value-consciousness is essentially transitive, implying an object which is evaluated. Our chosen term, liking, obviously possesses the same transitive implication. It might be suggested, perhaps, that 'being pleased with' is the basic state. But 'being pleased with' seems to be just a longer way of saying 'liking.'

Mr. Perry's term 'interest'—to take note of one further possibility—does not lie open to any of the above objections. It is transitive, it can refer to dispositions, and it is applicable both to the existent and the non-existent. On the other hand, the use to which this term has been put in the science of Psychology has left it with associations misleading in the present connection, and it has not the natural power, which the term 'liking' possesses, to suggest that favouring attitude of the subject mind which is absolutely fundamental. Moreover, it is a disadvantage that the term 'interest' is applied indifferently to the psychical state and to the object of the psychical state. And, finally, it would be inconvenient to be precluded from using the term 'interest' when we wished to signify that cognitive attentiveness which the term is commonly used to signify.

'Liking,' then, seems on the whole to

be the best term to express the basic element in the consciousness of value-for-self. We must now take up our task of tracing the manner in which the concept of value-for-self acquires for the reflective consciousness a much more specific meaning than mere 'objective of self's liking,' owing to the recognition of certain distinctions within objects of liking. I shall set out these distinctions in logical rather than historical order, beginning with the most simple and working towards the more complex.

The first distinction is the very elementary one between objects liked *more* and objects liked *less*. This distinction need not detain us. It introduces, in its crudest form, the distinction between major and minor values-for-self, corresponding to objects of major and minor liking respectively. It ought not, in strictness, to have any effect in modifying the meaning of the concept 'value-for-self'; although I shall have to point out later that it is not altogether certain that it does not in fact have some slight modifying influence.

The next distinction has greater importance. There are some objects that we like for themselves, others that we like only because they help in the attainment of objects liked for themselves. Recognition of this distinction leads us to make a distinction between *end* values-for-self and *instrumental* values-for-self, corresponding to objects of independent and dependent liking respectively. And with the emergence of this distinction the meaning of 'value-for-self' does begin to undergo definite modification. Since it is from end values that instrumental values derive all the value that they possess for us, it will be natural to recognise that it is only end values that have a direct claim to the title 'value.' In so far as this distinction is active in the mind, therefore, there will be a tendency to identify value-for-self not with object of *any* liking of the self, but with object of an *independent* liking of the self.

Our next distinction, one which has very important consequences, arises within the field of end values. It rests upon recognition of the fact that some end values have *also* instrumental value, being conducive to the attainment of certain other things liked for themselves, while other end values have from the same point of view a definite *dis*value. Thus ends like health and knowledge may be liked for themselves, but liked *further* because seen to contribute usefully to the attainment of many other liked things, whereas a good many things liked for themselves, e.g., idleness and gluttony, have quite obviously an opposite tendency. We may perhaps express the situation that arises by saying that end values fall roughly into two classes, according as their main tendency is to co-operate with or to obstruct the end values of the self as a whole.

Now the 'co-operative' end values, if we may so christen them, will certainly be accorded a much higher status as values-for-self than the 'obstructive' end values. But the precise nature of this 'higher status' is something which we must determine with a good deal of care, for in truth we meet here with a very important development in the meaning of the concept 'value-for-self.' There is no question, indeed, of any modification in principle of the original equation 'value-for-self' = 'liked by self.' But a complexity now reveals itself within the meaning of 'liked by *self*' which reacts profoundly upon the meaning of 'value-for-self.' For it now appears that 'liked by self' may mean either, on the one hand, to be an object of liking to the self as a whole, to the self as the unitary centre of its several likings—as in varying degrees is the case with what we have called the 'co-operative' end values—or it may mean, on the other hand, to be an object of liking to the self only in some very partial aspect of its being, and so inimical to the self's other likings as to be more properly called an object of *disliking* to the self as a whole—as in the case of the 'obstructive' end values. Now it can hardly be denied, I think, that it is in the former of these two conceptions of itself, i.e., in its being as the unitary centre of manifold likings, that the self recognises its essential selfhood to consist. Accordingly, it will be only those objects of liking which are harmonious, if not positively at least negatively, with the self's likings as a whole, objects which belong to the class of co-operative end values, or, at the least, of neutral end values, which will now be accepted by the self as genuinely representing what is 'liked by *self*; and it is they alone which will now be recognised as 'values-for-self.' It is evident that when this distinction has become operative in the mind many things previously regarded as values-for-self will present themselves quite definitely in the light of *dis*values: because, though in one sense still 'liked by self,' in a more profound sense of 'self' they are in antagonism to what is 'liked by self.'

The distinction which is now engaging us concerns our ultimate purpose so closely that I may be excused if, in spite of the limited space at my disposal, I dwell for a little upon its general principle. The general principle is, I think, neither obscure nor seriously debatable. The essence of the matter is just this, that as self-consciousness develops, and the self becomes conscious of itself as the unitary centre of manifold likings, the meaning of 'object of liking to self,' and consequently of 'value to self,' becomes deepened, and in a manner transformed. Whatever is now regarded as good or valuable for the self has got to be something that respects the systematic manifoldness that belongs to the nature of a self. 'Good-for-self' will now mean object not merely of an independent liking, but of an independent and *integral* liking of the self—an 'integral' liking being definable as one which is substantially consistent with the likings of the self as a whole.

We must note now, but more briefly, a further modification of the meaning of value-for-self which arises at the same level of reflective self-consciousness as that which we have just considered. At this same level, the self will become explicitly conscious of its perduring identity, conscious of itself as a relatively *abiding* subject. For a self which so understands its self-hood, an object of liking will tend to be regarded as fully deserving the title of object of the *self's* liking only in so far as the liking in question is of a relatively permanent and not a merely ephemeral character. It would appear, therefore, that the epithet 'relatively permanent' ought to be added to the epithets 'integral' and 'independent' in order to denote accurately the kind of object of liking which is on this developed plane of experience identified with 'value-for-self.'

There is just one other distinction which must, I think, add its quota of meaning to the concept 'value-for-self.' The immediately preceding determinations rested upon the self's consciousness of a distinction between a relatively real and a relatively unreal expression of self-hood. But self-consciousness leads to the recognition of a further distinction within self-hood, the distinction of the self as it is from the self as it is capable of becoming. We become aware of the self containing within itself possibilities of desirable development in a multitude of directions. Now when we consider the significance of this manifestation of our self-consciousness in its relation to the self's likings, we can see that the self will recognise (1) that there are many things which it does not now like, but which it is in principle possible for it to *come* to like; and (2) that among these things there are some which there is good reason to suppose that it is *worth while* coming to like, since we can even now see their nature to be such that the liking of them is in a high degree integral, and relatively permanent, as well as independent. Thus a person might very well have no present liking for scientific pursuits, or for music, but at the same time, because fully realising their fulfilment of the conditions required for a high degree of value-for-self to any self which does like them, he might *want* to like them. What will be the attitude of the value-consciousness towards such objects of prospective but unawakened liking, objects which it does not now like but would only, as it were, *like* to like? On the whole, it seems probable that their relation to the likings of the ideally developed self will bring them recognition as values-for-self in some sense. Just how much the concept of value-for-self must be modified thereby it is not easy to determine, and it is fortunate that, as will become apparent later, this particular modification has not the importance of its predecessors for the fulfilment of our ultimate purpose.

Now we have so far been studying only that branch of our value-consciousness which is connected with the self's consciousness of its *own* likes and dislikes. But man's life is lived in a social medium, and it is very certain that every self is aware that the other selves with whom it is in contact have their likes and dislikes also. To be conscious of a value-for-self relative to one's own likings is thus in principle to be conscious also of a value-for-others relative to others' likings. It must further become apparent at no very advanced level of reflection that likes and dislikes show a considerable amount of variation as between different persons, and that accordingly things which are values for A and B may very well be disvalues for the differently constituted persons C and D. But what must especially engage the attention of man as a member of a social group, of a body organised for a substantially common purpose, is not the values which are private to the individuals A and B and C and D, but the values that are *common* to all of them; the values which are values for *man*, rather than for this man or that man. Doubtless the 'manhood' or 'common human nature' to which reference is thus made will in early communities be interpreted exclusively in terms of the common human nature of the members of that community. But it is clear that this is a stage

destined to be superseded with the advance of civilisation. The growing sense of an universal human kinship can hardly fail to bring in its train a conscious interest in a human nature common to all men, and a consequent interest in the concept of a good which is good relatively not merely to the likings of this or that man, nor even to the likings of the typical man of this or that community, but rather good relatively to the likings of man as such, to the likings inherent in the common constitution of human nature.

It is, I think, altogether to be expected that when men have become 'kind-conscious' the concept of 'value for man as such' should evoke a very particular interest. Unlike the concept of value-for-self, it is conspicuously a concept of common interest, and thus an appropriate subject for the mutual interchange of ideas. What is good for the individual A is of great interest to A, but not as a rule of very much interest to individuals B, C and D. But what is good for man as man, in virtue of the common human nature shared by A, B, C and D alike, is a topic of interest to them all, a topic upon which they may pool their powers and their knowledge to mutual advantage. We might perhaps put it this way, that mankind will have little interest in 'subjective' goods *except* where the 'subject' in question is the human self as such.

I think we may regard it as natural, then, that just as our value-consciousness is interested in value-for-self, conceived on the basis of the self's likes and dislikes, so also it should be interested in value-for-man, conceived on the basis of the likes and dislikes inherent in human nature as such. And it seems fairly obvious that substantially the same distinctions whose recognition sharpens, and at the same time gives depth to, the meaning of good-for-self are equally applicable to the conception of good-for-man. The distinctions of major from minor likings, of independent from dependent likings, of integral from partial likings, and of relatively permanent from sporadic likings, all retain their significance when it is the conative constitution of the human self as such, rather than of the individual historic self, that is under consideration: and in a way strictly analogous to that already discussed in the case of good-for-self, the appreciation of these distinctions must issue in the recognition of good-for-man as equivalent not to *any* object of liking to human nature, but rather to 'object of an independent, integral, and relatively permanent liking of human nature.' Thus—to take a simple illustration which may help to elucidate the somewhat arid formula—knowledge would naturally come to be regarded as a good-for-man on the ground that man is so constituted that he has a liking for it which is entertained towards the object for itself, is compatible with his liking nature as a whole, and is relatively enduring.

One distinction appealed to in the determination of the meaning of good-for-self is, however, not here in point, *viz.* the distinction of present from prospective likings. It is not in point, because the meaning which human nature has for us at any time defines itself, as a matter of course, in terms of all that human nature has ever revealed itself to be, in its most ideally advanced quite as much as in its elementary manifestations. Accordingly, since the most developed human likings of which we have any conception will enter into what we mean by human nature, there will be no room here for a contrast between present and unawakened likings, appropriate as that distinction is to the case of a developing historic self.

As to the distinction of major from minor liking, it is not at first sight obvious whether the epithet 'major' ought not to be added to the qualifications of liking necessary to make an object of liking equivalent to 'good,' both in the case of good-for-self and in the case of good-for-man. Strictly, I do not think it ought to appear. On the other hand, it seems clear that if anyone were attempting to draw up a list of

'goods-for-man' (to confine ourselves to this issue), he would probably not be satisfied to include in the list an object for itself, liked integrally, and liked in a relatively permanent way, if it should happen that it was not *also* liked *much*. Perhaps, however, the explanation is really a very simple one, just the fact that any attempt to draw up a list of goods will tend naturally to limit its field to the major representatives of the class. On the whole, I think we should say that the question of major or minor liking has no bearing on the *meaning* of goodness, but has a good deal of influence in determining what things we select as typical examples of 'goods.'

We have reached the point, then, of seeing the meaning of good-for-man, for a developed consciousness, to be an 'object of an independent, integral, and relatively permanent liking of human nature.' I do not mean, of course, that these several determining characters are explicitly present in the minds of all persons who use, even significantly use, the concept 'good-for-man.' But I do maintain that this formula expresses the meaning of the concept which we must suppose to have been operative in men's minds throughout the gradual process of determining what things are good for man, if that process has been a work of intelligence at all. This is the meaning, I believe, which has underlain and guided, whether explicitly recognised or not, the unsystematic reflections of the value-consciousness of generations of men, reflections which have resulted in the now traditional acceptance by the civilised world of a more or less definite set of things as pre-eminently 'goods-for-man.'

But *are* there certain things that have received this public and traditional endorsement? The phrase 'good-for-man' is not a common phrase in ordinary discourse, and the critic may very reasonably ask what kind of value-judgment I have in mind when I speak of the value-consciousness of mankind having found expression in the endorsement of a definitive set of things as good-for-man. I answer—and here we come to the kernel of the matter—that the kind of judgment I have in mind is precisely the kind of judgment which is commonly supposed by the Objectivist to assert a good simple and unqualified, an 'intrinsic' good. When goodness is predicated of such things as knowledge or aesthetic experience, the Objectivist holds that we are using, or may be using, the term goodness in an absolutely simple, unrelational, unanalysable sense. I contend against this that the apparent simplicity is never a real simplicity; that actually there underlies the predication of goodness in all such cases the conception of a certain relationship between the things and the emotional nature of man as we know it, a relationship which is indispensable to the recognition of the things as good; and that this relationship is precisely expressed by saying that the things are objects of independent, integral, and relatively permanent liking to human nature.

This then is our hypothesis. And before considering the evidence in its favour it will be well to deal at once with an obvious objection. If people really mean 'good-for-man' in these judgments, why do they say just 'good'? The objection is, I think, less formidable than it appears. It seems appropriate, on reflection, that the relational qualification should tend to drop out where the relativity in question is to our common human nature. In the case of a quality which (as we claim to be the case with goodness) is naturally thought of as relative to persons in some sense, it will be necessary to add a relational phrase only where a *special* relativity to some *special* person or persons is intended. If *no* relativity is indicated, the natural presumption will be that the quality is relative not to any special party, but just to our common human nature. Hence the *omission* of the relational qualification may be said in such cases to serve exactly the same purpose as would be served by its *inclusion*. We might perhaps imagine a parallel case, to illustrate our point, in respect of colour-judgments. Even if we all believed, as many people do believe, that red is red only for man, we should continue to say 'this is red,' not 'this is red-for-man.' We should only feel the need of appending a relational qualification if the relativity was to an *individual:* as, e.g., a colour-blind person who was aware of his peculiarity might say 'this is red *to me.*' The omission of a relational qualification would imply that the relativity was merely to our common sensitive organisation.

Passing from this difficulty which meets us at the threshold, let us now consider the positive evidence that the formula I have reiterated does represent, in the sense of making fully explicit, what is really meant by good when that term is predicated in an ostensibly unqualified sense. The first and the chief point to which I wish to call attention is that the so-called 'intrinsic' goods of the Objectivist are precisely the kind of things that would come to be called just 'good' if our theory of the meaning given to goodness is correct. If goodness means the quality of being an object of independent, integral and relatively permanent liking to human nature, then the particular group of things which tradition has called just 'good,' and which the Objectivist declares therefore to be intrinsically good, is exactly the group of things that we should expect. Truth and Beauty, for example, in their more philosophical dress as knowledge and aesthetic experience, fall into line at once. Each has in a pre-eminent degree the characteristic of being an object of independent, integral, relatively permanent,—and we may properly add here, major—liking of human nature. And the same thing may be said of such goods as health and friendship, on whose behalf the common value-consciousness of mankind has also made high, though less high, claims. Pleasure, I agree, occupies a somewhat equivocal position for our formula. It is an object of human liking, of major liking, of independent liking, and of relatively permanent liking. But whether or not it is an object of *integral* liking, a liking consistent with the liking nature as a whole, depends entirely upon what *kind* of pleasure it is. But then is not this equivocal position of pleasure for our formula precisely the kind of position it occupies for the value-consciousness of mankind also? The general attitude towards pleasure would probably be expressed fairly enough by saying that it is regarded as good in so far as it is not seriously obstructive of other values. But if so, that would admirably fit in with our formula. For it would mean that wherever the pleasure was of such a kind that it could be an object of integral liking to man it would be a good; and if not of such a kind, not good. But that is just what would be maintained if our formula were operative.

Now this applicability of our formula to the so-called intrinsic goods is not, indeed, conclusive *proof* that our formula expresses what is really meant in these contexts by goodness. Nevertheless, I think we may say that if this is *not* what is meant by goodness, then the applicability of the formula is a very odd coincidence indeed. Actually, I think we are entitled to go further. I think we are entitled to say that the onus of proof now lies upon the Objectivist. For consider just where we stand. Our account started from a value-experience, admittedly subjectivist, which all must concede to be actual, and it proceeded from that basis to show, without any appeal to other than well-recognised psychical and other factors, how man would eventually come to pronounce as 'good,' without explicit relational qualification, whatever was an object of independent, integral, and relatively permanent liking to human nature. We then found that the very things which are in *fact* pronounced to be good in this way—the so-called 'intrinsic goods'—possess all the characteristics of our formula. The Objectivist, on the other hand, has to appeal to an unique kind of perception whose claim to be something real is still, at best,

sub judice, and whose strangely erratic behaviour even among its best friends is something of a scandal. Moreover, as was hinted earlier, the Objectivist is powerless to explain why so many mutually contradictory things have been called good in the same apparently unqualified way by different peoples in different ages—a phenomenon which is easily explicable on our view, since we can recognise the vast difference which different conditions of life and different levels of mental development must make to the things that are conceived to be objects of integral, independent and relatively permanent liking to human nature. It seems to me, therefore, that the onus of proof now lies upon the Objectivist, our present theory being one of greater *prima facie* probability. And I propose to devote most of what time remains to repelling objections to our theory, rather than to seeking for further positive support.

5

It will not, I think, present itself as a very serious objection to anyone that our formula is certainly not explicitly present in the minds of most of those who predicate goodness (in the context we have been considering). It seems fairly clear that a formula can accurately represent what persons really mean by good even though they have no recognisable version of the formula before them. In ordinary discourse we are very seldom indeed conscious of the full definitory meaning of the complex terms that we use; and yet, in so far as we are using the terms intelligently, that meaning is operative in and controlling our usage. I am glad here to be able to enlist the authority of Dr. Ross. 'It appears,' he writes, 'as if we cannot avoid recognising that there is such a thing as using a term which implicitly refers to a certain complex, while yet the complex is not explicitly present to our minds. And in principle this might, it seems, be true of good.' [8] After all, even in philosophical discourse, the valuable maxim 'define your terms' has to be applied with something less than absolute rigour if the argument is to advance at a tolerable pace at all.

But by what test, it may fairly be asked, are we to determine whether any particular complex, not explicitly before our minds when we use a term, is in fact implicitly present? Again I am well content with Dr. Ross's answer. 'If it is the correct definition,' he holds, 'what should happen is that after a certain amount of attention to it we should be able to say "Yes, that is what I meant by 'good' all along, though I was not clearly conscious till now that it *was* what I meant."' [9] The process of criticising proposed definitions, he adds, has two moments. A definition of a term must be rejected if (*a*) we are able to point to things of which the term is predicable and the definition not, or *vice versa;* or if (*b*) even when the denotations of the term and of the definition coincide (or when we cannot be sure that they do not), we can 'see that a proposed definition does not express what we *mean* by the term to be defined.' [10] This seems to me to be a valid and valuable statement of the situation, and I should make no objection whatever to the application of such a test to the formula I have put forward as representing judgments which 'at the first look' predicate intrinsic goodness. I am well aware, of course, that in Dr. Ross's judgment the application of the test proves fatal to *all* relational definitions of the nature of goodness. But while fully agreeing that it is fatal to the relational definitions which Dr. Ross actually cites, and which he appears to have alone before his mind, I must point out that our particular variety of relational definition does not appear in Dr. Ross's list at all—explicitly or implicitly.

It will be worth our while, however, to consider with some care Dr. Ross's criticism of relational definitions of goodness, or at least of the subjectivist group of relational definitions. For, while we are claiming exemption for our own particular formula, it is evident that Dr. Ross intends his criticism to have an exhaustive reference. On pages 80–83 he furnishes what, I take it, he regards as a systematic classification of those theories of the nature of goodness which make goodness depend upon a relation to subjective or psychological factors. He arranges them under two main heads, A and B. A consists of those theories which hold that a thing's being good means that some person has, or some persons have, some kind of *feeling* towards it, B of those theories which hold that what is meant is rather that some person *thinks,* or some persons *think,* the thing to be good. Upon the second group, B, Dr. Ross wastes few words; and, being in perfect accord with all that he says, I propose to waste even fewer by making no further reference to this type of theory. But we must follow Dr. Ross into his sub-division of group A, to which our own theory would most naturally belong, and which Dr. Ross allows to possess a much greater *prima facie* plausibility than the other group. The sub-division adopted will be best explained in its author's own words. 'Theories of this type,' he says, 'are divisible into those which identify goodness with the presence of some feeling (1) in at least one person, no matter who he is, (2) in the person who judges an object to be good, (3) in a majority of persons of some class or other—say persons belonging to a particular stage in the history of civilisation, (4) in a majority of mankind, or (5) in all mankind.' [11]

Now of course the most conspicuous feature of Dr. Ross's classification from our point of view is that it omits altogether the particular variety of type A which seems to ourselves to offer the true definition. For it need scarcely be pointed out that being an

---

[8] *The Right and the Good,* p. 93.
[9] *Ibid.*
[10] *Ibid.*

[11] *The Right and the Good,* pp. 82–83.

object of liking to human nature is by no means identical with being an object of liking either to all mankind or to a majority of all mankind—while much less is it identical with any of the other suggested formulae. Yet there is surely nothing unintelligible, or even strained, about the concept 'object of liking to *human nature.*' There are appropriate objects of liking to human nature just as there are appropriate objects to cat nature or dog nature. Cat nature is so constituted as to like stalking its prey and to dislike immersion in water. What is the difficulty about saying that human nature is so constituted as to like and dislike certain specific things also? Indeed, aren't we saying that kind of thing almost every day of our lives? And aren't our psychologists busily engaged at this very time in trying to ascertain just what the basic likes and dislikes of human nature are? And wasn't it the chief aim of the Greek moralist to determine what mode of life human nature was so constituted as in the end, and on the whole, to like best?

I hope, then, that no one will retort against me that while Tom, Dick or Harry can have likings, it is not possible to assign likings to what is not a person but an abstraction, *viz.*, human nature. If we are to take that view in earnest, then we ought likewise to insist, I presume, that *instincts* cannot intelligibly be assigned to human nature either, since, strictly speaking, it is only an actual living creature that can have an instinct. But I fancy that the critic would wish neither to forbid other people to speak, nor himself to refrain from speaking of 'the instincts of human nature.' In neither case is there any real difficulty about the meaning that is intended. Just as there are instincts which men have in virtue of their common human nature, so too there are likings which men have, or tend to come to have, in virtue of their common human nature.

But perhaps the best analogy for our usage is provided by the usage of the Greek philosophers in their search after man's *summum bonum.* Who is the 'man'

whose *summum bonum* is sought? Not surely any particular man, but just 'man as such,' the exemplar of our common human nature. The Greek moralist works with a *type man,* constituted by the conative, emotional, and intellectual proclivities believed to be common to human nature, sets him in a natural and social environment which, though inevitably relative to the age and place of the moralist, is made as little specific as possible, and seeks to determine what mode of life will afford the fullest satisfaction to a being so constituted and so conditioned. It is not anything essentially dissimilar, in my judgment, that mass opinion has been doing in the long process of constructing its list of 'goods for man.' The chief difference is due to the simple fact that in the one case the process is undertaken with scientific thoroughness and method, and in the other case not. That is why mass opinion is content with a set of pre-eminent *goods*, and does not concern itself with the deeper, and to ethical science vitally important, question of the relation of these goods to one another within the unity of *the good*. But so far as the concept of 'human nature' is concerned, the procedure seems fundamentally the same; and there seems no more difficulty in applying the concept in one case than in the other.

I must claim, then, that the subjectivist definition of good which I have placed before you is not to be put out of court on the score of being unintelligible, and I must insist that Dr. Ross's criticism of subjectivist theories is not exhaustive of the type so long as the classification upon which it is based ignores this particular variety. It *might* be the case, indeed, that the exclusion of it was only formal. That is, it might be the case that some of Dr. Ross's criticisms of the theories on his list are capable of being adapted, with more or less trifling modifications, to the destruction of our theory too. It is therefore of first-rate importance to observe that this is not even remotely the case—as anyone may assure himself by even a cursory inspection of the relevant pages of Dr. Ross's book.[12] His criticisms simply do not touch our theory at all. And this is not really surprising. For in spite of superficial resemblances, there is one highly important difference between our theory and any of those which Dr. Ross considers. Each of Dr. Ross's theories makes the goodness of a thing depend upon the feelings (we may say, for convenience, the 'likings') of *some definitive existing person or persons*. Now it is extremely easy to show, as Dr. Ross does clearly show, that when we say 'X is good' we are not, as these theories would imply, meaning to assign to X a quality so impermanent that its coming to belong to X, and its ceasing to belong to X, are contingent upon the mere shift of favour on the part of some particular person or persons. There is undoubtedly an implication of permanence and 'objectivity' about our more 'absolute' value-judgments which belies any such description. But if goodness is made relative, as we make it, to the likings not of definitive persons but of human nature as such, this implication is saved. If what we mean when (in these value-judgments) we say 'X is good' is that X is related in a certain way to the liking nature of *man*, we are not implying, nor indeed even allowing, that X's possession of goodness is at the mercy of the changing likes and dislikes of any persons whatsoever.

I want to turn next—and, I may add, finally—to a difficulty of quite a different kind. It would, naturally, be a crushing objection to our theory, as to any other relational theory of the nature of goodness, if the Objectivist were able to exhibit to us *just one thing* (other, of course, than moral virtue) whose goodness is beyond question underived from relationship to subjective liking or to anything else. Has this ever been achieved? I am going to argue here that no Objectivist has even come near to achieving it. There are, of course, in the writings of all Objectivist axiologists chap-

ters ostensibly directed to 'proving' some selected list of 'intrinsic' values. But close inspection will, I think, reveal a fatal flaw in these arguments. What we find in them is, as a rule, a very cogent demonstration that certain things are good irrespective of any relation to other *goods*, but it is merely *taken for granted*, on the basis of a prior attempted refutation in principle of subjectivist accounts of the nature of goodness, that these things are good irrespective of any relation to subjective feelings *also*. Hence if the prior 'refutation' be itself fallacious (as we have seen reason to believe must be maintained in Dr. Ross's case), the proof of the intrinsic value of particular good things will be fundamentally defective.

I shall illustrate once again by a reference to Dr. Ross's stimulating book. In his short chapter upon 'What things are good' Dr. Ross claims to be offering considerations which will assist the reader to apprehend virtue and knowledge and certain other things as each having a value absolutely in and for itself. What the reader in fact finds is that his arguments are one and all designed to demonstrate that the goodness of each of these goods is independent of any relationship to other goods, but that nothing whatsoever is done to show that the goodness in question is independent of a relationship to subjective feelings. The latter question is not, I think, affected one way or the other by a single word in the whole chapter. We may take the thoroughly typical argument whereby Dr. Ross seeks to persuade us of the intrinsic value of knowledge. He asks us[13] to 'suppose two states of the universe equal in respect of virtue and of pleasure and of the allocation of pleasure to the virtuous, but such that the persons in the one have a far greater understanding of the nature and laws of the universe than those in the other. Can any one doubt,' he goes on, 'that the first would be a *better* state of the universe?'

---

[12] *The Right and the Good*, pp. 83–84.

[13] *The Right and the Good*, p. 139.

Dr. Ross expects, and rightly expects, that this question will receive an affirmative answer. But I must point out that an affirmative answer does not carry with it a recognition of *intrinsic* value in knowledge. Dr. Ross has so constructed his hypothetical situation that an affirmative answer certainly entails the recognition that knowledge has a value which is not dependent upon a relationship to other *goods*. But, so far as his argument here is concerned, it must remain an entirely open question whether the value recognised is an 'objective' quality, or whether, on the other hand, it is dependent upon a relationship to subjective factors—such as, e.g., the likings of human nature. The terms of Dr. Ross's argument are such that no light at all can be shed upon this crucial issue.

How, one might ask, would Dr. Ross's argument require to be supplemented in order to become relevant to the question of the *objectivity* of the value of knowledge? It would, I think, be formally satisfactory if, in being invited to appraise the relative value of these two states of the universe, we were at the same time instructed to rule out from our minds all considerations arising from our familiarity with human likes and dislikes. Thus we should be obliged to suppose, for the sake of the argument, that there is no native impulse of curiosity in man which makes him come to like knowing for its own sake. If, fulfilling these conditions, we were to proceed to put to ourselves Dr. Ross's question, an affirmative answer *would*, I think, imply the recognition of a strictly 'intrinsic' value in knowledge.

But *should* we then be able to return an affirmative answer? It is a matter which each must decide for himself by personal experiment, but I feel convinced that, if the experiment be performed with due observance of the conditions, only a negative answer will be found possible. No legitimate ground remains, I believe, for judging the first state of the universe to be the better. Old emotional habits, like old cognitive

habits, die hard, and there is undoubtedly a great mass of prepossessions to be broken through before one can hope to return a fair answer. But I must leave the experiment with the reader, pausing only to draw attention to two pitfalls which seem especially liable to engulf the unwary. (1) We know that knowledge, even if it were not itself liked, would still be instrumental to a host of things that are liked, and this makes it difficult for us not to think of the state of the universe with knowledge as the 'better' state. But it is clear that the terms of the hypothesis make this consideration irrelevant. Reference to other goods, whether as 'objects of liking' or in any other sense, is definitely ruled out. (2) A good many of us are more deeply influenced than we are apt to realise by an inherited religious tradition which leads us to think of our faculties as given to us by God for use and development, so that it is in accord with the Will of God, and so far 'good,' that they should be exercised to the full. On this ground alone there is a powerful disposition in most of us to regard a state of the universe in which the faculty of knowledge finds active expression as better than a state in which it does not. Evidently, however, we are not, in making this judgment, recognising knowledge to be something 'good in itself.' We are merely recognising respect for the gifts of God, or obedience to the Divine Will, to be a duty.[14]

It appears to me, then, that Dr. Ross totally fails to demonstrate the objective

---

[14] It must be admitted that it is extremely difficult, in an ideal experiment such as that which we are here called upon to perform, to prevent one's value-judgments from being affected by the cross-currents of moral and religious duty. Many, perhaps most, educated persons, even apart from religious considerations, believe it to be their duty to develop their capacity for knowledge. On that account the conception of 'knowledge' is closely associated in their minds with the conception of 'goodness.' But clearly the effort has got to be made to abstract from the influence of this connection, if we are seeking to discover, by the device of experiment upon our value-responses, whether knowledge is good simply *as such*, in and by itself, as the Objectivist claims that it is.

goodness of his 'intrinsic goods,' and I am not able to conceive any other method likely to yield a different result. Dr. Moore's attempt fails for exactly the same reason as Dr. Ross's. His argument in Chapter VI of *Principia Ethica* depends essentially upon a prior supposed refutation of relational theories of the meaning of good in Chapter I; and, as we noted earlier, Dr. Moore is himself the latest recruit to the ranks of those who find the reasoning of Chapter I fallacious. I do not find, therefore, in Dr. Moore's attempted demonstration of intrinsic goods anything which places in serious jeopardy the central contention of this paper—the contention that there is nothing whatsoever, with the single exception of moral virtue, which does not derive its goodness from a relationship to subjective liking.

6

It is more than time that this paper drew to its belated close. Nevertheless, I must add just a few brief words upon a matter alluded to at an early stage of the paper, if I am to round off my theory with any pretence of completeness at all. It has been an implication of my argument that when we predicate value of morally virtuous conduct we mean something rather radically different by the term value from what we mean when we predicate value of anything else whatsoever. In the latter applications the meaning always involves an essential relation to human liking. In the former application no such reference is involved. Yet there clearly must be some common factor in the two meanings. Otherwise, why use the same term 'good' or 'valuable' in both cases? What is this common factor? What is the analogy between the usages which justifies us in employing common terms?

The correct answer, I think, is that all usages of the term 'good' signify at least this common feature in that to which good-

ness is attributed, *viz.*, that it is the object of what may perhaps least misleadingly be called a *pro*-attitude: just as that to which badness is attributed is always the object of a *contra*-attitude. An object of liking is quite obviously the object of a *pro*-attitude. But it is equally obvious, when we reflect upon it, that morally virtuous conduct is likewise the object of a *pro*-attitude. The latter *pro*-attitude is certainly not the same kind of *pro*-attitude as is entertained towards an object of mere liking. But a *pro*-attitude it undoubtedly is. The identity and the difference can probably be made most plainly apparent by reflecting upon the value-judgments ingredient in any simple case of so-called 'moral temptation,' in which the course we believe that we ought to follow is recognised to be incompatible with the course that we like best. Our mental attitudes towards the two courses are conspicuously different, but both of them are beyond question *pro*-attitudes. Indeed, if they were not, there could be no consciousness of inner conflict. It is equally certain, on the one hand, that the morally right course does not appeal to our mere 'liking,' and, on the other hand, that it does *appeal* to us. Its appeal is such, indeed, that it may be made by us the motive of our act, and thus be adopted as our 'end' in preference to that which we 'like best.'

If this is true, it appears that what we mean ultimately when we predicate goodness of moral virtue is that it is an object of approval or favour to the moral consciousness. Does this then imply, it may perhaps be asked, that even the goodness of moral virtue is in the last resort 'subjective,' consisting in a certain relationship to a state of consciousness? It is, I think, partly a question of the use of words. Most people, however, would probably agree that the moral consciousness, though it must be *in* a subject, is yet not 'subjective' in the same sense as desires and likings are 'subjective.' But I cannot now embark upon the long and arduous task of defining the true status within the self—much less within the whole scheme of things—of the moral conscious-ness. A fully adequate theory of value could not, I am sure, be dispensed from this obli-gation. But the pretensions of the present paper are more modest. I am content if I have established a *prima facie* case for the view that the meaning of value as applied to all the so-called intrinsic values with the exception of moral virtue involves an essen-tial relationship to human liking.

Method in Ethics

PAUL HENLE

Pragmatic philosophers have on the whole tended to treat problems of ethics as parallel to problems of knowledge. The object of this paper is, first, to make the parallel perfectly explicit and, second, to show that it is not peculiar to a pragmatic view but is compatible with any one of a wide range of epistemological and ethical positions. Within this range and for a considerable number of problems, at least, the aim is to set up a one-to-one correspondence between ethics and epistemology with the result that any conclusion from one discipline may be carried over to the other.

The method of reaching this conclusion is to consider the relation between pleasure and value. Sharp definitions of neither of these terms can be given, since in part the aim is to provide a method of determining the nature of these entities. The usual injunctions concerning the term "pleasure" are, however, necessary. It is not intended to refer exclusively, or even primarily, to physical pleasures, and there is no assumption that all pleasures, or even any of them, can be ranked on a single linear scale of magnitude.

Pursuant of this plan, too facile relationships of pleasure and value will be discarded in Section I, the parallel to epistemology will be established in Section II, some consideration of the ontology of eth-

Reprinted from the journal *Ethics* by Paul Henle by permission of The University of Chicago Press. Copyright 1943.

ics will be noted in Section III, and the problem of ethical choice will be examined in Section IV.

I

In general, this paper is in sympathy with naturalistic conceptions of value, holding that felt pleasures must be ethically important and that any attempt to disregard them leaves an ethical theory perhaps consistent in itself but utterly useless, since it creates an insoluble problem of ethical motivation. To build a whole ethical superstructure without answering the question, "What motive is there for doing good?" is to deprive ethical systems of any efficacy they might have and to reduce them to the status of an empty play of logical definitions and theorems, devoid of application, and not complex enough as logic to make them even interesting. And the only way of avoiding this result is to incorporate the problem of motivation within the theory of good itself in the manner of the ethical naturalists.

This paper, then, begins from a naturalistic position, though I am not at all sure it ends with one, for theories which equate good with a totality of pleasures or satisfactions, such as utilitarianism, are unworkable from two points of view. They answer problems neither of personal nor of social morality.

To consider first the case of personal morality. The answer to an ethical dilemma must be: "Do what will create most pleasure," either individual pleasure in the case of egoistic hedonism or pleasure of society in the case of utilitarianism. But this answer, in the one case as in the other, is likely to leave the problem unsolved, for the alternative which will create the greater pleasure depends on which can be shown to be more worth while. This is to say that pleasure is not an intrinsic characteristic of an activity, nor are pleasures relative merely to the actor, but they seem relative as well to the ideal they further or with which they are in conflict. To take a concrete case, consider the now familiar situation of a student faced with the alternatives of continuing his studies or enlisting in the army. To advise him to do what will cause the most pleasure is only to invite the reply: "If you can show that the paramount necessity is the defense of the country, then enlisting will bring most pleasure; but if you can show that this necessity is not imperative, or if you can show that the intellectual tradition should be continued at any cost, then continuing studies will bring the greater pleasure—but, until you show one or the other, your advice is useless."

Such a case, as well as the foregoing considerations, would seem to indicate that there are at least two components in pleasure, the one which might be termed immediate pleasure, resulting from an experience inherently satisfactory to the person experiencing it. Predominantly of this sort are the pleasures of coming upon an unexpectedly beautiful landscape or of smoking a cigarette. Another aspect of pleasure lies in accomplishing or furthering some purpose considered valuable for its own sake. Satisfactions of writing a book or taking an active part in some civic organization are of this latter sort. Often the two components of satisfaction may be evenly balanced, as in the satisfaction of viewing a landscape for the sake of which one has climbed a mountain or in the satisfaction of smoking after a full day's work. And in no case do we wish to suggest that the two aspects are experienced separately; rather they interpenetrate, fusing into a unitary experience whose dual character is revealed only in analysis. This is true even in the case in which the two elements have opposed values, as in the case in which the pleasure of a cigarette is tempered by the feeling that time is being wasted or in the case that the dreariness of writing is mitigated by the feeling of the importance of what is being written.

The point of these illustrations, then, is that, while immediate pleasures might conceivably be reckoned by some hedonistic scheme, the second group of pleasures are dependent on the acceptance of some underlying purpose, so that the problem cannot be decided in terms of pleasures alone. For the sake of clarity and in a manner which follows current usage, we shall refer to the second class of pleasures as *satisfactions*.

Again, on the side of social applications, a naturalistic ethics requires the employment of some sort of hedonistic calculus. Now it is generally recognized that such a calculus is very difficult to construct, too difficult for any precise applications; but what is less frequently recognized is that the calculus, even in theory, is impossible. The objection is not merely based on applications—it is no proper objection to contemporary physics, for example, that it would have great difficulty giving an accurate estimate of the number of electrons in this building—but rather that even under ideal conditions the calculus could not be applied. This may be seen from the most cursory attempt to sketch its workings.

A unit of pleasure would be required for this calculus, just as a unit of length is required for any calculus of distances. In the first case, as in the second, the unit must be arbitrary, and we might tentatively choose as our unit the amount of pleasure obtained from eating a bar of chocolate of specified size and composition. Of course, this pleasure varies with one's hunger, so, just as the meter bar is defined relative to conditions of temperature and pressure, the unit of pleasure must be defined relative to more complex conditions of health, previous taking of nourishment, and exertion since eating last. With the necessary restrictions of this sort we might, appropriately, name our unit of pleasure the "bentham." So far the difficulties have been merely technical, but, in the application of the standard, insuperable difficulties arise. We might list desires as being greater or less than a bentham, but there seems to be no way of giving meaning to the addition of pleasures. Is a pleasure of one bentham, combined with a pleasure of one bentham, a pleasure of two benthams? And, in any case, what might be meant by a pleasure of two benthams? Thus the scale would not be additive, and quantitative determinations become impossible.

Again, there might be people for whom the assimilation of the chocolate bar under the given conditions would provide neither pleasure nor displeasure, only profoundest apathy. Any pleasure measured by this scale would then appear to be infinite, and no comparison of values could be obtained.

Finally, if, in addition to the bentham, some other unit of pleasure were proposed, say the "wimpy," defined as the pleasure of eating a hamburger of specified dimensions and consistency under specified conditions, no transformation formula could be worked out to go from one method of measurement to the other. The conversion formulas would vary from person to person and from moment to moment. Of two courses of action, one might produce more pleasure measured in one sort of unit and the other measured by the other, so that which course of action were better would depend on which unit were chosen—surely an

undesirable condition and a *reductio ad absurdum* of any projected calculus of the sort required.[2]

Both, then, because of the failure to provide any means of reaching individual decisions and because of the theoretical difficulties inherent in any attempt to formulate the hedonistic calculus, the straightforward attempt to identify good with any sum of pleasures must be abandoned, and ethics would seem to be in the position of being able neither to avoid the notion of pleasure nor to dispense with it. In perhaps a different sense than Plato intended, the ethicist is in danger of being overcome by pleasure.

II

A workable theory of ethics would seem to require some sort of relationship between pleasures and purposes, and the difficulty in ethics lies in determining the nature of this relationship. Faced with this situation, it may be worth while to adopt a procedure similar to that of nineteenth-century physicists who were wont to construct mechanical models to serve as explanations in a variety of fields. In this case, of course, a mechanical model of ethical phenomena will not do, but an epistemological one may be of service. Epistemology is by no means a settled field, but it seems to me, at least, to be a field in which solutions have been more clearly thought out than in ethics, in which more ingenuity has been expended, and in which more complex struc-

---

[2] *e.g.*, suppose A and B are the only people involved in alternative courses of action, I and II. Suppose the pleasures involved to be the following:

Course I: $+3b$ for A, $-2b$ for B;
Course II: $-1b$ for A, $+3b$ for B;
Therefore, Course II is preferable.

Suppose for A, $1b, = 2w$; for B, $1b = \frac{1}{3}w$.
Course I: $+6w$ for A, $-\frac{2}{3}w$ for B;
Course II: $-2w$ for A, $+1w$ for B;
Therefore, Course I is preferable.

tures have been proposed than are to be found in ethics. Hence an analogy between theory of knowledge and ethics may be useful, though I do not think it will solve all problems.

This is not to say that ethics is derivative from epistemology or that theory of knowledge is logically prior to ethics but merely that a technique successful in the one field may advantageously be applied to the other. And this proposal is nothing new. After all, the method of attack in Kant's second *Critique* is a conscious imitation of that employed in the first.

The suggestion to be advanced here is that the relation of pleasures to ethical values is analogous to the relation of sense data to physical objects. It will be objected at once that there is no more disputed ground in epistemology than this relationship. This, of course, must be admitted, but it still may be the case that there is enough basic agreement on many topics to provide a fruitful analogy. That this is the case, we proceed to show by an enumeration of the points of agreement in epistemology.

We may begin by specifying the sense of the term "sense datum" required. The word is sometimes used with the significance of an isolated sound or patch of color; with the significance that Russell attached to the term "particulars" about thirty years ago.[3] It may also be used to indicate a complex of such data having a Gestalt character and interpreted as indicating some object. In this latter sense the term "appearance" might be more apt, except for its connotation of being "merely appearance." The latter sense is the one we shall employ.

At least six relations and distinctions may be indicated as involving sense data and physical objects.

1. The data are given in a sense in which the object itself is not. Depending on one's epistemological theory, the data may be parts of the object, effects of the object, or

signs of the object, but in any case they will be given with a kind of immediacy the object lacks. This is not to rule out the possibility of a direct, Bergsonian intuition of objects but merely to insist that this intuition, if it exists, is qualitatively different from the immediacy of sense data.

2. Because of this immediacy, the datum is subjective in a sense in which the object is not. Communication of the sheerly sensuous character of a datum is impossible, and there can be discourse only concerning the relations between data. An example of this is the well-known fact that if green appears to one man as red appears to another, they will agree as to what things are green and will never discover the difference.

3. The datum symbolizes the object. It may symbolize in the way in which an effect symbolizes its cause, or in which a part symbolizes the whole, depending on one's theory; but in any case the reference is there.

4. The datum may be modified by the hypotheses concerning the existence of a given object. Thus a person looking for a friend in a crowd is likely to mistake several people for him before the friend actually arrives. These false recognitions involve data, modified by the hypotheses.

5. By and large data are of little interest on their own account, but only because they are symbolic of, and related to, objects.

6. Finally, the data verify hypotheses concerning the existence of objects. The exact theory of this verification awaits satisfactory explanation, but at least the following factors would seem to be involved: (a) some sort of conception of the object, possibly vague; (b) expectations of the relation of this object to other objects; (c) expectations of the sort of sense data which would occur as a result of (b); (d) the final occurrence or failure of occurrence of these data. Thus, if I would verify the presence of a cat in the next room, I must know (a) something at least of what a cat is in

[3] *e.g.*, *Mysticism and Logic* (London, 1918), chap. vii.

order that (*b*) I may conjecture where the cat is likely to be discovered among the articles of furniture of the room. Otherwise I may fail to discover the cat because I sought it on the ceiling rather than on the floor. (*c*) I must form some expectation of what a cat would look like under these conditions, otherwise I may stare at the cat without recognizing it. Finally, (*d*) the required data may either actually appear or fail to appear.

It should be noted also that the data which are predicted of stage *c* need not be a literal imagination of those which actually appear at stage *d*. As a rule, the expectation is vague and permits of a variety of actual situations. The verification consists not in discovering a qualitative identity between expectations and presentations but rather in the fact that the data fit into an anticipated schema or pattern. The verification then consists in a fulfilment or disappointment of these fairly general expectations.

Other relations between data and objects might be suggested, but they are controversial and would depend upon one's epistemological views. Enough has been suggested, however, to introduce our parallel which would claim analogous relations between the following sets of entities:

In Epistemology	*In Ethics*
sense data	pleasures and displeasures
objects	values
hypotheses concerning existence of objects	aims or intentions
verification of hypotheses	realization of aims

In order to make the intended parallel clear, some explanation is required of the sense of the terms "value" and "aim." Sometimes the two are used synonymously, but the distinction intended is between what is aimed at, a certain goal, the value, and the belief that these values are to be found in a certain situation or course of conduct, the aim. The aim thus becomes a program for the realization of the value or a hypothesis concerning the value. There are senses in which the terms "ideal" and "good" are synonymous with "value" as used here, and in this same sense "envisagement of good" corresponds to "aim."

A further distinction is required. In the description of physical objects all affective and value characteristics are omitted. This is not to say that in actual perception the two groups of qualities can be separated, as, for example, it may be impossible for some poeple to view a snake without feeling disgust. Rather in the description of a snake the feelings accompanying the perception of it are neglected, so that two persons will agree that something is a snake even though one finds it admirable and another repulsive. Similarly, in our discussion of values it is necessary to neglect all except the affective or value characteristics, though, here again, this divorce is possible only in thought. Thus, if, as Plato suggests, the satisfactions of producing a poem and a child are at least generically similar, then these constitute the same value, or at least similar values.

It may be objected that values as suggested here constitute a highly Platonic realm of supernatural entities. Whether this constitutes an objection is, of course, a matter of debate, but it is sufficient for the present to indicate that no ontological status has been assigned to values and that everything said so far is compatible with a complete nominalism and materialism.

With so much by way of preamble, we may now proceed to make our parallel explicit:

1. Just as we saw that data are present in a sense in which objects are not, so pleasures and displeasures are present in a sense in which values are not. The pleasure may be looked on as a part of the value or as an effect of the value, corresponding to phenomenalist or realist views of the object, or the relation may be conceived in some other way; but in any case the pleas-

ure is given in a way in which the value is not.

In case the value is conceived as some transcendent good, it may permit of direct intuition, but, as in the case of objects, its immediacy will be of a different sort from that of pleasures.

2. Again, pleasures are completely subjective. Whether or not my pleasure on eating a well-cooked meal is qualitatively similar to yours is something which can never be determined, but in so far as they can be compared it is through the values to which they attach. This is less obvious on the ethical side than in the case of objects, because pleasures most often are not discussed directly but by means of the object to which they attach. The point may, however, be made clearer by way of an illustration. Suppose a book collector has just acquired a first edition of one of his favorite authors and, having exhibited his trophy, is trying to explain to a friend his satisfaction in possessing it. The friend believes that books are merely things to read and has no interest in first editions. The collector will have great difficulty in making his feeling clear unless, perchance, he discovers that the friend also is a collector, say of prints or match covers or autographs. Then it seems a fair inference that the values in the two cases are similar, if not the same, and the pleasure can be explained by showing its function in realizing the value, i.e., by comparing it to the pleasure of acquiring a desirable autograph.

3. The pleasure may symbolize the value, again by being a part of it or an effect of it, as was the case with sense data and objects.

4. Pleasures may be modified by their relations to aims. Thus a task which is in itself unpleasant may be considered pleasant because of its relation to some aim. This modification of pleasures by aims is probably even more widespread than the corresponding modification of data by theories about objects.

5. Again, to some extent at least, we have relatively little interest in pleasures merely as such but are interested in them in relation to aims. This would seem to be the force of the hypothetical example of the youth in the dilemma quoted in the preceding section. This also is the force of the oft-quoted paradox of hedonism.

6. Finally, the realization of a value is closely analogous to the verification of the existence of an object. Like verifications, realizations are never complete but always allow for a continuation of the process.

So far we have not distinguished pleasures and displeasures but have treated both as the ethical analogues of sense data. We have seen, however, that in their verificatory function, sense data constitute either fulfilment or disappointment. Hence, analogously, we may distinguish pleasures, as realizing an aim, from displeasures, as marking a failure of realization. The process of realization can be developed in strict parallel to the process of verification. There is required (a) the concept of some value to be realized. This concept, like the corresponding physical concept, may be and usually is vague. (b) There must be some envisagement of the physical conditions under which the value is to be attained; (c) there must be a schematic envisagement of the satisfactions to be attained through the realization of the value; and (d), finally, there is the occurrence of pleasures or displeasures which mark the actual realization. Thus, if the value aimed at be a pious life, it is necessary, as Socrates insisted, to have some conception of what piety is and essential, as Euthyphro pointed out, to know in what ways piety manifests itself in behavior, and equally essential, as neither one of them maintained, to know the satisfactions to be expected from piety. Only when this has been set forth can actual pleasures provide a realization of the value, piety, or displeasures a failure of realization.

As with the case of objects, failure of realization springs principally from two sources: from a failure to judge the circumstances under which the value is to be realized, point (b) above, or from a failure under the specified conditions to obtain the anticipated satisfactions. Conduct which is "idealistic" in the pejorative sense that connotes impracticality suffers from the first defect, and conduct which is "disappointing" suffers from the second—"disappointing" in the sense of having followed through a charted course of action without receiving the satisfaction expected from it.

Before concluding this parallel, one modification of it may be suggested. Contemporary logic, by its absence of distinction between common nouns and adjectives, has tended to soften the distinction between hypotheses regarding the existence of objects of a certain sort and hypotheses concerning the embodiment of qualities. If qualities are properly conceived, they may be substituted for objects in the epistemological side of the proposed parallel. This required view of qualities holds that they are not immediately given in sensation but that sense data are merely indicative of the presence of qualities. Thus a given sense datum would not be a presentation of the objective characteristic, red, but merely a clue to the presence of the quality.[4] This difference between sense data and qualities is roughly indicated by the difference between "The object looks red" and "This object is red." With such a conception of qualities, values are analogous to qualities; aims, to hypotheses concerning the presence of qualities, etc. I have, however, refrained from couching the analogy in these terms for two reasons: (1) this conception of qualities as transcending immediate sense experience does not have the prevalence it deserves and so might be confusing and (2) it is desirable to avoid even terminological confusion with the views of the British intuitionists that the good is a simple quality, where *quality* is employed in an immanent sense.

[4] Cf. C. I. Lewis, *Mind and the World Order* (New York, 1929), chap. v.

III

Thus far we have studiously avoided any commitment concerning the ontological status of values. By means of the parallel set forth in the preceding section, it is open to us to argue that there may be the same variety of theories concerning the nature of values as there are concerning the nature of objects. To enumerate a complete list would be both tedious and fruitless; a few of the more important varieties might, however, be considered.

We may begin with what might be termed ethical phenomenalism, the counterpart of epistemological phenomenalism. Such a view would hold that values are nothing more than groupings of pleasures and displeasures in much the same sense in which an ordinary phenomenalism would hold that objects are nothing more than groupings of sense data. The argument favoring the position would be the same in the two cases: in each case the more complex and remote entity is a construct out of the more immediately given. In each case any contrary position assumes the existence of entities without providing any means of verifying their existence. Such a view would provide a completely naturalistic theory of ethics, since the only ethical entities would be pleasures and displeasures and values constructed out of them. Such a view, however, would not be equivalent to ordinary hedonism in either its egoistic or its social forms, since the value is not merely an aggregate of quantitatively considered pleasures but a certain organization of them, in the same way that on a phenomenalist view an object is not a mere sum of sense data but the orderly appearance of data under specifiable conditions.

Again, in a manner comparable to a critical realist epistemology, it might be argued that affective states, though not parts of a value, are manifestations of it. On such a theory, the value would transcend pleasures and displeasures and be revealed by them symbolically. The value might even be taken to be the cause of the pleasures in somewhat the same sense that the object is taken to be the cause of sensations. Platonism in ethics seems to be a view of this kind.

The grounds for belief in such a view might be a claim of direct intuition of a value, similar to a Platonist's intuition of the good, or something which, by analogy to Santayana's terminology, one might call "moral faith," i.e., an instinctive belief that pleasures point beyond themselves and are revelatory of a different order of being. In the case of these ethical positions, the argument would be developed in a fashion parallel to the epistemological.

Again, just as it can be argued that every object requires a subject, so it can be argued that every value is a value for some mind. And just as not every object can be an object for each individual mind, so not every value can be a value for each individual mind, but an absolute valuer as well as an absolute knower must be posited. Just as every hypothesis is true in some degree, so every aim is in some degree realizable, and the most adequate aim, as the most adequate hypothesis, is the most comprehensive. Thus an ethical idealism might be built up, comparable to an epistemological idealism.

But enough of these sketches of ethical ontologies. The chief varieties, phenomenalistic, realistic, and idealistic, have been indicated, and the reader may be left to fill in the details or to develop his own epistemology of ethics. The foregoing considerations do not pretend to prove that a person holding a given epistemological view must hold the corresponding ethical view but merely that there is a presumption in favor of the analogue. The parallel drawn does not extend to all details, and there may be reasons for finding a position convincing in one field and not the other. Still, considerations which are thought to be decisive on the one side, in the absence of a special argument, should be convincing on the other.

IV

Thus far no attention has been given to the problem of choice or discrimination between aims, the question of what it means to say that one aim is "right" where another is "wrong."

If our analogy is to be carried out, two problems must be distinguished. First, there is the theoretical problem which is the problem of truth on the epistemological side. Just as there are correspondence, coherence, and pragmatic theories of truth, all involving relationships of hypotheses to objects, so on the ethical side one might speak of the correspondence of an aim with its value, the coherence of aims, and the possibility of realizing an aim. This ethical analogue of truth bears some resemblance to the use of the term "good." Certainly there are ethical theories which say an aim is good if it corresponds to an objectively existing value or that good consists in a synthesis of believed aims (just as truth is on an idealistic view a synthesis of believed hypotheses).

The more important problem, however, is not this problem of the nature of ethical goodness but the problem of making an actual choice. Given alternative aims, as in the case of our student who was undecided whether to enlist or to continue his studies, what criteria can and should influence his decision? Once again our analogy may be of service, and we may seek our answer by means of the parallel problem in epistemology: Given a concrete situation involving perplexity, how can and should one, in advance of verification, choose between alternative hypotheses? To take a simple illustration, if one is driving along a dark road at night and a small object dashes across it before the headlights, one may wonder just what sort of animal it is. The following considerations are relevant in reaching a decision:

1. The sense data themselves suggest certain hypotheses and rule out others. Thus the perceived data are compatible with the hypothesis of the animal's being a cat or a dog or a rabbit, but they definitely exclude its being a giraffe.

2. One's past experience and the general fund of human experience suggest hypotheses and eliminate others. Thus our knowledge of the habits of cats, dogs, and rabbits makes it probable that one was seen. On the other hand, unless one were driving in Madagascar, it would be exceedingly unlikely that the animal observed were an aye-aye, even though the observed sense data were entirely compatible with its being one.

The point might be stated in somewhat different terms: we project our hypotheses so as to preserve our past verifications. Every verification at the time it is made, of course, is absolute, not in the sense of being a complete verification but in the sense of being unequivocally a verification or not. Still, if subsequent judgments contradict a previous verification, we use these later judgments retroactively and hold that the prior verification was not really a verification at all. Thus if we were to assert that the animal observed were an aye-aye, we should have to sacrifice the verificatory force of all the observations which led to the generalization that aye-ayes are peculiar to Madagascar. Hence we avoid the judgment. The point might be summarized as follows: an experience which was verificatory at the time it occurred need not be so in retrospect, and we project new hypotheses, as far as possible, so as to conserve the verificatory aspect of these previous experiences.

3. There remains the problem of the choice of categories of classification, the problem of dividing the world into such classes as cats, dogs, and the like. In part at least the choice of such concepts is dictated by their applicability, by the fact that we do find objects which fit into them. It is of course entirely possible that a different set of concepts, making quite different divisions in the world, might have done equally well.[5]

These factors, then, are characteristic of any projection of hypotheses before the process of verification. As a psychological account of the making of judgments, there are no peculiar problems raised, but, largely for its ethical interest, we may raise the epistemological problem: Is there any source of error in these preliminary judgments before the actual verification? To point the problem. Suppose there are two motorists in the car, one of whom thinks a cat has been seen and the other a rabbit. Suppose, as is most probable, that they drive on without attempting to capture the animal. Is there any way in which the judgment of the one can be considered superior to that of the other, or is the question merely one of personal choice and opinion? A brief analysis of the factors enumerated above will show, I believe, that in part these factors admit of an objective evaluation, in part the matter is subjective.

To consider the first, that one man's data suggest a cat to him and the other's a dog to him, admits of no dispute, and neither needs nor is capable of any substantiation. To this extent the judgments are subjective. On the other hand, the powers of discrimination of each man are subject to investigation. How often is either confused in first impressions and, specifically, how often does either confuse cats and dogs? This question permits, ideally at least, of objective settlement.

There is another respect, also, though somewhat more subtle, in which an objectively determinable error might arise. One cannot doubt that what A saw looked to him like a cat, but does A know what a cat looks like under the circumstances? There

[5] For the development of this view see *ibid.*, Appen. E.

might be confusion not as to the nature of the presentation but as to whether or not the presentation is a case of looking like a cat. The adolescent who wonders whether or not he is in love is a case in point here. He knows exactly what his feelings are and can describe them in painful detail, but he is in doubt as to whether or not these constitute being in love. Presumably, though by indirect methods, such problems can be settled in an objective fashion.

With regard to the second point, the conservation of verifications: it can be decided on quite objective grounds what effect a new hypothesis would have on past verifications, since all that is at issue is a matter of logic—the consistency of accepted hypotheses with the one proposed.

On the third score, the possibility that different categories are involved, different modes of classification employed, it might be argued that no real difference is involved. If, for example, the problem is one of identifying an herb, and one person makes a conjecture as to its place in a botanical classification and another as to its place in a medicinal classification, there is no real dispute. Either person may be right or wrong independently of the other. If, however, it is proposed to verify the hypotheses, a clash may arise, since the verification of one may preclude the verification of the other. Thus to verify the place in the medicinal scheme it might be necessary to cut and steep the herb; to verify the botanical, to allow it to grow and flower. If only one specimen were available, the application of the two schemes would be mutually exclusive, and, assuming the two modes of classification to be equally successful, there would be no way of settling the dispute as to which was to be employed. Here would seem to be an irrational element in the procedure of verification.

It would appear, then, that in the tentative choice of hypotheses before verification has progressed there would be certain elements which are quite subjective and which cannot be said to be correct or incorrect. These are the appearance of the data themselves and, in some cases at least, the choice of the categories involved in hypotheses. On the other hand, the remaining factors—the discrimination of data, the knowledge of the appearance to be expected on the basis of some concept, and the probability of the hypotheses in terms of past experience—all are capable of objective determination.

To set up the analogy to ethics, as choices in ordinary knowledge are between hypotheses, so choices in ethics are between aims. As in the former case, we may distinguish the same three elements:

1. In adopting any aim, the present pleasures and displeasures are an index to the sort of values which may or may not be present in the situation. To take a simple illustration, a feeling of lack of accomplishment and time wasted may be an indication to a man that the aims at the values contained in planting his garden or beginning a major piece of work are realizable but that the aims at values contained in reading a detective story are not.

2. Parallel to the attempt to preserve previous verifications is the attempt to act in a manner as to preserve one's previous pleasures. This is not to deny that an activity experienced as pleasurable was pleasurable, and nothing can alter that fact. Similarly an activity which was experienced as verificatory was so experienced and nothing can alter the fact. But in retrospect, just as an experience may be remembered to have been verificatory when experienced but now may no longer have probative value, so an experience may be remembered to have been a source of pleasure but now may no longer be so. This is merely to admit the possibility of remorse. Just as we project present hypotheses, on the whole, along the pattern of previous ones to avoid renouncing our past verifications, so we project future aims along the lines of past ones in order to pre-

serve a pleasant memory of past pleasures. It is this reason, presumably, which makes it so much more difficult for an older man to change his set of aims than for a younger. He has so much more to lose. In Section I we distinguished between immediate pleasures and satisfactions derivative from the pursuit and accomplishment of an aim. It is presumably only the satisfactions and not the immediate pleasures which are lost in retrospect.

3. Just as we saw that there are possibilities of using different sets of categories to classify and describe phenomena, so there would appear to be the possibility of the same alternatives in the field of ethics. If we exclude for the moment theoretical ethics, we may consider ethical systems as ways of life, giving injunctions as to practical conduct. From this point of view we may notice the values which attach to a quiet sort of life given to studiously "cultivating one's own garden"—a life which consists in meticulous obedience to law but involves no wider interest in public affairs and no achievement of fame. From the ancient Epicurean point of view, these values are to be classified along with the values of contemplation of mild pleasures, of relative security, and the like. From Nietzsche's point of view, the value would be classified with the values inherent in slavery, mediocrity, and following the herd. It is entirely possible, of course, that the value has affinities with each of the sets of values in question, and to that extent there is no conflict between Epicurean and Nietzschean morals. When, however, one seeks to realize a given set of values, there the activities to be pursued on the basis of one classification conflict with those of another, and we have the split in morals. This is quite comparable to the conflict over methods of verification mentioned before.

Again, when we come to raise the question of which of these factors are capable of objective determination and which

remain subjective, the answers must be the same as before. The sort of aim which is indicated by a given state of pleasure or displeasure must remain subjective. The discrimination among such data is, however, a question and is subject to review. Mob action would seem to be a case in point. The group has some sort of feeling of pleasure or displeasure—indignation, elation, enthusiasm, or the like—but because of the circumstances often does not decide just what feeling it is and may act in a manner which it regrets.

Again, even if a feeling is properly discriminated, its indicative value may be questionable. Just as a youngster may doubt whether or not he is in love, so a student may think mistakenly on the basis of his liking for a given course that the aim of a scholarly life is realizable in his case, while actually he would find it completely unsatisfactory. Ideally, at least, such mistakes could be caught, and objectivity is possible here.

With regard to the second point, the conservation of satisfactions, objectivity is possible. The whole question is one of consistency of aims which in theory is simply a problem of logic. In practice, however, aims are considerably less articulate and well formulated than scientific hypotheses so that the task is a good deal more difficult.

The third factor involving conflicts arising from differences in ethical categories has already been discussed and, as in the epistemological case, appears to be subjective.

If this parallel holds, decisions as to ethical aims, like choices between scientific hypotheses, are in part based on objective grounds and are in part subjective. To the extent that such decisions involve an immediate taking of pleasures and displeasures as indicative of values and to the extent that they reflect classifications of values, they are subjective. To the extent that there is room for evaluating discriminations, for checking the reliability of evaluations, and for investigations of the consistency of aims, they are objective. To the extent that objective factors are involved, they may properly be called "right" and "wrong."

Ethical Absolutism and
the Ideal Observer

RODERICK FIRTH

The moral philosophy of the first half of the twentieth century, at least in the English-speaking part of the world, has been largely devoted to problems concerning the analysis of ethical statements, and to correlative problems of an ontological or epistemological nature. This concentration of effort by many acute analytical minds has not produced any general agreement with respect to the solution of these problems; it seems likely, on the contrary, that the wealth of proposed solutions, each making some claim to plausibility, has resulted in greater disagreement than ever before, and in some cases disagreement about issues so fundamental that certain schools of thought now find it unrewarding, if not impossible, to communicate with one another. Moral philosophers of almost all schools seem to agree, however, that no major possibility has been neglected during this period, and that every proposed solution which can be adjudged at all plausible has been examined with considerable thoroughness. It is now common practice, for example, for the authors of books on moral philosophy to introduce their own theories by what purports to be a classification and review of all *possible* solutions to the basic problems of analysis; and in many cases,

indeed, the primary defense of the author's own position seems to consist in the negative argument that his own position cannot fail to be correct because none of the others which he has mentioned is satisfactory.

There is one kind of analysis of ethical statements, however, which has certainly not been examined with the thoroughness that it deserves—the kind of analysis, namely, which construes ethical statements to be both absolutist and dispositional. In a paper entitled "Some Reflections on Moral-Sense Theories of Ethics,"[1] Broad has discussed a number of the most important features of this kind of analysis, and has even said that most competent persons would now agree that there are only two other theories about the meaning of ethical terms which are worth as much serious consideration. Yet there are many moral philosophers who leave no place for this kind of analysis in their classification of ethical theories, and many others who treat it unfairly by classifying it with less plausible proposals which are superficially similar. And what makes such carelessness especially unfortunate, is the fact that this kind of analysis seems to be capable of satisfying the major demands of certain schools of ethical thought which are ordinarily supposed to be diametrically op-

Reprinted from *Philosophy and Phenomenological Research*, XII, March 1952, by permission of the author and *Philosophy and Phenomenological Research*.

[1] C. D. Broad, *Proceedings of the Aristotelian Society*, N.S. Vol. XLV, pp. 131–136.

posed to one another. It is a kind of analysis, moreover, which may have been proposed and defended by several classical moralists;[2] and this is perhaps one good reason for giving it at least a small share of the attention which is now lavished on positions which are no more plausible.

The following discussion of absolutist dispositional analyses of ethical statements is divided into two parts. In the first part I have discussed some of the important characteristics which are common to all analyses of this general form. In the second part I have discussed some of the problems which would have to be solved in working out a concrete analysis of this kind, and I have made certain proposals about the manner in which such an analysis can best be formulated.[3]

PART ONE: CHARACTERISTICS OF THE ANALYSIS

1. It Is Absolutist

To explain the precise sense in which a dispositional analysis of ethical statements may be absolutist rather than relativist, it is helpful to begin by defining the two terms "relative statement" and "relativist analysis."

Speaking first about statements, we may say that any statement is relative if its meaning cannot be expressed without using a word or other expression which is egocentric. And egocentric expressions may be described as expressions of which the meaning varies systematically with the speaker. They are expressions which are ambiguous in abstraction from their relation to a speaker, but their ambiguity is conventional and systematic. They include the personal pronouns ("I," "you," etc.), the corresponding possessive adjectives ("my," "your," etc.), words which refer directly but relatively to spatial and temporal location ("this," "that," "here," "there," "now," "then," "past," "present," "future"), reflexive expressions such as "the person who is speaking," and the various linguistic devices which are used to indicate the tense of verbs. All of these egocentric expressions can apparently be defined in terms of the word "this."[4]

A moral philosopher is commonly called a relativist, and his analysis of ethical statements is said to be a relativist analysis, if he construes ethical statements to be relative. We may thus say, derivatively, that an analysis of ethical statements is relativist if it includes an egocentric expression, and if it is incompatible with any alternative analysis which does not include an egocentric expression.

It follows, therefore, that relativist analyses, no matter how much they may differ from one another, can always be conveniently and positively identified by direct inspection of their constituent expressions. Thus, to give a few examples, a philosopher is an ethical relativist if he believes that the meaning of ethical statements of the form "Such and such a particular act (x) is right" can be expressed by other statements which have any of the following forms: "*I* like x as much as any alternative to it," "*I* should (in fact) feel ashamed of myself if *I* did not feel approval towards x, and *I* wish that *other people* would too,"

---

[2] Adam Smith comes immediately to mind, but Hume can likewise be interpreted as accepting an absolutist dispositional analysis of "right." (*Vide*, e.g., F. C. Sharp, "Hume's Ethical Theory," *Mind*, N.S. Vol. XXX, pp. 53–56. But for a different interpretation of Hume, *vide* Broad, *Five Types of Ethical Theory*, pp. 84–93.) It is even possible to make out a case for including Kant in this list. (*Vide* Part II of this paper on the subject of ethical impartiality.) Sidgwick, although he denied that "right" is analyzable, seems not unwilling to accept an absolutist dispositional analysis of "good." (*Methods of Ethics*, 4th ed., p. 112, last sentence.)

[3] In this connection I am much indebted to Professor R. B. Brandt, with whom I have discussed the problems of moral philosophy at great length. He is not, of course, responsible for my errors.

[4] *Vide* Bertrand Russell, *An Enquiry into Meaning and Truth*, p. 134, and *Human Knowledge, Its Scope and Its Limits*, p. 92.

"Most people *now* living would feel approval towards x if they knew what they really wanted," "If *I* should perceive or think about x and its alternatives, x would seem to *me* to be demanding to be performed," "x is compatible with the mores of the social group to which *the speaker* gives his primary allegiance," and "x will satisfy a maximum of the interests of people *now* living or who *will* live *in the future*." Each one of these possible analyses contains an egocentric expression (which I have italicized). And it is evident that if any of these analyses were correct, it would be possible for one person to say that a certain act is right, and for another person (provided, in some cases, that he is not a member of the same social group, nor living at the same time) to say that that very same act is not right, without logically contradicting each other. This familiar characteristic of all relativist analyses is not *definitive* of relativism; it is, however, a necessary *consequence* of the fact that relativist analyses contain egocentric expressions.

We may now define an absolutist analysis of ethical statements as one which is not relativist.[5] The kind of analysis which I propose to discuss in this paper, therefore, is one which does not include an egocentric expression. It is a kind of analysis, I suspect, which is closely associated with relativism in the minds of many philosophers, but it is unquestionably absolutist and implies that ethical statements are true or false, and consistent or inconsistent with one another, without special reference to the people who happen to be asserting them.

2. It Is Dispositional

I shall say that a proposed analysis of ethical statements is dispositional if it con-

[5] It will be observed that according to these definitions a pure emotive theory of ethics is neither absolutist nor relativist. For absolutism and relativism are theories about the meaning of ethical *statements*, whereas a pure emotive theory denies, in effect, that there *are* any ethical statements (as contrasted with ethical exclamations, exhortations, etc.).

strues ethical statements to assert that a certain being (or beings), either actual or hypothetical, is (or are) disposed to react to something in a certain way. To say that a certain being is disposed to react in a certain way is to say that the being in question would react in that way under certain specifiable conditions. Thus a dispositional analysis of an ethical statement may always be formulated as a hypothetical statement of the kind which is commonly called a "contrary-to-fact conditional." A dispositional analysis of statements of the form "x is right," for example, might have the form: "Such and such a being, if it existed, would react to x in such and such a way if such and such conditions were realized."

During the past fifty years moral philosophers have given a good deal of attention to the evaluation of dispositional analyses which are *relativist*, and a comprehensive defense of one such relativist analysis can be found in the writings of Westermarck.[6] Westermarck believes, if I understand him, that the meaning of statements of the form "x is wrong," can be expressed by other statements of the form "The speaker tends to feel towards x (i.e., *would* feel in the absence of specifiable inhibiting factors), an emotion of disinterested moral disapproval which would be experienced by him as a quality or dynamic tendency in x." Although this analysis is considerably more sophisticated than many of the analyses which relativists have proposed, it is typical of a position to which absolutists have raised a number of closely-related, and by now very familiar, objections.

A dispositional analysis of ethical statements which was *absolutist* would not, of course, be open to the same objections. It would construe ethical statements in one of the following three ways: (1) as assertions about the dispositions of all *actual* (past, present, and future) beings of a cer-

[6] *Vide* especially *Ethical Relativity*, Ch. V. An equally interesting relativist dispositional analysis has been proposed by F. C. Sharp, *Ethics*, Appleton-Century, N. Y., 1928, Ch. VII.

tain kind; (2) as assertions about the dispositions of all *possible* beings of a certain kind (of which there might in fact exist only one or none at all), or (3) as assertions about the dispositions of a majority (or other fraction) of a number of beings (actual or possible) of a certain kind. It is evident that an analysis of any of these three types would include no egocentric expression, and would therefore construe ethical statements in such a way that they would be true or false, and consistent or inconsistent with one another, without special reference to the people who happen to be asserting them.

It is only the second of these three kinds of analysis which I propose to examine in this paper, for analyses of the other two types, it seems to me, are open to obvious and yet insuperable objections. An analysis of the first type would construe ethical statements to entail that there actually exists a being (perhaps God) whose dispositions are definitive of certain ethical terms. But this would mean that all ethical statements containing these ethical terms are necessarily false if such a being does *not* exist—a consequence which seems to be incompatible with what we intend to assert when we use ethical terms. And in my opinion an analysis of the third type would be even less plausible, because it would imply that ethical statements express judgments which can only be verified or refuted, at least theoretically, by statistical procedures. I shall not amplify these familiar arguments, however, since much of what I shall say about ethical analyses of the second type can be equally well applied to analyses of the other two types, and anyone who so wishes may easily make the necessary translations in reading the second part of this paper.

It will be convenient, throughout the following pages, to use the term "ideal observer" in speaking about a possible being of the kind referred to in an absolutist dispositional analysis. The adjective "ideal" is used here in approximately the same sense in which we speak of a perfect vacuum or a frictionless machine as ideal things; it is not intended to suggest that an ideal observer is necessarily *virtuous*, but merely that he is conceivable and that he has certain characteristics to an extreme degree. Perhaps it would seem more natural to call such a being an ideal *judge*, but this term could be quite misleading if it suggested that the function of an ideal observer is to pass judgment on ethical issues. As an ideal observer, of course, it is sufficient that he be capable of reacting in a manner which will determine by definition whether an ethical judgment is true or false. And it is even conceivable, indeed, that an ideal observer, according to some analyses, should lack some of the characteristics which would make it *possible* for him to pass judgment on ethical issues—which would mean, of course, simply that he would not be able to judge the nature of his own dispositions.

Using the term "ideal observer," then, the kind of analysis which I shall examine in this paper is the kind which would construe statements of the form "x is P," in which P is some particular ethical predicate, to be identical in meaning with statements of the form: "Any ideal observer would react to x in such and such a way under such and such conditions."[7]

This formulation may draw attention to the fact that a dispositional analysis which is absolutist may nevertheless be extensionally equivalent to one that is relativist. For the egocentric expression in a relativist analysis is often qualified by reference to ideal conditions (described in if-clauses), and it is evident that each of

---

[7] Lewis has proposed that dispositional analyses of "objective statements" be formulated with a "probability qualification." (*Vide An Analysis of Knowledge and Valuation*, pp. 235–243.) If such a qualification were introduced into the analysis of ethical statements, an absolutist dispositional analysis would have the form: "Under such and such conditions an ideal observer would *in all probability* react in such and such a way." For simplicity I shall not consider this alternative, but none of the conclusions reached in this paper will be incompatible with the introduction of such a probability qualification.

these qualifications limits the respects in which one speaker could differ from another if the reactions of each were relevant to the truth of his own ethical statement. Westermarck, for example, analyzes ethical statements not by reference simply to the feeling which the speaker would actually have if confronted with a particular act or situation, but by reference to the feelings which he would have *if* he were impartial and *if* certain inhibiting factors (e.g., fatigue) were absent. And if a relativist were to continue to add such qualifications to his analysis, he might eventually reach a point at which *any* speaker who met all these qualifications would have all the characteristics which an absolutist might wish to attribute to an ideal observer. In that case ethical statements, when analyzed, would be contrary-to-fact conditionals of the form: "If I were an ideal observer I would react to x in such and such a way under such and such conditions." And if the specified characteristics of an ideal observer were sufficient to insure, in virtue of the laws of nature, that all ideal observers would react in the same way, it is evident that the truth value of ethical statements, so interpreted, would not differ from their truth value if interpreted absolutistically as statements about *any* ideal observer. Intensionally, however, the two analyses would still differ: the relativist, unlike the absolutist, would still maintain that the egocentric reference is essential, and by this he would imply, as we have seen, that two different speakers cannot make ethical assertions which are logically incompatible.

Let us now consider briefly some of the derivative characteristics of an analysis which is both absolutist and dispositional.

3. *It Is Objectivist*

The adjectives "subjectivist" and "objectivist" are often used in a *logical* sense, and as synonyms, respectively, of the terms "relativist" and "absolutist"; in this sense, as we have seen, an analysis of the kind that we

are discussing is objectivist. To avoid duplication of meaning, however, I shall use the terms "subjectivist" and "objectivist" in a traditional *ontological* sense—in the sense in which Berkeley's analysis of all physical statements is subjectivist, and Descartes's analysis of some physical statements is objectivist. We may say, in this sense, that a proposed analysis of ethical statements is subjectivist if it construes ethical statements in such a way that they would all be false by definition if there existed no experiencing subjects (past, present, or future). An analysis may be called "objectivist," on the other hand, if it is not subjectivist. Thus it is evident that in this ontological sense, as well as in the logical sense, an analysis of the kind which we are discussing is objectivist: it construes ethical statements to be assertions about the reactions of an *ideal* observer—an observer who is conceivable but whose existence or nonexistence is logically irrelevant to the truth or falsity of ethical statements.

This fact that a dispositional analysis is objectivist, is obviously a reflection of the fact that ethical statements, according to such an analysis, may always be formulated as conditional statements in the subjunctive mood; they may always be construed, in other words, as asserting that if such and such *were* the case, such and such *would* be the case. Hypothetical statements of this kind are commonly called "contrary-to-fact conditionals," but since they are sometimes used in such a way that they may be true even though they are not contrary to fact, they are perhaps more aptly referred to as "independent-of-fact conditionals." As used in an absolutist dispositional analysis, for example, such statements are not intended to imply *either* that there exists, *nor* that there does not exist, a being who satisfies the description of an ideal observer; they are intended to imply, on the contrary, that the existence or non-existence of such a being is *irrelevant* to the truth of the statement. Since the subjunctive conditional has exactly the same function whether the analysis is absolutist or relativist, it is evident that objectivism and absolutism are logically independent characteristics of an analysis of ethical statements; thus Westermarck's analysis is objectivist and relativist, whereas the one which we shall be examining is objectivist and absolutist.

The fact that an analysis of ethical statements is objectivist, moreover, is independent of all questions concerning the kinds of things to which ethical terms can be correctly applied. Thus it might in fact be true that the term "good" can be correctly applied only to conscious states, and hence that all ethical statements of the form "x is good" would in fact be false if there existed no experiencing subjects. And similarly, it might in fact always be false to say that a given act is wrong if neither that act, nor any of its alternatives, has any effect on the experience of conscious beings. But such facts would be entirely compatible with an objectivist *analysis* of ethical statements, for to say that an analysis is objectivist is to say merely that the existence of experiencing subjects is not essential by *definition* to the truth of ethical statements. This distinction is important because the term "subjectivist" is sometimes applied to hedonism and to certain forms of pluralistic utilitarianism, on the ground that these theories attribute value only to states of consciousness, or that they regard actual productivity of these valuable states as the sole determinant of the rightness or wrongness of an act. It is evident, however, that philosophers who support these theories should not be said to accept a subjectivist analysis of ethical statements unless they believe—as some of them, of course, do not—that ethical terms must be *defined* by reference to the experience of actual beings.

4. *It Is Relational*

An analysis of ethical statements is *relational* if it construes ethical terms in such a way that to apply an ethical term to a particular thing (e.g., an act), is to assert that that thing is related in a certain way to some other thing, either actual or hypothetical. There is no doubt that an absolutist dispositional analysis is relational, since it construes ethical statements as asserting that a lawful relationship exists between certain reactions of an ideal observer and the acts or other things to which an ethical term may correctly be applied. But to avoid misunderstanding, this fact must be interpreted in the light of certain qualifying observations.

It should not be overlooked, in the first place, that if an absolutist dispositional analysis were correct, ethical statements would have the same form that statements about secondary qualities are often supposed to have. Not only phenomenalists and subjectivists, but many epistemological dualists, would agree that to say that a daffodil is yellow is to say something about the way the daffodil would appear to a certain kind of observer under certain conditions; and the analysis of ethical statements which we are considering is exactly analogous to this. Thus the sense in which an absolutist dispositional analysis is relational, is the very sense in which a great many philosophers believe that yellow is a relational property of physical objects; and to say that a statement of the form "x is right" is relational, therefore, is not necessarily to deny that the terms "right" and "yellow" designate equally simple properties.

But the analogy can be carried still further if a distinction is drawn between a relational and a non-relational sense of "yellow." Many philosophers believe that the adjective "yellow" has two meanings; they believe that it designates both a relational property of physical objects and a non-relational property of sense-data—a distinction corresponding roughly to the popular use of the terms "really yellow" and "apparently yellow." And it is quite possible not only that the term "right" is similarly ambiguous, but also that in one of its senses it designates a characteristic of human experience (apparent rightness) which in some important respect is just as simple and unanalyzable as the property of apparent yellowness. And thus we might even decide by analogy with the case of "yellow," that "really right" must be defined in terms of "apparently right"—i.e., that the experiencing of apparent rightness is an essential part of any ethically-significant reaction of an ideal observer.

And finally, it must be remembered that to call an absolutist analysis "relational," is not to imply that it construes the ethical properties of one thing to be dependent by definition on the *existence* of any other thing, either natural or supernatural. Since an ideal observer is a *hypothetical* being, no changes in the relationships of existent things would require us, for logical reasons alone, to attribute new ethical properties to any object, nor to revise any ethical judgment which we have previously made. For this reason an absolutist dispositional analysis is not open to one of the most familiar objections to relational analyses, namely, that such analyses construe the ethical properties of an object to be dependent on facts which seem quite clearly to be *accidental*—on the fact, for example, that certain actual people happen to have a certain attitude toward the object.[8]

5. *It Is Empirical*

If we define the term "empirical" liberally enough so that the dispositional concepts of the natural sciences may properly be called empirical, there is no doubt that an absolutist dispositional analysis of ethical statements *might* be empirical. Such an analysis would be empirical, for example, if the defining characteristics of an ideal

observer were psychological traits, and if the ethically-significant reactions of an ideal observer were feelings of desire, or emotions of approval and disapproval, or some other experiences accessible to psychological observation.

It might be somewhat less evident, however, that an absolutist dispositional analysis *must* be empirical. For most of the philosophers who maintain that ethical properties are non-natural, and that ethical truths are known by rational intuition, have admitted that ethical intuitions may be erroneous under certain unfavorable conditions, or else, if this is regarded as self-contradictory, that under certain conditions we may appear to be intuiting an ethical truth although in fact we are not.[9] And it might seem that to recognize the possibility of error in either of these two ways is to recognize a distinction between the property of apparent rightness and the property of real rightness—a distinction, as we have seen, which is sufficient to permit the formulation of an absolutist dispositional analysis.

On this issue, however, I think we must take the word of the rational intuitionists themselves, and if there is any one fact about which intuitionists agree, it is the fact that some ethical properties are neither introspectable nor analyzable. And from this fact it follows, necessarily, that their ethical theory is epistemologically dualist—i.e., that there is no formula, however complex, by which ethical statements can be translated into statements about experiences which confirm them. Intuitionists must admit, I believe, that they are able to assess the cognitive value of their ostensible intuitions by reference to the conditions under which these intuitions occur, and

---

[8] Since, according to an absolutist dispositional analysis, the truth or falsity of ethical statements is dependent on the laws of nature, ethical statements are not intuitively or logically necessary; they are necessary, however, in whatever sense the laws of nature are necessary.

[9] A. C. Ewing, for example, is willing to say that intuitions are sometimes false. (*Vide The Definition of Good*, pp. 27–9.) But Hastings Rashdall, for example, preferred to say that it is difficult to distinguish intuitions from "mere feelings or aversions which may be only prejudices due to inheritance or environment or superstition." (*Vide The Theory of Good and Evil*, Vol. I, pp. 211–213.)

they must admit that they would not be able to do this unless they had some conception of an ideal observer. Thus Ewing lists[10] four factors which are responsible for false intuitions: (1) lack of experience, (2) intellectual confusions, (3) failure to attend adequately to certain aspects of the situation, (4) psychological causes "such as those with which the psychoanalyst deals." And the very fact that Ewing can compile such a list is proof that he has some conception of an ideal observer whose definition excludes these four factors. But this fact does not make intuitionism any less dualist, of course, for Ewing and other intuitionists will maintain that in formulating these ideal conditions they are merely formulating a *test* for the validity of an ethical statement, and not an analysis of the statement.[11]

Even though we conclude that an absolutist dispositional analysis must be empirical, however, there is still considerable room for disagreement about the precise nature of the ethically-significant reactions of an ideal observer. It seems clear that these reactions, if the analysis is to be at all plausible, must be defined in terms of the kind of moral experience which we take to be evidence, under ideal conditions, for the truth of our ethical judgments. It is important to observe that experiences of this kind—which we may properly call "moral data"—cannot be states of moral *belief*. An absolutist dispositional analysis, like any other analysis which grants cognitive meaning to ethical sentences, would permit

us to say that we *do* have moral beliefs, and even that moral consciousness is *ordinarily* a state of belief. But if the ethically-significant reaction of an ideal observer were the belief (or judgment) that a certain act is right or wrong, it is evident that an absolutist dispositional analysis would be circular: it would contain the very ethical terms which it is intended to define.

In order to define an absolutist dispositional analysis, therefore, it is necessary to maintain that moral data are the moral experiences to which we appeal when *in doubt* about the correct solution of a moral problem, or when attempting to *justify* a moral belief. For the epistemic function of moral data, when defined in this way, will correspond to the function of color sensations in determining or justifying the belief that a certain material object is "really yellow." And in that case moral data could play the same role in the analysis of "right" that color sensations play in the analysis of "really yellow."

Now there are many debatable questions concerning the nature of moral data, and until these questions are answered it will not be possible to explain precisely what is meant by the "ethically-significant reactions" of an ideal observer. These questions are primarily psychological, however, and can easily be separated from other questions concerning the content of an absolutist dispositional analysis. And if it is possible to provide a satisfactory formulation of the other components of an absolutist dispositional analysis (especially the definition of "ideal observer") this formulation will be compatible with *any* phenomenological description of moral data.

One of the most salient differences of opinion, for example, concerning the nature of moral data, is the difference of opinion concerning what we may call their "phenomenal location." There are many philosophers, on the one hand, who maintain that moral data are primarily feelings, or emotions, or other elements of experience

---

[10] *Op. cit.*, p. 26.

[11] An empiricist could be expected to ask how the intuitionist can *know* that one particular set of conditions is preferable to another; for, if the intuitionist's position is correct, it is surely not inconceivable that any given pathological condition (e.g., any of "those with which the psychoanalyst deals") is especially conducive to, or even absolutely necessary for, correct intuiting. (Cf. Brandt, "The Significance of Differences of Ethical Opinion for Ethical Rationalism," *Philosophy and Phenomenological Research*, Vol. IV, No. 4, pp. 488–490.) If this creates a problem for the intuitionist, however, it is a kind of problem which he shares with epistemological dualists in general.

which appear in the deliberative consciousness of the moral judge as ostensible states of the judge himself. There seems to be a growing number of philosophers, on the other hand, who are equally empirical in their epistemology, but who maintain that the typical moral datum is an obligatoriness or "demand quality" which appears in the deliberative consciousness of the moral judge as an ostensible property of an envisaged act or goal.[12] But however important this difference of opinion may be, it is a difference of opinion about the nature of moral data and not about the logical or epistemological relationships between moral data and ethical statements; both of these positions are compatible, therefore, with the theory that ethical statements are statements about the dispositions of an ideal observer to experience moral data (whatever they may be) under certain specifiable conditions.

Whatever conclusion we might reach concerning the phenomenal location of moral data, it will still be necessary to distinguish very carefully between moral data themselves, which, under ideal conditions, are the *evidence* for moral beliefs, and the very similar experiences which may be the *consequences* of moral beliefs. This distinction would not be difficult to make if we were content to say that moral data are simply feelings of desire (or, correlatively, that moral data are "demand qualities" of *all* kinds). For there seems to be little reason to doubt that feelings of desire may occur in the absence of moral beliefs. But if we should wish to maintain, as many philosophers have done, that moral data are the emotions of moral approval and disapproval, it would be much harder to make the necessary distinction. As Broad has pointed out, those emotions of approval

and disapproval which we think of as specifically *moral* emotions, are the very ones "which appear *prima facie* to be felt towards persons or actions in respect of certain moral characteristics which they are believed to have."[13] So if these emotions are said to be the evidence for moral beliefs, there appears to be a vicious circle in the process by which moral beliefs are justified. And there appears to be a similar vicious circle in an absolutist dispositional analysis. For if moral emotions are experienced only as a consequence of moral beliefs or judgments, and if we refuse to attribute moral beliefs to an ideal observer in our analysis, then there is no reason to think that an ideal observer would experience any moral emotions at all. But if, on the other hand, we do attribute moral beliefs to an ideal observer, we should have to employ the very ethical terms (e.g., "right") which we are attempting to analyze. This fact, in one form or another, has provided the basis for many arguments in support of non-naturalist ethics.

But the difficulty, I believe, has been highly exaggerated. It cannot plausibly be denied that moral emotions are often (perhaps usually) felt as a consequence of moral beliefs—that we often feel approval, for example, toward those acts which we believe to be right. But this is merely to say, if an absolutist dispositional analysis is valid, that we often feel approval toward those acts which we think would produce approval in an ideal observer. The crucial question is whether it is possible to feel an emotion of moral approval toward an act when we are in *doubt* about whether it is right or wrong. And surely this *is* possible.[14] It is not uncommon, for example, to find ourselves feeling moral approval toward an act, and then to begin to wonder whether our reaction is *justified*: we might wonder, for example,

[12] *Vide,* e.g., W. Köhler, *The Place of Value in a World of Facts,* Ch. III. Elsewhere ("Sense-data and the Percept Theory," *Mind,* Vol. LVIII, N.S., No. 232, and Vol. LIX, N.S., No. 233) I have discussed in some detail the general philosophical significance of the view that such ostensible properties may be "objectively localized."

[13] "Some of the Main Problems of Ethics," *Philosophy,* Vol. XXI, No. 79, p. 115.

[14] I am assuming, of course, that an emotion of moral approval is not *defined* as an emotion of approval produced by a moral belief.

whether we are sufficiently familiar with "the facts of the case" or whether our emotions are being unduly influenced by some selfish consideration. At such times we may continue to experience the emotion of moral approval although in doubt about the rightness of the act. We may even attempt to rationalize our emotion by persuading ourselves that the act is right. In rare cases, indeed, we may even continue to experience the emotion although convinced that our reaction is *not* justified. (This is sometimes the case, for example, when people feel approval toward an act of retribution.) Consequently, unless apparent facts of this kind can be discounted by subtle phenomenological analysis, there is no epistemological objection to defining the ethically significant reactions of an ideal observer in terms of moral emotions.

Whether or not this is the correct way to define these reactions, however, is a psychological question which I shall not consider in this paper. There are other, more fundamental, questions concerning the content of an absolutist dispositional analysis, and it is these to which the remaining part of this paper will be devoted.

PART TWO: THE CONTENT OF THE ANALYSIS

If it is possible to formulate a satisfactory absolutist and dispositional analysis of ethical statements, it must be possible, as we have seen, to express the meaning of statements of the form "x is right" in terms of other statements which have the form: "Any ideal observer would react to x in such and such a way under such and such conditions." Thus even if we are not to discuss the nature of the ethically-significant reactions of an ideal observer in this paper, it might seem that we are nevertheless faced with two distinct questions: (1) What are the defining characteristics of an

ideal observer? and (2) Under what conditions do the reactions of an ideal observer determine the truth or falsity of ethical statements? I believe, however, that the second of these questions can be treated as part of the first. For it is evident that the conditions under which the ethically-significant reactions of an ideal observer might occur, could be relevant to the meaning of ethical statements only if they could affect an ideal observer in such a way as to influence his ethically-significant reactions. And since the influence of any such relevant conditions must therefore be *indirect*, it would always be possible to insure precisely the same reactions by attributing suitable characteristics directly to the ideal observer. If, for example, the absence of certain emotional stimuli is thought to be a relevant and favorable condition, this fact could be taken into account simply by specifying that the ideal observer is by definition unresponsive to such emotional stimuli. I think it will soon become clear, moreover, that this procedure yields a type of analysis which comes closer to expressing what we actually intend to assert when we utter ethical statements. But even if I am mistaken about this, it will not be prejudicial to any basic problem if we assume, for simplicity, that the second question may be reduced to the first, namely, What are the defining characteristics of an ideal observer?

Before attempting to answer this question, however, there are a few remarks which I think should be made about the implications and methodology of any such attempt to define an ideal observer.

It is important, in the first place, to view any attempt of this kind in proper perspective. It would undoubtedly be difficult to arrive at a rational conclusion concerning the plausibility of absolutist dispositional analyses in general, without first experimenting with various concrete formulations. At the present stage in the history of moral philosophy, however, it would be especially unfortunate if the inadequacies of some particular formulation were to prejudice philosophers against absolutist dispositional analyses in general. Any plausible formulation is certain to be very complex, and there is no reason to suppose that philosophers could ever reach complete agreement concerning all the details of an adequate analysis. But this in itself should not prevent philosophers from agreeing that this general *form* of analysis is valid. Nor would it necessarily be irrational for a philosopher to decide that this general form is valid, although he is dissatisfied even with *his own* attempts to formulate a concrete analysis.[15]

Ethical words, moreover, like all other words, are probably used by different people, even in similar contexts, to express somewhat different meanings; and a correct analysis of one particular ethical statement, therefore, may not be a correct analysis of another statement which is symbolized in exactly the same way but asserted by a different person. This kind of ambiguity is a familiar obstacle to all philosophical analysis, but it causes unusual difficulties when we attempt to evaluate a proposed dispositional analysis of ethical statements. Any such analysis, if it is at all plausible, is certain to assign a number of complex characteristics to an ideal observer, and to refer to complex psychological phenomena in describing the nature of his ethically-significant reactions. And assuming that ethical statements *can* be analyzed in this manner, there is no good reason to believe that all human beings, no matter what the extent of their individual development, and no matter what their past social environment, could analyze their ethical statements correctly by reference to precisely the same kind of ideal observer and precisely the same psy-

[15] Cf. A. C. Ewing's statement (*The Definition of Good*, p. 43) that he can "see" in advance that nobody will ever be able to produce a satisfactory empirical analysis of ethical statements. Similarly a philosopher might "see" that *only* an empirical analysis which is absolutist and dispositional could be satisfactory.

chological phenomena. If ther*e* *are* any irreducible differences in the intended meaning of ethical statements, some of these differences might not be discoverable, and most of them might be so slight that they could not be held responsible for differences of opinion concerning the proper analysis of ethical statements. Some of these differences in meaning, on the other hand, might be sufficiently large to be reflected in the formulation of philosophical analyses of ethical statements. And there is consequently a clear sense in which philosophers may appear to disagree about the analysis of ethical statements, although in fact, because ethical words are somewhat ambiguous, they are analyzing different statements and hence not disagreeing at all.

It would be a serious mistake, however, to confuse the kind of ambiguity to which I have just referred with the kind of ambiguity which is definitive of a relativist analysis. The ambiguity which is definitive of relativism, as we have seen, is conventional, systematic, and characteristic only of statements which contain an egocentric expression. The kind of ambiguity which we have just been discussing, on the other hand, is accidental, unsystematic, and characteristic in some degree of all symbols. Thus it is not ordinarily the intention of an ethical absolutist to maintain that the words which we use to express ethical statements have a unique semiotical capacity—the capacity, namely, to express exactly the same meaning no matter who utters them; in fact even those absolutists who believe that ethical words express simple, unanalyzable, concepts, could scarcely maintain that there is any conclusive evidence to show that an ethical word, no matter who employs it, always expresses the *same* unanalyzable concept. The thesis maintained by the absolutist as such, is simply that ethical statements are not *conventionally* ambiguous in a manner which would require them to be analyzed by means of an egocentric expression; and this thesis is quite consistent, of course, with the proposition that ethical statements are accidentally ambiguous—perhaps even more ambiguous, indeed, than most other statements.

In the light of this distinction, then, it seems clear that if two philosophers believe that they are in perfect agreement concerning the meaning of ethical statements—i.e., if they believe that their ability to communicate is not limited by accidental ambiguity—they may still be either relativists or absolutists. If they are relativists, and related to one another spatially, temporally, and socially in certain ways, they will believe that neither of them could assert an ethical statement which is logically inconsistent with any ethical statement asserted by the other. If they are absolutists, however, they will believe that they *can* contradict each other in their ethical statements. Thus the absolutist, unlike the relativist, believes that nothing stands in the way of the expression of cognitive disagreement about ethical matters except the accidental ambiguity which is characteristic of all symbols. And since the absolutist can consistently admit that this accidental ambiguity may be sufficiently great to prevent philosophers from agreeing on a concrete analysis of ethical statements, the apparent inadequacy of any particular analysis, such as the one which I shall propose, should not be considered as proof that the general form of an absolutist dispositional analysis is unsatisfactory.

It should also be kept in mind that the kind of analysis which we are seeking is one which would be an analysis of ethical statements in the sense (and probably only in the sense) in which hypothetical statements about the way a daffodil would appear to a "normal" observer are said to constitute an analysis of the material object statement "This daffodil is yellow." To attempt an analysis of this sense of the word "analysis" would lead to difficult problems far beyond the scope of this paper. But two points may be mentioned. First, an analysis

in this sense of the word is not required to be *prima facie* or "intuitively" equivalent to the analyzandum, and for this reason the surprising complexity of a proposed analysis is not a sufficient reason for rejecting it: thus the fact that a proposed analysis of "This daffodil is yellow" happens to refer to white light, a transparent medium, a neutral background, and a variety of physiological conditions of an observer, is not ordinarily thought to make the analysis unsatisfactory. And second, an analysis in this sense of the word is an analysis of the so-called "cognitive meaning" of ethical statements, and thus is not required to have the same emotive meaning as the analyzandum. Even if we should find a satisfactory analysis of ethical statements, therefore, we should still have to supplement this analysis by a theory of emotive meaning if we wished to take account of all the functions of ethical statements in actual discourse.

The method employed in formulating dispositional analyses—whether of "soluble" or "yellow" or "right"—is the method most aptly described as "pragmatic." In analyzing ethical statements, for example, we must try to determine the characteristics of an ideal observer by examining the procedures which we actually regard, implicitly or explicitly, as the rational ones for *deciding* ethical questions. These procedures, to mention just a few, might include religious exercises, the acquisition of certain kinds of factual information, appeals to a moral authority, and attempts to suppress one's emotions if they are thought to be prejudicial. Each of these procedures will suggest certain characteristics of an ideal observer, and there is reason to believe that the characteristics suggested by these various procedures will not be incompatible with one another: some of the characteristics which are likely to be attributed to a moral authority, for example, seem to be the very ones which we try to produce or to approximate in ourselves when we engage in religious exercises, or seek for factual information, or attempt to suppress emotions which we think are prejudicial.

This appeal to the procedures by which we judge or decide ethical questions, does not imply that the pragmatic method will force us to deny the important distinction, previously mentioned, between an ideal *observer* and an ideal *judge*: there is clearly no logical reason why a judge should have to *be* an ideal observer, or should even have to be closely similar to an ideal observer, in order to make correct judgments about the ethically-significant reactions of such a being. On the other hand, there cannot be much doubt that the ethically-significant reactions of an ideal observer must be psychological in nature, and that some of the evidence for the occurrence of these reactions could be directly accessible only to an ideal observer himself. It is for this epistemic reason that in practice we are likely to rate moral judges by reference to their similarity to an ideal observer. And it is to be expected, consequently, that any plausible description of an ideal observer will be a partial description of God, if God is conceived to be an infallible moral judge. But of course an ideal observer need not possess such characteristics as the power to create physical objects or even the power to reward and punish, if these characteristics appear to be irrelevant to God's capacities as a moral judge.

CHARACTERISTICS OF AN IDEAL OBSERVER

1. *He Is Omniscient With Respect to Non-Ethical Facts*

We sometimes disqualify ourselves as judges of a particular ethical question on the ground that we are not sufficiently familiar with the facts of the case, and we regard one person as a better moral judge than another if, other things being equal, the one has a larger amount of relevant

factual knowledge than the other. This suggests that an ideal observer must be characterized in part by reference to his knowledge of non-ethical facts. I say "non-ethical" because, as we have seen, the characteristics of an ideal observer must be determined by examining the procedures which we actually take to be the rational ones for deciding ethical questions; and there are many ethical questions (*viz.*, questions about "ultimate ethical principles") which cannot be decided by inference from ethical premises. This does not mean, of course, that an ideal observer (e.g., God) *cannot* have knowledge of ethical facts (facts, that is to say, about his own dispositions); it means merely that such knowledge is not *essential* to an ideal observer.

A difficulty seems to arise from the fact that in practice we evaluate the factual knowledge of a moral judge by reference to some standard of relevance, and regard one judge as better than another if, other things being equal, the one has more complete knowledge of all the facts which are *relevant*. But it is evident that a concept of relevance cannot be employed in *defining* an ideal observer. To say that a certain body of factual knowledge is not relevant to the rightness or wrongness of a given act, is to say, assuming that an absolutist dispositional analysis is correct, that the dispositions of an ideal observer toward the given act would be the same *whether or not* he possessed that particular body of factual knowledge or any part of it. It follows, therefore, that in order to explain what we mean by "relevant knowledge," we should have to employ the very concept of ideal observer which we are attempting to define.

Fortunately, however, we do not seem to think that a person is to any extent disqualified as a moral judge merely because he possesses factual information which we take to be *superfluous*. Our difficulty would be overcome, therefore, if we were simply to stipulate that an ideal observer is *omniscient* with respect to non-ethical facts, and so far as I can see the term "omniscient," when employed in this way, is neither extravagant nor mysterious. We apparently believe not only that the "facts of the case" are relevant to the objective rightness or wrongness of a particular act, but also that there is no point at which we could be logically certain that further information about matters of fact (e.g., further information about the consequences of the act), would be irrelevant. A satisfactory ethical analysis must be so formulated, therefore, that no facts are irrelevant *by definition* to the rightness or wrongness of any particular act. And this is the intent of the term "omniscient," for to say that an ideal observer is omniscient is to insure that no limits are put on the kinds or the quality of factual information which are available to influence his ethically-significant reactions.

Since omniscience implies complete knowledge of the *past* as well as the future, it might be wondered whether we are not being unnecessarily generous in attributing omniscience to the ideal observer. And it might seem that one's answer to this question will depend on one's views concerning the factors which determine whether an act is in fact right or wrong. Thus a philosopher whose position is not purely utilitarian (i.e., teleological), but to some extent deontological, might be expected to take one position; he might be expected to believe that certain events prior to the performance of an act (e.g., the making of contracts) are directly relevant to the objective rightness or wrongness of an act, in which case he would naturally wish to stipulate that the knowledge of an ideal observer extend to the past as well as the future. The typical utilitarian, on the other hand, believing that the past events are relevant only in so far as they affect the future, might be expected to deny that an ideal observer must have any knowledge about events occurring prior to the act which is being judged.

It seems clear, however, that this difference of opinion would exist only if the utilitarian wished to define rightness and wrongness in such a way that the thesis of utilitarianism followed analytically from his definitions, and most contemporary utilitarians maintain, I believe, that the thesis of utilitarianism is a synthetic proposition. What they would wish to say, therefore, if they accepted an absolutist dispositional analysis of ethical statements, is that an ideal observer, although he *is* by definition fully cognizant of all past events, would nevertheless have precisely the same ethically-significant reactions to a present act if by definition he were *not* cognizant of past events. Thus there is no reason why the utilitarian and the deontologist must disagree at this point about the analysis of ethical statements.

2. *He Is Omnipercipient*

We sometimes disqualify ourselves as judges of certain ethical questions on the ground that we cannot satisfactorily imagine or visualize some of the relevant facts, and in general we regard one person as a better moral judge than another if, other things being equal, the one is better able to imagine or visualize the relevant facts. Practical moralists have often maintained that lack of imagination is responsible for many crimes, and some have suggested that our failure to treat strangers like brothers is in large part a result of our inability to imagine the joys and sorrows of strangers as vividly as those of our siblings. These facts seem to indicate that the ideal observer must be characterized by extraordinary powers of imagination.

The imaginal powers of the ideal observer, to be sure, are very closely related to his omniscience, and the word "omniscience" has sometimes been used to designate an unlimited imagination of perception. But however we may decide to use the word "omniscience," the important point is simply that it is not sufficient for an ideal observer to possess factual knowledge in a manner which will permit him to make true factual judgments. The ideal observer must be able, on the contrary, simultaneously to visualize all actual facts, and the consequences of all possible acts in any given situation, just as vividly as he would if he were actually perceiving them all. It is undoubtedly impossible for us to imagine the experience of a being capable of this kind of universal perception, but in making ethical decisions we sometimes attempt to visualize several alternative acts and their consequences in rapid succession, very much *as though* we wished our decision to be based on a simultaneous perception of the alternatives. And in view of this fact, and the others which I have mentioned, it seems necessary to attribute universal imagination to an ideal observer, thus guaranteeing that his ethically-significant reactions are forcefully and equitably stimulated.

3. *He Is Disinterested*

We sometimes disqualify ourselves as judges of certain ethical questions on the ground that we cannot make ourselves impartial, and we regard one person as a better moral judge than another if, other things being equal, the one is more impartial than the other. This suggests that one of the defining characteristics of an ideal observer must be complete impartiality. But it is difficult to define the term "impartial" in a manner which will not make our analysis circular or be otherwise inconsistent with our purpose.

It is important, in the first place, not to confuse the impartiality of an ideal observer with the *uniformity* of his ethically-significant reactions. We are likely to think of a judge who is impartial as a judge who arrives at similar decisions in similar cases, and we may be tempted, therefore, to define an ideal observer as an observer whose ethically-significant reactions to two acts would always be the same if the two acts were alike in all ethically-relevant respects. But this will not do. For even if we could find a way to avoid circularity in defining "ethically-relevant respects," the characteristic which we should have analyzed would be more appropriately called "consistency" than "impartiality." And the fact that it is not self-contradictory to say that a person (e.g., a magistrate) is consistently partial, indicates that consistency and impartiality are not identical characteristics. Consistency, as we shall later see, *is* one of the characteristics of an ideal observer. But to say that an ideal observer is consistent is to say something about the uniformity of his ethically-significant reactions, whereas to say that he is impartial is to say something about the factors which *influence* his reactions.

When we try, however, to specify the kinds of factors which do and do not influence the decisions of an impartial judge, it is difficult to avoid interpreting the term "impartial" too broadly. For impartiality is so closely associated with the capacity for correct moral judgment, that we are likely to conclude that a judge lacks impartiality only if we believe that his decisions have been influenced by factors which *pervert* them—by factors, that is to say, which cause them to be incorrect. And whatever the justification for such reasoning may be when we are evaluating a moral judge, our analysis would evidently be circular if the term "impartial," as applied to an ideal observer, involved some concealed reference to a standard of correct moral judgment. It is difficulties of this kind which may have led Broad to remark that a philosopher who attempts this kind of dispositional analysis "is on a very slippery slope, and scarcely ever manages to avoid inconsistency. In defining his ideal he nearly always unwittingly introduces some characteristic which is in fact ethical, and thus fails . . . to define ethical characteristics in completely non-ethical terms."[16]

It is also difficult, on the other hand, to

---

[16] *Five Types of Ethical Theory*, p. 263.

avoid interpreting the term "impartial" too narrowly. There is a familiar sense of this term, for example, which seems to be well represented by Bentham's maxim that every man should count for one and none for more than one. In this sense of the term a man would be impartial, in making a decision about his duty in a given situation, if he gave equal consideration to the welfare of each person who could be affected by his acts, regardless of how the person happened to be related to him.[17] And the maxim that we should treat all men as our brothers, has likewise been interpreted to imply a rule of impartiality in this sense—i.e., to imply that there are no special relationships which justify giving more consideration to one person than to another. But to analyze ethical statements by reference to this kind of impartiality, would rule out, by very definition of the words "right" and "wrong," the moral theory (held by Ross and others) that the rightness or wrongness of an act is determined in part by irreducible obligations arising directly from certain personal relationships; such an analysis would entail, for example, that there is never any moral justification, other things (including the value of the consequences) being equal, for making a decision which favors one's mother or friend or creditor at the expense of a greater benefit to someone else. Most philosophers would probably agree, however, that a correct analysis of ethical statements would not entail any particular conclusions concerning material questions of this sort. The solutions to such questions, they would agree, are synthetic and must not be prejudiced by our definitions.

Now it seems to me that a large part of what we mean when we say that an ideal judge is impartial, is that such a judge will not be influenced by interests of the kind which are commonly described as "particular"—interests, that is to say, which are directed toward a particular person or thing but not toward other persons or things of the same kind; and in so far as this is what we mean by "impartiality," we can define the term without falling into either of the errors which we have been considering. For to say that an ideal observer is not influenced by particular interests, is to attribute to him a certain psychological characteristic which does not refer, either explicitly or implicitly, to a moral standard. Nor does it logically entail, on the other hand, either that an ideal observer would react favorably, or that he would react unfavorably, to an act which benefits one person at the expense of a greater benefit to another.

The term "particular interest," to be sure, is a difficult one to define, and raises problems about the nature of particularity which are beyond the scope of this paper; but I think that for present purposes it is not unreasonable to pass over these problems. Since ethical judgments are concerned, directly or indirectly, with acts, let us use "x" to denote the performance of a certain act by a certain agent. Let us first draw a distinction between the "essentially general properties" of x and the "essentially particular properties" of x. The properties of x which are essentially particular are those properties which cannot be defined without the use of proper names (which we may understand, for present purposes, to include egocentric particulars such as "I," "here," "now," and "this"); thus one of the essentially particular properties of x might be its tendency to increase the happiness of the citizens of the U.S.A. All other properties are essentially general; thus one of the essentially general properties of x might be its tendency to increase happiness. We may then say that a person has a positive particular interest in x if (1) he desires x, (2) he believes that x has a certain essentially particular property P, and (3) he would not desire x, or would desire it less intensely, if, his other beliefs remain-

[17] Impartiality in this sense has sometimes been equated with distributive justice. *Vide*, e.g., Rashdall, *The Theory of Good and Evil*, Vol. I, Ch. VIII.

ing constant, he did not believe that x had this property P.

It may seem that this definition makes a variety of logical and ontological assumptions, some of which can be questioned. But I think that the intent of the definition is clear enough, and that the distinctions which it requires must be made, in one form or another, by any adequate logic and ontology. The definition is intended to represent the characteristic which we have in mind when we say that a moral judge who lacks impartiality is one who is tempted to "sacrifice principle"—i.e., to judge one act in a manner in which he would not wish to judge other acts which he thought to be of the same kind. And the definition proposes, in effect, that to say in this context that two acts are thought to be "of the same kind," is to say that they are thought to have the same essentially general properties. It is quite likely, of course, that we never actually believe that any two acts *do* have the same essentially general properties; it is for this reason, indeed, that we find it so easy to rationalize and "make exceptions" when judging acts which affect ourselves, our children, or our country. But this fact does not affect the usefulness of the definition, because part (3) is formulated hypothetically in the subjunctive mood: whether or not a person has a particular interest, is something to be decided by inferring, as best we can, how he *would* react *if* his beliefs were altered in certain ways.

It is important to observe that a person should not be said to have a particular interest in a certain act (x) merely because his interest in x is a result of his belief that x is related in a certain way to a *unique particular*. Let us suppose, for example, that Crito wanted Socrates to escape from prison because he thought that Socrates was the wisest man who would ever live. Let us suppose, for simplicity, that Crito did not want the wisest of men to be killed by his fellow human beings, and that this was his *sole* reason for wanting Socrates to escape. Now in this case it would surely be a mistake to maintain that Crito was neces-

sarily influenced by a particular interest, for this would mean, if particular interests are excluded from an ideal observer, that the ethically-significant reactions of an ideal observer could *never* be influenced by the fact that a particular person or thing has a certain distinguishing property. And it is evident, I assume, that the ethical relevance or irrelevance of a fact of this sort cannot be decided merely by analyzing the meaning of ethical terms.

The crucial question about Crito's interest, therefore, is not whether it is an interest in the fate of a unique particular (Socrates), but whether the properties of Socrates which arouse this interest are essentially particular, i.e., properties which cannot be analyzed without the use of proper names. Two of the essentially particular properties which Crito might have attributed to Socrates are (A) being the wisest friend of Crito, and (B) being the most effective gad-fly in Athens. In a terminology suggested by Broad (following McTaggart), we may say that each of these is an "exclusive description" of Socrates. But Crito's interest, we are supposing, is a result of his belief that Socrates has the essentially general property (C) being wiser than any other man. In Broad's terminology this third property might also be an exclusive description of Socrates. But unlike the other two, this property is a "sufficient description," i.e., one which "refers to no merely designated particulars, but consists wholly of universals."[18] We may say, therefore, that Crito is interested in Socrates because of a certain sufficient description which he attributes to Socrates. For this reason his interest is no particular; it is an interest, so to speak, which he would have in *any* person whom he thought to be the wisest of all men. Interests of this kind, therefore, even though they are directed toward a particular person or thing, do not tend to make us impartial in our moral judgments.

Assuming now, that we have found a

[18] Broad, *Examination of McTaggart's Philosophy*, Vol. 1, p. 178.

satisfactory definition of "particular interest," we must still decide how to use this term in our analysis. Shall we say that an ideal observer is completely lacking in particular interests? Or shall we say simply that his ethically-significant reactions are uninfluenced by such interests, leaving open the possibility, so far as our analysis is concerned, that such interests might be present but in some sense "suppressed"? At first thought the latter statement seems to be adequate to represent our concept of an impartial moral judge, for we often admire such a judge precisely because we believe that he does have particular interests but that his desire to be impartial has counteracted their influence. On further reflection it will be discovered, however, that we cannot explain what it means to say that a judge is uninfluenced by particular interests, except by reference, directly or indirectly, to the manner in which he would react *if* he had no particular interests. And this seems to imply that the first alternative is ultimately unavoidable if our analysis is to be complete. I think we must conclude, therefore, that an ideal observer is entirely lacking in particular interests—that he is, in this sense, *disinterested*.

4. *He Is Dispassionate*

The concept of impartiality cannot be exhaustively analyzed in terms of interests, for an impartial judge, as ordinarily conceived, is a judge whose decisions are unaffected not only by his interests, but also by his emotions. This suggests that an ideal observer must be defined as a person who is in some sense dispassionate as well as disinterested. It is possible, to be sure, that the supposed effects of an emotion on our ethically-significant reactions, are always the effects of an accompanying or constituent interest; and if this were proved to our satisfaction, our conception of an ideal observer might be somewhat simplified. For our present purpose, however, this is irrelevant so long as it is generally believed that

moral nearsightedness or blindness can be caused by the typically passional features of an emotion. We are searching for an analysis of ordinary ethical statements, and it is not to be expected that such an analysis will reflect all those distinctions, or just those distinctions, which would be required for an adequate system of psychology.

It is possible to construct a definition of the term "dispassionate" which will correspond, point by point, with our definition of the term "disinterested." Thus we can define a "particular emotion" as one which is directed toward an object only because the object is thought to have one or more essentially particular properties. And we can say that an ideal observer is dispassionate in the sense that he is incapable of experiencing emotions of this kind—such emotions as jealousy, self-love, personal hatred, and others which are directed towards particular individuals as such. At present this seems to me to be the most satisfactory way of defining the term "dispassionate" as applied to an ideal observer.

It would also be possible, however, to go a good deal further and to say that an ideal observer is incapable of experiencing any emotions at all, thus bringing our conception of an ideal observer closer to Kant's conception of a "purely rational being." There is no corresponding alternative open to us for the definition of "disinterested," because it seems unlikely that an ideal observer who had no interests at all would ever have any ethically-significant reactions. But the issue is not so clear with respect to emotions, especially if the moral datum, and hence the ethically-significant reactions of an ideal observer, can be defined in terms of a non-emotional, ostensibly objective, "demand quality."[19] And even those who believe that the moral datum is emotional, could maintain that an exception needs to be made only for moral approval and disapproval, or other emotions constituting the ethically-significant reactions of an ideal observer.

[19] *Vide supra*, Part I, Section 5.

It might be maintained, to be sure, that there are certain emotions which are essential to an ideal observer, not because they constitute his ethically-significant reactions, but because they will influence these reactions in certain ways. And it should be observed that if this is an error, it is not a *logical* error, for precisely how an ideal observer should be defined can be determined only by analyzing the meaning of ethical statements. In fact, provided that we base our analysis on a direct examination of the meaning of ethical statements, it would not even be a logical mistake to attribute *virtues* to an ideal observer—to say, for example, that he has love and compassion for all human beings. It is true that love and compassion, assuming that they are truly virtues, are virtues only because of their relationship to certain ethically-significant reactions of an ideal observer—to those reactions, namely, by reference to which the ethical term "virtue" is defined; but virtues may be attributed to an ideal observer without circularity, of course, provided that we do not have to justify their attribution by reference to the fact that they are virtues. If, for example, the Christian conception of God has influenced our conception of an ideal observer, then, if an absolutist dispositional analysis is correct, it has influenced the very meaning of ethical statements. And if philosophers from a non-Christian culture have a somewhat different conception of an ideal observer, this fact implies nothing more surprising than that ethical statements possess the kind of ambiguity which I have called "accidental." Thus my reason for believing that it is not necessary to attribute such virtues as love and compassion to an ideal observer, is not that it would be a logical mistake to do so, but simply that I am not inclined to think that a man is necessarily a better moral judge, however superior as a person, merely because he possesses such virtues. The value of love and compassion to a judge, considered solely as a judge, seems to lie in the qualities of knowledge and disinterestedness which are so closely related to them; and these two qualities, as we have seen, can be independently attributed to an ideal observer.

5. *He Is Consistent*

Consistency is ordinarily regarded as one of the characteristics of a good judge, and this fact suggests that an ideal observer must be described in part as a being whose ethically-significant reactions are perfectly consistent with one another. But there are obstacles, as we shall see, to defining the relevant kind of consistency in a manner which avoids circularity and yet makes consistency an independent characteristic of an ideal observer.

When we say that the ethical decisions of a judge in two different cases are consistent with one another—or, correspondingly, that in two different situations the ethically-significant reactions of an ideal observer are consistent—we are evidently not passing judgment on the logic of any actual process of thought. There is an obvious sense, to be sure, in which a judge might accept consistent or inconsistent *premises* or use consistent or inconsistent *arguments* (either in reaching his decisions or in attempting to justify them); but when we assert that the two decisions of the judge are *themselves* consistent with one another, we intend to say something about a particular relationship between the two ethical statements which express the judge's final conclusions, and nothing, unless perhaps by insinuation, about the judge's processes of thought.

But it is also clear that we do not intend to say merely that these two ethical statements are *logically* consistent with one another. For since the two statements express ethical decisions about two different cases, they necessarily refer to different acts or events, and of course *any* two self-consistent statements are logically consistent with one another if they refer to different acts or events. Thus the kind of consistency which we have in mind must be "stronger" than logical consistency: we must mean to say that it is in some sense *possible* that the two statements are both true, but not merely that it is *logically* possible.

If this is so, however, the consistency or inconsistency of two ethical decisions must depend on the relationship of these decisions to certain general ethical principles which are conceived as restricting the "possible" combinations of ethical statements. And this conclusion is supported, I believe, by examination of the kind of reasoning which actually leads us to conclude that two decisions are consistent or inconsistent with one another. We might assert, for example, that a moral judge is inconsistent because in one case he decided in favor of act x rather than x', whereas in another case he decided in favor of y rather than y'; and if we assert this, an analysis of our reasoning would probably show that we are assuming that it is possible for x to be the right act only if a certain ethical principle (P) is true, whereas it is possible for y to be the right act only if P is false.[20] Our judgment that the two decisions are inconsistent, therefore, is based on the assumption that there is no *other* valid ethical principle (a certain principle Q, for example) which could in some way take precedence over P in one of the two cases.[21] We are not, to be sure, committing ourselves either to the belief that P is true or to the belief that P is false. But we *are* assuming that the facts of the two cases are not different in some respect which is ethically crucial. And to assume even this is to presuppose at least one ethical proposition, namely, that there is no valid ethical prin-

ciple (e.g., Q) which, together with P, could be used to justify *both* decisions.

I think we must conclude, therefore, that whenever we assert that the decisions of a moral judge in two different cases are consistent with one another, we are presupposing a certain amount of ethical knowledge. And this implies that our analysis would be circular if we made consistency of this kind one of the defining characteristics of an ideal observer.

There is, however, a much more limited kind of consistency which we might wish to attribute to an ideal observer. For if we agree that his ethically-significant reactions are stimulated by his imagination of a possible act, then, since an act may be imagined at any number of different times, there is nothing in our analysis up to this point which would logically require that an ideal observer always react in the same way even when he imagines one *particular* act (i.e., an act occurring at a particular time and place and hence having a certain particular set of alternatives). And if this appears to be a deficiency in our analysis, we could easily correct it by attributing a limited consistency to an ideal observer: we could define him, in part, as a being whose ethically-significant reactions to any particular act would always be exactly similar.

If we decide to do this, however, it is important to notice that consistency, when interpreted in this way, has a status very different from that of omniscience, disinterestedness, and the other defining characteristics of an ideal observer which we have so far considered. For according to the kind of absolutist analysis which we have been examining, ethical statements, as we have previously observed, are statements which depend for their truth or falsity on the existence of certain psychological laws; and if ethical statements are ever true, they are true only because we have defined an ideal observer in such a way that, in virtue of the relevant psychological laws, *any* ideal observer would react in the same way to a particular act. Thus in attributing om-

---

[20] We might reason, for example, that x could be right only if we have a special obligation toward those who have suffered for our sake, whereas y could be right only if we do *not* have such an obligation. In some cases, of course, the principle P might itself be a complex conjunction of ethical principles.

[21] There are at least two kinds of cases in which a principle Q might be said to "take precedence over" a principle P: (1) Cases in which P and Q are conflicting principles, each representing a "claim" against the agent, and (2) cases in which P is simply an incomplete statement of a more completely qualified principle, Q.

niscience, disinterestedness, and other such characteristics to an ideal observer, we are doing something of crucial importance for the kind of analysis which we are considering: we are eliminating from the personality of the ideal observer, so to speak, various factors which actually cause certain people to differ in their ethically-significant reactions from other people—such factors, for example, as selfish desires and ignorance of the facts of the case. And assuming that ethical statements *are* sometimes true, and absolutist dispositional analysis can be adequate only if such factors are completely eliminated from the personality of an ideal observer.

The characteristic of consistency, however, unlike omniscience, disinterestedness, and the others which we have discussed, does not eliminate some particular source of disagreement in ethical reactions. It is, on the contrary, a *consequence* of eliminating such disagreement, since any factor which could cause two different ideal observers to react in different ways to a particular act, could also cause one and the same ideal observer to react in different ways at different times. And this means, to put the matter bluntly, that if it is necessary to attribute consistency to an ideal observer in order to insure that he is psychologically incapable of reacting to the same act in different ways at different times, then we have simply failed to find all the *other* characteristics of an ideal observer which are necessary for the formulation of an adequate analysis. Thus an ideal observer will indeed be consistent if an adequate dispositional analysis can be formulated; but his consistency will be a derivative characteristic—a consequence of his other characteristics together with certain psychological laws.

6. *In Other Respects He Is Normal*

An examination of the procedures by which we attempt to decide moral questions, reveals that there are a great many conditions which we recognize, though not always explicitly, to be favorable or unfavorable for making valid moral judgments. Mild bodily exercise such as walking, the presence of other people trying to make similar decisions, and certain kinds of esthetic stimuli, have all been regarded by some people as favorable conditions, whereas mental fatigue, distracting sensory stimuli, and lack of experience, are generally regarded as unfavorable. It seems likely, however, that our analysis will take all these special conditions into account if we attribute such general characteristics as omniscience and disinterestedness to an ideal observer.

It seems fairly clear, on the other hand, that no analysis in terms solely of such general, and highly ideal, characteristics, could be fully adequate to the meaning of ethical statements. For however ideal some of his characteristics may be, an ideal observer is, after all, a *person;* and whatever may be true of the future, our conception of the personality of an ideal observer has not yet undergone the refining processes which have enabled theologians, apparently with clear conscience, to employ the term "person" in exceedingly abstract ways. Most of us, indeed, can be said to have a conception of an ideal observer only in the sense that the characteristics of such a person are implicit in the procedures by which we compare and evaluate moral judges, and it seems doubtful, therefore, that an ideal observer can be said to lack any of the determinable properties of human beings.

The determinate properties of an ideal observer, however, except for the ideal characteristics which we have so far discussed, are apparently not capable of precise definition. We may employ the customary linguistic device, to be sure, and say that the properties of an ideal observer cannot vary beyond the limits of "normality," but there are a number of reasons why it does not seem to be possible to define these limits satisfactorily. It is evident, for example, that normality is a gestalt concept, and that a certain trait which in abstraction might properly be called abnormal, could nevertheless contribute to a total personality which falls within the bounds of normality. And this fact by itself is sufficient to destroy any hope of defining the term "normal" by continuing to add specific characteristics to the ones which we have already attributed to an ideal observer. This difficulty, however, and the others which prevent us from formulating a satisfactory definition of "normal," are practical rather than theoretical, and they do not tend in the slightest degree to disprove the thesis that ethical statements are statements about an ideal observer and his ethically-significant reactions. There are analogous difficulties, moreover, in formulating a dispositional analysis of the statement "This is (really) yellow"; and I have yet to find any convincing reason, indeed, for believing that "yellow" can be defined dispositionally although "right" cannot.

'Good,' 'Right,' 'Ought,' 'Bad'

BRAND BLANSHARD

1. The attempt of analysts to find a meaning for 'good' which should be at once recognizable as its major meaning and also precise has led to such a variety of conflicting definitions that we were moved in the last chapter to try another approach. We would study how values arose in human experience and how they are connected with impulse and desire. Such a study might reveal features in goodness which were likely to elude direct analysis, but which analysis might confirm when once suggested. Has anything of the sort come to light?

It has. As was gradually disclosed in this study, 'good' is not the name of a simple abstraction, but is, on the contrary, a term with a complex meaning that has long roots in human nature and its history. It is a term like 'life' and 'mind', which are clear enough for practical purposes without examination, but whose definition, once it is attempted, takes us far. 'Good' has the meaning it does because we are the sort of beings we are. Human nature *is* essentially a set of activities directed toward ends, and human life is a striving toward these ends. As this striving, beginning in impulse, passes on into desire, it comes to have some awareness of its ends, but it never knows them wholly. Good is relative to this process of seeking. Only that would be good altogether which wholly satisfied by wholly fulfilling this end-seeking process. Anything else is good in the degree in which it thus fulfils and satisfies.

Before asking where this carries us by way of implications, let us see where it places us among the theories of the day. It requires us to take a middle course in controversies about the objectivity of goodness and its naturalness. As regards objectivity, it would agree with the emotivist that goodness does not belong to things in complete independence of attitudes and feelings about them; a thing is good because, and in so far as, it fulfils and satisfies. On the other hand, whether it does or would fulfil and satisfy is an objective fact about it, and the stress we have laid on fulfilment makes this a fundamentally different fact from that of merely being liked. As regards naturalism the theory again steers a middle course. The non-natural quality of goodness, even fittingness as a non-natural character, both of which have proved so hard for naturalists to detect, are no longer required. Whether an object does in fact fulfil and satisfy is something that can be determined without going outside nature as we conceive it. But then on the other hand we do not conceive human nature as naturalists commonly do. It is so thoroughly teleological that it cannot be understood apart from what it is seeking to become. What is good, then, in the sense of what would wholly fulfil and satisfy, is not to be determined by an empirical study of what men actually like, desire, or approve. That is evidence, to be sure; whatever does in fact fulfil and satisfy is good so far; but human desires, and there-

Reprinted with permission of The Macmillan Company from *Reason and Goodness* by Brand Blanshard. © by George Allen & Unwin, Ltd. 1961.

fore human good, run immeasurably beyond this. No such good is ever final.

2. Neither the analytic nor the genetic path to goodness is sufficient by itself. Any account of it that is to be acceptable, must be one upon which the two paths converge. The ascetic, reflecting fastidiously on the quality of his yearnings, may conclude that the good life lies in the repression of all 'animal impulse', but human nature will correct his theory by expunging him and his kind. He might say that extinction is not refutation, which is true enough. But most men would think, and rightly I suspect, that if a course of life is such as to invite extinction, there must be something wrong with the intuition that sponsors it. A proposal regarding the good which elicits a veto from human nature is doomed. On the other hand, goods recommended as 'natural' are themselves many and conflicting. The suggestion has been made, for example, that the ethical struggle is simply a continuation of the biological struggle, and that whoever is victor in that struggle, however 'red in tooth and claw', is best. It is to the credit of Huxley that when called upon to endorse the suggestion, he replied that men's ordinary sense of what 'good' meant put it out of court. Claimants to the role of natural must submit themselves, like others, to the judgment of this inner tribunal. Will our own theory of goodness pass its scrutiny?

The only way to tell is to bring cases before it and see. Take any case you will of experience regarded as intrinsically good, and ask yourself whether its goodness does not turn on two facts about it—first that it brings satisfaction in the form of some degree of pleasure, and second that it fulfils a want. Try it with any experience of love, of friendship, of intellectual insight, of sex, of beauty, of victory in contest, of success in skill or creation. Our suggestion is that both these characters, and only these, will be invariably there.

The most obvious objections to such an account are perhaps (1) that experience may be good when pleasure is absent, (2) that it may again be good when fulfilment is absent, and (3) that even when both are present, this does not give us what we *mean* by 'good'.

3. (1) We often call experiences valuable when they are not obviously pleasant. The bearing of suffering, a hard football game, the dangerous ascent of a mountain, the throes of examination, the vigil of the doctor with a patient critically ill, the personal or material loss that leaves one stronger, the mere cold bath of a cold morning—are not these good? But how could anyone call them pleasant?

It is true that all of these may plainly be goods, in the sense of instrumental goods. And no one who is not ready to take foul weather with fair in trying to reach ulterior ends is likely to reach them at all. But it is one thing to face pain and suffering hardily in the interest of such an end, and quite another thing to welcome them as goods in themselves. As for the experiences just mentioned: the examination and the doctor's vigil are cases of strain accepted as unavoidable means to a much desired result. The football game, the ascent of the mountain, and the cold bath are certainly not cases of unmixed pain; there are disagreeable elements in them, but also exhilaration, without which (or the consequences) the experiences would surely not be sought. As for the others, suffering and the shock of loss are not goods in themselves, however useful they may be in steeling one against the future. When people deliberately inflict pain on themselves, they generally do it as a means to an end perhaps imperfectly realized, such as the approval of a Deity or their own or others' admiration; to seek suffering for its own sake would be thought the sign of a morbid and disordered mind.

It may be said that experience may be good when, though not positively painful, its affective quality is merely neutral. But this is questionable. We saw long ago in considering the Stoics and Mill that with the loss of power to take satisfaction in the exercise of a faculty there goes also the sense that the exercise is worth maintaining. The total loss of this power is, to be sure, a rare affliction. Normally there is a mild satisfaction attending even the most prosaic activities of common life; and few people, however unhappy they call themselves, would prefer to be dead than alive. But if satisfaction does vanish completely from these activities, an apathy supervenes that, far from being the greatest of goods, as the Stoics hoped, is merely grey and insipid. 'All values are vain, unless we can feel, as well as see, their value. Knowledge without feeling is like an electric motor without current.'[1]

4. (2) Are there not valued experiences that, conversely, are pleasant without fulfilling any sort of want? Someone tells me a funny story, and I laugh; but I was not hungering for his funny story. Mozart hears the church bells at three, and takes an instant delight in them, but he could hardly have wanted them before first hearing them. I turn a corner on a mountain drive, and am confronted with a glorious sunset; but it is something I neither expected nor desired.

The objection is sound if it means that experiences found good are not always the object of preceding desires. Definite desire must draw its material from satisfied impulse, and impulse is at first exploratory and without definite guidance. But we are not straining language when we say that a want or need may exist without being in active and conscious exercise. Mozart may have a disposition to notice and respond to musical sounds before he hears them, and if he hears them with exceptional delight, we take that as evidence of the disposition. If he had been deaf, or tone-deaf, or as indisposed to respond to such things as the cow in the neighbouring field, he would have felt no interest in the bells and found no value in listening to them. It was be-

cause he did have a faculty and disposition, even though previously unawakened, that he responded as he did. So of our response to the humorous story and to the sunset at the turn of the road. If we lacked a sense of humour or a sense of beauty, such things would fall on deaf ears and blind eyes. These senses need not be in perpetual exercise. But unless they were there, the funniest of stories and the most gorgeous of sunsets would elicit nothing from us.

It may be said that at this rate every response will be the sign of a capacity and a disposition, and hence that no response will give more indication of their presence than another. But this latter conclusion does not follow. The sense of humour or of beauty is a matter of degree, so that one person's response to a given stimulus will be much more complete than another's. If our theory is true, we should expect that the person who could respond more completely would find more value in his response than a person of feeble sensibility. This, so far as we can tell, is just what happens.[2]

5. (3) It may be objected, again, that satisfaction and fulfilment may both be present in an experience and yet not give what we *mean* by calling it good. The proof is (a) that if this is really what we mean, then, regarding anything that we do not believe to possess these characters, we should be contradicting ourselves in calling it good, whereas in fact we should not; and (b) that, regarding an experience which we do know to be satisfactory and fulfilling, we can still ask with meaning whether it is good, whereas this would be impossible if having these characters was all we meant by good.

(a) The word 'good' has many meanings; Dr. Ewing has usefully distinguished ten of them.[3] And if a person says that there is nothing self-contradictory in calling the suffering of a serious illness a good thing, he may of course be right; such

---

[1] F. L. Lucas, *Literature and Psychology*, 261.

[2] See also below, Sec. 19.
[3] In *The Definition of Good*, Ch. 4.

suffering may be far from fulfilling or satisfying, and may still be *instrumentally*
good; to say this is no contradiction. But
that does not show that our definition is
wrong. All it shows is that there are other
senses of the word. The goodness we are
talking about is that which belongs to an
experience thought worth having in itself.
And if we are clear regarding such an experience as suffering that it neither fulfils
any impulse or demand of our nature nor
carries with it any feeling of satisfaction,
could we consistently ascribe to it this kind
of goodness? I do not think we could. In
calling it so we *should* be contradicting
our own belief. Of course we may use the
word without realizing quite what we mean
by it, so that when someone proposes this
meaning, our first impulse is to reject it.
But if when he goes on to ask whether we
should really apply the word where these
characters are seen to be absent, we have
to say No; we could not, consistently with
our meaning, say anything else. This objection to our definition turns into evidence in
its favour.

(b) Our analysis of goodness would
probably be called a naturalistic analysis.
As such, is it not open to the famous objection by which G. E. Moore dismissed all
naturalistic notions of goodness? Take any
such definition you will, said Moore—
length and breadth of life, being pleasant,
being the object of desire, being what we
desire to desire, or any other; could you
not meaningfully ask regarding something
known to have these qualities whether it is
good? If the question is meaningful at all,
your definition must be wrong. For if having the property in question is what 'good'
means, and you know the object to have it,
then you know the answer already, and to
ask what it is would be pointless. If 'good'
means pleasant, for example, you could not
honestly ask if pleasure was good, for that
would be asking whether pleasure is pleasant, which nobody in his senses would ask.
The fact that we *can* meaningfully ask
whether pleasure is good shows that 'good'

cannot *mean* merely pleasant. Similarly the
fact that we can meaningfully ask whether
that which fulfils and satisfies is good
shows that 'good' does not *mean* having of
these properties. That is the objection.

Now I think Moore's argument does
dispose of most naturalistic definitions of
'good'. But, as Mr. Frankena has shown,[4]
to say before examination that it disposes
of all of them is to beg the question. The
only way to tell whether a proposed definition will fit your meaning is to try it. And
we are quite ready to face this test. Take
any experience you wish that at once fulfils
a drive of human nature and brings pleasure or happiness with it, ask about this experience whether it is intrinsically worth
having, and we suggest that you have the
answer already. The experiences you would
naturally think of as meeting the requirements—the experiences of beauty, friendship, sex, play, creation, knowledge—are
those about which it is least possible to
have any genuine question as to their goodness. If these things are not good, what in
the world is?

A reader may protest, however, that he
does genuinely doubt whether they are
good. This may show indeed that we have
failed to catch the true meaning of the
term as he uses it. But it may equally show
something else. It may show simply that his
meaning is so indefinite that any crystalli-
zation of it into words would strike him as
failing to equate with what he had in
mind. If this is the case, his rejection of our
proposed meaning has no significance, for
he would reject any other definite suggestion with equal promptitude. A definition
of good is not to be dismissed merely because it fails to comport with a mental
cloud. One may argue, to be sure, that
good is indefinable not, as Moore believed,
because it is simple and unanalysable, but
because it is so amorphous and complex.
The term may be used to focus upon an
object a composite but nebulous mass of

[4] W. K. Frankena, 'The Naturalistic Fallacy',
Mind, Vol. 48 (1939), 473.

impulses, affects, emotions, and ideas of which no possible verbal formula would be admitted to give the equivalent. Press such reflections home, and one will soon be saying that no two people ever use the word with the same meaning, nor the same person twice. In a sense that is true. But unless we could go beyond this anarchy to some community of meaning, the business of dictionaries, of science, and indeed of ordinary intercourse would be at an end. No definition of 'good' will fit exactly the shifting wracks of meaning that float through our minds as we use it. All we claim for what we have proposed is that it gives the minimal common character that we assign to an experience in calling it worth while.

6. Without stopping to discuss the many less obvious difficulties, let us go on to ask why our theory commits us to regarding some other ethical terms. Granting for the moment, that an experience is good which satisfies and fulfils, what light does this throw on the meaning of 'right'? Our answer can be predicted readily enough. We have argued that there is no means for determining the right apart from the good. If one is to defend an action as right, one must do so by showing what it entails; and for us this means showing that it tends to bring into being as much good as any alternative. In the light of what we have seen about good, this means in turn that an action is right if, and only if, it tends to bring into being as much experience that is at once satisfying and fulfilling as any alternative action.

This somewhat awkward way of putting the case is required by certain facts of a technical kind. (a) Why not simply say that the right act is that which produces the *most* good? Because it is possible that the largest good should be attainable in several different ways. In that case to speak of *the* right act would be misleading, for any one of several acts would be right. We must therefore say that an act is right if it

tends to produce *not less than* the greatest good attainable.

(b) But why 'tends' to produce? Why not say simply 'produces'? Because in some cases this would have consequences that no one would care to accept. A child becomes suddenly ill and the anxious mother goes to the medicine closet for a remedy she has found effective in such cases. But a pharmacist has confused the labels, and she inadvertently gives the child a medicine that causes its death. Should we appraise the rightness or wrongness of her action here by its actual consequences? That is certainly not what we actually do. We appraise actions as right and wrong, not in virtue of their actual consequences, but in virtue of the consequences which we conceive that actions done in these circumstances and with this intention would normally produce. Hence the awkward phrase 'tends to produce'.

(c) Again, we have said, 'an action *is right if, and only if*, it tends', etc.; why not say 'rightness *means*' so-and-so? Because there has been a protracted and somewhat unprofitable controversy over whether productivity of good is what rightness actually means or whether it is merely a 'right-making characteristic'; and I should prefer at the moment not to get involved in the controversy. If a dogmatic answer to the question were called for, I should say that such productivity is not the meaning of right in the sense that it is the plain man's explicit meaning; but then I suspect that he has no sharply definite meaning in mind at all, and that this sense comports as well as any other with what he means.

Finally (d) we have spoken of our actions *bringing into being* certain goods or experiences; why not simply *producing* good consequences? There is generally no harm in saying this; but it has a danger that is perhaps worth averting. Not all the goods by which we appraise an action are necessarily results that follow it in time. Some of them may be states of mind, or relations between these, which are brought into being by the action but are simultaneous with it. The state of mind in which an act of justice, generosity, or loyalty to truth is done may itself be of value.

7. A right act, then, is one that tends to bring into being at least as much in the way of satisfying and fulfilling experience as would any available alternative. But experience for whom? For me, or you, or some third party? We can only answer that from the point of view of value, this query is irrelevant. We are often called upon, of course, to choose between producing goods for ourselves and goods for others, but the choice is in principle the same as in choosing between goods of our own. If what makes anything good is the fulfilment and satisfaction of impulse-desire, and a given experience of my neighbour's performs this office as well as one of my own, it is as good as my own, and in the reckoning of rights and duties must count as equal to it. Goodness is no respecter of persons, only of the potentialities of persons. If my neighbour's capacities are such as to carry him further than mine toward a rich and satisfying life, his life is more significant, more important, than mine. If the village fathers in Stratford had known what they had in a certain boy named William, outwardly very much like the Thomas, Richard, and Henry that sat on the benches beside him, and, knowing what they had, had been as ready to make of him a road-cleaner or a chimney-sweep as any of the others, they would have been acting neither in his interests, nor their own, nor the community's. Each of us is a quiverful of assorted arrows of desire. In general design these arrows are alike in all of us; we all undoubtedly have desires to know and love, to make things, to dominate, to be admired. But in some of us certain arrows are very long and others very short; in others these lengths are reversed; and the chances are that in no two of us is the combination of longs and shorts exactly the

same. But such as they are, we always shoot them at infinity. Each man blunders along after the good that his powers make possible for him, not knowing quite what these are, or how far they will carry him. Nevertheless, it is his potentiality of good that is the ground of his rights. We owe him duties because he has wants that our action may frustrate or fulfill. We do not feel called upon to provide educational facilities for our cows and horses, because they could get no good from them if we did. But if, when we are providing such things, we ignore deliberately the possibilities of any youth, however obscure, we are plainly failing in our duty. We may not be able to provide for all; we may have to leave some out entirely; there are no rights independent of circumstances. But we must at least *consider* the claims of all. I am not clear what is meant by the sacredness of human life as such, and should think the maintenance of hopeless imbeciles at the expense of normal persons a dubious practice morally. But there can be no doubt of the immorality of allowing people to come into existence and then denying the facts of their possibility and desire, and the right to consideration based on these facts. The dignity of man rests as much on what he might be as on what he is.

There may be readers disposed to complain that we have talked too much of non-moral goods, to the neglect of specifically ethical ones. But all goods are ethical goods. Any value or disvalue which, by being thrown into the scale, could affect a decision on right or wrong is of ethical moment. The good whose production makes an act right may be of any kind. The question whether to award a scholarship to X or Y is a moral problem, even though the capacities considered are intellectual only. The question whether, in one's will, one should leave money toward an art gallery, a college, or a playing field, is as truly a moral problem as the question whether one should tell a lie or break a promise. A question becomes a moral question at the moment when competing values, of any kind whatever, enter upon the scene.

8. To this account of the rightness of actions, and to all accounts that derive the right from the good, there is a formidable objection, which may as well be faced now. The rule we have proposed is the simple and sweeping one: So act as to bring about the greatest good. This rule, if valid at all, should be valid without exceptions, for if here and there it guided us wrongly, how could we rely on it anywhere? Now the deontologists hold that it does have exceptions.[5] They hold that the rule of the greatest good sometimes requires of us actions that would by general agreement be wrong. The two types of case most commonly adduced are those of promises and punishment.

Suppose I have borrowed some money from A, who is a man of means, and promised to return it on the first of the month. On that day, with the money in my pocket, I start out for A's house to repay him. I meet on the way a friend B, who is badly in need of help. I have the money in my pocket that would give him the help he needs. Should I give it to him? I call to mind my principle of producing the greatest good. Is it not probable that a greater good would be produced by my giving the money to the man in need than to my creditor who would not miss it? And yet is it not perfectly clear that men generally would have no patience with me if in this case I were to act on that principle? They would say that if I promised to pay, my first obligation was to keep my promise, not to give the money away, even to someone who would get more good out of it than my creditor. My obligation is not to produce the greatest good but to honour my engagement.

Now of course we agree with the deontologists that in such a case one ought

[5] For a statement and initial criticism of the deontologists' view, see Chapter VI above.

normally to keep the promise. We agree further that if an ethical theory is to be taken seriously, it must agree with ordinary responsible judgment about what is right and wrong, since what it is looking for is the ground on which that judgment is implicitly based. Where we cannot agree is in saying that keeping the promise in such cases would break the rule of the greatest good. We admit that it seems to do so. But we should hold that even in cases like this the reason for keeping the promise is the greater good involved in it.

Let us note, to begin with, that the deontologists themselves do not hold that one should keep one's promise though the heavens fall. If one's child has fallen suddenly ill, and can be saved only by an expensive prescription, and for this prescription the only available money is what was meant for one's creditor, they would agree that one should break one's promise and save one's child. Why? Because the good achieved by this course would outweigh the obligation to keep the promise. Yet the curious thing is that what is outweighed by this good is declared itself not to be a good at all; the obligation to keep my promise is not based on any good whatever that is entailed by such action. In throwing the prospective courses into the scales, I have on one side a foreseen good, on the other the keeping of a promise in which there is declared to be no good, but which is obligatory none the less. There is something strange about such a situation. Must there not be some good about keeping the promise that can be compared with, and in extreme cases outweighed by, the good of not keeping it?

9. Now for keeping an inconvenient promise there are many reasons which we do not commonly think of in the act of keeping it, but which come to light with a moment's thought. Most of them take the form of the evils we should bring about by not keeping it. In this case we should forfeit the confidence of our creditor; we should not only disappoint him, but leave

ourselves deeper in difficulty; we should encourage in ourselves an insidious habit which makes the meeting of obligations harder; above all, perhaps, we should lower in some measure the general confidence in promises—a serious matter, since the commerce of men with each other would grind to a stop if such confidence were destroyed. We all know these arguments. And yet they leave us dissatisfied. It does not seem difficult to meet them one by one by inventing special cases in which the breaking of a promise would involve none of these evils, while we should insist nevertheless on its being kept. Suppose the debt were a secret one; then public confidence would not be lowered by our default. Suppose we knew that our creditor had quite forgotten both loan and promise; then he would not be disappointed. Suppose we broke the promise after explicit calculation of the goods involved on both sides; then we need not worry about bad habits, for any habit we have initiated is a good one. These arguments all seem relevant. Yet they leave us cold. We watch the evils involved in promise-breaking disappearing one by one from before our eyes, and if the greatest good theory is right, we ought to find ourselves ready at the end to acclaim the promise-breaker and go ourselves and do likewise. But the fact is that we do not. We feel that there is something sophistical about this whole line of argument, and that in spite of all the evidence it adduces that we could break the promise with no ill results, we ought to keep it just the same.

10. Why is this? It is because we feel that in the rule of promise-keeping as such there is something of value that would be compromised by light-hearted violations of it, and that it is somehow illegitimate to consider the advantages and disadvantages in the particular case apart from the practice of which it is an instance. A long succession of moralists have obviously been moved by this conviction. Plato held that we cannot pass upon the rightness of a par-ticular act without taking into account the frame of life to which it belongs. Kant went so far as to hold that in considering whether to break a promise, the principle was all-important; to break a promise—any promise—was to subscribe to the view that promises could be broken at will, which was virtually to deny that there were such things at all. Joseph argues that in keeping a promise there is a good which deontologists fail to recognize, a good that lies in acting in accordance with the rule, and ultimately in the 'pattern of life' to which the rule itself belongs. These moralists are clinging tenaciously to an element in common thought that is clearly present and important. But the question is whether one can do justice to the importance of rules while still adhering to the principle of the greatest good.

I think one can. But to do so one must penetrate into the kind of choice which the plain man conceives himself as making in such a case. In deciding whether to keep a promise, he is not choosing between two particular acts whose particular effects provide the whole ground of choice between them. He is deciding whether a *kind* of conduct, a public practice, shall be maintained, and he feels that if he decided to break it, he would be voting against the practice itself, which he is most reluctant to do. He is reluctant because he feels that the practice is bound up in a vital way with his order of life, and that to undermine it would involve dimly-seen but far-reaching and disastrous consequences. In short, he refuses to consider the value of keeping this particular promise without considering the value of the practice of which it is an example. Is this mere confusion on his part?

11. That it is really not confusion has been ably argued by Mr. Rawls.[6] He points out that rules may be conceived in two very different ways. On the one hand a rule may be a summary of what has been

[6] John Rawls, 'Two Concepts of Rules', *Philosophical Review*, Vol. 64 (1955), 3–32.

decided in cases of a certain kind. When the community has considered the matter of promises, it has generally found keeping them to have better results than breaking them, and the rule records this verdict. If we do conceive the rule in this way, we may approach our particular problem with a free mind, and consider the case on its merits. We may find that the advantages lie where the rules would lead us to expect, and then we shall conform to it; or we may find that they lie on the other side, and then there is no call to conform to it, for the case is evidently one of the exceptions to which the rule does not apply. Now when the utilitarian is charged with holding lightly the rule of keeping promises, it is this statistical conception of rules that is attributed to him. And if this is all there is to a rule, the charge is true.

But it has too seldom been noticed, says Professor Rawls, that there is at work in our minds a very different idea of what a rule is. A rule may *define a practice*. In some very important areas of conduct, we can see that if everyone were to act on independent calculation, it would be impossible for anyone to count on how others would act, and the result would be a general uncertainty amounting perhaps to chaos. 'As an alternative one realizes that what is required is the establishment of a practice, the specification of a new form of activity; and from this one sees that a practice necessarily involves the abdication of full liberty to act on utilitarian and prudential grounds.'[7] One cannot even conceive correctly what keeping a promise is unless one sees it as part of a wider convention. To make a promise is to accept this convention; it is to say that one will *not* decide whether to keep the promise by appeals to its special effects in this case, but will be bound by the over-riding commitment. To decide the particular case as if it stood alone is to break this commitment; and to break the commitment is to strike at one of the main strands that bind society together.

For if I claim the privilege of deciding this case on its isolated merits, I must in mere consistency grant the same privilege to others, and their acceptance of that privilege would be disastrous. What is at stake is not merely the value of my act, but the value of the practice of which that act is a part.

12. One may illustrate this notion of a rule as a practice by analogy to a game.[8] Outside the game of baseball, a man may do something that looks very like sliding for a base, 'taking a called strike', or hitting a home run. But he is not really doing so. For these performances are by definition parts of a game and cannot occur except as the game is being played. And just as it is unreasonable for a man who hits a tennis ball a long way with a broomstick to claim that he has hit a home run, so it is unreasonable for a man who is playing the game to claim the freedom of the man who is not. By undertaking to play at all, he has given up that freedom and accepted the rules of the game. If after hitting a home run he decided that in this case it was best, all consequences considered, not to run the bases, his teammates would regard him not as a philosopher but as an idiot, and the umpire would quite rightly call him out. Now when we make a promise, we enter, so to speak, into a social game, of which promise-keeping is one of the rules. We cannot play that game and also choose whenever we wish *not* to play it, to pretend that we are as free to keep a promise or not as we are to take, or not to take, our umbrella. If we and others claimed that sort of freedom, the game would be at an end, which means that the sort of community we know would be at an end.

Of course we may decide not to play at all. If the player who has hit the home run sees that his small son in the stands is about to fall over the railing, he may decide to run to his aid rather than to run the bases. But that is not breaking a particular rule; it is temporarily forsaking the

---

[7] *Op. cit.*, 24.

[8] *Op. cit.*, 25.

game itself in the interest of what seems more important. That is what we do when we break a promise in the interest of some great alternative good. If, having promised to repay a debt, I find that if I repay it I shall not have the wherewithal to save the life of my child, I act of course in the child's interest. But that is not to treat keeping my promise as I would the taking of my umbrella. I am ready to break with the whole convention so far as it stands in the way of my doing this, or if one prefers, I am interpreting the convention itself as containing these built-in exceptions, and am quite willing that everyone else should interpret it that way also.

13. We said that when deontologists attacked the maxim of the greatest good, their most telling arguments were based on promises and punishment. We have considered promises. We shall delay over punishment only long enough to say that we should deal with it in the same way. The trump card is usually the judge who is tempted at a time of social strain to convict an innocent man for the sake of maintaining order in the community. It is argued that action in line with the greatest good would call for conviction of the innocent man, and that this is outrageous. Outrageous it certainly is. The judge is plainly not free to take this line, but the question is, Why not? Our answer is that the judgment of a court is not like taking an umbrella; it does not stand alone; by definition it is performed under rigid conditions. The court has been expressly appointed, and has given its pledge, to render judgment in accord with the evidence only, rejecting all appeals to expedience or advantage; to act otherwise in this case would betray the judicial system as a whole and indeed the wider official system of which this is a part. That was why the French people took the Dreyfus conviction so seriously, and why they were generally thought to be right in so doing. They felt by a sound instinct that what was at stake was more than the fate of a single officer,

more even than the reputation of the high command; it was the integrity of France on its official side.

We hold, then, that the maxim of the greatest good still stands. The cases adduced to overthrow it are cases out of context, and usually cases whose very description serves to reveal the missing context. When this is taken into account, the calculation that seemed to make for an anarchic looseness is seen to support that loyalty to principle which common sense so plainly feels. This does not mean that we recognize two different and independent ways of justifying an action, one by bringing it under a rule, and another by appealing to the good involved. We recognize only one way, the latter. But if we are to do justice to actual thought, we must take some actions as embodying practices which go beyond them, and which must be accepted or rejected as wholes.

14. We have been discussing what makes an action right, and we have implied from time to time that if we see an action to be right, it is our *duty* to do it. We must now ask what is meant by calling an action our duty. In the light of what has been said we can exclude some common suggestions. Duty is not a divine command, at least in essence, since it binds the atheist, who does not recognize a divine being, in exactly the same way as it binds the devotee. It is not a categorical imperative if that means that its commands have no regard to consequences or desires. Is it then what Kant described as a hypothetical imperative? To say so has often been supposed inconsistent with the rigour of duty. 'If you want health, then have a care for diet and exercise'; 'if you want friends, be considerate of others'. But then suppose you are the sort of eccentric who is indifferent to health and friendship; does not that mean that you are absolved from such duties? And are we not making duty likewise rest on the mere contingency of having certain impulse-desires?

We answer, and stress the answer, that

this is *not* a contingency, and that therefore with us too the command of duty is really categorical. A human nature that did not have these impulse-desires would not be human nature. Mind itself is a set of activities directed toward ends, and to halt or remove them would blot us out altogether. Look again at the theoretical impulse. This is an impulse which, as we have seen, is already at work in the most rudimentary perceptive judgment and is still there, pushing for completion, in the most complicated theories of physics or metaphysics. One could not carve this impulse out of man without annihilating him as man. His whole common-sense world may be regarded as a single complex judgment, elaborated through millenniums of pressure on the part of this central impulse. We could no more divest ourselves of this impulse and its work than we could leap off our own shadows. Even in denying that we have such an impulse, we are obviously exercising it. To cease to exercise it would be to cease to remember or expect or infer or even recognize; in short, it would be to resign from the world.

So of other central impulses, the aesthetic for example. The Gestaltists have shown us that we cannot really choose whether to be interested or not in certain forms or shapes, since nature has settled this for us; certain sounds carry emotional meaning from the start; in the rhythm of the drumbeat or the dance there is an appeal as ancient as the race. We can develop the interest or stunt it; we cannot remove it, or sensibly deny it is there. Some people have tried to rid themselves of the whole embarrassing problem of good by refusing to admit that there is such a thing, of any type whatever; there are things and happenings, but none of them is better or worse than any other. But if a man chooses to make this point, it is presumably because he regards it as better to make it than not, and then he is back with a grotesque suddenness in the world of values he is trying to escape.

Nature itself has thus determined that we should seek certain forms of self-fulfilment. It is only through the seeking of these ends that we have become what we are, only by continuing to seek them that we can become what we may be. The command to continue the search is thus addressed by human nature to itself: 'If you are to be what you want to be, and what you cannot help wanting to be, do this.' I am not, of course, suggesting that a person cannot help wanting to learn trigonometry or read Ruskin; I am suggesting that from his very constitution he does and must regard knowledge and beauty as goods to be pursued. He is so made as to desire them, and fulfilling and satisfying such desires is what 'good' means. And of course the fulfilment and satisfaction in which goodness consists are not mine alone, but those of anyone capable of them.

15. Now this gives the meaning of 'ought'. To say that I ought to do something is ultimately to say that if a set of ends is to be achieved, whose goodness I cannot deny without making nonsense of my own nature, then I must act in a certain way. There is of course no *compulsion* to act in this way. I am free to follow the lesser good if I choose. And if I do so choose, no outward penalty may overtake me. But 'the greatest penalty of wrongdoing', Plato said, 'is to grow into the likeness of the bad man', and that penalty is inescapable. The ethical ought is like the logical ought; indeed the logical ought is a special case of the ethical. The logical ought says, 'If you want to attain truth, think consistently'. It does not say that you cannot contradict yourself; we are all more or less experts in that ancient art. It only says that if you do contradict yourself, you will nullify the aim of your thinking because you cut yourself off from truth. The ethical ought is to desires generally what the logical ought is to the particular desire to know. It stands over them all; it is the voice not of this or that end, or of this or that possible good, but of *the* end, *the* good, to which all desire is directed, which all men alike are seeking. That is what

gives it its authority. It concentrates, in a sense, the whole weight of human hope and desire. I do not mean, of course, that what our sense of duty says at any moment is infallible; for it remains true enough, as Leslie Stephen said, that conscience is the voice of racial experience speaking in the individual ear, and regarding the particular prescriptions of duty, the race itself may be mistaken. But that there is some greatest good purchasable by my present act cannot be denied without stultification; if error comes, it comes in construing what this is. Our account leaves the fact of duty palpable and its supremacy secure. Duty is the imperative laid upon us by a *summum bonum* which is prescribed by human nature itself. As Butler said of conscience, 'if it had power, as it has authority, it would absolutely govern human life'. It speaks with so great an urgency because it is dimly felt to be representative of the hope and will of mankind.

16. Here a serious difficulty crops up. Does not our account do away with any distinctively *moral* good altogether? It seems to make of moral goodness, that is, dutifulness or the good will, something that is good merely as instrumental to other and non-moral goods. If it really does this, it is sharply at variance with much weighty teaching on this matter. Kant began *The Metaphysic of Morals* by saying that the only thing in the world that was good without qualification was the good will, by which he meant loyalty to duty as such; and moralists who differ from each other as widely as Rashdall and the deontologists agree that dutifulness is not only an intrinsic good, but the greatest of all such goods. Is this teaching to be rejected?

There is at least a genuine paradox in it. Duty, as we have seen, is always a duty to produce good; the goodness, then, of dutifulness, or the disposition to do one's duty, would seem to lie in its being the condition and promise of this good. But to make dutifulness itself a good, in the sense of something to be sought in its own right and independently of other goods, seems

unintelligent and hardly intelligible. If it is my duty to do my duty, it is because this latter duty is to produce some good, and unless it promised to do so, it would not be my duty at all. Thus the duty of being dutiful is not independent and self-justifying; it is derivative from the good that such regard for duty brings about. To make dutifulness, as Kant did, an end in itself, indeed the only end that ethics as such could recognize, is to leave the chain of duty hanging in the air, without any concrete good to which it can attach itself. Hence the curious emptiness of Kantian ethics. We are to go on cultivating and refining our sense of duty; we are to hold the moral law in awe above the starry heavens; we are to do our duty though those heavens fall; but if we venture to ask Kant *what* it is our duty to do, he can only repeat that we are to be dutiful; that is itself the good that morality is to aim at. Yet by itself it is a vacuous good. The very nature of duty is to aim beyond itself, and if it has nothing but itself to aim at, it can only stand despondently still. There can no more be a duty to act, if there is no good to attain by it, than to think if there is no truth to be won by thinking.

Are we to say, then, that dutifulness, the disposition to seek and do one's duty, is an extrinsic, not an intrinsic, good? No, that will hardly do either. The truth would seem to be that it is a mixture of the two. That it is an extrinsic good, and a very great one, is undeniable. Indeed it is probably the most important single fact about a man, since without it, opportunity, position, and powers may be useless or used for evil, while with it, we have the warrant that he will at least try to play his part in the world. In a sense it is more important than any of the goods it may lead him to realize, for it stands as guarantor of all of them. But there is no reason to deny that, on our theory, it may be an intrinsic good also. Such a good is for us the fulfilment and satisfaction of impulse-desire. Now while impulse-desires are commonly aimed at the goods that duty might produce, they can also be aimed at the perfection of the moral mechanism, so to speak, by which goods are engendered and judged. Just as a musician may transfer part of his interest from the music that he is playing to his technique in playing it, or a philosopher some of his interest from the solution of his problem to the logical skill required for solving it, so the person interested in achieving good for himself or others may come to take an interest in his own sensitiveness of distinction among goods and firmness in following what appears the best; he may pursue these as a distinct end. And so far as he finds fulfilment and satisfaction in the pursuit, moral goodness becomes a good, in the sense that knowledge and the experience of beauty are goods.

Nevertheless, on our view its primary goodness is, and should remain, extrinsic. This is not to make it unimportant, any more than to regard health as only extrinsically good is to make it unimportant. And it serves to suggest a genuine danger in making dutifulness an end in itself. Rashdall somewhere remarks that the moral sense is a sense of the relative importance of ends. That, I think, is the right way to conceive it. A healthy moral interest should be fixed rather upon the goods to be achieved than upon the mechanisms or attitudes of our own mind in achieving them. Moral obligation *is*, we saw, the claim upon us of ends appointed by our own nature. As Kant recognized, a perfectly healthy moral will—what he called the holy will, that is, one in which desire and the sense of duty exactly corresponded—would have no worries about the state of its conscience; it would simply do its duty with delight. It is even possible that a preoccupation with goodness should stand in the way of goods that would otherwise be achieved, just as an attempt at introspection when we have a certain desire will destroy the desire by diverting attention from its end. Moral goodness is one of

those priceless things, of which culture is another, that tend to wither away when placed in too bright a light. I have been told, indeed, that an eminent woman contemporary, having concluded early in life, that she was neither good-looking nor socially gifted, decided that she would go in for goodness, and I must admit that the result has been excellent. But if one looks more closely, one sees that far more is at work than the interest in goodness, for there is an absorbing interest also in the goods that she is busy about.

Without such enthusiasms, the mere devotion to goodness has something artificial about it, and even a touch of morbidity. Artificial, because of the unnaturalness of working laboriously to produce goods for which the worker has no heart. One likes to receive a gift from a friend when it is a testimony to his liking and his pleasure in one's own pleasure; one receives it gingerly when one knows that it springs from the sender's sense that he must do his duty, come what may; gifts without the giver are bare. In the preoccupation with moral goodness there is sometimes a touch of morbidity too. The man with sound health is more disposed to eat than to finger his pulse. It is probably the preacher, with his professional obligation to fix his eye upon goodness as such, and urge its claims, who feels the danger most acutely. A Greek of classic times would have been astonished and nonplussed at the Hebrew's concern over the state of his soul, and I suppose there is no parallel in other literatures to his passionate 'Create a clean heart within me', or to his passionate aversion to sin as 'the body of this death'. To deprecate this strain in our western culture or to depreciate its power to keep a refractory human nature in order would be absurd.

It is not absurd, however, to point out that without strong independent desires which it can stimulate and moderate, the pursuit of goodness as a state of the 'heart' may easily cross the line that separates health from morbidity. In Thomas à Kempis, in the *Theologia Germania*, in St. Theresa, in George Fox, in Amiel, in Kierkegaard, there is, of course, much that is noble; there is also something of the hothouse and the sick-room. When the emphasis in preaching is very strongly on the 'inward parts', as it is in the admirable sermons of James Martineau,[9] one gets, at times, the same sense of the need for opened windows; and in the continual stress on sin of some of the later Kierkegaardians—the insistence that the human will, even at its best, is one vast festering sore—we see the pursuit of goodness virtually turned against itself and eating out its own vitals. The prayer book confession that there is no health in us seems to me simply untrue, the relic of a theology committed to the doctrine of the fall, though perhaps if often enough repeated, it does tend to become true.

17. Besides the question of moral goodness, there is one other that our account of the good is sure to raise immediately, namely what is meant by evil. Like 'good', the term 'evil' is most ambiguous; it covers, if we may say so, a multitude of evils. When called upon to give examples, people would think of very different things. Some would mention Black Deaths and Great Fires and Lisbon earthquakes; others would name ignorance and ugliness; others, old age and death; others still, sin; some few, perhaps, would talk of the niggardliness of nature, and point out that most of the planet and indeed of the known universe is uninhabitable by man. Some of these evils fall outside our present interest, since they are clearly instrumental. Uninhabitable snowfields and deserts, epidemics, fires and earthquakes, are commonly called physical evils, but strictly speaking there are no such things. What are called so are instru-

[9] *Endeavours After the Christian Life*, and *Hours of Thought on Sacred Things*.

mental only; they are not bad in themselves; they induce experiences that are bad. Disease as a mere state or process within the body has nothing evil in it; neither does a big fire or a big wave or a barren soil. Most of the universe, as far as we can see, is neither good nor evil. When certain events in it directly give rise to suffering or privation, we call them bad by metonymy, because they are the immediate causes of what is intrinsically bad, namely conscious states or their relations. It is only with intrinsic evil that we are here concerned.

Now if goodness consists in the fulfilment and satisfaction of impulse-desire, one would expect evil to consist in one or other of the following things: (a) the failure of impulse-desire to reach its goal, (b) its active defeat or frustration, (c) the coercive presence of that from which impulse-desire is seeking to escape. We find all these types of evil illustrated in fact, and they seem between them to exhaust the types of intrinsic evil.

18. (a) Everyone has impulse-desires, strong or weak, for such things as knowledge, beauty, and easy relations with others. Suppose one conspicuously falls short of these; suppose, for example, that one is too stupid or too ignorant to enjoy any but the most elementary grasp of the world about him; we call such a state an evil. Why? Not because the man is actively suffering in any way or feels that he has anything to complain about; he may be extremely self-complacent. We call his state evil nevertheless, because it marks so evident a failure of the impulse-desire for knowledge to reach even a normal level of fulfilment; that it has not even gone far enough to become aware of its own failure does not better the situation. Again, we consider bad the sort of insensitivity that is content to live in a squalid litter, with no taste for order, no eye for beauty, no sense for the graces of speech or movement. Once more, when one hears of persons who

feel at the end of their lives that they have nothing to repent of, meaning that they have never done anything that would land them in jail, we feel again a failure that we must call evil, even though the agent may be unaware of it. Our own theory of good and evil covers such cases fully, in the sense that, in the light of it, we can see plainly why we call them bad. If good means the fulfilment and satisfaction of impulse-desire, these are evil because in this respect they are failures.

Since, in our view, there are two factors in goodness, fulfilment and satisfaction, it is conceivable that a given experience should fall short on one account, but not on the other; it might fulfil without satisfying, or satisfy without fulfilling. I think that approximations to both these states occur, and that when they do, we recognize that we have at best a defective good. We saw in discussing the passionless sage of the Stoics that much light of an intellectual kind may be achieved with very little of the satisfaction that such achievement commonly brings. We saw too that while such a state could not be called an evil, its value or goodness had largely vanished. Fortunately such states are abnormal and rather rare. In ordinary life the achievement of a desired end is the most certain of all things to bring satisfaction. On the other hand the mere continued possession of the end is no guarantee that the satisfaction will remain. When T. H. Huxley was awarded the medal of the Royal Society, he was in raptures; a little later he wrote: 'The thing that a fortnight ago (before I got it) I thought so much of, I give you my word I do not care a pin for. I am sick of it and ashamed of having thought so much of it, and the congratulations I get give me a sort of internal sardonic grin.'[10] Even such a prodigy of success as Goethe said of his life when he was an old man: 'at bottom it has been nothing but pain and burden and I can affirm that during the whole of my 75 years, I have not had four weeks of gen-

[10] *Life and Letters of T. H. Huxley*, I, 101.

uine well-being. It is but the perpetual rolling of a rock that must be raised up again forever.'[11] Frank Chapman Sharp thinks that such cases, in which the good seems to have vanished because, though the fulfilment is still there, the satisfaction in it has gone, show that the goodness lies in the satisfaction alone, and he ends as a hedonist.[12] But the inference is illicit. What such cases show is that satisfaction is essential to goodness, not that it is exclusively essential. Indeed, attentively considered, they seem to show that satisfaction *cannot* be the only factor. Suppose that the satisfaction felt by Huxley or Goethe in his own level of achievement was small (that it was really zero or less I take leave to question), can we say that the goodness of such lives is really no greater than that of other men with similarly low satisfaction but a tithe of their attainment? That is certainly at odds with what we actually think. We should say that the goodness of an experience was greater if the achievement or fulfilment was greater, even though the satisfaction remained the same. If the satisfaction actually went down as the fulfilment went up, a situation that is conceivable, I think we should be genuinely puzzled as to whether the experience was better or not; we should begin to talk in terms of comparative amounts. In any case our present point is clear, namely that a fulfilment that is without normal satisfaction is to that extent a defective good.

19. The same holds where there is satisfaction but low fulfilment. There appear to be diseased minds who live in a state of perpetual euphoria, cackling and cooing with idiot's delight over the little nothings of their daily round. In sheer satisfaction with themselves and the world, they would make the Huxleys and the Goethes seem like melancholiacs. If the hedonists were right, such a state would be highly desirable. But we certainly do not so

[11] Quoted by James, *Varieties of Religious Experience*, 137.
[12] See his *Ethics*.

regard it. We think, rather, that for an experience to be genuinely good, there must be not only satisfaction, but something worth taking satisfaction in, and the worth of this object will be measured, not by the satisfaction itself, but by the immanent standard of the activity involved, cognitive if it is an activity of knowing, aesthetic if one of appreciating, ethical if it involves diverse activities and ends. It is no doubt better that the idiot's life should be a perpetual grin than a perpetual groan, even if his life is a 'poem in praise of practically nothing'; but it would be very much better still if, answering to the delight, there were the sort of object that would fill a normal mind or engage a normal sensibility. Satisfaction, even great satisfaction, without the corresponding fulfilment is at best a defective good.

Indeed, even when fulfilment and satisfaction are both present, there is a point of view from which every life may be regarded as evil, and our theory renders such judgments, otherwise perverse and peevish, at least intelligible. It was the cheerful and courageous R. L. Stevenson who wrote, 'failure is the fate allotted'; 'our business is to continue to fail in good spirits.' 'Take the happiest man', said James, 'the one most envied by the world, and in nine cases out of ten his inmost consciousness is one of failure. Either his ideals in the line of his achievements are pitched far higher than the achievements themselves, or else he has secret ideals of which the world knows nothing, and in regard to which he invariably knows himself to be found wanting.'[13] The goodness of such achievements is clearly a matter of degree; and a climb that, regarded from below, is a triumph, may also, when seen from above, be a falling short. The two judgments are equally true. Goodness in its essence is relative to an endeavour, and any stage of that endeavour is called good or evil, depending on the point of the journey from which it is regarded. This is, or ought to

[13] *Varieties*, 137.

be, an embarrassing reflection to a theory that holds goodness to be a simple quality like yellow, which, in a given experience, is either present or absent. On the theory here offered, such a reflection is natural and inevitable.

20. (b) Besides evils of failure there are evils of frustration. Failure and frustration are perhaps the same thing in the end; they are both defeats that spring from a disproportion between inner power and outer circumstance. But what specially distinguishes failure is some deficiency in one's self; what distinguishes frustration is some marked untowardness of circumstance. We say that the inadvertent burning by Mill's maid of Carlyle's manuscript of *The French Revolution* was an evil; that Milton's blindness and Beethoven's deafness and Wilson's paralysis and Maupassant's insanity were evils; that the cutting off of Schubert and Shelley at thirty was evil; that the removal of Lincoln from the scene at the height of his power and usefulness was an evil. Why are these things called evils? Partly, no doubt, because of the loss of what would have been very valuable, but surely also because of the frustration of promise and endeavour. Death, though the common lot, is the greatest of evils because it writes such an uncompromising *Finis* to all our efforts. These estimates are what one would expect on our theory of good. If good consists in fulfilment and satisfaction, their frustration will be regarded, naturally and universally, as evil.

21. (c) What about ugliness, a foul smell, a grating noise, and above all, pain? Many reflective persons have tried to take evil as the privation of good, but it is hard to hold this convenient theory in the face of evils like these. Intense pain is certainly more than the absence of something; it is positive, and positively horrible. In such phrases as 'pleasure and pain', there is the suggestion that it is the same sort of experience as pleasure, only opposite in quality, which is of course untrue, since pain is not

an 'affection' like pleasure at all. It is a sensation, a sensation at times of appalling intensity, to which there is perhaps nothing corresponding among the experiences we call good. Again, the experience of a foul smell, or a jarring discord, or a finger-nail grating on a blackboard, is not a mere lack or absence, but something positive, something aggressively disagreeable. Such cases require us to hold, I think, that just as there are experiences marked out as natural ends by reason of their fulfilling impulse-desire, so there are others from which there is a natural aversion and desire to escape. Pain is the type and chief of such evils. At every level of sentience, it is something to be fled from. Instead of feeling satisfaction as the experience of it increases, one feels satisfaction in the degree of one's relief from it. The claim has been made that there are exceptions, that some people take satisfaction and pleasure in pain as others do in heard harmonies. In the east I have often seen fakirs pushing themselves about on beds of upturned nails. But I am unconvinced by such cases. There is no reason to think these men prefer pain; it is precisely because they regard it as an evil difficult to be borne that they think to curry favour with God and man by the hardihood with which they bear it. Nor is it necessary, I should suppose, to say that the masochist finds satisfaction in pain itself as distinct from all that may attend it in an abnormal mind—the obscure stimulations of sex, the relief of feelings of guilt, the thought of oneself as suffering in some imagined cause. There are strange cases like that of Albert Jay Chapman, who permanently crippled one hand by plunging it into a fire as a symbolic atonement for a wrong done; there is the large company of martyrs who faced pain almost eagerly; there are the people who give thanks sincerely for the discipline of pain. But it is mere muddle to think that these things settle the question whether in any case whatever pain *is* good, as opposed to productive of good results. If there is any case on record of a person

finding intense pain good in itself, I do not know of it. It may be said that the issue is pre-judged, since part of what we mean by pain in thus generalizing about it is that it is disliked. That may be true. But this is not all that we mean. Pain, as we have said, is not an affection primarily, but a sensation, with a content of its own.

It was argued in an earlier chapter that when we call a past pain evil, we do not mean to say merely that a pain occurred. But we found it hard to discriminate the pain from the badness or evil of it. I know of no satisfactory analysis of this distinction, and do not profess to have arrived at one. But it seems clear that when we say a painful experience is evil, we do not mean merely that what is painful is painful. We have seen that in describing an experience as intrinsically good we are saying that it satisfies and fulfils. In saying that it is evil, we say correspondingly that it flouts satisfaction or fulfilment or both. Pain flouts both, and it seems to have an added way of doing this that is peculiarly its own. (i) Pain, particularly if intense, makes a free and normal exercise of powers impossible; it tends to contract our being to one dreadful point. (ii) It carries with it dissatisfaction, that opposite of pleasure for which we have no convenient word, but which the Germans call *Unlust* as distinct from *Schmerz*. (iii) *Schmerz* or pain proper has a character of its own. Its evil is not exhausted by *Unlust* and frustration, though these are both there; and it is hence to be doubted whether an account of evil can precisely parallel an account of good. What makes an experience good is the satisfying fulfilment of faculty. What makes an experience bad is the flouting of such fulfilment with its attendant blight on satisfaction; but the blight may take more than one form. It may be the mere failure of satisfaction where this was normal or possible; it may be the presence of *Unlust*; or it may be the presence of pain.

22. (d) As for *moral* evil, the disposition to, or choice of, the worse rather than

the better, it is to be understood in the same way as moral goodness. We condemn it primarily because it is the potentiality and the generator of all kinds of other ills. There is a distinction between vice and the vices, just as there is between goodness and the virtues. A vice is a disposition either to produce evil in a particular way—indolence and carelessness are examples—or to produce evil of a particular kind, as mendacity and cruelty do. The vice that is opposed to moral goodness is the disposition toward the bad because it is bad. It is plain enough why we should regard these as evils, and the latter as by far the greater evil. Malice is a seed-plot for every kind of evil that the human will can produce. Anger and hatred are not necessarily malicious, for they may be directed only against what is harmful in other men, and thus tend to good rather than evil, though unhappily they are not as a rule so economically used. But a man who was malicious generally would be a standing enemy to every kind of good of everyone around him.

Some writers have questioned whether pure malice, either of the special or the general form, exists. I have already questioned whether anyone takes satisfaction in pain as such, but unfortunately it is harder to doubt that some people take a genuine satisfaction in inflicting it on others. As one reads Macaulay's account of Jeffreys, for example, one can scarcely resist his conclusion that this hateful creature showed 'the most odious vice which is incident to human nature, a delight in misery merely as misery'.[14] On our own theory we should expect that most such cases would be explicable in other ways than as examples of mere 'motiveless malignity', for example, as instances of the love of power accompanied by relative lack of fellow-feeling and imagination; and we should regard a man who took delight in inflicting misery when there was nothing to gain by it as not merely morally bad but as abnormally or inhu-

manly constructed, a monster lacking natural perception and sympathy. That, I think, is how we do feel. Furthermore, we should regard pure moral badness, the attitude that took as its motto 'Evil, be thou my good', as not really possible. It is hard to see how anyone could consistently take what we regard as the great evils as goods, or the great goods as evils; those goods are appointed for him by his nature as human. Even Iago, in deceiving, betraying and murdering, did not elect evil simply for evil's sake; his creator seems to have felt that this would make him unreal. Granting that Iago was thoroughly selfish, completely unsympathetic, and remarkably adroit, 'the most delightful thing to such a man would be something that gave an extreme satisfaction to his sense of power and superiority; and if it involved, secondly, the triumphant exertion of his abilities, and thirdly the excitement of danger, his delight would be consummated'.[15] Odious as Iago was, he was not a mere and pure devil.

23. Nor is anyone else. Our own theory of human nature is nearly the opposite of that which, founded on the myth of the fall, regards man as rotten at the core and utterly to be condemned except as divine grace, distributed on inscrutable principles, interposes to save him. He is, on the contrary, so made as to seek, inevitably and universally, a set of great goods; his whole life is a groping after them. Even the criminal, as Socrates saw, does not choose evil merely as evil; no one is such a complete fool and knave as to do that. When vicious and harmful acts spring, not from a rush of passion, as they often do, but from something that can be called a motive, the motive is never simply to work evil, conceived as such. Some twist of thought makes the worse appear the better reason; the act, looked at through the vapours of anger, fear, or jealousy, is seen in a false light; even sin, I have heard a theologian say, is 'an effort to be blessed

---

[14] *History of England*, Ch. IV.

[15] A. C. Bradley, *Shakespearean Tragedy*, 228.

in ways not approved by God'. If human nature is governed, as we hold it is, by certain powerful impulse-desires whose fulfilment and satisfaction provide the meaning of good, we should expect that there would be no such thing as moral badness, if that means a settled will toward the bad because of its badness, that choices of the bad as such would seldom or never occur, and that when they did seem to occur, they would generally turn out, on examination, to be choices of evil *sub specie boni*. All these expectations, I think, are confirmed by fact.

D. Ethical Non-Cognitivism

A Suggestion About Value [1]

W. H. F. BARNES

Value judgements in their origin are not strictly judgements at all. They are exclamations expressive of approval. This is to be distinguished from the theory that the value judgement, "A is good," states that I approve A. The theory that I am now putting forward maintains that "A is good," is a form of words expressive of my approval. To take an illustration:—When I say "I have a pain," that sentence states the occurrence of a certain feeling in me: when I shout "Oh!" in a certain way that is expressive of the occurrence in me of a certain feeling. We must seek then for the origin of value judgements in the expressions of approval, delight, and affection, which children utter when confronted with certain experiences.

If all so-called value judgements are, in principle, expressions of approval, then they will only possess meaning in so far as the society in which they are used is agreed on what things it approves. And then "good" and "value" will be terms which have meaning only by referring to the actual nature of the thing, not to any non-natural quality it possesses. Meanwhile it is worth while mentioning that many controversies arising out of value judgements *are* settled by saying, "I like it and

you don't, and that's the end of the matter." We are content to adopt this solution of the difficulty on matters such as food and drink, though even here we admit the existence of epicures and connoisseurs. Why are we not content to accept the same solution on all matters where value is concerned?

The reason we are not so content seems to lie in the fact that the action of one man dictated by his approval of something is frequently incompatible with the action of another man dictated by his approval of something. Life in a society leads us continually to transfer our approval to different objects. Reflection upon that life leads to still further modifications. It is this opposition between the approval of one man and that of others which lies at the bottom of controversies about value. If I maintain "A is good" against the contention "A is bad," my attempt to prove the truth of my statement is not really what it pretends to be. I point out details in A which are the object of my approval. By so doing I hope that my opponent, when he becomes aware of these, will approve A: and so be ready to say "A is good." But what I have done is not really to gain his assent to a proposition but to change his attitude from one of disapproval to one of approval towards A. All attempts to persuade others of the truth of value judgements are thus really attempts to make others approve the things we approve.

Reprinted from *Analysis*, I, 1933, by permission of the author and Basil Blackwell & Mott Ltd.

[1] This note is an extract from a paper of which the main topic was Hartmann's Ethics. The paper was read before the Jowett Society on November 8th, 1933.

241

Critique of Ethics

A. J. AYER

There is still one objection to be met before we can claim to have justified our view that all synthetic propositions are empirical hypotheses. This objection is based on the common supposition that our speculative knowledge is of two distinct kinds—that which relates to questions of empirical fact, and that which relates to questions of value. It will be said that "statements of value" are genuine synthetic propositions, but that they cannot with any show of justice be represented as hypotheses, which are used to predict the course of our sensations; and, accordingly, that the existence of ethics and aesthetics as branches of speculative knowledge presents an insuperable objection to our radical empiricist thesis.

In face of this objection, it is our business to give an account of "judgements of value" which is both satisfactory in itself and consistent with our general empiricist principles. We shall set ourselves to show that in so far as statements of value are significant, they are ordinary "scientific" statements; and that in so far as they are not scientific, they are not in the literal sense significant, but are simply expressions of emotion which can be neither true nor false. In maintaining this view, we may confine ourselves for the present to the case of ethical statements. What is said about

them will be found to apply, *mutatis mutandis,* to the case of aesthetic statements also.

The ordinary system of ethics, as elaborated in the works of ethical philosophers, is very far from being a homogeneous whole. Not only is it apt to contain pieces of metaphysics, and analyses of non-ethical concepts: its actual ethical contents are themselves of very different kinds. We may divide them, indeed, into four main classes. There are, first of all, propositions which express definitions of ethical terms, or judgements about the legitimacy or possibility of certain definitions. Secondly, there are propositions describing the phenomena of moral experience, and their causes. Thirdly, there are exhortations to moral virtue. And, lastly, there are actual ethical judgements. It is unfortunately the case that the distinction between these four classes, plain as it is, is commonly ignored by ethical philosophers; with the result that it is often very difficult to tell from their works what it is that they are seeking to discover or prove.

In fact, it is easy to see that only the first of our four classes, namely that which comprises the propositions relating to the definitions of ethical terms, can be said to constitute ethical philosophy. The propositions which describe the phenomena of moral experience, and their causes, must be assigned to the science of psychology, or sociology. The exhortations to moral virtue are not propositions at all, but ejaculations or commands which are designed to provoke the reader to action of a certain sort. Accordingly, they do not belong to any branch of philosophy or science. As for the expressions of ethical judgements, we have not yet determined how they should be classified. But inasmuch as they are certainly neither definitions nor comments upon definitions, nor quotations, we may say decisively that they do not belong to ethical philosophy. A strictly philosophical treatise on ethics should therefore make no ethical pronouncements. But it should, by giving an analysis of ethical terms, show what is the category to which all such pronouncements belong. And this is what we are now about to do.

A question which is often discussed by ethical philosophers is whether it is possible to find definitions which would reduce all ethical terms to one or two fundamental terms. But this question, though it undeniably belongs to ethical philosophy, is not relevant to our present enquiry. We are not now concerned to discover which term, within the sphere of ethical terms, is to be taken as fundamental; whether, for example, "good" can be defined in terms of "right" or "right" in terms of "good," or both in terms of "value." What we are interested in is the possibility of reducing the whole sphere of ethical terms to non-ethical terms. We are enquiring whether statements of ethical value can be translated into statements of empirical fact.

That they can be so translated is the contention of those ethical philosophers who are commonly called subjectivists, and of those who are known as utilitarians. For the utilitarian defines the rightness of actions, and the goodness of ends, in terms of the pleasure, or happiness, or satisfaction, to which they give rise; the subjectivist, in terms of the feelings of approval which a certain person, or group of people, has towards them. Each of these types of definition makes moral judgements into a sub-class of psychological or sociological judgements; and for this reason they are very attractive to us. For, if either was correct, it would follow that ethical assertions were not generically different from the factual assertions which are ordinarily contrasted with them; and the account which we have already given of empirical hypotheses would apply to them also.

Nevertheless we shall not adopt either a subjectivist or a utilitarian analysis of ethical terms. We reject the subjectivist view that to call an action right, or a thing good, is to say that it is generally approved of, because it is not self-contradictory to assert that some actions which are generally approved of are not right, or that some things which are generally approved of are not good. And we reject the alternative subjectivist view that a man who asserts that a certain action is right, or that a certain thing is good, is saying that he himself approves of it, on the ground that a man who confessed that he sometimes approved of what was bad or wrong would not be contradicting himself. And a similar argument is fatal to utilitarianism. We cannot agree that to call an action right is to say that of all the actions possible in the circumstances it would cause, or be likely to cause, the greatest happiness, or the greatest balance of pleasure over pain, or the greatest balance of satisfied over unsatisfied desire, because we find that it is not self-contradictory to say that it is sometimes wrong to perform the action which would actually or probably cause the greatest happiness, or the greatest balance of pleasure over pain, or of satisfied over unsatisfied desire. And since it is not self-contradictory to say that some pleasant things are not good, or that some bad things are desired, it cannot be the case that the sentence "x is good" is equivalent to "x is pleasant," or to "x is desired." And to every other variant of utilitarianism with which I am acquainted the same objection can be made. And therefore we should, I think, conclude that the validity of ethical judgements is not determined by the felicific tendencies of actions, any more than by the nature of people's feelings; but that it must be regarded as "absolute" or "intrinsic," and not empirically calculable.

If we say this, we are not, of course, denying that it is possible to invent a language in which all ethical symbols are definable in non-ethical terms, or even that it is desirable to invent such a language and adopt it in place of our own; what we are denying is that the suggested reduction of ethical to non-ethical statements is consistent with the conventions of our actual language. That is, we reject utilitarianism and subjectivism, not as proposals to replace our existing ethical notions by new ones, but as analyses of our existing ethical notions. Our contention is simply that, in our language, sentences which contain normative ethical symbols are not equivalent to sentences which express psychological propositions, or indeed empirical propositions of any kind.

It is advisable here to make it plain that it is only normative ethical symbols, and not descriptive ethical symbols, that are held by us to be indefinable in factual terms. There is a danger of confusing these two types of symbols, because they are commonly constituted by signs of the same sensible form. Thus a complex sign of the form "x is wrong" may constitute a sentence which expresses a moral judgement concerning a certain type of conduct, or it may constitute a sentence which states that a certain type of conduct is repugnant to the moral sense of a particular society. In the latter case, the symbol "wrong" is a descriptive ethical symbol, and the sentence in which it occurs expresses an ordinary sociological proposition; in the former case, the symbol "wrong" is a normative ethical symbol, and the sentence in which it occurs does not, we maintain, express an empirical proposition at all. It is only with normative ethics that we are at present concerned; so that whenever ethical symbols are used in the course of this argu-

ment without qualification, they are always to be interpreted as symbols of the normative type.

In admitting that normative ethical concepts are irreducible to empirical concepts, we seem to be leaving the way clear for the "absolutist" view of ethics—that is, the view that statements of value are not controlled by observation, as ordinary empirical propositions are, but only by a mysterious "intellectual intuition." A feature of this theory, which is seldom recognized by its advocates, is that it makes statements of value unverifiable. For it is notorious that what seems intuitively certain to one person may seem doubtful, or even false, to another. So that unless it is possible to provide some criterion by which one may decide between conflicting intuitions, a mere appeal to intuition is worthless as a test of a proposition's validity. But in the case of moral judgements, no such criterion can be given. Some moralists claim to settle the matter by saying that they "know" that their own moral judgements are correct. But such an assertion is of purely psychological interest, and has not the slightest tendency to prove the validity of any moral judgement. For dissentient moralists may equally well "know" that their ethical views are correct. And, as far as subjective certainty goes, there will be nothing to choose between them. When such differences of opinion arise in connection with an ordinary empirical proposition, one may attempt to resolve them by referring to, or actually carrying out, some relevant empirical test. But with regard to ethical statements, there is, on the "absolutist" or "intuitionist" theory, no relevant empirical test. We are therefore justified in saying that on this theory ethical statements are held to be unverifiable. They are, of course, also held to be genuine synthetic propositions.

Considering the use which we have made of the principle that a synthetic proposition is significant only if it is empirically verifiable, it is clear that the acceptance of an "absolutist" theory of ethics would undermine the whole of our main argument. And as we have already rejected the "naturalistic" theories which are commonly supposed to provide the only alternative to "absolutism" in ethics, we seem to have reached a difficult position. We shall meet the difficulty by showing that the correct treatment of ethical statements is afforded by a third theory, which is wholly compatible with our radical empiricism.

We begin by admitting that the fundamental ethical concepts are unanalysable, inasmuch as there is no criterion by which one can test the validity of the judgements in which they occur. So far we are in agreement with the absolutists. But, unlike the absolutists, we are able to give an explanation of this fact about ethical concepts. We say that the reason why they are unanalysable is that they are mere pseudo-concepts. The presence of an ethical symbol in a proposition adds nothing to its factual content. Thus if I say to someone, "You acted wrongly in stealing that money," I am not stating anything more than if I had simply said, "You stole that money." In adding that this action is wrong I am not making any further statement about it. I am simply evincing my moral disapproval of it. It is as if I had said, "You stole that money," in a peculiar tone of horror, or written it with the addition of some special exclamation marks. The tone, or the exclamation marks, adds nothing to the literal meaning of the sentence. It merely serves to show that the expression of it is attended by certain feelings in the speaker.

If now I generalise my previous statement and say, "Stealing money is wrong," I produce a sentence which has no factual meaning—that is, expresses no proposition which can be either true or false. It is as if I had written "Stealing money!!"—where the shape and thickness of the exclamation marks show, by a suitable convention, that a special sort of moral disapproval is the feeling which is being expressed. It is clear that there is nothing said here which can be true or false. Another man may disagree

with me about the wrongness of stealing, in a sense that he may not have the same feelings about stealing as I have, and he may quarrel with me on account of my moral sentiments. But he cannot, strictly speaking, contradict me. For in saying that a certain type of action is right or wrong, I am not making any factual statement, not even a statement about my own state of mind. I am merely expressing certain moral sentiments. And the man who is ostensibly contradicting me is merely expressing his moral sentiments. So that there is plainly no sense in asking which of us is in the right. For neither of us is asserting a genuine proposition.

What we have just been saying about the symbol "wrong" applies to all normative ethical symbols. Sometimes they occur in sentences which record ordinary empirical facts besides expressing ethical feeling about those facts: sometimes they occur in sentences which simply express ethical feeling about a certain type of action, or situation, without making any statement of fact. But in every case in which one would commonly be said to be making an ethical judgment, the function of the relevant ethical word is purely "emotive." It is used to express feeling about certain objects, but not to make any assertion about them.

It is worth mentioning that ethical terms do not serve only to express feeling. They are calculated also to arouse feeling, and so to stimulate action. Indeed some of them are used in such a way as to give the sentences in which they occur the effect of commands. Thus the sentence "It is your duty to tell the truth" may be regarded both as the expression of a certain sort of ethical feeling about truthfulness and as the expression of the command "Tell the truth." The sentence "You ought to tell the truth" also involves the command "Tell the truth," but here the tone of the command is less emphatic. In the sentence "It is good to tell the truth" the command has become little more than a suggestion. And thus the "meaning" of the word "good," in its ethical usage, is differentiated from that of the word "duty" or the word "ought." In fact we may define the meaning of the various ethical words in terms both of the different feelings they are ordinarily taken to express, and also the different responses which they are calculated to provoke.

We can now see why it is impossible to find a criterion for determining the validity of ethical judgements. It is not because they have an "absolute" validity which is mysteriously independent of ordinary sense-experience, but because they have no objective validity whatsoever. If a sentence makes no statement at all, there is obviously no sense in asking whether what it says is true or false. And we have seen that sentences which simply express moral judgements do not say anything. They are pure expressions of feeling and as such do not come under the category of truth and falsehood. They are unverifiable for the same reason as a cry of pain or a word of command is unverifiable—because they do not express genuine propositions.

Thus, although our theory of ethics might fairly be said to be radically subjectivist, it differs in a very important respect from the orthodox subjectivist theory. For the orthodox subjectivist does not deny, as we do, that the sentences of a moralizer express genuine propositions. All he denies is that they express propositions of a unique non-empirical character. His own view is that they express propositions about the speaker's feelings. If this were so, ethical judgements clearly would be capable of being true or false. They would be true if the speaker had the relevant feelings, and false if he had not. And this is a matter which is, in principle, empirically verifiable. Furthermore they could be significantly contradicted. For if I say, "Tolerance is a virtue," and someone answers, "You don't approve of it," he would, on the ordinary subjectivist theory, be contradicting me. On our theory, he would not be contradicting me, because, in saying that tolerance was a virtue, I should not be

making any statement about my own feelings or about anything else. I should simply be evincing my feelings, which is not at all the same thing as saying that I have them.

The distinction between the expression of feeling and the assertion of feeling is complicated by the fact that the assertion that one has a certain feeling often accompanies the expression of that feeling, and is then, indeed, a factor in the expression of that feeling. Thus I may simultaneously express boredom and say that I am bored, and in that case my utterance of the words, "I am bored," is one of the circumstances which make it true to say that I am expressing or evincing boredom. But I can express boredom without actually saying that I am bored. I can express it by my tone and gestures, while making a statement about something wholly unconnected with it, or by an ejaculation, or without uttering any words at all. So that even if the assertion that one has a certain feeling always involves the expression of that feeling, the expression of a feeling assuredly does not always involve the assertion that one has it. And this is the important point to grasp in considering the distinction between our theory and the ordinary subjectivist theory. For whereas the subjectivist holds that ethical statements actually assert the existence of certain feelings, we hold that ethical statements are expressions and excitants of feeling which do not necessarily involve any assertions.

We have already remarked that the main objection to the ordinary subjectivist theory is that the validity of ethical judgements is not determined by the nature of their author's feelings. And this is an objection which our theory escapes. For it does not imply that the existence of any feelings is a necessary and sufficient condition of the validity of an ethical judgement. It implies, on the contrary, that ethical judgements have no validity.

There is, however, a celebrated argument against subjectivist theories which our theory does not escape. It has been pointed out by Moore that if ethical statements were simply statements about the speaker's feelings, it would be impossible to argue about questions of value.[1] To take a typical example: if a man said that thrift was a virtue, and another replied that it was a vice, they would not, on this theory, be disputing with one another. One would be saying that he approved of thrift, and the other that *he* didn't; and there is no reason why both these statements should not be true. Now Moore held it to be obvious that we do dispute about questions of value, and accordingly concluded that the particular form of subjectivism which he was discussing was false.

It is plain that the conclusion that it is impossible to dispute about questions of value follows from our theory also. For as we hold that such sentences as "Thrift is a virtue" and "Thrift is a vice" do not express propositions at all, we clearly cannot hold that they express incompatible propositions. We must therefore admit that if Moore's argument really refutes the ordinary subjectivist theory, it also refutes ours. But, in fact, we deny that it does refute even the ordinary subjectivist theory. For we hold that one really never does dispute about questions of value.

This may seem, at first sight, to be a very paradoxical assertion. For we certainly do engage in disputes which are ordinarily regarded as disputes about questions of value. But, in all such cases, we find, if we consider the matter closely, that the dispute is not really about a question of value, but about a question of fact. When someone disagrees with us about the moral value of a certain action or type of action, we do admittedly resort to argument in order to win him over to our way of thinking. But we do not attempt to show by our

arguments that he has the "wrong" ethical feeling towards a situation whose nature he has correctly apprehended. What we attempt to show is that he is mistaken about the facts of the case. We argue that he has misconceived the agent's motive; or that he has misjudged the effects of the action, or its probable effects in view of the agent's knowledge; or that he has failed to take into account the special circumstances in which the agent was placed. Or else we employ more general arguments about the effects which actions of a certain type tend to produce, or the qualities which are usually manifested in their performance. We do this in the hope that we have only to get our opponent to agree with us about the nature of the empirical facts for him to adopt the same moral attitude towards them as we do. And as the people with whom we argue have generally received the same moral education as ourselves, and live in the same social order, our expectation is usually justified. But if our opponent happens to have undergone a different process of moral "conditioning" from ourselves, so that, even when he acknowledges all the facts, he still disagrees with us about the moral value of the actions under discussion, then we abandon the attempt to convince him by argument. We say that it is impossible to argue with him because he has a distorted or undeveloped moral sense; which signifies merely that he employs a different set of values from our own. We feel that our own system of values is superior, and therefore speak in such derogatory terms of his. But we cannot bring forward any arguments to show that our system is superior. For our judgement that it is so is itself a judgement of value, and accordingly outside the scope of argument. It is because argument fails us when we come to deal with pure questions of value, as distinct from questions of fact, that we finally resort to mere abuse.

In short, we find that argument is possible on moral questions only if some

[1] Cf. *Philosophical Studies*, "The Nature of Moral Philosophy."

system of values is presupposed. If our opponent concurs with us in expressing moral disapproval of all actions of a given type *t*, then we may get him to condemn a particular action A, by bringing forward arguments to show that A is of type *t*. For the question whether A does or does not belong to that type is a plain question of fact. Given that a man has certain moral principles, we argue that he must, in order to be consistent, react morally to certain things in a certain way. What we do not and cannot argue about is the validity of these moral principles. We merely praise or condemn them in the light of our own feelings.

If anyone doubts the accuracy of this account of moral disputes, let him try to construct even an imaginary argument on a question of value which does not reduce itself to an argument about a question of logic or about an empirical matter of fact. I am confident that he will not succeed in producing a single example. And if that is the case, he must allow that its involving the impossibility of purely ethical arguments is not, as Moore thought, a ground of objection to our theory, but rather a point in favour of it.

Having upheld our theory against the only criticism which appeared to threaten it, we may now use it to define the nature of all ethical enquiries. We find that ethical philosophy consists simply in saying that ethical concepts are pseudo-concepts and therefore unanalysable. The further task of describing the different feelings that the different ethical terms are used to express, and the different reactions that they customarily provoke, is a task for the psychologist. There cannot be such a thing as ethical science, if by ethical science one means the elaboration of a "true" system of morals. For we have seen that, as ethical judgements are mere expressions of feeling, there can be no way of determining the validity of any ethical system, and, indeed, no sense in asking whether any such system is true. All that one may legitimately

enquire in this connection is, What are the moral habits of a given person or group of people, and what causes them to have precisely those habits and feelings? And this enquiry falls wholly within the scope of the existing social sciences.

It appears, then, that ethics, as a branch of knowledge, is nothing more than a department of psychology and sociology. And in case anyone thinks that we are overlooking the existence of casuistry, we may remark that casuistry is not a science, but is a purely analytical investigation of the structure of a given moral system. In other words, it is an exercise in formal logic.

When one comes to pursue the psychological enquiries which constitute ethical science, one is immediately enabled to account for the Kantian and hedonistic theories of morals. For one finds that one of the chief causes of moral behaviour is fear, both conscious and unconscious, of a god's displeasure, and fear of the enmity of society. And this, indeed, is the reason why moral precepts present themselves to some people as "categorical" commands. And one finds, also, that the moral code of a society is partly determined by the beliefs of that society concerning the conditions of its own happiness—or, in other words, that a society tends to encourage or discourage a given type of conduct by the use of moral sanctions according as it appears to promote or detract from the contentment of the society as a whole. And this is the reason why altruism is recommended in most moral codes and egotism condemned. It is from the observation of this connection between morality and happiness that hedonistic or eudaemonistic theories of morals ultimately spring, just as the moral theory of Kant is based on the fact, previously explained, that moral precepts have for some people the force of inexorable commands. As each of these theories ignores the fact which lies at the root of the other, both may be criticized as being one-sided; but this is not the main objection to either of them. Their essential defect is that they treat propositions which refer to the causes and attributes of our ethical feelings as if they were definitions of ethical concepts. And thus they fail to recognise that ethical concepts are pseudo-concepts and consequently indefinable.

As we have already said, our conclusions about the nature of ethics apply to aesthetics also. Aesthetic terms are used in exactly the same way as ethical terms. Such aesthetic words as "beautiful" and "hideous" are employed, as ethical words are employed, not to make statements of fact, but simply to express certain feelings and evoke a certain response. It follows, as in ethics, that there is no sense in attributing objective validity to aesthetic judgments, and no possibility of arguing about questions of value in aesthetics, but only about questions of fact. A scientific treatment of aesthetics would show us what in general were the causes of aesthetic feeling, why various societies produced and admired the works of art they did, why taste varies as it does within a given society, and so forth. And these are ordinary psychological or sociological questions. They have, of course, little or nothing to do with aesthetic criticism as we understand it. But that is because the purpose of aesthetic criticism is not so much to give knowledge as to communicate emotion. The critic, by calling attention to certain features of the work under review, and expressing his own feelings about them, endeavours to make us share his attitude towards the work as a whole. The only relevant propositions that he formulates are propositions describing the nature of the work. And these are plain records of fact. We conclude, therefore, that there is nothing in aesthetics, any more than there is in ethics, to justify the view that it embodies a unique type of knowledge.

It should now be clear that the only information which we can legitimately derive from the study of our aesthetic and moral experiences is information about our own mental and physical make-up. We take note of these experiences as providing data for our psychological and sociological generalisations. And this is the only way in which they serve to increase our knowledge. It follows that any attempt to make our use of ethical and aesthetic concepts the basis of a metaphysical theory concerning the existence of a world of values, as distinct from the world of facts, involves a false analysis of these concepts. Our own analysis has shown that the phenomena of moral experience cannot fairly be used to support any rationalist or metaphysical doctrine whatsoever. In particular, they cannot, as Kant hoped, be used to establish the existence of a transcendent god.

Critique of Ayer

SIR DAVID ROSS

. . . There is one of the arguments put forward by the positivists which seems to me to provide, when reflected on, an argument in favour not only of the view that our ethical judgments are genuine judgments, but of the view that there are fundamental ethical judgments for which general agreement may be claimed. My. Ayer remarks[1] that, while his theory escapes many of the objections brought against subjectivistic theories in ethics, there is one which it does not escape. This is the argument[2] that such theories would make it impossible to argue about questions of value, which nevertheless we undoubtedly do. He admits that his own theory also would make it impossible to argue about questions of value; as he holds that such sentences as "thrift is a virtue" and "thrift is a vice" do not express propositions at all, he clearly cannot hold that they express incompatible propositions. If, then, he is to resist the argument in question, he must simply deny that in fact we ever do dispute about questions of value; for if we did dispute about things which on his theory we cannot dispute about, his theory would clearly be untrue. He boldly adopts the course to which he is logically forced, and denies that we ever do dispute about questions of value. And

he justifies this by saying that apparent disputes about questions of value are really disputes about questions of fact . . . [At this point Sir David quotes about two hundred words from Ayer's *Language, Truth and Logic*, pp. 163-6 (1936 edition), reprinted on pp. 242 ff. of the present volume.—Ed.] . . . It is perfectly true that, when we differ on a question of right or wrong, or of goodness or badness, it is by consideration of questions of fact—of the precise nature of the consequences or of the probable consequences, or of the motives involved—that we try to remove the difference of opinion on the moral question. And in doing so we betray the conviction that if we could get down to agreement about the facts of the case, we should find ourselves in agreement on the moral question; or in other words, that though we may differ in our moral judgments on some complicated case, we agree in our fundamental judgments as to what kinds of consequences ought to be aimed at and what kinds of motive are good. The more Mr. Ayer emphasizes this element in our discussion of moral questions, the more he pays tribute to the strength of this conviction; for unless we thought that if we could agree on the factual nature of the act we should probably agree on its rightness or wrongness, there would be no point in trying to reach agreement about its factual nature. And in the great majority of cases we find this confidence confirmed, by finding that we agree in our moral judgements when we agree about the facts. But

Reprinted from *The Foundations of Ethics* by Sir David Ross by permission of the Clarendon Press, Oxford. Copyright 1930.
[1] *Language, Truth, and Logic*, p. 163 (1936 edition).
[2] Professor Moore's argument, in *Philosophical Studies*, 333–4.

no doubt we sometimes fail to find agreement even then. We do not find, however, as Mr. Ayer claims, that no subject of dispute remains. We find, indeed, that there is no room for further *argument*; when we have come to some premiss which to us seems axiomatic, and which the other person denies, we can argue no further. But we do not find that all *difference of opinion* has vanished, and that we are left only with different feelings, one liking certain consequences or motives and another disliking them. We find ourselves still saying "this is good," and the person with whom we are speaking still saying "this is bad." And it is not by showing that *argument* ceases, but by showing that *difference of opinion ceases*, that Mr. Ayer could escape from Professor Moore's argument.

But indeed our adoption of the very practice which Mr. Ayer here describes is enough to refute his account of the nature of what are commonly called ethical judgments. He denies that they are judgments; he says they are mere expressions of liking or dislike. If that were all they are, why argue at all? What should we be trying to prove? Is *A* arguing to prove that he likes the given act, and *B* to prove that he dislikes it? Clearly not. *A* does not doubt that *B* dislikes it, nor *B* that *A* likes it; and if they did doubt, they would adopt quite different means of convincing one another, e.g. *A* by consistently seeking to do similar acts and *B* by consistently avoiding them. What they are attempting to do by the process Mr. Ayer describes is to convince each other that the liking, or the dislike, is justified, in other words that the act has a character that *deserves* to be liked or disliked, is good or is bad.

Ethical Judgements

A. J. AYER

The emotive theory of values, which is developed in the sixth chapter of this book, has provoked a fair amount of criticism; but I find that this criticism has been directed more often against the positivistic principles on which the theory has been assumed to depend than against the theory itself.[1] Now I do not deny that in putting forward this theory I was concerned with maintaining the general consistency of my position; but it is not the only ethical theory that would have satisfied this requirement, nor does it actually entail any of the non-ethical statements which form the remainder of my argument. Consequently, even if it could be shown that these other statements were invalid, this would not in itself refute the emotive analysis of ethical judgements; and in fact I believe this analysis to be valid on its own account.

Having said this, I must acknowledge that the theory is here presented in a very summary way, and that it needs to be supported by a more detailed analysis of specimen ethical judgements than I make any attempt to give.[2] Thus, among other things, I fail to bring out the point that the common objects of moral approval or disapproval are not particular actions so much as classes of actions; by which I mean that if an action is labelled right or wrong, or good or bad, as the case may be, it is because it is thought to be an action of a certain type. And this point seems to me important, because I think that what seems to be an ethical judgement is very often a factual classification of an action as belonging to some class of actions by which a certain moral attitude on the part of the speaker is habitually aroused. Thus, a man who is a convinced utilitarian may simply mean by calling an action right that it tends to promote, or more probably that it is the sort of action that tends to promote, the general happiness; and in that case the validity of his statement becomes an empirical matter of fact. Similarly, a man who bases his ethical upon his religious views may actually mean by calling an action right or wrong that it is the sort of action that is enjoyed or forbidden by some ecclesiastical authority; and this also may be empirically verified. Now in these cases the form of words by which the factual statement is expressed is the same as that which would be used to express a normative statement; and this may to some extent

Reprinted from *Language, Truth and Logic*, 1946, pp. 20–22, by permission of Victor Gollancz, Ltd. (From the new Preface to the 1946 edition.)

[1] Cf. Sir W. David Ross, *The Foundations of Ethics*, pp. 30–41 [reprinted in part, pp. 250–1 this volume].

[2] I understand that this deficiency has been made good by C. L. Stevenson in his book, *Ethics and Language*, but the book was published in America and I have not yet been able to obtain it. There is a review of it by Austin Duncan-Jones in *Mind*, October, 1945, and a good indication of Stevenson's line of argument is to be found in his articles on "The Emotive Meaning of Ethical Terms," *Mind*, 1937, "Ethical Judgements and Avoidability," *Mind*, 1938, and "Persuasive Definitions," *Mind*, 1938.

explain why statements which are recognized to be normative are nevertheless often thought to be factual. Moreover, a great many ethical statements contain, as a factual element, some description of the action, or the situation, to which the ethical term in question is being applied. But although there may be a number of cases in which this ethical term is itself to be understood descriptively, I do not think that this is always so. I think that there are many statements in which an ethical term is used in a purely normative way, and it is to statements of this kind that the emotive theory of ethics is intended to apply.

The objection that if the emotive theory was correct it would be impossible for one person to contradict another on a question of value is here met by the answer that what seem to be disputes about questions of value are really disputes about questions of fact. I should, however, have made it clear that it does not follow from this that two persons cannot significantly disagree about a question of value, or that it is idle for them to attempt to convince one another. For a consideration of any dispute about a matter of taste will show that there can be disagreement without formal contradiction, and that in order to alter another man's opinions, in the sense of getting him to change his attitude, it is not necessary to contradict anything that he asserts. Thus, if one wishes to affect another person in such a way as to bring his sentiments on a given point into accordance with one's own, there are various ways in which one may proceed. One may, for example, call his attention to certain facts that one supposes him to have overlooked; and, as I have already remarked, I believe that much of what passes for ethical discussion is a proceeding of this type. It is, however, also possible to influence other people by a suitable choice of emotive language; and this is the practical justification for the use of normative expressions of value. At the same time, it must be admitted that if the other person persists in maintaining his contrary attitude, without however disputing any of the relevant facts, a point is reached at which the discussion can go no further. And in that case there is no sense in asking which of the conflicting views is true. For, since the expression of a value judgment is not a proposition, the question of truth or falsehood does not here arise.

The Emotive Meaning
of Ethical Terms

C. L. STEVENSON

I

Ethical questions first arise in the form "Is so and so good?" or "Is this alternative better than that?" These questions are difficult partly because we don't quite know what we are seeking. We are asking, "Is there a needle in that haystack?" without even knowing just what a needle is. So the first thing to do is to examine the questions themselves. We must try to make them clearer, either by defining the terms in which they are expressed, or by any other method that is available.

The present paper is concerned wholly with this preliminary step of making ethical questions clear. In order to help answer the question "Is X good?" we must *substitute* for it a question which is free from ambiguity and confusion.

It is obvious that in substituting a clearer question we must not introduce some utterly different kind of question. It won't do (to take an extreme instance of a prevalent fallacy) to substitute for "Is X good?" the question "Is X pink with yellow trimmings?" and then point out how easy the question really is. This would beg the original question, not help answer it. On the other hand, we must not expect the substituted question to be strictly "identical" with the original one. The original

Reprinted from *Mind*, 46, 1937, by permission of the author and *Mind*.

question may embody hypostatization, anthropormorphism, vagueness, and all the other ills to which our ordinary discourse is subject. If our substituted question is to be clearer, it must remove these ills. The questions will be identical only in the sense that a child is identical with the man he later becomes. Hence we must not demand that the substitution strike us, on immediate introspection, as making no change in meaning.

Just how, then, must the substituted question be related to the original? Let us assume (inaccurately) that it must result from replacing "good" by some set of terms which define it. The question then resolves itself to this: How must the defined meaning of "good" be related to its original meaning?

I answer that it must be *relevant*. A defined meaning will be called "relevant" to the original meaning under these circumstances: Those who have understood the definition must be able to say all that they then want to say by using the term in the defined way. They must never have occasion to use the term in the old, unclear sense. (If a person did have to go on using the word in the old sense, then to this extent his meaning would not be clarified, and the philosophical task would not be completed.) It frequently happens that a word is used so confusedly and ambiguously that we must give it *several* defined meanings, rather than one. In this case only the whole set of defined meanings will be called "relevant," and any one of them will be called "partially relevant." This is not a rigorous treatment of *relevance*, by any means, but it will serve for the present purposes.

Let us now turn to our particular task—that of giving a relevant definition of "good." Let us first examine some of the ways in which others have attempted to do this.

The word "good" has often been defined in terms of *approval*, or similar psychological attitudes. We may take as typical examples: "good" means *desired by me* (Hobbes); and "good" means *approved by most people* (Hume, in effect).* It will be convenient to refer to definitions of this sort as "interest theories," following Mr. R. B. Perry, although neither "interest" nor "theory" is used in the most usual way.

Are definitions of this sort relevant?

It is idle to deny their *partial* relevance. The most superficial inquiry will reveal that "good" is exceedingly ambiguous. To maintain that "good" is *never* used in Hobbes's sense, and never in Hume's, is only to manifest an insensitivity to the complexities of language. We must recognize, perhaps, not only these senses, but a variety of similar ones, differing both with regard to the kind of interest in question, and with regard to the people who are said to have the interest.

But this is a minor matter. The essential question is not whether interest theories are *partially* relevant, but whether they are *wholly* relevant. This is the only point for intelligent dispute. Briefly: Granted

that some senses of "good" may relevantly be defined in terms of interest, is there some *other* sense which is *not* relevantly so defined? We must give this question careful attention. For it is quite possible that when philosophers (and many others) have found the question "Is X good?" so difficult, they have been grasping for this *other* sense of "good," and not any sense relevantly defined in terms of interest. If we insist on defining "good" in terms of interest, and answer the question when thus interpreted, we may be begging *their* question entirely. Of course this *other* sense of "good" may not exist, or it may be a complete confusion, but that is what we must discover.

Now many have maintained that interest theories are *far* from being completely relevant. They have argued that such theories neglect the very sense of "good" which is most vital. And certainly, their arguments are not without plausibility.

Only . . . what *is* this "vital" sense of "good"? The answers have been so vague, and so beset with difficulties, that one can scarcely determine.

There are certain requirements, however, with which this "vital" sense has been expected to comply—requirements which appeal strongly to our common sense. It will be helpful to summarize these, showing how they exclude the interest theories:

In the first place, we must be able sensibly to *disagree* about whether something is "good." This condition rules out Hobbes's definition. For consider the following argument: "This is good." "That isn't so; it's not good." As translated by Hobbes, this becomes: "I desire this." "That isn't so, for *I* don't." The speakers are not contradicting one another, and think they are, only because of an elementary confusion in the use of pronouns. The definition, "good" means *desired by my community*, is also excluded, for how could people from different communities disagree?[1]

* [The author has asked us, in republishing this paper, to add the note which follows: For a more adequate treatment of Hume's views see my *Ethics and Language* (Yale University Press, 1944), Chap. XII, Sect. 5. In the present paper the references to Hume are to be taken as references to the general *family* of definitions of which Hume's is typical; but Hume's own definition is somewhat different from any that is here specifically stated. Perhaps the same should be said of Hobbes.]

[1] See G. E. Moore's *Philosophical Studies*, pp. 332–334.

In the second place, "goodness" must have, so to speak, a magnetism. A person who recognizes X to be "good" must *ipso facto* acquire a stronger tendency to act in its favour than he otherwise would have had. This rules out the Humian type of definition. For according to Hume, to recognize that something is "good" is simply to recognize that the majority approve of it. Clearly, a man may see that the majority approve of X without having, himself, a stronger tendency to favour it. This requirement excludes any attempt to define "good" in terms of the interest of people *other* than the speaker.[2]

In the third place, the "goodness" of anything must not be verifiable solely by use of the scientific method. "Ethics must not be psychology." This restriction rules out all of the traditional interest theories, without exception. It is so sweeping a restriction that we must examine its plausibility. What are the methodological implications of interest theories which are here rejected?

According to Hobbes's definition, a person can prove his ethical judgments, with finality, by showing that he is not making an introspective error about his desires. According to Hume's definition, one may prove ethical judgments (roughly speaking) by taking a vote. *This* use of the empirical method, at any rate, seems highly remote from what we usually accept as proof, and reflects on the complete relevance of the definitions which imply it.

But aren't there more complicated interest theories which are immune from such methodological implications? No, for the same factors appear; they are only put off for a while. Consider, for example, the definition: "X is good" means *most people would approve of X if they knew its nature and consequences.* How, according to this definition, could we prove that a certain X was good? We should first have to find out, empirically, just what X was like, and what

[2] See G. C. Field's *Moral Theory,* pp. 52, 56–57.

its consequences would be. To this extent the empirical method, as required by the definition, seems beyond intelligent objection. But what remains? We should next have to discover whether most people would approve of the sort of thing we had discovered X to be. This couldn't be determined by popular vote—but only because it would be too difficult to explain to the voters, beforehand, what the nature and consequences of X really were. Apart from this, voting would be a pertinent method. We are again reduced to counting noses, as a *perfectly final* appeal.

Now we need not scorn voting entirely. A man who rejected interest theories as irrelevant might readily make the following statement: "If I believed that X would be approved by the majority, when they knew all about it, I should be strongly *led* to say that X was good." But he would continue: "*Need* I say that X was good, under the circumstances? Wouldn't my acceptance of the alleged 'final proof' result simply from my being democratic? What about the more aristocratic people? They would simply say that the approval of most people, even when they knew all about the object of their approval, simply had nothing to do with the goodness of anything, and they would probably add a few remarks about the low state of people's interests." It would indeed seem, from these considerations, that the definition we have been considering has presupposed democratic ideals from the start; it has dressed up democratic propaganda in the guise of a definition.

The omnipotence of the empirical method, as implied by interest theories and others, may be shown unacceptable in a somewhat different way. Mr. G. E. Moore's familiar objection about the open question is chiefly pertinent in this regard. No matter what set of scientifically knowable properties a thing may have (says Moore, in effect), you will find, on careful introspection, that it is an open question to ask whether anything having these properties is *good*. It is difficult to believe that this recurrent question is a totally confused one, or that it seems open only because of the ambiguity of "good." Rather, we must be using some sense of "good" which is not definable, relevantly, in terms of anything scientifically knowable. That is, the scientific method is not sufficient for ethics.[3]

These, then, are the requirements with which the "vital" sense of "good" is expected to comply: (1) goodness must be a topic for intelligent disagreement; (2) it must be "magnetic"; and (3) it must not be discoverable solely through the scientific method.

II

I can now turn to my proposed analysis of ethical judgments. First let me present my position dogmatically, showing to what extent I vary from tradition.

I believe that the three requirements, given above, are perfectly sensible; that there is some *one* sense of "good" which satisfies all three requirements; and that no traditional interest theory satisfies them all. But this does not imply that "good" must be explained in terms of a Platonic Idea, or of a categorical imperative, or of an unique, unanalyzable property. On the contrary, the three requirements can be met by a *kind* of interest theory. *But we must give up a presupposition which all the traditional interest theories have made.*

Traditional interest theories hold that ethical statements are *descriptive* of the existing state of interests—that they simply *give information* about interests. (More accurately, ethical judgments are said to describe what the state of interests is, was, or will be, or to indicate what the state of interests *would* be under specified circum-

stances.) It is this emphasis on description, on information, which leads to their incomplete relevance. Doubtless there is always *some* element of description in ethical judgments, but this is by no means all. Their major use is not to indicate facts, but to *create an influence*. Instead of merely describing people's interests, they *change* or *intensify* them. They *recommend* an interest in an object, rather than state that the interest already exists.

For instance: When you tell a man that he oughtn't to steal, your object isn't merely to let him know that people disapprove of stealing. You are attempting, rather, to get *him* to disapprove of it. Your ethical judgment has a quasi-imperative force which, operating through suggestion, and intensified by your tone of voice, readily permits you to begin to *influence*, to *modify*, his interests. If in the end you do not succeed in getting *him* to disapprove of stealing, you will feel that you've failed to convince him that stealing is wrong. You will continue to feel this, even though he fully acknowledges that you disapprove of it, and that almost everyone else does. When you point out to him the consequences of his actions—consequences which you suspect he already disapproves of—these *reasons* which support your ethical judgment are simply a means of facilitating your influence. If you think you can change his interests by making vivid to him how others will disapprove of him, you will do so; otherwise not. So the consideration about other people's interest is just an additional means you may employ, in order to move him, and is not a part of the ethical judgment itself. Your ethical judgment doesn't merely describe interests to him, it directs his very interests. The difference between the traditional interest theories and my view is like the difference between describing a desert and irrigating it.

Another example: A munition maker declares that war is a good thing. If he merely meant that he approved of it, he would not have to insist so strongly, nor

[3] See G. E. Moore's *Principia Ethica*, Chap. i. I am simply trying to preserve the spirit of Moore's objection, and not the exact form of it.

grow so excited in his argument. People would be quite easily convinced that he approved of it. If he merely meant that most people approved of war, or that most people would approve of it if they knew the consequences, he would have to yield his point if it were proved that this wasn't so. But he wouldn't do this, nor does consistency require it. He is not *describing* the state of people's approval; he is trying to *change* it by his influence. If he found that few people approved of war, he might insist all the more strongly that it was good, for there would be more changing to be done.

This example illustrates how "good" may be used for what most of us would call bad purposes. Such cases are as pertinent as any others. I am not indicating the *good* way of using "good." I am not influencing people, but am describing the way this influence sometimes goes on. If the reader wishes to say that the munition maker's influence is bad—that is, if the reader wishes to awaken people's disapproval of the man, and to make him disapprove of his own actions—I should at another time be willing to join in this undertaking. But this is not the present concern. I am not using ethical terms, but am indicating how they *are* used. The munition maker, in his use of "good," illustrates the persuasive character of the word just as well as does the unselfish man who, eager to encourage in each of us a desire for the happiness of all, contends that the supreme good is peace.

Thus ethical terms are *instruments* used in the complicated interplay and readjustment of human interests. This can be seen plainly from more general observations. People from widely separated communities have different moral attitudes. Why? To a great extent because they have been subject to different social influences. Now clearly this influence doesn't operate through sticks and stones alone; words play a great part. People praise one another, to encourage certain inclinations, and blame one another, to discourage others. Those of forceful personalities issue commands which weaker people, for complicated instinctive reasons, find it difficult to disobey, quite apart from fears of consequences. Further influence is brought to bear by writers and orators. Thus social influence is exerted, to an enormous extent, by means that have nothing to do with physical force or material reward. The ethical terms facilitate such influence. Being suited for use in *suggestion*, they are a means by which men's attitudes may be led this way or that. The reason, then, that we find a greater similarity in the moral attitudes of one community than in those of different communities is largely this: ethical judgments propagate themselves. One man says "This is good"; this may influence the approval of another person, who then makes the same ethical judgment, which in turn influences another person, and so on. In the end, by a process of mutual influence, people take up more or less the same attitudes. Between people of widely separated communities, of course, the influence is less strong; hence different communities have different attitudes.

These remarks will serve to give a general idea of my point of view. We must now go into more detail. There are several questions which must be answered: How does an ethical sentence acquire its power of influencing people—why is it suited to suggestion? Again, what has this influence to do with the *meaning* of ethical terms? And finally, do these considerations really lead us to a sense of "good" which meets the requirements mentioned in the preceding section?

Let us deal first with the question about *meaning*. This is far from an easy question, so we must enter into a preliminary inquiry about meaning in general. Although a seeming digression, this will prove indispensable.

III

Broadly speaking, there are two different *purposes* which lead us to use language.

On the one hand we use words (as in science) to record, clarify, and communicate *beliefs*. On the other hand we use words to give vent to our feelings (interjections), or to create moods (poetry), or to incite people to actions or attitudes (oratory).

The first use of words I shall call "descriptive"; the second, "dynamic." Note that the distinction depends solely upon the *purpose* of the *speaker*.

When a person says "Hydrogen is the lightest known gas," his purpose *may* be simply to lead the hearer to believe this, or to believe that the speaker believes it. In that case the words are used descriptively. When a person cuts himself and says "Damn," his purpose is not ordinarily to record, clarify, or communicate any belief. The word is used dynamically. The two ways of using words, however, are by no means mutually exclusive. This is obvious from the fact that our purposes are often complex. Thus when one says "I want you to close the door," part of his purpose, ordinarily, is to lead the hearer to believe that he has this want. To that extent the words are used descriptively. But the major part of one's purpose is to lead the hearer to *satisfy* the want. To that extent the words are used dynamically.

It very frequently happens that the same sentence may have a dynamic use on one occasion, and may not have a dynamic use on another; and that it may have different dynamic uses on different occasions. For instance: A man says to a visiting neighbor, "I am loaded down with work." His purpose may be to let the neighbor know how life is going with him. This would *not* be a dynamic use of words. He may make the remark, however, in order to drop a hint. This *would* be dynamic usage (as well as descriptive). Again, he may make the remark to arouse the neighbor's sympathy. This would be a *different* dynamic usage from that of hinting.

Or again, when we say to a man, "Of course you won't make those mistakes any more," we *may* simply be making a predic-

tion. But we are more likely to be using "suggestion," in order to encourage him and hence *keep* him from making mistakes. The first use would be descriptive; the second, mainly dynamic.

From these examples it will be clear that we can't determine whether words are used dynamically or not, merely by reading the dictionary—even assuming that everyone is faithful to dictionary meanings. Indeed, to know whether a person is using a word dynamically we must note his tone of voice, his gestures, the general circumstances under which he is speaking, and so on.

We must now proceed to an important question: What has the dynamic use of words to do with their *meaning*? One thing is clear—we must not define "meaning" in a way that would make meaning vary with dynamic usage. If we did, we should have no use for the term. All that we could say about such "meaning" would be that it is very complicated and subject to constant change. So we must certainly distinguish between the dynamic use of words and their meaning.

It does not follow, however, that we must define "meaning" in some nonpsychological fashion. We must simply restrict the psychological field. Instead of identifying meaning with *all* the psychological causes and effects that attend a word's utterance, we must identify it with those that it has a *tendency* (causal property, dispositional property) to be connected with. The tendency must be of a particular kind, moreover. It must exist for all who speak the language; it must be persistent and must be realizable more or less independently of determinate circumstances attending the word's utterance. There will be further restrictions dealing with the interrelations of words in different contexts. Moreover, we must include, under the psychological responses which the words tend to produce, not only immediately introspectable experiences but *dispositions* to react in a given way with appropriate stimuli. I hope to go into these matters in a subsequent essay.[4] Suffice it now to say that I think "meaning" may be thus defined in a way to include "propositional" meaning as an important kind.

The definition will readily permit a distinction between meaning and dynamic use. For when words are accompanied by dynamic purposes, it does not follow that they *tend* to be accompanied by them in the way mentioned above. E.g. there need be no tendency realizable more or less independently of the determinate circumstances under which the words are uttered.

There will be a kind of meaning, however, in the sense above defined, which has an intimate relation to dynamic usage. I refer to "emotive" meaning (in a sense roughly like that employed by Ogden and

Richards).[5] The emotive meaning of a word is a tendency of a word, arising through the history of its usage, to produce (result from) *affective* responses in people. It is the immediate aura of feeling which hovers about a word.[6] Such tendencies to produce affective responses cling to words very tenaciously. It would be difficult, for instance, to express merriment by using the interjection "alas." Because of the persistence of such affective tendencies (among other reasons) it becomes feasible to classify them as "meanings."

Just *what* is the relation between emotive meaning and the dynamic use of words? Let us take an example. Suppose that a man tells his hostess, at the end of a party, that he thoroughly enjoyed himself, and suppose that he was in fact bored. If we consider his remark an innocent one, are we likely to remind him, later, that he "lied" to his hostess? Obviously not, or at least, not without a broad smile; for although he told her something that he believed to be false, and with the intent of making her believe that it was true—those being the ordinary earmarks of a lie—the

---

[4] The "subsequent essay" became, instead, Chapter 3 of *Ethics and Language*, which among other points defends those that follow:

(1) When used in a generic sense that emphasizes what C. W. Morris calls the *pragmatic* aspects of language, the term "meaning" designates a tendency of words to express or evoke states of mind in the people who use the words. The tendency is of a special kind, however, and many qualifications are needed (including some that bear on syntax) to specify its nature.

(2) When the states of mind in question are cognitive, the meaning can conveniently be called *descriptive*; and when they are feelings, emotions, or attitudes, the meanings can conveniently be called *emotive*.

(3) The states of mind (in a rough and tentative sense of that term) are normally quite complicated. They are not necessarily images or feelings but may in their turn be further tendencies—tendencies to respond to various stimuli that may subsequently arise. A word may have a constant meaning, accordingly, even though it is accompanied, at various times that it is used, by different images or feelings.

(4) Emotive meaning is sometimes more than a by-product of descriptive meaning. When a term has both sorts of meaning, for example, a change in its descriptive meaning may not be attended by a change in emotive meaning.

(5) When a speaker's use of emotive terms evokes an attitude in a hearer (as it sometimes may not, since it has only a *tendency* to do so), it must not be conceived as merely adding to the hearer's attitude in the way that a spark might add its heat to the atmosphere. For a more appropriate analogy, in many cases, we must think rather of a spark that ignites tinder.

[5] See C. K. Ogden and I. A. Richards, *The Meaning of Meaning* (2nd ed. London, 1927). On p. 125 there is a passage on ethics which is the source of the ideas embodied in this essay.

[6] In *Ethics and Language* the phrase "aura of feeling" was expressly repudiated. If the present essay had been more successful in anticipating the analysis given in that later work, it would have introduced the notion of emotive meaning in some such way as this:

The emotive meaning of a word or phrase is a strong and persistent tendency, built up in the course of linguistic history, to give direct expression (quasi-interjectionally) to certain of the speaker's feelings or emotions or attitudes; and it is also a tendency to evoke (quasi-imperatively) corresponding feelings, emotions, or attitudes in those to whom the speaker's remarks are addressed. It is the emotive meaning of a word, accordingly, that leads us to characterize it as *laudatory or derogatory*—that rather generic characterization being of particular importance when we are dealing with terms like "good" and "bad" or "right and wrong." But emotive meanings are of great variety: they may yield terms that express or evoke horror, amazement, sadness, sympathy, and so on.

expression, "you lied to her," would be emotively too strong for our purposes. It would seem to be a reproach, even if we intended it not to be a reproach. So it will be evident that such words as "lied" (and many parallel examples could be cited) become suited, on account of their emotive meaning, to a certain kind of dynamic use—so well suited, in fact, that the hearer is likely to be misled when we use them in any other way. The more pronounced a word's emotive meaning is, the less likely people are to use it purely descriptively. Some words are suited to encourage people, some to discourage them, some to quiet them, and so on.

Even in these cases, of course, the dynamic purposes are not to be identified with any sort of meaning; for the emotive meaning accompanies a word much more persistently than do the dynamic purposes. But there is an important contingent relation between emotive meaning and dynamic purpose: the former assists the latter. Hence if we define emotively laden terms in a way that neglects their emotive meaning, we become seriously confused. *We lead people to think that the terms defined are used dynamically less often than they are.*

IV

Let us now apply these remarks in defining "good." This word may be used morally or nonmorally. I shall deal with the nonmoral usage almost entirely, but only because it is simpler. The main points of the analysis will apply equally well to either usage.

As a preliminary definition let us take an inaccurate approximation. It may be more misleading than helpful but will do to begin with. Roughly, then, the sentence "X is good" means *we like* X. ("We" includes the hearer or hearers.)

At first glance this definition sounds absurd. If used, we should expect to find the following sort of conversation: A. "This is good." B. "But I *don't* like it. What led you to believe that I did?" The unnaturalness of B's reply, judged by ordinary word usage, would seem to cast doubt on the relevance of my definition.

B's unnaturalness, however, lies simply in this: he is assuming that "we like it" (as would occur implicitly in the use of "good") is being used descriptively. This will not do. When "we like it" is to take the place of "this is good," the former sentence must be used not purely descriptively, but dynamically. More specifically, it must be used to promote a very subtle (and for the nonmoral sense in question, a very easily resisted) kind of *suggestion*. To the extent that "we" refers to the hearer it must have the dynamic use, essential to suggestion, of leading the hearer to *make* true what is said, rather than merely to believe it. And to the extent that "we" refers to the speaker, the sentence must have not only the descriptive use of indicating belief about the speaker's interest, but the quasi-interjectory, dynamic function of giving direct expression to the interest. (This immediate expression of feelings assists in the process of suggestion. It is difficult to disapprove in the face of another's enthusiasm.)

For an example of a case where "we like this" is used in the dynamic way that "this is good" is used, consider the case of a mother who says to her several children, "one thing is certain, *we all like to be neat.*" If she really believed this, she would not bother to say so. But she is not using the words descriptively. She is *encouraging* the children to like neatness. By telling them that they like neatness, she will lead them to *make* her statement true, so to speak. If, instead of saying "we all like to be neat" in this way, she had said "it's a good thing to be neat," the effect would have been approximately the same.

But these remarks are still misleading. Even when "we like it" is used for suggestion, it is not quite like "this is good." The latter is more subtle. With such a sentence as "this is a good book," for example, it would be practically impossible to use instead "we like this book." When the latter is used it must be accompanied by so exaggerated an intonation, to prevent its becoming confused with a descriptive statement, that the force of suggestion becomes stronger and ludicrously more overt than when "good" is used.

The definition is inadequate, further, in that the definiens has been restricted to dynamic usage. Having said that dynamic usage was different from meaning, I should not have to mention it in giving the *meaning* of "good."

It is in connection with this last point that we must return to emotive meaning. The word "good" has a laudatory emotive meaning that fits it for the dynamic use of suggesting favorable interest. But the sentence "we like it" has no such emotive meaning. Hence my definition has neglected emotive meaning entirely. Now to neglect emotive meaning serves to foster serious confusions, as I have previously intimated; so I have sought to make up for the inadequacy of the definition by letting the restriction about dynamic usage take the place of emotive meaning. What I should do, of course, is to find a definiens whose emotive meaning, like that of "good," simply does *lead* to dynamic usage.

Why did I not do this? I answer that it is not possible if the definition is to afford us increased clarity. No two words, in the first place, have quite the same emotive meaning. The most we can hope for is a rough approximation. But if we seek for such an approximation for "good," we shall find nothing more than synonyms, such as "desirable" or "valuable"; and these are profitless because they do not clear up the connection between "good" and favorable interest. If we reject such synonyms, in favor of nonethical terms, we shall be highly misleading. For instance "this is good" has something like the meaning of "I

do like this; do so as well." But this is certainly not accurate. For the imperative makes an appeal to the conscious efforts of the hearer. Of course he cannot like something just by trying. He must be led to like it through suggestion. Hence an ethical sentence differs from an imperative in that it enables one to make changes in a much more subtle, less fully conscious way. Note that the ethical sentence centers the hearer's attention not on his interests but on the object of interest, and thereby facilitates suggestion. Because of its subtlety, moreover, an ethical sentence readily permits counter-suggestion and leads to the give and take situation that is so characteristic of arguments about values.

Strictly speaking, then, it is impossible to define "good" in terms of favorable interest if emotive meaning is not to be distorted. Yet it is possible to say that "this is good" is *about* the favorable interest of the speaker and the hearer or hearers, and that it has a laudatory emotive meaning which fits the words for use in suggestion. This is a rough description of meaning, not a definition. But it serves the same clarifying function that a definition ordinarily does, and that, after all, is enough.

A word must be added about the moral use of "good." This differs from the above in that it is about a different kind of interest. Instead of being about what the hearer and speaker *like,* it is about a stronger sort of approval. When a person *likes* something, he is pleased when it prospers and disappointed when it does not. When a person *morally approves* of something he experiences a rich feeling of security when it prospers and is indignant or "shocked" when it does not. These are rough and inaccurate examples of the many factors which one would have to mention in distinguishing the two kinds of interest. In the moral usage, as well as in the nonmoral, "good" has an emotive meaning which adapts it to suggestion.

And now, are these considerations of

any importance? Why do I stress emotive meanings in this fashion? Does the omission of them really lead people into errors? I think, indeed, that the errors resulting from such omissions are enormous. In order to see this, however, we must return to the restrictions, mentioned in Section I, with which the typical sense of "good" has been expected to comply.

V

The first restriction, it will be remembered, had to do with disagreement. Now there is clearly some sense in which people disagree on ethical points, but we must not rashly assume that all disagreement is modeled after the sort that occurs in the natural sciences. We must distinguish between "disagreement in belief" (typical of the sciences) and "disagreement in interest." Disagreement in belief occurs when A believes p and B disbelieves it. Disagreement in interest occurs when A has a favorable interest in X and when B has an unfavorable one in it. (For a full-bodied disagreement, neither party is content with the discrepancy.)

Let me give an example of disagreement in interest. A. "Let's go to a cinema tonight." B. "I don't want to do that. Let's go to the symphony." A continues to insist on the cinema, B on the symphony. This is disagreement in a perfectly conventional sense. They cannot agree on where they want to go, and each is trying to redirect the other's interest. (Note that imperatives are used in the example.)

It is a disagreement in *interest* which takes place in ethics. When C says "this is good," and D says "no, it's bad," we have a case of suggestion and counter-suggestion. Each man is trying to redirect the other's interest. There obviously need be no domineering, since each may be willing to give ear to the other's influence; but each is

trying to move the other none the less. It is in this sense that they disagree. Those who argue that certain interest theories make no provision for disagreement have been misled, I believe, simply because the traditional theories, in leaving out emotive meaning, give the impression that ethical judgments are used descriptively only; and of course when judgments are used purely descriptively, the only disagreement that can arise is disagreement *in belief*. Such disagreement may be disagreement in belief *about* interests, but this is not the same as disagreement *in* interest. My definition does not provide for disagreement in belief about interests any more than does Hobbes'; but that is no matter, for there is no reason to believe, at least on common sense grounds, that this kind of disagreement exists. There is only disagreement *in* interest. (We shall see in a moment that disagreement in interest does not remove ethics from sober argument—that this kind of disagreement may often be resolved through empirical means.)

The second restriction, about "magnetism," or the connection between goodness and actions, requires only a word. This rules out only those interest theories that do *not* include the interest of the speaker in defining "good." My account does include the speaker's interest, hence is immune.

The third restriction, about the empirical method, may be met in a way that springs naturally from the above account of disagreement. Let us put the question in this way: When two people disagree over an ethical matter, can they completely resolve the disagreement through empirical considerations, assuming that each applies the empirical method exhaustively, consistently, and without error?

I answer that sometimes they can and sometimes they cannot, and that at any rate, even when they can, the relation between empirical knowledge and ethical judgments is quite different from the one that traditional interest theories seem to imply.

This can best be seen from an analogy. Let us return to the example where A and B could not agree on a cinema or a symphony. The example differed from an ethical argument in that imperatives were used, rather than ethical judgments, but was analogous to the extent that each person was endeavoring to modify the other's interest. Now how would these people argue the case, assuming that they were too intelligent just to shout at one another?

Clearly, they would give "reasons" to support their imperatives. A might say, "but you know, Garbo is at the Bijou." His hope is that B, who admires Garbo, will acquire a desire to go to the cinema when he knows what film will be there. B may counter, "but Toscanini is guest conductor tonight, in an all-Beethoven program." And so on. Each supports his imperative (*"let's do so and so"*) by reasons which may be empirically established.

To generalize from this: disagreement in interest may be rooted in disagreement in belief. That is to say, people who disagree in interest would often cease to do so if they knew the precise nature and consequences of the object of their interest. To this extent disagreement in interest may be resolved by securing agreement in belief, which in turn may be secured empirically.

This generalization holds for ethics. If A and B, instead of using imperatives, had said, respectively, "it would be *better* to go to the cinema," and "it would be *better* to go to the symphony," the reasons which they would advance would be roughly the same. They would each give a more thorough account of the object of interest, with the purpose of completing the redirection of interest which was begun by the suggestive force of the ethical sentence. On the whole, of course, the suggestive force of the ethical statement merely exerts enough pressure to start such trains of reasons,

since the reasons are much more essential in resolving disagreement in interest than the persuasive effect of the ethical judgment itself.

Thus the empirical method is relevant to ethics simply because our knowledge of the world is a determining factor to our interests. But note that empirical facts are not inductive grounds from which the ethical judgment problematically follows. (This is what traditional interest theories imply.) If someone said "close the door," and added the reason "we'll catch cold," the latter would scarcely be called an inductive ground of the former. Now imperatives are related to the reasons which support them in the same way that ethical judgments are related to reasons.

Is the empirical method *sufficient* for attaining ethical agreement? Clearly not. For empirical knowledge resolves disagreement in interest only to the extent that such disagreement is rooted in disagreement in belief. Not all disagreement in interest is of this sort. For instance: A is of a sympathetic nature and B is not. They are arguing about whether a public dole would be good. Suppose that they discovered all the consequences of the dole. Is it not possible, even so, that A will say that it is good and B that it is bad? The disagreement in interest may arise not from limited factual knowledge but simply from A's sympathy and B's coldness. Or again, suppose in the above argument that A was poor and unemployed and that B was rich. Here again the disagreement might not be due to different factual knowledge. It would be due to the different social positions of the men, together with their predominant self-interest.

When ethical disagreement is not rooted in disagreement in belief, is there *any* method by which it may be settled? If one means by "method" a *rational* method, then there is no method. But in any case there is a "way." Let us consider the above example again, where disagreement was due to A's sympathy and B's coldness. Must they end by saying, "well, it's just a matter of our having different temperaments"? Not necessarily. A, for instance, may try to *change* the temperament of his opponent. He may pour out his enthusiasms in such a moving way—present the sufferings of the poor with such appeal—that he will lead his opponent to see life through different eyes. He may build up by the contagion of his feelings an influence which will modify B's temperament and create in him a sympathy for the poor which did not previously exist. This is often the only way to obtain ethical agreement, if there is any way at all. It is persuasive, not empirical or rational; but that is no reason for neglecting it. There is no reason to scorn it, either, for it is only by such means that our personalities are able to grow, through our contact with others.

The point I wish to stress, however, is simply that the empirical method is instrumental to ethical agreement only to the extent that disagreement in interest is rooted in disagreement in belief. There is little reason to believe that all disagreement is of this sort. Hence the empirical method is not sufficient for ethics. In any case, ethics is not psychology, since psychology does not endeavor to *direct* our interests; it discovers facts about the ways in which interests are or can be directed, but that is quite another matter.

To summarize this section: my analysis of ethical judgments meets the three requirements for the typical sense of "good" that were mentioned in Section I. The traditional interest theories fail to meet these requirements simply because they neglect emotive meaning. This neglect leads them to neglect dynamic usage, and the sort of disagreement that results from such usage, together with the method of resolving the disagreement. I may add that my analysis answers Moore's objection about the open question. Whatever scientifically knowable properties a thing may have, it *is* always open to question whether a thing having these (enumerated) qualities is good. For to ask whether it is good is to ask for *influence*. And whatever I may know about an object, I can still ask, quite pertinently, to be influenced with regard to my interest in it.

VI

And now, have I really pointed out the "typical" sense of "good"?

I suppose that many will still say "no," claiming that I have simply failed to set down *enough* requirements that this sense must meet, and that my analysis, like all others given in terms of interest, is a way of begging the issue. They will say: "When we ask 'is X good?' we don't want mere influence, mere advice. We decidedly don't want to be influenced through persuasion, nor are we fully content when the influence is supported by a wide scientific knowledge of X. The answer to our question will, of course, modify our interests. But this is only because a unique sort of truth will be revealed to us—a truth that must be apprehended a priori. We want our interests to be guided by this truth and by nothing else. To substitute for this special truth mere emotive meaning and mere factual truth is to conceal from us the very object of our search."

I can only answer that I do not understand. What is this truth to be *about*? For I recollect no Platonic Idea, nor do I know what to *try* to recollect. I find no indefinable property nor do I know what to look for. And the "self-evident" deliverances of reason, which so many philosophers have mentioned, seem on examination to be deliverances of their respective reasons only (if of anyone's) and not of mine.

I strongly suspect, indeed, that any sense of "good" which is expected both to unite itself in synthetic a priori fashion with other concepts and to influence interest as well, is really a great confusion. I extract from this meaning the power of influence alone, which I find the only intelligible part. If the rest is confusion, however, then it certainly deserves more than the shrug of one's shoulders. What I should like to do is to *account* for the confusion—to examine the psychological needs which have given rise to it and show how these needs may be satisfied in another way. This is *the* problem, if confusion is to be stopped at its source. But it is an enormous problem and my reflections on it, which are at present worked out only roughly, must be reserved until some later time.

I may add that if "X is good" has the meaning that I ascribe to it, then it is not a judgment that professional philosophers and only professional philosophers are qualified to make. To the extent that ethics predicates the ethical terms of anything, rather than explains their meaning, it becomes more than a purely intellectual study. Ethical judgments are social instruments. They are used in a cooperative enterprise that leads to a mutual readjustment of human interests. Philosophers have a part in this; but so too do all men.

The Emotive Conception of Ethics and Its Cognitive Implications

C. L. STEVENSON

I

In discussing emotive meaning and its place in ethics, I wish to begin not with an analysis of the ethical terms but with a description of the practical situations in which they are used. And in particular I wish to deal with situations that involve a "personal decision."

I shall say that a man's ethical decision is "personal," as distinct from "interpersonal," when he makes it in the privacy of his own reflections. In judging what is good or bad, right or wrong, he is not consulting others and is not advising them but is merely settling the issues in his own mind. Such a decision is not, of course, typical of the whole of an ethical problem. Sooner or later any man is likely to let his personal problem become interpersonal: he will discuss it with others, either in the hope of revising his judgment in the light of what they say, or else in the hope of leading them to revise their judgments. But for brevity I must ignore the interpersonal aspects of the problem. I have dealt with them elsewhere in considering the methods that are available for resolving a disagreement in attitude; and in the present essay I think it may be of interest to view ethics from a somewhat different perspective.

My conception of a personal decision

Reprinted from *The Philosophical Review*, 69, 1950, by permission of the author and *The Philosophical Review*.

will not be new: I shall borrow most of it from John Dewey and the rest from such writers as Hobbes, Spinoza, and Hume. My hope is simply to see this old conception in a new relationship. Some may feel that an emotive analysis of ethics, of the sort I shall later defend, is too simple—that it must be insensitive, in particular, to the role of cognition in ethics. Now I think that is far from the case. So I shall take a conception of a personal decision which, by common consent, has cognitive elements that are highly complex; and I shall then endeavor to show that an emotive analysis, so far from ignoring them, is actually of interest in throwing them into sharper relief.

II

Suppose, then, that a man is making a personal decision about an ethical issue. Just what is he trying to do?

A part of my answer is this: he is trying to make up his mind whether to approve or disapprove of something. So at first—though, as we shall see, only at first—his attitudes have a more conspicuous role in his problem than do his thoughts or beliefs. So long as he is ethically undecided his attitudes are in a psychological state of *conflict*; half of him approves of a certain object or action, and the other half of him disapproves of it. And only when he has resolved his conflict, making his attitudes, at least in greater degree, speak with one voice, will he have made his decision. As we commonly put it, he is making up his mind about "what he really approves of."[1]

To see the cognitive aspects of such a decision we need look only a little further: When a man has conflicting attitudes he is virtually forced to think—to recall to mind whatever he knows about the alternatives before him and to learn as much more about them as he can. For between his thoughts and his attitudes there is an intimate relationship. A change in his thoughts is likely to *bring about* a change in his attitudes and, in particular, is likely to end or minimize his conflict by strengthening, weakening, or redirecting one of the attitudes involved. The man may not know this in the sense of holding it as an articulate theory of psychology, but at least he will act, in some degree, as if he knew it. Hence his problem of resolving his conflict will also be a problem of establishing, cognitively, the varied beliefs that may *help* him to resolve it.

Just how does this influence of thoughts upon attitudes take place? A full explanation, of course, is far more than I am prepared to undertake; but a small part of it is given by this familiar psychological principle: our approval of anything is strengthened or weakened depending on whether we approve or disapprove of its consequences. Suppose, for instance, that a man has conflicting attitudes toward X, and suppose that he later comes to believe that X causes Y. Now if he approves of Y (and for simplicity I shall consider that possibility only) he will thereupon approve of X more strongly. And his strengthened approval of X, outweighing the partial dis-

approval that he also has for it, will tend to make him resolve his conflict in X's favor.

The role of thought or cognitive inquiry in this example will be obvious: it establishes the ordinary causal proposition that X leads to Y. But we have still to explain why a belief of this proposition does anything more than satisfy a scientific curiosity. Why does it strengthen the man's approval of X? One cannot easily hold, I think, that the belief has any power *in itself* to do this. It strengthens the man's approval of X only because Y too is an object of his approval. If Y were indifferent to him he would feel that any question about the relation of X to Y was foreign to his problem. His reasoning serves, then, purely as an *intermediary* between his attitudes: by connecting his thought of X with his thought of Y it also connects his attitude toward X with his attitude toward Y, letting the one be reinforced by the other. And by serving as an intermediary—not this one time, of course, but over and over again—his reasoning fulfills an ethical function. It is an instance of "practical reason" in the only sense of that term that seems to me intelligible: it is ordinary reasoning made practical by its psychological context. But let us note, and with full attention, that its function remains an essential, pervasive one. Without such reasoning each attitude would be compartmentalized from the others, and the net result would not even be conflict, it would be psychological chaos.

When a personal decision in ethics is conceived in this way its cognitive elements are of the utmost variety. They belong not to some one science but rather to all sciences.

At first glance they may seem to belong exclusively to psychology, but in fact they do not. I have said, to be sure, that they spring from a conflict in attitudes, which in turn introduces beliefs that mediate between these attitudes and others; and that much can properly be described and explained by a psychologist. But a psychologist's problem is not the ethical prob-

---

[1] He is also deciding whether he wants others to *share* his approval—a point which I must here ignore for simplicity. There will also be an interplay, of course, between an individual's decision and the "mores" of his community, as I have explained in Essay XI, end of Sect. 5, and in *Ethics and Language*, p. 97.

lem that provides the *subject* of his study. The ethical problem lies in *resolving* the conflict, not in describing or explaining it. And the beliefs that help an individual to resolve it, though themselves psychological phenomena, are not beliefs *about* psychological phenomena, necessarily, and hence not beliefs whose *truth* is tested by psychologists. They may be beliefs about economic phenomena, political phenomena, sociological phenomena, physical phenomena, and so on; for all of these, being potentially the objects of an individual's attitudes, may have to be related to the given object that he is evaluating. Some of the beliefs, of course, *may* be about psychological phenomena, hence psychology is relevant to an ethical problem just as the other sciences are. But it simply takes its place *beside* these other sciences. It has no special privileges.

III

I have been discussing "ethics" in a broad sense of the term. I have not distinguished between a decision about what is *morally good* and a decision about what is simply *valuable*. Now such a distinction can obviously be made, and, although I have doubts as to whether it is very important, I suspect it deserves our passing attention. There are several ways of making it, the most important way, as I see it, depending on the sort of attitudes that are in question and hence on the sort of conflict that is being resolved.

Some of our attitudes are "peculiarly moral," in contrast not to those that are "immoral" but only to those that are "nonmoral." The peculiarly moral attitudes manifest themselves to introspection by feelings of guilt, remorse, indignation, shock, and so on, or else (when their object prospers rather than fails to prosper) by a specially heightened feeling of security and internal strength. These introspective mani-

festations, of course, are indicative of various other characteristics, of which I shall mention only one: When we act in accordance with a peculiarly moral approval we have a secondary approval, so to speak, which makes us proud to recognize our primary one. And when we yield to what we call "temptation"—or, in other words, when the strength of this peculiarly moral approval is outweighed by our nonmoral disapproval—we have a strong inclination to conceal our conduct from our introspection. When we cannot do this, as is often the case, we then have the sense of being victimized by forces which, in retrospect, we wish we had been able to control. "If we had the power to live our life over again," we say to ourselves in effect, "we should take care to inhibit these other attitudes before they had time to become ingrained into our personality."

Now when an individual has a conflict between one peculiarly moral attitude and another, and when he is attempting to make these attitudes, and only these, speak with one voice, then his personal decision, too, can be called "peculiarly moral," and will belong to "ethics" in a quite narrow sense of the term. But if some or all of the attitudes involved are not of this sort, then his decision, though still evaluative, is not "peculiarly moral" and belongs to "ethics" in a broad sense of the term only.

So the distinction in question can readily be made. But, as I have intimated, I suspect it of being unimportant. I doubt whether any of us will have much interest in a man's peculiarly moral decision unless it involves attitudes that predominate over his ordinary preferences. For suppose to the contrary: suppose that a monk has fully decided that it is his duty to be chaste. His peculiarly moral attitudes are not in conflict with one another; they direct him with one voice to follow the straight and narrow path. But suppose that his ordinary preferences constantly outweigh his peculiarly moral attitudes, leading him along a path that is not so straight and not so narrow. I suspect, in that case, that we shall be interested less in his code of morality than in his code of preference. In short, if ethics is to be "practical" philosophy and not a mockery of what is practical, it must be prepared to look beyond the peculiarly moral attitudes and consider all those other attitudes by which a man's conduct may be directed.

So in what follows I shall include as "ethical" any decision that makes an important difference to conduct—no matter whether the attitudes involved are peculiarly moral or not. But perhaps the reader need not reject my views even if he feels that I define "ethical" too broadly. For no matter whether a decision is peculiarly moral or simply preferential, it will involve the resolution of conflict; and it will also involve the many cognitive elements that I have mentioned—the many beliefs which, mediating between attitudes, become relevant to the conflict. So if the reader wishes to restrict the topic to peculiarly moral decisions, he will not, as I see it, be revealing new forces that influence their outcome; he will simply be viewing the forces I have mentioned in a smaller field of operation.

IV

Having discussed the nature of a personal decision I can now go on to the topic of ethical language. The point I wish to make is this:

An ethical analysis that puts emotive meaning to one side and pays attention only to descriptive meaning is very likely to *under*estimate the cognitive content of ethics. One of the main reasons, then, for paying attention to emotive meaning is that it enables one to avoid this error and to recognize the cognitive content in its full variety. Thus I wish to show that an emotive conception of ethics, so often criticized for depriving ethics of its thoughtful,

reflective elements, has actually just the opposite effect.

Let me begin by criticizing the non-emotive views. I cannot be at all complete, for many of my objections would depend upon my conception of interpersonal problems, whereas I must here limit my attention to those that are personal. But perhaps a partial criticism will be sufficient.

Consider the following statement, which is typical of the evolutionary school of analysis: *The degree to which anything is good or bad depends upon the degree to which it increases or decreases the power of society to win out in the struggle for survival.* I shall assume that this statement is in quasi-syntactical idiom and hence can be considered as a definition. Now what will be the effect of this definition, if it is introduced into a situation where any one of us, troubled by conflicting attitudes toward a given object or action, X, is trying to make an ethical decision?

There can be little doubt that it will introduce a *part* of what is cognitively relevant. It will lead us to inquire about the effects of X on social survival; and, since we may be presumed to have a strong approval of the latter, which will transfer to X if we find that X leads to it, our inquiry will be relevant to our conflict. But note that the definition will also do something else: it will lead us to suppose that the effect of X on social survival is *all* that we have to consider. And, if our problem is one of resolving a conflict, that may easily be false. As I have previously remarked the considerations relevant to resolving a conflict are of the greatest variety. So although the definition introduces certain topics it excludes others and ends with a conception of ethics that is cognitively impoverished.

That *other* cognitive topics are relevant is evident from this possibility: Having found that X would maximize social survival, suppose we also found that it would produce a society like that of Aldous Huxley in his *Brave New World*—a society that is secure enough, to be sure, but so lacking in poetic imagination that literature degenerates into the pithy but banal slogans of advertisers. I think most of us would begin to fear that the proposed X would purchase survival at too high a price: we should feel that the price, too, had to be reckoned with. And should anyone argue that the price was irrelevant, being foreign to the evolutionary definition of "good," I think we should answer: "So much the worse for the definition."

My objection holds not merely against this one definition but against any definition of the form, "'X is valuable' means that X is conducive to E," where E need not be social survival, but can be the social integration of interests, or the greatest happiness of the greatest number, or the maximal presence of a unique, indefinable quality, or any other impersonal aim. Such a definition implies that one need only, in making an evaluative decision about X, examine its consequences upon E. It implies that one need *not* examine the consequences of X upon things unrelated to E and need not examine the consequences of E itself. But in fact a person may have *doubts* as to whether E will resolve the conflict from which the need of his evaluative decision arose. He may wonder whether his approval of E is strong enough to outweigh his disapproval of the other consequences I have mentioned. Now the very possibility of these *doubts* shows that the definition is insensitive to the magnitude of his problem; for to settle the doubts he must examine these other consequences, which the definition declares to be irrelevant.

All but a very few nonemotive analyses, in my opinion, are open to an objection which, if not identical with this, is closely parallel to it. And I suspect that the analyses which are free from the objection immediately run into difficulties of another kind. For example:

Consider the definition, "'X is good' means the same as 'If I knew all about the nature and consequences of X, any conflict that I now may have about it would be resolved in its favor.'" This is a nonemotive definition; and, being made to order, as it were, to fit my conception of a personal decision, it is free from the above objection. But since it introduces the pronoun, "I," it does not make clear how two spectators can disagree: when one says "X is good" and the other says "X is not good" each is talking about himself and each may be telling the truth. An emotive conception, on the other hand, can easily avoid this difficulty, as I have shown elsewhere in contrasting disagreement in belief about attitudes with disagreement in attitude.[2] This point would lead us away from the personal to the interpersonal aspects of an ethical problem, however, so I shall keep within my prescribed limits and say no more about it.

The view of John Dewey, who has been so sensitive to the cognitive complexity of ethics, raises a somewhat different question. I am greatly indebted to Dewey, as this essay readily indicates. And yet I cannot believe that he has been successful in analyzing the ethical terms. He is content to say that they affect conduct and satisfaction by being predictive. But, since all predictive statements tend to affect conduct and satisfaction, and since not all of them, presumably, are ethical, we must ask what *sort* of predictions are in question. And to this Dewey gives no precise answer.

Nor do I see how Dewey could succeed—apart from introducing emotive meaning in the way I shall presently discuss—in repairing his analysis. The cognitive elements that are relevant to a conflict are no less varied than the attitudes between which they mediate. I should suppose, moreover, that they are different for different individuals; and I should suppose that, even for a given individual, they would vary with different problems. Now Dewey wants to pack all these elements into the very meaning of an ethical term:

[2] Essays I and II, pp. 1 ff. and 26 f., and *Ethics and Language*, chs. 1 and 8.

he wants them to be relevant to an ethical judgment *by definition*. But they are so complicated that he is unable to specify what they are. So he can give only the genus of a definition, without the needed differentiae.

V

Let me now turn to the more constructive part of this essay. I hope to show that emotive meaning is likely to succeed where cognitive meaning is likely to fail, that it will restore the thoughtful and reflective elements of ethics to their rightful place.

The precise definition of "emotive meaning" is itself a complicated matter; but the various details will not, I think, greatly affect the simple point I am about to make. So I shall assume that "emotive meaning," whatever else, refers to a tendency of certain words to express or evoke attitudes; and I shall assume that it is one thing to express or evoke attitudes and another thing to designate them. That is to say, the interjection, "alas," which expresses or evokes sorrow, functions rather differently from the noun "sorrow" itself, which designates sorrow.

It will be unnecessary for me to show, I trust, that the ethical terms have an emotive meaning—so long, that is, as I do not insist that it is their only sort of meaning. The controversy has been concerned not with this point but rather with the *importance* of their emotive meaning. It is to be mentioned only to be put to one side so that it will not distract us from what is really essential; or is it itself an essential factor?

When we limit attention to problems of the sort I have been emphasizing— evaluative decisions that a man makes in private rather than in discussions with other people—the emotive meaning of the ethical terms may at first seem trivial. It

may remind us merely that ethical decisions are sometimes attended by self-exhortation. Although self-exhortation is interesting enough, it is scarcely a matter to be dwelt upon.

There is another respect, however, in which attention to emotive meaning is more rewarding. It helps us, in cases where a man is making a decision, to see how his language reflects his problem—how it reflects his effort to make his attitudes speak with one voice. It does so in this simple way:

Suppose that the man first withholds such terms as "good" and "bad"; that he next uses them somewhat tentatively, or else alternates between the one term and the other; and that finally he uses one of them only, and with conviction. If we take his ethical terms as emotive, and hence as expressing his attitudes, we can easily explain the fact that they are verbal clues to the nature of his problem; for at first he has no unimpeded attitude to express, being in a state of conflict; and, as his attitudes speak more and more with one voice, he expresses them more and more freely.

Let me here emphasize a point that I feel to be of central importance. If we take the man's ethical terms as *expressing* his attitudes, we can become sensitive to the nature of his problem without difficulty. But if we take them as merely *designating* his attitudes, we are likely to miss the very aspect of his problem that makes it an evaluative one.

For suppose we were to insist that his ethical judgment was no more than attitude-designating, like the statement, "Careful introspection assures me that I approve of this." That would immediately suggest to us that the man's problem was one of describing his own state of mind and hence a problem in psychology. Whereas we have seen that it is something else. The man is trying to *resolve* a conflict, and the process of resolving it is much more complicated than the introspective process of describing it. In other words the attitude-designating terms would be twice removed from his problem; they would formulate beliefs that were *about* it. And by emphasizing *these* beliefs, instead of the many others that he is really concerned with, they would suggest that he is simply *looking at* his conflict. But in fact he is *living through* it and all the activities that attend its resolution, the task of looking at it being comparatively inessential.

To restore the correct emphasis, then, we must take the ethical terms not as attitude-designating but as attitude-expressing and hence as emotive. For in the latter capacity the terms are only once removed from the man's attitudes; they are related to his attitudes by a direct route and not by the indirect route of expressing beliefs about them. By causing us to look to the attitudes themselves, rather than to beliefs that do no more than describe them, emotive meaning frees us from the tendency of supposing that an evaluative decision is somehow an exercise in introspective psychology. It reminds us that the man's efforts throughout his decision are to change his very attitudes. He must actually make this change and not merely describe it as a self-conscious spectator, as if all the work were being done for him by somebody else.

Thus emotive meaning, once it is taken into account, makes us more sensitive to the nature of an ethical problem. And yet we have seen only its negative importance: we have seen only how it prevents us from making too much of the beliefs that are comparatively *inessential*—the individual's introspective beliefs that are *about* his attitudes. We have still to see how emotive meaning bears positively on cognition, how it introduces the beliefs that really are essential—those that *mediate between* an individual's attitudes and thus cause his attitudes to change.

I can best deal with this latter topic by taking a simple example. Suppose that a man says that X is good. By itself this is only a beginning; he is likely to go on, giving what are called *reasons* for this judgment. "It is good," he says, "because it leads to Y and Z." And if we ask him, "Are those the only reasons you need to consider?" he will be likely to say, "No, I suppose not." Perhaps he will then go on to consider other consequences of X, or of Y and Z. And so on.

This example, which simply puts an ethical judgment in its wider context, is sufficient to show that the cognitive elements in an ethical problem are well taken care of by statements that contain no ethical terms at all. They are taken care of by the *reasons for* the ethical judgment. The latter statements, though they do indeed, in such a context, deal with beliefs that mediate between attitudes, remain ordinary cognitive statements, open to all the tests of inductive or deductive logic. So the question that arises is this: since the reasons that attend the ethical judgment will introduce the cognitive issues, to what extent must their work be anticipated by the ethical judgment itself?

My answer is this: there can be no objection, so far as the cognitive richness of an ethical problem is concerned, to an analysis that delegates *all* the relevant beliefs to the reasons, allowing the judgment to keep none of them. I do not say that that is mandatory from a linguistic point of view, but I do say that it is feasible. For the important thing, after all, is that our language be conceived as introducing, in one way or another, the varied cognitive elements which an ethical problem does in fact bring with it. And how can an analysis be thought to impoverish ethics if, having recognized no cognitive elements in an ethical judgment itself, it immediately recognizes them among the reasons by which the ethical judgment can be supported?

To be sure, such an analysis must not stop at that point. It must explain why the ethical judgment, once made, introduces a situation to which the reasons become relevant. It must explain why the judgment feels naked, so to speak, when the reasons are not given. But that is easily explained, and the explanation simply takes us back to emotive meaning and to the living context in which the emotive terms are used.

A man's willingness to say that X is good, and hence to express his approval, will depend partly on his beliefs—his beliefs serving, as usual, to mediate between his attitude to X and his attitudes to other things. Unless he is rather less than a rational animal, then, he will not express his approval without stopping to think. And the reasons that he gives for his judgment enable him to formulate what he is stopping to think *about*. In that simple way the relation between his judgment and his reasons can be explained. His reasons do not "entail" his expression of approval, of course, or make it "probable." An expression of attitude cannot stand in these logical relationships to descriptive statements but only in causal relationships. But the reasons do make a difference: they help to determine whether the man will continue to make his judgment, or qualify it, or replace it by an unfavorable one. So they can be called "reasons" in a perfectly familiar sense of that term.

It is because the ethical terms are emotive, then, that they introduce the varied cognitive elements into an ethical problem. Although emotive meaning does not supply these elements by itself it introduces a situation that shows them to be relevant. This will be true if we take the ethical terms to be *purely* emotive. That is not, actually, my own view; but, since my own view cannot be briefly summarized, I shall be content to defend it by showing that even an extreme view is immune to an all too familiar objection. Whatever else the emotive conception of ethics may do it does not imply that evaluative decisions must be thoughtless.

Let me now argue that an emotive view cannot only be sensitive to the complexities of an ethical problem but is likely to be *more* sensitive to them than any nonemotive view.

If we think back on the nonemotive views I have criticized we can easily see that they too are trying to account for the reasons that support an ethical judgment. But how can they *relate* the judgment to the reasons? They cannot, of course, do this in the way I have done it, for they ignore emotive meaning from the start. So they do what at first glance seems plausible. They conceive of the judgment as somehow containing in its own meaning all the cognitive factors that the reasons deal with. They suppose that the reasons simply do over again, explicitly, the cognitive work that the judgment has done implicitly.

But this procedure, as we have seen, is an impossible one. The reasons are too complicated to permit it. So one of several things will happen. In attempting to make clear what an ethical judgment means a nonemotive analyst will have to leave something out; he will have to mention some too limited factor, like survival, and ignore all the others—thus impoverishing ethics. Or else he will be adequate to personal problems at the expense of ignoring interpersonal ones. Or else, like Dewey, he will be unable to complete his analysis. This last alternative is no less distressing than the others, in my opinion, since it gives the impression that the ethical terms are somehow unfit for use until all their meaning is specified and hence that they remain suspect until analysis achieves the impossible.

When the reasons are conceived as causally related to an *emotive* judgment, however, these difficulties vanish. The full set of reasons need not be "there" in the ethical judgment itself. We can add them piecemeal. And that is how, in practice, we do add them. For we do not know in advance all the reasons that will bear upon our problem, just as we do not know in advance the nature of our varied attitudes between which the reasons mediate. We progressively become aware of them as our evaluative decision gets under way.

VI

I have been limiting my attention to personal decisions, even though the *inter*personal aspects of ethics are of equal or greater importance. And as I have said I cannot here develop the latter topic. But I feel that I should make one remark about it to avoid stating the cognitive claims of an emotive ethics in an exaggerated form.

In making a personal decision a man is very likely to find that his reasons, if carefully developed, will resolve his conflict to a significant degree and hence lead him to a definite judgment. For the chance of his being evenly divided against himself, when all his attitudes come into play, is scarcely worth considering. In an interpersonal problem, however, the case may be different. When controversial, such a problem involves disagreement in attitude—which is roughly a conflict "writ large." Two men disagree in the sense that their attitudes cannot both be satisfied. Now will reasoning, by its causal effect on their attitudes, resolve such a disagreement and lead both men to value the same things?

I suspect that it often will, but I cannot be sure that it always will. For the question is a complicated, psychological one: If men come to share a great number of beliefs about X, will they have the same attitude to X? On a question of such magnitude it is difficult even to weigh the probabilities.

So in spite of the cognitive richness of the emotive conception of ethics, I cannot be sure that it will make all the questions of normative ethics theoretically open to a unique, reasoned answer. And perhaps the reader will consider that a ground for seeking some other conception of ethics. When seen only in relation to personal decisions,

he may say, the emotive conception of ethics seems defensible, but for interpersonal issues it is cognitively weak and must be rejected.

If that is his objection then I can only wonder what more acceptable analysis he can find. For however he may care to define the ethical terms, he will be able to mention nothing that I cannot recognize among the *reasons* that support an emotive judgment. And his subject matter either will or will not be an object of people's approval. To find out about this he must raise the complicated psychological question that I have just mentioned; and he too will not know the answer.

But perhaps the reader does not care whether his ethical subject matter is an object of approval. In that case he will have this to consider: having convinced certain men by reasoning that X is good, in his sense, he may find that in consequence they have a much greater desire to destroy X. His ethics may be totally "unsanctioned," as Bentham and Mill would say. But how could such an ethics be of interest to anybody? Why, indeed, would one study ethics at all, in preference to some pleasantly innocuous subject, like the stamp issues of Andorra? It will not help him to rest content in the assurance that all men *ought*, in his unsanctioned sense, to approve of what he finds good. They may admit that too, and thereupon take a special pride in doing what, in his sense, they oughtn't to do.

The uncertainty of a rationally obtainable convergence of attitudes will arise, then, for *any* ethics that actually works. And that being so, the seeming objection to the emotive conception is rather an objection to the complexities of social life. So I hold to my central thesis: the emotive conception of ethics, so far from depriving ethics of its thoughtful, reflective elements, in fact preserves them in all their variety.

Emotivism and Ethical Objectivity

CARL WELLMAN

To the casual observer, the language of ethics appears to be as objective as the language of science. We normally formulate ethical sentences in the declarative mood; we speak of them as true or false, and we expect them to be supported with adequate evidence. Traditional theories of ethics have usually accepted this appearance at its face value. However many and deep the disagreements between theological and secular ethicists or between intuitionists and naturalists, they all have agreed that ethical statements have a genuine claim to objective validity.

The emotive theory of ethics, explicitly or by implication, denies this claim to objectivity. Ayer openly proclaimed that normative utterances assert nothing at all and that there can be no dispute about ethical issues. Later emotivists, particularly Stevenson, qualified this subjectivism in various ways, but in the end they also insisted that ethical statements cannot be objective in the same way that factual statements are. More than any other feature, it is this subjectivism that has troubled the critics of emotivism. Hence, anyone who wishes to assess the achievements and limitations of the emotive theory of ethics would do well to confront this crucial question: Are ethical statements objective or subjective?

Reprinted from *American Philosophical Quarterly* V, April 1968, by permission of the author and *American Philosophical Quarterly*.

I

However one may decide to answer this question in the end, one must begin by recognizing that the language of ethics at least *appears* to be objective. Early forms of emotivism branded this appearance as sheer illusion and proclaimed the complete subjectivity of ethical utterances. Illusion or not, it must be explained even if it is to be explained away. If ethical utterances are really expressions of emotion or disguised commands, why are they not formulated in the exclamatory or imperative mood? If they are neither true nor false, why do we speak of them as such? If logic is inapplicable to them, what are ethical arguments? Stevenson recognized the urgency of such questions and, almost alone among the emotivists, discussed them with care and imagination. In fact, his writings[1] in ethical theory can profitably be read as an extended and systematic explanation of the appearance of objectivity in ethics.

(1) When one speaker says "this is good" and another says "no, it is bad," their utterances certainly seem to be incompatible. But if ethical sentences express and evoke emotions rather than stating facts,

[1] The various writings of Charles L. Stevenson will be referred to in this way: *Ethics and Language* (New Haven, 1944), as *EL*, *Facts and Values* (New Haven, 1963), as *FV*, and his essay "Ethical Fallibility" in *Ethics and Society*, ed. by Richard DeGeorge (Garden City, 1966), pp. 197–217, as *EF*.

their utterances are not logically inconsistent. How, then, can one explain the appearance of contradiction here? Stevenson does it by challenging the assumption that all disagreement requires logical incompatibility. Disagreement in belief involves an opposition of beliefs both of which cannot be true; disagreement in attitude involves an opposition of attitudes both of which cannot be satisfied. Two speakers disagree in attitude when they have opposed attitudes to the same object and when at least one of them has a motive for altering or calling into question the attitude of the other (*FV*, pp. 1–2). Although the two utterances "this is good" and "no, it is bad" are not logically inconsistent, they are still incompatible because they express a disagreement in attitude.

(2) Ethical disagreement typically leads to ethical dispute; that is, speakers who disagree in attitude usually argue more or less persistently with one another. But it is generally agreed that about matters of taste there is no disputing. If matters of ethics are equally subjective, why should ethical disputes arise? Stevenson's answer is twofold. The need for concerted social action requires that disagreements in attitude be resolved in a way which does not require that differences in taste be overcome, and we are more able to change attitudes by persuasion than we are to modify tastes of the palate by merely verbal means (*EL*, pp. 111–112). We dispute about ethical issues because ethical argument is both practically necessary and psychologically effective.

(3) Ethical sentences are normally formulated in the declarative rather than the exclamatory or imperative mood. But why do they have the grammatical structure of factual statements if their logical function is really to express and evoke attitudes? Although Stevenson has never discussed this question explicitly, he can answer it within his theoretical framework. On his analysis, ethical sentences have descriptive as well as emotive meaning. It

may well be the inclusion of this factual component that leads us to express ourselves in the declarative mood. Moreover, there are reasons to use this mood even with respect to the emotive component of ethical sentences. We tend to care more deeply and permanently about ethical matters than about the things which call forth exclamations or commands, and our attempts to influence others may be more effective if they are cloaked in the form of statements.

(4) In ordinary English we frequently speak of ethical sentences as true or false. But since attitudes cannot be true or false in anything like the sense that beliefs can, it would seem that the sentences which express and evoke our attitudes must necessarily be lacking in truth-value. How, then, can we properly apply the words "true" and "false" to ethical sentences? Originally Stevenson maintained that, although the descriptive component of ethical sentences is true or false, the emotive component cannot properly be said to have truth-value in the strict sense at all (*EL*, p. 154). Now, however, he admits that his earlier contention was misleading and holds that we can speak of ethical sentences in their entirety as true or false without any linguistic impropriety. In ordinary English, any sentence in the declarative mood may be said to be true or false, whether or not it asserts a fact, because the function of the word "true" is simply to repeat with emphasis the sentence to which it is applied (*FV*, pp. 214–217).

(5) In addition to statements, the language of ethics includes questions. Now a factual question expresses doubt about the nature of reality and is a request for information. But such uncertainty in belief cannot be central in a language whose primary function is to express and evoke attitudes. How, then, can an emotivist interpret the ethical questions we ask? Stevenson explains that ethical questions express personal uncertainty in attitude. This uncertainty arises from a conflict of atti-

tudes within the individual and poses the ethical problem of resolving this inner conflict (FV, pp. 56–58). An ethical question expresses the speaker's uncertainty in attitude, refers to the hearer's attitudes, and is a request for influence (EL, pp. 92–93). Hence, an ethical question like "is it good?" means roughly "do you approve of it, and shall I?"

(6) A speaker may wonder if he is mistaken in some ethical statement even when his conviction remains unshaken. But there can be no falsehood where there is no real objectivity, and there is no room for personal uncertainty as long as the individual has a single unwavering attitude. How can the emotivist explain our willingness to acknowledge our fallibility in ethics? Stevenson replies that a person who wonders whether some firm attitude of his may not be mistaken is really in doubt about the stability of his attitude. After all, any reasonable man recognizes that even his strongest attitude may have to be revised in the light of additional inquiry or discussion because he expects to find further reasons for or against his attitudes (EF, pp. 214–215). This readiness to reconsider in the future is quite consistent with the sincere expression and practical commitment to one's present attitude.

(7) Arguments like "this is good because this is a pleasure and all pleasures are good" seem to be formally valid. But if ethical statements express attitudes rather than assert propositions, how can logic apply to them at all? Stevenson holds that the canons of formal logic can be directly applied to some ethical arguments because of the descriptive meaning incorporated in ethical language (EL, p. 116). It is only insofar as ethical sentences go beyond descriptive meaning to express and evoke attitudes that logic loses its hold on them.

(8) We often argue about ethical issues. We give reasons for our own ethical conclusions and present evidence against the ethical statements of others. But since attitudes are lacking in truth-value, they

can hardly be proved true or false. How, then, is ethical reasoning possible? In part, Stevenson's answer has already been given. Ethical conclusions sometimes follow logically from a set of premises by virtue of the descriptive meaning of the statements involved. In all such cases, however, at least one of the premises must itself be an ethical statement (EL, p. 236). In those cases where ethical conclusions are inferred from purely factual premises, the premisses are related to the conclusion psychologically rather than logically (EL, pp. 112–113). Although the facts cited do not prove the attitude true, they do support it by reinforcing it (FV, p. 83). Therefore, it is always possible to defend an ethical statement by giving reasons for it.

(9) Not only is ethical reasoning possible, it is necessary. We customarily demand reasons for any ethical statement, and if the speaker cannot or will not support his utterance, we discount it as arbitrary or dogmatic. Since we do not expect a man to prove his exclamations, why is it necessary for him to defend his expressions of attitude? Stevenson replied that a man's willingness to express his approval or disapproval depends upon his beliefs about the object of his attitude and that no rational man will express his attitude without stopping to think. Hence, an ethical judgment "feels naked, so to speak, when the reasons are not given" (FV, p. 67).

(10) Reasons can and must be given for ethical statements, but not every reason is a good reason. With respect to any ethical conclusion, we distinguish between relevant and irrelevant facts. But if the connection between belief and attitude is purely psychological, our distinction cannot be a logical one. How can the emotivist analyze the notion of relevance in ethical reasoning? Stevenson seems to say that relevant facts are those which strengthen or weaken the attitudes of the hearer; reasons which are not likely to be effective in modifying the attitude in question are irrelevant (FV, p. 4). Thus the distinction be-

tween relevant and irrelevant considerations can be drawn in terms of psychological effectiveness.

(11) In ethics rational methods of persuasion are to be preferred to sheer propaganda or purely emotional rhetoric. For an emotivist, however, the appeal to facts is no more valid logically than emotional appeals or even distortion of the facts. Where logical canons are excluded, how can there be any measure of the goodness of a method of persuasion apart from psychological efficacy? Stevenson agrees that in most cases rational methods are preferable to nonrational ones and denies that he must base his case on rhetorical effectiveness alone. There are many reasons to choose rational methods of persuasion. The method of applying all the available information is good because it builds up a habit of inquiry and tends to result in stable attitudes; the method of ignoring awkward facts is bad because it can lead to resentment if discovered and often results in disorganized or disastrous conduct (*EL*, pp. 156–157 and *FV*, pp. 195–197).

(12) Even when the inferences go from factual premises to ethical conclusions, we speak of ethical arguments as "valid" or "invalid." But the emotivist denies that the canons of formal logic apply to such arguments at all. How can he explain our use of logical terms in an area where logic is inapplicable? Stevenson suggests that these words, at least as they are used in the context of ethics, are to be analyzed analogously to ethical words like "good" or "right." To ask which factual premises really justify an ethical conclusion is to ask a normative question, not to pose a neutral metaethical problem. Thus to claim that reason R would justify evaluative conclusion E is to make another evaluative judgment E' serving to evaluate the situation that would exist if R were the case (*FV*, pp. 87–89). For example, to say "the fact that it is pleasant is a valid reason to infer that it is good" is to commit oneself to saying "that object, if it were pleasant, would be good." Since judgments of validity in ethical reasoning turn out to be a special case of ethical judgments, the words "valid" and "invalid" have primarily emotive meaning. It makes perfectly good sense to apply these words to ethical arguments, for there are many reasons to approve or disapprove of an argument besides those supplied by formal logic.

There are at least twelve features of the language of ethics would suggest that it is an objective form of discourse—ethical utterances can be incompatible with one another, we dispute about ethical issues, ethical sentences are formulated in the declarative mood, we speak of them as true or false, we ask ethical questions, the individual may wonder if his ethical conviction is mistaken, some ethical arguments are formally valid, ethical reasoning is always possible, and it is usually necessary, we distinguish between relevant and irrelevant considerations, rational methods of persuasion are to be preferred to sheer propaganda, and we apply the terms "valid" and "invalid" to ethical arguments. Together, these various features give an appearance of objectivity that seems to count heavily against emotivism, the theory that primarily ethical sentences express and evoke emotions or attitudes. Some of the early emotivists, like Ayer, tried to deny or explain away this appearance of objectivity, but Stevenson has shown in a remarkable and impressive manner how a more complex and subtle emotivism can explain all of these awkward characteristics of ethical language.

II

Although Stevenson has taken great pains to explain the appearance of objectivity, he persists in denying any genuine objectivity to ethical statements. It is here that I wish to take issue with him. The obvious line of attack would be to point to some feature of the language of ethics which bears its objectivity so clearly on its face that any subjective interpretation becomes impossible. I must confess that I have been able to discover no such feature. Therefore, I cannot hope to refute emotivism with any conclusiveness.

Nevertheless, I am not prepared to accept emotivism and the subjectivism that it entails. Granted that Stevenson can explain the appearance of objectivity within his emotive theory of ethics, the mere fact that the appearance needs explaining is *prima facie* evidence against emotivism. The fact that so many aspects of ethical language appear to conflict with subjectivism is a reason to adopt an objective interpretation of ethical language, other things being equal. Moreover, not all explanations are equally adequate. Some explanations are theoretically simple; others are complicated, requiring many qualifications and *ad hoc* hypotheses. Some are natural and straightforward; others are strained or even perverse. Although I must admit with grudging admiration that Stevenson can explain every awkward fact about the language of ethics, I insist that he has not explained every fact as well as could be desired. Therefore, my argument will take the form of showing that at some points his explanations, although not clearly false, are still philosophically inadequate.

Let me begin with a minor, but revealing, problem. How can formal logic be applied to ethical arguments? Consider this syllogism:

Nothing that weakens people's sense of independence is good. A dole weakens people's sense of independence. Therefore, a dole is not good.

Stevenson maintains that this argument is formally valid and suggests that it be treated in accordance with the first pattern of analysis (*EL*, p. 116). But how can it be logically valid when the major premiss and the conclusions are ethical statements which express and evoke attitudes completely lacking in truth-value? Stevenson's reply is that these ethical statements also have descriptive meaning and that it is insofar as they express beliefs that the ordinary canons of logic apply to them. Very well, using the first pattern of analysis and considering only descriptive meaning, the argument amounts to this:

I disapprove of anything that weakens people's independence.
A dole weakens people's sense of independence.
Therefore, I disapprove of the dole.

Analyzed this way, the argument is formally valid, but it is no longer an ethical argument because its conclusion is not an ethical statement. What the argument establishes is a factual statement about the speaker's attitude, but it does nothing to establish the attitude expressed in the ethical conclusion "a dole is not good." As Stevenson himself insists, the whole point of ethical reasoning is to establish or call into question the attitudes, not the descriptive meanings, expressed in ethical conclusions (*EL*, p. 154). Thus it is only in the most uninteresting sense that formal logic applies to even the simplest and most straightforward ethical argument, for the validity of the argument does nothing whatsoever to establish the ethical import of the conclusion in question.

In fact, the situation is far worse than this. Stevenson now admits that no description of the speaker's attitude is built into the meaning of ethical statements (*FV*, pp. 210–212). Obviously this admission will require radical revision of the first pattern of analysis, but it is less obvious which modification Stevenson will elect. He might, as Moore suggested, simply delete the descriptive meaning from the first pattern, but then his explanation of how formal logic is applicable to some ethical arguments becomes entirely beside the point.

He can no longer say that the ordinary canons of logic apply to ethical arguments to the extent that they have descriptive meaning if he eliminates the descriptive meaning of ethical statements. If he tries to save his explanation of the validity of ethical syllogisms by ascribing some other descriptive meaning to ethical statements, it would seem that all ethical reasoning would then fall into the second pattern of analysis. Let us, therefore, consider this second pattern with some care.

Stevenson suggests (*EL*, p. 231) that second pattern arguments like the following are logically valid:

"Good" means "is conducive to social harmony."
His act was conducive to social harmony.
Therefore, his act was good.

Since logic is supposed to be applicable to ethical arguments only insofar as they have descriptive meaning, presumably we can disregard any emotive meaning the sentences in the argument may have. Thus interpreted, the major premiss simply establishes the descriptive meaning for the word "good," and the conclusion applies this word in its purely descriptive meaning only. On this interpretation, the definition enables us to infer the conclusion from the minor premiss because it assures us that the conclusion merely repeats the factual premiss in other words. This explains its validity well enough, but it also denudes the conclusion of any ethical import. Therefore, Stevenson has not explained how formal logic can apply to ethical arguments *as ethical* at all. The second pattern, in spite of its introduction of descriptive meaning through persuasive definitions, does nothing to explain how any genuinely ethical conclusion follows logically from any set of premisses, whether ethical or factual or both.

It may be objected that I have missed the whole point of a persuasive definition. Introducing a persuasive definition does enable one to infer an ethical conclusion just because a persuasive definition is not purely descriptive. Every such definition expresses an attitude and pleads a cause. Fine, but how does the ethical import of the definition get transferred to the conclusion of the argument? Put differently, is there any contradiction in accepting the attitude expressed in the persuasive definition and rejecting the attitude expressed in the conclusion of the argument? Stevenson remarks that if a person did not in fact approve of all and only those things to which the persuasive *definiens* were predicable, he would not accept the persuasive definition of "good" (*EL*, p. 230). Perhaps, but this is a contingent psychological generalization, not a logical truth. Thus, it does not show that there would be any *logical* inconsistency in accepting the persuasive definition together with the factual minor premiss and then rejecting the attitude expressed in the ethical conclusion. And as long as Stevenson insists on tying logical validity to descriptive meaning, he cannot appeal to the persuasiveness or emotive meaning of a definition to explain why ethical arguments in the second pattern are sometimes valid.

Only two options remain open to Stevenson. Either he must develop a wider conception of logic, or he must admit that logic is completely inapplicable to ethical arguments as ethical. It is implausible to maintain that ethical syllogisms are formally invalid simply because they are ethical. If "all men are mortal, all Greeks are men, therefore all Greeks are mortal" is valid because of its logical form rather than its subject-matter, it seems only logical to suppose that an argument of the same form remains valid when the descriptive predicates are replaced with ethical terms.

The other alternative is more attractive in itself and more in keeping with Stevenson's express statements. One might hold that the applicability of formal logic does not depend upon the descriptive meaning of the ethical terms but upon the meaning of logical words like "all," "some," "not," "or," and "is." I suspect that Stevenson could work out an explanation along these lines, but he has not done so as yet. The theory he now holds as to the nature of logic excludes the applicability of formal logic to any ethical argument. Moreover, if he does widen his conception of logic, he is in danger of cutting the ground out from under his case for subjectivism in ethics. He now argues that ethical statements cannot claim objective validity on the grounds that they have primarily emotive meaning and that logical reasoning is limited to descriptive meaning. Once he admits that validity is not tied to descriptive meaning, he must find some new basis for rejecting the objectivity of ethical statements.

A second, and more basic, problem that arises in evaluating the adequacy of Stevenson's emotivism is this: how can he analyze epistemic terms? We often speak of ethical statements as "true" or "false," and of ethical conclusions as "correct" or "incorrect." We apply the terms "valid" and "invalid" to ethical arguments and distinguish between "relevant" and "irrelevant" considerations when drawing ethical inferences. Other epistemic terms like "reasonable" or "groundless" are entirely normal in ethical discussions. How can an emotivist, who denies that ethical sentences have any real objectivity, explain our everyday use of these words?

In *Ethics and Language* Stevenson suggested that although the descriptive meaning of ethical sentences could be true or false in the usual sense, the emotive meaning is completely without truth-value. Therefore, it is philosophically misleading to call an ethical statement as a whole true or false (*EL*, p. 154). More recently he has admitted that we can introduce the words "true" and "false" into ethical discussions "with full linguistic propriety" (*FV*, p. 215) and that when we do so we are using these words in their ordinary and strictest sense (*FV*, pp. 217–219). In my opinion his more recent position is the more plausible one.

We certainly do apply the words "true" and "false" to ethical statements, and there is no compelling reason to think that we are stretching language when we do so. However, this admission is awkward for Stevenson. All of his arguments to prove that, apart from a few exceptions, ethical reasoning cannot be logically valid depend upon his assumptions that validity is tied to truth and that truth (in its strict sense) is inapplicable to ethical conclusions. Once the latter assumption is abandoned, all the arguments in ch. 7 of *Ethics and Language* must be given up also. This is not a chapter to be discarded lightly or replaced easily, for Stevenson's case against the objectivity of ethical statements rests squarely upon it. Moreover, if ethical conclusions are true or false in the same sense that factual statements are, then it would seem to follow that they have as good a claim to objectivity as factual statements do.

Stevenson is at pains to deny this seeming implication. He contends that one can infer nothing about the function, meaning, or objectivity of an utterance from the fact that it can be spoken of as true or false because the applicability of these terms is determined solely by grammatical structure (*FV*, pp. 216–217). I doubt this. The only example he gives of an utterance that has the grammatical structure of the declarative mood even though it does not function as a statement is "He's a stinker." Stevenson points out that one might reply "how true" or "that is simply not true" to this expression of emotion. What he does not point out is that it would be somewhat strained to reply "that is true" and very odd to respond "that is false." This reveals, I suspect, that the locutions "how true," and "that is not true" are sometimes used in ways that are only very loosely connected with the epistemological notion of truth. When one stops to consider other examples of declarative sentences that have noncognitive functions, it becomes even more evident that one cannot speak of every declarative utterance as true or false. A draftee might receive the order "You will report for induction at 8:00 A.M. on the 28th of September." I could say to my recalcitrant child "You shall obey me or I'll know the reason why." A borrower might say "I promise to repay you next Friday." The university catalogue might read "No student will at any time consume alcoholic beverages on the campus." My linguistic sense tells me that it would be improper and out of place to reply "that is true" or "that is false" in any of these cases. Therefore, I believe that more than grammatical structure is presupposed in applying these epistemic terms to sentences.

My own view is that this something more is a claim to rationality, that to call an utterance true is to claim that the reasons for it outweigh whatever considerations could be brought against it. In ch. 10 of *The Language of Ethics*,[2] I develop and defend the thesis that the epistemic terms "true" and "false" have critical meaning, that they function to make, press, withdraw, or concede the claim to rationality. If I am correct, Stevenson cannot admit that ethical statements have truth-value without conceding their objectivity and, by implication, abandoning his emotivism. Of course, I may not be correct. But surely Stevenson must explain his conception of truth more fully and give evidence that it is more adequate than its competitors if he is to maintain his present position.

The other pair of epistemic terms that I wish to examine is "valid" and "invalid." We often apply these words to ethical arguments, and there is no real reason to suppose that we are straining ordinary language when we do so. But how is Stevenson to explain this application of apparently logical categories when he maintains that in most ethical arguments the premisses are related to the conclusion psychologically rather than logically? In many passages he seems to say that the relevance or irrelevance of some consideration, and

thus the validity or invalidity of the argument, is simply a matter of its psychological effectiveness in modifying the attitude of the hearer (*EL*, p. 114 and *FV*, p. 4). This suggests that "valid" is a purely descriptive term meaning roughly "effective in persuading the hearer." In spite of the textual evidence for this interpretation, I doubt whether Stevenson really wishes to analyze the notion of validity this way. At times he explicitly denies that good reasons are simply those which influence the hearer (*EL*, pp. 156–157), and he insists that any judgment of the validity of an ethical argument is itself a normative judgment (*FV*, p. 89).

Probably he wants to give some sort of an emotive analysis of the terms "valid" and "invalid." Only in this way can he claim that judgments of validity are normative and still uphold his emotive theory of ethics. Possibly, "valid" means simply "good," so that to say that an argument is valid is primarily to approve of it. However, this suggestion does not seem very plausible as it stands because one sometimes wants to approve of an argument that he takes to be invalid. For example, one may approve of an illogical argument if it manages to persuade an emotionally upset man not to commit suicide. There are two ways in which Stevenson might move towards a more complex, and at the same time more plausible, analysis of ethical validity. He might limit the sort of attitudes that are expressed in judgments of validity. Just as "morally good" has a special sort of emotive meaning because it expresses a special sort of approval, moral approval, so "valid" might have a special sort of emotive meaning because, for example, it expresses only epistemic approval. Although Stevenson nowhere develops such an analysis, it is suggested by the way in which he marks off "interest in knowledge" from the many other kinds of interests which are involved in ethical discussions (*EL*, pp. 284–286). The other direction in which Stevenson might move is to incorporate some descrip-

² C. Wellman, *The Language of Ethics* (Cambridge, Mass., 1961).

tive meaning into judgments of validity. This would be in line with his version of emotivism and is even suggested by his discussion of the reasons why rational methods are usually to be preferred to irrational ones (*EL*, pp. 156–157). Thus he might say that "valid" means "in accordance with method of arguing *M*," where *M* is spelled out by specifying such things as avoiding logical inconsistency, not falsifying the facts of the case, using all available information. Just what descriptive meaning a speaker would build into his use of the term "valid" would, presumably, depend upon which methods he happens to approve. If Stevenson were to follow out the two directions I have indicated, the result would be something like this: "valid" means "in accordance with method of arguing *M*" and expresses a positive epistemic attitude.

What is one to say of such an emotive theory of logical terms? (1) Probably it could be worked out in detail and, if it were, would have much to recommend it. (2) Some such theory is essential to Stevenson's position unless he is prepared either to deny that we in fact apply logical terms to ethical arguments or abandon his view that the conclusions of these arguments lack objectivity. Therefore, until he works out his analysis of logical terms more fully, his theory is essentially incomplete. (3) To interpret logical terms like "valid" and "invalid" emotively would seem to infect logic with the same subjectivity that emotivism insinuates into ethics. Would Stevenson be willing to accept this consequence? Everything he says about logic, and science too, indicates that he regards these as very different from ethics in their genuine claim to objectivity. (4) Would Stevenson be willing to extend an emotive analysis to other epistemic terms like "true," "reasonable," or "correct"? If so, what becomes of objective truth in factual matters? If not, what are his criteria for distinguishing the two species of epistemic terms, the emotive and the non-emotive?

(5) We do not argue for or against judgments of validity in at all the way this analysis would imply. On this theory the valid argument is the one in accordance with the approved method, and when Stevenson gives examples of reasons for approving a method he always gives pragmatic considerations, such as, that using the method will not lead to disastrous consequences, that its use will create social harmony, etc. It does not seem to me that such pragmatic matters enter into our judgments of validity at all.

But this criticism leads to another basic problem in Stevenson's position. Do rational methods of argument have any privileged position in ethical discussion? It would almost seem that Stevenson would be forced to answer this question in the negative because all sorts of nonrational methods of persuasion were possible in ethics, many of these are rhetorically effective, and in most cases logical criticism of such methods is out of place. Moreover, he points out that in certain cases, as when dealing with the feeble-minded or emotionally upset or when there is no time for lengthy discussion, nonrational methods of persuasion are fully justified. Nevertheless, Stevenson insists that rational methods do have priority in ethical discussion because under normal circumstances these are the best methods. He supports this normative judgment with many reasons. If people's attitudes are formed in ignorance of the facts, their action is likely to be disorganized and blundering; and there is a considerable value in building up the habit of inquiry in most men (*EL*, pp. 156–157). Rational methods give a more permanent agreement and a more stable personal conviction than "rhapsody or exhortation" (*FV*, pp. 7–8). If one person discovers that another person has given him a one-sided presentation of the facts, he will resent this treatment (*FV*, p. 195). For the individual, it is better to consider both sides of the case both to avoid disastrous consequences when the resulting attitude is put into practice and to gain the intrinsic value paying attention to all the facts (*FV*, p. 196).

What disturbs me about this case for rational methods is that it is framed in purely pragmatic terms. One chooses rational methods because they are better, and they can be seen to be better by considering the value consequences of using or not using them. It is my contention that the privileged position of rational methods in ethical discussion is not simply a matter of their greater utility.

Any method is a method of doing something, and this relational aspect must not be overlooked in choosing a method. Shouting at a man may be a very good method of waking him up but a very poor method of putting him to sleep. Accordingly, we must ask what we are trying to do when we discuss ethical issues. If we are simply trying to persuade someone, then we do indeed have a choice between rational and nonrational methods. Looking at ethical arguing as a purely psychological matter of creating and reinforcing attitudes, Stevenson is probably right that the choice of methods is the pragmatic one to be determined by relative rhetorical effectiveness and various value consequences. But suppose that ethical arguing is thought of as establishing the truth of an ethical conclusion. Then the entire picture changes. One cannot ask whether rational or nonrational methods are the best means of proving a conclusion true, for nonrational methods do not really prove or disprove anything. The man who chooses rational over nonrational methods of ethical arguing is not simply choosing a better method to achieve the same end (persuasion) but the only possible method to achieve a very different end (knowledge of the truth). Why is this so? It is because to make a statement is to make an implicit claim to truth, a claim that the statement is supported by the weight of the evidence. And the only possible test of *this* claim is reasoning. Thus rational methods of ethical

arguing have a privileged position which is denied by Stevenson's emotive theory of ethics.

My contention rests, to be sure, upon my view that there is a claim to rationality built into ethical statements. Is there any real evidence that this is so? Well, one bit of evidence is the existence of ethical disagreement. Just because Stevenson denudes ethical statements of their claim to rationality he is unable to explain ethical disagreement. His suggestion is that two speakers disagree ethically when (a) their utterances express opposed attitudes to the same thing, and (b) at least one speaker has a motive to alter the attitude of the other (*EL*, p. 3).

Why is this second condition necessary? Probably because Stevenson recognizes that there are differences which do not involve any disagreement. Hence he says that where two people have opposed attitudes but neither has a sufficient motive to change the attitude of the other, they merely differ in attitude (*EL*, pp. 4–5). But this does not seem to be true. It often happens that two people argue strenuously about some ethical issue only to find that neither can convince the other. At this point both may give up and "agree to disagree." Although neither speaker any longer has a sufficient motive to try to change the attitude of the other, it does not seem to me that they have ceased to disagree. Or suppose that two speakers express opposed attitudes to something, one saying "it is good" and the other "no, it is bad," but that neither can be bothered even to try to convince the other. Do they thereby avoid disagreement? I think not. Their disagreement lies in the opposition of their attitudes; whether either has any real motive to overcome this opposition is quite another thing. Agreeing to disagree is not the same as merely differing.

Stevenson, however, cannot explain disagreement in terms of the opposition of attitudes, because he denies that there can be any logical opposition between attitudes. On his theory, the opposition is a practical one; the attitudes are opposed in that both cannot be satisfied (*FV*, p. 2). But surely opposed attitudes can often be satisfied together. If a man likes kippers for breakfast and his wife does not, they have opposed attitudes to the same fish. However, a practical solution is ready at hand. Let the man eat both kippers and let the wife breakfast on other food. In this way the opposition between the attitudes even furthers the practical cooperation; for if both liked kippers, they would have to fight over who is to get the larger portion. I am not suggesting that opposed attitudes never conflict in practice; far from it. Still, the opposition of attitudes does not consist in the impossibility of satisfying both, for there are fortunate cases in which opposed attitudes need not conflict in practice. In reality the opposition of ethical attitudes is logical. "This is good" and "no, it is bad" are opposed because, while the former claims implicitly that favor is the rational attitude to take towards the object, the latter claims that disfavor is the rational attitude. It is logically impossible for both of these claims to be correct; hence the ethical disagreement. Take away these claims, and no real disagreement remains; for it is about these incompatible claims that the speakers are disagreeing. Recognize these claims, and it follows that reasoning is essential to ethical argument in a way in which nonrational methods of persuasion are not. This privileged position of rational methods simply does not fit with the emotive theory of ethics.

A fourth, and final, problem that I see in emotivism is this: what is an ethical problem? Stevenson holds that an ethical problem arises from a conflict of attitudes and consists in the need to resolve this conflict. What answers to this need is a strong stable attitude, one which excludes all opposed attitudes from the person's mind and will continue to do so throughout further experience, additional information, and ex-

tended discussion. Accordingly, the purpose of ethical investigation is simply to achieve a fixed attitude towards some object or action.

Now it may be true that ethical problems usually arise from a conflict of attitudes, although Stevenson has admitted that this is not always so (*FV*, pp. 198). Still, it is not true that the problem consists in the need to resolve the conflict which poses it. The essence of a problem is doubt, and doubt is neither a conflict nor a need to resolve conflict, however closely it may be associated with both. Doubt is wondering whether or not some ethical judgment is correct. Drop out this epistemic notion of correctness and no problem remains. Stevenson has reduced an ethical problem to a conflict of attitudes to be lived through or a need to be satisfied, but essential to any genuine problem is the notion of a correct as opposed to incorrect solution.

That this notion of correctness is central to ethical problems can be seen in two ways. First, the notion of correctness brings with it the assumption that for any given problem there is one and only one correct solution. To have a problem involves taking it for granted both that there is a correct answer and that if two inconsistent answers present themselves, at least one of them must be mistaken. That this assumption, which is one of the defining characteristics of objectivity, does control our ethical thinking is seen by what happens when investigation or dispute breaks down. When a person has been unable to decide which answer to accept in the light of all the information he can get, he does not shrug his shoulders and conclude that there is no answer or that all answers are equally good. He admits that he cannot find the answer, but not that there is no answer to be found. Again, when two disputants continue to disagree after prolonged debate, neither regards the inconclusiveness of their argument as showing that both are correct or that there was no question of correctness in the first place. Each continues to insist that he is right and that, therefore, the other must be wrong.

Second, the notion of correctness brings with it the assumption that the correctness or incorrectness of a proposed answer is fixed independently of anyone's acceptance or rejection. In some sense the answer is there to be discovered; thinking cannot make it so. That this assumption, another of the defining characteristics of objectivity, defines the nature of an ethical problem can be seen by the way in which we draw the line between considerations which are and those which are not relevant to the solution of the problem. Only considerations which count for or against the correctness of a proposed answer are relevant; most considerations which bear simply on the firmness of the investigator's conviction are rejected as beside the point. Knowing that on matters of this kind I am so dogmatic and stubborn that nothing is likely to change my mind does nothing to reassure me about the correctness or adequacy of my answer to the question "Is euthanasia right?" If an ethical problem is nothing but the need to fix a firm attitude, as Stevenson contends, then whether or not a proposed answer is really a solution would depend primarily upon facts about the psychology of the speaker or thinker. Actually, these are quite irrelevant because a problem consists in doubt over the correctness of an ethical judgment, and this is entirely independent of what the person who makes this judgment does or will think on this issue.

It is my firm and fixed conviction that our ethical thinking is molded by these two assumptions, that there can be one and only one correct answer to any ethical question and that which answer is correct is independent of anyone's acceptance or rejection. Stevenson might concede that most people make these assumptions but go on to argue that they are mistaken in so doing. Nevertheless, as long as we *do* presuppose these things, our ethical language will reflect this fact. Possibly it would be better for us to discard our present language and speak and think about ethics in quite a different manner. In such a new language, however, ethical questions would not pose ethical problems; for a problem consists, not just in the need to resolve a conflict of attitudes, but in doubt over which resolution is the correct one. Because Stevenson rejects the notion of objective correctness in ethics, he misunderstands both personal uncertainty and ethical disagreement, for it is this over which the individual is uncertain and the group is disagreeing.

By now my conclusion will be as obvious as it is unexpected; I am right and Stevenson is wrong. I cannot help but admire the way in which he has explained the appearance of objectivity, but I must insist that this appearance is not an illusion and that ethical statements really are objectively true of false. There are many strong reasons to accept ethical emotivism, and it is not easy to provide an alternative analysis which will do justice to the language of ethics. I have not discussed either of these very relevant topics in this paper. What I have done is to argue that Stevenson't attempts to explain away the objectivity claimed by ethical statements are unavailing. If Stevenson's theory is found wanting, it can be taken for granted that all lesser forms of emotivism are inadequate also. However much emotivism has contributed to the development of ethical theory in this century, it is not the last word in ethics.

The Impasse in Ethics—
and a Way Out

BRAND BLANSHARD

I

Philosophy is sometimes thought the least progressive of intellectual disciplines. Some departments in the field still use an introductory textbook twenty-three centuries old. But however slowly philosophy moved in earlier times, its pace has been greatly accelerated in the years since the turn of the century. At that time there were at least two disciplines in the field that seemed to have reached some stability—logic and ethics. In a comparatively few years both subjects have been torn down and reconstructed from the foundations. In the first quarter of the century came *Principia Mathematica*, which did more, I suppose, to transform the theory and practice of logic than any other work since Aristotle. In the second quarter the same root-and-branch reconstruction was attempted in ethics.

Thirty years ago it looked as if ethics had entered on a period of Augustan calm. Something like general agreement seemed to be in sight. Paulsen in Germany, Janet in France, Moore, Rashdall, and McTaggart in Britain, Palmer, Fullerton, and Everett in America, all had been converging to-

Reprinted from Brand Blanshard, *The Impasse in Ethics and a Way Out*, Howison Lecture, 1954, University of California Publications in Philosophy, 28, pp. 92–112, by permission of the author and University of California Press.

ward the same position—described by Paulsen as "teleological ethics" and by Rashdall as "ideal utilitarianism." This position was attractively simple and clear cut. Of the two chief questions of ethics, What is good? and What is right? it held the first to be primary: if you knew what kinds of experience were most worth having, you could deduce what you ought to do; you ought to do whatever was needful to produce the largest amount of good.

How were you to tell what was good? Certainly not by argument; if you did not directly see that it was better to be happy than unhappy, no further evidence would help. This did not mean that there was anything irrational or arbitrary about your insights, any more than about saying that in a parallelogram the opposite sides must be equal. You saw by an intuition which was itself an act of intelligence that happiness *must* have this further character.

Was happiness the only kind of experience that was thus intrinsically good? No; by almost universal agreement, hedonism was rejected. Wisdom and beauty and love, for example, had a goodness that was clearly not exhausted by the happiness they brought with them. And what was this goodness that such experiences had in common? It was nothing sensible like yellow or sweet; it was not a natural quality at all if that meant something that could be observed and measured scientifically. Furthermore, it was so simple as to be beyond all logical analysis. It was one of those fundamental notions like time and existence about which we can say extraordinarily little, in spite of being perfectly familiar with them. The position could be summed up in its rule of practice: always so act as to produce the largest amount of intrinsic goodness, goodness being a simple nonnatural quality that belonged self-evidently to experiences of various kinds.

Now I do not think that the doctrine, put in this form, will stand. Nevertheless, if there is any ethical theory toward which we can claim a convergence of abler minds from Plato and Aristotle down, I think it is this; and what I want to consider is how much of it is left after the attacks of recent years. It has been subjected to three great waves of criticism which many think have swept it finally away. First came the attack of the deontologists, who held that the theory was mistaken in basing the right on the good. Then came the emotivists, with their contention that goodness was not a quality at all and therefore inhered in nothing. Lastly came the naturalists, who insisted that even if goodness were a quality it was a merely natural one, and therefore ethics must give up its pretensions to being anything more than a natural science. I lay no stress on the historical order of these criticisms. The three waves came so close together that, whatever their sequence, I feel free to deal with them in the order of convenience.

II

First, then, the deontologists. As early as 1912 H. A. Prichard of Oxford began a revolt against the ruling ethics in an article that later became famous, entitled "Does Moral Philosophy Rest on a Mistake?" His answer to this question was Yes. The mistake lay in connecting duty with interest or advantage, your own or anyone else's. The ideal utilitarians had argued that to ask what was your duty was to ask what would produce the greatest good. Prichard admitted that in some situations the answer to the second question would supply the answer to the first. If the problem, for example, was what sort of scholarship to endow, or what charity to support, it was only by knowing which would carry with it the greatest good that you could know which you ought to do. But suppose you had borrowed a book and promised to return it on a certain day; would the question what you ought to do be settled by knowing whether it would do more good to return it? Prichard said No. It might be greatly to your advantage to keep it; would that justify disregarding your promise? Obviously not; you should return it nevertheless. If your duty was not thus based on your own advantage, was it then based on the other man's? No again; for he might have forgotten the matter and felt no need of the book, so that your advantage in keeping it would not be counterbalanced by any disadvantage to him. Still, if you had promised to return it, return it you normally should. The man of conscience who has made a promise does not stop to calculate whether he or his friend or society is going to reap some profit from his living up to it. He thinks it his business to live up to it. If he is asked why, he does not turn to some balance sheet of consequences; he says he ought to keep the promise because he made it; period. In this, said Prichard, he is right. To justify keeping promises by hunting for profit in so doing is not only futile; it is wrong in principle, for it supposes that duty rests on prospective good, whereas we can often see plainly that something is our duty when we have no idea whether it will bring future good or not.

Prichard's essay was strangely disregarded, and, preoccupied with other problems, he let many years go by without pressing his case. But the case was taken up by two able colleagues, first by E. F.

Carritt and a little later by Sir David Ross, whose two books *The Right and the Good* and *Foundations of Ethics* are among the finest examples of lucid argument in ethical literature. Ross maintained that however plausible the rule might seem of pursuing the greatest good, it was open to the two most fatal objections that can be offered to an ethical rule: at times adherence to it was plainly wrong, and a times violation of it was plainly right. He held that of two prospective courses it was sometimes our duty to choose the one that, so far as we could see, would do less good and leave the world worse off. To utilitarians of every stripe this was a shocking thesis. Yet Ross held that, far from being bizarre or irresponsible, it was the requirement of ethical common sense. The strength of this surprising view will be clearer if we work it out in an example, and we may as well choose our example from a major virtue, justice.

In a certain town an outbreak of lawlessness takes the form of repeated brutal assaults. The epidemic has been growing rapidly, and the offenders have clearly been encouraged by the failure of the law to catch up with them. At last a certain X is apprehended. His record suggests that he is the ringleader; his connection with the latest crime seems clear; and he is brought for trial before a local judge. The case against him is overwhelming. There is only one circumstance that stands in the judge's way. He happens to know with certainty that the accused man, notorious offender and general pest that he is, in this particular case is not guilty. The judge happens, and he alone, to have caught a glimpse of him elsewhere at the time of the crime. What is the judge's duty? If duty were merely a matter of producing the greatest good, would he not have to reason as follows: "By convicting this man and dealing with him severely, I shall probably halt an epidemic of violence, and thus not only promote the common security but also, perhaps, save a number of lives. These are extremely important ends. What is to be set

against them? The suffering or at least loss of freedom of a man who is innocent of the crime alleged. But, after all, he richly deserves on other counts whatever he may get. Is not the suffering of such a man a small price to pay for the checking of lawlessness? . . . Ah, but then," the judge reflects, "am I not leaving out a most important consequence? What about respect for my court and for courts generally? If it became known that a judge might deliberately convict a man he knew to be innocent, people would lose confidence that courts would give them justice, that acquitted men were not really criminals, and convicts not really martyrs. Such a loss of confidence would be sheer disaster." But then he considers further. "What would produce the disaster is not my convicting this man but only a public knowledge of the facts, and it lies within my power whether this knowledge will ever get out. Only the culprit and I know the truth. As for him, nobody will believe him, no matter what he says. As for me, I need only keep silence. By giving my verdict against the culprit while locking one detail in my own mind, I can at once avert any discredit that might accrue to the court and promote the public security. And is not that the aim of courts anyhow?"

This is the sort of reasoning into which we are led, Ross believes, by the ethics of the greatest good of the greatest number. Can we accept it? He insists that we cannot, and surely we must agree with him. Here is a case in which we are far more certain of the wrongness of convicting an innocent man than of any theory on the other side; we should say that such an act was monstrous, let the theoretical chips fall where they may. "Very well," Ross would say, "let us see where exactly they do fall. You agree that convicting the man would be wrong?" "Of course." "You agree that a mere calculation of consequences would make it out to be right?" "Apparently so." "You agree that if the judge did justice in this case, the lawlessness would probably increase?" "Yes." "And that this would be a worse state of things than the alternative?" "Yes, I suppose so." "But the judge ought to do justice anyhow?" "Yes, clearly." "Well, then," Ross would conclude, "you have admitted my whole case. You have agreed that, in essence, duty has nothing whatever to do with producing the greater good, and that it may be a man's duty to choose a course that will make the world worse."

Now I must confess that, in spite of the argument, I find this conclusion incredible. I agree that the judge should acquit the innocent man; I cannot agree that in so doing he would be making the world worse. Where, then, is the error in Ross's reasoning? Some have tried to find it by throwing into the scale the judge's motive. They suggest that, even if convicting the innocent man did produce the better results, the deliberate intention of the judge was in itself an evil which must outweigh any later good. But this is futile. For what counts in a motive morally is the desire to do right, and it is conceivable that the judge, even in convicting an innocent man, did so out of a sincere regard for duty. He may have been muddled, but muddle is not sin. We should consider his action wrong nevertheless. Hence we cannot charge the wrongness of the action upon the badness of its motive. If we are to show, as against Ross, that its wrongness lies in any badness connected with it, that badness must lie neither in consequences merely, nor in the motive merely, nor in both together. Then where?

The person who gives a true answer to this question works, I think, under a disadvantage. He cannot point to any particular person, time, or place as the residence of the good he has in mind; and yet he is convinced that it is because of this good that justice should be done. Can he give any indication where it lies? Yes. Subject to an important word of later comment, it lies in the set of relations that justice would maintain between the judge, the prisoner, and the members of the community. The judge is installed by those members to serve as their intelligence and conscience in critical cases; his special business, to which he pledged himself in accepting office, is to give judgment in accordance with the evidence. Even if, in a given case, an unjust judgment should lead to consequences as good as those of a just one, the community in which justice is done is so far a better community. The giving of a verdict against the evidence, from whatever motives, would be a breach of faith not only with the prisoner but with the community as a whole. It would involve at once the breaking of multiple engagements, the telling to the public of an untruth, and the doing of grave injustice. Now the keeping of engagements, the telling of truth, and the doing of justice are essential parts of the community's plan of life. To violate them officially is to do far more than to injure a particular person; it is to challenge and disrupt this plan of life as a whole.

One may object that it will not disrupt this if the normal consequences are cut off. But most men will not be convinced. They will say that disruption may be a matter of logic as well as of consequences. To forsake engagements, truth, and justice whenever a prospect of particular advantage comes in view would be to weaken the claims of these things throughout the range of our conduct; it would tear a huge hole in the network of relations that makes society possible. This, I think, is what really halts the plain man when he is invited to abandon principle. It need not be any bad consequences on which he can put his finger, nor yet the importance of any one principle standing alone, for he is ready to admit that in extreme cases an untruth must be told or a promise broken. But even in these cases he violates principle with a reluctance that is inexplicable if principles are simply means to particular goods, and not wholly explicable even if they are taken, in Ross's way, as *prima facie* rules of right. What really moves us is the sense—a vague sense, admitted—of remoter repercussions, of what the breach of principle would mean for the fabric of our life as a whole, a sense that if what is proposed were admitted, it would bring down the house in which we are living about our ears. It is important, we should all agree, that a crime wave should be discouraged. But it is far more important to maintain those relations of honor, truthfulness, and justice which touch our lives at a thousand points and make a society like ours possible. If these things may be repudiated in their own peculiar shrine, then, to put it crudely, anything goes. The foundations of our communal life have caved in.

Ross denies this because he believes that, apart from its motives and its consequences, there is nothing good in right action. He says frankly that he "can see *no* intrinsic goodness attaching to the life of a community merely because promises are kept in it."[1] But I doubt whether he can keep to this, even in his own thinking. When he is criticizing the utilitarians, he offers a case that he regards as decisive. Take two communities in which the amount of happiness is the same, but which differ in one respect: in the first, the material goods of life are distributed justly; in the second, they are not. Ross argues that if the utilitarians are right it should make no difference which community we choose, whereas it is obvious that we ought to choose the former. I agree. But *why* ought we to choose it? If it is not because justice would produce more happiness, is it because justice is itself good? Ross could only say No; for in the mere doing of justice, as in the mere keeping of promises, he would find no good whatever. Is it then in the motives that would be at work in the first community but not in the second? No again; for we may suppose without inconsistency that in respect not only of happiness but also of loyalty to duty the two

communities are on the same level. Should we still choose the first? I am sure that Ross would say we should. But once more, why? The natural answer is surely, "Because the first community is better." But this he cannot say. We ought to choose the first, but for no reason at all. Though the first is not preferable, it is still our duty to prefer it.

Now, with great admiration for Ross's discernment, I cannot believe that if he were asked why he would prefer the one to the other, he would really be at his wit's end, and able to say only, "You ought because you ought." I think he would naturally say, "You ought because a just community is better than an unjust one." And if so, he would be admitting that even here the right derives from the good.

III

But the ideal utilitarian who thought that with this he had made out his case was to receive a jolting surprise. It was hard to be told by Prichard and Ross that his moral philosophy was based on a mistake. It was far more dismaying to be told that his subject did not exist at all, that there were no such things as judgments of good or evil, right or wrong. This was the startling intelligence that was given him, with an air of calm finality, by the new school of emotivists. To be sure, the emotivists were subjectivists; and he had met subjectivists before. He had read his Hume and his Westermarck, and was confident that the weapons which had removed such Apollyons as these from his path could deal with the pettier poltergeists that might appear in their train. Hume had argued that the rightness of an action meant only that society, viewing the action in the light of its consequences, felt an emotion of approval toward it. But if this were offered as an account of what people mean by "right," it obviously would not do. The social re-

[1] W. David Ross, *Foundations of Ethics* (Oxford, Clarendon Press, 1939), p. 142.

former insists that his cause is right, and goes on doing so while knowing only too well that it is jeered at by almost everyone. He could not possibly mean by its rightness that it now has general approval. Nor was Hume's case much strengthened by Westermarck, in spite of the prodigious array of anthropological scholarship brought to bear on it. According to Westermarck, the judgment of right or good was not a statement that society approved of something; it was the statement that one had approving feelings of one's own.

It was against this position that G. E. Moore, in his little book on ethics, offered arguments that came to be regarded as the definitive refutation of subjectivism. Moore pointed out that if a moral judgment states only how we feel about an act, we are landed in a nest of absurdities. It would follow that on moral matters we were virtually infallible, since we surely know how we feel about things. It would follow that no two persons could ever agree in moral judgment, since if Jones said an action was right all he meant was that he, Jones, had a certain feeling about it; if Smith made the same remark, all he meant was that he, Smith, had a certain feeling about it; and these were not the same assertions. Further, Jones and Smith could not contradict each other on these matters even if they tried. Smith's statement that an act was wrong would not contradict Jones's statement that it was right; it would merely record a different kind of feeling about it. And if there is anything clear about our discussions of moral problems, said Moore, it is that our beliefs do sometimes clash. A subjectivism which tells us that such beliefs never do or can clash has ruled itself out by its plain discordance with fact.

But now arose a kind of subjectivism undreamed of in Moore's philosophy. By agreement and difference he had meant agreement and difference in opinion; and, to anyone who did mean that, the view that when two men called an action right and wrong, respectively, they were not

contradicting each other must certainly seem absurd. But what if their difference was not one of opinion at all but a difference merely in attitude? Then these paradoxes about infallibility, agreement, and difference would never arise. This was the new line taken by the emotivists; ". . . sentences which simply express moral judgements," wrote Professor Ayer, "do not say anything. They are pure expressions of feeling and as such do not come under the category of truth and falsehood. They are unverifiable for the same reason as a cry of pain or a word of command is unverifiable—because they do not express genuine propositions."[2] The emotivists held, like Prichard, that moral philosophy had been based on a mistake, but the mistake was the more radical one of supposing our judgments on moral matters to be judgments at all. When Ross called an action right, they said, he was not stating a truth or even a falsehood; he was asserting nothing whatever; he was merely expressing a feeling of moral warmth toward the action. When G. E. Moore called the experience of beauty intrinsically good, he was not saying something about the experience, as he had always supposed he was, nor even about his own feeling, as Westermarck suggested. He was only exclaiming about it; he was saying "Hurrah for beauty!" The whole mass of our value judgments, every assertion of right or wrong, good or evil, beauty or ugliness, is thus removed at a stroke from the field of cognition into that of emotion.

This theory, which has been called the "boo-hurrah" theory of ethics, has been the most widely discussed ethical theory of the past two decades; and its acceptance in one form or another by Russell and Ayer in Britain, and by Carnap and Reichenbach in this country, has attracted respectful attention to it. Though it is not an American product, the fullest exposition of it must be

[2] Alfred J. Ayer, *Language, Truth and Logic* (2d ed.; London, Victor Gollancz, Ltd., 1948), pp. 108–109.

placed to the credit of an American, Charles L. Stevenson, of the University of Michigan.[3] No one will deny that if true, it is extremely important.

The ideal utilitarians held that we could weigh the goods and evils entailed by conduct against each other; indeed, that we could commonly see the superiority of certain goods to others to be self-evidently true, and this of course meant objectively true, in the sense that if persons differed about it they could not both be right. This implied, again, that at every moment of our waking lives there was some objectively right act that we should try to find and do. It implied that if two persons or two nations differed, there was always an objectively right course waiting, so to speak, to be discovered, and that tribunals had a ground on which to render impartial decisions. If the emotivists were correct, all this was an illusion. The Japanese felt enthusiasm about the attack at Pearl Harbor; we felt anger; but there was no ethical character in the act, and no good or evil in the consequence, that would justify either attitude, nor did it make sense to say that there was any truth to be discovered as to the rightness or wrongness of either side. As for the grounds on which an international court might base judgments of guilt, we could only say that they did not exist in fact, and could not even in theory. Such a court, if it tried to pronounce judgment, would only be expressing another and third feeling.

Can practical consequences of this kind be validly urged against the new ethical theory? I do not think so. I do think that acceptance of the theory would in fact discredit the notion of justice, interpersonal or international, and that this would have unfortunate practical consequences. But since I think that pragmatism too has been discredited, I do not believe that any theory can be overthrown by pragmatic considerations. The proposal must be dealt with, like

[3] *Ethics and Language* (New Haven, Yale University Press, 1944).

other theories, on the ground of its accordance or discordance with fact. Where does it stand in this respect?

It offers itself as a statement of what is meant by judgments of value. Does this signify what plain people actually mean, or what people mean after they have critically examined their ideas? The two meanings may of course be quite different. When the plain man says that grass is green, he does not mean that its being green depends on the accident of his seeing it; I think he assumes the green to be there whether anyone sees it or not. When the college student whose innocence has been corrupted by Berkeley says that grass is green, his meaning may be quite different, namely, that there is something out there, not itself green, which, when it works on his senses, makes him see green. Now emotivism has been careless about telling us which meaning it has in mind. If it is reporting the first kind of meaning, it has obviously missed the mark. When the plain man calls murder "wrong" or suffering "bad" he clearly does not imply that they would not be so apart from the accident of his being aware of them; he would be puzzled, if not shocked, by any such suggestion. He means to say something about murder and suffering themselves. But of course the plain man may mean something which, if considered in its implications, he would have no business to mean. The question then is whether the plain man's view, when considered in its implications, is the more consistent with what the rest of our thought and experience forces us to accept.

Now I think that it is the emotivist view which must yield. It would require us to abandon ways of thinking which are far better grounded than it is itself. Let me mention two of these which I have already put in words and in print, apparently with no effect, on Matthew Arnold's desperate principle that "what I say three times is true."

First, emotivism is irreconcilable with our way of thinking of past or future values. There is some plausibility in saying, as Christian Scientists do, that when we judge our present suffering to be bad, we are expressing our own attitude merely, and that if this attitude were changed, there would be no badness to express. There is somewhat less plausibility in saying that when we judge a current famine in India to be bad, we are saying nothing about the famine but only expressing our own feeling about it. But I submit that there is no plausibility at all in saying that when we judge the suffering in Buchenwald to have been bad, all we mean to express is our present feeling. On this interpretation, the suffering did in fact occur, but nothing that we now express when we call it bad could have belonged to the suffering when it occurred; for all the statement expresses is present feeling, and that did not come into being till after the suffering was over. According to this ingenious theory, nothing bad has ever occurred, or at least it is meaningless to say it has. To be sure, the record of the race has been full of things that we have always supposed to be major ills—disease, war, want, fear, frustration, to say nothing of the infinite silent suffering of the animal world. On the emotivist theory, it would literally be without meaning to say that any of this was bad when it occurred, since all that the term "bad" expresses is the present feeling of the speaker. I can only say that this seems to me absurd.

It may be replied that the absurdity lies in a misreading of the emotivist's theory. When he calls this past suffering "bad," a simple and sensible meaning is open to him, namely, that a hostile feeling was felt toward these things by the people of the time. But this, innocent enough on the surface, surrenders the whole emotivist case. For it admits that what was supposed to be a mere expression of feeling is in truth a judgment, a judgment about how people in fact felt in the past; that, like other judgments, it may be true or false; and hence that the emotivist view, which

denies this of value statements, is itself false. Thus the theory is in a dilemma. If it adheres to the view that value statements express present feeling only, then it cannot consistently say that anything evil has ever happened, which is absurd. If it takes the natural way of avoiding this absurdity, it contradicts itself.

Unfortunately its case is no better when it deals with the future; it cannot hold that anything good or evil ever will happen. Of course, in their role as sensible men, emotivists, like other people, talk occasionally of the good time that is coming. But as emotivists they must at once remind themselves that when they call it a "good" time, they are saying nothing that will characterize it when it comes; they are giving vent to their present feeling, that and nothing more. Since that present feeling is over with the moment, nothing expressed by the word "good" can belong to the future event. Now it may be that whenever we say that anything good or bad ever has happened or will happen, we are really talking nonsense. But for my own part, I find this less plausible than that this ingenious theory has somewhere gone off the track.

My second difficulty with emotivism is this: it renders all our attitudes arbitrary and groundless. Attitudes are divided by emotivists into pro- and anti-attitudes; when we call something good, we express a pro-attitude; when we call it bad, an anti-attitude. Now if we are asked why we take a pro-attitude toward something, we should no doubt answer that it is because of something good in the object which makes such an attitude appropriate. Why should we view with favor our children's happiness and cultivation, and with disfavor their ignorance and misery? The natural answer, surely, is that happiness and cultivation are good, and ignorance and misery bad. It would be arbitrary and groundless to favor something if there was nothing good about it, or to disfavor it if there was nothing bad. But from this natural answer the emotivist is cut off. For him the object is not favored because it is good; it is good, in the only legitimate sense, because it is favored. In itself, and apart from such favoring, it is perfectly neutral. There is nothing good in enlightenment or happiness or dutifulness which can make it appropriate to favor them, nothing bad in pain or disease or death that could justify aversion to them. The only good or evil is that with which we invest an object through the attitude itself. But this implies that we can never justify our approval or disapproval of anything, that no pro- or anti-attitude is more appropriate than any other, since all attitudes are equally without foundation in what is there.

For one who holds this view, I should suppose that the natural policy would be never to approve or disapprove of anything. But since that is hardly practicable, the most prudent line would surely be to call everything good, since this is all that is needed to make it good in the only sense in which anything is so. We are told that Walt Whitman was so well disposed toward the world that he could greet the Brooklyn telephone directory or a list of the Maine lakes with "whoops of blessing." I commend this attitude to the emotivists. If it seems somewhat undiscriminating, let us remember that in the nature of things there are no values to discriminate, and that it is a very short-sighted economy that settles for geese when it may as easily have swans.

The view of the emotivists that there is no such thing as an objective good seems, therefore, less convincing to me than the ancient and honorable prejudice that it does exist. So far, then, the great tradition in ethics, which holds that right action lies in producing the greatest good, remains still open to us.

IV

But now comes the third wave of criticism. It is directed at a side of the older theory that we have not considered, its distinction between the "is" and the "ought." When the ideal utilitarians concluded that duty lay in seeking not the greatest pleasure but the greatest good, they had on their hands the curiously baffling question what they meant by "good." This was a character owned in common by all good things, but what sort of character was it? Pleasure was a feeling that could be observed, but what was this rarefied something called "goodness," which was neither pleasure, nor knowledge, nor beauty, nor love, but an essence distilled from all of them?

Moore struggled for long with this question, and concluded that goodness is not a character in the "natural" world at all. When you perceive a rose, you can smell its sweetness, feel its softness, and see its shape and color, but when you say the experience is good, are you reporting another quality of the same kind? Clearly not, says Moore. All these other qualities are sensible, but no one has ever seen or otherwise sensed goodness, any more than he has seen the light that never was on sea or land. Very well, if we cannot sense it or point to it, perhaps we can specify it by defining it. But no, it turns out to be so simple that it cannot be dissected into parts, and is therefore beyond defining. Its meaning is perfectly clear; its presence is easy to recognize; it is almost as familiar to us as our hands and feet, but we cannot say what it is.

Here doubts begin to arise. To be sure, there are other familiar concepts that prove to be highly elusive when we try to pin them down—time, for example, and existence, and being awake. But these are all complex, while goodness is supposed to be simple. And if a term is at once simple and constantly on our lips, one would expect that what it refers to would be clear. Yet when moralists began to think about Moore's analysis, many of them had to report doubt whether they had ever known such a quality and indeed whether there was any such quality to know. It was a philosophic will-o'-the-wisp that dissolved when one tried to lay hold of it. These doubts were strengthened when, after a time, Moore himself began to doubt; at one point he confessed that he was as strongly drawn by the emotivist view as by his old view of goodness as a quality. Now if, when an analysis of a common meaning is offered, many or most qualified persons can find nothing in their thought that answers to the analysis, the criticism is inevitable that the analysis has failed to catch what is really meant.

With this criticism I agree. It is the first of the three criticisms of the older position with which I have been able to agree. Like many others, I find it hard to verify this nonnatural quality of goodness. But my difficulty goes beyond this; I think that goods and bads are more firmly rooted in human nature than the ideal utilitarians would admit. They refused to admit that in the meaning of good any part was played by the gratifying of human impulses, the satisfying of human needs, or the fulfilling of human desires. They conceded that these sometimes served as conditions of our finding something good, but the goodness never consisted of them even in part: it was a quite distinct nonnatural quality that supervened on these satisfactions. I cannot resist the conviction that the connection between goodness and fulfillment is more intimate than this. If that is a prejudice, it is at least one that is shared by a large and highly respectable company, which includes Plato, Aristotle, Aquinas, Hobbes, Spinoza, Hegel, Green, and Mill. They all held that the goodness of anything was so bound up with the fulfilling of needs or desires that such fulfillment entered into, and supplied in whole or part the very meaning of, goodness. In the present sense of the term they were all of them naturalists. I that sense I am a naturalist too.

Since the question involves analysis, may I venture a remark about this treacherous process? When Socrates set the fashion for Western thinkers in defining ethical terms, his method was a straightforward

one; perceiving that even when we were uncertain what a term meant, we could often point with confidence to varying examples of it, he proposed that we discover our meaning by asking what it was in virtue of which we recognized these as examples, and that we do this by bringing to light what they had in common. This is regarded by some present-day analysts as too crude a method; for it is possible, they say, to find a set of characters that is always present when goodness is present, and yet is not strictly what goodness means. The proof of this is that we may use the word "goodness" significantly without any explicit thought of the characters named; and further, that the question whether a thing could be good without these characters is not instantly seen to be meaningless.

I suggest that when analysis reaches this stage it has become so refined as to be self-defeating. Not only does the term "good" have no one meaning (Dr. Ewing has recently distinguished ten meanings), but even when used in the restricted sense of intrinsically good, I see no reason to think that its meaning is either clear or simple. Words are used very much as checks are used, to transfer accumulated stores, and the fact that no inventory is made of these at the time of transfer does not imply that the checks are irredeemable. Behind this term "good," which we bandy about so readily as a counter, there lies a massive wealth of meaning which for most purposes may be taken for granted, but which the analyst ignores at his peril. If he assumes that the word means only what is explicitly present whenever it is used, the result will be a triumph of precise and lucid superficiality, which must be repudiated at the first glimpse of what lies in its hinterland.

Very well, if goodness is not a quality but rather a complex of characters of which the word is merely the opening gate, what is included in this complex? Let me make such answer as I have to give with the help of a famous case in ethical history.

John Stuart Mill, you will recall, concluded that goodness meant pleasure. Hence any state of mind that was intrinsically good, whether an experience of beauty or of wisdom or of champagne, was good in the precise degree of its pleasantness. This led to an attractively simple solution of nearly all the problems of ethics, and Mill regarded it with some complacency. But when his friend Carlyle began to berate it as a "pig" philosophy, he had second thoughts. He asked himself the classic question: if he had to choose between the life of a pig, supported in the style to which Mr. Wodehouse's Empress of Blandings was accustomed, or an equal period in the life of a harassed and henpecked Socrates, would he elect the porcine bliss or the philosophic struggle? Could he put his hand on his heart and say that the pleasure of the Socratic life was certainly greater? No. Did he have the slightest doubt, however, that it would be better to be Socrates in any case? No again, Mill confessed, with that honesty and candor that made him so persuasive. But then what became of his theory that the good lay in pleasure alone? His answer, of course, was that though the Socratic life might not contain *more* pleasure than the other life, the pleasure it did contain was so much better, so much higher in quality, as to outweigh any deficit in quantity. By pretty general agreement, this did more credit to his heart than to his head. You cannot consistently say that, with their pleasantness equal, one experience is better than another, and also that their goodness lies in their pleasantness alone. It was all too clear that Mill was making two major mistakes at once: first, in identifying goodness with pleasure; second, in trying to combine this view with the admission that goodness was other than pleasure.

Several generations of teachers and students have triumphantly pointed out Mill's blunders. But many, even in doing so, have felt that his sane and honest mind had carried him very near to the truth. I own to being one of these. I am inclined to think that goodness consists in two components, both of which Mill more or less clearly recognized, and that if he had seen the parts they really play, his theory on this point would have been beyond cavil.

In the first place, he recognized that pleasure, or, as I prefer to call it, satisfaction, is present in every state of mind that is intrinsically good, and is inseparable from the goodness. This, I submit, remains true even if goodness is not exhausted by pleasure. Take one example. We who are in academic life call knowledge or understanding good. Suppose that at one stroke we could achieve what we are seeking, and have at our command all the knowledge and understanding of what James calls the "quarto and folio editions of mankind," but with this one proviso added, that we should find no pleasure, take no satisfaction, in it. Would it have any value for us? I am not asking whether we might still choose it for its consequences to ourselves or others; that is a wholly different question. I am asking whether it would have intrinsic value for us, and suggesting that it would not. Indeed, this answer has over and over again been forced upon those who tried to evade it. It was forced upon the Stoics, who, in seeking to rid themselves of feeling, found that as they lived more exclusively in the gray light of reason, everything else turned gray. It was forced upon Mill himself by the nervous collapse of his earlier years, when, having lost the power to enjoy as the result of intellectual overforcing, he found that the goods for which he was living had suddenly turned to dust and ashes. Enjoyment is not all there is to goodness; at this date there is no need to stop over that. But it is so essential to any experience we call good that if it vanishes, the value vanishes with it.

Secondly, Mill recognized that of two states which are equally pleasant one may be better than the other, and through the example he took he set our feet on the right road, though he somehow missed it himself. What is it that makes the life of Socrates more worth living than that of the pig, whether pleasanter or not? Surely not the quality of his pleasure, whatever that may mean, but something more obvious, something indeed that stares us in the face. *It is simply that in the mind of a great thinker we have a richer fulfillment of the faculties that make us men.* In respect to his intelligence, Socrates is more of a man than we are, more of what we want to be. The power, the need, the desire, to know is fundamental in all of us. Its presence at a certain level is a defining mark of human nature; the fulfillment in exceptional measure is what marks off the large mind from the little one.

The same fact marks off even a lowly human mind from the animal mind. Mill's essay appears to have been written before *The Origin of Species,* though it was published a year or two later. We see now, as he could not, that running through the whole development of mind, and determining its course, there is a continuous drive, or, rather, set of drives, of which human nature itself is only the most recent expression. One of these is the impulse to know, which is central in human nature because its roots run deep into animal nature. Even in the dimwitted four-footed cousin that Mill referred to, and in the midst of notorious appetites in other directions, it flickers up into a vagrant curiosity. In the higher apes it is far more active. In man, with his power to look before and after, it is more restless and inquiring still. And, despite Housman's gibe that the love of truth is the faintest of human passions, in a few men it burns up into a devouring, illuminating flame that seems to light up for miles ahead the road which intelligence must travel. Contact with such a mind is self-revelation; we seem to see for the first time that this is what we are really about, this is what we have been trying to do all along; we catch a glimpse, as Arnold would say, of "the hills where our life rose, and the sea where it goes." A great mind is a great mind because it does what we are all trying to do, only better. In sum, when

we say that it is better to be Socrates than ourselves, and ourselves than a fool, and a fool than a pig, we are saying that in Socrates we have a completer fulfillment of a set of drives or impulses that are continuous from one extreme to the other.

To say of an experience that it is intrinsically good means, then, two things: first, that it satisfies; and second, that it fulfills. Pleasure without fulfillment, as Aristotle saw, is hardly possible. Fulfillment without pleasure, as Mill saw, is valueless. Of two experiences that equally fulfill, the one we enjoy more is the better. Of two experiences that we equally enjoy, the one that fulfills more is the better. Of course fulfillment does not mean meeting our demands for enlightenment only; it means meeting all the other demands of our nature so far as they can be met without mutual suppression. The quiver of human nature is full of arrows of desire, big and little, desires that are fashioned from what we are, desires for food and drink and play and friends and things of beauty. If anything fulfills and satisfies such demands, it is *ipso facto* good; if it is utterly out of relation to such demands, no one would think of calling it good.

It may be said that there are impulses in human nature whose indulgence is evil, such as those of aggression and fear. But Professor Pepper has shown fine insight, I think, in pointing out that these are not drives with ends of their own; they are summoned up when other drives are frustrated, and are nature's means of intensifying these or safeguarding them. When they do get out of hand and must be suppressed, it is not because they are evil in themselves but because their fulfillment would block other fulfillments. The doctrine that men are naturally evil, so current in some theological circles, is thus the precise reverse of the truth. To fulfill and satisfy what nature prompts is not only good; it is what goodness means.

I have been speaking about goodness; but in thus conceiving goodness we are also defining the nature of duty. Moralists have taken a strange delight at times not only in making duty a "stern daughter of the voice of God" but also in placing it "at enmity with joy," in setting it up as a hard-faced, alien censor of the natural man and his interests. There are followers among us of that morbid prophet Kierkegaard who glory in the thought that duty may demand of us what common sense and reflection alike would brand as outrageous: "ours not to reason why, ours but to do and die." Against this reactionary irrationalism I would plead for the naturalness of duty. Duty is no unintelligible command laid on us from without. It is the voice of our own nature, the imperative of our own reason, telling us that if our central strivings and those of others, the ends that nature itself has set before us, are to be fulfilled, we must act thus and not otherwise. This is not to deprive duty of its force but to bring it home to us as authentic and reasonable. To the man who declines to recognize duty we offer not some dubious authority or a threat about the future, but a simple question or two. "Do you want health, understanding, friendship?" "Yes, of course; they are what make life worth while." "If it is good that you should have them, is there any ground for denying that it is good for others to have them?" "No." "Do you agree that course X is a necessary means if these things that make life worth living are to be achieved?" "Yes, so it appears." "Then you cannot reject course X without repudiating your own reason and the central demands of your own nature."

V

It is time to bring our threads together. We saw that the great tradition in ethics appeared to have ended in an impasse after two thousand years. The rule of that ethics was so to live as to produce the most good. This rule has been met in our day by three attacks: the first against its goal,

the second against its objectivity, the third against its notion of goodness. The first attack, delivered from Oxford, sought to show by such examples as that of the judge and the innocent man that it is sometimes our duty to produce less than the greatest good. To this I replied that the goods achieved by convicting innocence would be far outweighed by the evil of destroying the pattern of society in which justice was done. You may have felt when I made that reply that there was something dubious about it, that a pattern of society could hardly itself be intrinsically good. We have now seen that, strictly speaking, that is true, that nothing is good but consciousness, and consciousness in the joint form of the satisfaction and fulfillment of impulse. It is because the general satisfaction and fulfillment of our nature is bound up inextricably with a pattern of society in which justice is done that this pattern must be held inviolable. The right to freedom from arbitrary hurt to our persons, our possessions, our actions, or our name is one of the plainest conditions of that fullness of life in which its goodness is now seen to consist. To encourage those in power to violate that pattern at will for local expediencies is to seek a special good by an act which would in principle put all goods in jeopardy; it would be like the dog's dropping of its bone for the shadow in the river. There is, of course, nothing new in this contention. If I am not mistaken, it is a return to the vision of Plato, who held that in the end the justification of every act lay in its place in the form of the good life.

Is this life *objectively* good? Running alongside the great tradition which from Plato down has held that it was, there has been a secondary tradition, stretching from Callicles to Russell, which held that it was not, and that goodness is as variable as man's fluctuating feeling. We have seen that in the latest and probably most formidable shape which that theory has taken it conflicts with universal ways of thinking about right and wrong. But we saw when we turned to the third and final criticism that this theory is by no means groundless. Goodness *is* dependent on the feeling and impulse of conscious minds. It consists in the satisfaction and fulfillment of human nature. Does this destroy the objectivity of our judgments of good and evil? On the contrary, it provides a clear meaning for their objective truth and frees that truth from any dependence on individual thought or feeling. It bridges the chasm between fact and value. It enlists science, especially psychology, in the service of morals. It answers sensitively to our reflective judgments of better and worse. It naturalizes duty, and rationalizes its authority. It offers a standard responsive alike to men's deeper identities and to the surface differences of nature and desire. In a time when skepticism about personal morality and pessimism about international morality seem to be the order of the day, it holds that to be moral is in the end to be natural and reasonable and sane.

The Meaning of "Good"

PATRICK NOWELL-SMITH

A-Words and G-Words

If we examine the adjectives used in ordinary discourse we find that they exhibit a great variety of logical behaviour. The grammatical form of an adjective sometimes gives us a clue to its logical behaviour; for example adjectives in -ent, -ible, -ous, and -ic fall into families which differ logically from each other, and we can often tell something about the meaning of a new adjective from its termination in the same sort of way that a chemist could deduce something about a compound unknown to him from the fact that its name ended in -ite, -ate, or -ide. But termination is not an altogether reliable guide to logical behaviour. In the first place words that are not derived from Latin or Greek sources seldom have special terminations, but they do nevertheless fall into logical families; and secondly it is notorious that words in -ible and -able function in at least two different ways. To say that a man is eligible for parliament is to say that he can (constitutionally) be elected, that his election would not be barred by any disqualification such as insanity or a peerage; it is not to say that he ought to be elected or is worthy to be elected. On the other hand an eligible bachelor is not someone who can legally be married but someone worth marrying.

The classification of adjectives is nec-

essarily a tentative and inexact business, especially in a field where it has never been attempted by people whose interests are philosophical rather than philological; and for a start I shall distinguish three main types. Consider, for example, the following sentences:

The view from the top was extensive.
The view from the top was sublime.

The adjective 'sublime' does not form part of a description of the view, unless we insist on making all adjectives descriptive and thereby reduce the force of 'descriptive' to vanishing point. We could give an exhaustive description of the view by enumerating its contents, and if the list contained a large number of large objects this would entail that the view was extensive. The question whether the view was extensive or not is a question of empirical fact.[1] But the sublimity of the view is not part of its contents and no description of the view would logically entail the truth or falsity of 'the view was sublime'. It is just this that the argument against the Naturalistic Fallacy shows so clearly. Some philosophers have said that goodness is a 'consequential property', by which is meant that it is a property that something can have only if it

Reprinted from *Ethics* by Patrick Nowell-Smith, pp. 70–74, 160–182, by permission of the author and Penguin Books Ltd. Copyright 1954.

---

[1] 'Extensive' is not strictly a 'descriptive' word; for to say that a view is extensive is not to describe it. But it belongs to descriptive discourse and will do as an example as I am not interested in the logic of descriptive discourse for its own sake.

has certain other properties. But we have already seen that the link between goodness and the good-making properties is not a logical one; a special act of awareness is needed to apprehend it. The relation between 'sublime' and those features of a landscape in virtue of which we would call it sublime is of the same type.

Consider the following conversation:

A. When I got to the top, I saw the whole plain spread out beneath me and Nanga Parbat towering above it. A waterfall that must have been at least five hundred feet high cascaded down from near where I stood into the swirling waters of the Indus.
B. What a sublime (magnificent, stirring, awe-inspiring, wonderful, etc.) sight that must have been.

B uses the phrase 'must have been' to indicate that the sight was sublime *because* of the items in A's description; and A would have been surprised and hurt if B had said: "I don't think much of that". The connexion between their remarks is obviously not logical entailment; yet we feel that B's comment was the natural and appropriate one to make. And this is because he is evincing the natural, appropriate emotion. Most people would react to the description in the same way and not say that the view was mean or sordid or squalid.

Taking a cue from this situation I shall refer to words of the same family as 'sublime' as Aptness-words(A-words), because they are words that indicate that an object has certain properties which are apt to arouse a certain emotion or range of emotions. I use the word 'indicate' with deliberate vagueness and do not say, for example, that 'terrifying' could be defined in terms of 'causing fear'. Nor, for reasons that will appear later, can we say that 'sublime' or 'terrifying' just express the emotion of the speaker. A-words have a logic of their own which is different both from that of Descriptive-words (D-words) and from that of

exclamations or reports of one's feelings.

Consider, again, our use of the word 'weed'. The ordinary man (who is not a Berkeleian philosopher) takes, rightly or wrongly, an uncompromisingly realistic view of D-words, such as 'dandelion' and 'yellow.' He believes that even if there were no gardeners there would still be dandelions and that they would still be yellow. But, if there were no gardeners, would there still be weeds? To say that a dandelion is a weed is not like saying that it is a member of the order Compositae; and the difference does not lie only in the fact that 'weed' is an ordinary-language word. To say that dandelions are weeds is not to *classify* them at all. For the contrast between weeds and flowers (in that sense of 'flowers' in which flowers are contrasted with weeds) depends on the interests of gardeners. If there were no gardeners we should have no use for this contrast; and if the interests of gardeners changed, if, for example, dandelions came to be admired for their beauty, rarity, or medicinal properties, dandelions would cease to be weeds. A weed is, roughly, a plant that we wish to eradicate rather than to cultivate. If a man said that he liked cultivating groundsel we might think him odd; but if he said that he liked cultivating weeds, this would be *logically* odd and we should have to take him to mean that he liked cultivating those plants that others usually wish to eradicate. In this way we could remove the logical (but not the horticultural) oddness from what he says by making 'weed' into a descriptive expression.

For amateur and self-employed gardeners 'weed' is an A-word. But for a gardener who is employed by someone else its logic is quite different. He may have no interest in his job at all or he may *like* having plantains and dandelions on the lawn. For him, a weed is, roughly, any plant that he *ought* to eradicate, that it is his duty to eradicate whether he likes the plant or not, and the word 'weed' is a Gerundive-word

(G-word), roughly analogous to 'praise-worthy', 'note-worthy', 'laudable', 'damn-able', etc.[2]

The logical relationships between A-words, D-words, and G-words will be examined later. The present account is over-simplified and schematic since it is intended only to throw light on the question whether all adjectives 'stand for properties'. We might mark the differences by saying that they stand for different sorts of properties, aptness-properties, descriptive-properties, and gerundive-properties. But what is gained by this? 'Red', 'sublime', and 'laudable' are all adjectives and all obey the same grammatical rules; but we have seen that to say that they all stand for properties is to say more than this. It is to say that they fit in the same way into the same prescribed scheme of categories containing substances, properties, states, events, processes, and so on; and this in turn is to say that their logical behaviour is similar. But this is just what it is not. There is a logical oddness about cultivating weeds or being bored by a sublime view that is not present in cultivating dandelions or being bored by a view of St. Paul's. To mark the differences by saying that all adjectives stand for properties, but properties of different sorts, is to mark it in the wrong way. The intention is to mark logical differences, the method is that appropriate to marking logical similarities.

One of Moore's most important arguments seems to depend on ignoring the distinction between A-words and D-words. "Let us imagine one world exceedingly *beautiful*. Imagine it as beautiful as you can; put into it whatever on this earth you most admire. . . . And then imagine the *ugliest* world you can possibly conceive. Imagine it simply one heap of *filth*, containing everything that is most *disgusting* to us. . . . The only thing we are not entitled to imag-ine is that any human being ever has or ever, by any possibility, can, live in either, can ever see and enjoy the *beauty* of the one or hate the *foulness* of the other."[3] The conclusion that Moore thinks we must admit is that it would be better for the beautiful world than for the ugly world to exist, even though no one ever lived in either. But the words I have italicized are not purely descriptive and they cannot be understood to mean anything at all if the presence of human beings and their tastes and interests are excluded, as it must be to make Moore's point. If, for example, instead of using the word 'filth' we specified what the second world was to contain in the neutral language of chemistry it is not so obvious that, if there were no one to see or smell either world, the one would be better than the other. To imagine something as beautiful or ugly, admirable or disgusting, is already to 'react' to it.

'Good'

I

'Good' in the Context of Choice

We have seen that when 'good' is used in the context of choice there can be no logical gap between deciding that something is the best or better than its rivals and choosing it. This does not imply that there can be no discrepancy between the decision which is, on the face of it, not a performance of any kind but a judgement, and the choice; but it does imply that if there is such a discrepancy a special reason must be given for it. And we must now consider the role of such expressions as 'because it is a good one' and 'because it is the best' when they are used to explain why a man chose the thing he did.

The answer to the question 'Why did you choose that car?' might be a statement of fact ('because it has more leg-room') or

---

[2] A few more examples: A dress may be red, comfortable, and indecent. A ball may be a leg-break, tempting, and over-pitched. A man may be blue-eyed, amusing, and admirable.

[3] *Principia Ethica*, p. 83.

an A-sentence ('because it is more comfortable'); and I have already discussed
the contextual background in which such
answers can be given and taken as logically
complete explanations. In each case the car
must have some A-property and some ordinary, empirical properties on which its
A-property depends. While the factual
answer says what the empirical properties
are and contextually implies an A-property
without specifying what it is, the
A-sentence does the reverse. And each
answer implies a pro-attitude towards the
A-property concerned; otherwise it would
not be an answer to the question.

The answer 'because it is the best'
functions in a similar way, but with certain
important differences. In the first place it
does not just imply a pro-attitude; it expresses it. But it does not only do this. If
this were all I wanted to do I should have
to say 'because I happen to like it more
than the others'. It contextually implies
that I have reasons for my choice; but it
does not say what they are and therefore
does not explain my choice.

We are tempted to say that it gives the
best possible reason. After all, what better
reason could there be for choosing a car
than the fact that it was the best available
or the best that I could afford? What better
reason could there be for doing anything
than the belief that it is the best thing to
do?

The trouble is that the reason is *too*
good. It is like saying that I was frightened
because it was a terrifying experience; and,
as an explanation, it operates in much the
same way. Just as 'because it was terrifying' shows that my fear was not an unusual one and contextually implies that the
object had certain unspecified properties
by which people are usually frightened, so
'because it was the best' shows that my
choice was no passing whim, that it was
considered more or less carefully, that the
object had certain unspecified 'good-
making' properties, and that my choice was
not a peculiar one. Any of these contextual

implications could be expressly withdrawn,
especially, as we shall see, the last; but in
default of such withdrawal my audience
would be entitled to assume them. Just as a
G-sentence showed more plainly than an
A-sentence that advice was being given but
was less explicit about the reasons, so 'because it was the best' shows more plainly
that I was choosing but says even less
about the reasons.

In fact it says nothing about them at
all; it only implies that I have reasons. The
goodness of something is not one of the
properties for which I choose it. If it were,
it would make sense to ask why its superior
goodness was a reason for choosing it. To
ask a man who chose a car because it was
faster or more economical or had more
leg-room why he chose it is to display ignorance of people's purchasing habits; to
say to him "I know you thought it the best
car; but why did you choose it?" is logically odd.

The same logical ties that bind goodness so closely to choosing bind it also to
activities that are akin to choosing. A man
who says that he voted for a certain proposal because he thought it good has not
explained why he voted for it; he has
merely guarded himself against accusations
of flippancy, irresponsibility or indulging in
complicated machinations. And it is logically odd to say "I think it is an excellent
proposal, but I shan't vote for it." As we
saw, reasons could be given for this discrepancy, and the logical nexus between
thinking good and voting comes out in the
fact that we should feel entitled to infer
that there must be a special reason. To call
something good is, in a way, already to
vote for it, to side with it, to let others
know where I stand. But it does more than
this; it implies that I have reasons for cast-
ing my vote as I do.

'Good' in the Context of Advice

The considerations that apply to 'good' in
the context of choice apply equally in the

context of advice. And here again the subjectivist is right in connecting 'this is good' with the pro-attitude of the speaker. There is the same sort of absurdity in 'This is good, but I don't advise you to do it' as there is in 'This is the best course; but shall I take it?'. In the latter case the speaker both expresses a decision as to how he should act and in the same breath asks if he should; and in the former he gives advice and in the same breath retracts it. It would be equally odd if the hearer were to say "You have told me that it is the best course to take; but do you advise me to take it?"

The differences in the use of 'good' in advice and choice are due to the fact that the problem to be solved is now someone else's. The adviser is not making up his mind what to do, but helping someone else to make up his mind. And this difference brings with it another. The relevant pro-attitude is that of the audience. But in other respects the contextual implications are the same. To tell someone that something is the best thing for him to do is to advise him to do it, but not irresponsibly. The speaker implies that he has good reasons for his advice, that he knows what the problem is and that his advice is relevant. The same predictive and causal elements are present as in the case of A-sentences; and advice may, as before, be given disingenuously, improperly, mistakenly, or unfortunately if one or other of the contextual implications is absent.

II

Other Uses of 'Good'

I shall discuss the other uses of 'good' in the order in which they seem to diverge more and more from the fundamental use, which is to express or explain a preference.

(a) *Praising and Applauding.* Like choosing, these are performances, not statements; and, although in primary uses they do express the speaker's pro-attitude, they have other contextual implications which will be examined later. They can be done with or without words; but the gestures, handclapping and the like, which are used for praising have conventional, symbolic meanings. They mean what they do in the way that words mean, not in the way that clouds mean rain or cobras in the garden mean trouble. Virtue-words are words of praise; and relatively specific words like 'brave', 'honest', and 'generous' are also descriptive; for they describe a person's behaviour and predict the way in which he can be relied upon to behave in certain sorts of situation. They both praise and give the reason, what the praise is *for*. But 'good' does not do this. In cases where there are recognized standards that a man must reach to be worthy of praise they contextually imply that he has reached those standards; but they do not say what the standards are. 'Because it is a good one' does not explain why I praise something; but it does imply that the thing has certain unspecified properties for which I praise it. My praise was not casual or capricious.

(b) *Commending.* The verb 'to commend' is used in two ways. It may mean 'entrust to the care of'; but this sense is irrelevant, since 'good' is not used to commend in this sense. In the sense in which 'good' is used for commending it is akin to praising but has a more hortatory force. To commend something to someone is to advise him to choose it. The Oxford Dictionary, as we saw, calls 'good' "the most general adjective of commendation" in English; but it goes on to add "implying the existence in a high or at least satisfactory degree of characteristic qualities which are either admirable in themselves or useful for some purpose".

The form of this definition is interesting, since it brings out the difference between the job that the word is used for and the conditions limiting its use in a way that philosophers' definitions of 'good' never do.

The writer of the dictionary sees clearly that the word is used to do a job which is not 'stating' but commending and that the elements of objective fact which some philosophers insist on treating as part of its meaning are really part of the contextual background of its use. In the uses which follow this, contextual background looms larger and larger, so that in some uses the word 'good' almost comes to be a descriptive word, though, as we shall see, it never quite does this and in moral contexts it can never wholly lose its gerundive force or its pro-force.

(c) *Verdicts and Appraisals.* In chapter I we saw that moral language is not only used for choosing and advising, but also making moral judgements, which are not decisions to do something but verdicts or appraisals of something or somebody. Now appraisals are *judgements*, not just expressions of a man's own taste or preference; and it is this point that the Consequential Property Theory tries to bring out, but in a misleading way. When we judge something to be good we always judge it to be good in respect of some property, and it is a question of empirical fact whether it has this property or not. Thus to judge a wine to be good is not just to express a preference for it—and we shall see that it need not be to do this at all—; the judgement must be backed by my belief that it has a certain bouquet, body, and flavour, and these are objective qualities, since a man who found that he disagreed markedly from all the experts on these points would admit himself to be wrong. It is an essential feature of judgements that they are made by reference to standards or criteria; but it is necessary to be extremely careful in discussing the way in which the criteria are related to the verdict or appraisal.

Let us assume for the moment that the criteria used by experts at wine-tastings, horse-shows, beauty contests, and school examinations are agreed to be the proper criteria, though this will have to be questioned later. We might be tempted to say

that if the criteria for being a good X are that the X must have properties a, b, and c in some specifiable degree, then 'good X' simply means 'X which has the properties a, b, and c in the requisite degree'. But this will not do. For it is possible to understand what 'good X' means without knowing what the criteria are. Thus, if I do not know the criteria used at Crufts I could not tell a good dog (in this sense of 'good') from a bad one or pick out the best dog from a group. But this does not mean that I cannot understand what 'good dog' means in the way that I could not understand what 'mangy dog' meant if I did not know what 'mangy' meant. For I do know that if it is a good dog it must have in a fairly high degree those properties which are mentioned in the list of criteria for judging dogs, although I do not know what these properties are or to what degree a dog must have them to rate as 'good.'

The next two uses are special cases of the appraising use.

(d) *Efficiency.* When 'good' is predicated of any object (natural or artificial, animate or inanimate) that is used for a purpose it implies the presence in a relatively high degree of those properties that the object must have to do its job. But again it would be a mistake to say that 'good knife' just *means* 'knife that is sharp, easily handled, durable, etc.' The connexion between the properties which a knife must have to be efficient and its efficiency is an empirical one. We know from experience that a knife which has not got these properties at all just won't cut and that its relative efficiency at cutting depends on the degree to which it has these properties. Nor can we even say that 'good knife' means 'knife which cuts efficiently', because we could understand what 'good' means in the expression 'good knife' without knowing what knives were for. But 'good knife' (in this sense of 'good') does mean 'knife which has those properties (whatever they are) which a knife must have if it is to do its job efficiently (whatever that is)'.

(e) *Skill.* When we call a man a good lawyer, scholar, cricketer or liar, the use is similar to the 'efficiency' use except for the fact that, since these are men, the purpose concerned is their purpose, not the purpose they are used for. Just as we could not use 'good' to imply efficiency unless we agreed about what the object concerned is for, so we could not use it to imply skill unless there was something that was agreed to constitute success at the activity concerned. But, just as we cannot say that 'good' means 'efficient' in the one sense, so we cannot say that it means 'successful' in the other. In activities involving skill there are rules for achieving success which are such that we know from experience that unless a man applies them he is unlikely to be successful. Thus, if we know the rules for success at bridge or cricket we can predict, in a very general way, what a good bridge-player or cricketer will do; and in calling a man 'good' we imply that he applies or follows the rules. This implication can, of course, be expressly withdrawn because we know that people sometimes achieve success in very unorthodox ways. But 'good' never quite loses its gerundive force and if we call a man a good cricketer without intending to imply that his methods ought to be imitated we mislead our audience.

(f) *The descriptive use.* Like most words, 'good' can be used to mean 'what most people would call good'. A man who uses it may not be choosing, advising, defending a choice or piece of advice, or appraising, but referring to an object which he or others would call good if they were doing one of these. Thus I may call a wine good even if I am not competent to apply the criteria, just because I have heard the experts praise it.

This use belongs to descriptive discourse because it is a question of historical fact whether people do or do not call the object good, and that is what is being as-serted. It is necessarily a secondary use, since it would be impossible to use 'good' to mean 'what people call good' unless people called things good in primary ways. And 'good' is hardly ever used with this descriptive force alone. The speaker implies that he himself sides with those who call the thing good unless this implication is expressly withdrawn or obviously inadmissible in the context.

III

We must now consider the ways in which these uses of 'good' are connected with each other. It is clearly not an accident that the same word is used in all these different ways nor could this fact be explained in a purely historical, or philological way. 'Good' is *the* Janus-word *par excellence;* it is often used to do more than one job on one occasion and the logical connexions between the various jobs are what they are because the facts are what they are. It is also most emphatically an ordinary, non-technical word and it is a consequence of this that the logic of its use reflects empirical truths that hold only for the most part and admit of exceptions. For ordinary language, unlike mathematics, is not deliberately constructed by men who have a keen eye for consistency and rigour; it is not deliberately constructed at all but grows and changes in an environment in which the exceptional case can be and must be ignored. The contextual implications of any use of 'good' are many and varied and, on occasion, any of them can be withdrawn, a point which should make us suspicious of counter-examples. It is impossible to understand the actual uses of 'good' by considering artificial and exceptional situations because the logic of ordinary language does not cater for such situations.

But there is one element which seems

to be common to all cases. Although a man need have no comparisons in mind when he calls something 'good', such comparisons are always implied. He must, if challenged, be able to produce examples of descriptively similar things that he would call not so good. For example, we always praise something with a certain degree of warmth which lies somewhere on a scale between mild commendation and hysterical adulation. The word 'good' can be used to express almost any degree of warmth, but it must be less than that expressed in the same context by 'excellent' or 'superb' and greater than that expressed by 'fair' or 'tolerable'.

It is not difficult to understand the connexions between the more obviously performatory uses, praising, applauding, and commending; nor is it difficult to appreciate their intimate connexion with preference and choice. To praise is not to choose; but it is connected with choosing in that it would be odd for a man to choose the thing he was prepared to praise less highly or not at all. He must have special reasons for this, modesty for example, a sense of unworthiness to possess the 'better' thing or a desire that someone else should have it. Again, if a man habitually praises one pianist more highly than another we expect to find him attending the recitals of the former more regularly and to be more annoyed when he is prevented from going. But he might have been told that the second is really a better pianist and be trying to cultivate a taste for his performance. Explanations can be given of discrepancies between praising and choice; but in default of an explanation the connexion is contextually implied.

If, on a particular occasion, I call a man brave it would be logically odd to ask if I was in favour of what he did; for 'brave' is a praising word and by using it I show that I am in favour. Similarly, if I call courage a 'virtue' I show that I am, in a general way, in favour of courage, although

I might not always want to praise a brave deed. It is an empirical fact that men are, for the most part, in favour of the modes of conduct that they call (descriptively) brave, honest, or generous. But this pro-attitude is so widespread that these words are not pure descriptive words; they are terms of praise and merely a pro-attitude unless this is expressly withdrawn.

Now praising and applauding are activities which are often performed with the special purpose of encouraging the person concerned to continue in the same style, and hissing and booing are used with the opposite intention. Although the words and gestures employed in praising owe their encouraging force to convention, they have, granted the convention, a natural effect on the people praised. For it is an empirical fact that, except in special circumstances—for example, if the praise is considered impertinent—people enjoy being praised and are therefore likely to go on doing what they are praised for. Praising is logically tied to approval; for if we heard a man praise something we could not wonder whether he approved of it or not unless we suspected him of being disingenuous or ironical; and it is logically tied in the same way to encouraging. But, although it is an empirical fact that men tend to encourage and try to promote that of which they approve, we must as always, assume that men on the whole intend the natural consequences of their actions and therefore do not praise that which they would prefer to be otherwise. And this assumption is reflected in the fact that praising implies both approval and encouragement.

The same logical ties bind praising to advising; it would be logically odd to praise one candidate more highly than another and to go on to say that one was advising against his being given the job or the prize. Odd, but not impossible; for there might, as always, be special reasons for this.

The "characteristic qualities" which, according to the dictionary, are implied by the use of 'good' may be "either admirable in themselves or useful for some purpose". In contexts involving efficiency or skill it is the latter that we have in mind. In such contexts there need be no direct connexion between the performatory uses, which are all variations of 'preferring' or 'being on the side of', and the usefulness implied by 'good'. We may have no pro-attitude whatsoever towards the purpose for which something is used or the activity at which a man is skilful, as when we speak of a 'good cosh' or a 'good liar'. But there is still an indirect link with the pro-attitudes since 'good' in these contexts implies success, and 'success' is a pro-word. A man is not a good liar unless he fairly consistently achieves his aim.

Preference and Appraisal

But it is the connexions between the performatory uses and the verdict-giving, judging, or appraising use when the qualities on which the verdict is based are thought to be "admirable in themselves" that are the most important and the most difficult. I shall substitute 'preferable' for 'admirable', since admiration is itself a performance akin to praising and 'admirable' is therefore too narrow in scope to cover all appraisals other than those of efficiency or skill.

All the performatory uses contextually imply appraisal; for we have seen that it is improper to use 'good', at least in an impersonal formula, to express or defend a preference unless the preference is a considered one, based on reasons and not unusual. And to say that the preference is 'based on reasons' is to say that the speaker applied criteria or standards. It is not necessary that he should have done this deliberately; he may have done it automatically; but he must be able to defend his choice by an appeal to the standards which justify it.

But, although the performatory uses imply appraisal, it is not so clear that the converse is true. Indeed it is not true in any direct sense; appraisals often imply preference only in a roundabout way. For when 'good' is used to give a verdict it need neither express nor imply a pro-attitude on the part of the speaker. In such cases what a man is primarily doing with the word 'good' is applying those standards which are only contextually implied in the more subjective uses. Since 'good' is a Janus-word, he may, of course, be expressing his preferences or advising as well; but he need not be. The embittered schoolmaster may have no interest in the work of the examination candidates at all; he may even prefer stupidity to intelligence or have a private belief that the usual criteria for intelligence are quite wrong. Nevertheless he may still apply the grading words 'good', 'fair', 'poor', and so on in accordance with the accepted criteria either from conscientiousness or from habit or from fear of losing his job.

In the same way a professional taster of wine may dislike all wine or prefer the less good to the better; his judgement is based solely on the presence of those "characteristic qualities" which, as an expert, he is able to detect and knows to be among the criteria for 'good wine'. But even in these cases there is an indirect reference to choosing and advising which comes out when we turn from the question "What are the criteria in fact used for grading Xs?" to the question "Why do we have the criteria that we do?". Professional wine-tasters are, after all, business men or the employees of business men and, though their job may be to taste wine, they only have this job because wine is to be bought and sold. It is no accident that the criteria for 'good Xs' are connected with the Xs that people prefer or approve of more highly. The professional wine-taster may not *like* Chateau Lafite; but he uses criteria for judging wine under which it gets high marks because people are prepared to pay highly for wine which rates highly under these criteria, and they do this because they like it.

IV

Nature and Convention

The dictionary's phrase "admirable in themselves" is unfortunately ambiguous. In its context it is clear that 'in themselves' is contrasted with 'for a purpose', and that what the author has in mind is the familiar contrast between good-as-means and good-as-an-end. But 'in itself' is often used in philosophy with at least three other meanings. (a) It is sometimes used as a synonym for 'really' or 'objectively' to imply independence of human opinion or judgement of value. But, in discussing Moore's 'two worlds' argument I have already suggested that it is doubtful whether any sense can be given to the idea of something being good if there was no one to judge it good.

(b) It is sometimes used with a gerundive force. What is admirable or preferable in itself is what people ought to admire or prefer. But to use it in this way is not to comment on the use of 'good' but to make a value-judgement; and, if the author of the dictionary were thought to be using it in this way, he must be thought to subscribe himself to all the value-judgements he cites as examples of 'good'. (c) But 'good-in-itself' could also be used to mean 'naturally good,' to imply that the criteria or standards used for judging the goodness of something are not, like the criteria for a good postage stamp, dependent on human convention. It is this contrast that I propose to discuss.

We call a taste (or any other pro-attitude) a 'natural' one if (a) it is pretty general even among people of very different societies and if (b) most people do not have to learn to acquire it. It is impor-

tant to notice that both these criteria for what is 'natural' are extremely vague and that they both admit of exceptions. A taste for strawberries does not cease to be natural because Jones happens not to like them or because Smith did not like them at first. Benevolence and love of life are natural pro-attitudes, even though there are misanthropes and suicides.

The criteria used for appraising are partly natural and partly conventional. In music, for example, the criteria which critics apply to a composition or performance are conventional in that they vary in different cultures and it is necessary to learn what they are; and musical taste is also partly conventional in that it is not natural to like or admire a Bach fugue in the way that it is natural to like sweets or to love one's children. It may well be that no criteria or tastes are wholly conventional. Correlations can be found between the criteria employed and the physiological facts of hearing; for example we know that the musical intervals and key-relationships on which all western music is based and which enter into the criteria used for judging a musical composition are of a mathematically simple kind. And even in the case of the criteria used for judging dogs at Crufts, which are highly artificial, it is possible to trace historical connexions between the criteria now used and the criteria that were used when dogs were used for practical purposes; and these last were natural criteria in that the purposes, such as hunting and protection from wild animals, were based on natural pro-attitudes.

But in many cases the criteria now used are connected to natural criteria only through a long process of change and have become modified to such an extent that their original connexion with natural pro-attitudes has been entirely lost. And in such cases it often happens that we do not use the criteria we do because people have the pro-attitudes they have, but we have the pro-attitudes we have because the

criteria are what they are. It may be that
no one can now remember exactly why certain criteria were originally chosen to be
the standards of judging something to be
good or bad of its kind and that people are
now prepared to admire, praise, and pay
highly for objects because they conform to
the accepted criteria, rather than accepting
the criteria as 'proper' ones because, under
them, the things that they admire rate
highly. Taste is dictated by fashion, not
fashion by taste.

But such cases must (logically) be
secondary cases and it would therefore be
a mistake to cite them in proof of the contention that criteria are logically prior to
pro-attitudes. For unless there were primary cases in which we adopted criteria
because we already had a pro-attitude towards the objects that in fact rate highly
under them, it would be impossible to understand how the same set of words could
be used both in applying criteria and for
choosing, praising, and advising. It is only
because 'good' is used in applying criteria
in cases where we use the criteria we do
because our desires, interests, and tastes
are what they are that men can come to acquire a taste for what counts as 'good'
under the accepted criteria even in cases
where the original connexion between the
criteria and the taste has been lost. Advertisers and propagandists, arbiters of taste
and leaders of fashion could not (logically) stimulate new tastes and attitudes
by the reiterated use of criterion-applying language unless this language was also used for applying criteria in cases
where there are pre-existing tastes and attitudes. Without genuine enthusiasts there
could be no snobs.

In many cases, therefore, the answer to
the question 'Why do we use the criteria
for judging so-and-sos that we do?' may be
of a purely historical kind; the criteria are
traditional; they have been concocted and
moulded by interested parties, and so on.
But this sort of answer cannot be given in

all cases; there must be some cases in
which we use a set of criteria because, as
an empirical fact, they give higher ratings
to those objects which we prefer.

In discussing appraisals I assumed that
there was no difficulty about saying what
the proper criteria for judging Xs are or
about selecting the experts, leaders of fashion, or arbiters of taste; and it might seem
that these assumptions involve a vicious
circularity in the attempt to construe the
grading-scale of good, fair, poor, and bad
in terms of the standards used by experts.
But this is not so for two reasons. (a) In
some cases there are tests of competence
which are purely objective and empirical.
Some men, for example, have perfect pitch,
can detect minute musical intervals, can
recognize and accurately reproduce long
and complicated tunes and so on, while
others cannot; and these are matters of
fact. In judging their expertise we must,
of course, rely on the ability of other experts
to assess their competence; but the judgements of these experts is 'objective' because they fulfil the requirements for objective language discussed in chapter 4. It
is possible that one man might have a finer
ear than all other men, so that in a case in
which he said that two notes were slightly
different when everyone else said they
were the same he would be right and they
wrong. But if there were no indirect tests,
such as the appeal to readings of scales
and meters, for deciding whether he can
really detect these differences or is only
bluffing, and if those who honestly claimed
to be able to make fine discriminations did
not on the whole agree with each other, we
could not call their judgements 'objective'.

Now from the fact that a man is able
to make these fine discriminations or to
perform better than others in these objectively testable ways, it does not, of course,
follow that he is a good judge. For to say
that he is a good judge is either to state
that he is good at applying the accepted

criteria for what is good (which is different from being good at passing the objective tests) or to express approval of his judgements, to praise him, to encourage others to accept his judgements, and so on; and in most cases it is to do all these things at once. But, once again, the reason why we allow that, in a general way, the most technically competent people are the best judges lies in the facts. A man who is tone-deaf is unlikely to be able even to distinguish one piece of music from another and his value-judgements (if he makes them), are not likely to be consistent with each other; so that his value-judgements would be useless as a guide to others. A man who knows little Greek could not be a good judge of a piece of Greek prose. Consistency and fine discrimination are not sufficient conditions of good taste or moral insight, but they are necessary conditions if criteria are to be used for the purposes for which they are used.

(b) Secondly, the person who rejects the criteria usually employed or the verdict of the acknowledged experts may do so in two ways. He may simply refuse to be guided by them on the grounds that he happens not to like what is usually called good. But, if he goes further and says that the usual criteria are not *good* criteria, he is not just rejecting them; he is himself using criterion-applying language and he implies that he has second-order criteria for judging (and condemning) the usual first-order criteria.

To the questioning of criteria there is no end; but if we ask whether the criteria for judging Xs are *good* criteria we must, at whatever level we have reached, use criteria for deciding whether they are good or not. It is logically absurd to ask a question without knowing how the answers to it are to be judged to be good or bad answers. The appeal to criteria accepted by experts is not circular, but regressive; and the regress is not a vicious one since, although we *can* always question the criteria,

there is no practical or logical necessity to do so. The self-guaranteeing criteria so vainly sought by some moralists are neither possible nor necessary.

V

Non-Practical Appraisals

We often make appraisals in contexts where there is clearly no question of choosing or advising, for example moral judgements about historical or fictional characters. And this seems to involve a difficulty for theories which make appraisals logically dependent on pro-attitudes. Hutcheson and Hume, for example, tried to reduce moral judgements to expressions of feeling. They were not guilty of the Naturalistic Fallacy, since they were prepared to allow that moral approval and sympathy are special, moral feelings distinct from other types of feeling. But even this concession to the peculiarity of the moral use of language does not save them from an important objection that seems at first sight fatal to their case. Sentiments, as Hume noticed, seem to vary in rough proportion to the propinquity of their objects. We are not moved by the iniquity of remote historical characters as we are by those closer to us; and we feel more approval for and sympathy with those near to us than with those who are more remote. Yet our moral judgements do not vary in the same way. "We read Cicero now without emotion, yet we can still judge Verres to be a villain. According to Hume's theory our judgement must change as do our feelings. I do not feel indignation as strongly now about the German invasion of Czechoslovakia as I did at the time it happened; yet I do not judge the action to be less wrong than I did then, or the agents less criminal. . . . It is but a weak subterfuge to say we transport ourselves by the force of imagination into distant ages and countries, and consider the passions which we should have felt on contemplating these characters had we been contemporaries and had commerce with the persons. . . . I now feel completely indifferent to Verres, and know it. Yet, Hume tells me, when I judge Verres to have been a villain, I am so deceived by my imagination that I talk as if I felt a strong feeling of anger."[4]

Dr. Raphael's criticism is fatal to the theory that a man who makes a moral appraisal is always expressing a feeling; and a similar criticism could also be made of any theory which says that to appraise is always to praise, advise, commend, etc. On some occasions a man may be simply *applying* the criteria that he and others customarily use for these purposes. To call Verres a villain is to pass a verdict on him, to condemn him. Now the Moral Sense School were, I think, mistaken in construing moral approval and disapproval as *feelings,* since this suggests too strongly the analogy with itches, aches, and tickles. But they were right to connect moral appraisals and verdicts with approval and disapproval. For although a man who passes a verdict need not be expressing a pro- or con-attitude, we have seen that the criteria he uses are directly or indirectly linked with these attitudes; and in the case of moral judgements they must be linked in a special way that may be absent in other cases.

I said earlier that, although in other cases 'good' might lose its gerundive force, it cannot wholly do so when used to make moral appraisals. The reason is that, whatever may be the case with other types of appraisal, moral appraisals must be universal. Anyone who makes a moral appraisal even of a remote character must be willing to apply the same criteria universally. And it follows from this that he must be willing to apply them in practical contexts. If I am

[4] D. D. Raphael: *The Moral Sense,* pp. 88 and 91.

not prepared to condemn anyone whose behaviour is like that of Verres in all relevant respects, then, in calling Verres a villain, I am not making a genuine moral judgement; and the relevant respects are all of an empirical, objective kind. It would, of course, be trivial to include among them an objective property of villainy or moral turpitude; all that is necessary is that I should be prepared to condemn anyone who did the sort of thing that Verres is called a villain for having done, anyone who oppressed the poor, robbed the rich, took bribes, and cheated the treasury, and all for his own personal profit.

Moral appraisals are therefore connected with choosing and advising in a way that non-moral appraisals need not be. It is not logically odd to say "This is the better wine, but I prefer that"; but it is logically odd to say "This is the (morally) better course; but I shall do that."[5] And a man cannot be making a genuine moral judgement about Verres if he would himself be prepared to act on the same principles on which Verres acted and prepared to exhort others to do so. In condemning Verres he is not expressing any emotion; but he is affirming his own moral principles.

VI

Objective-Subjective

In chapter 6 I said that the distinction between "For what job is the word '. . .' used?" and "Under what conditions is it proper to use that word for that job?" throws light on the objective-subjective dispute.

As we should expect, both parties are

[5] This may sound surprising. We all know what it is to take what we know to be the morally worse course. I shall try to remove the air of paradox in chapter 18.

right. Just as the subjectivists are right in denying that A-words stand for special properties and explaining them in terms of people's reactions, so they are also right in connecting 'good' and 'bad' with people's desires, tastes, interests, approvals, and disapprovals. There is a logical absurdity about calling a play 'amusing' if the speaker believes that it never has amused anyone and never will; and there is the same logical absurdity in calling something 'good' without any direct or indirect reference to a pro-attitude. If the connexion between 'good' and the pro-attitude that is contextually relevant were not a logical one, a gap would emerge between calling something good on the one hand and deciding to choose it, choosing it or advising others to choose it on the other which would make these activities unintelligible. Moreover, the subjectivists are also right in connecting 'good' with the pro-attitudes of the speaker, at least in moral cases.

But the objectivists are also right. They are mistaken in denying the points made by the subjectivists above and in thinking that goodness must be a unique, non-natural property. It is sometimes argued that if there were no such property we could not account for the fact that we use the impersonal form 'this is good' rather than the personal form 'I approve of this', and those who use this argument are inclined to forget that we have an impersonal form 'this is nice' as well as the personal form 'I like it', so that niceness would have to be an objective property too.

It would indeed be puzzling to understand why we use these impersonal forms if we were just talking about or expressing our own approvals; but this argument does not show that we are talking about something else, still less that this must be a unique property. We can account for the objective formula, as we did in the case of 'nice', by saying (a) that 'X is good' is not only used in the context of choice and (b) that, when it is so used, it implies a great deal that is not implied by 'I approve of X' and is expressly denied by 'I happen to approve of X.' It implies that my approval is not an unusual one and that I could give reasons for it. It implies also—what is a matter of objective fact—that the object conforms to certain standards which are generally accepted.

It is sometimes argued that 'this is good' cannot just mean 'I approve of this' on the ground that we can say "I approve of this because it is good". Approval must therefore be an intellectual emotion which arises in us only when we recognize something to have the objective property 'goodness'. But it has never been clear what the connexion between the approval and the recognition of the property is supposed to be. Is it logically necessary that anyone who recognizes the property should feel approval or is it just an empirical fact that people who notice the property, and only they, have the feeling? Each of these answers involves insuperable difficulties; but if neither is correct we must find some other way of explaining the 'because' in 'I approve of X because it is good'.

The need for such an explanation vanishes when we see that this is not a reason-giving 'because' like that in 'I approve of Jones because he is kind to children' but more like 'I like Jones because he is likeable'. It rebuts the suggestion that I just 'happen to' approve of X and it implies that X has certain properties which make it worthy of my approval and that it conforms to the known standards for Xs.

The objectivist is right in drawing attention to the factual background which makes impersonal appraisals possible; but the facts which it contains are ordinary, empirical facts, not special, non-natural facts. Unlike the subjectivist (who tends to ignore the background altogether), he tries to include the background in the meaning of the word; and this, combined with the mistake of confusing practical and descriptive discourse, leads him into the vain pursuit of a single ingredient to which we always refer when we call something good.

VII

The Naturalistic Fallacy

We are now in a position to see why the moral philosophers of the past subordinated the critical or appraising uses of moral language to the practical uses. Each presupposes the other, but in a different way. The practical uses presuppose the appraising use in that we could not use 'good' as we do for choosing, advising, and praising if we did not employ criteria or standards; since we only use 'good' for these purposes *when* we are employing standards. Nevertheless people who did not know what standards were could do things recognizably like what we, who have standards, call choosing, advising, and praising. They would be very rudimentary performances, hardly deserving the names of choice, advice, and praise; but they could occur. We draw a distinction between 'good' and 'happen to like' which people without standards could not draw; and we, who have the distinction, would describe their activities in terms of what they 'happen to like', because they could not do anything that we would call 'choosing the best'. In this way the practical uses of 'good' imply the appraising use.

But the practical uses are logically prior to the appraising use in a much more fundamental way. Unless men had pro-attitudes, there could not be even rudimentary analogues of what we know as appraising, judging, or passing a verdict. For these involve the use of standards; and without pro-attitudes we should neither have any use for standards nor even be able to understand what a 'standard' was. We can imagine a world in which there was choosing, but no appraising and also a world in which there was classifying, sorting, and ordering (for example by size)

but no choosing; but, in a world in which there was no choosing, there could be no such thing as appraising or grading.

Ethical Naturalism is the attempt to trace logical connexions between moral appraisals and the actual pro- and con-attitudes of men, their desires and aversions, hopes and fears, joys and sorrows. One-track naturalistic theories always fail to do justice to the complexity both of the facts and of the logical connexions, since they suggest that there is only one thing towards which men have a pro-attitude, pleasure, or that all pro-attitudes are desires. And these theories are both psychologically and logically misleading.

Opponents of the Naturalistic Fallacy have pointed out the logical errors. It is true that gerundive and deontological words cannot be defined in terms of pleasure, desire, or even purpose; and I shall try to show how they are connected with these teleological concepts later. It is also true that gerundive judgements and value judgements do not follow logically from descriptive statements about what men like, enjoy, and approve of. But the reason for this is not that gerundive words and value words refer to special entities or qualities, but that a person who *uses* them is not, except in certain secondary cases, describing anything at all. He is not doing what psychologists do, which is to describe, explain, and comment on what people like, enjoy, and approve of; and he is not doing what moral philosophers do, which is to describe, explain, and comment on the way in which people use moral words; he is himself using moral language, expressing approval, praising, advising, exhorting, commending, or appraising.

The attack on the Naturalistic Fallacy is thus far justified. But the conclusion which is commonly drawn, that moral concepts are a special sort of concept which must be purged of all association with the 'merely empirical or phenomenal' concepts of enjoying, wanting, and approval is not justified. Psychology is not as irrelevant to ethics as some modern philosophers insist; for, although moral judgements do not follow from psychological statements, we cannot understand what the terms used in moral judgements mean unless we examine them in the context of their use; and they are used either directly to express a pro- or con-attitude or to perform some other task which beings who had no pro- or con-attitudes could not perform or even understand. The various ways in which 'good' is used are unintelligible unless they are directly or indirectly connected with choice; and I shall try to show later that the same applies to 'ought'.

Moral philosophy does not, therefore, "rest on a mistake". For the great philosophers were not primarily interested in the question whether deontological words could be analysed in terms of 'merely empirical' or 'natural' concepts. They believed that, human beings being what they are, there are certain types of activity that are in fact satisfactory to them and that it is possible empirically to discover what these are. No doubt they often made mistakes of fact, for example that of supposing that what is satisfactory to one man would be satisfactory to another; and they made mistakes of logic, for example that of supposing that 'good' could be extracted from its context and be said to mean the same as 'satisfactory'. But they do not seem to have been mistaken in their basic assumptions that the language of obligation is intelligible only in connexion with the language of purpose and choice, that men choose to do what they do because they are what they are, and that moral theories which attempt to exclude all consideration of human nature as it is do not even begin to be moral theories.

What Is a Value Judgement?

R. M. HARE

MEANING AND CRITERIA

It is a characteristic of 'good' that it can be applied to any number of different classes of objects. We have good cricket-bats, good chronometers, good fire-extinguishers, good pictures, good sunsets, good men. The same is true of the word 'red'; all the objects I have just listed might be red. We have to ask first whether, in explaining the meaning of the word 'good', it would be possible to explain its meaning in all of these expressions at once, or whether it would be necessary to explain 'good cricket-bat' first, and then go on to explain 'good chronometer' in the second lesson, 'good fire-extinguisher' in the third, and so on; and if the latter, whether in each lesson we should be teaching something entirely new—like teaching the meaning of 'fast dye' after we had in a previous lesson taught the meaning of 'fast motor-car'—or whether it would be just the same lesson over again, with a different example—like teaching 'red dye' after we had taught 'red motor-car'. Or there might be some third possibility.

The view that 'good chronometer' would be a completely new lesson, even though the day before we had taught 'good cricket-bat', runs at once into difficulties. For it would mean that at any one time our

Reprinted from *The Language of Morals* by R. M. Hare, 1952, by permission of the author and the Clarendon Press, Oxford. Pp. 95–97, 111–119, 121–133, 148-150.

learner could only use the word 'good' in speaking of classes of objects which he had learnt so far. He would never be able to go straight up to a new class of objects and use the word 'good' of one of them. When he had learnt 'good cricket-bat' and 'good chronometer', he would not be able to manage 'good fire-extinguisher'; and when he had learnt the latter, he would still be unable to manage 'good motor-car'. But in fact one of the most noticeable things about the way we use 'good' is that we are able to use it for entirely new classes of objects that we have never called 'good' before. Suppose that someone starts collecting cacti for the first time and puts one on his mantel-piece—the only cactus in the country. Suppose then that a friend sees it, and says 'I must have one of those'; so he sends for one from wherever they grow, and puts it on his mantel-piece, and when his friend comes in, he says 'I've got a better cactus than yours'. But how does he know how to apply the word in this way? He has never learnt to apply 'good' to cacti; he does not even know any *criteria* for telling a good cactus from a bad one (for as yet there are none); but he has learnt to use the word 'good', and having learnt that, he can apply it to any class of objects that he requires to place in order of merit. He and his friend may dispute about the criteria of good cacti; they may attempt to set up rival criteria; but they could not even do this unless they were from the start under no difficulty in using the word 'good'. Since, therefore, it is possible to use the word 'good' for a new class of objects without further instruction, learning the use of the word for one class of objects cannot be a different lesson from learning it for another class of objects—though learning the criteria of goodness in a new class of objects may be a new lesson each time. . . .

DESCRIPTION AND EVALUATION

There are two sorts of things that we can say about strawberries; the first sort is usually called *descriptive,* the second sort *evaluative.* Examples of the first sort of remark are, 'This strawberry is sweet' and 'This strawberry is large, red, and juicy'. Examples of the second sort of remark are 'This is a good strawberry' and 'This strawberry is just as strawberries ought to be'. The first sort of remark is often given as a reason for making the second sort of remark; but the first sort does not by itself entail the second sort, nor vice versa. Yet there seems to be some close logical connexion between them. Our problem is: 'What is this connexion?'; for no light is shed by saying that there is a connexion, unless we can say what it is.

The problem may also be put in this way: if we knew all the descriptive properties which a particular strawberry had (knew, of every descriptive sentence relating to the strawberry, whether it was true or false), and if we knew also the meaning of the word 'good', then what else should we require to know, in order to be able to tell whether a strawberry was a good one? Once the question is put in this way, the answer should be apparent. We should require to know, what are the criteria in virtue of which a strawberry is to be called a good one, or what are the characteristics that make a strawberry a good one, or what is the standard of goodness in strawberries. We should require to be given the major premiss. We have already seen that

we can know the meaning of 'good strawberry' without knowing any of these latter things—though there is also a sense of the sentence 'What does it mean to call a strawberry a good one?' in which we should not know the answer to it, unless we also knew the answer to these other questions. It is now time to elucidate and distinguish these two ways in which we can be said to know what it means to call an object a good member of its class. This will help us to see more clearly both the differences and the similarities between 'good' and words like 'red' and 'sweet'.

Since we have been dwelling for some time on the differences, it will do no harm now to mention some of the similarities. For this purpose, let us consider the two sentences 'M is a red motor-car' and 'M is a good motor-car' . . .

The first similarity between 'M is a red motor-car' and 'M is a good motor-car' is that both can be, and often are, used for conveying information of a purely factual or descriptive character. If I say to someone 'M is a good motor-car', and he himself has not seen, and knows nothing of M, but does on the other hand know what sorts of motor-car we are accustomed to call 'good' (knows what is the accepted standard of goodness in motor-cars), he undoubtedly receives information from my remark about what sort of motor-car it is. He will complain that I have misled him, if he subsequently discovers that M will not go over 30 m.p.h., or uses as much oil as petrol, or is covered with rust, or has large holes in the roof. His reason for complaining will be the same as it would have been if I had said that the car was red and he subsequently discovered that it was black. I should have led him to expect the motor-car to be of a certain description when in fact it was of a quite different description.

The second similarity between the two sentences is this. Sometimes we use them, not for actually conveying information, but for putting our hearer into a position subsequently to use the word 'good' or 'red' for giving or getting information. Suppose, for example, that he is utterly unfamiliar with motor-cars in the same sort of way as most of us are unfamiliar with horses nowadays, and knows no more about motor-cars than is necessary in order to distinguish a motor-car from a hansom cab. In that case, my saying to him 'M is a good motor-car' will not give him any information about M, beyond the information that it is a motor-car. But if he is able then or subsequently to examine M, he will have learnt something. He will have learnt that some of the characteristics which M has, are characteristics which make people—or at any rate me—call it a good motor-car. This may not be to learn very much. But suppose that I make judgements of this sort about a great many motor-cars, calling some good and some not good, and he is able to examine all or most of the motor-cars about which I am speaking; he will in the end learn quite a lot, always presuming that I observe a consistent standard in calling them good or not good. He will eventually, if he pays careful attention, get into the position in which he knows, after I have said that a motor-car is a good one, what sort of a motor-car he may expect it to be—for example fast, stable on the road, and so on.

Now if we were dealing, not with 'good', but with 'red', we should call this process 'explaining the meaning of the word'—and we might indeed, in a sense, say that what I have been doing is explaining what one means by 'a good motor-car'. This is a sense of 'mean' about which, as we have seen, we must be on our guard. The processes, however, are very similar. I might explain the meaning of 'red' by continually saying of various motor-cars 'M is a red motor-car', 'N is not a red motor-car', and so on. If he were attentive enough, he would soon get into a position in which he was able to use the word 'red' for giving or getting information, at any rate about motor-cars. And so, both with 'good' and with 'red', there is this process, which in the case

of 'red' we may call 'explaining the meaning', but in the case of 'good' may only call it so loosely and in a secondary sense; to be clear we must call it something like 'explaining or conveying or setting forth the standard of goodness in motor-cars'.

The standard of goodness, like the meaning of 'red', is normally something which is public and commonly accepted. When I explain to someone the meaning of 'red motor-car', he expects, unless I am known to be very eccentric, that he will find other people using it in the same way. And similarly, at any rate with objects like motor-cars where there is a commonly accepted standard, he will expect, having learnt from me what is the standard of goodness in motor-cars, to be able, by using the expression 'good motor-car', to give information to other people, and get it from them, without confusion.

A third respect in which 'good motor-car' resembles 'red motor-car' is the following: both 'good' and 'red' can vary as regards the exactitude or vagueness of the information which they do or can convey. We normally use the expression 'red motor-car' very loosely. Any motor-car that lies somewhere between the unmistakably purple and the unmistakably orange could without abuse of language be called a red motor-car. And similarly, the standard for calling motor-cars good is commonly very loose. There are certain characteristics, such as inability to exceed 30 m.p.h., which to anyone but an eccentric would be sufficient conditions for refusing to call it a good motor-car; but there is no precise set of accepted criteria such that we can say 'If a motor-car satisfies these conditions, it is a good one; if not, not'. And in both cases we could be precise if we wanted to. We could, for certain purposes, agree not to say that a motor-car was 'really red' unless the redness of its paint reached a certain measurable degree of purity and saturation; and similarly, we might adopt a very exact standard of goodness in motor-cars. We might refuse the name 'good motor-car' to any car that would not go round a certain race-track without mishap in a certain limited time, that did not conform to certain other rigid specifications as regards accommodation, &c. This sort of thing has not been done for the expression 'good motor-car'; but, as Mr. Urmson has pointed out, it has been done by the Ministry of Agriculture for the expression 'super apple'.[1]

It is important to notice that the exactness or looseness of their criteria does absolutely nothing to distinguish words like 'good' from words like 'red'. Words in both classes may be descriptively loose or exact, according to how rigidly the criteria have been laid down by custom or convention. It certainly is not true that value-words are distinguished from descriptive words in that the former are looser, descriptively, than the latter. There are loose and rigid examples of both sorts of word. Words like 'red' can be extremely loose, without becoming to the least degree evaluative; and expressions like 'good sewage effluent' can be the subject of very rigid criteria, without in the least ceasing to be evaluative.

It is important to notice also, how easy it is, in view of these resemblances between 'good' and 'red', to think that there are no differences—to think that to set forth the standard of goodness in motor-cars is to set forth the meaning, in all senses that there are of that word, of the expression 'good motor-car'; to think that 'M is a good motor-car' means neither more nor less than 'M has certain characteristics of which "good" is the name'.

It is worth noticing here that the functions of the word 'good' which are concerned with information could be performed equally well if 'good' had no commendatory function at all. This can be made clear by substituting another word, made up for the purpose, which is to be

[1] *Mind*, lix (1950), 152 (also in *Logic and Language*, ii, ed. Flew, 166).

supposed to lack the commendatory force of 'good'. Let us use 'doog' as this new word. 'Doog', like 'good', can be used for conveying information only if the criteria for its application are known; but this makes it, unlike 'good', altogether meaningless until these criteria are made known. I make the criteria known by pointing out various motor-cars, and saying 'M is a doog motor-car', 'N is not a doog motor-car', and so on. We must imagine that, although 'doog' has no commendatory force, the criteria for doogness in motor-cars which I am employing are the same as those which, in the previous example, I employed for goodness in motor-cars. And so, as in the previous example, the learner, if he is sufficiently attentive, becomes able to use the word 'doog' for giving or getting information; when I say to him 'Z is a doog motor-car', he knows what characteristics to expect it to have; and if he wants to convey to someone else that a motor-car Y has those same characteristics, he can do so by saying 'Y is a doog motor-car'.

Thus the word 'doog' does (though only in connexion with motor-cars) half the jobs that the word 'good' does—namely, all those jobs that are concerned with the giving, or learning to give or get, information. It does not do those jobs which are concerned with commendation. Thus we might say that 'doog' functions just like a descriptive word. First my learner learns to use it by my giving him examples of its application, and then he uses it by applying it to fresh examples. It would be quite natural to say that what I was doing was teaching my learner the *meaning* of 'doog'; and this shows us again how natural it is to say that, when we are learning a similar lesson for the expression 'good motor-car' (i.e. learning the criteria of its application), we are learning its meaning. But with the word 'good' it is misleading to say this; for the meaning of 'good motor-car' (in another sense of 'meaning') is something that might be known by someone who did not know the criteria of its application; he would know, if someone said that a motor-car was a good one, that he was commending it; and to know that, would be to know the meaning of the expression. Further, as we saw earlier (6.4), someone might know about 'good' all the things which my learner learnt about the word 'doog' (namely, how to apply the word to the right objects, and use it for giving and getting information) and yet be said not to know its meaning; for he might not know that to call a motor-car good was to commend it.

It may be objected by some readers that to call the descriptive or informative job of 'good' its *meaning* in any sense is illegitimate. Such objectors might hold that the meaning of 'good' is adequately characterized by saying that it is used for commending, and that any information we get from its use is not a question of meaning at all. When I say 'M is a good motor-car', my meaning, on this view, is to commend M; if a hearer gets from my remark, together with his knowledge of the standard habitually used by me in assessing the merits of motor-cars, information about what description of motor-car it is, this is not part of my meaning; all my hearer has done is to make an inductive inference from 'Hare has usually in the past commended motor-cars of a certain description' and 'Hare has commended M' to 'M is of the same description'. I suspect that this objection is largely a verbal one, and I have no wish to take sides against it. On the one hand, we must insist that to know the criteria for applying the word 'good' to motor-cars is not to know—at any rate in the full or primary sense—the meaning of the expression 'good motor-car'; to this extent the objection must be agreed with. On the other hand, the relation of the expression 'good motor-car' to the criteria for its application is very like the relation of a descriptive expression to its defining characteristics, and this likeness finds an echo in our language when we ask 'What do you mean,

good?', and get the answer 'I mean it'll do 80 and never breaks down'. In view of this undoubted fact of usage, I deem it best to adopt the term 'descriptive meaning'. Moreover, it is natural to say that a sentence has descriptive meaning, if the speaker intends it primarily to convey information; and when a newspaper says that X opened the batting on a good wicket, its intention is not primarily to commend the wicket, but to inform its readers what description of wicket it was.

It is time now to justify my calling the descriptive meaning of 'good' secondary to the evaluative meaning. My reasons for doing so are two. First, the evaluative meaning is constant for every class of object for which the word is used. When we call a motor-car or a chronometer or a cricket-bat or a picture good, we are commending all of them. But because we are commending all of them for different reasons, the descriptive meaning is different in all cases. We have knowledge of the evaluative meaning of 'good' from our earliest years; but we are constantly learning to use it in new descriptive meanings, as the classes of objects whose virtues we learn to distinguish grow more numerous. Sometimes we learn to use 'good' in a new descriptive meaning through being taught it by an expert in a particular field—for example, a horseman might teach me how to recognize a good hunter. Sometimes, on the other hand, we make up a new descriptive meaning for ourselves. This happens when we start having a standard for a class of objects, certain members of which we have started needing to place in order of merit, but for which there has hitherto been no standard. . . .

The second reason for calling the evaluative meaning primary is, that we can use the evaluative force of the word in order to *change* the descriptive meaning for any class of objects. This is what the moral reformer often does in morals; but the same process occurs outside morals. It may happen that motor-cars will in the near future change considerably in design (e.g. by our seeking economy at the expense of size). It may be that then we shall cease giving the name 'a good motor-car' to a car that now would rightly and with the concurrence of all be allowed that name. How, linguistically speaking, would this have happened? At present, we are roughly agreed (though only roughly) on the necessary and sufficient criteria for calling a motor-car a good one. If what I have described takes place, we may begin to say 'No cars of the nineteen-fifties were really good; there weren't any good ones till 1960'. Now here we cannot be using 'good' with the same descriptive meaning as it is now generally used with; for some of the cars of 1950 do indubitably have those characteristics which entitle them to the name 'good motor-car' in the 1950 descriptive sense of that word. What is happening is that the evaluative meaning of the word is being used in order to shift the descriptive meaning; we are doing what would be called, if 'good' were a purely descriptive word, redefining it. But we cannot call it that, for the evaluative meaning remains constant; we are rather altering the standard. This is similar to the process called by Professor Stevenson 'persuasive definition'; the process is not necessarily, however, highly coloured with emotion. . . .

Although with 'good' the evaluative meaning is primary, there are other words in which the evaluative meaning is secondary to the descriptive. Such words are 'tidy' and 'industrious'. Both are normally used to commend; but we can say, without any hint of irony, 'too tidy' or 'too industrious'. It is the descriptive meaning of these words that is most firmly attached to them; and therefore, although we must for certain purposes class them as value-words (for if we treat them as purely descriptive, logical errors result), they are so in a less full sense than 'good'. If the evaluative meaning of a word, which was primary, comes to be secondary, that is a sign that the standard to which the word appeals has

become conventional. It is, of course, impossible to say *exactly* when this has happened; it is a process like the coming of winter.

Although the evaluative meaning of 'good' is primary, the secondary descriptive meaning is never wholly absent. Even when we are using the word 'good' evaluatively in order to set up a new standard, the word still has a descriptive meaning, not in the sense that it is used to *convey* information, but in the sense that its use in setting up the new standard is an essential preliminary—like definition in the case of a purely descriptive word—to its subsequent use with a new descriptive meaning. It is also to be noticed that the relative prominence of the descriptive and evaluative meanings of 'good' varies according to the class of objects within which commendation is being given. We may illustrate this by taking two extreme examples. If I talk of 'a good egg', it is at once known to what description of egg I am referring—namely, one that is not decomposed. Here the descriptive meaning predominates, because we have very fixed standards for assessing the goodness of eggs. On the other hand, if I say that a poem is a good one, very little information is given about what description of poem it is—for there is no accepted standard of goodness in poems. But it must not be thought that 'good egg' is exclusively descriptive, or 'good poem' exclusively evaluative. If, as the Chinese are alleged to do, we chose to eat eggs that are decomposed, we should call that kind of egg good, just as, because we choose to eat game that is slightly decomposed, we call it 'well-hung' (compare also the expression 'good Stilton cheese'). And if I said that a poem was good, and was not a very eccentric person, my hearer would be justified in assuming that the poem was not 'Happy birthday to you!'

In general, the more fixed and accepted the standard, the more information is conveyed. But it must not be thought that the evaluative force of the word varies at all exactly in inverse proportion to the descriptive. The two vary independently: where a standard is firmly established and is as firmly believed in, a judgement containing 'good' may be highly informative, without being any the less commendatory. Consider the following description of the Oxford Sewage Farm:

> The method employed is primitive but efficient. The farm is unsightly, obnoxious to people dwelling near it, and not very remunerative, but the effluent from it is, in the technical sense, good.[2]

Now here, as may be seen by consulting handbooks on the subject, there are perfectly well-recognized tests for determining whether effluent is good or bad. One manual[3] gives a simple field test, and another[4] gives a series of more comprehensive tests which take up seventeen pages. This might tempt us to say that the word is used in a purely descriptive sense and has no evaluative force. But, although admittedly in calling effluent good in this technical sense we are commending it as effluent and not as perfume, we are nevertheless commending it; it is not a neutral chemical or biological fact about it that it is good; to say that it was bad would be to give a very good reason for sacking the sewage-farmer or taking other steps to see that it was good in future. The proper comment on such a lapse was made by a former Archbishop of York, speaking to the Congress of the Royal Sanitary Institute, 1912:

> There is now, I hope, no need of the trenchant eloquence of that noble-hearted pioneer of sanitary science, Charles Kingsley, to insist that it is not religion, but something more nearly approaching blasphemy, to say that an outbreak of disease is God's will being done,

when patently it is man's duty which is being left undone.[5]

It is true that, if the word 'good' in a certain sentence has very little evaluative meaning, it is likely that it has a fair amount of descriptive meaning, and vice versa. That is because, if it had very little of either, it would have very little meaning at all, and would not be worth uttering. To this extent the meanings vary inversely. But this is only a tendency; we may do justice to the logical phenomena by saying that 'good' normally has at least some of both sorts of meaning; that it normally has sufficient of both sorts taken together to make it worth uttering; and that, provided that the first two conditions are satisfied, the amounts of the two sorts of meaning vary independently.

There are, however, cases in which we use the word 'good' with no commendatory meaning at all. We must distinguish several kinds of such non-commendatory uses. The first has been called the *inverted-commas* use. If I were not accustomed to commend any but the most modern styles of architecture, I might still say 'The new chamber of the House of Commons is very good Gothic revival'. I might mean this in several senses. The first is that in which it is equivalent to 'a good example to choose, if one is seeking to illustrate the typical features of Gothic revival' or 'a good specimen of Gothic revival'. This is a specialized evaluative sense, with which we are not here concerned. I might mean, on the other hand, 'genuinely preferable to most other examples of Gothic revival, and therefore to be commended *within* the class of Gothic revival buildings, though not within the class of buildings in general'. With this sense, too, we are not now concerned; it is a commendatory use, with a limited class of comparison (8. 2). The sense with which we are concerned is that in which it means, roughly, 'the sort of Gothic revival building about which a certain sort of peo-

---

[2] *Social Services in the Oxford District,* p. 322.
[3] Kershaw, *Sewage Purification and Disposal,* pp. 213–14.
[4] Thresh, Beale, and Suckling, *The Examination of Waters and Water Supplies,* 6th ed.

[5] Kershaw, op. cit., p. 4.

ple—you know who —would say "that is a good building".' It is a characteristic of this use of 'good' that in expanding it we often want to put the word 'good' inside inverted commas; hence the name. We are, in this use, not making a value-judgement ourselves, but alluding to the value-judgements of other people. This type of use is extremely important for the logic of moral judgements, in which it has caused some confusion.

It is to be noticed that it is easiest to use 'good' in an inverted-commas sense when a certain class of people, who are sufficiently numerous and prominent for their value-judgements to be well known (e.g. the 'best' people in any field), have a rigid standard of commendation for that class of object. In such cases, the inverted-commas use can verge into an *ironic* use, in which not only is no commendation being given, but rather the reverse. If I had a low opinion of Carlo Dolci, I might say 'If you want to see a really "good" Carlo Dolci, go and look at the one in . . .'.

There is another use in which the absence of evaluative content is not sufficiently obvious to the speaker for us to call it either an inverted-commas or an ironic use. This is the *conventional* use, in which the speaker is merely paying lipservice to a convention, by commending, or saying commendatory things about, an object just because everyone else does. I might, if I myself had no preference at all about the design of furniture, still say 'This piece of furniture is of good design', not because I wished to guide my own or anyone else's choice of furniture, but simply because I had been taught characteristics which are generally held to be criteria of good design, and wished to show that I had 'good taste' in furniture. It would be difficult in such a case to say whether I was evaluating the furniture or not. If I were not a logician, I should not ask myself the questions which would determine whether I was. Such a question would be 'If some-

one (not connected in any way with the furniture trade), consistently and regardless of cost filled his house with furniture not conforming to the canons by which you judge the design of this furniture to be good, would you regard that as evidence that he did not agree with you?' If I replied 'No, I would not; for what furniture is of good design is one question, and what furniture one chooses for oneself is another', then we might conclude that I had not been really commending the design by calling it good, but only paying lip-service to a convention.

These are only some of the many ways in which we use the word 'good'. A logician cannot do justice to the infinite subtlety of language; all he can do is to point out some of the main features of our use of a word, and thereby put people on their guard against the main dangers. A full understanding of the logic of value-terms can only be achieved by continual and sensitive attention to the way we use them.

COMMENDING AND CHOOSING

It is now time to inquire into the reasons for the logical features of 'good' that we have been describing, and to ask why it is that it has this peculiar combination of evaluative and descriptive meaning. The reason will be found in the purposes for which it, like other value-words, is used in our discourse. . . .

I have said that the primary function of the word 'good' is to commend. We have, therefore, to inquire what commending is. When we commend or condemn anything, it is always in order, at least indirectly, to guide choices, our own or other people's, now or in the future. Suppose that I say 'The South Bank Exhibition is very good'. In what context should I appropriately say this, and what would be my purpose in so doing? It would be natural for me to say it to someone who was wondering whether to go to London to see the Exhibition, or, if he was in London, whether to pay it a visit. It would, however, be too much to say that the reference to choices is always as direct as this. An American returning from London to New York, and speaking to some people who had no intention of going to London in the near future, might still make the same remark. In order, therefore, to show that critical value-judgements are all ultimately related to choices, and would not be made if they were not so related, we require to ask, for what purpose we have standards.

It has been pointed out by Mr. Urmson that we do not speak generally of 'good' wireworms. This is because we never have any occasion for choosing between wireworms, and therefore require no guidance in so doing. We therefore need to have no standards for wireworms. But it is easy to imagine circumstances in which this situation might alter. Suppose that wireworms came into use as a special kind of bait for fishermen. Then we might speak of having dug up a very good wireworm (one, for example, that was exceptionally fat and attractive to fish), just as now, no doubt, sea-fishermen might talk of having dug up a very good lug-worm. We only have standards for a class of objects, we only talk of the virtues of one specimen as against another, we only use value-words about them, when occasions are known to exist, or are conceivable, in which we, or someone else, would have to choose between specimens. We should not call pictures good or bad if no one ever had the choice of seeing them or not seeing them (or of studying them or not studying them in the way that art sudents study pictures, or of buying them or not buying them). Lest, by the way, I should seem to have introduced a certain vagueness by specifying so many alternative kinds of choices, it must be pointed out that the matter can, if desired, be made as precise as we require; for we can specify, when we have called a picture a good one, within

what class we have called it good; for example, we can say 'I meant a good picture to study, but not to buy'.

Some further examples may be given. We should not speak of good sunsets, unless sometimes the decision had to be made, whether to go to the window to look at the sunset; we should not speak of good billiard-cues, unless sometimes we had to choose one billiard-cue in preference to another; we should not speak of good men unless we had the choice, what sort of men to try to become. Leibniz, when he spoke of 'the best of all possible worlds', had in mind a creator choosing between the possibilities. The choice that is envisaged need not ever occur, nor even be expected ever to occur; it is enough for it to be envisaged as occurring, in order that we should be able to make a value-judgement with reference to it. It must be admitted, however, that the most useful value-judgements are those which have reference to choices that we might very likely have to make.

It should be pointed out that even judgements about past choices do not refer merely to the past. As we shall see, all value-judgements are covertly universal in character, which is the same as to say that they refer to, and express acceptance of, a standard which has an application to other similar instances. If I censure someone for having done something, I envisage the possibility of him, or someone else, or myself, having to make a similar choice again; otherwise there would be no point in censuring him. Thus, if I say to a man whom I am teaching to drive 'You did that manoeuvre badly' this is a very typical piece of driving-instruction; and driving-instruction consists in teaching a man to drive not in the past but in the future; to this end we censure or commend past pieces of driving, in order to impart to him the standard which is to guide him in his subsequent conduct.

When we commend an object, our judgement is not solely about that particular object, but is inescapably about objects like it. Thus, if I say that a certain motor-car is a good one, I am merely saying something about that particular motor-car. To say something about that particular car, merely, would not be to commend. To commend, as we have seen, is to guide choices. Now for guiding a particular choice we have a linguistic instrument which is not that of commendation, namely, the singular imperative. If I wish merely to tell someone to choose a particular car, with no thought of the kind of car to which it belongs, I can say 'Take that one'. If instead of this I say 'That is a good one', I am saying something more. I am implying that if any motor-car were just like that one, it would be a good one too; whereas by saying 'Take that one', I do not imply that, if my hearer sees another car just like that one, he is to take it too. But further, the implication of the judgement 'That is a good motor-car' does not extend merely to motor-cars *exactly* like that one. If this were so, the implication would be for practical purposes useless; for nothing is exactly like anything else. It extends to every motor-car that is like that one in the *relevant* particulars; and the relevant particulars are its virtues—those of its characteristics for which I was commending it, or which I was calling good about it. Whenever we commend, we have in mind something about the object commended which is the reason for our commendation. It therefore always makes sense, after someone has said 'That is a good motor-car', to ask 'What is good about it?' or 'Why do you call it good?' or 'What features of it are you commending?' It may not always be easy to answer this question precisely, but it is always a legitimate question. If we did not understand why it was always a legitimate question, we should not understand the way in which the word 'good' functions.

We may illustrate this point by comparing two dialogues:

(1) X. Jones' motor-car is a good one.

Y. What makes you call it good?

X. Oh, just that it's good.

Y. But there must be some *reason* for your calling it good, I mean some property that it has in virtue of which you call it good.

X. No; the property in virtue of which I call it good is just its goodness and nothing else.

Y. But do you mean that its shape, speed, weight, manoeuvrability &c., are irrelevant to whether you call it good or not?

X. Yes, quite irrelevant; the only relevant property is that of goodness, just as, if I called it yellow, the only relevant property would be that of yellowness.

(2) The same dialogue, only with 'yellow' substituted for 'good' and 'yellowness' for 'goodness' throughout, and the last clause ("just as . . . yellowness') omitted.

The reason why X's position in the first dialogue is eccentric is that since, as we have already remarked, 'good' is a 'supervenient' or 'consequential' epithet, one may always legitimately be asked when one has called something a good something, 'What is good about it?' Now to answer this question is to give the properties in virtue of which we call it good. Thus, if I have said, 'That is a good motor-car' and someone asks 'Why? What is good about it?' and I reply 'Its high speed combined with its stability on the road', I indicate that I call it good in virtue of its having these properties or virtues. Now to do this is *eo ipso* to say something about other motor-cars which have these properties. If any motor-car whatsoever had these properties, I should have, if I were not to be inconsistent, to agree that it was, *pro tanto*, a good motor-car; though of course it might, although it had these properties in its favour, have other countervailing disadvantages, and so be, taken all in all, not a good motor-car.

This last difficulty can always be got over by specifying in detail why I called **the first motor-car a good one.** Suppose that a second motor-car were like the first one in speed and stability, but gave its passengers no protection from the rain, and proved difficult to get into and out of. I should not then call it a good motor-car, although it had those characteristics which led me to call the first one good. This shows that I should not have called the first one good either, if it too had had the bad characteristics of the second one; and so in specifying what was good about the first one, I ought to have added '. . . and the protection it gives to the passengers and the ease with which one can get into and out of it'. This process could be repeated indefinitely until I had given a complete list of the characteristics of the first motor-car which were required to make me allow it to be a good one. This, in itself, would not be saying all that there was to be said about my standards for judging motor-cars—for there might be other motor-cars which, although falling short to a certain extent in these characteristics, had other countervailing good characteristics; for example, soft upholstery, large accommodation, or small consumption of petrol. But it would be at any rate some help to my hearer in building up an idea of my standards in motor-cars; and in this lies the importance of such questions and answers, and the importance of recognizing their relevance, whenever a value-judgement has been made. For one of the purposes of making such judgements is to make known the standard.

When I commend a motor-car I am guiding the choices of my hearer not merely in relation to that particular motor-car but in relation to motor-cars in general. What I have said to him will be of assistance to him whenever in the future he has to choose a motor-car or advise anyone else on the choice of a motor-car or even design a motor-car (choose what sort of motor-car to have made) or write a general treatise on the design of motor-cars (which involves choosing what sort of motor-cars to advise other people to have

made). The method whereby I give him this assistance is by making known to him a standard for judging motor-cars.

This process has, as we have noticed, certain features in common with the process of defining (making known the meaning or application of) a descriptive word, though there are important differences. We have now to notice a further resemblance between showing the usage of a word and showing how to choose between motor-cars. In neither case can the instruction be done successfully unless the instructor is consistent in his teaching. If I use 'red' for objects of a wide variety of colours, my hearer will never learn from me a consistent usage of the word. Similarly, if I commend motor-cars with widely different or even contrary characteristics, what I say to him will not be of assistance to him in choosing motor-cars subsequently, because I am not teaching him any consistent standard—or any standard at all, for a standard is by definition consistent. He will say, 'I don't see by what standards you are judging these motor-cars; please explain to me why you call them all good, although they are so different'. Of course, I might be able to give a satisfactory explanation. I might say, 'There are different sorts of motor-cars, each good in its way; there are sports cars, whose prime requisites are speed and manoeuvrability; and family cars, which ought rather to be capacious and economical; and taxis, and so on. So when I say a car is good which is fast and manoeuvrable, although it is neither capacious nor economical, you must understand that I am commending it as a sports car, not as a family car'. But suppose that I did not recognize the relevance of his question; suppose that I was just doling out the predicate 'good' entirely haphazard, as the whim took me. It is clear that in this case I should teach him no standard at all.

We thus have to distinguish two questions that can always be asked in elucidation of a judgement containing the word 'good'. Suppose that someone says 'That is a good one'. We can then always ask (1) 'Good what—sports car or family car or taxi or example to quote in a logic-book?' Or we can ask (2) 'What makes you call it good?' To ask the first question is to ask for the class within which evaluative comparisons are being made. Let us call it the class of comparison. To ask the second question is to ask for the virtues or 'good-making characteristics'. . . .

That the descriptive meaning of the word 'good' is in morals, as elsewhere, secondary to the evaluative, may be seen in the following example. Let us suppose that a missionary, armed with a grammar book, lands on a cannibal island. The vocabulary of his grammar book gives him the equivalent, in the cannibals' language, of the English 'good'. Let us suppose that, by a queer coincidence, the word is 'good'. And let us suppose, also, that it really is the equivalent—that it is, as the *Oxford English Dictionary* puts it, 'the most general adjective of commendation' in their language. If the missionary has mastered his vocabulary, he can, *so long as he uses the word evaluatively and not descriptively,* communicate with them about morals quite happily. They know that when he uses the word he is commending the person or object that he applies it to. The only thing they will find odd is that he applies it to such unexpected people, people who are meek and gentle and do not collect large quantities of scalps; whereas they themselves are accustomed to commend people who are bold and burly and collect more scalps than the average. But they and the missionary are under no misapprehension about the meaning, in the evaluative sense, of the word 'good'; it is the word one uses for commending. If they were under such a misapprehension, moral communication between them would be impossible.

We have thus a situation which would appear paradoxical to someone who thought that 'good' (either in English or in the cannibals' language) was a quality-word like 'red'. Even if the qualities in peo-ple which the missionary commended had nothing in common with qualities which the cannibals commended, yet they would both know what the word 'good' meant. If 'good' were like 'red', this would be impossible; for then the cannibals' word and the English word would not be synonymous. If this were so, then when the missionary said that people who collected no scalps were good (English), and the cannibals said that people who collected a lot of scalps were good (cannibal), they would not be disagreeing, because in English (at any rate missionary English), 'good' would mean among other things 'doing no murder', whereas in the cannibals' language 'good' would mean something quite different, among other things 'productive of maximum scalps'. It is because in its primary evaluative meaning 'good' means neither of these things, but is in both languages the most general adjective of commendation, that the missionary can use it to teach the cannibals Christian morals.

Suppose, however, that the missionary's mission is successful. Then, the former cannibals will come to commend the same qualities in people as the missionary, and the words 'good man' will come to have a more or less common descriptive meaning. The danger will then be that the cannibals may, after a generation or two, think that that is the only sort of meaning they have. 'Good' will in that case mean for them, simply 'doing what it says in the Sermon on the Mount'; and they may come to forget that it is a word of commendation; they will not realize that opinions about moral goodness have a bearing on what they themselves are to *do*. Their standards will then be in mortal danger. A Communist, landing on the island to convert the people to *his* way of life, may even take advantage of the ossification of their standards. He may say 'All these "good" Christians— missionaries and colonial servants and the rest—are just deceiving you to their own profit.' This would be to use the word descriptively with a dash of irony; and he could not do this plausibly unless the standards of the Christians had become considerably ossified. Some of the ploys of Thrasymachus in the first book of Plato's *Republic* are very similar to this.

. . .Such vicissitudes of the word 'good' reflect accurately [this] sort of moral development. . . Moral principles or standards are first established; then they get too rigid, and the words used in referring to them become too dominantly descriptive; their evaluative force has to be painfully revived before the standards are out of danger. In the course of revival, the standards get adapted to changed circumstances; moral reform takes place, and its instrument is the evaluative use of value-language. The remedy, in fact, for moral stagnation and decay is to learn to use our value-language for the purpose for which it is designed; and this involves not merely a lesson in talking, but a lesson in doing that which we commend; for unless we are prepared to do this we are doing no more than paying lip-service to a conventional standard.

A Quasi-Naturalist Definition

RICHARD BRANDT

It seems worthwhile to consider a novel form of naturalistic definition. This definition, however, is so markedly different from other naturalistic definitions that we call it "quasi-naturalist." We shall explain the definition first.

Let us first agree to speak of a "corresponding attitude" for every ethical term. To "preferable" the attitude of preference will correspond; to "obligation" something like "feeling obligated" for the case of agents and "inclined to demand" for observers; and so on. Roughly what we mean by a "corresponding" attitude is the attitude someone justifiably has if some ethical statement is properly asserted by him. There can be further discussion, obviously, of the question of what attitude corresponds, in this sense, to any ethical term in which one happens to be interested.

The quasi-naturalist definition proposes that "x is E" (where E is some ethical term) means the same as "The E-corresponding attitude [which will be determined once we have specified the ethical term] to x satisfies all the conditions that would be set, as a general policy, for the endorsement of attitudes governing or appraising choices or actions, by anyone who was intelligent and factually informed and had thought through the problems of the possible different general policies for

Richard B. Brandt, ETHICAL THEORY: The Problems of Normative and Critical Ethics, © 1959. Reprinted by permission of Prentice-Hall, Inc., Englewood Cliffs, New Jersey. Pp. 265–269.

the endorsement of such attitudes." For example, "x is preferable to y" would mean "Preferring x to y satisfies all the conditions that would be set. . . ."[1]

This definition is properly classified as naturalist, because whether an "E-corresponding attitude" satisfies "all the conditions" can in the end be decided in principle by observation and the methods of science. In other words, the definition can be translated into the language of empirical science (p. 155). But it is also properly distinguished as "quasi-naturalist" in order to mark two important points. Some naturalist definitions, like the proposal that "x is worthwhile in itself" means "x is pleasant," have the consequence that important substantive ethical principles are true by definition (in this case "Something is worthwhile in itself if and only if it is pleasant"). The quasi-naturalist definition has no such implication. Second, other naturalist definitions, like the Ideal Observer theory, have the consequence that it is true by definition that a certain method must be used if true or valid ethical propositions are to be discovered. The quasi-naturalist definition, again, has no such implication, for in order to determine what ethical

---

[1] There is a point of vagueness in this definition, corresponding to one in the Qualified Attitude Method, which we shall discuss in the following chapter. There are also particular phrases in the definition that are vague. For example, when has one "thought through" the problems mentioned? But such vagueness is not necessarily an objection.

method will lead to valid ethical statements, it implies we must first ascertain what conditions would be set by an intelligent, informed person for the endorsement of attitudes of a certain kind.

It is no objection to this definition, as it is an objection to the Ideal Observer definition, that some people do not use the Qualified Attitude Method,* but, rather, a theological or utilitarian method. The reason for this is that someone's use of a theological method, for instance, may simply show that he believes that "all the conditions that would be set" include some condition having to do with the will of God.

These distinctive features of the quasi-naturalist definition are strong recommendations of it. Everyone is under the impression that whatever he is saying, when he makes an ethical statement, it is something which is correct or incorrect, valid or invalid. The quasi-naturalist definition has the desirable implication that this impression is correct. On the other hand, the definition is framed so as not to exclude, as necessarily irrelevant, any of the arguments actually used about particular ethical principles, or any of the debates about ethical method which strike us as seriously relevant.

Of course this definition must be able to survive criticisms of the kind that have been leveled at traditional naturalist definitions, in order to be acceptable as a reportive definition of ethical terms. It must also be able to stand up against the reasons that have been offered for the emotive theory (pp. 214-20). It is not clear, however, that any of these points is a serious objection to it. Of all the naturalistic definitions it seems decidedly the least open to objection.

A noncognitive theory. One may think, however, that the quasi-naturalist definition is too remote from our overt meanings to qualify as what we *mean* when we use ethical terms. It is, therefore, worthwhile to consider whether some form of noncognitive analysis of ethical language might be more satisfactory. Let us explore this.

First of all, however, we should remind ourselves that a noncognitivist need not deny that the Qualified Attitude Method is the "standard" method of evaluating ethical statements, or that good reasons can be given for following it, of the kind we offered. This is obvious, when we remind ourselves of the definition of "noncognitivism" (p. 205); this theory asserts only that ethical statements are best understood by likening them to some speech form different from fact statements, and that ethical terms are not property-referring at all—or at least that, if they do refer to properties, the fact is of secondary import for understanding ethical discourse. The noncognitivist's theory commits him in consistency only to saying that ethical statements certified by the Qualified Attitude Method need not be viewed as confirmed by evidence in the way in which the statements of the empirical sciences are confirmed, either in view of the meaning and function of ethical terms or in view of

---

* [*Editors' Note.* The Qualified Attitude Method is described in the immediately preceding section of the chapter. In it Professor Brandt suggests a method for resolving ethical disputes. Instead of simply asking "What is my attitude toward X?" the user of the Qualified Attitude Method considers what his attitude toward X would be *if* certain conditions are fulfilled; thus, his attitude toward X is *discounted* (1) if it is not impartial, (2) if it is not sufficiently informed as to the facts of the situation, (3) if it is a consequence of an abnormal state of mind such as anger, grief, fatigue, depression, etc., and (4) if its prompting would be incompatible with having a system of principles that are *consistent* with one another and *general* (in the sense of applying to all members of the class in question, and containing no proper names). The requirements of the Qualified Attitude Method are much the same as the criteria invoked by the Ideal Observer theory; but the Qualified Attitude Method differs from the Ideal Observer theory in that it makes no claim at all about the meaning of ethical terms (it is not committed, as the Ideal Observer theory is, to a naturalistic definition of ethical terms); it is neutral with regard to these meta-ethical theories, but claims only that there is a rational method—the one outlined by the Qualified Attitude Method—for resolving ethical disagreements.]

any other facts. Let us, for the sake of the argument, not contest this point.

There is a more questionable assertion that the noncognitivist may make, although he need not. This is that, even if most people are prepared to make an ethical statement only if they think it meets the conditions of the Qualified Attitude Method, and even if there are convincing reasons in support of so doing, the fact is unimportant and can be ignored—because whether people accept the Qualified Attitude Method as a standard for ethical reasoning and whether they are convinced by reasons that support its use is in the end a matter of their attitudes and not of sheer logic. This point, however, is mistaken. It leads the noncognitivist who accepts it to an insupportable neutrality in his own appraisal of methods in ethics—to the view that one is just as good as another. It leads him to overlook the fact that there are conclusive reasons for preferring one method of ethical deliberation to another. It leads him to overlook the fact that ethical thinking and debate are very similar to inductive reasoning—reasoning according to a "standard" form which can be supported by good reasons and to which there is no serious alternative.

Let us now suppose that the noncognitivist agrees that in the sense explained the Qualified Attitude Method is the "standard" method of ethical reflection, that following it can be supported by strong reason, and that on this account some ethical judgments—those which satisfy the conditions of the Method—have a correspondingly approved status. But will this affect his account of the *meaning and function* of ethical terms? Let us see how we can or must reconstruct his theory so as to allow for agreeing to these various things.

First, the noncognitivist can continue, without change, to say that the primary job of ethical language is noncognitive. He may say that the primary job is to advise, or to urge, or to express attitudes, or to express over-all moral or impartial attitudes

in the sense described in the preceding chapter, or some combination of these things. Perhaps he will say that there are different noncognitive jobs done by the same ethical words on different occasions. So much for the noncognitive side of ethical language.

We have seen that there is reason to recognize another aspect of ethical language. Toward the end of the preceding chapter we saw that many noncognitivists suggest that ethical language does not do *merely* a noncognitive job, or at least that it does such a job in a special way. It has been proposed that the use of ethical language has certain "contextual implications" or makes certain claims. What is *distinctive* of ethical language, it has been held, is the making of certain claims or the having of contextual implications of a special sort. But there were differences of opinion among noncognitivists about just what these claims or implications are.

On the basis of our argument so far, we are now in a position to make a proposal about an important one of these claims or implications. Our suggestion is *not* that ethical statements claim that the attitude (etc.) they express satisfies the conditions of the Qualified Attitude Method; it is not this, because we agree that some persons do not use this Method, and have not thought of the reasons which support it. Our suggestion is rather a weaker one; it is that ethical language *claims, of the attitude* (etc.) *which it expresses,* that it satisfies all the conditions which would be set, as a general policy for the endorsement of attitudes governing or appraising choices or actions, by anyone who was intelligent and factually informed and had thought through the problems of the possible different general policies for the endorsement of such attitudes. In other words, we suggest a noncognitivist should say that the use of ethical language makes a claim about the attitude it expresses, which is identical with part of what the quasi-naturalist definition says ethical terms assert. For instance, "It is desirable to do *x*" may be construed as (1) the expression of an over-all impartial preference (or, perhaps, as equivalent to "I advise you to do *x*"), and (2) as claiming or at least implying that favoring *x* is *justified* in the sense that it satisfies the conditions which would be set by intelligent persons, and so forth. Ethical statements, then, may be construed as both doing something and making a validity-claim of this sort.[2]

In order to distinguish the foregoing analysis clearly from the quasi-naturalist one, we must, of course, be clear about just what it is for a statement to make an assertion, and what are the criteria for deciding the content asserted by a given statement.

---

[2] We should notice that a philosopher might propose theories, like the three just formulated, not of ethical terms themselves, but of the term "justified." He might refuse to analyze ethical terms themselves, saying that we understand them well enough, but might propose any one of them for the term "justified" as applied to ethical statements.

Such a view is not very satisfactory. For we shall still want some view about ethical terms themselves. Moreover, there is no reason to think that such analyses of "justified" are any better established than corresponding analyses of ethical language itself.

Similarly, we must be clear what it is for a statement to express something, or to make a claim; and we must know what the criteria are for deciding what is expressed or claimed. Let us assume that the problems involved in clarifying all those things can be satisfactorily overcome.

Is there anything to choose between the quasi-naturalist analysis of ethical terms, and this noncognitivist account? Despite some reservations (particularly about whether such a noncognitivist can consistently say the noncognition function is *primary*), we prefer to say there is nothing to choose. On the contrary, we do assert that there is no insuperable objection to either one, and that one or the other of them is correct. For our future purposes, however, it is simpler to adopt the quasi-naturalist definition. We shall, therefore, in the future, talk as if this definition should be given preference. But, whenever we use it, it would be possible to make the same point by using the noncognitive theory just suggested. We believe there is no sound objection to the quasi-naturalist definition, but we have no quarrel with one who prefers the above noncognitive analysis instead.

Ethical Relativism

RICHARD BRANDT

A Greek philosopher who lived in the fifth century B.C., named Protagoras, seems to have believed two things: first, that moral principles cannot be shown to be valid for everybody; and second, that people ought to follow the conventions of their own group.[1] Something like this combination of propositions probably had been thought of before his time. Primitive people are well aware that different social groups have different standards, and at least sometimes doubt whether one set of standards can really be shown to be superior to others. Moreover, probably in many groups it has been thought that a person who conforms conscientiously to the standards of his own group deserves respect.

Views roughly similar to those of Protagoras may be classified as forms of *ethical relativism*. The term "ethical relativism," however, is used in different senses, and one should be wary when one comes across it. Sometimes one is said to be a relativist if he thinks that an action that is wrong in one place might not be in another, so that one is declared a relativist if he thinks it wrong for a group of Eskimos to strip a man of his clothing twenty miles

from home on January 1, but not wrong for a tribe at the equator. If "relativism" is used in this sense, then practically everyone is a relativist, for practically everyone believes that particular circumstances make a difference to the morality of an act—that, for instance, it is right to lie in some circumstances but wrong in others. Again, one is sometimes said to be a relativist if he asserts a pair of causal propositions: that different social groups sometimes have different values (ethical opinions) as a result of historical developments; and that an individual's values are near-replicas of the tradition of his group, however strongly he may feel that they are "his own" or that they are "valid" and can be supported by convincing reasons. We shall not use "ethical relativism" for either of these views, but reserve it for a theory at least fairly close to that of Protagoras.[2]

---

[2] It is useful to compare Protagoras' relativism with the special theory of relativity in physics. One implication of this theory is that measurements of certain physical quantities, like the temporal distance between two events, will come out differently for different frames of reference (one "frame of reference" being the set of observers having the same relative rectilinear motion). All the careful observations in *one* frame will give the *same* result; and in this sense there is a "right" answer for this frame. But different frames will have different "right" answers, and there is in principle no way of showing that one of these is the "really right" answer. However, certain quantities (like the spatio-temporal distance between two events) are absolutes, in the sense that careful measurements will give one right answer for everybody.

Richard B. Brandt, *Ethical Theory:* The Problems of Normative and Critical Ethics, © 1959. Reprinted by permission of Prentice-Hall, Inc., Englewood Cliffs, New Jersey. Pp. 271–284.
[1] For Protagoras' view, see Plato, *Theaetetus*, pp. 166ff.; and F. J. Copleston, *A History of Philosophy*, I (London: Burns Oates & Washbourne Ltd., 1956), pp. 87–90.

1. THE QUESTION: "ARE CONFLICTING ETHICAL OPINIONS EQUALLY VALID?"

The position of Protagoras, however, is somewhat vague, and if we are to assess it, we must sharpen it. It is also convenient to deal separately with its two parts. We shall begin with a restatement of the first part of his theory, and then assess it at some length; only then shall we consider the second half of his position. As we go on, we shall see that the first part of his theory is theoretically more interesting and important than the second. For this reason, we shall apply the term "ethical relativism" to any theory that agrees with our sharpened form of Protagoras' first point, irrespective of its attitude toward the second.

It is clarifying to substitute, in place of our initial statement of Protagoras' view, the following, as a brief formulation of the relativist thesis in ethics: *"There are conflicting ethical opinions that are equally valid."* But this formulation requires discussion in order to be clear.

The first thing to notice—although the fact will not be obvious until we have explained the phrase "equally valid"—is that the statement is *about* ethical opinions or statements, but is not an ethical statement itself. It is not like saying, "Nothing is right or wrong!" or "Some things are both right and wrong!" It is a metaethical theory.

Next, the statement is cautious. It does not say that no ethical opinions are valid for everybody. It says only that some ethical opinions are not more valid than some other ethical opinions that conflict with them.

Third, our relativist thesis is not merely the claim that different individuals sometimes in fact have conflicting ethical *opinions.* It does assert this, but it goes further. It holds that the conflicting ethical opinions are *equally valid.* We do not establish this merely by showing that people

disagree. Nor do we establish it by showing that individuals' ethical opinions are at least to some extent dependent on the cultural stream within which they stand. Everyone must agree to this—although everyone must also admit that somehow societies often spawn their own moral critics. Nor do we establish it by showing that the standards of a given society have their causes. Of course they do; and so do the scientific opinions in a given society, although we hardly think this necessarily impugns their universal validity.

Fourth, what do we mean by "conflicting ethical opinions"? We mean, of course, by an "opinion" the readiness to make a sincere statement. Thus, a person has an "ethical opinion" to the effect that a particular thing is right or wrong if he could, when asked, make without deception an ethical statement to the effect that that thing is right or wrong. (We explained how to identify an "ethical" statement in Chapter 1.) Now, suppose Mr. A makes an ethical statement, and Mr. B makes a different ethical statement. How shall we tell whether the two statements "conflict"? A sufficient condition of conflict is this: that both statements are about the *same subject* (we explain this in a moment), and the one applies to this subject an ethical predicate *P*, and the other applies to it the same ethical predicate prefaced by the English "not" or something that means or entails the same. For instance, one may say "is morally right" and the other may say "is not morally right," of the very same subject. But now, when do two ethical statements have the *same subject?* This is a more awkward question. We cannot test this just by observing the verbal forms. For instance, Thomas Jefferson said, approximately, "A revolution every few years is a fine thing." But suppose Karl Marx also said, "A revolution every few years is a fine thing." Could we assume that these two men were necessarily saying the same thing? Of course not. Or again, suppose

Mr. A, a resident of the South Pacific, says it is right to bury one's father alive on his sixtieth birthday, irrespective of his state of health; and suppose I say this is not right. Are we talking about the same thing? Not necessarily. The kind of situation Mr. A has in mind is likely to be very different from the kind of situation I have in mind. Perhaps he is assuming that the body one will have in the next world will be exactly like the kind one has just before departing this life (and hence, may think it advisable to depart before feebleness sets in); whereas I may think one has no further existence at all after one's earthly demise. He is talking about burying alive a father who will exist in the next world in a certain kind of body; and I am not. In this situation, it is only confusing to say that our ethical opinions "conflict." Let us say that two people are *talking about the same subject* only in the following situation. Let us suppose A and B make conflicting ethical predications about something or some kind of thing, ostensibly the same for both. But suppose further there is some property P that A more or less consciously believes this thing or kind of thing has, whereas B does *not* believe this. Further, let us suppose that if A *ceased* to believe this, he would cease to have the same ethical opinion about it but agree with B; and let us suppose that if B *began* to believe this (other things being equal), he would change his ethical opinion and agree with A. In this case, let us say that A and B are *not* appraising the same subject. But if there is no more-or-less conscious belief having the status described, then we shall say that they *are* talking about the same subject, and that their ethical opinions are conflicting.

But now, finally, what is the meaning of the phrase "equally valid"? In order to clarify this, let us draw a parallel with language we use in appraising scientific theories. Suppose we have two conflicting theories about natural phenomena. Each of these theories might explain a large part of the known facts, but not all of them, at least not very well. We might then say, "In the light of presently known facts, the two theories are equally plausible." On the other hand, we might make a more radical supposition. Suppose, when thinking about these theories, we make the daring forecast about future evidence, that when scientific investigation has been indefinitely prolonged and all possible experimental data are in, both of these theories will explain all the facts, and there will be no ground for a rational preference of one to the other, although parts of the two theories do contradict each other. In this case, we might say, although this sounds startling, "Although these theories are mutually contradictory in some respects, they are both *valid*." What a person who made such a statement would be saying is that the use of a refined inductive logic, on a complete set of experimental data, would support as strongly confirmed *both* of two conflicting theories. We need not argue whether in fact this case ever does or even could arise, but we can understand the possibility, and the important thing is the parallel with ethics. Now, the ethical relativist is not merely making the uninteresting claim, when he says two conflicting ethical statements are equally valid, that the two statements are equally plausible in the light of the facts known at present. He is saying something much more radical, about what would happen if one were testing these statements by the best possible ethical methodology, and in the light of a complete system of factual or nonethical knowledge. In other words, he is saying that the application of a "rational" method in ethics would support, equally, two conflicting ethical statements even if there were available a complete system of factual knowledge—or else that there is no "rational" method in ethics comparable to an ideal inductive method for empirical science.

I have used the phrase "rational method in ethics" as designating something roughly parallel in ethics to inductive logic in empirical science. This idea will be familiar to us from the preceding chapter, where we argued that the Qualified Attitude Method has this status.

We can now explain exactly what it means to say that two conflicting ethical statements are "equally valid." What it means to say this, is that *either* there is *no* unique rational or justified method in ethics, *or* that the use of the unique rational method in ethics, in the presence of an ideally complete system of factual knowledge, would still not enable us to make a distinction between the ethical statements being considered.

The ethical relativist asserts that there are at least *some* instances of conflicting ethical opinions that are equally valid in this sense.

There are more, and less, radical relativists. The more radical kind of relativist asserts that there are conflicting ethical opinions and that there is *no unique rational method in ethics*. To mark this, let us call him a "methodological relativist" or an "ethical skeptic." The less radical relativist does not say there is no unique rational method, but says that there are still some instances of conflicting ethical opinions that are equally valid. Let us call him a "nonmethodological relativist." We must look at the logic of, and the evidence supporting, these two kinds of relativism separately.

2. *METHODOLOGICAL RELATIVISM*

It would perhaps be better to call a "methodological" relativist a "skeptic" and not a relativist at all.[3] Nevertheless, it is es-

tablished usage to classify various writers, especially anthropologists, as "relativists," although they are methodological relativists in our sense. In order to avoid confusion, we shall follow this terminology.

In order to assess the truth of the theory, the first thing to decide is whether there *are* conflicting opinions about the *same* subject at all. It has been denied that there are. Karl Duncker, in an article in *Mind*, in 1939, questioned whether any anthropological evidence establishes that there are—and suggested that anthropologists had overlooked the fact that when different societies ostensibly advocate different moral principles (for example, the U.S.A., monogamy; Moslems, polygamy), they actually have different situations in mind. However, we have already assessed the evidence on this point (pp. 99-103), and concluded that there are conflicting ethical judgments even when speakers have the same situation in mind. So far, then, methodological relativism stands up.

But is the theory correct in its assertion that there is no unique rational method in ethics? Obviously it is not, if the argument of the preceding chapter is sound. We need not go over this ground again. The reader will by now have made up his mind whether or not this is the case.[4]

If the reader found the preceding chapter convincing, he may be puzzled by the fact that there are methodological relativists among social scientists. The reason is simple: the kind of theory we are suggesting is of a species that has only recently been proposed, and social scientists are un-

---

[3] Certainly this position is different from "relativism" in physics. In relativity physics, there are *correct* judgements for each frame of reference; only, it is impossible to say that one of these judgments (correct for its frame of reference) is really correct for everybody.

[4] Notice, however, that the acceptance of the quasi-naturalist definition leaves open the question of methodological relativism, for it might be that intelligent (and so on) persons would set *no* conditions for the endorsement of attitudes governing choices in community living. In this case, *every* attitude would pass, and there would be no ground for preferring one of two conflicting ethical statements to the other. The same is true for the noncognitive analysis we discussed.

familiar with it.[5] (Neither, for the most part, are they familiar with sophisticated forms of naturalism.) When they say that one ethical statement cannot be shown "objectively" to be more valid than another, what they mean, and all that they mean, is that one cannot show that ethical statements are confirmed or refuted by observation in *exactly the same way* as are hypotheses in science. They rightly see that "is desirable" must be tested in a way different from "is desired," and they conclude that ethical statements cannot be evaluated at all—overlooking the fact that tests appropriate for assessing ethical judgments may be somewhat distinctive, but none the less defensible, given their subject matter.

Moreover, many social scientists simply do not realize that their acceptance of inductive logic is no more "rational," in the sense of no more supportable by the canons of deductive logic, than is the "standard" method of ethical thinking. Yet, without qualms they make use of inductive logic—but at the same time condemn as "subjective" the appraisal of ethical statements, although in fact the "standard" method is warranted by reasons equally as good as those that can be adduced to support inductive reasoning in science. Presumably, as time goes on (and scientists become more familiar with the results of contemporary thinking about inductive logic and ethics), social scientists will cease making this irrational distinction.

The reader need not, incidentally, feel that he has to choose between what we have called the "standard" method, and methodological relativism. We might be mistaken about what the "standard" method is. It might very well be that there is one and only one method that would be used to resolve ethical issues by intelligent (and so on) people, but that it is somewhat different from the method we have described. The "methodological relativist" (as we have defined this term) is making a strong statement: he is saying that there is *no* method that is a "rational" method in the sense of being the one unique method that would be used to resolve ethical issues by intelligent (and so on) people. But there might well be such a method, even if it is not the one we have described.

Of the theories we have been considering in previous chapters, which ones are forms of methodological relativism and which are not? Clearly naturalism is not, for naturalists so construe the meaning of ethical statements that ethical statements have the same capacity to be confirmed by observation as do the statements of empirical science. There is one "unique rational method" for assessing ethical statements, and it is simply the method of inductive logic. Some of the naturalists, on the other hand, are nonmethodological relativists, for instance, Westermarck.[6]

The emotive theory, on the other hand, *as it is usually worked out*, belongs to the methodological relativist species. The whole concept of validity in ethics is

---

[5] A contributing factor is that some social scientists do not distinguish "relativism" in the sense of methodological or nonmethodological relativism as defined above from other senses of "relativism" (described on pp. 340–3). Hence, they think that the truth of one can be inferred from the truth of the other. Since relativism in the senses described on pp. 340–3 is doubtless true, one who does not make the proper distinctions naturally concludes that relativism in one or the other of the two senses now under consideration is also true. Such an inference is, of course, entirely unwarranted.

[6] Different "unique rational methods" vary in the extent to which they can succeed in resolving ethical disputes. There could well be a "method" —and it might well be the only method we could claim to be a "rational" method—that marked a few ethical judgments as definitely untenable, but gave us no help on the serious issues. In fact, this is the case with Westermarck's view. The unique method is the method of empirical science. But if ethical statements mean what Westermarck says they do (p. 166), the method can show that some ethical statements are unwarranted and false, but will not in all cases resolve ethical disputes in the sense of showing that only one of two conflicting statements, made by different people, is correct.

banned. The theory does not recognize any unique rational method of ethical deliberation; on the contrary, anything is allowed that is effective, that wins harmony of attitudes either interpersonally or intrapersonally. Indeed, ineffective reasoning is all right too, according to this theory; it merely *is* ineffective. As a result, there is no way in which any ethical conviction can be "objectively" criticized as being defective, incorrect, or erroneous.

On the other hand, the emotive theory *need* not be a species of methodological relativism. For instance, if it is held that ethical statements are expressions of over-all, impersonal attitudes, then an ethical statement may be "mistaken" if the speaker does not have the over-all, impersonal attitude he purports to have. Much the same is true if it is supposed that the use of ethical language has certain "contextual implications" or makes certain "claims," for then we can say that ethical statements are at least "misleading" if not "incorrect"—if the "contextual implications" or "claims" distinctive of ethical language are not satisfied.[7]

If the argument of the preceding chapter is correct, we have said, the methodological relativist is mistaken because there *is* a unique rational method in ethics. Worse still, it *may* be that he is *contradicting* himself if he both affirms methodological relativism *and* makes ethical statements (which the relativist presumably, like other men, will often do). Whether he is contradicting himself depends on what he means by his ethical statements. He certainly is contradicting himself if he means what the Ideal Observer form of naturalism (in its absolutist form) says ethical statements mean (p. 173).

The relativist of this variety need not, however, renounce engaging in ethical debate, or stop thinking that such debate is

[7] The reader should examine R. M. Hare, *The Language of Morals* (Oxford: Clarendon Press, 1952), p. 69, and P. H. Nowell-Smith, *Ethics* (Baltimore: Penguin Books, 1954), p. 319.

fruitful. Indeed, he may think that the major questions of normative ethics can be answered—not in the sense of finding a "right" answer for them, but in the sense that *agreement* is attainable. He can hold, as many social scientists do, that there are points of ethics about which there is universal agreement, common ground on the basis of which discussion and adjudication can fruitfully proceed. He may think there is a wide basis of agreement that can be extended further, by pointing out the implications—in view of known scientific facts—of commitments already made. For instance, agreement on a program of economic reform might be reached—starting from agreement that suffering is evil and to be avoided—by showing that these economic reforms are necessary means for avoiding suffering. Indeed, the methodological relativist can, in general, espouse ethical reasoning of the form licensed by "contextualism"; but no more than that.

3. NONMETHODOLOGICAL RELATIVISM: RELATIVISM "PROPER"

The second and less radical form of relativism agrees with the first form that there are conflicting ethical judgments about the same subjects; but it differs by holding that there is a unique rational method for answering ethical questions. It then goes on to assert that when we apply this method even to an ideally complete set of data, it sometimes happens that it is impossible to decide between conflicting ethical judgments. Practically, it is an important question how often and where this "sometimes" is; but we postpone this question for the moment. Is methodological relativism true or tenable?

We have already conceded the thesis it shares with the more radical view: that there are conflicting ethical judgments about the same subjects. But, where there are such conflicting judgments, are the judgments ever *equally valid*? This question is a difficult one. Indeed, it may be *in-consistent* to suppose that they ever are. We must consider this.

There are *some* metaethical theories that are consistent with nonmethodological relativism, with saying that conflicting judgments are sometimes equally valid. Take, for instance, the view of Westermarck. He is a naturalist and therefore thinks that the rational method for answering the questions of ethics is the method of science. On the other hand, he thinks that "x is wrong" means "I have a tendency to feel impartial resentment toward people who do things like *x*." Given his premises, is it consistent to be a relativist? That is, is it consistent to say that conflicting ethical statements are sometimes both "valid" in the sense permitted by his theory? Yes, for we can describe conditions in which conflicting statements would both be "valid." Suppose Jones and Smith are debating whether it is right to pluck a chicken alive, in order to secure a somewhat tastier dish. Jones says it is; Smith says it isn't. Now suppose Jones has been so conditioned that he really would tend to feel impartial resentment toward anyone who did this sort of thing. Further, suppose Smith, who was reared in South America, would not; he simply cannot get excited about whether chickens are plucked before or after they are killed, and in any case he is very fond of the taste of succulent chicken. In this situation, according to Westermarck's analysis, it really would be true and correct for Jones to say, "That is not wrong," and for Smith to say, "That is wrong." Perhaps this outcome suggests something wrong with Westermarck's analysis; but this is what his analysis implies, and there is nothing inconsistent about the reasoning or conclusion.

But it is inconsistent to assert nonmethodological relativism and also certain other metaethical theories: e.g., nonnaturalism, Perry's theory, the absolutist form of Ideal Observer theory.

The intriguing question for us is whether the thesis developed in the preceding chapter leads to the same conclusion.

The main burden of our previous chapter was this: (1) The Qualified Attitude Method is the "standard" method for evaluating ethical statements and can be defended by good reasons. (2) Ethical statements either assert or claim or imply that a corresponding attitude (for instance, preference in the case of judgments about what is preferable) meets all the conditions which would be set by informed, reflective people for the endorsement of attitudes governing choices in community living. Is the thesis of nonmethodological relativism inconsistent with either of these assertions? Let us consider them in order.

(1) Nonmethodological relativism is consistent with our conclusions about the Qualified Attitude Method if and only if it is logically possible for two conflicting ethical judgments both to satisfy the conditions of this Method. *Is* this logically possible? When we think of it we can see that in one respect our description of the Qualified Attitude Method was incomplete. It told us how each of us is to proceed in order to decide whether a given ethical judgment is valid—that it must jibe with our corresponding attitudes in so far as they need not be "discounted," and so on. But it did not make perfectly clear whether a person's ethical judgment is valid if it satisfies the tests as made by him but *not the tests as made by other persons*. One could make it a part of the Qualified Attitude Method that a judgment is satisfactory only if it meets the prescribed tests as performed by everyone. If, on the other hand, it is enough for the validity of a judgment made by a particular person, that it satisfy the tests as performed by him, then it is logically possible that conflicting judgments both be valid.

How shall we decide this matter? It is not easy to say what is "standard" practice. It is at least very infrequently that we think our judgment meets the conditions we have enumerated as parts of the Qual-ified Attitude Method, and at the same time think that a conflicting judgment by someone else meets the same conditions, as tested by him. So it is not easy to say whether, if we did think these things, we should feel free to assert our own ethical proposition. Nevertheless, we have ob-served above (p. 175) that there are per-sons who think there are great variations in moral beliefs, and who do not think it likely that *everybody's* judgments, however corrected or qualified, will necessarily agree on many issues. Still they are quite prepared to go ahead and make moral as-sertions as required by consonance with their own criticized attitudes. They think that a person can say, like Martin Luther, "Here *I* stand; I can do no other," irrespec-tive of information about the attitudes of others. So a formulation of the Qualified Attitude Method consistent with relativism has some support in ordinary thinking. Moreover, there are reasons for *recom-mending* such a formulation—reasons to the effect that adherence to an absolutist for-mulation would paralyze moral judgment by making it impossible to claim either a pro- or a con- judgment as justified in far too many cases. Therefore we shall not re-gard it as part of the Qualified Attitude Method that one's ethical judgment be found compatible with the discounted atti-tudes of *everybody*; what is required is only that it be compatible with the judge's *own* discounted attitudes. So far, then, it is consistent for us to assert that the Qualified Attitude Method is the proper test of ethi-cal judgments, and also to assert the thesis of nonmethodological relativism.

(2) We stumble into a logical dif-ficulty, however, when with this conclusion in mind we consider the consistency of nonmethodological relativism with our pro-posal that ethical statements assert or claim that a corresponding attitude meets all the conditions that would be set (and so on). The difficulty is as follows. Suppose Mr. A makes careful use of the Qualified Attitude Method, and as a result says, "*x* is desira-ble." And suppose Mr. B, after the same process, says, "*x* is undesirable." The view of the nonmethodological relativist is that this situation can really arise, that both parties really can have applied whatever unique rational method is available. But how can one person say *x* is desirable, and the other correctly deny this, *if our pro-posal about the meanings is correct?* At least, how can it be if what Mr. A is saying is, "Desiring *x*, *on the part of everybody*, meets the conditions...."? Surely this can-not be asserted if Mr. B's desiring of *x* does *not* meet the appropriate conditions at least as tested by Mr. B.

Evidently, if we are to be consistent relativists, we must not only have a specific understanding of the Qualified Attitude Method (as suggested above), but also a particular understanding of the quasi-naturalist definition. We must specify this definition in a relativist direction, just as the Ideal Observer theory has a relativist form (p. 173). We can say, to take "desira-ble" as an example, that "*x* is desirable" means "Desire for *x* on *my part* satisfies all the conditions that would be set ..." (and so on), with the understanding that the "set conditions" may be such that desire for *x* on the part of one person may meet them, and desire for non-*x* on the part of some other person may also meet them. With this emendation, the quasi-naturalist definition is brought even closer to the non-cognitivist counterpart described at the end of Chapter 10—the view that to say that "*x* is desirable" is (1) to express a desire for *x*, perhaps an overall impartial one, and (2) to claim or imply that the desire expressed satisfies all the conditions (and so on, as before).

If we are not prepared to understand the quasi-naturalist definition in some such manner, we must in consistency reject rela-tivism.

It makes little difference, for the topics we have to discuss beyond the present chapter, whether we make these specifications and adopt relativism, or do not make them and accept absolutism. The reasons for relativism are fairly weighty, but we shall see that the issue hardly arises in later contexts. In particular, it will not be necessary to distinguish relativist from absolutist forms of the quasi-naturalist definition in later discussions. We shall feel free to ignore the difference partly because nothing will turn on it, and because the relativistically-minded reader can supply the emendations without difficulty (except perhaps in Chapter 14, where the changes must be slightly more complex).

In order to continue the argument, let us assume that we are now agreed that it is *consistent* to adopt certain metaethical theories (and in particular approximately the one outlined in Chapter 10), and at the same time to be a nonmethodological relativist. Nevertheless, it may still be that non-methodological relativism is just plain *false*. We must now consider this possibility. How shall we decide this? Again, it depends on our metaethics. Take Westermarck's view. If the attitudes of all impartial persons were in agreement, then one person could never truly say, "I have an impartial tendency to feel resentment against the agent of acts like x," and at the same time someone else correctly say, of the same x, "I do *not* have an impartial tendency to feel resentment against the agent of acts like x." Then, according to Westermarck's definitions, one person could not truly say, "x is wrong," when another one could truly say, "x is not wrong." Hence, conflicting ethical statements would in fact never be "equally valid." Relativism would be false.

Similar reasoning must be used to decide whether relativism is true or false, if we adopt the view that the "rational" method in ethics is the Qualified Attitude Method. Essentially the issue is this: If one informed (and so on) attitude in fact never clashes with another attitude that is equally qualified, both of course being directed at the same act or thing, then one

person can never correctly claim, "x is wrong," when someone else can correctly say, "x is not wrong." *Valid* ethical statements would then never conflict; and relativism would be false.

Relativism is right, then, according to our theory (and Westermarck's), essentially if "qualified" (in the sense of not requiring to be "discounted") attitudes toward the same act or event can be conflicting.

Well, can they, or can they not? Or what should we believe?

The simplest way to answer these questions, of course, is just to find two individuals, both qualified in the relevant ways, and observe whether in fact one wants, abhors, feels obligated to do, demands from others, feels indignant or disgusted at, admires, or prefers things, actions, or events to which the other individual takes an opposite attitude. It is difficult, though, ever to be certain that such individuals are before us. How can we be sure that all the relevant facts are believed by both, and that neither needs to be disabused of false beliefs? How can we be sure that all the relevant considerations are present to the minds of both, with requisite vividness? Perhaps, of course, individuals on occasion may with reason be said to approximate to these conditions. It seems preferable, however, not to rest one's argument on such possible cases.

There is an indirect method for answering our question. Consider a parallel: that we feel free to make statements about how gases *would* behave at an absolute-zero temperature, although we have not actually observed gases in this state. Why? We draw inferences from relevant causal laws. The same is true in our case. If we have good reason to believe causal laws, to the effect that a person's attitudes are not a function solely of his information (or its vividness) and his state of personal needs or wishes (at the time) and his normalcy, then we have so much reason to think that "qualified" attitudes occasionally vary. If we happen to know precisely the nature of these laws, we may be able to specify the conditions under which such variation will occur. Psychological theory and experiment, then, are the most obvious source for an answer to our question.

Unfortunately, psychological theories do not provide a uniform answer to our question. Gestalt theory would lead us to believe that attitudes ("ought" experiences) to a situation will be identical, if the situation is identically understood, and personal needs and interests do not play a distorting or blinding role. Psychoanalytic theory and Hullian learning theory, however, provide a different answer. According to these theories, two attitudes, equally "qualified" in the sense of occurring in minds with equal information (and so on), can be conflicting, depending on the history of the development of the persons: their past identifications, their past rewards and punishments. The doctors, then, disagree. But how does the currently available experimental evidence look? Does it favor the view of either theory, on this particular point? To this our answer must be: There is no *certainly* correct reading of the evidence, but it *appears* to favor the relativist answer to our question, for there is some reason to think that fundamental orientations may be adopted from parents in early life, and that these may have a permanent influence on attitudes; that identifications, emotional relations with important figures in one's life, and feelings of security play a role in the development of one's values; that certain things or events maybe highly valued in compensation for the inaccessibility of other satisfactions at an earlier period, or as a result of deprivations. Then, if these things are true, we can specify some occurrences in the life of an individual that would have the effect that his attitudes now, whatever the information (and so on) of his present state of mind, would be different from what they would have been had his earlier experiences been different. Individuals with rele-

vantly different earlier experiences, then, may be expected to have different attitudes, despite identical qualifications with respect to knowledge, impartiality, and so forth.[8]

On the whole, then, the relativist is better able to claim the support of contemporary psychological theory and research than is his adversary. However, the issue is not closed.

The facts of anthropology are also relevant to our question, and in the following way. In the first place, we have already noticed (p. 109) that studies of cultural change in primitive societies suggest that facts like personal conflicts and maladjustments, the attitudes of one's close relatives (for example, whether favorably oriented toward White civilization), and personal success in achieving status in one's group or outside one's group (for example, with White men) play an important role in the development of the values of adults. This finding is some support for our reading of the observational evidence of psychology. In the second place, there is the fact that various groups have different values. The mere fact that different ethical standards exist in different societies, of course, by itself proves nothing relevant to our present problem. Nevertheless, something important is proved if the facts bear testimony that different standards can prevail even if different groups have the *same beliefs*

[8] We should not, however, overlook the possibility that an individual might, if he knew that an attitude of his was a result of some type of early experience (for example, a high valuation of knowledge being a result of the unsatisfactoriness of his personal relations at an earlier period of development), to some extent lose this attitude. In other words, perhaps self-understanding in the sense of understanding the genesis of one's own values is a fact relevant to what one's present attitudes will be. It is possible that any two individuals, otherwise equally "qualified," would in fact always have the same attitudes toward everything at the conclusion of a careful psychological treatment in which each acquired complete self-understanding. Is there evidence, from psychoanalysts or other specialists in personality theory, that points in this direction? The writer does not know.

about the relevant event or act, and if there is no reason to suppose that the group standards reflect group differences in respect of other "qualifications." (We must remember that attitudes common to a group cannot usually be discounted as being a result of personal interest or of an abnormal frame of mind.) The fact of variation of group standards, in these circumstances, would tend to show that attitudes are a function of such variables, that attitudes could differ even if our "ideal qualifications" were all met.

Is there such variation of group standards? We have seen that there is one area of ethical opinion where there is diversity in appraisal and at the same time possible identity of belief about the action—that about the treatment of animals. On the whole, primitive groups show little feeling that it is wrong to cause pain to animals, whereas the columns of *The New York Times* are testimony to the fact that many persons in the U.S.A. take a vigorous interest in what goes on in slaughterhouses. We have already mentioned some details about the attitudes of primitive groups (p. 103). Nevertheless, we cannot be sure that attitudes of the groups here in question really do fulfill our "qualifications" equally well. Primitive peoples rarely make pets of the animals they maltreat. There is at least some question whether they have a vivid imagination of what the suffering of an animal is like, comparable to that of the authors of letters to the *Times*. The writer has assured himself by personal investigation that there is no definite discrepancy between the Hopi *beliefs*, about the effects of maltreating animals, and those of what seems a representative sample of educated White Americans. Degrees of *vividness* of

belief, however, do not lend themselves to objective investigation, and it is not clear how we may definitely answer questions about them, either way. Perhaps the sanest conclusion is just to say that, as far as can be decided objectively, groups do sometimes make divergent appraisals when they have identical beliefs about the objects, but that the difficulties of investigation justify a healthy degree of skepticism about the conclusiveness of the inquiry.

The fact that objective inquiry is difficult naturally works both ways. It prevents us from asserting confidently that, where there are differences of appraisal, there is still identity of factual belief. But equally it prevents us from denying confidently that there is identity of belief, where appraisals differ.

The anthropological evidence, taken by itself, then, does not give a *conclusive* answer to our question. At the present time, the anthropologist does not have two social groups of which he can say definitely: "These groups have exactly the same beliefs about action A, on all points that could be seriously viewed as ethically relevant. But their views—attitudes—about the morality of the acts are vastly different." Whether, everything considered, the relativist reading of the facts is not the more balanced judgment, is another question. The writer is inclined to think it is the better judgment.

If we agree that the ethical standards of groups are not a function solely of their beliefs (or the vividness of these), it is reasonable to suppose that "ideally qualified" attitudes may well conflict with respect to the very same act or event. To say this is to say that there is reason to suppose that nonmethodological relativism is correct.

The Justification of Value Judgments: Rational Choice

PAUL TAYLOR

A. THE CONCEPT OF A WAY OF LIFE

I have defined a way of life as a hierarchy of value systems in which each system belongs to a different point of view. Since a value system is nothing but a set of standards and rules arranged according to their relative precedence, it follows that a way of life is simply an organization of different sets of standards and rules. These sets (value systems) are in turn arranged according to *their* relative precedence. How is their relative precedence determined? In order to answer this question we must first consider what it means for a value system to be relevant to a situation and to be in conflict with another value system. It is only when two value systems are both relevant to a situation and are in conflict with each other that one can be said to take precedence over the other.

In Chapter 5 I gave as an example a situation to which an aesthetic value system and an etiquette value system are irrelevant and to which a moral value system and a prudential value system are both relevant. It was a situation in which one's own life and the lives of others are in danger and one is confronted with the choice of whether to risk one's life to help others.

Paul W. Taylor, NORMATIVE DISCOURSE, © 1961. Reprinted by permission of Prentice-Hall, Inc., Englewood Cliffs, New Jersey.

Now the fact that aesthetic considerations and considerations of etiquette are not relevant to such a situation is a fact about a person's way of life. Another person with a different way of life might hold that they are. In the act of committing himself to a way of life, a person subscribed to the principle that, if his own life and the lives of others were in danger, it would be irrelevant to use the standards and rules of aesthetics or of etiquette in deciding what to do. Another person, in committing himself to a way of life, may have subscribed to the opposite principle. We cannot say whether such value systems "really" are relevant or irrelevant to the situation. We can only decide the question on the basis of a given way of life, and different ways of life will yield different answers.

What, then, does it mean to say that a value system is relevant to a situation? It is to say that, according to a certain way of life, the standards and rules of that system are to be used to guide the choices and regulate the conduct of those in the situation. And this means simply that the standards and rules in question include the situation in their range of application. According to the given way of life, it is legitimate and proper to judge the choices and conduct of people in the situation by the standards and rules of the value system. Conversely a value system is irrelevant when its standards and rules do not cover the situation in their range of application, and so cannot be used to judge choices or conduct in the situation.

It is possible for two value systems, each belonging to a different point of view, to be relevant to a situation but not to be in conflict. They do not conflict when it is possible for a person's choice and conduct to be in accordance with the standards and rules of both systems. Two relevant value systems are in conflict, on the other hand, when a person's adopting one system in the situation prevents him from adopting the other, that is, when the standards or rules of one system are in conflict with those of the other. From Chapter 3 we know that one standard conflicts with another when a feature of something which is good-making according to one will be bad-making according to the other. That is, in so far as an object fulfills one standard it fails to fulfill the other. And we know that one rule conflicts with another when acts which are right according to one are wrong according to the other. There are different degrees to which two value systems may be in conflict, depending on how many of the standards and rules of one are in conflict with those of the other.

That two different value systems can be relevant to a situation and not in conflict may be illustrated as follows. Suppose we are judging a painting from two points of view, the aesthetic and the econ-omic. When we judge it aesthetically, we apply the standards of a certain aesthetic value system we have adopted. When we judge it economically, we are interested in its worth as an investment and we apply the standards of an economic value system we have adopted. The painting may be aesthetically good and also a good invest-ment; it may be aesthetically bad but a good investment; it may be aesthetically good but a bad investment; or it may be both aesthetically bad and a bad invest-ment. The two value systems are thus logi-cally independent of each other. They may be said to be divergent, but not to be in conflict. Even when they diverge (i.e., when the painting is judged as aestheti-cally good and economically bad, or vice versa) that which *makes* the painting aesthetically good is not that which *makes* it economically bad. In other words, the features of the painting which are good-making characteristics from the aesthetic point of view are not the same features which are bad-making characteristics from the economic point of view. As a result, our judgment that the painting is beautiful does not entail that we buy it, and our judgment that it is a bad investment does not entail that we find it aesthetically dis-pleasing. Since the aesthetic system and the economic system are not logically con-nected, to increase (or decrease) the aes-thetic value of something is not *eo ipso* to increase (or decrease) its economic value, although there may be a causal relation be-tween the two. Therefore they cannot be in conflict. For an example of two value sys-tems in conflict, I would cite the case dis-cussed above, where one's own life and the lives of others are in danger. Here a moral value system may indeed conflict with a value system of self-interest, since to act from self-interest would *involve* acting im-morally (i.e., violating a moral rule), and acting morally would *involve* sacrificing one's own interests.

It should be noted that the decision as to whether two value systems conflict in a given situation does not depend on a way of life, but on the nature of the value sys-tems themselves. They conflict when their constituent standards and rules conflict, re-gardless of the way of life that contains them. It is true that conflict does not arise unless the way of life allows the two value systems to be relevant to the same situa-tion. But once this is so, then whether or not they conflict is not determined by a way of life.

Let us now suppose that two value systems are in conflict. If we ask which sys-tem takes precedence over the other, it is to the principles of a way of life that we must refer for an answer. Different ways of life will entail different answers. According to one, value system V will take precedence over value system V'; according to another, V' will take precedence over V. There is nothing in the value systems themselves which renders them superior (or inferior) to others. We cannot show that a moral value system always or necessarily takes precedence over a prudential value system, for example, merely by examining the value systems themselves. We cannot even show this by analyzing the two points of view to which the value systems belong. The canons of reasoning which define one point of view do not stipulate that any value system which is guided by them shall be superior to any value system guided by another set of canons. Such a stipulation can only be made outside all points of view, as a principle to which one subscribes as part of one's way of life. Thus we cannot say that the moral point of view takes precedence over the prudential point of view unless we have committed ourselves to a way of life in which a moral value system takes precedence over a prudential value system whenever the two conflict. The mere fact that the one system is moral does not *make* it take precedence over another system. Indeed, there is at least one way of life, actually practiced by a culture, which does not claim superiority on behalf of its moral system over the value system of prudence or self-interest. This is the culture of the Navaho Indians. (This has been argued by John Ladd in *The Structure of a Moral Code*. Cambridge, Mass.: Harvard University Press, 1957, esp. pp. 212-213 and pp. 292-296.) However, for the Navaho there is perhaps no conceivable conflict between morality and prudence, in light of "the general Navaho presumption that the welfare of others is a necessary condition of one's own welfare." (*Ibid.*, p. 296.)

The commitment to a way of life involves the decision to *make* one value system take precedence over another when they are in conflict. Since each value system that is part of a way of life belongs to a different point of view, it may be thought that the commitment to a way of life also decides which *point of view* shall take precedence over another. But the most we can say is that a way of life determines indirectly the relative precedence of points of view. We can speak of one point of view (say, the moral) taking precedence over another point of view (say, the prudential), but only in the sense that, given a situation in which a person must decide between acting morally and acting in his self-interest, the person's way of life determines that the moral system takes precedence over the prudential system. In another situation, or with another way of life, it might be the case that self-interest will take precedence over morality. Thus we cannot ask, "Does one point of view in general take precedence over another?" We can only ask "Does this particular value system belonging to one point of view take precedence over that particular value system belonging to another point of view?" And this question can be answered only relatively to a way of life. However, under special conditions it would be possible to make a generalization, albeit a somewhat misleading one, concerning the relative precedence of points of view. Suppose, for example, that there is one way of life which is always preferred to every other way of life on the basis of a rational choice. And suppose that, according to this way of life, whenever a moral value system conflicts with a prudential value system the moral system takes precedence. We might then say, still somewhat misleadingly, that the moral point of view takes precedence over the point of view of self-interest. (The relative precedence of points of view is discussed further in Section B of Chapter 11.)

In summary, to commit oneself to a way of life is to subscribe to certain principles. These principles are of two types:

principles of relevance and principles of relative precedence. When we subscribe to a principle of the first type, we *decide* which value systems shall be relevant to a certain kind of situation and which shall not. In choosing a way of life we *make* a given system relevant or not relevant to a given situation. Similarly, when we subscribe to a principle of the second type, we *decide* that one value system shall take precedence over another in a situation where they conflict and to which they are both relevant. In choosing a way of life we stipulate the relative precedence of our value systems. Thus we cannot answer the question why a certain value system is relevant or why it takes precedence over another. We can only say that these simply are the principles to which we subscribe in virtue of the fact that we are committed to a particular way of life. In the very act of committing ourselves, we make value system V relevant to situation S and we make value system V take precedence over value system V'. We cannot give reasons for claiming that V is relevant to S or that V takes precedence over V'. We can only say we have chosen that way of life. Such a choice is our *ultimate normative commitment*. The only kind of reasons which can be given to justify the principles of a way of life are reasons which justify the way of life as a whole. As we shall see, such reasons consist in showing that the way of life is rationally chosen.

Variation in ways of life depends on the particular principles of relevance and relative precedence which define each. From this variation in ways of life themselves, we can distinguish another kind of variation—a variation in *commitments* to a way of life. Thus we may classify varying commitments according to (a) their degree of coherence and stability, (b) their degree of depth, (c) their degree of conventionality or unconventionality, and (d) their degree of explicitness.

(a) I have been speaking up to now as if everyone commits himself to just one way of life, striving to live by its principles and to realize its ideals throughout his life. The fact is, however, that individuals vary widely in the coherence and stability of their ultimate commitments. In a society at large, there will always be a more or less definite way of life to which most members of the society have been committed by being brought up within it. They have not committed themselves as a matter of choice, but have been committed by others. If they remain uncritical and conventional in their outlook, they will have a coherent and stable way of life. But there will be individuals who for one reason or another will come to doubt the way of life in which they have been brought up. They might then choose a new way of life which will be just as coherent and stable as the way of life of their society. On the other hand, they might become disillusioned with their new way of life. They might shortly find themselves committed to another, which again might turn out to be unsatisfactory to them. To the extent that a person's commitments are in this way temporary and constantly changing, to that extent they lack coherence and stability. The extreme of incoherence and instability is reached when an individual has no way of life of his own. He lives without principles or ideals. Whatever standards and rules he does follow are not organized into unified value systems. He lacks second-order norms by which to determine the relative precedence of other norms. And he applies his norms inconsistently, sometimes having pro-attitudes toward the very same things which at other times are the objects of his con-attitudes. From this extreme there is a continuum of commitments of increasing coherence and stability until we arrive at a single, all-embracing, permanent way of life, in which the value systems of all points of view are integrated in a consistent hierarchy.

(b) Commitments to ways of life may

vary not only in degree of coherence and stability, but also in degree of depth or throughness. A strong-minded, deeply convinced, thoroughly committed person will strive to live according to his way of life under all circumstances. He will exert every effort to fulfill its ideals, even at great cost to his own comfort or safety. A person who is not deeply committed to a way of life will be only weakly motivated to live by its principles and ideals, and will frequently fail to adhere to the standards and rules involved in it when it is not to his immediate advantage. (I shall consider depth of commitment further in Chapter 12.)

(c) Commitments to ways of life also vary in degree of conventionality or unconventionality, according to their agreement or disagreement with the way of life of the general culture or times. An individual's way of life is conventional to the extent that it agrees with the way of life of his family, of his religious background, of his economic and social class, and of the various groups to which he belongs. (We shall see that the conventionality or unconventionality of a way of life has nothing to do with whether it can be rationally chosen.)

(d) Another dimension in which commitments to ways of life vary is in their degree of explicitness. A person might live fully in accordance with the ideals and principles of a way of life and yet not be able to *tell* someone what they are. Such a person would be unable to make his way of life explicit; he could not articulate, either to himself or to others, his basic beliefs and "values." We might say of him that he lives *as if* he believed in certain ideals and principles. His commitment is implicit, not explicit. Another person might be able to state clearly and coherently what his way of life is. If he is of a certain bent and has certain abilities, he might even write out his "philosophy of life" in a book. He might also preach it to others and try to get them to become committed to it. He might accordingly be proclaimed a prophet or wise

man, or else (depending on the social conditions of his time and on the nature of his way of life) a fanatic, a crank, a reformer, or a demagogue.

B. ABSOLUTISM AND RELATIVISM

Having considered what it means to be committed to a way of life, we are now prepared to continue our inquiry into the justification of value judgments. We have reached the fourth and final stage of such justification: the rational choice of a way of life. We have seen that the commitment to a way of life is an ultimate commitment. If we ask someone to justify his value judgments and he appeals to standards or rules, and if we ask him for reasons for accepting his standards or rules and he validates them, and if we then ask him to justify his entire value system and he vindicates it, he must finally refer to his whole way of life. There he takes his final stand. The question now before us is: How can this ultimate commitment itself be justified? This question, it seems to me, lies at the heart of the controversy between absolutism and relativism in values.

No one has brought out more clearly the fact that commitment to a way of life is an ultimate commitment than R. M. Hare. In the following passage Mr. Hare gives his account of the justification of decisions and principles. (The term "principles" covers not only what I have referred to as standards and rules, but also what I have called the ideals and principles of a way of life.)

. . . A complete justification of a decision would consist of a complete account of its effects, together with a complete account of the principles which it observed, and the effects of observing those principles. . . . Thus, if pressed to justify a decision completely, we have to give a complete specification of the way of life of which it is a part. This complete specification it is impossible in practice to give; the nearest attempts are those given by the great religions, especially those which can point to historical persons who carried out the way of life in practice. Suppose, however, that we can give it. If the inquirer still goes on asking 'But why *should* I live like that?' then there is no further answer to give him, because we have already, *ex hypothesi*, said everything that could be included in this further answer. We can only ask him to make up his own mind which way he ought to live; for in the end everything rests upon such a decision of principle. He has to decide whether to accept that way of life or not; if he accepts it, then we can proceed to justify the decisions that are based upon it; if he does not accept it, then let him accept some other, and try to live by it. (R. M. Hare, *The Language of Morals*, p. 69.)

We have considered a somewhat parallel situation with regard to the vindication of value systems. There, however, an appeal is made to "principles" in a wider context, for we found that a value system can be vindicated in terms of the ideals of a whole way of life. But there is no such wider context to refer to when we are asked to justify a way of life itself. Hare says that we can only ask the person to try to live by it. But is there no way to show that one person's choice of a way of life is more *intelligent* or *enlightened* than another's? Hare himself argues that the choice of a way of life is not an *arbitrary* decision.

To describe such ultimate decisions as arbitrary, because *ex hypothesi* everything which could be used to justify them has already been included in the decision, would be like saying that a complete description of the universe was utterly unfounded, because no further fact could be called upon in corroboration of it. This is not how we use the words 'arbitrary' and 'unfounded.' Far from being arbitrary, such a decision would be the most well-founded of decisions, because it would be based upon a consideration of everything upon which it could possibly be founded. (*Ibid.*, p. 69.)

In light of these remarks, it would seem that there is at least one condition for rationality in making a "decision of principle" to commit oneself to a whole way of life, namely the condition that one *know* what is involved in all the alternative ways of life among which one is choosing. I shall later specify what I consider to be the necessary and sufficient conditions for a rational choice among ways of life, and this condition will be included among them. Before doing this, however, it is important to clarify the general nature of a rational choice.

The context in which I am dealing with such a choice is the context of justifying a value judgment. My purpose is to make clear the logic of our reasoning when our value judgments are consistently challenged. In setting forth the conditions of a rational choice among ways of life, I shall not be trying to describe a situation of choice which would actually confront someone in everyday life. I shall be constructing a concept of a rational choice in the abstract. This concept is designed to answer the question, "What sort of commitment to a way of life would anyone on reflection be willing to call a justified one?" The question is not, "How do people actually come to commit themselves to a way of life?" Nor is it, "What would be the psychological grounds (causes) for a person's choice if he actually were confronted with alternative ways of life among which he were asked to choose?"

The philosophical question with which we are concerned arises only when we try to push back our defense or support of a value judgment as far as it will go—to its ultimate foundations, as it were. The logic of our thinking moves step by step from the judgment to a standard or rule, from a standard or rule to higher standards or rules, from those to the highest standards or rules within the framework of validation, from there to the whole value system which sets that framework, and from there to the whole way of life in terms of which the value system is vindicated. Here we stop, until we notice that there are many different and conflicting ways of life. We see that if we commit ourselves to one we will be able to justify our value judgment, but that if we commit ourselves to another we will be able to show that our value judgment is unjustified. It is then that we ask ourselves if all ways of life are equally justified. Is it not possible to give good reason for accepting one way of life rather than another?

The issue raised here is that which many philosophers call the issue between relativism and absolutism. Are values relative or absolute? If we can trace the logical foundations of our value judgments back to our commitment to a certain way of life but cannot justify this commitment itself, then all values are said to be relative. They are relative to our way of life. (More accurately, they are relative to our value systems, and our value systems are themselves relative to our way of life.) This relativistic position holds that, if we find (as we do) that different societies and cultures have conflicting ways of life, then the struggle between them is a matter of brute force, unless they voluntarily decide to tolerate each other's differences. No rational choice can be made between them. If one has a moral code (i.e., a moral value system) which contradicts the moral code of the other—so that acts of a certain sort are right in the one culture and wrong in the other—we cannot talk about acts of that sort being "really" right or "really" wrong. They *are* right (not merely believed to be right) in one culture and wrong in the other. Good reasons can be given *for* doing the acts, if one accepts the supreme norms of the value systems as vindicated by the way of life of the first culture. Similarly, good reasons can be given *against* doing the same acts in the framework of the way of life of the second culture. Since good reasons cannot be given in support of one whole way of life rather than the other, any "good reasons" are relative to value systems and finally to ways of life. They are valid only in so far as one adopts a cer-

tain value system and with it a certain way of life.

We cannot escape this kind of relativism by arguing that the canons of reasoning which define normative points of view are equally as rational as the canons of reasoning which define the scientific, the mathematical, and the historical points of view. It is true that just as we can explicate the canons of reasoning that govern the latter and thereby reveal the ideal of rationality implicit in those ways of thinking, so we can explicate the canons of reasoning which govern the various normative points of view and thereby disclose the ideal of rationality implicit in them. The relativist can grant this and still claim that our inability to justify a whole way of life opens the way for skepticism, and destroys the rationality of normative thinking *as a whole*. His argument is based on the fact that the canons of reasoning which govern the scientific, the mathematical, and the historical points of view are independent of whatever way of life a scientist, a mathematician, or a historian may be committed to. A physicist will appeal to the same sort of evidence to confirm a hypothesis whether he be a Hindu or a Christian, a Communist or a Capitalist. But the reasons which he appeals to in trying to justify his *value judgments* will vary according to the way of life he is committed to. Unless his way of life can itself be justified, the reasons which he gives will not make a universal claim on all men. The relativist would have to admit that, on the levels of verification and validation, taking a certain point of view would entail the same rules of valid inference and relevance for everyone, no matter what his way of life may be. Hence *to this extent* a person can claim rationality on behalf of his way of justifying value judgments. It is only when we reach the level of vindicating a whole value system that the skeptical power of relativism is felt. At this level we can no longer appeal to the universality of our canons of reasoning as a sufficient ground for claiming that the justification of value judgments is a rational process. The universal canons at this level are the rules of valid inference which define the process of vindication itself. That is, they are the rules according to which we justify a value system by showing that it has contributive and instrumental value to a way of life. *But such rules allow for the same value system to be both justified and unjustified*, since a value system which has contributive and instrumental value to one way of life can have contributive and instrumental disvalue to another.

Under the relativist's assumption that ways of life cannot rationally be justified, it seems we must make an important, indeed a damaging, qualification in our claim to *know* what is good or bad, right or wrong. We must admit that such knowledge varies from way of life to way of life, whereas scientific, mathematical, and historical knowledge do not. This difference is sufficient to make us doubtful about using the word "knowledge" at all in connection with value judgments. A similar doubt arises concerning our use of the words "true" and "false." A value system may be vindicated in one culture and an opposite or conflicting value system may be vindicated in another culture, since each culture embodies a different way of life. This seems to imply that a given value judgment may be true in one culture and false in another. Indeed, it is possible to define valuational relativism as the view that no value judgment is simply true or simply false, but is only true *for* someone (or *for* some group or culture), and false *for* someone else (or *for* some other group or culture). Nobody would say this about scientific, mathematical, or historical statements. A scientific, mathematical, or historical statement is simply (absolutely, genuinely) true or false. To say that it is true *for* someone means only that someone believes it or *thinks* it is true. Value judgments may also be said to be true for someone in this sense. But this is not what the relativist is getting

at when he makes such a claim. He means that the truth of a value judgment is relative to someone's (or some group's or culture's) way of life in such a way that the same judgment will be false relative to another person's (or group's or culture's) way of life.

Valuational absolutism, on the other hand, claims that a value judgment is simply true or false, not true or false *for* someone. It is true when it can be shown to be justified, false when it can be shown to be unjustified. It is shown to be justified when it is verified by appeal to a standard or rule which can be validated within a value system, which in turn is vindicated by reference to a way of life, *and this way of life can rationally be preferred to all others*. If the way of life which vindicates the value system can rationally be shown not to be preferable to some other way of life, then the value judgment is false. To say that the judgment is true or false is to say that it is *really* true or false, quite aside from whether or not people think so. Of course its truth or falsity does depend on a given value system, but not all value systems are equally justified. Some may be vindicated in terms of a nonrational way of life. Hence value systems do not fully provide a justification for a value judgment. A value judgment is *completely* justified (i.e., it is as justified as it can be) when the value system within the framework of which it is verified and validated is itself vindicated by reference to a *rational* way of life. Only such a value judgment can be claimed to be really true. Its truth in some respects will be different from scientific and mathematical truth, although, like the latter, it will be independent of cultural variation. A value judgment will be true even though its truth is not recognized by a whole culture (just as "The earth is a globe" was true even when people thought that the earth was flat).

For the valuational absolutist, what is the difference between the truth of value judgments and the truth of scientific or mathematical statements? The answer lies in how they are justified. Scientific and mathematical statements are completely justified in terms of the canons of valid reasoning set by the scientific and mathematical points of view. To decide to take such a point of view is to decide to reason in a certain way, that is, according to certain rules of inference. What is found to be intellectually acceptable according to these rules will be designated as true; what is found, under the same rules, to be intellectually unacceptable will be false. The canons of reasoning which govern the complete justification of a value judgment, on the other hand, require the steps of vindication and rational choice. These latter do not correspond to any steps used in verifying scientific statements or in proving mathematical statements. The verification and validation of value judgments are carried out within the framework of a value system according to the canons of reasoning which define a normative point of view; they may be compared generally with empirical verification and deductive reasoning in nonnormative points of view. But as we have seen, the value system referred to in the verification and validation of value judgments must itself be justified. The method used is that of a pragmatic test, which in turn makes reference to a way of life. There is no similar test and no similar reference in scientific and mathematical reasoning.

C. THE CONCEPT OF A RATIONAL CHOICE

I shall now proceed to give the argument for valuational absolutism. To do so, I shall try to explicate the concept of a rational choice among ways of life, and thereby show that the preference for one way of life rather than another is not arbitrary. This is the fourth and final stage in the total justification of a value judgment. It can be accomplished by showing that when-

ever anyone is confronted with a situation in which he is to choose between a given way of life and other ways of life, and whenever that situation satisfies the necessary conditions for a rational choice, the given way of life will be chosen in preference to any other.

The necessary conditions for a rational choice among ways of life must be specified. I suggest that these conditions may be grouped under three general headings: conditions of freedom, conditions of enlightenment, and conditions of impartiality. I shall say that a choice is rational *to the extent that* it is free, enlightened, and impartial. Each of these conditions sets up an ideal. No actual choice can ever be completely free, completely enlightened, or completely impartial. Hence no choice actually made among alternative ways of life can be fully rational. As I have already pointed out, the concept of a rational choice is the concept of an ideal. In describing it, I am trying to explicate one of the canons of rationality—to state what *would* be considered by anyone to be a rational choice, *if* such a choice were ever to occur under ideal conditions. I am not trying to describe any actual choice made by someone. All that is necessary for ultimately justifying a value judgment is that a *meaning* be given to the concept of rational choice that will make explicit the assumptions underlying the way a fully rational person would think in the given context. My claim here is that *to the extent that* any actual choice fulfills the conditions of rationality which I shall state, *to that extent* it justifies the way of life chosen and consequently can be used to justify a value judgment. I shall now specify the conditions of rationality under the three headings mentioned.

1. *Conditions of freedom.* A choice is free to the extent that:

(a) *The choice is not decisively determined by unconscious motives.* That is, if unconscious motives do have a role as psychological determinants of the person's choice, their role is not decisive. What *is* decisive will be given in the fourth condition of freedom, stated below under (d).

(b) *The choice is not at all determined by internal constraint.* That is, the person who makes the choice is under no element of compulsion, whether of irresistible impulse or extreme desire. He is calm and collected, in complete control of himself.

(c) *The choice is not at all determined by external constraint.* That is, there is nothing in the physical or social environment of the person to compel him to make a choice. So far as the physical environment is concerned, the person is not in any immediate physical danger and does not have to suffer any immediate physical harm when he makes his choice. (Some of the ways of life among which he is choosing, however, might entail more physical danger and suffering than others.) So far as the social environment is concerned, no social pressure is being brought to bear on him to choose one alternative rather than another. No one is goading him, threatening him, or trying to intimidate him. He is not under any form of coercion or duress.

(d) *The choice is decisively determined by the person's own preference.* That is, his choice follows upon his preference, though in order that his choice be rational *his preference must be enlightened and impartial* (as spelled out below). To say that a choice is free is not to say that it is uncaused or undetermined. It is rather to say that the choice is the result of, and hence determined by, the individual's making up his own mind about the matter. I do not call this process *deliberation*, however. Deliberation is evaluation, and all evaluation is made according to standards or rules. We are concerned here with a preference, not an evaluation. There are no standards or rules to appeal to, since we are dealing with a choice among whole ways of life and all standards and rules are included in these. If we were to appeal to a standard or rule, we would be presuppos-

ing a way of life in making the choice, and therefore our choice would not be a choice among ways of life.

2. *Conditions of enlightenment.* A choice is enlightened to the extent that:

(a) *The nature of each way of life is fully known.*

(b) *The probable effects of living each way of life are fully known.*

(c) *The means necessary to bring about each way of life* (i.e., what is required to enable a person to live each way of life) *are fully known.*

There are three kinds of knowledge involved in *each* of these conditions: intellectual knowledge, imaginative knowledge, and practical knowledge. Intellectual knowledge of a way of life includes all the empirical knowledge necessary for a complete and accurate *description* of the way of life itself, of the probable effects of living according to it, and of the necessary means for bringing it about. Such knowledge must provide us with answers to a whole series of questions. What is it like for a person (or group, or culture) to live the way of life? What are the ideals of the way of life; what vision of the *summum bonum* does it embody? What value systems are relevant to different sorts of situations and what value systems take precedence over others in those situations? What would be the psychological and social consequences of a person's (or group's, or culture's) living that way of life? What physical, social, and psychological conditions must be realized before a person (or group, or culture) would be able to live the way of life?

In addition to the knowledge that the empirical sciences must provide, intellectual knowledge of the *nature* of a way of life must also include philosophical knowledge. We must know the canons of reasoning that constitute the point of view to which any value system in the way of life belongs. What are the rules of relevance and the rules of valid inference which govern the justification of judgments, standards and rules within the framework of each value system? That is, according to what criteria is a reason a relevant reason or a good reason in such justification?

Intellectual knowledge of a way of life, in short, consists of all the scientific and philosophical knowledge that can possibly enlighten us concerning the value systems and the points of view which constitute it. A person does not make a rational choice among ways of life, however, if he merely has intellectual knowledge of them. Imaginative knowledge is also necessary. He must be able to *envisage* what it is like to live each way of life. He must be able, by imagination, to convey himself into each way of life and experience it vicariously. Short of actually having lived a way of life, there are four particularly effective means for developing this imaginative knowledge: through personal contact with people who live the way of life, through the reading of history, biography, and to a lesser extent anthropology and sociology, through the study of religion, and through appreciation of the fine arts.

When one has personal friends or acquaintances who live a certain way of life, or better, lives among people who follow it, one's imaginative insight into it is increased, even if one does not share that way of life with them. Constant contact with people makes us subtly aware of their interests, attitudes, points of view, and aspirations, so that we can sense intuitively the way they look upon the world. The closer we get to people and the better we come to know them, the deeper becomes our understanding of their way of life.

We can also increase our ability to envisage a way of life by reading the history of peoples who have embodied it in their culture, or by reading a biography of an individual whose life exemplifies it to a high degree. This is especially helpful when the historian or biographer is sympathetic to the way of life. If an individual's letters, essays, and speeches have been published,

reading these will also help to convey to us his way of life. Anthropological and sociological studies of whole cultures or of subcultural groups sometimes can be used to the same effect. Thus Margaret Mead's writings on Samoa can help us to imagine the Samoan way of life, and sociological studies of New York City's juvenile gangs can make us vividly aware of their way of life.

Each of the established religions of a society is itself a total way of life and a sensitive reading of its sacred texts and other scriptures will to some extent enable a person who does not practice it to imagine what it is like to practice it. The detailed investigations of scholars in comparative religion can also help a nonbeliever envisage what it is like to have a particular religion and to experience life from its point of view. Of course one can have *full* knowledge of a religion only if he himself practices it, that is actually lives the way of life which is the religion. This is what I have called "practical knowledge," and I shall consider it more fully below. My only claim here is that the sensitive reading of the literature of a religion can *aid* us in coming to an imaginative grasp of its meaning, even if we do not practice it or believe in it. It is necessary in addition to purely scientific and philosophical knowledge about the practices and beliefs of the religion if a rational preference for the religion over another way of life (or for another way of life over the religion) is to be made.

The critical analysis and appreciation of art has long been recognized as a way to deepen our understanding not only of an artist's personal outlook but also of the whole spirit of an age or the general world view of a culture. The music, the painting and sculpture, the dance, the architecture, the drama, and the literature of a culture all present to us the way of life of the culture. A thorough understanding of works of art in these various forms brings us to an imaginative awareness of a way of life which no scientific or philosophical knowledge, however complete, could yield. One of the most interesting aspects of a great novel, poem, or drama, for example, is the way its author creates a world in which certain fundamental attitudes, points of view, and ways of life are expressed. A novelist, poet, or dramatist does not necessarily attempt to persuade us to accept *his* world outlook or way of life. He confronts us with one, or sometimes several, for our imaginative contemplation. And his work often reflects the entire world view which underlies his social milieu and cultural background. Reading a novel or poem, watching a drama or ballet, listening to music, looking at painting, sculpture, and architecture all can give us a direct insight, an intuitive grasp, of a way of life. Thus we gain an envisagement of what it is like to live a way of life which we ourselves may never have lived.

The third kind of knowledge which we must have if our choice among ways of life is to be ideally enlightened is knowledge by acquaintance, or what I have designated "practical knowledge." A person has this kind of knowledge of a way of life when he actually has lived it. This means that he has been inspired by the ideals of the way of life and that he has adopted the appropriate value systems relevant to given situations. We recall that adopting a value system involves both reasoning in a certain way and living in a certain way. To have practical knowledge of a way of life is to know what it is like to live it because one has conducted his thinking and his behavior in accordance with the value systems of which it is comprised. In the case of a religion, one has practical knowledge of it when one has been a believer, has practiced it, has actively and sincerely participated in its form of worship. Although such knowledge by acquaintance can be one of the best means of enlightening ourselves about ways of life, it should be noted that a person who lives a way of life might not be able intellectually or imaginatively to

see it as a unified whole. He may be too involved in it to have the kind of detached understanding which can come from an outsider's intellectual or imaginative knowledge of it. A second limitation of practical knowledge is that we can come to know very few ways of life by means of it. One cannot just decide to "try out" a way of life as an experiment and live it for a few months or even a few years. A person must be educated in a certain way, and sometimes must receive special training, to come to the point where he can accept a way of life and commit himself wholly to it. It should further be noted that, at the time of the rational choice itself, the person who makes the choice must not be committed to any of the ways of life among which he is choosing. But this brings us to the third set of conditions for a rational choice.

3. *Conditions of impartiality.* A choice is impartial to the extent that:

(a) *The choice is disinterested.* That is, the choice is not at all determined by bribes, by exercise of favoritism, by desire to protect one's privileges (or those of one's family, friends, or class), or by any emotional prejudices on the part of the person who makes the choice. For example, if a person is influenced by anti-Semitism he cannot possibly make a rational choice between the way of life of Judaism and some other way of life. And this holds regardless of how much intellectual or imaginative knowledge he might possess of Judaism.

There is one condition that can *guarantee* the complete disinterestedness of the choice, and I therefore include it among the conditions of a rational choice. (It was suggested to me by Professor John Hospers.) We can eliminate entirely the element of self-interest in a choice by stipulating that the person who makes the choice *not* know what position he himself would have in any chosen way of life, if it were to be realized on earth. Like the souls in Book X of Plato's *Republic*, his future destiny would be *decided by lot.* Thus there would be no possibility that the person was influenced by desire for personal advantage or protection of special privileges in making his choice. For he would have no idea which way of life would be more in his self-interest to choose.

(b) *The choice is detached or objective.* By this I mean that it is a choice among ways of life other than that in which the person who makes the choice was brought up and other than that to which he is committed at the time of choice. The latter condition must be included for the obvious reason that we are asking a person to state his preference for one way of life over others. If he is already committed to a way of life and yet (under the second set of conditions) knows about other ways of life, his preference is set in advance. He will prefer his own way of life to the others. Such a person is not in a position to make a choice at all, to say nothing of a rational choice.

The first qualification, however, deserves to be examined at greater length. A rational choice among certain ways of life can be made only by those who were not brought up within the framework of any one of those ways of life. For it is impossible entirely to escape the influence of early childhood, when we were given rules to follow and standards to fulfill and all the pro-attitudes and con-attitudes that go with success or failure in doing this. Although, as we shall see when we come to the third condition of impartiality, a person need not be *biased* as a result of his being brought up in one way of life, he will always be under its influence. Consequently his choice among ways of life which include that one will never be truly impartial. In order to insure the maximum degree of impartiality, then, the following conditions of "detachment" or "objectivity" must hold. Let us assume that a person was brought up in a way of life, A, so that he is not qualified to make a rational choice between way of life A and way of life B, or between way of life A and way of life C. But (*if all other conditions of a rational choice are sa-*

tisfied) he is qualified to make a rational choice between B and C. Similarly, a person brought up in B cannot make a rational choice between A and B or between B and C, but he can between A and C. And one brought up in C can choose between A and B, but not between A and C or B and C. Now suppose all persons who were brought up in ways of life C, D, E, F, G . . . etc., were to make a rational choice between A and B, and suppose that they all preferred A to B. Then under the assumption that *in each case all the conditions of rationality were satisfied*, we may conclude that way of life A is more justified than way of life B. This judgment is strengthened to the extent that ways of life C, D, E, F, G, etc., are very different from one another and from both A and B. The judgment is strengthened even more if persons brought up in B, upon satisfying all the other conditions of a rational choice but this one, were to prefer A to B.

It might be objected that, no matter how free and enlightened the choice is, and no matter how disinterested are the persons making the choice, it is still not a truly impartial choice. For a person brought up in C will prefer A to B because A is more *similar* to C than is B. And the same for those brought up in D, E, F, G, etc. In each case A is more similar and B is less similar to the way of life in which the person was brought up, and for that reason the person always has a slight bias toward A and away from B. The influence of early childhood is ever-present and therefore impartiality is never attained. Indeed, it is unattainable. In order to face this objection, I set one additional condition of impartiality.

(c) *The choice is unbiased.* In order to minimize the impact of early childhood environment upon a rational choice, I stipulate not only that the person making the choice must not have been brought up in one of the ways of life among which he is choosing (the condition of detachment), but I also stipulate that the person was not *indoctrinated into* or *conditioned blindly* to accept the way of life in which he was brought up. To put it positively, a choice is unbiased to the extent that (i) the person's upbringing was nonauthoritarian, (ii) the person's education was liberal, and (iii) the person's experience of life up to the time of choice was of considerable variety, richness, and depth.

All children are brought up within the framework of some standards and rules. But there is a great difference between being conditioned to an unquestioning acceptance of standards and rules and being brought to see the reasons behind such standards and rules. When the standards are imposed and the rules laid down in an authoritarian manner by the parents, the child learns blind obedience and rigid conformity. When the parents impose standards and lay down rules in a nonauthoritarian manner (and they must impose *some* standards, lay down *some* rules, or else the child will have no guidance), the parents encourage the child to question the standards and rules and to ask that they be justified. The parents' answers will at first, of course, be given in a relatively simple way, for instance, in terms of the usefulness of the standards and rules in accomplishing this or that specific purpose. Nonauthoritarian parents will also try to develop in the child, as he grows older, an ability to make "decisions of principle," that is, to make up his own mind whether to follow a rule or standard or to make an exception to it in a given situation, or to decide to reject the rule or standard entirely. A nonauthoritarian upbringing enables a child as he grows older to justify his value judgments and his standards and rules, and finally to choose his own way of life (which may or may not be the same as that of his parents). As a mature person he will be able to change his way of life when social, economic, political, domestic and other conditions of his life demand such a change.

A similar contrast can be found in the difference between indoctrination and education. To be *educated within* the framework of a society's way of life is not necessarily to be *indoctrinated into* that way of life. Indoctrination is a deliberate manipulation of the mind of a child, an attempt to produce unquestioned belief in one way of life and a blind rejection of all others. Education, on the other hand, is a process of giving the child tools of criticism as well as of adjustment. As the child matures, his education becomes more liberal, presenting him with value systems and ways of life which are foreign to his own. At the same time his mind is trained to think critically about his own way of life, so that he is forced to make up his own mind about issues on which he finds he must take a stand, or about controversies on which he finds he must take sides. The society which not only permits, but encourages, its members to criticize its own foundations (value systems) is in no sense a society which indoctrinates its members.

Finally, we may contrast the life of a person who has been brought up in a uniform culture, where he meets only people who have the same outlook and opinions as he does and whose value systems are the same as his, where he remains in one occupation all his life, never travels either to foreign countries or to other areas of his native land, reads no books, remains protected from any great suffering, and never goes through any deeply emotional experiences—we may contrast such a life with that of a person who meets and gets to know people of varied backgrounds and from all walks of life, who travels widely, reads a great deal, and has a generally varied and rich experience of life. Although both of these persons are, in some very general sense, "children of their culture," the latter is much less a child of his culture than the former. In the same way, an educated person is much less a child of his culture than an indoctrinated person, and a person with a nonauthoritarian upbringing than one with an authoritarian upbringing.

To the extent that a person in these various ways is *not* a child of his culture, to that extent he is better able to make an impartial choice among ways of life which exclude the one he was brought up in. And to that extent he will not automatically prefer the way of life which is most similar to that of his childhood. Thus, although total absence of bias cannot be guaranteed, we can in this way minimize it.

These, then, are the conditions which define an ideal rational choice among ways of life. It is a choice which is totally free, totally enlightened, and totally impartial. No one is ever in a situation where he can actually make such a choice. We are never confronted with alternative ways of life under these ideal conditions. But that is not to the point. The real question is this. What *would* make a reason for committing ourselves to a way of life a *good* reason? My answer, in sum, is that such a reason is to be found in the situation I have described—where we find that more and more people brought up in a variety of ways of life tend more and more to prefer one particular way of life to all others, when their preference results from a free, enlightened, and impartial choice. What better reason *could* there be for committing ourselves to a way of life?

I have tried only to show that it makes sense to talk about a rational choice among ways of life, and that therefore the relativist's position is not tenable. In justifying our value systems we can go beyond vindicating them in terms of a way of life. We can ask that the way of life itself be justified. It will always be impossible *in practice* to know with certainty which way of life is more justified than any other, since the conditions of an ideal rational choice are such that it is difficult even to approximate them. But it is *theoretically* possible to do so, and therefore *meaningful* to speak of a rationally chosen way of life. Although we can never be certain whether one way of life is rationally preferable to another, we can reach a probable knowledge of this in the following way. We can say that, to the extent that choices become more and more rational and to the extent that more

and more people who make such choices tend to prefer a way of life A to a way of life B, then *to that extent it is reasonable for anyone to accept A as preferable to B.* Such acceptance must remain tentative only. It must be open to revision in the light of further choices under conditions which more closely approximate those of an ideal rational choice. But it provides the best *available* way of knowing whether A really is preferable to B.

It might be objected that no such agreement could ever be reached, even if all the conditions of a rational choice were fully realized. For it is always possible that variations in temperament among people will result in variations in their preference for ways of life. Thus even choices made under ideal conditions of rationality will be subject to the disagreements among romanticists and classicists, doers and thinkers, rationalists and mystics, dogmatists and skeptics, optimists and pessimists, conservatives and radicals, seekers of happiness and doers of duty. This possibility must be admitted, but it does not destroy the concept of a rational choice as such. It merely leaves open the question—which would have to be left open even without this consideration—whether increase in rationality of choice leads to agreement among the choosers. All that we can say is that, *if* under the conditions of a rational choice there was a tendency among choosers to agree that way of life A is preferable to way of life B (whether or not the choosers were of the same temperament), then we would have just that much reason to conclude that A is more justified than B. That such a tendency would be made manifest as ideal conditions of rational choice were more and more closely approximated must remain an open question.

D. WHY BE RATIONAL?

There is one difficulty involved in this attempt to define a rational choice among ways of life which, if not satisfactorily met, undercuts the entire project. Have I not imposed my own way of life upon the concept of a rationally preferable way of life by stipulating just these conditions of rationality and not others? In other words, am I not begging the question by giving conditions for a rational choice which are themselves part of a way of life? Am I not merely presupposing a way of life and working within its framework, rather than taking a standpoint outside all ways of life? And in that case how do I know that the way of life I am presupposing is itself preferable to all others? Until I have shown that it is so, I cannot claim that the conditions which I specify for a rational choice really do justify one way of life rather than another. On the other hand, if I try to establish the preferability of this presupposed way of life by appeal to a rational choice, I am arguing in a circle, for the conditions of a rational choice are part of that way of life itself.

My answer is to deny that the conditions of a rational choice are part of a way of life. For they are the conditions which I presume *anyone*, in *any* way of life, would accept as defining a rational choice, in the ordinary sense of the word "rational." If people on reflection would not be willing to accept these conditions, I would not say they were making a mistake. Nor would I continue to impose my conditions upon them. I would ask them what conditions *they* would give for defining a rational choice. If they offered some which I had not thought of and which did seem (to me and to them) to elucidate further our ordinary meaning of being rational in making choices, then these new conditions would go into the definition. Would they not then be imposing *their* way of life upon the concept of rational choice? The answer is no, because the concept of a rational choice is independent of all ways of life. Even if two persons were committed to very different ways of life, both would have to admit that, *if* a rational choice *were* to be made between their two ways of life, it would have to be a free, enlightened, and impar-

tial choice. Or else it would have to be a choice under other conditions which better elucidate what a rational choice means.

But whatever the conditions, they cannot change when the way of life being judged changes. This follows from the very meaning of the word "rational." If the choice is to be a rational one, it must at least have properties of rationality which do not vary with the ways of life among which the choice is being made. Thus it must always be possible for a person to admit that a rational choice was made and yet another way of life was preferred to his own. To test the preferability of one's own way of life by the method of rational choice always presupposes the possibility that the test will turn out negative. For otherwise it is no test at all. One would have set up the conditions of a "rational choice" (the test conditions) in such a way that one's own way of life would always come out on top. To vary the conditions so that they always bring about this result is a sign that the choice is *not* rational. For it is an essential part of the meaning of rationality that its conditions not vary with what is being judged.

In specifying the conditions of a rational choice, then, no particular way of life is involved. All that is involved is an attempt to make explicit the idea which we all have (no matter what may be our way of life) when we reflect about what an ideally rational choice among ways of life would be. I have spelled out what I think it would be. It is for others to challenge my account and to improve upon it. The conditions I have specified are, I think, an accurate explication of the meaning of the word "rational" in this context. Consequently I believe that any person would have to admit that this is what a rational choice consists in, even if making such a choice would result in other ways of life being preferred to his own.

Furthermore, if my explication of rational choice is correct, then any person would have to agree with it, even though his own way of life denied freedom of choice to people, prevented enlightened choices from being made, and did not develop impartiality in people. It does not follow, however, that his way of life would never be preferred to others when a rational choice among them was made. We do not know what actual ways of life would be preferred when rational choices were made, and *there is no necessity that the preferred ways of life have the same characteristics as the rational choice itself.* The concept of a rational choice is not logically connected with the *content* of any particular way of life. I am not imposing the content of my own way of life upon others when I explicate the conditions of rationality in terms of freedom, enlightenment, and impartiality. If one should ask me, "Why ought I to accept your conditions of rationality?", my answer would be, "They are not *my* conditions of rationality, but yours too. Is this not what *you* would mean by an ideally rational choice?" If the reply is negative, then the way is open for further explication of a rational ideal common to both of us, with both of us trying to make our explication correct.

Perhaps behind the foregoing objection is a deeper (but more confused) one. Suppose a person grants that, as far as he is concerned, my explication of a rational choice is correct. He admits that I have shown what being ideally rational means in the context of choosing among ways of life. But he then raises the following objection. "Let us assume way of life A is rationally preferred to way of life B, that is, A is rationally chosen—in the sense you have specified—over B. Why does it follow that I should live according to A rather than B? I grant that A is rationally *preferred* to B. But why is the way of life which *is* preferred the way of life which *ought to be* preferred? Do not answer that it is because the preference is based on a rational choice. I already know it is based on a rational choice. I am asking why I ought to follow a rational choice. My question concerns the claim that a rational choice has

upon me. Why ought I to live the way of life that is rationally chosen? To put it all in a nutshell, why be rational?"

This is a huge muddle. The confusion becomes apparent when we ask ourselves what sort of answer the person wants. What reply could possibly satisfy him? I shall try to disentangle this confusion by discussing four points:

1. The distinction between (a) giving a correct explication of a rational choice among ways of life and (b) giving reasons for trying to be rational in explicating a rational choice.

2. The distinction between (a) and (b) on the one hand, and, on the other, (c) giving reasons for the validity of the argument that "A ought to be preferred to B" follows from "A is preferred to B on the basis of a rational choice."

3. The distinction between (c) and (d) giving reasons for the validity of the argument that "One ought to live according to way of life A" follows from "Way of life A is rationally chosen over all others."

4. The distinction between (c) and (d) on the one hand, and, on the other, (e) giving reasons for committing oneself to try to discover which way of life is rationally chosen over all others.

1. If someone asks why he *should* live the way of life that is rationally chosen, one possible reply is that the question is beside the point. In defining (explicating) the conditions of a rational choice I am not trying to argue that people ought to live the rationally chosen way of life. I am only trying to state what a rational choice *means*, regardless of whether or not people actually want to live a rationally chosen way of life. I am not saying they ought to want to do this. If people do want to live according to the most justified way of life, they must first know which way of life is most justified. In my explication of a rational choice I am trying to state how we find out what that way of life is. My explication will be of little interest to those who do not want to discover the most justified

way of life. But if my explication is a correct explication, it will be of help to those who have such an aim. The aim is to find out how to discover what it means to live rationally, that is, according to the most justified way of life. But in carrying out my explication I am not imposing this aim or this further purpose upon anyone. Nor am I claiming that anyone ought to have such an aim or purpose. So the question "Why be rational?" is simply irrelevant to the attempt to explicate the method for finding the most justified way of life.

But this reply might not satisfy the objector. He might make the following rejoinder. "My question 'Why be rational?' is not entirely irrelevant, for I can ask it about your explication itself. If you are trying to give a rational account of the method for finding the most justified way of life, as you say you are, then what reasons are there for accepting your account? Suppose I do not accept it. You may claim that in that case I would not be rational. But why be rational here?"

There is a confusion in this rejoinder which stems from a failure to distinguish between the demand for reasons for preferring a way of life and the demand for reasons for accepting an account of such reasons. The first demand is expressed in the question: (a) What are good reasons for preferring one way of life to another? The answer to this question lies in the attempt to *explicate* what it means to be ideally rational in preferring one way of life to another. Let us suppose an answer is offered, such as the answer I have proposed in the concept of a rational choice. Then the second question is asked: (b) Why should the canons of reasoning governing this answer be accepted? Let us see how this question arises.

It may be that the concept of a rational choice as I have defined it does not provide a correct or accurate explication of justifying a way of life. I may have failed in my attempt to answer question (a) and I am perfectly willing to be criticized on

that account. But any such criticism must itself be governed by the canons of reasoning that govern correct explication. The person who makes the criticism is seeking a correct explication and therefore must accept the canons of reasoning which define the philosophical point of view (as distinct from the scientific, the mathematical, and the various normative points of view). *Within* that point of view he may carry on arguments concerning the acceptability of answers to question (a). But the question "Why be rational?" does not arise within such a rational framework.

How, then, does it arise? The questioner may explain that he means as follows: "When I ask 'Why be rational?' I am demanding reasons for anyone's placing himself within a rational framework, like that of the philosophical point of view. I am not asking for reasons within a rational framework. I am outside a point of view and am asking why I should take the point of view and so have my thinking governed by its canons of reasoning. 'Why be rational?' means 'Why take the philosophical point of view (or any point of view, for that matter)?'"

Here the questioner wants to be given reasons for accepting the canons of reasoning which govern a proposed explication. These are the canons of the philosophical point of view. What sort of reasons could we give? I submit that only one sort of reason can be given: *If* we want to live the most justified way of life, or *if* we want to answer question (a), then taking the philosophical point of view is indispensable. If a person did not care to live the most justified way of life, or if he were not interested in trying to find out what that way of life is, or if he did not want a valid procedure for finding out what that way of life is, then it would be pointless (in the present context) to take the philosophical point of view. Taking that point of view is a necessary means to the three ends just mentioned. Unless a person takes that point of view he cannot achieve any of them. But if he does not seek them, no reasons can be given for his taking the point of view. We cannot argue that he *ought* to seek those ends without assuming the canons of reasoning of some point of view which the objector is also willing to assume. Since he has stated his unwillingness to be placed within any point of view, no argument can be given that will make a claim to his assent. In short, if his question "Why be rational?" is a demand for reasons for taking *any* point of view, then it is logically impossible to answer his question. In order to answer the question "Why?" we must give reasons, and giving reasons is a process of thought governed by canons of reasoning that define some point of view. Since no such canons are accepted, no reasons can be given.

Further reflection on this situation makes us doubtful about just what the difficulty is. If it is logically impossible to give an answer to a question, is there actually any question to be answered? In the present case an answer to the question is logically impossible because the questioner has deliberately refused to accept the conditions required for giving an answer. It is the questioner himself who has made his question unanswerable. It is hardly surprising, then, to discover that we cannot give any answer that will satisfy him. Indeed, must we not conclude that no genuine question is being asked? For the words "Why be rational?" can have meaning only if reasons can be given for being rational. But no such reasons are allowed under the conditions set by the questioner. Thus in asking the question he is demanding reasons and at the same time making it impossible to satisfy the demand. The conclusion we are forced to draw is that he does not know what he is saying. He is merely pronouncing words in an interrogative form outside of any possible context for their use.

On the other hand, suppose the questioner does want to live the most justified way of life, or wants to find out what such a life would be. In these circumstances he has very good reasons for taking the philosophical point of view. For only by doing so will he be able to discover which way of life (if any) is the most justified. We might call this a pragmatic justification (vindication) of the philosophical point of view, although this must not be confused with vindicating value systems which belong to normative points of view.

2. But perhaps the foregoing discussion has missed the principal point of the objection. What is being objected to is our saying that a person *ought* to prefer a way of life because it has been shown to be rationally chosen over other ways of life. Would we not be falling into the naturalistic fallacy? (A full account of the naturalistic fallacy will be given in Chapter 9.) From the fact that people rationally prefer one way of life to another we infer that we ought to prefer it. Is this not going from "is" to "ought"? We might reply that if a person does not prefer what is rationally preferred, he is not rational. The question then pops up, "Why be rational?" Here the challenge means, "Why ought one to prefer a way of life which, under conditions of a rational choice, actually is preferred over other ways of life?"

A reply would have to provide good reasons for going from "A is rationally preferred to B" to "A ought to be preferred to B." Is there not a fallacy in this inference? I do not think so, for the following reason. When we say that A is rationally preferred to B, we mean that whenever the conditions of a rational choice hold, A is preferred to B. Let us assume that the conditions as I have specified them do correctly explicate the justification of a way of life (and this assumption is not now in question). Then it would follow that A is more justified than B. This means that there are better reasons for choosing A than for choosing B. If a person, knowing this, were still to prefer B to A, his preference would be a paradigm of an irrational choice. The person might want to persist in his choice nevertheless, claiming that he honestly does prefer B to A. There is no logical error in his doing this, so long as he does not claim that he has good reasons, or is being rational, in doing it. He is saying in effect that he does not care to be rational about this matter. But then he must not ask "Why be rational?" For as soon as he asks "Why?" he is demanding reasons and thus presupposing rationality. To ask such a question is to speak as if only a rational answer will be acceptable. But in the present situation he already knows what a rational preference is (namely, the preference of A over B) and that his own preference runs counter to the rational one. What more does he need to know? Again his question appears to be outside any contexts for its possible use.

3. We may further distinguish between the question (c) "What are good reasons for going from 'A is rationally preferred to B' to 'A ought to be preferred to B'?" and a very similar question (d) "What are good reasons for going from 'A is rationally preferred to all other ways of life' to 'Everyone ought to live in accordance with A'?" Question (d) is, I think, the basic question that is in the back of many people's minds when they ask "Why be rational?" In asking this they want to know why anyone ought to do what he already knows to be rationally justified. Why should one's action be motivated by one's knowledge of the good? I shall now try to show that this is an empty question.

To say that someone already knows that an act, X, is rationally justified is to say that he knows there are good reasons for doing X. Thus he already has good reasons for doing X. Why, then, should he ask for such reasons? He might say that he knows X is the rational thing to do but he wants to know why he ought to do the rational thing. He wants to know, in other words, by what rule of logic we can go from "X is the rational thing to do" to "X ought to be done." The answer is that both statements mean the same thing, namely that there are good reasons for doing X. As I shall point out in Part II, the word "ought" is here being used prescriptively, and this contextually implies that there are good reasons for doing the act prescribed. To prescribe act X by saying "X ought to be done" is contextually to imply that there are good reasons for doing X. Now if a person wants to know why he ought to do X, he is asking for good reasons for doing X. But in the case at hand he acknowledges that he has good reasons for doing X. Hence his question is empty. It can only be "answered" by uttering a tautology: "There are good reasons for doing an act which you have good reasons for doing." Or: "It is rational to do what is rationally justified." Or: "It is rational to be rational."

The same considerations apply if we demand good reasons for living a way of life which is acknowledged to be rationally justified. If a person knows that a way of life is rationally chosen and is therefore as justified as it can be, then he knows why he ought to live it. Indeed, he already has the very best reasons for living it. This renders the demand for good reasons otiose. No further reasons can be given for him to live the way of life, since *ex hypothesi* he already has the best reasons for living it. But then he does not *need* any further reasons.

4. It was mentioned under point 1 that when a person *wants* to know how a way of life can be justified, he must assume that taking a rational point of view toward the problem is itself justified. Canons of reasoning (in this case canons of philosophical reasoning) must be accepted in any attempt to solve the problem. So if he seeks an answer to his problem, he cannot demand reasons for taking the philosophical point of view. He cannot ask "Why be rational?" since he already presupposes the justification of being rational in seeking an answer to his problem. Now he might seek an answer to his problem purely from intellectual curiosity. He might not be interested in justifying his own way of life. He might simply want to know whether anyone's way of life can be justified and if so,

how. It would then be perfectly consistent for him to find out how a way of life can be justified and then not try to justify his own nor try to live in accordance with a justified one.

Suppose, on the other hand, that a person wants to know how a way of life can be justified in order to discover whether his own is justified and in order to live in accordance with a justified one. And let us suppose that such a person, on learning of the method of rational choice, accepts it as a correct explication of how a way of life can be justified. Then suppose he asks "Why ought I to try to live in accordance with the rationally chosen way of life?" We must now be puzzled about what his question can mean. Can he be serious in asking it? For he is already committed to trying to live in accordance with a justified way of life. And his question cannot mean "What makes a way of life justified?", since he accepts the concept of a rational choice as providing a correct answer to this. His question is rather, "Granted that a rationally chosen way of life is a justified one, why ought I to try to live in accordance with it?" But if he is interested in finding out how a way of life can be justified in order to live in accordance with a justified one, then he knows he is committed to living a rationally chosen one, since this makes it justified. Hence he cannot be serious in demanding reasons for living such a way of life. He is already trying to do so.

The person might then make the following move, in explaining his question. He might say, "It is true that I am already committed to living a rationally chosen way of life because I want to live in accordance with a justified one. But it seems to me that my commitment is without reason. I am asking if there are any reasons for committing myself in the way that I have. It is true that I am now trying to live rationally, but I want to know what reasons can be given for my (or anyone's) decision to try to live rationally."

This question is quite different from the one discussed under point 1. For the person is not demanding reasons for taking the philosophical point of view. He already knows that taking this point of view is necessary if he is to find out how a way of life can be justified and so find out which way of life to try to live in accordance with. His question is rather about his end of trying to live in accordance with a justified way of life. He wants to know if any reasons can be given for seeking such an end. Moreover, his question is not the question discussed under point 3. He is not asking why he should live a rationally chosen way of life. He knows why—because it is rationally chosen. He sees that this is an empty demand, since he acknowledges that a person who knows that his way of life is rationally chosen already has all the reasons he can possibly have for living that way of life. The question he is concerned with is not why a person should live a justified way of life, but why a person should try to find out what way of life is justified in the first place, and why he should seek a justified way of life in order to try to live in accordance with it. In other words, why not simply disregard the problem, or seek some other end?

How can such a question be answered? It would seem that if a person did not care about finding a rational way of life or did not want to try to live in accordance with one, nothing could be said to show that he was unjustified in his attitudes. It would seem that no reasons could be given *against* his lack of commitment to seeking a rational way of life, and also that no reasons could be given *for* such a commitment. Either a person cares about such things or he does not, and that is all there is to be said on the matter.

Yet something more can be said. In the first place, we can point out that a person who is not interested in finding a rational way of life or in trying to live in accordance with it cannot give reasons *for* his lack of commitment (or for his commitment to other ends). Nor can he give reasons *against* the commitment of a man who does want to find out which way of life is most justified and who does care about living in accordance with it. In the second place, it is possible to interpret the question, "Why try to find a rational way of life, and why have the purpose of trying to live in accordance with it?" as a way of asking to be *convinced* or *persuaded* that one is right in making these commitments. Like the person who asks "Why be moral?" and wants as an answer to be inspired to fulfill moral standards and to follow moral rules (i.e., to adopt a moral value system), the questioner here wants to be moved to be more deeply committed to his basic goals. He wants to have his attitudes strengthened, to be encouraged, to be given support in his endeavors. Can such a demand be satisfied? I think there are two general methods which can be used. We might try to convince him intellectually or we might try to persuade him emotionally. It must be understood that the first method is not a matter of proof. We cannot give reasons from which it follows that a person is right in being committed to seeking a rational way of life. We can, however, ask him to review his commitment in light of alternative commitments. We can ask him to think what a justified way of life is—that it is the way of life which a person would have the best reasons for living. If he says he already knows this (as we acknowledge that he does), we can only invite him to think about it more deeply, to pay more attention to what it is he is seeking when he seeks a rational way of life, and to be fully aware of what it means not to care about seeking a rational way of life. Finally, however, we must leave it up to him. He must *choose* whether to seek a rational way of life or not. He makes no logical error in choosing not to seek it, but if he chooses not to, he must not expect to find a way of life which he can justify when it is challenged. If, on the other hand, he does want to find that way of life which can best be defended rationally against attack, then in the very fact

that he wants to do this lies his commitment. He has made his choice, for to try to find such a way of life is already to seek the end he now wishes to be encouraged to seek.

This is about all we can do in an intellectual way to answer his question. What can we do in the way of emotional appeals? In order to persuade the person emotionally that he is right in seeking his end we must use techniques (such as praise, rewards, pointing at inspiring examples, and so on) which would be effective in strengthening his motivation to seek the end. This is not, strictly speaking, to *answer* his question. But it is to respond to his question in such a way (if we are successful) as to satisfy him. The outcome of this process is that he no longer asks the question. And this is not because we have silenced him. Our procedure does not involve preventing him from *uttering* a question that is still in his mind. Rather, we put to rest the inner doubt. He no longer asks the question *to himself*. He has come to have a strong, stable disposition to try to find a rational way of life in order to live in accordance with it. He no longer demands that he be justified in having this disposition.

This completes my account of the justification of value judgments. Throughout the discussion I have taken the philosophical point of view and so committed myself to approaching the question as rationally as I could. But this commitment to rationality was not my *ultimate commitment*, for one can always give reasons for taking the philosophical point of view. These reasons would constitute a pragmatic justification (vindication) of taking that point of view. They would point out that it is a necessary means to a certain end we have chosen. If our end is to learn as much as we can about what it means to be rational in justifying value judgments, then taking the philosophical point of view is indispensable for achieving our end. The *ultimate* commitment is our deciding to seek this end.

Throughout my discussion of the justification of value judgments, I have assumed that the reader shares with me not only this commitment, but also the acceptance of the philosophical point of view which such a commitment requires. Within the framework set by the canons of reasoning of that point of view, the reader may wish to criticize what I have to say about the justification of value judgments. But he cannot criticize me for taking that point of view on the grounds that when I state what it is to be rational in justifying value judgments I am assuming canons of rationality and therefore arguing in a circle. For the canons of the philosophical point of view only govern the correctness of an *explication* of the rules of reasoning used in justifying value judgments. Those canons are not themselves *used* in justifying value judgments. (The canons of normative points of view, however, are so used.) My explication of the justification of value judgments may well be incorrect at many points and I am open to criticism on that account. But whatever criticism is made, it must be made from within the framework of the philosophical point of view. And the one who offers such criticism is ultimately committed to the same ideal as that to which I am committed—to learn as much as possible about what it means to be rational in justifying value judgments.

We must distinguish this philosophical ideal from the practical ideal of actually trying to live a rational life. The philosophical ideal requires only that we be rational in our intellectual inquiry into what it means to live a rational life (including what it means to be rational in the justification of our value judgments). The practical ideal requires that we be rational in all of life. The philosophical ideal is to find out *whether* value judgments can be justified and, if so, *how*. The practical ideal is to find out *which* value judgments are justified and to live in accordance with them. This means trying to fulfill the standards and follow the rules that verify our value judgments and that constitute the value systems of a rationally chosen way of life. Is the commitment to live this way of life an ultimate commitment? Yes, if we mean by "ultimate" that no further justificatory reasons can be given for making the commitment.

Someone might now triumphantly conclude, "You see, it is all *ultimately* absurd. We finally come to the point where we must commit ourselves without reason. Push reason far enough and you will arrive at unreason. All our ultimate commitments, being ultimate, are arbitrary. Thus we might as well toss a coin to decide whether to live a rational or a nonrational way of life. In the end they are equally nonrational. No reasons can be given for deciding in favor of a rational life rather than a nonrational life. It is impossible to answer the question 'Why not live a nonrational life?' So both rational and nonrational ways of life are on an equal footing. The choice between them is arbitrary, unfounded, and absurd."

The reply to this objection should now be obvious. It is the very reply I have made (under point 3 above) to the person who demands that reasons be given for living a rational life. No reasons *can* be given, it is true. But no reasons *need* be given. For knowing that a certain way of life is rational is knowing that one is wholly justified in committing oneself to it. To know that it is rational is already to have all the reasons one could possibly have for living it. As Mr. Hare pointed out in a passage I have quoted, the decision to commit oneself to a way of life which is rationally chosen over other ways of life (each of which must be fully known for the choice to be enlightened and hence rational) is the most reasonable, least arbitrary, and best founded decision of all. It is the decision to live the way of life one is most justified in living, all things considered.

Aren't Moral Judgments "Factual"?

MARTIN E. LEAN

In this paper I am concerned with the question of how moral terms and judgments may be regarded in terms of the notions of factual matter or judgment, value matter or judgment, objective, subjective, and other such kindred terms and notions. What I have done is to see how strong a case I can make for holding, in the face of some of the well-known argumentative moves for the contrary view, that moral terms are genuine factual predicates and moral judgments are factual in character. This task I first set for myself some ten years ago when, as my contribution to a program at Columbia University memorializing G. E. Moore (under whom I had been privileged to study there some years before) I elected to see what could be made of his position about this. His position—to which he steadfastly adhered despite the most cogent and persuasive arguments of the relativists, logical positivists, linguistic analysts and emotivists—was, it will be recalled, precisely that moral judgments are factual and that moral disagreements between people can and do involve moral judgments that stand to each other in the relation of genuine logical contradiction.

It was not a position with which I then agreed, and it would have been easier and more comfortable to have flourished a new cadenza on the more fashionable tune of the time, to play picador to, e.g., Prof. C. L.

Reprinted from *The Personalist,* Vol. 51.

A shorter version of this paper was presented at a philosophical meeting held at Columbia University in 1959 in commemoration of G. E. Moore.

Stevenson's matador, than to essay the role of champion in behalf of a position so obviously déclassé. But Moore was dead and the vividness of his courageously steadfast honesty and carefulness was especially large before me, and indeed before all who had known him and were gathering to honor his memory. And so I dared to raise a lance and try a round in behalf of an unpopular cause.

Now Moore himself, it will be remembered, did very little more than to assert the thesis that moral judgments are factual, and to reiterate it insistently. It did not to him, apparently, seem to need argument. His main concern was to descry and decry what he named the naturalistic fallacy, and to argue the indefinability, unanalysability and logical simplicity of the quality "good." I am not here primarily concerned with these issues. My concern rather is with what case can be made for the view that moral judgments are factual. The fact is that what began for me as no more than a dedicated exercise became a posture of conviction. The more I sought to see what moves could be made to and from Moore's position, my realization grew that he had a game with vastly more potential than I had previously been in the frame of mind to appreciate. I had been persuaded by the fashion of the times, by arguments more in the nature of lawyers' briefs than of accurate and justly weighed presentations of the facts and issues pro and con, and perhaps by psychological considerations too messy and irrelevant to be dredged here.

What I have produced is, I dare say, but another lawyer's brief, arguing the other side. I trust that it will be understood that I do not claim it is the way Moore would have argued it. Indeed I have reason to believe that he would have either rejected or eschewed or at least have been extremely dubious about some of my arguments. But two things perhaps may be said for what I have done. First it is not a mere reiteration of the old thesis but an argument; and an argument that does not appeal to the old-fashioned gambits of question-begging intuition, divine revelation, or the like. Rather it attempts, successfully or not, to make the thesis respectable in contemporary terms. And the second thing that may be said for doing what I have done is this. As Aristotle reminded Nichomachus, his son, in advising him about aiming at the Golden Mean, the carpenter in straightening the warped board exerts pressure oppositely, to the other extreme, in seeking to bring the board to true. So I, in wrestling with the warp which seems to me now to be clearly present in the currently fashionable and uncritically received view about moral judgments, have exerted pressure to the opposite extreme. Perhaps your opposing pressure now to my argument will contribute to our getting the matter straight and true.

I

It has become the dominant and prevailing view in meta-ethics that moral terms are not really factual predicates, and that moral judgments are not factual. This is the view, more or less, of Thrasymachus in the *Republic* and of the Sophist Protagoras, for example, in ancient times; of David Hume in more modern times; and it is plainly the argument of the ethical relativists from Edward Westermarck on, and of their more fashionable contemporary cousins: the logical positivists, the linguistic analysts and the persuasive-emotivists. Moral expressions and judgments, however sophisticated, and however disguised they may be by their occurrence in the grammatically indicative mood, are nonetheless of the logical and ontological status of primitive tribal taboos. They are inter-culturally relative, and intra-culturally evaluative and attitudinal, hortatory and imperative, emotive and exclamatory, subjective in their application and in no sense factual. Whatever is irreducibly factual about moral evaluations, over and above the plain fact that people make them, resides in or consists of the extraneous other-than-moral factual features of the situations in which or about which the moral evaluations are made.

The argument for this general view seems to rest mainly on two premises: First, that individuals and indeed whole societies can and to a considerable extent do disagree and even differ radically in their moral assessments; and second, that there is no operational definition or specifiable criterion of application for moral terms, and hence no effective rational procedure for settling disagreements or differences in their use.

In this paper I want to examine each of these two premises for truth and relevance. What is the extent and nature of moral disagreement and difference?

Does such disagreement and difference, so far as it does exist, unambiguously and necessarily imply either relativism or emotivism? Is there no rational technique for resolving or explaining such disagreements and differences? Is it essential to a term's being deemed a factual predicate that there be precise, specifiably discernible criteria for its application? Is it essential to a judgment's being deemed factual that there be an effective rational decision procedure for resolving disagreement and establishing truth?

Now, to begin with, it can hardly be maintained that there is not widespread disagreement and difference in moral evaluations, or that, on the other hand, there are definitional criteria for moral terms and decision methods for moral judgments. But this being granted, we are also obliged to acknowledge that there is likewise an appreciable amount of agreement among people in their moral evaluations, that people do learn to use moral terms with recognizable consistency, and that there are rational moves by which people argue their moral evaluations. And if this also be granted (as I think it must) then I can set the theme of my argument by pointing to these two sets of facts. For it seems to me logically obvious that if the former set of facts constitutes an argument (however inconclusive) *against* the thesis that moral terms are proper factual predicates and that moral judgments are factual, then by the same token the latter set of facts should constitute at least a *prima facie* argument *for* that thesis. So is the battle joined. Those who would maintain the thesis that moral judgments are factual must account for the facts of moral disagreement and divergence; and they must also take account of the lack—nay, more, the seeming impossibility—of effective definition and decision criteria. Those who would deny the thesis, on the other hand, must account in some other way for the amount and kind of agreement, and the reconciliation techniques, that do exist.

It seems to be a feature of the historical dialectic of the problem that relatively little has been done with the latter obligation in recent years, even by—what shall we call them?—the absolutists or objectivists, whose cause it would serve. The best that the latter seem to have been able to muster, in answering the case of the relativists or emotivists and pressing their own, have been metaphysically and logically dubious appeals to theological revelation, or seemingly question-begging intuition, or (though I would say that this is not wholly irrelevant) some form of "naturalism."

I propose therefore to begin with a consideration of the fact of widespread agreement in moral judgment, rather than of disagreement (which I shall come to later).

There are two obvious ways in which the fact of widespread agreement among people in their particular moral assessments might be accounted for. One explanation is that the moral terms are genuine factual predicates, and that moral judgments are thereby factual in a relevant and significant respect. The other is that our moral terms are predicates in a merely grammatical respect, pseudo-predicates ontologically, but our judgments nonetheless coincide because we learn them rote-fashion, from childhood on, as a sort of moral catechism—just as the members of a primitive tribe learn the rituals and taboos, and thereafter heed and chant them in unison, and react with emotion whenever and to whatever they are applied.

Now it seems to me patent that the complexity of the phenomena of moral judgment discourse simply cannot be accounted for on this latter view. I do not deny, of course, that there is this process of societal inculcation of moral concern in its members. Nor do I deny that particular precepts may be and often are taught in uncritical rote fashion, commonly in a religious context, and that the whole may acquire for us complex affective associations of the most varied sort. What I challenge is only that this account is adequate to all the facts. But before turning to this, I want to consider for a moment the logical relevance of the whole account in terms of rote-learning to the issue of whether or not moral judgments are factual.

It is surprising how readily philosophers fall into the trap of supposing that the "tribal taboo" account of moral agreement implies (or entitles one to say) that moral judgments are not factual. Let us suppose (what is surely not the case either, for that matter) that all the particular taboos in a given set have no other property in common, are bound together by no other principle than that they have been singled out and called "taboo" by the tribal priests. So that to say that a particular form of behavior is "taboo" would be to say nothing more than that it is one of the proscribed forms of behavior on this arbitrary list. The term "taboo" would then function somewhat as do proper names, which designate or denote particulars without describing or characterizing them—except in certain derivative and incidental ways. (E.g., in terms of acquired emotional associations, or in terms of developing convention, or the like—as the proper name "Mary" is a female's name, or as we all seem to be able to understand what it means to say of a political leader that "He's no Winston Churchill," or "He's a veritable Hitler.")

The point is this. Surely the mere fact that an arbitrarily and whimsically selected set of particulars has arbitrarily been designated by an otherwise meaningless sound or mark in no way negates that anyone who grasps and accepts the arbitrary convention, and subsequently identifies the particular or set by this term, thereby makes a *factual* judgment—and if the identification be correct, then a *true* judgment. (I am not prepared to go all the way with those linguistic philosophers who have said that knowing what something is is simply knowing its correct name. But I think it is undeniable that the converse—so far as it goes, which is admittedly not very far—is certainly true.)

Thus, even if moral judgments were no more than taboo-identifications, or proper-name identifications, they would still be factual. "That is Tom Jones" is a factual judgment and is either true or false. It could even be a *true* judgment if Tom were an illegitimate foundling child, having neither biological nor adoptive relationship to any family named Jones, and had been assigned this name quite arbitrarily. Moreover, to say "That is Tom Jones" is not to make the still more trivial statement "If that is the person I think it is, then it is (i.e., his name is) Tom Jones" (a statement, that is, which ventures no more than

a memory-claim judgment about a proper name). To say "That is Tom Jones" is surely to claim at least both that the individual is the one that the speaker takes him to be, and that that is his name. Similarly, to say that "Taking the tribal god's name in vain is taboo" is to express a relatively complex factual judgment which is either true or false, regardless of the origin of this particular taboo for the particular tribe, and regardless of the origin or the word-concept "taboo." And to say of a specific action in a specific instance that "In doing that he violated the taboo," would be to make a factual judgment of a still more complex type.

By the same token, even if the "tribal-taboo" or "catechism" account of moral judgments were the whole story, this would not deprive them of their rightful classification as factual judgments, judgments which not only may call for the responses "I agree," or "I disagree," but which also properly take the semantic adjectives "true" and "false." Thus, the statements "Wanton killing is wrong" and "It was wrong to kill him when he was plainly surrendering" clearly express factual judgments. They are either false or (as I submit all of us who have learned to use moral terms and sentences recognize in this instance) *true.* To be sure, some really interesting and very difficult questions remain: What more, if anything (other than that it is a moral fact) can we say about the nature of the fact that we are recognizing when we correctly judge and identify something as being wrong, or, as the case may be, right? How, if at all, can the word-concepts in which we make our moral judgments be analysed—and if they cannot be, why not? What social or other empirical factors generate and affect our moral discernments?

But wherever these quests might lead us, it is a sheer mistake to suppose that the taboo-catechism account implies that moral judgments are not factual. Failure to recognize this obvious logical point seems to me a howler on a par with the one introduced by David Hume (and alas since perpetuated) when he made the distinction between "matters-of-fact" and "relations-of-ideas"—as though it were not a *fact* that two and two make four, or *true* that every debtor has a creditor. (The admirable Hume, it may be noted in passing, also contributed his part to the vulgar confusions which he decried in discussions of ethics—but that is another story.) The question of what kind of facts or truths logical facts or truths and moral facts or truths are, and how they are discovered or determined, is a different question. *That* they are facts or truths is simply not in question.

Thus far I have been discussing the taboo-catechism type of explanation for the degree of consensus that does obtain in moral discourse, and the mistake in the common supposition that such an account implies that moral judgments are not factual in character. I turn now to the alternative explanation: that moral terms are genuine factual predicates. In this connection I shall in due course take up the question of the moral *dis*agreement that exists. And I shall also consider (what it may be noted I have stated but not yet discussed) the inadequacy of the taboo-catechism account as an explanation for all the phenomena of moral discourse.

On the view that moral terms are genuine factual predicates, moral judgments are factual in more than the respect in which they would be, as I have shown, even if the taboo-catechism account were the whole story. That story, so far as it goes, need not be discarded on the present view, it should be appreciated. It could hardly be denied that, whatever else we may say of them, moral terms are predicates of incalculably great social importance—like such undisputedly genuine factual predicates or "dangerous," illegal," "public property," and innumerable others. Think of teaching a child the meaning of such expressions as "It's very hot," or "It's very sharp," or "That doesn't belong to

you," casually, in a merely matter-of-fact tone. Indeed it is hardly conceivable that we should *not* be taught all such pragmatically important predicates in appropriately affective fashion in childhood, or that we should not be assiduously catechized and reinforced ever after in their proper use, by such social forces and instruments as our families, the church, the school, the state, the mass media of communication, and by each other.

There are, on the other hand, two things that I think the simple taboo-catechism cannot adequately account for, and that the present view does. They are, moreover, two things that do not merely count negatively *against* the simple taboo-catechism view, but also count positively *for* the genuine factual predicate view regarding moral terms. What they are, in fact, are the selfsame two types of moral phenomena that we have been discussing: the moral agreement which people exhibit, on the one hand; and their moral disagreement on the other. I hasten to resolve the paradox.

How could moral *dis*agreement support the genuine factual predicate view? The kind of disagreement to which I here refer is not the disagreement or difference that is said to exist between societies (which I shall consider later), but the disagreement between individuals within a given society. Moreover, I do not mean the "disagreement" of the plainly amoral or immoral individuals in the given society. For these individuals are clearly and simply either ignorant, or indifferent, or wilfully recalcitrant with respect to the moral issue, and cannot properly be said to be disagreeing. And in any case their defection from the ranks is easily explainable in terms compatible with the taboo-catechism theory as well as with the present one—e.g., poor, improper, or total lack of family training, alienation of the individual from his family or of the family from the rest of society, and the like. Nor do I mean the kind of absurd defection expressed in the not uncommon but logically silly statement that "nothing is *really* right or wrong"—where the speaker seems not to notice that he is operating with the very concepts he would reject.

The kind of disagreement which I do mean is that which occurs among conventionally moral men, men committed to the moral concern, who are in agreement in the rest of their moral utterances to an extent sufficient to indicate that they are speaking the same language. I mean, moreover, the kind of disagreement that cannot be settled by recourse to some simple list of precepts or injunctions, but which can occur between two individuals who are perfectly familiar with and in substantial agreement about these, and who even agree about what most other people would say about the issue in question. Two such individuals can still continue to argue the issue. Each raises considerations and presents reasons which the other can recognize to be relevant and will try to rebut or assimilate. What are we to make of this?

On the taboo-catechism account, such a debate must surely be a logical absurdity if not an impossibility. But clearly such debates can and do in fact occur. Morally concerned men, men who have been properly inculcated with the particular tribal taboos or the specifics of the moral catechism of their society (allowing for the moment that this is what moral utterances express), men who accept and concur in the main body of these, may come to challenge one of them, thus: "Is it *really* wrong?" Or alternatively: "Is it *always* wrong?" Clearly, if "right" and "wrong" meant no more than "is on the list" or "is contrary to what is on the list," such challenges would make no sense, short of a wholesale rejection of the entire sense of "taboo." But many thoughtful, morally concerned men have meaningfully asked themselves questions of this kind, challenging some particular "received" moral rule, or some particular customary interpretation or application of such a rule. And of this, it seems to me, we

can make sense only on the premiss that moral terms are genuine factual predicates. For I submit that there is a clearly discernible logic in the way men argue their moral disagreements. To say that the whole dispute resides in disagreement about the non-moral facts, or that it arises from simple vagueness, obscurity, ambiguity or equivocation with respect to the key terms, or that the terms have no meaning with respect to the case disputed but only refer to the feelings of the disputants, is simply not to do justice to the facts in all their variety and subtlety. For if this were all that there was to it, how is it that disputants can agree as to what is and what is not a morally relevant reason or consideration in the argument, and how are they able to recognize and agree as to what empirical questions it would be pertinent and helpful to have the answer to?

It is of course a two-edged fact that there should be moral disagreement between individuals within a given society, let alone divergences among different societies. Else it would not have been supposed to be a *prima facie* argument against the thesis that moral terms are factual semantic predicates and that moral judgments are factual. Thus far I have only shown that it has the other, less commonly recognized edge. I shall turn presently to the question of how moral disagreement and divergence may be reconciled with my thesis. I want first to say something more about the facts of moral agreement. Just above I argued that even in their moral disagreements people in disputing exhibit a meeting of minds that cannot adequately be accounted for on the simple taboo-catechism view. I want now to argue the inadequacy of this view for the plain facts of moral agreement as well, and to show why I think these facts imply the thesis I am defending.

It is clear enough from the very characterization how the simple taboo-catechism view, as I am calling it, is supposed to account for the fact that people in a given society do agree widely in their moral assessments. Let us look more carefully at the facts. I think that if we are not blinded by an *a priori* commitment to the taboo-catechism view, we must in honesty admit that it does not really accommodate all the facts. From the mere rote-learning of an arbitrary set of simple injunctions, identified in a finite set of learning instances, and connected by no other principle than their inclusion under an otherwise undefined and cognitively meaningless label, obviously it should not be possible for two people to exceed chance in coming independently to agreement about new precepts or new cases. But it seems to me clearly the case that the moral assessments in which people in a given society, judging independently, agree, go far beyond the level, quantitatively and qualitatively, of the specific precepts and examples in which they may have been mutually catechized in childhood. However much people do also disagree, the extent of their agreement, as well as of their ability to resolve initial disagreement in terms of exceedingly subtle considerations which disagreeing parties nonetheless recognize as relevant, seems to me certainly to exceed the expectation of chance—which would appear to be the explanation of these phenomena on which we should be obliged to depend if moral predicates lacked semantic reference.

Imagine, by analogy, how we should fare if we tried to teach a totally color-blind child the use of the color words, or the color-shade words, or even the word "color" itself (assuming we used samples that had been equated for reflective intensity, saturation, and surface texture). Imagine (by way of still closer analogy) how we should fare in teaching any child the color words if there were not something uniquely and recognizably common to all the shades of a given color, and about all the different colors. Could we if that were the case expect him to identify independently (as children can) a new color *as* a color, or a new shade as a shade of an al-

ready familiar generic color? Would not the child be mystified?

So imagine trying to teach a child the use of the moral terms if there were nothing that one could expect him to discern in common among the diverse moral precepts, or among the varied examples in terms of which a given one is taught. How would this be possible, and especially how would it be possible that he could by himself discern the moral features in new and increasingly more complex types of circumstances, and initiate new and subtle judgments of his own?

Let us consider what it is for a term to have semantic reference and for a judgment to be factual in character. In a certain perhaps Pickwickian but nonetheless illuminating sense, every factual assertion expresses what, to mark the Pickwickian respect, and to distinguish it from what is normally understood by the words "judgment of comparison," I shall here term an "*extrinsic* judgment of comparison." What is normally meant by the phrase "judgment of camparison" are those which have some such explicit form as "this is like, or different from, or larger than that." These we might describe by way of contrast as *intrinsically* comparative judgments, for it is their essence and distinction that they refer to one thing in comparison with another. Moreover, they express the comparison *explicitly*, in contrast with those which, while analysis reveals them to be intrinsically comparative, express a more obscure or *implicit* sort of comparison. I have in mind here such judgments as "He improved the situation," and especially the more subtle cases such as "That weighs ten pounds," or "The specific heat of that compound is 2.38"—at the bottom of which, of course, are comparisons or ratios.

Now the respect in which *all* judgments may be regarded as reflecting a comparison is perhaps not wholly unlike the respect in which these last, more subtle kinds of cases do so—weight, specific heat, mass, atomic number, hard, soft, and the like. Yet obviously it must be a different respect. For it is a respect, I am saying, in which *all* judgments reflect comparisons. What is this respect?

In order to judge in a present instance that something is or is not the case, it is clear that we must *previously* have experienced (or in some way based on our experience have been informed about) the *kind* of thing that we are judging the present something to be, or not to be, a case of. Correspondingly, to judge that a particular expression is semantically appropriate to describe a present case, we must previously have experienced (or have been informed about) the kind of case to which it is semantically appropriate. Thus in judging that the situation before us is of a specified character and semantically warrants a given verbal expression, we are in effect judging—recognizing, that is—that the situation is, in the relevant respects, like the situations in which we previously encountered that property and learned to use that semantically appropriate expression. And if the situation is indeed recognizably of that character, then what we have judged and said to be the case *is* the case, is *so*, is true, is a *fact*.

It should of course be understood that in presenting this perspective about all judgment and all assertive utterance I need not hold any such naive view as that we learn all our words and concepts in terms of a specifiable set of unarguably paradigm cases at specifiable times in our lives. Nor am I suggesting, what is also patently contrary to the facts, that whenever we judge something or employ an expression we must do so self-consciously, or go through any conscious or even unconscious steps, or hold up in our heads some paradigm image. The point I am making about all judgment and assertive utterance is a logical not a psychological one.

To judge that the man on the left is taller is indubitably a comparative judgment of the normal sort, even though I need not attend to anything but the two individuals when I make it. I need not be self-conscious nor entertain any images or other thoughts about standards of linear measurement or of verbal propriety. My judging, here, except in well-known special kinds of circumstances, normally does not consist in anything more than simply looking, noticing, and perhaps saying. Yet obviously the logic of what has occurred when someone asserts that the man on the left is taller involves what in an undeniable respect we must acknowledge to be a judgment of comparative height. In the same way, then, I would argue that consideration reveals that the logic of the whole enterprise of judging and asserting, including the intrinsically and explicitly comparative judgments normally identified as such, rests on what in an undeniable further and special respect we must acknowledge to be implicit comparison.

Consider now moral judgments. We learn in childhood and subsequently to use moral terms by experiencing their use in concrete situations. As with all simple terms learned early in our linguistic life, we learn them ostensively—i.e., not by their being analysed or verbally defined for us, and not, moreover, as self-conscious exercise in vocabulary building, but rather by experiencing their use in practical connection with the very kinds of things, properties or situations to which they pertain. And to put it succinctly, albeit admittedly crudely, this experience of their use is what they mean to us.

Our early use of such terms, at least, is of course a kind of conditioned response, a rote use. By the very import of "rote," even consistent rote use of an expression is obviously not a guarantee of meaning understood; nor, to be sure, does it establish that an expression is not being used as a proper name, but designates for the user an identifiable characterizing property or kind of situation predicable in a factual judgment. All *this* is established only when the individual is able to use the expression in new situations which are not simple total duplications of the rote-learned cases; and when in these new cases the individual's use, and equally important, his withholding or denying of use where that is appropriate, coincides beyond chance with that of others who independently employ the expression. And this, I am maintaining, is precisely the situation we have with respect to our moral terms and judgments.

II

Lest my argument seem to be no more than a *tour de force* resting solely on the admittedly technical (though I insist sound) point of what it means to be a factual predicate and a factual judgment, I need to say something more about the troublesome business of moral disagreement and divergence, and about our inability to resolve this by established definitions and decision procedures.

It is, also, true that moral differences may and frequently do persist after the disputants are talked out. The disputants disengage, either morally indignant or sadly, but in either case not knowing what more to do or say—and perhaps even admitting that there is nothing more that can be done or said. In this respect moral disputes are like disputes of taste—and *de gustibus non est disputandum* we all know. Or do we? Perhaps so about *de gustibus*, and perhaps not. That is another pickle. The point I want to make here is that the facts of moral differences are not at all difficult to reconcile with the thesis I am advancing. For to hold that moral terms are learnable genuine predicates with semantic significance is not to deny that the property or properties they designate may be extremely subtle and (whether or not it is itself a simple property) dependent on complex factors, and therefore difficult to apply

with rigor or certainty in many or even most cases—though quite easy to apply in some. (Consider the simple—and I might add "non-natural"—property of entailment, or of contradiction, which is easy to perceive in some propositional sets, and extremely difficult to decide in others.)

Are we really prepared to classify as non-factual *all* issues for which there is no acknowledged method of conclusively establishing truth and resolving dispute? Surely if there were no pre-judgment of the case, no other reasons—or causes—persuading us that moral terms are not genuine predicates and moral judgments not factual, this lack of a decision method would not of itself lead us to that conclusion. How many, really, of our predicates and judgments, outside of mathematics and, less certainly, the quantitative natural sciences, are determinable by universally acknowledged operational definitions and decision techniques? Many, most, perhaps even all of our everyday concepts are to some degree vague and ill-defined; and hence so must our judgments be. Few of them permit of unequivocal test even where there is agreement in application, nor of resolution where there is not.

Though we tend not to focus on this, we may realize when we do that with many of the predicates and judgments that we do not hesitate to classify as factual, it is by no means a foregone conclusion that the class of borderline cases must be smaller than the class of clear-cut ones. Consider such notoriously vague and loose, but nonetheless admittedly factual terms as: "useful," "plausible," "justifiable," "rational," "intelligent," "witty," "clear," "strong," "healthy," "real motive," and so on, just about *ad infinitum*. Is it not the case with these that disputes and borderline instances are almost the rule rather than the exception? And that operational criteria and decision procedures are not only lacking but peculiarly inappropriate?

The strange thing is that while some

may deplore the use of such terms for some purposes (though one can hardly dispense with them in the ordinary everyday circumstances of living and speaking), there is not the same inclination here, as there is with moral terms, to say that they are not in fundamental character factual predicates. Even the fact that they are value terms—a fact, incidentally, which is seldom noticed in this connection—does not militate against their being classified as factual. Although, as we do with judgments about the guilt of a defendant in a murder trial, we may be inclined to say that judgments in terms of these predicates are merely opinions, we do not feel inclined to say that what we judge in terms of them are themselves purely matters of opinion or personal taste, rather than of fact, any more than we say that the actual guilt or innocence of the defendant is a matter only of opinion and not of fact, just because we lack conclusive evidence and are obliged to rely on opinion judgment as to what the fact is. What is more, we do not feel inclined to say this about these other somewhat vague and loose terms even though with them, unlike the question of the actual guilt of the defendant in the murder trial, where we might have witnessed the crime, we have no clear picture, or even no picture at all, of what conclusive evidence or demonstration might be for them.

It must be recognized, moreover, that as with most judgments we make about other matters that are unquestionably matters of fact, many matters of non-moral fact are at least very relevant to the moral assessments we make in particular cases. There are important questions of empirical fact that we wish to consider in coming to a decision: questions of fact about the past, the present and the future; questions about the causal relations of these facts, and about what the consequences of certain occurrences or courses of action might be. And there are questions of a non-empirical sort that we also take into account, concerning the internal consistency, entailment and compatibility of our values, aims and particular moral assessments, with respect to each other and to certain modes of conduct. Clearly such matters as the foregoing may be difficult to ascertain, judge or interpret with any degree of certainty. And it may be difficult to keep them in mind in full and clear array so that they may contribute their relative weights to the vector resultant that is our considered moral judgment. Being for the most part imponderables, matters we can judge only with qualitative as opposed to quantitative probability, moreover, they are morally determining considerations about which reasonable men of moral concern might differ. And since what they decide about these non-moral factors will affect the weight which they give them in coming to a particular moral assessment, it is hardly surprising that people should differ about that particular moral assessment—just as even experts may do in certain domains of engineering or economic investigation in which subtly complex and indeterminable parameters may upset the best-laid plans and predictions.

Why should it not be the case, moreover—indeed, I would insist it often is—that a man is just plain wrong in a particular moral assessment he makes—even in relatively simple and clear-cut cases where most people perceive the issues clearly and agree. Our moral judgments and their implications for conduct connect closely with our desires, attitudes, fears, and the like, and it is obvious that our moral judgment will therefore be susceptible to extraordinary distorting pressures. It is common knowledge that a person's moral judgment and conduct may be affected—just as his objectivity about other matters may be—by such distorting field forces as sexual desire, parental and filial love, friendship, and concern with implications for his own past and future conduct and his present self-esteem. Everyone knows that, even without explicit persuasion, censure, threat, or the like from his fellow men, a man may come, through subsequent reflection, and perhaps through new experiences, to reconsider an earlier moral judgment.

As a concrete non-moral illustration of how technical difficulties and even personal considerations may affect our ability to come to confident decision and agreement about a clearly factual matter, consider the issue whether the net effect of limited Social Security taxation and payments is beneficial or deleterious to the nation's economy. Here is a question that produces heated disagreement among experts, and defies resolution. For it is simply not possible to isolate the net economic effect of this program, either in the present or in the future, amidst all the other determining forces. It can hardly be denied that the program has some net effect upon the economy as a whole, even if it be the case that it contributes opposing forces which equate to zero. However imprecise and non-operational the notion of "beneficial for the nation's economy" may be, it is not, of course, without factual content. There are some fiscal moves of a major sort that produce unmistakeable effects upon the economy. But with the factual issue of the effect of Social Security we must be content with opinion, demonstration being impossible. Individual experience, differences in economic theories held, differences in the assessment of past and present factors that likewise defy exact measurement—and, no doubt, political outlook and personal sympathies as well—all contribute to the experts' opinions. And the opinions differ. The implication of this for moral opinion should be clear.

An obvious reply to this line of argument is that with such a notion as something's being economically beneficial or deleterious, it is possible, in some simpler cases, at least, to define and show just what is meant; whereas this seems not to be possible with moral predicates. Other putatively factual predicates may be vague, imprecise, lacking in operational criteria or decision procedure for their application

and for settling either sharp or border-line case disputes. But they are not "mystical," not wholly indefinable in other terms, as the moral terms seem to be. The properties that these other terms designate can be singled out and made explicit when we wish to demonstrate to another—perhaps to someone first learning the term—what they mean.

My answer to this is two-fold. First, so far as the moral terms are concerned, the situation is not quite so mystical and unanalysable as this argument makes it out to be. And second, it is simply not the case that we deny "factuality" to judgments that we make on the basis simply of total wholistic inspection of a situation without employing specifiable or even discernible criteria.

Admittedly my first point will not sustain too much weight. The moral terms do seem to be peculiarly recalcitrant with respect to analysis, or even, except within a very narrow range, to synonymous definition. Yet for the record we should remember that in making a moral assessment we do not do so without examining the facts of the situation. Just as in aesthetic judgments, whatever be *their* logical character, we do not say the blank wall exhibits the artistic quality, but that the painting does, so we recognize moral features in situations, not in introspection nor *in vacuo*. When the painting is different, so may the reaction be. Similarly, in moral contexts we know what kinds of facts to look for, and we recognize exculpating and inculpating circumstances when we discover them. And just as the aesthetically practised are not bewildered by the variety of genres or of particular paintings that may evoke similar appreciation or criticism, nor at a loss as to how at least to begin to resolve seeming incompatibilities of judgment, so we find that in the moral sphere not just anything evokes our moral approval, but only certain recognizably distinctive classes of acts. We are seldom surprised by new judgments we find ourselves or others making. And even when we are, or when we disagree with others, we know how to go about tying the disputed case to the old ones in which we had agreement. So much for this point.

Let us consider now whether judgments made on wholistic inspection, without specifiable or discernible criteria, can possibly be termed "factual."

I have been arguing that in learning to use the moral terms, we do learn to recognize a distinct property (or set of properties), however unable we may be to articulate it in other words. It may be, as G. E. Moore held, a simple, unique and unanalysable quality (in this respect—though only in this respect—like the quality designated by the color-word "yellow"). It may be—what need not be incompatible with what Moore held—a peculiarly abstract property of actions and situations that are relationally complex and many-faceted. But it is clearly something that we are taught to recognize in the learning cases of childhood without its being explicitly defined or isolated for our discernment within the concrete contexts in which it is exemplified. Inasmuch as this seems to some to be too mystical, it is worthwhile to compare it with one or two other cases involving a learned ability to recognize a property which can only be shown but not explicitly isolated, discerned, or pointed out.

I shall begin with the interesting and relatively unfamiliar case of the remarkable skill of the expert chicken-sexers in egg hatcheries. (This example I owe to Douglas Gasking, of the University of Melbourne, who used it to make a point [not about ethics] with which I do not wholly agree. I do not know whether he would agree with my use of it here.) These individuals are trained to discriminate the sex of newborn chicks—something which cannot otherwise be done with chicks of this age, short of dissection or some other economically unfeasible method, but which is important, in the economics of egg hatcheries, to do as early as possible. Inasmuch as

the trainees cannot be shown specifically what the distinguishing features are, even by those already possessing the skill, a devious training procedure is resorted to that is found to be effective. The procedure employed is singularly reminiscent of the way in which one seems of necessity to have to teach or learn the use of moral, aesthetic and mental terms—and perhaps it would not be inaccurate to say that it is the way in which one does in fact learn most language concepts, even when explicit definition or specification is possible.

The trainee is shown repeatedly and in succession color photographs of, say, a thousand baby chicks which had been banded at birth with a code number, and which had subsequently, when sufficiently grown, been checked for gender. Unable to discern or to be shown any principle of correlation between the appearance of the photographed chicks and the subsequent verified sex differentiation, the trainee calls out his arbitrary guess, and in Skinnerian programmed-learning fashion, is immediately reinforced or discouraged in his guess "judgment" by being told what the actual finding for the particular chick was. Without ever learning themselves to specify just what the correlated features are, some trainees in time acquire a consistent skill of discrimination that, while not perfect, well exceeds the chance performance of the control groups which the untrained provide.

There are, of course, many analogous examples: the change-makers in the Automat restaurants in New York City, who are able to grab up precisely twenty nickels, without looking, from a coin well, and shove them confidently *en masse*, without counting, at the patron who presents a dollar bill. Manufacturing industries are sprinkled with individuals who comparably become human discriminating machines without being able to isolate criteria. And then there are the calculating prodigies, and especially the idiot savants. But we really need not go so far afield. The fact is, if one only attends, that in so many of our everyday abilities, including the use of word-concepts, we learn, discriminate, accommodate, and act, all without conscious or explicit criteria even when these exist.

The examples I have cited are all of course of the type in which there is an unambiguous and, as we say, "objective" criterion of verification or success. Obviously it would have been pointless and question-begging to cite any other kind for the purpose of establishing that there exists the learning phenomenon and genuine use skill that I wanted to show. But it may now be objected that it is just the lack of such success criteria for moral discrimination cases that is the crux. Well, we have discussed how much it is lacking and how much it is not. Looking at the matter the other way around, is it true that all matters that we consider factual are tied to such an unambiguous, unmistakable, unarguable, "objective" criterion of proof as the matter of chick gender? Perhaps it is not very persuasive to cite aesthetic judgments. The same people are likely to balk. But surely it is only a scientific fanatic who would want to maintain that the everyday psychological judgments we make about human conduct, motives and rationality, or about the plausibility of an explanation, or the non-numerical probability of a given occurrence, are all merely subjective and whimsical and devoid of objective or factual character simply because they concern matters for which we lack criteria of conclusive validation, and which are dependent upon the preponderant considered agreement of otherwise rational men, and of subsequent events. Only think what so stringent a criterion for the notion of "factual" would imply for such statements as "I am (he is) experiencing a visual after-image"; or "He is obviously thinking such and such," or "afraid of such and such"; or even (especially before the complicating advent of the wave-length theory of physical color—which surely did not first endow such judgments with factual character) for so plain and simple a judgment as "This is red."

III

I want finally to say something about the relevance of the anthropological data adduced by the ethical relativists. The fact is, this argument goes, that not only do people within a given social structure, and in the same general place and historical period, disagree in their particular moral assessments, while generally participating in a common moral dialogue, but even more significantly, people in different cultures, or at different places, or in different times and circumstances, have held opposite moral values on a total societal scale. And this, it is argued, shows that moral judgments, however sophisticated, are nonetheless all no more than expressions of tribal custom—the *ethos*, the *mores* of the culture.

Now I have already discussed the facts of *intra*-cultural moral disparity, and I shall not say anything more here about that other than to point out that some of the arguments cited in that connection clearly apply also, *mutatis mutandis*, to *inter*-cultural differences. There is no justification for ruling out *a priori* the possibility that men at other times or at other places may be morally blind or insensitive or unsophisticated, just as they may be with respect to their scientific knowledge and methods. Nor is there reason to rule out that men in another society at an earlier time or place, like men at the same general time and place on the contemporary scene (the Nazis, for example) may be immoral, or egregiously wrong in their moral self-assurance—misled, deceived, even self-deceived, by the same sorts of forces, even though on a larger scale, that can distort the judgment of individuals or smaller groups within our own society.

There is, moreover, in any case a certain *non sequitur* that is present in this relativist argument: the mere fact (if it is a plain fact) that moral predicates have had different denotations for different people at different times and places neither entails nor implies that the terms are semantically empty nor that they are merely emotive and subjective, nor even that they have undergone a change in connotation. For there are of course many words of undeniably clear, constant and "objective" significance, whose denotative applicability is variable—whether variable in a simple and relatively systematic way, as with such words as "I," "mine," "here," "now," etc., or variable in the more complex and contingent way that such terms as "useful," or "new" are, or as is the word "fit,' for example, applied to one and the same pair of shoes in one's childhood and in one's full growth. Thus, with respect to the moral terms, it is entirely possible, so far as I can see to the contrary, that the simple and indefinable property designated (if it is indefinable) should be such a subtle and complexly relational one—thus giving rise to radical change in denotation in appropriately different circumstances.

It may very well be, moreover, that the degree of moral variation in different cultures is not so great as advertised by the relativists, or as it might *prima facie* seem. It has been suggested by other anthropological investigators that close attention to the apparent differences would reveal that they exist because of ignorance or disagreement about the non-moral facts as between the investigator and the society he is investigating. The differences noted may be due in the given society to a failure to perceive or appreciate causal and logical connections; a failure that may be induced by the blind pull of custom and tradition, or the blinding power of primitive ritual and belief. Does a primitive Eskimo society which sets its weak and elderly adrift on an ice floe to die, when the tribe is confronted with a critical survival situation, really differ from us in their morality? Are we not on occasion faced with similar moral deci-

sions? And if the primitive society takes to itself the comforting belief that the departed suffering souls will go to another realm in which there will be comfort for them too—or even merely to the unfeelingness of extinction—are their moral judgments hopelessly irreconcilable with ours?

IV

Finally, I would call attention to the question-begging nature of the argument of the relativists insofar as it rests on the citation of anthropological and historical data. The fallacy to which I refer is so patent in the relativist argument that it is difficult to believe that it should have gone unnoticed in meta-ethical discussion—though apparently it has. Let us see what it is.

It should be noted, to begin with, that in speaking of other societies, especially primitive societies, we are confronted not only with an alien culture, but with an alien language as well. In the Trobriand Island moral system, we may be told, it is regarded as right and proper to do this or that—let us call it "X"—which is considered morally reprehensible in our culture. Now if X were the single exception, or one of the few differences with respect to what in our society and language community we mean by "moral" issues, the tack we might adopt is to look for special explanatory circumstances, or else simply to decry it as an example of error, inconsistency or the like. This need not trouble us logically. What is logically queer, I submit, is an account of a society which is described as differing *radically* from ours in its "morality." Let us see why.

Ordinarily, to determine that a word-concept in another society's language has the same meaning as one in ours, we must compare their use of their term with our use of ours. This may be done essentially in two ways: either by comparing direct, ostensive, concrete denotative uses, or by comparing other verbal behavior. This other verbal behavior may be either directly and explicitly about the use of the initial word concept at issue, or about other matters that may, at least for us, be sufficiently closely related to the initial word-concept for us to be able to decide.

Now insofar as moral discourse is a distinctive discourse, and its terms do ultimately defy analysis or definition in terms of non-moral equivalents, as appears to be the case, it seems clear that there is no other guarantee of inter-linguistic synonymy of word-concepts in this sphere than ostensive identity. We are obliged, in short, to rely on equivalence of the classes of denotational instances. And to the extent that there is denotational divergence in the use of the word-concept in question, from our use of the putative equivalent in our language, to that extent there is *prima facie* reason to doubt that the two word-concepts correspond. And if there are simply no expressions or systems of expressions in that alien language that are applied in sufficient coextension with our moral discourse, is this not good reason to suspect—even to conclude—that that society simply lacks the word-concepts that we identify under the label "moral"?

With respect to concrete physical phenomena, material objects, properties, behavior and the like, we should normally expect that the absence of semantically applicable word-concepts would be well-correlated, even if not perfectly so, with lack of attention to the given physical phenomena, even if those phenomena should be otherwise perceptibly present. The Eskimos, we are told, while they have no general word equivalent to our word "snow," have numerous words, each designating a variety of this substance that, in its variety, plays an important role in the Eskimo life. We have but one word, and unless we are skiing enthusiasts, are most of us insensitive to the perceptible variety in which snow may exist. It should be even less surprising, I submit, that where the word-concept that is lacking in a given society's language refers to a relational property of a subtle, sophisticated, highly abstract sort, there will in that society be an absence of concern with, or even a total lack of awareness of that property.

It is axiomatic that verbal ambiguity is most pernicious where the equivocal uses are closely similar. Parallelly, two distinct concepts are more susceptible of conflation when they are sufficiently close as to have considerable denotative applicability in common. (Consider the denotative similarity of "mass" and "weight," for instance; or of "speed," "velocity" and "acceleration.")

Now no one, I think, would be inclined to say that the Trobriand Islanders had a different conception or standard of *kindliness* from ours because (assuming they did do this, and did it moreover without some quaint belief as to its beneficial effect upon the victim) they went about kicking dogs or helpless humans. We should not say this was their idea of kindliness even if they did the kicking with what might be described as a beatific smile, such as a missionary might exhibit in performing for them what we should identify as a kindly act. But it does seem to be an especially attractive trap for the unwary that such distinct things as what is common behavior in a given society, or what is accepted, encouraged, approved, and rewarded, on the one hand, and on the other, what is regarded as moral, happen to be closely related—as they are in our society, or at least as we (morally) say they ought to be.

Nonetheless they are distinct concepts, and we can and do distinguish them in thought and word—as I just have. Why then should we succumb so readily to the argument of the relativists who cite anthropological data? We might as well speak of radically different and incompatible systems or scientific method, as of radically different and incompatible systems or standards of morality. Even the very phrase, "*system* of morality," as the anthropological relativist employs it in arguing that morals are nothing but the *mores* or customs of tribes and ethics nothing but *ethos* or culture, gives away the question-begging approach that he employs in examining primitive or other societies for their morality. What he does is simply to look at their conduct, and to see how they react to each other's conduct. This, he has already decided, is all that morality is.

What he discovers, of course, is what is taboo in that society and what is not; what is and is not accepted, encouraged, approved and rewarded; and perhaps what words in their language are related to all of this. But does he discover their *moral values*? What reason other than the question-begging one do we have for plainly attributing the concept of morality to such people at all?

III
Theories of Normative Ethics

A. What Things Have Value?
B. What Acts Are Right?

Multiple Intrinsic Goods

G. E. MOORE

Is it true that one whole will be intrinsically better than another, whenever and only when it contains more pleasure, no matter what the two may be like in other respects? It seems to me almost impossible that any one, who fully realizes the consequences of such a view, can possibly hold that it *is* true. It involves our saying, for instance, that a world in which absolutely nothing except pleasure existed—no knowledge, no love, no enjoyment of beauty, no moral qualities—must yet be intrinsically better—better worth creating—provided only the total quantity of pleasure in it were the least bit greater, than one in which all these things existed *as well as* pleasure. It involves our saying that, even if the total quantity of pleasure in each was exactly equal, yet the fact that all the beings in the one possessed in addition knowledge of many different kinds and a full appreciation of all that was beautiful or worthy of love in their world, whereas *none* of the beings in the other possessed any of these things, would give us no reason whatever for preferring the former to the latter. It involves our saying that, for instance, the state of mind of a drunkard, when he is intensely pleased with breaking crockery, is just as valuable, in itself—just as well worth having, as that of a man who is fully realizing all that is exquisite in the tragedy of King Lear, provided only the mere quantity of pleasure in both cases is the same. Such instances might be multi-

plied indefinitely, and it seems to me that they constitute a *reductio ad absurdum* of the view that intrinsic value is always in proportion to quantity of pleasure. Of course, here again, the question is quite incapable of proof either way. And if anybody, after clearly considering the issue, does come to the conclusion that no one kind of enjoyment is ever intrinsically better than another, provided only that the pleasure in both is equally intense, and that, if we *could* get as much pleasure in the world, without needing to have any knowledge, or any moral qualities, or any sense of beauty, as we can get *with* them, then all these things would be entirely superfluous, there is no way of proving that he is wrong. But it seems to me almost impossible that anybody, who does really get the question clear, should take such a view; and, if anybody were to, I think it is self-evident that he would be wrong.

It may, however, be asked: If the matter is as plain as this, how has it come about that anybody ever has adopted the view that intrinsic value *is* always in proportion to quantity of pleasure, or has ever argued, as if it were so? And I think one chief answer to this question is that those who have done so have *not* clearly realized all the consequences of their view, partly because they have been too exclusively occupied with the particular question as to whether, in the case of *the total consequences* of *actual* voluntary actions, degree of intrinsic value is not always in proportion to quantity of pleasure—a question which, as has been admitted, is, in itself, much more obscure. But there is, I think, another reason, which is worth mentioning, because it introduces us to a principle of great importance. It may, in fact, be held, with great plausibility, that no whole can ever have any intrinsic value *unless* it contains some pleasure; and it might be thought, at first sight, that this reasonable, and perhaps true, view could not possibly lead to the wholly unreasonable one that intrinsic value is always *in proportion* to quantity of pleasure: it might seem obvious that to say that nothing can be valuable *without* pleasure is a very different thing from saying that intrinsic value is always *in proportion* to pleasure. And it is, I think, in fact true that the two views are really as different as they seem, and that the latter does not at all follow from the former. But, if we look a little closer, we may, I think, see a reason why the latter should very naturally have been *thought* to follow from the former.

The reason is as follows. If we say that no whole can ever be intrinsically good, *unless* it contains some pleasure, we are, of course, saying that if from any whole, which is intrinsically good, we were to subtract all the pleasure it contains, the remainder, whatever it might be, would have no intrinsic goodness at all, but must always be either intrinsically *bad*, or else intrinsically indifferent: and this (if we remember our definition of intrinsic value) is the same thing as to say that this remainder actually *has* no intrinsic goodness at all, but always *is* either positively bad or indifferent. Let us call the pleasure which such a whole contains, A, and the whole remainder, whatever it may be, B. We are then saying that the whole A+B is intrinsically good, but that B is *not* intrinsically good at all. Surely it seems to follow that the intrinsic value of A+B cannot possibly be greater than that of A by itself? How, it may be asked, could it possibly be otherwise? How, by adding to A something, namely B, which has *no* intrinsic goodness at all, could we possibly get a whole which has *more* intrinsic value than A? It may

naturally seem to be self-evident that we could not. But, if so, then it absolutely follows that we can never increase the value of any whole whatever except by adding *pleasure* to it: we may, of course, *lessen* its value, by adding other things, e.g. by adding pain; but we can never *increase* it except by adding pleasure.

Now from this it does not, of course, follow strictly that the intrinsic value of a whole is always *in proportion* to the quantity of pleasure it contains in the special sense in which we have throughout been using this expression—that is to say, as meaning that it is in proportion to the *excess* of pleasure over pain, in one of the five senses explained in Chapter I. But it is surely very natural to think that it does. And it *does* follow that we must be wrong in the reasons we gave for disputing this proposition. It does follow that we must be wrong in thinking that by adding such things as knowledge or a sense of beauty to a world which contained a certain amount of pleasure, without adding any more pleasure, we could increase the intrinsic value of that world. If, therefore, we are to dispute the proposition that intrinsic value *is* always in proportion to quantity of pleasure we must dispute this argument. But the argument may seem to be almost indisputable. It has, in fact, been used as an argument in favour of the proposition that intrinsic value *is* always in proportion to quantity of pleasure, and I think it has probably had much influence in inducing people to adopt that view, even if they have not expressly put it in this form.

How, then, can we dispute this argument? We might, of course, do so, by rejecting the proposition that no whole can ever be intrinsically good, *unless* it contains some pleasure; but, for my part, though I don't feel certain that this proposition *is* true, I also don't feel at all certain that it is *not* true. The part of the argument which it seems to me certainly can and ought to be disputed is another part—namely, the assumption that, where a whole contains two factors, A and B, and one of these, B, has no intrinsic goodness at all, the intrinsic value of the whole cannot be *greater* than that of the other factor, A. This assumption, I think, obviously rests on a still more general assumption, of which it is only a special case. The general assumption is: That where a whole consists of two factors A and B, the amount by which its intrinsic value exceeds that of one of these two factors must always be equal to that of the other factor. Our special case will follow from this general assumption: because it will follow that if B be intrinsically *indifferent*, that is to say, if its intrinsic value = 0, then the amount by which the value of the whole A+B exceeds the value of A must also = 0, that is to say, the value of the whole must be precisely *equal* to that of A; while if B be intrinsically *bad*, that is to say, if its intrinsic value is less than 0, then the amount by which the value of A+B will exceed that of A will also be less than 0, that is to say, the value of the whole will be *less* than that of A. Our special case does then follow from the general assumption; and nobody, I think, would maintain that the special case was true without maintaining that the general assumption was also true. The general assumption may, indeed, very naturally seem to be self-evident: it has, I think, been generally assumed that it is so: and it may seem to be a mere deduction from the laws of arithmetic. But, so far as I can see, it is *not* a mere deduction from the laws of arithmetic, and, so far from being self-evident, is certainly untrue.

Let us see exactly what we are saying, if we deny it. We are saying that the fact that A and B *both* exist together, together with the fact that they have to one another any relation which they do happen to have (when they exist together, they always must have *some* relation to one another; and the precise nature of the relation certainly may in some cases make a great difference to the value of the whole state of things, though, perhaps, it need not in all

cases)—that these two facts *together* must have a certain amount of intrinsic value, that is to say must be either intrinsically good, or intrinsically bad, or intrinsically indifferent, and that the amount by which this value exceeds the value which the existence of A would have, if A existed quite alone, *need* not be equal to the value which the existence of B would have, if B existed quite alone. This is all that we are saying. And can any one pretend that such a view necessarily contradicts the laws of arithmetic? Or that it is self-evident that it cannot be true? I cannot see any ground for saying so; and if there is no ground, then the argument which sought to show that we can never add to the value of any whole *except* by adding pleasure to it, is entirely baseless.

If, therefore, we reject the theory that intrinsic value is always in proportion to quantity of pleasure, it does seem as if we may be compelled to accept the principle that *the amount by which the value of a whole exceeds that of one of its factors is not necessarily equal to that of the remaining factor*—a principle which, if true, is very important in many other cases. But, though at first sight this principle may seem paradoxical, there seems to be no reason why we should not accept it; while there are other independent reasons why we should accept it. And, in any case, it seems quite clear that the degree of intrinsic value of a whole is *not* always in proportion to the quantity of pleasure it contains.

But, if we do reject this theory, what, it may be asked, can we substitute for it? How can we answer the question, what kinds of consequences are intrinsically better or worse than others?

We may, I think, say, first of all, that for the same reason for which we have rejected the view that intrinsic value is always in proportion to quantity of pleasure, we must also reject the view that it is always in proportion to the quantity of any other *single* factor whatever. Whatever single kind of thing may be proposed as a measure of intrinsic value, instead of pleasure—whether knowledge, or virtue, or wisdom, or love—it is, I think, quite plain that it is not such a measure; because it is quite plain that, however valuable any one of these things may be, we may always add to the value of a whole which contains any one of them, not only by adding more of that one, but also *by adding something else instead*. Indeed, so far as I can see, there is no characteristic whatever which always distinguishes every whole which has greater intrinsic value from every whole which has less, *except* the fundamental one that it would always be the duty of every agent to prefer the better to the worse, if he had to choose between a pair of actions, of which they would be the *sole* effects. And similarly, so far as I can see, there is no characteristic whatever which belongs to all things that are intrinsically *good* and only to them—except simply the one that they all *are* intrinsically good and *ought* always to be preferred to *nothing at all*, if we had to choose between an action whose sole effect would be one of them and one which would have no effects whatever. The fact is that the view which seems to me to be true is the one which, apart from theories, I think every one would naturally take, namely, that there are an *immense variety* of different things, *all* of which are intrinsically good; and that though all these things may perhaps have some characteristic *in common*, their variety is so great that they have none, which, *besides* being common to them all, is also *peculiar* to them—that is to say, which never belongs to anything which is intrinsically bad or indifferent. All that can, I think, be done by way of making plain what kinds of things are intrinsically good or bad, and what are better or worse than others, is to classify some of the chief kinds of each, pointing out what the factors are upon which their goodness or badness depends. And I think this is one of the most profitable things which can be done in Ethics, and

one which has been too much neglected hitherto. But I have not space to attempt it here.

I have only space for two final remarks. The first is that there do seem to be two important characteristics, which are *common* to absolutely all intrinsic goods, though not peculiar to them. Namely (1) it does seem as if nothing can be an intrinsic good unless it contains *both* some feeling and *also* some other form of consciousness; and, as we have said before, it seems possible that amongst the feelings contained must always be some amount of pleasure. And (2) it does also seem as if every intrinsic good must be a complex whole containing a considerable variety of different factors—as if, for instance, nothing so simple as pleasure by itself, however intense, could ever be any good. But it is important to insist (though it is obvious) that neither of these characteristics is *peculiar* to intrinsic goods: they may obviously *also* belong to things bad and indifferent. Indeed, as regards the first, it is not only true that many wholes which contain both feeling and some other form of consciousness are intrinsically bad; but it seems also to be true that nothing can be intrinsically bad, *unless* it contains some feeling.

The other final remark is that we must be very careful to distinguish the two questions (1) whether, and in what degree, a thing is *intrinsically* good and bad, and (2) whether, and in what degree, it is capable of adding to or subtracting from the intrinsic value of a whole of which it forms a part, from a third, entirely different question, namely (3) whether, and in what degree, a thing is *useful* and has good *effects*, or *harmful* and has *bad* effects. All three questions are very liable to be confused, because, in common life, we apply the names 'good' and 'bad' to things of all three kinds indifferently: when we say that a thing is 'good' we may mean either (1) that it is intrinsically good or (2) that it adds to the value of many intrinsically good wholes or (3) that it is useful or has good effects; and similarly when we say that a thing is bad we may mean any one of the three corresponding things. And such confusion is very liable to lead to mistakes, of which the following are, I think, the commonest. In the first place, people are apt to assume with regard to things, which really are very good indeed in senses (1) or (2), that they are scarcely any good at all, simply because they do not seem to be of much *use*—that is to say, to lead to *further* good effects; and similarly, with regard to things which really are very bad in senses (1) or (2), it is very commonly assumed that there cannot be much, if any, harm in them, simply because they do not seem to lead to *further* bad results. Nothing is commoner than to find people asking of a good thing: What *use* is it? and concluding that, if it is no use, it cannot be any good; or asking of a bad thing: What harm does it do? and concluding that if it *does* no harm, there cannot be any harm *in* it. Or, again, by a converse mistake, of things which really are very useful, but are not good at all in senses (1) and (2), it is very commonly assumed that they *must* be good in one or both of these two senses. Or again, of things, which really are very good in senses (1) and (2), it is assumed that, because they are good, they cannot possibly do harm. Or finally, of things, which are neither intrinsically good nor useful, it is assumed that they cannot be any good at all, although in fact they are very good in sense (2). All these mistakes are liable to occur, because, in fact, the degree of goodness or badness of a thing in any one of these three senses is by no means always in proportion to the degree of its goodness or badness in either of the other two; but if we are careful to distinguish the three different questions, they can, I think, all be avoided.

Why Not Hedonism? A Protest

RALPH MASON BLAKE

In current discussions of ethical theory it has become the tradition to treat hedonism on the more or less definite assumption that its rejection is a foregone conclusion. Its falsity is so thoroughly taken for granted that it is thought possible to dispose of its claims in very short order indeed. It is usually treated with ill-disguised contempt as an antiquated heresy that has so long since been definitely refuted that its truth can scarcely be contemplated as a genuine possibility at all. Its "fallacies" are summarily pointed out, in a few brief pages, and we are hurried on to a consideration of theories more worthy of the attention of a mature mind.

I find this state of affairs extremely unsatisfactory. For my own part, I may as well say at once, I accept the hedonistic position. If there are any serious difficulties in the way of such acceptance, I very much wish to know what they are. The current "refutations" seem to me for the most part simply puerile—so much so, indeed, that I should feel a sense of shame in proposing to discuss them seriously were it not for the scandalous fact that they are still solemnly repeated and piously deferred to. Perhaps it is some such sense of shame that keeps Mr. Santayana, who, almost alone among contemporary writers, adopts a fully hedonistic position, from dealing with the current objections. Mr. Santayana, however, prefers in general to expound rather than argue his philosophy, and the truth of

hedonism in particular doubtless seems to him so evident that he cannot bring himself to any careful consideration of the alleged difficulties. The occasion therefore seems ripe for such a discussion, and it is something of the sort which, in summary fashion, I propose to undertake.

Let it first be clearly understood, however, that in attempting to defend hedonism from its critics I am by no means concerned with the *integral* defense of any historical hedonistic system. By hedonism I do not mean Epicureanism, or Benthamism, or the doctrines of J. S. Mill. There is not the slightest difficulty in showing, and it has in fact been demonstrated *ad nauseam,* that these historic theories are one and all infected with serious fallacies and gross errors. I believe, however, that there is a set of fundamental principles which, whether or not it has ever been held in this precise form by any of the classical proponents of hedonism, at any rate seems to have been more or less approximated by each of them; that this set, moreover, will be recognized as undoubtedly constituting a hedonistic system; and, finally, that *this* hedonistic system is by no means to be disposed of by the simple device of showing that it has usually been inadequately stated, defended by fallacious arguments, and combined with inconsistent or erroneous principles.

This central core of hedonistic doctrine has been most clearly and completely disengaged from its various historical accompaniments not by any advocate of the theory, but, oddly enough, precisely by its

Reprinted from the journal *Ethics,* 1926, by R. M. Blake by permission of The University of Chicago Press.

acutest critic, Mr. G. E. Moore (in his *Ethics,* Home University Library). Ignoring all complications and refinements of interpretation, the bare essentials of this view can be stated in a highly compressed form in seven propositions. Of these the first two are simple preliminary definitions of terms. They are as follows:

(1) To say of a thing that it is *intrinsically* good means that it would be good even if it existed quite alone, without any accompaniments or effects whatever.

(2) To say of a thing that it is *ultimately* good, or good *for its own sake,* means (a) that it is intrinsically good, and (b) that it contains no part which is not intrinsically good.

The next three propositions are definitions of moral concepts. They are not peculiar to hedonism as such, but characterize it as *teleological,* rather than as a *formalistic* system of ethics. (For this distinction, cf. Paulsen's *System of Ethics,* Book II, Chapter 1.) These propositions are as follows:

(3) To call a voluntary act *wrong* means that the total consequences of some other action possible to the agent under the circumstances form a whole which is intrinsically better than the whole formed by the total consequences of the act in question.

(4) To call a voluntary act *right* means that it is not wrong.

(5) To call a voluntary act a *duty* for a given agent, or to say that the agent *ought* to perform it, means that, among the acts possible to the agent under the circumstances, the total consequences of the act in question form a whole which is intrinsically better than the whole formed by the total consequences of any of the other possible acts.

The next proposition also is not necessarily peculiar to hedonism as such. It amounts to a denial of Mr. Moore's principle of "organic unity" (cf. his *Principia Ethica*), and might form a part of a non-hedonistic system. This principle is as follows:

(6) The intrinsic value of a whole is always in proportion to the amount of ultimate value which it contains.

The last proposition is the characteristic and peculiar thesis of hedonism:

(7) Pleasurable consciousness is always ultimately good (or good for its own sake); and nothing else is ever ultimately good.

And now for the current objections. Most of these, I think it will be readily seen, simply do not touch at all the theory previously stated. So far as it is concerned, they are completely beside the mark. For example, much ink is still expended on the refutation of *psychological hedonism,* i.e., the once fashionable theory that the sole human motive is the desire for pleasure. (Cf., e.g., Dewey's constant recurrence to this subject in his *Human Nature and Conduct.*) In view of the fact that no serious thinker, so far as I know, now holds any such theory, this ink is simply wasted. The doctrine was, of course, accepted by most of the hedonists of the past, and was indeed frequently put forward by them as a proof of the truth of their ethical theory. Its falsity is, however, now generally recognized, and its uselessness as a basis for demonstration of the ethical theory fully admitted. It evidently forms no part of the doctrine previously stated, and is in no way implied thereby. Discussion of it is therefore wholly irrelevant to any living issue.

But even those who recognize the irrelevance of psychological hedonism sometimes formulate and criticize ethical hedonism in a way which is almost equally irrelevant. Hedonists hold—so the matter is frequently put—that even though the desire for pleasure is not actually the sole human motive, yet nevertheless it *ought* to be. Thus Miss Calkins tells us (*The Good Man and the Good,* p. 73) that "according to this theory the proper, though not the invariable, object of the morally willing self is pleasure." And according to Mr. Joad (*Common-Sense Ethics,* p. 13; cf. p. 15) "although other things besides pleasure may be desired, pleasure is the only thing that ought to be desired." Now, whether or not such a doctrine has actually formed a part of the hedonistic systems in the past, it certainly ought to be plain that it is by no means an *essential* feature of such a system. Not only is it not in any way implied in the foregoing propositions, but on any reasonable view of things would seem even to be excluded thereby. For according to these principles to say that no man *ought* ever to desire anything other than pleasure means that the total consequences of a desire for something other than pleasure *never* form a whole which contains more pleasurable experience than does the whole formed by the total consequences of any other possible desire; and to most observers of human life this statement seems to be plainly false. Hence, indeed, the familiar "hedonistic paradox" to the effect that "pleasure to be got must be forgot"—a paradox which may certainly be quite consistently accepted by hedonists. The fact that hedonists judge the value of acts by reference to their consequences in pleasure by no means commits them to the view that such consequences are best attained by making them directly the sole motive and the sole object of human desire. Nobody makes any scruple of admitting that such a valuable end as health, for example, is not best attained by making it a direct and constant object of conscious concern. It should therefore not surprise us to find that the like is true also of other valuable ends. In fact, I am not familiar with any system of ethics in which it is held that desire for the ultimate end proposed by the system should be made the sole human desire. Why then should it be supposed that hedonists alone are bound to maintain such a doctrine?

As for the connection of hedonism with egoism, it might seem superfluous at this late date to insist that hedonists need in no way be adherents of egoism. Yet this confusion still to some extent persists, even among writers who ought to know very much better. Thus Professor Muncterberg

seems to have supposed that a hedonist can consistently regard any given act as constituting for him a duty only provided he can view it as resulting in a preponderance of pleasure for himself; for he argues against hedonism as follows (*Eternal Values*, p. 39): "When we will the morally good, we do indeed wish that the good also give us joy, but we know that it is not good simply because it gives us pleasure. . . . Even if we acknowledge the pleasure in the minds of other human beings as goal for our moral action, the moral self is not therefore based on pleasure. . . . We feel it our duty to serve the pleasure of others, but this duty cannot itself come into question as a pleasure. We may submit to it with pleasure, but we do not submit to it because it gives us pleasure." But need a hedonist maintain that our duty must needs be a pleasure in the doing?

Mr. Joad also thinks it an inconsistency in a hedonist to admit "that the individual can, and ought to, desire something which may have no relation to his own pleasure, namely, the good of the community" (op. cit., p. 15); for he tells us not only that Mill's implicit admission of this doctrine involved him in inconsistencies, but also that "these inconsistencies in Mill are important, and I have dwelt on them at some length because they demonstrate the impracticability of maintaining, even with the best will in the world, that pleasure is the only thing of value . . . They reveal themselves most completely in Mill's work, but they are implied in any form of utilitarian hedonism." (Op. cit., p. 16.) I should very much like to have it pointed out just *how* the rejection of egoism implies any inconsistency in such a form of utilitarian hedonism as that outlined above.

Another classical line of attack upon hedonism consists in elaborate criticism of the so-called *hedonistic calculus*. If the rightness or wrongness of actions depends upon the degree to which a greater or less "quality of pleasure" is realized in their consequences, then, in order definitely to determine upon the rightness or wrongness of any action, we must be able somehow to predict the consequences of various actions and to estimate the relative "quantities of pleasure" involved. Now no one would deny, I suppose, that it is no easy matter to forecast the future, especially in such a complicated sphere as that of human conduct and its effects; nor will anyone be disposed to doubt that there are grave difficulties involved in the determination and comparison of quantities of pleasure and displeasure. I cannot here enter into the details of this question, but it ought to be clearly understood that precisely similar difficulties affect *any teleological system* of ethics whatever. Every such system makes the value of actions depend upon the quantity of good which they succeed in realizing; every such system holds that some actions are better than others; that some realize more and some less good. In every such system, therefore, some sort of "calculus" is necessary, and I find it very difficult to understand how it can be any easier to determine such quantitative questions as are here involved in terms of "satisfaction of desire" or "harmony" or "self-realization" than it is in terms of pleasure and displeasure. Hedonists have at least made a resolute attempt to deal with this aspect of the matter. I fail to see how any teleological system can view such an attempt as superfluous; and I am not aware that any system has made the attempt with more earnestness or with greater success than hedonism.

Professor Dewey is one of those who make much of the defects of the "calculus" as an objection to hedonism. But I cannot help thinking that he interprets the doctrine in a manner that is highly artificial and unreal. He seems to suppose that in the view of hedonists the calculus can be applied with perfect mathematical precision to the determination of results of individual acts severally, and that, too, with absolute accuracy and certainty of result. (*Human Nature and Conduct,* pp. 50-51.)

This seems to me something of a caricature of the hedonistic view. I venture to think that even Bentham and Mill, who no doubt entertained somewhat exaggerated notions with regard to the applicability of the calculus, never went to anything like such lengths. And what is Professor Dewey's own conclusion with regard to the calculus? He tells us that

the problem of deliberation is not to calculate future happenings, but to appraise present proposed action. We judge present desires and habits by their tendency to produce certain consequences ... The future outcome is not certain ... But its tendency (i.e., the tendency of the fire which Professor Dewey uses as an example) is a knowable matter, what it will do under certain circumstances. And so we know what is the tendency of malice, charity, conceit, patience. We know by observing their consequences, by recollecting what we have observed, by using that recollection in constructive imaginative forecasts of the future, by using the thought of future consequences to tell the quality of the act now proposed. (*Human Nature and Conduct,* pp. 206–7.)

Precisely. And I believe that this is very much the sort of thing that the hedonist means by his despised "calculus."

But, it will perhaps be said, we cannot trust men to guide their actions by any such calculus. The vast majority of mankind are incapable of judging with any accuracy concerning the consequences of their acts; they can neither foresee them all nor correctly estimate their value. So far as this is true, however, it is true on *any* teleological system. And in any such system it is only so far as some such calculus can more or less roughly be carried out that any knowledge of the rightness or wrongness of actions can be attained. Where the estimate fails we must be content to remain in ignorance. Those who are incapable of guiding themselves must, as in other matters, be guided and taught by those possessed by more adequate vision.

"But in the crisis of decision a man cannot be expected always to delay action until he has completed such a calculation of consequences." In truth, no one expects him to do so. As well expect a man on every practical problem of mathematics to calculate his logarithms afresh. In ordinary practice the mathematician relies upon his logarithmic tables. Just so in practical action are we guided by more or less explicitly formulated codes of action, systems of general rules which we take to be the result of past experience, and to embody a measure of wisdom and foresight. We do not question the validity or the value of a method of calculating logarithms because not every Tom, Dick, and Harry is capable of performing it, nor because in practice we follow the results of past calculations. Similar considerations should apply to the calculus of pleasures.

"But a calculus of pleasures can give no definite result. What is one man's meat is another man's poison. What is happiness to one man is unhappiness to another." This, of course, simply means that *what gives* pleasure to one man fails to give it to another. This is certainly a fact which must be taken into account by any theory, but if the sources of pleasure thus vary from man to man, is it not so also with the sources of any ultimate good which one may choose? Are the sources of "satisfactions of desire" or of "self-realization" any less diverse and conflicting? Hedonism here again appears to be no worse off than any other teleological system.

Professor Albee (*History of English Utilitarianism*, p. 274) puts the argument a little differently:

A direct computation of the consequences of actions, in terms of happiness or unhappiness, can never afford the foundation for a scientific Ethics, not merely, or principally, because experience shows that individuals derive pleasure and pain, as the case may be, from very different things; but because it is absolutely certain, on general principles, that every advance in morality involves a **shifting** of the scale of hedonistic values. Otherwise expressed, individuals and nations are con-

stantly, if generally slowly, discarding one scale of hedonistic values for another, previously assumed to be ultimate, and this in proportion to the development of moral character. Reduced to its lowest terms, this means that hedonistic values vary as moral character varies.

It is difficult to see that this way of stating the matter makes things really any harder for the hedonist. It is true that men's judgments regarding the sources or causes of pleasure are subject to frequent change, but so are the judgements with regard to the source of any sort of ultimate value. It is true that as men change they derive pleasure from different things and in different degrees than formerly. But whatever theory of ultimate value is adopted, it seems likely that changes in human thought and character or in other conditions of life will bring with them similar alterations in the sources of value. The mere fact that changes in *moral character* constitute one cause of such alterations in the sources of value seems to introduce no essentially novel difficulty into the argument; and in any case the fact would remain the same and the difficulty equal on any theological theory whatever.

But arguments based on the difficulties of the calculus do not exhaust the case against hedonism. There is no stopping the chorus of objections. "A state of unbroken pleasure would not really be pleasant. A continuous heaven of constant enjoyment would be intolerable boredom." Such an objection surely represents mere confusion of thought. How can pleasure be unpleasant? How can enjoyment be boredom? "But uninterrupted pleasure is an ideal which is impossible of attainment in any actual human life. It is a mere chimera." Or, as Professor Rogers puts the point: "That at which a sensible human being aims is no unimaginable state of the intensest possible pleasure unaccompanied by pain. . . . Rational satisfaction is no dream of an undisturbed and impossibly complete state of felicity." (*Theory of Ethics*, pp.

49-50.) But what hedonist has asserted the attainability of such an ideal? Are hedonists, then, wholly ignorant of the conditions of human life? In truth they are not so foolish as to maintain the attainability of any such perfect consummation, or to counsel attempts to realize the impossible. What they hold is simply that the intrinsic value of any state of affairs is in proportion to the amount of pleasurable experience it contains, and that human effort should be so directed as to make this amount *as great as possible*. No overstrained idealism is implied. A hedonist may, indeed, consistently also be a pessimist. We should not forget that the truth of pessimism has often been argued from hedonistic premises.

But then, says Professor Rogers, "in practice the only clear meaning, therefore, that a 'sum of pleasures' carries is this, that I want my life to be a continuous series of satisfied moments lasting as long as possible. But this is pretty much an empty platitude, which throws almost no light at all on what constitutes satisfaction at any given moment." (Op. cit., p. 48.) But is it to be expected of any theory of the nature of the ultimate end that it should automatically reveal the particular means to that end? For Professor Rogers "that at which a sensible human being aims is ... the realization that he is making the most of life that is possible for him, with his particular interests and limitations, to make, considering the means at his disposal." (p. 50) How much light does this way of formulating the end throw upon "what constitutes satisfaction at any given moment"?

The interesting feature of Professor Rogers' case is that *de facto* he comes very near, despite his protests, to being a hedonist himself—if only he were not so desperately afraid of the name. "Only when we can point to pleasure," he writes, "is the judgment of value felt to be justified." (p. 31) "No aim will be called reflectively a good aim unless it tends to result in pleasure." (p. 38) But still he will not be called a hedonist. He does not "intend to say that

mere pleasurableness by itself is a good. Pleasantness as such is not good because pleasantness does not exist by itself; a good is concrete, and pleasantness merely an abstract quality." But, may we ask, what hedonist attaches any value to mere "pleasantness" as an abstract universal? It is, of course, only concrete pleasurable experience which he values.

Professor Dewey finds it a fundamental defect in utilitarianism that it thinks "of the good to which intelligence is pertinent as consisting in future pleasures and pains." This, in his view, involves a "catastrophe." He emphasizes the "contrast between such conceptions of good and of intelligence and the facts of human nature according to which good, happiness, is found in the present meaning of activity, depending upon the proportion, order, and freedom introduced into it by thought as it discovers objects which realize and unify otherwise contending elements." (p. 212) Professor Dewey's thought, here and elsewhere, seems to be that utilitarian hedonism unduly emphasizes satisfactions to be realized in a distant and none too certain future at the expense of the happiness to be gained in the present through the solution of immediate conflict; that it unduly exalts remote and more or less doubtful advantages at the expense of present fruition (cf. p. 265). That such a tendency to some extent may have operated in the history of utilitarianism I will not deny. But I see not the slightest reason to suppose that such an emphasis is the only one which can be consistently adopted by one who accepts the hedonistic position.

Professor Calkins rejects hedonism because of the "narrowness" of its conception of the good. "'Why then,' the non-hedonist protests to the hedonist, 'why do you exclude activity and thought from your conception of the good, or the ultimate end, why do you limit this chief good to happiness alone?'" (*The Good Man and the Good*, p. 76.) The very asking of this question, it appears, is sufficient to refute hedonism, for without more ado Professor Calkins continues on the next page, "Now that the hedonistic answer to this question is discredited, we turn, naturally enough, to anti-hedonistic doctrines." And what do we find? "It is already clear that only one qualitative theory of the good can escape challenge for its narrowness. This is the doctrine which describes the good not in terms of any one kind of consciousness, as pity, loyalty, wisdom, or happiness, but as inclusive of all these experiences and of all others which people wish or will for themselves" (p. 78). But is it really so clear that there is no "narrowness" here? Might we not ask, with a pertinence equal to that of the non-hedonist's former inquiry, "Why do you exclude things not wished or willed from your conception of the good? Why do you limit the ultimate end to things wished or willed alone?" It is, of course, evident that *any* theory of the end must distinguish between what is ultimately good and what is not, and must therefore inevitably suffer from this form of "narrowness."

Many criticisms of hedonism reduce to most elementary misunderstandings of the hedonistic distinction between pleasurable experience as *intrinsic* and *ultimate* good, and moral value as a species of extrinsic or *instrumental* good. Thus A. E. Taylor writes (*Problem of Conduct*, p. 327): "A man is not morally good because his career has been marked by extraordinary cases of good luck, nor is the life of one of the lower animals to be reckoned morally good because it may contain a vast number of pleasant moments." But hedonists, of course, do not say that *moral* goodness consists in enjoyment of pleasure; for them enjoyment is an *extrinsic* value derived from the fact that certain actions and dispositions *result in* consequences which are more pleasurable than the results of other acts and dispositions. The same confusion is apparent also in Taylor's treatment of the question, Is the good always pleasant? He interprets this to mean "Is the morally good or *right* act always accompanied by more

pleasure than a wrong act?" To the question so stated no hedonist would dream of giving an affirmative answer. Professor Fullerton also gives a criticism of hedonism based on this same misunderstanding. After quoting Bentham to the effect that all pleasure is in itself good, even the pleasure a malicious man "takes at the thought of the pain which he sees, or expects to see, his adversary undergo," he asks, "Can the pleasure of a malignant act properly be called *morally* good at all?" (*A Handbook of Ethical Theory*, p. 224; cf. p. 240.) This question being answered in the negative, Bentham's position is considered to be refuted. But, as we have seen, no hedonist dreams of maintaining that pleasant experience is *in itself* a *moral* good. In fact, for hedonism nothing whatever is in itself, i.e., intrinsically, a moral good.

Another favorite procedure of the critics is based upon the fact that hedonists have often professed to give demonstrative *proofs* of the truth of their theory. These attempted demonstrations are examined and found to be inconclusive, or positively fallacious. Hedonism, it is thus discovered, has "failed to prove its case," and we pass on to consider the alternative theories. Now let us admit at once that the fundamental principles of hedonism are incapable of demonstration. So far as I can see, the critics are quite right in rejecting all the alleged proofs that have ever been offered, and I know of nothing that can be set in their place. But how stands the case with the alternative theories? Is it possible to give a demonstration of *their* fundamental principles? Their advocates scarcely pretend that it is. These alternatives are accepted, not because of any rigorous proof of their truth, but on quite other grounds. The fact that hedonism "fails to prove its case" in itself certainly constitutes no proof of the truth of any other theory. The truth of the matter seems to be that no theory of ethics, *in so far as it is a question of ultimate ends*, is susceptible of "proof" in the strict sense. In fact, even Bentham and Mill were on occasion prepared to admit as much. Thus Bentham says of the fundamental principle of hedonism, "Is it susceptible of any direct proof? It should seem not; for that which is used to prove everything else, cannot itself be proved." (Selby-Bigge, *British Moralists,* Vol. I, Sec. 364.) And Mill also remarks: "To be incapable of proof by reasoning is common to all first principles." (*Utilitarianism,* Everyman Library edition, p. 32.) Unfortunately, however, Mill nevertheless attempted, in his fourth chapter, precisely such a proof as he had here stated to be impossible. His lack of success is certainly not surprising.

Fundamental ethical principles, in fact, as Mr. Moore so properly insists, are accepted or rejected on intuitive grounds. The most that any adherent of any ethical system can do by way of persuading another to accept his theory is to state its fundamental principles as clearly and adequately as possible, to take care that these are properly interpreted, and that the issues are not obscured by any confusion with irrelevant or inconsistent doctrines, to exhibit the implications of these principles and their consistency or inconsistency with other human beliefs, and then simply appeal to the reflective judgement of his hearer. If the latter, having once clearly understood the principles and their implications, thereupon rejects them, then *cadit quaestio.*

For my own part, when I subject to such a test the fundamental principles of hedonistic ethics, they appear to me to ring true. Indeed, it seems to me to be actually self-evident that all pleasurable experience is ultimately good. It does *not* seem to me self-evident that *nothing but* pleasurable experience is ever ultimately good; but much careful reflection has hitherto failed to reveal anything else which *does* seem to me ultimately good. Again, it is not self-evident to me that the intrinsic value of a whole is necessarily always in proportion to the amount of ultimate good which it contains; but in every instance which I have

ever considered it has always seemed to me that this is actually the case. Consequently I am forced to adopt a hedonistic position. If other men judge these matters differently I know of no way of "refuting" them; but, on the other hand, I have never been able to see that any of the considerations advanced in opposition to hedonism constitute a refutation of *it.*

From what has been said, however, it is obvious that there may be perfectly *legitimate* criticisms of hedonism—those, namely, which consist simply in presenting for judgment "hard cases" concerning which it is thought that the only conclusion consistent with hedonistic principles will nevertheless, on careful reflection, be rejected. But such criticisms, however legitimate in method, have never actually seemed to me in the least conclusive. Such force as they at first sight sometimes appear to have always turns out to arise, so far as I can see, from some confusion of thought which still clouds the issue. Once these confusions are cleared away, I never seem to find in these "hard cases" anything incompatible with the truth of hedonism.

Any adequate consideration of this phase of the matter would lead us too far afield to allow of our undertaking it on the present occasion with any degree of fullness. I shall therefore simply illustrate the way in which it seems to me possible to dispose of such hard cases by the examination of a few upon which Mr. Moore chiefly depends, and which I hope will be more or less typical. The following is an instance which he believes will persuade us that even wholes containing no pleasure may be intrinsically valuable: "Let us imagine one world exceedingly beautiful. Imagine it as beautiful as you can . . . and then imagine the ugliest world you can possibly conceive. Imagine it simply one heap of filth" (*Principia Ethica,* p. 8), and then suppose that no one ever can or does receive pleasure or displeasure from either world in any respect or degree whatever. "Would it not be well to do what we could to produce the beautiful world rather than the other?" Would not the former be intrinsically better than the latter? Now I ask myself whether this case does not derive most of its apparent force from the circumstance that the reader who makes the imaginative comparison very naturally revolts from the image of the ugly world and at the same time takes pleasure in the thought of the beautiful world, and that he neglects explicitly to notice and discount this fact. I also ask myself whether the reader is not influenced, and his judgement unconsciously perverted, by the fact that we can scarcely compare these two imaginary worlds without the thought that the beautiful world obviously possesses greater pleasure-producing potentialities than the ugly one; by the fact that it is difficult to compare these two imaginary worlds without reference to the consideration that the one world provides, for any conscious being that might sometime be introduced upon the scene, a better basis for enjoyment than does the other. Once I carefully notice and discount such sources of bias, I entirely fail, for my own part, to see the superior value in the beautiful world.

Another of Mr. Moore's examples—one of those which to his mind "constitute a *reductio ad absurdum* of the view that intrinsic value is always in proportion to quantity of pleasure," is as follows. If this hedonistic principle is true, it "involves our saying . . . that a world in which absolutely nothing except pleasure existed—no knowledge, no love, no enjoyment of beauty, no moral qualities—must yet be intrinsically better—better worth creating—provided only the total quantity of pleasure in it were the least bit greater, than one in which all those things existed *as well as* pleasure." (*Ethics*, pp. 237, 238.) This instance seems almost deliberately framed to confuse the issue; for it is very difficult in considering the matter to remember that, if we are not illegitimately to introduce into our second world an additional increment of pleasure, by "enjoyment of beauty" we

must here distinctly mean merely *contemplation* of beauty, wholly divorced from any element of pleasure. Moreover, it is difficult to keep our minds wholly free from the thought of the greater hedonic potentialities of a world possessing so many elements which in our experience are fruitful sources of enjoyment, as compared with a world from which these sources are eliminated. Once I clear my mind from such confusing associations, however, I feel no further difficulty in reaching the hedonistic conclusion.

Mr. Moore also points out that the hedonistic theory compels us to assert that "the state of mind of a drunkard, when he is intensely pleased with breaking crockery, is just as valuable, in itself—just as well worth having, as that of a man who is fully realizing all that is exquisite in the tragedy of King Lear, provided only the mere quantity of pleasure in both cases is the same" (p. 238). Here again, once I carefully abstract from all tacit reference to the differing promise and potentiality of these two states of mind, from all larger thought of their vastly differing significance for the total lives of these men and their fellows, I find myself quite clearly committed to the hedonistic view of the matter.

I thus do quite clearly embrace the conclusion which Mr. Moore thinks self-evidently mistaken, "that if we *could* get as much pleasure in the world, without needing to have any knowledge, or any moral qualities, or any sense of beauty, as we can get *with* them, then all these things would be entirely superfluous" (p. 238). But I also quite as heartily agree with Mr. Moore that "the question is quite incapable of proof either way" (p. 238), and that "if anybody, after clearly considering the issue, does come" to the contrary conclusion, "there is no way of proving that he is wrong" (p. 238). My point simply is that there is no short and easy way with hedonism, and that the cavalier way in which it is commonly treated is wholly unreasonable and unjust.

Intrinsic Value

MONROE C. BEARDSLEY

I

Many philosophers apparently still accept the proposition that there is such a thing as intrinsic value, i.e., that some part of the value of some things (objects, events, or states of affairs) is intrinsic value. John Dewey's attack seems not to have dislodged this proposition, for today it is seldom questioned. I propose to press the attack again, in terms that owe a great deal to Dewey, as I understand him.

The predicates (1) "... has intrinsic value," (2) "... is intrinsically valuable," and (3) "... is intrinsically desirable," will be used interchangeably—not for the sake of elegant variation, but because each permits idiomatic constructions that bring out different features of what I take to be the same concept. "Desirable" associates with "to desire," which will be convenient to have available at a later stage of the argument. (No doubt "valuable" and "to value" are similarly related, but the latter is not free from the suggestion of reflective appraisal.) On the other hand, the noun "value" is useful because we can speak of "a value" and "a kind of value." "Value" lends itself more readily than "desirability" to such adjectival qualifications as "cognitive value" and "moral value."

Two phrases are the most often used in defining "intrinsic value": "for its own sake" and "in itself." Their meanings are

close, but not identical, and the second seems more satisfactory than the first.

We might say that something is intrinsically valuable, in some degree, if it is valuable for its own sake, and that if it has value for the sake of something else, then its intrinsic value, if any, is that which would remain if that other-regarding value were subtracted. One inconvenience of this definition can be brought out as follows: A sheet of postage stamps has been misprinted—the central figure, say, is inverted. The stamps derive part of their value from their rarity. Is one of these stamps valuable, in part, for its own sake? Well, its value is not for the sake of anything else—if we speak of its philatelic value, not its market value. But is this value then intrinsic? It seems strange to say this when it can be taken away, without altering the stamp at all, simply by having the Post Office Department print a few hundred million more copies. Since its rarity is a relational property, there is a sense in which the rare stamp is valuable not for the sake of anything else, either. It might be replied that, even if the issue becomes plentiful, the philatelic value of each individual stamp is not destroyed, but only reduced; rarity cannot transform an object with no value into one with value; it can only increase certain sorts of value in things that already have some degree of it. Still, that part of the stamp's philatelic value that is supplied by rarity seems to be neither intrinsic nor extrinsic, if these are defined as "for its own sake" and "for the sake of something else" respectively.

Reprinted from *Philosophy and Phenomenological Research*, XXVI, Sept. 1965, pp. 1–17, by permission of the author and the publisher.

401

The second definition of "intrinsic value" is that proposed by G. E. Moore in his paper on "The Conception of Intrinsic Value." Suppose we can distinguish between the internal and external properties of a thing, that is between (1) its qualities and inner relations, and (2) its relations to other things. Then the value that depends upon a thing's internal properties alone is its intrinsic value; the value that depends (wholly or partly) upon a thing's external properties is its extrinsic value. The intrinsically good thing is "good in itself." Moore states the definition this way:

To say that a kind of value is "intrinsic" means merely that the question whether a thing possesses it, and in what degree it possesses it, depends solely on the intrinsic nature of the thing in question.[1]

It is this definition of intrinsic value that leads to Moore's thought-experiment in *Principia Ethica*. To decide the question "What things have intrinsic value"?, he says,

it is necessary to consider what things are such that, if they existed *by themselves*, in absolute isolation, we should yet judge their existence to be good.[2]

If the intrinsic value of a thing is independent of its relationship to anything else, it cannot be destroyed by the removal of everything else. Moore holds that only by applying this test can we sort out intrinsic from extrinsic value with clarity and confidence.

Some puzzles in Moore's definition of "intrinsic nature" have been further discussed by him and by others.[3] One difficulty is to explain how intrinsic goodness can be a property dependent solely on the intrinsic properties of things, without itself

being an intrinsic property—this explanation is needed to fix the status of goodness as a "nonnatural property." Another is to decide whether dispositional properties are to be called internal or external, and to dispose of a certain element of arbitrariness or conventionality in the classification of some properties as dispositional. In the case of the most self-contained and self-sufficient of the valuable objects we are acquainted with—that is, works of art—the internal-external distinction has an immediate appeal. Thus we tell people to listen to the music "itself" and pay no attention to anything outside it, such as objects it might suggest or the biography of the composer. And the so-called "Formalist" has been known to assert that the (aesthetic) value of a painting depends on internal properties alone (lines, shapes, and colors) and owes nothing to its representational relationship to the world outside it. But even if these notions are regarded as acceptable, serious questions can be raised about the sharpness and decisiveness of the internal-external distinction.

And it is no doubt for this reason, as well as for others, that most contemporary value-theorists have concluded that if anything is intrinsically valuable it is not an external object, but an experience or psychological state. At best, the work of art could only be said to have "inherent value" (in C. I. Lewis's terminology), if exposure to it can result in an aesthetically enjoyable experience. The distinction between internal and external properties seems clearer when applied to experiences. Of course, intentionality—a reference to other states of mind or to the external world—must be taken as internal to the experience itself; but neither an ostensible memory of a past pleasure nor the expectation of a future one is causally dependent upon the occurrence of those pleasures, and so, theoretically at least, we can conceive any short stretch of conscious life apart from its antecedents and consequents. And apparently we can ask whether it has intrinsic value.

[1] *Philosophical Studies*, London 1922, p. 260.
[2] *Principia Ethica*, Cambridge University 1903, p. 187; cf. *Ethics*, London 1947, pp. 42, 101.
[3] See C. D. Broad, "G. E. Moore's Latest Published Views on Ethics," *Mind* LXX (1961), pp. 435–57.

I take it that to say that something is valuable is to say that it deserves to be valued; and to say that something is desirable is to say that it is worthy of being desired. Now when we add "intrinsically" to, say, "desirable," how does it fit into the definiens? Does "X is intrinsically desirable" mean

(1) "X is intrinsically worthy of being desired" (that is, by definition, "X is worthy-of-being-desired on account of its internal properties alone")?

Or does it mean

(2) "X is worthy of being intrinsically desired" (that is, by definition, "X is worthy of being-desired-on-account-of-its-internal-properties-alone")?

I have puzzled over the relationship between these two expressions, and find that I can only understand the former in terms of the latter. For if X's desirability depends on its internal properties alone, then these must be the properties that ought to be, or deserve to be, desired; and what ought to be the case is that X is desired on account of these internal properties.

Thus in order to attach a sense to "intrinsically desirable" we must first attach a sense to "intrinsically desired." And there is, I think, no trouble about this. For there is an evident psychological distinction between desiring something on account of its internal properties alone, and desiring it on account of its relationships to other things. The distinction is not easy to apply, because in most of our desires, care for the thing itself and concern for what will come of it are thoroughly mixed. But we can pretty well fix the extremes: at the one end, the candy that the child in the grocery store wants, and screams for, and evidently would count the world well lost for; at the other end, the pieces of string and bits of cellophane that we instantly discard, once we have secured the goods they serve to wrap. And we can use Moore's test with some success to make the psychological

distinction, by asking a person, for example, to think what he would choose to do if he had only a short time on earth, with limitless resources and no obligations to others. The child no doubt would gorge himself on candy, but nobody would pore over chewing-gum wrappers.

So I would like to allow, and exploit, the term "to desire intrinsically." But of course it does not follow automatically that because we can attach "intrinsically" to "desire," we therefore attach it to "desirable." There are obviously other adverbs that go with "desired," but not with "desirable" (for example, "eagerly," "strongly," and "widely"). An argument must be made out to show that things can be intrinsically desirable as well as intrinsically desired.

II

The question, then, is this: What good reasons are there, if any, for believing that there is such a thing as intrinsic value? Since this proposition is seldom considered to be in need of elaborate proof, formal arguments are difficult to collect. I can only discover three such arguments: (1) an argument from definition, (2) a dialectical demonstration, and (3) an attempt at empirical confirmation.

(1) *The Argument from Definition.* In the view of some thinkers, the existence of intrinsic value can be simply shown in this way: Some extrinsic value is instrumental value, which is defined as follows:

"X has instrumental value" means "X is conducive to something that has intrinsic value." (Call this Definition A.)

I have selected the loose term "conducive to," in order to avoid some distinctions that we do not need at present. Thus if Y is an end to which X is a means, or a whole of which X is a necessary part, then X is conducive to such intrinsic value as Y possesses. Obviously, if we accept Definition A, we are as committed to the existence of intrinsic value as we are to the existence of instrumental value—however long the chain of conduciveness may be.

But must we accept this definition? In order for Y to confer its value on X, when X is conducive to Y, it is certain that Y must have some value to confer, but whether that value is intrinsic or instrumental does not matter as far as X is concerned. So the following alternative definition should be acceptable:

"X has instrumental value" means "X is conducive to something that has value." (Call this Definition B.)

The Arguer from Definition rejects Definition B. It is all right if the key term in the definiens, "value," can be defined by itself, without reference to intrinsic value. But the word "value," he might contend, is necessarily an ellipsis; it cannot stand by itself. Up to this point I have been speaking as though value is a genus with two species, so that value can be defined first and then divided by Moore's test. And it is true that in describing that test, Moore speaks as though we could first know that an object has a certain total value, before going on to discover how much of that total is intrinsic, and how much extrinsic. But this, according to the Arguer from Definition, is all misleading. The terms "extrinsic value" and "intrinsic value," despite the noun they share, do not name coordinate species of a genus, but designate two very different concepts, one of which is derivative from the other.[4] And Moore's own way of speaking agrees with this interpretation, on occasion. For example, he speaks[5] as

though the phrase "good as a means" (i.e., having instrumental value) is synonymous with the phrase "a means to good" (i.e., conducing to intrinsic value). Being good as a means is not a way of being good—the instrumentally valuable thing is not a valuable instrument, strictly speaking, but an instrument of value. And similarly,

To have value merely as a part is equivalent to having no value at all, but merely being a part of that which has it.[6]

This line of thought would issue in the rejection of my Definition B. For it seems to show that instrumental value can only be defined in terms of intrinsic value; so that the existence of the former automatically entails the existence of the latter.

Nevertheless, it seems to me that the word "value" does have a meaning by itself, and does mark out a genus. We can sensibly ascribe value as such to things, and this is even more clearly true of "desirable" and "worth having."[7] The terms "good as a means" and "good as an end in itself," if they may be taken as synonymous with "instrumental good" and "intrinsic good," suggest that the distinction is between two *grounds* of goodness, not two *senses*. This is the position assumed by Moore in his *Ethics* when he asserts that

saying a thing is intrinsically good . . . means it would be a good thing that the thing in question should exist, even if it existed *quite alone*, without any further accompaniments or effects whatever.[8]

For here "intrinsically good" is defined by means of "a good thing." If this is a correct procedure, Definition B is acceptable, and the Argument from Definition fails.

(2) *The Dialectical Demonstration* is closely connected with the Argument from Definition, but deserves exhibition on its own. I think of it as logically parallel to the

---

[4] "Intrinsic" and "extrinsic," in the convenient terminology of Austin Duncan-Jones, would then be "sense-discriminating," rather than "concept-modifying," adjectives (see "Intrinsic Value: Some Comments on the Work of G. E. Moore," *Philosophy* XXXIII (1958), pp. 240–73, esp. pp. 261–62).

[5] *Principia Ethica*, p. 24.

[6] *Ibid.*, p. 35.

[7] See Duncan-Jones, pp. 257–58.

[8] *Ethics*, p. 42.

First Cause argument for the existence of God. "Instrumentally valuable" is a relational concept—X borrows its value from Y, or Y confers its value upon X. If the value Y confers is itself instrumental, so that it is merely passed along from Z, then where does Z get its value? In the last analysis, something must (according to this argument) possess its value in itself, or nothing can get any value.[9] So the existence of any instrumental value proves the existence of some intrinsic value, just as the occurrence of any event is said to prove the existence of a First Cause.

To align the Demonstration of intrinsic value with the venerable First Cause argument may lend it prestige, but may also suggest its faults. As Kant showed, the First Cause argument projects a certain kind of ideal explanation that cannot be completed if the causal series has no beginning term. That is, if to explain an event, X, requires not only that we assign cause, W, but that we assign an *explained* cause, then the ideal explanation of X would involve the explanation of all its causal antecedents; and if these have no first term, no such explanation can be given. Similarly, the Dialectical Demonstration of intrinsic value projects a certain kind of ideal justification that cannot be completed if the series of means and ends has no last term. That is, if to justify ascribing a value to X requires not only that we show it is a means to Y, but also that we justify ascribing a value to Y, and if there is no stopping point, no such ideal justification can be given. But ordinary justification, like ordinary causal explanation, involves no such infinite regress.

The Dialectical Demonstration cannot be a pure formal demonstration, for, unless the Argument from Definition is valid, it cannot be proved strictly self-contradictory to assert the existence of instrumental value

but deny the existence of intrinsic value. The Demonstration must rather be thought of as applying to our *knowledge* of value. Premise 1: We know, or have good reason to believe, that some things are instrumentally valuable. Premise 2: We could not know this unless we knew some things to be intrinsically valuable. Conclusion: We know some things to be intrinsically valuable. Now, Premise 1 seems to me clearly true. But the conclusion seems to me quite clearly false. The paradoxical feature of our value-knowledge is just that we have a good deal of sound knowledge about instrumental values, but are in considerable doubt about intrinsic values. Philosophers have disputed, and still dispute, about whether pleasure is an intrinsic value, and, if so, whether it is the only intrinsic value; and it is significant that as ordinary people we have not had to wait upon the settlement of these issues before discovering a great many valuable things nearer to hand. We must have some way of knowing that in many concrete situations it is better for a person to be healthy than sick, without knowing whether that is because it is intrinsically best for him to maximize his net positive hedonic quality, or realize his potentialities, or cultivate a good will, or whatever.

The apparent hopelessness of resolving problems about instrumental value without knowing antecedently what, if anything, intrinsic value may be, can be cleared away, I believe, if we go back to the concrete contexts of value-problems.[10] When we are in the position of having to decide what is valuable, or more valuable, we are in Dewey's "problematic situation," and such a situation is one in which certain ends are in grave doubt and others are (on that occasion) taken as temporarily fixed. If the value of everything in the situation were in

[9] Cf. Hume's argument that "something must be desirable on its own account," *Inquiry Concerning the Principles of Morals*, N.Y.: Liberal Arts Press, 1957, p. 111.

[10] Here I want to acknowledge my debt to Sidney Hook's essay on "The Desirable and Emotive in Dewey's Ethics," in his collection, *John Dewey: Philosopher of Science and Freedom*, N.Y. 1950.

question at once, nothing could be decided at all, and indeed no problem could even be conceived; only in terms of certain tentatively-held values, can we decide, or even ask, whether other things are valuable or not. There must be a basis on which it is reasonable for us to pick out salient elements in the situation, and assign them probable values, without transforming the task of assignment into another problematic situation, thus endlessly postponing a decision. A state of affairs such as good health, for example, has retained its eligibility through earlier problems and experiences; its value has survived them, in the sense that up to this point health does not seem to have interfered with our pursuits, but a lack of it from time to time has not only contributed to the rise of difficult problems, but has limited our capacity to resolve them. We need not suppose that health is an intrinsic good, or that it is always good, or even that we are necessarily right in taking it to be good on the present occasion—but we do have rational justification for supposing that it has positive value that ought to be taken into consideration now.

This is the merest sketch of a way of looking at the problem of evaluation. The gist of it is that reasonable decisions about instrumental values do not presuppose, or wait upon, previous reasonable decisions about intrinsic values (even if such decisions were possible, which I shall argue—in the next section—they are not). So there is no infinite regress in a purely instrumentalist theory of value.

(3) *The Empirical Confirmation.* Some writers on the theory of value have not relied on eother of the *a priori* forms of argument that I have just considered, but have held that the existence of intrinsic value is attested by direct experience. One of the most carefully considered theories is that of C. I. Lewis. He distinguishes three kinds of value-predication, of which the basic kind is the "expressive statement," having a form like "This is good," where

"this" refers to immediate presentations in experience.[11] Expressive statements report "value-apprehensions" or "direct findings of value-quality in what is presented,"[12] and are therefore incorrigible.[13]

. . . It will hardly be denied that there is what may be called "apparent value" or "felt goodness," as there is seen redness or heard shrillness. And while the intent to formulate just this apparent value-quality of what is given, without implication of anything further, encounters linguistic difficulties, surely it will not be denied that there are such immediate experiences of good and bad to be formulated.[14]

It is this immediate value-quality that Lewis calls intrinsic value, and that imports intrinsic value into those experiences that possess it. To it all forms of value-judgment are ultimately anchored. And because it is only in experiences that we are directly acquainted with such qualities, only experiences can, strictly speaking, have intrinsic value. When an object enables us to "realize" intrinsic value in experience, by being directly presented to us, the object has "inherent value," which is a form of extrinsic value.[15] "The goodness of a good *object* is a potentiality for the realization of goodness in experience."[16]
We have suggested—and intend to abide by—distinction between intrinsic and extrinsic values by reference to the question, "Is that which is valued, valued *for its own sake* or for the sake of something else?"[17]

What is most surprising in Lewis's characterization of this value-quality, is the way he employs alternately, and indifferently, the two expressions that other phi-

[11] *Theory of Knowledge and Valuation,* LaSalle, Ill., 1946, p. 374.
[12] *Ibid.,* p. 365.
[13] *Ibid.,* p. 375.
[14] *Ibid.,* pp. 374–75.
[15] *Ibid.,* pp. 386–87, 391.
[16] *Ibid.,* p. 389.
[17] *Ibid.,* p. 385.

losophers have been at such pains to keep distinct: "valuable in itself" and "valued in itself."

There are passages in which Lewis seems to suggest that being valuable and being valued may not be the same thing, since one of them may be evidence of the other. Here being liked is an *index* of being

Such appellations as these—"liked" or "disliked," "wanted" or "unwanted," "good" or "bad," as addressed to the directly presented—are better indices of the immediately valuable or disvaluable than others.[18]

intrinsically valuable, hence not identical to it (though the force of this distinction is certainly much blunted by putting "good" and "bad" in with "liked" and "disliked"). And later he says, in the antecedent of a concessive conditional, that "liking and disliking are decisive of immediate value,"[19] again as though there might be an evidential relationship between being immediately liked and being intrinsically valuable. But in Lewis's prevailing usage, "valuable" is simply reduced to "liked," or "likeable," and "*per se* desirable" only means "*per se* desired." The normative element in "value" is completely lost sight of.

It is intrinsic desiredness that Lewis substitutes for intrinsic desirability. Thus he speaks of "the likeability and dislikeability of things; their directly gratifying quality or the opposite,"[20] and says that "value-disvalue is that mode or aspect of the given or the contemplated to which desire and aversion are addressed."[21] These remarks suggest that when he speaks of "desirability," he means only "likeability," and when he speaks of "finding value-qualities" he means only finding something that excites desire or aversion. But in that case, Lewis has not really shown that the existence of intrinsic desirability (in the usual sense) is confirmed in immediate experience.[22]

Charles A. Baylis[23] explicates "intrinsic good" as what is "worthy of existence entirely apart from any extrinsic value it may have" (an interesting example of reversing the order of definitions proposed in the Argument from Definition above). And he explicates "worthy of existence" by saying

that anything which has this characteristic ought, *ceteris paribus*, to exist rather than not, that it would be better for it to exist, and that anyone who can bring it into being ought to do so unless there is something preferable he can do instead.[24]

Like W. D. Ross, in short, he makes "intrinsic value" entail a conditional ought-sentence, a prima facie obligation. He then goes on to say that "the best initial evidence . . . we could have" for ascribing intrinsic value to something

is that we find ourselves *prizing* things of that kind, *i.e.*, liking, approving, desiring, preferring, and commending them, for their own qualities (rather than because of their relations to other valuable things) in circumstances where to the best of our searching knowledge we are making no mistake in our cognition of them. Such evidence gives us an initial probability that what we thus prize is intrinsically good.[25]

Since Baylis agrees with Lewis that only experiences can be intrinsically good, his position contrasts interestingly with Lewis's

[18] *Ibid.*, p. 404.
[19] *Ibid.*, p. 410.
[20] *Ibid.*, p. 418.
[21] *Ibid.*, p. 403.

[22] Cf. Duncan-Jones: "I do not think that worth-havingness is more or less the same as pleasantness or enjoyableness" (*op. cit.*, p. 266), because "worth having" involves an element of "deliberation." And cf. John Dewey: "To pass from immediacy of enjoyment to something called 'intrinsic value' is a leap for which there is no ground" (*Theory of Valuation*, International Encyclopedia of Unified Science, Vol. II, No. 4, Chicago 1939, p. 41).
[23] "Grading, Values, and Choice, *Mind* LXVII (1958): 485–501.
[24] *Ibid.*, p. 494.
[25] Baylis, *op. cit.*, pp. 494–95.

on the question of our knowledge of intrinsic value. For Lewis, the desiring of a mental state, while it is occurring (i.e., the enjoyment of it), is conclusive evidence of its desirability. For Baylis, it is only "initial evidence," the probative force of which is then to be increased

by making repeated examinations of things of the same kind under circumstances which vary just enough to guard against the kinds of cognitive error which might occur.[26]

It seems to me that Baylis gives two completely unrelated accounts of intrinsic value, and only makes them seem the same by passing so swiftly from one to the other. Up to the middle of his paper, all characterizations of intrinsic value are in terms of words like "worthy," "better," and "ought"—and it clearly retains its normative character. But when he comes to his thesis that particular well-conducted prizings constitute *evidence* for intrinsic value, a quite different characterization takes over.

The attribution of intrinsic goodness to an experience is like the attribution of an ideally defined, but not actually observable, physical property, *e.g.*, weighing precisely one pound, to an object.[27]

Weighing exactly one pound is explicated in terms of being equal in weight to a standard pound; and the latter turns out to be a complicated conditional about what would happen under ideal weighing conditions (admitting that the ideal conditions cannot all be specified). Thus "X weighs exactly one pound" means (approximately) "X would be found to be one pound in weight by an Ideal Weigher, under Ideal Conditions, with an Ideal Scale, etc., etc." And similarly, "X has intrinsic value" turns out to be equivalent to a complex conditional to the effect that X would be prized by an Ideal Observer, defined by all the necessary accoutrements and qualifications of such an individual.[28]

[26] *Ibid.*, p. 495.
[27] *Ibid.*, p. 497.
[28] *Ibid.*, p. 499.

I do not propose to take up the Ideal Observer theory here, or related proposals for defining intrinsic value, such as have been very carefully worked out by Roderick Firth and Richard Brandt.[29] Yet I hesitate to set aside so important a position without more careful consideration. Essentially, my view of it can be put in the form of a dilemma. When "X has intrinsic value" is defined in terms of the attitude, or desires, or satisfactions, of an Ideal Observer, the specified characteristics of the Ideal Observer either do or do not include any normative concepts. If the Ideal Observer is defined wholly in nonnormative terms, as one who is is omniscient, impartial, etc., etc., then (1) statements about the Ideal Observer can be confirmed by reports of my own prizings, under controlled conditions, but (2) it will remain an open question, in Moore's sense, whether the Ideal Observer actually desires what is desirable; and from the statement that something is desired by the Ideal Observer, nothing follows about what deserves to exist, or to be done. On the other hand, if normative terms are smuggled into the definition of the Ideal Observer—so that he is defined in effect as one who knows intrinsic value when he sees it—then (1) it does follow that I ought to desire, as far as I can, what the Ideal Observer desires, but (2) statements about the desires of the Ideal Observer can no longer be empirical hypotheses, and cannot be confirmed, or given initial probability, by reports of any actual desirings or prizings; from the statement that a certain musical experience is found prizeworthy by an Ideal Observer, no predictions can be derived about my prizings or disprizings.

I conclude that the existence of intrinsically valuable things, including mental

[29] See Firth, "Ethical Absolutism and the Ideal Observer," *Philosophy and Phenomenological Research* XII (March 1952): 317–45; Firth and Brandt, "The Definition of an 'Ideal Observer' Theory in Ethics," *ibid.* XV (March 1955): 407–23; Richard Henson, "On Being Ideal," *Philosophical Review* LXV (1956): 389–400; and Richard Brandt, *Ethical Theory*, Englewood Cliffs, 1959, ch. 10.

states, cannot be made certain by direct experience, or probable by inductive inference from direct experience.

It is interesting, by the way, that Paul Taylor, in his recent book, rejects the Argument from Definition, and holds that "a world where all values were extrinsic, the value of one thing depending on the value of another whose value in turn depends on the value of something else, *ad infinitum*," is not logically impossible, nor even unimaginable.[30] In his view, it is an empirical fact about our world that all extrinsic values ultimately do go back to intrinsic ones. But it seems to me that Taylor, for all his care, mixes the desirable and the desired as Lewis and Baylis do. Thus, in describing the "world in which instrumental and contributive values did *not* depend on intrinsic value," he says that in such a world

No one would do anything for its own sake, simply because he found personal enjoyment in it. It would be a world of "practical people" who knew how to get things done but had no reason for getting one thing done rather than another.[31]

But this is a caricature of a world in which all values are extrinsic. For, in the first place, the question whether people "do anything for its own sake" is not at all the question whether there is intrinsic value; the world without intrinsic value (that is, our world) is a world in which people may often do something for its own sake, and may experience many enjoyments, but they cannot *justify* doing something for its own sake by simple appeal to enjoyment. And in the second place, a world in which all values are instrumental would be precisely a world in which every correct value-judgment could be supported by a reason, and so there would always be a "reason for getting one thing done rather than another."

[30] *Normative Discourse*, N.Y. 1961, p. 26.
[31] *Ibid.*, p. 32.

III

I now turn from the arguments for the thesis that there exists at least one thing with intrinsic value, to my argument against this thesis. It is that the concept of intrinsic value is inapplicable—that even if something has intrinsic value, we could not know it, and therefore that it can play no role in ethical or aesthetic reasoning.

Richard Brandt has remarked that "X is desirable" means the same as "Desiring X is justified."[32] What "desirable" adds to "desired" is this claim to justifiability. But the only way this claim can be made good is by considering X in the wider context of other things, in relation to a segment of a life or of many lives. Thus the term "intrinsic desirability" pulls in two directions: the noun tells us to look farther afield, the adjective tells us to pay no attention to anything but X itself.

This implicit contradiction in the concept of intrinsic value can, in theory, be removed on one epistemological assumption. If we could detect the presence of intrinsic value by immediate intuition—in the way Moore claimed to know that the satisfactions of personal relationship and of artistic beauty are the highest intrinsic values available to human beings[33]—then we would not require reasons in order to know it. If we ask why the experience of a good painting has intrinsic value, the answer will be "It contains (or is characterized by) aesthetic enjoyment."[34] And if we then ask why aesthetic enjoyment is intrinsically valuable, we have reached an end. For no further reasons can be given, so long as we are confined, in answering, to the experience itself. We can only say that it is self-evident to some cognitive faculty that is equipped to grasp the self-evidence of such truths as this. I cannot honestly appeal to

[32] *Op. cit.*, p. 30.
[33] *Principia Ethica*, p. 188.
[34] Supposing there is such a special sort of enjoyment; see my paper on "The Discrimination of Aesthetic Enjoyment," *British Journal of Aesthetics*, III (1963), pp. 291–300.

such intuitive apprehensions of intrinsic value, when I do not possess them myself. But I can fairly question whether others are mistaken in thinking that they possess them. The familiar arguments against ethical intuitionism will not be reviewed in detail here. Since intuition is a last resort as a way of resolving the problems of value theory, it is fatal that ethical intuitions conflict; that criteria cannot be given for distinguishing correct from incorrect ones; and that the alleged analogies with other types of *a priori* knowledge (mathematical, for example) break down. It can never be a necessary truth that any particular instance of aesthetic enjoyment is desirable, since later experience may reveal that it was not in fact desirable at all; therefore it can never be a necessary truth that any particular instance of aesthetic enjoyment is *intrinsically* desirable; therefore no *general* or *universal* proposition about the connection of aesthetic enjoyment and intrinsic value can be necessary; and therefore, there is no necessary truth about the intrinsic value of aesthetic enjoyment to be grasped by intuition.

Brandt gives an excellent example for discussion:

Consider a child who is swinging, in a rapturous state of enjoyment. We shall probably think that being in this state of mind (and perhaps body) is worthwhile for itself alone. To be in a state of rapturous enjoyment of the experience of swinging is for one's state of mind to have an intrinsic property, on account of which the child's experience is desirable. So we shall say that the child's experience is of intrinsic worth.[35]

Now, how could one justify the assertions that this experience is (a) intrinsically desirable and (b) desirable? If intrinsic desirability is in question, we can only say, "It is an experience containing the rapturous enjoyment of swinging." But it would be odd if we were content to accept this as

a sufficient reason for saying that the experience is intrinsically desirable, when we would not accept it as a sufficient reason for saying that the experience is desirable. For to support the latter statement, we would need at least to say that in the first place the swinging doesn't do the child any harm (it is an innocent pleasure), and that there is nothing else more important for him to be doing at this time. Otherwise we should not say that this particular experience of swinging is desirable at all. But as soon as we bring in these considerations making the desirability of this experience depend in part upon the lack of unwanted consequences and upon the comparison of this action with other possible actions, then the desirability we have defended is no longer intrinsic, but extrinsic.

When we call a thing "desirable," it seems to me, we claim to place it in a larger perspective; we suggest that alternatives have been considered, and the desirable thing selected with a view to its implications and connections. And this is the trouble with Moore's test, and all such artificial desert-island ethical models. Let us suppose the child has only a few minutes to live, because the world is about to come to an end, and he is rapturously swinging; and suppose anything else you like, to close off other alternatives. He wants to swing, he is ecstatic about it. Of course we are not going to call him in to do his homework, or worry about his catching cold. Suppose we narrow his opportunities to two, swinging or doing some unpleasant alternative, like washing the dishes. We are asked to choose which he shall do, and we say, "Let him swing!" Are we then conceding that the enjoyment of swinging has intrinsic value? I do not think so.

It is essential to distinguish between two propositions about this one-minute-to-live version of Moore's test:

(1) There is no reason for the child not to swing on this occasion, if he wants to and enjoys it.

[35] *Op. cit.*, p. 303.

(2) There is reason to say that the child's swinging enjoyment on this occasion is intrinsically desirable.

The situation we have artificially set up is designed to make the first proposition true. But this is a very different proposition from the second, which is what the example is supposed to prove.

What can be shown by the swinging example is that we can imagine cases in which there could be nothing to make a particular experience undesirable—neither intrinsic nor extrinsic reasons. But once we deliberately set aside all extrinsic factors, there is nothing to argue about, either for or against. No reason can be given why the child should not swing if he wishes, and since he does not need a reason for doing what he already wants to do, reasons do not come into the picture at all. In normal everyday life, with its continuities and connections, the fact that he desires to swing would raise the question of its desirability—but it would not settle that question, of course. It would also assign the burden of proof. When the child expresses, or evinces, the desire to swing, the next question is whether any reasons can be given against the satisfaction of this desire (of course, if such reasons are given against it, it will then be in order to see whether reasons can be given for it). What makes the artificial situation artificial is just that it rules out any possible reasons against swinging, and so prevents any real problem from arising. I accept the spirit (though not every word) of a remark by William James, which is quoted with approval by William Frankena in his recent book on ethics:

Take any demand, however slight, which any creature, however weak, may make. Ought it not, for its own sake, to be satisfied? If not, prove why not.[36]

[36] *Essays in Pragmatism*, N.Y. 1948, p. 73; see William Frankena, *Ethics*, Englewood Cliffs 1963, p. 38.

If not, why not? That is exactly what I mean by the burden of proof.

And I think that this concept of the burden of proof is very important in many problems. We say that in a criminal trial the burden of proof lies upon the prosecution. An aprioristic philosopher might express the situation this way: "In criminal trials, there is an antecedent probability that the accused is innocent." Then the question would arise in the philosophy of law: how can that antecedent probability of innocence be established? And hopeless problems would appear. Is it a pragmatic postulate? Is it self-evident? Is it intuited by a special sense of justice? Is it deducible from theological premises about the nature of man? But all these questions would be beside the point. And I think the same thing holds for intrinsic value. The child wants to swing. It is a mistake to say that this fact gives initial probability to the proposition that the pleasure of swinging has intrinsic value. And it is a mistake to say that the pleasure he gets in swinging *justifies* the act of swinging. Say rather that his wanting to swing raises the question whether it would be justified for him to swing, but as long as no reason can be given *against* it, the swinging does not *require* any justification.

The value-judgment, "This act of swinging is desirable," is best thought of as an answer to a question, a solution of a problem. But so long as the child wants to swing, and in the nature of the case there can be no objection, there is no problem to be solved. To say that "beauty is its own excuse for being" is to say that beauty *needs* no excuse for being.

The artificial dead-end situation dreamed up according to Moore's instructions is essentially misleading. But some real-life situations may seem to approximate it. There are occasions when we want to say things like: "You'll find Mammoth Cave well worth seeing in itself," or "Go ahead and eat the ice cream cone; it's tasty," or "Forget business. Relax. Just have a good time." Borrowing a Deweyan term, let us call these "consummatory judgments"—they point out that something can be enjoyed for its own sake, they locate sources and occasions of intrinsic enjoyment in food, art, etc. They do not seem to be judgments of extrinsic value: they are hedged about in such a way as apparently to recommend a course of action without considering consequences at all. Are they, then, really judgments of intrinsic value?

I think this inference would be mistaken. Consummatory judgments are better interpreted not as value-judgments but as statements to the effect that no judgment is required, because there is no conflict of values, no occasion for deliberation and choice. "Go ahead and swing" surely has to be based on a preliminary survey of the situation: the rope looks safe, the child's stomach is not easily upset; there is no homework in the offing; there are no visiting children who should have the first turn on the swing, etc. Once we know these facts we can adopt a vacation point of view, and, when the child asks politely, or simply starts running toward the swing, we say, "Go ahead." This is not a judgment of intrinsic value at all, but a kind of *nihil obstat*. If some contrary reason loomed, we would have to stop and think, and decide. Consummatory judgments are then judgments of a metalinguistic order. "No reason why you shouldn't if you want to," is the basic formula.

In closing, I should like to pay my respects to John Dewey once more. I am always frustrated in reading Dewey, trying to separate the enormously good points from the confusing ones. Much of Dewey's famous attack on intrinsic value is really concerned with something else, namely ends-in-themselves (as opposed to ends-in-view). What he exposes over and over again is the danger of fixing on goals without reasonable regard to their means and consequences, and he is convinced that the belief in intrinsic value fosters this fixation, with its attendant train of ills: fanaticism, utopianism, opportunism, and the rest. But of course it does not logically follow that if there are intrinsically valuable things then there are necessarily ends-in-themselves. The world might be full of things that have intrinsic value, but whose intrinsic value is always outweighed by harmful effects. This would be the opposite of F. H. Bradley's description of Leibniz's universe, when he said it was the best of all possible worlds but everything in it was a necessary evil. The means might be delightful, but the ends always awry. It is only in Moore's artificial isolation that a thing with intrinsic value would necessarily be an end, and a great part of Dewey's concern should have been allayed by assurance that from the fact that a thing would be an end in isolation it does not follow that it would be an end in the context of human life. Nevertheless, I believe Dewey was also right in rejecting intrinsic value and that this part of his theory has important ethical and social consequences, too. To connect the desirable and the desired, to connect values with human needs and wishes, is indeed the task of a naturalistic theory of value. But to make this connection prematurely, through an indentification of intrinsic value with immediate enjoyments, encourages a dangerously one-sided approach to human problems. For then desires, which provide the data and conditions of value-problems, and set some of the limits within which solutions are to be found, are taken as something more final than they really are, rather than as states of affairs that may themselves have to be transformed. And reasoning about values may become too exclusively a matter of balancing interests, and finding ways to satisfy existing and conflicting wants, rather than an inquiry into their conditions in the natural and social environment. When we recognize the essential relatedness of all value, this helps to remind us that in the deepest and most poignant conflicts in ourselves or in our society, it is often desires themselves that must be transformed if lives are to be freed and fulfilled.

The Good of Man

G. H. VON WRIGHT

1. The notion of the good of man, which will be discussed in this chapter, is the central notion of our whole inquiry. The problems connected with it are of the utmost difficulty. Many things which I say about them may well be wrong. Perhaps the best I can hope for is that what I say will be interesting enough to be worth a refutation.

We have previously (Ch. III, sect. 6) discussed the question, what kind of being has a good. We decided that it should make sense to talk of the good of everything, of the *life* of which it is meaningful to speak. On this ruling there can be no doubt that man *has* a good.

Granted that man has a good—what *is* it? The question can be understood in a multitude of senses. It can, for example, be understood as a question of a *name*, a verbal equivalent of that which we *also* call 'the good of man'.

We have already (Ch. I, sect. 5) had occasion to point out that the German equivalent of the English substantive 'good', when this means the good of man or some other being, is *das Wohl*. There is no substantive 'well' with *this* meaning in English. But there are two related substantives, 'well-being' and 'welfare'.

A being who, so to speak, 'has' or 'enjoys' its good, is also said to *be well* and, sometimes, to *do well*.

The notion of being well is related to the notion of health. Often 'to be well' means exactly the same as 'to be in good,

bodily and mental, health'. A man is said to be well when he is all right, fit, in good shape generally. These various expressions may be said to refer to minimum requirements of enjoying one's good.

Of the being who does well, we also say that it flourishes, thrives, or prospers. And we call it happy. If health and well-being primarily connote something privative, absence of illness and suffering; happiness and well-doing again primarily refer to something positive, to an overflow or surplus of agreeable states and things.

From these observations on language three candidates for a name of the good of man may be said to emerge. These are 'happiness', 'well-being', and 'welfare'.

The suggestion might be made that 'welfare' is a comprehensive term which covers the whole of that which we also call 'the good of man' and of which happiness and well-being are 'aspects' or 'components' or 'parts.' It could further be suggested that there is a broad sense of 'happiness', and of 'well-being', to mean the same or roughly the same as 'welfare'. So that, on *one* way of understanding them, the three terms could be regarded as rough synonyms and alternative names of the good of man.

The suggestion that 'the good of man' and 'the welfare of man' are synonymous phrases I accept without discussion. That is: I shall use and treat them as synonyms. (Cf. Ch. I, sect. 5; also Ch. III, sect. 1.)

It is hardly to be doubted that 'happiness' is sometimes used as a rough synonym of 'welfare'. More commonly, however, the two words are *not* used as synonyms. Happiness and welfare may, in fact, become

Reprinted from *The Varieties of Goodness* by Georg Henrik von Wright, by permission of the author and Routledge & Kegan Paul. New York: Humanities Press Inc. Copyright 1963.

distinguished as two concepts of different logical category or type. We shall here mention three features which may be used for differentiating the two concepts logically.

First of all, the two concepts have a primary connexion with two different forms of the good. One could say, though with caution, that happiness is a *hedonic*, welfare again a *utilitarian* notion. Happiness is allied to pleasure, and therewith to such notions as those of enjoyment, gladness, and liking. Happiness has no immediate logical connexion with the beneficial. Welfare again is primarily a matter of things beneficial and harmful, *i.e.* good and bad, for the being concerned. As happiness, through pleasure, is related to that which a man enjoys and likes, in a similar manner welfare, through the beneficial, is connected with that which a man wants and needs. (Cf. Ch. I, sect. 5.)

Further, happiness is more like a 'state' (state of affairs) than welfare is. A man can become happy, be happy, and cease to be happy. He can be happy, and unhappy, more than once in his life. Happiness, like an end, can be achieved and attained. Welfare has not these same relationships to events, processes, and states *in time*.

Finally, a major logical difference between happiness and welfare is their relation to *causality*. Considerations of welfare are essentially considerations of how the doing and happening of various things will causally affect a being. One cannot pronounce on the question whether something is good or bad for a man, without considering the causal connexions in which this thing is or may become embedded. But one can pronounce on the question whether a man is happy or not, without necessarily considering what were the causal antecedents and what will be the consequences of his present situation.

The facts that happiness is primarily a hedonic and welfare primarily a utilitarian notion. and that they have logically different relationships to time and to causality, mark the two concepts as being of that

which I have here called 'different logical category or type'. It does not follow, however, that the two concepts are logically entirely unconnected. They are, on the contrary, closely allied. What then is their mutual relation? This is a question, on which I have not been able to form a clear view. Welfare (the good of a being) is, somehow, the broader and more basic notion. (Cf. Ch. III, sect. 12.) It is also the notion which is of greater importance to ethics and to a general study of the varieties of goodness. Calling happiness an 'aspect' or 'component' or 'part' of the good of man is a non-committal mode of speech which is not meant to say more than this. Of happiness I could also say that it is the consummation or crown or flower of welfare. But these are metaphorical terms and do not illuminate the logical relationship between the two concepts.

2. By an end of action we shall understand anything, *for the sake of which* an action is undertaken. If something, which we want to do, is not wanted for the sake of anything else, the act or activity can be called an *end in itself*.

Ends can be intermediate or ultimate. Sometimes a man wants to attain an end for the sake of some further end. Then the first end is *intermediate*. An end, which is not pursued for the sake of any further end, is *ultimate*. We shall call a human act *end-directed*, if it is undertaken either as an end in itself or for the sake of some end.

What is an ultimate end of action is settled by the last answer, which the agent himself can give to the question, *why* he does or intends to do this or that. It is then understood that the question 'Why?' asks for a reason and not for a causal explanation of his behaviour. (Cf. Ch. IV, sect. 8.)

In the terms which have here been introduced, we could redefine Psychological Hedonism as the doctrine that every end-directed human act is undertaken, ultimately, for the sake either of attaining some pleasure or avoiding something unpleasant. The doctrine again that every end-directed human act is undertaken, ultimately, for the sake of the acting agent's happiness we shall call Psychological Eudaimonism. A doctrine to the effect that every end-directed act is ultimately undertaken for the sake of the acting agent's welfare (good) has, to the best of my knowledge, never been defended. We need not here invent a name for it.

Aristotle sometimes talks[1] as though he had subscribed to the doctrine of psychological eudaimonism. If this was his view, he was certainly mistaken and, moreover, contradicting himself. It would be sheer nonsense to maintain that every chain of (non-causal) questions 'Why did you do this?' and answers to them must terminate in a reference to happiness. The view that man, in everything he does, is aiming at happiness (and the avoidance of misery) is even more absurd than the doctrine that he, in everything he does, is aiming at pleasure (and the avoidance of pain).

I said that, if Aristotle maintained psychological eudaimonism, he was contradicting himself. (And for this reason I doubt that Aristotle wanted to maintain it, though some of his formulations would indicate that he did.) For Aristotle also admits that there are ends, other than happiness, which we pursue for their own sake. He mentions pleasure and honour among them.[2] Even 'if nothing resulted from them, we should still choose each of them', he says.[3] On the other hand, those other final ends are sometimes desired, *not* for their own sake, but for the sake of something else. Whereas happiness, Aristotle thinks, is *never* desired for the sake of anything else.[4] Pleasure, *e.g.* pleasant amusement, can be desired for relaxation, and relaxation for the sake of continued activity.[5] *Then* pleasure is not a final end.

I would understand Aristotle's so-called eudaimonism in the following light:

among possible ends of human action, *eudaimonia* holds a unique position. This unique position is *not* that *eudaimonia* is the final end of all action. It is that *eudaimonia* is the only end that is never anything except final. It is of the nature of *eudaimonia* that it cannot be desired for the sake of anything else. *This* is, so Aristotle seems to think, why *eudaimonia* is the highest good for man.[6]

It is plausible to think that a man can pursue, *i.e.* do things for the sake of promoting or safeguarding, his own happiness only as an ultimate end of his action. A man can also do things for the sake of promoting or safeguarding the happiness of some other being. It may be thought that he can do this only as an intermediate end of his action. The idea has an apparent plausibility, but is nevertheless a mistake. The truth seems to be that a man can pursue the happiness of others either as intermediate *or* as ultimate end.

The delight of a king can be the happiness of his subjects. He gives all his energies and work to the promotion of this end. Maybe he sacrifices his so-called 'personal happiness' for the good of those over whom he is set to rule. Yet, if this is what he likes to do, it is also that in which his happiness consists. To say this is not to distort facts logically. But to say that the king sacrifices himself for the sake of becoming happy and not for the sake of making others happy, would be a distortion. It would be a distortion similar to that of which psychological hedonism is guilty, when it maintains that everything is done for the sake of pleasure, on the ground that all satisfaction of desire may be thought intrinsically pleasant.

Can a man's *welfare* be an end of his own action? The question is equivalent to asking, whether a man can ever be truly

---

[1] See, *e.g.*, *Ethica Nicomachea* (*EN*), 1094a 18–21, 1095a 14–20, and 1176b 30–31.

[2] *EN*, 1097b 1–2. See also 1172b 20–23.

[3] *EN*, 1097b 2–3.

[4] *EN*, 1097b 1 and again 1097b 5–6.

[5] Cf. *EN*, 1176b 34–35.

[6] There is no phrase in Aristotle's ethics which corresponds to our phrase 'the good of man'. *Eudaimonia* (happiness, well-being) Aristotle also calls the best or the highest good. The notion of a *summum bonum*, however, is not identical with the notion of the good of man as we use it here. But the two notions may be related.

said to do things for the sake of promoting or protecting his own good. It is not quite clear which is the correct answer.

On the view which is here taken of the good of a being, to do something for the sake of promoting one's own good, means to do something *because* one considers doing it *good for* oneself. And to do something for the sake of protecting one's own good means to do something *because* one considers neglecting it bad for oneself.

For all I can see, men sometimes do things for the reasons just mentioned. This would show that a man's welfare *can be* an end of his own action.

Yet the good of a being as an end of action is a very peculiar sort of 'end'. Normally, an end of action is a state of affairs, something which is 'there', when the end has been attained. But welfare is not a state of affairs. (Cf. the discussion in section 1.) For this reason I shall say that welfare, the good of a being, can only in an *oblique* sense be called an end of action.

Obviously, the reason why a man does something, which he considers good for himself, is not always and necessarily *that* he considers doing it good for himself. Similarly, the reason why a man does something, which he considers bad for him to neglect, is not always and necessarily *that* he considers neglecting it bad for himself. This shows that a man's own welfare is not always an ultimate end of his action. It also shows that a man's own welfare is not always an end of his action at all. It does not show, however, that a man's own welfare is sometimes an intermediate end of his action. Whether it *can* be an intermediate end, I shall not attempt to decide. If the answer is negative, it would follow that, when a man's own welfare is an end of his action, it is necessarily an ultimate end.

Sometimes a man does something because he considers doing it good for another being, and neglects something because he considers doing it bad for another being. It is obvious that another man's good can be the *intermediate* end of a

man's action. The reason why the master takes heed to promote and protect the welfare of his servants, can be that he expects them to serve him more efficiently if they thrive and are happy. Then his servants' welfare is an intermediate end of the master's. It may be suggested that, when the end of a man's action is another being's welfare, then it is necessarily an intermediate end. This suggestion, I think, is false. We shall return to the topic later (Chapter IX), when discussing egoism and altruism.

Beings can be handled or treated as means to somebody's ends. This is the case, *e.g.*, with domestic animals and slaves. Philosophers have sometimes entertained the idea that beings could also be treated as 'ends' or 'ends in themselves'. It is not clear what it means to say that a being, *e.g.* a man, is an 'end in itself'. But treating a man as an end in itself *could mean*, I suggest, that we do certain things because we consider them good for that man (and for no other ulterior reason) and abstain from doing certain things because we consider them bad for that man. In other words: whenever a being's good is an ultimate end of action, that being is treated as an end in itself. A man can treat other men thus, but also himself. That men *should be* thus treated is an interesting view of the nature of moral duty. We shall briefly talk of this in Chapter X.

In the next five sections of the present chapter we shall be dealing with various aspects of the concept of happiness and in the last five sections with questions relating to the concept of welfare.

3. Happiness, we said, is a hedonic notion. It is, of course, not *the same* as pleasure. Nor can it be defined, as has been suggested, as 'pleasure and the absence of pain'.

Moralists who have written about happiness have sometimes associated the notion more intimately with one, sometimes with another, of the three principal 'forms' of pleasure, which we have in this book distinguished. One could, accordingly, speak of three types of *ideals of happiness* or of the happy life.

The first I shall call *Epicurean ideals*. According to them, 'true happiness' derives above all from *having* things which please. 'Pleasure' need not here be understood in the 'grosser' sense of sensuous pleasure. It includes the enjoyment of agreeable recollections and thoughts, of good company, and of beautiful things. Moore's position in *Principia Ethica* can, I think, be called an Epicureanism in this broad sense.

Can a man find happiness entirely in passive pleasure? *i.e.* can following an Epicurean recipe of living make a man completely happy? I can see no *logical* impossibility in the idea. If a man's supreme desire happened to be to secure for himself a favourable balance of passive pleasure over passive 'unpleasure', *i.e.* of states he enjoys over states he dislikes, and if he were successful in this pursuit of his, then the Epicurean recipe of living would, by definition, make him happy. It may be argued—from considerations pertaining to the contingencies of life—that the chances are strongly against his succeeding. It may also be argued—this time from considerations pertaining to the psychology of human nature—that very few men are such pleasure-lovers that the supreme thing they want for themselves in life is a maximum of passive pleasure. But the facts—if they be facts—that Epicurean ideals are risky and not very commonly pursued throughout a whole life, must not induce us to deny that a man—if there be such a man—who successfully pursued such ideals was genuinely happy and flourishing. To deny this would be to misunderstand the notions of happiness and the good of man and would be symptomatic, I think, of some 'moralistic perversion'.

The second type of ideals of the happy life probably comes nearer than the Epicurean ideals to something which the classical writers of utilitarianism had in mind. It seems to me true to say that the utilitarians thought of happiness, not so much in terms of passive pleasure, as in terms of satisfaction of desire. Happiness, on such a view, is essentially contentedness—an equilibrium between needs and wants on the one hand and satisfaction on the other.

Yet one of the great utilitarians—protesting against unwanted consequences of a view which he was himself, though not wholeheartedly, defending—made the famous *dictum*, 'It is better to be a human being dissatisfied than a pig satisfied'. I am not a utilitarian myself. But I would like to protest, in a sense, against Mill's remark. The ultimate reason why it is *not good* for man to live like a pig, is that the life of a pig *does not satisfy* man. The *dissatisfied* Socrates, to whom Mill refers, we may regard as a symbol of man in search of a better and therewith more satisfying form of life. If his cravings were all doomed to be nothing but 'vanity and the vexation of spirit', then to idealize the dissatisfied Socrates would be to cherish a perverted view of the good life.

If one adopts the view that happiness is essentially an equilibrium between desire and satisfaction, one may reach the further conclusion that the safest road to happiness is to have as few and modest wants as possible, thus minimizing the chances of frustration and maximizing those of satisfaction. This recipe of happiness I shall call *the ascetic ideal* of life.[7] When carried to the extreme, this ideal envisages complete happiness in the total abnegation of all desire whatsoever.

Asceticism, in this sense, can be termed a *crippled* view of happiness. In order to see in which respect it is crippled, it is helpful to consider the contrary of happiness, *i.e.* unhappiness or misery. It would seem that there is a more direct connexion between unhappiness and dissatisfaction of desire than there is between happiness and

[7] Asceticism as an abnegation of worldly desire for the sake of the good of the soul must be distinguished from that which I here call asceticism as an ideal of life. To the first, asceticism is no 'end' or 'value' in itself, but an exercise and preparation for the good life.

satisfaction. Frustration of desire is a main source of unhappiness. Never or seldom to get that for which one is craving, never or seldom to have a chance of doing that which one likes to do, *this* is above all what makes a man miserable.

To call extreme asceticism a crippled ideal is to accuse it of a logical mistake. This is the mistake of regarding happiness as the *contradictory*, and not as the *contrary*, of unhappiness. By escaping frustration a man escapes unhappiness—provided, of course, that it does not befall him in the form of such affliction, which accident or illness or the acts of evil neighbours may cause him. The man of *no* wants, if there existed such a creature, would not be unhappy. But it does not follow that he would be happy.

The third type of ideals of the happy life which I wanted to mention here, seeks happiness neither in passive pleasure nor in the satisfaction of desire, but in that which we have called active pleasure, *i.e.* the pleasure of doing that on which we are keen, which for its own sake we like *doing*. In the activities which we are keen on doing, we aim at technical goodness or perfection. (See Ch. II, sect. 12.) The better we are in the art, the more do we enjoy practising it, the happier does it make us. Therefore, the more talented we are by nature for an art, the more can the development of our skill in it contribute to our happiness.

It may be argued—chiefly against Epicureanism I should think—that the pleasures of the active life are those which are best suited to secure the attainment of lasting happiness. It is more risky to be, for one's well-being, dependent upon things we *have* or *get* than upon things we *do* (or *are*). That is: it is more risky to seek happiness in passive than in active pleasure. There is probably a great deal of truth in the argument. But it would certainly be wrong to think that the road to happiness through an active life was completely risk-free.

4. The factors which determine whether a man will become happy, we shall call *conditions* of happiness. Of such conditions one may distinguish three main groups. Happiness, we shall say, is conditioned partly by *chance* or luck, partly by innate *disposition,* and partly by *action*. 'Action' here means action on the part of the individual concerned himself. That which is *done to* a man may, for present purposes, be counted as chance-factors conditioning his happiness.

Illness can befall a man or he can become bodily or mentally injured without any fault of his own. If such misfortune assumes a certain permanence, it may affect a man's happiness adversely. It may do so either as a cause of pain or as a cause of frustration of desire or because it prevents the victim from engaging in activity which, for its own sake, he enjoys. However, luck may also favour a man's good. The benefit a person draws from good friends or good teachers or financial benefactors has, partly if not wholly, the character of luck. It is something which life has in store for some men but not for others to make them happier, independently of their own doings and precautions.

It is an aspect of that which we called the ascetic ideal of life, that man is well advised to *make* himself as independent as possible of chance and luck as conditions of his happiness. This he can try to do in various ways: by hardening himself to sustain pain, by withdrawing from political and social engagements, or by not aspiring too high even in those activities, which he enjoys for their own sake. The belief that a man could make himself altogether independent of external factors affecting his good, is a conceit peculiar to certain 'ascetic' and 'stoic' attitudes to life. It overrates man's possibilities of conditioning his happiness and peace of mind by assuming a certain attitude to contingencies.

The innate dispositions of happiness have to do both with bodily health and with mental equipment and temper. A man of weak health is more exposed to certain risks of becoming unhappy than a man of good health. A man of many talents has more resources of happiness than a man of poor gifts. A man of good temper and cheerful outlook will not let adversities frustrate his efforts as easily as the impatient and gloomy man. To the extent that such temperamental dispositions can be developed or suppressed in a man, they fall under those conditions of happiness which a man controls through his action.

Human action, which is relevant to the happiness of the agent himself, is of two types. Action of the first type are things which the agent does, measures which he takes for the sake of promoting or protecting his happiness. Such action is *causally* relevant to his happiness. Action of the second type are things which the agent does or practises for their own sake, as ends in themselves, *i.e.* simply because he wants to do or likes to do them and for no other reason. Action in which a man delights one could call *constitutive* of his happiness, 'parts' of his happiness.

Now it may happen that action, which is thus constitutive of a man's happiness, *also* affects his happiness causally. It may affect his happiness promotingly, but also affect it adversely. For example: a man is immensely fond of playing various games. He plays and enjoys playing them all day long. In so doing he neglects his education and his social duties and maybe his health too. Thus the very same thing, which is constitutive of his happiness, may, by virtue of its consequences, accumulate clouds of unhappiness over the agent's head, while he is rejoicing in this thing. This possibility is responsible for the major complications, which are connected with a man's own action as a conditioning factor of his happiness and welfare generally.

5. When is a man happy? It is obvious that a man can be truly called happy, even though many painful and unpleasant things have happened to him in the course of his life. But not if he never had any pleasures. What must the preponderance of the pleasant over the unpleasant be, if he is still to be called happy?

Here it is helpful to consider the states which we call gladness and sadness. They occupy a kind of intermediate position between happiness and unhappiness on the one hand, and pleasure and its contrary on the other hand. It may be suggested that pleasant and unpleasant experiences and activities are constitutive of gladness and sadness in a manner similar to that in which states of joy and depression are constitutive of happiness and unhappiness. A man can be glad although he has a toothache, and he can be a happy man even though he chances to be very sad for a time. But he could not be glad if he had no pleasures to compensate such pains as he may have at the time of his gladness; and he cannot be happy if he is not *on the whole* more glad than sad. But we cannot tell exactly what must be the balance.

Pleasure, joy, and happiness are things of increasing degrees of permanence and resistance to changes. Something can please a man without cheering him up, and cheer him up without making him happy. Something can be a terrible blow to a man and make him sad, but whether it makes him unhappy is another matter.

Consider, for example, a man whom we call happy and who is hit by a sudden blow of bad luck, say, the loss of a child in an accident. He will experience painful agonies and extreme sadness. 'News of the disaster made him dreadfully unhappy,' we might say, thinking of these emotional effects on him. If, however, we were to say that the news made him *an unhappy man*, we should be thinking not only, or maybe even not at all, on those emotional effects, but on effects of a less immediate showing and of a longer lasting. If we can say of him some such things as, 'For years after he was as paralysed; none of the things, which used to delight him, gave him pleasure any longer,' or 'Life seemed to have lost meaning for him,—for a time he even contemplated suicide,' then the accident made him *unhappy* as distinct from merely *sad*. But whether things, bearing on the distinction, can be truly said of the man, is not to be seen in an inkling.

Analogous things can be said about changes in the reverse direction. A piece of news, say of an unexpected inheritance, can make a man jump with joy. But whether it makes him *happy* as distinct from merely *glad* can only be seen from effects of a longer lasting and less obvious showing on his subsequent life.

Should we say 'the *whole* of his subsequent life'? I think not. Happiness is neither a momentary state nor is it a sum total to be found out when we close our life's account. A man can *become* happy, *be* happy, and *change* from happy to unhappy. Thus, in the course of his life, a man can be both happy and unhappy. And he can be happy and unhappy more than once. (See section 1.)

We could make a distinction between a happy *man* and a happy *life* and regard the second as a thing of wider scope. This would make it possible to say of somebody that he had a happy life although, for some time, he was a most unhappy man.

6. A judgment to the effect that some being is happy or is not happy or is unhappy we shall call an *eudaimonic* judgment.

I think it is illuminating to compare the logic of the eudaimonic judgment to the logic of the statement 'This is pleasant'. Of the sentence 'This is pleasant' we said that it conceals a logical form. (See Ch. IV, sect. 6.) It suggests that pleasantness is a property which we attribute to some object or state, whereas in fact to judge something pleasant is to verbalize a relationship in which the judging subject stands to this thing. To judge something hedonically good is to manifest an *attitude*, one could also say, to certain things (activities, sensations, the causes of sensations). The logically most adequate form of the verbalization is therefore, it seems, the relational

form 'I like this' or some similar relational form.

In an analogous sense the sentence 'He is happy' may be said, I think, to conceal a logical form. It suggests a view of happiness as a property which the happy individual exhibits—which shines forth from him. Whereas, in fact, to be happy is to be in a certain relationship. A relationship to what? it may be asked. A relationship to one's circumstances of life, I would answer. To say 'He is happy' is similar to saying 'He likes it', the 'it' not meaning this or that particular thing or activity but, so to speak, 'the whole thing'. One could also say, 'He likes his life as it is.'

On this view, if a man says of himself 'I am happy,' he manifests in words an attitude which he takes, or a relationship, in which he stands, to his circumstances of life. Happiness is *not* in the circumstances —as it were awaiting the judgment—but springs into being with the relationship. (Just as hedonic goodness does not reside in the taste of an apple, but in somebody's liking the taste of an apple.) To judge oneself happy is to pass judgment on or value one's circumstances of life.

To say 'He is happy' can mean two different things. It can mean that the man, of whom we are talking, is in the relationship to his circumstances which, if *he* were to verbalize his attitude, he could express in the words 'I am happy'. Then 'He is happy' is not a value-judgment. It is a true or false statement to the effect that a certain subject values certain things, *i.e.* his circumstances of life, in a certain way. We could also call it a statement to the effect that a certain valuation *exists* (occurs, takes place).

Quite often, however, 'He is happy' is not a judgment about that which *he is* at all, but about that which *we should be*, if we happened to be in his circumstances. 'He is happy' then means roughly, 'He *must be* happy, *viz.* considering the circumstances he is in.' Such judgments are often an expression of envy. To say with conviction, 'Happy is he, who ...' is usually to pronounce on that which we think would make ourselves happy.

We shall henceforth disregard the case, when the third person judgment 'He is happy' is only a disguise for our own valuations and thus really is a first person judgment.

7. On the view which I am defending here, judgments of happiness are thus very much like hedonic judgments. The third person judgments are true or false. In them is judged that so-and-so is or is not pleased with his circumstances of life. They are judgments *about* valuations—and therefore are no value-judgments. The first person judgments are not true or false. They *express* a subject's valuations of his own circumstances. They are genuine value-judgments, and yet in an important sense of 'judgment' they are no judgments.

Ultimately, a man is himself judge of his own happiness. By this I mean that any third person judgment which may be passed on his happiness, depends for its truth-value on how *he himself* values his circumstances of life. This is so independently of whether he verbalizes his attitude in a first person judgment or not.

In *a* sense, therefore, a man's own verdict 'I am happy' or 'I am unhappy', should he happen to pass it, will be final—whatever we may think *we* should say, if we were in his circumstances. We must never make the presence or absence of circumstances, which would determine our own first person judgments of happiness, the *criteria* of truth of third person judgments.

What may make it difficult to see clearly this 'subjectivity' of the notion which we are discussing, is the fact that not every man is the best and most competent judge of his *prospects* of happiness. A man may strongly want to do something, think his life worthless if he is not allowed this thing. But another, more experienced man, may warn him that, if he follows his immediate impulses, he will in the end be-

come a most miserable wretch. The more experienced man may be right. But the criterion, which proves him right, is *not* the mere fact that certain things—illness, destitution, and what not—befall this other man as a predicted consequence of his folly and wickedness. The criterion is that these consequences make that other man unhappy. If our fool accepts the consequences with a cheerful heart, the wise man cannot insist that he must be right. He cannot do so on the ground, say, that those same consequences would have made him, or most people, miserable. Nor can he pretend that the lightsome fellow is 'really' unhappy, though unaware of his own misery.

But cannot a man be mistaken in thinking that he *is* happy? In a sense he can *not*, but in another he *can*. 'He says he is happy, but in fact he is *not*' can express a true proposition. But does not the truth of this proposition entail that the person who professes to be happy is lying? And is this not uninteresting? The answer is that, beside uninteresting lies, there exist profoundly interesting lies in the matters, which we are now discussing. First person judgments of happiness can be insincere, and insincerity may be regarded as a species of lying.

The same, incidentally, holds good for first person hedonic judgments too. A youngster may profess to like the taste of tobacco, which in fact he detests, just for the sake of showing off. He may even make himself believe this, in some involved and twisted sense of 'believe'. A polite man may say he likes the taste of a wine merely to please his host. The insincerity of such first person judgments may be relatively easy to unmask.

In the case of first person judgments of happiness and misery, the problem of sincerity is most difficult—both psychologically and conceptually. I shall not here try to penetrate its logical aspects, which I find very bewildering. (I am not aware of any satisfactory discussion of the topic in the literature.) I shall make a shortcut through the difficulties and only say this much in conclusion:

However thoroughly a man may cheat himself with regard to his own happiness, the criterion of cheating or insincerity must be that *he* admits the fraud. A judgment is insincere when the subject 'in his innermost self' admits that it is not as he says it is. If his lips say 'I am happy' and he is not, then in his heart he must already be saying to himself 'I am not happy'. He, as it were, does not hear the voice of his heart. These are similes, and I am aware of the temptation to misuse them. (They are the same sort of similes that are used and misused in psychoanalysis—the similes of the subconscious, the super-ego, etc.) What I mean by them could perhaps be said most plainly as follows: The fact that first person judgments of happiness can be insincere must not be allowed to conflict logically with the fact that whether a person is happy **or not** depends upon *his own* attitude to his circumstances of life. The supreme judge of the case *must be* the subject himself. To think that it could be otherwise is false objectivism.

8. Judgments of the beneficial and the harmful, *i.e.* of that which is good or bad for a man, involve two components. We have called them the *causal* and the *axiological* component. (See Ch. III, sect. 5.) We must now say some words about each of them.

When something happens, *i.e.* the world changes in a certain respect, there will usually also be a number of subsequent changes, which are bound (by socalled 'natural necessity') to come about, once the first change took place. These subsequent changes we here call the *consequences* of the first change. If the first change is of that peculiar kind which we call a human act, then the subsequent changes are *consequences of action*. The change or changes upon which a certain further change is consequent (*i.e.* the consequence of which this further change is) we shall call the *cause(s)* of this further change.

Most things which happen, perhaps all, would not have happened, *unless* certain antecedent changes had taken place in the world. These antecedent changes we shall call the *causal prerequisites or requirements* of the subsequent change. They are sometimes also called 'necessary causes'. The necessary causes may be, but need not be, 'causes' in the sense defined above.

These explanations are very summary. Not least of all considering the importance to ethics of the notion of consequences of action, it is an urgent *desideratum* that the logic of causal relationships be better elaborated than it is. We shall not, however, attempt this here. Only a few observations will be added to the above.

The notions both of consequences and of prerequisites and of causes of a change are relative to the further notion of a *state of the world*. Thus, *e.g.*, a change which is required in order to effect a certain change in the world as it is to-day, may not be required in order to effect this same change in the world as it is to-morrow.

It is sometimes said that every event (change) 'strictly speaking' has an infinite number of consequences throughout the whole of subsequent time, and that for this reason we can never know for certain which all the consequences of a given event are. These statements, if true at all, hold good for some different notion of consequence, but not for the notion with which we are here dealing. Exactly what could be meant by them is not clear. Yet we need not dismiss them as nonsense. When, for example, something which happens to-day is said to be a consequence of something which took place hundreds of years ago, what is meant is perhaps that, if we traced the 'causal history' of this event of to-day we should find among its 'causal ancestry' that event of hundreds of years ago. Here the notions of causal ancestry and causal history could be defined in terms of *our* notions of cause, consequence, and prerequisite and yet it need not follow that, if an event belongs to the causal ancestry of another event, the first must be a cause or prerequisite of the second or the second a consequence of the first. For example: Let event *b* be a consequence (in our sense) of event *a* and a causal prerequisite (in our sense) of event *c*. It would then be reasonable to say that event *a* is a 'causal ancestor' of event *c*, or that tracing the 'causal history' of *c* takes us to *a*. In some loose sense of the words, *a* may be said to be a 'cause' of *c* and *c* a 'consequence' of *a*. But in the more precise sense, in which we are here employing the terms, *a* is not (necessarily) a cause of *c*, nor *c* (necessarily) a consequence of *a*.

The causes and consequences of things which happen, are often insufficiently known and therefore largely a matter of belief and conjecture. Sometimes, however, they *are* known to us. The statement, should it be made, that they *cannot* ('in principle') be known either is false or applies to some different notions of cause and consequence from ours.

By knowledge of the causes and consequences of things which happen, I here mean knowledge relating to *particulars*. An example would be knowledge that the death of N. N. was due to a dose of arsenic, which had been mixed into his food. Such knowledge of particulars is usually grounded on knowledge of general propositions–as for example that a dose of arsenic of a certain strength will (unless certain counteracting causes intervene) 'inevitably' kill a man. Whether all such knowledge of particulars is grounded on general knowledge, we shall not discuss.

When in the sequel we speak of *knowledge* of the causes and consequences of things, or of known causes and consequences, 'knowledge' is short for 'knowledge or belief' and 'known' for 'known or believed'. The consequences which are known (*i.e.* known or believed) at the time when the thing happens, we shall also call *foreseen* consequences.

So much for the causal component involved in judgments of the beneficial and the harmful. We now turn to the axiological component. A preliminary task will here be to clarify the notions of a *wanted* and an *unwanted* thing.

9. The notion of a wanted thing, which I shall now try to explain, is not the same as that of an end of action. I shall call it the notion of being *wanted in itself*. How things which are wanted in themselves, are related to things which are wanted as ends of action, will be discussed presently. Correlative with the notion of being wanted in itself is the notion of being *unwanted in itself*. 'Between' the two falls a notion, which we shall call the notion of being *indifferent in itself*.

The notion of being wanted in itself is the nearest equivalent in my treatment here to the notion of *intrinsic value* in Moore and some other writers. Moore, when discussing the notion of intrinsic worth, often resorts to a logical fiction which, *mutatis mutandis*, may be resorted to also for explaining the meaning of a thing being wanted, unwanted, or indifferent 'in itself'.

This fiction is that of a preferential choice between two alternatives. A major difficulty is to formulate the terms of the choice correctly for the purpose of defining the axiological notions under discussion. (Moore's explanation of intrinsic value in terms of betterness of alternatives cannot be regarded as *logically* satisfactory—apart from questions of the meaningfulness of the very notion.[8]) Our proposal here of a solution to the problem is tentative only.

Assume you were offered a thing X which you did not already possess. Would you then rather take it than leave it, rather have it than (continue to) be without it? The offer must be considered apart from questions of causal requirements and of consequences. That is: considerations of things which you will have to do in order to get X, and of things which will happen to you as a consequence of your having got the thing X must not influence your choice. If then you would rather take X than leave

[8] See *Ethics*, pp. 42–44 and, in particular, Moore's reply to his critics in *The Philosophy of G. E. Moore*, pp. 554–557.

it, X is *wanted in itself*. If you have the opposite preference, X is *unwanted in itself*.
If you have no preference, X is *indifferent
in itself*.

As readily noted, the ideas of the in itself wanted and unwanted, which we have
thus tried to explain in terms of a fictitious
preferential choice, are necessarily relative
to a *subject*. Nothing is wanted or unwanted 'in itself', if the words 'in itself' are
supposed to mean 'apart from any rating or
valuing subject'. The words 'in itself' mean
'causal prerequisites and consequences
apart'. A thing, which for one subject is a
wanted thing, may be regarded as unwanted by another subject. A thing, furthermore, which is wanted *now*, may be
unwanted at another time—the subject
being the same. The notion of being
wanted or unwanted in itself is thus relative, not only to a subject, but also to a particular time in the life of this subject.

Moore did not think that intrinsic
value was relative to subject and time. In
this respect his 'objectivist' notion of the intrinsically good and bad differs from our
'subjectivist' notion of the in itself wanted
and unwanted.

It is important to note that from our
definition of the in itself wanted, unwanted, and indifferent it does not follow
that, if X is wanted in itself, then not-
X (the absence of X) is unwanted in itself.
That not-X is wanted, unwanted, and indifferent in itself corresponds, on our definitions, to the following set of preferences:

Consider a thing X, which you have.
Would you rather get rid of it than retain
it, rather be without it than (continue to)
possess it? The proposal must be considered apart from things which you will have
to do in order to get rid of X and from
things which will happen to you as a
consequence of your having got rid of X.
Then not-X is wanted in itself, if you prefer
to get rid of X, unwanted in itself, if you
prefer to retain X, and indifferent in itself,
if you have no preference.

10. Anything which is an—intermediate
or ultimate—end of action, can be called a
good (for the subject in pursuit of the end).
(Cf. above Ch. I, sect. 5 and Ch. III, sect.
1.) Anything which is an end of action, can
also be said to be *a wanted thing*.

Also every thing, which is wanted in
itself, can be called a good (for the subject
to whom it is wanted). And every thing,
which is unwanted in itself, can be called a
bad (for the subject who shuns it).

Ends of action and things wanted in
themselves thus both fall under the category 'goods'. Ends of action also fall under
the category 'things wanted'.

The question may be raised, how ends
of action and things wanted in themselves
are mutually related. The question is complicated and I shall not discuss it in detail.
It is reasonable to think that only things,
which are attainable through action, *can be*
ends of action. 'Craving for the moon' is
not aiming at an end. But things other than
those which are attainable through action,
can be wanted in themselves—sunshine on
a chilly day, for example. The only simple
relationship between ends of action and
things wanted in themselves, which I can
suggest, is that ultimate ends of action are
also things wanted in themselves.

Intermediate ends of action are either
things wanted in themselves or things indifferent in themselves or, not infrequently,
things unwanted in themselves. To get the
in itself unwanted can never be an ultimate
end of action, since the assumption that it
is involves a contradiction. But to escape
the in itself unwanted sometimes is an ultimate end of action. The unwanted is that
which we shun, except when occasionally
we pursue it as intermediate end for the
sake of something else or suffer it as a necessary prerequisite of something coveted.

When a man gets something which is,
to him, wanted in itself, without having
pursued it as an end, we shall say that this
wanted thing *befalls* him. Similarly, when a
man gets something which is, to him, un-

wanted in itself and which he has not pursued as an intermediate end, we shall say that this thing befalls him.

The question may be raised whether a thing which befalls or happens to a man can appropriately be said to be 'wanted'. 'Wanted' in English has many meanings and must therefore be used with caution. Sometimes it means 'desired', sometimes 'needed', sometimes 'wished for'. When the wanted thing is an end of action, the nearest equivalent to 'wanted' is 'desired'. Perhaps things which happen to a man and which satisfy our explanation of the in itself wanted, should better be called 'welcome'. They are things we 'gladly accept' or are 'happy to get'. Often we just call them 'good'. When I here call them 'wanted', it is by contrast to 'unwanted', which word is certainly correctly used for shunned things that befall or happen to a man.

11. Consider something, which an agent pursues as an ultimate end. Assume that he gets it. Attaining the end is usually connected with a number of things as its causal prerequisites and a number of other things as its consequences. Of the things which are thus causally connected with his end, some are perhaps known and others not known to the agent. Some, moreover, may be known to him already at the time when he pursues the end, others become known to him after he has attained it. That is: their causal relationship to the end is (becomes) known to him.

The thing which the agent pursues as an ultimate end, is to him a good and something he wants in itself. Of those things again which are causally connected—either as prerequisites or as consequences—with his attainment of the end, some are wanted in themselves (by him), others are unwanted in themselves (by him), others indifferent in themselves (to him). The sum total of those things, which are unwanted in themselves, we shall call the *price*, which the agent has to pay for the attainment of his ultimate end.

This notion of 'price', be it observed, includes consequences as well as causal prerequisites. On this definition of the notion, not only those things which the agent has to endure, in order to get his wanted thing, but also those which he has to suffer as a consequence of having got it, count as part of that which he has to *pay* for the good. One can define the notion of a price in different ways—for other purposes. This is how we define the notion for present purposes.

For anything which is wanted in itself, the question may be raised: Is this good worth its price? The question can be raised *prospectively*, with a view to things which have to be gone through as a consequence of starting to pursue this good as an end, or it can be raised *retrospectively*, with a view to things already suffered.

To answer the question whether a certain good is (was) worth its price, is to pass a value-judgment. It is to say of something, a good, that it is better or worse, more or less worth, than something else, its price. How shall this value-judgment be properly articulated?

I think we must resort here, for a second time, to the logical fiction of a preferential choice. We said (in section 9) that things which we do not have, are wanted in themselves when, ignoring their causes and consequences, we would rather get them than continue to be without them, and unwanted in themselves when we would rather continue to be without them than get them. This question of taking or leaving, having or being without, we can also raise for things, *considering their causes and consequences*. A correct way of presenting the choice which we should then be facing, is, I think, as follows:

Assume that X is something, which is not already in our world (life), *i.e.* is something which we do not already possess or which has not already happened or which we have not already done. Would we then want X to become introduced into our world (life), considering also the causal prerequisites of getting (doing) X and the consequences of having got (done) X? Or would we prefer to continue to be without X? In making up our mind we should also have to consider the causal prerequisites and the consequences of *not* having this change in our world (life). It may, for example, be necessary for us to take some in itself unwanted action to prevent X from coming into existence, if we wish to avoid having X, and it may be necessary for us to forsake some other in itself wanted thing Y as a consequence of *not* having had X.

We introduce the symbol 'X+C' for the complex whole, consisting of X and those other things, which are causally connected with it either as prerequisites or as consequences of its coming into being, *i.e.* of the change from not-X to X. The symbol 'not-X+C'' shall stand for the complex whole, consisting of the absence of X and the presence of those things which are causally connected, either as prerequisites or as consequences, with the continued absence of X.

The question which is presented for consideration in the fictitious preferential choice we are discussing, is whether we should prefer X+C to not-X+C' or whether we should have the reverse preference or whether we should be indifferent (have no preference).

Let the answer to the proposal be that we should rather have than continue to be without X, *i.e.* prefer X+C to not-X+C'. Then we shall say that X+C or the complex whole, consisting of X and the causal prerequisites and consequences of the coming into being of X, is a *positive constituent* of our good (welfare). Of the thing X itself we say that it is *good for us* or *beneficial*. This we say of X independently of whether X is wanted or unwanted or indifferent in itself.

Let the answer to the proposal be that we should rather continue to forego than have X, *i.e.* prefer not-X+C' to X+C. Then

we shall say that X+C is a *negative constituent* of our good. Of the thing X itself we say that it is *bad for us* or *harmful*. This we say independently of whether X is wanted or unwanted or indifferent in itself.

The answer can, of course, also be that we should be indifferent to the alternatives. Then X+C is neither a positive nor a negative constituent of our good, and X is neither beneficial nor harmful.

Let us call X the *nucleus* of that complex whole, which consists of X and the causal prerequisites and consequences of the coming into existence of X. We could then say that the things which are beneficial or harmful, good or bad for a man, are nuclei of those complex causal wholes, which are positive or negative constituents of his good (welfare).

We can now state the conditions for answering the question whether a certain good is worth its 'price'. When a certain causal whole is a positive constituent of our good *and* its nucleus is a thing, which is wanted in itself, then we say that this thing or good *is* worth its price. When, however, the whole is a negative constituent of our good, *although* its nucleus is a thing, which is wanted in itself, then we say that this thing or good is *not* worth its price.

From our definitions of the beneficial and the harmful it does *not* follow that, if not-X is harmful, then X is beneficial, and *vice versa*. If, however, not-X is harmful, then X will be called *needed*. The needed is that, the lack or loss of which is a bad thing, an evil. The needed and the harmful are opposed as contradictories, *in the sense* that the contradictory of the needed is harmful, and *vice versa*. The beneficial and the harmful are opposed as contraries.

To provide a being with that which is beneficial for it is to *promote* its welfare. To provide it with that which it needs and to take care that it does not lose the needed is to *protect* its welfare. Things (acts, events) which are protective of a being's welfare are good for the being in the sense of 'good for' which can also be rendered by 'useful', but not in that sense of 'good for' which we call 'beneficial'. (Cf. Ch. III, sect. I.)

12. The preferential choice, in the terms of which we have defined the notions of the beneficial and the harmful, we have called a 'logical fiction'. That it is a fiction implies two things. First, it implies that we are talking of how a man *would choose*, if he were presented with the choice, and not of what he actually chooses. Secondly, it implies that we assume the causal component involved in the value-judgment to be *completely known* to the subject at the time of the choice. This second assumption entails that there are no imperfections in the subject's knowledge which are such that, if they were detected and corrected, the subject would revise his preferences.

Thus, on our definitions, the answer to the question whether a certain thing is good or bad for a man, is independent of the following two factors: First, it is independent of whether he (or anybody else) *judges* or does not judge of the value of this thing for him. Secondly, it is independent of what he (and everybody else) happens to *know* or not to know about the causal connexions of this thing. Yet, in spite of this independence of judgment and knowledge, the notions of the beneficial and the harmful are in an important sense *subjective*. Their subjectivity consists in their dependence upon the *preferences* (*wants*) of the subject concerned.

Considering what has just been said, it is clear that we must distinguish between that which *is* good or bad for a man and that which *appears*, *i.e.* is judged or considered or thought (by himself or by others), to be good or bad for him.

Any judgment to the effect that something is good or bad for a man is based on such knowledge of the relevant causal connexions which the judging subject happens to possess. Since this knowledge may be imperfect, the judgment which he actually passes may be different from the judgment which he would pass, if he had perfect knowledge of the casual connexions. When there is this discrepancy between the actual and the potential judgment, we shall say that a man's *apparent* good is being mistaken for his *real* good.

Of certain things it is easier to judge correctly whether they are good or bad for us, than of certain other things. This means: the risks of mistaking our apparent good for our real good are sometimes greater, sometimes less. It is, on the whole, easier to judge correctly in matters relating to a person's health than in matters relating to his future career. For example: the judgment that it will do a man good to take regular exercise is, on the whole, safer than the judgment that it will be better for him to go into business than study medicine. Sometimes the difficulties to judge correctly are so great that it will be altogether idle and useless to try to form a judgment.

Sometimes we know for certain that a choice, which we are facing, is of great *importance* to us in the sense that it will make considerable *difference* to our future life, whether we choose the one or the other of two alternatives. An example could be a choice between getting married or remaining single or between accepting employment in a foreign country or continuing life at home. But certainty that the choice will make a great difference is fully compatible with uncertainty as to whether the difference will be for good or for bad. The feeling that our welfare *may* become radically affected by the choice, can make the choice very agonizing for us.

Also of many things in our past, which we did not deliberately choose, we may know for certain that they have been of great importance to us in the sense that our lives would have been very different, had these things not existed. This could be manifestly true, for example, of the influence which some powerful personality has had on our education or on the formation of our opinions. We may wonder whether it was not bad for us that we should have been so strongly under this influence. Yet, if we know only that our life would have been very different but cannot at all imagine *how* it would have been different, we may also be quite incompetent to form a judgment of the beneficial and harmful nature of this factor in our past history.

It is a deeply impressive fact about the condition of man that it should be difficult, or even humanly impossible, to judge confidently of many things which are known to affect our lives importantly, whether they are good or bad for us. I think that becoming *overwhelmed* by this fact is one of the things which can incline a man towards taking a religious view of life. 'Only God knows what is good or bad for us.' One could say thus—and yet accept that a man's welfare is a subjective notion in the sense that it is determined by what *he* wants and shuns.

13. Are judgments of the beneficial or harmful nature of things objectively true or false? When we try to answer this question, we must again observe the distinction between a first person judgment and a third person judgment. (Cf. Ch. IV, sect. 5 and this chapter, sections 6 and 7.)

When somebody judges of something that it is (was, will be) good or bad for somebody else, the judgment is a third person judgment. It depends for its truth-value on two things. The one is whether certain causal connexions are as the judging subject thinks that they are. The other is whether certain valuations (preferences, wants) of another subject are as the judging subject thinks that they are. Both to judge of causal connexions and to judge of the valuations of other subjects is to judge of empirical matters of fact. The judgment is 'objectively' true or false. It is, properly speaking, not a value-judgment, since the 'axiological' component involved in it is not a valuation but a judgment *about* (the existence or occurrence of) valuations.

The case of the first person judgment is more complicated. Its causal component is a judgment of matters of fact. In this re-

spect the first person judgment is on a level with the third person judgment. Its axiological component, however, is a valuation and not a judgment about valuations. With regard to this component the judgment cannot be true or false. There is no 'room' for mistake concerning its truth-value. In this respect the first person judgment of the beneficial and the harmful is like the first person hedonic or eudaimonic judgment.

Although the first person judgment cannot be false in its axiological component, it can be *insincere*. The problem of sincerity of judgments concerning that which is good or bad for a man is most complicated. It is intimately connected with the problems relating to the notions of *regret* and of *weakness of will*. A few words will be said about them later.

A subject can also make a statement about his own valuations in the past or a conjecture about his valuations in the future. Such a statement or conjecture is, logically, a third person judgment. It is true or false both in its causal and in its axiological component.

Whether a judgment is, *logically*, a first person judgment, cannot be seen from the person and tense of its grammatical form alone. A man says 'This will do me good'. In saying this he could be anticipating certain consequences and *expressing* his valuation of them. But he could also be anticipating certain consequences and *anticipating* his valuation of them. In the first case, the judgment he makes is of the kind which I here call a first person judgment of the beneficial or harmful nature of things. In the second case, the judgment is (logically) a third person judgment. The subject is speaking *about* himself, *i.e.* about his future valuations.

Sometimes a judgment of the beneficial or the harmful is clearly anticipative both of consequences and of valuations. Sometimes it is clearly anticipative with regard to consequences and expressive with regard to valuations. But very often, it seems, the status of the judgment is not clear even to the judging subject himself. The judgment may contain *both* anticipations *and* expressions of valuations. Perhaps it is true to say that men's judgments of what is good or bad for themselves tend on the whole to be anticipative rather than expressive with regard to valuations.

The distinction between the *apparent* and the *real* good, it should be observed, can be upheld both for third person and for first person judgments of the beneficial and the harmful. In this respect judgments of the beneficial and the harmful differ from hedonic and eudaimonic judgments. (For the two last kinds of judgment the distinction vanishes in the first person case, *i.e.* in the genuine value-judgments.) Because of the presence of the causal component in the judgment, a subject can always be mistaken concerning the beneficial or the harmful nature of a thing—even when there is no 'room' for mistake with regard to valuation.

14. A man's answer to the question whether a certain good is worth its price or whether a thing is beneficial or harmful, may undergo alterations in the course of time. Such alterations in his judgments can be due either to changes in his knowledge of the relevant causal connexions or to changes in his valuations. For example: a man attains an end, which he considers worth while to have pursued, until years afterwards he comes to realize that he had to pay for it with the ruin of his health. Then he revises his judgment and *regrets*.

There are two types of regret-situation relating to choices of ends and goods in general. Sometimes the choice can, in principle if not in practice, be repeated. To profess regret is then to say that one would not choose the same thing again next time, when there is an opportunity. But sometimes the choice is not repeatable. The reason for this could be that the consequences, of which one is aware and which are the ground for one's regret, continue to operate throughout one's whole life. There is no opportunity of making good one's folly in the past by acting more wisely in the future. Then to express regret is to pass judgment on one's *life*. It is like saying: If I were to live my life over again, I would, when arrived at the fatal station, act differently.

The value-judgments of regret and no-regret, like hedonic judgments and judgments of happiness, are neither true nor false. But they may be sincere or insincere. A person can say that he regrets, when in fact he does not, and he can stubbornly refuse to admit regret which he 'feels'. How is such insincerity unmasked? For example in this way: If a man, after having suffered the consequences, says he regrets his action, but on a new occasion repeats his previous choice, then we may doubt whether his remorse was not pretence only. He was perhaps annoyed at having had to pay so much for the coveted thing and therefore said it was not worth it, but at the bottom of his heart he was pleased at having got it. These are familiar phenomena.

Yet to think that a repetition of the professed folly were a sure sign of insincere regret, would be to ignore the complications of the practical problems relating to the good of man. A good, if strongly desired in itself and near at hand, may be a temptation to which a man succumbs, when the evil consequences are far ahead and the recollection of having suffered them in the past is perhaps already fading. There is no logical absurdity in the idea that a man sincerely regrets something as having been a mistake, a bad choice with a view to his welfare, *i.e.* with a view to what he 'really' wants for himself, and yet wilfully commits the same mistake over again, whenever there is an opportunity.

When a man succumbs to temptation and chooses a lesser immediate good, *i.e.* thing wanted in itself, rather than escapes a greater future bad, *i.e.* thing unwanted in itself, then he is acting wilfully against the

interests of his own good. It is in such situations that those features of character
which we call *virtues*, are needed to safeguard a man's welfare. We shall talk about
them later (in Chapter VII).

That a man can do evil to himself
through ignorance of the consequences of
his acts or through negligence is obvious.
That he can also harm himself through
akrasia or weakness of will has a certain appearance of paradox. He then, as it were,
both wants and does not want, welcomes
and shuns, one and the same thing. When
viewed in the short perspective, 'prerequisites and consequences apart', he wants it;
when viewed in the prolonged perspective
of the appropriate causal setting, he shuns
it. One could say that, if he lets himself be
carried away by the short perspective, then
he was not capable of viewing *clearly* his
situation in the long perspective. Or one
could say that, if a man has an *articulated
grasp* of what he wants, he can never harm
himself through weakness of will. But saying this must not encourage an undue optimism about man's possibilities of acting in
accordance with cool reasoning.

Utilitarianism

G. E. MOORE

I

Ethics is a subject about which there has been and still is an immense amount of difference of opinion, in spite of all the time and labour which have been devoted to the study of it. There are indeed certain matters about which there is not much disagreement. Almost everybody is agreed that certain kinds of actions ought, as a general rule, to be avoided; and that under certain circumstances, which constantly recur, it is, as a general rule, better to act in certain specified ways rather than in others. There is, moreover, a pretty general agreement, with regard to certain things which happen in the world, that it would be better if they never happened, or, at least, did not happen so often as they do; and with regard to others, that it would be better if they happened more often than they do. But on many questions, even of this kind, there is great diversity of opinion. Actions which some philosophers hold to be generally wrong, others hold to be generally right, and occurrences which some hold to be evils, others hold to be goods.

And when we come to more fundamental questions the difference of opinion is even more marked. Ethical philosophers have, in fact, been largely concerned, not with laying down rules to the effect that certain ways of acting are generally or always right, and others generally or always wrong, nor yet with giving lists of things which are good and others which are evil, but with trying to answer more general and fundamental questions such as the following. What, after all, is it that we mean to say of an action when we say that it is right or ought to be done? And what is it that we mean to say of a state of things when we say that it is good or bad? Can we discover any general characteristic, which belongs in common to absolutely *all* right actions, no matter how different they may be in other respects? and which does not belong to any actions except those which are right? And can we similarly discover any characteristic which belongs in common to absolutely all 'good' things, and which does not belong to any thing except what is a good? Or again, can we discover any single reason, applicable to all right actions equally, which is, in every case, *the* reason why an action is right, when it is right? And can we, similarly, discover any reason which is *the* reason why a thing is good, when it is good, and which also gives us the reason why any one thing is better than another, when it is better? Or is there, perhaps, no such single reason in either case? On questions of this sort different philosophers still hold the most diverse opinions. I think it is true that absolutely every answer which has ever been given to them by any one philosopher would be denied to be true by many others. There is, at any rate, no such consensus of opinion among experts about these fundamental ethical questions, as there is about many fundamental propositions in Mathematics and the Natural Sciences.

Reprinted from *Ethics* by G. E. Moore, Chaps. 1 and 2, by permission of Oxford University Press. Copyright 1912.

Now, it is precisely questions of this sort, about every one of which there are serious differences of opinion, that I wish to discuss in this book. And from the fact that so much difference of opinion exists about them it is natural to infer that they are questions about which it is extremely difficult to discover the truth. This is, I think, really the case. The probability is, that hardly any positive proposition, which can as yet be offered in answer to them, will be strictly and absolutely true. With regard to *negative* propositions, indeed, —propositions to the effect that certain positive answers which have been offered, are false,—the case seems to be different. We are, I think, justified in being much more certain that some of the positive suggestions which have been made are *not* true, than that any particular one among them *is* true; though even here, perhaps, we are not justified in being *absolutely* certain.

But even if we cannot be justified either in accepting or rejecting, with absolute certainty, any of the alternative hypotheses which can be suggested, it is, I think, well worth while to consider carefully the most important among these rival hypotheses. To realize and distinguish clearly from one another the most important of the different views which may be held about these matters is well worth doing, even if we ought to admit that the best of them has no more than a certain amount of probability in its favour, and that the worst have just a possibility of being true. This, therefore, is what I shall try to do. I shall try to state and distinguish clearly from one another what seem to me to be the most important of the different views which may be held upon a few of the most fundamental ethical questions. Some of these views seem to me to be much nearer the truth than others, and I shall try to indicate which these are. But even where it seems pretty certain that some one view is erroneous, and that another comes, at least, rather nearer to the

truth, it is very difficult to be sure that the latter is strictly and absolutely true.

One great difficulty which arises in ethical discussions is the difficulty of getting quite clear as to exactly what question it is that we want to answer. And in order to minimize this difficulty, I propose to begin, in these first two chapters, by stating one particular theory, which seems to me to be peculiarly simple and easy to understand. It is a theory which, so far as I can see, comes very near to the truth in some respects, but is quite false in others. And why I propose to begin with it is merely because I think it brings out particularly clearly the difference between several quite distinct questions, which are liable to be confused with one another. If, after stating this theory, we then go on to consider the most important objections which might be urged against it, for various reasons, we shall, I think, pretty well cover the main topics of ethical discussion, so far as fundamental principles are concerned.

This theory starts from the familiar fact that we all very often seem to have a choice between several different actions, any one of which we might do, if we chose. Whether, in such cases, we really do have a choice, in the sense that we ever really *could* choose any other action than the one which in the end we do choose, is a question upon which it does not pronounce and which will have to be considered later on. All that the theory assumes is that, in many cases, there certainly are a considerable number of different actions, any one of which we could do, *if* we chose, and between which, therefore, in *this* sense, we have a choice; while there are others which we could not do, even if we did choose to do them. It assumes, that is to say, that in many cases, *if* we had chosen differently, we should have acted differently; and this seems to be an unquestionable fact, which must be admitted, even if we hold that it is never the case that we *could* have chosen differently. Our theory assumes, then, that many of our actions are under the control of our wills, in the sense that *if*, just before we began to do them, we had chosen not to do them, we *should* not have done them; and I propose to call all actions of this kind *voluntary* actions.

It should be noticed that, if we define voluntary actions in this way, it is by no means certain that all or nearly all voluntary actions are actually themselves chosen or willed. It seems highly probable that an immense number of the actions which we do, and which we *could* have avoided, *if* we had chosen to avoid them, were not themselves willed at all. It is only true of them that they are 'voluntary' in the sense that a particular act of will, just before their occurrence, would have been sufficient to *prevent* them; not in the sense that they themselves were brought about by being willed. And perhaps there is some departure from common usage in calling all such acts 'voluntary.' I do not think, however, that it is in accordance with common usage to restrict the name 'voluntary' to actions which are quite certainly actually willed. And the class of actions to which I propose to give the name—all those, namely, which we could have prevented, *if*, immediately beforehand, we had willed to do so—do, I think, certainly require to be distinguished by some special name. It might, perhaps, be thought that almost all our actions, or even, in a sense, *absolutely* all those, which properly deserve to be called 'ours,' are 'voluntary' in this sense: so that the use of this special name is unnecessary: we might, instead, talk simply of 'our actions.' And it is, I think, true that almost all the actions, of which we should generally think, when we talk of 'our actions,' are of this nature; and even that, in some contexts, when we talk of 'human actions,' we do refer exclusively to actions of this sort. But in other contexts such a way of speaking would be misleading. It is quite certain that both our bodies and our minds constantly do things, which we certainly could not have prevented, by merely

willing just beforehand that they should not be done; and some, at least, of these things, which our bodies and minds do, would in certain contexts be called actions of ours. There would therefore be some risk of confusion if we were to speak of 'human actions' generally, when we mean only actions which are 'voluntary' in the sense I have defined. It is better, therefore, to give some special name to actions of this class; and I cannot think of any better name than that of 'voluntary' actions. If we require further to distinguish from among them, those which are also voluntary in the sense that we definitely willed to do them, we can do so by calling these 'willed' actions.

Our theory holds, then, that a great many of our actions are voluntary in the sense that we could have avoided them, *if*, just beforehand, we had chosen to do so. It does not pretend to decide whether we *could* have thus chosen to avoid them; it only says that, *if* we had so chosen, we should have succeeded. And its first concern is to lay down some absolutely universal rules as to the conditions under which actions of this kind are *right* or *wrong*; under which they *ought* or *ought not* to be done; and under which it is our *duty* to do them or not to do them. It is quite certain that we do hold that many voluntary actions are right and others wrong; that many ought to have been done, and others ought not to have been done; and that it was the agent's duty to do some of them, and his duty not to do others. Whether any actions, except voluntary ones, can be properly said to be right or wrong, or to be actions which ought or ought not to have been done, and, if so, in what sense and under what conditions, is again a question which our theory does not presume to answer. It only assumes that these things *can* be properly said of some voluntary actions, whether or not they can also be said of other actions as well. It confines itself, therefore, strictly to voluntary actions; and with regard to these it asks the following questions. Can we discover any characteristic, over and above the mere fact that they *are* right, which belongs to absolutely *all* voluntary actions which are right, and which at the same time does not belong to any except those which are right? And similarly: Can we discover any characteristic, over and above the mere fact that they are wrong, which belongs to absolutely *all* voluntary actions which are wrong, and which at the same time does not belong to any except those which are wrong? And so, too, in the case of the words 'ought' and 'duty,' it wants to discover some characteristic which belongs to *all* voluntary actions which *ought* to be done or which it is our duty to do, and which does not belong to any except those which we ought to do; and similarly to discover some characteristic which belongs to *all* voluntary actions which ought *not* to be done and which it is our duty *not* to do, and which does not belong to any except these. To all these questions our theory thinks that it can find a comparatively simple answer. And it is this answer which forms the first part of the theory. It is, as I say, a *comparatively* simple answer; but nevertheless it cannot be stated accurately except at some length. And I think it is worth while to try to state it accurately.

To begin with, then, this theory points out that all actions may, theoretically at least, be arranged in a scale, according to the proportion between the *total* quantities of pleasure or pain which they *cause*. And when it talks of the *total* quantities of pleasure or pain which an action causes, it is extremely important to realize that it means quite strictly what it says. We all of us know that many of our actions do cause pleasure and pain not only to ourselves, but also to other human beings, and sometimes, perhaps, to animals as well; and that the effects of our actions, in this respect, are often not confined to those which are comparatively direct and immediate, but that their indirect and remote effects are sometimes quite equally important or even

more so. But in order to arrive at the *total* quantities of pleasure or pain caused by an action, we should, of course, have to take into account absolutely *all* its effects, both near and remote, direct and indirect; and we should have to take into account absolutely *all* the beings, capable of feeling pleasure or pain, who were at any time affected by it; not only ourselves, therefore, and our fellow-men, but also any of the lower animals, to which the action might cause pleasure or pain, however indirectly; and also any other beings in the Universe, if there should be any, who might be affected in the same way. Some people, for instance, hold that there is a God and that there are disembodied spirits, who may be pleased or pained by our actions; and, if this is so, then, in order to arrive at the *total* quantities of pleasure or pain which an action causes, we should have, of course, to take into account, not only the pleasures or pains which it may cause to men and animals upon this earth, but also those which it may cause to God or to disembodied spirits. By the *total* quantities of pleasure or pain which an action causes, this theory means, then, quite strictly what it says. It means the quantities which would be arrived at, if we could take into account absolutely *all* the amounts of pleasure or pain, which result from the action; no matter how indirect or remote these results may be, and no matter what may be the nature of the beings who feel them.

But if we understand the total quantities of pleasure or pain caused by an action in this strict sense, then obviously, theoretically at least, six different cases are possible. It is obviously theoretically possible in the first place (1) that an action should, in its total effects, cause some pleasure but absolutely no pain; and it is obviously also possible (2) that, while it causes both pleasure and pain, the total quantity of pleasure should be *greater* than the total quantity of pain. These are two out of the six theoretically possible cases; and these two may be grouped together by saying that, in both of them, the action in question causes an *excess* of pleasure over pain, or *more* pleasure than pain. This description will, of course, if taken quite strictly, apply only to the second of the two; since an action which causes no pain whatever cannot strictly be said to cause more pleasure than pain. But it is convenient to have some description, which may be understood to cover both cases; and if we describe no pain at all as a *zero* quantity of pain, then obviously we may say that an action which causes some pleasure and no pain, does cause a *greater* quantity of pleasure than of pain, since any positive quantity is greater than zero. I propose, therefore, for the sake of convenience, to speak of both these first two cases as cases in which an action causes an *excess* of pleasure over pain.

But obviously two other cases, which are also theoretically possible, are (1) that in which an action, in its total effects, causes some pain but absolutely no pleasure, and (2) that in which, while it causes both pleasure and pain, the total quantity of *pain* is greater than the total quantity of *pleasure*. And of both these two cases I propose to speak, for the reason just explained, as cases in which an action causes an *excess* of *pain* over *pleasure*.

There remain two other cases, and two only, which are still theoretically possible; namely (1) that an action should cause absolutely no pleasure and also absolutely no pain, and (2) that, while it causes both pleasure and pain, the total quantities of each should be exactly equal. And in both these two cases, we may, of course, say that the action in question causes *no* excess either of pleasure over pain or of pain over pleasure.

Of absolutely every action, therefore, it must be true, in the sense explained, that it either causes an excess of pleasure over pain, or an excess of pain over pleasure, or neither. This threefold division covers all the six possible cases. But, of course, of any two actions, both of which cause an excess

of pleasure over pain, or of pain over pleasure, it may be true that the excess caused by the one is *greater* than that caused by the other. And, this being so, all actions may, theoretically at least, be arranged in a scale, starting at the top with those which cause the *greatest* excess of pleasure over pain; passing downwards by degrees through cases where the excess of pleasure over pain is continually smaller and smaller, until we reach those actions which cause no excess either of pleasure over pain or of pain over pleasure: then starting again with those which cause an excess of pain over pleasure, but only the smallest possible one; going on by degrees to cases in which the excess of pain over pleasure is continually larger and larger; until we reach, at the bottom, those cases in which the excess of pain over pleasure is the greatest.

The principle upon which this scale is arranged is, I think, perfectly easy to understand, though it cannot be stated accurately except in rather a complicated way. The principle is: That any action which causes an excess of pleasure over pain will always come higher in the scale *either* than an action which causes a *smaller* excess of pleasure over pain, *or* than an action which causes no excess either of pleasure over pain or of pain over pleasure, *or* than one which causes an excess of pain over pleasure; That any action which causes no excess either of pleasure over pain or of pain over pleasure will always come higher than any which causes an excess of pain over pleasure; and finally That any, which causes an excess of pain over pleasure, will always come higher than one which causes a *greater* excess of pain over pleasure. And obviously this statement is rather complicated. But yet, so far as I can see, there is no simpler way of stating quite accurately the principle upon which the scale is arranged. By saying that one action comes higher in the scale than another, we may mean any one of these five different things; and I can find no simple expression which will really apply quite accurately to all five cases.

But it has, I think, been customary, among ethical writers, to speak loosely of any action, which comes higher in this scale than another, for any one of these five reasons, as causing *more* pleasure than that other, or causing a *greater balance* of pleasure over pain. For instance, if we are comparing five different actions, one of which comes higher in the scale than any of the rest, it has been customary to say that, among the five, this is the one which causes a *maximum* of pleasure, or a *maximum balance* of pleasure over pain. To speak in this way is obviously extremely inaccurate, for many different reasons. It is obvious, for instance, that an action which comes lower in the scale may actually produce much more pleasure than one which comes higher, provided this effect is counteracted by its *also* causing a much greater quantity of pain. And it is obvious also that, of two actions, one of which comes higher in the scale than another, *neither* may cause a balance of pleasure over pain, but both actually more pain than pleasure. For these and other reasons it is quite inaccurate to speak as if the place of an action in the scale were determined either by the total quantity of pleasure that it causes, or by the total balance of pleasure over pain. But this way of speaking, though inaccurate, is also extremely convenient; and of the two alternative expressions, the one which is the most inaccurate is also the most convenient. It is much more convenient to be able to refer to any action which comes higher in the scale as simply causing *more pleasure*, than to have to say, every time, that it causes *a greater balance of pleasure over pain.*

I propose, therefore, in spite of its inaccuracy, to adopt this loose way of speaking. And I do not think the adoption of it need lead to any confusion, provided it is clearly understood, to begin with, that I am going to use the words in this loose way. It must, therefore, be clearly understood that, when, in what follows, I speak of one ac-

tion as causing more pleasure than another, I shall not mean strictly what I say, but only that the former action is related to the latter in one or other of the five following ways. I shall mean that the two actions are related to one another either (1) by the fact that, while both cause an excess of pleasure over pain, the former causes a greater excess than the latter; or (2) by the fact that, while the former causes an excess of pleasure over pain, the latter causes no excess whatever either of pleasure over pain, or of pain over pleasure; or (3) by the fact that, while the former causes an excess of pleasure over pain, the latter causes an excess of pain over pleasure; or (4) by the fact that, while the former causes no excess whatever either of pleasure over pain or of pain over pleasure, the latter does cause an excess of pain over pleasure; or (5) by the fact that, while both cause an excess of pain over pleasure, the former causes a smaller excess than the latter. It must be remembered, too, that in every case we shall be speaking of the *total* quantities of pleasure and pain caused by the actions, in the strictest possible sense; taking into account, that is to say, absolutely *all* their effects, however remote and indirect.

But now, if we understand the statement that one action causes more pleasure than another in the sense just explained, we may express as follows the first principle, which the theory I wish to state lays down with regard to right and wrong, as applied to voluntary actions. This first principle is a very simple one; for it merely asserts: That a voluntary action is right, whenever and only when the agent could *not,* even if he had chosen, have done any other action instead, which would have caused more pleasure than the one he did do; and that a voluntary action is wrong, whenever and only when the agent *could,* if he had chosen, have done some other action instead, which would have caused more pleasure than the one he did do. It must be remembered that our theory does not assert that any agent ever could have *chosen* any

other action than the one he actually performed. It only asserts, that, in the case of
all voluntary actions, he *could* have acted
differently, *if* he had chosen: not that he
could have made the choice. It does not assert, therefore, that right and wrong depend upon what he could *choose*. As to
this, it makes no assertion at all: it neither
affirms nor denies that they do so depend.
It only asserts that they do depend upon
what he could have done or could do, *if* he
chose. In every case of voluntary action, a
man could, *if* he had so chosen just before,
have done at least one other action instead.
That was the definition of a voluntary action: and it seems quite certain that many
actions are voluntary in this sense. And
what our theory asserts is that, where
among the actions which he could thus
have done instead, *if* he had chosen, there
is any one which would have caused more
pleasure than the one he did do, then his
action is always wrong; but that in all
other cases it is right. This is what our
theory asserts, if we remember that the
phrase 'causing more pleasure' is to be understood in the inaccurate sense explained
above.

But it will be convenient, in what follows, to introduce yet another inaccuracy
in our statement of it. It asserts, we have
seen, that the question whether a voluntary
action is right or wrong, depends upon the
question whether, among all the other actions, which the agent could have done instead, *if* he had chosen, there is or is not
any which would have produced more
pleasure than the one he did do. But it
would be highly inconvenient, every time
we have to mention the theory, to use the
whole phrase 'all the other actions which
the agent could have done instead, *if* he
had chosen.' I propose, therefore, instead to
call these simply 'all the other actions
which he *could* have done,' or 'which were
possible to him.' This is, of course, inaccurate, since it is, in a sense, not true that he
could have done them, if he could not have
chosen them: and our theory does not pretend to say whether he *ever* could have

chosen them. Moreover, even if it is true
that he could *sometimes* have chosen an
action which he did not choose, it is pretty
certain that it is not always so; it is pretty
certain that it is *sometimes* out of his
power to choose an action, which he certainly could have done, *if* he had chosen. It
is not true, therefore, that *all* the actions
which he could have done, *if* he had chosen, are actions which, in every sense, he
could have done, even if it is true that
some of them are. But nevertheless I propose, for the sake of brevity, to speak of
them all as actions which he *could* have
done; and this again, I think, need lead to
no confusion, if it be clearly understood
that I am doing so. It must, then, be clearly
understood that, when, in what follows, I
speak of all the actions which the agent
could have done, or all those open to him
under the circumstances, I shall mean only
all those which he could have done, *if* he
had chosen.

Understanding this, then, we may state
the first principle which our theory lays
down quite briefly by saying: 'A voluntary
action is right, whenever and only when no
other action possible to the agent under the
circumstances would have caused more
pleasure; in all other cases, it is wrong.'
This is its answer to the questions: What
characteristic is there which belongs to *all*
voluntary actions which are right, and *only*
those among them which are right? And
what characteristic is there which belongs
to *all* those which are wrong, and *only* to
those which are wrong? But it also asked
the very same questions with regard to two
other classes of voluntary actions—those
which *ought* or ought *not* to be done, and
those which it is our *duty* to do or not to
do. And its answer to the question concerning these conceptions differs from its
answer to the question concerning right
and wrong in a way, which is, indeed, comparatively unimportant, but which yet deserves to be noticed.

It may have been observed that our
theory does *not* assert that a voluntary action is right only where it causes *more*

pleasure than any action which the agent could have done instead. It confines itself to asserting that, in order to be right, such an action must cause at least *as much* pleasure as any which the agent could have done instead. And it confines itself in this way for the following reason. It is obviously possible, theoretically at least, that, among the alternatives open to an agent at a given moment, there may be two or more which would produce precisely *equal* amounts of pleasure, while all of them produced more than any of the other possible alternatives; and in such cases, our theory would say, *any one* of these actions would be perfectly right. It recognizes, therefore, that there may be cases in which no single one of the actions open to the agent can be distinguished as *the* right one to do; that in many cases, on the contrary, several different actions may all be equally right; or, in other words, that to say that a man acted rightly does not necessarily imply that, if he had done anything else instead, he would have acted wrongly. And this is certainly in accordance with common usage. We all do constantly imply that sometimes when a man was right in doing what he did, yet he might have been equally right, if he had acted differently: that there may be several different alternatives open to him, none of which can definitely be said to be wrong. This is why our theory refuses to commit itself to the view that an action is right only where it produces *more* pleasure than any of the other possible alternatives. For, if this were so, then it would follow that no two alternatives could ever be *equally* right: some one of them would always have to be *the* right one, and all the rest wrong. But it is precisely in this respect that it holds that the conceptions of 'ought' and of 'duty' differ from the conception of what is 'right.' When we say that a man 'ought' to do one particular action, or that it is his 'duty' to do it, we do imply that it would be wrong for him to do anything else. And hence our theory holds that, in the case of 'ought' and 'duty' we

may say, what we could not say in the case of 'right,' namely, that an action ought to be done or is our duty, only where it produces *more* pleasure than any which we could have done instead.

From this distinction several consequences follow. It follows firstly that a voluntary action may be 'right' without being an action which we 'ought' to do or which it is our 'duty' to do. It is, of course, always our duty to act rightly, in the sense that, if we don't act rightly, we shall always be doing what we ought not. It is, therefore, true, in a sense, that whenever we act rightly, we are always doing our duty and doing what we ought. But what is not true is that, whenever a particular action is right, it is always our duty to do that particular action and no other. This is not true, because, theoretically at least, cases may occur in which some other action would be quite equally right, and in such cases, we are obviously under no obligation whatever to do the one rather than the other: whichever we do, we shall be doing our duty and doing as we ought. And it would be rash to affirm that such cases never do practically occur. We all commonly hold that they do: that very often indeed we are under no positive obligation to do one action rather than some other; that it does not matter which we do. We must, then, be careful not to affirm that, because it is always our duty to act rightly, therefore any particular action, which is right, is always also one which it is our duty to do. This is not so, because, even where an action is right, it does not follow that it would be wrong to do something else instead; whereas, if an action is a duty or an action which we positively ought to do, it always would be wrong to do anything else instead.

The first consequence, then, which follows, from this distinction between what is right, on the one hand, and what ought to be done or is our duty, on the other, is that a voluntary action may be right, without being an action which we ought to do or which it is our duty to do. And from this it follows further that the relation between 'right' and what ought to be done is not on a par with that between 'wrong' and what ought *not* to be done. Every action which is wrong is also an action which ought not to be done and which it is our duty not to do; and also, conversely, every action which ought not to be done, or which it is our duty not to do, is wrong. These three negative terms are precisely and absolutely coextensive. To say that an action is or was wrong, is to imply that it ought not to be, or to have been, done; and the converse implication also holds. But in the case of 'right' and 'ought,' only one of the two converse propositions holds. Every action which ought to be done or which is our duty, is certainly also right; to say the one thing of any action is to imply the other. But here the converse is not true; since, as we have seen, to say that an action is right is *not* to imply that it ought to be done or that it is our duty: an action may be right, without either of these two other things being true of it. In this respect the relation between the positive conceptions 'right' and 'ought to be done' is not on a par with that between the negative conceptions 'wrong' and 'ought not to be done.' The two positive conceptions are not coextensive, whereas the two negative ones are so.

And thirdly and finally, it also follows that whereas every voluntary action, without exception, must be either right or wrong, it is by no means necessarily true of every voluntary action that it either ought to be done or ought not to be done,—that it either is our duty to do it, or our duty not to do it. On the contrary, cases may occur quite frequently where it is neither our duty to do a particular action, nor yet our duty not to do it. This will occur, whenever, among the alternatives open to us, there are two or more, any one of which would be equally right. And hence we must not suppose that, wherever we have a choice of actions before us, there is always some one among them (*if* we could only find out which), which is *the* one which we

ought to do, while all the rest are definitely wrong. It may quite well be the case that there is no one among them, which we are under a positive obligation to do, although there always must be at least one which it would be right to do. There will be one which we definitely *ought* to do, in those cases and those cases only, where there happens to be *only* one which is right under the circumstances—where, that is to say, there are not several which would all be equally right, but some one of the alternatives open to us is *the* only right thing to do. And hence in many cases we cannot definitely say of a voluntary action either that it was the agent's duty to do it nor yet that it was his duty not to do it. There may be cases in which none of the alternatives open to us is definitely prescribed by duty.

To sum up, then: The answer which this theory gives to its first set of questions is as follows. A characteristic which belongs to all right voluntary actions, and only to those which are right, is, it says, this: That they all cause at least *as much* pleasure as any action which the agent could have done instead; or, in other words, they all produce *a* maximum of pleasure. A characteristic which belongs to all voluntary actions, which *ought* to be done or which it is our *duty* to do, and only to these, is, it says, the slightly different one: That they all cause *more* pleasure than any which the agent could have done instead; or, in other words, among all the possible alternatives, it is they which produce *the* maximum of pleasure. And finally, a characteristic which belongs to all voluntary actions which are wrong, or which ought not to be done, or which it is our duty not to do, and which belongs only to these, is, in all three cases the same, namely: That they all cause *less* pleasure than some other action which the agent could have done instead. These three statements together constitute what I will call the first part of the theory; and, whether we agree with them or not, it must, I think, at least be admitted that they are propositions of a very fundamental nature and of a very wide range, so that it would be worth while to know, if possible, whether they are true.

But this first part of the theory is by no means the whole of it. There are two other parts of it, which are at least equally important; and, before we go on to consider the objections which may be urged against it, it will, I think, be best to state these other parts. They may, however, conveniently form the subject of a new chapter.

II

In the last chapter I stated the first part of an ethical theory, which I chose out for consideration, not because I agreed with it, but because it seemed to me to bring out particularly clearly the distinction between some of the most fundamental subjects of ethical discussion. This first part consisted in asserting that there is a certain characteristic which belongs to absolutely *all* voluntary actions which are right, and *only* to those which are right; another closely allied characteristic which belongs to *all* voluntary actions which ought to be done or are duties, and *only* to these; a third characteristic which belongs to *all* voluntary actions which are wrong, ought not to be done, or which it is our duty not to do, and *only* to those voluntary actions of which these things are true. And when the theory makes these assertions it means the words 'all' and 'only' to be understood quite strictly. That is to say, it means its propositions to apply to absolutely every voluntary action, which ever has been done, or ever will be done, no matter who did it, or when it was or will be done; and not only to those which actually have been or will be done, but also to all those which have been or will be *possible,* in a certain definite sense.

The sense in which it means its propo-

sitions to apply to *possible,* as well as actual, voluntary actions, is, it must be remembered, only if we agree to give the name 'possible' to all those actions which an agent *could* have done, *if* he had chosen, and to those which, in the future, any agent will be able to do, *if* he were to choose to do them. Possible actions, in this sense, form a perfectly definite group; and we do, as a matter of fact, often make judgments as to whether they would have been or would be right, and as to whether they ought to have been done in the past, or ought to be done in the future. We say, 'So-and-so ought to have done this on that occasion,' or 'It would have been perfectly right for him to have done this,' although as a matter of fact, he did not do it; or we say, 'You ought to do this,' or 'It will be quite right for you to do this,' although it subsequently turns out, that the action in question is one which you do not actually perform. Our theory says, then, with regard to all actions, which were in this sense possible in the past, that they *would have been* right, if and only if they *would* have produced a maximum of pleasure; just as it says that all actual past voluntary actions *were* right, if and only if they *did* produce a maximum of pleasure. And similarly, with regard to all voluntary actions which will be possible in the future, it says that they will be right, if and only if they *would* produce a maximum of pleasure; just as it says with regard to all that will actually be done, that they will be right, if and only if they *do* produce a maximum of pleasure.

Our theory does, then, even in its first part, deal, in a sense, with possible actions, as well as actual ones. It professes to tell us, not only which among actual past voluntary actions *were* right, but also which among those which were possible *would have been* right if they had been done; and not only which among the voluntary actions which actually will be done in the future, *will* be right, but also which among those which will be possible, *would* be right, if they *were* to be done. And in doing this, it does, of course, give us a criterion, or test, or standard, by means of which we could, theoretically at least, discover with regard to absolutely every voluntary action, which ever either has been or will be either actual or possible, whether it was or will be right or not. If we want to discover with regard to a voluntary action which was actually done or was possible in the past, whether it was right or would have been right, we have only to ask: Could the agent, on the occasion in question, have done anything else instead, which would have produced more pleasure? If he could, then the action in question was or would have been wrong; if he could not, then it was or would have been right. And similarly, if we want to discover with regard to an action, which we are contemplating in the future, whether it would be right for us to do it, we have only to ask: Could I do anything else instead which would produce more pleasure? If I could, it will be wrong to do the action; if I could not, it will be right. Our theory does then, even in its first part, profess to give us an absolutely universal *criterion* of right and wrong; and similarly also an absolutely universal *criterion* of what ought or ought not to be done.

But though it does this, there is something else which it does not do. It only asserts, in this first part, that the producing of a maximum of pleasure is a characteristic, which did and will belong, *as a matter of fact*, to all right voluntary actions (actual or possible), and only to right ones; it does not, in its first part, go on to assert that it is *because* they possess this characteristic that such actions are right. This second assertion is the first which it goes on to make in its second part; and everybody can see, I think, that there is an important difference between the two assertions.

Many people might be inclined to admit that, whenever a man acts wrongly, his action always does, on the whole, result in greater unhappiness than would have ensued if he had acted differently; and that when he acts rightly this result *never* en-

sues: that, on the contrary, right action always does in the end bring about at least as much happiness, on the whole, as the agent could possibly have brought about by any other action which was in his power. The proposition that wrong action always *does*, and (considering how the Universe is constituted) always *would*, in the long run, lead to less pleasure than the agent could have brought about by acting differently, and that right action never *does* and never *would* have this effect, is a proposition which a great many people might be inclined to accept; and this is all which, in its first part, our theory asserts. But many of those who would be inclined to assent to this proposition, would feel great hesitation in going on to assert that this is *why* actions are right or wrong respectively. There seems to be a very important difference between the two positions. We may hold, for instance, that an act of murder, whenever it is wrong, always does produce greater unhappiness than would have followed if the agent had chosen instead some one of the other alternatives, which he could have carried out, *if* he had so chosen; and we may hold that this is true of all other wrong actions, actual or possible, and never of any right ones: but it seems a very different thing to hold that murder and all other wrong actions are wrong, when they are wrong, *because* they have this result—*because* they produce less than the possible maximum of pleasure. We may hold, that is to say, that the fact that it does produce or would produce *less* than a maximum of pleasure is absolutely always a *sign* that a voluntary action is wrong, while the fact that it does produce or would produce a maximum of pleasure is absolutely always a *sign* that it is right; but this does not seem to commit us to the very different proposition that these results, besides being *signs* of right and wrong, are also the *reasons* why actions are right when they are right, and wrong when they are wrong. Everybody can see, I think, that the distinction is important; although I think it is often overlooked in ethical discussions. And it is precisely this distinction which separates what I have called the first part of our theory, from the first of the assertions which it goes on to make in its second part. In its first part it only asserts that the producing or not producing a maximum of pleasure are, absolutely universally, *signs* of right and wrong in voluntary actions; in its second part it goes on to assert that it is *because* they produce these results that voluntary actions are right when they are right, and wrong when they are wrong.

There is, then, plainly some important difference between the assertion, which our theory made in its first part, to the effect that all right voluntary actions, and only those which are right, do, *in fact*, produce a maximum of pleasure, and the assertion, which it now goes on to make, that this is *why* they are right. And if we ask why the difference is important, the answer is, so far as I can see, as follows. Namely, if we say that actions are right, *because* they produce a maximum of pleasure, we imply that, provided they produced this result, they *would* be right, *no matter what other effects they might produce* as well. We imply, in short, that their rightness does *not* depend at all upon their other effects, but *only* on the quantity of pleasure that they produce. And this is a very different thing from merely saying that the producing a maximum of pleasure is always, as a matter of fact, a *sign* of rightness. It is quite obvious, that, in the Universe as it is actually constituted, pleasure and pain are by no means the only results of any of our actions: they all produce immense numbers of other results as well. And so long as we merely assert that the producing a maximum of pleasure is a *sign* of rightness, we leave open the possibility that it is so only because this result does always, as a matter of fact, happen to coincide with the production of *other* results; but that it is partly upon these other results that the rightness of the action depends. But so soon as we assert that actions are right, *because* they

produce a maximum of pleasure, we cut away this possibility; we assert that actions which produced such a maximum *would* be right, even if they did not produce any of the other effects, which, as a matter of fact, they always do produce. And this, I think, is the chief reason why many persons who would be inclined to assent to the first proposition, would hesitate to assent to the second.

It is, for instance, commonly held that some pleasures are higher or better than others, even though they may not be more pleasant; and that where we have a choice between procuring for ourselves or others a higher or a lower pleasure, it is generally right to prefer the former, even though it may perhaps be less pleasant. And, of course, even those who hold that actions are only right because of the quantity of pleasure they produce, and not at all because of the quality of these pleasures, might quite consistently hold that it is *as a matter of fact* generally right to prefer higher pleasures to lower ones, even though they may be less pleasant. They might hold that this is the case, on the ground that higher pleasures, even when less pleasant in themselves, do, if we take into account all their further effects, tend to produce more pleasure on the whole than lower ones. There is a good deal to be said for the view that this does actually happen, as the Universe is actually constituted; and that hence an action which causes a higher pleasure to be enjoyed instead of a lower one, will in general cause *more* pleasure in its *total* effects, though it may cause *less* in its immediate effects. And this is why those who hold that higher pleasures are in general to be preferred to lower ones, may neverthless admit that mere quantity of pleasure is always, *in fact*, a correct *sign* or *criterion* of the rightness of an action.

But those who hold that actions are only right, *because* of the quantity of pleasure they produce, must hold also that, *if* higher pleasures did not, in their total effects, produce *more* pleasure than lower ones, then there *would* be no reason what-ever for preferring them, provided they were not themselves more pleasant. *If the sole* effect of one action were to be the en-joyment of a certain amount of the most bestial or idiotic pleasure, and the *sole* effect of another were to be the enjoyment of a much more refined one, then they must hold that there would be no reason whatever for preferring the latter to the former, provided only that the mere quan-tity of pleasure enjoyed in each case were the same. And if the bestial pleasure were ever so slightly more pleasant than the other, then they must say it would be our positive duty to do the action which would bring it about rather than the other. This is a conclusion which does follow from the assertion that actions are right *because* they produce a maximum of pleasure, and which does not follow from the mere asser-tion that the producing a maximum of pleasure is always, *in fact,* a sign of right-ness. And it is for this, and similar reasons, that it is important to distinguish the two propositions.

To many persons it may seem clear that it *would* be our duty to prefer some pleasures to others, even if they did not en-tail a greater *quantity* of pleasure; and hence that though actions which produce a maximum of pleasure are perhaps, *in fact,* always right, they are not right *because* of this, but only because the producing of this result does in fact happen to coincide with the producing of other results. They would say that though perhaps, in fact, actual cases never occur in which it *is* or would be wrong to do an action, which produces a maximum of pleasure, it is easy to *imagine* cases in which it *would* be wrong. *If,* for instance, we had to choose between creat-ing a Universe, in which all the inhabit-ants were capable only of the lowest sen-sual pleasures, and another in which they were capable of the highest intellectual and aesthetic ones, it would, they would say, plainly be our duty to create the latter rather than the former, even though the

mere quantity of pleasure enjoyed in it were rather less than in the former, and still more so if the quantities were equal. Or, to put it shortly, they would say that a world of men is preferable to a world of pigs, even though the pigs might enjoy as much or more pleasure than a world of men. And this is what our theory goes on to deny, when it says that voluntary actions are right, *because* they produce a maxi-mum of pleasure. It implies, by saying this, that actions which produced a maximum of pleasure *would* always be right, no matter what their effects, in other respects, might be. And hence that it *would* be right to cre-ate a world in which there was no intelli-gence and none of the higher emotions, rather than one in which these were pres-ent in the highest degree, provided only that the mere quantity of pleasure enjoyed in the former were ever so little greater than that enjoyed in the latter.

Our theory asserts, then, in its second part, that voluntary actions are right when they are right, *because* they produce a maximum of pleasure; and in asserting this it takes a great step beyond what it as-serted in its first part, since it now implies that an action which produced a maximum of pleasure always *would* be right, no mat-ter how its results, in other respects, might compare with those of the other possible alternatives.

But it might be held that, even so, it does not imply that this would be so *abso-lutely unconditionally.* It might be held that though, in the Universe as actually constituted, actions are right *because* they produce a maximum of pleasure, and hence their rightness does not at all depend upon their *other* effects, yet this is only so for some such reason as that, in this Universe, all conscious beings do actually happen to desire pleasure; but that, if we could imag-ine a Universe, in which pleasure was not desired, then, in such a Universe, actions would *not* be right because they produced a maximum of pleasure; and hence that we cannot lay it down absolutely unconditionally that in all conceivable Universes any voluntary action would be right whenever and only when it produced a maximum of pleasure. For some such reason as this, it might be held that we must distinguish between the mere assertion that voluntary actions are right, when they are right, *because* they produce a maximum of pleasure, and the further assertion that this *would* be so in all conceivable circumstances and in any conceivable Universe. Those who assert the former are by no means necessarily bound to assert the latter also. To assert the latter is to take a still further step.

But the theory I wish to state does, in fact, take this further step. It asserts not only that, in the Universe as it is, voluntary actions are right *because* they produce a maximum of pleasure, but also that this would be so, *under any conceivable circumstances*: that if any conceivable being, in any conceivable Universe, were faced with a choice between an action which would cause more pleasure and one which would cause less, it would *always* be his duty to choose the former rather than the latter, no matter what the respects might be in which his Universe differed from ours. It may, at first sight, seem unduly bold to assert that any ethical truth can be absolutely unconditional in this sense. But many philosophers have held that some fundamental ethical principles certainly are thus unconditional. And a little reflection will suffice to show that the view that they may be so is at all events not absurd. We have many instances of other truths, which seem quite plainly to be of this nature. It seems quite clear, for instance, that it is not only true that twice two do make four, in the Universe as it actually is, but that they necessarily would make four, in any conceivable Universe, no matter how much it might differ from this one in other respects. And our theory is only asserting that the connexion which it believes to hold between rightness and the production of a maximum of pleasure is, in this respect,

similar to the connexion asserted to hold between the number two and the number four, when we say that twice two are four. It asserts that, if any being whatever, in any circumstances whatever, had to choose between two actions, one of which would produce more pleasure than the other, it always would be his duty to choose the former rather than the latter: that this is absolutely unconditionally true. This assertion obviously goes very much further, both than the assertion which it made in its first part, to the effect that the producing a maximum of pleasure is a *sign* of rightness in the case of all voluntary actions, that ever have been or will be actual or possible, and also than the assertion, that in the Universe, as it is actually constituted, actions are right, when they are right, *because* they produce a maximum of pleasure. But bold as the assertion may seem, it is, at all events, not impossible that we should know it to be true.

Our theory asserts, therefore, in its second part: That, if we had to choose between two actions, one of which would have as its sole or total effects, an effect or set of effects, which we may call A, while the other would have as its sole or total effects, an effect or set of effects, which we may call B, then, *if* A contained more pleasure than B, it always would be our duty to choose the action which caused A rather than that which caused B. This, it asserts, would be absolutely *always* true, *no matter what A and B might be like in other respects*. And to assert this is (it now goes on to say) *equivalent* to asserting that any effect or set of effects which contains more pleasure is always *intrinsically better* than one which contains less.

By calling one effect or set of effects *intrinsically better* than another it means that it is better *in itself*, quite apart from any accompaniments or further effects which it may have. That is to say: To assert of any one thing, A, that it is *intrinsically* better than another, B, is to assert that if A existed *quite alone*, without any accompaniments or effects whatever—if, in short, A constituted the whole Universe, it would be better that such a Universe should exist, than that a Universe which consisted solely of B should exist instead. In order to discover whether any one thing is *intrinsically* better than another, we have always thus to consider whether it would be better that the one should exist *quite alone* than that the other should exist *quite alone*. No one thing or set of things, A, ever can be *intrinsically* better than another, B, unless it would be better that A should exist quite alone than that B should exist quite alone. Our theory asserts, therefore, that, wherever it is true that it would be our *duty* to choose A rather than B, if A and B were to be the sole effects of a pair of actions between which we had to choose, there it is always also true that it would be *better* that A should exist quite alone than that B should exist quite alone. And it asserts also, conversely, that where-ever it is true that any one thing or set of things, A, is intrinsically better than an-other, B, there it would always also be our duty to choose an action of which A would be the sole effect rather than one of which B would be the sole effect, if we had to choose between them. But since, as we have seen, it holds that it never could be our duty to choose one action rather than another, unless the total effects of the one contained more pleasure than that of the other, it follows that, according to it, no ef-fect or set of effects, A, can possibly be in-trinsically better than another, B, *unless* it contains more pleasure. It holds, therefore, not only that any one effect or set of effects, which contains more pleasure, is al-ways intrinsically better than one which contains less, but also that no effect or set of effects can be intrinsically better than another *unless* it contains more pleasure.

It is plain, then, that this theory as-signs a quite unique position to pleasure and pain in two respects; or possibly only in one, since it is just possible that the two propositions which it makes about them are not merely equivalent, but absolutely iden-tical—that is to say, are merely different ways of expressing exactly the same idea. The two propositions are these. (1) That if any one had to choose between two ac-tions, one of which would, in its total effects, cause more pleasure than the other, it always would be his duty to choose the former; and that it never could be any one's duty to choose one action rather than another, unless its total effects contained more pleasure. (2) That any Universe, or part of a Universe, which contains more pleasure, is always intrinsically better than one which contains less; and that nothing can be intrinsically better than anything else, unless it contains more pleasure. It does seem to be just possible that these two propositions are merely two different ways of expressing exactly the same idea. The question whether they are so or not simply depends upon the question whether, when we say, 'It would be better that A should exist quite alone than that B should exist quite alone,' we are or are not saying exactly the same thing, as when we say, "Suppos-ing we had to choose between an action of which A would be the sole effect, and one of which B would be the sole effect, it would be our duty to choose the former ra-ther than the latter.' And it certainly does seem, at first sight, as if the two proposi-tions were not identical; as if we should not be saying exactly the same thing in asserting the one, as in asserting the other. But, even if they are not identical, our theory asserts that they are certainly *equivalent*: that, whenever the one is true, the other is cer-tainly also true. And, if they are not identi-cal, this assertion of equivalence amounts to the very important proposition that: An action is right, only if no action, which the agent could have done instead, would have had intrinsically better results; while an action is wrong, only if the agent *could* have done other action instead whose total results would have been intrinsically better. It certainly seems as if this proposition were not a mere tautology. And, if so, then we must admit that our theory assigns a unique position to pleasure and pain in two respects, and not in one only. It asserts, first of all, that they have a unique relation to right and wrong; and secondly, that they have a unique relation to *intrinsic value*.

Our theory asserts, then, that any whole which contains a greater amount of pleasure, is always intrinsically better than one which contains a smaller amount, no matter what the two may be like in other respects; and that no whole can be intrinsically better than another unless it contains more pleasure. But it must be remembered that throughout this discussion, we have, for the sake of convenience, been using the phrase 'contains more pleasure' in an inaccurate sense. I explained that I should say of one whole, A, that it contained more pleasure than another, B, whenever A and B were related to one another in either of the five following ways: namely (1) when A and B both contain an excess of pleasure over pain, but A contains a greater excess than B; (2) when A contains an excess of pleasure over pain, while B contains no excess either of pleasure over pain or of pain over pleasure; (3) when A contains an excess of pleasure over pain, while B contains an excess of pain over pleasure, (4) when A contains no excess either of pleasure over pain or of pain over pleasure, while B does contain an excess of pain over pleasure; and (5) when both A and B contain an excess of pain over pleasure, but A contains a smaller excess than B. Whenever in stating this theory, I have spoken of one whole, or effect, or set of effects, A, as containing more pleasure than another, B, I have always meant merely that A was related to B *in one or other of these five ways*. And so here, when our theory says that every whole which contains a greater amount of pleasure is always intrinsically better than one which contains less, and that nothing can be intrinsically better than anything else unless it contains more pleasure, this must be understood to mean that any whole, A, which stands to another, B, in *any one* of

these five relations, is always intrinsically better than B, and that no one thing can be intrinsically better than another, unless it stands to it in *one or other* of these five relations. And it becomes important to remember this, when we go on to take account of another fact.

It is plain that when we talk of one thing being 'better' than another we may mean any one of five different things. We may mean either (1) that while both are positively good, the first is better; or (2) that while the first is positively good, the second is neither good nor bad, but indifferent; or (3) that while the first is positively good, the second is positively bad; or (4) that while the first is indifferent, the second is positively bad; or (5) that while both are positively bad, the first is less bad than the second. We should, in common life, say that one thing was 'better' than another, whenever it stood to that other in any one of these five relations. Or, in other words, we hold that among things which stand to one another in the relation of better and worse, some are positively good, others positively bad, and others neither good nor bad, but indifferent. And our theory holds that this is, in fact, the case, with things which have a place in the scale of *intrinsic* value: some of them are intrinsically good, others intrinsically bad, and others indifferent. And it would say that a whole is intrinsically good, whenever and only when it contains an excess of pleasure over pain; intrinsically bad, whenever and only when it contains an excess of pain over pleasure; and intrinsically indifferent, whenever and only when it contains neither.

In addition, therefore, to laying down precise rules as to what things are intrinsically *better* or *worse* than others, our theory also lays down equally precise ones as to what things are intrinsically *good* and *bad* and *indifferent*. By saying that a thing is intrinsically good it means that it would be a good thing that the thing in question should exist, even if it existed *quite alone,* without any further accompaniments or effects whatever. By saying that it is intrinsically bad, it means that it would be a bad thing or an evil that it should exist, even if it existed quite alone, without any further accompaniments or effects whatever. And by saying that it is intrinsically indifferent, it means that, if it existed *quite alone*, its existence would be neither a good nor an evil in any degree whatever. And just as the conceptions 'intrinsically better' and 'intrinsically worse' are connected in a perfectly precise manner with the conceptions 'right' and 'wrong,' so, it maintains, are these other conceptions also. To say of anything, A, that it is 'intrinsically good,' is equivalent to saying that, if we had to choose between an action of which A would be the sole or total effect, and an action, which would have absolutely no effects at all, it would always be our duty to choose the former, and wrong to choose the latter. And similarly to say of anything, A, that it is 'intrinsically bad,' is equivalent to saying that, if we had to choose between an action of which A would be the sole effect, and an action which would have absolutely no effects at all, it would always be our duty to choose the latter and wrong to choose the former. And finally, to say of anything, A, that it is 'intrinsically indifferent' is equivalent to saying that, if we had to choose between an action, of which A would be the sole effect, and an action which would have absolutely no effects at all, it would not matter which we chose: either choice would be equally right.

To sum up, then, we may say that, in its second part, our theory lays down three principles. It asserts (1) that anything whatever, whether it be a single effect, or a whole set of effects, or a whole Universe, is *intrinsically good*, whenever and only when it either is or contains an excess of pleasure over pain; that anything whatever is *intrinsically bad*, whenever and only when it either is or contains an excess of pain over pleasure; and that all other things, no matter what their nature may be, are intrinsi-

cally indifferent. It asserts (2) that any one thing, whether it be a single effect, or a whole set of effects, or a whole Universe, is intrinsically *better* than another, whenever and only when the two are related to one another in one or other of the five following ways: namely, when either (*a*) while both are intrinsically good, the second is not so good as the first; or (*b*) while the first is intrinsically good, the second is intrinsically indifferent; or (*c*) while the first is intrinsically good, the second is intrinsically bad; or (*d*) while the first is intrinsically indifferent, the second is intrinsically bad; or (*e*) while both are intrinsically bad, the first is not so bad as the second. And it asserts (3) that, if we had to choose between two actions one of which would have intrinsically better total effects than the other, it always would be our duty to choose the former, and wrong to choose the latter; and that no action ever can be right *if* we could have done anything else instead which would have had intrinsically better total effects, nor wrong, *unless* we could have done something else instead which would have had intrinsically better total effects. From these three principles taken together, the whole theory follows. And whether it be true or false, it is, I think, at least a perfectly clear and intelligible theory. Whether it is or is not of any practical importance is, indeed, another question. But, even if it were of none whatever, it certainly lays down propositions of so fundamental and so far-reaching a character, that it seems worth while to consider whether they are true or false. There remain, I think, only two points which should be noticed with regard to it, before we go on to consider the principal objections which may be urged against it.

It should be noticed, first, that, though this theory asserts that nothing is *intrinsically* good, unless it is or contains an excess of pleasure over pain, it is very far from asserting that nothing is *good*, unless it fulfills this condition. By saying that a thing is *intrinsically good*, it means, as has been explained, that the existence of the thing in question *would* be a good, even if it existed quite alone, without any accompaniments or effects whatever; and it is quite plain that when we call things 'good' we by no means always mean this: we by no means always mean that they *would* be good, even if they existed quite alone. Very often, for instance, when we say that a thing is 'good,' we mean that it is good *because of its effects*; and we should not for a moment maintain that it *would* be good, even if it had no effects at all. We are, for instance, familiar with the idea that it is sometimes a good thing for people to suffer pain; and yet we should be very loth to maintain that in all such cases their suffering *would* be a good thing, even if nothing were gained by it—if it had no further effects. We do, in general, maintain that suffering is good, only *where* and *because* it has further good effects. And similarly with many other things. Many things, therefore, which are not 'intrinsically' good, may nevertheless be 'good' in some one or other of the senses in which we use that highly ambiguous word. And hence our theory can and would quite consistently maintain that, while nothing is *intrinsically* good except pleasure or wholes which contain pleasure, many other things really are 'good'; and similarly that, while nothing is *intrinsically* bad except pain or wholes which contain it, yet many other things are really 'bad.' It would, for instance, maintain that it is *always* a good thing to act rightly, and a bad thing to act wrongly; although it would say at the same time that, since actions, strictly speaking, do not *contain* either pleasure or pain, but are only accompanied by or causes of them, a right action is *never intrinsically* good, nor a wrong one *intrinsically* bad. And similarly it would maintain that it is perfectly true that some men are 'good,' and others 'bad,' and some better than others; although no man can strictly be said to *contain* either pleasure or pain, and hence none can be either intrinsically good or intrinsically bad or intrinsically better than

any other. It would even maintain (and this also it can do quite consistently), that events which are *intrinsically* good are nevertheless very often bad, and intrinsically bad ones good. It would, for instance, say that it is often a very bad thing for a man to enjoy a particular pleasure on a particular occasion, although the event, which consists in his enjoying it, may be intrinsically good, since it contains an excess of pleasure over pain. It may often be a very bad thing that such an event should happen, because it *causes* the man himself or other beings to have less pleasure or more pain in the future, than they would otherwise have had. And for similar reasons it may often be a very good thing that an intrinsically bad event should happen.

It is important to remember all this, because otherwise the theory may appear much more paradoxical than it really is. It may, for instance, appear, at first sight, as if it denied all value to anything except pleasure and wholes which contain it—a view which would be extremely paradoxical if it were held. But it does *not* do this. It does not deny all value to other things, but only all *intrinsic* value—a very different thing. It only says that none of them *would* have any value if they existed quite alone. But, of course, as a matter of fact, none of them do exist quite alone, and hence it may quite consistently allow that, as it is, many of them do have very great value. Concerning kinds of value, other than intrinsic value, it does not profess to lay down any general rules at all. And its reason for confining itself to intrinsic value is because it holds that this and this alone is related to right and wrong in the perfectly definite manner explained above. Whenever an action is right, it is right only if and because the total effects of no action, which the agent could have done instead, would have had more *intrinsic* value; and whenever an action is wrong, it is wrong only if and because the total effects of some other action, which the agent could have done instead, would have had more *intrinsic* value. This proposition, which is true of *intrinsic* value, is not, it holds, true of value of any other kind.

And a second point which should be noticed about this theory is the following. It is often represented as asserting that pleasure is the only thing which is *ultimately* good or desirable, and pain the only thing which is *ultimately* bad or undesirable; or as asserting that pleasure is the only thing which is good *for its own sake*, and pain the only thing which is bad *for its own sake*. And there is, I think, a sense in which it does assert this. But these expressions are not commonly carefully defined; and it is worth noticing that, if our theory does assert these propositions, the expressions '*ultimately* good' or 'good *for its own sake*' must be understood in a different sense from that which has been assigned above to the expression '*intrinsically* good.' We must not take '*ultimately* good' or 'good *for its own sake*' to be synonyms for '*intrinsically* good.' For our theory most emphatically does *not* assert that pleasure is the only thing *intrinsically* good, and pain the only thing *intrinsically* evil. On the contrary, it asserts that any whole which *contains* an excess of pleasure over pain is *intrinsically* good, no matter how much else it may contain besides; and similarly that any whole which contains an excess of pain over pleasure is *intrinsically* bad. This distinction between the conception expressed by '*ultimately* good' or 'good *for its own sake*,' on the one hand, and that expressed by '*intrinsically* good,' on the other, is not commonly made; and yet obviously we must make it, if we are to say that our theory does assert that pleasure is the only *ultimate* good, and pain the only *ultimate* evil. The two conceptions, if used in this way, have one important point in common, namely, that both of them will only apply to things whose existence *would* be good, even if they existed quite alone. Whether we assert that a thing is 'ultimately good' or 'good for its own sake' or 'intrinsically good,' we are always asserting that it would be good, even if it existed quite alone. But the two conceptions differ in respect of the fact that, whereas a whole which is 'intrinsically good' may contain parts which are *not* intrinsically good, i.e. *would* not be good, if they existed quite alone; anything which is 'ultimately good' or 'good for its own sake' can contain no such parts. This, I think, is the meaning which we must assign to the expressions 'ultimately good' or 'good for its own sake,' if we are to say that our theory asserts pleasure to be the *only* thing 'ultimately good' or 'good for its own sake.' We may, in short, divide intrinsically good things into two classes: namely (1) those which, while as wholes they are intrinsically good, nevertheless contain some parts which are not intrinsically good; and (2) those, which either have no parts at all, or, if they have any, have none but what are themselves intrinsically good. And we may thus, if we please, confine the terms 'ultimately good' or 'good for their own sakes' to things which belong to the second of these two classes. We may, of course, make a precisely similar distinction between two classes of intrinsically bad things. And it is only if we do this that our theory can be truly said to assert that nothing is 'ultimately good' or 'good for its own sake,' except pleasure; and nothing 'ultimately bad' or 'bad for its own sake,' except pain.

Such is the ethical theory which I have chosen to state, because it seems to me particularly simple, and hence to bring out particularly clearly some of the main questions which have formed the subject of ethical discussion.

What is specially important is to distinguish the question, which it professes to answer in its first part, from the much more radical questions, which it professes to answer in its second. In its first part, it only professes to answer the question: What characteristic is there which does actually, *as a matter of fact*, belong to all right voluntary actions, which ever have been or will be done in this world? While, in its second part, it professes to answer the much more fundamental question: What characteristic is there which *would* belong to absolutely any voluntary action, which was right, in any conceivable Universe, and under any conceivable circumstances? These two questions are obviously extremely different, and by the theory I have stated I mean a theory which does profess to give an answer to *both*.

Whether this theory has ever been held in exactly the form in which I have stated it, I should not like to say. But many people have certainly held something very like it, and it seems to be what is *often* meant by the familiar name 'Utilitarianism,' which is the reason why I have chosen this name as the title of these two chapters. It must not, however, be assumed that any-

body who talks about 'Utilitarianism' *always* means precisely this theory in all its details. On the contrary, many even of those who call themselves Utilitarians would object to some of its most fundamental propositions. One of the difficulties which occurs in ethical discussions is that no single name, which has ever been proposed as the name of an ethical theory, has any absolutely fixed significance. On the contrary, every name may be, and often is, used as a name for several different theories, which may differ from one another in very important respects. Hence, whenever anybody uses such a name, you can never trust to the name alone, but must always look carefully to see exactly what he means by it.

Utilitarian Generalization

DAVID LYONS

Sometimes an act is criticized just because the results of everyone's acting similarly would be bad. The *generalization test*, 'What would happen if everyone did the same?' is often used in raising such criticisms; and a principle warranting the criticism is of the following kind:

> (G1) If the consequences of everyone's doing a certain sort of thing would be undesirable, then it would be wrong for anyone to do such a thing.

This principle is clearly teleological (utilitarian) since in appealing to it, in determining whether acts are wrong, we consider only desirable and undesirable effects—their utility. It is also a generalization principle: the consequences of a general practice (everyone's doing the same) are considered; a particular act is assessed as an act of that kind; and thus the verdict applies to all such acts. Such a principle may therefore be called a form of *utilitarian generalization*.

Challenges employing the generalization test are not uncommon in everyday moral argument. The significance of the test has, however, puzzled philosophers. Thus the subject is of some interest in its own right. But the generalization test has philosophical importance today primarily because it has been associated with the forms of utilitarian generalization, and because these principles, in turn, have seemed to accomplish certain moral tasks

Reprinted from *Forms and Limits of Utilitarianism* by David Lyons by permission of the author and the Clarendon Press, Oxford. Copyright 1964.

on strictly utilitarian grounds which other forms of utilitarianism fail to do.

Our main subject then is this family of principles—their logic and their substantive import: the members of the family; how they compare with the more traditional kind of utilitarian principle; how they may properly be applied. Moreover, I shall use this inquiry—the methods of analysis which I shall adopt and the conclusions that are reached—as a basis for examining a much-heralded recent theory in this tradition, rule-utilitarianism. I shall relate all these principles to considerations of justice and fairness—to show that the apparent force of the generalization test requires appeal to more than utility.

In this first chapter I shall identify and characterize utilitarian generalization, suggest difficulties and issues, sketch an historical framework, and indicate the dimensions within this class of principles.

A. TWO KINDS OF UTILITARIANISM

'Oh look!' she said, pointing off to the right. 'The apples are ripe in that orchard. Let's stop and pick some.'

'No. . . .' He drove on, more slowly. 'I don't think we should. Suppose everyone did that!'

'Don't be silly—not everyone will. And the few we'd take wouldn't be missed.'

'But that's beside the point. If we can do it then so can anyone else. And if everyone did the same . . .'

And if everyone did the same, if every passer-by picked as he chose, this grower (or perhaps all growers) would suffer irretrievable losses. Moreover, he might ask himself: 'Does it pay to take such care of my orchards if others are to pick them bare?' Thus, his incentive could be undermined and future production could thereby be damaged. Or he might be obliged, at considerable cost, to post guards and erect fences that would mar the now pleasant landscape.

If such contingencies were the ground for our moralizer's objection, then he was employing the generalization test. He was appealing to a form of utilitarian generalization, such as (G1).

Notice how our moralizer did not argue. He did not claim that the grower would suffer hardship or loss as a result of the small expropriation proposed by his companion. Nor did he say that such hardship or loss would indirectly flow from the act, as a result of their example inciting others to do likewise, sparking a chain reaction leading to a devastation of the orchard. Nor did he maintain that in doing such a thing he and his companion were disposing themselves to act in future in ways which ultimately would have bad consequences. Finally, our moralizer did not mention the contingency, the outside chance that others would in fact do the same and that, under the circumstances, this act might contribute to a bad state of affairs.

That is to say, the moralizer did not argue that the over-all effects of the one act would be undesirable (or worse than those of some alternative) and that this was the reason against taking some apples. He might have argued in this way while still appealing to utility. But such an argument rests upon applying the test of utility in a radically different way—in what I shall call a *simple utilitarian* way.

Simple utilitarian considerations are those that concern all the effects of the particular act in question (or the effects of

that act as compared with those of the alternative acts). If the moralizer had appealed to such considerations he would have asked, 'What will happen if *this* act is performed?' and not 'What would happen if *everyone* did the *same*?'

In contrast, *general* utilitarian considerations concern the total effects that *could* be produced if all acts similar to the one in question, which could be performed, actually were performed. That is, in applying a form of utilitarian generalization, we describe the particular act in some way, thus marking off a class of acts, which could be performed, that are similar in the respects specified. We do not assume that others will do the same. We are only to suppose that the kind of act specified is generally practised and to evaluate the effects of this hypothesized practice.

These two kinds of utilitarianism—simple and general—are distinguishable in two respects: (1) the manner in which value-criteria, the tests for utility, are applied to acts, and (2) the generality of the judgements derivable. In the case of simple utilitarianism, (1) value-criteria are applied to the effects of particular acts taken separately, and (2) judgements concern only particular acts. The rightness or wrongness of a particular act depends upon the value of its effects, i.e. upon its *simple utility*; or alternatively upon the value of its effects as compared with the values of the effects of the alternative acts, i.e. upon its *relative simple utility*. In the case of utilitarian generalization, on the other hand, (1) value-criteria are applied only to what I shall call the *tendency* of an act, i.e. to the effects of everyone's doing the same sort of thing; and (2) the judgements directly derivable concern a class of acts that are similar in the specified way, each one determined as right or wrong or obligatory, or prima facie so, as the case may be. The rightness or wrongness of a particular act here depends upon the value of its tendency, i.e. upon its *generalized utility*; or alternatively upon the value of its tendency as compared with the values of the tendencies of the alternatives, i.e. upon its *relative generalized utility*.

The generalization test occurs in various familiar linguistic shapes and often incorporates the substance of the matter at hand. Thus we may have:

What if everyone dodged the draft?

Suppose everyone lied just to suit his own convenience?

But suppose everyone failed to pay his taxes!

What would happen if *no one* bothered to vote?

When such objections are made, many kinds of disagreement can arise. For example:

(1) 'Well, what *would* happen? The question you pose is more complex than it may appear. The total effects of everyone's doing what I propose to do may be quite different, qualitatively different, from the effects of this one act. If people haven't generally acted in this way before, we may not know, we may have no reliable idea of, what consequences would result.'

The particular details of the factual problems suggested here will not be considered in this study. We are concerned with the general nature of these principles, and this will lead us to examine some empirical (causal) phenomena. But we shall not be concerned with the specific applications of the principles, and thus not generally with the practical problems of getting the required information and correctly inferring judgements from the principles on the basis of that information.

The practical problems here are akin to, though more complex than, a set of difficulties faced in applying simple utilitarianism. In that case the implications of a given principle depend upon *all* the effects (all the utilities and disutilities) of individual acts, no matter how remote or indirect they may be. Such practical obstacles to success in discovering what a given principle actually implies are compounded in the case of utilitarian generalization, for there one is concerned, not with all the effects of one act, but with all the effects of every one of a class of similar acts, supposing that all are performed.

(2) 'But would the results be as bad as you suggest? Would they be bad at all? How do you judge so? Why in that way?'

This value-theoretic set of problems, in practice linked with (1), will not concern us either. I am distinguishing two features of a teleological or utilitarian theory and dealing with one only. We are leaving value-theory aside and shall concentrate upon the structure of utilitarianism—how the value-criteria are to be applied. Thus we shall not ask 'What are the criteria of intrinsic goodness?' or 'What things are desirable (undesirable)?' or 'How can we decide what is a desirable goal?' We shall consider only questions related to differences in utilitarian theories such as the differences between simple and general utilitarian considerations. We are doing so because some have thought that a mere difference in structure along these lines results in a substantive difference in the implications of utilitarian principles.

But if we do not concern ourselves with value-criteria, and therefore set no restrictions upon them at all, this will allow us to call certain theories 'utilitarian' even though they might not ordinarily be so called. For example, 'self-realizationist' teleological theories might be counted as utilitarian; and is this not a confusion to be avoided? The answer is, that we need not be concerned with such distinctions. It is merely a terminological—and partly historical—point, which principles we choose to call 'utilitarian'. The forms of utilitarian generalization and also the species of rule-utilitarianism that we shall examine are, in fact, usually supposed to be applied in conjunction with universalistic value-criteria (where the interests of each person count equally), and these theories may therefore be counted as 'utilitarian' in one restricted sense. Bue we are not assuming that a utilitarian theory is necessarily hedonistic, for example (i.e. based upon a pleasure principle), and we need impose no other evaluative restrictions.

The reason some have been concerned to restrict value-criteria used in conjunction with 'utilitarian' principles is that by adopting certain *ad hoc* valuations the utilitarian seems to escape at least some of the traditional criticisms of his theory. Thus, as we shall see, the 'ideal' utilitarian can claim that just distributions are intrinsically good (and unjust distributions intrinsically evil) and thereby attempt to assimilate justice to utility and in that way accommodate utilitarianism to a class of criticisms based on appeals to justice. But, as I shall argue in the last chapter, even this move will take the utilitarian only so far and not far enough. For what the utilitarian cannot allow is that some value related to the rightness or wrongness of acts is characteristic of acts of certain kinds, e.g. unfair acts, independently of their effects.

The only condition we must impose is that, when principles are compared, the value-criteria employed in conjunction with them must of course be (whatever else they are) identical. This will tacitly be assumed—for our arguments, as opposed to illustrative examples, will be strictly schematic, requiring no specification of value-criteria.

The following issues will receive attention in the immediately succeeding chapters:

(3) 'What is the force of "everyone" in your objection? Who is to count? Surely not everyone, for not everyone will have occasion to do this kind of act. Shall we consider merely those who will pass by this orchard, or all those who will pass by all similar orchards? Or shall we consider only those who will notice the apples? Or perhaps only those who will be strongly tempted to take some? How do we decide which class to consider? How does one show that a particular method of selection is not arbitrary?'

Similarly:

(4) 'What are we to count as the same sort of action? And how do we decide? Shall we consider "picking apples" or "stealing apples"? Shall we mention that no one is looking or that there will be many left when we have taken some?'

The latter two sets of problems are more fundamental than (1) and (2), for any defensible application of utilitarian generalization presupposes answers to the questions raised.

(5) 'But of course not everyone will do the same. To suppose that they will is to suppose falsely. And to act upon such a false supposition intentionally is to mislead oneself regarding the circumstances—and therefore the effects—of one's act—a very *un*utilitarian thing to do.'

(6) 'But of course few others will do the same. Therefore the evil will not be produced anyway, regardless of what I do, so my act cannot be wrong.'

(7) 'But of course most others will do the same. Therefore the evil will be produced anyway, regardless of what I do, so my act cannot be wrong.'

(8) 'My act itself will not have bad effects. And I am responsible for my acts alone, not for what others will or might do. Thus there is no utilitarian ground against my acting this way—regardless of what others do.'

These objections involve a set of related misunderstandings regarding utilitarian generalization which none the less suggest real problems as to the relevance of the behaviour of others. We shall deal with the relevance of others' behaviour in some detail.

(9) 'Granted that this is an act of the kind you specify; but there are also important differences. This is a special case which deserves special consideration (or indulgence).'

And finally:

(10) 'What does it matter? Why should I consider such an objection at all?'

B. DEVELOPMENT OF THE NEW UTILITARIANISM

Until recently, the notion of *generalization* in ethics was not normally associated with *utility*. Generalization has had two primary associations: the principle of generality and Kant's ethical doctrines.

The principle of generality—otherwise called, e.g. the principle of impartiality or equity—merely asserts that moral considerations have a universal character or 'bindingness'. A common formula for this notion is 'Treat like cases alike'—and, as we understand, 'Treat relevantly different cases differently.' More particularly, we may say: if it is right (or wrong) for someone to do a certain kind of thing, then it is likewise right (or wrong) for anyone to do a similar thing. Sometimes, the principle is understood as requiring that moral criticism and justification turn upon rules and principles—or at least turn upon general reasons.

The principle of generality thus has a minimal content. It says nothing about *which* acts are right or wrong, nor *why* some are right and others wrong; nothing about which are to be regarded as similar and which as different, nor why they may be so regarded. In this sense, it is a formal principle (thus, sometimes called the formal principle of justice): it tells us about morality, about the generality of moral considerations, but not about their content, nothing about the rightness or wrongness of acts as such. One might say that it concerns the correctness or soundness of moral reasoning as distinct from the direct assessment of acts (or of other moral subjects).

The Kantian notion of generalization (or of universalizability) is not, on the other hand, strictly formal. Kant's theory directly concerns the assessment of moral subjects (in this case, the maxims of actions, e.g. 'Do such and such' or 'In such and such circumstances, do so and so'); it concerns the application of first-order moral terms such as 'good', and it presuma-bly provides a ground or criterion for their ascription. The test is for the universalizability of a maxim, i.e. whether the maxim of one's act could possibly become a 'universal law' and whether an ideal rational agent could consistently will that it become a universal law.

Clearly, neither notion of generalization is at all related to utility. It would therefore be misleading to speak of utilitarian generalization as 'Kantian' simply because it involves a notion of generalization.

The earliest, pioneering study of a form of utilitarian generalization was made by C. D. Broad two generations ago. ('On the Function of False Hypotheses in Ethics', *International Journal of Ethics* xxvi (April 1916), 377–97.) Broad considered the more common negative form, that which concerns only the *un*desirable effects of general practices. He pointed out that such a principle is normally applied when it is as certain as possible that not everyone will do the same—that the general practice will not actually occur. The supposition (hypothesis) that everyone will do the same is normally counterfactual. Thus Broad called arguments based on the generalization test 'the method of false hypothesis' or of 'false universalisation' in ethics. He argued that such a principle when viewed as strictly utilitarian was paradoxically most *un*utilitarian, since it required acting upon a 'false account of the circumstances'. This led him towards an 'ideal' utilitarian position. We shall examine these arguments in their turn.

Broad's study neither represented nor occasioned a movement in moral philosophy. It developed as a critique of one common method of moral reasoning which presented obvious difficulties. It is understandable, then, that for two decades after Broad's unfavourable review utilitarian generalization was largely ignored by academic philosophers.

Meanwhile, utilitarianism came under severe attack. Actually, criticism was directed at simple utilitarianism—or at the predominant form of it, *Act-Utilitarianism*. For at that time the distinction between simple and general utilitarianism was unnoticed, and thus Act-Utilitarianism was taken as the paradigm theory.

Roughly speaking (as I shall explain), Act-Utilitarianism is the theory that one should always perform acts the effects of which would be at least as good as those of any alternative. These are right actions; all others are wrong. It is one's duty, or over-all obligation, to perform right acts only; and thus if one act has the best consequences, that act is *the* thing to be done. In our terminology, this grounds the moral assessment of acts upon their relative simple utilities. This theory has otherwise been called 'crude', 'extreme', or 'direct' utilitarianism—although these terms have also been used rather generally with regard to simple utilitarianism.

Admittedly, the classical utilitarian theories might not properly be characterized as purely simple utilitarian. None the less, partly through the influence of G. E. Moore (*Principia Ethica* and *Ethics*), in this century the traditional variety had come to be viewed as simple utilitarian, and Act-Utilitarianism as a coherent formulation of the predominant traditional theory.

Admittedly, there were differences among utilitarians during the first three or four decades of this century—concerning value-theory (e.g. hedonistic versus 'ideal' utilitarians); concerning the scope of moral considerations (positive versus negative utilitarians); concerning responsibility (whether actual or probable consequences should be considered); and so on—but these differences developed within the confines of simple utilitarianism.

Thus, while outside criticisms have mainly been directed against Act-Utilitarianism, their point has been that utility is not the sole (or perhaps not at all a) determinant of right action. These criticisms have had two related aspects. First, counter-examples were offered, examples of purportedly strong obligations, the exist-

ence or strength of which could supposedly not be accounted for by Act-Utilitarians. Criticisms have, for example, turned upon purported 'prima facie obligations' such as those of fidelity, obligations resting more upon past acts or circumstances than upon the effects of present and future acts. It has been claimed that Act-Utilitarianism cannot adequately account for our obligations to keep our promises, to repay our debts, to tell the truth, to punish the guilty and protect the innocent. In particular, it has been held that a really wrong act can appear right on Act-Utilitarian grounds, just because a condition of secrecy shrouds the act. And it is supposed that a condition of secrecy should not weaken our obligations.

In the second place, it has been argued that utilitarians cannot account for certain perfectly good elements of moral reasoning. We often appeal to moral laws or rules or principles—or at the very least to good reasons—in defending particular judgements. We sometimes justify our acts, for example, by saying 'Because I *promised* I would'—or, less typically, by appealing to a principle that promises *ought* to be kept. Such considerations are not obviously utilitarian. How can a utilitarian account for them?

These criticisms may have served to resuscitate philosophic interest in utilitarian generalization. In any event, R. F. Harrod in 1936 offered a 'revised utilitarianism' based upon general acceptance of the main criticisms of Act-Utilitarianism and an attempt to accommodate them. ('Utilitarianism Revised', *Mind*, xlv (April 1936), 137–56.) Instead of scuttling utilitarianism, Harrod sought a new variety. His theory was identical with Act Utilitarianism in every respect except that the relative generalized rather than the relative simple utility of an act was always to be considered.

Harrod's proposal—including some quite important and original arguments which we shall examine—aroused no immediate interest. This was due, perhaps, to the rise of logical positivism with its associated ethical doctrines: normative ethics appeared to some to be an illegitimate (or at most a psychological) inquiry. Moral philosophers became preoccupied with the nature of ethics and ethical language at the expense of other questions. Not until after the Second World War did the programme of revitalizing utilitarianism by means of revising it come to be entertained widely and seriously.

The post-war period brought with it the new utilitarianism. This has been called 'modified', 'restricted', and 'indirect' utilitarianism and, increasingly, *rule-utilitarianism*. The principal idea has been to apply the test of utility, not to the effects of an act itself, but rather to its tendency or to a rule under which the act falls.

Sometimes these new terms are applied to particular theories (such as Harrod's); sometimes the terms have, confusingly, been applied generically. It has been confusing because there are different varieties of utilitarian generalization and of rule-utilitarianism, just as there are different varieties of simple utilitarianism. We shall examine some of these intrafamilial differences presently. For the present, let us note that there is some difference and some kinship between utilitarian generalization and rule-utilitarianism. The former makes no direct reference to rules. By rule-utilitarianism I shall mean that kind of theory according to which the rightness or wrongness of particular acts can (or must) be determined by reference to a set of rules having some utilitarian defence, justification, or derivation. Note, however, that particular rules may be assessed by means of a variant generalization test, 'What would happen if everyone observed rule *R*?', and sets of rules may be evaluated by inquiring, 'What would happen if everyone observed Rules R^1, R^2, . . . , R_n?'

One source of rule-utilitarianism is the notion of *good reasons* in ethics and the appeal to moral rules or principles. Analyses

of moral reasoning have stratified it into several 'levels': first, the justification of particular judgements about the rightness or wrongness of an act by reference to a good reason pro or con kinds of acts, or by reference to a moral rule; secondly, the validation of such reasons or rules by reference to higher-order rules or principles or criteria; and perhaps third (there are variations here), the vindication or ultimate defence of these higher rules, principles, or criteria. (See, e.g., H. Feigl, 'Validation and Vindication', in W. Sellars and J. Hospers, *Readings in Ethical Theory* [New York: Appleton-Century-Crofts, Inc., 1952], pp. 667–80; K. Baier, *The Moral Point of View* [Ithaca, New York: Cornell University Press, 1958]; P. W. Taylor, *Normative Discourse* [Englewood Cliffs, New Jersey: Prentice-Hall, 1961].) Now when the first-order rules (or reasons) are grounded upon a second-order criterion of utility, we have rule-utilitarianism.

To complicate matters, however, the most notable early theories, such as Toulmin's, had impure second-order criteria, not strictly utilitarian. Toulmin placed a special premium upon the social acceptance of rules as opposed to their utilities. (S. E. Toulmin, *An Examination of the Place of Reason in Ethics* [Cambridge, England: Cambridge University Press, 1950].) This impurity in the rule-utilitarian tradition is one reason for coining the new label, 'utilitarian generalization'. But, as I have said, the latter also involves no direct reference to rules.

Another mode of argument intending to lead towards rule-utilitarianism or towards utilitarian generalization is based upon the time-honoured method of appealing to example. By showing that the new type of principle does not fall prey to the traditional criticism, the counter-examples originally offered against utilitarianism in general are vitiated. There is a dialectic involved here which I shall comment on presently. The following examples illustrate one frequent aspect of the argument, that of the revisionistic against the traditional utilitarian:

(1) Should one bother to vote when it is inconvenient to do so? One knows, generally, that his single ballot will not be especially significant; therefore, the direct effects of voting and of not voting will hardly be different, if at all. And, regarding indirect effects, while one's absence from the polls will (let us assume) not be noticed by others, and therefore will not influence their behaviour, it would on the other hand be more convenient not to vote.

If we tally up the score, it appears that an Act-Utilitarian must hold that it would be wrong to vote under such circumstances, since the over-all effects of voting are worse than those of abstaining. Thus it seems that mere inconvenience provides a reason overriding whatever good reason we ordinarily have to vote. And this, many would hold, is simply not so.

An Act-Utilitarian can, of course, object that our facts are mistaken, that we have weighed the utilities incorrectly, that we have overlooked certain pernicious indirect effects. Here innumerable argumentative complications can arise which, for our present purposes, we need not consider. Let us assume, for the sake of the immediate argument, that there can be such a case of voting that, because of inconvenience, would be wrong on the Act-Utilitarian account.

Now some would hold this as a case against Act-Utilitarianism. It is supposed that one has a good reason for voting that is stronger than Act-Utilitarianism suggests: mere inconvenience (as opposed to serious suffering or hardship) does not provide a sufficient countervailing reason. And, considering the generality of the Act-Utilitarian theory, if the theory is wrong in one case it cannot be accepted; it is not an adequate account of the rightness or wrongness of actions.

The rule-utilitarian—or better, the proponent of utilitarian generalization—might accept these criticisms and yet not reject utilitarianism. He would argue that most voters face a similar predicament, each finding it inconvenient to cast his singly indecisive ballot. If each reasoned in the Act-Utilitarian way he would decide against voting. But what would happen if everyone who found it inconvenient to vote failed to vote? Since, as we are supposing, most will find it inconvenient to vote, very few would then vote; consequently, the wrong man could be elected; or worse still, the mass abstentions might seriously harm the electoral system which is, in the long run, of great importance to all. And this evil would far outweigh the total inconvenience which could be avoided by abstaining. Thus, if *one* abstained, the balance of utility would be positive; no harm would be done, and inconvenience would be avoided. But if *everyone* who found it inconvenient to vote abstained, the over-all effects would be bad, much worse than if all those had voted and suffered the inconveniences. Only when the general practice is considered—and not always when the individual act is considered separately—can we take into account certain undesirable consequences. Only by appealing to utilitarian generalization can certain undesirable consequences be avoided.

But it might be objected that this is illusory. For if others do not act in the condemned way, e.g. if others do vote even when it is inconvenient, the undesirable consequences in question will not materialize whatever one does. And conversely, no matter what one does, if others do not vote the evil will be produced. The proponent of utilitarian generalization is then pressed to different reasons for urging that utilitarian generalization is none the less a tenable moral principle while Act-Utilitarianism is not. He then argues that a valid moral principle is one that everyone can hold and act upon. If everyone followed Act-Utilitarianism, certain bad consequences would result that could be avoided if everyone in fact acted according to utilitarian generalization. We shall put a fuller perspective upon arguments like these later on, in the third and fourth chapters.

(2) Suppose now that one lives in a town in which racial segregation is the brutally enforced rule, and in which the prospects of changing the oppressive system are quite slim. How should one take these facts into account? One who contravenes the segregation rules endangers his family and friends, jeopardizes his home and livelihood, perhaps removes himself from further activity in the community. For example, fairly certain dangers face a racially mixed group even if they gather at one's home, and face someone who vigorously agitates for reform. The good results of such unorthodox behaviour will (let us suppose) be far outweighed by the vengeful harm done those who refuse to acquiesce in the rules.

It may therefore be argued that Act-Utilitarianism counsels inactivity in such a case—or at least that one refrain from activities which expose one or others to danger.

A proponent of utilitarian generalization might argue, however, that if everyone were to continue to acquiesce, if everyone failed to take the risks entailed by defying and seeking to change the rules, then the suffering imposed by the system would continue unabated. But if, on the other hand, everyone were to run the risks, very desirable consequences would result, far outweighing individual sacrifices which might be made, since the joint effort would be sufficient to change the system.

Again, we have an example suggesting a peculiar divergence between the two kinds of utilitarianism. But the main interest in this case is that personal sacrifice is involved, and that the proponent of utilitarian generalization would hold that, if such sacrifice were called for by his principle, then it must be suffered. Notice, however, that if one or only a few take the risks and suffer the burdens, that will not be sufficient to produce the good that could be produced by (or to eliminate the evil that

could be eliminated by) everyone's doing the same. None the less, it appears that no part of the generalization test concerns what others actually are doing or will do. Thus, these applications of utilitarian generalization make that sort of principle appear quite *un*utilitarian. For the generalizer appears to surrender that hard-headed practicality which has been the hall-mark of utilitarianism. He is not supposed to be concerned with the actual effects of his acts, but only with the conjectured effects of an hypothesized general practice. He may have to accept the sacrifice, in accordance with his principle, on the false supposition that others will do the same.

How should one act? Should one refuse to doff one's hat before the tyrant's statue, knowing that if one acts alone one will suffer as a result and that no appreciable good will come of it, and knowing also that others will not refuse to doff their hats? Are there social situations, political régimes, in which one simply ought not to acquiesce? The relevance of the present cases to these questions is that utilitarian generalization appears to provide a utilitarian ground for disobedience, a utilitarian ground for seemingly *un*utilitarian but—shall we say?—morally imperative acts. We shall have to examine whether our examples mislead us, whether this is really a utilitarian argument after all. (These issues will arise in the last chapters.)

Let us now consider such examples in the light of the relevant developments in moral philosophy. A three-sided conflict has accompanied the rise of the new utilitarianism. In the first place, critics of utilitarianism have claimed that it cannot account for certain reliable moral beliefs or data. (These arguments, as we have noted, have mainly been directed against simple utilitarianism, although they have also been extended to apply against general utilitarianism. And there have been attacks on the latter by simple utilitarians. However, criticisms of general utilitarianism have either been based on peculiarities of particular theories or presentations of them, or rest upon an inadequate grasp of the nature of utilitarian generalization. We can, therefore, ignore this aspect of the debate.)

Secondly, simple utilitarians have attempted to reject or accommodate the criticisms. They may claim that the charges are based upon factual error or evaluative oversight; they may go so far as to claim that the charges are based upon moral error; or they may qualify simple utilitarianism, patching it up to meet the objections. Finally, the proponents of utilitarian generalization (or of rule-utilitarianism) generally accept the traditional criticisms of simple utilitarianism while claiming that these are ineffective against their new theories.

Thus, examples such as those I have outlined are supposed to establish the superiority of the new to the old utilitarianism. But what is our method and what are our criteria for criticizing and comparing alternative moral theories? I shall not go into this general question extensively, but I shall deal (in Chapter IV) with a characteristic argument purporting to show the superiority of the new utilitarianism.

It should be obvious, however, that any attempt to displace simple by general (or rule-) utilitarianism presupposes a positive answer to the following questions: Are there in fact any substantive differences between these theories? If so, between which ones? And are these differences in the requisite directions?

Utilitarians have generally failed to examine these questions. Instead their arguments develop along the lines already suggested. A proponent of the new utilitarianism accepts, as (most probably) correct, judgements or generalizations, about particular acts or kinds of acts, that seem inconsistent with simple utilitarianism. Or he accepts, as (most probably) correct, rules or reasons that are used in criticizing or justifying acts but which are

prima facie unutilitarian. For example, he may agree with the critics that the strength of one's obligations to keep one's promises (or to tell the truth) is greater than the relative simple utility of promise-keeping (or veracity) would make it appear. In this respect, some hard moral data are more or less assumed—are held less vulnerable to criticism than simple utilitarianism. But it must be observed that the supposed inconsistency of such data with simple utilitarianism is not rigorously substantiated. For any such argument requires that we pin down the facts of the case and specify value-criteria; but some crucial facts are often assumed and the assessment of effects is left at a most intuitive level.

The argument against simple utilitarianism therefore suffers from inconclusiveness. Some such looseness in argument cannot perhaps be avoided, but it is compounded when the revisionistic utilitarian claims—on the basis of sweeping factual assumptions and without specifying value-criteria—that the new theory can indeed account for the data in question.

These comments may appear harsh and unfair, calling for rigour where rigour is impossible. Let us then accept the rough and ready factual and evaluative considerations. One general issue remains: why should we suppose that it makes any difference to assess acts as acts of certain kinds (or as instances of rules) instead of separately? What positive ground do we have—apart from the more or less roughly hewn examples—for making this supposition? This is the issue I shall emphasize: whether in fact the new utilitarianism offers an alternative.

There are certain obstacles to arriving at a firm answer to this question, obstacles arising from the wide variations possible upon the several utilitarian themes. Simple utilitarianism, as we shall see, takes many substantively different forms. Act-Utilitarianism is but one such form—or perhaps it is a genus within the simple utilitarian family, having its own species. As I have mentioned, rule-utilitarianism is often admixed with non-utilitarian elements. Moreover, the reference to rules involves various special conditions depending upon how the rules are characterized. It is impossible, therefore, to make a wholesale comparison between the old and the new utilitarianisms in determining what difference it makes just to structure a utilitarian theory one way rather than the other.

The simplest and most fundamental comparison that can be made is between simple utilitarianism and utilitarian generalization, for these two kinds of principle are defined precisely by reference to such a difference in structure. We shall therefore ask: What difference does it make to apply the test of utility to an act in respect of its generalized instead of its simple utility? What different results are entailed by asking 'What would happen if everyone did the same?' rather than 'What will happen if this act is performed?' And in this way, while directly determining the substantive relations between simple and general utilitarianism, we can begin to sketch the relative position of the rule-utilitarianism as well.

C. THE DIMENSIONS OF THE PRINCIPLES

In comparing the two kinds of utilitarianism, we must take care to exclude extraneous factors. Various forms of the two kinds differ substantively, but these differences arise from features with which we are not primarily concerned. For example, Act-Utilitarianism, based unrestrictedly upon the relative simple utilities of acts, differs substantively from those negative versions of utilitarianism which limit our attention to undesirable consequences. On a negative theory, the term 'wrong' can be applied only to those acts that have undesirable consequences on the whole. Thus, according to Act-Utilitarianism, but not according to negative theories, there can be acts with good consequences on the whole which are none the less wrong—so long as their consequences are not as good as those of some alternative.

Here is a difference within the simple utilitarian family itself that could obtrude into our basic comparison. We can eliminate this possible source of confusion by comparing only what I shall call *analogous* principles, i.e. principles that differ only in those respects that distinguish the two kinds of utilitarianism generically.

Consider the following two principles:

(G1) If the consequences of everyone's doing a certain sort of thing would be undesirable, then it would be wrong for anyone to do such a thing.

(S1) If the consequences of a particular act would be undesirable, then it would be wrong for that act to be performed.

These principles are analogous (they form an analogous pair) since they differ only in the relevant respects. They may be viewed in this way:

(G1') If the generalized utility of an act (viewed as an act of a certain kind) is negative, then every act of that kind is wrong.

(S1') If the simple utility of an act is negative, then that act is wrong.

It will be helpful now to indicate some respects in which these principles (and any other two analogous principles) are similar. I shall emphasize three: strength, quality, and gradation.

(a) Strength. A principle is *weak* or *strong* according as it does or does not include the *ceteris paribus* condition, 'other things being equal' or its equivalent. No such qualification is to be found in (G1) or (S1); they are both strong, having this truth-functional structure:

$$\text{If } p \text{ then } r.$$

Here 'r' is a judgement concerning the particular act or the kind of act in question. For the derivation of such a judge-ment (i.e. its justification on the basis of such a principle), it is sufficient that the utilitarian condition, 'p', be satisfied.

These principles differ from otherwise similar but weak forms that yield merely prima facie judgements against acts when the same respective conditions are fulfilled. Thus, the weakened version of (S1) is:

(S2) If the consequences of a particular act would be undesirable, then it would be wrong, other things being equal, for that act to be performed.

In (S2), satisfaction of the initial clause is not a sufficient wrong-making condition, but merely one part of a sufficient con-dition. In other words, whereas in (S1) the negative simple utility of an act is a suffi-cient condition for the wrongness of that act, in (S2) it is not sufficient.

This distinction may be viewed in still another way. A principle is weak or strong according as it provides prima facie (i.e. good but not necessarily sufficient) reasons or conclusive (i.e. sufficient) reasons for or against taking or refraining from courses of atcion. A *good reasons* equivalent of (S2) is:

(S2′) If the consequences of a particular act would be undesirable, then there is a *good* reason against that act being performed.

And (S1) would be rendered, by extending the good reasons idiom:

(S1′) If the consequences of a particular act would be undesirable, then there is a *conclusive* reason against that act being performed.

There are also strong and weak forms of utilitarian generalization (as, indeed, there may be for any kind of principle). One particularly important example is the weakened version of (G1):

(G2) If the consequences of everyone's doing a certain sort of thing would be undesirable, then it would be wrong for anyone to do such a thing without a reason or justifica-tion.

This is essentially Marcus Singer's 'generalization argument', which is, of course, merely one of a number of forms of utilitarian generalization. (M. G. Singer, *Generalization in Ethics* (New York: Alfred A. Knopf, 1961).) The qualification 'without a reason or justification' has been preserved from Singer's formulation, al-though some of the rest is slightly revised into our terminology. It should be observed that this qualification is the equivalent of 'other things being equal' in weakening the principle and thereby limiting the judge-ments derivable.

While the formulation of a *ceteris paribus* condition is immaterial, of rather more interest is the effect of such a clause upon the truth-functional structure of principles. Weak principles may be analysed in the following manner:

If *p* and *q*, then *r*.

That is, the *ceteris paribus* condition may be viewed as part of the antecedent, as a second condition which must be satisfied if the unqualified judgement 'r' is to be deriv-able or justifiable. For if only the main utilitarian condition 'p' is satisfied, then the sort of judgement derivable is a weakened or conditional one. Thus, in applying the strong (G1), we may find that the gen-eralized utility of lying just to suit one's convenience is negative. This satisfies the sole condition, and is thereby sufficient for deriving the judgement, 'It would be wrong for anyone to do such a thing (i.e. lie just to suit one's convenience).' But in applying the weak (G2) in the same case, if we merely satisfy the same condition with-out certifying that other things *are* equal, then we cannot derive the unqualified judgement; we are entitled to derive mere-ly this conditional one: 'If other things are equal, then it would be wrong for anyone to do such a thing.'

(If we view *ceteris paribus* principles in this way, we find that 'prima facie right' and 'prima facie wrong' are definable in terms of 'right' and 'wrong' respectively.

And this suggests that the notion of a 'good reason' can be defined in terms of 'conclusive reason'. I am not sure that theorists who employ concepts like 'prima facie right' and 'good reason' will find this result attractive. Moreover, inserting the *ceteris paribus* condition in the antecedent is to some extent unidiomatic. Indeed, this is but the beginning of a catalogue of potential problems. In general, an analysis of any of these principles—strong or weak—in truth-functional terms may be overly simple and inadequate. Also, there may be grounds for questioning whether there is a radical difference between the sense of the *ceteris paribus* condition in principles and its sense in derived judgements. But I offer this tentative outline of a sketch of *ceteris paribus* principles and judgements in the hope that difficulties merely touched upon here will attract the attention of others. I do not believe that my presentation affects the main arguments to be advanced below.)

The forms of utilitarian generalization can also be cast in the good reasons mould. For example, (G2) becomes:

(G2′) If the consequences of everyone's doing a certain sort of thing would be undesirable, then everyone has a good reason against doing such a thing.

We may note, finally, that the difference between strong and weak principles is substantive. Two principles identical in every respect but that one has and the other lacks a *ceteris paribus* condition have different particular implications. Let us suppose that the main utilitarian condition 'p' is satisfied. Then an unconditional judgement is derivable from the strong principle, and this judgement simply cannot be overridden. That is, if we assume the correctness of the strong principle, we cannot admit any conflict between the strong judgements derivable therefrom and other judgements. If the conflicting judgements are both strong, we have moral incompatibility. And unless moral reason-

ing is essentially incoherent, this is an unacceptable state of affairs; one principle or the other (assuming the two conflicting judgements are derived from different principles) *must* be incorrect. On the other hand, if one of the conflicting judgements is weak (derived from a weak principle), it simply carries no weight against a strong, conclusive judgement. Accordingly, if our original principle was weak, the judgements derivable are weak, and therefore they are simply compatible with any other judgements. They are overridden by conflicting strong judgements, and they must somehow be weighed against conflicting weak judgements. This is a substantive difference. And this is another topic to which we shall return.

(b) *Quality.* A principle is *positive* or *negative* according as its application does or does not admit our taking into account positive good that could be produced as well as evil that could be avoided. Negative principles are restrictive: they limit our attention to overall consequences that are undesirable—pain, hardship, suffering, frustration, inconvenience—and require us to don blinders against the utility of acts above some assumed norm or level. This level may sometimes be obscure, but the general distinction seems sound. It is a distinction strongly urged by the proponents of negative utilitarianism.

We may be tempted to render positive and negative principles symmetrically. It may seem, for example, that the positive counterpart of (G1) is:

If the consequences of everyone's doing a certain sort of thing would be *desirable*, then it would be wrong for anyone to *fail to do* such a thing.

But this would inadequately capture the import of a positive principle. For just as negative principles are intended to be restrictive, so positive principles must be inclusive, comprehending losses as well as gains in utility by treating one as the opposite of the other. (Utilitarians agree that evil should be avoided; but negative utilitarians would restrict the scope of relevant consequential considerations. Thus, we should formulate the positive counterpart of (G1) as:

(G3) If the consequences of everyone's doing a certain sort of thing would be desirable, then it would be wrong for anyone to fail to do such a thing; and if the consequences of everyone's doing a certain sort of thing would be undesirable, then it would be wrong for anyone to do such a thing.

As I have already argued, the distinction between positive and negative principles has substantive ramifications. Thus, the first half of (G3) is not redundant—it has implications apart from those of (G1).

One possible misapprehension about the quality of a principle should be mentioned. It should not be supposed that positive principles yield only 'positive' judgements, i.e. judgements for acts, and that negative principles yield only 'negative' judgements, i.e. judgements against acts. Since negative principles are the more restrictive of the two kinds, the point can most sharply be made with respect to them. Negative principles can yield judgements for or against acts, depending upon such factors as how the act is described. For example, if the results of everyone's refraining from voting would be *un*desirable, then on the basis of (G1) we can infer that it would be wrong for anyone to refrain from voting; and this means that everyone should vote, that everyone has a conclusive reason *for* voting. The nature of the verdict depends as much upon the formulation of the issue (the description of the act) as upon the facts of the case and which principle is applied. This example suggests how we shall interpret the variant generalization test, 'What would happen if *no one* did that?'—employing the 'right'-'wrong' and act-alternative dichotomies. But more on that later.

(*c*) *Gradation.* A principle is *comparative* or *non-comparative* according as it does or does not incorporate some requirement of comparing the utility of an act with the utilities of its alternatives. That is, a comparative principle concerns relative utilities, whereas a non-comparative principle does not. The former involves taking into account differences in degree as well as differences in the quality of utilities.

In the case of strong utilitarian principles, the lack of a comparative feature entails significant defects; in applying such a principle under certain circumstances, anomalous results can be gotten. For example, the strong, negative, non-comparative (S1) provides a conclusive reason against performing any act that has undesirable effects on the whole—it would classify any such act as (simply and unequivocally) wrong. It sometimes does happen, however, that one's alternatives are limited to acts each of which has undesirable effects on the whole. Ordinarily, we would say that one ought to choose the least evil. But (S1) implies that any such act would be wrong. Not in this or that respect wrong, or tending to be wrong, or prima facie wrong—but *wrong*. But not every alternative can be wrong.

Such a case can be set right *ad hoc* if we regard the undesirable effects below a certain degree as unavoidable and therefore not to be counted—thus making at least one act have an indifferent utility. This would avoid the immediate difficulty. The degree would change from case to case. But then we would require another *ad hoc* ruling to cover the application of strong, positive, non-comparative principles in cases where more than one act has desirable effects on the whole—the other edge of the sword. And of course such problems would arise in connexion with utilitarian generalization, concerning the tendencies of acts.

We should therefore want to append to various principles a condition to the following effect: 'unless there is no alternative the consequences of which (or: the consequences of the general performance of which) would be less undesirable (or: more desirable) than those of the act (or: of the kind of act) in question'. Such a condition would transform a non-comparative into a comparative principle.

For our purposes, however, we need not carry along this cumbersome clause. I shall illustratively refer mainly to the two particular forms of utilitarian generalization that have acquired most importance. These two principles are the weak, negative, non-comparative (G2)—Singer's 'generalization argument'—and a strong, positive, comparative form—roughly, Jonathan Harrison's 'modified utilitarianism' and R. F. Harrod's 'revised utilitarianism'. (See J. Harrison, 'Utilitarianism, Universalisation, and Our Duty to Be Just', *Proceedings of the Aristotelian Society,* liii [1952–3], 105–34.)

The latter principle is roughly (G3) plus a comparative qualification, which might be formulated in this way:

> (G4) If the consequences of everyone's doing a certain sort of thing would be better (i.e. more desirable) than the consequences of everyone's doing each of the alternatives, then it would be wrong for anyone to fail to do such a thing; and if the consequences of everyone's doing a certain sort of thing would be worse (i.e. less desirable) than the consequences of everyone's doing some alternative, then it would be wrong for anyone to do such a thing.

This is excessively complex. Neither clause in fact stresses the quality of consequences; what is at stake is the relative generalized utilities of acts. Given the comparative feature and the exhaustiveness and mutual exclusiveness of 'right' and 'wrong', the first clause becomes otiose.

According to this principle, an act is wrong if its generalized utility is less than that of some alternative. This serves to pick out, from every set of alternatives, a class of right acts. There may be several such acts, with equally desirable tendencies, no alternative of which has a better tendency; or there will be one act the tendency of which is better than any other of the original set. The principle can therefore be compressed into a simpler but full formulation as follows:

> (G4) If the consequences of everyone's doing a certain sort of thing would be worse than those of some alternative, then it would be wrong for anyone to do such a thing.

The analogous form of simple utilitarianism is the reason for the importance of (G4); it may accordingly be formulated:

> (S4) If the consequences of a particular act would be worse than those of some alternative, then it would be wrong for that act to be performed.

According to this principle, an act is wrong if its simple utility is less than that of some alternative. Whatever else holds for (G4) holds, *mutatis mutandis,* for (S4).

This simple utilitarian principle will be recognized as roughly that of Act-Utilitarianism. The first difference between this principle and that of Act-Utilitarianism is the former's compatibility with certain non-utilitarian considerations that are not compatible with Act-Utilitarianism. For the latter is a complete and homogeneous theory in the sense that it admits the relative simple utilitarian considerations of (S4) but *only* those considerations. (S4) on the other hand could be part of a heterogeneous theory which, for example, provided moral grounds for choosing among right acts, i.e. among alternative acts with the highest equally valuable effects. Therefore, to achieve our first approximation of Act-Utilitarianism, we should replace the initial 'If' in (S4) with 'If and only if'. I shall refer to the resulting principle as (AU).

This sort of modification can be imposed upon any other simple or general utilitarian form. If (G4) were so modified, we would have a homogeneous relative general utilitarian theory of obligation strictly analogous to Act-Utilitarianism. This will be referred to as (GU).

Other modifications might be made in this resultant Act-Utilitarian principle. The most important of these are the probability qualifications, e.g. where an act is assessed according to its probable instead of its actual effects. I shall comment on these briefly.

I have noted three dimensions of utilitarian principles: strength, quality, and gradation. Within these dimensions as I have sketched them, we can construct eight analogous pairs of principles—or sixteen, if we allow for the strengthening transformation based upon changing 'If' to 'If and only if'. It is possible, however, to make finer distinctions. One type is within the probability dimension. All the principles we have considered so far take into account the actual effects of acts, as opposed to their probable or expectable or foreseeable or even intended consequences. The probabilistic variants will not be considered here, for several reasons.

In the first place, it is difficult to formulate a probability qualification, partly because there are alternative approaches to its conception (especially when intentions come in), partly because there are various ways of calculating probabilities. Secondly, it would be extremely difficult to develop some of the arguments I shall hazard below if probabilities were generally considered, if only because the arguments would be that much more complex.

Moreover, one may be unconvinced that probability qualifications are really desirable. What is the point of including such conditions? Often, the avoidance of a morally untenable position. Since the effects of a particular act are so complex and far-reaching, with perhaps completely unexpected, unexpectable, not to say unintended ramifications, one cannot generally be expected to know the actual effects of acts. A man must therefore generally govern his conduct on the basis of what is most likely to happen (or what can reasonably be expected to happen, or what he intends to accomplish—or what have you). If we tie the rightness of acts to their actual effects, we aim too high, requiring of a man more than he can reasonably be expected to deliver. It would be unreasonable to claim that Jones ought to have done x because x had the best effects, when we are aware that Jones could not have known this and that he acted according to his best lights. If we tell him that he should have done x, i.e. that it was wrong not to have done x, we are telling him that he ought to have done what he could not necessarily do. But we cannot demand that he act upon the basis of the actual effects of acts, for we cannot require that he know (or even feel certain of) their actual effects.

This approach suggests, however, a conflation of two distinguishable kinds of moral considerations. Our subject, on the one hand, is the rightness or wrongness of acts. Another kind of moral consideration—outside the scope of this inquiry—relates to the moral worth of persons: questions of responsibility, of praise and blame, of morally justified expectations regarding others' behaviour, of morally defensible deliberation. The criteria involved in these two kinds of considerations may be very different. While a theory of obligation—concerning the rightness or wrongness of acts—might hold that Jones ought not to have done x, i.e. that x is a wrong thing to have done, this theory is compatible with a theory about the moral worth of persons which holds that Jones is not blameworthy for having done x. The question whether Jones could have known that x was—'objectively', or all things considered—a wrong thing to do may have no bearing upon Jones's error in doing x.

In any event, our simple, non-probabilistic principles may be qualified, if necessary, with some probability condition. We may view the principles that we shall consider below as raw material admitting further refinement. Accordingly, it may be helpful to regard the succeeding chapters as to this extent not a full study of utilitarian generalization, but a basic sketch.

The second point of divergence between (S4)—or (AU)—and some approaches to Act-Utilitarianism, concerns the value-criteria which may be employed in conjunction with this kind of principle. We are, as I have said, simply disregarding questions in value-theory proper. This renders our conclusions the more general.

Finally, a note on terminology. I am using a simplified first-order normative vocabulary based upon the terms 'right' and 'wrong'. It is irrelevant here whether these are the central notions in ordinary moral reasoning; they serve quite well, I believe, in conveying the substance of utilitarianism. In this context, I take it that 'right' (in the sense of conclusively right, and not merely right other things equal) is mutually exclusive with 'wrong' (in the sense of conclusively wrong). And these terms are exhaustive of the possibilities—although finer distinctions can be made. That is to say, we are supposing that while acts may be in this respect right and in that respect wrong, any particular act (or any act which falls under the purview of moral considerations of this sort) is *either* right *or* wrong. In other words, two judgements concerning a particular act z, one of which asserts that x is right and the other of which asserts that x is wrong, are morally incompatible. If we are not unwilling to use such terms in ethics, we can say that a theory which implies morally incompatible judgements is inconsistent. Thus, in accordance with modern utilitarian usage, I shall say that 'right' is equivalent to 'not wrong' and 'wrong' to 'not right'. I would not myself argue that every act is in fact either right or wrong, as these terms are normally used. But the usage we shall make of these

terms is to some extent technical, in the context of a very general type of normative theory.

Secondly, I take it that judgements are substantively different or non-equivalent only when they cannot be transformed into identical judgements by means of the linguistic moves suggested in the foregoing; otherwise they are substantively identical or equivalent.

Thirdly, at the risk of excessive caution, I shall note that in speaking of *the effects of* an act I intend to include *all* the effects; in speaking of *the tendency of* an act I intend to include *all* the effects resulting from *everyone's* doing acts of the sort specified. In speaking of the *utilities* of an act (simple or generalized), I intend to include all value which is teleologically attributable to that act (or to the acts of the kind in question), i.e. the net-balance of desirable or undesirable consequences. This manner of speaking presupposes, of course, that particular acts are discrete and identifiable, and that they can in some way be distinguished from their consequences. This presupposition is problematic, but I do not see how we can avoid it in working within the framework of utilitarianism.

I shall use the terms 'act' and 'action' indifferently. In general, I shall use lower-case letters, $x, y, \ldots$ to stand for particular acts, and upper-case letters, $A, B, C, \ldots$, as place-holders for descriptions of acts (kinds of acts). One or two other special terms will be introduced in their appropriate settings.

And now we can properly formulate the issue involved in our comparison of simple utilitarianism and utilitarian generalization. We shall be concerned to determine whether there can be a condition of extensional non-equivalence (non-equivalence, for short) between analogous forms of the two kinds of principle. Non-equivalence obtains if, and only if, analogous principles do not always yield substantively identical (equivalent) judgements with respect to particular acts.

On one view, the judgements which are directly derivable from the forms of utilitarian generalization are themselves general, relevant to acts of certain kinds. But particular judgements are in turn derivable from such general ones by means of a mediating premiss that a particular act is of the kind specified in the general judgement. In principle, it is these particular judgements ultimately derivable from the forms of utilitarian generalization which are to be substantively compared with the particular judgements directly derivable from the analogous forms of simple utilitarianism.

For example, we can perhaps derive from (G1) this general judgement: 'It would be wrong for anyone to lie just to suit his convenience' (on the supposition that the tendency of lying just to suit one's convenience is undesirable). Noting that the particular act in question is such an act—can properly be so described—we derive a conclusive judgement against the act. And if the analogous simple utilitarian principle, (S1), does not yield an equivalent, a substantively identical, conclusive judgement against the same act, a condition of non-equivalence obtains.

The Moral Point of View

KURT BAIER

Throughout the history of philosophy, by far the most popular candidate for the position of the moral point of view has been self-interest. There are obvious parallels between these two standpoints.* Both aim at the good. Both are rational. Both involve deliberation, the surveying and weighing of reasons. The adoption of either yields statements containing the word 'ought.' Both involve the notion of self-mastery and control over the desires. It is, moreover, plausible to hold that a person could not have a reason for doing anything whatsoever unless his behavior was designed to promote his own good. Hence, if morality is to have the support of reason, moral reasons must be self-interested, hence the point of view of morality and self-interest must be the same. On the other hand, it seems equally obvious that morality and self-interest are very frequently opposed. Morality often requires us to refrain from doing what self-interest recommends or to do what self-interest forbids. Hence morality and self-interest cannot be the same points of view.

1. SELF-INTEREST AND MORALITY

Can we save the doctrine that the moral point of view is that of self-interest? One way of circumventing the difficulty just mentioned is to draw a distinction between two senses of 'self-interest,' shortsighted and enlightened. The short-sighted egoist always follows his short-range interest without taking into consideration how this will affect others and how their reactions will affect him. The enlightened egoist, on the other hand, knows that he cannot get the most out of life unless he pays attention to the needs of others on whose good will be depends. On this view, the standpoint of (immoral) egoism differs from that of morality in that it fails to consider the interests of others even when this costs little or nothing or when the long-range benefits to oneself are likely to be greater than the short-range sacrifices.

This view can be made more plausible still if we distinguish between those egoists who consider each course of action on its own merits and those who, for convenience, adopt certain rules of thumb which they have found will promote their long-range interest. Slogans such as 'Honesty is the best policy,' 'Give to charity rather than to the Department of Internal Revenue,' 'Always give a penny to a beggar when you are likely to be watched by your acquaintances,' 'Treat your servants kindly and they will work for you like slaves,' 'Never be arrogant to anyone—you may need his services one day,' are maxims of this sort. They embody the "wisdom" of a given society. The enlightened long-range egoist may adopt these as rules of thumb, that is, as *prima-facie* maxims, as rules which he will observe unless he has good evidence

Reprinted from Chapter 8 of Kurt Baier: *The Moral Point of View*. © 1958 by Cornell University. Used by permission of Cornell University Press.

* [The point of view of morality and the point of view of self-interest.]

that departing from them will pay him better than abiding by them. It is obvious that the rules of behavior adopted by the enlightened egoist will be very similar to those of a man who rigidly follows our own moral code.

Sidgwick appears to believe that egoism is one of the legitimate "methods of ethics," although he himself rejects it on the basis of an "intuition" that it is false. He supports the legitimacy of egoism by the argument that everyone could consistently adopt the egoistic point of view. "I quite admit that when the painful necessity comes for another man to choose between his own happiness and the general happiness, must as a reasonable being prefer his own, i.e. it is right for him to do this on my principle."[1] The consistent enlightened egoist satisfies the categorical imperative, or at least one version of it, 'Act only on that maxim whereby thou canst at the same time will that it should become a universal law.'

However, no "intuition" is required to see that this is not the point of view of morality, even though it can be universally adopted without self-contradiction. In the first place, a consistent egoist adopts for all occasions the principle 'everyone for himself' which we allow (at most) only in conditions of chaos, when the normal moral order breaks down. Its adoption marks the return to the law of the jungle, the state of nature, in which the "softer," "more chivalrous" ways of morality have no place.[2]

This point can be made more strictly. It can be shown that those who adopt consistent egoism cannot make moral judgments. Moral talk is impossible for consistent egoists. But this amounts to a *reductio ad absurdum* of consistent egoism.

Let B and K be candidates for the presidency of a certain country and let it be granted that it is in the interest of either to be elected, but that only one can succeed. It would then be in the interest of B but against the interest of K if B were elected, and vice versa, and therefore in the interest of B but against the interest of K if K were liquidated, and vice versa. But from this it would follow that B ought to liquidate K, that it is wrong for B not to do so, that B has not "done his duty" until he has liquidated K; and vice versa. Similarly K, knowing that his own liquidation is in the interest of B and therefore anticipating B's attempts to secure it, ought to take steps to foil B's endeavors. It would be wrong for him not to do so. He would "not have done his duty" until he had made sure of stopping B. It follows that if K prevents B from liquidating him, his act must be said to be both wrong and not wrong—wrong because it is the prevention of what B ought to do, his duty, and wrong for B not to do it; not wrong because it is what K ought to do, his duty, and wrong for K not to do it. But one and the same act (logically) cannot be both morally wrong and not morally wrong. Hence in cases like these morality does not apply.

This is obviously absurd. For morality is designed to apply in just such cases, namely, those where interests conflict. But if the point of view of morality were that of self-interest, then there could never be moral solutions of conflicts of interest. However, when there are conflicts of interest, we always look for a "higher" point of view, one from which such conflicts can be settled. Consistent egoism makes everyone's private interest the "highest court of appeal." But by 'the moral point of view' we *mean* a point of view which is a court of appeal for conflicts of interest. Hence it cannot (logically) be identical with the point of view of self-interest. Sidgwick is, therefore, wrong in thinking that consistent egoism is one of the "legitimate methods of ethics." He is wrong in thinking that an "intuition" is required to see that it is not the correct moral point of view. That it is not can be seen in the same way in

---

[1] Henry Sidgwick, *The Methods of Ethics*, 7th ed. (London: Macmillan and Co., 1907), pref. to the 6th ed., p. xvii.

[2] See below, Chapter Twelve, section 3.

which we can "see" that the Court of Petty Sessions is not the Supreme Court.

2. MORALITY INVOLVES DOING THINGS ON PRINCIPLE

Another feature of consistent egoism is that the rules by which a consistent egoist abides are merely rules of thumb. A consistent egoist has only one supreme principle, to do whatever is necessary for the realization of his one aim, the promotion of his interest. He does not have principles, he has only an aim. If one has adopted the moral point of view, then one acts on principle and not merely on rules of thumb designed to promote one's aim. This involves conforming to the rules whether or not doing so favors one's own or anyone else's aim.

Kant grasped this point even if only obscurely. He saw that adopting the moral point of view involves acting on principle. It involves conforming to rules even when doing so is unpleasant, painful, costly, or ruinous to oneself. Kant, furthermore, argued rightly that, since moral action is action on principle (and not merely in accordance with rules of thumb), a moral agent ought not to make exceptions in his own favor, and he interpreted this to mean that moral rules are absolutely inflexible and without exceptions. Accordingly he concluded that if 'Thou shalt not kill' states a moral rule, then any and every act correctly describable as an act of killing someone must be said to be morally wrong.

Kant also saw that this view required him to reject some of our deepest moral convictions; we certainly think that the killing of a man in self-defense or by the hangman is not morally wrong. Kant was prepared to say that our moral convictions are wrong on this point. Can we salvage these moral convictions? The only alternative, to say that acting on principle does not require us not to make exceptions in

our own favor, seems to be equally untenable.

It is therefore not surprising that many philosophers have abandoned Kant's (and the commonsense) view that the moral rightness of an act is its property of being in accordance with a moral rule or principle. Thus, the deontologists claim that rightness is a simple property which we can "see" or "intuit" in an act, and the utilitarians, that rightness is a complex property, namely, the tendency of an act to promote the greatest happiness of the greatest number. But, as is well known, these accounts are not plausible and lead to considerable difficulties.

However, this whole problem arises only because of a confusion, the confusion of the expression 'making an exception to a rule' with the expression 'a rule has an exception.' As soon as this muddle is cleared away, it can be seen that Kant is right in saying that acting on principle implies making no exception in anyone's favor, but wrong in thinking that therefore all moral rules must be absolutely without exception.

'No parking in the city' has a number of recognized exceptions which are part of the rule itself, for example, 'except in the official parking areas,' 'except in front of a parking meter,' 'except on Saturday mornings and after 8 P.M. every day.' A person who does not know the recognized exceptions does not completely know the rule, for these exceptions more precisely define its range of application. A policeman who is not booking a motorist parking in front of a parking meter is not granting exemption to (making an exception in favor of) this motorist. On the contrary, he is administering the rule correctly. If he did apply the no-parking rule to the motorist, *he* would be applying it where *it* does not apply, because this is one of the recognized exceptions which are *part* of the rule. On the other hand, a policeman who does not book a motorist parking his vehicle in a prohibited area at peak hour on a busy day is making an exception in the motorist's favor. If he does so because the man is his friend, he illegitimately grants an exemption. If he does so because the motorist is a doctor who has been called to attend to a man lying unconscious on the pavement, this is a "deserving case" and he grants the exemption legitimately.

Apply this distinction to the rules of a given morality. Notice first that moral rules differ from laws and regulations in that they are not administered by special administrative organs such as policemen and magistrates. Everyone "administers" them himself. Nevertheless, it makes sense to speak of making exceptions in one's own favor. For one may refuse to apply the rule to oneself when one knows that it does apply, that is to say, one may refuse to observe it even when one knows one should. And what is true of making exceptions in one's own favor is true also of making them in favor of someone else. It is almost as immoral to make exceptions in favor of one's wife, son, or nephew as in favor of oneself.

When we say, therefore, that a person who has killed a burglar in self-defense has not done anything wrong, we are not making an exception in the houseowner's favor. It is much nearer the truth to say that, in our morality, the rule 'Thou shalt not kill' *has several recognized exceptions*, among them 'in self-defense.' We can say that a man does not know fully our moral rule 'Thou shalt not kill' if he does not know that it has, among others, this exception.

Like other rules of reason, our moral convictions are so only presumptively.[3] Killing is wrong *unless* it is a killing in self-defense, killing by the hangman, killing of an enemy in wartime, accidental killing, and possibly mercy killing. If it is one of these types of killing, then it is *not* wrong.

Even if it is one of the wrongful acts of killing, it is so only *prima facie*, other things being equal. For there may have been an overriding moral reason in favor of

killing the man, for example, that he is about to blow up a train and that this is the only way of stopping him.

One further point should be made to avoid misunderstanding. Unlike laws and regulations, moral rules have not been laid down by anyone. Knowing moral rules cannot, therefore, involve knowing exactly what a certain person has enjoined and forbidden and what exceptions he has allowed, because there is no such person. In the case of regulations and laws, it was precisely this knowledge which enabled us to draw the distinction between saying that someone was granting an exception and saying that he was merely applying the rule which, for cases of this sort, provided for an exception. Our distinction seems to collapse for moral rules.

However, the answer to this is simple. When a magistrate is empowered to make exceptions or grant exemptions in "deserving cases," the question of what is a "deserving case" is not of course answered in the regulation itself. If it were, the magistrate would not be exercising his power to grant exemption, but would simply apply the regulation as provided in it. How, then, does the magistrate or policeman know what is a deserving case? The doctor who parks his car in a prohibited spot in order to attend to an injured man is such a case, namely, a *morally deserving* case. The principles in accordance with which policemen or magistrates grant exemptions to existing regulations are moral principles. In the case of moral rules, there cannot be any distinction between exceptions which are part of the rule and deserving cases. *Only* deserving cases can be part of the moral rule, and *every* deserving case is properly part of it. Hence while in the case of laws and regulations there is a reason for going beyond the exceptions allowed in the regulation itself (when there is a morally deserving instance), in the case of moral rules there is no such reason. For all deserving cases are, from the nature of the case, part of the moral rule itself. Hence it is never

[3] See above, Chapter Two, sections 5 and 6.

right to make an exception to a moral rule in anyone's favor. Kant is therefore quite right in saying that it is always wrong to make exceptions to moral rules in one's own favor (and for that matter in anyone else's), but he is wrong in thinking that this makes moral rules inflexible.

All this follows from the very nature of moral principles. They are binding on everyone alike quite irrespective of what are the goals or purposes of the person in question. Hence self-interest cannot be the moral point of view, for it sets every individual one supreme goal, his own interest, which overrules all his other maxims.

3. MORAL RULES ARE MEANT FOR EVERYBODY

The point of view of morality is inadequately characterized by saying that *I* have adopted it if *I* act on principles, that is, on rules to which I do not make exceptions whenever acting on them would frustrate one or the other of my purposes or desires. It is characterized by greater universality than that. It must be thought of as a standpoint from which principles are considered as being acted on *by everyone*. Moral principles are not merely principles on which a person must always act without making exceptions, but they are principles *meant for everybody*.

It follows from this that the teaching of morality must be completely universal and open. Morality is meant to be taught to all members of the group in such a way that everyone can and ought always to act in accordance with these rules. It is not the preserve of an oppressed or privileged class or individual. People are neglecting their duties if they do not teach the moral rules to their children. Children are removed from the homes of criminals because they are not likely to be taught the moral rules there. Furthermore, moral rules must be taught quite openly and to everybody

without discrimination. An esoteric code, a set of precepts known only to the initiated and perhaps jealously concealed from outsiders, can at best be a religion, not a morality. 'Thou shall not eat beans and this is a secret' or 'Always leave the third button of your waistcoat undone, but don't tell anyone except the initiated members' may be part of an esoteric religion, but not of a morality. 'Thou shalt not kill, but it is a strict secret' is absurd. 'Esoteric morality' is a contradiction in terms. It is no accident that the so-called higher religions were imbued with the missionary spirit, for they combine the beliefs of daemons and gods and spirits characteristic of primitive religions with *a system of morality*. Primitive religions are not usually concerned to proselytize. On the contrary, they are imbued with the spirit of the exclusive trade secret. If one thinks of one's religion as concentrated wisdom of the life revealed solely to the *chosen* people, one will regard it as the exclusive property of the club, to be confined to the elect. If, on the other hand, the rules are thought to be for everyone, one must in consistency want to spread the message.

The condition of universal teachability yields three other criteria of moral rules. They must not, in the first place, be "self-frustrating." They are so if their purpose is frustrated as soon as everybody acts on them, if they have a point only when a good many people act on the opposite principle. Someone might, for instance, act on the maxim 'When you are in need, ask for help, but never help another man when he is in need.' If everybody adopted this principle, then their adoption of the second half would frustrate what obviously is the point of the adoption of the first half, namely to get help when one is in need. Although such a principle is not self-contradictory—for anybody could consistently adopt it—is is nevertheless objectionable from the moral point of view, for it could not be taught openly to everyone. It would then lose its point. It is a parasitic principle, useful to anyone only if many people act on its opposite.

The same is true of "self-defeating" and "morally impossible" rules. A principle is self-defeating if its point is defeated as soon as a person lets it be known that he has adopted it, for example, the principle 'Give a promise even when you know or think that you can never keep it, or when you don't intend to keep it.' The very point of giving promises is to reassure and furnish a guarantee to the promisee. Hence any remark that throws doubt on the sincerity of the promiser will defeat the purpose of making a promise. And clearly to *let it be known* that one gives promises even when one knows or thinks one cannot, or when one does not intend to keep them, is to raise such doubts. And to say that one acts on the above principle is to imply that one may well give promises in these cases. Hence to reveal that one acts on this principle will tend to defeat one's own purpose.

It has already been said that moral rules must be capable of being taught openly, but this rule is self-defeating when taught openly, for then everyone would be known to act on it. Hence it cannot belong to the morality of any group.

Lastly, there are some rules which it is literally impossible to teach in the way the moral rules of a group must be capable of being taught, for example, the rule 'Always assert what you think not to be the case.' Such *morally impossible* rules differ from self-frustrating and self-defeating rules in that the latter could have been taught in this way, although it would have been quite senseless to do so, whereas the former literally cannot be so taught. The reason why the above rule cannot be taught in this way is that the only possible case of acting on it, doing so secretly, is ruled out by the conditions of *moral teaching*.

(1) Consider first someone secretly adopting this rule. His remarks will almost always mislead people, for *he will be taken to be saying what he thinks true*, whereas he *is* saying the opposite. Moreover, in most cases what he thinks (and not what he says) will be true. Thus, it will usually be the case that p is true when he says 'not-p,' and not-p when he says 'p,' whereas people will take it that p is true when he says 'p', and not-p when he says 'not-p.' Thus communication between him and other people breaks down, since they will almost always be misled by him whether he wishes to mislead them or not. The possibility of communication depends on a speaker's ability *at will* to say either what he thinks to be the case or what he thinks not to be the case. Our speaker cannot communicate because by his principle he is forced to mislead his hearers.

Thus, anyone secretly adopting the principle 'Always assert what you think not to be the case' cannot communicate with others since he is bound to mislead them whether he wants to or not. Hence he cannot possibly teach the principle to anybody. And if he were to teach the principle without having adopted it himself, then, although he would be understood, those who adopted it would not. At any rate, since moral teaching involves teaching rules such as the taught may openly avow to be observing, this case is ruled out. A principle which is taught for secret acceptance only cannot be embodied in a *moral* rule of the group.

(2) Of course, people might soon come to realize what is the matter with our man. They may discover that in order not to be misled by what he says they have only to substitute 'p' for 'not-p' and vice versa. But if they do this, then they have interpreted his way of speaking, not as a reversal of the general presumption that one says what one thinks is the case (and not the opposite), but as a change of the use of 'not.' In his language, it will be said, 'not' has become an affirmation sign, negation being effected by omitting it. Thus, if communication is to be possible, we must interpret as a change in usage what is intended as the reversal of the presumption that every assertion conveys what the assertor believes to be the case.

If everyone were, by accident, to

adopt simultaneously and secretly our principle 'Always assert what you think is not the case,' then, for some time at least, communication would be impossible. If, on the other hand, it were adopted openly, then communication would be possible, but only if the adoption of the principle were to be accompanied by a change in the use of "not" which would completely cancel the effect of the adoption of the principle. In that case, however, it can hardly be said that the principle has been adopted.

(3) The case we are considering is neither (1) nor (2). We are considering the open teaching of the principle 'Always assert what you think is not the case,' for open acceptance by everybody, an acceptance which is not to be interpreted as a change in the use of 'not.' But this is nonsense. We cannot all *openly* tell one another that we are always going to mislead one another in a certain way and insist that we must continue to be misled, though we know how we could avoid being misled. I conclude that this principle could not be embodied in a rule belonging to the morality of any group.

These points are of general interest in that they clarify some valuable remarks contained in Kant's doctrine of the categorical imperative. In particular they clarify the expression "can will" contained in the formulation 'Act so that thou *canst will* thy maxim to become a universal law of nature.' "Canst will" in one sense means what I have called "morally possible." Your maxim must be a formula which is morally possible, that is, which is logically capable of being a rule belonging to the morality of some group, as the maxim "Always lie" is not. No one *can* wish that maxim to be a rule of *some morality*. To say that one is wishing it is to contradict oneself. One cannot wish it any more than one can wish that time should move backwards.

The second sense of "can will" is that in which no rational person can will certain things. Self-frustrating and self-defeating moral rules are not morally impossible, they are merely senseless. No rational person could wish such rules to become part of any morality. That is to say, anyone wishing that they should, would thereby expose himself to the charge of irrationality, like the person who wishes that he should never attain his ends or that he should (for no reason at all) be plagued by rheumatic pains throughout his life.

The points just made also show the weakness of Kant's doctrine. For while it is true that someone who acts on the maxim 'Always lie' acts on a morally impossible one, it is not true that every liar necessarily acts on that maxim. If he acts on a principle at all, it may, for instance, be 'Lie when it is the only way to avoid harming someone,' or 'Lie when it is helpful to you and harmful to no one else' or 'Lie when it is entertaining and harmless.' Maxims such as these can, of course, be willed in either of the senses explained.

4. MORAL RULES MUST BE FOR THE GOOD OF EVERYBODY

The conditions so far mentioned are merely formal. They exclude certain sorts of rule as not coming up to the formal requirements. But moral rules should also have a certain sort of content. Observation of these rules should be *for the good of everyone alike*. Thrasymachus' view that justice is the advantage of the stronger, if true of the societies of his day, is an indictment of their legal systems from the moral point of view. It shows that what goes by the name of morality in these societies is no more than a set of rules and laws which enrich the ruling class at the expense of the masses. But this is wrong because unjust, however much the rules satisfy the formal criteria. For given certain initial social conditions, formal equality before the law may favor certain groups and exploit others.

There is one obvious way in which a rule may be for the good of everyone alike, namely, if it furthers the common good. When I am promoted and my salary is raised, this is to my advantage. It will also be to the advantage of my wife and my family and possibly of a few other people—it will not be to the advantage of my colleague who had hoped for promotion but is now excluded. It may even be to his detriment if his reputation suffers as a result. If the coal miners obtain an increase in their wages, then this is to the advantage of coal miners. It is for their common good. But it may not be to the advantage of anyone else. On the other hand, if production is raised and with it everyone's living standard, that is literally to everyone's advantage. The rule 'Work harder,' if it has these consequences, is for the common good of all.

Very few rules, if any, will be for the common good of everyone. But a rule may be in the interest of everyone alike, even though the results of the observation of the rule are not for the common good in the sense explained. Rules such as 'Thou shalt not kill,' 'Thou shalt not be cruel,' 'Thou shalt not lie' are obviously, in some other sense, for the good of everyone alike. What is this sense? It becomes clear if we look at these rules from the moral point of view, that is, that of an independent, unbiased, impartial, objective, dispassionate disinterested observer. Taking such a God's-eye point of view, we can see that it is in the interest of everyone alike that everyone should abide by the rule 'Thou shalt not kill.' From the moral point of view, it is clear that it is in the interest of everyone alike if everyone alike should be allowed to pursue his own interest provided this does not adversely affect someone else's interests. Killing someone in the pursuit of my interests would interfere with his.

There can be no doubt that such a God's-eye point of view is involved in the moral standpoint. The most elementary teaching is based on it. The negative version of the so-called Golden Rule sums it up: 'Don't do unto others as you would not have them do unto you.' When we teach children the moral point of view, we try to explain it to them by getting them to put

themselves in another person's place: 'How would you like to have that done to you!' 'Don't do evil,' the most readily accepted moral rule of all, is simply the most general form of stating this prohibition. For doing evil is the opposite of doing good. Doing good is doing for another person what, if he were following (self-interested) reason, he would do for himself. Doing evil is doing to another person what it would be contrary to reason for him to do to himself. Harming another, hurting another, doing to another what he dislikes having done to him are the specific forms this takes. Killing, cruelty, inflicting pain, maiming, torturing, deceiving, cheating, rape, adultery are instances of this sort of behavior. They all violate the condition of "reversibility," that is, that the behavior in question must be acceptable to a person whether he is at the "giving" or "receiving" end of it.

It is important to see just what is established by this condition of being for the good of everyone alike. In the first place, anyone is doing wrong who engages in nonreversible behavior. It is irrelevant whether he knows that it is wrong or not, whether the morality of his group recognizes it or not. Such behavior is "wrong in itself," irrespective of individual or social recognition, irrespective of the consequences it has. Moreover, every single act of such behavior is wrong. We need not consider the whole group or the whole of humanity engaging in this sort of behavior, but only a single case. Hence we can say that all nonreversible behavior is morally wrong; hence that anyone engaging in it is doing what, prima facie, he ought not to do. We need not consider whether this sort of behavior has harmful consequences, whether it is forbidden by the morality of the man's group, or whether he himself thinks it wrong.

The principle of reversibility does not merely impose certain prohibitions on a moral agent, but also certain positive injunctions. It is, for instance, wrong—an omission—not to help another person when he is in need and when we are in a position to help him. The story of the Good Samaritan makes this point. The positive version of the Golden Rule makes the same point more generally: 'Do unto others as you would have them do unto you.' Note that it is wrong—not merely not meritorious—to omit to help others when they are in need and when you are in a position to help them. It does not follow from this, however, that it is wrong not to promote the greatest good of the greatest number, or not to promote the greatest amount of good in the world. Deontologists and utilitarians alike make the mistake of thinking that it is one, or the only one, of our moral duties to "do the optimific act." Nothing could be further from the truth. We do not have a duty to do good to others or to ourselves, or to others and/or to ourselves in a judicious mixture such that it produces the greatest possible amount of good in the world. We are morally required to do good only to those who are actually in need of our assistance. The view that we always ought to do the optimific act, or whenever we have no more stringent duty to perform, would have the absurd result that we are doing wrong whenever we are relaxing, since on those occasions there will always be opportunities to produce greater good than we can by relaxing. For the relief of suffering is always a greater good than mere enjoyment. Yet it is quite plain that the worker who, after a tiring day, puts on his slippers and listens to the wireless is not doing anything he ought not to, is not neglecting any of his duties, even though it may be perfectly true that there are things he might do which produce more good in the world, even for himself, than merely relaxing by the fireside.

5. UPSETTING AND RESTORING THE MORAL EQUILIBRIUM

So far, we have considered only primary moral rules, that is, those which prohibit or enjoin certain types of behavior, such as 'Thou shalt not kill,' 'Thou shalt not steal,' 'Thou shalt help thy neighbour when he is in need of your help,' and so on. Secondary rules of morality are those which prohibit or enjoin certain types of behavior in response to some "upset of the moral balance," for example, 'An eye for an eye, a tooth for a tooth,' 'Let him who is free from guilt throw the first stone,' 'One good turn deserves another.'

What is it to "upset the moral balance"? The moral balance is preserved when everyone is "strictly minding his own business." Plato was right in connecting morality with minding one's own business; he was wrong only in his explanation of the connection. Minding one's own business and not interfering with anyone else are not all there is to morality, though it is true that when everyone minds his own business the moral equilibrium is maintained. This equilibrium can be upset in two quite different ways. I may behave in a manner which upsets the moral balance against me or in my favor. I may accumulate a moral debit or credit account; the first when I do what I ought not to do, the second when I do "more than my duty"; the first when I violate a "rule of duty," the second when I observe a "rule of supererogation." When, for example, I kill someone, steal something, am cruel to someone, or commit adultery, I am accumulating a moral debit balance. If, on the other hand, at great risk to myself I save someone's life or make great financial sacrifices for the sake of a good cause, I am acquiring a moral credit balance. It is for cases of this sort that the secondary moral rules are devised. Primary moral rules define what it is, morally speaking, to mind one's own business, to preserve the moral equilibrium. Secondary moral rules indicate what is to be done by whom when the balance has been upset.

Secondary moral rules are determined by the concept of desert, of positive or negative moral merit. They state what a person deserves, that is, ought to get or have done to him, as a result of the upset of the moral balance. A person who has not upset the moral balance deserves nothing. He has neither positive nor negative moral merit.

The aim of a morality is to prevent the upsetting of the moral equilibrium by violation of "rules of duty" and to encourage it by the observation of "rules of supererogation." At the same time, the methods of deterring and encouraging potential rule breakers must not themselves interfere with the primary rules. The secondary rules are therefore seen as designed to "restore the moral balance." They have the object of deterring or encouraging rule breakers, but also of bringing the process to an end. When the balance is "restored," the secondary rules no longer apply.

Take first the case of preventing violations of duty. An obvious, if crude, way of "restoring the moral equilibrium" is provided by the institution of revenge. The person injured returns the harm. The supreme principle governing such secondary rules is 'One bad turn deserves another.' This has the serious disadvantage that it is difficult to "restore" the moral equilibrium. Since revenge is itself the infliction of harm on an individual, the secondary rule applies again. In the institution of the vendetta or the blood fued, what is designed to discourage violations of primary moral rules in fact leads to endless mutual harming.

The substitution of punishment for revenge remedies this drawback. The infliction of hardship on the wrongdoer is taken out of the hands of the injured person or his aggrieved relations and handed over to a disinterested official. By making a ceremony of it, it is clearly indicated that this is not intended as merely the infliction of harm on an individual, but as the application of a secondary moral rule designed to "restore" the moral balance. The object of the practice is to deter future wrongdoers. The infliction of hardship on a given individual is justified by his prior violation of a primary moral rule. There is now no aggrieved person left. Punishment has restored the moral equilibrium. The wrong-doer has expiated, atoned for, his wrong. Everyone has a clean slate again. It is wrong for the aggrieved to continue to harbor a grudge, to refuse to forgive the wrongdoer.

The situation is somewhat different in the case of an upset of the moral balance by observing (not breaking) a rule of supererogation. Obviously, the point of these rules is that they should be observed rather than broken, although observing them (not breaking them) constitutes an upset of the moral equilibrium. Such breaches of the moral equilibrium are desirable. In order to encourage them, we have secondary rules of morality, guided by the general principle 'One good turn deserves another.' We say that a person who engages in works of supererogation thereby acquires moral desert or merit.

However, in the case of the personal requital of a good turn, there is nothing undesirable about the unending reciprocation of such good turns. It is desirable that the person who received the returns of gratitude should in turn feel grateful. There is, therefore, no reason why the state should take personal reciprocations out of the hands of the recipients and put communal rewards in their place. 'Mine is the vengeance' has a point; 'Mine is the gratitude' has not.

There are two conceptions which belong in this secondary field of morality, but which have usually been assigned to the primary field, obligation and justice. When we say that we are under an obligation to someone, we mean that we ought to restore the moral equilibrium by "discharging our obligation." To discharge one's obligations *is* to restore the moral equilibrium. Doing so terminates the special moral relationship created between two people by the upset of the moral balance which gave rise to the obligation. To say that killing is wrong or that one ought not to kill is to say something that does not involve the secondary field of morality. To say that one ought to discharge one's obligations is to say something that does. Many confusions and paradoxes could have been avoided if this distinction had been clearly grasped.

Justice is a moral concept involving the secondary field of morality. For 'doing justice' means 'giving to everyone what he deserves,' that is, restoring the moral equilibrium by the appropriate action—giving a reward, repaying a debt, passing sentence, administering punishment, and the like. Plato's examination of morality in the Republic is vitiated by his failure to distinguish between the primary notions of rightness and wrongness and the secondary notion of justice.

6. SOCIAL MORALITY

We have so far considered absolute morality only. As we have noted, the moral point of view is characterized by a formal and a material condition. The formal condition is this: a man cannot be said to have adopted the moral point of view unless he is prepared to treat the moral rules as principles rather than mere rules of thumb, that is, to do things *on principle* rather than merely to act purposively, merely for himself or some favored group. The material condition is this: the rules must be for the good of everyone alike. This does not mean that they must be for the common good of all human beings, past, present, and future, for such a condition would be impossible to satisfy. Its meaning can be elucidated by setting forth the criteria of saying that a rule is for the good of everyone alike. As far as absolute morality is concerned, only one condition must be satisfied, namely, that these rules should be "reversible," that is, not merely for the good of the agent, but at least not detrimental to the persons who are affected by the agent's behavior.

An examination of social conditions will yield some further criteria of 'being for the good of everyone alike.' A society is more than just a number of individuals living in a certain area and behaving in ways directly affecting others, such as killing, maiming, and robbing. Life in society involves a social framework which multiplies the points of contact between individuals and which can transform the effects of a man's behavior on his fellow men. Within a given social framework, behavior may be harmful which is not, from its nature, the infliction of harm on another. It may be harmful only if and because a great many people in that society engage in it. No harm is done if one person walks across the lawn. But the lawn is ruined if everyone does. No harm is done if one person uses the gas. But if everyone uses it during peak hours, then the gas supply may break down, and everyone will be adversely affected.

That such behavior is morally objectionable is widely recognized. We acknowledge that it is, by the well-known formula 'You can't do that; what if everyone did the same!' Kant thought of it as the core of his categorical imperative, 'Act only on that maxim whereby thou canst at the same time will that it should become a universal law.' This is precisely what we "cannot will" in the cases in question. Although it is not true that, as Kant put it, a will willing such a maxim to become a universal law would, literally, contradict itself, nevertheless, in making such a maxim a universal law, one would enjoin people to do evil, and such a law would obviously be wrong.

It is, however, important to distinguish behavior which is "nonuniversalizable" from behavior that is "nonreversible." The latter can be seen to be wrong in itself, irrespective of the consequences and of how many people engage in it. This is not so in the case of nonuniversalizable behavior. There we have to consider the consequences, and not merely of a single act but of a great many of them. There is nothing wrong in itself with putting one straw on the camel's back, but one of them will be the last.

What exactly does this prove? That no one is allowed to lay even one straw on the camel's back? That every act of this kind is wrong? Surely not. Before we can say that any act of this sort is wrong, a number of conditions must be satisfied.

In the first place, all concerned must be equally entitled to behave in the nonuniversalizable way. It would, for instance, be most undesirable if everyone had dinner at 6:30 P.M., for all the nation's service would then come to a standstill at that time. But it cannot follow from this that eating at 6:30 P.M. is wrong for everyone. It cannot follow because the argument applies equally for any time, and it must be all right to eat at some time. Of course, there is no serious problem here. Not everyone is equally entitled to have his dinner at 6:30 P.M. Those who are on duty at that time must have it before or after or while they are attending to their duties.

There are further conditions. If everyone were celibate all his life, mankind would die out, or, at any rate, the number would soon be so seriously reduced as to make life unbearable. Those who do not find the prospect of the end of the human race upsetting will have to admit that the return to primitive conditions is undesirable. Again, if everyone suddenly stopped smoking, drinking, gambling, and going to the pictures, some states might go bankrupt and this would be undesirable. All the same, it can hardly be true that abstinence in matters of sex, smoking, drinking, gambling, and visits to the cinema can be wrong in any and every case, even though we are surely all equally entitled to refrain from these ways of spending our time.

There must, therefore, be a further condition. Everyone must not only be equally entitled to engage in these forms of activity, but people must also be inclined to do so. There would have to be a real danger that, unless they are stopped somehow, many will engage in this sort of behavior. People are lazy, so they will not go to the polling booth or make the detour round the newly planted lawn. People like picking flowers, so they will destroy the rare wild flowers. People want to heat their rooms, so they will want to use their radiators during peak hours. But there is no great danger that they will all go celibate, or give up smoking and drinking.

This point, by the way, shows that nonuniversalizability cannot be adduced to show that suicide is wrong. Suicide is no more wrong than celibacy and for the same reason. People are less keen in suicide even than on celibacy. There is no danger of the race dying out. In fact, all over the world people are so keen on procreation that the suicide rate could go up a long way before anyone need be alarmed. Of course if, one day, life and sex were to become burdens to all of us and if, nevertheless, it really is desirable that the race should go on, then reckless suicide or slothful celibacy might become morally wrongful types of conduct. Until then, those weary of life and sex need not have a bad conscience about their uncommon indulgences.

There is one further point in this. To say that it is wrong to walk across the lawn or switch on the gas during peak hours, provided (a) it would have undesirable consequences *if* everyone did it, (b) we are all equally entitled to do it, and (c) doing it is an indulgence, not a sacrifice, amounts to saying that since refraining from doing these things is a sacrifice such a sacrifice for the common good should not be demanded of one or a few only, but equally of all, even if a universal sacrifice is not needed. Since no one is more entitled than anyone else to indulge himself and since *all* cannot do so without the undesirable consequences which no one wants, *no one* should be allowed to indulge himself.

Now the conditions are complete. If the behavior in question is such that (i) the consequences would be undesirable if everyone did it, (ii) all are equally entitled to engage in it, and (iii) engaging in this sort of behavior is an indulgence, not a sacrifice, then such behavior *should be prohibited by the morality of the group.*

But now suppose that it is not prohibited. Is it wrong all the same? Kant certainly thought so. I think he is mistaken. For since, by indulging in the behavior in question, I am not actually doing any harm, my behavior is not wrong in itself, but only when taken in conjunction with that of others. I cannot prevent the evil by refraining. Others must refrain too. In the case of nonreversible behavior, *my action alone* is the cause of the evil. I can avoid the evil if I refrain. In the case under discussion, however, if I have reason to suppose that the others will not refrain, I surely have reason not to refrain either, as my only reason for refraining is my desire to avoid causing the evil consequences. If these cannot be avoided, I have no reason not to indulge myself. If the grass is not going to grow anyway, why should I make the detour?

It is no good arguing that I am not entitled to do wrong just because other people might or probably would. For I am not doing wrong. I have no moral reason for the sacrifice. I need no justification or excuse, for my behavior is wrong only *if I have no reason to think* that others will refuse to make the sacrifice. If I have reason to think they will refuse to make it, then I have reason to think that my own sacrifice will be in vain; hence I have reason against making it.

Of course, if the results are *very* undesirable and my sacrifice is *very* small and I am not certain what the others will do, I should take the risk of making the sacrifice even if it turns out to have been in vain. But, otherwise, reason will support the opposite course.

The situation is different if the morality or the custom or the law of the group does already contain a rule forbidding such behavior. If there is such a rule, then the behavior is wrong, for such a rule has the backing of morality. As we have said, a group ought to have rules forbidding nonuniversalizable behavior. And when there is such a rule, then the community has regulated behavior of this sort and I ought to do my share toward the success of the regulation.

I should like to add one word about the morality of individual initiative in these matters. Some people think that individuals should go ahead with a good example and not wait until the rule-making powers of the group are used. Others argue that this is putting too great a burden on the public-spirited. Thus, compulsory military service with exemptions granted to those engaged in important national industries is said by some to be fairer, volunteering for national service is said by others to be morally preferable. I can see no reason for the latter view. It may indeed seem preferable from the military point of view, for it may be argued that volunteers are better soldiers. But there is no reason why if keenness is wanted volunteers should not have preferential rights to serve in the army rather than in industry. On the other hand, there is no reason why the sacrifices involved in the defense of their country should be borne only by those who are taking their moral responsibilities seriously, and no reason why those who are not should benefit gratuitously. In the absence of argument showing that the method of individual initiative yields a more efficient army, the other seems to me preferable and, in any case, obviously fairer. Hesitation to use the lawmaking force of the community is understandable, for such use may endanger individual freedom, but often this hesitation is supported on the grounds of the moral preferability of individual sacrifice and initiative. Such arguments seem to me unsound.

What Makes Right Acts Right?

SIR DAVID ROSS

The real point at issue between hedonism and utilitarianism on the one hand and their opponents on the other is not whether 'right' means 'productive of so and so'; for it cannot with any plausibility be maintained that it does. The point at issue is that to which we now pass, *viz.* whether there is any general character which makes right acts right, and if so, what it is. Among the main historical attempts to state a single characteristic of all right actions which is the foundation of their rightness are those made by egoism and utilitarianism. But I do not propose to discuss these, not because the subject is unimportant, but because it has been dealt with so often and so well already, and because there has come to be so much agreement among moral philosophers that neither of these theories is satisfactory. A much more attractive theory has been put forward by Professor Moore: that what makes actions right is that they are productive of more *good* than could have been produced by any other action open to the agent.[1]

This theory is in fact the culmination of all the attempts to base rightness on productivity of some sort of result. The first form this attempt takes is the attempt to base rightness on conduciveness to the advantage or pleasure of the agent. This

theory comes to grief over the fact, which stares us in the face, that a great part of duty consists in an observance of the rights and a furtherance of the interests of others, whatever the cost to ourselves may be. Plato and others may be right in holding that a regard for the rights of others never in the long run involves a loss of happiness for the agent, that 'the just life profits a man.' But this, even if true, is irrelevant to the rightness of the act. As soon as a man does an action *because* he thinks he will promote his own interests thereby, he is acting not from a sense of its rightness but from self-interest.

To the egoistic theory hedonistic utilitarianism supplies a much-needed amendment. It points out correctly that the fact that a certain pleasure will be enjoyed by the agent is no reason why he *ought* to bring it into being rather than an equal or greater pleasure to be enjoyed by another, though, human nature being what it is, it makes it not unlikely that he *will* try to bring it into being. But hedonistic utilitarianism in its turn needs a correction. On reflection it seems clear that pleasure is not the only thing in life that we think good in itself, that for instance we think the possession of a good character, or an intelligent understanding of the world, as good or better. A great advance is made by the substitution of 'productive of the greatest good' for 'productive of the greatest pleasure.'

Not only is this theory more attractive than hedonistic utilitarianism, but its logical relation to that theory is such that the latter could not be true unless *it* were true,

Reprinted from *The Right and the Good* by Sir David Ross by permission of the Clarendon Press, Oxford. Copyright 1930.

[1] I take the theory which, as I have tried to show, seems to be put forward in *Ethics* rather than the earlier and less plausible theory put forward in *Principia Ethica*. For the difference, cf. my pp. 8–11.

while it might be true though hedonistic utilitarianism were not. It is in fact one of the logical bases of hedonistic utilitarianism. For the view that what produces the maximum pleasure is right has for its bases the views (1) that what produces the maximum good is right, and (2) that pleasure is the only thing good in itself. If they were not assuming that what produces the maximum *good* is right, the utilitarians' attempt to show that pleasure is the only thing good in itself, which is in fact the point they take most pains to establish, would have been quite irrelevant to their attempt to prove that only what produces the maximum *pleasure* is right. If, therefore, it can be shown that productivity of the maximum good is not what makes all right actions right, we shall *a fortiori* have refuted hedonistic utilitarianism.

When a plain man fulfils a promise because he thinks he ought to do so, it seems clear that he does so with no thought of its total consequences, still less with any opinion that these are likely to be the best possible. He thinks in fact much more of the past than of the future. What makes him think it right to act in a certain way is the fact that he has promised to do so—that and, usually, nothing more. That his act will produce the best possible consequences is not his reason for calling it right. What lends colour to the theory we are examining, then, is not the actions (which form probably a great majority of our actions) in which some such reflection as 'I have promised' is the only reason we give ourselves for thinking a certain action right, but the exceptional cases in which the consequences of fulfilling a promise (for instance) would be so disastrous to others that we judge it right not to do so. It must of course be admitted that such cases exist. If I have promised to meet a friend at a particular time for some trivial purpose, I should certainly think myself justified in breaking my engagement if by doing so I could prevent a serious accident or bring relief to the victims of one. And the sup-

porters of the view we are examining hold that my thinking so is due to my thinking that I shall bring more good into existence by the one action than by the other. A different account may, however, be given of the matter, an account which will, I believe, show itself to be the true one. It may be said that besides the duty of fulfilling promises I have and recognize a duty of relieving distress,[2] and that when I think it right to do the latter at the cost of not doing the former, it is not because I think I shall produce more good thereby but because I think it the duty which is in the circumstances more of a duty. This account surely corresponds much more closely with what we really think in such a situation. If, so far as I can see, I could bring equal amounts of good into being by fulfilling my promise and by helping some one to whom I had made no promise, I should not hesitate to regard the former as my duty. Yet on the view that what is right is right because it is productive of the most good I should not so regard it.

There are two theories, each in its way simple, that offer a solution of such cases of conscience. One is the view of Kant, that there are certain duties of perfect obligation, such as those of fulfilling promises, of paying debts, of telling the truth, which admit of no exception whatever in favour of duties of imperfect obligation, such as that of relieving distress. The other is the view of, for instance, Professor Moore and Dr. Rashdall, that there is only the duty of producing good, and that all 'conflicts of duties' should be resolved by asking 'by which action will most good be produced?' But it is more important that our theory fit the facts than that it be simple, and the account we have given above corresponds (it seems to me) better than either of the simpler theories with what we really think, *viz.* that normally promise-keeping, for example, should come before benevolence, but

---

[2] These are not strictly speaking duties, but things that tend to be our duty, or *prima facie* duties. Cf. pp. 19–20.

that when and only when the good to be produced by the benevolent act is very great and the promise comparatively trivial, the act of benevolence becomes our duty.

In fact the theory of 'ideal utilitarianism,' if I may for brevity refer so to the theory of Professor Moore, seems to simplify unduly our relations to our fellows. It says, in effect, that the only morally significant relation in which my neighbours stand to me is that of being possible beneficiaries by my action.[3] They do stand in this relation to me, and this relation is morally significant. But they may also stand to me in the relation of promisee to promiser, of creditor to debtor, of wife to husband, of child to parent, of friend to friend, of fellow countryman to fellow countryman, and the like; and each of these relations is the foundation of a *prima facie* duty, which is more or less incumbent on me according to the circumstances of the case. When I am in a situation, as perhaps I always am, in which more than one of these *prima facie* duties is incumbent on me, what I have to do is to study the situation as fully as I can until I form the considered opinion (it is never more) that in the circumstances one of them is more incumbent than any other; then I am bound to think that to do this *prima facie* duty is my duty *sans phrase* in the situation.

I suggest 'prima facie duty' or 'conditional duty' as a brief way of referring to the characteristic (quite distinct from that of being a duty proper) which an act has, in virtue of being of a certain kind (e.g. the keeping of a promise), of being an act which would be a duty proper if it were not at the same time of another kind which is morally significant. Whether an act is a duty proper or actual duty depends on *all* the morally significant kinds it is an in-

stance of. The phrase 'prima facie duty' must be apologized for, since (1) it suggests that what we are speaking of is a certain kind of duty, whereas it is in fact not a duty, but something related in a special way to duty. Strictly speaking, we want not a phrase in which duty is qualified by an adjective, but a separate noun. (2) 'Prima' *facie* suggests that one is speaking only of an appearance which a moral situation presents at first sight, and which may turn out to be illusory; whereas what I am speaking of is an objective fact involved in the nature of the situation, or more strictly in an element of its nature, though not, as duty proper does, arising from its *whole* nature. I can, however, think of no term which fully meets the case. 'Claim' has been suggested by Professor Prichard. The word 'claim' has the advantage of being quite a familiar one in this connexion, and it seems to cover much of the ground. It would be quite natural to say, 'a person to whom I have made a promise has a claim on me,' and also, 'a person whose distress I could relieve (at the cost of breaking the promise) has a claim on me.' But (1) while 'claim' is appropriate from *their* point of view, we want a word to express the corresponding fact from the agent's point of view—the fact of his being subject to claims that can be made against him; and ordinary language provides us with no such correlative to 'claim.' And (2) (what is more important) 'claim' seems inevitably to suggest two persons, one of whom might make a claim on the other; and while this covers the ground of social duty, it is inappropriate in the case of that important part of duty which is the duty of cultivating a certain kind of character in oneself. It would be artificial, I think, and at any rate metaphorical, to say that one's character has a claim on oneself.

There is nothing arbitrary about these *prima facie* duties. Each rests on a definite circumstance which cannot seriously be held to be without moral significance. Of *prima facie* duties I suggest without claim-

---

[3] Some will think it, apart from other considerations, a sufficient refutation of this view to point out that I also stand in that relation to myself, so that for this view the distinction of oneself from others is morally insignificant.

ing completeness or finality for it, the following division.[4]

(1) Some duties rest on previous acts of my own. These duties seem to include two kinds, (a) those resting on a promise or what may fairly be called an implicit promise, such as the implicit undertaking not to tell lies which seems to be implied in the act of entering into conversation (at any rate by civilized men), or of writing books that purport to be history and not fiction. These may be called the duties of fidelity. (b) Those resting on a previous wrongful act. These may be called the duties of reparation. (2) Some rest on previous acts of other men, i.e. services done by them to me. These may be loosely described as the duties of gratitude.[5] (3) Some rest on the fact or possibility of a distribution of pleasure or happiness (or of the means thereto) which is not in accordance with the merit of the persons concerned; in such cases there arises a duty to upset or prevent such a distribution. These are the duties of justice. (4) Some rest on the mere fact that there are other beings in the world whose condition we can make better in respect of virtue, or of intelligence, or of pleasure. These are the duties of beneficence. (5) Some rest on the fact that we can improve our own condition in respect of virtue or of intelligence. These

are the duties of self-improvement. (6) I think that we should distinguish from (4) the duties that may be summed up under the title of 'not injuring others.' No doubt to injure others is incidentally to fail to do them good; but it seems to me clear that non-maleficence is apprehended as a duty distinct from that of beneficence, and as a duty of a more stringent character. It will be noticed that this alone among the types of duty has been stated in a negative way. An attempt might no doubt be made to state this duty, like the others, in a positive way. It might be said that it is really the duty to prevent ourselves from acting either from an inclination to harm others or from an inclination to seek our own pleasure, in doing which we should incidentally harm them. But on reflection it seems clear that the primary duty here is the duty not to harm others, this being a duty whether or not we have an inclination that if followed would lead to our harming them; and that when we have such an inclination the primary duty not to harm others gives rise to a consequential duty to resist the inclination. The recognition of this duty of non-maleficence is the first step on the way to the recognition of the duty of beneficence; and that accounts for the prominence of the commands 'thou shalt not kill,' 'thou shalt not commit adultery,' 'thou shalt not steal,' 'thou shalt not bear false witness,' in so early a code as the Decalogue. But even when we have come to recognize the duty of beneficence, it appears to me that the duty of non-maleficence is recognized as a distinct one, and as *prima facie* more binding. We should not in general consider it justifiable to kill one person in order to keep another alive, or to steal from one in order to give alms to another.

The essential defect of the 'ideal utilitarian' theory is that it ignores, or at least does not do full justice to, to the highly personal character of duty. If the only duty is to produce the maximum of good, the question who is to have the good—whether it is myself, or my benefactor, or a person

---

[4] I should make it plain at this stage that I am *assuming* the correctness of some of our main convictions as to *prima facie* duties, or, more strictly, am claiming that we *know* them to be true. To me it seems as self-evident as anything could be, that to make a promise, for instance, is to create a moral claim on us in someone else. Many readers will perhaps say that they do *not* know this to be true. If so, I certainly cannot prove it to them; I can only ask them to reflect again, in the hope that they will ultimately agree that they also know it to be true. The main moral convictions of the plain man seem to me to be, not opinions which it is for philosophy to prove or disprove, but knowledge from the start; and in my own case I seem to find little difficulty in distinguishing these essential convictions from other moral convictions which I also have, which are merely fallible opinions based on an imperfect study of the working for good or evil of certain institutions or types of action.

[5] For a needed correction of this statement, cf. pp. 22–23.

to whom I have made a promise to confer that good on him, or a mere fellow man to whom I stand in no such special relation—should make no difference to my having a duty to produce that good. But we are all in fact sure that it makes a vast difference.

One or two other comments must be made on this provisional list of the divisions of duty. (1) The nomenclature is not strictly correct. For by 'fidelity' or 'gratitude' we mean, strictly, certain states of motivation; and, as I have urged, it is not our duty to have certain motives, but to do certain acts. By 'fidelity,' for instance, is meant, strictly, the disposition to fulfil promises and implicit promises *because we have made them.* We have no general word to cover the actual fulfilment of promises and implicit promises *irrespective of motive;* and I use 'fidelity,' loosely but perhaps conveniently, to fill this gap. So too I use 'gratitude' for the returning of services, irrespective of motive. The term 'justice' is not so much confined, in ordinary usage, to a certain state of motivation, for we should often talk of a man as acting justly even when we did not think his motive was the wish to do what was just simply for the sake of doing so. Less apology is therefore needed for our use of 'justice' in this sense. And I have used the word 'beneficence' rather then 'benevolence,' in order to emphasize the fact that it is our duty to do certain things, and not to do them from certain motives.

(2) If the objection be made, that this catalogue of the main types of duty is an unsystematic one resting on no logical principle, it may be replied, first, that it makes no claim to being ultimate. It is a *prima facie* classification of the duties which reflection on our moral convictions seems actually to reveal. And if these convictions are, as I would claim that they are, of the nature of knowledge, and if I have not misstated them, the list will be a list of authentic conditional duties, correct as far as it goes though not necessarily complete. The

list of *goods* put forward by the rival theory is reached by exactly the same method—the only sound one in the circumstances—*viz.* that of direct reflection on what we really think. Loyalty to the facts is worth more than a symmetrical architectonic or a hastily reached simplicity. If further reflection discovers a perfect logical basis for this or for a better classification, so much the better.

(3) It may, again, be objected that our theory that there are these various and often conflicting types of *prima facie* duty leaves us with no principle upon which to discern what is our actual duty in particular circumstances. But this objection is not one which the rival theory is in a position to bring forward. For when we have to choose between the production of two heterogeneous goods, say knowledge and pleasure, the 'ideal utilitarian' theory can only fall back on an opinion, for which no logical basis can be offered, that one of the goods is the greater; and this is no better than a similar opinion that one of two duties is the more urgent. And again, when we consider the infinite variety of the effects of our actions in the way of pleasure, it must surely be admitted that the claim which *hedonism* sometimes makes, that it offers a readily applicable criterion of right conduct, is quite illusory.

I am unwilling, however, to content myself with an *argumentum ad hominem,* and I would contend that in principle there is no reason to anticipate that every act that is our duty is so for one and the same reason. Why should two sets of circumstances, or one set of circumstances, not possess different characteristics, any one of which makes a certain act our *prima facie* duty? When I ask what it is that makes me in certain cases sure that I have a *prima facie* duty to do so and so, I find that it lies in the fact that I have made a promise; when I ask the same question in another case, I find the answer lies in the fact that I have done a wrong. And if on reflection I find (as I think I do) that neither of these reasons is reducible to the other, I must not on any *a priori* ground assume that such a reduction is possible.

An attempt may be made to arrange in a more systematic way the main types of duty which we have indicated. In the first place it seems self-evident that if there are things that are intrinsically good, it is *prima facie* a duty to bring them into existence rather than not to do so, and to bring as much of them into existence as possible. It will be argued in our fifth chapter that there are three main things that are intrinsically good—virtue, knowledge, and, with certain limitations, pleasure. And since a given virtuous disposition, for instance, is equally good whether it is realized in myself or in another, it seems to be my duty to bring it into existence whether in myself or in another. So too with a given piece of knowledge.

The case of pleasure is difficult; for while we clearly recognize a duty to produce pleasure for others, it is by no means so clear that we recognize a duty to produce pleasure for ourselves. This appears to arise from the following facts. The thought of an act as our duty is one that presupposes a certain amount of reflection about the act; and for that reason does not normally arise in connexion with acts towards which we are already impelled by another strong impulse. So far, the cause of our not thinking of the promotion of our own pleasure as a duty is analogous to the cause which usually prevents a highly sympathetic person from thinking of the promotion of the pleasure of others as a duty. He is impelled so strongly by direct interest in the well-being of others towards promoting their pleasure that he does not stop to ask whether it is his duty to promote it; and we are all impelled so strongly towards the promotion of our own pleasure that we do not stop to ask whether it is a duty or not. But there is a further reason why even when we stop to think about the matter it does not usually present itself as a duty: *viz.* that, since the performance of most of our duties involves the giving up of some pleasure that we desire, the doing of duty and the getting of pleasure for ourselves come by a natural association of ideas to be thought of as incompatible things. This association of ideas is in the main salutary in its operation, since it puts a check on what but for it would be much too strong, the tendency to pursue one's own pleasure without thought of other considerations. Yet if pleasure is good, it seems in the long run clear that it is right to get it for ourselves as well as to produce it for others, when this does not involve the failure to discharge some more stringent *prima facie* duty. The question is a very difficult one, but it seems that this conclusion can be denied only on one or other of three grounds: (1) that pleasure is not *prima facie* good (i.e. good when it is neither the actualization of a bad disposition nor undeserved), (2) that there is no *prima facie* duty to produce as much that is good as we can or (3) that though there is a *prima facie* duty to produce other things that are good, there is no *prima facie* duty to produce pleasure which will be enjoyed by ourselves. I give reasons later[6] for not accepting the first contention. The second hardly admits of argument but seems to me plainly false. The third seems plausible only if we hold that an act that is pleasant or brings pleasure to ourselves must for that reason not be a duty; and this would lead to paradoxical consequences, such as that if a man enjoys giving pleasure to others or working for their moral improvement it cannot be his duty to do so. Yet it seems to be a very stubborn fact, that in our ordinary consciousness we are not aware of a duty to get pleasure for ourselves; and by way of partial explanation of this I may add that though, as I think, one's own pleasure is a good and there is a duty to produce it, it is only if we *think* of our own pleasure not as simply our own pleasure, but as an objective good, something that an

[6] pp. 135–8.

impartial spectator would approve, that we can think of the getting it as a duty; and we do not habitually think of it in this way.

If these contentions are right, what we have called the duty of beneficence and the duty of self-improvement rest on the same ground. No different principles of duty are involved in the two cases. If we feel a special responsibility for improving our own character rather than that of others, it is not because a special principle is involved, but because we are aware that the one is more under our control than the other. It was on this ground that Kant expressed the practical law of duty in the form 'seek to make yourself good and other people happy.' He was so persuaded of the internality of virtue that he regarded any attempt by one person to produce virtue in another as bound to produce, at most, only a counterfeit of virtue, the doing of externally right acts not from the true principle of virtuous action but out of regard to another person. It must be admitted that one man cannot compel another to be virtuous; compulsory virtue would just not be virtue. But experience clearly shows that Kant overshoots the mark when he contends that one man cannot do anything to *promote* virtue in another, to bring such influences to bear upon him that his own response to them is more likely to be virtuous than his response to other influences would have been. And our duty to do this is not different in kind from our duty to improve our own characters.

It is equally clear, and clear at an earlier stage of moral development, that if there are things that are bad in themselves we ought, *prima facie*, not to bring them upon others; and on this fact rests the duty of non-maleficence.

The duty of justice is particularly complicated, and the word is used to cover things which are really very different—things such as the payment of debts, the reparation of injuries done by oneself to another, and the bringing about of a distribution of happiness between other people

in proportion to merit. I use the word to denote only the last of these three. In the fifth chapter I shall try to show that besides the three (comparatively) simple goods, virtue, knowledge, and pleasure, there is a more complex good, not reducible to these, consisting in the proportionment of happiness to virtue. The bringing of this about is a duty which we owe to all men alike, though it may be reinforced by special responsibilities that we have undertaken to particular men. This, therefore, with beneficence and self-improvement, comes under the general principle that we should produce as much good as possible, though the good here involved is different in kind from any other.

But besides this general obligation, there are special obligations. These may arise, in the first place, incidentally, from acts which were not essentially meant to create such an obligation, but which nevertheless create it. From the nature of the case such acts may be of two kinds—the infliction of injuries on others, and the acceptance of benefits from them. It seems clear that these put us under a special obligation to other men, and that only these acts can do so incidentally. From these arise the twin duties of reparation and gratitude.

And finally there are special obligations arising from acts the very intention of which, when they were done, was to put us under such an obligation. The name for such acts is 'promises'; the name is wide enough if we are willing to include under it implicit promises, i.e. modes of behaviour in which without explicit verbal promise we intentionally create an expectation that we can be counted on to behave in a certain way in the interest of another person.

These seem to be, in principle, all the ways in which *prima facie* duties arise. In actual experience they are compounded together in highly complex ways. Thus, for example, the duty of obeying the laws of one's country arises partly (as Socrates contends in the *Crito*) from the duty of gratitude for the benefits one has received from it; partly from the implicit promise to obey which seems to be involved in permanent residence in a country whose laws we know we are *expected* to obey, and still more clearly involved when we ourselves invoke the protection of its laws (this is the truth underlying the doctrine of the social contract); and partly (if we are fortunate in our country) from the fact that its laws are potent instruments for the general good.

Or again, the sense of a general obligation to bring about (so far as we can) a just apportionment of happiness to merit is often greatly reinforced by the fact that many of the existing injustices are due to a social and economic system which we have, not indeed created, but taken part in and assented to; the duty of justice is then reinforced by the duty of reparation.

It is necessary to say something by way of clearing up the relation between *prima facie* duties and the actual or absolute duty to do one particular act in particular circumstances. If, as almost all moralists except Kant are agreed, and as most plain men think, it is sometimes right to tell a lie or to break a promise, it must be maintained that there is a difference between *prima facie* duty and actual or absolute duty. When we think ourselves justified in breaking, and indeed morally obliged to break, a promise in order to relieve someone's distress, we do not for a moment cease to recognize a *prima facie* duty to keep our promise, and this leads us to feel, not indeed shame or repentance, but certainly compunction, for behaving as we do; we recognize, further, that it is our duty to make up somehow to the promisee for the breaking of the promise. We have to distinguish from the characteristic of being our duty that of tending to be our duty. Any act that we do contains various elements in virtue of which it falls under various categories. In virtue of being the breaking of a promise, for instance, it

tends to be wrong; in virtue of being an instance of relieving distress it tends to be right. Tendency to be one's duty may be called a parti-resultant attribute, i.e. one which belongs to an act in virtue of some one component in its nature. *Being* one's duty is a toti-resultant attribute, one which belongs to an act in virtue of its whole nature and of nothing less than this.[7] This distinction between parti-resultant and toti-resultant attributes is one which we shall meet in another context also.[8]

Another instance of the same distinction may be found in the operation of natural laws. *Qua* subject to the force of gravitation towards some other body, each body tends to move in a particular direction with a particular velocity; but its actual movement depends on all the forces to which it is subject. It is only by recognizing this distinction that we can preserve the absoluteness of laws of nature, and only by recognizing a corresponding distinction that we can preserve the absolutness of the general principles of morality. But an important difference between the two cases must be pointed out. When we say that in virtue of gravitation a body tends to move in a certain way, we are referring to a causal influence actually exercised on it by another body or other bodies. When we say that in virtue of being deliberately untrue a certain remark tends to be wrong, we are referring to no causal relation, to no relation that involves succession in time, but to such a relation as connects the various attributes of a mathematical figure. And if the word 'tendency' is thought to suggest too much a causal relation, it is better to talk of certain types of act as being *prima facie* right or wrong (or of different persons as having different and possibly conflicting claims upon us), than of their tending to be right or wrong.

Something should be said of the relation between our apprehension of the

[7] But cf. the qualification in p. 33, n. 2.
[8] Cf. pp. 122–3.

prima facie rightness of certain types of act and our mental attitude towards particular acts. It is proper to use the word 'apprehension' in the former case and not in the latter. That an act, *qua* fulfilling a promise, or *qua* effecting a just distribution of good, or *qua* returning services rendered, or *qua* promoting the good of others, or *qua* promoting the virtue or insight of the agent, is *prima facie* right, is self-evident; not in the sense that it is evident from the beginning of our lives, or as soon as we attend to the proposition for the first time, but in the sense that when we have reached sufficient mental maturity and have given sufficient attention to the proposition it is evident without any need of proof, or of evidence beyond itself. It is self-evident just as a mathematical axiom, or the validity of a form of inference, is evident. The moral order expressed in these propositions is just as much part of the fundamental nature of the universe (and, we may add, of any possible universe in which there were moral agents at all) as is the spatial or numerical structure expressed in the axioms of geometry or arithmetic. In our confidence that these propositions are true there is involved the same trust in our reason that is involved in our confidence in mathematics; and we should have no justification for trusting it in the latter sphere and distrusting it in the former. In both cases we are dealing with propositions that cannot be proved, but that just as certainly need no proof.

Some of these general principles of *prima facie* duty may appear to be open to criticism. It may be thought, for example, that the principle of returning good for good is a falling off from the Christian principle, generally and rightly recognized as expressing the highest morality, of returning good for evil. To this it may be replied that I do not suggest that there is a principle commanding us to return good for good and forbidding us to return good for evil, and that I do suggest that there is a positive duty to seek the good of all men. What

I maintain is that an act in which good is returned for good is recognized as *specially* binding on us just because it is of that character, and that *ceteris paribus* any one would think it his duty to help his benefactors rather than his enemies, if he could not do both; just as it is generally recognized that *ceteris paribus* we should pay our debts rather than give our money in charity, when we cannot do both. A benefactor is not only a man, calling for our effort on his behalf on that ground, but also our benefactor, calling for our *special* effort on *that* ground.

Our judgements about our actual duty in concrete situations have none of the certainty that attaches to our recognition of the general principles of duty. A statement is certain, i.e. as an expression of knowledge, only in one or other of two cases: when it is either self-evident, or a valid conclusion from self-evident premisses. And our judgements about our particular duties have neither of these characters. (1) They are not self-evident. Where a possible act is seen to have two characteristics, in virtue of one of which it is *prima facie* right, and in virtue of the other *prima facie* wrong, we are (I think) well aware that we are not certain whether we ought or ought not to do it; that whether we do it or not, we are taking a moral risk. We come in the long run, after consideration, to think one duty more pressing than the other, but we do not feel certain that it is so. And though we do not always recognize that a possible act has two such characteristics, and though there *may* be cases in which it has not, we are never certain that any particular possible act has not, and therefore never certain that it is right, nor certain that it is wrong. For, to go no further in the analysis, it is enough to point out that any particular act will in all probability in the course of time contribute to the bringing about of good or of evil for many human beings, and thus have a *prima facie* rightness or wrongness of which we know nothing. (2) Again, our judgements about our particular duties are not logical conclusions from self-evident premises. The only possible premisses would be the general principles stating their *prima facie* rightness or wrongness *qua* having the different characteristics they do have; and even if we could (as we cannot) apprehend the extent to which an act will tend on the one hand, for example, to bring about advantages for our benefactors, and on the other hand to bring about disadvantages for fellow men who are not our benefactors, there is no principle by which we can draw the conclusion that it is on the whole right or on the whole wrong. In this respect the judgement as to the rightness of a particular act is just like the judgement as to the beauty of a particular natural object or work of art. A poem is, for instance, in respect of certain qualities beautiful and in respect of certain others not beautiful; and our judgement as to the degree of beauty it possesses on the whole is never reached by logical reasoning from the apprehension of its particular beauties or particular defects. Both in this and in the moral case we have more or less probable opinions which are not logically justified conclusions from the general principles that are recognized as self-evident.

There is therefore much truth in the description of the right act as a fortunate act. If we cannot be certain that it is right, it is our good fortune if the act we do is the right act. This consideration does not, however, make the doing of our duty a mere matter of chance. There is a parallel here between the doing of duty and the doing of what will be to our personal advantage. We never *know* what act will in the long run be to our advantage. Yet is is certain that we are more likely in general to secure our advantage if we estimate to the best of our ability the probable tendencies of our actions in this respect, than if we act on caprice. And similarly we are more likely to do our duty if we reflect to the best of our ability on the *prima facie* rightness or wrongness of various possible acts in virtue

of the characteristics we perceive them to have, than if we act without reflection. With this greater likelihood we must be content.

Many people would be inclined to say that the right act for me is not that whose general nature I have been describing, *viz.* that which if I were omniscient I should see to be my duty, but that which on all the evidence available to me I should think to be my duty. But suppose that from the state of partial knowledge in which I think act A to be my duty, I could pass to a state of perfect knowledge in which I saw act B to be my duty, should I not say 'act B was the right act for me to do'? I should no doubt add 'though I am not to be blamed for doing act A.' But in adding this, am I not passing from the question 'what is right' to the question 'what is morally good'? At the same time I am not making the *full* passage from the one notion to the other; for in order that the act should be morally good, or an act I am not to be blamed for doing, it must not merely be the act which it is reasonable for me to think my duty; it must also be done for that reason, or from some other morally good motive. Thus the conception of the right act as the act which it is reasonable for me to think my duty is an unsatisfactory compromise between the true notion of the right act and the notion of the morally good action.

The general principles of duty are obviously not self-evident from the beginning of our lives. How do they come to be so? The answer is, that they come to be self-evident to us just as mathematical axioms do. We find by experience that this couple of matches and that couple make four matches, that this couple of balls on a wire and that couple make four balls; and by reflection on these and similar discoveries we come to see that it is of the nature of two and two to make four. In a precisely similar way, we see the *prima facie* rightness of an act which would be the fulfilment of a particular promise, and of another which would be the fulfilment of another promise, and when we have reached sufficient maturity to think in general terms, we apprehend *prima facie* rightness to belong to the nature of any fulfilment of promise. What comes first in time is the apprehension of the self-evident *prima facie* rightness of an individual act of a particular type. From this we come by reflection to apprehend the self-evident general principle of *prima facie* duty. From this, too, perhaps along with the apprehension of the self-evident *prima facie* rightness of the same act in virtue of its having another characteristic as well, and perhaps in spite of the apprehension of its *prima facie* wrongness in virtue of its having some third characteristic, we come to believe something not self-evident at all, but an object of probable opinion, *viz.* that this particular act is (not *prima facie* but) actually right.

In this respect there is an important difference between rightness and mathematical properties. A triangle which is isosceles necessarily has two of its angles equal, whatever other characteristics the triangle may have—whatever, for instance, be its area, or the size of its third angle. The equality of the two angles is a parti-resultant attribute.[9] And the same is true of all mathematical attributes. It is true, I may add, of *prima facie* rightness. But no act is ever, in virtue of falling under some general description, necessarily actually right; its rightness depends on its whole nature[10] and not on any element in it. The reason is that no mathematical object (no figure, for instance, or angle) ever has two characteristics that tend to give it opposite resultant characteristics, while moral acts

often (as every one knows) and indeed always (as on reflection we must admit) have different characteristics that tend to make them at the same time *prima facie* right and *prima facie* wrong; there is probably no act, for instance, which does good to any one without doing harm to some one else, and *vice versa*.

Supposing it to be agreed, as I think on reflection it must, that no one *means* by 'right' just 'productive of the best possible consequences,' or 'optimific,' the attributes 'right' and 'optimific' might stand in either of two kinds of relation to each other. (1) They might be so related that we could apprehend *a priori*, either immediately or deductively, that any act that is optimific is right and any act that is right is optimific, as we can apprehend that any triangle that is equilateral is equiangular and *vice versa*. Professor Moore's view is, I think, that the coextensiveness of 'right' and 'optimific' is apprehended immediately.[11] He rejects the possibility of any proof of it. Or (2) the two attributes might be such that the question whether they are invariably connected had to be answered by means of an inductive inquiry. Now at first sight it might seem as if the constant connexion of the two attributes could be immediately apprehended. It might seem absurd to suggest that it could be right for any one to do an act which would produce consequences less good than those which would be produced by some other act in his power. Yet a little thought will convince us that this is not absurd. The type of case in which it is easier to see that this is so is, perhaps, that in which one has made a promise. In such a case we all think that *prima facie* it is our duty to fulfil the promise irrespective of the precise goodness of the total consequences. And though we do not think it is necessarily our actual or absolute duty to do so, we are far from thinking that any, even the slightest, gain in the value of the total

---

[9] Cf. pp. 28, 122–3 [in *The Right and the Good*].
[10] To avoid complicating unduly the statement of the general view I am putting forward, I have here rather overstated it. Any act is the origination of a great variety of things many of which make no difference to its rightness or wrongness. But there are always many elements in its nature (i.e. in what it is the origination of) that make a difference to its rightness or wrongness, and no element in its nature can be dismissed without consideration as indifferent.

[11] *Ethics*, 181.

consequences will necessarily justify us in doing something else instead. Suppose, to simplify the case by abstraction, that the fulfilment of a promise to A would produce 1,000 units of good[12] for him, but that by doing some other act I could produce 1,001 units of good for B, to whom I have made no promise, the other consequences of the two acts being of equal value; should we really think it self-evident that it was our duty to do the second act and not the first? I think not. We should, I fancy, hold that only a much greater disparity of value between the total consequences would justify us in failing to discharge our *prima facie* duty to A. After all, a promise is a promise, and is not to be treated so lightly as the theory we are examining would imply. What, exactly, a promise is, is not so easy to determine, but we are surely agreed that it constitutes a serious moral limitation to our freedom of action. To produce the 1,001 units of good for B rather than fulfil our promise to A would be to take, not perhaps our duty as philanthropists too seriously, but certainly our duty as makers of promises too lightly.

Or consider another phase of the same problem. If I have promised to confer on A a particular benefit containing 1,000 units of good, is it self-evident that if by doing some different act I could produce 1,001 units of good for A himself (the other consequences of the two acts being supposed equal in value), it would be right for me to do so? Again, I think not. Apart from my general *prima facie* duty to do A what good I can, I have another *prima facie* duty to do him the particular service I have promised to do him, and this is not to be set aside in consequence of a disparity of good of the order of 1,001 to 1,000, though a much greater disparity might justify me in so doing.

[12] I am assuming that good is objectively quantitative (cf. pp. 142–4), but not that we can accurately assign an exact quantitative measure to it. Since it is of a definite amount, we can make the *supposition* that its amount is so-and-so, though we cannot with any confidence *assert* that it is.

Or again, suppose that A is a very good and B a very bad man, should I then, even when I have made no promise, think it self-evidently right to produce 1,001 units of good for B rather than 1,000 for A? Surely not. I should be sensible of a *prima facie* duty of justice, i.e. of producing a distribution of goods in proportion to merit, which is not outweighed by such a slight disparity in the total goods to be produced.

Such instances—and they might easily be added to—make it clear that there is no self-evident connexion between the attributes 'right' and 'optimific.' The theory we are examining has a certain attractiveness when applied to our decision that a particular act is our duty (though I have tried to show that it does not agree with our actual moral judgements even here). But it is not even possible when applied to our recognition of *prima facie* duty. For if it were self-evident that the right coincides with the optimific, it should be self-evident that what is *prima facie* right is *prima facie* optimific. But whereas we are certain that keeping a promise is *prima facie* right, we are not certain that it is *prima facie* optimific (though we are perhaps certain that it is *prima facie* bonific). Our certainty that it is *prima facie* right depends not on its consequences but on its being the fulfilment of a promise. The theory we are examining involves too much difference between the evident ground of our conviction about *prima facie* duty and the alleged ground of our conviction about actual duty.

The coextensiveness of the right and the optimific is, then, not self-evident. And I can see no way of proving it deductively; nor, so far as I know, has any one tried to do so. There remains the question whether it can be established inductively. Such an inquiry, to be conclusive, would have to be very thorough and extensive. We should have to take a large variety of the acts which we, to the best of our ability, judge to be right. We should have to trace as far as possible their consequences, not only for the persons directly affected but also for those indirectly affected, and to these no limit can be set. To make our inquiry thoroughly conclusive, we should have to do what we cannot do, *viz.* trace these consequences into an unending future. And even to make it reasonably conclusive, we should have to trace them far into the future. It is clear that the most we could possibly say is that a large variety of typical acts that are judged right appear, so far as we can trace their consequences, to produce more good than any other acts possible to the agents in the circumstances. And such a result falls far short of proving the constant connexion of the two attributes. But it is surely clear that no inductive inquiry justifying even this result has ever been carried through. The advocates of utilitarian systems have been so much persuaded either of the identity or of the self-evident connexion of the attributes 'right' and 'optimific' (or 'felicific') that they have not attempted even such an inductive inquiry as is possible. And in view of the enormous complexity of the task and the inevitable inconclusiveness of the result, it is worth no one's while to make the attempt. What, after all, would be gained by it? If, as I have tried to show, for an act to be right and to be optimific are not the same thing, and an act's being optimific is not even the ground of its being right, then if we could ask ourselves (though the question is really unmeaning) which we ought to do, right acts because they are right or optimific acts because they are optimific, our answer must be 'the former.' If they are optimific as well as right, that is interesting but not morally important; if not, we still ought to do them (which is only another way of saying that they *are* the right acts), and the question whether they are optimific has no importance for moral theory.

There is one direction in which a fairly serious attempt has been made to show the connexion of the attributes 'right' and 'optimific.' One of the most evident facts of our moral consciousness is the sense which

we have of the sanctity of promises, a sense which does not, on the face of it, involve the thought that one will be bringing more good into existence by fulfilling the promise than by breaking it. It is plain, I think, that in our normal thought we consider that the fact that we have made a promise is in itself sufficient to create a duty of keeping it, the sense of duty resting on remembrance of the past promise and not on thoughts of the future consequences of its fulfilment. Utilitarianism tries to show that this is not so, that the sanctity of promises rests on the good consequences of the fulfilment of them and the bad consequences of their non-fulfilment. It does so in this way: it points out that when you break a promise you not only fail to confer a certain advantage on your promisee but you diminish his confidence, and indirectly the confidence of others, in the fulfilment of promises. You thus strike a blow at one of the devices that have been found most useful in the relations between man and man—the device on which, for example, the whole system of commercial credit rests— and you tend to bring about a state of things wherein each man, being entirely unable to rely on the keeping of promises by others, will have to do everything for himself, to the enormous impoverishment of human well-being.

To put the matter otherwise, utilitarians say that when a promise ought to be kept it is because the total good to be produced by keeping it is greater than the total good to be produced by breaking it, the former including as its main element the maintenance and strengthening of general mutual confidence, and the latter being greatly diminished by a weakening of this confidence. They say, in fact, that the case I put some pages back[13] never arises—the case in which by fulfilling a promise I shall bring into being 1,000 units of good for my promisee, and by breaking it 1,001 units of good for some one else, the

---

[13] p. 34 [in *The Right and the Good*].

other effects of the two acts being of equal value. The other effects, they say, never are of equal value. By keeping my promise I am helping to strengthen the system of mutual confidence; by breaking it I am helping to weaken this; so that really the first act produces $1,000 + x$ units of good, and the second $1,000 - y$ units, and the difference between $+ x$ and $- y$ is enough to outweigh the slight superiority in the *immediate* effects of the second act. In answer to this it may be pointed out that there must be *some* amount of good that exceeds the difference between $+ x$ and $- y$ (i.e. exceeds $x+y$); say, $x+y+z$. Let us suppose the *immediate* good effects of the second act to be assessed not at 1,001 but at $1,000 + x + y + z$. Then its net good effects are $1,000 + x + z$, i.e. greater than those of the fulfilment of the promise; and the utilitarian is bound to say forthwith that the promise should be broken. Now, we may ask whether that is really the way we think about promises? Do we really think that the production of the slightest balance of good, no matter who will enjoy it, by the breach of a promise frees us from the obligation to keep our promise? We need not doubt that a system by which promises are made and kept is one that has great advantages for the general well-being. But that is not the whole truth. To make a promise is not merely to adopt an ingenious device for promoting the general well-being, it is to put oneself in a new relation to one person in particular, a relation which creates a specifically new *prima facie* duty to him, not reducible to the duty of promoting the general well-being of society. By all means let us try to foresee the net good effects of keeping one's promise and the net good effects of breaking it, but even if we assess the first at $1,000 + x$ and the second at $1,000 + x + z$, the question still remains whether it is not our duty to fulfil the promise. It may be suspected, too, that the effect of a single keeping or breaking of a promise in strengthening or weakening the

fabric of mutual confidence is greatly exaggerated by the theory we are examining. And if we suppose two men dying together alone, do we think that the duty of one to fulfil before he dies a promise he has made to the other would be extinguished by the fact that neither act would have any effect on the general confidence? Any one who holds this may be suspected of not having reflected on what a promise is.

I conclude that the attributes 'right' and 'optimific' are not identical, and that we do not know either by intuition, by deduction, or by induction that they coincide in their application, still less that the latter is the foundation of the former. It must be added, however, that if we are ever under no special obligation such as that of fidelity to a promisee or of gratitude to a benefactor, we ought to do what will produce most good; and that even when we are under a special obligation the tendency of acts to promote general good is one of the main factors in determining whether they are right.

In what has preceded, a good deal of use has been made of 'what we really think' about moral questions; a certain theory has been rejected because it does not agree with what we really think. It might be said that this is in principle wrong; that we should not be content to expound what our present moral consciousness tells us but should aim at a criticism of our existing moral consciousness in the light of theory. Now I do not doubt that the moral consciousness of men has in detail undergone a good deal of modification as regards the things we think right, at the hands of moral theory. But if we are told, for instance, that we should give up our view that there is a special obligatoriness attaching to the keeping of promises because it is self-evident that the only duty is to produce as much good as possible, we have to ask ourselves whether we really, when we reflect, *are* convinced that this is self-evident, and whether we really *can* get rid of our view that promise-keeping has a bindingness independent of productiveness of maximum good. In my own experience I find that I cannot, in spite of a very genuine attempt to do so; and I venture to think that most people will find the same, and that just because they cannot lose the sense of special obligation, they cannot accept as self-evident, or even as true, the theory which would require them to do so. In fact it seems, on reflection, self-evident that a promise, simply as such, is something that *prima facie* ought to be kept, and it does *not*, on reflection, seem self-evident that production of maximum good is the only thing that makes an act obligatory. And to ask us to give up at the bidding of a theory our actual apprehension of what is right and what is wrong seems like asking people to repudiate their actual experience of beauty, at the bidding of a theory which says 'only that which satisfies such and such conditions can be beautiful.' If what I have called our actual apprehension is (as I would maintain that it is) truly an apprehension, i.e. an instance of knowledge, the request is nothing less than absurd.

I would maintain, in fact, that what we are apt to describe as 'what we think' about moral questions contains a considerable amount that we do not think but know, and that this forms the standard by reference to which the truth of any moral theory has to be tested, instead of having itself to be tested by reference to any theory. I hope that I have in what precedes indicated what in my view these elements of knowledge are that are involved in our ordinary moral consciousness.

It would be a mistake to found a natural science on 'what we really think,' i.e. on what reasonably thoughtful and well-educated people think about the subjects of the science before they have studied them scientifically. For such opinions are interpretations, and often misinterpretations, of sense-experience; and the man of science must appeal from these to sense-experience itself, which furnishes his real data. In ethics no such appeal is possible. We have no more direct way of access to the facts about rightness and goodness and about what things are right or good, than by thinking about them; the moral convictions of thoughtful and well-educated people are the data of ethics just as sense-perceptions are the data of a natural science. Just as some of the latter have to be rejected as illusory, so have some of the former; but as the latter are rejected only when they are in conflict with other more accurate sense-perceptions, the former are rejected only when they are in conflict with other convictions which stand better the test of reflection. The existing body of moral convictions of the best people is the cumulative product of the moral reflection of many generations, which has developed an extremely delicate power of appreciation of moral distinctions; and this the theorist cannot afford to treat with anything other than the greatest respect. The verdicts of the moral consciousness of the best people are the foundation on which he must build; though he must first compare them with one another and eliminate any contradictions they may contain.

It is worth while to try to state more definitely the nature of the acts that are right. We may try to state first what (if anything) is the universal nature of *all* the acts that are right. It is obvious that any of the acts that we do has countless effects, directly or indirectly, on countless people, and the probability is that any act, however right it be, will have adverse effects (though these may be very trivial) on some innocent people. Similarly, any wrong act will probably have beneficial effects on some deserving people. Every act therefore, viewed in some aspects, will be *prima facie* right, and viewed in others, *prima facie* wrong, and right acts can be distinguished from wrong acts only as being those which, of all those possible for the agent in the circumstances, have the greatest balance of *prima facie* rightness, in those respects in which they are *prima facie* right, over their *prima facie* wrongness, in those respects in which they are *prima facie* wrong—*prima facie* rightness and wrongness being understood in the sense previously explained. For the estimation of the comparative stringency of these *prima facie* obligations no general rules can, so far as I can see, be laid down. We can only say that a great deal of stringency belongs to the duties of 'perfect obligation' —the duties of keeping our promises, of repairing wrongs we have done, and of returning the equivalent of services we have received. For the rest, ἐν τῇ αἰσθήσει ἡ κρίσις.[14] This sense of our particular duty in particular circumstances, preceded and informed by the fullest reflection we can bestow on the act in all its bearings, is highly fallible, but it is the only guide we have to our duty.

When we turn to consider the nature of individual right acts, the first point to which attention should be called is that any act may be correctly described in an indefinite, and in principle infinite, number of ways. An act is the production of a change in the state of affairs (if we ignore, for simplicity's sake, the comparatively few cases in which it is the maintenance of an existing state of affairs; cases which, I think, raise no special difficulty). Now the only changes we can *directly* produce are changes in our own bodies or in our own minds. But these are not, as such, what as a rule we think it our duty to produce. Consider some comparatively simple act, such as telling the truth or fulfilling a promise. In the first case what I produce directly are movements of my vocal organs. But what I think it my duty to produce is a true view in some one else's mind about some fact, and between my movement of my vocal organs and this result there intervenes a series of physical events and events in his mind. Again, in the second case, I may have promised, for instance, to return a

book to a friend. I may be able, by a series of movements of my legs and hands, to place it in his hands. But what I am just as likely to do, and to think I have done my duty in doing, is to send it by a messenger or to hand it to his servant or to send it by post; and in each of these cases what I *do* directly is worthless in itself and is connected by a series of intermediate links with what I do think it is my duty to bring about, *viz.* his receiving what I have promised to return to him. This being so, it *seems* as if what I *do* has no obligatoriness in itself and as if one or other of three accounts should be given of the matter, each of which makes rightness not belong to what I do, considered in its own nature.

(1) One of them would be that what is obligatory is not *doing* anything in the natural sense of producing any change in the state of affairs, but *aiming at* something—at, for instance, my friend's reception of the book. But this account will not do. For (*a*) to aim at something is to act from a motive consisting of the wish to bring that thing about. But we have seen[15] that motive never forms part of the content of our duty; if anything is certain about morals, that, I think, is certain. And (*b*) if I have promised to return the book to my friend, I obviously do not fulfil my promise and do my duty merely by aiming at his receiving the book; I must see that he actually receives it. (2) A more plausible account is that which says I must do that which is likely to produce the result. But this account is open to the second of these objections, and probably also the first. For in the first place, however likely my act may seem, even on careful consideration, and even however likely it may in fact be, to produce the result, if it does not produce it I have not done what I promised to do, i.e. have not done my duty. And secondly, when it is said that I ought to do what is likely to produce the result, what is *probably* meant is that I ought to do a certain thing as a result of the wish to produce a

[14] 'The decision rests with perception.' Arist. *Nic. Eth.* 1109 b 23, 1126 b 4.

[15] pp. 5–6 [in *The Right and the Good*].

certain result, and of the thought that my act is likely to produce it; and this again introduces motive into the content of duty. (3) Much the most plausible of the three accounts is that which says, 'I ought to do that which will actually produce a certain result.' This escapes objection (*b*). Whether it escapes objection (*a*) or not depends on what exactly is meant. If it is meant that I ought to do a certain thing from the wish to produce a certain result and the thought that it will do so, the account is still open to objection (*a*). But if it is meant simply that the reason why I ought to do it is that it will produce a certain result, objection (*a*) is avoided. Now the account in its second form is that which utilitarianism gives. It says what is right is certain acts, not certain acts motivated in a certain way; and it says that acts are never right by their own nature but by virtue of the goodness of their actual results. And this account is, I think, clearly nearer the truth than one which makes the rightness of an act depend on the goodness of either the *intended* or the *likely* results.

Nevertheless, this account appears not to be the true one. For it implies that what we consider right or our duty is what we do *directly*. It is this, e.g. the packing up and posting of the book, that derives its moral significance not from its own nature but from its consequences. But this is *not* what we should describe, strictly, as our duty; our duty is to fulfil our promise, i.e. to put the book into our friend's possession. This we consider obligatory in its own nature, just because it is a fulfilment of promise, and not because of *its* consequences. But, it might be replied by the utilitarian, I do not do this; I only do something that leads up to this, and what I do has no moral significance in itself but only because of its consequences. In answer to this, however, we may point out that a cause produces not only its immediate, but also its remote consequences, and the latter no less than the former. I, therefore, not only produce the immediate movements of parts of my body but also my friend's reception of the book, which results from these. Or, if this be objected to on the grounds that I can hardly be said to have produced my friend's reception of the book when I have packed and posted it, owing to the time that has still to elapse before he receives it, and that to say I have produced the result hardly does justice to the part played by the Post Office, we may at least say that I have *secured* my friend's reception of the book. What I do is as truly describable in this way as by saying that it is the packing and posting of a book. (It is equally truly describable in many other ways; e.g. I have provided a few moments' employment for Post Office officials. But this is irrelevant to the argument.) And if we ask ourselves whether it is *qua* the packing and posting of a book, or *qua* the securing of my friend's getting what I have promised to return to him, that my action is right, it is clear that it is in the second capacity that it is right; and in this capacity, the only capacity in which it is right, it is right by its own nature and not because of its consequences.

This account may no doubt be objected to, on the ground that we are ignoring the freedom of will of the other agents—the sorter and the postman, for instance—who are equally responsible for the result. Society, it may be said, is not like a machine, in which event follows event by rigorous necessity. Some one may, for instance, in the exercise of his freedom of will, steal the book on the way. But it is to be observed that I have excluded that case, and any similar case. I am dealing with the case in which I secure my friend's receiving the book; and if he does not receive it I have not secured his receiving it. If on the other hand the book reaches its destination, that alone shows that, the system of things being what it is, the trains by which the book travels and the railway lines along which it travels being such as they are and subject to the laws they are subject to, the postal officials who handle it being such as they are, having the motives they have and being subject to the psychological laws they are subject to, my posting the book was the one further thing which was sufficient to procure my friend's receiving it. If *it* had not been sufficient, the result would not have followed. The attainment of the result proves the sufficiency of the means. The objection in fact rests on the supposition that there can be unmotived action, i.e. an event without a cause, and may be refuted by reflection on the universality of the law of causation.

It is equally true that non-attainment of the result proves the insufficiency of the means. If the book had been destroyed in a railway accident or stolen by a dishonest postman, that would prove that my immediate act was not sufficient to produce the desired result. We get the curious consequence that however carelessly I pack or dispatch the book, if it comes to hand I have done my duty, and however carefully I have acted, if the book does not come to hand I have not done my duty. Success and failure are the only test, and a sufficient test, of the performance of duty. Of course, I should deserve more praise in the second case than in the first; but that is an entirely different question; we must not mix up the question of right and wrong with that of the morally good and the morally bad. And that our conclusion is not as strange as at first sight it might seem is shown by the fact that if the carelessly dispatched book comes to hand, it is not my duty to send another copy, while if the carefully dispatched book does not come to hand I must send another copy to replace it. In the first case I have not my duty still to do, which shows that I have done it; in the second I have it still to do, which shows that I have not done it.

We have reached the result that my act is right *qua* being an ensuring of one of the particular states of affairs of which it is an ensuring, *viz*, in the case we have taken, of my friend's receiving the book I have promised to return to him. But this answer requires some correction; for it refers only to the *prima facie* rightness of my act. If to be a fulfilment of promise were a sufficient ground of the rightness of an act, all fulfilments of promises would be right, whereas it seems clear that there are cases in which some other *prima facie* duty overrides the *prima facie* duty of fulfilling a promise. The more correct answer would be that the ground of the actual rightness of the act is that, of all acts possible for the agent in the circumstances, it is that whose *prima facie* rightness in the respects in which it is *prima facie* right most outweighs its *prima facie* wrongness in any respects in which it is *prima facie* wrong. But since its *prima facie* rightness is mainly due to its being a fulfilment of promise, we may call its being so the salient element in the ground of its rightness.

Subject to this qualification, then, it is as being the production (or if we prefer the word, the securing or ensuring) of the reception by my friend of what I have promised him (or in other words as the fulfilment of my promise) that my act is right. It is not right as a packing and posting of a book. The packing and posting of the book is only incidentally right, right only because it is a fulfilment of promise, which is what is directly or essentially right.

Our duty, then, is not to do certain things which will produce certain results. Our acts, at any rate our acts of special obligation, are not right because they will produce certain results—which is the view common to all forms of utilitarianism. To say that is to say that in the case in question what is essentially right is to pack and post a book, whereas what is essentially right is to secure the possession by my friend of what I have promised to return to him. An act is not right because it, being one thing, produces good results different from itself; it is right because it is itself the production of a certain state of affairs. Such production is right in itself, apart from any consequence.

But, it might be said, this analysis applies only to acts of special obligation; the utilitarian account still holds good for the acts in which we are not under a special obligation to any person or set of persons but only under that of augmenting the general good. Now merely to have established that there *are* special obligations to do certain things irrespective of their consequences would be already to have made a considerable breach in the utilitarian walls; for according to utilitarianism there is no such thing, there is only the single obligation to promote the general good. But, further, on reflection it is clear that just as (in the case we have taken) my act is not only the packing and posting of a book but the fulfilling of a promise, and just as it is in the latter capacity and not in the former that it is my duty, so an act whereby I augment the general good is not only, let us say, the writing of a begging letter on behalf of a hospital, but the producing (or ensuring) of whatever good ensues therefrom, and it is in the latter capacity and not in the former that it is right, if it is right. That which is right is right not because it is an act, one thing, which will produce another thing, an increase of the general welfare, but because it is itself the producing of an increase in the general welfare. Or, to qualify this in the necessary way, its being the production of an increase in the general welfare is the salient element in the ground of its rightness. Just as before we were led to recognize the *prima facie* rightness of the fulfilment of promises, we are now led to recognize the *prima facie* rightness of promoting the general welfare. In both cases we have to recognize the *intrinsic* rightness of a certain type of act, not depending on its consequences but on its own nature.

Universal Prescriptivism

R. M. HARE

2.6. An illuminating way of approaching the thesis which I am maintaining (namely universal prescriptivism) is to look upon it as retaining what is sound in descriptivism (natural and non-natural), and adding to it an account of the other essential element in the meaning of moral judgements, the prescriptive. The truth in naturalism is that moral terms do indeed have descriptive meaning. It is not the only element in their meaning, and it is therefore misleading to refer to it, as do the naturalists, as *the* meaning of a moral term; but in virtue of possessing this descriptive meaning moral judgements are universalizable, and naturalism has the merit of implying this.

Another way of putting the point is this: both naturalism and my own view lay great stress on the fact that, when we make a moral judgement about something, we make it *because* of the possession by it of certain non-moral properties. Thus both views hold that moral judgements about particular things are made for reasons; and the notion of a reason, as always, brings with it the notion of a rule which lays down that something is a reason for something else. Both views, therefore, involve universalizability. The difference is that the naturalist thinks that the rule in question is a descriptive meaning-rule which exhausts the meaning of the moral term used; whereas in my own view the rule, though it is very analogous to a descriptive meaning-rule, and though, therefore, it is quite legitimate to speak of the 'descriptive

Reprinted from *Freedom and Reason* by R. M. Hare by permission of the author and the Clarendon Press, Oxford.

meaning' of moral terms, does not exhaust their meaning (*LM* 7.1 ff). For a naturalist, therefore, the inference from a non-moral description of something to a moral conclusion about it is an inference whose validity is due solely to the meaning of the words in it. The rule permitting the inference would be simply the descriptive meaning-rule for the moral term used, and to accept such a rule would be simply to accept a meaning for the moral word. Conversely, if the meaning of the moral word be once understood, there can, for the naturalist, be no departing from the inference-rule; it is impossible to refuse the conclusion of the inference without altering the meaning of the word. But for me the position is different. Since the 'descriptive meaning' of moral terms does not exhaust their meaning, the other element in their meaning can make a difference to the logical behaviour of these terms in inferences. This is the point at issue in the controversy about whether an 'ought' can be derived from an 'is'.

2.7. It is now time, therefore, to ask what effect the introduction of the additional, prescriptive element in their meaning has upon the logical character of moral words.[1] I shall not try at this stage to de-

[1] It must be emphasized that it is not part of my thesis that moral words are used prescriptively *in all contexts*; and it makes sense to call them 'moral' even when they are not so used. But on the prescriptive uses the other uses depend (4.2, 5.6 ff; *LM* 7.5, 9.3, 11.3). 'Prescriptive' is to be understood here in a wide sense to include permissions (10.5). Thus the statement that an act is morally permissible is in this sense prescriptive. The logical relations between prescriptions and permissions are too complex to be dealt with here.

fine the word 'prescriptive'. Its meaning will not become clear until much later. But let us start by supposing that we have a word which carries the descriptive meaning of some value-word, but lacks its prescriptive meaning. Such a word would be, in its logical character, just like an ordinary descriptive word. To know how to use it, we should have to know to what kind of things it was properly applied, and no more. Now let us suppose that we try to *add* prescriptive meaning to such a word, thereby, according to my theory, recreating the original value-word. Let us, to take the same example as I used in *LM* 7.2, coin the word 'doog' to carry the descriptive meaning of the word 'good as used in the sentence 'He is a good man', without its prescriptive meaning. Let us first notice, as before, that the statement 'X is a doog man' will be universalizable. Anybody who makes it will be committed to the view that some man who was exactly like X, or like him in the relevant respects, would also be a doog man; and the relevant respects would be simply those which the descriptive meaning-rule for the word 'doog' specified.

Now what happens if we try to add prescriptive meaning to such a word? The inevitable consequence of such an addition is that the descriptive meaning-rule becomes more than a mere meaning-rule. Since our value-word 'good' is to be used with the same descriptive meaning as 'doog' the *content* of the rule will remain the same; but its logical character will change. The rule will still say that it is proper to apply the word 'good' to a certain kind of man; but in saying this (in enunciating the rule) we shall be doing more than specifying the meaning of the word. For in saying that it is proper to call a certain kind of man good (for example a man who feeds his children, does not beat his wife, &c.) we are not just explaining the meaning of a word; it is not mere verbal instruction that we are giving, but something more: *moral* instruction. In learning

that, of all kinds of man, *this* kind can be called good, our hearer will be learning something synthetic, a moral principle. It will be synthetic because of the added prescriptiveness of the word 'good'; in learning it, he will be learning, not merely to use a word in a certain way, but to commend, or prescribe for imitation, a certain kind of man. A man who wholeheartedly accepts such a rule is likely to *live*, not merely *talk*, differently from one who does not. Our descriptive meaning-rule has thus turned into a synthetic moral principle.

This change brings other consequences with it. To illustrate them, let us consider the context of the words' use in more detail. I have so far been assuming that the society which is using these expressions 'good man' and 'doog man' has very inflexible standards of human excellence, and that therefore no question arises of the descriptive meaning of either word changing. But in the real world standards of human excellence change (for example, on the wrongness of wife-beating);[2] and therefore, if the expression 'good man' is to be used (as it is) to express changing standards, its logical character has to be such as to allow for this. This is done by making the prescriptive meaning of the word primary, and its descriptive meaning secondary.

It is not *necessary* that a value-word should be treated in this way. There are other moral words whose prescriptive meaning is secondary to their descriptive: for example 'industrious' (*LM* 7.5), 'honest', and 'courageous'. Let us imagine a society which places a negative value upon industry; there seem to be such societies in the world, in which the industrious man is regarded as a mere nuisance. Such a society could never (if it spoke English) express its moral standards by using the word 'industrious', like us, for commending peo-

[2] See G. M. Trevelyan, *English Social History*, p. 65: 'But the "lordship" was held [in the fifteenth century] to be vested in the husband, and when he asserted it by fist and stick, he was seldom blamed by public opinion.'

ple, only with a totally different descriptive meaning—i.e. commending them for totally different qualities, for example that of doing as little work as possible. If they did that, we should say that they had changed *the meaning* of the English word 'industrious'. The descriptive meaning of 'industrious' is much too firmly attached to the word for this sort of thing to be allowed; these people would be much more likely to use the word in its normal descriptive meaning, but neutrally or pejoratively; i.e. to give it no, or an adverse, prescriptive meaning.

But it is not so mandatory, though it is possible, to treat the word 'good', like the word 'industrious', as one whose descriptive meaning is primary (*LM* 7.5). If we came to disapprove of industry, we should not stop calling the industrious man industrious; but, if we had previously called him a good man because, among other virtues, he was industrious, we should, if we came to disapprove of his industry very much, stop calling him good. This is because the commendation which is the prescriptive force of the word 'good' is more firmly attached to it than any part of its descriptive meaning; we should therefore be likely to keep the word 'good' as a prescriptive word (part of our vocabulary of commendation), and alter its descriptive meaning.

It is useful to have in our language both secondarily evaluative words like 'industrious' and primarily evaluative words like 'good'; and we should therefore be suspicious, if any philosopher seeks to persuade us that we ought in the interest of concreteness to neglect the study of words like 'good' and concentrate on words like 'industrious' and 'courageous' (10.1). The object of such a manœuvre might be to convince us that *all* moral words have their descriptive meaning irremovably attached to them; but, fortunately for the usefulness of moral language in expressing changing standards, this is not so. To take this line would be to give an account of moral language which is, so far as it goes, true, but

not sufficiently general (in the sense in which Newtonian mechanics is not sufficiently general). The account would suffice for the moral language of an irrevocably closed society, in which a change in moral standards was unthinkable; but it does not do justice to the moral language of a society like our own, in which some people sometimes think about ultimate moral questions, and in which, therefore, morality changes. Orwell's Newspeak in *1984* was a language so designed that in it dangerous thoughts could not be expressed. Much of Oldspeak is like this too—if we want, in the Southern States, to speak to a negro as an equal, we cannot do so by addressing him as a nigger; the word 'nigger' incapsulates the standards of the society, and, if we were confined to it, we could not break free of those standards. But fortunately we are not so confined; our language, as we have it, *can* be a vehicle for new ideas.

2.8 It must be noticed that the mere fact that the descriptive meanings of moral words can alter does not distinguish them from ordinary descriptive words. All words can alter their meaning; dictionaries are full of sub-headings which begin 'Obs.'. And even in the case of words in current use their meanings vary from occasion to occasion within at times quite wide limits. And there is 'family resemblance' and 'open texture' and all that. Some people have been misled into thinking that, since descriptive words have these features, and since what has caused a lot of the trouble with value-words is their shifting descriptive meanings, the trouble can be cleared up without distinguishing between the two classes of words. The premisses of this inference are perfectly true, but the conclusion misses the point. Value-words *are* indeed like descriptive words, both in that they have descriptive meanings, and in that the descriptive meanings of both are alterable, flexible, and so on. So, if we cared to concentrate on the resemblances between the two classes of words, and ignore their differences, we could call them all 'descriptive words', meaning by this 'words having descriptive meaning'. But to do this would be to neglect an important (indeed essential) part of the meaning of moral and other value-words; and the philosopher who wishes to do justice to this will have to be more careful in choosing his terminology.

The terminology to which I have myself tried to be consistent is the following. An expression which, in a certain context, has descriptive meaning and no other, I call a descriptive term, word, or expression, as used in that context; one which has prescriptive meaning (whether or not it also has descriptive meaning) I call a prescriptive term; and one which has both kinds of meaning I call an evaluative term. A value-judgement or evaluative judgement is a judgement in which such a term is used; on the other hand the mention of an evaluative term inside quotation marks, or similarly 'insulated', does not make a judgement evaluative. Not all moral judgements are value-judgements (*LM* 11.3). In *The Language of Morals* I used the words 'evaluative meaning' for the prescriptive meaning of evaluative expressions. This had some advantages, as being a less question-begging expression which did not presuppose that what gave these terms their evaluative meaning was their prescriptivity; but in the end it turned out to be in the interests of clarity to make this, in effect, true by definition (LM 11.2; 5.7); and so in the present context I feel at liberty to use the words 'prescriptive meaning' which do carry this presupposition, and are somewhat clearer in that they avow it. To give examples of the use of these terms: 'red', in most contexts, is a descriptive term (though not when used of communists by conservatives); 'good' is, as typically used, an evaluative term, and so are 'right' and 'ought'.[3] These terms are primarily evalua-

tive; words like 'industrious', 'honest', and 'courageous' are, as explained above, secondarily evaluative. All words which are evaluative (whether primarily or secondarily) are also prescriptive; but there are expressions which are prescriptive but not evaluative (because they do not carry descriptive meaning as well). The ordinary singular imperative—or rather, to be strictly accurate, its 'neustic' (*LM* 2.1)—is of this kind.

Now the philosophers to whom I referred just now point out (rightly) that value-words are like ordinary descriptive words in that they both have descriptive meanings, which are, moreover, alterable and flexible in both cases. But the purpose of using the term 'evaluative' is not to deny that value-words have descriptive meaning; that is readily admitted, and arguments which seek to prove that they have descriptive meaning are not arguments against my position, which allows this. Nor are arguments designed to show that we can use the words 'true' and 'false' of value-judgements, or that we can speak of 'describing' somebody as a good man. We can say these things of any judgement which has descriptive meaning, provided that it is its descriptive meaning that we are adverting to. Nor do I wish to deny that the descriptive meanings of value-words are alterable and flexible; that this is so fits in very well with my thesis. I am not asserting that value-words are in this respect different from descriptive words. What I am asserting is that the character of what happens when the descriptive meaning of a value-word changes is profoundly affected by the fact that it has prescriptive meaning as well as descriptive.

---

[3] Some writers use the words 'evaluative' and 'value-judgement' in a narrower sense than this. They call judgements containing the word 'good' and some similar words 'evaluative' or 'value-judgements', and distinguish these from judgements containing the words 'right', 'wrong',

'ought', and the like, which they call 'normative judgements'. These two classes certainly need to be distinguished for some purposes, as we shall see; and this is a useful way of doing it. But since I have used the word 'evaluative' in its wide sense hitherto, it would be confusing to use it in a different sense from now on; I shall therefore continue to use it to cover 'ought' and 'right' as well as 'good'.

This can be clarified by means of a simple example. Let us suppose (to use an example which is current) that two people differ in where they draw the line between a 'bush' and a 'tree'. It is possible to imagine situations (for example if bushes are to be cut down but trees left standing) in which such a verbal difference might lead to important misunderstandings. But these misunderstandings could be cleared up quite easily by means of an agreement on the use of the word. In agreeing to draw the line in a certain place they would not be settling anything except a question of meaning—a verbal question. Wherever the line is drawn, the same instructions as before can be unambiguously given: e.g. 'Cut down all bushes below 15 ft. high with the lowest branch less than 3 ft. from the ground'. So classifying something as a bush does not *by itself* entail a prescription to cut it down.

I wish to contrast such a case of purely verbal difference with a case of a *moral* difference, thereby showing that typical moral disputes are not purely verbal, as on a naturalist account they would be, provided that the non-moral facts were agreed. Let us suppose that two people know all about the income-tax laws, and know, specifically, that a certain method of tax avoidance is perfectly legal; and let us suppose that they know all about the precise tax situation of somebody who is proposing to use this means of avoiding tax. One of them may say 'That would be wrong; it would be going too far; there are ways of avoiding tax that are morally perfectly legitimate (for example by claiming deduction on account of a dependent relative, if you have one); but this proposal goes beyond what I can condone'. But the other may say, 'In my view this proposal cannot be condemned on moral grounds; there *are* methods of tax avoidance which, though legal, I would condemn, but this is not one of them; in my view there is nothing wrong about it'. Now it is obvious that these two people cannot clear up their difference, as in the 'bush' case, by a verbal

agreement to use the word 'wrong' to cover certain cases and not others (*LM* 3.5). It follows that the rules which these two people are using for determining the application of the word 'wrong' cannot be merely descriptive meaning-rules, although they do, among other functions, determine the descriptive meaning of the term. They are rules having moral substance; in accepting one or the other of them the disputants would be committing themselves, not merely to a certain use of a word, but to a matter of moral principle. So when we 'flex' our moral words, we have regard, not merely to matters of mere convenience in communication, but to substantial questions of morality.

3. *PRINCIPLES*

3.1. I sought in the preceding chapter to explain in what sense moral judgements are universalizable. The explanation may be summed up as follows: they are universalizable in just the same way as descriptive judgements are universalizable, namely the way which follows from the fact that both moral expressions and descriptive expressions have descriptive meaning; but in the case of moral judgements the universal rules which determine this descriptive meaning are not mere meaning-rules, but moral principles of substance. In this chapter, I am going to consider various other ways in which moral judgements might be said to be universal or universalizable —mainly in order to avoid future misinterpretation by indicating to which of these views I subscribe and to which I do not.

It is, first of all, most important to distinguish the logical thesis which I have been putting forward from various *moral* theses with which it is easy to confuse it. I said above (2.7) that, because of universalizability, a person who makes a moral judgement commits himself, not merely to a meaning-rule, but to a substantial moral principle. The thesis of universalizability itself, however, is still a logical thesis. It is very important not to confuse the thesis of universalizability with the substantial moral principles to which, according to it, a person who makes a moral judgement commits himself.

By a 'logical' thesis I mean a thesis about the meanings of words, or dependent solely upon them. I have been maintaining that the meaning of the word 'ought' and other moral words is such that a person who uses them commits himself thereby to a universal rule. This is the thesis of universalizability. It is to be distinguished from *moral* views such as that everybody ought always to adhere to universal rules and govern all his conduct in accordance with them, or that one ought not to make exceptions in one's own favour. The logical thesis has, as we shall see, great potency in moral arguments; but for that very reason it is most important to make clear that it is no more than a logical thesis—for otherwise the objection will be made that a moral principle has been smuggled in disguised as a logical doctrine (10.3). In order to clarify this point I am going to take the two moral views just mentioned and show that they do not follow from the logical thesis, unless they themselves are interpreted in such a way as to be analytic (i.e. not to enjoin any one line of conduct rather than another). In the latter case, obviously, there would be no objection to deriving them from the logical thesis, because the accusation of smuggling in substantial moral principles could not then be raised.

3.2. Let us first consider the moral principle that everybody ought always to adhere to universal rules and govern all his conduct in accordance with them. The nature of this principle is best examined by asking what would constitute a breach of it. On one interpretation, it is impossible to break such a principle; for, given a description of a person's life, it is always, analytically, possible to find *some* universal rules according to which he has lived—if

only the rule 'Live thus: . . .' followed by a minute description, in universal terms, of how he has lived.

To avoid this trivialization of the principle we are considering, let us stipulate that a man is not to be said to have *adhered* to a rule, nor to have *governed his conduct in accordance with it,* unless he has in some sense had the rule before his mind (at any rate from time to time) and unless his conduct has in some sense been motivated by the desire to conform to it. Now on this interpretation, a man would be breaking the principle that everybody ought always to adhere to universal rules, and govern all his conduct in accordance with them, if he did something on some whim without considering any rule involved in the action. Does it follow from my logical thesis that such a person acts wrongly? Not in the least, it would seem; for the thesis does not say that a person who maintained that one ought always, in this man's circumstances, to act as he did, would be committing any logical fault, and still less does it say that the man himself is committing any *moral* fault. If, on a whim, I give a blind beggar a coin, this does not, according to the logical thesis of universalizability, stop my action being right; for it may be that one ought always to give alms to blind beggars—or even that one ought always to give alms to them without reflection. I do not wish to argue for or against such rules, but only to point out that they do not contravene my logical thesis. A person who acted thus without reflection could not, indeed, be thinking that this was the right thing to do; for that would involve consideration (in some sense) of a rule or principle; but he could do the right thing all the same. In the same way, one may use a word rightly without thinking whether it is the right word; but if one does think whether it is, one has thereby raised a question of principle: Is this the way the word is rightly used?

Offences against the thesis of universalizability are logical, not moral. If a person says 'I ought to act in a certain way, but nobody else ought to act in that way in relevantly similar circumstances', then, on my thesis, he is abusing the word 'ought'; he is implicitly contradicting himself. But the logical offence here lies in the *conjunction* of two moral judgements, not in either one of them by itself. The thesis of universalizability does not render self-contradictory any single, logically simple, moral judgement, or even moral principle, which is not already self-contradictory without the thesis; all it does is to force people to choose between judgements which cannot both be asserted without self-contradiction. And so no moral judgement or principle of substance follows from the thesis alone. Furthermore, a person may act, on a number of different occasions, in different ways, even if the occasions are qualitatively identical, without it following from the thesis that all, or that any particular one, of his actions must be wrong. The thesis does not even forbid us to say that *none* of the man's actions are wrong; for it is consistent with the thesis that the kinds of actions he did in the kind of situations described were morally indifferent. What the thesis does forbid us to do is to make different moral judgments about actions which we admit to be exactly or relevantly similar. The thesis tells us that this is to make two logically inconsistent judgements.

We might conceivably interpret the principle that one ought always to govern one's behaviour in accordance with universal rules as simply a denial, *en bloc*, of all such self-contradictory conjunctions of moral judgements. So interpreted, the principle becomes, like all denials of self-contradictions, analytic. It does not make much difference whether we say that it is a second-order statement about the logical properties of moral judgements, or that it is a first-order, but analytic, moral judgement. It could be put in either of these forms without substantially altering its character.

The same treatment can be given to the principle that one ought not to make exceptions in one's own favour. If this is interpreted merely as a denial that it can be the case that I ought to act in a certain way, but that others in relevantly similar circumstances ought not, then the principle is analytic (a repetition in other words of the logical thesis), and no moral judgement of substance follows from it. But if it is interpreted to mean that a man who acts in a certain way, while maintaining that others ought not so to act, is always *acting* wrongly, then not only is the principle synthetic, but most of us would dissent from it; for the man may well be acting rightly, though the moral judgement that he makes about other people's actions is inconsistent with the judgement (if he makes it) that his own action is right. At any rate, the man's *action* cannot be a breach of the thesis of universalizability, although what he *says* may be; and this is what we should expect if, as I have been maintaining, it is a logical thesis and not a substantive moral principle.

I shall not go into detail concerning other possible moral principles which might be confused with the thesis of universalizability. Two famous ones may, however, be just mentioned. The first is the 'Golden Rule', if put in the form of a moral principle: One ought to treat others as one would wish them to treat oneself. If this were rewritten to read ' . . . as others *ought* to treat oneself', then the same sort of account can be given of it as of the principles we have just discussed. By suitable interpretation, it can be made analytically true according to the universalist thesis; on other interpretations it becomes synthetic, but does not then follow from the thesis. If the word 'wish' is left in, the principle is obviously synthetic, and equally obviously does not follow from the thesis (6.9).

The second principle which may be mentioned is the Kantian one, which we may put in the form 'I ought never to act except in such a way that I can also will that my maxim should become a universal law'.[4] This, too, is capable of different interpretations; but it will be wisest, in a book of this character, while acknowledging a very great debt to Kant, to avoid becoming entangled in the spider's web of Kantian exegesis. If Kant is interpreted as meaning that a man who says that he ought to act in a certain way, but says 'Let others not act in this same way', is guilty of an implicit contradiction, then the Kantian principle is a way of stating a consequence of the logical thesis of universalizability. In this interpretation, *willing* (which is one of Kant's most elusive notions) is treated as roughly equivalent to *assenting to an imperative*, in the sense, not itself entirely clear, of *LM* 2.2. There is also a problem about the word 'can'; what I should wish to say about this will become apparent later (6.9, 10.4 f.). But it is a difficult enough task to make my own views clear to the reader, without trying to do the same for Kant's.

In general, I may anticipate my future argument by saying this: it looks at first sight as if we have a choice between two positions: (1) that the thesis of universalizability is itself a moral principle and therefore can have substantial moral consequences; and (2) that it is only a logical principle from which nothing of moral substance can follow, and that therefore it is useless for purposes of moral reasoning. It is the last clause ('it is useless ...') which is here mistaken. Later, I shall try to show that, though the thesis is not a substantial moral principle but a logical one, and though, therefore, nothing moral follows from it by itself, it is capable of very powerful employment in moral argument when combined with other premisses (6.3 ff.). So the dilemma is a false one—though this has not prevented its being often used.

3.3. Having made it clear that univer-

salism, as I am maintaining it, is a logical and not a moral thesis, I shall now try to remove certain sources of confusion as to its precise import. First of all, it may very well be asked whether this is a doctrine about *moral* uses of words only, or whether it is a doctrine about evaluative words in general.[5] The answer which I wish to give to this question is a somewhat complicated one, since we have to steer between at least two errors. It is a doctrine about evaluative words in general, but one which requires careful qualification. If we take as an example the word 'ought', it seems to me that, whatever the type of 'ought'-judgement that is being made (moral, aesthetic, technical, &c.) the judgement is universalizable (8.2).

This is one reason why the word 'ought' cannot be used in making legal judgements; if a person has a certain legal obligation, we cannot express this by saying that he *ought* to do such and such a thing, for the reason that 'ought'-judgements have to be universalizable, which, in the strict sense, legal judgements are not. The reason why they are not is that a statement of law always contains an implicit reference to a particular jurisdiction; 'It is illegal to marry one's own sister' means, implicitly, 'It is illegal in (e.g.) England to marry one's own sister'. But 'England' is here a singular term, which prevents the whole proposition being universal; nor is it universalizable, in the sense of committing the speaker to the view that such a marriage would be illegal in any country that was otherwise like England. It is therefore impossible to use 'ought' in such a statement. The moral judgement that one *ought* not to marry one's sister is, however, universal; it implies no reference to a particular legal system.

It is even more necessary to distinguish 'ought'-judgements from ordinary *imperatives* in respect of universalizability. If,

---

[4] Kant, *Groundwork of the Metaphysic of Morals*, 2nd ed., p. 17 (tr. H. J. Paton, p. 70).

[5] I must admit that what I said on this point in *Aristotelian Society*, lv (1954/5), 298, was worse than misleading.

when the squad gets to the end of the parade-ground, the serjeant says 'Left wheel', this does not commit him (on pain of being accused of having changed his mind) to giving the same order, rather than 'Right wheel', on similar occasions in the future. But if, in a tactical exercise, the instructor says 'The situation being what it is, you ought to attack on the left', he will have changed his mind if, the next time this same exercise is gone through with a new group of cadets, he says 'The situation being what it is, you ought to attack on the right'. By 'changed his mind', I mean 'said something which is inconsistent with what he said before'.

Though, however, some philosophers have gone much too far in assimilating 'ought'-judgements (of all sorts) to simple imperatives, it may be that some people do sometimes use the word 'ought' when they should more properly have used a plain imperative, in order to give an instruction without any thought of reasons or grounds. Plain imperatives do not *have* to have reasons or grounds, though they normally do have; but 'ought'-judgements, strictly speaking, would be being misused if the demand for reasons or grounds were thought of as out of place—though the reasons need not be ulterior ones; some universal moral judgements already incorporate all the reasons they need or can have (*LM* 4.4).

Nevertheless, it may be that there is a debased use of 'ought' in which it is equivalent to a simple imperative (though I must confess that I have come across such a use only in the writings of philosophers). Just in case, however, there is such a use, it is convenient to put the matter in the following way: In by far the majority of judgements containing the word 'ought', it has the sense that requires them to be universalizable; there *may* be some peripheral cases where it does not have this sense; but at any rate in its *moral* uses (with which we are chiefly concerned) it always does. The word 'moral' plays here a far smaller role than I was at one time

tempted to assign to it. It is the logic of the word 'ought' in its typical uses that requires universalizability, not that of the word 'moral'; the word 'moral' needs to be brought in only in order to identify one class of the typical uses, and that with which as moral philosophers we are most concerned. This means that the ambiguity of the word 'moral', which is notorious, need not worry us at this point. For in whichever of its current senses the word is being used, it suffices to exclude those peripheral uses of 'ought' (if they exist), in which it is not universalizable.

3.4. I now turn to the most serious of the misinterpretations to which universalism is subject. It is common to hear objection made to it on the ground that it implies that there are certain rather simple general moral principles which, in some unexplained sense, *exist* antecedently to the making of any moral judgement, and that all we have to do whenever we make such a judgement is to consult the relevant principle and, without more ado, the judgement is made. Such a doctrine would be that of a very hidebound moralist, whose moral principles were a set of copy-book headings.[6] This account of the matter differs from that which I wish to give in a number of respects. First of all, it is not clear what is meant in this context by speaking of moral principles 'existing'; but even if they (in some sense) exist, I am sure that they do not always exist *antecedently*, so that all we have to do is to consult them. This is made sufficiently clear by considering almost any case of serious moral perplexity—for example Sartre's well-known case of the young man who was in doubt whether to join the Free French forces or to stay and look after his widowed mother.[7] Sartre uses the example in order to make the point that in such cases no antecedently 'existing' principle

[6] See further *Aristotelian Society*, lv (1954/5), 309f.

[7] J.-P. Sartre, *L'Existentialisme est un Humanisme* (1946), pp. 39 ff. (tr. in W. Kaufmann (ed.), *Existentialism*, pp. 295 f.)

can be appealed to (*qui peut en decider a priori; aucune morale inscrite ne peut le dire*).[8] We have to consider the particular case and make up our minds what are its morally relevant features, and what, taking these features into account, ought to be done in such a case. Nevertheless, when we do make up our minds, it is about a matter of principle which has a bearing outside the particular case. Sartre himself is as much of a universalist as I am, in the sense in which I am, to judge by the little book in which this example occurs.[9] He has also on occasion himself given his public support to universal moral principles.[10]

Secondly, the principles which are adhered to in making moral judgements are seldom very simple or general, at any rate when the judgements are made by intelligent people who have had any wide experience of life. It is most important here to distinguish between what may be called *universality* and *generality*, although these terms are often enough used interchangeably. The opposite of 'general' is 'specific'; the opposite of 'universal' is 'singular'—though the existence of the term 'particular', contrasted with both 'universal' and 'singular', introduces complications into which we do not need to enter. It will suffice for our purposes if we explain the terms informally in the following way. It will be remembered that we explained the notion of universalizability by reference to the term 'descriptive meaning'. Any judgement which has descriptive meaning must be universalizable, because the descriptive meaning-rules which determine this meaning are universal rules. But they are not necessarily general rules. A descriptive

meaning-rule says that we can use a certain predicate of anything of a certain kind. And it is obvious that in the case of some descriptive predicates we shall have to go into a great deal of detail in order to specify what kind—if indeed this is formulable in words at all. Let the reader try specifying exactly what he means by a word like 'primitive', even in some particular context, and he will see what I mean. He will find that in order to distinguish it from other words such as 'archaic', 'unsophisticated', &c., he will have to enter into a great deal of detail, and may end up by having recourse to examples. Yet these are properly universal predicates. Other expressions create somewhat different difficulties owing to their complexity; in order to define the word 'barquentine' it is no use saying that it is a kind of vessel, nor even a kind of sailing-vessel; 'barquentine' is a very much less *general* term than 'vessel', yet both are equally, *universal* terms. Now universalism is not the doctrine that behind every moral judgement there has to lie a principle expressible in a few general terms; the principle, though universal, may be so complex that it defies formulation in words at all. But if it were formulated and specified, all the terms used in its formulation would be universal terms.

If I make a moral judgement about something, it must be because of some feature of the thing; but this feature may be one which requires much detail for its specification. It must be noticed that generality and specificity are, unlike universality and singularity, matters of degree. This enables us to put the difference between the two pairs of terms quite simply by means of examples. The moral principle 'One ought never to make false statements' is highly general; the moral principle 'One ought never to make false statements to one's wife' is much more specific. But both are universal; the second one forbids *anyone* who is married to make false statements to his wife. It should be clear from these explanations that the thesis of univer-

[8] Op. cit., p. 42 (Kaufmann, p. 296); cf. p. 47 (Kaufmann, p. 298), where the point is the same.
[9] Cf. op. cit., pp. 31–32, 70–78 (Kaufmann, pp. 293, 304–6): 'I bear the responsibility of the choice which, in committing myself, also commits the whole of humanity'; 'In this sense we may say that there is a human universality, but it is not something given; it is being perpetually made'; '[The young man] was obliged to invent *the law* for himself' (my italics).
[10] See *The Times*, 21 Sept. 1960, p. 10.

salizability does not require moral judgements to be made on the basis of highly general moral principles of the copy-book-heading type. As I explained in *LM* 3.6 and 4.3, our moral development, as we grow older, consists in the main in making our moral principles more and more specific, by writing into them exceptions and qualifications to cover kinds of cases of which we have had experience. In the case of most people they soon become too complicated to admit of formulation, and yet give tolerably clear guidance in familiar situations. It is, indeed, always possible for a situation to arise which calls for a qualification of the principle; but, unless a person is plunged suddenly into an environment quite different to that in which he has grown up, this is likely to happen less and less as he grows older, because the situations which he encounters will more often resemble ones which he has encountered, and thought morally about, before.

3.5. The logic of moral language is not restrictive with regard to the generality or specificity of our moral principles. It allows them to be highly general and simple, or highly specific and complicated, according to the temperament of the person who holds them. This may be seen by considering some extreme cases. There might be one man who acquired early in life a few very short moral prohibitions, and stuck rigidly to these, while regarding everything not falling under them as equally permissible. Another man might accumulate a series of moral principles as complicated as the Law of Moses (whether or not he could formulate them), and still be adding qualifications until his dying day.

There is a great difference between people in respect of their readiness to qualify their moral principles in new circumstances. One man may be very hidebound; he may feel that he knows what he ought to do in a certain situation as soon as he has acquainted himself with its most general features, without examining it at all closely to see whether it has any special features which would call for a different judgement. Another man may be more cautious (some people are even pathologically cautious in this respect); he will never make up his mind what he ought to do, even in a quite familiar situation, until he has scrutinized every detail of it to make sure that he can really subsume it under the principles that seem at first sight most relevant.

If some British admirers of the Existentialists were to be followed, we should all be like the latter person; we should say to ourselves that people, and the situations in which they find themselves, are unique, and that therefore we must approach every new situation with a completely open mind and do our moral thinking about it *ab initio*. This is an absurd prescription, only made plausible by concentrating our attention, by means of novels and short stories, on moral situations of extreme difficulty and complexity, which really do require a lot of consideration. It is important to realize that there are moral problems of this kind; but if *all* moral questions were treated like this, not only should we never get round to considering more than the first few that we happened to encounter, but any kind of moral development or learning from experience would be quite impossible. What the wiser among us do is to think deeply about the crucial moral questions, especially those that face us in our own lives; but when we have arrived at an answer to a particular problem, to crystallize it into a not too specific or detailed form, so that its salient features may stand out and serve us again in a like situation without need for *so much* thought. We may then have time to think about *other* problems, and shall not continually be finding ourselves at a loss about what we ought to do.

3.6. We have here, as so often in philosophy, to steer between two mistakes. It is unfortunate that terminological confusions tend often to drive us into one or the other. The expressions 'moral principle', moral rule', and the like are often interpreted in such a way that the rules or principles referred to have to be highly general. There are two main ways of achieving this. One is that of confining 'principles', as so restricted, to a relatively minor role in our moral thought. A man may make most of his moral decisions on grounds or for reasons which, though falling under the definition of 'universal principle' that I have been using, are insufficiently general to be called 'principles' in the restricted sense. He may reserve this word for what he calls 'matters of principle'—as when we say 'I make it a matter of principle *never* to come between husband and wife'. The purpose of making something a matter of principle, in this sense, is to avoid doing any moral thinking about particular cases.

There are sometimes justifications for this. It may be that the situations falling under the principle are such as leave no time for careful consideration of their particular features. It may be that such consideration is thought of as itself wrong (as perhaps in the instance just quoted; we may feel that to delve into other people's marital relations, as would be necessary if we were going to form a just judgement on them, would be an intolerable piece of interference). Or it may be that we have learnt from experience that, while we are engaged in a situation of a certain kind, moral thought is subject to recurrent pitfalls which in the heat of the moment it is difficult to avoid. For example, our natural kindness of heart, or desire to avoid scenes, may lead us to decisions which we subsequently come to think wrong. Or, in cases where we are in authority, we may think that arguments for treating a particular case in an exceptional way can always be devised by the ingenious; and that for this and other reasons, if an exception is made in one case (even though, because it is a hard one, there are reasons for doing so) there will be no end to the exceptions that will have to be made in less deserving cases. To use a frivolous example from a

recent broadcast programme: if the hotel manager allows the old lady to have her Pekinese on her lap in the lounge, then there will be no stopping people bringing in Great Danes and Wolfhounds and knocking over the tables; so he makes it a matter of principle to allow no dogs in the lounge.

A more serious example is provided by the question, whether it is ever legitimate to use torture in police interrogations. A police officer might determine as a matter of principle never to use it; and I should approve of his doing so. This is not, however, because I think it logically impossible that situations should arise in which, by a form of moral reasoning such as I can now accept (similar to that outlined later in this book), I could satisfy myself that torture ought to be used. It is in fact very easy to imagine such situations: suppose, for example, that a sadistic bacteriologist has produced and broadcast an infectious bacillus which will cause a substantial part of the world's population to die of a painful disease; and that he alone knows the cure for the disease. I should certainly not condemn the police if they tortured him to make him reveal it. But when I say that I approve of a police officer accepting it as a matter of principle not to use torture, I do not mean to deny that fantastic cases could be thought up in which it would be legitimate; what I mean is that, although a completely watertight set of moral principles covering all logically possible circumstances (if there could be such a thing, which is unlikely) would include a clause to allow an exception in such cases, it is unlikely to be possible in practice for a police officer (however intelligent and sensitive) to do the moral thinking which would be necessary to distinguish such cases from others, superficially similar, in which the principle forbidding torture ought to be adhered to; and it would be dangerous for him to try, because in the sort of circumstances in which torture is sometimes advocated and practised it is extremely difficult to think clearly and to consider all sides of the case. Moreover, in cases which actually occur—as contrasted with those which are logically possible—I hold, having seen the sort of things that happen, that the ill effects on society of this insidious evil are always such as far to counterbalance any good that might come of it, even if the most important consideration, the suffering of the victim, be left out of account. I have, therefore, no hesitation at all in saying that police officers, however desperate the circumstances, ought to make it a matter of principle never even to contemplate such methods.

The sort of consideration of hypothetical and fantastic cases which I have implicitly condemned is to be distinguished from that quite different use of hypothetical cases in moral reasoning which we shall later see to be both necessary and useful (6.8, 9.4, 11.7). It is always legitimate, in order to apply to moral argument the requirement of universalizability, to imagine hypothetical cases which really are, apart from the fact that the roles of the people concerned are reversed, precisely similar in the relevant respects to the actual case being considered; and this may properly be done, however fantastic the assumptions that have to be made, in matters which do not affect the moral issue, in order to make the hypothetical case seem possible. This perhaps holds even for people faced with urgent practical problems, provided that they have time to think at all; and most of us should, when we have time to think, think more about such matters. Indeed, there is nothing to prevent moral philosophers in their studies considering cases which fall outside even this limit—which, that is to say, are in their morally relevant particulars quite dissimilar from cases which are likely actually to occur. It may not be so useful to do this, as to consider cases in which the morally relevant features of actual cases are reproduced; but it may all the same be instructive. But for people in situations which expose them to a

particular moral danger, it may sometimes be best to put altogether out of their minds the possibility of exceptions to a principle. It is a very difficult matter to decide just when it is right to make something 'a matter of principle' in this way—it depends so much on the circumstances and on the psychology of particular people. But we cannot say that it is never right.

We clearly do sometimes use the word 'principle' in this sense, though it should be equally clear that this is not the way in which I have been using it. Burke, strangely to our ears, uses the word 'prejudice' ironically in a favourable sense for the same kind of thing: 'Prejudice is of ready application in the emergency; it previously engages the mind in a steady course of wisdom and virtue, and does not leave the man hesitating in the moment of decision, sceptical, puzzled and unresolved. Prejudice renders a man's virtue his habit, and not a series of unconnected acts. Through just prejudice, his duty becomes a part of his nature.'[11] All but a few philosophers would commend a man for making some of his decisions in the way Burke advocates; but a few of us (and probably not Burke) would think it right for *all* decisions to be made in this way.

Another, and less laudable, way of achieving generality in our moral principles is to treat them as a set of general maxims to which, in some sense (perhaps only verbally) we subscribe; we may as often as not, in our actual particular moral judgements, depart from them, but they form the background of our moral thinking (its mythology, we might almost say). Perhaps, though, a man whose moral 'principles' are like this is freed from the charge of hypocrisy (at the cost of incurring another charge of woolly thinking) by the fact that his principles are expressed in very vague terms, so that by judicious interpretation of them he can square his set of moral principles as a whole with any moral judgement

[11] *Reflections on Revolution in France* (1815 ed.), vol. v, p. 168.

that he finds himself making. As a practical guide to action such a set of principles has small value, because, at any rate in difficult cases, a wide variety of actions can be called conformable to them. Another expedient is to interpret the principles themselves strictly and precisely, but to adjust and vary (how?) the 'weight' which we give to them in particular circumstances. It is not, however, as a guide to action that such principles are attractive, but rather because they give a certain 'tone' to the moral life; a man can call himself a man of principle, while making his actual moral judgements in particular cases in the way that most of us do.

3.7. It is very easy, in revulsion from this caricature of moral thinking, to fall into the opposite error of abandoning principles altogether. Sometimes this idea is put in the form of a proposal to abandon *morality*; 'morality' and 'moral principles' and 'moral rules' seem somehow tainted; a young man, especially, may see in them the Victorian furniture that he has inherited from his grandparents, to be discarded as soon as convenient. This reaction is very understandable, and in itself praiseworthy. In so far as moral principles are thought of as something inherited and external—as not accepted by a man himself as a guide to his actions (with the responsibility for fitting them to new situations), they are dead things. The mistake lies in supposing that moral principles have *got* to be like this. The remedy for it is to be clear about the sense in which we are using the words; and I shall therefore now set out the way in which I think they can most helpfully be used, if we are to make morality again (as the military writers say) 'operational'.

First of all, let us be clear that a moral principle has not got to be highly general or simple, or even formulable in words, though it has got to be universal (in the sense already explained). Secondly let us insist that a man is not to be said to accept a moral principle unless he is making a serious attempt to *use* it in guiding his partic-

ular moral judgements and thus his actions. These two requirements are, as will be recognized, the two central theses of this book—that moral principles have to be universal, and that they have to be prescriptive. The latter of them compels us to look for principles that we can sincerely adhere to; the former insists that these should really be moral principles and not the *ad hoc* decisions of an opportunist. It will be seen in Chapter 6 how these two features taken together supply us with a most powerful lever in moral arguments. And this is the sort of principle that we all actually use in our moral thinking, the more so as we gain experience.

Let us consider for a moment what it is for a man to be *wise*—to be the sort of a person to whom we naturally turn for advice when faced with a moral difficulty. The word 'wise' is obviously evaluative; we shall not, on reflection, call a man wise unless we agree with the content of the moral advice he has given us—after we have seen the consequences of carrying it out, or disregarding it. But what is it in a man which leads us to expect that we shall be able, after the event, to say that his advice was wise? If I were seeking for advice in such a situation, I should look first for a man who had himself experienced difficulties of an analogous sort to mine. But this would not be enough; for the quality of the thought that he had given to these situations might have been poor. I should look also for a man of whom I could be sure that in facing moral questions (his own or mine) he would face them as questions of moral principle and not, for example, as questions of selfish expediency. This means that I should expect him to ask, of his own actions, 'To what action can I commit myself in this situation, realizing that, in committing myself to it, I am also (because the judgement is a universalizable one) prescribing to *anyone* in a like situation to do the same—in short, what can I will to be a universal law?' (5.5, 6.2). If I could find a man whom I knew to have been confronted with difficult choices, and whom, at the same time, I could expect to have had the courage to ask moral questions about them (not, to use Sartre's words, to 'conceal from himself the anguish'[12] of universalization), then that would be the man whose advice I should gladly seek, if it were moral advice that I wanted. And I should not expect him to produce quickly some simple maxim; he would, no doubt, find it extremely hard to formulate in words any universal proposition to cover the case. But I should be sure that he would consider the particular case and sympathetically in all its details, and after doing that try to find a solution to which I could commit, not only myself, but, as Sartre again puts it, 'the whole of humanity'.[13]

3.8. This is perhaps the best point at which to guard against another common misinterpretation of universalism. It is thought that a universalist must inevitably be a busybody; for if, as he maintains, a moral judgement about my own case implies a similar judgement about similar cases in which other people are involved, then must not a universalist be a person who is always passing moral judgements on other people, and is not this a pretentious and insufferable thing to do? But first of all, to make a moral judgement about somebody else's action is not necessarily to go about proclaiming to him and to other people that he has acted well or ill. It is possible, and usually tactful, to keep one's moral opinions to oneself. But this answer to the objection does not go deep enough. A more important answer is that all the universalist is committed to in making a moral judgement is to saying that *if* there is another person in a similar situation, then the same judgement must be made about his case. Since we cannot know everything about another actual person's concrete situation (including how it strikes him, which may make all the difference), it is nearly

always presumptuous to suppose that another person's situation is exactly like one we have ourselves been in, or even like it in the relevant particulars. If the other person asks us for advice, what we shall do, if we are sensible, is to question him very carefully about his situation; and if, after this careful and sympathetic inquiry, it appears that his situation has a good deal in common with one which has faced us, or if we are imaginative and sympathetic enough to be able to enter into his situation even without such previous experience, then we may have something in the way of moral advice that we can give him. And this advice, though based on careful examination of the specific details of the case, will have to be such as we could give in *any* similar case.

3.9. I wish, lastly, to clear up a pair of more elementary confusions. The first is that of taking 'universal' to mean 'universally accepted'. A moral principle would be universal, in this sense, if everybody in the world subscribed to it. It will be obvious that at any rate not all moral principles are universal in this sense, since there is widespread disagreement about many important moral questions; and I hope that it will be equally obvious that it is not in this sense that I am using the word. In any case, it is far from clear what relevance it has for moral philosophy whether or not there are moral principles which are universally accepted; it seems to me that *securus judicat orbis terrarum* is a pernicious maxim in morals, because it combines the vices of relativism with a plausibly absolutist ring. But to discuss this would be to digress.

The second confusion is more difficult to clear up. Suppose that somebody argues as follows: according to the universalist, when a man makes a moral judgement he is committed to saying that anybody who says something different about a similar case is wrong; therefore, according to the universalist, toleration in moral matters is impossible. In order to understand this matter clearly, it is necessary to distinguish

---

[12] Op. cit., p. 32 (Kaufmann, p. 293).
[13] Op. cit., p. 74 (Kaufmann, p. 305); see above, p. 38, n. 3.

between thinking that somebody else is wrong, and taking up an intolerant attitude towards him. The universalist is committed to a denial of relativism (which is in any case an absurd doctrine);[14] he holds that if anybody disagrees with me about a moral question, then I am committed to disagree-

ing with him, unless I change my mind. This appears a harmless enough tautology, and need hardly trouble the universalist. But the universalist is not committed to persecuting (physically or in any other way) people who disagree with him morally. If he is the sort of universalist that I am, he will realize that our moral opinions are liable to change in the light of our experience and our discussion of moral questions with other people; therefore, if another person disagrees with us, what is called for is not the suppression of his opinions but the discussion of them, in the hope that, when he has told us the reasons for his, and we for ours, we may reach agreement. Universalism is an ethical theory which makes moral argument both possible and fruitful; and it enables us to understand what toleration is, as we shall later see.

[14] Relativism, subjectivism, emotivism, and other such doctrines (none of which I hold) have become so inextricably confused with one another in philosophical writings as to make the term 'objectivism'—which is used indiscriminately to contrast with all these views, in all of their many forms—totally useless as a tool of serious inquiry. The confusion is increased by supposing, as many do, that anybody who is not what I have called a 'descriptivist' cannot be an 'objectivist' and must therefore be a 'relativist' or a 'subjectivist' or an 'emotivist', or all three—which, or in what senses, is seldom clear. For a crude and elementary attempt to sort matters out, see my article 'Ethics' in *Concise Encyclopedia of Western Philosophy and Philosophers*, ed. J. O. Urmson.

The Trivializability of Universalizability

DON LOCKE

Analytic ethics can easily be a frustrating business. We would like very much to arrive at substantial ethical conclusions, but these seem to be ruled out by the very nature of the subject. So it is not surprising that some hope, by reflecting on the essential nature of moral judgment, moral praise and blame, to arrive at formal principles which, while not embodying any particular moral content, nevertheless have some practical bearing on moral argument and moral opinion. One such principle would seem to be the principle that we must—logically must, must if we are to be judging morally in the first place—treat like cases alike. The only trouble is that as soon as any weight is put on this principle it seems to collapse into the shattering triviality that cases are alike, morally or in any other respect, unless they are different. In this paper I want to argue that Professor R. M. Hare's recent ingenious attempt to put forward a thesis of universalizability (in *Freedom and Reason* [Oxford, 1963], abbreviated to *FR*) suffers precisely this fate.

I

What, to begin with, does it mean to say that moral judgments are universalizable?

To say that a judgment is universal is to say that it applies to everything covered by the subject term, so to say that it is universalizable is, presumably, to say that it can be applied to everything covered by the subject term. If "This child ought to obey his parents" is universalizable, then it can be applied to all children; to say that it is universalizable is to say that all children ought to obey their parents.

Yet this cannot be quite right. I may say of a man who has promised to be home by eight o'clock that he ought to be home by eight, but in saying this, as a moral judgment, I certainly do not commit myself to saying that all men ought to be home by eight. Rather I commit myself to saying that all men who promise to be home by eight ought to be. So to universalize a moral judgment is to pass from saying that a particular thing is good or bad, right or wrong, ought or ought not be done, to saying that all things of a certain kind (a kind of which this one is an instance) are good or bad, right or wrong, ought or ought not be done. The particular thing is good or bad, and so forth, because it falls under some moral principle; the reason this child ought to obey his parents is that all children ought to obey their parents, and the reason this man ought to be home by eight is that all men ought to do what they promise to do. Thus to universalize a moral judgment is to state a principle from which that particular judgment can be derived, in the sense that the particular judgment

[1] Reprinted from *The Philosophical Review*, LXXVIII, Jan. 1968, pp. 25–44 by permission of the author and *The Philosophical Review*.

would not be true unless that principle were true. In other words, the thesis of universalizability is, at least to begin with, the thesis that particular moral judgments presuppose moral principles.

Hare's argument is that this universalizability of moral judgments is a matter of logic, and that although nothing of importance follows from this logical fact by itself, important consequences do follow once universalizability is joined to certain other facts, about moral judgments and about us. He begins by saying that the universalizability of moral judgments is simply a logical consequence of the fact that they possess "descriptive meaning." Moral judgments, like "This is good," are universalizable in precisely the same way that descriptive judgments, like "This is red," are universalizable. "If a person says that a thing is red, he is committed to the view that anything which was like it in the relevant respects would likewise be red. The relevant respects are those which, he thought, made it true that the first thing was red; in this particular case, they amount to one respect only: its red colour" (*FR*, p. 11). Thus the judgment "This is red" is universalizable in that we can pass from it to the "principle" that anything which is like it in being red is red. And if the judgment "This is good" is universalizable in precisely the same way, as Hare says it is, then this means that we can pass from "This is good" to the "principle" that anything which is like it in being good is good.

There are three things to notice about this. First, it is as trivial as trivial can be, whether we are dealing with the universalizability of descriptive judgments or with the universalizability of moral judgments —although Hare thinks that the thesis is "not so trivial" (*FR*, p. 12) when applied to moral judgments. Second, this universalizability is not just a feature of judgments which possess descriptive meaning; it is a feature of any judgment which is capable of being true or false. If a judgment P is true in a certain state of affairs S then any state of affairs which was like S in the relevant respects (those which make P true) would likewise be a state of affairs in which P was true. Of course it may be that Hare does not wish to deny this, since the examples he gives of things which are not universalizable —for example, decisions, desires, imperatives—are not things which are capable of being true or false. The judgment "I have decided to do x," on the other hand, is universalizable in the present sense. Still, if this is what Hare meant, it is surprising that he did not save himself a lot of trouble by simply defining "judgment with descriptive meaning" as "judgment capable of being true or false." Third, the fact that moral judgments are universalizable in this sense does nothing to show that particular moral judgments presuppose moral principles, for the simple reason that "Anything which is like this in being good is good" is not a moral principle.

Hare is thinking along these lines. If something is red or a husband or good, then there must be something X which makes it true to say that it is red or a husband or good, such that if anything else possessed X it too would be red or a husband or good. So from the fact that something is red or a husband or good, we can derive the principle that all things which are X are red or husbands or good. In the case of descriptive terms, like "red" or "husband," the principle that all X's are red, and that all X's are husbands, will be a truth of logic; but with prescriptive terms, like "good," the principle that all things which are X are good will, thanks to this prescriptivity, be a substantial, a synthetic, moral principle. But what Hare forgets is that the X which makes it true to say that this thing is red or a husband is the fact that it is red or a married male—that is, a husband. Indeed, if the X in question did not logically entail being red or being a husband, then the claim that all X's are are red or husbands could not be a truth of logic at all. So if moral judgments are, in the same sense, universalizable, what follows from the fact that this is good is only that all things which are X are good, where being X logically entails being good.

We need to distinguish, as Hare does not, between two interpretations of the claim that if something A is Y, there must be something X which makes it true to say that A is Y, such that if anything else were X it too would be Y. On the one hand, we can take the relationship between X and Y to be a logical relation, so that it is a matter of logic, that A's being X makes A Y. In this case the principle "All X's are Y's" will be a necessary, analytic truth— or if you prefer, a meaning rule. But on the other hand, we can take the relationship between X and Y to be a factual relation, so that it is a matter of fact, not of logic, that A's being X makes A Y. In this case the principle "All X's are Y's" will be a contingent, synthetic truth—or, among moral judgments, a moral principle. Hare passes from the claim that if a thing is red it must possess features, even if only the color red itself, which make it correct to call it red, to the claim that if a thing is good there must be something, logically independent of the fact that it is good, which makes it good. Now to assert that if A is Y there must be something which, as a matter of logic, makes A Y is to assert that if the term "Y" can be applied to anything there must be rules governing its application, even if the rule is only "Whatever is Y is Y." This is what is as trivial as trivial can be. But to assert that if A is Y there must be something which *as a matter of fact* makes A Y is to assert what is traditionally known as the Principle of Sufficient Reason. Which is not so trivial.

Thus the reason the universalizability of moral judgments yields synthetic moral principles, and not mere meaning rules, is not, as Hare thinks, that moral terms are prescriptive. It is that the universalizability in question is not the universalizability of "to say that something is red is to say that it is of a certain kind, and so to imply that anything which is of that kind is red"

(FR, p. 11); but the universalizability of "if something is red there is some reason why it is red" ("To universalise is to give the reason," FR, p. 5). The claim is that if a thing is good or bad, right or wrong, ought or ought not be done, there must be some contingently sufficient reason why it is, where a contingently sufficient reason is a reason R such that anything which is R is, *ceteris paribus*, good or bad, right or wrong, and so forth, this being a contingent and not a logical truth. This contingent truth that anything which is R is good will be the moral principle presupposed by the particular moral judgment that this thing is good.

II

The question of whether moral judgments are universalizable, in Hare's sense, now becomes the question of whether the Principle of Sufficient Reason applies in ethics. Indeed, if Hare's claim that his universalizability thesis is a logical thesis is to be upheld, the question is whether it is a fact of logic that the Principle of Sufficient Reason applies in ethics. For Hare's arguments to this effect we have to turn to Chapter 5, Section 2, of his *Language of Morals* (Oxford, 1952; abbreviated to LM).

The argument there is that goodness is what has been called a "supervenient" or "consequential" property. If someone says that X is good and Y is not, and yet denies that there is any other difference between X and Y, then we will know that something has gone wrong with his use of the word "good." In *Freedom and Reason*, Hare says, "He must either produce (or at least admit the existence of) some principle which makes him hold different moral opinions about apparently similar cases, or else admit that the judgments he is making are not moral ones" (p. 102). I think he would say that this holds of all evaluative judgments, and not just moral ones. By itself this argument is little more than persuasive —what we need is some account of why the logic of evaluative terms should be like this—but nevertheless it persuades me. It does seem that if one thing is good and another not, there must, as a matter of logic, be some difference between them which explains why one is good and the other not.

Let us agree, then, that the Principle of Sufficient Reason applies in ethics as a matter of logic, that if something is good then there must be some reason why it is good—which is to say that particular moral judgments, like "This is good," presuppose moral principles of the form "Whatever is like this in certain respects is also good." This conclusion has, indeed, been challenged on the grounds that one need not think of one's own moral views as binding on others, but I doubt whether this is a valid objection. Let us take the standard example of Sartre's student who was uncertain whether he ought to leave occupied France and join the Free French in the attempt to liberate his country, or whether he ought to stay with his mother and protect her. The main point of this example for Sartre is that previously formulated and accepted principles are of no help in this situation. The student accepts that one ought to act for one's country and that one ought to protect one's parents, but this tells him nothing when, as here, the principles point in opposite directions. The student has to decide *for himself* what, in such a situation, is the right thing to do, and in this sense he, as Sartre would put it, chooses his own morality—although it is worth remembering that this happens only because antecedently accepted principles have come into conflict. The point of this example for us is rather different. The question is whether, in deciding that he ought to join the Free French, in deciding that his country takes precedence over his family, the student is adopting a principle which will apply equally to anyone who is in his situation. Or is he merely

saying that this is what *he* ought to do, whereas perhaps others ought to act differently, even in a situation precisely like this? To put it in the sort of terms that Sartre might favor: in deciding that he ought to join the Free French, is the student legislating only for himself, or is he legislating for all humanity?

Hare's view is that, if he is not to be misusing the word "ought," the student must be legislating for everyone; if he has decided that the reasons for joining the Free French outweigh the reasons for staying with his mother, then he has decided that they do so no matter who is placed in this position. Of course, the student might say, "Matters are so evenly balanced here that it is impossible to say which of the two you ought to do. I have decided to join the Free French, but other people may well decide differently." But once the student has decided that he *ought* to join the Free French, then he has decided that this is the right decision, and that anyone who decides differently has decided wrongly. This view of the matter is certainly tempting, but so too is the opposite view, which has been argued by Alisdair MacIntyre: "Someone faced with such a decision might choose either to stay or to go without attempting to legislate for anyone else in a similar position. He might decide what to do without being willing to allow that anyone else who chose differently was blameworthy" ("What Morality Is Not," *Philosophy*, 32 [1957], p. 325). MacIntyre suggests the further example of the conscientious objector who says, "I ought to abstain from participation in war, but I cannot criticize or condemn responsible nonpacifists."

The first thing to notice about this is that the point at issue is not, as MacIntyre suggests, whether in deciding that I ought to do Y I decide that anyone who, in the same situation, acts differently is *blameworthy*; but whether in deciding that I ought to do Y I decide that anyone who, in the same situation, acts differently is *acting wrongly.* For I will not blame someone for doing what I regard as wrong if I believe that he is entitled to his opinion that what he does is right, just as I do not blame people who hold different, and I believe mistaken, moral views from me on such contentious matters as abortion and the war in Vietnam. Thus the conscientious objector might say, "I do not blame responsible nonpacifists, but I think that what they do is wrong." And Sartre's pupil might say, "Since the situation is so difficult I would not blame someone who acted differently from me, although I would think that his decision and his action were wrong." All this is quite consistent with Hare's universalizability thesis.

In order for these examples to count against Hare, the conscientious objector would have to say, "I believe that I ought not take part in the war, but someone else in my situation might quite correctly think otherwise"; and Sartre's pupil would have to say, "I have decided that I ought to join the Free French, but someone else in the same situation might quite correctly decide that he ought to stay with his mother." This may seem harder to defend, but it is still defensible. Indeed, interpreted in one way, it is something that many people would agree with. For Sartre's pupil might say, "I believe that I ought to join the Free French but if, in a situation like mine, you sincerely believe that you ought to stay with your mother, then that is what you ought to do—you ought to act differently, even though your situation is the same as mine." But notice that this does not count against Hare's universalizability thesis, for there is still a reason why Sartre's student ought to join the Free French, while someone else ought not—namely, that Sartre's student sincerely believes that this is what he ought to do. The student's decision presupposes the principle that, in a situation like this, one ought to do what one believes one ought to do, which means that if different people think differently then they ought to act differently. The principle is, in other words: in a situation like this, follow your conscience.

The claim is not that if I ought to do X then there is some reason why anyone ought to do X, but that if I ought to do X then there is some reason why I ought to do X (Principle of Sufficient Reason), such that anyone else to whom that reason applies ought also to do X (logical consistency). For example, Hare says, "Offences against the thesis of universalizability are logical, not moral. If a person says 'I ought to act in a certain way, but nobody else ought to act in that way in relevantly similar circumstances,' then, on my thesis, he is abusing the word 'ought'; he is implicitly contradicting himself" (*FR*, p. 32). This, he says, is a feature not specifically of moral judgments, but of any judgment using the word "ought." So let us take an example where "ought" is not used morally, as when I say, "I ought to go and see *Hamlet* before the season finishes." At first sight it seems that I am not at all committed to saying that anyone else in my situation ought to see it, too; my decision is a purely personal one and I am not "legislating" for anyone else. Nevertheless, I have some reason for thinking I ought to see *Hamlet*—for example, that I will enjoy it—and by "relevantly similar circumstances" Hare must mean, whether he realizes it or not, circumstances where the same reason applies. So the point is that if I think I ought to see *Hamlet* because I would enjoy it, then I will think that anyone else who would enjoy it ought, for the same reason, to see it, too. A reason is a reason for anyone for whom it is a reason, but this is not to say what is obviously false, that a reason for one person is a reason for anyone, that all reasons apply equally to everyone.

Thus the universalizability that Hare argues for is immune from MacIntyre's criticisms. But it may still be that the universalizability which Hare actually holds is not, for he continually states his view in terms of "same situation" or "same circumstances," as if he took the thesis to be that if A ought to do X then anyone, no matter who he is, in the same *objective* state of affairs ought also to do X. MacIntyre has given us good reason for doubting this claim. Thus Hare says, for example, "It is . . . characteristic of desires that they are not universalisable. . . . To want something does not commit the wanter to wanting other people, in the same circumstances, to have it" (*FR*, p. 157), as if the universalizability of moral judgments meant that thinking that you ought to do something commits you to thinking that other people, in the same circumstances, ought to do it also. Again, "All that the universalist is committed to in making a moral judgment is to saying that *if* there is another person in a similar situation, then the same judgment must be made about his case" (*FR*, pp. 48-49). Then (p. 154) Hare considers the good-health idealist who says to himself, "I ought to get out of bed now," without wanting to say that everyone else (of a similar age, and so forth) ought to get out of bed, too. Hare says, "This may be only a hypothetical 'ought'; he may mean merely that if he wants to live up to his ideal, he ought . . . ," as if the possibility that it is a categorical "ought" would conflict with the claim that all "oughts" are universalizable. But this "ought" can be categorical without this committing the good-health idealist to believing that everybody in his situation ought to leap out of bed. For the universal principle presupposed by his "ought" may be "Everyone with the good-health ideal ought to leap out of bed now." This would conflict with the universalizability thesis only if the thesis were that "oughts" apply universally, irrespective of the individual's particular interests, beliefs, and opinions. But Hare has given us no argument for such a thesis, and MacIntyre's arguments count against it.

In other words, Hare has established that if something ought to be done, then anything to which the same reason applies ought also, *ceteris paribus*, to be done. He

has not established that different people ought in the same situations to do the same thing, for the fact that they are different people might mean that the reasons which apply to them are different—as with Sartre's example, or with the good-health idealist, or with my thinking that I ought to see *Hamlet*.

III

In *Freedom and Reason*, Hare insists that the moral principles presupposed by particular moral judgments may be of any kind whatsoever: "On my view, there is absolutely no content for a moral prescription that is ruled out by logic or by the definition of terms." But in an earlier article, "Universalizability" (*Proceedings of the Aristotelian Society* [1954-55]; abbreviated to *U*), he had held that moral principles must, *qua* moral principles, be of a particular kind which, following Ernest Gellner, he called *U*-type. In *Freedom and Reason* he describes what he originally said as "worse than misleading" by which he means, I take it, that it is false. So it might seem that Hare has changed his mind about whether moral principles must be *U*-type principles. But in fact this is not so.

A *U*-type principle is one which contains no singular terms, no proper names, or definite descriptions, but is couched solely in general—Hare would prefer to say universal—terms. A singular term is one which refers to, or is defined by reference to, a particular thing or things, as "English" is defined by reference to England. Thus for Hare "being English" is not a universal; we will see how this misleads him. The first thing to notice is the difference between a judgment's being universal and its being *U*-type. "All Lockes are muddle-headed philosophers" is a universal proposition, but it is not *U*-type because it contains the proper name "Locke." In "Universalizability," Hare seemed to be aware of this distinction; he holds that all principles are universal, but that moral principles differ from others in being U-type principles: "I cannot be accused . . . of making my thesis [that moral judgments are U-type valuations] analytic in virtue of the meaning of the word 'reason'; for I see no grounds in common language for confining the word 'reason' to reasons involving U-type rules. I shall, however, argue later that it is analytic in virtue of the meaning of the word 'moral'" (U, p. 298). But in *Freedom and Reason* Hare ignores this distinction: "'England' is here a singular term, which prevents the whole proposition from being universal" (p. 36) or "The second part of this proposition contains no singular terms, and can therefore be called properly universal" (p. 11). So Hare thinks that all principles, being universal, will be U-type, and hence that the assumption that moral principles are universal in this sense—that is, are U-type principles—puts no restriction on the content of moral principles. In the next section we shall question the assumption that not all principles are universal, but for a start it is clear that not all principles are U-type, as Hare himself has shown. "I do not claim . . . that the rule or maxim which is involved in giving a reason is always of type U . . . . 'It resulted in an improvement in Great Britain's balance of payments' might be given as a reason for an action by someone who would only think it a reason if it improved *Great Britain's* balance of payments, not if it improved the balance of payments of some other country, however similar qualitatively" (U, pp. 297-298).

The question is, then, whether Hare was right in thinking that *moral* principles must be U-type principles. His argument (U, pp. 304 ff.) was that we could not understand a person's claim to be making a moral judgment—for example, that you ought not to do that—unless he were prepared to say that other similar people in other similar situations ought not do it either. This argument fails to establish the conclusion. Suppose I say, "You ought not do that," and, when asked why, say, "Because you are an Englishman." I happen to believe that the English are, by virtue of being English, a race subject to specially high moral standards, which do not apply to other lesser beings. I accept, as a moral principle, that Englishmen ought not to do things like that—for example, kiss one another when they score goals at soccer—though I see nothing wrong with members of other nationalities doing it. My principle is a universal principle, in the sense that it applies to all Englishmen, but it is not a U-type principle because it contains what Hare would consider a singular term, "Englishmen." Nevertheless, when I say that you ought not to do that, I am prepared to say that other similar people—that is, other Englishmen—ought not to do it either. So Hare's argument against the possibility of a moral principle which is not of type U does not apply against this moral principle, which is not of type U. No doubt Hare would say that my "You ought not to do that" cannot be a moral judgment unless I am prepared to say it applies to everyone who is like Englishmen. That is, if on some far-distant planet we were to come across people who were born in a country which is in all respects precisely like England then, if my principle is to be a moral principle, I would have to say that they, too, ought not kiss one another when they score goals. But it is clear that my saying "Englishmen ought not kiss one another when they score goals" does not necessarily commit me to applying this same principle to these other people. I may say that no matter how like the English these people happen to be, they are still not English, and in a matter like this that makes all the difference. Perhaps I would be regarded as inconsistent in not extending my principle to cover these *nouveaux* English, but my inconsistency would not be a logical inconsistency; it would be more like putting sugar in your tea one day and not the next. But the important point is that if I extend my principle to cover these nouveaux English *I am* extending it; my original principle did not cover them, it applied only to the genuine English, and it was no less a moral principle for that.

Thus Hare's argument does not establish that a moral principle must be a *U*-type principle. What it does seem to establish is that a moral principle must be a universal principle, in that "I ought not to do that" implies "A person like me in circumstances of this kind ought not to do that kind of thing when the other people involved are the sort of people they are" (*U*, p. 305). We can now see how, in *Freedom and Reason*, Hare comes to assume that any principle, moral or not, must be *U*-type, and why he describes his earlier argument as "worse than misleading." He sees that, in the sense in which his argument shows moral principles to be universal, all principles are universal, and so the argument cannot demonstrate a difference between moral and nonmoral principles. But, in *Freedom and Reason*, he fails to notice the distinction between "universal" and "*U*-type," and so he thinks that his original argument shows not just that moral judgments presuppose universal principles, but that they presuppose *U*-type principles. In the end, as Professor D. H. Munro has pointed out (in a review of *FR*, *Australasian Journal of Philosophy*, 42 [1964], p. 125), Hare seems to be saying that since "It is illegal to marry one's own sister" is not universalizable (it contains an implicit reference to a particular jurisdiction), it must lack descriptive meaning (cf. *FR*, p. 36)!

IV

Why should Hare have wanted to say that moral principles must be *U*-type? The main reason people have wanted to insist that moral judgments are universalizable is that they hope to show that it is a logical

truth, and therefore something that can be established by a theory-neutral analytic ethics, that we ought not to make exceptions in our own favor: I cannot, logically cannot, claim an obligation for others that would not apply to me, nor a right for myself that would not apply to others. Morality, we might say, is no respecter of persons. Less metaphorically, moral principles do not make exceptions of particular individuals just because they happen to be those particular individuals. If a moral principle applies or does not apply to a particular person, it is not because he is that particular person, but because he possesses some feature or combination of features which could, at least in principle, be possessed by others. It does not matter *who* you are; what counts is only the general—Hare would prefer to say the universal—features of you and your situation.

Now I think it is clear that this thesis is not one which is logically true, either in virtue of what we mean by a *principle* or in virtue of what we mean by a *moral* principle. Rather the claim that morality is no respecter of persons is itself a substantial moral claim which some might not accept. Someone might well believe in the divine rights of kings, and believe that his king is the only monarch in whom these rights are invested. "The king and only the king," he says, "has the right to deprive his subjects of their lives." This, he believes, is a moral truth and one which applies to only the one person; the king alone has the right to take human life. Here is a moral principle which makes an exception of a particular individual. Indeed, here is a principle, and a moral one at that, which does not seem to be universal.

It might be said that "The king may deprive his subjects of their lives" is implicitly universal, despite the fact that it begins with a "the" and not an "all," in that it says, in effect, that *all* kings have this right. But for a start I see no reason in logic why someone should restrict the application of this principle to this particular king, and not apply it to his predecessors and successors. Or, if this seems implausible, suppose someone to believe that there will and can be only one Christ, and that this Christ has rights and duties which no one else can have. "Christ was alone in having a duty to die for us" is not even implicitly universal, if being universal means being of the form "All *X*'s are *Y*'s."

Hare's argument has been, however, that particular moral judgments presuppose universal moral principles, in that if anything is, for example, good, there will be some principle of the form "Everything like this in the relevant respects is good" which states the reason why this thing is good. Thus, if the king alone has this right to deprive people of their lives there must be some reason why he has it—for example, that, as king, he derives it from God. If Christ alone has this duty to die for us there must be some reason why he has this duty—for example, that he was the Son of God and so alone was in a position to die for us. But in what sense do these reasons provide us with *universal* moral principles? "Everyone (anyone) who is king has this right," "Everyone (anyone) who is the Son of God has this duty," may be universal in form, but they still apply to only one person. Inasmuch as there is only one king, only one Son of God, these principles precisely do make exceptions of particular people.

The point is that even if moral judgments do, as a matter of logic, presuppose reasons, no limit has been set on what can be offered as a reason. All the argument has shown is that if I believe that I am morally privileged, then I must be able to offer reasons why I am thus privileged—for example, that I am the author of "The Trivializability of Universalizability." No doubt this reason is morally unacceptable; no one will accept this fact as morally relevant. But to say this is to import a moral element into an argument supposed to be purely logical. All that is required by logic

is that I offer some reason; whether you find my reason morally acceptable is neither here nor there. My reason generates the "universal" moral principle "Everyone like me in being the author of this article has these special rights," but since I am the only person who wrote it—and though others may write similar articles with the same name, no one else can write *this* article—the principle is only formally universal; it still applies to only one person.

The error is obvious enough. Once we say that moral principles are universal principles, we will naturally think of them as applying to everyone, as allowing no exceptions. Thus, for example, Bernard Mayo: "Secondly, it [a moral judgment] must be universalizable in the sense that it applies not only to me but to you; not only to you but to me; not only to us but to everybody; this is involved in speaking of *moral* principles as opposed to maxims or private policies" (*Ethics and the Moral Life* [New York, 1958], p. 91). Yet the plain fact is that not all moral principles do apply to everyone. "Wives ought to honor and obey their husbands" does not apply to me, and "Thou shalt not commit adultery," taken strictly, does not apply to anyone who is not married. What is true, of course, is that these principles apply to anyone who is a wife, to anyone who is married, and principles containing singular terms are no different in this respect; "Englishmen ought not do that" applies to anyone who is English. These principles apply universally in the sense that they would apply to anyone *if* he were a wife, if he were married, if he were an Englishman. The point is merely that any principle, moral or not, *U*-type or not, applies to anyone who falls within its scope, under its range of application. Which is yet another triviality.

If it is false to say that all moral principles apply to everyone, and trivial to say that all moral principles apply to everyone who falls within their range of application, what of the claim that moral principles apply to people irrespective of who they are? This would be correct only if it were true that moral principles cannot contain references to particular items and individuals—that is, if moral principles must be *U*-type principles. But this, as we have seen, is precisely what Hare does not establish; he merely takes it for granted because he does not distinguish "*U*-type" from "universal." All that has been shown is that moral principles must be universal in the trivial sense of applying to everyone and everything that they apply to.

V

All this may seem unfair to Hare. For his avowed position in *Freedom and Reason* is that the universalizability of moral judgments sets no limit on their possible content. Rather, when coupled with the fact that moral judgments are prescriptive and that there are, in fact, limits to what most of us are prepared to prescribe for ourselves, the universalizability of moral judgments sets a limit to what we can honestly and sincerely assert as a moral judgment. If someone says that, in a particular case, something ought to be done, then he himself must be prepared to do that same thing, should he find himself in the same situation or one which is similar in the relevant respects. If he is not prepared to, then he cannot be making a genuine moral claim; indeed, he must be misusing the word "ought." "What circumscribes . . . moral prescriptions . . . is, on my theory, not . . . a verbal restriction on the content of moral judgments; it is rather the desires and inclinations of the human race" (*FR*, p. 195).

Thus the fact that there are limits to what we are prepared to prescribe for ourselves—and, for Hare, to prescribe something for oneself is to do it if one can —does set a limit to what any ordinary nonfanatical person will be willing to offer

as a moral prescription. For example, if I want to say that Jews ought to be exterminated or that homosexuals ought to be imprisoned, then I must be prepared to accept extermination or imprisonment for myself, should I turn out to be a Jew or a homosexual. Only what Hare calls a fanatic would go to this extreme; such people "must e.g. want to get rid of Jews more than they themselves want to live; or they must want to lock up homosexuals more than they want to be at liberty themselves" (*FR*, p. 197).

Someone might say, "I believe that Jews ought to be exterminated, and therefore that if I were a Jew I too ought to be exterminated. But this doesn't mean that if I were a Jew I would accept extermination. For if I were a Jew I would not believe that Jews ought to be exterminated. What this shows is not that there is something wrong with my moral beliefs, but that there is something wrong with Jews— that they are too stupid or insensitive to recognize what is morally right." Hare has an answer to this. The question is not what I would or would not be prepared to do if I were in some situation S, but what I am or am not, here and now, prepared to commit myself to doing should I find myself in situation S. We ask not "What *would* you say or feel or think, or how *would* you like it, if you were he?" but "What *do* you say (*in propria persona*) about a hypothetical case in which you are in his position?" (*FR*, p. 108).

Now this theory of moral reasoning presupposes that moral judgments are universalizable in a further sense which we have not so far discussed. For the form of the argument presupposes that it is always possible to construct at least a hypothetical case in which the moral principles in question apply to the person who was originally applying them to someone else. This means that, despite Hare's claim that he is not setting limits to the content of moral judgments, moral principles cannot admit of exceptions being made of particular people

—or else it would be comparatively easy to avoid having a particular principle used against oneself. But more than that, it also means that it must always be possible to apply *any* moral principle to *anyone*, at least in a hypothetical case. We have already seen that not all moral principles do apply to everyone; "Englishmen ought not to kiss one another when they score goals" does not apply to me. But it *could* be applied to me; it would apply to me *if* I were English.

Nevertheless, not all moral principles are hypothetically applicable in this way. True, "Wives ought to honor and obey their husbands" would apply to me *if* I were a wife. But in so far as this condition is not one which I could satisfy, this principle is not one which can be applied to me (*in propria persona*), even in a hypothetical situation. It is not necessary to labor this defect in Hare's argument. The point has been made, elegantly, by C. C. W. Taylor (review of *FR, Mind*, 14 [1965], p. 287):

How would Hare's argument deal with a white man who said "Africans who have been brought up in a tribal society, whose moral outlook is consequently quite different from ours, who don't accept European standards of culture, education etc. are not worth the slightest moral consideration, but should be treated simply as chattels by their white masters"? There is no point in saying to this man, suppose him to be a South African farmer of Dutch descent, moderate means, secondary school education and rigid Calvinist principles, "What do you, Heinrick Potgeiter, say of a hypothetical situation in which *you*, Heinrick Potgeiter, are in the situation of such an African?" For what can count as being in the situation of such an African other than having not only the physical characteristics but also the upbringing, outlook, sympathies and interests of such an African? And what is this other than actually being such an African? But what is the sense of the supposition that a white farmer of Dutch descent etc., might in certain circumstances be an African of a totally different educational level and moral and social outlook? Surely the only sense is that the farmer has come to be another person. But the whole force of the argument depended on the assumption that the person in the hypothetical situation and the person required to legislate for that situation should be *the same* person.

The important point for Hare is not so much that moral principles do not admit of exceptions being made of particular people but, more generally, that moral principles can always be applied to anyone. Unfortunately this is not so, and no doubt the word "universal" is to blame once again (notice, for example, *FR*, p. 107: "If it is a universal property, then, because of the meaning of the word 'universal,' it is a property which might be possessed by another case in which he played a different role"). Moral principles may be universal in the sense of applying to everything of the particular sort, though this universality becomes trivial when there is and can be only one thing of that sort. They are not universal in the sense of being applicable to everyone. Indeed, as Taylor shows, this does not follow even if it is shown that moral principles must necessarily be *U*-type principles.

VI

We began by asking what it means to say that moral judgments are universalizable. Predictably enough, we have found that it might mean several different things. In particular, to say that "A ought to do X" is universalizable might mean:

(1) that it presupposes some logical truth, dependent upon a meaning rule, to the effect that anything which is Y ought to be done (since if X ought to be done there must be some feature or combination of features Y which, as a matter of meaning or logic, makes X something which ought to be done);

(2) that it presupposes some synthetic moral principle to the effect that anything which is Y ought to be done (since if X ought to be done there must be some feature or combinations of features Y which, as a matter of fact as opposed to a matter of logic, makes X something which ought to be done);

(3) that it presupposes some universal principle (since any principle, moral or otherwise, will be universal in some sense);

(4) that it presupposes some U-type moral principle (since if the principle were not U-type, if it contained some singular terms, it would not be a universal principle);

(5) that it presupposes some moral principle which applies to anyone and everyone (since a universal or U-type principle applies to anyone and everyone);

(6) that it presupposes some moral principle which cannot allow exceptions to be made of particular people just because they happen to be those particular people (since a universal or U-type principle applies equally to all);

(7) that it presupposes some moral principle which could be applied to anyone and everyone (since a universal or U-type principle could be applied to anyone and everyone).

My argument has been as follows:

(1) is a necessary consequence of the fact that moral judgments can be true or false, and is therefore a logical truth, but also a trivial one.

(2) is a necessary consequence of the fact that the Principle of Sufficient Reason applies to moral truths, and in so far as this is a consequence of the logic of moral terms, as I believe it is, so far thesis (2) is

also a logical truth. It may also be trivial, but it is not so trivial as (1).

(3) is a logical truth only if "universal" means "applying to everything it applies to," in which case it too is utterly trivial. Otherwise it is false, so long as "The Son of God alone had a duty to die for us" is a possible moral judgment.

(4) is also false, so long as "Englishmen ought not to kiss one another when they score goals" is a possible moral judgment.

(5) is also false, so long as "Wives ought to honor and obey their husbands" is a possible moral judgment.

(6) may well be true, though as a matter of fact rather than a matter of logic. Or rather it is true as a matter of morals, since it is in itself a substantial moral claim, not in the sense of setting limits to what is good or bad, right or wrong, and so forth, but in the sense of setting limits on what considerations can be accepted as morally relevant.

(7) is false, so long as there are some morally relevant properties which cannot be possessed by a particular people.

Hare's errors seem to spring originally from his loose and idiosyncratic use of "universal." The most that his argument shows is that if we make exceptions we must have reasons for making them. But as a thesis about the logic of moral judgments, it sets no limits whatsoever to what those reasons might be. If I want to, I can always find some reason why you ought to do X while I need not, or why I may do X while you ought not, though if I do this often enough my moral opinions are going to look odd or my moral judgments insincere, or both. Nevertheless, though sticks and stones may break my bones, logic cannot hurt me.

Generalization in Ethics

MARCUS SINGER

INTRODUCTORY

Section 1. The question "What would happen if everyone did that?" is one with which we are all familiar. We have heard it asked, and perhaps have asked it ourselves. We have some familiarity with the sort of context in which it would be appropriate to ask it. Thus we understand that it is either elliptical for or a prelude to saying, "If everyone did that, the consequences would be disastrous," and that this is often considered a good reason for concluding that one ought not to do that. The situations in which this sort of consideration might be advanced are of course exceedingly diverse. One who announces his intention of not voting in some election might be met by the question, "What would happen if no one voted?" If no one voted, the government would collapse, or the democratic system would be repudiated, and this is deemed by many to indicate decisively that everyone should vote. Again, one who disapproves of another's attempts to avoid military service might point out: "If everyone refused to serve, we would lose the war." The members of a discussion group, which meets to discuss papers presented by members, presumably all realize that each should take a turn in reading a paper, even one who may not

want to and prefers to take part in the discussions only, because if everyone refused the club would dissolve, and there would be no discussions. This sort of consideration would not be decisive to one who did not care whether the club dissolved. But it undoubtedly would be decisive to one who enjoys the meetings and wishes them to continue.

Each of these cases provides an example of the use or application of a type of argument which I propose to call *the generalization argument:* "If everyone were to do that, the consequences would be disastrous (or undesirable); therefore, no one ought to do that." Any argument of the form "The consequences of no one's doing that would be undesirable; therefore everyone ought to do that" is also, obviously, an instance of the generalization argument. It is this line of argument, and considerations resembling it, that will be at the very center of this inquiry.

The basic problem about the generalization argument (which can be thought of indifferently as either an argument or a moral principle) is to determine the conditions under which it is a good or valid one, that is to say, the conditions under which the fact that the consequences of *everyone's acting* in a certain way would be undesirable, provides a good reason for concluding that it is wrong for anyone to act in that way. For there are conditions under which the generalization argument is obviously not applicable, and it is necessary to determine just what they are. The instances presented above are ones in which the consideration of the consequences of everyone's acting in a certain way seems clearly relevant to a moral judgment about that way of acting. But there are others in which this sort of consideration is just as clearly irrelevant. For instance, while "humanity would probably perish from cold if everyone produced food, and would certainly starve if everyone made clothes or built houses,"[1] it would be absurd to infer from this that no one ought to produce food or to build houses.

It might be thought that this is a counterexample, which proves the generalization argument to be invalid or fallacious generally. To argue that you ought not to do something because of what would happen if *everyone* did, though it is somewhat like arguing that you ought not to do something because of what would happen if you do, is also quite different. On the pattern of, "If you were to do that the consequences would be disastrous, therefore you ought not to do that," we can argue, "If everyone were to do that the consequences would be disastrous, therefore not everyone ought to do that." But the transition from "not everyone ought to do that" to "no one ought to do that," from "not everyone has the right" to "no one has the right," seems surely fallacious. It is like saying that no one has red hair because not everyone does. Yet this transition, or something very much like it, is essential to the generalization argument.

But there is actually no fallacy involved in the generalization argument, though there may be in particular applications of it. For it is not always a fallacy to argue from "some" to "all," and the belief that it is always fallacious is merely a prejudice arising out of a preoccupation with certain types of statements. It is a fact of

[1] Morris R. Cohen, *The Faith of a Liberal* (New York: Henry Holt and Company, 1946), p. 86.

logic that if any one argument of a certain form is invalid then all arguments of that form are invalid, and this is the principle underlying the use of counterexamples. Yet it involves an inference from "some" to "all." It is true that the generalization argument involves an inference from "not everyone has the right" to "no one has the right," from "it would not be right for everyone" to "it would not be right for anyone." This inference, however, is mediated, and therefore qualified, by the principle that *what is right (or wrong) for one person must be right (or wrong) for any similar person in similar circumstances.* For obvious reasons I shall refer to this principle as "the generalization *principle*," even though it has traditionally been known as the principle of fairness or justice or impartiality.

The generalization principle is not likely to be regarded as fallacious. Yet it has frequently been regarded as vacuous and hence devoid of significant application. This also is not so, and the best way of showing this is by showing how it can be significantly and usefully applied. The generalization argument presupposes and consequently depends upon the generalization principle, and the generalization principle is certainly of considerable interest in its own right. So the next chapter will be devoted to determining the meaning and importance of this principle. This will involve a consideration of the meaning and function of the qualification "similar persons in similar circumstances," and this in turn will provide us with the basis for determining its connections with moral judgment and moral reasoning.

My examination of the generalization *argument* will follow this, and my method here, for the most part, will be to consider a number of fairly plausible objections to it and to show that they are not decisive. This will take us some distance towards the formulation of the conditions under which the generalization argument is valid. ....

CHAPTER IV:
THE GENERALIZATION
ARGUMENT

The generalization argument has the general form: "If everyone were to do x, the consequences would be disastrous (or undesirable); therefore no one ought to do x." It will be convenient to refer to any particular argument of this or some equivalent form as an instance, or application, of the generalization argument. Any actual instance of this argument may of course appear with many variations of wording. One might merely ask the question, "What would happen if everyone did that?" or "How would you like it if everyone did that?" This sort of argument, however, underlies the use of such questions. But there is actually no great difficulty in identifying instances of this argument. The major problem is that of determining its rational force, both in the general case and in particular applications.

As we have seen, there are certain conditions under which this argument is applicable, and certain conditions under which it is not. Some applications of this argument are fallacious, and some are not. Thus the basic problem about the generalization argument is to determine the conditions under which it is valid. To say that this argument is *valid* under certain conditions is to say that, under those conditions, the proposition that the consequences of everyone's acting in a certain way would be undesirable provides good reason for concluding that it is wrong to act in that way.

The statement that an application of the argument must meet certain conditions in order to be valid presupposes that the form of the argument itself is not invalid, that the argument is not invalid altogether. If the form of the argument were itself fallacious, there could be no question of distinguishing valid applications from invalid ones, for it would be invalid in every instance. And if this were the case, then the fact that it would be disastrous if everyone acted in a certain way could have no bearing on the question whether it is wrong to act in this way. It would be a fact with no moral relevance.

When stated in this way, the idea that the generalization argument is invalid in every instance should sound somewhat less plausible. Nevertheless, it is supported by the fact that the argument certainly appears to involve a formal fallacy, that of arguing from "not everyone" to "no one," or from "some" to "all." If it does, then while it might still be an effective means for persuasion, it could have no claim on rational conviction.

But this is a case in which grammatical form is a misleading guide to logical form. It is true that the generalization argument involves an inference from a statement of the form "Not everyone ought to do that" to one of the form "no one ought to do that," and thus may be said to involve an inference from "some" to "all." This is precisely why I have called it the generalization argument. But, as should by now be clear, it is not true that this sort of inference is always fallacious. It would be fallacious to argue that, since not everyone loves music, no one loves music. It is not necessarily fallacious to argue that, since not everyone ought to act in a certain way, therefore no one ought to act in that way. The difference is that in the latter case we are dealing with moral judgments, and the inference from "not everyone ought" to "no one ought" is mediated, and hence qualified, by the generalization *principle*.

That the generalization principle is involved in the generalization argument is no doubt obscured by the fact that in applications of the argument the qualification "all similar persons in similar circumstances" is left inexplicit. But in valid applications of the argument this restriction is either implicitly understood from the context or is indicated by various linguistic devices. For example, the argument "everyone ought to vote because if no one voted the government would collapse" is evidently meant to apply only to those legally permitted to vote. This condition on the argument I shall call that of *restricted universality*, and I shall go on to discuss it presently. Before doing so, however, it will be useful to set forth with some precision the various steps involved in the generalization argument, in order to illustrate more clearly its logical structure. For the generalization principle is not the only principle involved in it. Let us consider, then, the anatomy of the generalization argument.

Section 1. The argument involves, in the first place, the principle, "If the consequences of A's doing x would be disastrous, then A ought not to do x." The term "disastrous" is a stronger term than is actually necessary for the statement of this principle, as are such roughly synonymous terms as "terrible" and "catastrophic." It can be replaced by the somewhat weaker and more general term "undesirable." The consequences of an act can be undesirable without being disastrous. But if they are disastrous then they are undesirable. Thus this principle, which I shall call the *principle of consequences,* can be stated as follows: (I) If the consequences of A's doing x would be undesirable, then A ought not to do x." This is, obviously, equivalent to "If the consequences of A's *not* doing x would be undesirable, then A ought to do x." It is not, however, equivalent to "If the consequences of A's doing x would be desirable, then A ought to do x." I doubt very much whether the latter proposition is true (and whether it is or not will be discussed in Chapter VII). At any rate, it is no part of the generalization argument.

The principle of consequences is a necessary ethical or moral principle. It is necessary not only in the sense that its denial involves self-contradiction. It is necessary also in the sense that like the generalization principle, it is a necessary presupposition or precondition of moral rea-

soning. There can be sensible and fruitful disagreement about matters within the field delimited by it, but there can be no sensible or fruitful disagreement about the principle itself. We might say that, like the generalization principle, it is both necessary and fundamental.

I do not wish to imply that anyone ever has seriously questioned or denied this principle. It may be that no has done so, at least explicitly; though there are probably many instances in which it has been denied by implication, just as there are unquestionably many cases in which it has been violated or disregarded. Yet the principle can be misunderstood, especially if the term "undesirable" is not properly understood. This term may be interpreted in either of two senses, with the consequence that there are two ways of interpreting the principle. Though these two ways are consistent with each other, they should be kept distinct.

One sense of "undesirable" is that of "undesirable on the whole." On this interpretation, the principle does not mean that if *some* of the consequences of A's doing x would be undesirable then A ought not to do x. It is perfectly consistent with it for some of the consequences of an act to be desirable and others to be undesirable, or for them to be undesirable in some respects but not in others. And it may well be that while some of the consequences of an act are undesirable, it is not undesirable, on the whole, for the act to be done. For the desirable consequences may *outweigh* the undesirable ones. Or it may be that the consequences of A's not doing x would be worse (more undesirable) than the consequences of his doing it.

In the second sense of "undesirable" it does not have this proviso of "on the whole." On this interpretation, the fact that some of the consequences of A's doing x would be undesirable is a reason for asserting that A ought not to do x, but it is not a conclusive reason. On the basis of this fact one could reasonably presume that it would be wrong for A to do x.[2] This presumption can be rebutted by showing that not all the consequences are undesirable, and that the undesirable consequences are outweighed by (are less important than) the desirable ones; in other words, by showing that the consequences of A's doing x would not be undesirable on the whole. Thus a more adequate, because less elliptical, statement of the principle, on this interpretation, would be: If the consequences of A's doing x would be undesirable, then A ought not to do x *without a reason or justification.* Such statements as "A ought to do x" are usually elliptical in this way.

These brief remarks should make it clear that this principle assumes a good deal less than might at first glance be supposed. It does not by itself determine the meaning of the term "undesirable," or what is desirable or undesirable, or how the various consequences of an action are to be weighed against each other in order to determine whether they are undesirable on the whole. Agreement on the principle is quite consistent with disagreement on these latter questions. Indeed, without agreement on the principle, disagreement on these other matters would have no point.

Now this first step in the generalization argument is the basis for the second, which is a generalization from it: (2) If the consequences of everyone's doing x would be undesirable, then not everyone ought to do x.[3]

It is at the third step of the argument that the generalization principle comes into play: (3) If not everyone ought to do x, then no one ought to do x. This can of course be stated in the alternative form: If it is wrong for everyone to do x, then it is wrong for anyone to do x. Note that I have left unstated the necessary qualifications.

All of these steps are actually telescoped in the generalization argument itself, which is obviously deducible from (2) and (3); If the consequences of everyone's doing x would be undesirable, then no one ought to do x.

It may be useful to display in one place, in slightly different language, this deduction of the generalization argument from the generalization principle and the principle of consequences. The principle of consequences (C) states that: If the consequences of A's doing x would be undesirable, then A does not have the right to do x. The following principle (GC) is what I call a generalization from C: If the consequences of everyone's doing x would be undesirable, then not everyone has the right to do x. Now the generalization principle (GP) may be stated as follows: If not everyone has the right to do x, then not anyone (no one) has the right to do x. The generalization argument (if the consequences of everyone's doing x would be undesirable, then no one has the right to do x) clearly follows from GP and GC.

Some remarks on this deduction are now in order. In the above generalization from the principle of consequences, (GC), "everyone" is treated collectively, not distributively. The hypothesis "If the consequences of everyone's acting in a certain way would be undesirable" differs from "If

---

[2] I am using the expressions "A ought not to do x," "It would be wrong for A to do x," and "A has no right to do x," synonymously, and I should say that this is in general conformity with their ordinary use. Thus I am treating "A ought to do x," as equivalent to "It would be wrong for A not to do x," and "A has no right not to do x." Note that the contradictory of "A ought to do x" is not "A ought not to do x," which is rather its contrary (for neither may hold), but "A has the right not to do x" (or "A need not do x").

[3] Since expressions like "not everyone ought" and "no one ought" can be deceptive, perhaps it should be said here that I definitely do not mean by "not everyone ought" the same as "not everyone is *required*," but rather "not everyone has the

right" or "it would not be right for everyone." Similarly, by "no one ought" I do not mean "no one is required, or has the duty," but rather "no one has the right," or "it would not be right for *anyone*." (If one perfers to translate "not everyone ought to do x" by "it ought not to be the case that everyone does x," I can see no objection to it, except that it is not very idiomatic, and I cannot see that it is helpful.)

the consequences of *each and every act* of that kind would be undesirable." The latter implies that each and every act of that kind would be wrong. This is the true logical generalization of the principle of consequences, but it is not the one intended, nor is it particularly important.

Thus GC has as its consequent "not everyone ought to do *x*," instead of "everyone ought not to do *x*," because supposedly if not everyone does *x*, the undesirable consequences that would result from everyone's doing it would be avoided. Hence the generalization argument does not imply that the consequences of each and every act of the kind mentioned would be undesirable. By reason of the generalization principle it implies that each and every act of that kind may be presumed to be wrong. Yet from the fact that an act is wrong it does not follow that its consequences would be undesirable.

The generalization argument is to be distinguished from what may be called the *generalized principle of consequences:* If the consequences of doing *x* would be undesirable (in general, or usually), then it is wrong (in general) to do *x*. Here "*x*" refers, not to a specific action, but to a kind of action. The consequences of lying are usually undesirable; hence lying is usually wrong. The generalized principle of consequences refers to the *individual consequences* of actions of a certain kind. The generalization argument refers to the *collective consequences* of everyone's acting in a certain way. These are not always the same.

From the fact that the generalization principle is involved in the generalization argument, in the way shown, it follows that all the qualifications required by the former are required by the latter. They are therefore necessary for any application of the argument to be valid. The first is that of restricted universality, the restriction to "every similar person in similar circumstances." The second is the elliptical nature of the conclusion that no one has the right

to do *x*. As I mentioned once before, the form of the generalization principle especially appropriate for the proper understanding of the generalization argument is: If not everyone ought to act or be treated in a certain way, then no one ought to act or be treated in that way *without a reason or justification*. A more adequate statement of the generalization argument, therefore, is: If the consequences of everyone's acting or being treated in a certain way would be undesirable, then no one ought to act or be treated in that way *without a reason*. In other words, whoever acts in a way in which it would be undesirable for everyone to act must justify his conduct. The fact that it would be undesirable for everyone to act in that way provides a presumptive reason, and not a conclusive one, for the judgment that his conduct is wrong. One can justify oneself, or show that one is an exception, by showing that one's circumstances are relevantly different from those in which the act is wrong.

But the discussion of the procedures by which one can justify his (or someone else's) acting in a way in which it would be undesirable for everyone to act, or in which it would be generally wrong to act, may be left for later on. What I propose to do now is to consider in somewhat greater detail the condition of restricted universality. . . .

Section 3. When people begin to admonish me that if everyone did as I did, etc., I answer that "humanity would probably perish from cold if everyone produced food, and would certainly starve if everyone made clothes or built houses."[4]

[4] Morris R. Cohen, *The Faith of a Liberal* (New York: Henry Holt and Company, 1946), p. 86. Part of the sentence just prior to the one quoted in the text is: "It would be a poor world if there were no diversity of function to suit the diversity of natural aptitudes." This is true; it does not follow that we have here a valid counterexample to the generalization argument. Cf. Cohen's *Reason and Nature* (New York: Harcourt, Brace and Company, 1931), p. 433: "Nor is there any force in the argument that lying is morally bad because it cannot be made universal. The familiar argument, 'If everybody did so and so . . .' applies

This certainly has the appearance of a genuine counterexample to the generalization argument. Since the consequences of everyone's producing food would be undesirable, on the pattern of the generalization argument it would seem to follow that it is wrong for anyone to do so, and this, of course is absurd.

But this actually does not follow, and the generalization argument does not at all have this consequence. For consider what would happen if no one produced food. If no one produced food, everyone would starve. Hence on the same line of reasoning it might be argued that everyone ought to produce food. The argument that no one ought to produce food because of what would happen if everyone did can thus be met by the counterargument that everyone ought to produce food because of what would happen if no one did. A valid application of the generalization argument, however, cannot be met by such a counterargument. The argument that everyone ought to vote because of what would happen if no one did cannot be rebutted in this way.

In a case in which the consequences of everyone's acting in a certain way would be undesirable, while the consequences of no one's acting in that way would also be undesirable, I shall say that the argument can be *inverted*. Thus the argument is invertible with respect to producing food, building houses, and making clothes. Now in order for the generalization argument to have a valid application with respect to some action it is necessary that it not be invertible with respect to that action. In other words, an argument of the form, "Since the consequences of everyone's doing x would be undesirable, no one ought to do x," is valid only if it is not the case that the consequences of no one's doing x would also be undesirable.

This condition on the validity of the generalization argument is not something *ad hoc*, devised just to meet this kind of case, though even if it were, this would be no objection to it. It is another of those conditions implicitly understood but not explicitly stated, and can readily be incorporated into the statement of the argument: "If the consequences of everyone's doing x would be undesirable, while the consequences of no one's doing x would not be undesirable, then no one has the right to do x." This of course also holds in the form: "If the consequences of no one's doing x would be undesirable, while the consequences of everyone's doing x would not be undesirable, then everyone ought to do x." It is important to remember that the restrictions already discussed apply here also. The conclusion that no one has the right to do x is elliptical for "no one has the right to do x *without a reason*." Furthermore, the terms "everyone" and "no one" involved here are restricted in their scope. Thus, fully stated, incorporating all the restrictions so far discussed, the generalization argument may be stated: "If the consequences of every member of K's doing x in certain circumstances would be undesirable, while the consequence of no member of K's doing x (in those circumstances) would not be undesirable, then no member of K has the right to do x (in such circumstances) without a special reason."

The condition of restricted universality deserves special mention in this context. The terms "everyone" and "no one" must have the same restrictions on their scope in any one application of the argument. For an application of the argument may be invertible, or may seem to be so, if the term "no one" is used with a wider extension than "everyone," or if "everyone" is used with a wider extension than "no one." Such a situation can arise in the following manner. Suppose (1) that if everyone were to act in a certain way the consequences would be undesirable, and (2) that if no one were to act in that way the conse-

---

just as well to baking bread, building houses, and the like. It is just as impossible for everybody to tell lies all the time as to bake bread all the time or to build houses all the time."

quences would be undesirable. Such a case so far conforms to the condition under which the argument is invertible, and hence invalid. However, it may be that in (1) "everyone" is restricted to the members of a certain class K, while in (2) "no one" is not restricted to the members of this class but has a wider range, so that it means, say, "no one at all." In such a case the argument is not really invertible. In order for it to be invertible it is necessary for the consequences of every member of K's acting in that way and the consequences of no member of K's acting in that way both to be undesirable. It may very well be true of some kind of action that the consequences of no one *at all* acting in that way would be undesirable while the consequences of no member of a certain class acting in that way would not be.

Consider a concrete case. Suppose an attempt is made to invert the argument, "Everyone ought to vote, since the consequences would be disastrous if no one voted." To attempt to invert this argument is to raise the question of what would happen if everyone voted. "If everyone were to vote, this would mean that idiots, imbeciles, infants, illiterates, incompetents, lunatics, and public enemies would vote. And it would be just as bad if all these people were to vote as it would be if no one were to vote at all." But this has not the slightest tendency to show that the original argument is invalid. One who claims that everyone ought to vote, because of what would happen if no one did, does not mean that everyone in the universe, including idiots, illiterates, lunatics, and Martians, ought to vote. The conclusion that everyone ought to vote is restricted to the same class or classes of persons to which the term "no one," in the premise, is restricted. This is obviously, or is obviously meant to be, the class of persons of which it is true that if none of them voted the consequences would be disastrous, and does not include imbeciles, infants, or lunatics. For of these people it is not true that if none of them

voted the consequences would be disastrous; on the contrary, it would be disastrous if all such people did vote or attempt to vote. (It may be noted that this is normally the consideration invoked in order to justify legal restrictions on the right to vote.) Such people furthermore are not usually among those legally permitted to vote. Yet the argument is certainly restricted to those who are legally permitted to vote in the election in question, though it is hardly necessary for this condition to be made explicit in concrete applications. No one can justly be held responsible for not voting in an election in which he has no legal right to vote, even if there are good grounds for holding that he ought to have this right. (The question whether a law is just, is distinct from the question whether it ought to be broken; though the two are related, an answer to the one is not an automatic answer to the other.) This restriction would be even more obvious if the original premise were phrased "If everyone refused to vote . . ." instead of "If no one voted . . ." For one who is not permitted or has no opportunity to do something cannot sensibly be said to have refused to do so. This argument is therefore not invertible.

It follows that not every application of the generalization argument is invertible, and therefore that this condition is not a trivial one.

Section 5. The generalization argument is invertible with respect to certain actions because there is something wrong in the way they are described. In the cases just considered the actions were described in too general a way. An opposite inadequacy is at the root of another class of invalid applications of the argument.

"If everyone ate at six o'clock there would be no one to perform certain essential functions, things that must be attended to at all times, and so on, with the net result that no one would be able to eat at six or any other time, and with various other undesirable consequences." Does it follow that no one has the right to eat at six o'clock? If it did, we should have a genuine counterexample to the generalization argument.

The important point to notice here is that this argument in no way depends on the exact time specified. If we could argue that no one has the right to eat at six, we could argue that no one has the right to eat at five, or at seven, or at three minutes past two, and so on. We could therefore argue that no one has the right to eat at any time, and this would mean that no one has the right to eat.

In such a case as this the argument may be said to be *reiterable*. Thus the argument is reiterable whenever it is applied to some action arbitrarily specified, as part of its description, as taking place at some particular time, or at some particular place, or by some particular person, or in relation to some particular person or thing. To take another example: 'If everyone were to eat in this restaurant it would get so crowded that no one would be able to do so . . . ; therefore no one ought to eat in this restaurant." The reference to *this* restaurant is not essential here; the same argument would apply to *that* one, and to any other one. The argument can obviously be reiterated for every restaurant, and its consequence would be not just that no one ought to eat at this or that restaurant but that no one ought to eat at any restaurant. And the same argument would apply not only to restaurants but to any place or location whatsoever. Hence in this case also the implication would be that no one ought to eat. Furthermore, note that there is no need to restrict ourselves to eating in order to obtain examples of reiterable arguments. Any action, such as walking, talking, sleeping, or drinking—even doing nothing at all—when particularized in this way, will do as well.

This last point should have indicated that such examples as these can have no rational force as counterexamples. Any instance of the generalization argument that

is reiterable is invalid. For any instance of the generalization argument that is reiterable is also invertible. Note that the instances just given, which are clearly representative ones, are just as clearly invertible. The argument from "not everyone has the right to eat at six o'clock" to "no one has the right to eat at six o'clock," since it can be reiterated for any time, implies "no one has the right to eat." But what would happen if no one ate? If no one were to eat the consequences would be just as undesirable, presumably, as if everyone were to eat at the same time.

Still there is a clear-cut difference between those instances of the argument that are reiterable, and therefore invertible, and those that are invertible without being reiterable. In the latter instances the actions are described in too general a way. In the former instances the descriptions of the actions are not general enough—the actions are described in too particularized a way. In these cases particular details of the action that are really arbitrary and inessential are treated as though they were essential. These specified details—in the cases considered, the specification of the exact time and place of an action—are shown to be arbitrary, and hence not essential, by the fact that the argument can be reiterated with respect to them. There may be cases in which the exact time or place of an action is morally relevant. In these cases the argument would not be reiterable with respect to time or place, and this is the test of whether such details are essential. In the instances presented above, these details are inessential (arbitrary, irrelevant) because the argument does not depend on them, and this is shown by the fact that it can be reiterated with respect to them. The same argument applies for any given selection of time or place, and hence for every time or place.

It should be evident that the instances of reiterable arguments just given are in all important respects representative of an indefinitely large class of similar instances that might be advanced as counterexamples to the generalization argument. A few further candidates would be the following: "What would happen if everyone tried to sit in the front row?" "What would happen if everyone went to the circus today?" "What would happen if everybody tried to crowd into Times Square on New Year's Eve?" and so on. Since these are all reiterable, in one way or another, they are all invalid applications of the generalization argument, and thus provide no reason to suppose that the actions referred to are wrong. Of course, though all of these instances are invertible, not all of them are invertible directly. Yet, since the reference to a particular type of action is no more essential in these instances than the reference to the particular time or place of the action, on the same line of reasoning we could argue with equal cogency that no one ought ever to do anything at all, and this is further evidence that every application of the generalization argument that is reiterable is invertible and hence invalid.

Section 7. There is one other objection to the generalization argument, one which is, oddly enough, fairly popular, that must be disposed of. I shall only mention it here, and save extended discussion of it for the sequel (Chapter VI, section 4). It is simply irrelevant to reply, "Not everyone *will* do it." It is irrelevant because the argument does not imply or presuppose that everyone will. It may be the case, and in most cases almost certainly is, that not everyone will do the act in question; but the generalization argument in no way denies this. What the argument implies is that if A has the right to do something, then everyone else, or everyone similar to A in certain respects, has this same right in a similar situation; and therefore if it would be undesirable for everyone to have this right, then A cannot have such a right. Incidentally, this is not to say that if the consequences of everyone's acting in a certain way would be undesirable, then the consequences of some particular individual's acting in this way

would be undesirable. The consequences of any particular act of this kind, considered by themselves, may be beneficial. But this makes no difference. What has to be shown is how A is an exception. Now one is not shown to be an exception by the fact that the consequences of his acting in a certain way would not be the same as the consequences of everyone's acting in that way. Neither is one shown to be an exception by the fact that not everyone will act in that way. For, since everyone could argue in the same way, what such facts would show is that everyone is an exception, which is strictly nonsense.

Another curious misconception is one that has just been alluded to. This is to interpret the generalization argument as implying that if the consequences of everyone's doing some act would be undesirable, then the consequences of *anyone's* doing that act would be undesirable. This latter statement is so obviously false that it ought to be obvious that it is no part of the generalization argument. Yet apparently it is not. This misconception is actually the basis of a whole essay on the subject, which confidently claims that the argument "bristles with difficulties," that it has very "modest and doubtful functions," and that "most of its alleged uses . . . are sheerly fallacious . . . often where we cannot prove a fallacy we can see that there is very likely to be one and can produce no clear case where it is quite certain that no fallacy lurks."[5] These claims are not surprising, given the assumptions from which they start. They are nevertheless very wide of the mark, and that they do rest on the misinterpretation mentioned is clearly shown by such a passage as the following:

[5] C. D. Broad, "On the Function of False Hypotheses in Ethics," *The International Journal of Ethics*, vol. XXVI (April 1916), pp. 377–97 at 397. The generalization argument, ostensibly, is here called, variously, the "principle of false universalisation," the "principle of false generalization," the "argument from false universalisation," and the "argument from false generalisation." Given the argument in the text, however, these names themselves are all false.

The result of one man's action may be very small, and it may be impossible for him to see by contemplating it alone whether it be good, bad, or indifferent. But he may be able to see that a great number of such actions would produce a result of the same kind as a single one but of much greater magnitude, and that this result would be unmistakably good or bad. If he has reason to suppose that the goodness or badness of the results of a large number of similar actions is the sum of the goodness or badness of the results of the separate actions, he will be able to conclude as to the moral quality of his own proposed action though it was not obvious on mere inspection.[6]

But the procedure here detailed, which is described as "the use of the principle of false generalization as a moral microscope," is not at all an application of the generalization argument, and it is no function of the argument to determine the consequences of a particular act of a certain kind. To ask "What would happen if everyone did what you proposed to do?" though it implies that your doing it must be *wrong*, is not to imply that the *consequences* of your doing it must be bad. The consequences of your doing it may be good. Yet this possibility is actually ruled out in advance by this interpretation of the argument, since what it presupposes is that an act can be wrong only if its consequences would be undesirable.[7] This assumption is certainly false.

[6] *Ibid.*, p. 382. Cf. pp. 385–86, where this same interpretation is again very clearly brought out: "It may be said that the argument is to show that A's abstention must be wrong though its badness is not obvious on inspection, because a large number of precisely similar abstentions would have admittedly bad results. But it is surely easy to see that this argument is here a very feeble one. It is quite true that A's abstention *would* have bad consequences if it took place together with the abstention of a great many other people. But it does not in the least follow that it *will* have any bad consequences if it takes place together with but few other abstentions." The confusion between the morality of an act and the evaluation of its consequences is here self-evident.

[7] Cf. *ibid.*, p. 394, where it is stated unmistakably that 'We have all along assumed that the rightness or wrongness of an action depends wholly on its actual or probable consequences."

The confusion involved here is aptly brought out in the following passage:

You cannot argue from the fact that the *co-existence* of this motive in a great many people would lead to bad results that its existence in any particular person will lead to bad results. . . . It is very easy to commit a gross fallacy here. This is to confuse the two statements "the motive *m* frequently leads to bad results" and "the frequency of the *m* would lead to bad results." From the former we could conclude that any particular instance of the motive is likely to lead to bad results; from the latter we can conclude nothing of the sort. . . .[8]

This is very true, and the distinction presented is a most useful one, most usefully put. But it is one that can also apply to actions. Thus: (1) the action *a* frequently leads to bad results; (2) the frequency of the action *a* would lead to bad results. Now this first statement is connected with the principle of consequences, in its generalized form—indeed, it is but another statement of it—and from it we can conclude that any instance of the action *a* is likely to have bad results, and hence that any instance of the action *a* is likely to be wrong. The second statement, however, is connected, not with the principle of consequences, but with the generalization argument, and is actually an alternative statement of its premise. This gives us a good way of stating the confusion noted above. For the generalization argument does not imply that if the frequency of the action *a* would lead to bad results, then the action *a* frequently leads to bad results. Neither does it imply that if the frequency of the action *a* would lead to bad results, then any instance of the action *a* is likely to have bad results. The second statement, as well as the generalization argument, does imply that any instance of the action *a* may be presumed to be wrong. But, to repeat, this is not to imply that any instance of the action is likely to have bad consequences. . . .

[8] *Ibid.*, p. 396.

CHAPTER V:
MORAL RULES AND PRINCIPLES

Section 2. So far I have been discussing moral rules, and have said little about how they differ from moral principles. A moral rule states that a certain kind of action is generally wrong (or obligatory), and leaves open the possibility that an act (or omission) of that kind may be justifiable. Thus moral rules do not hold in all circumstances; they are not invariant; in a useful legal phrase, they are "defeasible." Moral principles, however, hold in all circumstances and allow of no exceptions: they are invariant with respect to every moral judgment and every moral situation. They are thus "indefeasible." A further point of difference between rules and principles is that principles are always relevant, whereas rules are not. For example, the rule against lying is not relevant to a situation in which lying is not involved, and the rule against killing is not relevant where killing is not involved. Moral principles, however, are relevant in every moral situation, in every situation in which a moral question arises. It is evident that such principles, at least in most instances, are bound to be somewhat more abstract than moral rules, though they are not necessarily less definite.[9]

---

[9] Some other conceptions of moral principles that have recently been presented may be worth mentioning. K. Baier, for example, in "Decisions and Descriptions," *Mind*, vol. LX (April 1951), p. 199, says: "Moral principles and moral laws differ from moral rules in that the former need not be recognized. ... A moral law or principle becomes a moral rule by becoming recognized." This seems to me no more than verbal legislation, without much chance of passing. P.H. Nowell-Smith, *Ethics* (London: Penguin Books, 1954), regards a moral principle as a "disposition to choose," and speaks of adopting, changing and choosing to change one's moral principles (pp. 306–14). I know of no sense in which a principle can be adopted or chosen, and this is reinforced by the consideration that it is "logically odd" to speak of someone's adopting or choosing different motives or dispositions. (Notice that to "choose to change one's moral principles" would, on this view, be to

The principle of a rule can be thought of as analogous to the intent of a piece of legislation, which is the purpose it was designed to achieve, and hence the reason for its existence. Situations are constantly arising in which the literal or strict interpretation of a rule would be contrary to its intent or purpose. This is, in fact, the basis of the distinction between the spirit and the letter of the law. In such situations the rule ought not to be applied. Thus, though one can have *some* understanding of a rule without understanding its intent, for an adequate understanding of the rule one should know the intent behind it. Only so can exceptions to it be made with justice and revisions of it made with intelligence. For a perfect understanding of a rule, one should, ideally, understand how it fits into the system of rules and the system of purposes they are designed to further. Now a similar point applies to moral rules and principles. One can have some understanding of a moral rule without understanding how to apply moral principles. But for an adequate understanding of a rule one must know the principles on which it is based—to put it another way, the reasons on which it is established. This is one reason why reflection on morality is essential to morality.

Let us now consider some examples of moral principles. The generalization argument is one. The generalization principle is another. A third is what I have called the *principle of consequences:* "If the consequences of A's doing x would be undesirable, then A ought not to do x." A fourth principle, obviously similar to the third, is: "It is always wrong to cause unnecessary

---

"choose to change one's dispositions to choose.") So I regard this as just another instance of verbal legislation. This is not to imply that there is nothing to be said for these ways of defining moral principles; it implies that there is very little. The basic ambiguity in the term "principle," from which these varying views derive ("principle" is often used in the sense of "motive," and was originally used in the sense of "fundamental source" or "origin"), is well brought out by Whewell, *The Elements of Morality*, Bk. II chap. IV, p. 117.

suffering." Let us call this the *principle of suffering*. A fifth principle concerns the character of moral rules and follows from what has already been said about them: "Any violation of a moral rule must be justified." This principle, which is an obvious and immediate consequence of the generalization argument, may be called the *principle of justification*.

A little reflection suffices to show that it is impossible for any of these principles to conflict, though they are all closely related, and this is a further important difference between moral rules and principles.

Yet it might be supposed that there is a possibility of a conflict between the generalization argument and the principle of consequences. For the consequences of an action in a particular case might be undesirable, while the consequences of the general performance of that sort of action might not be undesirable, and this would seem to give us incompatible results. So it is advisable to examine this possibility.

Suppose, then, that if A were to do x the consequences would be undesirable; it follows, on the principle of consequences, that A ought not to do x. Suppose, also, that if no one were to do x, the consequences would be undesirable; it would seem to follow, on the basis of the generalization argument, that everyone, including A, ought to do x. But there are two possibilities here: (1) if everyone were to do x, the consequences would also be undesirable; or (2) if everyone were to do x, the consequences would not be undesirable. In the first case, the generalization argument is invertible, and nothing follows from it. So in this case the conclusion from the principle of consequences prevails, and A ought not to do x. In the second case, there must be something distinctive about A, or the circumstances in which he is placed, to explain this difference between the consequences of his performing such an action and the consequences of everyone's performing it. If everyone similar to A did x in

a similar situation, the consequences would be undesirable, and so in this case also it follows that A ought not to do x.

I conclude from this that there is no possibility of a conflict between these two principles, and hence that there is no possibility of a conflict between any of them. Since the appearance of conflict arises out of an insufficiently detailed specification of circumstances, it can always be dispelled, and this does not have the consequence of creating a class of situations to which they are inapplicable. But there are some important points to be noted about each of the last three principles I have listed, as well as about moral principles in general, and it is the intention of the following remarks to bring these out.

1. The principle of consequences states that, if the consequences of A's doing x would be undesirable, then A ought not to do x; and I have already pointed out that this is equivalent to, "If the consequences of A's *not* doing x would be undesirable, then A ought to do x." Now it might be supposed that a case can arise in which these two statements of the principle could come into conflict, in which, in other words, this principle can lead to conflicting results. Suppose that the consequences of A's doing x would be undesirable, and also that the consequences of A's not doing x would be undesirable, and that these consequences would be equally undesirable. What follows then?

It should be noted that in most cases where one might appear to be in such a situation as this the circumstances are not exactly the same—the circumstances under which the consequences of doing x would be undesirable will be different from the circumstances under which the consequences of not doing x would be undesirable—and hence the contradiction is easily avoided. So let us imagine that the circumstances are exactly the same, and that we are referring to one and the same occasion. The condition that leads to the difficulty, then, is the one that the consequences are *equally* undesirable. Apart from this condition, the situation described would correspond almost exactly with the situation that almost always exists when two rules conflict, and one has to choose "the lesser of two evils." Apart from this condition, one's action (either of doing x or not doing x) could be justified on the ground that its consequences would not be undesirable *on the whole*, given the relevant facts about the situation, since the consequences of the alternative action would be *worse*. In the situation described, however, this possibility is closed. Since this is so, it is evident that these equally undesirable "consequences" are not actually the consequences of A's action. By hypothesis, these "consequences" are *inevitable*, no matter what A does. This does not mean that they will be exactly the same, no matter what A does, though this is a distinct possibility. What it means is that, under these peculiar circumstances, it does not matter what A does— these "consequences" are no more the consequences of A's action than they are of what B does, of what C does, or of what anyone does. Such a situation would be one beyond human control, and questions of right and wrong are as out of place as they would be in connection with an earthquake or a hurricane. What A might justly be blamed for is for getting into such a predicament in the first place. But this is something else again, and it is clear that the supposition that we have just examined constitutes no objection to this principle or to anything I have said about it. . . .

CHAPTER VI: THE APPLICATION OF THE GENERALIZATION ARGUMENT

Section 3. I have been arguing that "not everyone will do it" is neither an objection to the generalization argument nor a justification of a course of conduct that may otherwise be presumed to be wrong, and that

the fact that one may know or believe that others will not act in that way has no bearing on the situation. At the same time, I pointed out that there are cases where the circumstances or characteristics of others *are* relevant in the application of the generalization argument, that some applications of the argument presuppose that not everyone is in certain circumstances or has certain characteristics. It is now necessary to recognize that there are situations in which the *behavior* of others is also relevant. Suppose, not that not everyone will act in the way in question, or that most people will not, which is certainly the most common type of situation; but that everyone, or practically everyone, *is* acting in that way. Such situations are by no means nonexistent. Such situations are ones in which ordinary moral rules and practices are not generally observed, in which people generally, or else the members of a relatively well-defined group, can be counted on to lie, steal, cheat, or kill, or do anything else they think they can get away with. Let us call such situations "state of nature situations." Any reader of Hobbes will understand the reason why. In such situations there seems no point in asking, "What would happen if everyone acted in that way?" For practically everyone already is acting in that way, and the situation already is undesirable. Now what ought one to do in such a situation? Is one under any obligation to conform to ordinary moral rules in dealing with people who do not themselves observe them? "Suppose that I live in a society in which the spoken word is seldom to be relied on or men go about in constant fear of their lives . . . . What is my obligation?"[10] Does the generalization argument apply here? If so, how?

In order to answer such questions we must determine more precisely what the

[10] R.F. Harrod, "Utilitarianism Revised," *Mind*, vol. XLV (April 1936), p. 151. See also J. Harrison, "Utilitarianism, Universalisation, and Our Duty to be Just," *Aristotelian Society Proceedings*, N.S. vol. LIII (London: Harrison & Sons. Ltd., 1953), pp. 125–30.

situation is. The situation I am envisaging is not one of utter chaos, of unrestricted and ever increasing enmity and violence, or of a war to the death of "every man against every man." Such a state could certainly not exist for long, supposing it could exist at all, and, indeed, can hardly be imagined. At best—or at worst—the chaos could be only partial. As Hume has pointed out, in examining much the same hypothesis, "Whether such a condition of human nature could ever exist, or if it did, could continue so long as to merit the appellation of a *state,* may justly be doubted. Men are necessarily born in a family-society, at least; and are trained up by their parents to some rule of conduct and behavior."[11] The situation, then cannot be one in which absolutely everyone generally or almost always violates the fundamental rules of morality, or, in other words, in which absolutely everybody habitually lies to everybody else, or attempts to cheat, steal from, or kill everybody else, or does whatever he wants to whenever he wants to and thinks he can get away with it. *This* would be absolute chaos—a situation in which everybody was insane. It is true that in such a situation there could be no question of right and wrong, and thus no question of applying the generalization argument. But neither could there be any question about anything else. Our supposition, therefore, in order to serve as the basis for a problem, must be considerably restricted.

Let us suppose, then with Hume,

that it should be a virtuous man's fate to fall into the society of ruffians, remote from the protection of laws and government; what con-

duct must he embrace in that melancholy situation? He sees such a desperate rapaciousness prevail; such a disregard to equity, such contempt of order, such stupid blindness to future consequences, as must immediately have the most tragical conclusion, and must terminate in destruction to the greater number, and in a total dissolution of society to the rest. He, meanwhile, can have no other expedient than to arm himself, to whomever the sword he seizes, or the buckler, may belong: To make provision of all means of defence and security: And his particular regard to justice being no longer of use to his own safety or that of others, he must consult the dictates of self-preservation alone, without concern for those who no longer merit his care and attention.[12]

Hume's particular brand of utilitarianism, it is evident, leads him to the conclusion that since, in a situation of this type, the rules of justice or morality are of no use, they are therefore suspended or inapplicable, and the implication of this is that, in such a situation, one is justified in doing anything. This, I shall argue, is not the case. In such a situation one is justified in doing whatever is necessary to the preservation of one's own life, person, or property, or those of one's friends and allies, and therefore is justified in taking whatever steps are clearly necessary for this purpose. But this clearly is not a justification for doing anything whatsoever; the rules of morality, therefore, are not altogether inapplicable. And if we consider the matter more closely we shall see that the generalization argument is not either.

What I am imagining is that one is in a situation in which he has to confront or have dealings with a group of people who habitually lie to him whenever they deem it to their advantage, or would cheat, steal, assault, torture, or even kill under these same conditions. Would it be right or wrong for him to act in the same ways toward them, for him to treat them as they would treat him? Now it is true that there *seems* no point in asking, in connection

---

[11] David Hume, *An Enquiry Concerning the Principles of Morals,* L. A. Selby-Bigge, ed. (2nd ed.; Oxford: The Clarendon Press, 1902), sec. iii, part i. p. 190. Hume adds: "But this must be admitted, that, if such a state of mutual war and violence was ever real, the suspension of all laws of justice, from their absolute inutility, is a necessary and infallible consequence." For reasons to be given, I do not think that this is true, in any sense in which it means something different from saying that the "laws of justice" are not in fact observed.

[12] *Ibid.,* p. 187.

with such situations, "What would happen if everyone acted in that way?" For it seems as if everyone, or practically everyone, already is acting in that way, and the situation already is undesirable. But this is only what seems! It is not true that the generalization argument is inapplicable here. What is true is that it is not applicable in an unrestricted manner, and from this it does not follow that it is not applicable at all. That certain other people are acting or may reasonably be expected to act in certain ways is part of the context in which the generalization argument is applied. To put it another way, that certain other people are acting in ways in which it would be undesirable for everyone to act, in ways that are generally wrong, is part, and an essential part, of the circumstances in which one is acting. Thus the question whether one has, say, the right to lie to them, is not about lying simply, but about lying as a means of self-defense or self-preservation. One has the right to lie as a means to the preservation of one's own life or person or property, or in defense of those of others, provided that it really is necessary to do so or may reasonably be considered so. For if everyone *in such circumstances* were to do this, the consequences would not be undesirable. Indeed, it may be that this is the only way of ending this abysmal state of things, and if it is, it is one's duty to do so, and to attempt to bring about a situation in which law and order prevails. It may be necessary to fight fire with fire, force with force, and deception with deception. But in the nature of the case the advantage one would gain by replying in kind must be only temporary, so long as the situation continues; one's primary duty, therefore, must be to attempt to change the situation. Yet from the fact that one has no right to take unfair advantage of others, it does not follow that anyone is under the obligation of allowing others to take unfair advantage of him.

(This, incidentally, is the basis of society's right against criminals. What is called "punishment" is primarily a means to the preservation of society, and though it may justly be made to serve other purposes, this is its primary justification. But this is by no means a wholesale justification of any punishment that may in fact be meted out, of all the devices that have been used as punishments, or of the laws of every society. For it does nothing to answer the question whether a society or government is worth preserving, and it is clear that not all of them are.)

This, however, does not justify unrestricted lying, theft, or violence. The argument presented merely establishes the right of self-defense, and does not give anyone a general right to do these things, a right to do them whenever he pleases. In general, one would have the right to do these things only to those who would do them to oneself or to others, and then only as a means of self-defense. Of course, there are exceptions to this rule also, but I cannot see that even these reasons would ever justify such things as rape or pillage. Furthermore, though one may have the right to kill as a means to the preservation of one's own or someone else's life, and consequently may also cheat, lie, or steal in order to achieve the same purpose, it does not follow that one would have the right to kill or assault or injure another who would merely attempt to gain some advantage over one by lying or cheating. For in this case the means is disproportionate to the end and goes beyond what the end would justify. It would seem, then, that some gradations of priority can be set up among the actions here enumerated.

It may be wondered why the actions of others should be relevant here and not in other situations, why the fact that other people are acting, or may be expected to act, in certain ways can be a relevant difference in one's circumstances, while the fact that not everyone will act in certain ways is not. The answer is that if it were not for this fact, that others are behaving in certain immoral ways or are disregarding moral rules, the question whether one has the right to act towards them in the same way would not arise. This fact both defines the situation as a state of nature situation and generates the question. There would be no such problem if it were not for this. In other situations, on the other hand, this is not the case. The fact that "not everyone will do it" can only lead me to suppose that I can get away with it, or that the consequences will not be so terrible, and not that I have a right to do it.

A state of nature situation, in short, is just a generalization of a situation in which one has to defend oneself or help another, and everything said about it would apply to a situation involving just two people. A has no right to lie to B, but A has the right to lie to B in self-defense.

The state of nature situations considered so far may be characterized, generally, as those in which certain people, or the members of a certain group, habitually violate certain fundamental moral rules, in such a way and in such numbers as to bring instability, disorder, and uncertainty into society. As we have seen, one who for any reason finds himself in the midst of a "society" of thieves or murderers or maniacs is in such a situation. This general description is also exemplified in the relations existing between the criminal elements of a society on the one hand, and its police or law-abiding elements on the other—between any society and its underworld—as well as the relations between two warring groups or nations. But there will be many variations depending on the exact nature of the situations and the nature of the opposition between the groups. Now, however, what we have to notice is that this term can usefully be extended to cover situations in which there is merely no established practice or convention or tradition, or in other words, no local rule, governing people's actions on a certain matter, and yet there ought to be one. It can be said that there ought to be such a rule when, in order for action to be effective in achieving

some desirable end, or in the elimination of some intolerable evil, it must be organized, at least sufficiently so for one to have reasonable assurance that others in one's situation will join in the effort. And it must be a sufficient number of others, for, by hypothesis, the situation is one in which one person alone, or too small a group, cannot expect to achieve the aim of the activity. Only so can there be reasonable assurance that the aim will be achieved, and without this the risks, either of failure or reprisal, may be too great to make such action sensible. Of course, some people can afford to take such risks, but not everyone can.

Suppose you are a worker who is contemplating going out on strike, either in protest against miserable working conditions or to attain a living wage, and suppose that there is no union to organize the activities of workers. Unless you are fortunate enough to possess some skill that makes you indispensable to your employer or that will enable you to find other employment easily, you are clearly in such a situation. Or suppose you are a teacher who, on moral grounds, objects to being required to sign a "loyalty oath." Whether loyalty oaths are good or bad is not the question here. Suppose, for the sake of argument, that they are bad, and that no one ought to sign one or be required to sign one. Yet, unless a sufficient number of other teachers in your institution or school system or state also refuse to sign, your refusal is likely to lead to nothing but the loss of your job, and may also prevent you from obtaining another. If you are sufficiently well known and respected, your refusal may possibly have some good effects and you may possibly be able to afford to refuse. But it is unlikely that you are. It is clear that what is needed here is some degree of organization and mutual understanding, but this does not always exist and is not always attainable.

Now what should one do in such situations as these? That there ought to be, in such cases, some rule or agreement in terms of which activity can be organized and people enabled to count on the support of others, is easily established by the application of the generalization argument, by a procedure we have already examined. But suppose there is no such rule. What should one do then? One thing that seems clear is that even without some assurance that others in the same circumstances will join in one's action, it is not, generally, wrong for one to do so oneself. One would, as a rule, have a right to do so, if one wants to take the risk or thinks it worth taking. Yet one also has a right not to, since one has no duty to sacrifice oneself for others if the sacrifice has no reasonable expectation of achieving its end. Hence it is largely a matter of prudence here. But it is not wholly so, for one may and very often will have obligations to others, say to support one's family, that would be inconsistent with imprudent action. For these reasons, among others, I do not think that the question here is one to which any general answer can be given. Each case must be considered in its own right, and will reveal complications that any general solution must gloss over. Hence, I do not think that even any general presumption can be established. It does not follow, however, that the generalization argument is inapplicable in such situations. With suitable restrictions and qualifications, it is, and where it is not, the question is not one of morality, but of what course is the most prudent or likely to prove the most effective.

Suppose the question is whether the government should be resisted, or even be overthrown. It must be emphasized that this question has no tint of appropriateness unless the government is intolerably bad or has enacted despotic or repressive laws of an intolerable nature. Even so, as we have seen, the presumption is against it, and this presumption is especially strong if there are legal or constitutional means, as there are in our system, for repealing or changing the law, or eliminating those in power. Even without such provisions the presumption is still against rebellion, for the consequences of general rebellion will generally be worse than the consequences of general obedience. Nevertheless, there are circumstances in which this presumption can be outweighed and rebellion justified. Some governments not only have no right to exist, but may be so bad as not to be worth preserving even if the consequences of rebellion would be a long period of anarchy and terror. It might be argued in certain circumstances that if everyone refused to obey the law it would either be repealed or the government would collapse, and that this, on the whole, would be a good thing, or at least undesirable, whereas if everyone were to obey the law or help keep the government in power the consequences would be on the whole distinctly undesirable. There are circumstances in which this might hold, and if it does, then it is one's duty to break the law, unless one has, as one might, some special reason for not doing so. But suppose it is known that others will continue to obey the law, even though it is oppressive, that they have been so cowed into submissiveness as to make disobedience or rebellion futile; and suppose further that anyone who refuses to obey the law will be shot and that the members of his family will be sold into slavery. What should one do then? If the facts mentioned are truly the facts of the case, then the situation is really intolerable, and it would seem that one's only hope is to conform to the law while attempting to organize resistance. If this hope should be taken away, then one's situation is absolutely hopeless, and any general advice would be both presumptuous and dangerous. At this point the matter would no longer be one of right and wrong.

Before leaving this topic there is one point that needs special emphasis. It is not every occasion on which others are violating the rules of society, or acting immorally, that gives one the right to do so as well. The fact that other people are engaging in smuggling, or the breaking of rationing restrictions, does not mean that anyone has the *right* to do so, and consequently does not mean that I have. Similarly, if I live in a society in which the majority regularly persecute or intimidate some minority group, in which intolerance and bigotry are generally practiced and generally approved of (that is to say, practiced and approved of by the majority of people or by a highly articulate and powerful minority), this does not give me the right to do so as well, and it certainly does not mean that I have any duty to do so. It is only if my conforming to the rules would be obviously and dangerously imprudent, only if it would place me in a perilous or precarious position, or would lead to great and avoidable harm, that it would be right for me to break them. For here it can be said that if everyone in circumstances similar to mine were to break the rules, the consequences would not be disastrous. Indeed, they might be disastrous otherwise.

Generalization Arguments

J. HOWARD SOBEL

The question, "What if everyone were to do that?" has long been prominent in practical discourse. Recently it has received considerable theoretical treatment which includes a book by Marcus George Singer,[1] who feels that the argument which underlies it is central and decisive in moral reasoning.

The object of the present essay is to develop several logical points that are crucial to an understanding of generalization arguments. To this end two claims made by Mr. Singer will be criticized. The first concerns two principles: the *principle of the generalization argument,*

If the consequences of A's doing *x* would be undesirable, then no one ought to do *x*, i.e., everyone ought not to do *x*;

and *the principle of consequences,*

If the consequences of A's doing *x* would be undesirable, then A ought not to do *x*.

According to Mr. Singer these two principles[2] cannot conflict.[3] I shall argue that this no-conflict thesis is false.

Reprinted from *Theoria*, 31, 1965, pp. 32–60, by permission of the author and *Theoria*.

[1] Marcus George Singer, *Generalization in Ethics* [New York: Alfred A. Knopf, 1961].

[2] These principles each have several versions. For example, the following are two versions of the principle of the generalization argument:

If the consequences of no one's doing *x* would be undesirable, then everyone ought to do *x*.

If the consequences of everyone's not doing *x* would be undesirable, then everyone ought to do *x*.

Cf. Singer, pp. 4, 61, and 66.

The second claim to be criticized is that the principle of the generalization argument can be derived from the principle of consequences taken in conjunction with a version of *the generalization principle,*[4] viz.:

If someone whose case is like A's ought not to do *x*, then no one whose case is like A's ought to do *x.*, i.e., every such person ought not to do *x*.[5]

There are good reasons for thinking that this claim is also false.

Before taking up these two claims, it is necessary to set out one of Mr. Singer's preliminary conclusions concerning generalization arguments. This will be done in Section I. Section II will be directed to his no-conflict proposition, and Section III will concern the putative derivation.

[3] Cf. Richard B. Brandt, "Toward a Credible Form of Utilitarianism", Section 3; *Morality and the Language of Conduct*, edited by Hector-Neri Castañeda and George Nakhnikian [Detroit, Wayne State University Press, 1963]. Richard A. Wasserstrom, *The Judicial Decision*, Stanford University Press, [Stanford, 1961], Chapter 6. Brandt and Wasserstrom maintain that act-utilitarianism cannot conflict with a kind of rule-utilitarianism.

[4] Cf. C. D. Broad, "On the Function of False Hypotheses in Ethics", *International Journal of Ethics*, Vol. XXVI (April, 1916), p. 392. A. C. Ewing, "What Would Happen if Everybody Acted Like Me?", *Philosophy*, Vol. XXVII (January, 1953), pp. 20 and 23. A. K. Stout, "But Suppose Everyone Did the Same", *Australasian Journal of Philosophy*, Vol. XXXII (May, 1954), pp. 20–21.

[5] Mr. Singer uses "no one ought" synonymously with "no one has the right", and thus, I suppose, he uses it synonymously with "everyone ought not". Cf. p. 65, nn. 1 and 2.

I

When we ask, "What would happen if everyone did that?" we usually do not mean to be asking what would happen if *everyone* did that. The question is rather, "What would happen if everyone did that who was similar to you and in similar circumstances?" And even this is not quite right since we are only interested in certain similarities. The question, fully spelled out, seems to be, "What would happen if everyone did that who was similar to you in relevant respects and who was in circumstances similar to yours in relevant respects?" Thus, to the question, "What would happen if no one voted?" responses such as, "But I am not well", and "But the polls are so far away", are ordinarily relevant; while a response such as "But my favorite color is chartreuse", is ordinarily irrelevant. Mr. Singer refers to this feature of the generalization argument as its usually implicit restricted universality.

The restricted universality of the generalization argument suggests a number of questions concerning the concept of relevancy, but we can proceed without posing them. It is sufficient for present purposes to observe that the following principle is obviously true:

If the consequences of A's doing x would be undesirable, then the consequences of anyone's doing x whose case is like A's in relevant respects would be undesirable.

This principle is true if the undesirability of the consequences of A's doing x is a relevant feature of A's case. Whatever else is said concerning the concept of relevancy in the present context, what this principle says is hardly disputable. I mention it only because it plays a role in my discussion of Mr. Singer's defense of his no-conflict proposition.

II

2.1 Mr. Singer says that the principle of consequences and the principle of the generalization argument can never conflict. Every case of apparent conflict is said to arise out of an insufficiently detailed specification of circumstances; once the generalization argument is properly formulated, it and the principle of consequences will necessarily concur in their directives. Here is the argument:

Suppose, then, that if A were to do x the consequences would be undesirable; it follows, on the principle of consequences, that A ought not to do x. Suppose, also, that if no one were to do x, consequences would be undesirable; it would seem to follow, on the basis of the generalization argument, that everyone, including A, ought to do x. But there are two possibilities here: (1) if everyone were to do x, the consequences would also be undesirable; or (2) if everyone were to do x, the consequences would not be undesirable. In the first case, the generalization argument is invertible, and nothing follows from it. So in this case the conclusion from the principle of consequences prevails, and A ought not to do x. *In the second case, there must be something distinctive about A, or the circumstances in which he is placed, to explain this difference between the consequences of his performing such an action and the consequences of everyone's performing it. If everyone similar to A did x in a similar situation, the consequences would be undesirable,* and so in this case also it follows that A ought not to do x. I conclude from this that there is no possibility of a conflict between these two principles . . . Since the appearance of conflict arises out of an insufficiently detailed specification of circumstances, it can always be dispelled.[6]

It is the second possibility that interests me. Mr. Singer argues that under this possibility, just as under the first one, it follows that A ought not to do x. But it is

[6] Singer, pp. 105–6. (Italics added.)

not clear precisely how he reaches this conclusion.

Perhaps Mr. Singer would admit the following expansion of his argument. "Since the consequences of A's doing x would be undesirable, it follows that if everyone whose case is like A's did x the consequences would be undesirable; *and* it also follows that if no one whose case is like A's did x the consequences would *not* be undesirable. So in this case the generalization argument is not invertible and it concurs with the principle of consequences: they both entail that A ought not to do x." But perhaps Mr. Singer would expand as follows: "Since A's doing x would be undesirable, it follows that it would be undesirable in terms of consequences for everyone whose case is like A's to do x. But in this case there are two possibilities concerning the consequences of no one's doing x: (1) if no one whose case is like A's did x, the consequences would be undesirable; and (2) if no one whose case is like A's did x, the consequences would not be undesirable. Under the first possibility, the generalization argument is invertible, and the principle of consequences prevails. Under the second possibility, the principle of consequences and the generalization argument concur. Under either possibility, it follows that A ought not to do x."

Which of these two expansions Mr. Singer would prefer is a matter which need not be settled here. We can concentrate on an inference that is crucial to the argument on *any* interpretation, viz.: Since the consequences of A's doing x would be undesirable, if everyone similar to A did x in a similar situation, the consequences would be undesirable.

2.2   Before doing this I should like to point out that whether or not his argument is sound, it is curious that Mr. Singer employs it. He maintains that the generalization argument is central and decisive in moral reasoning and that it is the fundamental principle of morality. [7] But if his defense of the no-conflict proposition is correct, it not only establishes that the two principles can never conflict; it also establishes, or rather it can be turned to establish, that whenever the principle of the generalization argument applies, the principle of consequences also applies, and in a like sense. But if this were so, the generalization argument, far from being fundamental in moral reasoning, would in every case be theoretically superfluous; one could rely on the less problematic principle of consequences. [8]

It is clear that Mr. Singer's argument has this unwanted implication. Suppose that the generalization argument applies and that if everyone whose case is like A's were to do x the consequences would be undesirable. By Mr. Singer's argument, the consequences of A's doing x would also be undesirable: the principle of consequences would apply as well. For if the consequences of A's doing x would *not* be undesirable there would have to be "something distinctive about A, or the circumstances in which he is placed, to explain this difference between the consequences of his performing such an action and the consequences of everyone's performing it." But we have supposed there is nothing distinctive about A's case since we have considered only the consequences of everyone's doing x whose case is like A's. Thus, if his argument shows that the generalization argument cannot conflict with the principle of consequences, it also shows, or can be turned to show, that the generalization argument always concurs with that principle and thus is theoretically superfluous. Actually, neither

---

[7] Singer, p. viii.

[8] The generalization argument might still be construed as a practical aid in the application of the principle of consequences—as a sort of "moral microscope"—but this would still leave the principle of consequences fundamental and theoretically sufficient which is not Mr. Singer's view.

conclusion has been established. As I shall show, Mr. Singer's argument for his no-conflict proposition is not sound.

2.3 According to Mr. Singer,

(1) The consequences of A's doing x would be undesirable.

entails

(2) The consequences of everyone's doing x—everyone whose case is like A's—would be undesirable.

His argument for the no-conflict thesis rests on this supposed entailment. But (1) does not entail (2). I assumed in Section I that (1) does entail,

(3) The consequences of anyone's doing x—anyone whose case is like A's—would be undesirable.

And, for purposes of the discussion, this assumption will be continued. But (2) and (3) are distinct and logically independent statement forms, and though (1) entails (3) it does not entail (2).

That (2) and (3) are distinct statement forms, is obvious enough. (2) says that the *general* doing of x would have undesirable consequences; (3) says that *any* doing of x would have undesirable consequences. (2) is concerned with a general practice (i.e., everyone's doing x); (3) is concerned with particular actions. [9] But though it is obvious that (2) and (3) are distinct, it is not so obvious that they are logically independent. Two cases are sufficient to establish this independence: one in which a statement of form (2) is true while a statement of form (3) is false; and one in which a statement of form (3) is true while a statement of form (2) is false. The first case concerns disarmament.

[9] For brevity, the qualifying phrase, "whose case is like A's", will often be left implicit.

Imagine the following world: There are three nations, each is armed, and there is an effective balance of power. No nation will intentionally start a war. But if the world remains armed, in five years there will be an accident which will lead to a disastrous general war. Unfortunately, no nation is going to disarm and the disaster is coming. This is in part due to the fact that the nations do not trust each other and will not accomplish a disarmament agreement and arrange for its effective implementation: There is no machinery for secure international co-operation, and none will be developed within the next five years. Each nation is convinced that if it were to disarm it would do so alone, and that this would disrupt the balance of power and precipitate the war that all fear. So no nation is going to disarm. And this shared conviction is correct; any nation's disarming would precipitate a holocaust. Of course, if *every* nation were to disarm, war would be averted. This fact too is common knowledge.

In this world all nations are exactly alike in so far as questions of disarmament are concerned, and in this world the consequences of any given nation's disarming would be undesirable. Consider an arbitrarily selected nation A. Would the consequences of A's disarming be undesirable? Compare them with the consequences of A's remaining armed. One might insist that in remaining armed A contributes to the armed state of the world and thus shares in that most undesirable consequence which will in five years follow from this armed state. This is a highly suspicious contention—it would be hard to say just what contribution A makes—but let us grant it: let us grant that A's remaining armed is possessed of undesirable consequences, namely, its share of the war to come in five years. It is clear that these consequences are more than counter-balanced by the undesirable effects which would attend A's disarming, for if A were to disarm, the disruption of the balance of power would bring about a general war *now*. Even if we allow that A's remaining armed will be possessed of some undesirable consequences, there is no doubt that the consequences of A's disarming would be even more undesirable. There is no doubt that the consequences of A's disarming would be undesirable on the whole. And what we have said of A applies, of course, to any nation, since A is any arbitrarily selected nation. So, the consequences of any nation's disarming would be undesirable; and not only from a narrowly national point of view, but also from a quite altruistic and international point of view.

What of the consequences of *every* nation's disarming? Would they be undesirable? It is clear that they would not be. If every nation were to disarm, war would be averted. This is certainly not an undesirable consequence. And it would not be difficult to fill in the description of the case in a way which made it clear that the best possible consequences would result from every nation's disarming; they could be rendered better than the consequences of any other pattern of armament behavior for the community.

Thus we have a case in which the consequences of anyone's (i.e., any nation's) doing *x* (i.e., disarming) would be undesirable, though the consequences of everyone's doing *x* would not be undesirable. This case shows that (3) does not entail (2). It incidentally also shows that (1) does not entail (2).

The second case concerns voting in a large national election. The situation is as follows: There are ninety million registered voters, sixty-five million of whom are going to vote. The vote will be divided almost entirely between the two major parties, one party receiving approximately thirty-five million votes, the other receiving approximately thirty million votes. Finally, the voting behavior of an average voter has no effect on the voting behavior of anyone else. What is the position of an

average registered voter? Would the consequences of his voting be undesirable? We begin by noting that whether or not he votes he will not contribute *at all* to his candidate's success or failure; his candidate will win or lose, as the case may be, whether or not he casts his vote. His candidate does *not* need his vote. But, of course, if he votes his vote will enter into the vote his candidate receives as well as into the votes cast in the election. Armed with this tautology one might go on to insist that his vote would contribute to his candidate's "cause" and to the "health of democratic institutions", though it is a bit hard to believe in the reality of these contributions. It is said that "every little bit counts", but when votes in a national election are in question this may not be true. The fact is that his vote would never be missed. It would be impossible in practice to determine the character or the extent of his contribution: if he makes one, it is incalculably small and elusive. His voting will not have appreciably desirable consequences. Will it have any undesirable consequences? Since he is a typical registered voter, we can assume that he finds voting slightly inconvenient and bothersome, and that he could use the time that he would spend voting in some other way that would be definitely, even if only mildly, constructive. Weighing the definite loss incurred by voting against the incalculable and unspecifiable contribution to his candidate's cause and the health of democratic institutions, we can conclude that the consequences of his voting would be somewhat undesirable. On the other hand, the consequences of his *not* voting but doing something constructive instead would *not* be undesirable. Of course, what I have said holds for *any* average registered voter. And since it is fair to assume that the consequences of every average registered voter's not voting but doing something constructive instead would be undesirable, we have a case in which the consequences of everyone's (i.e., every average registered voter's) doing x (i.e., not voting but doing something constructive instead) would be undesirable, even though the consequences of anyone's doing x would not be undesirable. This case shows that (2) does not entail (3); it also shows that (2) does not entail (1). The disarmament and voting cases taken together show that (2) and (3) are logically independent, and that (1) and (2) are also logically independent.

2.4 There is an objection to my two cases that can be formulated most simply in connection with the disarmament case. In this case I stipulated that if any nation were to disarm it would do so alone. This stipulation made it plausible that the consequences of any nation's disarming would be undesirable. But it may look as though this stipulation introduced a fatal difficulty. If A were to disarm it would do so alone; this apparently is a relevant feature of A's case. But if it is, how can I ask what would happen if every nation whose case is like A's were to disarm? Surely, one might say, in the world described it is *impossible* for every such nation to disarm.

But it is not impossible for every nation like A to disarm—though, as a matter of fact, not every nation like A is going to disarm. The class of nations is completely determinate; it includes just those nations that would disarm alone if they were to disarm. And I can ask what would happen if all of these nations were to disarm, for the following conditional makes good sense:

(4) If every nation that is like A., i.e., every nation that, for one thing, would disarm alone if it were to disarm, were to disarm; then the consequences would not be undesirable.

The antecedent of (4) will not be fulfilled; it is contrary-to-fact and this is clear on its face. But its fulfillment is not impossible. It is not as if I were attempting to say what would happen if every nation that is like A were both to disarm and not disarm.

Suppose there are two red figures and two blue figures on a blackboard, and nothing else. I cannot say that if the red figures *are* blue, then all the figures are blue. And I cannot say that if the red figures were both (completely) red and (completely) blue, then all the figures would be blue. But I can say that if the red figures were blue instead of red, then all the figures would be blue. Of course, it is clear that the antecedent of this last conditional is not fulfilled, but this is not to say that its fulfillment was impossible: we know what it would be like for the red figures to be blue instead of red.

There is nothing contradictory about my identifying a number of nations as nations that would disarm alone if they were to disarm, and then considering what would happen if all of the identified nations were to disarm. In fact, I could even identify the nations as nations that are not going to disarm, and then consider what would happen if they *were* to disarm. The conditionals so framed have antecedents which show on their faces that they are contrary-to-fact. But they are not contrary-to-logic: we know what it would be like for them to be fulfilled, even though we know that they will not be fulfilled.

But problems remain. The best way to raise and resolve them is through a consideration of another objection to my disarmament case, an objection very closely related to the first objection. Though what was wanted was *one* case in which the consequences of anyone's doing x would be undesirable *and* in which the consequences of everyone's doing x would not be undesirable, it may seem that I in fact presented *two* cases, one for each proposition. In other words, it may seem that the specifications for the disarmament case are not compatible, that they cannot be taken as specifying a single case.

The disarmament case is supposed to

be specified by the following six statements:

(i)   There are three nations.

(ii)   No nation is going to disarm.

(iii)   A war will occur in five years.

(iv)   If any nation were to disarm, it would do so alone.

(v)   If any nation were to disarm, war would result.

(vi)   If every nation were to disarm, war would be averted.

The question is, are these statements compatible?

It may not be immediately obvious that (v) and (vi) are compatible, but recollection of (iv) should suffice to make it obvious. Given (iv) it is easy to imagine that (v) should be true. But what about (vi)? Well, it is hard to imagine *any* case in which (vi) is false. If all nations disarm, how could there be a war? What would it be fought with?

So (v) and (vi) can both be true; for example, it is easy to imagine them both being true if (iv) is true. But is it possible for (iv) and (vi) both to be true? One might argue that it is not possible for them both to be true because (iv), taken with (i), entails that the antecedent of (vi) *cannot* be fulfilled, which in turn entails that given (iv) and (i), (vi) will be neither true nor false. But (iv) and (i) do not entail that the fulfillment of the antecedent of (vi) is impossible. It is clear that it is *logically* possible for every nation to disarm, that every nation will disarm is not *logically* false. Furthermore, there is *no* sense of "possible" in which (iv) taken with (i) entails that it is not possible for every nation to disarm. It is true that since, if any nation were to disarm, it would do so alone (and since there are three nations), not every nation *will* disarm. Universal disarmament *is* ruled out by (i) and (iv), but they do not entail that it is in *any* sense *impossible*. Suppose that I am not going to watch TV tonight, because my wife is not going to watch TV tonight. That is, suppose I am not going to

watch TV tonight because I know that *if I were to, I would do so alone,* and I do not like to watch TV alone. It would follow from the underlined statement alone that my wife and I *will* not watch TV together tonight, but there is no sense of "cannot" in which it would follow that we *cannot* watch TV together tonight. Similarly, (iv) and (i) do not entail that universal disarmament is in any sense impossible, even though they do entail that it is not going to take place. To conclude, (iv) and (vi) can both be true, so (v) and (vi) can both be true and are compatible. Thus it is clear that (i) through (vi) are compatible and *can* be taken as specifying a single case.

I have considered two closely related objections to my two cases. Another and separate objection to these cases is that in each the agents' certainty about what their fellows will do is ignored. Whether nation A ought not to disarm depends on how sure that nation is that no other nation would follow suit; and whether it would be unreasonable for a person to vote depends on how sure he is that his vote would make no difference. Since I ignore questions of certainty, my cases may seem to be incompletely drawn and thus inconclusive. But, this objection is not cogent. It is, in fact, wholly irrelevant for it supposes that I am interested in what nation A *ought* to do, or in what it would be *reasonable* for a registered voter to do. But my present interest is only in the *desirability* of certain sets of consequences, and this will not be a function of the knowledge, beliefs, or attitudes of the agents except in ways for which allowance has already been made (e.g., the fact of mutual distrust figures in the determination of the disastrous consequences of any nation's disarming).

2.5 The conclusion stands. (2) and (3) are logically independent: A general practice which would have undesirable consequences can consist entirely of particular actions whose consequences would not be undesirable (e.g., everyone's not voting); and, conversely, a general practice which would not have undesirable consequences can consist entirely of particular actions whose consequences would be undesirable (e.g., every nation's disarming). [10] It may seem strange that the consequences of a general practice can differ evaluatively from the consequences of the actions that would constitute it, but most of this strangeness disappears when one attends to a certain difference between the procedures for evaluating the consequences of general practices and those of particular actions.

To evaluate the consequences of a general practice such as every nation's disarming, one first asks what would happen if every nation were to disarm, i.e., one asks what the world would be like if every nation were to disarm. It is also necessary to know what would happen if no nation were to disarm, as well as what would happen if two nations were to disarm while two nations remained armed, etc. If E is the general practice which consists of every nation's disarming, and N and S are the *only* possible alternative patterns of group behavior, one begins by asking: What would happen if E, if N, and if S? Then, one determines the differences if any, between what would happen if E; and what would happen if N; and if S. Next, these differences are evaluated. The consequences of E are said to be undesirable only if

[10] That general practices and their constituent particular actions are evaluatively independent is not a discovery of mine. Hume, speaking of the "social virtues of justice and fidelity" remarks that "the result of the individual acts is here, in many instances, directly opposite to that of the whole system of actions; and the former may be extremely hurtful, while the latter is, to the highest degree, advantageous". *An Enquiry Concerning the Principles of Morals*, Appdx. III. Similarly, R. F. Harrod states, "There are certain acts which when performed on n similar occasions have consequences more than n times as great as those resulting from one performance . . . an act [can be] expedient in the circumstances . . . inexpedient when done by all in precisely similar circumstances". "Utilitarianism Revised", *Mind*, Vol. XLV (April, 1936), p. 148.

one of these differences would be undesirable, that is, only if what would happen if every nation were to disarm (E) would be *worse* than what would happen if either no nation were to disarm (N) or what would happen if some but not all nations were to disarm (S). Here is a necessary condition for the undesirability of these consequences. We need not decide whether it is also a sufficient condition.

The procedure for the evaluation of the consequences of a particular action is in many respects quite similar. Thus, we first ask what would happen if Mr. A were to vote, what would happen if he stayed home and rested, what would happen if he stayed home and read a book, etc. In general, if v is the action whose consequences are to be evaluated and r and b are the only possible alternatives to this action, we ask what would happen if Mr. A did v, did r, and did b. Differences are then determined and evaluated just as in the case of a general practice.

How do these two evaluation procedures differ? One important difference relates to their first steps. While we ask similar questions (viz., "What would happen if . . .?"), the considerations relevant to their answers display an important difference. Thus, in determining what would happen if nation A were to disarm, one would want to know what other nations would do if A were to disarm. In contrast, in determining what would happen if every nation were to disarm, one has no interest in what any nation would do, disarm or not disarm, under "this or that" contingency: What nations would do if a given nation were to disarm is necessarily irrelevant to what would happen if they were all to disarm. Stated more generally, the two questions, "What would happen if A were to do x?", and "What would happen if everyone were to do x?", differ in this: What various agents would do (x or not x) in various situations in which nations may find themselves can be relevant to the first question; such information is necessarily irrelevant to the second question. Given this difference in the very first phases of the evaluations, it is not at all surprising that the consequences of a general practice can differ evaluatively from the consequences of its constituent particular actions.

2.6 The logical independence of (2) and (3) has been established and explained, and (2) and (1) have also been shown to be logically independent. Mr. Singer's defense of his no-conflict proposition has been shown to involve an error, and we now have very good reasons for thinking that the two principles can conflict: certainly they seem to conflict in both the voting and disarmament cases. In the voting case the consequences of anyone's voting would be undesirable, though the consequences of no one's voting would also be undesirable: Apparently the principle of consequences says, "Do not vote!" while the generalization argument says, "Vote!" In the disarmament case the consequences of nation A's disarming would be undesirable, while the consequences of every nation's remaining armed would also be undesirable: Apparently the principle of consequences says, "Do not disarm!" while the generalization argument says, "Do not remain armed!", that is, "Disarm!" Since there is no reason for distrusting these apparent conflicts, the conclusion to be drawn is that the two principles *can* conflict.

And once it is seen that the generalization argument can conflict with the principle of consequences, it is no longer possible to be complacent about its validity; it becomes necessary to *show* that it is valid, and to explain why it should even sometimes take precedence over the principle of consequences, assuming that it sometimes should.

Generalization arguments *can* call for actions which would have undesirable consequences: they *can* conflict with straightforward appeals to consequences. But how can I permit myself to be moved by them

in such cases? When considering consequences, shouldn't I attend exclusively to consequences that I can do something about, i.e., to consequences of *my* actions? If it is agreed that the consequences of my doing *x* would be undesirable, shouldn't this settle the case against *x* at least in so far as arguments from consequences are concerned? It would certainly be very strange if arguments from what would happen if *no one* were to do *x* should sometimes take precedence over arguments from what would happen if *I* were to do *x*, when the issue is what *I* ought to do.

A. C. Ewing has given a clear and effective statement of the problem. Observing that the generalization argument is "often accepted in preference to the straightforward utilitarian criterion where the two seem to conflict", he then asks "whether this can ever be rationally justified"; and points out that,

prima facie the use of the [argument] seems very hard to defend. Why on earth should I be debarred from doing something, not because my doing it produces bad consequences, but because, if everybody did it, which I know will not be the case, the consequences *would* be bad? How can it be relevant to cite against an action not the results likely to accrue from it, but results which would accrue if something else happened that certainly will not happen?[11]

III

3.1 "You ask why you should attend to what would happen if everyone behaved as you. The answer, though it needs spelling out, lies in the fact that what you ought to do everyone ought to do. It is a logical truth that what is right for one is right for all, and once the force of this tautology is appreciated the validity of the

[11] A. C. Ewing, "What Would Happen if Everybody Acted Like Me?", *Philosophy*, Vol. XXVII (January, 1953), p. 17.

generalization argument ceases to be a problem and become obvious."

No approach to the generalization argument is more promising or more popular than this one. Variants of it have been presented by a number of authors; the one provided by Mr. Singer is especially detailed. He sees that the principle of the generalization argument does not follow from the generalization principle alone, but he contends that it can be derived from the generalization principle together with the principle of consequences; and indeed if his derivation were in order, he would have gone some way towards its establishment. The principles used as premises *are* less problematic than the principle to be derived: so the derivation would have improved the position of the argument, even though it would still be necessary to deal with the fact that the generalization argument can conflict with the principle of consequences. But Mr. Singer's derivation is not in order, and there is no obvious way of removing its defects.

He begins with the principle of consequences:[12]

> (5) If the consequences of A's doing x would be undesirable, then A ought not to do x.

Then Mr. Singer derives what he calls a generalization from (5):

> (6) If the consequences of everyone's doing x—everyone whose case is like A's—would be undesirable, then someone whose case is like A's ought not to do x.

(This is not Mr. Singer's wording, but I am convinced it is his sense. He puts "not everyone ought to do x" where I put "someone ought not to do x". However, though these expressions are not ordinarily interchangeable, he apparently intends them to be in his usage. He insists

that "not everyone ought to do x" is different from "everyone ought not to do x", and states that he uses "not everyone ought to do x" synonymously with "not everyone has the right to do x". This latter insistence entails that he does *not* use "not everyone ought to do x" synonymously with "everyone ought not to do x together". It is clear that what Mr. Singer means by "not everyone ought to do x" can be more naturally expressed by "someone ought not to do x" and I have formulated his argument accordingly. But even if Mr. Singer would not endorse my formulation, it presents a defense of the generalization argument which is at least very similar to his. And it has the virtue of focusing attention on complexities of "someone" that are as important to the subject as are the more often discussed complexities of "everyone". But I am convinced that Mr. Singer would accept my formulation of his argument, and in what follows I shall assume this without further comment.)

Next a version of the generalization principle is introduced:

> (7) If someone whose case is like A's ought not to do x, then everyone whose case is like A's ought not to do x.

And finally, from (6) and (7), the principle of the generalization argument is deduced:

> (8) If the consequences of everyone's doing x—everyone whose case is like A's—would be undesirable, then everyone whose case is like A's ought not to do x.

The weak point in this demonstration is the move from (5) to (6). Mr. Singer says that (5) entails (6), but the character of the entailment is not made clear. He speaks of (6) as a generalization from (5), but, as he observes, the style of this generalization is not a familiar one. We are told that "the true logical generalization of the principle of consequences" would be,

> (9) If the consequences of each and every person's doing of x would be undesirable, then each and every person ought not to do x.[13]

And (9) does follow from (5). Furthermore, (9) (given a non-empty universe of persons) entails,

> (10) If the consequences of each and every person's doing of x would be undesirable, then someone ought not to do x.

However, as Mr. Singer would insist, (10) is not to be confused with (6). The hypothesis of (6) is concerned with the consequences of a general practice, while the hypothesis of (10) is concerned with the consequences of the particular acts that would make up the general practice. It would, however, be easy to confuse (10) and (6) since one and the same sentence form can be used to express both of these statement forms, viz.:

"If the consequences of everyone's doing x would be undesirable, then someone ought not to do x."

Thus, it is possible to derive from (5) something that can *look* like (6), and if the ambiguity involved is not noted this can be taken for a derivation of (6) itself.

Another (bad) reason for thinking that (5) entails (6) would rest on the belief that,

> (2) The consequences of everyone's doing x would be undesirable

entails,

> (3) The consequences of anyone's doing x would be undesirable.

13 Singer, p. 66.

If (2) entailed (3), then (9) which follows from (5) would in turn entail (6). But then, as was shown in Section II, (2) does *not* entail (3).

A third and related (bad) reason for thinking that (5) entails (6) would rest on the belief that (2) entails,

> (11) There is at least one person such that the consequences of his doing x would be undesirable.

Given this entailment you could be sure that if the consequences of everyone's doing x would be undesirable, then the consequences of someone's doing x would be undesirable. And from (5) it would follow that this someone ought not to do x. But (2) does not entail (11). The consequences of everyone's doing x can be undesirable even though there is not one person such that the consequences of his doing x are undesirable. The voting case shows this.

Three plausible though defective reasons for thinking that (5) entails (6) have been noted. But since none of them can be definitely attributed to Mr. Singer, it is still not clear why he thinks that (5) entails (6). One possibility is that he does *not* think that (5) entails (6). Perhaps his true view, despite expressions to the contrary, is that (6) is "in the spirit" of (5) and that it can be seen to be true "in the light" of (5) even though it is not strictly entailed by (5). This possibility must be explored.

3.2 According to the principle of consequences, if the consequences of someone's doing x would be undesirable, then that person ought not to do x: the point is that the cited undesirable consequences ought to be avoided. But then if the consequences of everyone's doing x would be undesirable, it seems that, in order to avoid these undesirable consequences, at least some person or persons ought not to do x. Statement form (6) has as its consequent that someone ought not to do x, instead of "everyone ought not to do x," because supposedly if not everyone does x the undesirable consequences that would result from everyone's doing it would be avoided.[14]

Surely it cannot be alright for everyone to do something which would result in undesirable consequences if done by everyone. In such a case someone ought not to do this thing; in fact, enough people ought not to do it to avoid the undesirable consequences.

This line of reasoning is persuasive, but on reflection it is not conclusive and in fact it can be seen to beg the question. Recall that generalization arguments can conflict with the principle of consequences: the consequences of everyone's doing x can be undesirable even though the consequences of anyone's not doing x are also undesirable. Thus in the disarmament case, though it would be undesirable for every nation to remain armed, it would also be undesirable for any nation not to remain armed, i.e., to disarm. In such cases it seems quite possible that it would be alright for each agent to do x, even though disaster will result if x is done by everyone. In the disarmament case it *seems* alright for each nation to remain armed, since this is its best course of action (i.e., the action with the best consequences) given the world in which it finds itself. And one cannot argue, in the context of a defense of generalization arguments, that it is *not* alright for each nation to act in this way, since disaster will result from all nations' acting in this way, for *this is what is to be shown.*

3.3 The initial plausibility of the defense of the generalization argument that is under discussion derives in large part from the fact that "someone ought [not] to do x" has several distinct senses which are *in different ways* unsuited for use in the defense.

In order to serve in the present defense of the generalization argument, "someone ought [not] to do x" must be used in (6) and in (7) in a sense that (a) entails that everyone ought [not] to do x, i.e., that is "universalizable"; and that (b) is entailed by the statement that the consequences of no one's [everyone's] doing x would be undesirable, i.e., that is entailed by the premise of the generalization argument. But though there are senses of "someone ought" that clearly possess feature (a), and at least one sense that seems to possess feature (b), I know of no sense that clearly possesses both features. And, furthermore, in order to maintain that any sense of this phrase possesses both features (as it must if it is to serve in the present defense of the generalization argument) it seems necessary *first* to establish that the generalization argument is valid. An examination of three senses of "someone ought" will serve to substantiate this claim.

First, "someone ought to do x" can be used in the sense of,

(12) There is at least one person such that he ought not to do x.

"Someone ought" has what can be called a *simple existential* sense, and when used in this sense it is clearly universalizable. If there is at least one person such that he ought to do x, then everyone who is in relevant respects like any such person ought to do x. However, though it is clear that this sense of "someone ought" possesses feature (a), it is not clear that it possesses feature (b). *Perhaps,* if it would be undesirable in terms of consequences for no one to do x, then it follows that there is at least one person who ought to do x. But since it could also be undesirable in terms of consequences for any given person to do x, this entailment is not an obvious one; and it is in fact essentially *what is at issue,* as I have already recalled in Section 3.2. To entertain the possibility

[14] Singer, p. 67.

that generalization arguments are not valid is to entertain the possibility that there may not be even one person who ought to do *x* despite the fact that if no one were to do *x*, the consequences would be undesirable.

Second, "someone whose case is like A's ought to do *x*" can of course be used synonymously with,

(13) Anyone whose case is like A's ought to do *x*.

If "someone ought" is taken in this sense, then it is certainly universalizable; in this sense it makes a statement which clearly entails the statement made by "everyone ought", since it makes the very same statement. But reading the phrase in this way renders problematic its entailment by the premise of the generalization argument. Perhaps the entailment holds, but that it does is not obvious, and whether or not it does is identical with the question whether or not generalization arguments are valid. If "someone" in (6) is replaced by "anyone", (6) becomes identical with the principle of the generalization argument, and therefore cannot without circularity be used in its defense.

Third, there is a very important sense of "someone ought to do *x*" that I *believe* [15] is entailed by the fact that the consequences of no one's doing *x* would be undesirable. Suppose that I am at a party, chatting with several people grouped around a painting. The conversation has turned to the painting on the wall. Suddenly there is one of those lulls that are so awkward, and I feel that I must say something to hold up my end of the conversation. Knowing nothing about art but not wanting to change the subject completely, I say, "Someone ought to straighten it". A sufficient ground for my judgment, however lame it might be as a conversational gambit, seems to be that

it would be undesirable for no one to straighten it: Since the painting is crooked and this state of affairs is undesirable, someone ought to straighten it. In saying that someone ought to straighten the painting, I seem to be saying no more than that *the painting ought to be straightened;* and this would follow simply from the fact that it would be undesirable for it to remain crooked, i.e., undesirable for it not to be straightened, i.e., undesirable for no one to straighten it. So this sense of "someone ought" seems to possess feature (b); that is, it is entailed by the premise of the generalization argument. But does it possess feature (a)? Does it entail that *everyone* (who is standing in front of the painting) ought to straighten the painting?

One (bad) reason for thinking that this "someone ought" is *not* universalizable would be that it is compatible with "not everyone ought": The last thing I may want is for everyone to work on straightening the painting. I might well say, "Someone ought to straighten the painting, but not everyone, please!": But this fact does not show that this "someone ought" is not universalizable, i.e., that it does not entail that everyone ought. When I say "but not everyone", I imply that I feel that everyone ought not to try to straighten the picture together or all at the same time; and this is compatible both with the view that the picture ought to be straightened by someone, *and* with the view that everyone has a good reason for straightening it and thus ought in a sense to straighten it. As has been noted recently, "everyone" is complex: it has what has been called a *collective* use in which it is replaceable by something like "everyone together" or "everyone at once", and a *distributive* use in which it is replaceable by "anyone". [16] The "everyone" in "but not everyone, please!" is collec-

---

[15] The reason for my reservation is indicated in footnote 17.

[16] A. Phillips Griffiths, "The Generalisation Argument: A Reply to Mr. Braybrooke", *Analysis*, Vol. 23 (April, 1963), pp. 113–115.

tive, and the "everyone", in the universalization is distributive.

Another (bad) reason for thinking
that this "someone ought" is *not* universalizable, would consist in the supposed fact
that in this use it entails that there is no
one who ought to straighten the painting.
Suppose that each of us finds heights disagreeable, and that straightening the
painting would require climbing a ladder.
Each of us might agree that it would be desirable for the painting to be straightened,
even though not one of us felt that *he* ought
to do the job. "Why me?", each of us
might ask, and our questions would go unanswered. So it *seems* that though someone ought to straighten it, since only one
person is needed and any person will do,
there is no *one* who ought to straighten it.
But again an error is involved. The fact is
that there is no one *in particular* who
ought to straighten the painting, but this
could be so because *each* of us ought
to straighten it. In such a case lots
might be drawn, not to select someone to
do a job that no one *ought* to do, but rather
to select someone to do a job which no one
wants to do and which *everyone* ought to
do.

So it seems that this third sense of
"someone ought" may be universalizable,
but the question remains whether it *is* universalizable. In the painting case I believe
it is true both that someone ought to
straighten the painting and that everyone
ought to straighten it. Since it would be
desirable for the painting to be straightened, someone ought to straighten it; and
since anyone can straighten it by himself
(assumed for this case), each and every
person has a reason for straightening the
painting; and hence there is a sense in
which each and every person ought to
straighten the painting.

So in this case it is true both that
someone ought to straighten the painting
and that everyone ought to straighten it,
but this is not to say that the former entails the latter. In fact, there seems little

reason to think that it does. A crucial
feature of this case is that anyone can
straighten the painting by himself, and
rather than say that "everyone ought to
straighten it" follows from "someone ought
to straighten it", perhaps we should say
only that in this case "everyone ought"
follows from "someone ought" *coupled with*
the statement that anyone can remedy the
situation by himself (anyone can straighten
this picture by himself). It is still possible that "everyone ought" does not follow
from "someone ought" *by itself;* a slightly
different case enforces this possibility.

It would take three of us to straighten
a painting; if anyone were to try to shift
it by himself, he would drop it. And each
of us knows the others well enough to know
that even if he were to try to straighten
it, no one would help him. In this case one
could argue that although it is true that
someone ought to straighten the painting,
there is no sense in which it is true that
each of us ought to straighten it. [17] In
fact, it could be argued that there is not
one of us who ought to engage in straightening it since such an effort on the part
of any one of us would be quixotic and
under the circumstances disastrous. And
this argument would stand *unless* we were
to assume that since the consequences of
no one's taking steps to straighten the
painting would be a crooked painting, each
of us ought to take steps to straighten
it (though the painting fall in the process).

[17] *Perhaps* careful speakers would say "some of
us" rather than "someone", since more than one
person is needed. If so, then the "someone ought
to do *x*" under discussion does *not* possess feature
(b); it is not entailed by "if no one were to do *x*
the consequences would be undesirable", though it
is entailed by this *coupled with* the statement that
these consequences can be avoided by the action
of one man. Furthermore, if the "someone ought"
under discussion is necessarily singular in the
manner suggested, then it *does* possess feature
(a)—it is universalizable. *However,* I believe that
this "someone ought to do *x*" is not necessarily
"singular". It is, I think, often interchangeable
with "*x* ought to be done": When we use "someone ought to do *x*" in the sense under discussion,
we say, I think, that *x* ought to be done by *one*
person or by *some*.

But once again this cannot be assumed; *it is what is to be shown.* Even if the present use of "someone ought" is universalizable, that it is cannot be claimed in the course of a defense of the generalization argument; this becomes clear when we consider cases in which, though it would be undesirable in terms of consequences for no one to do *x*, no man can forestall these undesirable consequences by doing *x* by himself. And such cases are of course supremely relevant to a discussion of generalization arguments. Undesirable consequences that one man can avoid do not call for generalization arguments. It is the occasional necessity for joint action and co-operation that provides a use for the generalization argument, that makes for its conflicts with the principle of consequences, and that renders its justification difficult. [18]

What is needed for the present defense of the generalization argument is a sense of "someone ought to do *x*" that, prior to an establishment of the generalization argument, can be shown to combine features (a) and (b). Three senses have been examined, none of which satisfies this condition. The first two clearly possess feature (a), but before one could say that they possess feature (b) it would be necessary to show that the generalization

argument is valid. The third as I have said seems to possess feature (b), but cannot be shown to possess feature (a) prior to the establishment of the generalization argument. Evidently, there are senses of "someone ought to do *x*" that clearly possess feature (a), and there is at least one sense that seems to possess feature (b); but it is likely that there is no sense which can be shown to possess both of these features prior to a demonstration that the generalization argument is valid. In other words, there seems to be no way in which "someone ought" can be understood in (6) and (7) such that *both* (6) and (7) can be shown to be true prior to the establishment of (8), though there is a sense of the phrase which seems to make (6) true (my third sense), and there is a sense of the phrase which makes (7) true (my first sense, as well as my second). Much of the initial plausibility of the defense of the generalization argument under discussion derives, I believe, from the possibility of equivocating on "someone ought".

3.4 Mr. Singer has not shown that the principle of the generalization argument can be derived from the principle of consequences coupled with the generalization principle. Furthermore, it seems that no attempt along the lines of his could succeed: (6) seems to be incurably unsuited to its task. And it must now be added that any defense of the principle of the generalization argument that uses the principle of consequences, will impose restrictions on their interpretations and will raise special problems.

The principle of consequences and the generalization argument can conflict; this was shown in Section II. Thus they cannot both be *conclusive* principles. If both principles are true, at least one of them must yield something less than completely unqualified ought-judgments. Otherwise, in cases of conflict, two judgments of the following forms would both be true:

[18] Mr. Singer makes a crucial mistake when he says that the consequent of (6) takes the form it does "because supposedly if not everyone does *x* the undesirable consequences that would result from everyone's doing it would be avoided" (p. 67). But the fact is that the undesirable consequences will only be avoided if *enough* persons do not do *x*. And I believe that Mr. Singer's use of the word "supposedly" is an indication that he was aware of this fact. He probably reasoned in this way: Since the undesirable consequences will be avoided if *enough* persons do not do *x*, *x* ought not to be done by one or some persons, i.e., *someone* ought not to do *x*; and since *someone* ought not to do *x*, there is at least one person such that he ought not to do *x*. But there seems to be no sense of "someone ought" in which *both* of these inferences are unproblematic; for example, if "someone" is used in my third sense only the first inference is evident, and if it is used in my first sense only the second inference is evident.

A ought to do x

and

A ought not to do x.

But this is impossible. When conclusive and unqualified "oughts" are involved,

A ought not to do x

entails,

It is not the case that A ought to do x.

Taken in the conclusive sense, "ought" and "ought not" express logical contraries. Both may be false (perhaps there is no one thing that A ought to do), but not both can be true. And so the principle of consequences and the generalization argument cannot both be *conclusive* ought-principles. At least one must be a qualified ought-principle, e.g., a *presumptive* principle of the form,

If *p*, then *presumably* A ought to do x.

or a prima facie principle of the form,

If p, then A ought to do x *other things being equal.*

If there are reasons for thinking that A ought to do x, it is still possible that A ought not to do x. And if A has a reason for doing x and thus ought to do x other things being equal, it is still possible that A ought not to do x. But if there definitely are conclusive reasons for doing x—then it cannot be the case that A ought not to do x.

So anyone who employs the principle of consequences in defense of the principle of the generalization argument, in fact, anyone who endorses both principles, must concede that at least one of them is not a conclusive principle. There are three possibilities. Perhaps *neither* principle is a conclusive ought-principle. If so, then in the conflict cases one must expect that sometimes the principle of consequences will prevail and that sometimes the generalization argument will prevail. Thus, though it be somewhat paradoxical, one must expect that at least sometimes a person ought to do a thing even though if everyone like him were to do this sort of thing the consequences would be undesirable. Maybe the generalization argument (or the principle of consequences) will *always* prevail in cases of conflict, but prior to an indication of the precise character of their qualifications one must expect that neither will prevail over the other in *all* cases of conflicts.

A second possibility is that though the principle of consequences is a conclusive principle, the principle of the generalization argument is not. If this is the case, the principle of consequences prevails in *all* conflict cases, and there will be occasions (more occasions than one should expect under the first possibility) when a person ought to do a thing even though it would be undesirable in terms of consequences for everyone like him to do this thing.

A third possibility is that though the principle of the generalization argument is a conclusive principle, the principle of consequences is not. In this case, the somewhat paradoxical implications of the first two possibilities do not obtain. It should be noted, however, that this alternative is probably not open to one who wants to use the principle of consequences in a defense of the generalization argument; it is hard to see how a non-conclusive principle could play a role in the establishment of a conclusive one. It should also be noted that, of the three alternatives, the present one assigns the greatest importance to the generalization argument *and* makes its justification most urgent. [19]

---

[19] Of the three possible positions, Mr. Singer selects the second. He holds that the principle of consequences can be interpreted in such a way that it is a conclusive principle (p. 64). And he maintains that a completely adequate and explicit statement of the principle of the generalization argument ends with the phrase "without a reason". Since Mr. Singer does not think that the two principles can conflict, he is not struck by the relatively minor role that he assigns to the generalization argument, and he is not aware of the somewhat paradoxical aspects of his position.

The relations between our two principles are apparently complex and many matters remain to be discussed. But this much is clear: these principles cannot both be conclusive principles, and *if* (though I think it unlikely) the principle of consequences plays a role in the establishment of the principle of the generalization argument, then at least this latter principle is not a conclusive one, and one should expect that at least sometimes a person ought to do a thing even though it would be undesirable for everyone like him to do this thing.

CONCLUSION

The principle of consequences and the principle of the generalization argument can conflict; this was shown in Section II. And it is unlikely that the principle of consequences can be used in a defense of the generalization argument. Mr. Singer has not shown that it can be so used, and there are reasons for thinking that no attempts along the lines of his will prove more successful. These points were argued in Section III.

But of course, even if the principle of consequences plays no role in the validation of the generalization argument, this argument may still be valid. There are other approaches to it that deserve exploration. Perhaps, for example, it should be understood as an appeal to fairness. Nonetheless, though nothing established in this essay shows that the generalization argument is not valid, it is clear that its validity cannot simply be affirmed. Some demonstration or defense is rendered imperative by the fact that it can conflict with straightforward appeals to consequences. And it is of course possible that no good defense of the generalization argument is available: it may be just a time-honored fallacy.

IV

Rights, Justice, Punishment, and Responsibility

On Natural Rights

RALPH MASON BLAKE

At various times in the history of moral and political philosophy the concept of natural rights has played an important and prominent rôle in the thoughts of men. It has frequently, indeed, been the central and dominating idea of a whole system. At other periods, however—and it is through one of these that we seem at present to be passing—it has fallen out of favor. In many quarters it seems just now to be regarded as an outworn and exploded superstition of the past, and any appeal to the idea is looked upon as evidence of an antiquated and unenlightened approach to the problems of the day. We may well ask ourselves, however, whether an idea of such vitality, appealed to at times, indeed, by the most diverse schools of thought as giving warrant to their views, and constantly reappearing in men's minds just when it seemed once more finally to have been got rid of, does not really embody some important notion which it would be useful to preserve and dangerous to lose sight of. It is this question which I propose here to examine.

It would be admitted, I suppose, that, speaking generally, "rights" are correlative with "duties" and are defined by laws. Thus, if we start with the positive law, whether constitutional or statutory, we find that there are many positive laws which define "rights" vested in certain individuals or groups of individuals (one of

which groups may be society as a whole), and impose duties correlative with these rights upon other individuals or groups of individuals (or again upon society as a whole). The rights so defined seem usually to be of the nature of *claims* which their possessors may legitimately (i.e., in accordance with the law) make upon others, claims, therefore, which always imply some correlative duty on the part of these others. Thus if in accordance with the law a laborer, upon the performance of labor, has a right to the wages for which he contracted, this means that he may legitimately *claim* the sum agreed upon, and that it is the legal *duty* of the employer to satisfy this claim by paying the wage. Or again, if a man has a legal right to the exclusive enjoyment of a certain piece of property, this means that he may lawfully claim immunity from any interference on the part of others with such exclusive enjoyment, and that it is the legal duty of these others to refrain from such interference. It thus appears that positive laws may, on occasion, give rise to positive legal rights and duties; and such rights as thus arise seem to be of the nature of certain liberties or freedoms which their possessors may legitimately exercise.

The traditional conception of "natural" rights, whatever its other content, seems at least always to be that of a system of "rights" having a deeper and more fundamental character than any merely legal rights, of a system of rights possessing an ultimate and objective validity

Reprinted from *The International Journal of Ethics* (later renamed *Ethics*), 1925–26, pp. 86–96, by Ralph Mason Blake by permission of The University of Chicago Press.

not derived from their relation to any system of positive law. Natural rights, as their name indicates, are supposed to be based instead upon a law of nature itself, independent of any positive enactments of men, and of a higher validity. It is therefore considered possible to contrast merely legal rights with natural rights, and in case of conflict to assert the superior claims of the latter. Just as positive rights are derived from positive laws and correlated with legal duties, so natural rights are conceived to be based upon the "natural law," prescribed by the very nature of things, and to be correlated with certain natural duties. And, like legal rights, natural rights appear usually in the form of *claims*, often to some freedom, immunity, or privilege, made legitimate by this "law of nature."

But now this conception of a "law of nature" is certainly not entirely clear. It merits further examination. Among what are commonly known as laws of nature are certain generalizations of physical, chemical, or biological phenomena. These in fact are what we nowadays have chiefly in mind when we speak of natural law, or of the laws of nature. But these laws, it is fairly clear, are precisely not what are in question when it is a matter of determining rights. Laws of nature, in this sense of the term, do not tell us in the least what is right or what ought to be; they merely describe for us, without reference to matters of value, how natural phenomena as a matter of fact actually do occur. They thus explicitly abstract from the whole question as to whether the natural occurrences which they describe embody any sort of right or justice.

The natural laws from which natural rights could be supposed to arise must therefore be of quite another sort. They must *not* abstract from matters of value, but must instead deal primarily therewith. They must be statements of what claims various individuals or groups of individuals *ought* to be privileged to make. Not,

then, from natural physical laws, but only from natural *moral* laws can natural rights be conceived to arise—from the principles of *natural morality*, if one may be permitted to employ so unfashionable a term.

And now it is necessary to point out a very significant difference between the conception of a "law" in the sense of a fundamental principle of natural morality, and a law in the sense of a positive law or legal precept. The latter is in essence a *command* or imperative issued by some competent authority and backed by the force of some sanction, some penalty or reward to accrue from the authority in question, whether this authority be state, church, public opinion, or the customs of society. Natural moral laws, on the other hand, are not necessarily to be thought of as commands or precepts issued by any authority whatever. If they chance to be backed by some authority, that is conceived to be a wholly accidental circumstance. Nor are they necessarily enforced by any sanctions whatever. A positive law issued by no authority is a contradiction in terms. Laws of nature, on the other hand, are conceived to be independent of any authority. They remain what they are and retain their entire validity whether any authority commands them and enforces them with penalties or not. A law of nature *may* be enacted into a positive law— indeed many have held that in default of enactment by any human authority they must be conceived to form part of the positive law of God, and to be enforced by supernatural sanctions. But the very conception of a law of nature is that it does not derive its being or its validity from any enactment or positive command whatever, but would remain valid even if every positive law were to contravene it. It is not only independent of positive laws, it is also deeper and more fundamental than they, and possessed of a higher validity.

The conception of a "natural law" from which natural rights and natural duties are derived is, then, the conception of a principle stating that the claim to such and such liberties, freedoms, or privileges ought to be vested in such and such individuals or groups of individuals, a principle which is to remain true and valid no matter what the positive law of any authority may decree, and by which any positive law which contravenes it may be condemned as contrary to natural right and justice—as constituting a violation of natural rights. And by calling these principles "laws of nature" it is implied that they are prescribed and determined by the very nature of things and are therefore independent of any choice or arbitrary decree, human or divine.

Not only, however, are such natural laws conceived as prescribed by nature herself, and as therefore superior to any arbitrary decree or enforcing sanction; they are also thought of as constituting eternal and immutable principles, as possessed of no merely temporary validity, but as remaining permanently valid—so long at least as the present order of nature shall continue in its general features to remain substantially what it now is. It might perhaps be admitted that other principles may be "laws of nature" for beings other than human, placed in a different general scheme of things; but such laws of nature as affect us human beings are conceived to be permanently valid truths for this our world, lasting unchanged so long as it shall last. Moreover, such laws of nature are conceived as being not only permanent in time, but as being also universally applicable in place. Inasmuch as they are determined by the general nature of things, it is held that they must be valid for all men everywhere, whether as a matter of fact all men have always recognized or acted upon their validity or not. And finally these natural laws are held to be *rational* laws, that is to say, principles which right reason, reflecting upon the order of nature, must necessarily discover to be generally valid.

And now, if it be admitted that these are the features which form the core of the ideas of natural laws, and of natural rights and duties based upon such laws, as these ideas have commonly been conceived, we may well ask ourselves whether there actually is or even conceivably can be any such thing as a "law of nature" in this sense of the term. In what sense, namely, can "nature" or "the nature of things" determine laws as to what claims ought to be vested in certain individuals or groups of individuals, and as to what duties ought in turn to be imposed upon others? And at first sight we may well doubt whether anything of the sort is at all possible, for when we turn to history we find the most diverse and incompatible opinions, not only as to what these "natural rights" and these "laws of nature" as a matter of fact *are*, but also as to the very way in which "nature" is supposed to supply these principles or standards. The conception of "living according to nature," according to natural right and justice as opposed to and deeper than merely legal, customary, or conventional standards, has played a central part in many different philosophies; but the difficulty is that it has supplied so many and such diverse standards—many of them mutually incompatible. Thus Aristotle found the "natural" in the rational standard of the mean, and in all that distinguishes man as a rational animal from the brutes; the Epicureans, on the other hand, found the "natural" precisely in that which men share with the brutes— the tendency to seek pleasurable and to avoid painful experiences. Thus Hobbes found the natural man to be actuated only by the egoistic will to power, whilst to Rousseau he appeared as a model of innocent peaceableness and sympathetic affection. It seems impossible to bring any real order out of such a chaos, and the attempt to find any standard of "what ought to be" from a contemplation of "nature" may thus well appear to be wholly futile.

And in fact, as this attempt has usually been conceived, it really is futile. I do not believe it to be possible to derive any principles with regard to what ought to be, any principles of "natural morality" or "laws of nature," from a contemplation, no matter how earnest, disinterested and thoroughgoing, of the facts of nature, as these are reported to us by the ordinary descriptive sciences of nature. There is no road to the derivation of such principles from the consideration, taken merely in themselves, of the truths of physics or astronomy, or even of those of biology, psychology, or history. The reason for this impossibility seems to be that from "nature" as it is studied in any of these sciences all matters of *value* have from the beginning been carefully excluded. The physicist, the astronomer, the biologist and the psychologist simply abstract from the value aspects of the phenomena which they study. They do not even ask the question—and *a fortiori* do not succeed in answering it—whether this or that phenomenon with which they are dealing is good or bad, right or wrong, just or unjust—all such matters are left entirely to one side. And since a consideration of values is no part of the task of these sciences, no principles concerning values can possibly be derived from or determined by their results. The "nature" which they study is the natural order deliberately considered apart from any of the values which it may embody, and nature in this abstract sense can determine no standards. When we consider nature apart from value we have already deprived ourselves of any basis for rationally preferring one part of nature or one tendency manifested in nature to any other. We cannot deduce, solely from the fact that physical or psychological laws are what they are, any principles as to what ought to be.

But let us now note that if values are left out of the "nature" studied by these sciences, it by no means follows that values are not also themselves a part of the natural order, if that order be only considered in a less partial and abstract fashion, nor that this value aspect of the natural order may not itself legitimately be made the object of a rational consideration. Reflexion upon human experience in the world discerns certain phases of it as "good" and certain others as "bad." We find thus as a matter of fact that the world of "nature" contains distinctions of value as an actual part of itself; and from an impartial consideration of these value aspects of the natural order it is not so entirely chimerical to hope or to expect that some principles or standards may be derived.

If we ask what are the primary or fundamental "values" of human experience, as discerned by such a consideration, I think that we can give a reply which will represent a very considerable measure of agreement on the part of contemporary students of the subject. It seems, namely, to be very widely held nowadays that intrinsic positive value attaches only to those conscious experiences which can be described as experiences of "happiness" or of "satisfaction," and that negative value, on the other hand, attaches only to conscious experiences of "unhappiness," "misery," or "dissatisfaction." The exact determination of the meaning of these phrases is of course still to a considerable extent a matter of dispute. There are, on the whole, two main schools of interpretation. According to the one, happiness and unhappiness consist respectively in the psychological states of feeling called pleasure and displeasure, whereas, according to the other they consist rather in what is called "fulfilment of interest or desire"—a matter which often goes under the name (implying also certain modifications of the view) of "self-realization." But in spite of the theoretical difference here indicated there appears to be such a very close connection in practical human experience between experiences of pleasure and experiences of fulfilment of interest, that the two theories seem bound in the end to come out practically at very much the same point.

In any case, if we admit that this widely accepted view, for instance, in one or the other of its divergent interpretations is correct, we are supplied at once with principles of value. And such principles, if they or anything like them be true, are not merely "ethical standards" imposed on the natural order from without. In fact they are genuinely *natural* standards. It seems to me, for example, that the proposition "misery is in itself an evil," or the proposition "happiness is in itself a good," is as much a truth about the natural order of things as is the proposition "fire burns," or "grass is green." Now from such principles of value we can derive principles of conduct. We can say, for instance, that what any person or group of persons "ought" to do is simply whatever will produce a greater balance of happiness over misery than any other alternative that is before him, and conversely, that what he "ought not" to do, or what it would be "wrong" for him to do, is just whatever would produce a lesser balance of positive over negative values—having in view, of course, the effects of his actions upon the experience of all conscious beings whatsoever. Doubtless all these conceptions lead to great difficulties when we try to apply them to the details of practical conduct; but I believe that we can and do guide ourselves more or less effectively by reference to such principles, and at any rate the principles themselves seem clear enough.

Now supposing principles of conduct to be determined in this way, it seems to me that they would rightly be called "natural principles," for they would be determined by "natural" standards—by standards, that is, which have a validity of their own, independent of the arbitrary command or prohibition of any authority whatever. They would be "natural laws" or the laws of "natural morality," and "natural rights" would be simply those "rights," those freedoms or privileges, which any individual "ought," in the sense defined, to be allowed to claim, i.e., in the sense that to allow these claims is a condition of the realization of the natural standard of, say, the increase of happiness and the decrease of misery or unhappiness. They would be claims which would be valid because they would rest upon the validity of a "natural law," because they would be prescribed by the very "nature of things."

In accordance with our previous discussion of the meaning of "natural rights" we must add, however, that "natural laws," so far as they are to define natural rights, must be principles of permanent, and not of merely transitory, validity, and furthermore that they must be such as are valid for all men everywhere. In other words, the truly natural rights must be those claims, liberties, and privileges the possession of which by the person or persons in question will continue, so long at least as human nature and the laws of the physical universe remain substantially what they now are, to constitute permanent and general conditions of human happiness.

But now, finally, *are* there any such natural rights, and, if so, what in particular are they? I believe that it is reasonable to hold that there are in this sense natural rights. We can scarcely doubt that there are certain general features of the physical order, of the psychological nature of man, and of the association of men in social and political aggregations, which have been, and will so far as we can see for a long time continue to be, permanent forces to be reckoned with in the human pursuit of happiness. And it seems reasonable to hold, these factors being what they are, and the values of human experience being also what they are, that so long as all these factors of the situation remain the same there will be certain permanent and general conditions for the attainment of values, and that some of these conditions will take the form of the allotment to certain individuals or groups of individuals of certain claims, privileges, and freedoms which all others shall be bound to respect. I shall not, however, attempt to say what in particular any such natural rights may be. In fact, I regard the determination of natural rights rather as a problem awaiting solution than as anything as yet at all fully or satisfactorily determined. But I do at least regard it as a legitimate problem, and as one which there is some fair hope of solving. Indeed, I suppose that sociologists and political scientists, however unwilling they may be to state the problem in the terms which we have here employed, are already, at least in some measure, approximating to its solution.

What has brought the notion of natural rights into general, and as it seems to me undeserved, contempt has, I think, been the almost universal assumption on the part of those who have believed in them that the "natural rights of man" and the "laws of nature" on which they are based are readily discoverable either by a simple consideration of traditional commands and prohibitions, or by some short and easy method of insight or immediate intuition. Rather, their determination must be the result of long and careful investigation and experiment. And the defenders of natural rights have also made other serious errors. They have usually conceived of natural rights too abstractly, as if each stood quite on its own basis, independent of and indifferent to every other. On the contrary, natural rights must form a *system* of carefully interrelated and mutually adjusted rights and duties. And finally, natural rights have too often been thought of as vested in certain individuals apart from all reference to society and the interests of society. The very definition of a "right" should be sufficient to dispose of such a notion. A right is a claim which ought to be allowed to an individual in view of the general welfare. Allowed by whom? We can only answer, "By society." A claim upon what? Upon the forbearance and support of others. Society is implied at every turn.

Rights

SIR DAVID ROSS

A general discussion of right or duty would hardly be complete without some discussion, even if only a brief one, of the closely related subject of rights. It is commonly said that rights and duties are correlative, and it is worth while to inquire whether and, if at all, in what sense this is true. The statement may stand for any one, or any combination, of the following logically independent statements:

(1) A right of A against B implies a duty of B to A.
(2) A duty of B to A implies a right of A against B.
(3) A right of A against B implies a duty of A to B.
(4) A duty of A to B implies a right of A against B.

What is asserted in (1) is that A's having a right to have a certain individual act done to him by B implies a duty for B to do *that* act to A; (2) asserts the converse implication; what is meant by (3) is that A's having a right to have a certain act done to him by B implies a duty for A to do *another* act to B, which act may be either a similar act (as where the right of having the truth told to one implies the duty of telling the truth) or a different sort of act (as where the right to obedience implies the duty of governing well); (4) asserts the converse implication.

Of these four propositions the first appears to be unquestionably true; a right in one being against another is a right to treat or be treated by that other in a certain way, and this plainly implies a duty for the other to behave in a certain way. But there is a certain consideration which throws doubt on the other three propositions. This arises from the fact that we have duties to animals and to infants. The latter case is complicated by the fact that infants, while they are not (so we commonly believe) actual moral agents, are potential moral agents, so that the duty of parents, for instance, to support them may be said to be counterbalanced by a duty which is not incumbent on the infants at the time but will be incumbent on them later, to obey and care for their parents. We had better therefore take the less complicated case of animals, which we commonly suppose not to be even potential moral agents.

It may of course be denied that we have duties to animals. The view held by some writers is that we have duties concerning animals but not to them, the theory being that we have a duty to behave humanely to our fellow men, and that we should behave humanely to animals simply for fear of creating a disposition in ourselves which will make us tend to be cruel to our fellow men. Professor D. G. Ritchie, for instance, implies that we have not a duty to animals except in a sense like that in which the owner of an historic house may be said to have a duty to the house.[1] Now the latter sense is, I suppose, purely metaphorical.

From *The Right and the Good* by Sir David Ross, pp. 197–203, by permission of the Clarendon Press, Oxford.

[1] *Natural Rights*, 108.

We may in a fanciful mood think of a noble house as if it were a conscious being having feelings which we are bound to respect. But we do not really think that it has them. I suppose that the duty of the owner of an historic house is essentially a duty to his contemporaries and to posterity; and he may also think it is a duty to his ancestors. On the other hand, if we think we ought to behave in a certain way to animals, it is our of consideration primarily for *their* feelings that we think we ought to behave so; we do not think of them merely as a practising-ground for virtue. It is because we think their pain a bad thing that we think we should not gratuitously cause it. And I suppose that to say we have a duty to so-and-so is the same thing as to say that we have a duty, grounded on facts relating to them, to behave in a certain way towards them.

Now if we have a duty to animals, and they have not a duty to us (which seems clear, since they are not moral agents), the first and last of our four propositions cannot both be true, since (4) implies that a duty of men to animals involves a right of men against animals, and (1) implies that this involves a duty of animals to men, and therefore (4) and (1) together imply that a duty of men to animals involves a duty of animals to men. And since the first proposition is clearly true, the fourth must be false; it cannot be true that a duty of A to B necessarily involves a right of A against B. Similarly, the second and third propositions cannot both be true; for (2) and (3) taken together imply that a duty of men to animals involves a duty of animals to men. But here it is not so clear which of the two propositions is true; for it is not clear whether we should say that though we have a duty to animals they have no right against us, or that though they have a right against us they have no duty to us. If we take the first view, we are implying that in order to have rights, just as much as in order to have duties, it is necessary to be a moral agent. If we take the second view,

we are implying that while only moral agents have duties, the possession of a nature capable of feeling pleasure and pain is all that is needed in order to have rights. It is not at all clear which is the true view. On the whole, since we mean by a right something that can be justly claimed, we should probably say that animals have not rights, not because the claim to humane treatment would not be just if it were made, but because they cannot make it. But the doubt which we here find about the application of the term 'rights' is characteristic of the term. There are other ways too in which its application is doubtful. Even if we hold that it is our duty not merely to do what is just to others but to promote their welfare beyond what justice requires, it is not at all clear that we should say they have a right to beneficent treatment over and above what is just. We have a tendency to think that not every duty incumbent on one person involves a right in another.

This characteristic of our way of thinking about rights has been fastened upon by theory. Green, for instance, divides the whole region of duty into three parts: (1) moral duties which involve no rights on the other side, (2) obligations involving such rights, both obligations and rights being included in the *jus naturae* and being such as *should* be legally recognized, (3) legal obligations involving legal rights on the other side.[2] He describes the rights in class (2)—what I will for brevity call moral rights—as sharing with legal rights the characteristic of depending for their existence on some form of general recognition. The recognition in the latter case consists in the making of a law; in the former it consists simply in a general state of public opinion. Now it is plainly wrong to describe either legal or moral rights as depending for their existence on their recognition, for to recognize a thing (in the sense in which 'recognize' is here used) is

[2] *Principles of Political Obligation*, §§ 10, 11.

to recognize it as existing already. The promulgation of a law is not the recognition of a legal right, but the creation of it, though it may imply the recognition of an already existing moral right. And to make the existence of a *moral* right depend on its being recognized is equally mistaken. It would imply that slaves, for instance, acquired the moral right to be free only at the moment when a majority of mankind, or of some particular community, formed the opinion that they ought to be free, i.e. when the particular person whose conversion to this view changed a minority into a majority changed his mind. Such a view, of course, cannot be consistently maintained, and we find Green implying in successive sections that social recognition is indispensable to the existence of rights,[3] and that the slave has a right to citizenship though this right is not recognized by society.[4] In the latter passage we see the true Green, the passionate lover of liberty, reacting against the theory of the previous page. Some may think that slavery is not wrong; but every one will admit that there are certain forms of treatment of others which are wrong and which the sufferer has the right to have removed, whether this right is recognized by society or not.

There is, however, to be found in Green another view which is less clearly false. According to this, the existence of a right is made to depend not on the recognition of *it* but on the recognition of a power in the person in question to seek an end common to all the citizens of a community.[5] This avoids the patent error of making the existence of a right depend on its being recognized to exist. Yet like the former view it makes a moral right depend not on the nature of a given person and his relations to his fellows, but on what people think about them, i.e. on what a majority of the community think about them. But though the existence of *legal* rights depends on the degree of enlightenment of the community, the existence of moral rights plainly does not, but on the nature and relations of the persons concerned.

Green's theory seems to have arisen as follows. He starts his historical survey with Hobbes and Spinoza, both of whom identify right with power. A *legal* right *may* be identified with a certain kind of power; it is the power of getting certain things not by one's own brute force but by the aid of the law. Green seems to have tried to get a theory of moral rights by making a similar amendment of the bare identification of right with power; and he accordingly identifies them with the power of getting certain things not by one's own brute force nor by the aid of the law but by the aid of public opinion; instead of saying, what is surely evident, that a moral right is not a power at all. Yet there are elements in his account which point to a truer theory; e.g. 'a "right" is an ideal attribution ("ideal" in the sense of not being sensibly verifiable).'[6] Now whether a given society recognizes a particular right is, I take it, sensibly verifiable in the sense in which Green here insists that a right is not. What is not sensibly verifiable is whether the society is justified in recognizing the right, and this depends on whether the right is there antecedently to society's recognition of it. Thus the insistence that a right is not sensibly verifiable points to an objective theory of rights; but unfortunately Green follows this clue no farther.

If we eliminate the possibility of holding that animals have rights, by saying that only that which has a moral nature can have a right, our main doubt with regard to the correlation of rights and duties is on the question whether there is a right to

---

[3] 'A claim to which reality is given by social recognition, and thus implicitly a right' (§ 139). Cf. 'This recognition of a power, in some way or other, as that which should be, is always necessary to render it a right' (§ 23). 'Rights are made by recognition. There is no right "but thinking makes it so"' (§ 136).

[4] § 140 implies that the slave's right to citizenship is founded on his possessing a common human consciousness with the citizens of the state.

[5] Cf. e.g. §§ 25, 26.

[6] § 38.

beneficence. It is obvious that a man has a right to just treatment, and it is commonly agreed that he has a right to have promises made to him fulfilled; it is less generally agreed that he has a right to beneficent treatment, even when it is admitted that it is our duty to treat him beneficently.

Some would even say that to treat others beneficently is to go beyond our duty. But probably this statement rests on a mere confusion. We usually oppose justice to *benevolence*. But while treating a man justly is commonly understood to mean doing certain things to him (paying our debts to him, and the like), irrespective of the spirit in which we do them, treating him benevolently obviously means doing certain things to him from goodwill. And it is rightly felt that there is a great difference between the two things, and it is found natural to say that the one implies, and the other does not, a right on the other side, and (by some people) even to say that the one is a duty and the other is not. But if we will distinguish between doing what is just and doing it in the spirit of justice, and between doing what is beneficent and doing it in the spirit of beneficence, then (in accordance with the principle that it is always acts, and not acts from a certain motive, that are our duty) it is clear that it is not our duty to act in the spirit of justice, any more than in the spirit of beneficence, and that it *is* our duty to do what is beneficent, as it is our duty to do what is just.

If we are clear on this point, our main objection to saying that the other person has a right to beneficence disappears. I do not say that our whole objection disappears; for there hangs about the notion of a 'right' the notion of its being not only something which one person should in decency respect but also something which the other person can in decency claim, and we feel that there is something indecent in the making of a *claim* to beneficence.

These doubts about the application of the term 'right' appear to spring from the fact that 'right' (the noun) does not stand

for a purely moral notion. It began, I suppose, by standing for a legal notion, and its usage has broadened out so as to include certain things that cannot be claimed at law; but its usage has not yet broadened out so much as to become completely correlative to duty. Once we start on the process of broadening it out, however, there seems to be no secure resting-place short of this.

Returning now to the four propositions about the correlativity of duties and rights, it seems that with regard to the second proposition, 'A duty of B to A implies a right of A against B' (which has latterly been the subject of our dicussion), we should say (1) that this is not true when A is not a moral agent, and (2) that it is true when A is a moral agent (even if the duty be the duty of beneficent action). And since our only doubt about the third proposition, 'A right of A against B implies a duty of A to B,' arises from our doubt whether animals have not rights, if we agree that animals have not rights we need not doubt the truth of this proposition. It is this proposition, above all, that has been maintained by those who have insisted on the correlativity of rights and duties; for this was maintained essentially against the belief that men have 'natural rights' in a state of nature in which they have no duties.

A further problem, however, awaits us, *viz.* whether a failure to do one's duty involves a corresponding loss of right. Or rather, as we have found the meaning of 'rights' more doubtful than that of 'duties,' it will be more profitable to omit any reference to rights, and put our question in the form, "if A fails in his duty to B, does that put an end to B's duty to A?' In some cases we seem to be clear that this is so. If a tradesman sends me goods inferior to those I chose in his shop, I am not morally, any more than legally, bound to pay him the full price; I may return the goods and pay nothing, or (with his consent) keep them and pay a lower price. And in general any duty arising out of a contract is cancelled by non-fulfilment of the corresponding duty on the other side. In other cases we are not so clear. It is not so generally agreed, for instance, that if A tells lies to B, B is justified in telling lies to A. Two blacks, we say in such a case, do not make a white. Yet the peculiar stringency of the duty of veracity seems to spring from an implicit understanding that language shall be used to convey the real opinions of the speakers, and it would seem that a failure to carry out the understanding on one side makes it no longer binding on the other; and we should have small patience with an habitual liar who insisted on strict veracity in others. It must be admitted that a man who has deceived me has destroyed what would have been the main reason for its being my duty to tell him the truth. But we should probably hesitate to say that by his breach of the implicit understanding my duty to tell him the truth has been entirely destroyed, as by the tradesman's breach of contract my duty to pay him has been destroyed. Various reasons help to account for this. For one thing, it is likely that by deceiving a liar I may indirectly deceive innocent people; for another, the consequences for my own character are likely to be particularly dangerous. But the main reason probably lies elsewhere. Before the contract was made between my tradesman and me, there was no duty incumbent on me of paying him this sum of money. I had a general duty to promote the good of all men, but there was no obvious reason for supposing that this could be best done by transferring this sum of money to him. But even before the implicit undertaking to tell the truth was established I had a duty not to tell lies, since to tell lies is *prima facie* to do a positive injury to another person. Since this duty does not rest on contract, it is not abolished by the breach of contract, and therefore while a person who has been deceived by another is justified in refusing to answer his questions, he is not justified in telling him lies. Yet that this forms only a small part of the stringency of the duty of truthfulness may be inferred from the leniency with which we should judge deceit, in a case in which no implicit undertaking to tell the truth has been established, e.g. when a civilized man deceives a savage whom he has just met for the first time, or *vice versa,* or when one of two savages belonging to different tribes deceives the other. Deceit is much more venial in such a case, because the offender has no reason to suppose that the other is not deceiving, or going to deceive, *him.*

Taking, then, the obvious division between duties arising out of contract and those that arise otherwise, we must say that while the former are cancelled by breach of the contract on the other side, the latter are not cancelled by the bad behaviour of the other person. It would also seem, from a consideration of our actual moral judgments, that the former type of duty is the more stringent of the two.

Now the distinction between the rights corresponding to duties that arise out of contract, and the rights corresponding to other duties, may be quite suitably expressed as a distinction between contractual and natural rights, and the notion of natural rights as a distinct class may thus be vindicated, if it be cut free from the belief which has been so often bound up with it, that there are rights in a state of nature, i.e. in a state in which there are no duties. Such a belief is made possible for Hobbes only by a complete confusion between rights and powers, amounting to an express identification of the two.

Justice as Fairness

JOHN RAWLS

1. It might seem at first sight that the concepts of justice and fairness are the same, and that there is no reason to distinguish them, or to say that one is more fundamental than the other. I think that this impression is mistaken. In this paper I wish to show that the fundamental idea in the concept of justice is fairness; and I wish to offer an analysis of the concept of justice from this point of view. To bring out the force of this claim, and the analysis based upon it, I shall then argue that it is this aspect of justice for which utilitarianism, in its classical form, is unable to account, but which is expressed, even if misleadingly, by the ideas of the social contract.

To start with I shall develop a particular conception of justice by stating and commenting upon two principles which specify it, and by considering the circumstances and conditions under which they may be thought to arise. The principles defining this conception, and the conception itself, are, of course, familiar. It may be possible, however, by using the notion of fairness as a framework, to assemble and to look at them in a new way. Before stating this conception, however, the following preliminary matters should be kept in mind.

Throughout I consider justice only as a virtue of social institutions, or what I shall call practices.[1] The principles of justice are

regarded as formulating restrictions as to how practices may define positions and offices, and assign thereto powers and liabilities, rights and duties. Justice as a virtue of particular actions or of persons I do not take up at all. It is important to distinguish these various subjects of justice, since the meaning of the concept varies according to whether it is applied to practices, particular actions, or persons. These meanings are, indeed, connected, but they are not identical. I shall confine my discussion to the sense of justice as applied to practices, since this sense is the basic one. Once it is understood, the other senses should go quite easily.

Justice is to be understood in its customary sense as representing but *one* of the many virtues of social institutions, for these may be antiquated, inefficient, degrading, or any number of other things, without being unjust. Justice is not to be confused with an all-inclusive vision of a good society; it is only one part of any such conception. It is important, for example, to distinguish that sense of equality which is an aspect of the concept of justice from that sense of equality which belongs to a more comprehensive social ideal. There may well be inequalities which one concedes are just,

---

Reprinted from *The Philosophical Review*, 1955, pp. 164–194, by permission of the author and *The Philosophical Review*.

[1] I use the word "practice" throughout as a sort of technical term meaning any form of activity specified by a system of rules which defines offices, roles, moves, penalties, defenses, and so on, and which gives the activity its structure. As examples one may think of games and rituals, trials and parliaments, markets and systems of property. I have attempted a partial analysis of the notion of a practice in a paper "Two Concepts of Rules" *Philosophical Review* LXIV (1955) 3–32.

or at least not unjust, but which, nevertheless, one wishes, on other grounds, to do away with. I shall focus attention, then, on the usual sense of justice in which it is essentially the elimination of arbitrary distinctions and the establishment, within the structure of a practice, of a proper balance between competing claims.

Finally, there is no need to consider the principles discussed below as *the* principles of justice. For the moment it is sufficient that they are typical of a family of principles normally associated with the concept of justice. The way in which the principles of this family resemble one another, as shown by the background against which they may be thought to arise, will be made clear by the whole of the subsequent argument.

2. The conception of justice which I want to develop may be stated in the form of two principles as follows: first, each person participating in a practice, or affected by it, has an equal right to the most extensive liberty compatible with a like liberty for all; and second, inequalities are arbitrary unless it is reasonable to expect that they will work out for everyone's advantage, and provided the positions and offices to which they attach, or from which they may be gained, are open to all. These principles express justice as a complex of three ideas: liberty, equality, and reward for services contributing to the common good.[2]

The term "person" is to be construed variously depending on the circumstances. On some occasions it will mean human individuals, but in others it may refer to na-

tions, provinces, business firms, churches, teams, and so on. The principles of justice apply in all these instances, although there is a certain logical priority to the case of human individuals. As I shall use the term "person," it will be ambiguous in the manner indicated.

The first principle holds, of course, only if other things are equal: that is, while there must always be a justification for departing from the initial position of equal liberty (which is defined by the pattern of rights and duties, powers and liabilities, established by a practice), and the burden of proof is placed on him who would depart from it, nevertheless, there can be, and often there is, a justification for doing so. Now, that similar particular cases, as defined by a practice, should be treated similarly as they arise, is part of the very concept of a practice; it is involved in the notion of an activity in accordance with rules.[3] The first principle expresses an analogous conception, but as applied to the structure of practices themselves. It holds, for example, that there is a presumption against the distinctions and classifications made by legal systems and other practices to the extent that they infringe on the original and equal liberty of the persons participating in them. The second principle defines how this presumption may be rebutted.

It might be argued at this point that justice requires only an equal liberty. If, however, a greater liberty were possible for all without loss or conflict, then it would be irrational to settle on a lesser liberty. There

---

[2] These principles are of course well-known in one form or another and appear in many analyses of justice even where the writers differ widely on other matters. Thus if the principle of equal liberty is commonly associated with Kant (see *The Philosophy of Law*, tr. by W. Hastie, Edinburgh, 1887, pp. 56 f.), it may be claimed that it can also be found in J. S. Mill's *On Liberty* and elsewhere, and in many other liberal writers. Recently H. L. A. Hart has argued for something like it in his paper "Are There Any Natural Rights?," *Philosophical Review*, LXIV (1955), 175–191. The injustice of inequalities which are not won in return for a contribution to the common advantage

is, of course, widespread in political writings of all sorts. The conception of justice here discussed is distinctive, if at all, only in selecting these two principles in this form; but for another similar analysis, see the discussion by W. D. Lamont, *The Principles of Moral Judgment* (Oxford, 1946), ch. v.

[3] This point was made by Sidgwick, *Methods of Ethics*, 6th ed. (London, 1901), Bk. III, ch. v, sec. 1. It has recently been emphasized by Sir Isaiah Berlin in a symposium, "Equality," *Proceedings of the Aristotelian Society*, n.s. LVI (1955–56), 305 f.

is no reason for circumscribing rights unless their exercise would be incompatible, or would render the practice defining them less effective. Therefore no serious distortion of the concept of justice is likely to follow from including within it the concept of the greatest equal liberty.

The second principle defines what sorts of inequalities are permissible; it specifies how the presumption laid down by the first principle may be put aside. Now by inequalities it is best to understand not *any* differences between offices and positions, but differences in the benefits and burdens attached to them either directly or indirectly, such as prestige and wealth, or liability to taxation and compulsory services. Players in a game do not protest against there being different positions, such as batter, pitcher, catcher, and the like, nor to there being various privileges and powers as specified by the rules; nor do the citizens of a country object to there being the different offices of government such as president, senator, governor, judge, and so on, each with their special rights and duties. It is not differences of this kind that are normally thought of as inequalities, but differences in the resulting distribution established by a practice, or made possible by it, of the things men strive to attain or avoid. Thus they may complain about the pattern of honors and rewards set up by a practice (e.g., the privileges and salaries of government officials) or they may object to the distribution of power and wealth which results from the various ways in which men avail themselves of the opportunities allowed by it (e.g., the concentration of wealth which may develop in a free price system allowing large entrepreneurial or speculative gains).

It should be noted that the second principle holds that an inequality is allowed only if there is reason to believe that the practice with the inequality, or resulting in it, will work for the advantage of *every* party engaging in it. Here it is important to stress that *every* party must gain

from the inequality. Since the principle applies to practices, it implies that the representative man in every office or position defined by a practice, when he views it as a going concern, must find it reasonable to prefer his condition and prospects with the inequality to what they would be under the practice without it. The principle excludes, therefore, the justification of inequalities on the grounds that the disadvantages of those in one position are outweighed by the greater advantages of those in another position. This rather simple restriction is the main modification I wish to make in the utilitarian principle as usually understood. When coupled with the notion of a practice, it is a restriction of consequence,[4] and one which some utilitarians, e.g., Hume and Mill, have used in their discussions of justice without realizing apparently its signi-

[4] In the paper referred to above, footnote 2, I have tried to show the importance of taking practices as the proper subject of the utilitarian principle. The criticisms of so-called "restricted ultilitarianism" by J. J. C. Smart, "Extreme and Restricted Utilitarianism," *Philosophical Quarterly,* VI(1956), 344–354, and by H. J. McCloskey, "An Examination of Restricted Utilitarianism," *Philosophical Review,* LXVI (1957), 466–485, do not affect my argument. These papers are concerned with the very general proposition, which is attributed (with what justice I shall not consider) to S. E. Toulmin and P. H. Nowell-Smith (and in the case of the latter paper, also, apparently, to me); namely, the proposition that particular moral actions are justified by appealing to moral rules, and moral rules in turn by reference to utility. But clearly I meant to defend no such view. My discussion of the concept of rules as maxims is an explicit rejection of it. What I did argue was that, in the *logically special* case of practices (although actually quite a common case) where the rules have special features and are not moral rules at all but legal rules or rules of games and the like (except, perhaps, in the case of promises), there is a peculiar force to the distinction between justifying particular actions and justifying the system of rules themselves. Even then I claimed only that restricting the utilitarian principle to practices as defined strengthened it. I did not argue for the position that this amendment alone is sufficient for a complete defense of utilitarianism as a general theory of morals. In this paper I take up the question as to how the utilitarian principle itself must be modified, but here, too, the subject of inquiry is not all of morality at once, but a limited topic, the concept of justice.

ficance, or at least without calling attention to it.[5] Why it is a significant modification of principle, changing one's conception of justice entirely, the whole of my argument will show.

Further, it is also necessary that the various offices to which special benefits or burdens attach are open to all. It may be, for example, to the common advantage, as just defined, to attach special benefits to certain offices. Perhaps by doing so the requisite talent can be attracted to them and encouraged to give its best efforts. But any offices having special benefits must be won in a fair competition in which contestants are judged on their merits. If some offices were not open, those excluded would normally be justified in feeling unjustly treated, even if they benefited from the greater efforts of those who were allowed to compete for them. Now if one can assume that offices are open, it is necessary only to consider the design of practices themselves and how they jointly, as a system, work together. It will be a mistake to focus attention on the varying relative positions of particular persons, who may be known to us by their proper names, and to require that each such change, as a once for all transaction viewed in isolation, must be in itself just. It is the system of practices which is to be judged, and judged from a general point of view: unless one is prepared to criticize it from the standpoint of a representative man holding some particu-

lar office, one has no complaint against it.

3. Given these principles one might try to derive them from a priori principles of reason, or claim that they were known by intuition. These are familiar enough steps and, at least in the case of the first principle, might be made with some success. Usually, however, such arguments, made at this point, are unconvincing. They are not likely to lead to an understanding of the basis of the principles of justice, not at least as principles of justice. I wish, therefore, to look at the principles in a different way.

Imagine a society of persons amongst whom a certain system of practices is *already* well established. Now suppose that by and large they are mutually self-interested; their allegiance to their established practice is normally founded on the prospect of self-advantage. One need not assume that, in all senses of the term "person," the persons in this society are mutually self-interested. If the characterization as mutually self-interested applies when the line of division is the family, it may still be true that members of families are bound by ties of sentiment and affection and willingly acknowledge duties in contradiction to self-interest. Mutual self-interestedness in the relations between families, nations, churches, and the like, is commonly associated with intense loyalty and devotion on the part of individual members. Therefore, one can form a more realistic conception of this society if one thinks of it as consisting of mutually self-interested families, or some other association. Further, it is not necessary to suppose that these persons are mutually self-interested under all circumstances, but only in the usual situations in which they participate in their common practices.

Now suppose also that these persons are rational: they know their own interests more or less accurately; they are capable of tracing out the likely consequences of adopting one practice rather than another; they are capable of adhering to a course of

[5] It might seem as if J. S. Mill, in paragraph 36 of Chapter v of *Utilitarianism*, expressed the utilitarian principle in this modified form, but in the remaining two paragraphs of the chapter, and elsewhere, he would appear not to grasp the significance of the change. Hume often emphasizes that *every* man must benefit. For example, in discussing the utility of general rules, he holds that they are requisite to the "well-being of every individual"; from a stable system of property "every individual person must find himself a gainer in balancing the account. . . ." "Every member of society is sensible of this interest; everyone expresses this sense to his fellows along with the resolution he has taken of squaring his actions by it, on the conditions that others will do the same." *A Treatise of Human Nature,* Bk. III, Pt. II, Section II, paragraph 22.

action once they have decided upon it; they can resist present temptations and the enticements of immediate gain; and the bare knowledge or perception of the difference between their condition and that of others is not, within certain limits and in itself, a source of great dissatisfaction. Only the last point adds anything to the usual definition of rationality. This definition should allow, I think, for the idea that a rational man would not be greatly downcast from knowing, or seeing, that others are in a better position than himself, unless he thought their being so was the result of injustice, or the consequence of letting chance work itself out for no useful common purpose, and so on. So if these persons strike us as unpleasantly egoistic, they are at least free in some degree from the fault of envy.[6]

Finally, assume that these persons have roughly similar needs and interests, or needs and interests in various ways complementary, so that fruitful cooperation amongst them is possible; and suppose that they are sufficiently equal in power and ability to guarantee that in normal circumstances none is able to dominate the others. This condition (as well as the other) may seem excessively vague; but in view of the conception of justice to which the argument leads, there seems no reason for making it more exact here.

Since these persons are conceived as engaging in their common practices, which are already established, there is no question of our supposing them to come together to deliberate as to how they will set these practices up for the first time. Yet we can imagine that from time to time they

[6] It is not possible to discuss here this addition to the usual conception of rationality. If it seems peculiar, it may be worth remarking that it is analogous to the modification of the utilitarian principle which the argument as a whole is designed to explain and justify. In the same way that the satisfaction of interests, the representative claims of which violate the principles of justice, is not a reason for having a practice (see sec. 7), unfounded envy, within limits, need not be taken into account.

discuss with one another whether any of them has a legitimate complaint against their established institutions. Such discussions are perfectly natural in any normal society. Now suppose that they have settled on doing this in the following way. They first try to arrive at the principles by which complaints, and so practices themselves, are to be judged. Their procedure for this is to let each person propose the principles upon which he wishes his complaints to be tried with the understanding that, if acknowledged, the complaints of others will be similarly tried, and that no complaints will be heard at all until everyone is roughly of one mind as to how complaints are to be judged. They each understand further that the principles proposed and acknowledged on this occasion are binding on future occasions. Thus each will be wary of proposing a principle which would give him a peculiar advantage, in his present circumstances, supposing it to be accepted. Each person knows that he will be bound by it in future circumstances the peculiarities of which cannot be known, and which might well be such that the principle is then to his disadvantage. The idea is that everyone should be required to make *in advance* a firm commitment which others also may reasonably be expected to make, and that no one be given the opportunity to tailor the canons of a legitimate complaint to fit his own special condition, and then to discard them when they no longer suit his purpose. Hence each person will propose principles of a general kind which will, to a large degree, gain their sense from the various applications to be made of them, the particular circumstances of which being as yet unknown. These principles will express the conditions in accordance with which each is the least unwilling to have his interests limited in the design of practices, given the competing interests of the others, on the supposition that the interests of others will be limited likewise. The restrictions which would so arise might be thought of as those a person would keep in mind if he were designing a practice in which his enemy were to assign him his place.

The two main parts of this conjectural account have a definite significance. The character and respective situations of the parties reflect the typical circumstances in which questions of justice arise. The procedure whereby principles are proposed and acknowledged represents constraints, analogous to those of having a morality, whereby rational and mutually self-interested persons are brought to act reasonably. Thus the first part reflects the fact that questions of justice arise when conflicting claims are made upon the design of a practice and where it is taken for granted that each person will insist, as far as possible, on what he considers his rights. It is typical of cases of justice to involve persons who are pressing on one another their claims, between which a fair balance or equilibrium must be found. On the other hand, as expressed by the second part, having a morality must at least imply the acknowledgment of principles as impartially applying to one's own conduct as well as to another's, and moreover principles which may constitute a constraint, or limitation, upon the pursuit of one's own interests. There are, of course, other aspects of having a morality: the acknowledgment of moral principles must show itself in accepting a reference to them as reasons for limiting one's claims, in acknowledging the burden of providing a special explanation, or excuse, when one acts contrary to them, or else in showing shame and remorse and a desire to make amends, and so on. It is sufficient to remark here that having a morality is analogous to having made a firm commitment in advance; for one must acknowledge the principles of morality even when to one's disadvantage.[7] A man whose

moral judgments always coincided with his interests could be suspected of having no morality at all.

Thus the two parts of the foregoing account are intended to mirror the kinds of circumstances in which questions of justice arise and the constraints which having a morality would impose upon persons so situated. In this way one can see how the acceptance of the principles of justice might come about, for given all these conditions as described, it would be natural if the two principles of justice were to be acknowledged. Since there is no way for anyone to win special advantages for himself, each might consider it reasonable to acknowledge equality as an initial principle. There is, however, no reason why they should regard this position as final; for if there are inequalities which satisfy the second principle, the immediate gain which equality would allow can be considered as intelligently invested in view of its future return. If, as is quite likely, these inequalities work as incentives to draw out better efforts, the members of this society may look upon them as concessions to human nature: they, like us, may think that people ideally should want to serve one another. But as they are mutually self-interested, their acceptance of these inequalities is merely the acceptance of the relations in which they actually stand, and a recognition of the motives which lead them to engage in their common practices. *They* have no title to complain of one another. And so provided that the conditions of the principle are met, there is no reason why they should not allow such inequalities. Indeed, it would be short-sighted of them not to do so, and could result, in most cases, only from their being dejected by the bare knowledge, or perception, that others are better situated. Each person will, however, insist on an ad-

---

[7] The idea that accepting a principle as a moral principle implies that one generally acts on it, failing a special explanation, has been stressed by R. M. Hare, *The Language of Morals* (Oxford, 1952). His formulation of it needs to be modified, however, along the lines suggested by P. L. Gardi-

ner, "On Assenting to a Moral Principle," *Proceedings of the Aristotelian Society*, n.s. LV (1955), 23–44. See also C. K. Grant, "Akrasia and the Criteria of Assent to Practical Principles," *Mind*, LXV (1956), 400–407, where the complexity of the criteria for assent is discussed.

vantage to himself, and so on a common advantage, for none is willing to sacrifice anything for the others.

These remarks are not offered as a proof that persons so conceived and circumstanced would settle on the two principles, but only to show that these principles could have such a background, and so can be viewed as those principles which mutually self-interested and rational persons, when similarly situated and required to make in advance a firm commitment, could acknowledge as restrictions governing the assignment of rights and duties in their common practices, and thereby accept as limiting their rights against one another. The principles of justice may, then, be regarded as those principles which arise when the constraints of having a morality are imposed upon parties in the typical circumstances of justice.

4. These ideas are, of course, connected with a familiar way of thinking about justice which goes back at least to the Greek Sophists, and which regards the acceptance of the principles of justice as a compromise between persons of roughly equal power who would enforce their will on each other if they could, but who, in view of the equality of forces amongst them and for the sake of their own peace and security, acknowledge certain forms of conduct insofar as prudence seems to require. Justice is thought of as a pact between rational egoists the stability of which is dependent on a balance of power and a similarity of circumstances.[8] While the previous account is connected with this tradition, and with its most recent variant, the theory of games,[9] it differs from it in several important respects which, to forestall misinterpretations, I will set out here.

First, I wish to use the previous conjectural account of the background of justice as a way of analyzing the concept. I do not want, therefore, to be interpreted as assuming a general theory of human motivation: when I suppose that the parties are mutually self-interested, and are not willing to have their (substantial) interests sacrificed to others, I am referring to their conduct and motives as they are taken for granted in cases where questions of justice ordinarily arise. Justice is the virtue of practices where there are assumed to be competing interests and conflicting claims, and where it is supposed that persons will press their rights on each other. That persons are mutually self-interested in certain situations and for certain purposes is what gives rise to the question of justice in practices covering those circumstances. Amongst an association of saints, if such a community could really exist, the disputes about justice could hardly occur; for they would all work self-

---

[8] Perhaps the best known statement of this conception is that given by Glaucon at the beginning of Book II of Plato's *Republic*. Presumably it was, in various forms, a common view among the Sophists; but that Plato gives a fair representation of it is doubtful. See K. R. Popper, *The Open Society and Its Enemies*, rev. ed. (Princeton, 1950), pp. 112–118. Certainly Plato usually attributes to it a quality of manic egoism which one feels must be an exaggeration; on the other hand, see the Melian Debate in Thucydides, *The Peloponnesian War*, Book V, ch. VII, although it is impossible to say to what extent the views expressed there reveal any current philosophical opinion. Also in this tradition are the remarks of Epicurus on justice in *Principal Doctrines*, XXXI-XXXVIII. In modern times elements of the conception appear in a more sophisticated form in Hobbes *The Leviathan* and in Hume *A Treatise of Human Nature*, Book III, Pt. II, as well as in the writings of the school of natural law such as Pufendorf's *De jure naturae et gentium*. Hobbes and Hume are especially instructive. For Hobbes's argument see Howard Warrender's *The Political Philosophy of Hobbes* (Oxford, 1957). W. J. Baumol's *Welfare Economics and the Theory of the State* (London, 1952), is valuable in showing the wide applicability of Hobbes's fundamental idea (interpreting his natural law as principles of prudence), although in this book it is traced back only to Hume's *Treatise*.

[9] See J. von Neumann and O. Morgenstern, *The Theory of Games and Economic Behavior*, 2nd ed. (Princeton, 1947). For a comprehensive and not too technical discussion of the developments since, see R. Duncan Luce and Howard Raiffa, *Games and Decisions: Introduction and Critical Survey* (New York, 1957). Chs. VI and XIV discuss the developments most obviously related to the analysis of justice.

lessly together for one end, the glory of God as defined by their common religion, and reference to this end would settle every question of right. The justice of practices does not come up until there are several different parties (whether we think of these as individuals, associations, or nations and so on, is irrelevant) who do press their claims on one another, and who do regard themselves as representatives of interests which deserve to be considered. Thus the previous account involves no general theory of human motivation. Its intent is simply to incorporate into the conception of justice the relations of men to one another which set the stage for questions of justice. It makes no difference how wide or general these relations are, as this matter does not bear on the analysis of the concept.

Again, in contrast to the various conceptions of the social contract, the several parties do not establish any particular society or practice; they do not covenant to obey a particular sovereign body or to accept a given constitution.[10] Nor do they, as in the theory of games (in certain respects a marvelously sophisticated development of this tradition), decide on individual strategies adjusted to their respective circumstances in the game. What the parties do is to *jointly* acknowledge certain *principles* of appraisal relating to their common *practices* either as already established or merely proposed. They accede to standards of judgment, not to a given practice; they do not make any specific agreement, or bargain, or adopt a particular strategy. The subject of their acknowledgment is, therefore, very general indeed; it is simply the acknowledgment of certain principles of judgment, fulfilling certain general conditions, to be used in criticizing the arrangement of their common affairs. The relations of mutual self-interest between the parties

who are similarly circumstanced mirror the conditions under which questions of justice arise, and the procedure by which the principles of judgment are proposed and acknowledged reflects the constraints of having a morality. Each aspect, then, of the preceding hypothetical account serves the purpose of bringing out a feature of the notion of justice. One could, if one liked, view the principles of justice as the "solution" of this highest order "game" of adopting, subject to the procedure described, principles of argument for all coming particular "games" whose peculiarities one can in no way foresee. But this comparison, while no doubt helpful, must not obscure the fact that this highest order "game" is of a special sort.[11] Its significance is that its var-

[10] For a general survey see J. W. Gough, *The Social Contract*, 2nd ed. (Oxford, 1957), and Otto von Gierke, *The Development of Political Theory*, tr. by B. Freyd (London, 1939), Pt. II, ch. ii.

[11] The difficulty one gets into by a mechanical application of the theory of games to moral philosophy can be brought out by considering among several possible examples, R. B. Braithwaite's study, *Theory of Games as a Tool for the Moral Philosopher* (Cambridge, 1955). On the analysis there given, it turns out that the fair division of playing time between Matthew and Luke depends on their preferences, and these in turn are connected with the instruments they wish to play. Since Matthew has a threat advantage over Luke, arising purely from the fact that Matthew, the trumpeter, prefers both of them playing at once to neither of them playing, whereas Luke, the pianist, prefers silence to cacophony, Matthew is allotted 26 evenings of play to Luke's 17. If the situation were reversed, the threat advantage would be with Luke. See pp. 36 f. But now we have only to suppose that Matthew is a jazz enthusiast who plays the drums, and Luke a violinist who plays sonatas, in which case it will be fair, on this analysis, for Matthew to play whenever and as often as he likes, assuming, of course, as it is plausible to assume, that he does not care whether Luke plays or not. Certainly something has gone wrong. To each according to his threat advantage is hardly the principle of fairness. What is lacking is the concept of morality, and it must be brought into the conjectural account in some way or other. In the text this is done by the form of the procedure whereby principles are proposed and acknowledged (Section 3). If one starts directly with the particular case as known, and if one accepts as given and definitive the preferences and relative positions of the parties, whatever they are, it is impossible to give an analysis of the moral concept of fairness. Braithwaite's use of the theory of games, insofar as it is intended to analyze the concept of fairness, is, I think, mistaken. This is not, of course, to criticize in any way the theory of

ious pieces represent aspects of the concept of justice.

Finally, I do not, of course, conceive the several parties as necessarily coming together to establish their common practices for the first time. Some institutions may, indeed, be set up *de novo;* but I have framed the preceding account so that it will apply when the full complement of social institutions already exists and represents the result of a long period of development. Nor is the account in any way fictitious. In any society where people reflect on their institutions they will have an idea of what principles of justice would be acknowledged under the conditions described, and there will be occasions when questions of justice are actually discussed in this way. Therefore if their practices do not accord with these principles, this will affect the quality of their social relations. For in this case there will be some recognized situations wherein the parties are mutually aware that one of them is being forced to accept what the other would concede is unjust. The foregoing analysis may then be thought of as representing the actual quality of relations between persons as defined by practices accepted as just. In such practices the parties will acknowledge the principles on which it is constructed, and the general recognition of this fact shows itself in the absence of resentment and in the sense of being justly treated. Thus one common objection to the theory of the social contract, its apparently historical and fictitious character, is avoided.

5. That the principles of justice may be regarded as arising in the manner described illustrates an important fact about them. Not only does it bring out the idea

---

games as a mathematical theory, to which Braithwaite's book certainly contributes, nor as an analysis of how rational (and amoral) egoists might behave (and so as an analysis of how people sometimes actually do behave). But it is to say that if the theory of games is to be used to analyze moral concepts, its formal structure must be interpreted in a special and general manner as indicated in the text. Once we do this, though, we are in touch again with a much older tradition.

that justice is a primitive moral notion in that it arises once the concept of morality is imposed on mutually self-interested agents similarly circumstanced, but it emphasizes that, fundamental to justice, is the concept of fairness which relates to right dealing between persons who are cooperating with or competing against one another, as when one speaks of fair games, fair competition, and fair bargains. The question of fairness arises when free persons, who have no authority over one another, are engaging in a joint activity and amongst themselves settling or acknowledging the rules which define it and which determine the respective shares in its benefits and burdens. A practice will strike the parties as fair if none feels that, by participating in it, they or any of the others are taken advantage of, or forced to give in to claims which they do not regard as legitimate. This implies that each has a conception of legitimate claims which he thinks it reasonable for others as well as himself to acknowledge. If one thinks of the principles of justice as arising in the manner described, then they do define this sort of conception. A practice is just or fair, then, when it satisfies the principles which those who participate in it could propose to one another for mutual acceptance under the afore-mentioned circumstances. Persons engaged in a just, or fair, practice can face one another openly and support their respective positions, should they appear questionable, by reference to principles which it is reasonable to expect each to accept.

It is this notion of the possibility of mutual acknowledgment of principles by free persons who have no authority over one another which makes the concept of fairness fundamental to justice. Only if such acknowledgment is possible can there be true community between persons in their common practices; otherwise their relations will appear to them as founded to some extent on force. If, in ordinary speech, fairness applies more particularly to practices in which there is a choice whether to engage or not (e.g., in games, business competition), and justice to practices in which there is no choice (e.g., in slavery), the element of necessity does not render the conception of mutual acknowledgment inapplicable, although it may make it much more urgent to change unjust than unfair institutions. For one activity in which one can always engage is that of proposing and acknowledging principles to one another supposing each to be similarly circumstanced; and to judge practices by the principles so arrived at is to apply the standard of fairness to them.

Now if the participants in a practice accept its rules as fair, and so have no complaint to lodge against it, there arises a prima facie duty (and a corresponding prima facie right) of the parties to each other to act in accordance with the practice when it falls upon them to comply. When any number of persons engage in a practice, or conduct a joint undertaking according to rules, and thus restrict their liberty, those who have submitted to these restrictions when required have the right to a similar acquiescence on the part of those who have benefited by their submission. These conditions will obtain if a practice is correctly acknowledged to be fair, for in this case all who participate in it will benefit from it. The rights and duties so arising are special rights and duties in that they depend on previous actions voluntarily undertaken, in this case on the parties having engaged in a common practice and knowingly accepted its benefits.[12] It is not, however, an obligation which presupposes a deliberate performative act in the sense of a promise, or contract, and the like.[13]

An unfortunate mistake of proponents of the idea of the social contract was to suppose that political obligation does require some such act, or at least to use language which suggests it. It is sufficient that one has knowingly participated in and accepted the benefits of a practice acknowledged to be fair. This prima facie obligation may, of course, be overridden: it may happen, when it comes one's turn to follow a rule, that other considerations will justify not doing so. But one cannot, in general, be released from this obligation by denying the justice of the practice only when it falls on one to obey. If a person rejects a practice, he should, so far as possible, declare his intention in advance, and avoid participating in it or enjoying its benefits.

This duty I have called that of fair play, but it should be admitted that to refer to it in this way is, perhaps, to extend the ordinary notion of fairness. Usually acting unfairly is not so much the breaking of any particular rule, even if the infraction is difficult to detect (cheating), but taking advantage of loop-holes or ambiguities in rules, availing oneself of unexpected or special circumstances which make it impossible to enforce them, insisting that rules be enforced to one's advantage when they should be suspended, and more generally, acting contrary to the intention of a practice. It is for this reason that one speaks of the sense of fair play: acting fairly requires more than simply being able to follow rules; what is fair must often be felt, or perceived, one wants to say. It is not, however, an unnatural extension of the duty of fair play to have it include the obligation which participants who have knowingly accepted the benefits of their common practice owe to each other to act in accordance with it when their performance falls due; for it is usually considered unfair if someone accepts the benefits of a practice but refuses to do his part in maintaining it. Thus one might say of the tax-dodger that he violates the duty of fair play: he accepts the benefits of government but will not do

---

[12] For the definition of this prima facie duty, and the idea that it is a special duty, I am indebted to H. L. A. Hart. See his paper "Are There Any Natural Rights?," *Philosophical Review*, LXIV (1955), 185 f.

[13] The sense of "performative" here is to be derived from J. L. Austin's paper in the symposium, "Other Minds," *Proceedings of the Aristotelian Society*, Supplementary Volume (1946), pp. 170–174.

his part in releasing resources to it; and members of labor unions often say that fellow workers who refuse to join are being unfair: they refer to them as "free riders," as persons who enjoy what are the supposed benefits of unionism, higher wages, shorter hours, job security, and the like, but who refuse to share in its burdens in the form of paying dues, and so on.

The duty of fair play stands beside other prima facie duties such as fidelity and gratitude as a basic moral notion; yet it is not to be confused with them.[14] These duties are all clearly distinct, as would be obvious from their definitions. As with any moral duty, that of fair play implies a constraint on self-interest in particular cases; on occasion it enjoins conduct which a rational egoist strictly defined would not decide upon. So while justice does not require of anyone that he sacrifice his interests in that *general position* and procedure whereby the principles of justice are proposed and acknowledged, it may happen that in particular situations, arising in the context of engaging in a practice, the duty of fair play will often cross his interests in the sense that he will be required to forego particular advantages which the peculiarities of his circumstances might permit him to take. There is, of course, nothing surprising in this. It is simply the consequence of the firm commitment which the parties may be supposed to have made, or which they would make, in the general position,

together with the fact that they have participated in and accepted the benefits of a practice which they regard as fair.

Now the acknowledgment of this constraint in particular cases, which is manifested in acting fairly or wishing to make amends, feeling ashamed, and the like, when one has evaded it, is one of the forms of conduct by which participants in a common practice exhibit their recognition of each other as persons with similar interests and capacities. In the same way that, failing a special explanation, the criterion for the recognition of suffering is helping one who suffers, acknowledging the duty of fair play is a necessary part of the criterion for recognizing another as a person with similar interests and feelings as oneself.[15] A person who never under any circumstances showed a wish to help others in pain would show, at the same time, that he did not recognize that they were in pain; nor could he have any feelings of affection or friendship for anyone; for having these feelings implies, failing special circumstances, that he comes to their aid when they are suffering. Recognition that another is a person in pain shows itself in sympathetic action; this primitive natural response of compassion is one of those responses upon which the various forms of moral conduct are built.

Similarly, the acceptance of the duty of fair play by participants in a common practice is a reflection in each person of the recognition of the aspirations and interests

[14] This, however, commonly happens. Hobbes, for example, when invoking the notion of a "tacit covenant," appeals not to the natural law that promises should be kept but to his fourth law of nature, that of gratitude. On Hobbes's shift from fidelity to gratitude, see Warrender, *op. cit.*, pp. 51–52, 233–237. While it is not a serious criticism of Hobbes, it would have improved his argument had he appealed to the duty of fair play. On his premises he is perfectly entitled to do so. Similarly Sidgwick thought that a principle of justice, such as every man ought to receive adequate requital for his labor, is like gratitude universalized. See *Methods of Ethics*, Bk. III, ch. v, Sec. 5. There is a gap in the stock of moral concepts used by philosophers into which the concept of the duty of fair play fits quite naturally.

[15] I am using the concept of criterion here in what I take to be Wittgenstein's sense. See *Philosophical Investigations* (Oxford, 1953); and Norman Malcolm's review, "Wittgenstein's *Philosophical Investigations*," *Philosophical Review*, LXIII (1954), 543–547. That the response of compassion, under appropriate circumstances, is part of the criterion for whether or not a person understands what "pain" means, is, I think, in the *Philosophical Investigations*. The view in the text is simply an extension of this idea. I cannot, however, attempt to justify it here. Similar thoughts are to be found, I think, in Max Scheler, *The Nature of Sympathy*, tr. by Peter Heath (New Haven, 1954). His way of writing is often so obscure that I cannot be certain.

of the others to be realized by their joint activity. Failing a special explanation, their acceptance of it is a necessary part of the criterion for their recognizing one another as persons with similar interests and capacities, as the conception of their relations in the general position supposes them to be. Otherwise they would show no recognition of one another as persons with similar capacities and interests, and indeed, in some cases perhaps hypothetical, they would not recognize one another as persons at all, but as complicated objects involved in a complicated activity. To recognize another as a person one must respond to him and act towards him in certain ways; and these ways are intimately connected with the various prima facie duties. Acknowledging these duties in *some* degree, and so having the elements of morality, is not a matter of choice, or of intuiting moral qualities, or a matter of the expression of feelings or attitudes (the three interpretations between which philosophical opinion frequently oscillates); it is simply the possession of one of the forms of conduct in which the recognition of others as persons is manifested.

These remarks are unhappily obscure. Their main purpose here, however, is to forestall, together with the remarks in Section 4, the misinterpretation that, on the view presented, the acceptance of justice and the acknowledgment of the duty of fair play depends in every day life solely on there being a *de facto* balance of forces between the parties. It would indeed be foolish to underestimate the importance of such a balance in securing justice; but it is not the only basis thereof. The recognition of one another as persons with similar interests and capacities engaged in a common practice must, failing a special explanation, show itself in the acceptance of the principles of justice and the acknowledgment of the duty of fair play.

The conception at which we have arrived, then, is that the principles of justice may be thought of as arising once the constraints of having a morality are imposed upon rational and mutually self-interested parties who are related and situated in a special way. A practice is just if it is in accordance with the principles which all who participate in it might reasonably be expected to propose or to acknowledge before one another when they are similarly circumstanced and required to make a firm commitment in advance without knowledge of what will be their peculiar condition, and thus when it meets standards which the parties could accept as fair should occasion arise for them to debate its merits. Regarding the participants themselves, once persons knowingly engage in a practice which they acknowledge to be fair and accept the benefits of doing so, they are bound by the duty of fair play to follow the rules when it comes their turn to do so, and this implies a limitation on their pursuit of self-interest in particular cases.

Now one consequence of this conception is that, where it applies, there is no moral value in the satisfaction of a claim incompatible with it. Such a claim violates the conditions of reciprocity and community amongst persons, and he who presses it, not being willing to acknowledge it when pressed by another, has no grounds for complaint when it is denied; whereas he against whom it is pressed can complain. As it cannot be mutually acknowledged it is a resort to coercion; granting the claim is possible only if the party can compel acceptance of what the other will not admit. But it makes no sense to concede claims the denial of which cannot be complained of in preference to claims the denial of which can be objected to. Thus in deciding on the justice of a practice it is not enough to ascertain that it answers to wants and interests in the fullest and most effective manner. For if any of these conflict with justice, they should not be counted, as their satisfaction is no reason at all for having a practice. It would be irrelevant to say, even if true, that it resulted in the greatest satisfaction of desire. In tallying up the merits of a practice one must toss out the satisfaction of interests the claims of which are incompatible with the principles of justice.

6. The discussion so far has been excessively abstract. While this is perhaps unavoidable, I should now like to bring out some of the features of the conception of justice as fairness by comparing it with the conception of justice in classical utilitarianism as represented by Bentham and Sidgwick, and its counterpart in welfare economics. This conception assimilates justice to benevolence and the latter in turn to the most efficient design of institutions to promote the general welfare. Justice is a kind of efficiency.[16]

Now it is said occasionally that this form of utilitarianism puts no restrictions on what might be a just assignment of rights and duties in that there might be circumstances which, on utilitarian grounds, would justify institutions highly offensive to our ordinary sense of justice. But the classical utilitarian conception is not totally unprepared for this objection. Beginning with the notion that the general happiness can be represented by a social utility function consisting of a sum of individual utility functions with identical weights (this being the meaning of the maxim that each counts for one and no more than one),[17] it is commonly assumed that the utility functions of individuals are similar in all essential respects. Differences between individuals are ascribed to accidents of education and upbringing, and they should not be taken into account. This assumption, coupled with that of diminishing marginal utility, results in a prima facie case for equality, e.g., of equality in the distribution of income during any given period of time, laying aside indirect effects on the future. But even if utilitarianism is interpreted as having such restrictions built into the utility function, and even it it is supposed that these restrictions have in practice much the same result as the application of the principles of justice (and appear, perhaps, to be ways of expressing these principles in the language of mathematics and psychology), the fundamental idea is very different from the conception of justice as fairness. For one thing, that the principles of justice should be accepted is interpreted as the contingent result of a higher order administrative decision. The form of this decision is regarded as being similar to that of an entrepreneur deciding how much to produce of this or that commodity in view of its marginal revenue, or to that of someone distributing goods to needy persons ac-

---

[16] While this assimilation is implicit in Bentham's and Sidgwick's moral theory, explicit statements of it as applied to justice are relatively rare. One clear instance in *The Principles of Morals and Legislation* occurs in ch. x, footnote 2 to section XL: ". . . justice, in the only sense in which it has a meaning, is an imaginary personage, feigned for the convenience of discourse, whose dictates are the dictates of utility, applied to certain particular cases. Justice, then, is nothing more than an imaginary instrument, employed to forward on certain occasions, and by certain means, the purposes of benevolence. The dictates of justice are nothing more than a part of the dictates of benevolence, which, on certain occasions, are applied to certain subjects . . . ." Likewise in *The Limits of Jurisprudence Refined*, ed. by C. W. Everett (New York, 1945), pp. 117 f., Bentham criticizes Grotius for denying that justice derives from utility; and in *The Theory of Legislation*, ed. by C. K. Ogden (London, 1931), p. 3, he says that he uses the words "just" and "unjust" along with other words "simply as collective terms including the ideas of certain pains or pleasures." That Sidgwick's conception of justice is similar to Bentham's is admittedly not evident from his discussion of justice in Book III, ch. v. of *Methods of Ethics*. But it follows, I think, from the moral theory he accepts. Hence C. D. Broad's criticisms of Sidgwick in the matter of distributive justice in *Five Types of Ethical Theory* (London, 1930), pp. 249–253, do not rest on a misinterpretation.

[17] This maxim is attributed to Bentham by J. S. Mill in *Utilitarianism*, ch. v, paragraph 36. I have not found it in Bentham's writings, nor seen such a reference. Similarly James Bonar, *Philosophy and Political Economy* (London, 1893), p. 234 n. But it accords perfectly with Bentham's ideas. See the hitherto unpublished manuscript in David Baumgardt, *Bentham and the Ethics of Today* (Princeton, 1952), Appendix IV. For example, "the total value of the stock of pleasure belonging to the whole community is to be obtained by multiplying the number expressing the value of it as respecting any one person, by the number expressing the multitude of such individuals" (p. 556).

cording to the relative urgency of their wants. The choice between practices is thought of as being made on the basis of the allocation of benefits and burdens to individuals (these being measured by the present capitalized value of their utility over the full period of the practice's existence), which results from the distribution of rights and duties established by a practice.

Moreover, the individuals receiving these benefits are not conceived as being related in any way: they represent so many different directions in which limited resources may be allocated. The value of assigning resources to one direction rather than another depends solely on the preferences and interests of individuals as individuals. The satisfaction of desire has its value irrespective of the moral relations between persons, say as members of a joint undertaking, and of the claims which, in the name of these interests, they are prepared to make on one another;[18] and it is this value which is to be taken into account by the (ideal) legislator who is conceived as adjusting the rules of the system from the center so as to maximize the value of the social utility function.

It is thought that the principles of justice will not be violated by a legal system so conceived provided these executive decisions are correctly made. In this fact the principles of justice are said to have their derivation and explanation; they simply express the most important general features of social institutions in which the administrative problem is solved in the best way. These principles have, indeed, a special urgency because, given the facts of human nature, so much depends on them; and this explains the peculiar quality of the moral feelings associated with justice.[19] This assimilation of justice to a higher order executive decision, certainly a striking conception, is central to classical utilitarianism; and it also brings out its profound individualism, in one sense of this ambiguous word. It regards persons as so many *separate* directions in which benefits and burdens may be assigned; and the value of the satisfaction or dissatisfaction of desire is not thought to depend in any way on the moral relations in which individuals stand, or on the kinds of claims which they are willing, in the pursuit of their interests, to press on each other.

7. Many social decisions are, of course, of an administrative nature. Certainly this is so when it is a matter of social utility in what one may call its ordinary sense: that is, when it is a question of the efficient design of social institutions for the use of common means to achieve common ends.

---

[18] An idea essential to the classical utilitarian conception of justice. Bentham is firm in his statement of it: "It is only upon that principle [the principle of asceticism], and not from the principle of utility, that the most abominable pleasure which the vilest of malefactors ever reaped from his crime would be reprobated, if it stood alone. The case is, that it never does stand alone; but is necessarily followed by such a quantity of pain (or, what comes to the same thing, such a chance for a certain quantity of pain) that the pleasure in comparison of it, is as nothing: and this is true and sole, but perfectly sufficient, reason for making it a ground for punishment" (*The Principles of Morals and Legislation*, ch. ii, sec. iv. See also ch. x, sec. x, footnote 1). The same point is made in *The Limits of Jurisprudence Defined*, pp. 115 f. Although much recent welfare economics, as found in such important works as I. M. D. Little, *A Critique of Welfare Economics*, 2nd ed. (Oxford, 1957) and K. J. Arrow, *Social Choice and Individual Values* (New York, 1951), dispenses with the idea of cardinal utility, and uses instead the theory of ordinal utility as stated by J. R. Hicks, *Value and Capital*, 2nd ed. (Oxford, 1946), Pt. I, it assumes with utilitarianism that individual preferences have value as such, and so accepts the idea being criticized here. I hasten to add, however, that this is no objection to it as a means of analyzing economic policy, and for that purpose it may, indeed, be a necessary simplifying assumption. Nevertheless it is an assumption which cannot be made in so far as one is trying to analyze moral concepts, especially the concept of justice, as economists would, I think, agree. Justice is usually regarded as a separate and distinct part of any comprehensive criterion of economic policy. See, for example, Tibor Scitovsky, *Welfare and Competition* (London, 1952), pp. 59–69, and Little, *op. cit.*, cs. vii.

[19] See J. S. Mill's argument in *Utilitarianism*, ch. v, pars. 16–25.

In this case either the benefits and burdens may be assumed to be impartially distributed, or the question of distribution is misplaced, as in the instance of maintaining public order and security or national defense. But as an interpretation of the basis of the principles of justice, classical utilitarianism is mistaken. It *permits* one to argue, for example, that slavery is unjust on the grounds that the advantages to the slaveholder as slaveholder do not counterbalance the disadvantages to the slave and to society at large burdened by a comparatively inefficient system of labor. Now the conception of justice as fairness, when applied to the practice of slavery with its offices of slaveholder and slave, would not allow one to consider the advantages of the slaveholder in the first place. As that office is not in accordance with principles which could be mutually acknowledged, the gains accruing to the slaveholder, assuming them to exist, cannot be counted as in *any* way mitigating the injustice of the practice. The question whether these gains outweigh the disadvantages to the slave and to society cannot arise, since in considering the justice of slavery these gains have no weight at all which requires that they be overridden. Where the conception of justice as fairness applies, slavery is *always* unjust.

I am not, of course, suggesting the absurdity that the classical utilitarians approved of slavery. I am only rejecting a type of argument which their view allows them to use in support of their disapproval of it. The conception of justice as derivative from efficiency implies that judging the justice of a practice is always, in principle at least, a matter of weighing up advantages and disadvantages, each having an intrinsic value or disvalue as the satisfaction of interests, irrespective of whether or not these interests necessarily involve acquiescence in principles which could not be mutually acknowledged. Utilitarianism cannot account for the fact that slavery is always unjust, nor for the fact that it would be recognized as irrelevant in defeating the accusa-

tion of injustice for one person to say to another, engaged with him in a common practice and debating its merits, that nevertheless it allowed of the greatest satisfaction of desire. The charge of injustice cannot be rebutted in this way. If justice were derivative from a higher order executive efficiency, this would not be so.

But now, even if it is taken as established that, so far as the ordinary conception of justice goes, slavery is always unjust (that is, slavery by definition violates commonly recognized principles of justice), the classical utilitarian would surely reply that these principles, as other moral principles subordinate to that of utility, are only generally correct. It is simply for the most part true that slavery is less efficient than other institutions; and while common sense may define the concept of justice so that slavery is unjust, nevertheless, where slavery would lead to the greatest satisfaction of desire, it is not wrong. Indeed, it is then right, and for the very same reason that justice, as ordinarily understood, is usually right. If, as ordinarily understood, slavery is always unjust, to this extent the utilitarian conception of justice might be admitted to differ from that of common moral opinion. Still the utilitarian would want to hold that, as a matter of moral principle, his view is correct in giving no special weight to considerations of justice beyond that allowed for by the general presumption of effectiveness. And this, he claims, is as it should be. The every day opinion is morally in error, although, indeed, it is a useful error, since it protects rules of generally high utility.

The question, then, relates not simply to the analysis of the concept of justice as common sense defines it, but the analysis of it in the wider sense as to how much weight considerations of justice, as defined, are to have when laid against other kinds of moral considerations. Here again I wish to argue that reasons of justice have a *special* weight for which only the conception of justice as fairness can account. Moreover, it belongs to the concept of justice that they do have this special weight. While Mill recognized that this was so, he thought that it could be accounted for by the special urgency of the moral feelings which naturally support principles of such high utility. But it is a mistake to resort to the urgency of feeling; as with the appeal to intuition, it manifests a failure to pursue the question far enough. The special weight of considerations of justice can be explained from the conception of justice as fairness. It is only necessary to elaborate a bit what has already been said as follows.

If one examines the circumstances in which a certain tolerance of slavery is justified, or perhaps better, excused, it turns out that these are of a rather special sort. Perhaps slavery exists as an inheritance from the past and it proves necessary to dismantle it piece by piece; at times slavery may conceivably be an advance on previous institutions. Now while there may be some excuse for slavery in special conditions, it is never an excuse for it that it is sufficiently advantageous to the slaveholder to outweigh the disadvantages to the slave and to society. A person who argues in this way is not perhaps making a wildly irrelevant remark; but he is guilty of a moral fallacy. There is disorder in his conception of the ranking of moral principles. For the slaveholder, by his own admission, has no moral title to the advantages which he receives as a slaveholder. He is no more prepared than the slave to acknowledge the principle upon which is founded the respective positions in which they both stand. Since slavery does not accord with principles which they could mutually acknowledge, they each may be supposed to agree that it is unjust: it grants claims which it ought not to grant and in doing so denies claims which it ought not to deny. Amongst persons in a general position who are debating the form of their common practices, it cannot, therefore, be offered as a reason for a practice that, in conceding these very claims that ought to be denied, it nevertheless meets existing interests more effectively. By their very nature the satisfaction of these claims is without weight and cannot enter into any tabulation of advantages and disadvantages.

Furthermore, it follows from the concept of morality that, to the extent that the slaveholder recognizes his position vis-à-vis the slave to be unjust, he would not choose to press his claims. His not wanting to receive his special advantages is one of the ways in which he shows that he thinks slavery is unjust. It would be fallacious for the legislator to suppose, then, that it is a ground for having a practice that it brings advantages greater than disadvantages, if those for whom the practice is designed, and to whom the advantages flow, acknowledge that they have no moral title to them and do not wish to receive them.

For these reasons the principles of justice have a special weight; and with respect to the principle of the greatest satisfaction of desire, as cited in the general position amongst those discussing the merits of their common practices, the principles of justice have an absolute weight. In this sense they are not contingent; and this is why their force is greater than can be accounted for by the general presumption (assuming that there is one) of the effectiveness, in the utilitarian sense, of practices which in fact satisfy them.

If one wants to continue using the concepts of classical utilitarianism, one will have to say, to meet this criticism, that at least the individual or social utility functions must be so defined that no value is given to the satisfaction of interests the representative claims of which violate the principles of justice. In this way it is no doubt possible to include these principles within the form of the utilitarian conception; but to do so is, of course, to change its inspiration altogether as a moral conception. For it is to incorporate within it principles which cannot be understood on the basis of a higher order executive decision aiming at the greatest satisfaction of desire.

It is worth remarking, perhaps, that this criticism of utilitarianism does not depend on whether or not the two assumptions, that of individuals having similar utility functions and that of diminishing marginal utility, are interpreted as psychological propositions to be supported or refuted by experience, or as moral and political principles expressed in a somewhat technical language. There are, certainly, several advantages in taking them in the latter fashion.[20] For one thing, one might say that this is what Bentham and others really meant by them, at least as shown by how they were used in arguments for social reform. More importantly, one could hold that the best way to defend the classical utilitarian view is to interpret these assumptions as moral and political principles. It is doubtful whether, taken as psychological propositions, they are true of men in general as we know them under normal conditions. On the other hand, utilitarians would not have wanted to propose them merely as practical working principles of legislation, or as expedient maxims to guide reform, given the egalitarian sentiments of modern society.[21] When pressed they might well have invoked the idea of a more or less equal capacity of men in relevant respects if given an equal chance in a just society. But if the argument above regarding slavery is correct, then granting these assumptions as moral and political principles makes no difference. To view individuals as equally fruitful lines for the allocation of benefits, even as a matter of moral principle, still leaves the mistaken notion that the satisfaction of desire has value in itself irrespective of the relations between persons as members of a common practice, and irrespective of the claims upon one another which the satisfaction of interests represents. To see the error of this idea one must give up the conception of justice as an executive decision altogether and refer to the notion of justice as fairness: that participants in a common practice be regarded as having an original and equal liberty and that their common practices be considered unjust unless they accord with principles which persons so circumstanced and related could freely acknowledge before one another, and so could accept as fair. Once the emphasis is put upon the concept of the mutual recognition of principles by participants in a common practice the rules of which are to define their several relations and give form to their claims on one another, then it is clear that the granting of a claim the principle of which could not be acknowledged by each in the general position (that is, in the position in which the parties propose and acknowledge principles before one another) is not a reason for adopting a practice. Viewed in this way, the background of the claim is seen to exclude it from consideration; that it can represent a value in itself arises from the conception of individuals as separate lines for the assignment of benefits, as isolated persons who stand as claimants on an administrative or benevolent largesse. Occasionally persons do so stand to one another; but this is not the general case, nor, more importantly, is it the case when it is a matter of the justice of practices themselves in which participants stand in various relations to be appraised in accordance with standards which they may be expected to acknowledge before one another. Thus however mistaken the notion of the social contract may be as history, and however far it may overreach itself as a general theory of social and political obligation, it does express, suitably interpreted,

[20] See D. G. Ritchie, *Natural Rights* (London, 1894), pp. 95 ff., 249 ff. Lionel Robbins has insisted on this point on several occasions. See *An Essay on the Nature and Significance of Economic Science*, 2nd ed. (London, 1935), pp. 134–43, "Interpersonal Comparisons of Utility: A Comment," *Economic Journal*, XLVIII (1938), 635–41, and more recently, "Robertson on Utility and Scope," *Economica*, n.s. XX (1953), 108 f.

[21] As Sir Henry Maine suggested Bentham may have regarded them. See *The Early History of Institutions* (London, 1875), pp. 398 ff.

an essential part of the concept of justice.[22]

8. By way of conclusion I should like to make two remarks: first, the original modification of the utilitarian principle (that it require of practices that the offices and positions defined by them be equal unless it is reasonable to suppose that the representative man in *every* office would find the inequality to his advantage), slight as it may appear at first sight, actually has a different conception of justice standing behind it. I have tried to show how this is so by developing the concept of justice as fairness and by indicating how this notion involves the mutual acceptance, from a general position, of the principles on which a practice is founded, and how this in turn requires the exclusion from consideration of claims violating the principles of justice. Thus the slight alteration of principle reveals another family of notions, another way of looking at the concept of justice.

Second, I should like to remark also that I have been dealing with the *concept* of justice. I have tried to set out the kinds of principles upon which judgments concerning the justice of practices may be said to stand. The analysis will be successful to the degree that it expresses the principles involved in these judgments when made by competent persons upon deliberation and reflection.[23] Now every people may be

supposed to have the concept of justice, since in the life of every society there must be at least some relations in which the parties consider themselves to be circumstanced and related as the concept of justice as fairness requires. Societies will differ from one another not in having or in failing to have this notion but in the range of cases to which they apply it and in the emphasis which they give to it as compared with other moral concepts.

A firm grasp of the concept of justice itself is necessary if these variations, and the reasons for them, are to be understood. No study of the development of moral ideas and of the differences between them is more sound than the analysis of the fundamental moral concepts upon which it must depend. I have tried, therefore, to give an analysis of the concept of justice which should apply generally, however large a part the concept may have in a given morality, and which can be used in explaining the course of men's thoughts about justice and its relations to other moral concepts. How it is to be used for this purpose is a large topic which I cannot, of course, take up here. I mention it only to emphasize that I have been dealing with the concept of justice itself and to indicate what use I consider such an analysis to have.

---

[22] Thus Kant was not far wrong when he interpreted the original contract merely as an "Idea of Reason"; yet he still thought of it as a *general* criterion of right and as providing a general theory of political obligation. See the second part of the essay, "On the Saying 'That may be right in theory but has no value in practice'" (1793), in *Kant's Principles of Politics*, tr. by W. Hastie (Edinburgh, 1891). I have drawn on the contractarian tradition not for a general theory of political obligation but to clarify the concept of justice.

[23] For a further discussion of the idea expressed here, see my paper, "Outline of a Decision Procedure for Ethics," in the *Philosophical Review*, LX (1951), 177–197. For an analysis, similar in many respects but using the notion of the ideal observer instead of that of the considered judgment of a

competent person, see Roderick Firth, "Ethical Absolutism and the Ideal Observer," *Philosophy and Phenomenological Research*, XII (1952), 317–345. While the similarities between these two discussions are more important than the differences, an analysis based on the notion of a considered judgment of a competent person, as it is based on a kind of judgment, may prove more helpful in understanding the features of moral judgment than an analysis based on the notion of an ideal observer, although this remains to be shown. A man who rejects the conditions imposed on a considered judgment of a competent person could no longer profess to *judge* at all. This seems more fundamental than his rejecting the conditions of observation, for these do not seem to apply, in an ordinary sense, to making a moral judgment.

Problems of Distributive Justice

NICHOLAS RESCHER

THE TASK OF A THEORY OF DISTRIBUTIVE JUSTICE

The task of a theory of distributive justice is to provide the machinery in terms of which one can assess the relative merits or demerits of a distribution, the "assessment" in question being made from the moral or ethical point of view. Its objective is to establish a *principle* by which the "assessment" of alternative possible distributions can be carried out.[1]

It is clearly not sufficient that a principle of distributive justice should tell us only about the ideal distribution, the very best of possible alternatives. For to apply any such principle in practice we must know which of several feasible non-ideal alternatives is to be preferred: we must know not only what is *the best*, but must be able to determine—in the great majority of cases, at any rate—which of several alternative possibilities is the "better." A principle of evaluation is not adequate if it merely depicts a theoretical ideal that we cannot apply in practice to determine which of several putative possibilities comes "closer to the ideal." (How far has the beginner come toward learning how to evaluate bridge hands when he is told that the ideal holding consists of the four aces,

[1] Henry Sidgwick, *The Methods of Ethics* (7th ed., London: Macmillan, 1907), p. 270.

the four kings, the four queens, and a jack?)

What is needed is something to which writers on ethics—and, for that matter, writers on economics also—have been loath to address themselves, *a criterion of merit for suboptimal alternatives.* The evaluation criterion of an adequate theory of distributive justice must be capable not simply of absolute *idealization* (i.e., of telling us what the ideal is), but also of relative evaluation (i.e., of telling us which of several possible alternatives is to be regarded as the most satisfactory).

Distributive justice—exactly like punitive justice—can be brought to realization only in *this* world, that is, in an imperfect world populated by imperfect men. A perfectly just system of punitive justice would apprehend, process, and punish all and only the guilty, and would ignore, leave unprocessed and unpunished, all and only the innocent. But any realizable system will be such that it cannot fail to depart from the ideal in several ways (say, by catching some of the innocent and by letting escape some of the guilty). And these modes of injustice are interrelated and interlocked: as we modify the system to avoid injustices of the one kind, we *ipso facto* increase those of another. In evaluating alternative procedures in criminal law and law enforcement we have to be prepared to make choices among the realizable, and thus less-than-ideal, alternatives; exactly the same is true in evaluating socio-economic arrangements with respect to their accordance with or violation of the principles of distributive justice.

THE PRINCIPLE OF UTILITY

We shall base our inquiry into the principle of distributive justice upon an investigation of the doctrine of utilitarianism. This doctrine is founded upon the *principle of utility*, which asserts that utility (or, if you wish, simply the good things of this life) should be distributed according to the rule of "the greatest good of the greatest number." Exact as it sounds, this classic principle is imprecise and indeed inadequate. The first objective of our discussion is to exhibit these shortcomings in considerable detail. And when the necessary emendations are made, the resulting position will be such that the label "utilitarian" (as usually construed) can be pinned to it only with serious reservations and qualifications, if at all. We shall use this critique of the principle of utility to illustrate the very complex and inherently problematic character of the concept of distributive justice.

Some of the classical utilitarians have taken the principle of utility to relate to human actions in general, and not to be confined specifically to distributions of goods. Insofar as the majority of human actions have consequences affecting others favorably or unfavorably, they "distribute" utilities (or disutilities) to the parties concerned. So regarded, all actions affecting others become "distributions of utilities," and the principle of utility can be applied, thus widening its scope from that of a mere principle of distributive justice to a general criterion of right action in human conduct. For the present, however, we must take a limited view of the principle of utility, without reference to its oft maintained role as a criterion of right action in human conduct. We shall resist—at any rate for the time being—this expansion of its scope, confining its application to genuine distri-

butions. But at a later stage of the inquiry we shall return to the conception of the principle of utility as a general arbiter in ethics.

THE PRINCIPLE OF UTILITY IS A TWO-FACTOR CRITERION

Suppose that some three particular persons, Messrs A, B, and C, can be given the utility shares (a), (b), and (c), respectively, in accordance with either Scheme I or Scheme II:[2]

Share	Scheme I	Scheme II
(a)	3 units	2 units
(b)	3	2
(c)	3	6

Which scheme represents the superior mode of distribution? Scheme II yields "the greater good": it distributes ten units as compared with the nine of its rival. Scheme I yields a greater advantage in goods for "the greater number": two persons gain by its adoption and only one loses. The example brings out the fact that *the principle of utility is a two-factor criterion* ("greater good," "greater number"), and that these two factors can in given cases work against one another. There is thus nothing in the principle of utility itself to help us in making—let alone in dictating a particular outcome of—a choice between Scheme I and Scheme II. The principle unqualified is patently incomplete as an effective means for deciding between alternative distributions of a good.

Some utilitarians have, at least seemingly, gone from a two-factor to a one-factor criterion, placing their sole reliance upon "the greater good," dropping the last

---

[2] We are to think of the indicated shares here *not* as representing marginal utility increments added to an otherwise fixed initial amount, but as the *total resultant* utility distribution after whatever distributing mechanism may be supposed operative has done its work.

four words from the utilitarian formula. (Bentham himself inclined to this view in his later days,[3] reasoning, along lines shortly to be described, that the greater good *requires* greater numbers.) But despite its greater logical tidiness, the view that the eligibility of a proposed action with its consequent distribution of utility turns solely on the *total* good involved, without any regard whatsoever to the *pattern of its distribution,* is pretty obviously unacceptable. On the other hand, it would obviously not do to place, in a burst of democratic enthusiasm, an *exclusive* reliance on "the greater number."[4] For consider the distributions:

Share	Scheme I	Scheme II
(a)	5 units	4 units
(b)	5	4
(c)	5	3
(d)	1	3
(e)	1	3

Doubtless the greater number of recipients would opt for Scheme I and would vote for its adoption as against Scheme II, but it is doubtful (to say the least) that the first mode of division is to be preferred. In such cases, even the most ardent of democratic theoreticians have ever seen fit to safeguard the interests of minorities in ways that preclude an automatic adoption of schemes of type I.[5]

One traditional objection to utilitarianism articulated along these lines is presented in the choice between a less populous world with a higher per capita average utility, and a more populous world with a lower per capita average utility, say between:

Scheme 1

```
┌──────┐
│ (c)  │
├──────┤
│ (b)  │
├──────┤
│ (a)  │
└──────┘
```

Scheme 2

```
┌──────┐
│ (f)  │
├──────┤
│ (e)  │
├──────┤
│ (d)  │
├──────┤
│ (c)  │
├──────┤
│ (b)  │
├──────┤
│ (a)  │
└──────┘
```

A contemplation of these alternatives should force an adherent of the principle of utility to decide whether by "the greatest good" he is to mean the greatest *total* good or the greatest good *per capita* (i.e., the greatest *average* good). That proto-utilitarian William Paley wrote:

A larger portion of happiness is enjoyed amongst *ten* persons, possessing the means of healthy subsistence, than can be produced by five persons, under every advantage of power, affluence, and luxury . . . ; it follows, that the quantity of happiness in a given district, although it is possible it may be increased the number of inhabitants remaining the same, is chiefly and most naturally affected by alteration of the numbers: that, consequently, the decay of population is the greatest evil that a state can suffer; and the improvement of it the object which ought, in all countries, to be aimed at, in preference to every other political purpose whatsoever.[6]

Other—and nowadays surely more common—sentiments go the other way. Thus C. D. Broad writes:

---

[3] Compare F. Y. Edgeworth, *Mathematical Psychics,* pp. 117–118. Edgeworth strongly endorses the alteration, remarking: "The principle of greatest happiness may have gained its popularity, but lost its meaning, by the addition '*of the greatest number.*'"

[4] We wholly ignore the ambiguity that is singled out by the question "Greater number of *what?*" i.e., do we have an anthropocentric form of utilitarianism, where only humans (perhaps better, *intelligent creatures*) count, or a universalistic form, where other sentient beings are also included?

[5] It is important to qualify by safeguards of this sort the *census* technique by which D. Braybrooke and C. E. Lindblom seek to replace the classic utilitarian *calculus* in their recent book, *A Strategy of Decision* (New York: The Free Press of Glencoe, 1963).

[6] William Paley, *The Principles of Moral and Political Philosophy* (7th edn., London: Baldwin & Co., 1790), Vol. II, Book VI, ch. 2, pp. 346–347. Bentham, Godwin, and most early utilitarians side with Paley here. See E. Halévy, *The Growth of Philosophic Radicalism,* tr. Mary Morris, pp. 218–221. Compare also Henry Sidgwick, *The Methods of Ethics,* pp. 415–416.

If Utilitarianism be true it would be one's duty to try to increase the numbers of a community, even though one reduced the average total happiness of the members, so long as the total happiness in the community would be in the least increased. It seems perfectly plain to me that this kind of action, so far from being a duty, would quite certainly be wrong.[7]

A "UTILITY FLOOR" IS NEEDED

Let us try the effect of one facile amendment of the principle of utility. One of the standard textbook objections to the principle is presented by the following variant of the previous example:

Scheme 1	Scheme 2
	(c)
(c)	(b)
(b)	
(a)	(a)

Here Scheme II not only yields "the greater good," but works to the advantage of "a greater number," since two of the three people involved are obvious beneficiaries of its adoption. But is it reasonable that we should in *all* such cases be prepared to sacrifice an "individual interest" in "the general benefit," as the principle of utility says we must do? The answer to this question cannot be other than *no!* We would surely not want to subject one individual to unspeakable suffering to give some insignificantly small benefit to many others (even an innumerable myriad of them).[8] Actual privation offends our sense of justice in a more serious way than do mere inequities.

These considerations suggest adding to the principle of utility another qualifying

clause, a "principle of catastrophe-prevention" stipulating a minimal *utility floor* for all individuals below which no one should be pressed. The principle at issue may be regarded as being more or less built in to the very conception of a genuinely "minimally acceptable" share of good. For we would not conceive of a given level in just *this* way unless we were prepared to do battle for the rule that an exalted priority should be given to reducing to the lowest feasible number the people who receive less than this share. We might thus add to the initial principle the proviso: *provided that nobody receives less of "the good" than a certain (i.e., some plausible) minimum amount.* Clearly one of the most basic elements of our concept of justice is to minimize the number of persons in a state of genuine *deprivation* regarding their share in the available pool of utility. Diminishing the number of those who simply do not have enough is a more fundamental element of the concept of justice than diminishing the gap between the "haves" and the "have-nots."[9] And although the idea of an

---

[7] C. D. Broad, *Five Types of Ethical Theory* (London: Routledge & Kegan Paul, 1930), p. 250.

[8] A somewhat out-of-the-way example of this line of reasoning is provided by the argument of some modern theologians that creation as a whole is not worthwhile if it has the consequence of eternal damnation for some creatures.

[9] "There is a bottom level of instrumental good (money, or in this instance, food) below which equality is useless because it is equality in nothingness, or something so near to nothingness that it would be of no use to any of the recipients. No good would be achieved by requiring equality under such conditions. On the one hand, a person who said, "I know we'll all starve, but we must share equally anyway' would really be running the equality principle into the ground! Precisely the same thing has been alleged of a socialistic economy: though it provides near-equality, the incentive is so low and, human nature being what it is, the system is inevitably so inefficient that after a while there will not be much left to divide equally: we shall have what has been called a state of 'splendidly equalized destitution.' *If* it could be shown that an economy characterized by equal distribution produced this result, such an economy would be almost as useless to its members as the situation of ten men on the ice floe sharing substarvation rations." John Hospers, *Human Conduct* (New York: Harcourt, Brace & World, 1961), p. 428. (This and the following excerpts from John Hospers, *Human Conduct*, are reprinted with the permission of the publisher.) On the conception of a utility floor, see also B. de Jouvenel, *The Ethics of Redistribution*, pp. 23–24 and 85–88.

acceptable minimum level has traditionally been stressed primarily in survival contexts, the idea has long been applied in such other connections as, for example, education.

The utilitarians of the eighteenth and early nineteenth centuries recognized and accepted this principle, and it led them to abandon, in the economic (but not the political) sphere, the egalitarianism to which they were otherwise committed:

> If the Utilitarians rejected absolute equalitarianism, it was not because they considered society as naturally hierarchical, but because they thought the quantity of subsistence actually available was not sufficient to allow all the individuals actually existing to live . . . [adequately].[10]

Apart from some such qualification, the principle of utility is clearly deficient. It is perfectly conceivable that at some historical juncture an institution of slavery, for example, could conduce to the greater good of a greater number; but we shall not be prepared to let this fact count decisively on its behalf. Again, considerations of a cognate sort led to the economic doctrine that an economy must afford every participant a "living wage."[11]

AN EQUITY PRINCIPLE IS NEEDED

But the amendment proposed in the preceding section will not of itself suffice. For even when one inserts such a "utility floor" for the purpose of catastrophe-prevention, one does not provide for cases of the fol-

---

[10] E. Halévy, *The Growth of Philosophic Radicalism*, tr. Mary Morris, p. 502.

[11] For a detailed historical and ethical treatment of the living-wage concept, see John A. Ryan, *A Living Wage* (New York: Macmillan, 1906; 2nd edn., 1920).

lowing sort. We have now to do with five people, Messrs. A, B, C, D, and E, whose respective utility shares for two schemes of distribution are represented by (a), (b), (c), (d), and (e).

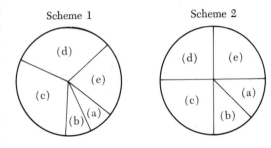

Let it be supposed that the acceptable minimal level is just exactly represented by the shares (a) and (b) on Scheme I, so that there is no question of anyone's being pressed "beneath the floor." Also the *total amounts* of utility (represented by the sizes of the two circles) may be supposed to be the same. Now the principle of utility dictates the preferability of Scheme I, since it assumes "the greater good of the greater number" of persons involved, viz., the recipients of shares (c)—(e). But even a rudimentary sensitivity to equity and justice revolts against this conclusion. For why should the hapless recipients of shares (a)—(b) be pressed to the floor in order to make the "rich" who receive (c)—(e) yet richer?

What is clearly needed, over and above the aforementioned utility floor, is some added principle of equity in the distribution of utility shares, some reference to the central tendency of utility allocations that will take equitableness into account. A reasonable (and in other contexts familiar) procedure might be *a rule of least square deviation from the average*. The adoption of such an equity principle would iron out difficulties of the type illustrated by the previous example.

Consider such a case as that of choosing between giving Messrs A, B, C, D, and

E one of the following utility distributions:

Share	Scheme I	Scheme II
(a)	7 units	6 units
(b)	7	6
(c)	7	6
(d)	2	10
(e)	2	12

From the angle of *total* utility, Scheme II is superior. But Scheme I gives "the greater number" of persons (viz., 3 of them) a greater utility share than they would have in Scheme II. Also, from the standpoint of central tendency, Scheme I is superior (the sum of the squares of deviations from the average is 30 for Scheme I but 32 for Scheme II). But, on the other hand, in adopting Scheme II in place of Scheme I, Messrs *A*, *B*, and *C* are each made to undergo *a trivially small sacrifice in utility in order that a substantial benefit can accrue to D and E*. It is clear that *if the claims of the individuals concerned are equal*, Scheme II is definitely to be preferred.[12]

Consider the alternative schemes of utility allocation in which Messrs *X*, *Y*, and *Z* get shares (a), (b), and (c), respectively:

Share	Scheme I	Scheme II
(a)	5 units	9 units
(b)	6	1 (= the "floor")
(c)	10	12

Note that Scheme II represents the greater good (22 units as compared with 21), and represents a greater good for a greater number (viz., Messrs *X* and *Z* are compara-

[12] The point that we may prefer the distribution of a lesser total with greater equality is developed with force and clarity in John Hospers, *Human Conduct*, pp. 428–429. It is, of course, based on a fundamental commitment diametrically opposed to the hard-nosed maximize-the-total-and-distribution-be-damned line of utilitarianism espoused by F. Y. Edgeworth, who held that J. S. Mill "darkens the subject (as many critics seem to have felt), by imposing a condition of equality of distribution" (*Mathematical Psychics*, p. 118).

tive beneficiaries in its adoption). But is Scheme II unqualifiedly preferable and its selection morally mandatory—regardless of who it is that is doing the selecting? (We tend to react differently if the choice of the second scheme is made by *Y* rather than by *X*.[13] The doctrinaire utilitarian has to write this difference in reaction off to foolish sentimentality.) Actually, the adoption of an equity principle of the sort under discussion would rationalize the selection of the first—patently fairer—allocation scheme. One could implement the principle by introducing the idea of an "effective average" which would discount the actual average by some function of the deviations from it (say by half of the standard deviation[14]). The concept of an effective average will be treated in greater detail in the next section.

It deserves to be stressed again at this point that we are dealing with distributions of "utility" viewed retrospectively, and not with distributions of some storable good viewed prospectively. In the distributions we are concerned with there is (by hypothesis) no question of redistribution (utility cannot be alienated or transferred, and even if it could, this would be precluded by our retroactive approach). This is important, because in ruling out redistributions we also rule out mutual agreements to reallocate in the common interest. If we were dealing with, say, money rather than utility, then consider, in this changed light, the case of a choice between giving Messrs *A*, *B* and *C* shares (a), (b), and (c) respectively:

Share	Scheme I	Scheme II
(a)	3 units	10 units
(b)	3	1
(c)	3	1

[13] Compare W. D. Ross, *Foundations of Ethics*, pp. 72, 75.
[14] This formula would yield an effective average of 5.9 for Scheme I and of 5.8 for Scheme II.

Our own preference on the basis of the preceding discussion is for Scheme I (where the "effective average" is 3) over Scheme II ("effective average" is 1.9). But, of course, if redistribution were possible, A would work out a "mutual assistance pact" with B and C to make a payoff of 3 units to each of them for going along with the adoption of Scheme II, thereby in effect bringing into the picture

Share	Scheme III
(a)	4 units
(b)	4
(c)	4

which is clearly preferable to either of the preceding schemes by *any* reasonable standard (ours not excluded). The distributor who would adopt Scheme II over against I with a view to laying the basis for a shift to III could plausibly be said to serve the interests of distributive justice. The considerations upon which our preference for I over II is based must be understood to include the ruling out of such a shift to (the nonenvisaged) alternative III.

In this way, it may be seen that the considerations of our discussion—while not in principle restricted to "utility," but applicable more generally—rest essentially on the stipulation that the set of alternative distributions under comparative evaluation be postulated as complete, without any widening of the range of alternatives by the possibility of redistribution.

THE CONCEPT OF AN EFFECTIVE AVERAGE

In the preceding section we introduced the concept of an effective average (EA):

EA=average−½σ (standard deviation from the average)

The role of this concept is simple: paradig-

matically, it is to systematize the intuitive feeling that of the two distributions Scheme

Share	Scheme I	Scheme II
(a)	2 units	1 unit
(b)	2	1
(c)	2	3
(d)	2	3
(e)	2	3

I is superior from the angle of distributive justice to Scheme II, this being so despite the facts (1) that Scheme I yields a lesser average share (2 as contrasted with 2.2 units) and (2) that in contrasting Scheme I with Scheme II, there are two 1-unit losers as compared with three 1-unit gainers, so that Scheme II yields the greater good of a greater number. From the standpoint of our "effective average," however, the advantage lies with Scheme I (2.00 as contrasted with 1.71). The purpose of this section is to exhibit some significant features of this concept of an effective average.

The key feature of the effective average as a criterion for comparison is that it can underwrite the preferability of one distribution to another without requiring that the preferred distribution be a Pareto improvement upon its competitor. Moreover, it provides a systematic grounding for two seemingly competing intuitions as to the nature of distributive justice, viz., that in certain cases inequalities can "pay for themselves" by resulting in a situation that conduces to the general good, and, moreover, that "a lower average income, with greater equality, may make a happier society than a higher average income with less."[15] An example of the second sort of

[15] R. H. Tawney, *Equality* (4th edn., London: Allen & Unwin, 1952), p. 129. The concept of an effective average thus serves (but more effectively) the same equalizing purpose that is served by the idea of a (utility) *ceiling*, in analogy with that of a *floor*, introduced by B. de Jouvenel. See his *The Ethics of Redistribution*, pp. 23–28, 86–87.

situation has just been provided. An illustration of the first sort of situation is:

Share	Scheme I	Scheme II
(a)	3 units	2.9 units
(b)	3	4
(c)	3	4
(d)	3	4
(e)	3	4

One qualification must immediately be made. The EA is a meaningful basis of comparison, and should in fact be regarded as being defined, only when it is not too far removed from the average—say, when EA lies within 50 per cent of the actual average A. This means that we must have

$$EA \geq \tfrac{1}{2} A$$

or equivalently, since $EA = A - \tfrac{1}{2} \sigma$ (where $\sigma =$ the standard deviation from the average), we must have

$$\sigma < A$$

that is, the standard deviation from the average is no larger than the average itself. Only under this condition should the conception of an "effective average" be applied. Thus such distributions as

Share	Scheme I	Scheme II
(a)	0 units	0 units
(b)	0	1
(c)	3	8

have no EA on this basis. In the case of very uneven distributions, when an EA is not defined, other tools must be employed. We shall not pursue the matter further here.

Compare the distributions:

Share	Scheme I	Scheme II
(a)	2 units	0 units
(b)	2	3
(c)	2	3

Share	Scheme III	Scheme IV
(a)	x units	3 units
(b)	3	3
(c)	3	3

It is reasonably plain on the basis of intuitive considerations that Scheme I is preferable to Scheme II (since it divides the same total more equitably) and that Scheme IV is preferable to Scheme I (since everyone fares uniformly better by it). Now when $x = 0$, then III = II; and when $x = 3$, then III = IV. The question thus arises: As x is increased from 0 to 3, at what value of x does III become preferable to I? Our EA calculation yields this value as $x = 1.24$. The reader is invited to measure this result against his own intuitions, realizing that in such a matter, as elsewhere, intuition is not a precision instrument yielding exact results.

An interesting use of the concept of an effective average is its application to the analysis of income distribution data. Consider the tabulation given below, derived from two sources: (1) U.S. Bureau of the Census, *Historical Statistics of the United States* (Washington, D.C., 1960), and (2) *idem., Statistical Abstract of the United States*, 86th edn. (Washington, D.C., 1965):

Average income for families and unattached individuals in the USA
(In 1,000's of 1950 dollars)

Year	Actual Average Amount	% increase over 1929	Effective Average Amount	% increase over 1929
1929	3.36	0	1.61	0
1941	3.66	9%	1.81	12%
1950	4.44	32%	2.33	45%
1962	5.78	72%	3.10	93%

The fact of a significant disparity in the distribution of income is revealed by the discrepancy between the actual and the effective average. On the other hand, the comparative lessening of this disparity is indicated by the significantly more rapid increase of the effective average as compared with the actual average.

Our contention is that an EA measure

of this sort, when defined, appears to provide a good basis of comparison, and thus an acceptable solution of the "meshing problem" in the relative assessment of the merit of greater or lesser *amounts* versus greater or lesser *equity* in alternative distributions.

THE NEED FOR A SOLUTION TO THE "MESHING PROBLEM"

In the face of the considerations adduced so far, it might seem plausible to adopt the *maximin criterion* of choice, giving preference to that alternative distribution which has the largest minimum share.[16] But consider the following two distribution schemes (with, say, 1 unit as the utility "floor"):

Share	Scheme I	Scheme II
(a)	1.9 units	7 units
(b)	3.1	3
(c)	3	2
(d)	3	2
(e)	3	2
(f)	3	2
(g)	3	2

Scheme II has the greater minimum, but is, pretty obviously, not to be preferred to Scheme I.[17]

Suppose we are confronted with the choice between two alternative schemes of utility allocation, as follows:[18]

[16] This is not a version but a revision of utilitarianism. Its sole advocate known to me is (apparently) Marcus G. Singer. See pp. 202–203 of his *Generalization in Ethics* (New York: Alfred A. Knopf, 1961).

[17] An analogous counterexample will serve against the *minimax criterion* that minimizes the maximum. A somewhat greater (but still finite) amount of ingenuity is needed to provide a counterexample to the maximin-cum-minimax combination of these two principles.

[18] I adapt this example from A. C. Ewing, "Political Differences," *The Philosophical Quarterly*, XIII (1963), 333–343 (see p. 338). Note that the numbers here represent numbers of people, and not utility units as in preceding charts.

Share	Scheme I	Scheme II
Made very happy	30 people	20 people
Made fairly happy	20	40
Made rather unhappy	45	35
Made very unhappy (i.e., pushed "below the floor")	5	5

Here, if Scheme I is adopted, the total number of happy people is decreased by 10, as compared with Scheme II, but the number of people made very happy is increased comparably. It is clear that *if the claims of the individuals are equal* we are still confronted with a possible conflict between "greater good" on the one hand and "greater number" on the other. For the orthodox utilitarian, this gap remains to be bridged—or perhaps simply faced and accepted as irresolvable at the theoretical level.

The problem was stated with model clarity by John Hospers in his ethics textbook:

The twentieth-century utilitarians . . . have always interpreted the classical utilitarians as meaning that one should aim at the largest total quantity of intrinsic good, with no qualifications or additions saying that quantity of good is to be sacrificed when a more nearly equal distribution can thereby be achieved. (Why then did Bentham and Mill include the phrase "for the greatest number"? Probably to insure that every person was included in the calculations of the greatest total quantity.) Our problem, then, is this: does this classical utilitarian account of the matter (largest total quantity of good, with everybody being figured into the total) need revision in the light of the principle of equal distribution which we have said is included in our idea of justice?

Most thoughtful people, it seems, desire both ideals to be achieved: they would like to have a society in which the largest total *amount* of good is present, and if they had to choose between a society containing more good and a society containing less, they would unhesitatingly choose the first. Similarly, however, they would like to have a society in which good is, as nearly as possible, *equally distributed* (with exceptions we shall take up in the next section); and if they had to choose between a society in which good was equally distributed and one in which there were glaring inequalities, they would choose the first. The question is, what is to be done when the two ideals conflict? Are we—as the classical utilitarians would say, or at any rate as we are taking them to mean—always to select the alternative that contains the maximum total quantity of good, irrespective of its distribution? Or are we, as the supporters of justice would say, to select the alternative that contains the most nearly equal distribution of good, regardless of the amount? Or are we somehow to mediate between the two views by considering *both* principles and by believing that the right act should embody them both—the greatest total possible good that is compatible with the most nearly equal distribution thereof? It is probably fair to say that most people, once they have thought of it, would consider the third alternative—the one bringing in both principles—to be the best.[19]

This "meshing problem" of balancing the total amount of good at issue in a given putative distribution against the fairness of the distribution in cases where these two desiderata cut against one another is one which utilitarians (and nonutilitarians, for that matter) have never resolved satisfactorily. However, its analysis seems to be a pressing task for an adequate substantive theory of distributive justice. Our proposed concept of an *effective average* is offered as a tentative step toward its solution. Be this as it may, the analysis has, I believe, established one important and essentially negative result. The principle of utility cannot of itself play the part of a final arbiter in a selection among alternative distributions. The application of the principle involves choices among alternatives whose resolution requires recourse to a further and at least equally fundamental principle.

As Sidgwick already clearly saw ..., the principle of utility fails us in its purported role as an ultimate recourse because we cannot avoid choices among alternative modes of implementing the utilitarian principle itself, choices, therefore, of such a character that they cannot in the nature of things be settled by the principle itself.

THE QUESTION OF CLAIMS

Thus far we have emphasized what might be called the domestic difficulties of the principle of utility (greater good *versus* greater number). But there are also its foreign difficulties vis-à-vis the concepts of fairness and equity. These may be illustrated by contrasting the following two utility allocations:

Share	Scheme I	Scheme II
(a)	4 units	4 units
(b)	4	3
(c)	4	3
(d)	1	2

From the orthodox utilitarian standpoint, all the advantages lie with Scheme I: (i) It represents the greater *total* good (13 contrasted with 12 units) and the greater *average* good (3.25 as contrasted with 3.00 units). (ii) It represents a "greater good for a greater number" since two individuals are beneficiaries (1-unit beneficiaries) of its adoption and only one individual is the loser (1-unit loser) thereby. But on the other hand, *supposing that the individuals who are to be recipients of these four shares all have equal claims*, a very positive point of merit on the part of Scheme II must be recognized: it is significantly more equitable.[20] If one is prepared, in cases

[19] John Hospers, *Human Conduct*, p. 426. Note that any such defect in the utilitarian principle of distribution affects the rule-version just as much as the act-version of the theory.

[20] For Scheme I, the sum of the squares of the deviations from the average is 6.75. For Scheme II this factor only amounts to 2. The "effective average" for Scheme I is 2.60 contrasted with 2.65 for Scheme II. As a matter of incidental interest, it is worth noting that if this same general pattern of

such as this, to give weight to the fairness of distributions, even when this goes against the factors operative in the principle of utility ("greater good," "greater number"), one is, in effect, abandoning this principle as the ultimate arbiter in matters of distributive justice by introducing a wholly new consideration of which the principle takes no account.

The point we are making here is certainly not new, being one of the standard objections to utilitarianism on the part of nineteenth-century critics. Herbert Spencer put the matter as follows:

"Everybody to count for one, nobody for more than one." Does this mean that, in respect of whatever is proportioned out, each is to have the same share whatever his character, whatever his conduct? Shall he if passive have as much as if active? Shall he if useless have as much as if useful? Shall he if criminal have as much as if virtuous? If the distribution is to be made without reference to the natures and deeds of the recipients, then it must be shown that a system which equalizes, as far as it can, the treatment of good and bad, will be beneficial. If the distribution is not to be indiscriminate, then the formula disappears. The something distributed must be apportioned otherwise than by equal division. There must be adjustment of amounts to deserts; and we are left in the dark as to the mode of adjustment—we have to find other guidance.[21]

In the case of an unequal group of

the distribution at issue is extended to involve a greater number of other people, the type-I distribution becomes preferable. For example, contrast:

Share	Scheme I	Scheme II
(a)	4 units	4 units
(b)	4	3
(c)	4	3
(d)	4	3
(e)	4	3
(f)	1	2

Now Scheme I is preferable to II since its *effective average* is the larger (2.9 as against 2.7).

[21] Herbert Spencer, *The Data of Ethics* (New York: D. Appleton & Co., 1879), sec. 84.

claims, the difficulties grow more acute than ever. Here we would in general have to confront a given schedule of (legitimate) claims and a set of alternative distributions among which to effect a (rationally defensible) preferential selection. An example would be as follows:

Individuals involved	Schedule of claims
A	4
B	4
C	8

Alternative Distributions

Scheme I	Scheme II	Scheme III
5 units	8 units	1 unit
5	4	5
6	4	10

In such a case we would (at any rate as long as the total amounts being distributed are the same[22]) clearly prefer that distribution which has the least sum of squares-of-differences-from-the-schedule, that is, Scheme I in the example. But what in the case of a tie by this criterion, as in the example:

Individuals	Claims
A	2
B	3
C	4

Distributions

Scheme I	Scheme II
3 units	0 units
1	4
2	2

Here we would surely prefer the intrinsically more equitable distribution, that is, the one with the larger effective average—i.e., Scheme I.

The standpoint at which we have thus arrived supports the charge of shortcomings that we had earlier found it necessary to make against the utilitarian standard for

[22] Cases in which this condition is not satisfied are treated in ch. 5.

assessing distributions. The principle is involved in an internal fission which leads to the need for further choices in its application in certain cases. These choices, being choices that arise in the *application of* the utilitarian principle, cannot be settled by the principle itself. They require an outside appeal—to such concepts as equity or fairness in accommodating claims—and in this way point to the fact that the utilitarian standard must be viewed as representing one factor among others. It simply will not do to regard the principle of utility as an ultimate and complete basis for a theory of distributive justice. Furthermore, we have found the direction in which one must look to find those necessary further factors of distributive justice, namely, considerations of equity in the accommodation of claims.[23] The focus of attention must thus shift to this matter of claims.

THE PROBLEM OF CLAIMS AND DESERT

If the claims of the individuals concerned are equal: an absolutely crucial, and to this point wholly ignored, cluster of considerations lurks in this clause.

Let us suppose Mr. *A* to be the very personification of virtue and Mr. *B* the embodiment of vice. And consider two schemes of utility allocation giving these two individuals the shares (a) and (b) respectively:

Scheme 1   Scheme 2

On the basis of the principle of utility above, taking account only of the total utility and the arithmetic of its distribution, there is nothing whatever to choose between these schemes. This upshot is patently unpalatable from a moral standpoint.

But worse is yet to come. Let us add to the *dramatis personae* of the preceding example also a Mr. *C*, who puts Mr. *B* quite into the shade in point of nastiness. Consider now the utility-allocation schemes:

Share	Scheme I	Scheme II
(a)	4 units	1 unit
(b)	2	2
(c)	1	5

If the principle of utility is our sole guide, there is patently nothing to do but adopt Scheme II in preference to its alternative. Crude and unreconstructed utilitarianism thus seems prepared to do substantial violence to elemental considerations of justice and common-sense morality.

From this standpoint it becomes clear that the *decisive and fatal* objection to any straightforward adoption of the classical principle of utility as a rule of distribution is this: it leaves wholly out of account that essential reference to claims, merit, and desert without which no theory of distributive justice fulfills the requisite for serious consideration.[24] In taking into account only the characteristics of the distribution of goods—"greatest good," "greatest number"—naive utilitarianism (and unsophisticated welfare economics) decisively to its detriment rides roughshod over the distinguishing claims of individuals. The emphasis of the "intuitionist" and "deontologist" opponents of classical utilitarianism

[23] When Saint Paul wrote "Masters, give unto your servants that which is just and equal" (Colossians 4:1), the "equal" at issue is not to be construed as "equal to what all the others get" but as "equal to his deserts."

[24] The point is cogently urged by W. D. Ross in *Foundations of Ethics*, pp. 76–77. No one, of course, denies that the classical utilitarians made—from the very start—certain rudimentary allowances for the principle of justice; as in Bentham's formula, "everybody to count for one, and nobody for more than one."

upon the moral sense of justice was (as we see it) thoroughly well placed.[25]

THE CLASSICAL UTILITARIANS ON CLAIMS

Utilitarians have realized from the beginning that justice could prove a stumbling block in the path of their theory. Bentham himself wrote:

But justice, what is it that we are to understand by justice: and why not happiness but justice? What happiness is, every man knows, because, what pleasure is, every man knows, and what pain is, every man knows. But what justice is—this is what on every occasion is the subject-matter of dispute. Be the meaning of the word *justice* what it will, what regard is it entitled to otherwise than as a means to happiness.[26]

Justice, according to Bentham, is an inherently obscure notion that must not be permitted to retard the pursuit of happiness.[27]

Classical utilitarians (in particular, Mill), ever fully alive to difficulties of this sort, struggled manfully with their resolution. Their argument, in brief, was as follows: "If goods are distributed unjustly, the 'normal expectations' of men are frustrated and the natural order of society undermined, with a resulting detriment to the general good." An unjust distribution, it is argued, is one that may in some cases seem to serve utilitarian purposes but cannot in

[25] A thoroughgoing dyed-in-the-wool utilitarian (such as J. J. C. Smart?) would of course not look at the matter in this light. For him what we regard as the deliverances of "the moral sense of justice" are but the misguided intimations of outmoded sentimentality. As Smart put the matter in correspondence: "Someone who feels strongly that the utilitarian principle is correct will of course judge our commonsense moral feelings by the principle, not vice-versa."

[26] Bentham, *Constitutional Code*, ch. 16, sec. 6.

[27] But compare Herbert Spencer's cogent objection that the history of this subject indicates no greater (and possibly less) consensus regarding the meaning of *happiness* than of *justice* (*The Data of Ethics*, sec. 60).

the nature of things actually do so: the unjust can never be truly utile. We may therefore regard justice as naturally derivative from utility and subordinate to it.

It is interesting to observe that this line of argument is an exact counterpart to Cicero's attempt (in our motto from *De Officiis*) to subordinate utility (expediency) to justice. An unjust act, he argues, can merely *seem* expedient, but cannot in the nature of things actually be so: the truly utile can never be unjust. We may therefore regard utility as naturally derivative from justice and subordinate to it.

Both lines of argumentation fall back upon essentially the same specious distinction between a *true* utility that must square with justice and a merely *seeming* utility that may be in conflict with it. Both positions take comfort in the same comforting illusion that "in the final analysis," utility and justice must—somehow—come to terms of agreement.

Suppose we look at a distribution from the retrospective angle—with the supposition that "all returns are in," and that *all the correct allowances have been made* for frustrations, disappointments, etc.— and that *then* we are to choose between the two alternative schemes for a utility allocation among 100 persons:

	Scheme I	
	Persons made happy	*Persons made unhappy*
"Deserving"	0	10
"Undeserving"	90	0

	Scheme II	
	Persons made happy	*Persons made unhappy*
"Deserving"	70	5
"Undeserving"	5	20

Surely the naively utilitarian espousal of Scheme I violates our natural sense of justice.

The classical utilitarians are on the side of the angels on this issue: they yield to no one in their eagerness to give considerations of justice and desert their appropriate weight. Their error, I believe, is not one of wrongheadedness, but—prior to Sidgwick—of self-delusion in convincing themselves that this desideratum can somehow be derived as a *strict consequence* of the principle of utility. The position of orthodox utilitarianism on this point was already taken up by that proto-utilitarian (indeed rule-utilitarian) David Hume, who argued at great length and with great fervor that "the rules of equity or justice depend entirely on the particular state and condition, in which men are placed, and owe their origin and existence to that UTILITY, which results to the public from their strict and regular observance" so that "the necessity of justice to the support of society is the SOLE foundation of that virtue."[28]

Sidgwick faced the problem squarely:

It is evident that there are many different ways of distributing the same quantum of happiness among the same number of persons; in order, therefore, that the utilitarian criterion of right conduct may be as complete as possible, we ought to know which of these ways is to be preferred. . . . Now the Utilitarian formula seems to supply no answer to this question: at least we have to supplement the principle of seeking the greatest happiness on the whole by some principle of Just or Right distribution of this happiness. The principle which most Utilitarians have either tacitly or expressly adopted is that of pure equality. . . .[29]

What Sidgwick fails to stress with the emphasis it demands is that such a recourse to a principle of justice is not a matter of removing a minor incompleteness in the principle of utility, but the introduction of another, importantly new type of consideration that can even cut against considerations of utility and that requires systematic coordination with the principle of utility. To hold Sidgwick's position consistently requires not a supplementation, but an *abandonment* of the classical, one-track utilitarianism.[30]

One must distinguish between the immanent and the transeunt goodness of alternative distributions of any type of good. Its *immanent* (or internal) goodness is determined by the goodness or merit of the entire distribution itself (i.e., the goodness of the pattern of distribution). Analogously, the *immanent* goodness of a hypothetical universe is fixed by the amount of the goodness *in* it, and its *transeunt* goodness is fixed by the amount of the goodness *of* it. And, as our examples have shown, these two things are not to be identified.[31] Indeed, it is crucial for the theory of distributive justice that they be kept carefully distinct. Yet defenses of the utilitarian theory sometimes slip over from one kind of goodness to the other. Even G. E. Moore (in Section Seventeen of *Principia Ethica*) moves from "It will increase the goodness *of* the world if I do X rather than not" to "It will increase the goodness *in* the world if I do X rather than not." (Only thus does he obtain his principle [Section Eighty-nine] that "The assertion, 'I am morally bound to perform this action' is identical with the assertion, 'This action will produce the greatest possible amount of good in the universe.'") Moore is able to lay to rest the difficulties which immediately crop up only by means of his "principle of organic unity," which justifies the claim that the goodness *in the universe as a whole* need not be correlated in any fixed way with the goodness *in the several constituent elements of the universe*. In this way he is able to salvage the needed distinction between immanent and transeunt good-

[28] In Section III, "Of Justice," and Appendix II of *An Enquiry Concerning the Principles of Morals*; compare also Part II of Book III, "Of Justice and Injustice," of the *Treatise of Human Nature*.

[29] *The Methods of Ethics*, Book IV, ch. 1, sec. 2.

[30] Actually, Sidgwick's principal departure from the utilitarian position is in the direction of egoism, in adding a principle of self-interest to the utilitarian principle of public interest.

[31] The distinction was clearly drawn by C. D. Broad, *Five Types of Ethical Theory*, p. 252.

ness. As against this principle of Moore's, our direct emphasis on the merit of distributions avoids any (unsought for and unwarranted) inference that somehow the goodness of the present in whole may be secured at the expense of that present in the parts, and that in distinguishing between immanent and transeunt goodness we are moving in the direction of a doctrine of something akin to *raison d'etat*.

CLAIM-EQUALIZATION

But cannot the utilitarian principle be reformulated so as to meet this line of objection? Let it be admitted that the original formulation of the principle contains a hidden assumption. It tacitly supposes that *the individuals at issue are indifferent in respect of claims*—that their merit is the same, that their desert regarding the allocation of utility is identical.

There seems to be little harm in this if viewed as a limiting restriction for the applicability of the principle. (No harm, that is, for anything other than the serviceability of the principle of utility, which now becomes even in principle confined to a very restricted group of cases.) Viewed as an assumption about "the way things are," it of course does gross violence to the facts of life.

Cannot the utilitarian principle of distribution readily be patched up to take account of the legitimate claims of the individuals concerned? Suppose that some amount of a good is to be divided among several persons: what part of it can Mr. X legitimately lay claim to as his portion? The principle of utility provides a ready answer (but only one). It is this: Consider the share that falls to X's lot in that distribution which achieves the objective of assuring "the greatest good of the greatest number," and then take as X's proper share his share in *this* distribution. (If there are

several such distributions, I would suppose that X cannot on the basis of the principle of utility properly *claim* more than the minimum of his alternative shares.)

But this is paper-towel reasoning: it won't wash. For with this view of claims, it does not help the utilitarian one jot to take claims into account. It is clear that the proportioning of shares to claims leaves exactly the *status quo ante* when the claims are tailored to fit the shares. There would be a vitiating circularity in the procedure of doling out claims as determined in terms of the public interest—that is, by considerations of utility—and then going on to maintain that we utilitarians accommodate justice by satisfying claims.

THE ROLE OF DESERVINGNESS

Even with the indicated claim-equalization assumption, the principle of utilitarianism continues to be in difficulties. For consider the following alternative divisions of utility shares among three *thoroughly but equally undeserving* individuals of exactly identical status with respect to claims:

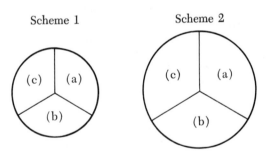

It seems clear to me that common sense would balk at the principle of utility's (automatic) option for Scheme II.

The doctrinaire utilitarian's insistence upon the maximization of happiness as the sole and exclusive consideration is misguided. Would many reasonable men prefer to our world another just exactly like it except in one sole respect—that Adolf Hitler's share of happiness is larger (at no one's expense)? [32]And yet this hypothetical world answers precisely to the utilitarian's prescript of a "greater happiness of a greater number." Unreconstructed utilitarianism is surely wrong at this point: happiness maximization (or utility maximization) is not a good in itself—and certainly does not serve the interests of justice—regardless of *how* it is maximized. One has to build into the principle of utility not only an equal claims qualification, but also the qualification that the individuals involved are all "deserving."

I have heard the following objection: "But the example is one in which the deprivation of happiness *ex hypothesi* serves no purpose, such as making others happier from *Schadenfreude*, or leading an evildoer to 'mend his ways,' or 'serving as a lesson' *pour encourager les autres*. Surely, however, one must endorse the principle that there should be as much happiness as possible in the world, unless some definite constructive purpose is served by its diminution." The principle is plausible but does not cut against the case in hand, for a constructive purpose *is* present here, viz., "to make the world a juster one."[33] Happiness

in our view is not an unconditional good, regardless of how arrived at. Suppose *A* inflicts an injury upon *B*. There is an act *X* which prevents the (otherwise automatic) penalty upon *A*—thus increasing the total happiness in the world—but (be it supposed) has no other causal effects upon the welfare of men. The performance of the act *X* would then, in our view, be a deed of saintly merit *if done by B*, but one of near-demonic demerit if done by some "outsider" *C*.[34]

SHARES MUST BE BASED UPON CLAIMS

However ardently one may espouse the dictum that "all men are created equal," i.e., come into the world with exactly the same status regarding claims, merit, and desert, there is no gainsaying that this situation is radically altered once men begin to *act*. Human actions—or at any rate, the great bulk of them—are inherently claim-modifying: they bring into being assets and liabilities, and engender merit and demerit. Surely nobody would want to hold that when the prize is to be awarded, there is no difference in the claims of the winner and the losers. Surely nobody would want to say that when the payroll is disbursed, the employer should be governed by the rule of "the greatest happiness of the greatest number," indifferent to the question of who are his workmen and who are not. Life is replete with "claim-creating circumstances" typified by the making (and breaking) of promises and contracts; in the nature of things, most distributions are of the functional sort that is unavoidably claim-responsive. "The greatest good of the greatest number, *always recognizing that the resulting distribution of goods and evils should be commensurate with the legiti-*

[32] Note that *punishment* is not at issue here, for it is the specific infliction of unpleasantness in response to an act of wrongdoing that the subject has committed, and must therefore be part of the causal sequence of developments.

[33] J. S. Mill was (I think) prepared to concede this point: ". . . it is universally considered just that each person should obtain that (whether good or evil) which he *deserves*; and unjust that he should obtain a good, or be made to undergo an evil, which he does not deserve. This is, perhaps, the clearest and most emphatic form in which the idea of justice is conceived by the general mind. As it involves the notion of desert, the question arises, what constitutes desert? Speaking in a general way, a person is understood to deserve good if he does right, evil if he does wrong; and in a more particular sense, to deserve good from those to whom he does or has done good, and evil from those to whom he does or has done evil. The precept of returning good for evil has never been regarded as a case of the fulfillment of justice, but as one in which the claims of justice are waived, in obedience to other considerations." *Utilitarianism*, ch. 5.

[34] On this point, compare W. D. Ross, *The Right and the Good*, p. 22.

mate claims of the individuals at issue"—
surely some such "proportionality qualification" is crucial and cannot be dispensed
with. The "principle of utility" cannot be a
serious candidate for a principle of distribution when its formulation does not take
account of the desert (merit, legitimate
claims) of the individuals involved.

In a fundamental sense the concept of
justice involves that of proportion: *congrui-
tas ac proportionalitas quaedam.*[35] Discussions of distributive justice cannot ignore
Aristotle's emphasis[36] that in a just distribution, shares must be proportioned to desert or merit (*kata axian*) in terms of the
relevant claims of the respective recipients.[37]

In taking this position, we must avoid
tempting misunderstandings. It is *not* being
said that it is not just to pay a debt to a
morally wicked person. (The indebtedness
is wholly definitive of the claims at issue,
and the moral character of the creditor is
entirely irrelevant to these claims.) Nor is
it being said that the state is not to treat all
as "equal before the law," but should accord preferential treatment to morally superior individuals. (As long as its subjects
comport themselves within "the limits of
the law," it is perfectly appropriate for the
state to regard their moral character as irrelevant in point of claim-establishment as
regards the sorts of distributions at issue.)
In short, it is to be stressed that our thesis

that *a just distribution must be based upon
claims* is to be construed in such a way that
the *legitimate claims* in question are relevant and appropriate with respect to the
distribution at issue.

What is the "Pure Principle of Distributive Justice"? According to a formula once
proposed by Sidgwick, justice is the similar
and injustice the dissimilar treatment of
similars. But *this* formulation of an "equity
principle" as being merely a matter of
adherence to the rule *Treat likes alike!* is
clearly inadequate, because it encompasses
only a part of the story. Let us consider six
persons: *A1* and *A2* both very (but
equally) undeserving, *B1* and *B2* both
highly (but equally) deserving, and *C1*
and *C2* both moderately deserving. And
let us consider a distribution that allocates
to *A1* and *A2* large (but equal) shares of
utility, to *C1* and *C2* modest (equal) shares,
and to *B1* and *B2* both minute (and equal)
shares. Obviously this distribution satisfies
the injunction of a similar treatment of similars, but it is, just as obviously, grossly unjust. The "equity principle" under consideration must be supplemented by a "proportionality principle" that the shares of the
distribution be proportionate to claims.[38]

The search for a principle of justice is
thus brought back to the Roman jurists'
dictum that the definitive principle of justice is inherent in the dictum *suum cuique
tribuere,* "to give each his own," or to Sim-
onides' dictum *to ta opheilomena hekastōi
apodidonai dikaion esti,* "to give what is
owed to each is just" (see Plato, *Republic*
331d ff.). But what, from the standpoint of
distributive justice, can be said to be "his
own"? Plainly the answer is "what he deserves," i.e., a share ideally equal—and in
any event, in general proportional—to his

---

[35] *Leibniz: Juris ac aequi elementa,* in *Mittei-
lungen aus Leibnizens ungedruckten Schriften,* ed.
G. Mollat (Leipzig, 1893), pp. 22 ff.

[36] *Nicomachean Ethics* V. 5, 1130b31–33, and
V. 6, 1131a20–27. Cf. W. D. Ross, *Aristotle* (5th
edn.), pp. 210–211.

[37] "It is often held by theologians that in the
next world all the accounts will be set straight,
that everyone will receive just what he deserves,
and that therefore there will be 'perfect justice.'
Kant, in fact, used this position as an argument for
immortality: the moral law requires justice (apportionment of reward to desert), and in this world
justice often does not triumph; therefore there
must be a life after this one in which it does. As
an argument, most philosophers agree that this one
is not successful. But at least it is a testimonial to
the widespread and deep-seated desire for justice."
John Hospers, *Human Conduct,* pp. 433–434.

[38] I do not mean to suggest that Sidgwick did
not recognize this fact; he certainly was well
aware of it: "the proposition 'that men ought to be
rewarded in proportion to their deserts' . . . would
be commonly held to be the true and simple principle of distribution in any case where there are
no claims arising from Contract or Custom to
modify its operation" (*The Methods of Ethics,* 7th
edn., p. 279).

legitimate claims. (Even this must be adapted to the case of indivisible goods.) And of course it is not just moral deservingness in general that is at issue here, but functional deservingness determined with respect to the defining conditions of the distribution at issue.

In saying that the issue of distributive justice cannot be properly broached, let alone resolved, without taking *claims* into account, we must not be interpreted as holding that the claims at issue are merely the purely legal claims and "rights" enshrined in positive law. Here, as elsewhere, the distinction between the merely legal and the genuinely just is operative, and the claims and rights at issue are certainly meant to include those whose foundation is of a moral rather than exclusively legal nature.

A fatal defect of naive utilitarianism is its incapacity to provide adequate accommodation for the pivotal facet of *justice*. No acceptable ethical theory can articulate its principle of choice among alternative distributions of goods and evils in abstraction from a consideration of the legitimate claims of the individuals at issue. But on utilitarian grounds, rights and duties, claims and obligations are always *sub judice* and always vulnerable. They are always insecure precisely because they are always at the mercy of utilitarian considerations. For the naive utilitarian, justice and obligation are always provisional matters, subject to possible subordination to considerations of utility.

To say this is not to deny that in many or most cases what sorts óf things are to count as legitimate claims may be established by a utilitarian (i.e., rule-utilitarian) approach. What is denied is that claim-establishing considerations must inevitably pass such a utilitarian test under pain of being counted as illegitimate. Obligations are obligations, and claims, claims, in a basic and primary way, irrespective of the utilitarian expediency of honoring them as such. To use an analogy: Exactly as the

utilitarian question of whether or not "honesty is the best policy" is simply irrelevant to the moral status of honesty, so the utilitarian expediency of recognizing proper claims is irrelevant to their legitimacy as claims and to the injustice of action in their despite.

But notice how far we have now departed from exclusive reliance upon the principle of utility. We have simply demoted considerations of "greatest good" and "greatest number," refusing them a preeminent status as the sole and solitary factors operative in the first instance, by coordinating them with considerations of justice. We speak advisedly of a *coordination* of considerations of utility with those of distributive justice because neither is, in our judgment, the sole ultimate criterion to which the other is to be subordinated systematically.

It is not hard to see that to hold that considerations of utility and of justice must lead to the same conclusion is to think both wishfully and carelessly. That proto-utilitarian Bernard de Mandeville illustrated graphically in his *Fable of the Bees* that considerations of utility (general welfare) and of justice can come into head-on conflict. The uncompromising utilitarian should be prepared—with Mandeville (and perhaps J. J. C. Smart?)—to brush considerations of justice wholly aside whenever they conflict with the principle of utility. For him, justice counts only when it is serviceable as a means to the maximization of utility; in other cases it is an obstacle to be brushed conveniently aside. Anyone seriously and fundamentally committed to some principle of justice cannot be a doctrinaire utilitarian. To say this is not, of course, to say that considerations of justice must never be tempered by considerations of utility—it does not lead to that stern dictum *Fiat justitia ruat caelum*, taking but a small step in its direction. For it is crucial in this context to realize that justice has two importantly different contraries: injustice on the one hand, and on the other, that "more than justice" represented by mercy, compassion, generosity, and works of supererogation generally. It would only be in the latter category of deviations from justice that utilitarian considerations can properly be accorded room for play.

OUR STRICTURES APPLICABLE NOT ONLY TO "ACT-UTILITARIANISM" BUT ALSO TO "RULE-UTILITARIANISM"

The standard objection against "act-utilitarianism"(that the act to be preferred on grounds of the "greatest good of greatest number" principle may be patently improper by involving blatant violation of a moral rule—e.g., giving property entrusted for safekeeping to a needy indigent rather than restoring it to its rightful owner) applies also to rule-utilitarianism. For a rule or practice that (as best we can tell) may assure the greatest good to the greatest number may *also* be equally unacceptable in an analogous way; e.g., group punishment of persons whose "guilt" of an offense of a given type is based upon some form of association, or punishment based upon the application of *ex post facto* laws, could (very possibly) prove under specifiable sets of circumstances to be a policy of demonstrable social advantage. J. S. Mill writes: "The principle, therefore, of giving

to each what they deserve, that is, good for good, as well as evil for evil, is not only included within the idea of Justice as we have defined it, but is a proper object of that intensity of sentiment which places the Just, in human estimation, above the simply Expedient."[39] What Mill fails to recognize is that this position is, in the final analysis, simply incompatible with utilitarianism—even the rule-utilitarianism he himself espouses.[40]

[39] *Utilitarianism*, ch. 10.

[40] The classic exponent of the position is, of course, David Hume. Two very able recent statements of rule-utilitarianism are: S. E. Toulmin, *The Place of Reason in Ethics* (London: Cambridge University Press, 1950), and P. H. Nowell-Smith, *Ethics* (London: Penguin Books, 1954). Compare also John Rawls, "Two Concepts of Rules," *The Philosophical Review*, LXIV (1955), 3–32. For a critical discussion of rule-utilitarianism (or "restricted utilitarianism") see J. J. C. Smart, "Extreme and Restricted Utilitarianism," *The Philosophical Quarterly*, V (1956), 344–354, as well as this author's *An Outline of a System of Utilitarian Ethics* (Victoria: Melbourne University Press, 1961). Smart cogently marshals the arguments against restricted utilitarianism, and is aware of (but undaunted by) the fact that the "restricted" theory is vulnerable to rejections of the kind usually urged against the "extreme" view which the restrictions were designed to circumvent. However, the difficulties encountered by restricted utilitarianism are taken by Smart to drive us back to an extreme, unrestricted utilitarianism rather than as scoring against the utilitarian position *tout court*. The uncompromisingly anti-utilitarian position (in the manner of W. D. Ross) has found an able exponent in H. J. McCloskey, "An Examination of Restricted Utilitarianism," *The Philosophical Review*, LXVI (1957), 466–485, and "A Note on Utilitarian Punishment," *Mind*, LXXII (1963), 599.

Punishment

SIR DAVID ROSS

In connexion with the discussion of rights it is proper to consider a question which has always interested and usually puzzled moralists, and which forms a crucial example for the testing of moral theories—the question of punishment. A utilitarian theory, whether of the hedonistic or of the 'ideal' kind, if it justifies punishment at all, is bound to justify it solely on the ground of the effects it produces. The suffering of pain by the person who is punished is thought to be in itself a bad thing, and the bringing of this bad thing into the world is held to need justification, and to receive it only from the fact that the effects are likely to be so much better than those that would follow his non-punishment as to outweigh the evil of his pain. The effects usually pointed to are those of deterrence and of reformation. In principle, then, the punishment of a guilty person is treated by utilitarians as not different in kind from the imposition of inconvenience, say by quarantine regulations, on innocent individuals for the good of the community. Or again, if a state found to be prevalent some injury to itself or to its members that had not been legislated against, and proceeded to punish the offenders, its action would in principle be justified by utilitarians in the same way as its punishment of offenders against the law is justified by them, *viz.* by the good of the community. No doubt the state would

From *The Right and the Good* by Sir David Ross by permission of the Clarendon Press, Oxford.

have greater difficulty in justifying its action, for such action would produce bad consequences which the punishment of law-breakers does not. But the difference would be only in degree. Nay more, a government which found some offence against the law prevalent, and in its inability to find the offenders punished innocent people on the strength of manufactured evidence, would still be able to justify its action on the same general principle as before.

Plain men, and even perhaps most people who have reflected on moral questions, are likely to revolt against a theory which involves such consequences, and to exclaim that there is all the difference in the world between such action and the punishment of offenders against the law. They feel the injustice of such action by the state, and are ready to say, in the words imputed to them by Mr. Bradley: 'Punishment is punishment, only when it is deserved. We pay the penalty because we owe it, and for no other reason; and if punishment is inflicted for any other reason whatever than because it is merited by wrong, it is a gross immorality, a crying injustice, an abominable crime, and not what it pretends to be. We may have regard for whatever considerations we please—our own convenience, the good of society, the benefit of the offender; we are fools, and worse, if we fail to do so. Having once the right to punish, we may modify the punishment according to the useful and the pleasant; but these are external to the matter, they cannot give us a right to punish, and nothing can do that but criminal desert.'[1]

There is one form of utilitarian view which differs in an important respect from that above ascribed to utilitarians. Professor Moore admits the possibility, which follows from his doctrine of organic unities, that punishment may not need to be justified merely by its *after*-effects. He points out[2] that it may well be the case that though crime is one bad thing and pain another, the union of the two in the same person may be a less evil than crime unpunished, and might even be a positive good. And to this extent, while remaining perfectly consistent with his own type of utilitarianism, he joins hands with intuitionists, most of whom, at any rate, would probably hold that the combination of crime and punishment is a lesser evil than unpunished crime.

Most intuitionists would perhaps take the view that there is a fundamental and underivative duty to reward the virtuous and to punish the vicious. I am inclined to diverge from this view. Two things seem to me to be clear: that we have a *prima facie* duty to do this, and that a state of affairs in which the good are happy and the bad unhappy is better than one in which the good are unhappy and the bad happy. Now if the first of these is an underivative fact, the two facts are logically unconnected. For it can be an underivative fact only if the intuitionist view is true, and if that view is true the superiority of the one state of affairs over the other cannot follow from the duty of producing it, since on the intuitionist view there are duties other than the duty of producing good. But an intuitionist may with propriety perform the reverse derivation; he may derive the *prima facie* duty of reward and punishment from the superiority of the state of affairs produced, since he may—and, as I think, must—admit that if a state of affairs is better than its alternatives there is a *prima facie* duty to produce it if we can. The duty of reward

and punishment seems to me to be in this way derivative. It can be subsumed under the duty of producing as much good as we can; though it must be remembered that the good to be produced in this case is very different from the other goods we recognize (say virtue, knowledge, and pleasure), consisting as it does in a certain relative arrangement of virtue, vice, pleasure, and pain.

But if we hold that there is this duty, it must be admitted that it is one which it is very difficult for us to see our way to performing, since we know so little about the degrees of virtue and vice, and of happiness and unhappiness, as they occur in our fellow men. And in particular there are two grave objections to holding that the principle of punishing the vicious, for the sake of doing so, is that on which the state should proceed in its bestowal of punishments.

(1) What we perceive to be good is a condition of things in which the total pleasure enjoyed by each person in his life as a whole is proportional to his virtue similarly taken as a whole. Now it is by no means clear that we should help to bring about this end by punishing particular offences in proportion to their moral badness. Any attempt to bring about such a state of affairs should take account of the whole character of the persons involved, as manifested in their life taken as a whole, and of the happiness enjoyed by them throughout their life taken as a whole, and it should similarly take account of the virtue taken as a whole, and of the happiness taken as a whole, of each of the other members of the community, and should seek to bring about the required adjustments. In the absence of such a view of the whole facts, the criminals that a retributive theory of state punishment would call on us to punish for the sake of doing so may well be persons who are more sinned against than sinning, and may be, quite apart from our intervention, already enjoying less happiness than a perfectly fair distribution would allow them. The offences which the state legislates

---

[1] *Ethical Studies,* ed. 2, 26–7.
[2] *Principia Ethica,* 214.

against are only a small part of the wrong acts which are being done every day, and a system which punishes not all wrong acts, but only those which have been forbidden by law, and does not attempt to reward all good acts—such an occasional and almost haphazard system of intervention does not hold out any good hope of promoting the perfect proportionment of happiness to virtue. Nor would it be in the least practicable for the state to attempt the thorough review of the merit and the happiness of all its members, which alone would afford a good hope of securing this end.

(2) Even if it were practicable, it is by no means clear that it is the business of the state to aim at this end. Such a view belongs, I think, to an outworn view of the state, one which identifies the state with the whole organization of the community. In contrast to this, we have come to look upon the state as the organization of the community for a particular purpose, that of the protection of the most important rights of individuals, those without which a reasonably secure and comfortable life is impossible; and to leave the promotion of other good ends to the efforts of individuals and of other organizations, such as churches, trade unions, learned and artistic societies, clubs. Now it cannot, I think, be maintained that the apportionment of happiness to merit is one of the essential conditions to the living of a reasonably secure and comfortable life. Life has gone on for centuries being lived with reasonable security and comfort though states have never achieved or even attempted with any degree of resolution to effect this apportionment. And in fact for the state to make such an attempt would seriously interfere with its discharge of its proper work. Its proper work is that of protecting rights. Now rights are (as we have seen) rights to be treated in certain ways and not to be treated in certain ways from certain motives; what the state has to take account of, therefore, is not morally bad actions, but wrong acts, and it has to take account of them in such a way as to diminish the chance of their repetition.

And this attempt would only be interfered with if the state were at the same time trying to effect a proportionment of happiness to moral worth in its members. The latter task, involving as it would a complete review of the merit and happiness of all its members, would involve leaving the punishment for each offence undetermined by law, and to be determined in the light of all the circumstances of each case; and punishment so completely undetermined in advance would be quite ineffective as a protector of rights.

But to hold that the state has no duty of retributive punishment is not necessarily to adopt a utilitarian view of punishment. It seems possible to give an account of the matter which retains elements in punishment other than that of expediency, without asserting that the state has any duty properly defined as the duty of punishing moral guilt. The essential duty of the state is to protect the most fundamental rights of individuals. Now, rights of any human being are correlative to duties incumbent on the owner of rights, or, to put it otherwise, to rights owned by those against whom he has rights; and the main element in any one's right to life or liberty or property is extinguished by his failure to respect the corresponding right in others.[3] There is thus a distinction in kind which we all in fact recognize, but which utilitarianism cannot admit, between the punishment of a person who has invaded the rights of others and the infliction of pain or restraint on one who has not. The state ought, in its effort to maintain the rights of innocent persons, to take what steps are necessary to prevent violations of these rights; and the offender, by violating the life or liberty or property of another, has lost his own right to have his life, liberty, or property respected, so that the state has no *prima facie* duty to spare him, as it has a *prima facie* duty to spare the innocent. It is morally at liberty to injure him as he has injured others, or to inflict any lesser injury

[3] Cf. pp. 54–5.

on him, or to spare him, exactly as consideration both of the good of the community and of his own good requires. If, on the other hand, a man has respected the rights of others, there is a strong and distinctive objection to the state's inflicting any penalty on him with a view to the good of the community or even to his own good. The interests of the society may sometimes be so deeply involved as to make it right to punish an innocent man 'that the whole nation perish not.' But then the *prima facie* duty of consulting the general interest has proved more obligatory than the perfectly distinct *prima facie* duty of respecting the rights of those who have respected the rights of others.

This is, I believe, how most thoughtful people feel about the affixing of penalties to the invasion of the rights of others. They may have lost any sense they or their ancestors had that the state should inflict retributive punishment for the sake of doing so, but they feel that there is nevertheless a difference of kind between the community's right to punish people for offences against others, and any right it may have to inconvenience or injure innocent people in the public interest. This arises simply from the fact that the state has a *prima facie* duty not to do the latter and no such duty not to do the former.

We can, I think, help ourselves towards an understanding of the problem by distinguishing two stages which are not usually kept apart in discussions of it. The infliction of punishment by the state does not, or should not, come like a bolt from the blue. It is preceded by the making of a law in which a penalty is affixed to a crime; or by the custom of the community and the decisions of judges a common law gradually grows up in which a penalty is so affixed. We must, I think, distinguish this stage, that of the affixing of the penalty, from that of its infliction, and we may ask on what principles the state or its officials should act at each stage.

At the earlier stage a large place must

be left for considerations of expediency. We do not claim that laws should be made against all moral offences, or even against all offences by men against their neighbours. Legislators should consider such questions as whether a given law would be enforced if it were made, and whether a certain type of offence is important enough to make it worth while to set the elaborate machinery of the law at work against it, or is better left to be punished by the injured person or by public opinion. But even at this stage there is one respect in which the notion of justice, as something quite distinct from expediency, plays a part in our thoughts about the matter. We feel sure that if a law is framed against a certain type of offence the punishment should be proportional to the offence. However strong the temptation to commit a certain type of offence may be, and however severe the punishment would therefore have to be in order to be a successful deterrent, we feel certain that it is unjust that very severe penalties should be affixed to very slight offences. It is difficult, no doubt, to define the nature of the relation which the punishment should bear to the crime. We do not see any *direct* moral relation to exist between wrong-doing and suffering so that we may say directly, such and such an offence deserves so much suffering, neither more nor less. But we do think that the injury to the inflicted on the offender should be not much greater than that which he has inflicted on another. Ideally, from this point of view, it should be no greater. For he has lost his *prima facie* rights to life, liberty, or property, only in so far as these rested on an explicit or implicit undertaking to respect the corresponding rights in others, and in so far as he has failed to respect those rights. But laws must be stated in general terms, to cover a variety of cases, and they cannot in advance affix punishments which shall never be greater than the injury inflicted by the wrongdoer. We are therefore content with an approximation to what is precisely just. At the same time we recognize that this, while it is a *prima facie* duty, is not the only *prima facie* duty of the legislator; and that, as in the selection of offences to be legislated against, so in the fixing of the penalty, he must consider expediency, and may make the penalty more or less severe as it dictates. His action should, in fact, be guided by regard to the *prima facie* duty of injuring wrongdoers only to the extent that they have injured others, and also to the *prima facie* duty of promoting the general interest. And I think that we quite clearly recognize these as distinct and specifically different elements in the moral situation. To say this is not to adopt a compromise between the intuitionist and the utilitarian view; for it can fairly be plain that one of the duties we apprehend intuitively is that of promoting the general interest so far as we can.

When the law has been promulgated and an offence against it committed, a new set of considerations emerges. The administrator of the law has not to consider what is the just punishmnet for the offence, nor what is the expedient punishment, except when the law has allowed a scale of penalties within which he can choose. When that is the case, he has still to have regard to the same considerations as arose at the earlier stage. But that, when the penalty fixed by law is determinate, this and no other should be inflicted, and that, when a scale of penalties is allowed, no penalty above or below the scale should be inflicted, depends on a *prima facie* duty that did not come in at the earlier stage, *viz.* that of fidelity to promise. Directly, the law is not a promise: it is a threat to the guilty, and a threat is not a promise. The one is an undertaking to do or give to the promisee something mutually understood to be advantageous to him; the other, an announcement of intention to do to him something mutually understood to be disadvantageous to him. Punishment is sometimes justified on the ground that to fail to punish is to

break faith with the offender. It is said that he has a right to be punished, and that not to punish him is not to treat him with due respect as a moral agent responsible for his actions, but as if he could not have helped doing them. This is, however, not a point of view likely to be adopted by a criminal who escapes punishment, and seems to be a somewhat artificial way of looking at the matter, and to ignore the difference between a threat and a promise.

But while the law is not a promise to the criminal, it is a promise to the injured person and his friends, and to society. It promises to the former, in certain cases, compensation, and always the satisfaction of knowing that the offender has not gone scot-free, and it promises to the latter this satisfaction and the degree of protection against further offences which punishment gives. At the same time the whole system of law is a promise to the members of the community that if they do not commit any of the prohibited acts they will not be punished.

Thus to our sense that *prima facie* the state has a right to punish the guilty, over and above the right which it has, in the last resort, of inflicting injury on any of its members when the public interest sufficiently demands it, there is added the sense that promises should *prima facie* be kept; and it is the combination of these considerations that accounts for the moral satisfaction that is felt by the community when the guilty are punished, and the moral indignation that is felt when the guilty are not punished, and still more when the innocent are. There may be cases in which the *prima facie* duty of punishing the guilty, and even that of not punishing the innocent, may have to give way to that of promoting the public interest. But these are not cases of a wider expediency overriding a narrower, but of one *prima facie* duty being more obligatory than two others different in kind from it and from one another.

"The Justification of Punishment"

ANTONY FLEW

I

I want to discuss philosophically, to glance at the logic of, the parts of this expression "the justification of punishment" and then to draw from this discussion one or two morals for discussions of the justification of punishment. This paper is based on one originally given to the Scots Philosophy Club at its Aberdeen meeting in 1953, as the third part of a symposium on *The Justification of Punishment* (no inverted commas).

II

(*a*) *Punishment.* (i) This term is both vague and 'open-textured' (Waismann).[1] Vague; because in several directions there is no sharp line drawn at which we must stop using it: when does punishment of the innocent or illegal punishment cease to be properly called punishment at all? (Here we must beware the scholasticism which F. P. Ramsey attacked in Wittgenstein, when the latter insisted that we *cannot* think illogically. For though there does come a point at which 'thinking' is so illogical, 'punishment' so wayward, that we should refuse to call them thinking or punishment at all, there is nevertheless a wide margin

of toleration. And of course, as usual when we say there comes *a point at which*, what we really mean is that there comes *a twilight zone after which*.) Open-textured; because many questions of its applicability could arise over which even full knowledge of current correct usage might leave us at a loss. Not because this case fell within a more or less recognized No-Man's-Land of vagueness across which no sharp line had been drawn but because it was of a sort which had simply not been envisaged at all: would it be punishment if no effort was made or even pretended to allocate the 'punishments' to the actual offenders, but only to ensure that the total of hangings, say, balanced the total of murders; irrespective of who was hung? (See Ernest Bramah[2] on thus "preserving equipoise within the Sacred Empire.") A third feature, which partly overlaps both the other two, is that several logically independent criteria are involved. Ideally these are all simultaneously satisfied, but there is no strict unanimity rule here to paralyze action: so the word may be applied, and correctly, where one criterion is definitely not satisfied (and not merely where, through its vagueness, there is doubt as to whether it is or is not satisfied).

Once these features, which this concept shares with so many others, are recognized it becomes clear that it would be well as a prelude to possible discussions of the ethics of punishment to list the criteria. This usually useful preliminary is in this

Reprinted from *Philosophy*, XXIX, October 1954, pp. 291–307, by permission of the author and *Philosophy*.

[1] *Logic and Language.* (Edited Antony Flew), Vol. I, pp. 119–20.

[2] *The Wallet of Kai Lung, Kai Lung's Golden Hours,* and *Kai Lung Unrolls His Mat.*

case exceptionally important. Both because there is—since ideas here have certainly developed and are still changing and controversial—every reason to expect there are minority users of the word "punishment": that some people will insist that certain elements are essential which others will not so regard. And because in ethical controversy the temptation to produce from up one's sleeve at later stages in the argument apparently decisive definitional jokers is very strong: and can only be removed by making clear from the start what is and what is not to be involved in the central notions.

In listing the criteria satisfied by what, without honorific intentions,[3] we may call a standard case of punishment, in the primary sense of the word, we have to realize: both—as we have already mentioned—that there are some non-standard users with their private variations on this primary use; and that there are secondary uses of the word (with which those intending to discuss the ethics of punishment are not directly concerned); and that it is correctly applied even by standard users in its primary sense to non-standard cases of punishment, i.e. cases in which not all the criteria are satisfied, but which because of its vagueness the word can cover.

I am going to present my remarks here as *proposals*. Not because I regard them as arbitrary; for on the contrary they are based on what I take to be the general or at least the dominant tendencies in current usage; though I shall not give as many illustrations as would otherwise be necessary, because Mabbott has already done a large part of this work, in his "Punishment" (in *Mind* 1939: this is quite the most valuable article I know on this subject). But because it needs sometimes to be emphasized that no philosophical analysis of the meaning of any term worth so analysing can ever leave things exactly as they were—however conservative the intentions and protestations of its protagonists. For it

must necessarily tend to change the meaning for us and our usage of the terms it analyses—ideally by precisifying it and making clear its implications.

(ii) I *propose*, therefore, that we take as parts of the meaning of "punishment", in the primary sense, at least five elements. *First*, it must be an evil, an unpleasantness, to the victim. By saying "evil"—following Hobbes—or "unpleasantness" not "pain", the suggestion of floggings and other forms of physical torture is avoided. Perhaps this was once an essential part of the meaning of the word, but for most people now its employment is less restricted. Note in this connection the development of an historically secondary use of the word; as applied first to a battering in boxing, then extended to similar situations in other sports where there is no element of physical pain (e.g. as an equivalent to "trouncing", of bowling in cricket).

Second, it must (at least be supposed to) be for an offence. A term in an old-fashioned public school, though doubtless far less agreeable than a spell in a modern prison, cannot be called a punishment, unless it was for an offence (unless perhaps the victim was despatched there for disobedience at home. Conversely, as Mabbott most usefully stresses, if a victim forgives an offender for an injury which was also an offence against some law or rule, this will not necessarily be allowed as relevant to questions about his punishment by the institution whose law or rule it is. A mnemonic in the 'material mode of speech': "Injuries can be forgiven; crimes can only be pardoned".

Third, it must (at least be supposed to) be of the offender. The insistence on these first three elements can be supported by straightforward appeal to the *Concise Oxford Dictionary*, which defines "punish" as "cause (offender) to suffer for an offence".

Notice here that though it would be pedantic to insist *in single cases* that people (logically) cannot be punished for what they have not done; still a *system* of

---

[3] There is, for instance, nothing honorific in saying that this car is a standard model; not 'custom built' or bespoke.

inflicting unpleasantness on scapegoats— even if they are pretended to be offenders—could scarcely be called a system of punishment at all. Or rather—to put it more practically and more tolerantly—if the word "punishment" is used in this way, as it constantly is, especially by anthropologists and psychoanalysts,[4] we and they should be alert to the fact that it is then used in a metaphorical, secondary, or non-standard sense: in which it necessarily has appropriately shifted logical syntax (that is: the word in this case carries different implications from those it carries in a standard case of its primary sense). A likely source of trouble and confusion.

Fourth, it must be the work of personal agencies. Evils occurring to people as the result of misbehaviour, but not by human agency, may be called penalties but not punishments: thus unwanted children and venereal disease may be the (frequently avoided) penalties of, but not the punishments for, sexual promiscuity. To the extent that anyone believes in a personal God with strong views against such sexual behaviour, to that extent he may speak of these as divinely instituted punishments (though, allowing the linguistic propriety of this, the fact that so often the punishments fall on the innocent and can be escaped by the guilty should give pause still).

(Note here. First the distinction often and usefully made—but rarely noticed even by those making it—between the 'natural' penalties *of* and the prescribed penalties *for* such and such conduct (gout *of* port-bibbing: free kicks *for* fouls). Second, that the expression "to the extent that" is peculiarly appropriate to beliefs about God and a quasi-personally sustained moral order in the universe: for with most people these

meander somewhere between complete conviction and complete disbelief; and hence to offer the present distinctions between the uses of "punishment", "penalty of" and "penalty for" as if these were already completely given in present (correct) usage would be seriously to misdescribe the confused situation which actually confronts us.)

Fifth, in a standard case punishment has to (be at least supposed to) be imposed by virtue of some special authority, conferred through or by the institutions against the laws or rules of which the offence has been committed. Mabbott brought this out clearly. A parent, a Dean of a College, a Court of Law, even perhaps an umpire or a referee, acting as such, can be said to impose a punishment; but direct action by an aggrieved person with no pretensions to special authority is not properly called punishment, but revenge. (Vendetta is a form of institutionalized revenge between families regarded as individuals.) Direct action by an unauthorized busybody who takes it upon himself to punish, might be called punishment—as there is no unanimity rule about the simultaneous satisfaction of all the criteria—though if so it would be a non-standard case of punishment. Or it might equally well be called pretending (i.e. claiming falsely) to punish. The insistence on these fourth and fifth criteria can be supported by appeal to the *Oxford English Dictionary* which prefaces that same definition as that given in the C.O.D. with "As an act of superior or public authority".

Besides these five positive criteria I *propose* negatively that we should not insist: *either* that it is confined to either legal or moral offences, but instead allow the use of the word in connection with any system of rules or laws—State, school, moral, trades union, trade association, etc.; *or* that it cannot properly be applied to morally or legally questionable cases to which it would otherwise seem applicable, but instead allow that punishments, say, under

---

[4] Cf. e.g. J. C. Flugel, *Population, Psychology, and Peace*, pp. 70–1. "Another germane example is the stigma of 'illegitimacy', and this example illustrates the important fact that the punishment or suffering in question need not necessarily be endured by the culprit" and "There is such a thing as vicarious punishment."

retrospective or immoral laws may be called punishments, however improper or undesirable the proceedings may be in other respects. Laxity in both these directions conforms with normal usage; while in the second it has the merit of separating ethical from verbal issues.

I shall say nothing about "collective punishment" except that: while no doubt the original unit on which punishment was inflicted was not the individual but the family, tribe, village, clan, or some other group; nevertheless for most of us today "collective punishment" is somehow metaphorical or secondary: it is a matter of regarding a group as an individual, for certain purposes.[5]

(b) *Justification.* This term is multiply relational. A justification has to be of A, rather than B, against C, and to or by reference to D; where A is the thing justified, B the possible alternative(s), C the charge(s) against A, and D the person(s) and/or principle(s) to whom and/or by reference to which the justification is made. The variables may have more than one value even in one context: there may, for instance, be more than one charge. But they do not all have to be given *definite* values *explicitly*. Indeed the point of saying all this lies precisely in the fact that in most cases of justification the values of some of the variables are given only implicitly by the context, and perhaps rather indefinitely too: hence, just as in the notorious case of motion, it is possible to overlook (some of the implications of) the relational nature of the concept. The alternative(s), for instance, may be unstated and even very hazily conceived: but that there must be at least one alternative is brought

out by considering that "There is no alternative" is always either a sufficient justification or a sufficient reason for saying that the question of justification does not arise. Finally, and most important—again compare the case of motion—the reference point, the fourth variable (the person(s) or principle(s) by reference to which justification is made) has the same rather indefinite value implicit in most actual contexts: the value "(whom I consider reasonable people, and what (*fundamentally*) they agree on".

Presumably this has contributed to the use of "justification" as a near synonym for "reason for". Which in turn has been a very minor determinant of the modern fashion—for which there is much to be said—of presenting moral philosophy as an enquiry into what are and are not *good reasons* in ethics. But note here. First, that the word "justification" may, even in contexts where all the variables have the same values, be used in two relevantly different ways: either implying that the proposed justification is or not implying that it is morally or otherwise acceptable to the user; in the latter case if it is *very* unacceptable the word may be put in protest quotes. (*Mutatis mutandis* the same is true of "reason".) Second, that this mode of presentation tends to conceal the existence of really radical ethical disagreements. This point has been pressed in a critical notice of S. E. Toulmin's *The Place of Reason in Ethics* by J. Mackie (*Australasian Journal of Philosophy* 1951). Presumably Toulmin would answer, on Kantian lines, that he was elucidating the *nature of ethics as such*: from which the fact that certain reasons were relevant and good, and others irrelevant and bad, followed necessarily. This would imply that those who seem to be doing ethics but admit different reasons to that extent cannot be doing ethics at all, or at least are very unreasonable people: by definition. Which is perhaps fair enough: providing that steps are taken to bring out just what must be involved in re-

---

[5] Compare here (*a*) K. R. Popper's examination of the appropriateness and limitations of the metaphor involved in regarding rogue states as criminals: *Open Society*, Vol. I, pp. 242 ff. (*b*) the Nuremberg Trials: a colossal effort to discover what the guilt of the Nazi régime amounted to in terms of the particular guilt of particular Germans. This point I owe, like so much else, to Mabbott, privately, and later to his *The State and the Citizen.*

jecting the definitions implicitly accepted by Toulmin, and that many would reject some of the implications of these definitions, and that their position in so doing is monstrous. To say this last is abandoning pure analysis to take sides, as all men must, in a struggle: making a normative, participant's utterance; and not a purely analytic, neutral's observation.

(c) *The*. The assumption behind the use of the definite article is that there is one and only one (unless the whole expression is interpreted, as it rarely is, as strictly equivalent to "justifying punishment"). This is questionable twice over, at two levels: first, because the variables admit of various values—what would serve as justification against one charge and for a Roman Catholic could be simply irrelevant against another and for an atheist humanist; and, second, because in any one context (i.e. where the same values are given to all the variables) there may be two logically separate acceptable justifications both independently sufficient. And surely this is not merely possible but likely: for the fields of human causation, motivation, and justification are precisely those in which 'overdetermination' (Freud) is most common. (An action is said to be *overdetermined* when at least two motives were at work to produce it, either of which alone would have been sufficiently strong to do so separately. The concept, *mutatis mutandis*, obviously can and should also be applied to matters of causation and justification.)

III

We come now to some applications of ideas suggested in our outline examination of the parts of the expression "the justification of punishment" to ethical discussions of the justification of punishment. We shall do this mainly by reference to Mabbott's paper, mentioned above; but we shall have an eye to other contributions,

especially those made to the Aberdeen symposium, also mentioned above.

(a) *Theorizing and justifying.*— Traditionally, views about the circumstances, the severity, and the forms in which punishment is justified—and why—have been presented as *theories* of punishment. Sometimes the metaphor has been developed by speaking of justification as providing "a theory to square with the facts (our moral convictions)".[6] This idiom seems to me radically misguided. First, because it conceals the essentially relational character of justification, which makes it an entirely different sort of thing from theorizing in the positive sciences (see II(*b*) above): suggesting, for instance, that the work of justification *could* be completed finally, for ever, and for everyone.

Second, because it misrepresents questions of value as questions of fact or philosophy: and insofar as these 'theories' are intended as justifications it is wrong to present them as enquiries into why we do, or what are our reasons for doing, what we do. Mabbott begins "I propose ... to defend a retributive theory and to reject absolutely all utilitarian considerations from its justification" (p. 152). In supporting this he writes: "The view that a judge upholds a bad law in order that law in general should not suffer is indefensible" (p. 157). This piece of judicial psychology is irrelevant: surely not "upholds" but "should uphold" is meant. It is quite difficult enough to disentangle factual, ethical, and analytical questions without adopting an idiom which obscures the differences between these, and encourages such confusing slips as this one.

Third, because it conceals the dynamic character of fruitful ethical discussion about justification. It suggests that two men embarking on such a discussion must start from a static, given, unalterable set of "facts" (their moral principles or convictions) and go on thrashing out together the

[6] One of the Aberdeen symposiasts.

implications in this field of these principles. Whereas in fact these "facts" (convictions) are often modified in the course of the discussion itself: just because that brings out unacceptable implications of or reveals unnoticed inconsistencies between these "facts" (convictions). (Compare the mistake made by Aristotle in *Nichomachean Ethics*, III. iii. (1112A18ff.), where his account of deliberation is similarly static and over-formal: tending, except at § 13 (1112B25-27), to overlook that men, being imperfect seers of implications and not omniscient, are often led to modify their objectives in the course of and in the light of deliberation about the means to reach these.)

Fourth, because it embodies and hides certain questionable assumptions: that "our moral convictions" are in agreement, and that they are unchanging. Both are false. Though in both cases, of course, it depends a lot on whom "our" is referring to. But with the former assumption, even taking British professional philosophers as the us-group, it is difficult to believe that debate about the ethics of contraception, abortion, homosexuality, and suicide, would not reveal differences both in the weight given to different admitted *prima facie* obligations, and even perhaps in what were admitted as obligations at all. For instance, if I may follow one bit of unconventionality, the mentioning of such subjects in connection with philosophical ethics, by another, the mention of religious gulfs—the Roman Catholics among us are surely committed to the (at least almost) unconditional repudiation of all these as always morally wrong; and this not as purely religious tabu but as a matter of natural (as opposed to revealed) obligation. In the case of the latter assumption, one would hope that some of the moral convictions of us especially are open to alteration by argument.

Both assumptions are peculiarly questionable in connection with punishment.

Not merely do the ethical views of different people differ pretty considerably, as we can see from the continuing arguments about the proper purpose, justification, and reform of punishment; but the same person often holds inconsistent views at different times or even at the same time. Who of us can manage to be consistent about the relative weight of retributive and utilitarian considerations: and this not merely because we are always being tempted to give more weight to the former than we should in a cool hour adjudge proper, whenever we are emotionally involved against the offender; but also because even in cool hours it is so hard to be sure and steady about difficult particular concrete problems of conduct.

(*b*) *Punishment as necessarily retributive.*—"Why should he be punished?" asks about the punishment of a particular person on a particular occasion. This is the type of question with which Mabbott was concerned: he formulated his problem as "Under what circumstances is the punishment of some particular person justified, and why?" (p. 152); and gave the answer "The only justification for punishing any man is that he has broken a law" (p. 158). This is supposed to be a retributive view and to be an ethical matter: as is made clear in the sentence already quoted "I propose to defend a *retributive* theory, and to reject absolutely all utilitarian considerations from its *justification* (my italics). Which would lead us to expect arguments, or at least assertions, to the effect that the vicious (or the criminal) deserve, and ought to be made, to suffer for their wickedness (crimes): without regard to the public advantage of such a system. But—to my mind fortunately—this is not at all what we are given. Roughly: insofar as Mabbott's view can be called retributive it is not a justification (satisfactory or otherwise),[7] and inso-

---

[7] Significantly, C. W. K. Mundle at Aberdeen and in a revised version of his paper to be published in the *Philosophical Quarterly* was unable to recognize Mabbott as a fellow retributionist.

far as any sort of justification is offered it is ideal (not hedonistic) utilitarian.

(i) Unfortunately, Mabbott never makes clear how far he is appealing to the meanings of words and how far to "our moral convictions": the confusion is easy for the latter are often incapsulated in the former; and expressions like "what we should say" are ambiguous as between moral and linguistic propriety. But it does seem as if his answer to his main question is intended to depend upon the very meaning of the word "punishment". Yet insofar as this is so he is not really offering a justification, based on retributive ethical claims; but a necessary truth drawn from, and elucidating the meaning of, "punishment".

It is interesting to compare here the position of F. H. Bradley: "Punishment is punishment only where it is deserved. We pay the penalty because we owe it, and for no other reason. If punishment is inflicted for any other reason whatever than because it is merited by a wrong, it is a gross immorality, a crying injustice, an abominable crime." (*Ethical Studies*, pp. 26-7.) This is similar to but not the same as Mabbott's position. Not the same; because Mabbott "dissents from most upholders of the retributive theory—from Hegel, from Bradley, and from Dr. Ross" (*loc. cit.*, p. 154) on the grounds that the essential link is between "crime" and "punishment" and not between "doing wrong" and "punishment". Similar; because both are confusing necessary truths with ethical claims: if Bradley's first and second sentences express necessary truths then the ethical claims made in the third are out of place; for if this is so, then however gross the immorality, crying the injustice and abominable the crime it *cannot* be punishment at all if it is not both deserved and paid because owed.

Furthermore, not only is Mabbott's "retributive justification"—insofar as it rests on an appeal to the meaning of "punishment"—not what it pretends to be, but this appeal itself cannot be made out completely. First, because while a *system* of 'punishing' people who had broken no laws could not be called a system of punishment, the term "punishment" is sufficiently vague to permit us to speak *in single cases and providing these do not become too numerous* (if they do become too numerous then *ipso facto* the use, the meaning, of "punishment" has changed) of punishing a man who has broken no law (or even done no wrong). This objection might be met by saying that the term already is more precise than we have allowed, or by now deciding to make it so. The effect of adopting the latter alternative—like that of all such manoeuvres with meanings—would be of course to shift and not to solve the *ethical* problems. (Consider the Rousseauian dialogue: Q. I know how to recognize the General Will: but is it always morally sound? A. The General Will is always upright—by definition. Q. But now how do I recognize it—so defined?) Second, because Mabbott wrote that "the *only justification* for punishing any man is that he has broken a law" (my italics); and it is surely impossible to draw the italicized point out of the present meaning of "punishment". One can only say that the question "Did he do it?" is always relevant to the question "Ought he to be punished?", or even that it is the only question which is always, because *necessarily*, relevant: appealing for this to the meaning of "punishment" as "an evil inflicted on an offender for an offence". But we cannot maintain that there is a contradiction involved in attempting to justify a single punishment for any reason other than that the victim has broken a law. Of course, this objection too could be met by a suitable adjustment of the meaning of "punishment"; though this adjustment would be both greater and harder to defend than that required to meet the former objection; and it would likewise involve a (not necessarily undesirable) shifting of any *ethical* problems, which cannot be dealt with by any manoeuvres with definitions.

(ii) Insofar as Mabbott's solution to

his problem is intended as an ethical claim it is open to grave objections. Taken in this way it is a claim that, while it does make sense to speak both of punishing those who have broken no law and of doing so for other reasons than this (with other justifications than this); the *sole* and *always requisite true* justification is that the victim has committed an offence. (Mabbott did not add "sufficient": presumably in order to allow for the possible justifiability of pardons and unjustifiability of enforcing certain laws.)

The objections both depend on what might be canonized as The Principle of the Multiplicity of Ethical Claims. Everyone who is not a one-track fanatic—which Mabbott emphatically is not—recognizes as *prima facie* valid grounds of obligation several ethical rules or claims: (indeed it might be said that a creature recognizing one and only one was not doing ethics at all, even fanatically). But to recognize several rules or claims which are logically independent is to open the way to both overdetermination and conflict: for it is to concede that it is at least logically possible that there can be circumstances both such that in them one claim reinforces another; and such that obeying one claim means disobeying another, satisfying one involves overriding another. And, fortunately in the former case, notoriously in the latter, with the set of claims which people actually do recognize, such circumstances do occur.

The objection to saying that the *sole* justification for punishing someone is that he has committed an offence is that Mabbott and almost everyone else would in fact allow that a punishment in certain circumstances was overdetermined in its justification—was justified twice over. Certainly: because, though Mabbott claims to "reject absolutely all utilitarian considerations from its justification", he is prepared to appeal to these to justify *systems* of punishment. But if a *system* is to be justified even partly on such grounds, some cases within that system must be partly justi-

fiable on the same grounds: the system surely could not have effects which no case within it contributed. (See III(*c*) below.)

The objection to saying that this justification is *always* requisite is that, if you allow any moral claims other than that only offenders ought to be punished, then in certain circumstances one of these might be conceded to have overriding force; and hence to justify the punishment of an innocent man; and hence to show that this retributive justification is not always requisite. Unless, of course, you are prepared to insist that no one who has not committed an offence ought ever to be 'punished' for it: though the heavens fall. And though it is probably true that the evil effects of such injustice will almost always outweigh the good; still, unless we can believe in some Providential guarantee that this is *always* so we cannot accept such a claim, and at the same time accept other claims which logically might sometimes override it,—the claim for instance to do what one can to prevent the fall of the heavens or some similar catastrophe.

We shall not argue further for these objections or provide illustrations: because Mabbott would no doubt be willing to admit them; and because this paper is in any case primarily concerned only with the prolegomena to ethical discussion. But one easy but mistaken assumption calls for notice: to show that something is just (or unjust) is not always and necessarily to show that it is justified (or unjustified); in spite of the common root and similar appearance of the words "just" and "justification". The sentence before "The only justification for punishing any man is that he has broken a law" was "Any criminal punished for any one of these reasons (*pour encourager les autres*, etc.—A.F.) is certainly unjustly punished". But the former is no sort of restatement of the latter: something may be just but open to all sorts of (moral or legal) objections; (and of course something may be just and it may be possible to justify it on further grounds). Again on p. 154 Mabbott seems to be making the same assumption, where he argues that even the most excellent consequences cannot "prove the punishment was just": for though this is true, they may nevertheless be conceded to *justify* the injustice.

(iii) A third interpretation of Mabbott's solution, which is perhaps nearest to what he actually had in mind when he wrote (as opposed to what he perhaps, or really, or ought to have, meant) is that "The only justification for punishing any man is that he has broken a law" amounts to an assertion that, if we are considering the punishment of a particular person on a particular occasion *and are accepting that the penal system is generally all right*, the sole consideration relevant to the question "Would it be justified or not?" is "Did he commit an offence for which this is the penalty prescribed?" (Omitting for the sake of simplicity and with Mabbott, questions of extenuation and excuse.) Whereas if we are considering the merits of a particular law, or the advantages of having a system of laws, or of a penal enforcement of those laws (as opposed perhaps to psychiatric enforcement by the compulsory treatment of offenders); then other and, particularly, utilitarian considerations are relevant.

This interpretation involves the most important distinction, which it is one of the chief merits of Mabbott's paper to underline, between systems and particular cases within those systems.[8] He criticizes, for instance, a writer who "confuses injustice within a penal system with the wrongfulness of a penal system" (p. 160) and later maintains that "it is essential to a legal system that the infliction of a particular punishment should *not* be determined by the good *that particular punishment* will do either to the criminal or 'society'. . . . One may consider the merits of a legal system or of a credit system but the acceptance of

either involves the surrender of utilitarian considerations in particular cases as they arise" (pp. 162-3).

The first objection to the position thus interpreted is that what Mabbott is saying in the passage just quoted is only *necessarily* true in the great majority not in all, particular cases: for there is no *contradiction* involved in saying that you accept a system but propose nevertheless to allow an occasional exception. This notion of "necessary truth in a great majority of cases" sounds scandalous and contradictory. It is perhaps a stumbling block; but it is not contradictory. It is just what is often needed in and appropriate to the "informal logic"[9] of the vague, elastic, concepts of everyday discourse (as opposed to the strict rigid "p" and "q" and "triangle" of the formal disciplines of mathematics and symbolic logic). It might have been used in II(*a*) above to make the point that, in the present meaning of "punishment" it is not incorrect to speak of punishment where one or other criterion for what we called a standard case of punishment is not satisfied, so long as these exceptional cases remain exceptional: we might have said that it is necessarily true in the great majority of cases that a punishment satisfies each (and all) of the criteria listed.

This being so, it is not possible to say that anyone accepting that there ought to be a system has committed himself to saying that utilitarian considerations are *necessarily* irrelevant to this or that particular case. The most that can be said—and this is very well worth saying—is that such a person is thereby committed to the surrender of utilitarian considerations in particular cases *as a rule*, a rule to which there can be exceptions. But, unfortunately, exceptional cases do not arrive labelled as such: so it is always open to someone to say that *this* is

---

[8] cf Hume *EPM* App. III 256.

[9] This phrase is borrowed from G. Ryle, "Ordinary Language", in *Philosophical Review*, April 1953: an invaluable exposition of the actual views and assumptions of those philosophers who "care what dustmen say".

the case where an exception ought to be made.

Mabbott's short way with misplaced utilitarianism, therefore, will not work. His mistake here can be seen as yet one more example of our perennial and pervasive failure to realize that the concepts of everyday discourse have not, and, if they are to do the sort of jobs they are needed to do, cannot have, the sharp outlines and rigidity of the concepts of the calculi of mathematics. Since this short way will not work perhaps it would be wise to re-examine, in a parallel excursus of our own, the sort of move which he handles so toughly in his *Excursus on Indirect Utilitarianism.*

"When I am in funds and consider whether I should pay my debts or give the same amount to charity, I must choose the former because repayment not only benefits my creditor ... but also upholds the general credit system" (pp. 155-6). "The view that a judge upholds ("ought to uphold"?—A.F.) a bad law in order that law in general should not suffer is indefensible" (p. 157.) Mabbott has two arguments against these appeals to the *indirectly* utilitarian (ethical) advantages of keeping promises, enforcing laws, repaying debts, in cases either where the *direct* results seem unlikely to be the best from a utilitarian point of view or where the *indirect* benefits may increase the balance of *direct* advantage. First, with Ross, he claims that the indirect consequences of single breaches of rules have been exaggerated. Second, with great emphasis as supposedly decisive, he claims that the indirect disadvantages of breaches are the consequences of people getting to know of the breaches, not of the breaches as such. "It follows that indirect utilitarianism is wrong in all such cases. For the argument can always be met by 'Keep it dark'" (p. 157).

But this, too, is too short a way with dissenters. The first claim is perhaps all very well; but, of course, a series of exceptions in single cases can add up to the effective abandonment of a general rule: and Mabbott himself is emphatic about the possible utilitarian advantages of having even a bad system of laws rather than no system at all. A beach is made up of single grains of sand. The second claim too is sound enough, but again the "indirect utilitarian" could argue that while the occurrence of single exceptions can, as a matter of fact, be kept dark (although it is almost impossible in *this* particular case to be sure that we shall succeed in suppression) it is, as a matter of fact, impossible to hush up the occurrence of a large number of exceptions: and large numbers are made up by the accumulation of units.

Of course such indirect utilitarian arguments[10]—depending as they do on *contingent* facts, about the actual effects upon the maintenance of a system of particular breaches of the prescriptions of that system, and about the possibilities of hushing up the occurrence of such breaches, cannot show that it is never and *necessarily* impossible to justify, upon utilitarian principles, the making of an exception by a breach of the prescriptions of a system, which can itself be justified upon utilitarian principles. To adapt one of Mabbott's own examples: suppose someone, having willed his property to be disposed of by a friend in accordance with private oral instructions, makes that friend promise to devote the money to a futile purpose; then, especially if the friend were the only witness of the making of that promise, even when all possible weight had been given to indirect utilitarian considerations of the importance of maintaining the system of promise-keeping and confidence in promises made; still it might be that the balance of good, on utilitarian principles, was overwhelm-

---

[10] It is the possibility of such indirect utilitarian arguments which ensures that properly thought out utilitarianisms are self-regulating doctrines. See I. M. Crombie "Social Clockwork" in D. M. MacKinnon's *Christian Faith and Communist Faith* (Macmillan, 1953), especially pp. 109f.

ingly on the side of breaking this particular promise, diverting the money to a beneficent purpose, and keeping the matter dark. Mabbott takes this as the *reductio ad absurdum* of any utilitarianism (ideal or hedonistic or what have you). Perhaps it is paradoxical, and perhaps it is repugnant to the present moral convictions of many or even most of us. But still a utilitarian might very well accept and even glory in the paradox: insisting that this was precisely the sort of case in which "our moral convictions" ought to be reformed.

"Reform" is surely a key word here: for at any rate the classical Utilitarians were concerned not merely with the reform of institutions but with the reform of ethical ideas and ethical reasoning. Mill's *Utilitarianism* is devoted to deciding "the controversy respecting the criterion of right and wrong" ("Everyman", p. 1): and phrases like "a test of right and wrong" (p. 2), "the moral standard set up by the theory" (p. 6), and "the utilitarian standard" significantly recur again and again. "Though the application of the standard may be difficult, it is better than none at all: while in other systems, the moral laws all claiming independent authority, there is no common umpire entitled to interfere between them" (p. 24). Mill refuses "to enquire how far the bad effects of this deficiency have been mitigated in practice, or to what extent the moral beliefs of mankind have been vitiated or made uncertain by the absence of any distinct recognition of an ultimate standard" (p. 8): but his phrasing makes clear his belief that there was a need for reform which he was hoping to meet. The burden of his charge against "the intuitive school of ethics" and of the corresponding claim for its "inductive" rival rests on the failure of the one and the success of the other in producing the test or standard required. And the acceptance of this alone makes possible a corresponding reform in ethical reasoning: "Whether happiness be or be not the end

to which morality should be referred—that it should be referred to an *end* of some sort, and not left in the dominion of vague feeling or inexplicable internal conviction, that it be made a matter of reason and calculation, and not merely of sentiment, is essential to the very idea of moral philosophy; is, in fact, what renders argument or discussion of moral questions possible" (Essay on *Bentham*).[11]

To return to the objections to Mabbott's solution in its third interpretation. The second objection is that on examination this resolves itself into one or the other of, or a confusion of, the other two. For either it amounts to saying that punishment is necessarily retributive, in the sense in which this thesis has already been examined and explained (in III (*b*) (*i*) above): the assertion that the sole consideration relevant to the question "Would it be justifiable to punish him?" is "Did he commit an offence for which this is the penalty prescribed?"; depending—allegedly—upon the very meaning of "punishment". Or it amounts to the same thing as the ethical claim (examined in III(*b*) (ii) above) that the sole and always requisite true justification for punishing a man is that he has committed the appropriate offence: but masquerading as a piece of logic (see II (*b*) above on *good reasons* in ethics). Decisions as to what is and is not to be allowed to be relevant in ethical discussions can—when the consideration concerned is not *necessarily relevant* (cf. III(*b*) (i) *ad*

[11] Perhaps we should emphasize here that, of course, Mill (though not Bentham) was very insistent indeed about the great importance of "secondary principles", and the proposed reform did not consist in or include anything so monstrous as the suggestion that we should "endeavour to test each individual action directly by the first principle" (p. 22). There is no need to expatiate here, in view of J. O. Urmson's recent powerful attack on these and other popular misconceptions of Mill (*Philosophical Quarterly*, 1953). But for a grim warning of the results of accepting this suggestion which Mill was not making, see Arthur Koestler's *Darkness at Noon*, on the Party "travelling without ethical ballast". Here the self-regulator—see footnote above—was not in use.

fin)—themselves be value decisions. Consider how my (really ethical) refusal to take into account the effects on, say, Egyptians or negroes of my actions could be given a logical look by saying that these are *irrelevant*: by refusing to admit as any sort of *reason* in any discussion about the right thing to do any statement of the form "That would harm E, an Egyptian, or N, a negro".[12]

To sum up this section (III(*b*)): the upshot is that in general there must be a 'retributive' element in punishment, inasmuch as punishments to be punishments must be of an offender for an offence; though this is not a matter of universal logical necessity but only of 'necessary truth in the great majority of cases', since there can be occasional exceptions. Mabbott's main mistakes were, I think: first, to insist that punishment is *necessarily and always* 'retributive' in this (non-ethical) sense; second, to think that such a supposedly necessary truth about punishment (or anything else) could constitute a retributive or any other sort of moral justification of it (or anything else). To attempt to justify from the concept alone is like trying to prove existence from the concept alone—The Ontological Argument. Though there is this at least to be said for it: that if "our moral convictions" are to be accepted as the arbiter, then the attempt to justify from the concept alone will amount to an appeal to the popular moral convictions incapsulated in ordinary language.

(c) *Overdetermination.*—Sometimes it seems to be assumed that there must be an inconsistency in justifying the adoption and enforcement of a law or a system of laws by *both* utilitarian *and* retributive appeals. But there is no necessary inconsistency in this, any more than there is in having advocated the nationalization of coal but now opposing the nationalization of chemicals or cement: though of course the people making these appeals or combining these policies may say other things, or offer supporting reasons, which do involve them in inconsistency. Thus, having a law against murder, or against any other sort of behavior which is reckoned to be wrong whether it is made illegal or not, can be defended *both* on the grounds that this makes for commodious living and against lives nasty, brutish, and short *and* on the grounds that it makes for wicked men getting their deserts. (I suspect that not only would most people resort to both sorts of arguments, but that Mill too would have done so— though he would have said that any "secondary principle" of retribution for ill-desert had *ultimately* to be justified by reference to the "first principle", the "Greatest Happiness Principle". I cannot hope to make good the historical claim here: but I refer again to Urmson's most excellent paper; and to the fact that Mill made "the turning point of the distinction between morality and simple expediency" that for wrong-doing "a person ought to be punished" (*loc. cit.*, p. 45).)

Perhaps philosophers have been misled into this assumption by undertaking to find a general comprehensive justification for all justified punishments; deceptively described as "a theory of punishment". This must commit them to producing: either an ethical claim which is to be insisted on in every case and to which no exceptions whatever will be admitted; or a necessary truth which obtains the universality required only at the cost of ceasing to be any sort of ethical justification.

IV

We have tried in this paper to bring out the main features of the logic of the expression "the justification of punishment"; and to apply the lessons to one outstanding

---

[12] "Mr. Lyttelton has helped to force through a federation based on the admitted policy of regarding African political opinions as irrelevant" (*Observer*, 23/8/53).

paper about the justification of punishment. We have not attempted, except insofar as was absolutely necessary, incidentally, to do any actual justification on our own account. Indeed the entire paper may be considered as prolegomena only: except that they are prolegomena of the sort which suggest that the latter enterprise—in the form of a comprehensive and universal enquiry as opposed to either a series of piecemeal jobs done in particular contexts or the attempt to find generally useful principles to which there will be occasional exceptions—was misconceived.

Free-Will and Psychoanalysis

JOHN HOSPERS

O Thou, who didst with pitfall and with gin
Beset the Road I was to wander in,
    Thou wilt not with Predestined Evil round
Enmesh, and then impute my Fall to Sin!
                —Edward FitzGerald,
    The Rubaiyat of Omar Khayyam.

It is extremely common for nonprofessional philosophers and iconoclasts to deny that human freedom exists, but at the same time to have no clear idea of what it is that they are denying to exist. The first thing that needs to be said about the free-will issue is that any meaningful term must have a meaningful opposite: if it is meaningful to assert that people are not free, it must be equally meaningful to assert that people *are* free, whether this latter assertion is in fact true or not. Whether it is true, of course, will depend on the meaning that is given the weasel-word "free." For example, if freedom is made dependent on indeterminism, it may well be that human freedom is nonexistent. But there seem to be no good grounds for asserting such a dependence, especially since lack of causation is the furthest thing from people's minds when they call an act free. Doubtless there are other senses that can be given to the word "free"—such as "able to do anything we want to do"—in which no human beings are free. But the first essential point about which the denier of freedom must be clear

Reprinted from Section 2 and part of Section 3 of the article "Meaning and Free-Will," *Philosophy and Phenomenological Research*, X, 1950 by permission of the publisher.

is *what* it is that he is denying. If one knows what it is like for people not to be free, one must know what it *would* be like for them to *be* free.

Philosophers have advanced numerous senses of "free" in which countless acts performed by human beings can truly be called free acts. The most common conception of a free act is that according to which an act is free if and only if it is a *voluntary* act. But the word "voluntary" does not always carry the same meaning. Sometimes to call an act voluntary means that we can do the act if we choose to do it: in other words, that it is physically and psychologically possible for us to do it, so that the occurrence of the act follows upon the decision to do it. (One's decision to raise his arm is in fact followed by the actual raising of his arm, unless he is a paralytic; one's decision to pluck the moon from the sky is not followed by the actual event.) Sometimes a voluntary act is conceived (as by Moore[1]) as an act which would not have occurred if, just beforehand, the agent had chosen not to perform it. But these senses are different from the sense in which a voluntary act is an act resulting from *deliberation*, or perhaps merely from *choice*. For example, there are many acts which we could have avoided, if we had chosen to do so, but which we nevertheless did not *choose* to perform, much less *deliberate* about them. The act of raising one's leg in the process of taking a step while out for a

[1] *Ethics*, pp. 15–16.

walk, is one which a person could have avoided by choosing to, but which, after one has learned to walk, takes place automatically or semi-automatically through habit, and thus is not the result of choice. (One may have chosen to take the walk, but not to take this or that step while walking.) Such acts are free in Moore's sense but are not free in the sense of being deliberate. Moreover, there are classes of acts of the same general character which are not even covered by Moore's sense: sudden outbursts of feeling, in some cases at least, could not have been avoided by an immediately preceding volition, so that if these are to be included under the heading of voluntary acts, the proviso that the act could have been avoided by an immediately preceding volition must be amended to read "could have been avoided by a volition or series of volitions by the agent *at some time in the past*"—such as the adoption of a different set of habits in the agent's earlier and more formative years.

(Sometimes we call *persons*, rather than their acts, free. Stebbing, for example, declares that one should never call acts free, but only the doers of the acts.[2] But the two do not seem irreconcilable: can we not speak of a *person* as free *with respect to a certain act* (never just free in general) if that *act* is free—whatever we may then go on to mean by saying that an act is free? Any statement about a free act can then be translated into a statement about the doer of the act.)

Now, no matter in which of the above ways we may come to define "voluntary," there are still acts which are voluntary *but which we would be very unlikely to think of as free*. Thus, when a person submits to the command of an armed bandit, he may do so voluntarily in every one of the above senses: he may do so as a result of choice, even of deliberation, and he could have avoided doing it by willing not to—he could, instead, have refused and been shot.

The man who reveals a state secret under torture does the same: he could have refused and endured more torture. Yet such acts, and persons in respect of such acts, are not generally called free. We say that they were performed *under compulsion*, and if an act is performed under compulsion we do not call it free. We say, "He wasn't free because he was forced to do as he did," though of course his act was voluntary.

This much departure from the identification of free acts with voluntary acts almost everyone would admit. Sometimes, however, it would be added that this is all the departure that can be admitted. According to Schlick, for example,

Freedom means the opposite of compulsion; a man is *free* if he does not act under *compulsion*, and he is compelled or unfree when he is hindered from without in the realization of his natural desires. Hence he is unfree when he is locked up, or chained, or when someone forces him at the point of a gun to do what otherwise he would not do. This is quite clear, and everyone will admit that the everyday or legal notion of the lack of freedom is thus correctly interpreted, and that a man will be considered quite free . . . if no such external compulsion is exerted upon him.[3]

Schlick adds that the entire vexed free-will controversy in philosophy is so much wasted ink and paper, because compulsion has been confused with causality and necessity with uniformity. If the question is asked whether every event is caused, the answer is doubtless yes; but if it is whether every event is compelled, the answer is clearly no. Free acts are uncompelled acts, not uncaused acts. Again, when it is said that some state of affairs (such as water flowing downhill) is necessary, if "necessary" means "compelled," the answer is no; if it means merely that it always happens that way, the answer is yes: universality of application is confused with compul-

---

[2] *Philosophy and the Physicists*, p. 212.

[3] *The Problems of Ethics*, Rynin translation, p. 150.

sion. And this, according to Schlick, is the end of the matter.

Schlick's analysis is indeed clarifying and helpful to those who have fallen victim to the confusions he exposes—and this probably includes most persons in their philosophical growing-pains. But *is* this the end of the matter? Is it true that all acts, though caused, are free as long as they are not compelled in the sense which he specifies? May it not be that, while the identification of "free" with "uncompelled" is acceptable, the area of compelled acts is vastly greater than he or most other philosophers have ever suspected? (Moore is more cautious in this respect than Schlick; while for Moore an act is free if it is voluntary in the sense specified above, he thinks there may be another sense in which human beings, and human acts, are not free at all.[4]) We remember statements about human beings being pawns of their early environment, victims of conditions beyond their control, the result of causal influences stemming from their parents, and the like, and we ponder and ask, "Still, are we really free?" Is there not something in what generations of sages have said about man being fettered? Is there not perhaps something too facile, too sleight-of-hand, in Schlick's cutting of the Gordian knot? For example, when a metropolitan newspaper headlines an article with the words "Boy Killer is Doomed Long before He Is Born,"[5] and then goes on to describe how a twelve-year-old boy has been sentenced to prison for the murder of a girl, and how his parental background includes records of drunkenness, divorce, social maladjustment, and paresis, are we still to say that his act, though voluntary and assuredly *not* done at the point of a gun, is free? The boy has early displayed a tendency toward sadistic activity to hide an underlying masochism and "prove that he's a man"; being coddled by his mother only worsens this tendency, until, spurned by a girl in his attempt on her, he kills her—not simply in a fit of anger, but calculatingly, deliberately. Is he free in respect of his criminal act, or for that matter in most of the acts of his life? Surely to ask this question is to answer it in the negative. Perhaps I have taken an extreme case; but it is only to show the superficiality of the Schlick analysis the more clearly. Though not everyone has criminotic tendencies, everyone has been moulded by influences which in large measure at least determine his present behavior; he is literally the product of these influences, stemming from periods prior to his "years of discretion," giving him a host of character traits that he cannot change now even if he would. So obviously does what a man is depend upon how a man comes to be, that it is small wonder that philosophers and sages have considered man far indeed from being the master of his fate. It is not as if man's will were standing high and serene above the flux of events that have moulded him; it is itself caught up in this flux, itself carried along on the current. An act is free when it is determined by the man's character, say moralists; but what if the most decisive aspects of his character were already irrevocably acquired before he could do anything to mould them? What if even the degree of will power available to him in shaping his habits and disciplining himself now to overcome the influence of his early environment is a factor over which he has no control? What are we to say of this kind of "freedom"? Is it not rather like the freedom of the machine to stamp labels on cans when it has been devised for just that purpose? Some machines can do so more efficiently than others, but only because they have been better constructed.

It is not my purpose here to establish this thesis in general, but only in one specific respect which has received comparatively little attention, namely, the field referred to by psychiatrists as that of unconscious motivation. In what follows I shall restrict my attention to it because it illus-

⁴ *Ethics*, Chapter 6, pp. 217 ff.
⁵ *New York Post*, Tuesday, May 18, 1948, p. 4.

trates as clearly as anything the points I wish to make.

Let me try to summarize very briefly the psychoanalytic doctrine on this point.[6] The conscious life of the human being, including the conscious decisions and volitions, is merely a mouthpiece for the unconscious—not directly for the enactment of unconscious drives, but of the compromise between unconscious drives and unconscious reproaches. There is a Big Three behind the scenes which the automaton called the conscious personality carries out: the id, an "eternal gimme," presents its wish and demands its immediate satisfaction; the super-ego says no to the wish immediately upon presentation, and the unconscious ego, the mediator between the two, tries to keep peace by means of compromise.[7]

To go into examples of the functioning of these three "bosses" would be endless; psychoanalytic case books supply hundreds of them. The important point for us to see in the present context is that *it is the unconscious that determines what the conscious impulse and the conscious action shall be.* Hamlet, for example, had a strong Oedipus wish, which was violently counteracted by super-ego reproaches; these early wishes were vividly revived in an unusual adult situation in which his uncle usurped the coveted position from Hamlet's father and won his mother besides. This situation evoked strong strictures on the part of

Hamlet's super-ego, and it was this that was responsible for his notorious delay in killing his uncle. A dozen times Hamlet could have killed Claudius easily; but every time Hamlet "decided" not to: a free choice, moralists would say—but no, listen to the super-ego: "What you feel such hatred toward your uncle for, what you are plotting to kill him for, is precisely the crime which you yourself desire to commit: to kill your father and replace him in the affections of your mother. Your fate and your uncle's are bound up together." This paralyzes Hamlet into inaction. Consciously all he knows is that he is unable to act; this conscious inability he rationalizes, giving a different excuse each time.[8]

We have always been conscious of the fact that we are not masters of our fate in every respect—that there are many things which we cannot do, that nature is more powerful than we are, that we cannot disobey laws without danger of reprisals, etc. We have become "officially" conscious, too, though in our private lives we must long have been aware of it, that we are not free with respect to the emotions that we feel—whom we love or hate, what types we admire, and the like. More lately still we have been reminded that there are unconscious motivations for our basic attractions and repulsions, our compulsive actions or inabilities to act. But what is not welcome news is that our very acts of volition, and the entire train of deliberations leading up to them, are but façades for the expression of unconscious wishes, or rather, unconscious compromises and defenses.

A man is faced by a choice: shall he kill another person or not? Moralists would say, here is a free choice—the result of deliberation, an action consciously entered into. And yet, though the agent himself does not know it, and has no awareness of

---

[6] I am aware that the theory presented below is not accepted by all practicing psychoanalysts. Many non-Freudians would disagree with the conclusions presented below. But I do not believe that this fact affects my argument, as long as the concept of unconscious motivation is accepted. I am aware, too, that much of the language employed in the following descriptions is animistic and metaphorical; but as long as I am presenting a view I would prefer to "go the whole hog" and present it in its most dramatic form. The theory can in any case be made clearest by the use of such language, just as atomic theory can often be made clearest to students with the use of models.

[7] This view is very clearly developed in Edmund Bergler, *Divorce Won't Help,* especially Chapter I.

[8] See *The Basic Writings of Sigmund Freud,* Modern Library Edition, p. 310 . (In *The Interpretation of Dreams.*) Cf. also the essay by Ernest Jones, "A Psycho-analytical Study of Hamlet."

the forces that are at work within him, his choice is already determined for him: his conscious will is only an instrument, a slave, in the hands of a deep unconscious motivation which determines his action. If he has a great deal of what the analyst calls "free-floating guilt," he will not; but if the guilt is such as to demand immediate absorption in the form of self-damaging behavior, this accumulated guilt will have to be discharged in some criminal action. The man himself does not know what the inner clockwork is; he is like the hands on the clock, thinking they move freely over the face of the clock.

A woman has married and divorced several husbands. Now she is faced with a choice for the next marriage: shall she marry Mr. A, or Mr. B, or nobody at all? She may take considerable time to "decide" this question and her decision may appear as a final triumph of her free will. Let us assume that A is a normal, well-adjusted, kind, and generous man, while B is a leech, an impostor, one who will become entangled constantly in quarrels with her. If she belongs to a certain classifiable psychological type, she will inevitably choose B, and she will do so even if her previous husbands have resembled B, so that one would think that she "had learned from experience." Consciously, she will of course "give the matter due consideration," etc., etc. To the psychoanalyst all this is irrelevant chaff in the wind—only a camouflage for the inner workings about which she knows nothing consciously. If she is of a certain kind of masochistic strain, as exhibited in her previous set of symptoms, she *must* choose B: her super-ego, always out to maximize the torment in the situation, seeing what dazzling possibilities for self-damaging behavior are promised by the choice of B, compels her to make the choice she does, and even to conceal the real basis of the choice behind an elaborate façade of rationalizations.

A man is addicted to gambling. In the service of his addiction he loses all his money, spends what belongs to his wife, even sells his property and neglects his children. For a time perhaps he stops; then, inevitably, he takes it up again. The man does not know that he is a victim rather than an agent; or, if he sometimes senses that he is in the throes of something-he-knows-not-what, he will have no inkling of its character and will soon relapse into the illusion that he (his conscious self) is freely deciding the course of his own actions. What he does not know, of course, is that he is still taking out on his mother the original lesion to his infantile narcissism, getting back at her for her fancied refusal of his infantile wishes—and this by rejecting everything identified with her, namely education, discipline, logic, common sense, training. At the roulette wheel, almost alone among adult activities, chance —the opposite of all these things—rules supreme; and his addiction represents his continued and emphatic reiteration of his rejection of Mother and all she represents to his unconscious.

This pseudo-aggression of his is of course masochistic in its effects. In the long run he always loses; he can never quit while he is winning. And far from playing in order to win, rather one can say that his losing is a *sine qua non* of his psychic equilibrium (as it was for example with Dostoyevsky): guilt demands punishment, and in the ego's "deal" with the super-ego the super-ego has granted satisfaction of infantile wishes in return for the self-damaging conditions obtaining. Winning would upset the neurotic equilibrium.[9]

A man has wash-compulsion. He must be constantly washing his hands—he uses up perhaps 400 towels a day. Asked why he

[9] See Edmund Bergler's article on the pathological gambler in *Diseases of the Nervous System* (1943). Also "Suppositions about the Mechanism of Criminosis," *Journal of Criminal Psychopathology* (1944) and "Clinical Contributions to the Psychogenesis of Alcohol Addiction," *Quarterly Journal of Studies on Alcohol*, 5:434 (1944).

does this, he says, "I need to, my hands are dirty"; and if it is pointed out to him that they are not really dirty, he says "They feel dirty anyway, I feel better when I wash them." So once again he washes them. He "freely decides" every time; he feels that he must wash them, he deliberates for a moment perhaps, but always ends by washing them. What he does not see, of course, are the invisible wires inside him pulling him inevitably to do the thing he does: the infantile id-wish concerns preoccupation with dirt, the super-ego charges him with this, and the terrified ego must respond, "No, I don't like dirt, see how clean I like to be, look how I wash my hands!"

Let us see what further "free acts" the same patient engages in (this is an actual case history): he is taken to a concentration camp, and given the worst of treatment by the Nazi guards. In the camp he no longer chooses to be clean, does not even try to be—on the contrary, his choice is now to wallow in filth as much as he can. All he is aware of now is a disinclination to be clean, and every time he must choose he chooses not to be. Behind the scenes, however, another drama is being enacted: the super-ego, perceiving that enough torment is being administered from the outside, can afford to cease pressing its charges in this quarter—the outside world is doing the torturing now, so the super-ego is relieved of the responsibility. Thus the ego is relieved of the agony of constantly making terrified replies in the form of washing to prove that the super-ego is wrong. The defense no longer being needed, the person slides back into what is his natural predilection anyway, for filth. This becomes too much even for the Nazi guards: they take hold of him one day, saying "We'll teach you how to be clean!" drag him into the snow, and pour bucket after bucket of icy water over him until he freezes to death. Such is the end-result of an original id-wish, caught in the machinations of a destroying super-ego.

Let us take, finally, a less colorful, more everyday example. A student at a university, possessing wealth, charm, and all that is usually considered essential to popularity, begins to develop the following personality-pattern: although well taught in the graces of social conversation, he always makes a *faux pas* somewhere, and always in the worst possible situation; to his friends he makes cutting remarks which hurt deeply—and always apparently aimed in such a way as to hurt the most: a remark that would not hurt A but would hurt B he invariably makes to B rather than to A, and so on. None of this is conscious. Ordinarily he is considerate of people but he contrives always (unconsciously) to impose on just those friends who would resent it most, and at just the times when he should know that he should not impose: at 3 o'clock in the morning, without forewarning, he phones a friend in a near-by city demanding to stay at his apartment for the weekend; naturally the friend is offended, but the person himself is not aware that he has provoked the grievance ("common sense" suffers a temporary eclipse when the neurotic pattern sets in, and one's intelligence, far from being of help in such a situation, is used in the interest of the neurosis), and when the friend is cool to him the next time they meet, he wonders why and feels unjustly treated. Aggressive behavior on his part invites resentment and aggression in turn, but all that he consciously sees is others' behavior towards him—and he considers himself the innocent victim of an unjustified "persecution."

Each of these acts is, from the moralist's point of view, free: he chose to phone his friend at 3 a.m.; he chose to make the cutting remark that he did, etc. What he does not know is that an ineradicable masochistic pattern has set in. His unconscious is far more shrewd and clever than is his conscious intellect; it sees with uncanny accuracy just what kind of behavior will damage him most, and unerringly forces him into that behavior. Consciously, the student "doesn't know why he did it"—he gives different "reasons" at different times, but they are all, once again, rationalizations cloaking the unconscious mechanism which propels him willy-nilly into actions that his "common sense" eschews.

The more of this sort of thing one observes, the more he can see what the psychoanalyst means when he talks about *the delusion of freedom*. And the more of a psychiatrist one becomes, the more he is overcome with a sense of what an illusion this free will can be. In some kinds of cases most of us can see it already: it takes no psychiatrist to look at the epileptic and sigh with sadness at the thought that soon this person before you will be as one possessed, not the same thoughtful intelligent person you knew. But people are not aware of this in other contexts, for example when they express surprise at how a person whom they have been so good to could treat them so badly. Let us suppose that you help a person financially or morally or in some other way, so that he is in your debt; suppose further that he is one of the many neurotics who unconsciously identify kindness with weakness and aggression with strength, then he will unconsciously take your kindness to him as weakness and use it as the occasion for enacting some aggression against you. He can't help it, he may regret it himself later; still, he will be driven to do it. If we gain a little knowledge of psychiatry, we can look at him with pity, that a person otherwise so worthy should be so unreliable—but we will exercise realism too, and be aware that there are some types of people that you cannot be good to; in "free" acts of their conscious volition, they will use your own goodness against you.

Sometimes the persons themselves will become dimly aware that "something behind the scenes" is determining their behavior. The divorcee will sometimes view herself with detachment, as if she were some machine (and indeed the psychoana-lyst does call her a "repeating-machine"): "I know I'm caught in a net, that I'll fall in love with this guy and marry him and the whole ridiculous merry-go-round will start all over again."

We talk about free will, and we say, for example, the person is free to do so-and-so if he can do so *if* he wants to—and we forget that his wanting to is itself caught up in the stream of determinism, that unconscious forces drive him into the wanting or not wanting to do the thing in question. The analogy of the puppet whose motions are manipulated from behind by invisible wires, or better still, by springs inside, is a telling one at almost every point.

And the glaring fact is that it all started so early, before we knew what was happening. The personality-structure is inelastic after the age of five, and comparatively so in most cases after the age of three. Whether one acquires a neurosis or not is determined by that age—and just as involuntarily as if it had been a curse of God. If, for example, a masochistic pattern was set up, under pressure of hyper-narcissism combined with real or fancied infantile deprivation, then the masochistic snowball was on its course downhill long before we or anybody else knew what was happening, and long before anyone could do anything about it. To speak of human beings as "puppets" in such a context is no idle metaphor, but a stark rendering of a literal fact: only the psychiatrist knows what puppets people really are; and it is no wonder that the protestations of philosophers that "the act which is the result of a volition, a deliberation, a conscious decision, is free" leave these persons, to speak mildly, somewhat cold.

But, one may object, all the states thus far described have been abnormal, neurotic ones. The well-adjusted (normal) person at least is free.

Leaving aside the question of how clearly and on what grounds one can distinguish the neurotic from the normal, let me use an illustration of a proclivity that everyone would call normal, namely, the decision of a man to support his wife and possibly a family, and consider briefly its genesis, according to psychoanalytic accounts.[10]

Every baby comes into the world with a full-fledged case of megalomania—interested only in himself, acting as if believing that he is the center of the universe and that others are present only to fulfill his wishes, and furious when his own wants are not satisfied immediately no matter for what reason. Gratitude, even for all the time and worry and care expended on him by the mother, is an emotion entirely foreign to the infant, and as he grows older it is inculcated in him only with the greatest difficulty; his natural tendency is to assume that everything that happens to him is due to himself, except for denials and frustrations, which are due to the "cruel, denying" outer world, in particular the mother; and that he owes nothing to anyone, is dependent on no one. This omnipotence-complex, or illusion of non-dependence, has been called the "autarchic fiction." Such a conception of the world is actually fostered in the child by the conduct of adults, who automatically attempt to fulfill the infant's every wish concerning nourishment, sleep, and attention. The child misconceives causality and sees in these wish-fulfillments not the result of maternal kindness and love, but simply the result of his own omnipotence.

This fiction of omnipotence is gradually destroyed by experience, and its destruction is probably the deepest disappointment of the early years of life. First of all, the infant discovers that he is the victim of organic urges and necessities: hunger, defecation, urination. More important, he discovers that the maternal breast, which he has not previously distinguished from his own body (he has not needed to, since it was available when he wanted it), is not

a part of himself after all, but of another creature upon whom he is dependent. He is forced to recognize this, e.g., when he wants nourishment and it is at the moment not present; even a small delay is most damaging to the "autarchic fiction." Most painful of all is the experience of weaning, probably the greatest tragedy in every baby's life, when his dependence is most cruelly emphasized; it is a frustrating experience because what he wants is no longer there at all; and if he has been able to some extent to preserve the illusion of non-dependence heretofore, he is not able to do so now—it is plain that the source of his nourishment is not dependent on him, but he on it. The shattering of the autarchic fiction is a great disillusionment to every child, a tremendous blow to his ego which he will, in one way or another, spend the rest of his life trying to repair. How does he do this?

First of all, his reaction to frustration is anger and fury; and he responds by kicking, biting, etc., the only ways he knows. But he is motorically helpless, and these measures are ineffective, and only serve to emphasize his dependence the more. Moreover, against such responses of the child the parental reaction is one of prohibition, often involving deprivation of attention and affection. Generally the child soon learns that this form of rebellion is profitless, and brings him more harm than good. He wants to respond to frustration with violent aggression, and at the same time learns that he will be punished for such aggression, and that in any case the latter is ineffectual. What face-saving solution does he find? Since he must "face facts," since he must in any case "conform" if he is to have any peace at all, he tries to make it seem as if he himself is the source of the commands and prohibitions: the *external* prohibitive force is *internalized*—and here we have the origin of conscience. By making the prohibitive agency seem to come from within himself, the child can "save face"—as if saying, "The prohibition

[10] E.g., Edmund Bergler, *The Battle of the Conscience*, Chapter I.

comes from within me, not from outside, so I'm not subservient to external rule, I'm only obeying rules I've set up myself," thus to some extent saving the autarchic fiction, and at the same time avoiding unpleasant consequences directed against himself by complying with parental commands.

Moreoever, the boy[11] has unconsciously never forgiven the mother for his dependence on her in early life, for nourishment and all others things. It has upset his illusion of non-dependence. These feelings have been repressed and are not remembered; but they are acted out in later life in many ways—e.g., in the constant deprecation man has for woman's duties such as cooking and housework of all sorts ("All she does is stay home and get together a few meals, and she calls that work"), and especially in the man's identification with the mother in his sex experiences with women. By identifying with someone one cancels out in effect the person with whom he identifies—replacing that person, unconsciously denying his existence; for the man, identifying with his early mother, playing the active role in "giving" to his wife as his mother has "given" to him, is in effect expressing the denial of his mother's existence, a fact which is narcissistically embarrassing to his ego because it is chiefly responsible for shattering his autarchic fiction. In supporting his wife, he can unconsciously deny that his mother gave to him, and that he was dependent on her giving. Why is it that the husband plays the provider, and wants his wife to be dependent on no one else, although twenty years before he was nothing but a parasitic baby? This is a face-saving device on his part: he can act out the reasoning "See, I'm not the parasitic baby, on the contrary I'm the provider, the giver." His playing the provider is a

constant face-saving device, to deny his early dependence which is so embarrassing to his ego. It is no wonder that men generally dislike to be reminded of their babyhood, when they were dependent on woman.

Thus we have here a perfectly normal adult reaction which is unconsciously motivated. The man "chooses" to support a family—and his choice is an unconsciously motivated as anything could be. (I have described here only the "normal" state of affairs, uncomplicated by the well-nigh infinite number of variations that occur in actual practice.)

Now, what of the notion of responsibility? What happens to it on our analysis?

Let us begin with an example, not a fictitious one. A woman and her two-year-old baby are riding on a train to Montreal in mid-winter. The child is ill. The woman wants badly to get to her destination. She is, unknown to herself, the victim of a neurotic conflict whose nature is irrelevant here except for the fact that it forces her to behave aggressively toward the child, partly to spite her husband whom she despises and who loves the child, but chiefly to ward off super-ego charges of masochistic attachment. Consciously she loves the child, and when she says this she says it sincerely, but she must behave aggressively toward it nevertheless, just as many children love their mothers but are nasty to them most of the time in neurotic pseudo-aggression. The child becomes more ill as the train approaches Montreal; the heating system of the train is not working, and the conductor pleads with the woman to get off the train at the next town and get the child to a hospital at once. The woman refuses. Soon after, the child's condition worsens, and the mother does all she can to keep it alive, without, however, leaving the train, for she declares that it is absolutely necessary that she reach her destination. But before she gets there the child is dead. After that, of course, the mother grieves, blames herself, weeps hysterically,

---

[11] The girl's development after this point is somewhat different. Society demands more aggressiveness of the adult male, hence there are more super-ego strictures on tendencies toward passivity in the male; accordingly his defenses must be stronger.

and joins the church to gain surcease from the guilt that constantly overwhelms her when she thinks of how her aggressive behavior has killed her child.

Was she responsible for her deed? In ordinary life, after making a mistake, we say, "Chalk it up to experience." Here we should say, "Chalk it up to the neurosis." *She* could not help it if her neurosis forced her to act this way—she didn't even know what was going on behind the scenes, her conscious self merely acted out its assigned part. This is far more true than is generally realized: criminal actions in general are not actions for which their agents are responsible; the agents are passive, not active—they are victims of a neurotic conflict. Their very hyper-activity is unconsciously determined.

To say this is, of course, not to say that we should not punish criminals. Clearly, for our own protection, we must remove them from our midst so that they can no longer molest and endanger organized society. And, of course, if we use the word "responsible" in such a way that justly to hold someone responsible for a deed is by definition identical with being justified in punishing him, then we can and do hold people responsible. But this is like the sense of "free" in which free acts are voluntary ones. It does not go deep enough. In a deeper sense we cannot hold the person responsible: we can hold his neurosis responsible, but *he is not responsible for his neurosis*, particularly since the age at which its onset was inevitable was an age before he could even speak.

The neurosis is responsible—but isn't the neurosis of part of *him*? We have been speaking all the time as if the person and his unconscious were two separate beings; but isn't he one personality, including conscious and unconscious departments together?

I do not wish to deny this. But it hardly helps us here; for what people want when they talk about freedom, and what

they hold to when they champion it, is the idea that the *conscious* will is the master of their destiny. "I am the master of my fate, I am the captain of my soul"—and they surely mean their conscious selves, the self that they can recognize and search and introspect. Between an unconscious that willy-nilly determines your actions, and an external force which pushes you, there is little if anything to choose. The unconscious is just *as if* it were an outside force; and indeed, psychiatrists will assert that the inner Hitler (your super-ego) can torment you far more than any external Hitler can. Thus the kind of freedom that people want, the only kind they will settle for, is precisely the kind that psychiatry says that they cannot have.

Heretofore it was pretty generally thought that, while we could not rightly blame a person for the color of his eyes or the morality of his parents, or even for what he did at the age of three, or to a large extent what impulses he had and whom he fell in love with, one *could* do so for other of his adult activities, particularly the acts he performed voluntarily and with premeditation. Later this attitude was shaken. Many voluntary acts came to be recognized, at least in some circles, as compelled by the unconscious. Some philosophers recognized this too—Ayer[12] talks about the kleptomaniac being unfree, and about a person being unfree when another person exerts a habitual ascendancy over his personality. But this is as far as he goes. The usual examples, such as the kleptomaniac and the schizophrenic, apparently satisfy most philosophers, and with these exceptions removed, the rest of mankind is permitted to wander in the vast and alluring fields of freedom and responsibility. So far, the inroads upon freedom left the vast majority of humanity untouched; they began to hit home when psychiatrists began to realize, though philosophers did

[12] A. J. Ayer, "Freedom and Necessity," *Polemic* (September-October 1946), pp. 40–43.

not, that the domination of the conscious by the unconscious extended, not merely to a few exceptional individuals, but to all human beings, that the "big three behind the scenes" are not respecters of persons, and dominate us all, even including that *sanctum sanctorum* of freedom, our conscious will. To be sure, the domination by the unconscious in the case of "normal" individuals is somewhat more benevolent than the tyranny and despotism exercised in neurotic cases, and therefore the former have evoked less comment; but the principle remains in all cases the same: the unconscious is the master of every fate and the captain of every soul.

We speak of a machine turning out good products most of the time but every once in a while it turns out a "lemon." We do not, of course, hold the product responsible for this, but the machine, and via the machine, its maker. Is it silly to extend to inanimate objects the idea of responsibility? Of course. But is it any less so to employ the notion in speaking of human creatures? Are not the two kinds of cases analogous in countless important ways? Occasionally a child turns out badly too, even when his environment and training are the same as that of his brothers and sisters who turn out "all right." He is the "bad penny." His acts of rebellion against parental discipline in adult life (such as the case of the gambler, already cited) are traceable to early experiences of real or fancied denial of infantile wishes. Sometimes the denial had been real, though many denials are absolutely necessary if the child is to grow up to observe the common decencies of civilized life; sometimes, if the child has an unusual quantity of narcissism, every event that occurs is interpreted by him as a denial of his wishes, and nothing a parent could do, even granting every humanly possible wish, would help. In any event, the later neurosis can be attributed to this. Can the person himself be held responsible? Hardly. If he engages in activities which are a menace to society, he must be put into prison, of course, but responsibility is another matter. The time when the events occurred which rendered his neurotic behavior inevitable was a time long before he was capable of thought and decision. As an adult, he is a victim of a world he never made—only this world is inside him.

What about the children who turn out "all right"? All we can say is that "it's just lucky for them" that what happened to their unfortunate brother didn't happen to them; *through no virtue of their own* they are not doomed to the life of unconscious guilt, expiation, conscious depression, terrified ego-gestures for the appeasement of a tyrannical super-ego, that he is. The machine turned them out with a minimum of damage. But if the brother cannot be blamed for his evils, neither can they be praised for their good; unless, of course, we should blame people for what is not their fault, and praise them for lucky accidents.

We all agree that machines turn out "lemons," we all agree that nature turns out misfits in the realm of biology—the blind, the crippled, the diseased; but we hesitate to include the realm of the personality, for here, it seems, is the last retreat of our dignity as human beings. Our ego can endure anything but this; this island at least must remain above the encroaching flood. But may not precisely the same analysis be made here also? Nature turns out psychological "lemons" too, in far greater quantities than any other kind; and indeed all of us are "lemons" in some respect or other, the difference being one of degree. Some of us are lucky enough not to have a gambling-neurosis or criminotic tendencies or masochistic mother-attachment or overdimensional repetition-compulsion to make our lives miserable, but most of our actions, those usually considered the most important, are unconsciously dominated just the same. And, if a neurosis may be likened to a curse of God, let those of us, the elect, who are enabled to enjoy a measure of life's happiness without the hell-fire of neurotic guilt, take this, not as our own achievement, but simply for what it is—a gift of God.

Let us, however, quit metaphysics and put the situation schematically in the form of a deductive argument.

1. An occurrence over which we had no control is something we cannot be held responsible for.

2. Events E, occurring during our babyhood, were events over which we had no control.

3. Therefore events E were events which we cannot be held responsible for.

4. But if there is something we cannot be held responsible for, neither can we be held responsible for something that inevitably results from it.

5. Events E have as inevitable consequence Neurosis N, which in turn has an inevitable consequence Behavior B.

6. Since N is the inevitable consequence of E and B is the inevitable consequence of N, B is the inevitable consequence of E.

7. Hence, not being responsible for E, we cannot be responsible for B.

In Samuel Butler's Utopian satire *Erewhon* there occurs the following passage, in which a judge is passing sentence on a prisoner:

It is all very well for you to say that you came of unhealthy parents, and had a severe accident in your childhood which permanently undermined your constitution; excuses such as these are the ordinary refuge of the criminal; but they cannot for one moment be listened to by the ear of justice. I am not here to enter upon curious metaphysical questions as to the origin of this or that—questions to which there would be no end were their introduction once tolerated, and which would result in throwing the only guilt on the tissues of the primordial cell, or on the elementary gases. There is no question of how you came to be wicked, but only this—namely, are you wicked or not? This

has been decided in the affirmative, neither can I hesitate for a single moment to say that it has been decided justly. You are a bad and dangerous person, and stand branded in the eyes of your fellow countrymen with one of the most heinous known offenses.[13]

As moralists read this passage, they may perhaps nod with approval. But the joke is on them. The sting comes when we realize what the crime is for which the prisoner is being sentenced: namely, consumption. The defendant is reminded that during the previous year he was sentenced for aggravated bronchitis, and is warned that he should profit from experience in the future. Butler is employing here his familiar method of presenting some human tendency (in this case, holding people responsible for what isn't their fault) to a ridiculous extreme and thereby reducing it to absurdity.

Assuming the main conclusion of this paper to be true, is there any room left for freedom?

This, of course, all depends on what we mean by "freedom." In the senses suggested at the beginning of this paper, there are countless free acts, and unfree ones as well. When "free" means "uncompelled," and only external compulsion is admitted, again there are countless free acts. But now we have extended the notion of compulsion to include determination by unconscious forces. With this sense in mind, our question is, "With the concept of compulsion thus extended, and in the light of present psychoanalytic knowledge, is there any freedom left in human behavior?"

If practicising psychoanalysts were asked this question, there is little doubt that their answer would be along the following lines: they would say that they were not accustomed to using the term "free" at all, but that if they had to suggest a criterion for distinguishing the free from the unfree, they would say that a person's

[13] Samuel Butler, *Erewhon* (Modern Library edition), p. 107.

freedom is present *in inverse proportion to his neuroticism*; in other words, the more his acts are determined by a *malevolent* unconscious, the less free he is. Thus they would speak of *degrees* of freedom. They would say that as a person is cured of his neurosis, he becomes more free—free to realize capabilities that were blocked by the neurotic affliction. The psychologically well-adjusted individual is in this sense comparatively the most free. Indeed, those who are cured of mental disorders are sometimes said to have *regained their freedom*: they are freed from the tyranny of a malevolent unconscious which formerly exerted as much of a domination over them as if they had been the abject slaves of a cruel dictator.

But suppose one says that a person is free only to the extent that his acts are *not unconsciously determined at all*, be the unconscious benevolent *or* malevolent? If this is the criterion, psychoanalysts would say, most human behavior cannot be called free at all: our impulses and volitions having to do with our basic attitudes toward life, whether we are optimists or pessimists, tough-minded or tender-minded, whether our tempers are quick or slow, whether we are "naturally self-seeking" or "naturally benevolent" (and *all the acts consequent upon these things*), what things annoy us, whether we take to blondes or brunettes, old or young, whether we become philosophers or artists or businessmen—all this has its basis in the unconscious. If people generally call most acts free, it is not because they believe that compelled acts should be called free, it is rather through not knowing how large a proportion of our acts actually are compelled. Only the comparatively "vanilla-flavored" aspects of our lives—such as our behavior toward people who don't really matter to us—are exempted from this rule.

These, I think, are the two principal criteria for distinguishing freedom from the lack of it which we might set up on the basis of psychoanalytic knowledge. Conceivably we might set up others. In every case, of course, it remains trivially true that "it all depends on how we choose to use the word." The facts are what they are, regardless of what words we choose for labeling them. But if we choose to label them in a way which is not in accord with what human beings, however vaguely, have long had in mind in applying these labels, as we would be doing if we labeled as "free" many acts which we know as much about as we now do through modern psychoanalytic methods, then we shall only be manipulating words to mislead our fellow creatures.

The Humanitarian Theory of Punishment

C. S. LEWIS

In England we have had a controversy about Capital Punishment. I do not know whether a murderer is more likely to repent and make a good end on the gallows a few weeks after his trial or in the prison infirmary thirty years later. I do not know whether the fear of death is an indispensable deterrent. I need not, for the purpose of this article, decide whether it is a morally permissible deterrent. Those are questions which I propose to leave untouched. My subject is not Capital Punishment in particular, but that theory of punishment in general which the controversy showed to be almost universal among my fellow-countrymen. It may be called the Humanitarian theory. Those who hold it think that it is mild and merciful. In this I believe that they are seriously mistaken. I believe that the "Humanity" which it claims is a dangerous illusion and disguises the possibility of cruelty and injustice without end. I urge a return to the traditional or Retributive theory not solely, not even primarily, in the interests of society, but in the interests of the criminal.

According to the Humanitarian theory, to punish a man because he deserves it, and as much as he deserves, is mere revenge, and therefore, barbarous and immoral. It is maintained that the only legitimate motives for punishing are the desire to deter others by example or to mend the criminal. When this theory is combined, as frequently happens, with the belief that all crime is more or less pathological, the idea of mending tails off into that of healing or curing and punishment becomes therapeutic. Thus it appears at first sight that we have passed from the harsh and self-righteous notion of giving the wicked their deserts to the charitable and enlightened one of tending the psychologically sick. What could be more amiable? One little point which is taken for granted in this theory needs, however, to be made explicit. The things done to the criminal, even if they are called cures, will be just as compulsory as they were in the old days when we called them punishments. If a tendency to steal can be cured by psychotherapy, the thief will no doubt be forced to undergo the treatment. Otherwise, society cannot continue.

My contention is that this doctrine, merciful though it appears, really means that each one of us, from the moment he breaks the law, is deprived of the rights of a human being.

The reason is this. The Humanitarian theory removes from Punishment the concept of Desert. But the concept of Desert is the only connecting link between punishment and justice. It is only as deserved or undeserved that a sentence can be just or unjust. I do not here contend that the ques-

Reprinted from *Res Judicatae*, VI, 1953, pp. 224–230, by permission of the publisher.

tion "Is it deserved?" is the only one we can reasonably ask about a punishment. We may very properly ask whether it is likely to deter others and to reform the criminal. But neither of these two last questions is a question about justice. There is no sense in talking about a "just deterrent" or a "just cure." We demand of a deterrent not whether it is just but whether it will deter. We demand of a cure not whether it is just but whether it succeeds. Thus when we cease to consider what the criminal deserves and consider only what will cure him or deter others, we have tacitly removed him from the sphere of justice altogether; instead of a person, a subject of rights, we now have a mere object, a patient, a "case."

The distinction will become clearer if we ask who will be qualified to determine sentences when sentences are no longer held to derive their propriety from the criminal's deservings. On the old view the problem of fixing the right sentence was a moral problem. Accordingly, the judge who did it was a person trained in jurisprudence; trained, that is, in a science which deals with rights and duties, and which, in origin at least, was consciously accepting guidance from the Law of Nature, and from Scripture. We must admit that in the actual penal code of most countries at most times these high originals were so much modified by local custom, class interests, and utilitarian concessions, as to be very imperfectly recognizable. But the code was never in principle, and not always in fact, beyond the control of the conscience of the society. And when (say, in eighteenth-century England) actual punishments conflicted too violently with the moral sense of the community, juries refused to convict and reform was finally brought about. This was possible because, so long as we are thinking in terms of Desert, the propriety of the penal code, being a moral question, is a question on which every man has the right to an opinion, not because he follows this or that profession, but because

he is simply a man, a rational animal enjoying the Natural Light. But all this is changed when we drop the concept of Desert. The only two questions we may now ask about a punishment are whether it deters and whether it cures. But these are not questions on which anyone is entitled to have an opinion simply because he is a man. He is not entitled to an opinion even if, in addition to being a man, he should happen also to be a jurist, a Christian, and a moral theologian. For they are not questions about principle but about matter of fact; and for such *cuiquam in sua arte credendum*. Only the expert "penologist" (let barbarous things have barbarous names), in the light of previous experiment, can tell us what is likely to deter: only the psychotherapist can tell us what is likely to cure. It will be in vain for the rest of us, speaking simply as men, to say, "but this punishment is hideously unjust, hideously disproportionate to the criminal's deserts." The experts with perfect logic will reply "but nobody was talking about deserts. No one was talking about *punishment* in your archaic vindictive sense of the word. Here are the statistics proving that this treatment deters. Here are the statistics proving that this other treatment cures. What is your trouble?"

The Humanitarian theory, then, removes sentences from the hands of jurists whom the public conscience is entitled to criticize and places them in the hands of technical experts whose special sciences do not even employ such categories as rights or justice. It might be argued that since this transference results from an abandonment of the old idea of punishment, and therefore, of all vindictive motives, it will be safe to leave our criminals in such hands. I will not pause to comment on the simple-minded view of fallen human nature which such a belief implies. Let us rather remember that the "cure" of criminals is to be compulsory; and let us then watch how the theory actually works in the mind of the Humanitarian. The immediate starting point of this article was a letter I read in one of our Leftist weeklies. The author was pleading that a certain sin, now treated by our laws as a crime, should henceforward be treated as a disease. And he complained that under the present system the offender, after a term in gaol, was simply let out to return to his original environment where he would probably relapse. What he complained of was not the shutting up but the letting out. On his remedial view of punishment the offender should, of course, be detained until he was cured. And of course the official straighteners are the only people who can say when that is. The first result of the Humanitarian theory is, therefore, to substitute for a definite sentence (reflecting to some extent the community's moral judgment on the degree of ill-desert involved) an indefinite sentence terminable only by the word of those experts—and they are not experts in moral theology nor even in the Law of Nature—who inflict it. Which of us, if he stood in the dock, would not prefer to be tried by the old system?

It may be said that by the continued use of the word punishment and the use of the verb "inflict" I am misrepresenting Humanitarians. They are not punishing, not inflicting, only healing. But do not let us be deceived by a name. To be taken without consent from my home and friends; to lose my liberty; to undergo all those assaults on my personality which modern psychotherapy knows how to deliver; to be re-made after some pattern of "normality" hatched in a Viennese laboratory to which I never professed allegiance; to know that this process will never end until either my captors have succeeded or I grown wise enough to cheat them with apparent success—who cares whether this is called Punishment or not? That it includes most of the elements for which any punishment is feared—shame, exile, bondage, and years eaten by the locust—is obvious. Only enormous ill-desert could justify it; but ill-desert is the very conception which the

Humanitarian theory has thrown overboard.

If we turn from the curative to the deterrent justification of punishment we shall find the new theory even more alarming. When you punish a man *in terrorem*, make of him an "example" to others, you are admittedly using him as a means to an end; someone else's end. This, in itself, would be a very wicked thing to do. On the classical theory of Punishment it was of course justified on the ground that the man deserved it. That was assumed to be established before any question of "making him an example" arose. You then, as the saying is, killed two birds with one stone; in the process of giving him what he deserved you set an example to others. But take away desert and the whole morality of the punishment disappears. Why, in Heaven's name, am I to be sacrificed to the good of society in this way?—unless, of course, I deserve it.

But that is not the worst. If the justification of exemplary punishment is not to be based on desert but solely on its efficacy as a deterrent, it is not absolutely necessary that the man we punish should even have committed the crime. The deterrent effect demands that the public should draw the moral, "If we do such an act we shall suffer like that man." The punishment of a man actually guilty whom the public think innocent will not will not have the desired effect; the punishment of a man actually innocent will, provided the public think him guilty. But every modern State has powers which make it easy to fake a trial. When a victim is urgently needed for exemplary purposes and a guilty victim cannot be found, all the purposes of deterrence will be equally served by the punishment (call it "cure" if you prefer) of an innocent victim, provided that the public can be cheated into thinking him guilty. It is no use to ask me why I assume that our rulers will be so wicked. The punishment of an innocent, that is, an undeserving, man is wicked only if we grant the traditional view that righteous punishment means deserved punishment. Once we have abandoned that criterion, all punishments have to be justified, if at all, on other grounds that have nothing to do with desert. Where the punishment of the innocent can be justified on those grounds (and it could in some cases be justified as a deterrent) it will be no less moral than any other punishment. Any distaste for it on the part of a Humanitarian will be merely a hang-over from the Retributive theory.

It is indeed, important to notice that my argument so far supposes no evil intentions on the part of the Humanitarian and considers only what is involved in the logic of his position. My contention is that good men (not bad men) consistently acting upon that position would act as cruelly and unjustly as the greatest tyrants. They might in some respects act even worse. Of all tyrannies a tyranny sincerely exercised for the good of its victims may be the most oppressive. It may be better to live under robber barons than under omnipotent moral busybodies. The robber baron's cruelty may sometimes sleep, his cupidity may at some point be satiated; but those who torment us for our own good will torment us without end for they do so with the approval of their own conscience. They may be more likely to go Heaven yet at the same time likelier to make a Hell of earth. Their very kindness stings with intolerable insult. To be "cured" against one's will and cured of states which we may not regard as disease is to be put on a level with those who have not yet reached the age of reason or those who never will; to be classed with infants, imbeciles, and domestic animals. But to be punished, however severely, because we have deserved it, because we "ought to have known better," is to be treated as a human person made in God's image.

In reality, however, we must face the possibility of bad rulers armed with a Humanitarian theory of punishment. A great many popular blue prints for a Christian society are merely what the Elizabethans called "eggs in moonshine" because they assume that the whole society is Christian or that the Christians are in control. This is not so in most contemporary States. Even if it were, our rulers would still be fallen men, and therefore, neither very wise nor very good. As it is, they will usually be unbelievers. And since wisdom and virtue are not the only or the commonest qualifications for a place in the government, they will not often be even the best unbelievers. The practical problem of Christian politics is not that of drawing up schemes for a Christian society, but that of living as innocently as we can with unbelieving fellow-subjects under unbelieving rulers who will never be perfectly wise and good and who will sometimes be very wicked and very foolish. And when they are wicked the Humanitarian theory of punishment will put in their hands a finer instrument of tyranny than wickedness ever had before. For if crime and disease are to be regarded as the same thing, it follows that any state of mind which our masters choose to call "disease" can be treated as crime; and compulsorily cured. It will be vain to plead that states of mind which displease government need not always involve moral turpitude and do not therefore always deserve forfeiture of liberty. For our masters will not be using the concepts of Desert and Punishment but those of disease and cure. We know that one school of psychology already regards religion as a neurosis. When this particular neurosis becomes inconvenient to government, what is to hinder government from proceeding to "cure" it? Such "cure" will, of course, be compulsory; but under the Humanitarian theory it will not be called by the shocking name of Persecution. No one will blame us for being Christian, no one will hate us, no one will revile us. The new Nero will approach us with the silky manners of a doctor, and though all will be in fact as compulsory as the *tunica molesta* or Smithfield or Tyburn, all will go on within the unemotional therapeutic sphere where words like "right" and "wrong" or "freedom" and "slavery" are never heard. And thus when the command is given, every prominent Christian in the land may vanish overnight into Institutions for the Treatment of the Ideologically Unsound, and it will rest with the expert gaolers to say when (if ever) they are to re-emerge. But it will not be persecution. Even if the treatment is painful, even if it is life-long, even if it is fatal, that will be only a regrettable accident; the intention was purely therapeutic. Even in ordinary medicine there were painful operations and fatal operations; so in this. But because they are "treatment," not punishment, they can be criticized only by fellow-experts and on technical grounds, never by men as men and on grounds of justice.

This is why I think it essential to oppose the Humanitarian theory of punishment, root and branch, wherever we encounter it. It carries on its front a semblance of mercy which is wholly false. That is how it can deceive men of good will. The error began, perhaps, with Shelley's statement that the distinction between mercy and justice was invented in the courts of tyrants. It sounds noble, and was indeed the error of a noble mind. But the distinction is essential. The older view was that mercy "tempered" justice, or (on the highest level of all) that mercy and justice had met and kissed. The essential act of mercy was to pardon; and pardon in its very essence involves the recognition of guilt and ill-desert in the recipient. If crime is only a disease which needs cure, not sin which deserves punishment, it cannot be pardoned. How can you pardon a man for having a gumboil or a club foot? But the Humanitarian theory wants simply to abolish Justice and substitute Mercy for it. This means that you start being "kind" to people before you have considered their rights, and then force upon them supposed kindnesses which they in fact had a right to refuse, and finally kindnesses which no one but you will recognize as kindnesses and which the recipient will feel as abominable cruelties. You have overshot the mark. Mercy, detached from Justice, grows unmerciful. That is the important paradox. As there are plants which will flourish only in mountain soil, so it appears that Mercy will flower only when it grows in the crannies of the rock of Justice: transplanted to the marshlands of mere Humanitarianism, it becomes a man-eating weed, all the more dangerous because it is still called by the same name as the mountain variety. But we ought long ago to have learned our lesson. We should be too old now to be deceived by those humane pretensions which have served to usher in every cruelty of the revolutionary period in which we live. These are the "precious balms" which will "break our heads."

The Humanitarian Theory of Punishment

J. J. C. SMART

I wish to discuss one or two logical points which arise out of C. S. Lewis's article on "The Humanitarian Theory of Punishment"[1] . . . Lewis has got at cross purposes with himself in a way very similar to that in which Intuitionists and Utilitarians in moral philosophy have often entangled themselves when arguing about the nature of obligation.

Consider these two sorts of questions: (1) "Ought Smith to leave his wife?" "Ought I to return this book?" "Ought I to drive on this side of the road?" and (2) "Are our present marriage customs for the best?" "Is the institution of promise making a good one?" "Ought we to have a rule of the road and if so what?" I shall call the first sort of questions "first-order questions" and the second sort of questions "second-order questions". We can now say, roughly, that the Intuitionists were right when they dealt with the first-order questions, but hopelessly at sea when they dealt with the second-order questions, while the Utilitarians were able to talk a great deal of sense when they discussed the second-order questions but were most strained and unplausible when they dealt with the first-order questions. The dispute in moral philosophy was so fruitless because each had (roughly) the right answer to one sort of question but not to the other. No one in his senses would weigh up the social consequences of returning a book he has borrowed: there is a moral rule that plainly covers the case and so he knows immediately what he should do. It is about *rules* and *social institutions* that we ask the Utilitarian type of question, not about individual actions.

Of course in exceptional cases we have to think as Utilitarians about individual actions. This is either when rules conflict or when there is no rule that covers the case in question. But by and large we just "see" what to do in the individual cases (we have been brought up so to do): it is only when we consider the effect of certain rules or institutions on society as a whole, when we consider modifying or augmenting these rules and institutions, that the Utilitarian pattern of thought becomes appropriate. Philosophers like Butler and Kant are at their happiest when discussing how we deal with the first-order type of question, those like Bentham and Mill when dealing with the second-order type of question. (Though note that Butler in one place[2] seems to say that God made our consciences as He did because *He* is a Utilitarian, even if we must not be. And I myself believe, rather heretically, that only a slight rephrasing of Kant is needed in order to turn him into a Utilitarian about *rules*.)

Reprinted from *Res Judicitae* by permission of the author and *Res Judicitae.*
[1] 6 *Res Judicitae*, 224–30.

[2] *Dissertation upon the Nature of Virtue*, § 8.

Bentham's Utilitarian methods of argument work smoothly when he is considering rules (legislation) but he is quite silly where he tries to talk in the same way about individual actions. The point, then, is this, that it is not a question of intuitionism or utilitarianism but of *both* (in different places). The actions which we "see" to be right are those which come under rules we have been trained to obey: the justification of the rules, but not, in general, of the individual actions, is utilitarian.

I have sketched out the above theory of morals (which you can find more fully worked out in Toulmin's book *The Place of Reason in Ethics*) because it appears to me that theories of punishment have got at cross purposes in a precisely similar way to that in which the intuitionists and utilitarians get into cross purposes about right and wrong.

From the point of view of the legislator, we ask: "Is this the best punishment to assign for this type of offence?" It seems to me that the only way in which this question can be rationally discussed is the utilitarian way: that is by considering the consequences for society of adopting or not adopting the penal law in question. What other type of argument is relevant? Admittedly one could appeal to Scripture, but the New Testament was not intended as a text-book of penology, and some of the penal ideas of the Old Testament are barbarous. Certainly if we knew that God had said that such-and-such was the law we should adopt we should be foolish not to adopt it. But how does God know that it is the best law? God is rational and must have argued rationally to His decision. How else, then, than by arguing in the way *we* should, if we were rational, that is, in the Utilitarian way? (Cf. Butler again.) There is something else that Lewis might put in the place of Utilitarian argument: an appeal to the Law of Nature. I do not know what this is. But I think I know what the use of the expression "Law of Nature" is. It is this: "this is the Law of Nature" =

"this is the rule that ought to be adopted", said by someone who wishes to disguise his own dogmatism and to conceal the fact that he is either unable or too lazy to search for a rational (i.e. a Utilitarian) justification of the proposed measure.

From a Utilitarian point of view, then, we discuss a measure by asking "Will this measure or will some alternative one tend most to promote the well-being of society?" If the proposed measure is a penal law there seem to be only three ways in which it can be of value:

(1)   To deter people;
(2)   To protect society by eliminating or removing criminals;
(3)   To reform the criminal.

The first two of these are by far the most important. It is not always possible to reform the criminal. And I should say that (1) is of greater importance than (2). Lewis discusses (1) and (3) but ignores (2). There may be other ways in which the institution of punishment may benefit society and which could be cited to justify it. I do not know of any. It might be argued that punishment satisfies the desire of certain members of the society for revenge. However, the desire for revenge is something which is perhaps better left unsatisfied. It is difficult to believe that society would not be happier if it thought less about revenge. Moreover I do not see how the principle of revenge itself could possibly be justified. "If we adopt the principle 'An eye for an eye and a tooth for a tooth' we will make society happier." How?

We see then that Utilitarian considerations are relevant in discussing what penal legislation we should adopt. But just as in the case of rightness, analysed earlier in this paper, we find a totally different situation when we come to the individual action, the action of the judge or magistrate. The judge or magistrate must not argue as a Utilitarian, save *per accidens* where the law leaves some margin for choice, when deciding what punishment to impose. The just punishment for murder is death. That is, death is the punishment laid down by law. It is totally beside the point for the judge to argue about what action, in this particular instance, would promote the greatest general happiness.

I now make the following suggestion. A lot of what Lewis says is perfectly true. As judges or magistrates we must not think as Utilitarians. But this has not the slightest bearing on the question of whether *legislation* should or should not be governed by Utilitarian criteria. Lewis lays stress on the concept of Desert, and it is here, in the thinking of the judge or magistrate, that this concept comes in. The concept of Desert is quite inapplicable so far as the thinking of the legislator is concerned. Ordinarily we know what is meant by "the deserved punishment". It is that laid down by law. But how can "desert" have a meaning when we discuss what punishment the law ought to lay down? If we try to apply the idea of desert here we are either driven back on to Lewis's personal preferences ("I should like to see murderers hanged", say) or we have to fall back on some crude equation of punishment with amount of damage done: an eye for an eye. Why the damage-retribution equation should be thought a sound principle of legislation I do not know. I do not see how it could possibly be justified. Why should society be happier if we adopt this principle? Indeed it is quite easy to see that society will be happier if we do *not* adopt this principle.

To sum up: Lewis shows quite clearly that we do not always think about punishment in the Utilitarian way. My reply is that it is when we think of ourselves in the situation of magistrates that we are quite right not to think as Utilitarians. In this situation we are concerned with the first-order questions. But it is in considering the penal laws themselves, in considering the second-order questions, that we must think as Utilitarians. Lewis's argument derives a great deal of its plausibility from confusing the first-order and second-order questions.

Determinism and Moral Perspectives

ELIZABETH L. BEARDSLEY

Can determinists find a satisfactory rationale for moral praise and blame? On this question, determinists themselves have long been divided. Although the affirmative answer has enjoyed the status of a majority opinion, the negative answer has at times found very effective support. The force of the negative answer emerges clearly in certain recent writings, in which writers sympathetic to determinism vigorously defend the thesis that determinism removes from the concepts of moral praiseworthiness and blameworthiness all legitimate application whatsoever.[1]

The negative answer to the question posed here is unsatisfactory, I think; but in some ways it is preferable to the affirmative answer as the latter is usually given

and supported. In this paper, I shall argue that judgments of moral praise and blame, affirmative as well as negative, can be made within the framework of determinism, provided that we accept a more complex account of these judgments and their foundations than is ordinarily supplied or assumed. I shall maintain that judgments concerning the presence or absence of moral praiseworthiness and blameworthiness are made from several different standpoints, which I shall call "moral perspectives." My primary purpose is to show how an understanding of these perspectives and their relations can contribute substantially toward relieving the tension widely felt (even by some who are reluctant to admit it) to exist between determinism and certain of our basic ethical concepts.

The terms "praise" and "blame" will be used here with the meaning of "moral praise" and "moral blame." Praise and blame will be treated as correlative concepts such that, for everything that is said about one, a corresponding statement about the other could be made, though it will usually be unnecessary to make it. The term "affirmative judgment of praise" will be used to refer to any explicit attribution of praiseworthiness to a person. A "negative judgment of praise" is an explicit denial that a person is praiseworthy. The general term "judgment of praise" will refer indifferently to either an affirmative or

Reprinted from *Philosophy and Phenomenological Research*, XXI, 1960, pp. 1–20, by permission of the author and *Philosophy and Phenomenological Research*.

[1] See Paul Edwards, "Hard and Soft Determinism," and John Hospers, "What Means This Freedom?", both in Sidney Hook, *Determinism and Freedom* (New York University Press, 1958); also W. I. Matson, "On the Irrelevance of Free-will to Moral Responsibility," *Mind*, Vol. LXV (1956), pp. 489–497. Although these writers frame their argument more explicitly in terms of the concept of moral responsibility than in terms of moral praiseworthiness and blameworthiness, the application to the latter concepts is clear. Matson's chief thesis, that libertarianism can validate the concept of moral responsibility no more successfully than determinism can, will not be dealt with in the present paper; the part of his article which bears most directly on what I shall have to say is found in sections 2 and 3.

a negative judgment of praise, and similarly for "judgment of blame." Judgments of praise and blame will be treated here as assertions which are true or false, and not as acts which may be useful or useless to perform.

DETERMINIST VIEWS OF PRAISE AND BLAME

Before discussing judgments of praise and blame, it will be helpful to consider briefly certain moral judgments of a different kind. The standpoint from which we affirm or deny that acts are objectively right or wrong I shall call the "perspective of objective rightness or wrongness." A judgment of objective rightness or wrongness is a judgment made about an act, not an agent; and it does not carry with it any implication about the praiseworthiness or blameworthiness of an agent. Statements like "Smith's act was objectively right, but he deserves no praise for it" not only are self-consistent, but are often true; objectively right acts can be committed inadvertently, or from reprehensible motives.

The judgment that an act is objectively right furnishes insufficient evidence for a judgment that its agent is praiseworthy, because certain key facts concerning the causal antecedents of the right act remain to be supplied. The objective rightness or wrongness of an act does not depend in any way on its causal antecedents, but on other considerations, such as its consequences (for teleologists), or its harmony with the will of God, moral rules, or the like (for formalists). It is therefore appropriate to call this perspective a "noncausal" one, for it takes no account of whether an act had causal antecedents of one kind rather than another, or indeed had completely determining causal antecedents at all.

Most philosophers, I think, would agree that the use of the moral perspective of objective rightness or wrongness pre-

sents no particular problem for the determinist. It is true that certain libertarians have apparently seen something profoundly incongruous in the application of any normative predicates at all to the constituent parts of a determined universe; but this line of thought has persuaded so few that it may be disregarded.

Much less harmony prevails among philosophers who have reflected on the relation between determinism and the concepts of moral praise and blame. Libertarians, of course, maintain that because the truth of determinism would invalidate affirmative judgments of praise and blame, determinism is false, and criteria for praiseworthiness and blameworthiness must include the requirement that an agent should have performed his act "freely." Though determinists are united in rejecting the conclusion of the libertarian argument as false, they differ sharply concerning the acceptability of the conditional premise.

Among leading determinists who believe that valid affirmative judgments of praise and blame can be made, a fairly clear account of the criteria for praiseworthiness and blameworthiness seems to have emerged. I shall call those who subscribe to this account "Group I determinists." Details of the account vary, but a substantial area of agreement remains. It is commonly held that if an agent has acted wrongly, without external constraint ("voluntarily"), without ignorance of relevant facts, and from a motive or because of a trait that is undesirable, then, and only then, the agent deserves blame for his act.[2] Similar conditions are held to govern praiseworthiness.[3]

Group I determinists deny that there is anything here to conflict with the truth

[2] I have found the presentation of this general position by P. H. Nowell-Smith in *Ethics* (London, 1954), particularly helpful here.

[3] Note that the terms "blameworthy" and "praiseworthy" have not been defined here and that no definitions of these terms will be offered in this paper.

of determinism. They point out that those who make judgments of praise and blame must indeed attend to several key factors among the causal conditions that produced the acts whose agents are judged. But any *other* causal conditions that may have been present, and, in particular, antecedents of antecedents, are to be completely disregarded. Moral praisers and blamers, on this view, are simply not concerned with the nature, or even the existence, of such additional factors. Determinism is thus fully compatible with attributions of praiseworthiness and blameworthiness.[4]

To determinists of a second group—"Group II determinists"—this account seems seriously oversimplified.[5] They contend that the same reasoning which leads us to withhold praise and blame from agents whose acts were committed involuntarily will, when combined with the thesis of determinism, lead on inexorably to the conclusion that no one ever deserves praise or blame for anything. They are haunted by the knowledge that many of the causal antecedents of acts have not been investigated by those who mete out praise and blame on the grounds specified above; and most particularly they are haunted by the knowledge that not all of the causal antecedents of voluntary acts are voluntary acts. Thus they come to believe that no distinction between "voluntary" and "involuntary" acts that a determinist can consistently make can sustain the moral weight that it must bear if we are to judge men praiseworthy or blameworthy. How, they ask, could we ever be justified in blaming or praising someone

for a voluntary act and not an involuntary one, when we know full well that even the voluntary act can be traced back to causes—environmental or hereditary—belonging to a world the agent never made?

I believe that there are elements of truth in each of these brands of determinism, and I shall try to show that this is the case.

THE PERSPECTIVE OF MORAL WORTH

Surely there is no doubt that the conditions for praiseworthiness and blameworthiness set forth in the Group I determinist's account do in fact constitute one important and familiar standard according to which we make judgments of praise and blame. It is highly convenient to introduce a special term for the characteristic of moral value that may be said to belong to an agent who has performed an act that meets the conditions specified. I shall say that an agent has "positive moral worth" if and only if he has acted rightly, voluntarily, with knowledge of relevant facts, and from a desire that is bad in its situation.[6] The term "moral worth" will be used to refer to either positive or negative moral worth indifferently, and the standard by which agents are judged to have moral worth (positive or negative) will be called the "standard of moral worth." Elsewhere [7] I have discussed certain features of the concept of moral worth in some detail, and have indicated how conditions for the

---

[4] Many would argue, of course, that determinism is much more than merely "compatible" with these judgments, since we cannot speak of an agent's act as "his" act or as arising "from" a motive or trait, unless determinism is assumed to be true. This argument will be deliberately set aside here.

[5] My distinction between "Group I" and "Group II" determinism is plainly very similar to Edwards' distinction between "soft" and "hard" determinism. See Edwards, *op. cit.*, and also Edwards and Pap, *A Modern Introduction to Philosophy* (Free Press, 1957), p. 380.

[6] I prefer to formulate this last condition in terms of a "desire" rather than of a "trait," because we sometimes make judgments of this kind without having sufficient evidence to ascertain the presence of a trait; but this point is not of central importance here.

[7] "Moral Worth and Moral Credit," *The Philosophical Review*, Vol. LXVI (1957), pp. 304–328. In the present treatment I have left the term "moral worth" undefined, and I have also introduced it here to refer to any attribute of agents who are praiseworthy or blameworthy *for* acts rather than to refer to an attribute of acts themselves.

presence of degrees of moral worth may be set up.

A "judgment of moral worth," which may be affirmative or negative, is a judgment in which moral worth is asserted to be present or absent. We must of course distinguish between a negative judgment of positive moral worth ("Agent A is not morally worthy for act A") and an affirmative judgment of negative moral worth ("Agent Y is morally unworthy for his act B").

I shall call the standpoint from which we make judgments of moral worth the "perspective of moral worth." This is plainly not a wholly non-causal perspective, as is the perspective of objective rightness or wrongness. Because *some* (a strictly limited set) of the circumstances causally relevant to the performance of an act are taken into account when the moral worth of its agent is being judged, this perspective may accurately be called a "causally limited" perspective. The factors taken into account in making judgments from this moral perspective will be termed the "worth-determining" factors.

Group II determinists are likely to feel that the introduction of the term "moral worth" is unobjectionable, and perhaps even useful, provided that judgments of moral worth are not held to imply judgments of praise or blame. Thinkers of this group may be disposed to admit that human beings do indeed have a strong psychological tendency to experience positive feelings when confronted by the gestalt agent-performing-act-under-conditions-for-positive-moral-worth, and to experience negative feelings when confronted by the corresponding negative gestalt. They may contend that, since these feelings cannot be rationally justified, human beings had better try to eliminate them from their psyches as soon as possible. The fact that there is no reason to believe that this has ever been accomplished is not likely to daunt them. In any case, the important point, for the Group II determinist, is that

we should avoid the confusion of believing that persons who happen to form part of the pleasant or unpleasant gestalts just mentioned deserve praise or blame for what they do. Because the crucial distinction between voluntary and involuntary acts is bound to collapse in the end, no one ever deserves praise or blame. Perhaps judgments of praise and blame *are* made from the perspective of moral worth, but they *should* not be.[8]

To this the Group I determinist will reply that, since the conditions for "moral worth" were originally taken directly from an analysis of conditions for praiseworthiness and blameworthiness, it is highly arbitrary, to say the very least, to attempt to purge judgments of moral worth of all association with judgments of praise and blame. Moreover, he will continue, the assertion that human beings have "feelings" which are merely "positive" or "negative," when they encounter persons exhibiting positive or negative moral worth, is decidedly misleading. The "feelings" referred to consist of definite reactions of a specific sort, to which are added, for most moral judges, quite explicit reflective convictions. Human beings feel—and reserve—a very special kind of approval and disapproval for those members of their species who perform acts that have certain salient features. Furthermore, the majority of those who have reflected on the matter' seem to have been convinced that approval and disapproval of this special kind are reactions to which the persons in question have a morally justified claim. It is this claim which is put forth in affirmative judgments of praise and blame. In view of these considerations, a heavy burden of

[8] It is convenient to speak of the point at issue between the Group I and Group II determinists as concerned primarily with the validity of *affirmative* judgments of praise and blame; and I occasionally do this. But it should be understood that the Group II determinist in fact equally denies the validity of any *negative* judgment of praise (or blame) which is made with the assumption that the class of persons who deserve praise (or blame) is not vacuous.

proof rests on the Group II determinist, who proposes to eliminate from moral discourse all affirmative judgments of praise and blame. This burden, the Group I determinist charges, has not been effectively sustained.

The Group I determinist will go on to admit readily that, among those features which an act must have if its agent is to merit praise or blame, the requirement that it be voluntary is indeed crucial. But, he will say, to establish voluntariness we need examine only certain of the immediate causal ancestors of an act.[9] Considerations about more remote causal forebears are as irrelevant here as information about a man's grandparents would be if proffered in reply to a query about his parents. Therefore it is the case, not only that we *do* make judgments of praise and blame from the perspective of moral worth, but that this procedure is entirely legitimate, and is not threatened by determinism. Thus, concludes the Group I determinist, the problem of praise and blame has been solved.

The Group I determinist may seem, on the face of it, to have had the better of the argument in the exchange just described. He is right, I think, in maintaining that judgments of praise and blame, affirmative as well as negative, have an extremely strong claim to be retained in moral discourse. He is right, also, in insisting that the distinction between voluntary and involuntary acts which is needed for affirmative judgments of praise and blame can be made by determinists. Finally, he is right in holding that what has been called here the "standard of moral worth" is the standard on which

many affirmative and negative judgments of praise and blame are based.

Where the Group I determinist is wrong is in his tacit assumption that *all* judgments of moral praise and blame are made from the perspective of moral worth, and that when a man has been judged praiseworthy or blameworthy from this perspective there is nothing more to say about his moral claim to be praised or blamed for the act under consideration. The truth, as I shall go on to try to show, is much less simple than this. There is indeed a network of causes stretching out in all directions, far beyond the worth-determining factors on which the Group I determinists so resolutely fix their minds. Moreover, these other causal factors are by no means without moral significance. We cannot hope to set up a genuinely effective defense against the Group II determinist's harsh view of what that significance is, unless some other way of doing justice to these additional causal factors can be found.

THE PERSPECTIVE OF MORAL CREDIT

I want now to examine a second moral perspective from which we appraise agents. It is necessary to explain the operation of this perspective somewhat more fully than was the case for moral worth, because it has received little attention from ethical theorists.

When we examine our affirmative and negative judgments of praise and blame, we find that many are made by the standard of moral worth; but we also find, I think, that many are not. A second standard of appraisal often comes into operation after a judgment based on moral worth has been made, when we go on to ask further questions about the individual situation of an agent who has performed an act for which he is judged morally worthy or unworthy. Here individual cir-

[9] If it should be said that so-called "voluntary" acts are not *really* voluntary after all, the Group I determinist would reply in the fashion of Flew, in the latter's discussion of the expression "acting freely." See A. Flew, "Divine Omnipotence and Human Freedom," in Flew and Macintyre, *New Essays in Philosophical Theology* (Macmillan, 1955), pp. 149–151.

cumstances which facilitated or hampered the performance of the act are taken into account. What we do, that is, is to investigate factors which made the performance of a certain act by a certain agent particularly "easy" or "difficult" for *him*. On the basis of this information, a further judgment of praise or blame is made.

How do we ascertain that the performance of act A by agent X was "easy" or "difficult"? Not by endeavoring to estimate the intensity of his subjective feelings of effort. What is needed here is an objective correlate;[10] and this, I think, is provided by the concept of circumstances *favorable* or *unfavorable* to the performance of a certain act, i.e., circumstances in whose presence the performance of such an act is either more or less likely to occur than it is in their absence. Given that an act is one for which its agent has positive or negative moral worth, a judgment is made to the effect that the balance of known circumstances causally relevant to the performance of that act was favorable or unfavorable. We try to decide, that is, whether, in view of all the things we know about him, it was antecedently probable that a certain act should have been performed by its agent. If an agent has performed an act for which he has positive moral worth, and if it was antecedently improbable that he should have performed this act, then he is praiseworthy by our new standard as well as by the standard of moral worth. We say that such an act was performed "in spite of obstacles" or "against odds." Similar remarks, of course, could be made regarding blameworthiness as judged by this new standard; and it is convenient at times, though somewhat unidiomatic, to speak of an act for which an agent is morally unworthy and which was antecedently improbable as having also been performed "against odds."

To those who deny that the perform-

ance against odds of an act for which the agent is morally worthy or unworthy earns for that agent special praise or blame the only answer can be an invitation to look again, more closely, at the moral appraisals we all make. Evidence confirming the view defended here can be found on all sides. For example, it was maintained not long ago by Auxiliary Bishop Joseph M. Marling of the Roman Catholic Church that the presence of severe neurosis in certain Catholic saints could be admitted, since it not only did not detract from the saintliness, but actually contributed to it, in that a neurosis constitutes a serious obstacle to the achievement of spiritual perfection.[11]

There are strong reasons, I think, for maintaining that the criteria for moral appraisals now being examined constitute a standard separate and distinct from the standard of moral worth. The alternative "single-standard" view (the belief that both sets of criteria can be combined into one complex standard) appears to be widely, though casually, held; but I think it is mistaken. My reasons for this conclusion have been given elsewhere.[12]

By our second standard, then, an agent X is praiseworthy for his act A to some degree if and only if: (1) X has positive moral worth to some degree for A, and (2) X's situation at the time of performing A included among the known circumstances a preponderance or balance of circumstances (other than the amount of "effort" put forth by the agent) which are reasonably judged to be unfavorable to the performance of the act. Similar conditions govern the presence of blameworthiness as judged by this second standard. Agents who perform acts under the conditions for praiseworthiness just specified will be said to have "positive moral credit" for their

---

[10] There will not, however, be an exact correlation between felt intensity of effort and the criterion proposed.

[11] See *Time*, Vol. LXVIII (August 27, 1956), for an account of an address by Auxiliary Bishop Joseph M. Marling of Kansas City, Mo., to the Guild of Catholic Psychiatrists.

[12] E. L. Beardsley, *op. cit.*, especially pp. 309–315.

acts. Like moral worth, moral credit may be present in either a positive or a negative form. A "judgment of moral credit" is an assertion or denial that an agent possesses positive or negative moral credit.[13]

The moral perspective from which judgments of moral credit are made may be called the "perspective of moral credit," and judgments of praise and blame based on the moral credit standard may also be said to be made from this perspective. In order to judge from the perspective of moral credit, we investigate the causal antecedents of an act more extensively than is done for judgments made from the perspective of moral worth. Any instance of any kind of factor which can reasonably be judged to be an unfavorable or favorable circumstance for a given kind of act is potentially a "credit-determining" factor for any agent performing an act of that kind, even though in common practice, to be sure, not all potential credit-determining factors are investigated before judgments are made. The perspective of moral credit, accordingly, may be called a "causally extended" perspective, as compared with our causally limited perspective of moral worth, and our noncausal perspective of objective rightness or wrongness.

Judgments made from the perspective of moral credit supplement judgments made from the perspective of moral worth. They do not supplant them, any more than judgments about the objective rightness or wrongness of acts are supplanted by judgments about the moral worth of their agents. The latter are selfcontained judgments, perfectly satisfactory and significant in their own right. Nevertheless, the perspective of moral credit does set limits to the perspective of moral worth, in that it is important for those who make judgments by the moral worth standard to remember that such judgments do not give us the

whole moral truth about an agent. Even when we do not actually go on to ascertain the moral credit-rating of an agent to whom we ascribe positive or negative moral worth, we must bear in mind that further questions along such lines *could* be asked. Judgments of praise and blame made from the perspective of moral worth will be made less dogmatically, with less show of finality, by those who understand that there is another moral perspective from which an individual can be judged. But those who make judgments from the perspective of moral credit must not forget the importance of the perspective of moral worth. Judges who constantly focus their attention on the "ease" or "difficulty" with which something was accomplished need to be reminded at times, to look at the quality of the moral accomplishment itself. Neither of these two moral perspectives can be said to be superior to the other.

It seems clear that the use of the perspective of moral credit is fully compatible with determinism.[14] And the identification of this new standpoint of moral appraisal as a separate moral perspective lends needed strength to the philosophical position of determinism, principally by revealing it to be less dogmatic and impersonal than it is often taken to be. In a more detailed treatment of these matters, the advantages to determinism of recognizing judgments of praise and blame based on moral credit could be explained more fully.

In the end, however, the convinced Group II determinist will always reply that the effort to set up a perspective of moral credit cannot salvage judgments of praise and blame. He will maintain that judgments of praise and blame based on moral credit are ultimately no more compatible with determinism than are judgments of

---

[13] See *ibid.* for a detailed discussion of the concept of moral credit and its relation to moral worth. Here I leave "moral credit" undefined, and use it to refer to an attribute of agents rather than of acts.

[14] It may be said, I think correctly, that the account of moral credit given here actually presupposes a determinist position, since reliable causal generalizations about human behavior underlie the estimates of probability on which judgments of moral credit, in large part, depend.

praise and blame based on moral worth.[15] As before, he may look tolerantly, or even benevolently, on the procedure of setting up a "perspective of moral credit," just so long as judgments of praise and blame are kept out of the picture. Again his reaction springs from his awareness of additional causal factors, this time of causal factors lying behind those taken into account from the perspective of moral credit. The Group II determinist will say that, although those who make judgments based on moral credit may make extensive inquiries into the factors causally relevant to human acts, sooner or later, because of the limits of time or energy or human knowledge, they must bring their investigations to a close. And when they do, they will not have told the whole causal story; and the part that will remain untold will invalidate judgments of praise and blame made from this moral perspective.

I believe that this charge can be answered, but I want to show first how it might be supported. Let us consider a comparison between two individuals, Jones and Smith. Jones has performed an act having a high degree of positive moral worth in spite of very unfavorable circumstances, whereas Smith, confronted by essentially the same kind of circumstances and placed in a very similar situation, has performed an act having a much lower degree of positive moral worth. It is clear that Jones possesses a higher degree of positive moral credit for his act than does Smith for his,[16] since the circumstances and situation constitute greater obstacles for Jones' act than for Smith's.

Now, no matter how strong our psychological tendency to feel a greater admiration for the achievement of Jones, such

an attitude, the Group II determinist would claim, is not justifiable. For moral credit is ascribed on the basis of finding that a preponderance of the *known* circumstances in an agent's situation was unfavorable to the performance of a given act. Judgments of moral credit deal with acts whose performance was improbable; nevertheless, they deal with acts that *were* performed, events that *happened*. If determinism is true, these happenings were caused. Therefore for each act for which an agent possesses moral credit there must exist also a cluster of one or more unknown circumstances causally relevant to the performance of the act, and a preponderance of *these* circumstances must have been favorable, rather than unfavorable. It is all very well, then, to judge that Jones performed under great odds an act for which he is morally worthy; but such a judgment is superficial and unstable. For, if determinism is true, these vaunted "odds" disappear upon examination; and Jones is seen to have done only what the causal factors in his situation, unknown as well as known, brought forth. So did Smith, and so do we all. How then can praise and blame by the standard of moral credit be justified?

It is evident that this reasoning is too cogent to be set aside. At the close of the preceding section, it was asserted that the causal factors not dealt with in judgments of moral worth were nevertheless morally significant, and would have to be taken care of in some other way. Many of these "left-over" causal factors have now been shown to provide a basis for judgments of praise and blame made from a second moral perspective, the perspective of moral credit. But the Group II determinist now reminds us that behind even the credit-determining factors lie still others, and that these too have a moral significance that cannot be lightly dismissed. His interpretation of the moral significance of this most distant range of causal factors is, as we have seen, simply that they invalidate all

[15] I disregard here the fact that the Group II determinist would also say that the perspective of moral credit inherits what he takes to be the deficiencies of the perspective of moral worth, since judgments of moral worth are presupposed by judgments of moral credit.

[16] On degrees of praiseworthiness by the standard of moral credit, see E. L. Beardsley, *op. cit.*, p. 319.

affirmative judgments of praise and blame. In the remainder of this paper, I shall try to show that another interpretation is possible, and that it is to be preferred.

THE PERSPECTIVE OF ULTIMATE MORAL EQUALITY

In the course of our discussion, we have now sorted out three groups of factors causally relevant to human behavior: worth-determining factors, credit-determining factors, and what may be called "ultimate" causal factors, which are simply those factors that are left out of account when we make judgments based on moral worth and moral credit. If determinism is true, we may be said to know, for any given act, *that* there are ultimate causal factors. But we do not know *what* they are: if we did know they would take their place among the potential credit-determining factors for the act in question. It is strange that this shadowy group of unknown circumstances should be morally so significant; but I think that there is no doubt that their moral significance is real.

When we are mindful of the existence of the ultimate causal factors, we look at human beings and their acts in a special way. This was brought out by the example of Jones and Smith. When we look at persons in this special way, they are seen to be equals, as far as their claims to moral praise and blame are concerned, or, rather, they are seen to have passed beyond any point at which discriminations of praise-worthiness or blameworthiness are applicable. Seen in this way, all men are members of a moral or spiritual democracy. This is a realm lying behind our distinctions of moral worth and moral credit, a realm in which each is simply the person he is. When we take into account the full range of factors causally relevant to human acts, we must regard human beings as a flock without goats and without sheep.

I propose to say that this special way

of looking at persons, in the light of the existence of ultimate causal factors for their behavior, constitutes another moral perspective. This I shall call the "perspective of ultimate moral equality." From this perspective we look at persons and their acts in the widest possible causal contexts, contexts without limits of any kind. Therefore we may call this a "causally unlimited" perspective. As a moral perspective it is, of course, strikingly different in some respects from the others that we have examined. Judgments made from the perspective of moral worth and the perspective of moral credit are judgments of discrimination. This is obvious in the case of comparative judgments, but it is also true of noncomparative ones. Our interest in knowing that X possesses positive moral worth for his honest act, and Y negative moral credit for his cowardly one, stems in large part from the fact that there are honest acts whose agents do not possess positive moral worth, and cowardly acts whose agents earn no negative moral credit. Judgments of praise and blame based on moral worth and moral credit are answers to questions which can in principle be answered either affirmatively or negatively.

This is not true of judgments made from the perspective of ultimate moral equality. Here all are on the same moral footing: none has any ultimate claim to praise or blame, and the judgments made from this perspective are all negative. No matter what acts a person has performed, all that we can say of him from this final moral perspective is that he deserves no praise for what he has done, or that he deserves no blame.

The statement "X is not ultimately praiseworthy for A" is a negative judgment of praise made from the perspective of ultimate moral equality, whereas "Y is not ultimately blameworthy for B" is a negative judgment of blame made from the same perspective. Judgments of praise and blame made from this perspective will here be limited in scope to persons whose acts have earned for them moral worth or moral credit. That is to say, the statement "X is not ultimately praiseworthy for A" will be permissible if and only if A is an act for which X possesses either positive moral worth or positive moral credit. And the truth-condition for this statement can be stated very briefly: the statement is true if and only if A has ultimate causes. Similarly, "Y is not ultimately blameworthy for B" is permissible if and only if B is an act for which Y possesses negative moral worth or negative moral credit, and true if and only if B has ultimate causes.

But, if determinism is true, we know of any event that it has ultimate causes, and we know this without any specific investigation. The behavior of all men is causally determined, and the nature of what we have called the "ultimate" causes is equally unknown in each case. This eradication of all distinctions in the causal status of acts erases all distinctions in the moral status of their agents. Therefore in one way it can never be news that Brown does not ultimately deserve praise for his kind deed, or that Robinson does not ultimately deserve blame for his unkind one.

In another way, however, these assertions *are* news, and important news. The fact that Brown and Robinson are ultimately moral equals is a vital part of the whole moral truth about them. Compare the situation for a factual account.[17] In factual descriptions of human beings we are interested in the qualities in which they differ, to be sure; but we are also interested in the qualities in which they are alike. For some purposes, and in some contexts, the similarities may be legitimately disregarded; but this does not mean that they can always be left out of account. Sometimes they are more significant

than the differences, and they are never more significant than they become when we are in danger of assuming that the differences tell the whole factual story. So it is with moral appraisals of human beings. For the whole moral story, judgments of praise and blame based on moral worth and moral credit need to be supplemented by judgments made from the perspective of ultimate moral equality.

Because this is true, we are justified in regarding the perspective of ultimate moral equality as a genuinely "moral" perspective, even though it eradicates moral discriminations. The knowledge that when persons are viewed in relation to the ultimate causal factors of their behavior moral discriminations no longer apply to them is a piece of moral knowledge, at least in being knowledge about moral matters. It is curious that as we go from a causally limited perspective to a causally extended one we increase our power to make moral discriminations, whereas when we come to a causally unlimited perspective these moral discriminations stop altogether. But the knowledge that this is so is moral knowledge, and it has important bearings on the rest of our moral knowledge.

The relation that holds between the perspective of ultimate moral equality and the other moral perspectives from which judgments of praise and blame are made is analogous in certain ways to the relation between the perspective of moral credit and that of moral worth. Judgments based on moral credit, as we have seen, set limits to judgments based on moral worth. Similarly, the knowledge that human beings can be viewed from a perspective which will show them to be morally equal will remind those who make judgments based on moral worth and moral credit that these judgments of moral inequality do not tell the whole story about the individuals being judged. This knowledge, in turn, will affect the attitudes of those who have it: they will regard themselves

---

[17] By this manner of speaking I do not mean to rule out the possibility that a naturalistic account of the meaning of basic ethical terms can be given.

and each other with more tolerance than before. Feelings of admiration, contempt, guilt, and pride, will all be experienced more moderately by those who know that no man is ever the *first* cause of evil or good deeds, or *finally* responsible for winning or losing when confronted by moral odds. But this is not to say that such feelings will not be experienced at all, or that they should not be.

For the perspective of ultimate moral equality cannot give us the whole truth about the praiseworthiness and blameworthiness of human beings either. The fact that X has negative moral worth for his act, or that Y has positive moral credit for his, is not cancelled by saying that X does not ultimately deserve blame, or that Y does not ultimately deserve praise. We value in a special way those whose acts meet the standards of moral worth and moral credit, and this is something that we cannot change. As Spinoza saw, it is true—even in a determined universe—that "we desire to form for ourselves an idea of man upon which we may look as a model of human nature."[18] The idea of a man who performs a right act voluntarily, knowingly, and from a good desire, and the idea of a man who, when confronted by odds, can still do these things—these *are* the models we have formed. Conformity to these patterns is what we regard as worthy of praise, and deviation from them in certain ways is what we regard as worthy of blame. We cannot feel about persons who thus conform or deviate as we do about animals or inanimate objects which measure up or fail to measure up to certain other standards. All this being so, judgments of praise and blame based on moral worth and moral credit are not only legitimate but vitally necessary parts of moral discourse. They are answers to questions that we cannot help asking.

The full moral truth about a man and his act, then, might run as follows: that he deserves a low degree of praise for it by

the standard of moral worth, a high degree of praise for it by the standard of moral credit, and ultimately no praise for it when he is judged from the perspective of ultimate moral equality. There is no reason why the three statements cannot be true simultaneously. Also, these perspectives seem to be genuinely coordinate, and complementary: we need them all. And, if we distinguish between moral perspectives, we shall be able to avoid the doubling of metaphysical perspectives which Kant found necessary in order to reconcile causality and morality. It is easier to regard a man as blameworthy from one point of view but not from another than to say that his act is both caused and uncaused.

The acquiring of moral wisdom, at least as far as moral appraisals are concerned, does not consist only in learning how to make sound judgments from each moral perspective. It consists also in learning under what circumstances each of the moral perspectives should be used—a large and fundamental problem that cannot be dealt with here.[19] Here let us note only that most of the questions about the praiseworthiness and blameworthiness of human beings that are actually asked are questions to which the appropriate answer is a judgment based on moral worth or one based on moral credit. Writers on ethics[20] have pointed out that we feel something peculiarly objectionable in an attempt by a wrongdoer to exculpate himself on the ground that all his acts were caused and therefore he deserves no blame. Here an inquiry into his blameworthiness is launched from one moral perspective and a reply is made from another. But moral

---

[18] B. Spinoza, *Ethics* (Oxford Press, 4th ed., 1930), p. 179.

[19] One important question to consider in this connection is whether it is ever justifiable to employ the perspective of ultimate moral equality when thinking of one's own future acts and their moral status. Some reflections which bear on this question (though they are not expressed in the language of the present paper) are offered by H. Fingarette in his interesting article "Psychoanalytic Re-Evaluation," *Philosophy and Phenomenological Research,* Vol. XVI (1955–1956), pp. 18–29.

[20] See, for example, Nowell-Smith, *op. cit.*, pp. 297–300.

perspectives, however coordinate, are certainly not interchangeable. Questions about praiseworthiness or blameworthiness should be answered from the perspective from which they are asked, whenever it is possible to tell what this is. Sometimes it will be appropriate, and even very desirable, to add to this answer a judgment from another moral perspective; but often it will not be. Particular caution must be exercised in advancing judgments made from the perspective of ultimate moral equality. These are illuminating. and even inspiring, when made in the right context, and by those who know how to make accurate discriminations by the standards of moral worth and moral credit. Otherwise they are apt to seem shallow, and somehow sentimental, or cheap.[21]

SOME OBJECTIONS AND REPLIES

The account which has been given of the perspective of ultimate moral equality and its relation to our other perspectives of praise and blame seems likely to arouse objections from all sides. Three of these appear to me to be particularly striking, and in this concluding section I shall try to reply briefly to each one in turn.

(1) The first objection that I shall consider is one that will be raised by Group II determinists. Some of what has been said in the preceding will presumably be acceptable to members of this group; but they will want to know how it can be maintained that the perspective of ultimate moral equality is merely *one* of several perspectives from which agents are appraised. It is rather *the* moral perspective, which, because of its special nature,

invalidates all others. It is superior to the others because it is broader in its scope. This is the only perspective that is causally unlimited, the only one from which we view acts in the context of *all* their causes, unknown as well as known. And since we are seeing more broadly, it follows that we are seeing more accurately.

The answer here must be that it is not clear that this does follow. Do we see "better" from a height that takes in a large part of the surrounding territory? The only reply can be "Yes and no." Details which are not seen from a height spring back into view when we climb back down and look at objects in the context of a smaller part of their surroundings; and things which looked alike from above manifest striking differences when seen from a position farther down. In this case, one standpoint does not reveal the "real nature" of the objects better than another one does.

But we must not be lured into pressing our optical metaphor of "perspectives" too far. In any case, the Group II determinist may wish to support his basic contention—that the perspective of ultimate moral equality has a privileged status—in another way. He may claim that it will be impossible, psychologically, for those who have viewed persons from the perspective of ultimate moral equality to go on making the same old judgments of praise and blame from other perspectives. How, he will ask, can we throw ourselves into the task of sorting the worthy from the unworthy, the creditable from the discreditable, when we know that from another standpoint these distinctions will disappear altogether? Will not the view from every perspective but that of ultimate moral equality take on the aspect of something unreal, a mirage without power to deceive for more than a moment?

Part of the answer here is that we cannot, indeed, make moral discriminations in exactly the "same old" way, and that we cannot "throw ourselves" into the sorting and grading processes with quite

[21] Judgments made from the perspective of ultimate moral equality are most effective when directed to individuals whose moral credit has been ascertained, as well as their moral worth. If we go directly from the perspective of moral worth to the perspective of ultimate moral equality without passing through the perspective of moral credit, it appears that something important has been left out.

the zeal of those who have never seen human beings as ultimate moral equals. The
difference, however, will be in the quality
and intensity of the emotions accompanying judgments of praise and blame based
on moral worth and moral credit. The
judgments themselves will go on being
made; human acts will go on being looked
at in causal contexts of varying scope. Our
models of human nature, in short, will go
on being used. To see whether it is psychologically possible to return from the
perspective of ultimate moral perspectives,
no determinist needs to look farther than
his own experience. It is in truth not possible to do anything else.

(2) A second objection is likely to be
raised by certain libertarians. It is the
charge that our so-called "perspective of
ultimate moral equality" is ignoble and
degrading. Such a perspective, it will be
said, affords a particularly deplorable example of the levelling tendency which
seeks to destroy standards of merit in all
areas. Plato's charge against political democracy—that it makes equals of unequals
—applies a thousandfold to the "moral
democracy" that is claimed to be visible
from this distorting perspective. The moral
world is hierarchical to the core; to remove
the sheep and the goats from the moral
landscape is to destroy it. So runs this
second charge.

The answer to it divides into two
parts. The first point to be made is that
moral discriminations have not been permanently eradicated. Viewed from the
other moral perspectives (which, as we
have seen, are not eliminated by the perspective of ultimate moral equality), the
moral landscape swims back into our ken
with sheep and goats intact. Moreover, it
is sometimes more appropriate to look at
the moral world in this way.

But some will feel that this part of the
answer is not enough: that it is wrong
ever to see all persons as moral equals.
Now even though one may be deeply convinced that the perspective of ultimate

moral equality, far from being ignoble, is
—when appropriately used—exalted and
inspiring, it is not altogether easy to know
how to argue for this conviction. One may
point to the increase in compassion, tolerance, equanimity, that come to those who
know how to look at themselves and each
other on occasion from the perspective of
ultimate moral equality. But it may conceivably be said in reply that these are
regarded as benefits only by persons who
are antecedently convinced that determinism is, as a matter of fact, true. This reply
is not without force. That portion of
Spinoza's defense of determinism which
shows "what service to our own lives a
knowledge of this doctrine is" has not lost
its power to move determinists; but what
power do his words have over others? If
all our acts go back to ultimate causes,
then we should indeed look at all human
beings with compassion and tolerance; but
what if they do not? Libertarians may contend that compassion and tolerance are not
spiritual goods if these attitudes are
directed toward humans who, because they
have misused their freedom, simply do not
deserve to be pitied or tolerated. And
equanimity in the face of moral iniquity
is nothing but extreme moral callousness,
particularly unforgivable, it will be said,
when the wrongdoer is oneself.

It may prove impossible to disabuse
some extreme libertarians of their conviction that human beings should never be
regarded as being all morally equal. But
it is hard to believe that most people, whatever their metaphysical beliefs, will not
find something to which they can respond
positively in the attitudes engendered by
the perspective of ultimate moral equality.
The making of all our judgments of praise
and blame with less finality, less assurance
that they represent the whole truth, must
seem to many an end to be welcomed.[22]
Religious teachings which have kept be-

[22] This end is particularly desirable for those
more sweeping judgments in which persons are
praised or blamed, not for specified acts, but for

fore our eyes the view from something like the perspective of ultimate moral equality ("There but for the grace of God go I") have performed a great service for our moral outlook.[23]

(3) Finally, I want to take note of the contention—in which those of all metaphysical persuasions will doubtless heartily concur—that this account of praise and blame is simply too complicated to be acceptable. How could the average unspeculative mortal ever find his way among such a bewildering variety of moral perspectives? How could he ever make a judgment of praise or blame?

In reply to these questions, two points must be made. First, a single moral judgment arrived at from a single moral perspective is not necessarily made more complicated by the present account than by other accounts.[24] But, secondly, it must be admitted that difficulties do arise when a moral judge is asked to remember that other moral perspectives exist and set limits to the one that he is using at any given time, and when he is asked, as he sometimes must be, to decide on the moral perspective that should be used in a particular situation. We have seen that moral wisdom, on the present view, consists not merely in the ability to make correct moral appraisals from a single perspective, but also in the ability to correlate the per-

spectives, and, on occasion, to choose among them.

It may well be that few attain this kind of wisdom, yet it is by no means clear that it cannot be attained by unspeculative persons. Perhaps such persons can and do make concrete judgments of moral praise and blame in a balanced and large-minded way, keeping the various relevant considerations in due proportion, and governing their own attitudes accordingly, despite a lack of any grasp of a theoretical basis for what they are doing. But, if it should turn out that we cannot really evade the conclusion that the present account makes moral wisdom harder for an unspeculative person to attain, this conclusion would not necessarily vitiate the account. Why should it not be the case that moral wisdom demands considerable resources of intellect as well as of character?

In this paper, I have been arguing that the question with which we began, "Can determinists find a rationale for moral praise and blame?", can be answered affirmatively. I have tried to show, however, that the unrecognized assumption behind the typical and influential affirmative answers that have been given—the assumption that judgments of praise and blame are made from a single moral perspective—is mistaken. I have maintained that those determinists who give a negative answer to our original question have caught sight of some important truths that the others have missed. In the end, however, with their attempts to set up the perspective of ultimate moral equality as the sole valid perspective for judgments of praise and blame, they have fallen into the same fundamental error as the others. One group eternally confronts the other with the question "How can you deny that human beings can be said to be praiseworthy and blameworthy, in view of the fact that they commit acts that are right or wrong, and at the same time done voluntarily, knowingly, and from good or bad desires?" To which the second group incessantly

---

their whole characters. Space limitations have precluded the consideration of such judgments here; but their treatment forms an important part of a more detailed examination of moral perspectives.

[23] Note that, even though the grace of God may be regarded as being "freely" given, in so far as it is held to constitute a causal determinant of human action, it is treated as essentially similar to what have here been called "ultimate causes." Of considerable interest for further study would be a comparison of the perspective of ultimate moral equality—here described in purely naturalistic terms—with such religious concepts as "equality in the sight of God."

[24] Indeed, the distinction between moral worth and moral credit makes it possible to give a simpler account of the judgments made by each standard than the account which proponents of the single standard view would have to give if their position were adequately worked out.

hurls back a question of its own: "How can you assert that human beings can be said to be praiseworthy or blameworthy, in view of the fact that their acts, like all other events, are wholly subject to causal laws, and must be traced back, in the end, to factors wholly beyond the agents' control?" The account given here, which may be called the "theory of multiple moral perspectives," is designed to help put an end to this durable impasse. I have tried to show that the first group is speaking from the perspective of moral worth, while the second replies from the perspective of ultimate moral equality. Both perspectives are valid; but each perspective is incomplete.

Three moral perspectives are necessary, I have contended, if we are to tell the whole about the praiseworthiness and blameworthiness of human beings. One of these, the perspective of ultimate moral equality, takes form as a consequence of assuming determinism to be true; but its adoption is not without moral and spiritual benefits. The other perspectives can be exhibited in an examination of judgments of praise and blame conducted quite independently of any determinist assumptions; and we can then see that determinism is— at the very least—fully compatible with the use of these moral perspectives. It seems to me that considerable work remains to be done in clarifying and refining these concepts and principles, and in exploring their implications in many directions. But if the claims made here are in essentials justified, it follows that determinists need not feel that old familiar uneasiness when confronted by the concepts of moral praise and blame. On the contrary, it may be that we stand here on solid ground.

V

Ethics and Psychology

Reasons and Causes

S. I. BENN
RICHARD PETERS

Problems connected with freedom and determinism are best clarified by examining what we wish to convey when we say that an action is 'determined'. For there are two different things, which are often confused, which 'determined' can mean. Firstly, there is what we might call 'causal explicability' and, secondly, 'unavoidability'. Many people have failed to distinguish these two very different strands in the meaning of the term 'determined', and they have often thought that 'determined' involves *both* of these things. When we say that our behaviour is determined, therefore, it is often assumed both that our behaviour has causes and that it is unavoidable. Let us, therefore, consider these two strands in the meaning of 'determinism' in turn, and we can then later show that simply because our behaviour has causes it does not necessarily follow that it is unavoidable.

(A) CAUSAL EXPLICABILITY

Determinism to a scientist conveys the general proposition that every event has a cause. Whether this general proposition is true is a very difficult question to decide, but it is certainly assumed to be true by

Reprinted from *Social Principles and the Democratic State* by S. I. Benn and Richard Peters by permission of the authors and George Allen & Unwin Ltd. The American edition is entitled *Principles of Political Thought*.

most scientists. To say that an event has a cause is to say that there are universal laws together with statements about initial conditions prevailing at particular times, and that from these two together we can predict an event which we call an 'effect'. For example, given that under the conditions x,y,z, iron expands when it is heated, and given that the conditions x,y,z prevail and that this is a case of iron being heated, we can make the prediction that iron will expand. Here we have a typical causal relation. The so-called 'cause' is then the event referred to in the statement of initial conditions. And these conditions are regarded as being *sufficient* to explain the effect, if it is a full-blooded causal *explanation*.

Have we such relations in human affairs? The initial difficulty about saying that we have is that it is difficult to maintain that there are any psychological or sociological laws which would enable us to make such definite predictions. There are also difficulties connected with our knowledge of particular situations which constitute the initial conditions; for when we are dealing with stones and bodies falling, their past history is scarcely part of the present situation. But when we are dealing with human beings, their past history is very much part of the present situation, and it is very difficult to know whether a given case is really of the type to which the particular law we have in mind applies. Nevertheless, there are some generalizations in psychology and the social sciences which are reasonably well established. They do not enable us to make detailed predictions; they merely enable us to state the sort of thing that will *tend* to happen under certain typical conditions. In this respect psychology is in no worse plight than other sciences like meteorology. The difficulties arise from the complexity of the subject-matter, and, it might be argued, can be remedied in time.

If, however, we look more closely at these so-called laws in psychology we find, in the main, that they do not give sufficient explanations of human *actions,* of what human beings do deliberately, knowing what they are doing and for which they can give reasons. Freud's brilliant discoveries, for instance, were not of the causes of *actions* like signing contracts or shooting pheasants; rather they were of things that *happen* to a man like dreams, hysteria, and slips of the tongue. These might be called 'passions' more appropriately than 'actions', and in this respect they are similar to what we call 'fits of passion' or 'gusts of emotion'. Men do not dream or forget a name 'on purpose' any more than they are deliberately subject to impulses or gusts of emotion. One class of laws in psychology, then, gives causal explanations which seem sufficient to account for what *happens* to a man, but not for what he does.

There is another class of laws, however, which concern not what happens to men, but what they do—their actions, performances and achievements. But such laws state necessary rather than sufficient conditions. We have in mind here the contributions made by physiological psychologists and those who have studied cognitive skills like learning, remembering, and perceiving. Part of what we mean by such terms is that human beings attain a norm or standard. Remembering is not just a psychological process; for to remember is to be *correct* about what happened in the past. Knowing is not just a mental state; it is to be sure that we are *correct* and to have *good grounds* for our con-

viction. To perceive something is to be *right* in our claims about what is before our eyes; to learn something is to *improve* at something or to get something *right.* All such concepts have norms written into them. In a similar way, as we have previously argued,[1] a human action is typically something done in order to bring about a result or in accordance with a standard. Such actions can be said to be done more or less intelligently and more or less correctly only because of the norms defining what are ends and what are efficient and correct means to them. It follows that a psychologist who claims that such performances depend on antecedent physiological conditions or mental processes, can at the most be stating necessary conditions. For processes, of themselves, are not appropriately described as correct or incorrect, intelligent or stupid. They only become so in the context of standards laid down by men. As Protagoras taught, nature knows no norms. It may well be true that a man cannot remember without part of his brain being stimulated, or that learning is a function, in part, of antecedent 'tension'. But the very meaning of 'remembering' and 'learning' precludes a sufficient explanation in these sorts of naturalistic terms.

Furthermore the problem of the freedom of the will arose mainly in connection with a type of action that is palpably different from a mere movement or process—an action that is preceded by deliberation and choice. For, roughly speaking, a 'willed action' was usually taken to mean [2] one in which we think before we act, when we make up our minds in terms of considerations which are relevant to the matter in hand before we act. There are difficulties about developing

---

[1] See Chapter 1.
[2] Whether the concept of 'a willed action' is a useful or clear one is another matter. Reference is here made to traditional controversies about freedom of the will such as that between Hobbes and Bishop Bramhall. (See R. S. Peters, *Hobbes,* 1956, pp. 178–89.)

causal laws for actions of this type which are additional to those already stated about actions in general. Such difficulties are similar to those which the social scientist, as well as the psychologist, has in predicting what human beings will do. This is connected with the fact that into the human being's deliberations about what he is going to do will be introduced considerations about what he is likely to do, which the social scientist may have published. A scientist may discover a causal law connecting the properties of clover with a certain effect upon the digestive organs of sheep. But, when he publishes his findings, the sheep cannot take account of them and modify their behaviour accordingly. But with men it is different. Many causal connections discovered by psychologists may only hold good provided that the people whose actions are predicted in accordance with the law remain ignorant of what it asserts. And it is practically impossible to ensure that this is the case. So, if people know the causes on which a prediction of a certain type of behaviour is based, and if they deliberate before acting, they may do something different from what is predicted, just because they recognize these causes. A prediction may thus be valid only on the assumption that the people concerned remain unconscious of the causes on which it is based. Otherwise it may be no more than a warning.

But why cannot causal explanations *also* be given of such informed deliberations which precede actions? We are here confronted with the difficulty of accounting for *logical* thought in causal terms, of giving a causal explanation for rational actions done after deliberation which involves logically relevant considerations. This is an extreme case of the difficulty already cited of giving sufficient explanations in causal terms for actions and performances which involve norms and standards. Yet, as has already been pointed out, such premeditated actions are particularly important in the free-will controversy, as the exercise

of 'will' has usually been associated with rational deliberation before acting. When a man is solving a geometrical problem and his thoughts are proceeding in accordance with certain logical canons, it is logically absurd to suggest that any causal explanation in terms of movements in his brain, his temperament, his bodily state, and so on, is sufficient *by itself* to explain the movement of his thought. For logical canons are normative and cannot be sufficiently explained in terms of states and processes which are not. Of course there are any number of necessary conditions which must be taken account of. A man cannot think *without* a brain, for instance. But any *sufficient* explanation would have to take account of the *reasons* for his actions. We would have to know the rules of chess, for instance, which gave some *point* to a chess-player's move. Indeed we would only ask for the cause of a chess-player's behaviour if he did something which could not be explained in terms of the rules of chess and the objective at which he was aiming. If, for instance, he refrained from taking his opponent's queen, when this was the obvious and the best move, we might ask 'What made him do that?' and we would be asking for a causal explanation, like 'he was tired'. But this would now be an explanation of what *happened* to him, not of what he did deliberately. We would not ask for such an explanation if there was an obvious reason for his move.[3]

This example can be generalized and the point made that behaviour is usually explicable not because we know its causes, but because people act in accordance with

[3] Of course the category of 'action' is much wider than that of premeditated action, though it may be co-extensive with that of 'rationality'. For this covers the sort of things for which a man could have a reason—i.e. which fall under what we call the purposive rule-following model. Premeditated action is a particular case of action where action is *preceded* by rehearsals and deliberation; but often reasons can be given by people for what they do even though they do not deliberate *before* they act.

certain known rules and conventions and adopt appropriate means to objectives which are accepted as legitimate goals. We know why a parson is mounting the pulpit not because we know much about the causes of his behaviour but because we know the conventions governing church services. We would only ask what were the causes of his behaviour if he fainted when he peered out over the congregation or if something similar *happened* to him. Most of our explanations of human behaviour are couched in terms of a purposive, rule-following model, not in causal terms. Moral behaviour, above all other sorts, falls into this purposive, rule-following category. For, as Aristotle put it in his *Ethics*, it is not a man's passions which are the object of moral appraisal nor his capacity to be subject to such passions; rather we praise or blame a man for what he does about his passions, for the extent to which he controls or fails to control them in various situations. Deliberation and choice may not precede every action, but habits are set up as a result of such deliberation and choice. It is for the exercise of such habits that men are praised and blamed—for the ends which they seek and for the means which they adopt to bring about their ends. Punishment, too, as we have pointed out, presupposes that men can foresee the consequences of their actions and that they can learn to avoid those to which penalties are attached. Praise and blame, reward and punishment, act as rudders to steer human actions precisely because men deliberate and choose and can be influenced by considerations of consequences. There is a radical difference between actions of this sort and cases where things happen to a man—where he acts 'on impulse', has a dream, a vision, or lapse of memory, or where he is afflicted by a feeling of nausea or hysterical paralysis. Questions of the 'freedom of the will' do not arise where things happen to a man; only where a man acts and can be praised or blamed, punished or rewarded for what he does. Yet

it is precisely in these cases of human actions, as distinct from passions, that causal explanations seem inappropriate as sufficient explanations.

Two sorts of objection might be mounted against this attempt to limit the role of causal explanations of human behaviour. In the first place it might be said that by substituting concepts like rule-following and the pursuit of objectives we were in fact introducing other sorts of causes. Now the word 'cause' can be used in this very wide sense. But the terminological question is largely irrelevant; for two sorts of explanations which are logically quite different would then be included under the enlarged concept of 'cause'. To follow rules, to take steps which are seen to be necessary to reach some sort of objective, to see the point of something, these may be 'causes'; but they are causes in quite a different sense of 'cause' from things like stomach contractions, brain lesions, acute pains, and so on. The types of explanation must be distinguished whether we use the term 'cause' to cover both or not. And certainly seeing the point of something is quite different—even if it is called a 'cause'—from the causes prevalent in the physical world. In the early days of the determinist controversy philosophers like Spinoza and Kant used the term 'self-determined' to distinguish rational actions from those which could be explained in terms of mechanical causes like movements of the brain and body. Indeed Kant's suggestion that man lives in two worlds, and is subject to two different sorts of causation, is a metaphysical way of bringing out the logical distinction between these two sorts of explanation.

The second objection is the suggestion that all reasons might be rationalizations— a smoke screen for what we are going to do anyway. We are, as it were, pushed by causes in the mechanical, physical sense, whatever we do; but sometimes we throw up an elaborate smoke screen of excuses which make no difference to what we in fact do. If, however, we say that *all* reasons are rationalizations, we make no difference between the behaviour of an obsessive or a compulsive and that of a rational man. If a compulsive believes that his hands are covered in blood and spends his time continually washing them, no relevant considerations will make any difference to his behaviour. All the known tests fail to show blood; yet he still goes on washing his hands. But a civil servant making a complex decision about policy does not proceed like this. He will change his mind and alter policy in the light of relevant considerations. Indeed it is only because people *sometimes* alter their behaviour because of relevant considerations that it makes any *sense* to talk of rationalizations as well as of reasons. A term like 'rationalization', which casts aspersions on the reasons given for action, is a verbal parasite. It flourishes because there *are* cases of genuine reasons with which rationalizations can be contrasted. Thus even if all behaviour has causes, in the sense of *necessary* conditions, there are objections to saying that all behaviour—especially rational behaviour—can be *sufficiently* explained by causes of the sort suggested by physical scientists, and by mechanistic philosophers like Hobbes.

Whether this means that there is *also* a case for freedom depends on whether 'free' can be equated, in any of its various senses, with 'not sufficiently explained in causal terms'. Kant and Spinoza, who spoke of self-determinism in the case of rational action, claimed that this is the proper sense in which men could be said to be free. A man is free or self-determined, they said, in so far as his behaviour is explained in terms of his rational decisions rather than in terms of purely mechanical causes. Such causes were viewed as movements which somehow pushed or impelled a man to act. In other words there was an implied contrast between rational actions and those which occurred as the result of some sort of internal push which acted as a quasi-

constraint on a man. And this notion, that a man was somehow the victim of internal forces, fitted in very well with the other meaning of 'determined' which suggested that there was some sort of *unavoidability* about a man's actions.

(B) UNAVOIDABILITY

If a man is told that his actions have causes, he will probably agree. But if he is told that they are causally determined, he will demur. He will not complain about the verbal redundancy of the assertion but will picture himself somehow as a prisoner or a victim. This illustrates our contention that the concept of 'determinism' conveys more than the suggestion that behaviour has causes, or that it can be *sufficiently* explained in terms of its causal antecedents. To most people to say that actions are determined conveys the suggestion that they are unavoidable, that the individual in question cannot *help* doing what he does. Furthermore, it is often assumed that wherever causes can be found for a man's actions, then also his actions are unavoidable. And it has been argued, as a corollary, that once the causes of an action are known, blame and punishment are absurd.

This assumption that any action for which causes can be produced is therefore unavoidable is surely a mistake occasioned by the peculiar circumstances of the rise of science. It so happened that scientific advance, which consisted in the discovery of far-reaching causal laws, coincided with the widespread theological doctrine of predestination and with the metaphysical picture of the universe as a vast piece of clockwork in which human beings, like cog-wheels, were pushed on in a set pattern of movement. God, as it were, constructed the clock and set it going. If the clock could be seen as a whole, men could see what the future had in store for them and what movements determined that their fate should be this and no other. Causal discoveries revealed the springs and levers which pushed men towards their appointed destiny. The tacit assumption therefore developed that wherever causes could be found for actions, they were also unavoidable. Causes, being pictured always as internal pushes and pulls, were thought somehow to compel a man. And this picture suggests compulsion whether such causes are properly to be regarded as necessary or as sufficient conditions for human action. Men were therefore regarded as being not free because they were the victims of a peculiar internal sort of compulsion exercised by the causes of their behaviour. They were thus not able to avoid doing what they did.

Reasons and Causes

A. J. AYER

It is now almost a commonplace among philosophers that motives are not causes. But this is not to say that it is true.

Why is it thought to be true? There are various reasons, not all of them of equal weight. The most simple of them is that motives operate *a fronte* whereas causes operate *a tergo;* to put it crudely, that causes push while motives pull. A more sophisticated argument is that cause and effect are distinct events: so, if the motive for an action caused it, it would have to be a separate occurrence which preceded the action or at any rate accompanied it; but in many, perhaps in most, cases of motivated actions, such separate occurrences are simply not discoverable; the specification of the motive is part of the description of the action, not a reference to anything outside it, and certainly not a reference to any distinct event. Thirdly, it is argued that in the scientific sense of 'cause', which is what is here in question, even singular causal statements are implicitly universal; to say that one particular event is the cause of another is to imply that events of these types are invariably connected by a causal law: this is not true, however, of statements in which a motive is assigned for some particular action; such a statement does not imply that whenever people have motives of the kind in question they act in a similar manner, or that whenever

From *Man As a Subject for Science* by A. J. Ayer, 1964, pp. 12–26. Reprinted by permission of The Athlone Press and the author.

actions of that type are performed they are done from the same sort of motive. Finally, a point is made of the fact that motivated action often consists in following or attempting to follow a rule; that is to say, the action may be one to which normative criteria are applicable; the question arises whether it has been performed correctly; but this means, so it is argued, that we somehow impoverish the motive if we regard it merely as a cause.

Let us now examine these arguments in turn. The first of them need not detain us long. If the contention is that purposive behaviour is to be accounted for, not as the response to any past or present stimulus, but rather in terms of the future state of affairs towards the realization of which the behaviour is directed, the argument fails for the simple reason that there may not in fact be any such future state of affairs. Even if men generally succeed in fulfilling their purposes, they do sometimes fail, and the explanation of their embarking on the action must be the same whether the purpose is fulfilled or not. But this is enough to rule the end out of court as a determinant of the action. I do not share the qualms that some people feel about the idea of an event's being pulled into existence by one that does not yet exist, for these metaphors of pushing and pulling must not be taken too seriously; there is no great difficulty in regarding an earlier event as a function of a later one. But however little we are influenced by the metaphor, we cannot think it possible that an event may be pulled into existence by one that never exists at all.

But this, it may be said, is to take an unfairly naïve view of the argument. Its point is not that purposive behaviour is to be explained in terms of its actual achievement but rather that it has to be understood as tending towards a certain end, whether or not this end is actually attained. A general may not succeed in winning his battle, a chess player may not succeed in mating his opponent, but in order to make sense of their manoeuvres, we have to know that these are their aims. If we want to explain behaviour of this kind, the question which we have to ask is not what impels it but where it is directed; and the same applies at all levels down to the rat, or even the mechanical rat, in the maze.

This is all very well, but does it not concede the point at issue? For what is now singled out as the explanatory fact is not the end towards which the behaviour is directed, considered as a future event, but rather the agent's having this as his aim. The suggestion is that the agent behaves as he does because he has a conscious or unconscious need or desire for such and such a state of affairs to be realized. And why should not this be said to impel him?

At this point, the first argument dissolves into the second. For the answer which will be given to our last question is that very often these desires and needs do not exist independently of the behaviour which they are supposed to impel. No doubt there are cases in which a man is impelled to action by a felt desire for the end which he believes that the action will secure him, but even in many cases in which an agent would be said to be conscious of his purpose, his action is not preceded by any psychological occurrence which could figure as his desire for the end in question. His consciousness of his purpose, in so far as it is anything apart from his behaviour, may just consist in his ability to say what it is, if the occasion for this arises; it is not required

that he should actually have formulated it even to himself. If the agent is not conscious of his purpose, it is still less likely that he will have had any distinctive experience which can be identified as the felt desire or need for the end towards which his action is directed. In such cases we may indeed conceive of the agent's desire as an unconscious mental state which drives him to act as he does; if we have a materialistic outlook, we may identify his desire or his need with some physical state of his organism; but to have recourse in this way to the unconscious or to physiology is to put up a theory which may account for the agent's having the motive that he has rather than to offer an analysis of what the motive is. What it provides at best is a problematic explanation of the existence of the motive; but what is wanted here, and what it does not provide, is an account of the motive as being itself an explanation of the action which it governs.

Again this is all quite true, but it proves very little. If one starts with the assumption that motives can cause the actions which they motivate only if they are 'ghostly thrusts', that is only if they take the form of distinctive experiences which precede or accompany the action, then indeed this argument will show that motives need not be causes. But the assumption is unjustified. It is true that a cause must be distinguishable from its effect, but there are other ways in which a motive can be independent of the action which it motivates than by figuring as a distinct experience, or even as an element in a psychoanalytical or physiological theory. The reason why we say that an action is done from such and such a motive may be no more than that the agent behaves or is disposed to behave in a certain fashion; but the point is that the description of the behaviour which constitutes his having the motive need not be identical with, or even include, a description of the action to which his having the motive leads him. On the contrary, if the assignment of the motive did not refer to something other than the action, if it did not associate the action with anything else at all, it is hard to see how it could have any explanatory force: merely to redescribe a phenomenon is not in any way to account for it. Yes it is, someone may say, if the redescription tells us more about the phenomenon; the assignment of a motive is explanatory in the sense that it enlarges our description of the action; it fills in an important gap in the story. But at this stage the dispute becomes merely verbal. If anyone wishes to give such a wide interpretation to the concept of an action that the motive from which the action is done is counted as a part of it, well and good: this is not perhaps a very felicitous usage, but it is manageable. The point still remains that if the initial description of the action does not include a reference to the motive, then the provision of this reference does link the behaviour which has been described to something beyond it, whether it be a distinctive experience or, as is more commonly the case, a further item or pattern of actual or potential behaviour; and it is only because it does this that the reference to the motive is explanatory. Indeed, this would seem to be the main characteristic of explanations in terms of motive, or more generally in terms of purpose. They serve to establish a lawlike connection between different pieces of behaviour.

This may operate in various ways. The simplest level of purposive behaviour is that which is ascribed to a homoeostatic system. The behaviour of the system on any given occasion is seen as exemplifying a uniform tendency to maintain equilibrium; it is purposive just in the sense that under varying conditions it operates so as to attain the same end-state. Much the same applies to the case of the animal, or the machine in the maze; what makes its behaviour purposive is that its agitation habitually continues until it emerges from the maze; in this instance the directional aspect of the behaviour is underlined by the fact that the individual trials may be stages in a process of learning, in which case they are related in a lawlike fashion to one another. If the animal is given a reward for its success, its appetite for the reward may be a measurable causal factor in the process of its training. The sense in which the animal looks for the reward, and so may be said to have this as its motive, is just that its behaviour would not be quite what it is if the reward had not been given to it on previous occasions. When it comes to simple human actions like putting on an overcoat to go out on a winter's day, our explanation derives its force from some such presupposition as that people in general under conditions of this kind do what they can to protect themselves against the cold. That this is the agent's motive on this particular occasion, rather than, say, a desire to appear well dressed, may indeed be discoverable only through his own avowal of it. But then his disposition to make this avowal, at any rate to himself, is a causal condition of his action. If he were not disposed to make it, then he would not in these circumstances be acting as he does. Otherwise there is no ground for concluding that this is his motive. In a more complicated case, like that of the general planning his battle, the general's desire for victory, if that is in fact his motive, may be exhibited in a fairly wide range of behaviour apart from his conduct of this particular engagement. And here again, if the assignment of the motive is to have any explanatory force, we must be in a position to say that unless he behaved, or was disposed to behave, in these other ways he would not in the circumstances be planning the battle in the way that he does.

In all this there is little that is controversial. No one would deny that purposive behaviour fitted into some sort of pattern, and it seems pretty obvious that the assignment of motives could not be explanatory unless some lawlike connections were indicated by it. What may, however, still be disputed is that these connections are causal. It may be contended that the rough regularities in behaviour, which are all that we have seen to be required for the applicability of a purposive explanation, do not fit the standard model of the relation of cause and effect.

Once more this is partly a question of terminology. If we construe the causal relation in a strictly Humean fashion so that its terms can only be distinct events, then the objection holds. For we have seen that in many quite typical cases the motive may be present in the form of a disposition which, though distinct from the behaviour which it motivates, is still not exactly a distinct event. It seems to me, however, that even from the point of view of doing justice to the ordinary, let alone the scientific, use of causal language, this conception of the causal relation may be too restrictive. For one thing, we often want to be able to regard the absence of some circumstance as a causal factor, that is, to admit negative as well as positive conditions, and even this does not fit tidily into the Humean scheme. I have, of course, no quarrel with Hume's fundamental idea that causation must in the end be a matter of regular concomitance, but I suggest that causal relations should be regarded as holding between facts rather than events, where 'fact' is understood in the wide sense in which true propositions of any form can be taken as expressing facts. This involves no sacrifice, since in any cases where it is appropriate these causal statements about facts can be translated into statements about events; it merely extends the field of causal relations a little more widely. Then the sense in which an agent's motive may be said to be the cause of the action which it motivates is that given certain conditions the fact that the agent performs the action is inferable from the fact that he has the motive in virtue of a causal law.

But just as the first of the arguments which we listed dissolved into the second, so, if I am right in what I have just been saying, the second dissolves into the third; for now the question arises whether there really are such causal laws. On the face of it, it seems at least very doubtful. As I said when I first referred to this argument, it is surely possible for someone to act from a given motive on a particular occasion without its being the case either that whenever anyone has a motive of this kind he acts in this way, or that whenever anyone acts in this way he does so from this kind of motive. No doubt there must be some degree of regularity in the way in which motives lead to actions, for us to find the connection intelligible. If people hold very queer beliefs, they may indeed take means to a given end that others would not take; in this sense the connection between motive and action may even be quite idiosyncratic. It remains true, however, that people in general do what they believe will enable them to achieve their ends, and that these beliefs, though they may be false, are usually backed by a fair amount of evidence. The result is that there is at least a tendency for similar motives to be correlated with similar actions. This tendency is especially marked in the case of standing motives. The range of behaviour which we are prepared to ascribe to jealousy, or greed, or ambition is fairly narrow. Even so, it will be objected, such tendencies, at their very strongest, fall a long way short of being causal laws.

All this is true, but possibly not decisive; for it may be that we are looking for our causal laws in the wrong place. The point from which I think that we should start is that when a man is said to have acted in consequence of having such and such a motive, it is implied at least that if he had not had this motive he would not in the particular circumstances have acted as he did. But this is to say that the existence of the motive is taken to be a necessary condition of the action; not indeed a necessary condition of anyone's performing the action at any time, or even of the agent's performing it at any time, but a necessary condition of his performing it at just this juncture. The question then arises whether it is also taken to be part of a sufficient condition, and this is not easy to answer. The ground for arguing that it must be is that otherwise the ascription of the motive would not properly account for the action; we should have to allow that even granting the agent's motive and the rest of the attendant circumstances, including all the other aspects of the agent's mental and physical condition at that time, we could not entirely rely on the action's taking place; and to this extent its occurrence will still be unexplained and indeed inexplicable. There may, however, be those who are prepared to accept this consequence, so long as they can hold that there is a high probability in this situation of the action's taking place: that is, they may be satisfied with the hypothesis that if the situation were repeated a great number of times the action would take place very much more often than not. But since this leaves an element of arbitrariness, in that we have no answer to the question why it should ever not take place, it seems preferable to make the stronger claim, unless it can be shown to be untenable. The suggestion then would be that whenever an agent can properly be said to have acted exclusively from a given motive, the circumstances must be such that in any situation of this kind, indispensably including the presence of such a motive, an action of this kind invariably follows.

It is clear that if so strong a claim as this is to be made to appear even plausible, a great deal will have to be included in the situation, both in the way of positive and negative conditions. We must, however, avoid including so much detail in the description either of the situation or the action that our claim becomes trivial; our ground for saying that there is an invariable connection between situations and actions of the sorts in question must be not that either the situation or the action is unique. In other words, the types of fact which our laws connect must be envisaged as repeatable.

But where are these connections to be found? Surely it is idle to maintain that these laws exist if we are unable to produce any examples. Well, perhaps we can produce examples of a rather humble kind. Let us begin with the hypothesis that whenever a person has a desire for the existence of a state of affairs S and believes that it is immediately in his power to bring about S by performing the action A, but not by any other means, and there is no state of affairs S^1 such that he both prefers the existence of S^1 to that of S and believes it to be immediately in his power to bring about S^1, but not conjointly with S, then unless he is prevented he will perform the action A. This is not quite a tautology, since the existence of the agent's desire is supposed to be established independently of his taking any steps to satisfy it. On this account, indeed, it may even not be unconditionally true: there may be cases of inhibition which would have to be specially provided for. But even if this difficulty can be overcome, the hypothesis still falls short of what we want because its consequent is subject to a general proviso: the person who satisfies the antecedent will perform the action A unless he is prevented. The question is whether this proviso can be dispensed with.

The way to dispense with it would be to list all the things that might prevent the action from being done, and insert them in the antecedent in the form of negative conditions. This would seem indeed to be an impossible undertaking at this level of generality: we could hardly hope to draw up an exhaustive list of negative conditions which would at this point apply to any action whatsoever. But in its application to particular instances, our general hypothesis will in any case dissolve into a number of more specific ones, according to the nature of the case: and once the relevant type of action and perhaps also certain features in the situation of the agent have been specified, it does not seem to me obvious that the list of negative conditions cannot be completed. Thus if the action is one which involves making a certain sort of hand movement, there may be a finite number of types of bodily disorder which would prevent it from being carried out; if it involves handling certain physical objects, there may be a finite number of ways in which they could become intractable; if the condition of the agent is specified, the types of psychological impediment to which he is then subject may again be finite in number: and if the number of these various factors is so limited, there seems to be no compelling reason to hold that they cannot be discovered and listed.

Of course we shall have no guarantee that the list is complete; but then we do not have such a guarantee in the case of laws of any other type. However carefully a generalization is formulated it must at least remain conceivable that it holds only under certain further conditions which we have failed to specify. Technically, if there are found to be such conditions, the generalization is falsified, though sometimes we prefer to regard it as having been incompletely stated. I do not, however, agree with those who would read into every generalization of law a *ceteris paribus* clause which tacitly protects it from being falsified through the operation of factors which the proponent of the generalization did not foresee. No doubt it is too much to require, as John Stuart Mill did, that causal laws should hold unconditionally, if this is understood to imply that they would still be true no matter what else were true; for one law often depends upon others, so that its truth would not be preserved if these other laws were false. It is, however, not too much to require that the law should hold under any circumstances whatever that actually arise. If the field which it is designed to cover is restricted, this limitation can and should be made explicit.

If *ceteris paribus* clauses were allowable, the task of finding laws in the sphere of human action would be very much easier, but as our example has shown, these provisos would only increase the laws' security at the expense of their scientific interest. Even as it is, our hypothesis contained a stipulation which would often not be satis-

fied. It is by no means invariably true that when someone is aiming at a given end he believes that there is only one means of attaining it which it is immediately in his power to realize. Very often he will be presented with a choice of such means, so that it needs to be explained why he selects one of them rather than the others. I have no doubt that a number of examples could be found in which I should not know how this was to be done, but I suggest that quite a lot of cases would be covered by the following hypothesis: whenever the antecedent of our first hypothesis is satisfied, with the difference that the agent believes that it is immediately in his power to bring about S not only by performing the action A but also by performing the action A^1, but that he cannot perform both, then if he believes that A and A^1 are equally efficacious in bringing about S, but prefers what he expects to be the other consequences of A to those which he expects of A^1, he will, unless he is prevented, perform the action A. Again, if this is not to be tautologous, there must be evidence for his preferring the other expected consequences of A to those of A^1, independently of the fact that he does perform A, but I think it fair to assume that this will usually be available. Our hypothesis does not, of course, commit us to holding that whenever an agent has a choice between actions of the kind A and A^1 as means to a given type of end S, he will choose A. A man may well decide to walk to work on one occasion and take a taxi on another. But then the assumption is that there is a change in the circumstances, in the state of his health or his finances or the weather or some other combination of factors, which will sufficiently account for the variations in his preference. I admit, however, that until a set of such hypotheses has been formulated and tested, the degree of strength that we can attribute to generalizations about human conduct remains an open question.

The most that I would claim at this stage is that the difference between these generalizations and those that can be found to govern other natural phenomena is nowhere more than a difference of degree. What I have tried to show, in arguing that motives may be causes, is that there is no warrant for regarding explanation in terms of motives as something of a different order from the explanations that occur in the physical sciences. There is nothing about human conduct that would entitle us to conclude *a priori* that it was in any way less lawlike than any other sort of natural process.

But what of the argument that human actions conform to rules, that we are often more interested in judging whether and how far they are up to standard than in discovering how they came about? I cannot see that it is relevant. From the fact that we can estimate an action in terms of its conforming to a rule, it no more follows that the performance of the action is not causally explicable than it follows that the appearance of a rainbow is not causally explicable from the fact that it can be made the subject of an aesthetic judgement. To explain something causally does not preclude assessing it in other ways. But perhaps the suggestion is merely that to relate an action to a rule is one way of accounting for it, and, in the present state of our knowledge, a better way of accounting for it than trying to subsume it under dubious causal laws. I cannot even agree with this because I think that it presents us with a false antithesis. The only reason why it is possible to account for the performance of an action by relating it to a rule is that the recognition of the requirements of the rule is a factor in the agent's motivation. He may attach a value in itself to performing a certain sort of action correctly; he may see its correct performance as a means towards some further end; or it may be a combination of the two. In any event this is as much a causal explanation as any other explanation in terms of motive. The invocation of rules adds nothing to the general argument.

The same applies, in my view, to the argument that actions most often need to be understood in terms of their social contexts. A great deal is made by some philosophers of the fact that an action is not a mere physical movement. It has a significance which depends not only on the agent's intention and motive, but very frequently also on a complex of social factors. Think of the social norms and institutions that are involved in such commonplace actions as signing a cheque, signalling that one is going to turn when one is driving a car, saluting a superior officer, playing a card, shaking hands with someone to whom one has just been introduced, waving good-bye to a friend. To represent these merely as different sorts of hand-movements, which of course they also are, is to miss their significance; it is indeed to fail to represent them in their character as actions.

All this is true, except that it seems to be an arbitrary question what we are to regard as constituting an action: whether, for example, we choose to say that the motorist's action is one of putting out his hand or one of signalling that he is going to turn. Earlier on, I referred to the action of drinking a glass of wine as an instance of the way in which the same action can have a different significance in different social contexts: it would have been no less, but also no more correct if I had described this as an instance of the way in which the same physical process can in such different contexts become a different action. Wherever we decide to draw the line between the characterization of an action and the assessment of its significance, the point remains that the physical movement has to be interpreted, and that in order to interpret it correctly it will often be necessary to understand its social as well as its personal implications.

But if we grant this point, what follows? Certainly not, as the philosophers who lay stress upon it seem to think, that these actions cannot be explained in causal terms. For when it comes to accounting for an action, the only way in which the social context enters the reckoning is through its influence upon the agent. The significance of the action is the significance that it has for him. That is to say, his idea that this is the correct, or expedient, or desirable thing to do in these circumstances is part of his motivation; his awareness of the social context and the effects which this has on him are therefore to be included in the list of initial conditions from which we seek to derive his performance of the action by means of a causal law. Whether such laws are discoverable or not may be an open question; but the fact that these items figure among the data has no important bearing on it.

That human behaviour has a point or meaning, in this sense, is not even an argument against the materialist thesis that it is all physiologically determined. This thesis is indeed highly speculative; we are very far from having a physiological theory which would account for people's actions in specific detail, let alone from being in a position to apply one. But if the motives which impel men to act are, let us say, projections of the state of their brains, there is no reason why this should not apply to their social responses as much as to anything else. But surely no purely physiological account could be an adequate description of an action. Obviously it could not; even if the study of the agent's brain could give us all the information that we needed beyond the observation of his physical movements, we should still have to decode it. But this is not an objection to holding that actions can be explained in these terms, any more than the fact that to talk about wave-lengths is not to describe colours is an objection to the science of optics. This also shows that even if I am wrong in assimilating motives to causes, it will not follow from this alone that human behaviour is not entirely subject to causal explanation. For the fact that we can explain an action in one manner by referring to the agent's motive leaves it a fully

open question whether it cannot also be explained more scientifically in terms, say, of a physiological theory.

None of this settles the issue of determinism. I do not indeed think that it can be settled at this level, since I agree with those who hold that it should not be interpreted as an *a priori* question. It is of course true that not every event in human history could in fact be predicted. Not only would the making of each prediction itself then have to be predicted, and so *ad infinitum*, but as Professor Popper and others have rightly pointed out, it would follow that no one could ever have a new idea. But however comforting this may be to those who dislike conceiving of themselves as subjects for science, it does not go any way to prove that not all events in human history are susceptible of lawlike explanations. The strength of the determinists lies in the fact that there seems to be no reason why the reign of law should break down at this point, though this is an argument which seemed more convincing in the age of classical physics than it does today. The strength of the indeterminists lies in the fact that the specific theories which alone could vindicate or indeed give any substance to their opponents' case have not yet been more than sketched, though this is not to say that they never will be. Until such theories are properly elaborated and tested, I think that there is little more about this topic that can be usefully said.

A philosophical question which I have not here discussed, partly because I do not think that I have anything new to say about it, is whether the denial of determinism is implied in our usual ascriptions of moral and legal responsibility. In common with many other philosophers I used to hold that it was not, that in this respect the antithesis between the claims of free will and determinism was illusory, but in so far as this is a question of what people actually believe, I now think it more likely that I was wrong. This is indeed a matter for a social survey which, as I said before, would probably not yield a very clear result. I should, however, expect it to indicate that if it were shown to them that a man's action could be explained in causal terms, most people would take the view that he was not responsible for it. Since it is not at all clear why one's responsibility for an action should depend on its being causally inexplicable, this may only prove that most people are irrational, but there it is. I am indeed strongly inclined to think that our ordinary ideas of freedom and responsibility are very muddle-headed: but for what they are worth, they are also very firmly held. It would not be at all easy to estimate the social consequences of discarding them.

Remarks on Psychological Hedonism

C. D. BROAD

We can now deal with the question whether Psychological Hedonism be itself true. Let us begin with certain undoubted facts which must be admitted. The belief that a future experience will be pleasant is *pro tanto* a motive for trying to get it, and the belief that it will be painful is *pro tanto* a motive for trying to avoid it. Again, the felt pleasantness of a present pleasant experience is *pro tanto* a motive for trying to make it last, whilst the felt painfulness of a present experience is *pro tanto* a motive for trying to make it stop. The question is whether the expected pleasantness of a future experience is the only feature in it which can make us want to get it, whether the felt pleasantness of a present experience is the only feature in it which can make us want to prolong it, whether the expected painfulness of a future experience is the only feature in it which can make us want to avoid it, and whether the felt painfulness of a present experience is the only feature in it which can make us want to get rid of it.

I must begin with one explanatory remark which is necessary if the above proposition is to be taken as a perfectly accurate statement of Psychological Hedonism. No sane Psychological Hedonist would deny that a pleasure which is believed to be longer and less intense may be preferred for its greater duration to one

From *Five Types of Ethical Theory* by C. D. Broad, 1930. Reprinted by permission of Routledge & Kegan Paul Ltd. New York: Humanities Press Inc.

which is believed to be shorter and more intense. Nor would he deny that a nearer and less intense pleasure may be preferred for its greater nearness to a more intense but remoter pleasure. And this implies that duration and remoteness are in some sense factors which affect our desires as well as pleasantness and painfulness. This complication may be dealt with as follows. There are certain determinable characteristics which every event, as such, must have. Date of beginning and duration are examples. There are others which an event may or may not have. Pleasantness, colour, and so on, are examples. Let us for the present call them respectively "categorial" and "non-categorial" determinable characteristics of events. Then the accurate statement of Psychological Hedonism would be as follows. No non-categorial characteristic of a present or prospective experience can move our desires for or against it except its hedonic quality; but, granted that it has hedonic quality, the effect on our desires is determined jointly by the determinate form of this and by the determinate forms of its categorial characteristics.

Now, so far as I am aware, no argument has ever been given for Psychological Hedonism except an obviously fallacious one which Mill produces in his *Utilitarianism*. He says there that "to desire" anything and "to find" that thing "pleasant" are just two different ways of stating the same fact. Yet he also appeals to careful introspection in support of Psychological Hedonism. Sidgwick points out that, if Mill's statement were true, there would be no more need of intro-spection to decide in favour of the doctrine than there is need for introspection to decide that "to be rich" and "to be wealthy" are two different expressions for the same fact. But, as he also points out, Mill is de-ceived by a verbal ambiguity. There is a sense of "please" in English in which the two phrases "X pleases me" and "I desire X" stand for the same fact. But the verb "to please" and the phrase "to be pleasant" are not equivalent in English. In the sense in which "X pleases me" is equivalent to "I desire X" it is not equivalent to "I find X pleasant." If I decide to be martyred rather than to live in comfort at the expense of concealing my opinions, there is a sense in which martyrdom must "please me" more than living in comfort under these condi-tions. But it certainly does not follow *ex vi termini* that I believe that martyrdom will be "more pleasant" than a comfortable life of external conformity. I do not think that "pleasantness" can be defined, or even de-scribed unambiguously by reference to its relations to desire. But I think we can give a fairly satisfactory ostensive definition of it as that characteristic which is common to the experience of smelling roses, of tasting chocolate, of requited affection, and so on, and which is opposed to the characteristic which is common to the experiences of smelling sulphuretted hydrogen, of hearing a squeaky slate-pencil, of being hurt, of un-requited affection, and so on. And it is certainly not self-evident that I can desire *only* experiences which have the character-istic thus ostensively defined.

I think that there is no doubt that Psy-chological Hedonism has been rendered plausible by another confusion. The experi-ence of having a desire fulfilled is always *pro tanto* and for the moment pleasant. So, whenever I desire anything, I foresee that if I get it I shall have the pleasure of fulfilled desire. It is easy to slip from this into the view that my motive for desiring X is the pleasure of fulfilled desire which I foresee that I shall enjoy if I get X. It is clear that

this will not do. I have no reason to antici-pate the pleasure of fulfilled desire on get-ting X unless I already desire X itself. It is evident then that there must be *some* desires which are not for the pleasures of fulfilled desire. Let us call them "primary desires," and the others "secondary." Butler has abundantly shown that there must be some primary desires. But, as Sidgwick rightly points out, he has gone to extremes in the matter which are not logically justi-fied. The fact that there must be primary desires is quite compatible with Psycholog-ical Hedonism, since it is quite compatible with the view that all primary desres are for primary pleasures, i.e., for pleasures of taste, touch, smell, etc., as distinct from the pleasures of fulfilled desire. Still, introspect-tion shows that this is not in fact so. The ordinary man at most times plainly desires quite directly to eat when he is hungry. In so doing he incidentally gets primary plea-sures of taste and the secondary pleasure of fulfilled desire. Eventually he may be-come a *gourmand*. He will then eat because he desires the pleasures of taste and he may even make himself hungry in order to enjoy the pleasures of fulfilled desire.

There is a special form of Psychological Hedonism of which Locke is the main exponent. This holds that all desire can be reduced to the desire to remove pain or uneasiness. The one conative experience is aversion to present pain, not desire for future pleasure. The position is as follows. When I am said to desire some future state X this means that the contemplation by me of my non-possession of X is painful. I feel an aversion to this pain and try to remove it by trying to get X. Since in the case of some things the contemplation of my non-possession of them is painful, whilst in the case of others it is neutral or pleasant, the question would still have to be raised as to why there are these differences. Perhaps the theory under discussion should not be counted as a form of Psychological Hedo-nism unless it holds that my awareness of the absence of X is painful if and only if I believe that the possession of X would be pleasant. This is in fact Locke's view, though he adds the proviso that my uneasiness at the absence of X is not necessarily proportional to the pleaure which I believe I should get from the possession of X. We will therefore take the theory in this form.

As regards the first part of the theory Sidgwick points out that desire is not usually a painful experience, unless it be very intense and be continually frustrated. No doubt desire is an unrestful state, in the sense that it tends to make us change our present condition. It shares this characteristic with genuine pain. But the difference is profound. When I feel aversion to a present pain I simply try to get rid of it. When I feel the unrest of desire for a certain object I do not simply try to get rid of the uneasiness; I try to get that particular object. I could often get rid of the feeling far more easily by diverting my attention from the object than by the tedious and uncertain process of trying to gain possession of it. As regards the second part of the theory, it seems plain on inspection that I may feel uneasiness at the absence of some contemplated object for other reasons than that I believe that the possession of it would be pleasant. I might feel uncomfortable at the fact that I am selfish, and desire to be less selfish, without for a moment believing that I should be happier if I were more unselfish.

The Psychological Hedonist, at this stage, has two more lines of defence: (a) He may say that we unwittingly desire things only in respect of their hedonic qualities, but that we deceive ourselves and think that we desire some things directly or in respect of other qualities. It is plain that this assertion cannot be proved; and, unless there be some positive reason to accept Psychological Hedonism, there is not the faintest reason to believe it. (b) He may say that our desires were originally determined wholly and solely by the hedonic qualities of objects; but that now, by association and other causes, we have come to desire certain things directly or for other reasons. The case of the miser who has come by association to desire money for itself, though he originally desired it only for its use, is commonly quoted in support of this view. Mill, in his *Utilitarianism*, deals with the disinterested love of virtue on these lines. Sidgwick makes the following important observations on this contention. In the first place it must be sharply distinguished from the doctrine that the original *causes* of all our desires were previous pleasant and painful experiences. The question is what were the original *objects* and *motives* of desire, not what kind of previous experiences may have *produced* our present desires. Secondly, the important question for ethics is what we desire here and now, not what we may have desired in infancy or in that pre-natal state about which the Psycho-analysts, who appear to be as familiar with the inside of their mother's womb as with the back of their own hands, have so much to tell us. If Ethical Hedonism be the true doctrine of the good, it is no excuse for the miser or the disinterested lover of virtue that they were sound Utilitarians while they were still trailing clouds of glory behind them. Lastly, such observations as we can make on young children point in exactly the opposite direction. They seem to be much more liable to desire things directly and for no reason than grown people. No doubt, as we go further back it becomes harder to distinguish between self-regarding and other impulses. But there is no ground for identifying the vague matrix out of which both grow with one rather than with the other.

I think that we may accept Sidgwick's argument here, subject to one explanation. It may well be the case that what very young children desire is on the whole what will in fact give them immediate pleasure, and that what they shun is what will in fact give them immediate pain; though there are plenty of exceptions even to this. But there is no ground to suppose that they think of the former things as likely to be pleasant, and desire them *for that reason*; or that they think of the latter things as likely to be painful, and shun them *for that reason*. It is unlikely that they have the experience of desiring and shunning for a reason at all at the early stages. And, if this be so, their experiences are irrelevant to Psychological Hedonism, which is essentially a theory about the reasons or motives of desire.

(2, 3) Psychological Hedonism is now refuted, and the confusions which have made it plausible have been cleared up. It remains to notice a few important general facts about the relations of pleasure and desire and of pain and aversion. (*a*) Just as we distinguish between the pleasure of fulfilled desire and other pleasures, such as the smell of roses, so we must distinguish between the pain of frustrated desire and other pains, such as being burnt. And just as there are secondary desires for the pleasures of fulfilled desire, so there are secondary aversions for the pain of frustrated desire. Secondary aversions presuppose the existence of primary aversions, and it is logically possible that all primary aversions might be directed to pains. But inspection shows that this is not in fact the case. (*b*) Among those pleasures which do not consist in the experience of fulfilled desire a distinction must be drawn between passive pleasures, such as the experience of smelling a rose, and the pleasures of pursuit. A great part of human happiness consists in the experience of pursuing some desired object and successfully overcoming difficulties in doing so. The relations of this kind of pleasure to desire are somewhat complicated. The pleasure of pursuit will not be enjoyed unless we start with at least some faint desire for the pursued end. But the intensity of the pleasure of pursuit may be out of all proportion to the initial intensity of the desire for the end. As the pursuit goes on the desire to attain the end grows in inten-

sity, and so, if we attain it, we may have enjoyed not only the pleasure of pursuit but also the pleasure of fulfilling a desire which has become very strong. All these facts are illustrated by the playing of games, and it is often prudent to try to create a desire for an end in order to enjoy the pleasures of pursuit. As Sidgwick points out, too great a concentration on the thought of the pleasure to be gained by pursuing an end will diminish the desire for the end and thus diminish the pleasure of pursuit. If you want to get most pleasure from pursuing X you will do best to try to forget that this is your object and to concentrate directly on aiming at X. This fact he calls "the Paradox of Hedonism."

It seems to me that the facts which we have been describing have a most important bearing on the question of Optimism and Pessimism. If this question be discussed, as it generally is, simply with regard to the prospects of human happiness or misery in this life, and account be taken only of passive pleasures and pains and the pleasures and pains of fulfilled or frustrated desire, it is difficult to justify anything but a most gloomy answer to it. But it is possible to take a much more cheerful view if we include, as we ought to do, the pleasures of pursuit. From a hedonistic standpoint, it seems to me that in human affairs the means generally have to justify the end; that ends are inferior carrots dangled before our noses to make us exercise those activities from which we gain most of our pleasures; and that the secret of a tolerably happy life may be summed up in a parody of Hegel's famous epigram about the Infinite End,* *viz.*, "the attainment of the Infinite End just consists in preserving the illusion that there is an End to be attained."

---

* *Die Vollführung des unendlichen Zwecks ist so nur die Täuschung aufzuheben, als ob er noch nicht vollführt sei.*

Duty and Interest

H. A. PRICHARD

In seeking a subject for an inaugural lecture, I have tried to find one which, without raising too technical issues, is near enough to every one to be of general interest and yet would be considered by philosophers still sufficiently controversial to deserve consideration. This subject I hope I have found in the relation between duty and interest. The topic is, of course, well worn. Nevertheless anyone who considers it closely will find that it has not the simple and straightforward character which at first sight it appears to possess.

A general but not very critical familiarity with the literature of Moral Philosophy might well lead to the remark that much of it is occupied with attempts either to prove that there is a necessary connexion between duty and interest or in certain cases even to exhibit the connexion as something self-evident. And the remark, even if not strictly accurate, plainly has some truth in it. It might be said in support that Plato's treatment of justice in the *Republic* is obviously such an attempt, and that even Aristotle in the *Ethics* tries to do the same thing, disguised and weak though his attempt may be. As modern instances, Butler and Hutcheson might be cited; and to these might be added not only Kant, in whom we should perhaps least expect to find such a proof, but also Green.

When we read the attempts referred to we naturally cannot help in a way wishing them to succeed; and we might express our wish in the form that we should all like

From H.A. Prichard, *Duty and Interest*, 1928, pp. 3–29, by permission of the Clarendon Press, Oxford.

to be able to believe that honesty is the best policy. At the same time we also cannot help feeling that somehow they are out of place, so that the real question is not so much whether they are successful, but whether they ought ever to have been made. And my object is to try to justify our feeling of dissatisfaction by considering what these attempts really amount to, and more especially what they amount to in view of the ideas which have prompted them. For this purpose, the views of Plato, Butler, and Green, may, I think, be taken as representative, and I propose to concentrate attention on them.

One preliminary remark is necessary. It must not be assumed that what are thus grouped together as attempts either to prove or to exhibit the self-evidence of a connection between duty and interest are properly described by this phrase, or even that they are all attempts to do one and the same thing. And in particular I shall try to show that the attempts so described really consist of endeavours based on mutually inconsistent presuppositions, to do one or another of three different things.

On a casual acquaintance with the *Republic*, we should probably say without hesitation that, apart from its general metaphysics, what it is concerned with is justice and injustice, and that, with regard to justice and injustice, its main argument is an elaborate attempt, continued to the end of the book, to show in detail that if we look below the surface and consider what just actions really consist in and also the nature of the soul, and, to a minor degree, the nature of the world in which we have to act, it will become obvious, in spite of appearance to the contrary, that it is by acting justly that we shall really gain or become happy.

Further, if we were to ask ourselves, 'What are Plato's words for right and wrong?'—and plainly the question is fair—we should have in the end to give as the true answer what at first would strike us as a paradox. We should have to allow that Plato's words for right and wrong are not to be found in such words as χρῆ or δεῖ and their contraries, as in χρῆ δίκαιον εἶναι or ὄυτνινα τρόπον χρῆ ζῆν, where the subject is implied by the context to be τὸν μέλλοντα μακάριον ἔσεσθαι, but in δίκαιον and ἄδικον themselves. When he says of some action that it is δίκαιον, that is his way of saying that it is right, or a duty, or an act which we are morally bound to do. When he says that it is ἄδικον, that is his way of saying that it is wrong. And in the sense in which we use the terms 'justice' and 'injustice,' it is less accurate to describe what Plato is discussing as justice and injustice than as right and wrong. Our previous statement, therefore, might be put in the form that Plato is mainly occupied in the *Republic* with attempting to show it is by doing our duty, or what we are morally bound to do, that we shall become happy.

This is the account of his object which we are more particularly inclined to give if we chiefly have in mind what Socrates in the fourth Book is made to offer as the solution of the main problem. But this solution is preceded by an elaborate statement of the problem itself, put into the mouth of Glaucon and Adeimantus; and if we consider this statement closely, we find ourselves forced to make a substantial revision of this account of Plato's object. Glaucon and Adeimantus make it quite clear that whatever it is that they are asking Socrates to show about what they refer to as justice, their object in doing so is to obtain a refutation of what may be called the Sophistic theory of morality. Consequently, if we judge by what Glaucon and Adeiman-

tus say, whatever Plato is trying to prove must be something which Plato would consider as affording a refutation of the Sophistic theory. But what is this theory as represented by Plato? It almost goes without saying that in the first instance men's attitude towards matters of right and wrong is an unquestioning one. However they have come to do so, and in particular whether their doing so is due to teaching or not, they think, and think without having any doubt, that certain actions are right and that certain others are wrong. No doubt in special cases, they may be doubtful; but, as regards some actions, they have no doubt at all, though to say this is not the same as to say that they are certain. But there comes a time when men are stirred out of this unquestioning frame of mind; and in particular the Sophists, as Plato represents them, were thus stirred by the reflection that the actions which men in ordinary life thought right, such as paying a debt, helping a friend, obeying the government, however they differed in other respects, at least agreed in bringing directly a definite loss to the agent. This reflection led them to wonder whether men were right in thinking these actions duties, i.e. whether they thought so truly. Then, having failed to find indirect advantages of these actions which would more than compensate for the direct loss, i.e. such advantages as are found in what we call prudent actions, they drew the conclusion that these actions cannot really be duties at all, and that therefore what may roughly be described as the moral convictions which they and others held in ordinary life were one gigantic mistake or illusion. Finally, they clinched this conclusion by offering something which they represented as an account of the origin of justice, but which is really an account of how they and others came to make the mistake of thinking these actions just, i.e. right.

This is the theory which on Plato's own showing he wants to refute. It is a theory about certain actions, and, on his own showing, what he has to maintain is the opposite theory about these same actions. But how, if our language is to be accurate, should these actions be referred to? Should they be referred to as *just*, i.e. right, actions, or should they be referred to as those actions which in ordinary life we *think* just, i.e. right? The difference, though at first it may seem unimportant, is really vital. In the unquestioning attitude of ordinary life we must either be *knowing* that certain actions are right or not knowing that they are right, but doing something else for which 'thinking them right' is perhaps the least unsatisfactory phrase. There is no possibility of what might be suggested as a third alternative, *viz.* that our activity is one of thinking, which in instances where we are thinking truly is also one of knowing. For, as Plato realized, to think truly is not to know, and to discover that in some particular case we were thinking truly is not to discover that in doing so we were knowing. Moreover, when we are what is described as reflecting on the activity involved in our unquestioning attitude of mind, we are inevitably thinking of it as having a certain definite character, and, in so thinking of it, we must inevitably be implying either that the activity is one of knowing or that it is not. For we must think of this attitude either as one of thinking, or as one of knowing, and if we think of it as one of thinking, we imply that it is not one of knowing, and *vice versa*. In fact, however we think of the activity, we are committed one way or the other. Now the Sophists clearly implied that this unquestioning attitude is one of thinking and not one of knowing; for it would not have been sense to maintain that those actions which in ordinary life we know to be right are really not right. Their theory, then, must be expressed by saying that those actions which in ordinary life we think, and so do not know, to be right are not really right. Consequently Plato also, since he regards this as the theory to be refuted, is implying that in ordinary life we think, and do not know, that certain actions are right, and that, to this extent, he agrees with the Sophists. And for this reason, if we are to state accurately the problem which he is setting himself, we must represent it as referring not to *just* actions but to those actions which he and others in ordinary life *think* just.

It is clear then that when Plato states through the medium of Glaucon and Adeimantus the problem which he has to solve, he is guilty of an inaccuracy, which, though it may easily escape notice, is important. For Glaucon and Adeimantus persistently refer to the actions of which they ask Socrates to reconsider the profitableness as just and unjust actions, whereas they should have referred to them as the actions which men in ordinary life think just and unjust.

I shall now take it as established that when we judge from Plato's own statement of his problem, worked out as it is by reference to the Sophists, we have to allow that he is presupposing that ordinarily we do not know but think that certain actions are right and that he is thinking of his task as that of having to vindicate the truth of these thoughts against the Sophists' objection. And this is what must be really meant when it is said that Plato's object is to vindicate *morality* against the Sophistic view of it, for here 'morality' can only be a loose phrase for our ordinary moral thoughts or convictions.

Glaucon and Adeimantus, however, do not simply ask Socrates to refute the Sophistic view; they ask him to do so in a particular way, which they imply to be the only way possible, *viz.* by showing that if we go deeper than the Sophists and consider not merely the gains and losses of which they take account, *viz.* gains and losses really due to the reputation for doing what men think just and unjust, but also those which these actions directly bring to the man's own soul, it will become obvious that it is by doing what we think just that we shall really gain. And so far as the rest of the *Republic* is an attempt to satisfy this request, this must be what it is an attempt to show.

Now on a first reading of the *Republic*, it is not likely to strike us that there is anything peculiar or unnatural about this part of the request. Just because Plato takes for granted that this is the only way to refute the Sophists, we are apt in reading him to do the same, especially as our attention is likely to be fully taken up by the effort to follow Plato's thought. But if we can manage to consider Plato's endeavour to refute the Sophists with detachment, what strikes us most is not his dissent from their view concerning the comparative profitableness of the actions which men think just and unjust—great, of course, as his dissent is—but the identity of principle underlying the position of both. The Sophists in reaching their conclusion were presupposing that for an action to be really just, it must be advantageous; for it was solely on this ground that they concluded that what we ordinarily think just is not really just. And what in the end most strikes us is that at no stage in the *Republic* does Plato take the line, or even suggest as a possibility, that the very presupposition of the Sophists' arguments is false, and that therefore the question whether some action which men think just will be profitable to the agent has really nothing to do with the question whether it is right, so that Thrasymachus may enlarge as much as he pleases on the losses incurred by doing the actions we think just without getting any nearer to showing that it is a mere mistake to think them just. Plato, on the contrary, instead of urging that the Sophistic contention that men lose by doing what they think just is simply irrelevant to the question whether these actions are just, throughout treats this contention with the utmost seriousness; and he implies that unless the Sophists can be met on their own ground by being shown that, in spite of appearances to the contrary, these actions will really be for the good of the agent, their conclusion that men's moral convictions are mere conventions must be allowed to stand. He therefore, equally with the Sophists, is implying that it is impossible for any action to be really just, i.e. a duty, unless it is for the advantage of the agent.

This presupposition, however, as soon as we consider it, strikes us as a paradox.

For though we may find ourselves quite unable to state what it is that does render an action a duty, we ordinarily think that, whatever it is, it is not conduciveness to our advantage; and we also think that though an action which is a duty may be advantageous it need not be so. And while we may not be surprised to find the presupposition in the Sophists, whose moral convictions are represented as at least shallow, we are surprised to find it in Plato, whose moral earnestness is that of a prophet. At first, no doubt, we may try to mitigate our surprise by emphasizing the superior character of the advantages which Plato had in mind. But to do this does not really help. For after all, whatever be meant by the 'superiority' of the advantages of which Plato was thinking, it is simply as advantages that Plato uses them to show that the actions from which they follow are right.

Yet the presupposition cannot simply be dismissed as obviously untrue. For one thing, any view of Plato's is entitled to respect. For another, there appear to be moments in which we find the presupposition in ourselves. There appear to be moments in which, feeling acutely the weight of our responsibilities, we say to ourselves, 'Why *should* I do all these actions, since after all it is others and not I who will gain by doing them?'

Moreover, there at least seems to be the same presupposition in the mind of those preachers whose method of exhortation consists in appeal to rewards. When, for instance, they commend a certain mode of life on the ground that it will bring about a peace of mind which the pursuit of worldly things cannot yield, they appear to be giving a resulting gain as the reason why we ought to do certain actions, and therefore to be implying that in general it is advantageousness to ourselves which renders an action one which we are bound to do. In fact the only difference between the view of such preachers and that of the Sophists seems to be that the former, in view of their theological beliefs, think that the various actions which we think right will have certain specific rewards the existence of which the Sophists would deny. And the identity of principle underlying their view becomes obvious if the preacher goes on to maintain, as some have done, that if he were to cease to believe in heaven, he would cease to believe in right and wrong. Again, among philosophers, Plato is far from being alone in presupposing that an action, to be right, must be for the good or advantage of the agent. To go no further afield than a commentator on Plato, we may cite Cook Wilson, whose claim to respect no one in Oxford will deny, and who was, to my mind, one of the acutest of thinkers. In lecturing on the *Republic* he used to insist that when men begin to reflect on morality they not only demand, but also have the right to demand, that any action which is right must justify its claim to be right by being shown to be for their own good; and he used to maintain that Plato took the right and only way of justifying our moral convictions, by showing that the actions which we think right are for the good of the society of which we are members, and that at the same time the good of that society *is* our good, as becomes obvious when the nature of our good is properly understood.

Moreover Plato, if he has been rightly interpreted, does not stand alone among the historical philosophers in presupposing the existence of a necessary connexion between duty and interest. At least Butler, whose thoughtfulness is incontestable, is with him. In fact in this matter he seems at first sight only distinguished from Plato by going further. In a well-known passage in the eleventh *Sermon*, after stating that religion always addresses itself to self-love when reason presides in a man, he says: 'Let it be allowed, though virtue or moral rectitude does indeed consist in affection to and pursuit of what is right and good, as such; yet that when we sit down in a cool hour, we can neither justify to ourselves this or any other pursuit, till we are convinced that it will be for our happiness, or at least not contrary to it.'

Here, if we take the phrase 'justify an action to ourselves' in its natural sense of come to know that we ought to do the action by apprehending a reason why we ought to do it, we seem to have to allow that Butler is maintaining that in the last resort there is one, and only one, reason why we ought to do anything whatever, *viz.* the conduciveness of the action to our happiness or advantage. And if this is right, Butler is not simply presupposing but definitely asserting a necessary connexion between duty and interest, and going further than Plato by maintaining that it is actually conduciveness to the agent's interest which renders an action right.

Nevertheless, when we seriously face the view that unless an action be advantageous, it cannot really be a duty, we are forced both to abandon it and also to allow that even if it were true, it would not enable us to vindicate the truth of our ordinary moral convictions.

It is easy to see that if we persist in maintaining that an action, to be right, must be advantageous, we cannot stop short of maintaining that it is precisely advantageousness and nothing else which renders an action right. It is impossible to rest in the intermediate position that, though it is something other than advantageousness which renders an action right, nevertheless an action cannot really be right unless it is advantageous. For if it be held that an action is rendered a duty by the possession of some other characteristic, then the only chance of showing that a right action must necessarily be advantageous must consist either in showing that actions having this other characteristic must necessarily be advantageous or in showing that the very fact that we are bound to do some action, irrespectively of what renders us bound to do it, necessitates that we shall gain by doing it. But the former alternative is not possible. By 'an action' in this context must be meant an activity by which a man brings certain things about. And if the characteristic of an action which renders it right does not consist in its bringing about an advantage to the agent, which we may symbolize by 'an X,' it must consist in bringing about something of a different kind, which we may symbolize by 'a Y,' say, for the sake of argument, an advantage to a friend, or an improvement in someone's character. There can, however, be no means of showing that when we bring about something of one kind, e.g. a Y, we must necessarily bring about something of a different kind, e.g. an X. The nature of an action as being the bringing about a Y cannot require, i.e. necessitate, it to be also the bringing about an X, i.e. to have an X as its consequence; and whether bringing about a Y in any particular case will bring about an X will depend not only on the nature of the act as being the bringing about a Y, but also on the nature of the agent and of the special circumstances in which the act is done. It may be objected that we could avoid the necessity of having to admit this on one condition, viz. that we knew the existence of a Divine Being who would intervene, where necessary, with rewards. But this knowledge would give the required conclusion only on one condition, viz. that this knowledge was really the knowledge that the fact of being bound to do some action itself necessitated the existence of such a Being as a consequence. For if it were the knowledge of the existence of such a Being based on other grounds, it would not enable us to know that the very fact that some action was the bringing about a Y itself necessitated that it would also be the bringing about an X, i.e. some advantage to the agent. No doubt if we could successfully maintain not only that an action's being the bringing about a Y necessitated its being a duty, but also that an action's being a duty necessitated as a consequence the existence of a Being who would reward it, we could show that an action's being the bringing about a Y necessitated its being rewarded. But to maintain this is really to fall back on the second alternative; and this alternative will, on consideration, turn

out no more tenable than the first. It cannot successfully be maintained that the very fact that some action is a duty necessitates, not that the agent will *deserve* to gain—a conclusion which it is of course easy to draw, but that he *will* gain, unless it can be shown that this very fact necessitates, as a consequence, the existence of a being who will, if necessary, reward it. And this obviously cannot be done.

No doubt Kant maintained, and thought it possible to prove, not indeed that the obligation to do *any* action, but that the obligation to do a *certain* action, involves as a consequence that men will gain by carrying out their obligations.[1] In effect he assumed that we know that one of our duties is to endeavour to advance the realization of the highest good, *viz.* a state of affairs in which men both act morally, i.e. do what they think right, purely from the thought that it is right, and at the same time attain the happiness which in consequence they deserve. And he maintained that from this knowledge we can conclude *first* that the realization of the highest good must be possible, i.e. that so far as we succeed in making ourselves and others more moral, we and others will become proportionately happier; and *second* that, therefore, since the realization of this consequence requires, as the cause of the world in which we have to act, a supreme intelligent will which renders the world such as to cause happiness in proportion to morality, there must be such a cause. But his argument, although it has a certain plausibility, involves an inversion. If, as he rightly implied, an action can only be a duty if we *can* do it, and if we can only even in a slight degree advance a state of affairs in which a certain degree of morality is combined with a corresponding degree of happiness, *provided* there be such a supreme cause of nature, it will be impossible to know, as he assumed that we do, that to advance this state of affairs is a duty, *until*

---

[1] Kant, *Critique of Practical Reason* (Bk. II, ii. § 5). [Abbott's Translation, pp. 220–9.]

we know that there is such a supreme cause. So far, therefore, from the connexion which he thought to exist between right action and happiness being demonstrable from our knowledge of the duty in question, knowledge of the duty, if attainable at all, will itself require independent knowledge of the connexion.

We are therefore forced to allow that in order to maintain that for an action to be right, it must be advantageous, we have to maintain that advantageousness is what renders an action right. But this is obviously something which no one is going to maintain, if he considers it seriously. For he will be involved in maintaining not only that it is a duty to do whatever is for our advantage but that this is our only duty. And the fatal objection to maintaining this is simply that no one actually thinks it.

Moreover, as it is easy to see, if we were to maintain this, our doing so, so far from helping us, would render it impossible for us to vindicate the truth of our ordinary moral convictions. For wherever in ordinary life we think of some particular action as a duty, we are not simply thinking of it as right, but also thinking of its rightness as constituted by the possession of some definite characteristic other than that of being advantageous to the agent. For we think of the action as a particular action *of a certain kind,* the nature of which is indicated by general words contained in the phrase by which we refer to the action, e.g. *'fulfilling* the *promise* which we made to X yesterday,' or *'looking after* our *parents.'* And we do not think of the action as right *blindly,* i.e. irrespectively of the special character which we think the act to possess; rather we think of it as being right in virtue of possessing a particular characteristic of the kind indicated by the phrase by which we refer to it. Thus in thinking of our keeping our promise to X as a duty, we are thinking of the action as rendered a duty by its being the keeping of our promise. This is obvious because we should never, for instance, think of using as an illustration of an action which we think right, telling X what we think of him, or

meeting him in London, even though we thought that if we thought of these actions in certain other aspects we should think them right. Consequently if we were to maintain that conduciveness to the agent's advantage is what renders an action right, we should have to allow that any of our ordinary moral convictions, so far from being capable of vindication, is simply a mistake, as being really the conviction that some particular action is rendered a duty by its possession of some characteristic which is not that of being advantageous.

The general moral is obvious. Certain arguments, which would ordinarily be referred to as arguments designed to prove that doing what is right will be for the good of the agent, turn out to be attempts to prove that the actions which in ordinary life we think right will be for the good of the agent. There is really no need to consider in detail whether these arguments are successful; for even if they are successful, they will do nothing to prove what they are intended to prove, *viz.* that the moral convictions of our ordinary life are true. Further the attempts arise simply out of a presupposition which on reflection anyone is bound to abandon, *viz.* that conduciveness to personal advantage is what renders an action a duty. What Plato should have said to the Sophists is: 'You may be right in maintaining that in our ordinary unquestioning frame of mind we do not know, but only think, that certain actions are right. These thoughts or convictions may or may not be true. But they cannot be false for the reason which you give. You do nothing whatever to show that they are false by urging that the actions in question are disadvantageous; and I should do nothing to show that they are true, if I were to show that these actions are after all advantageous. Your real mistake lies in presupposing throughout that advantageousness is what renders an action a duty. If you will only reflect you will abandon this presupposition altogether, and then you yourself will withdraw your arguments.'

I next propose to contend that there is

also to be found both in Plato and Butler, besides this attempt to show that actions which we *think* right will be for our good, another attempt which neither of them distinguishes from it and which *is* accurately described as an attempt to prove that *right* actions will be for our good. I also propose to ask what is the idea which led them to make the attempt, and to consider whether it is tenable.

When Plato raises the question 'What is justice?' he does not mean by the question 'What do we *mean* by the terms "justice" and "just," or, in our language, "duty" and "right"?,' as we might ask 'What do we mean by the term "optimism," or again, by the phrase "living thing"?' And as a matter of fact if he had meant this, he would have been raising what was only verbally, and not really, a question at all, in that any attempt to ask it would have implied that the answer was already known and that therefore there was nothing to ask. He means 'What is the characteristic the possession of which by an action necessitates that the action is just, i.e. an act which it is our duty, or which we ought, to do?' In short he means 'What renders a just or right action, just or right?'

Now this question really means 'What is the characteristic common to particular just acts which renders them just?' And for anyone even to *ask* this question is to imply that he already *knows* what particular actions are just. For even to *ask* 'What is the character common to certain things?' is to imply that we already *know* what the things are of which we are wanting to find the common character. Equally, of course, any attempt to *answer* the question has the same implication. For such an attempt can only consist in considering the particular actions which we know to be just and attempting to discover what is the characteristic common to them all, the vague apprehension of which has led us to apprehend them to be just. Plato therefore, both in representing Socrates as raising with his hearers the question 'What is justice?' and also in representing them all

as attempting to answer it, is implying, whether he is aware that he is doing so or not, that they all know what particular acts are, and what particular acts are not, just. If on the contrary what he had presupposed was that the members of the dialogue think, instead of knowing, that certain actions are just, his question—whether he had expressed it thus or not—would really have been, not 'What *is* justice?,' but 'What do we *think* that justice is?'; or, more clearly, not 'What renders an act just?' but 'What do we think renders an act just?.' But in that case an answer, whatever its character, would have thrown no light on the question 'What is justice?'; and apart from this, he is plainly not asking 'What do we *think* that justice is?.'

As has been pointed out, however, the view which Plato attributes to the Sophists presupposes that ordinary mankind, which of course includes the members of the dialogue, only thinks and does not know that certain actions are just. Therefore, when Plato introduces this view as requiring refutation and, in doing so, represents the members of the dialogue as not questioning the presupposition, he ought in consistency to have made someone point out that in view of the acceptance of this presupposition Socrates' original question 'What is justice?' required to be amended to the question 'What do we think that justice is?.' But Plato does not do so. In the present context the significant fact is that even after he has introduced the view of the Sophists he still represents the question to be answered as being 'What is justice?,' and therefore still implies that the members of the dialogue know what is just in particular. Even in making Glaucon and Adeimantus ask Socrates to refute the Sophists, what he, inconsistently, makes them ask Socrates to exhibit the nature of it not the acts which men think just but just acts. And when Plato in the fourth book goes on to give Socrates' answer, which, of course, is intended to express the truth, he in the same way represents Socrates as offering, and the others as accepting, an account of the nature of *just* acts, *viz.* that they consist in conferring those benefits on society which a man's nature renders him best suited to confer, and then makes Socrates argue in detail that it is *just* action which will be profitable. In doing so he is of course implying, inconsistently with the implication of his treatment of the Sophists' view, that the members of the dialogue, and therefore also mankind in ordinary life, *know* what is just in particular. For in the end the statement 'Justice is conferring certain benefits on society' can only mean that conferring these benefits is the characteristic the vague apprehension of which in certain actions leads us to know or apprehend them to be just; and the acceptance of this statement by the members of the dialogue must be understood as expressing their recognition that this characteristic is the common character of the particular acts which they already know to be just.

It therefore must be allowed that, although to do so is inconsistent with his view of the way in which the Sophistic theory has to be refuted, Plato is in the fourth book (and of course the same admission must be made about the eighth and ninth) endeavouring to prove that *just*, i.e. *right*, action, will be for the good or advantage of the agent.

Given that this is what Plato wants to prove in the fourth book, the general nature of what he conceives to be the proof is obvious. His idea is that if we start with the knowledge of what right actions consist in, *viz.*, to put it shortly, serving the state, and then consider what the effects of these and other actions will be by taking into account not only the circumstances in which we are placed, but also the various desires of the human soul and the varying amounts of satisfaction to which the realization of these objects will give rise, it will be obvious that it is by doing what is right that, at any rate in the long run, we shall become happy.

Now a particular proof of this kind, such as Plato's, naturally provokes two comments. The first is that there is no need to consider its success in detail, since we know on general grounds that it must fail. For it can only be shown that actions characterized by being the bringing about things of one kind, in this case benefits to society, will always have as their consequence things of another kind, in this case elements of happiness in the agent, provided that we can prove, as Plato makes no attempt to do, the existence of a Being who will intervene to introduce suitable rewards where they are needed. The second is that though the establishment of this conclusion, whether with or without the help of theological arguments, would be of the greatest benefit to us; since we should all be better off if we knew it to be true, yet it differs from the establishment of the corresponding conclusion against the Sophists in that it would throw no light whatever on the question 'What is our duty in detail, and why?' And this second comment naturally raises the question which seems to be the important one to ask in this connexion, *viz.* 'Why did Plato think it important to prove that right action would benefit the agent?'

The explanation obviously cannot be simply, or even mainly, that the combination in Plato of a desire to do what is right and of a desire to become happy led him to try to satisfy himself that by doing what is right he would be, so to say, having it both ways. The main explanation must lie in a quite different direction. There is no escaping the conclusion that when Plato sets himself to consider not what *should*, but what *actually does* as a matter of fact, lead a man to act, when he is acting deliberately, and not merely in consequence of an impulse, he answers 'The desire for some good to himself and that only.' In other words we have to allow that, according to Plato, a man pursues whatever he pursues simply as a good to himself, i.e. really as something which will give him satisfaction, or, as perhaps we ought to say, as an element in what will render him happy. In the *Republic* this view comes to light in the sixth book. He there speaks of τὸ ἀγαθόν as that which every soul pursues and for the sake of which it does all it does, divining that it is something but being perplexed and unable to grasp adequately what it is; and he goes on to say of things that are good (τὰ ἀγαθὰ) that while many are ready to do and to obtain and to be what only *seems* just, even if it is not, no one is content with obtaining what *seems* good, but endeavours to obtain what is *really* good. It might be objected that these statements do not bear out the view which is attributed to Plato, since Plato certainly did not mean by an ἀγαθόν a source of satisfaction or happiness to oneself. But to this the answer is that wherever Plato uses the term ἀγαθά (goods) elsewhere in the *Republic* and in other dialogues, such as the *Philebus,* the context always shows that he means by a good a good to oneself, and, this being so, he must really be meaning by an ἀγαθόν, a source of satisfaction, or perhaps, more generally, a source of happiness. The view, however, emerges most clearly in the Gorgias, where Plato, in order to show that rhetoricians and tyrants do not do what they really wish to do, maintains that in all actions alike, and even when we kill a man or despoil him of his goods, we do what we do because we think it will be better for us to do so.

Now if we grant, as we must, that Plato thought this, we can find in the admission a natural explanation of Plato's desire to prove that just action will be advantageous. For plainly he passionately wanted men to do what is right, and if he thought that it was only desire of some good to themselves which moved them in all deliberate action, it would be natural, and indeed necessary, for him to think that if men are to be induced to do what is just, the only way to induce them is to convince them that thereby they will gain or become better off.

In Butler also we are driven to find the same attempt to prove that right action will benefit the agent, and to give the same explanation. The proper interpretation of the most important part of the statement quoted from Butler is not very easy to discover. What he says is that when we sit down in a cool hour we can neither justify to ourselves the pursuit of what is *right* and *good,* as such, or any other pursuit, till we are convinced that it will be for our happiness or at least not against it. Here a puzzle arises from the fact that whereas by referring to certain of the actions which we have to justify to ourselves as the pursuit of what is *right,* he inevitably implies that we already *know* them to be right, yet by speaking of our having to justify them to ourselves, i.e. apparently to prove to ourselves that they are right, he seems to imply that we do *not* know them to be right. The interpretation given earlier evaded the puzzle by tacitly assuming that Butler was using the term 'right' loosely for what we think, and so do not know, to be right. But it may well be asked whether the assumption was justified. And if we consider the statement in reference to the *Sermons* generally, we seem bound to conclude that Butler was really maintaining two different, and indeed inconsistent, doctrines without realizing their difference, the one involving that the word 'right' is here used strictly, and the other involving that it is not. When Kant contrasts the two kinds of statement containing the word 'ought' which he designated as Categorical and Hypothetical Imperatives, he implies, although he does not expressly state, that the term 'ought' is being used in the two kinds of statement in radically different senses. In a Categorical Imperative, he implies, 'ought' has the ordinary moral sense in which it is co-extensive with 'duty,' and 'morally bound.' In a Hypothetical Imperative it has the purely non-moral sense of proper in respect of being the thing which is conducive to our purpose, whether that purpose be the object of some special desire which is moving us, e.g. as when we wash in order to become clean, or whether it be our happiness, as when we make friends in order to become happy. Corresponding to these two senses of the term 'ought,' there will be two senses of 'justifying a certain action,' the one moral and the other not. We may mean by the phrase proving to ourselves that it is a duty to do the action, or we may mean proving to ourselves that the act is the proper one to do in respect of its being the act which will lead to the realization of our purpose.

Now if we understand Butler's word 'right' to be a loose phrase for what in ordinary life we *think* to be right, we can understand him to be using 'justify' in the moral sense of 'justify,' without having to admit that he is involved in contradiction. We can understand him to be saying that in order to know that some action which we ordinarily think to be right is right, we must first prove to ourselves that it will be for our happiness, or at least not against it; and we shall then be representing him as explicitly maintaining what the Sophists and Plato, in seeking to refute them, presupposed. On the other hand if we understand Butler to be using the term 'right' strictly, we can only avoid attributing to him the self-contradictory view already referred to by understanding him to be using the term 'justify' in the non-moral sense. For while he would be involved in contradiction if he maintained that even where we knew that some action is right, we still need to prove to ourselves that we ought in the moral sense to do it, he would not be so involved, if he maintained instead that what we still need is to prove to ourselves that we ought to do it in the non-moral sense. Now the general drift of what Butler says of conscience, and especially his statement that it carries its own authority with it, implies that he considered that in ordinary life we *know* and do not *think* that certain actions are right; and if we judge by this, we must understand Butler to be here using 'right' strictly, and to be maintaining that even when we know that we morally ought to do something, we still need to know that we ought to do it in the non-moral sense of its being conducive to our purpose, and that therefore, since

our happiness is our purpose, we still need to know that it will conduce to our happiness. But if we think that this is what Butler is maintaining, we have to allow that the explanation of his maintaining it can only be the same as that given with regard to Plato. For if we ask '*Why*, according to Butler, when we already know that doing some action is a duty, do we still require to know that we ought to do the action in the non-moral sense of "ought"?,' the answer can only be 'Because otherwise we shall not do the action.' And the implication will be that when, to use Butler's phrase, we sit down in a cool hour, i.e. when we are not under the influence of impulses, the only thing we desire, and therefore the only purpose we have, is our own happiness, and that therefore we shall do whatever we do only in order that we may become happy. The general drift of his *Sermons*, however, and more especially his statement that it is manifest that nothing can be of consequence to mankind or any creature but happiness shows that Butler actually thought this. We have therefore to attribute to Butler side by side with the view already attributed to him, and undistinguished from it, a view which is inconsistent with it and is really the second view already attributed to Plato, viz. that even though we know certain actions to be right, we must have it proved to us that they will be for our good or happiness, since otherwise, as we act only from desire of our own happiness, we shall not do them.

I propose now to take it as established (1) that both Plato and Butler in a certain vein of thought are really endeavouring to prove that right actions, in the strict sense of 'right actions,' will be for the agent's advantage; (2) that their reason for doing so lies in the conviction that even where we know some action to be right, we shall not do it unless we think that it will be for our advantage; and (3) that behind this conviction lies the conviction of which it is really a corollary, viz. the conviction that desire for some good to oneself is the only motive of deliberate action.

But are these convictions true? For if it can be shown that they are not, then at least Plato and Butler's reason for trying to prove the advantageousness of right action will have disappeared.

The conviction that even where we know some action to be right, we shall not do it unless we think we shall be the better off for doing it, of course, strikes us as a paradox. At first no doubt we are apt to mis-state the paradox. We are apt to say that the conviction, implying as it does that we only act out of self-interest, really implies that it is impossible for us to do anything which we ought to do at all, since if we did some action out of self-interest we could not have done anything which was a duty. But to say this is to make the mistake of thinking that the motive with which we do an action can possibly have something to do with its rightness or wrongness. To be morally bound is to be morally bound to *do* something, i.e. to bring something about; and even if it be only from the lowest of motives that we have brought about something which we ought to have brought about, we have still done something which we ought to have done. The fact that I have given A credit in order to spite his rival B, or again, in order to secure future favours from A, has, as we see when we reflect, no bearing whatever on the question whether I ought to have given A credit. The real paradox inherent in the conviction lies in its implication that there is no such thing as moral goodness. If I give A credit solely to obtain future favours, and even if I gave him credit either thinking or knowing that I ought to do so, but in no way directly or indirectly influenced by my either so thinking or knowing, then even though it has to be allowed that I did something which I was morally bound to do, it has to be admitted that there was no moral goodness whatever about my action. And the conviction in question is really what is ordinarily called the doctrine that morality needs a sanction, i.e. really the doctrine that, to stimulate a man into doing some action, it is not merely insufficient but even useless to convince him that he is morally bound to do it, and that, instead, we have to appeal to his desire to become better off.

Now we are apt to smile in a superior way when in reading Mill we find him taking for granted that morality needs a sanction, but we cannot afford to do so when we find Butler, and still more when we find Plato, really doing the same thing. Moreover when Plato and Butler maintain the doctrine that lies at the back of this conviction, *viz.* the doctrine that we always aim at, i.e. act from the desire of, some good to ourselves, they are in the best of company. Aristotle is practically only repeating the statement quoted from the sixth book of the *Republic* when he says in the first sentence of the *Ethics,* that every deliberate action seems to aim at something good, and that therefore the good has rightly been declared to be that at which all things aim. For this to become obvious it is only necessary to consider what meaning must be attributed to the term ἀγαθόν in the early chapters of the *Ethics.* Again, to take a modern instance, Green says: 'The motive in every imputable act for which the agent is conscious on reflection that he is answerable, is a desire for personal good in some form or other. . . . It is superfluous to add good to *himself,* for anything conceived as good in such a way that the agent acts for the sake of it, must be conceived as *his own* good, though he may conceive it as his own good only on account of his interest in others, and in spite of any amount of suffering on his own part incidental to its attainment.'[2] Moreover the doctrine seems plausible enough, if we ask ourselves in a purely general way 'How are we to be led into doing something?.' For the natural answer is: 'Only by thinking of some state of affairs which it is in my power to bring about and by which I shall become better off than I am now; and the answer implies that only in this way shall we come to

[2] *Prolegomena to Ethics,* § § 91–2.

desire to do an action, and that, unless we desire to do it, we shall not do it.

Nevertheless it seems difficult, and indeed in the end impossible, to think that the doctrine will stand the test of instances. It seems impossible to allow that in what would usually be called disinterested actions, whether they be good or bad, there is not at least some element of disinterestedness. It strikes us as absurd to think that in what would be called a benevolent action, we are not moved at least in part by the desire that someone else shall be better off and also by the desire to *make* him better off, even though we may also necessarily have, and be influenced by, the desire to have the satisfaction of thinking that he is better off and that we have made him so. It seems equally absurd to maintain that where we are said to treat someone maliciously, we are not moved in part by the desire of his unhappiness and also partly by the desire to *make* him unhappy. Again when we are said to be pursuing scientific studies without a practical aim, it seems mere distortion of the facts to say that we are moved solely by the desire to have the satisfaction of knowing some particular thing and not, at least in part, by the desire to know it. And we seem driven to make a similar admission when we consider actions in which we are said to have acted conscientiously.

In this connexion it should be noted that the doctrine under consideration, *viz.* that our motive in doing any action is desire for some good to ourselves to which we think the action will lead, has two negative implications. The first is that the thought, or, alternatively, the knowledge, that some action is right has no influence on us in acting, i.e. that the thought, or the knowledge, that an action is a duty can neither be our motive nor even an element in our motive. The existence of this implication is obvious, since if our motive is held to be the desire for a certain good to ourselves, it is implied that the thought that the action is a duty, though present, is neither what moves us, nor an element in what

moves us, to do the action. The second implication is that there is no such thing as a *desire* to do what is right, or more fully, a desire to do some action in virtue of its being a duty. The existence of this second implication is also obvious, since if such a desire were allowed to exist, there would be no reason for maintaining that when we do some action which we think to be a duty, our motive is necessarily the desire for a certain good to ourselves. The truth of the doctrine could therefore be contested in one of two alternative ways. We might either deny the truth of the former implication; or, again, we might deny the truth of the latter. The former is, of course, the line taken by Kant, at any rate in a qualified form. He maintained in effect that the mere thought that an action is a duty, apart from a desire to do what we ought to do—a desire the existence of which he refused to admit—is at any rate in certain instances the motive, or at least an element in the motive, of an action. No doubt he insisted that the existence of this fact gave rise to a problem, and a problem which only vindication of freedom of the will could resolve; but he maintained that the problem was soluble, and that therefore he was entitled to insist on this fact. Now this method of refutation has adherents and at first sight it is attractive. For it seems mere wild paradox to maintain that in no case in which we do what we think of as right, do we ever in any degree do it *because* we think it right; and to say that we do some action *because* we think it right seems to imply that the thought that it is right is our motive. Again the statement seems natural that where we are said to have acted thus, we obviously did not want to do what we did but acted against our desires or inclinations. Nevertheless we are, I think, on further reflection bound to abandon this view. For one reason, to appeal to a consideration of which the full elucidation and vindication would take too long, the view involves that where we are said to have done some action because we thought it right, though we had a motive for what we did, we had no purpose in doing it. For we really mean by our purpose in doing some action that the *desire* of which for its own sake leads us to do the action. Again, if we face the purely general question 'Can we really do anything whatever unless in some respect or other we desire to do it?' we have to answer 'No.' But if we allow this, then we have to allow that the obvious way to endeavour to meet Plato's view is to maintain the existence of a desire to do what is right. And it does not seem difficult to do so with success. For we obviously are referring to a fact when we speak of someone as possessing a sense of duty and, again, a strong sense of duty. And if we consider what we are thinking of in these individuals whom we think of as possesssing it, we find we cannot exclude from it a desire to do what is a duty, as such, or for its own sake, or, more simply, a desire to do what is a duty. In fact it is hard to resist the conclusion that Kant himself would have taken this line instead of the extreme line which he did, had he not had the fixed idea that all desire is for enjoyment. But if we think this—as it seems we must —we, of course, have no need to admit the truth of Plato's reason for trying to prove that right actions must be advantageous. For if we admit the existence of a desire to do what is right, there is no longer any reason for maintaining as a general thesis that in any case in which a man knows some action to be right, he must, if he is to be led to do it, be convinced that he will gain by doing it. For we shall be able to maintain that his desire to do what is right, if strong enough, will lead him to do the action in spite of any aversion from doing it which he may feel on account of its disadvantages.

It may be objected that if we maintain the existence of a desire to do what is right, we shall become involved in an insoluble difficulty. For we shall also have to allow that we have a desire to become well off or happy, and that therefore men have two radically different desires, i.e. desires the object of which are completely incommensurable. We shall therefore be implying that in those instances—which of course must exist—in which a man has either to do what is right or to do what is for his happiness he can have no means of choosing which he shall do, since there can be no comparable characteristic of the two alternative actions which will enable him to choose to do the one rather than, or in preference to, the other. But to this objection there is an answer which, even if it be at first paradoxical, is in the end irresistible, *viz.* that in connexion with such instances it is wholly inappropriate to speak of a *choice*. A choice is, no doubt, necessarily a choice between comparable alternatives, e.g. between an afternoon's enjoyment on the river and an afternoon's enjoyment at a cinema. But it is purely arbitrary to maintain that wherever we have two alternative courses of action before us we have necessarily to *choose* between them. Thus a man contemplating retirement may be offered a new post. He may, on thinking it over, be unable to resist the conclusion that it is a duty on his part to accept it and equally convinced that if he accepts it, he will lose in happiness. He will either accept from his desire to do what is right in spite of his aversion from doing what will bring himself a loss of happiness, or he will refuse from his desire of happiness, in spite of his aversion from doing what is wrong. But whichever he does, though he will have *decided* to do what he does, he will not have *chosen* to do it, i.e. chosen to do it in preference to doing the alternative action.

For the reasons given I shall treat it as established that, though there is to be found in Plato and Butler what is really an attempt to prove that right action is advantageous, the question of its success or failure can be ignored, since the attempt is based on a fundamental mistake about actual human nature.

A Criticism of Kant

G. C. FIELD

. . . Kant, then, has not succeeded in the task he set himself. He thought that the nature of goodness or rightness could be derived from the conception of a rational being. If, as we have seen to be the case, his attempt thus to derive it was unsuccessful, the reason must be sought in one or both of two possible directions. On the one hand, it may be that he had not really understood what was involved in the nature of a rational being. On the other, he may have been mistaken in thinking that it was connected in this way with the conception of goodness or rightness. It would be well, perhaps, if we want to see which alternative to accept, to examine the conception of a rational being a little more closely.

A rational being, of course, is a being endowed with reason. But what is reason? Whatever else it is, it is in the first place a cognitive faculty of the conscious being, it is something in us which enables us to know something. We shall probably best distinguish it from other cognitive faculties by the kind of object that we know by it. Kant would say, for instance, that reason was that which enabled us to know universal and necessary truths. But however we distinguish it, the important point is that it is a form of knowing. As applied to actions, it tells us facts about the actions, it tells us the kind of action each one is. And we are here face to face with the

From G. C. Field, *Moral Theory*, 1921, pp. 46–51, by permission of Methuen & Company, Ltd., London, publishers.

crucial question, "Can reason be practical?" Or, in other words, "Can a knowledge of the nature of an action by itself move us to take that action?" Kant thought that it could: it is essential to his whole position. And if he is wrong in this, we have discovered the fundamental fallacy of his theory.

Let us try to realize the point of view of those who would hold that on this fundamental point Kant was wrong. We may, to begin with, set against Kant's view the dictum of Aristotle. The intellect by itself moves nothing, has no motive force. Or, in other words, the mere knowing that an action, or anything else, is of such-and-such a kind cannot possibly move us to act.

The point is of such vital importance that we must elaborate this point of view a little further. In the elementary stages of reflection, it might seem to us that this was obviously at variance with certain observable facts. We may say that the would-be criminal knows that if he commits a murder, he will be hanged. This knowledge is enough to make him refrain from doing so, however much he may want to. I know, when I am ill, that a certain medicine will make me well, and therefore I take it, however unpleasant it may be. Here we have cases of knowledge moving us to action. The argument is really a very superficial one, and only worth mentioning because it helps to illustrate and emphasize the view against which it is directed. For the point is, of course, that it is not the mere knowledge that moves us to action at all. If the criminal did not mind being hanged, if I am absolutely indifferent whether I get well or not, then the knowledge would have no effect on our action one way or another. The reason why the knowledge moves us to action is that it is the knowledge that that particular kind of action will have an effect that we want or desire. But the bare knowledge that a particular action is of a certain kind or will have a certain effect has no influence on us unless we have an interest in that effect or that kind of action, unless, that is, we have some feeling towards it. In short, action of any kind will not take place without the presence of a desire or some element of feeling or emotion. So that if we were pure reason without any desire or feelings, we should not, as Kant thought, act in a particular way, but we should simply not act at all.[1]

If this is true, Kant's fallacy lies in thinking that just the bare knowledge that an action is of a certain kind is sufficient to move us to do that action. Why that may sound plausible, at first hearing, is that when we speak of the kind of action we are apt to include in the meaning of that phrase the effect the action has on us: thus, for instance, we may speak of pleasant and unpleasant actions as being different kinds of actions, though the difference lies not necessarily at all in the actions themselves but simply in the effect they have on us. But Kant, of course, is careful to avoid this confusion. When he speaks of the kind of action, he means simply what the action is in itself, apart from its effects on us or any relation to our feelings.

In the light of this, we can get a clearer

view of the place of reason in action and the real meaning of reasonable action. Practical reason will mean for us what it meant for Aristotle, who first used the phrase: that is, the ability to discover what will be the best means to an end which we want to attain. The essence of unreasonable action will lie in doing something which will defeat our own ends: for instance, in doing something in obedience to an immediate desire which will hinder the attainment of something else which we really want more. Practical reason will really be the capacity of finding means to ends.

We can apply the same consideration to the meaning of the term "ends." In that connexion we may recall the passage where Kant argues that all rational beings must be ends in themselves, because each one regards himself as an end. And as they are all rational beings, what holds of one must hold of the others. So that they must all be ends in themselves. However ready we may be to accept the valuable practical consequences that Kant draws from the principle we should probably all feel that the argument as it stands is singularly unconvincing. And, in the light of the above consideration, we begin to see the reason for that. For it becomes clearer that the argument really rests on a confusion about the sort of fact that being an end really is. Being an end is not, in our ordinary use of the term, a fact about things like being a human being or being green or being a triangle, a fact about the thing itself, a fact which belongs to the thing in its own right. Being an end is not really a fact about the thing at all. My end in ordinary speech means my object or purpose, what I am aiming at or trying to get at or want or desire. It is made an end by being wanted, and if I cease to want it it ceases to be my end. If no one wants it any longer, it ceases to be an end at all. That is, there is strictly no such thing as an end in itself unless we are going to attach an entirely new meaning to the word. Being an end implies some relation to the desires or pur-

[1] We might express this in Kantian terms by saying that the reason cannot be free in his sense. If our reason acts, it acts according to certain laws of its own nature, no doubt. But to start it acting it needs an efficient cause, just as much as natural objects do, in this case, some form of desire or feeling. So far, therefore, is reason from supplying a possible motive for action, that it cannot itself act without a previous desire or feeling to set it in motion.

poses of some conscious being: and a thing is made an end by this relation. It follows, then, that nothing can be just an end: it could only be an end for someone, the purpose or desire of some conscious being. And there would, of course, be nothing self-contradictory in the view that each conscious being might have a different end, or that the same thing might be an end for one being and not for another.

The same consideration would apply, surely, to a conception like that of value. We should ask whether value must not be value for someone, whether we do not find that, if we are to think of value at all, we must think of it as essentially related to our feelings or the feelings of some conscious being or beings. This, at any rate, is our ordinary use of it. And ultimately we shall begin to ask ourselves whether we may not be finally forced to say the same of a wider conception like that of good. If we are, we shall have to say that our conception of good necessarily contains in itself a reference to some conscious being. We shall not be able to allow any such ideas as that of good, which was just good and not good for some being. Good would be found to be essentially related to and in some way dependent on the wishes or desires or feelings of some conscious being.

The Kantian would, of course, object here that Kant had already considered the claims of the desires and feelings and given reasons for rejecting them. In the first place, he had argued that to make goodness depend on desires or feelings, would make it something uncertain and fluctuating, because some people might desire a thing and others not, or the same person might desire it at one time and not at another. This is certainly a weighty objection, and will have to be considered at length later. Here it will suffice to suggest a possible line on which it might be met: that is, if we developed the idea of some end which every conscious being, by its very nature, must and would desire, if it only realized what it was. We shall meet

with this conception later. In the second place he had argued that such a view would make what we desired not good in itself but only as a means to an end. Here we can only say that Kant, doubtless largely under the influence of a faulty psychology, seems to fail to realize the possibility or the true meaning of anything being desired purely for its own sake. Finally it would be argued that such a view would not give us a thing good in itself, because its goodness would depend upon something else outside of it, namely, our desire of or feeling towards it. This we should readily admit. And we should reply that we do not and cannot recognize the existence or possibility of any such thing as good in itself in that sense, out of all relation to anything else. It simply has no meaning for us. And if it had, it would make goodness something of no interest or importance to us, and of no possible influence upon our actions.

With this, we really return to the point from which Kant started. We shall remember that one of the assumptions on which he seemed to base his theory was that which was expressed by saying that if a thing is really good, it must be good in itself. If that appealed to us at first as a reasonable statement of our own ordinary ideas, it was only because we had not yet realized what it really meant. When we did realize this, instead of accepting it as a correct starting-point, we should be more inclined to describe it as the fundamental fallacy of Kant, as indeed of many other writers. Goodness, we should say now, is not a quality which belongs to things in themselves, quite apart from their effect on or their relation to us [2] or some conscious being. If it were, it could only be

[2] Of course, in a sense, as we have seen, Kant does make goodness related to us, because it is an essential quality of rational beings. But that merely means that we, in so far as we are rational, are the things which have this quality. It is obviously a very different thing from asserting that goodness itself consists in a relation to us or to any conscious being. And nothing short of this will satisfy the above criticism.

related to us as an object of cognition. And if it were simply an object of cognition, something that we merely knew without having any feeling towards it, it could not move us to action, or indeed be of any practical interest or importance to us at all.

There are many other objections to Kant's view. But if the argument has been correct, we have found his fundamental fallacy in the false assumptions from which he starts. They are really two in number. He starts from the assumption that what is good must be good in itself, apart from all relations to anything else. And in consequence of this he is forced to assume that the mere intellectual apprehension of the fact is sufficient to move us to action. The other assumptions which we have ascribed to him follow from these two or are different forms which they take. But, if our argument has been at all correct, we must maintain against this that the simple intellectual apprehension, the bare knowledge of anything can never move us to action. And consequently his idea of a good in itself is incompatible with one of the most deeply recognized characteristics of the moral fact, namely, that it is somehow a reason for action.

Obligation and Motivation in Recent Moral Philosophy

WILLIAM K. FRANKENA

This paper will be concerned with a problem about the analysis of judgments of moral obligation, that is, of judgments in which an agent is said, by himself or others, to have a certain moral duty or obligation in a certain situation or kind of situation. It will not offer an analysis of such judgments, but will occupy itself with a study of a particular opposition between two points of view as to their analysis. The character of this opposition may be indicated as follows. Many moral philosophers have said or implied that it is in some sense logically possible for an agent to have or see that he has an obligation even if he has no motivation, actual or dispositional, for doing the action in question; many others have said or implied that this is paradoxical and not logically possible. The former are convinced that no reference to the existence of motives in the agent involved need be made in the analysis of a moral judgment; the latter are equally convinced that such a reference is necessary there.

Roughly, the opposition in question is between those who regard motivation as external and those who regard it as internal to obligation. We may, therefore, borrow W. D. Falk's labels and call the two points of view externalism and internalism,

respectively.[1] It should be noted, then, that the question is not whether or not moral philosophers may or must introduce the topic of motivation. Externalists have generally been concerned about motivation as well as about obligation; they differ from their opponents only about the reason for this concern. Internalists hold that motivation must be provided for because it is involved in the analysis of moral judgments and so is essential for an action's being or being shown to be obligatory. Externalists insist that motivation is not part of the analysis of moral judgments or of the justification of moral claims; for them motivation is an important problem, but only because it is necessary to persuade people to act in accordance with their obligations.

Again, the issue is not whether morality is to be practical. Both parties agree that it is to be practical in the sense of governing and guiding human behavior. That is, it should supply the rules of human practice, and it should not do this out of idle curiosity, but with a real concern for their being followed. But the one party insists that judgments of obligation must be practical in the further sense that their being efficacious in influencing behavior is

[1] See W. D. Falk, " 'Ought' and Motivation," *Proceedings of the Aristotelian Society*, N.S. XLVIII (1947–48), 137. The older term "rigorism" would do for externalism, but it has no good opposite for present purposes.

From *Essays in Moral Philosophy*, ed. A. I. Melden, by permission of the University of Washington Press and the author.

somehow logically internal to them, and the other denies this. The question is whether motivation is somehow to be "built into" judgments of moral obligation, not whether it is to be taken care of in some way or other.[2]

Here is an old and basic issue. It may be regarded as involved in Aristotle's critique of Plato's Idea of the Good, and is certainly present in Hume's polemic against cognitivists and rationalists in ethics. It is different from, and to a considerable extent cuts across, the issues which have been discussed so much recently (intuitionism versus naturalism, cognitivism versus noncognitivism, humanism versus supernaturalism, relativism versus absolutism, deontologism versus teleologism), for proponents of almost every one of these embattled points of view can be found on either side in this controversy. Indeed, I am disposed to think that it is more basic than most of these other issues, since answers to it are often taken as premises for settling them, for example they are frequently taken by naturalists and noncognitivists as premises for refuting intuitionism.

Yet, ancient and fundamental as it may be, this opposition has seldom been made explicit or studied in its own right, even in recent times when so many of the other oppositions which were latent in earlier moral philosophy have been underlined and debated. Its ghost was raised and given something like form by H. A. Prichard, but only, as he vainly hoped, to be laid forever.[3] R. M. Blake and Falk are perhaps the only others to make a separate study of it.[4] For the rest, however, the opposing positions involved have simply been assumed, it **seems to me**, without adequate analysis or defense. Hence it is my purpose here to call attention once more to this issue, to consider its present status, and to do something to clarify it and the methods by which it is to be settled.

My sympathies have always been with the first of the two positions described. It has not seemed to me inconceivable that one should have an obligation and recognize that one has it and yet have no motivation to perform the required act. But I am less sure of this than I used to be, and shall therefore explore the problem now with the goal, not of arriving at any final conclusions, but of taking some steps in that direction. I shall not proceed, however, by making an independent study of the matter, but by reviewing analytically and critically a number of passages and discussions in the literature of the last two or three decades.

I

Externalism may take various forms, as has been indicated. Intuitionism, holding that obligation is indefinable and nonnatural, is the most striking example of it, and internalism has cropped out most frequently in refutations of intuitionism. But many other views have held that moral judgments can be analyzed without any reference to the conations of the agent involved,[5] for instance, any form of naturalism which regards "I ought to do B" as equivalent to "B is approved by most people" or "B is conducive to the greatest general happiness," and any form of noncognitivism which identifies moral requirements with social or divine imperatives.[6] For all such theories, obligation

---

[2] I owe this use of the phrase "built into" to my colleague C. L. Stevenson.

[3] *Duty and Interest* (Oxford: Oxford University Press, 1928).

[4] R. M. Blake, "The Ground of Moral Obligation," *International Journal of Ethics*, XXXVIII (1928), 129–40. Blake was especially concerned about the "internalism," as I call it, of the idealistic ethics of self-realization. See also Falk, " 'Ought' and Motivation," and articles cited below. H. Reiner in *Pflicht und Neigung* (Meisenhiem: Westkulturverlag A. Hain, 1951) is dealing with a somewhat different problem.

[5] Notice, the question here is about a reference to the interests of the *agent* spoken of, not the interests of the *speaker*.

[6] Not all theological theories of obligation are externalistic, for theologians often hold or imply that "the moral law" is law or is obligatory

represents a fact or requirement which is external to the agent in the sense of being independent of his desires or needs.

Against them, internalists have a number of arguments which are more or less related and which they usually attribute to Hume, sometimes correctly. It is to a study of these arguments that the first main part of this paper will be devoted. In all of them the theme is that externalism has a problem about motivation, and is therefore false. The first to be considered is an argument by G. C. Field to the effect that, if an obligation represents an external fact about an agent in the sense explained above, then its presence entails no "reason for action."[7] But it is "one of the most deeply recognized characteristics of the moral fact" that it is in itself and necessarily "a reason for acting." Therefore the views of Kant, Moore, and other externalists are false.

We need not question Field's claim (1) that, if an action is obligatory, this is a reason for doing it, since an externalist can accept it. But Field assumes in his discussion (2) that a reason for action is a motive, and this may well be doubted. It seems to me, at any rate, that we must distinguish two kinds of reasons for action, "exciting reasons" and "justifying reasons," to use Hutcheson's terms.[8] When A asks, "Why should I give Smith a ride?" B may give answers of two different kinds. He may say, "Because you promised to," or he may say, "Because, if you do, he will remember you in his will." In the first case he offers a justification of the action, in the second a motive for doing it. In other words, A's "Why should I . . . ?" and "Why

ought I . . . ?" are ambiguous questions. They may be asking for an ethical justification of the action proposed, or they may be asking what motives there are for his doing it. "Should" and "ought" likewise have two meanings (at least) which are prima facie distinct: a moral one and a motivational one.

Thus a motive is one kind of reason for action, but not all reasons for action are motives. Perhaps we should distinguish between reasons for acting and reasons for regarding an action as right or justified. It is plausible to identify reasons for acting with motives, i.e., with considerations which will or may move one to action, and perhaps this is why Field assumes that all reasons are motives, but it is not plausible to identify motives with reasons for regarding an action as morally right or obligatory. At any rate, there is a prima facie distinction to be made between two senses of "ought" and two kinds of reasons, and, if this distinction is valid, then Field's case as he states it collapses. For then an externalist can reply that (1) is obviously true only if "reason" means "justifying reason" and not "motivating reason," and that (2) is true only if "reason" means "motivating reason"; and he may go on to claim that "obligation" is ambiguous, being indeed susceptible of an internalist analysis in its motivational sense, but not in its moral sense. He may even contend that the plausibility of internalism rests on a failure to make this distinction.

The internalist, then, must either show that the above distinction is invalid, which Field does not do, shift to a different argument, or move the entire discussion to another level.

---

because it is divinely *sanctioned* (i.e. because it is made to our interest to obey), not merely because it is commanded by God.

[7] *Moral Theory* (London: Methuen & Co., 1921), pp. 51, 52, 56 f.

[8] Cf. F. Hutcheson, "Illustrations on the Moral Sense" (1728), section 1, in *British Moralists*, ed. L. A. Selby-Bigge (2 vols.; Oxford: Clarendon Press, 1897), I, 403 f.

II

W. T. Stace and others use a similar argument against intuitionism and Platonism, contending boldly that, on any such analysis of "A ought to do B," A can admit that he ought to do B without its following that he has an *obligation* to do B. Stace's version of this contention may be paraphrased as follows.[9] On an externalist analysis of judgments of obligation, such a judgment merely asserts a kind of fact, simple or complex, natural or nonnatural. Then, even if the judgment "A ought to do B" is true, it does not follow that A has any obligation to *act,* any *practical* obligation, but only an obligation to *believe.* Why should he do anything about B? An obligation to act follows only if A desires to do something about it, and then it follows from this desire alone. Moreover, he may not desire to do anything about it, and then he has no obligation of any sort to act. But a moral judgment necessarily entails an obligation to act; therefore externalist theories are false.

This argument, which seems so plausible to Stace, has always been puzzling to me. Let us begin, as he does, by supposing that a moral judgment is just a statement of some kind of "external" fact. Then one cannot admit such a fact about oneself, and still ask sensibly if one has a moral obligation to act. For to admit the fact is then to admit the obligation. One cannot in that case ask, "Why morally ought I do the act in question?" except to gain an insight into the *grounds* of the admitted obligation. One can still ask, "Why should I do the act?" but only if one is using "should" in the sense in which one is asking for motivation, or in some third sense. No doubt, as Stace says, one *will* do it only if he desires to do what has the given kind of "external" characteristic. Then one's desire obliges him in the sense of moving him. But the admitted moral judgment asserts a *moral* obligation nonetheless, and whether one will in fact perform the act in question

or not does not bear on his having this obligation. Even if one may not desire to do what is right (i.e., what has the characteristic referred to by "right" on our hypothesis),[10] this does not change the fact that one has a moral obligation; it means only that one has no motivation, at least occurrently. That one has no moral obligation does not follow unless having an obligation entails having a motive. But this Stace does not show, and it is obviously true only in one sense of "obligation."

In fact, it is clear that Stace is assuming that to have an obligation is to have a motive, just as Field did, and his argument is essentially the same, though verbally different. And again the answer is that, until the contrary is shown, one must distinguish between two senses of "should" or "ought." For, if this distinction is valid, it can be claimed that Stace's argument reduces to this: even if I ought in one sense, it does not follow that I ought in the other sense, which is true but refutes no one. Stace, like Field, has failed to observe or consider the possible ambiguity of "should."

What he has noticed is that one apparently can ask, "Why should I do what I morally ought to do (if this represents some fact independent of my interests)?" But one can ask this sensibly only if "should" and "morally ought" are used in different senses. One cannot ask, "Why morally ought I to do what I morally ought to do?" even if "morally ought" does stand for an objective property. But neither can one ask, "Why should I do what I morally ought to do?" if "I should" and "I morally ought" *both* mean "I have a motive" or "It is necessary for my happiness," as they do on Stace's own view. For the question to be sensible, "I should" and "I morally ought" must have distinct meanings, what-

[9] W. T. Stace, *The Concept of Morals* (New York: Macmillan Co., 1937), pp. 41–43.

[10] That one may fail to feel any disposition whatsoever to do what is right cannot simply be asserted, for it is to make an important claim about human nature even on an externalist view.

ever these are; and, while one may entail motivation, the other need not.

III

The fullest and most recent version of this argument is to be found in P. H. Nowell-Smith's book.[11] He remarks with interest that the intuitionists "have but repeated Hume's argument" about the gap between the *is* and the *ought* in refuting naturalistic theories.[12] Then he goes on to contend that intuitionism itself may be disposed of by essentially the same argument, namely, that it likewise fails to bridge the gap; and in making this striking contention good he elaborates the argument that, no matter what "fact," natural, metaphysical, or non-natural, one may establish about an action, it will still not follow that one ought to do the action.

The intuitionist's answer to the question "Why should I be moral?"—unless, like Prichard, he rejects it as a senseless question—is that, if you reflect carefully, you will notice that a certain act has two characteristics, (a) that of being obligatory and (b) that of producing a maximum of good or of being a fulfil-

ment of a promise . . . etc. . . . But suppose all this has taken place. . . . Does it follow that I ought to do the action . . . ? . . . a world of non-natural characteristics is revealed to us by a . . . faculty called *"intuition."* . . . And from statements to the effect that these exist no conclusions follow about what I *ought to do.* A new world is revealed for our inspection . . . it is mapped and described in elaborate detail. No doubt it is all very interesting. If I happen to have a thirst for knowledge, I shall read on . . . But what if I am not interested? Why should I do anything about these newly-revealed objects? Some things, I have now learnt, are right and others wrong; but why should I do what is right and eschew what is wrong?

Of course the question "Why should I do what I see to be right?" is . . . an absurd one. . . . But . . . [this question], which [is] absurd when words are used in the ordinary way, would not be absurd if moral words were used in the way that intuitionists suppose . . . if "X is right" and "X is obligatory" are construed as statements to the effect that X has the non-natural characteristic of rightness or obligatoriness, which we just "see" to be present, it would seem that we can no more deduce "I ought to do X" from these premises than we could deduce it from "X is pleasant" or "X is in accordance with God's will."

This passage needs discussion here, even at the risk of some repetition. To begin with, it seems to me that Nowell-Smith is confusing two arguments, both suggested by Hume.[13] One says that conclusions involving "ought" cannot be derived from premises involving only "is" and not "ought." The other says something like this: conclusions involving "ought" cannot be derived from premises stating only *truths*, natural or nonnatural, even if one of these truths is what is meant by an ought-statement. Now it is the first of these

---

[11] *Ethics* (London: Penguin Books, 1954), pp. 36–43. Nowell-Smith is a noncognitivist, not a cognitivist as Field and Stace are. There are similar arguments in A. J. Ayer, "On the Analysis of Moral Judgments," *Horizon*, IX (1949), 171 ff.; Alf Ross, "The Logical Status of Value Judgments," *Theoria*, XI (1945), 203–8; R. C. Cross, "Virtue and Nature," *Proceedings of the Aristotelian Society*, N.S. L (1949–50), 123–37; H. Reichenbach, *The Rise of Scientific Philosophy* (Berkeley and Los Angeles: University of California Press, 1954), chap. xvii; R. M. Hare, *The Language of Morals* (Oxford: Clarendon Press, 1952), pp. 30, 79–93, 171; and elsewhere. I do not discuss these writers, however, because they may not be advancing quite the same argument; they seem to be insisting not so much that moral judgments are motivating as that they are prescriptive. Hence they may not be internalists. But, if they are, then what I say will apply to them, too.

[12] A. N. Prior says that Hume was but repeating Cudworth! Cf. *Logic and the Basis of Ethics* (Oxford: Clarendon Press, 1949), p. 33.

[13] The famous passage in Hume (*Treatise*, Bk. III, Pt. I, section 1), often appealed to lately, can be read as stating either of these arguments, but they must not be confused. He himself seems to distinguish it from the more obviously internalistic argument given a few pages earlier; hence he may intend it only in the first sense.

which is used by the intuitionists against their opponents, and *it* cannot be turned against them. For its point is valid even if ought-statements assert truths as the intuitionists claim, provided only that the truths they assert are different from those asserted by any is-statements. Insofar, then, as Nowell-Smith is trading on whatever validity this argument possesses, his case against intuitionism breaks down. It is the other argument on which he must rely.

This one is harder to deal with. We must first eliminate another point on which Nowell-Smith seems to trade. He supposes that "X is obligatory" stands for a nonnatural property and then argues that it does not follow that I ought to do X. Of course, it does not follow that I ought to do X, since it was not specified for whom X is obligatory. Let us take "I have an obligation to do" instead, and let us suppose that it asserts a fact about me and X, natural or nonnatural. Then the argument is that, even if it is true, it does not follow that I have an obligation to do X. Whether this is correct or not, however, depends on the meaning of "I have an obligation to do X" when it appears after the words "it does not follow." [14] If it here also stands for the fact in question, as cognitivists hold and as we are for the moment supposing, then it does follow that I have an obligation to do X, for the "conclusion" simply repeats the "premise."

Nowell-Smith may, of course, reply that no truth, natural or nonnatural, can entail an *obligation*. My point has been that it can *if* an obligation is a certain fact, as cognitivists claim. Nowell-Smith may go on to contend that an obligation is not identical with *any* such fact, but then he must show this independently, and cannot do so by the present argument. His contention may seem plausible when it is applied to naturalistic theories, as intuitionists

have always thought. But it is not obviously true, if one does not identify obligation and motivation, that an obligation cannot be identical with any peculiar kind of "fact" such as the intuitionist believes in, for he claims that it is such a peculiar "fact" precisely to account for its obligatoriness. He has, as it were, built obligatoriness into his "fact." Possibly this cannot be done or is too pat a solution, as Nowell-Smith suggests. But this must be shown independently; Nowell-Smith must argue directly that such a fact is inconceivable or is not what is meant by "obligation," remembering as he does so the prima facie distinction introduced above. For if it is conceivable and is what is meant by "obligation," his present argument is not cogent.

The real reason why Nowell-Smith thinks that no set of truths or facts entails my having an obligation to act is, of course, the fact that he implicitly assumes that my having an obligation implies my having a motive. This comes out when he says about the intuitionist's brave nonnatural world, "But what if I am not interested?" And again the answer is that, while there is a sense in which having an obligation equals having an interest, there is prima facie another sense in which it may stand for a truth of another kind, natural or not. It is true that motivation will not follow logically from this truth (though it may follow causally from a recognition of it); [15] it will not follow any more than "Y is a fellow traveler" follows from "Y is tickled pink." In this sense Nowell-Smith's point is correct. I can contemplate all the facts pointed out by the intuitionists and externalists and still ask sensibly, "Ought I?" if I am asking about motivation. But it may still be nonsense to ask, "Ought I?" in the moral sense, as the cognitivist would claim.

Here Nowell-Smith insists that, when words are used in the ordinary way, it is absurd to ask of an act which it is admittedly right for me to do, "Why should I

[14] As G. E. Moore pointed out in his reply to me. *The Philosophy of G. F. Moore*, ed. P. A. Schilpp (Evanston and Chicago: Northwestern University, 1942), pp. 567 ff.

[15] As H. D. Aiken has pointed out. See below.

do it?" And of course it is, if "should" is used in its moral sense. But in this sense, the intuitionist may contend, his usage involves no gap either, as we have been seeing. It is only if "should" is used in its motivation-seeking sense that he must allow that there is a gap, and in this sense, he may claim, there really is a gap, which is not noticed because of an ambiguity in the word "should" as it is ordinarily used.

Again, then, it becomes apparent that the internalist must either challenge this distinction between two uses of "should," or show independently that "should" implies motivation even in its moral use.

IV

The internalist arguments discussed above depend on the claim that obligation and its recognition entail the existence of motivation, but they depend on it indirectly, through an identification of a reason for acting, or of an obligation to act, with a motive for doing so. Frequently, however, the internalists make this claim in so many words, and conclude directly that externalistic theories are mistaken. Thus Field argues against Moore that "the moral fact" is in itself and necessarily of interest to us when apprehended, but this it cannot be on Moore's view, and therefore Moore's view is false.[16] Likewise for all forms of externalism. Suppose we take Field's first premise in a psychological sense, as asserting (1) that, if one acknowledges an obligation to do something, then it is psychologically impossible for him not to have some tendency to do it, and (2) that his recognizing his obligation by itself produces this tendency. Then it can be denied with some plausibility, for not everyone's moral experience witnesses to the truth of either of these assertions, let alone of both of them. But suppose it is true. Must an ex-

ternalist give up his position? Only if we can add two further premises: (3) that, no matter what external fact we may become acquainted with, it is always psychologically possible for us to be indifferent to it, and (4) that "the bare knowledge of anything can never move us to action." Now (4) is plausible, as Field shows at some length in attacking "the Kantian fallacy." But most externalists would admit that knowledge can move us to action only by awakening an already existing desire, in this case, perhaps, a desire to do the right.[17] As for (3), it is obviously false, since there are external facts to which, given the conative natures we have, we cannot remain wholly indifferent. And, this being the case, an externalist like Moore might insist that we are so constituted that we cannot be wholly cold in the presence of the particular external fact which he regards as constituting obligation—a claim which Field does nothing to disprove.

However this may be, Field gives us no grounds for accepting his premise that the recognition of an obligation is by itself and necessarily a motive. He seems simply to infer this from the fact that such recognition is by itself necessarily a reason for action. But we have seen that, at least prima facie, "reason" is ambiguous here, and something may be a reason without thereby being a motive. Field must then show that his assertion is true independently of any possible confusion between two senses of "reason," which he does not do. And, if he is not going in for the longer kind of reasoning to be described in our last section, he must show that it is true in a logical sense, as asserting that it is logically impossible to have an obligation to which one is indifferent.

Another use of the argument occurs in C. L. Stevenson's important first article,[18]

---

[16] *Moral Theory*, pp. 56 f.

[17] Cf., e.g., W. D. Ross, *The Right and the Good* (Oxford: Clarendon Press, 1930), pp. 157 f.
[18] "The Emotive Meaning of Ethical Terms," *Mind*, N.S. XLVI (1937), 16.

where he employs it against "any attempt to define ethical terms without reference to the interests of the speaker"—in favor, not of an internalistic cognitive theory, as in Field and Stace, but of an emotive one. Stevenson contends, among other things, that ethical terms "must have, so to speak, a magnetism," and that any analysis of them must provide for this. By saying they have magnetism he means that "a person who recognizes X to be 'good' [or 'obligatory'] must *ipso facto* acquire a stronger tendency to act in its favor than he otherwise would have had." He then writes:

This rules out the Humian type of definition. For according to Hume, to recognize that something is "good" is simply to recognize that the majority approve of it. Clearly, a man may see that the majority approve of X without having, himself, a stronger tendency to favour it.

The same reasoning, of course, will rule out intuitionism and other forms of externalism. On all such views, to assent to a moral judgment is to assent to a fact which involves no reference to one's interests; therefore this assent does not *ipso facto* or necessarily lead to a stronger tendency to favor the action in question.

This is essentially Field's argument over again, as Stevenson himself recognizes. The crucial premises are two: (1) that anyone who assents to a moral judgment must *ipso facto* or necessarily acquire a stronger tendency to do the action in question, and (2) that assenting to a fact which involves no reference to one's own interests will in no case *ipso facto* or necessarily produce such a tendency. Now these statements may be understood in a *causal* or psychological sense. But, if so, they should be shown to be true before they are used to rule out entire theories. The first is certainly not obvious in the case of all kinds of ethical judgments; it may be true of value-judgments but is it

true of all ought-judgments? That it is seems particularly doubtful if we must distinguish between two kinds of ought-statements, for then one kind might be incitive in tendency and the other not; yet Stevenson takes no account of the possibility of such a distinction. Again, as was just said, it is hard to believe that in the case of every "external fact" about an action it is *psychologically* possible for us to be indifferent to it. If this were so we could have no "primary appetites" in Butler's sense; all of our interests would be washingwomen taken in each other's laundry. But, if there are interests whose objects are "external," then Hume can plausibly claim that it is a psychological law of human nature that we invariably feel *some* tendency to do what we believe the majority to approve, or an intuitionist that it is psychologically necessary that we pursue a nonnatural right or good, as Plato thought.

Now Stevenson does nothing to refute such psychological theories. He must, then, be thinking that assenting to a moral judgment in some sense *logically* entails its having a tendency to affect one's action— that an analysis of a person's moral judgment or recognition that something is obligatory must in some way involve a reference to his tendencies to do the action in question. That is, motivation must be "built into" the analysis of ethical utterances. This dictum, however, cannot simply be assumed, if the issue is not to be begged, especially if the distinction referred to earlier holds. Moreover, it is ambiguous. It may mean that a reference to the agent's desires is to be built into the *descriptive* meaning of ethical judgments, or it may mean that part of what is meant by *assenting* to a moral judgment is a disposition to respond accordingly. The first of these alternatives is taken by Field and Falk [19] but rejected by Stevenson. The second, as

[19] Cf. Also D. C. Williams, "The Meaning of Good," *Philosophical Review*, XLVI (1937), 416–23.

we shall see in a later section, can be accepted by an externalist.

V

A somewhat novel form of the present argument has been advanced by H. D. Aiken in a well-known article.[20] He maintains (1) that judgments of obligation are normative in the sense that they influence the will and determine conduct, and (2) that "the relation between cognition and motivation, on any theory of motivation whatever, is a causal, not a logical, relation"; and he concludes that all "descriptivist" analyses of judgments of obligation are therefore mistaken, whether naturalistic or nonnaturalistic (including internalistic forms of naturalism such as those of Field and Stace). (2) is an important point and needed to be made, but it may be admitted. (1) is a premise already familiar to us in other forms, but, whereas his predecessors regard it as empirical, Aiken makes it analytic. He defines a judgment of obligation as one which influences conduct "by whatever means." This, however, has a curious effect, namely, that what are usually called ethical judgments may not be judgments of obligation in his sense since they will be so only if they influence the will. But then, even if his argument shows that his "judgments of obligation" cannot be descriptively analyzed, it proves nothing about the so-called moral judgments with which the rest of us have been concerned.

Aiken is tacitly assuming that judgments of the form "A should . . . ," "B ought . . . ," and so forth, in the uses with which we are concerned, are all causally efficacious, at least normally, and so fall

[20] "Evaluation and Obligation," *Journal of Philosophy*, XLVII (1950), 5–22. See also "The Authority of Moral Judgments," *Philosophy and Phenomenological Research*, XII (1951–52), 513. A similar view is present in A. Moore, "A Categorical Imperative?" *Ethics*, LXIII (1952–53), 235–50, to which my criticisms also apply.

under what he calls "judgments of obligation." This may be doubted, especially if we keep in mind our distinction between two kinds of "should" sentences, but let us accept it for the sake of the argument. Then his conclusion still does not follow. For a judgment that causally affects behavior may be susceptible of a cognitivist analysis, and even of an externalistic one. That is, a statement may be a "judgment of obligation" and yet be descriptive. For its moving power may be due wholly to the information, natural or nonnatural, which it conveys to our desires. If I say to you as we cross the street, "There is a car coming," my statement will influence your actions, and it may do so simply in its informative capacity (given your desire to live). Then it will be a "judgment of obligation" and yet be capable of a descriptivist and externalist analysis.

The matter may be put thus. Consider "I ought to do X" in any safely ethical use. The question is whether or not this is to be given an internalistic analysis. Aiken does give us such an analysis of the metasentence, " 'I ought to do X' is normative." But this is not an analysis of the sentence, "I ought to do X," itself, and so all of the standard theories about its analysis remain open. It is, however, this sentence which constitutes our problem; we want to know the function or meaning of "obligatory" as it is used in, "It is obligatory on me to do X," not in, " 'It is obligatory on me to do X' is obligatory." Aiken's attempt to sidestep the dispute about ethical sentences is no doubt a laudable one; the moral of my critique is only that, if one does sidestep it, one must not draw any conclusions about it, as he seems to do.

VI

The above kinds of argument against externalism all depend on the claim that obligation or judgments of obligation somehow entail motivation, perhaps directly, perhaps by identifying motivation and reasons for acting or by identifying motivation and obligation to act. I have tried to dispose of each argument individually, but my main point has been that there is a prima facie distinction to be made between moral or justifying reasons and exciting or motivating ones, or between moral and nonmoral obligation; that this distinction is usually neglected by internalists when they use such arguments; and that if this distinction is valid the arguments lose their cogency. For then the externalist can reply that, while there is a motivational sense of "ought" which *is* "internal," there is another sense of "ought" which is moral and which may be "external" for all that has been shown so far.

In making this point I have but echoed an old intuitionist refrain, which to my knowledge was first sung by Samuel Clarke and last by R. M. Blake, but which may also be sung by nonintuitionists. Clarke, observing the rising conflict between internalism and externalism of his day, distinguishes "the truest and formallest obligation," which is moral, from "the Dread of Superior Power and Authority, and the Sanction of Rewards and Punishments . . . which is . . . really in itself only a *secondary* and *additional* Obligation, or *Inforcement* of the first." Then he remarks that a failure to notice this ambiguity of the term "obligation" has blinded some writers to the (externalist)truth that "the original *Obligation* of all . . . is the eternal *Reason* of Things. . . ." He says drily, in parentheses, ". . . the ambiguous use of which word [Obligation], as a *Term of Art,* has caused some Perplexity and Confusion in this Matter"—the perplexity and confusion being, of course, in the minds of the internalists.[21] It seems to me, as it seemed to him and to Blake, that neglect of this ambiguity has been a serious mistake in recent moral philosophy.

Even if the distinction is valid, however, it does not follow that internalism is false, but only that externalism may be true if it cannot be refuted on grounds other than those so far considered. One may admit the distinction and still claim that both kinds of judgment of obligation, the moral as well as the nonmoral, are susceptible of an internalistic analysis. In fact, some recent internalists do distinguish moral from nonmoral obligation in one way or another, though apparently without seeing that the above kind of argument does not establish the internality of the moral ought, when this is distinguished from the nonmoral one. It may then be held that, independently of such a distinction and of the above arguments, it can be shown that moral obligation is internal. We must now in the second main part of this paper take up some considerations that seem calculated to show this.

It will be helpful, first, to sort out a number of propositions that internalists have held or may be holding, particularly since they have rarely been distinguished in the literature. All of the above writers, and many others, are convinced that having or acknowledging an obligation to do something involves having, either occurrently or dispositionally, some motivation for doing it; and they infer that externalism is false. But this proposition can be taken to assert several things, namely: (1) that the state of having an obligation includes or is identical with that of being motivated in a certain way; (2) that the statement, "I have an obligation to do B," means or logically entails the statement, "I have, actually or potentially, some motivation for doing B"; [22] (3) that the reasons that justify a judgment of obligation include or are identical with the reasons that prove the existence of motivation to act accordingly; (4) that the reasons that justify a judgment of obligation include or are identical with those that *bring about* the existence of motivation to act accordingly; (5) that, although justifying a moral

[21] Cf. *British Moralists,* II, 16.

[22] Or, "It is to my interest to do B," or, "B is conducive to my self-realization."

judgment does not include giving exciting reasons for acting on it, it presupposes the existence, at least potentially, of such excitement; (6) that *saying* or being *said* to have an obligation presupposes one's having motives for doing the action in question; (7) that *assenting* to an obligation entails feeling or having a disposition to feel at least some inclination to act in the way prescribed; or (8) that one can know or "see" or think that one has a certain obligation only when one is in a favorable conative state with respect to performing the act in question.

Even these formulations are not very rigorous, but perhaps they will suffice to make clearer the opposition we are discussing. The externalist is concerned to deny (1) through (4), which the internalist will assert. If they are true, externalism is untenable. However, as far as I can see, the internalists have not shown them to be true to such a degree that they can be safely used as premises for refuting externalism; indeed, they are plausible only when the distinction between two senses of "ought" and "reason" that we have been stressing is not borne in mind.

As for (5) through (8), an externalist may accept them, though they may also be denied with some plausibility (and would be denied by a really "compleat" externalist). It is obvious that he can admit (8), for it makes only a psychological assertion about the conditions of moral insight; in fact, (8) is maintained by such externalists as Scheler and Hartmann.[23] (5), as we shall see, may also be agreed to by an externalist, though only if "presupposes" is understood in some psychological or "contextual" sense, and not in a strictly logical one.

The arguments to be dealt with here generally involve (1), (6), or (7), and we may take first those that use (1) in some form or other. In one of them Falk appeals to the familiar principle that "I

[23] Cf. also H. Reiner, *Pflicht und Neigung*.

morally ought" implies "I can," adding that "I can" implies "I want to (in the sense that I have, at least dispositionally, some motivation for doing)," and then drawing an internalist conclusion.[24] Suppose we admit, though both claims may be disputed, that "I morally ought" in all its senses implies "I can," and that "I can" implies "I want to." Even then this argument will be cogent only if the "implies" involved is a logical one in both cases. But is it in " 'I can' implies 'I want to'?" To say, "I cannot whistle a tune while standing on my head, unless I feel some inclination to do so," is perhaps an odd thing to say about an odd bit of behavior, but it seems at most to state a physical fact, not a logical necessity. One may, of course, so define "I can" as to include "I have some impulse to," but it is not obvious that one should, and it is not clear that "ought" implies "can" as so defined.

But *"ought implies can"* need not be construed as asserting a strict logical implication. It may plausibly be understood as saying: (a) moral judgments "presuppose," "contextually imply," or "pragmatically imply" that the agent is able to act as proposed or is believed to be, but do not assert or state that he is; or (b) the *point of uttering* moral judgments disappears if the agents involved are not able to act as proposed or at least believed to be; or (c) it would be morally wrong to insist that an agent ought to do a certain action, if he is or is thought to be unable to do it. If Kant's dictum is interpreted in one of these ways the externalist need have no fear, for then it will not serve to refute him.

VII

In a somewhat similar argument, Aiken reasons that obligation presupposes respon-

[24] Cf. "Morals without Faith," *Philosophy*, XIX (1944), 7; "Obligation and Rightness," *Philosophy*, XX (1945), 139.

sibility and that this presupposes motivation:

Hume's argument can be stated in another . . . way. We assume that no person can be held morally responsible for actions which he did not willingly perform. We do not address such judgments as "Killing is wrong" to cyclones. . . . In short, we regard only responsible beings as moral or immoral. But . . . responsibility *presupposes* a motive for or interest in any act for which a person is held "responsible." If this is so, the very notions of "moral" and "immoral" involve a reference to feeling or sentiment; and every moral judgment states or implies such a reference.

Aiken then asserts that this argument "disqualifies all theories whatever which . . . deny that moral categories are to be construed in terms of human feeling or interest. . . ."[25] In another place he claims that obligation and desire are intimately related, "For . . . it is doubtful whether the term ['ought'] is ever properly applied to anything save motivated activity." Here too he takes this conviction as a criterion to be met "by any adequate analysis of 'ought'."[26]

Now, the argument from obligation to responsibility to motivation is like the argument from obligation to ability to motivation, and the same points hold about it. Instead of repeating, then, let us take up the conviction that moral obligation and judgment presuppose motivation. It does seem correct to say that my having moral duties implies that *others* have desires and feelings, but this externalists need not deny. It is also plausible to hold that my having duties, or being a moral agent whose acts are right or wrong, presupposes *my* having interests and motives. To this extent Aiken is, in my opinion, correct.

[25] *Hume's Moral and Political Philosophy* (New York: Hafner Publishing Co., 1948), p. xxxi.
[26] "A Pluralistic Analysis of the Ethical 'Ought,'" *Journal of Philosophy*, XLVIII (1951), 497.

But an externalist can agree, and still insist that, although one can ascribe obligation only to a motivated being, to ascribe an obligation to such a being is not to talk about his motives but to assert some external fact about him.

More crucial is Aiken's further claim that A's having an obligation to do B presupposes his having not only interests *überhaupt* but, directly or indirectly, an interest in doing B (though not necessarily a predominant one). If this means that A's having a duty to do B logically entails his having an interest in doing B, or that establishing his obligation to do B logically entails showing him that he has such an interest or producing such an interest in him, it may be denied. A man who is seeking to determine if he has a duty to do a certain deed need not look to see if he has any motives for doing it, and he cannot claim that he does not have the duty simply on the ground that he finds no supporting motivation. Aiken may reply that, nevertheless, A's having an obligation to do B in some sense presupposes his having a concern to do B, at least dispositionally, and I am inclined to agree that it does, but only in the sense that *ascribing* this duty to A "contextually" or pragmatically implies that, if A sees he has it, he will have some concern to perform it (6). This, however, does not mean that A's having this concern is a condition of his having a duty to do B, and it can be admitted by an externalist. In *Principia Ethica* Moore says, "If I ask whether an action is *really* my duty or *really* expedient, the predicate of which I question the applicability to the action in question is precisely the same. In both cases I am asking, 'Is this event the best on the whole that I can effect?'" Yet, although "duty" and "expedient" have the same conceptual meaning for Moore, he maintains that there is a difference in their use, "duty" being applied to those useful actions "which it is more useful to praise and to enforce by sanctions, since they are actions which there is a temptation to omit." [27] Then "B is A's duty" *means,* "B is the best thing on the whole that A can do," but it *presupposes* that A is tempted not to do it. Perhaps moral judgments only presuppose motivation in a similar sense.

VIII

Two other considerations seem to have been regarded as showing that having an obligation entails having a corresponding motivation. One is a conviction that a man cannot have an obligation unless he accepts it as such and "beats responsive and not irresponsive to the claim" in what James calls the "everlasting ruby vaults" of his heart.[28] This is expressed in the following quotation from Falk: ". . . Even the commands of God could only constitute moral obligations for somebody who considered it a *law unto himself* to respect what God bids him to do." [29] Now it does seem in some sense correct to say that a man cannot actually have a moral duty if he does not see and accept it. At the same time, this is an odd thing to say unless we are using "duty" in two senses, for we are saying that A has no duty to do B if he does not recognize that he has a duty to do B. The same double usage occurs in the sentence, "You ought to do what you think you ought to do." The matter can be cleared up by using the distinction, long accepted by externalists, between what one *subjectively* ought to do and what one *objectively* ought to do. The point, then, is that A subjectively ought to do B only

if he accepts this as his obligation. It still may be, however, that B would be objectively right for him to do anyway. In fact, when a man thinks that something is his duty, what he thinks is that it is a duty independently of his thinking so (and independently of his wanting to do it); and when he asks what his duty is, he implies that he has a duty that he does not yet recognize, and what he is seeking to know, as it were, is what it would have been his duty to do even if he had not discovered it. Thus there is a sense in which one has a moral obligation even if one does not recognize it as such.

It has also been insisted by internalists that the moral will is autonomous, and R. M. Blake believed that this doctrine should be repudiated by externalists as incompatible with the existence of any categorical imperative. Nowell-Smith is especially persistent in asserting such autonomy. ". . . The feature which distinguishes moral obligations from all others is that they are self-imposed. . . ." "The questions 'what shall I do?' and 'what moral principles should I adopt?' must be answered by each man for himself; that at least is part of the connotation of the word 'moral'." [30] In spite of what Blake says, it is hard entirely to reject this "moral protestantism," as Margaret Macdonald has called it,[31] common as it is to Kant, existentialism, and Nowell-Smith. But I am not persuaded that a recognition of autonomy necessarily leads to internalism. In areas outside of ethics we also believe in autonomy, e.g., in our scientific beliefs, and, in "religious protestantism," in our theological beliefs. Yet here the "facts" in which we freely believe or disbelieve are "external" ones—facts which are independent of us but about which we are nevertheless left to make up our own minds. It may then be that obligations are external facts of a simi-

[27] See G. E. Moore, *Principia Ethica* (Cambridge: Cambridge University Press, 1903), pp. 169–70.

[28] W. James, "The Moral Philosopher and the Moral Life," in *The Will to Believe* (New York: Longmans, Green & Co., 1897), p. 196. James is inconsistent on this point, for he also says that a man has an obligation as soon as someone else makes a demand on him.

[29] "Obligation and Rightness," p. 147.

[30] *Ethics,* pp. 210, 320.

[31] Cf. *Philosophical Analysis,* ed. M. Black (Ithaca: Cornell University Press, 1950), p. 220.

lar sort. Certainly intuitionists and naturalists can allow us the same kind of autonomy in ethics that we claim in science and religion, without thereby going over to the enemy. They may hold that what we objectively ought to do is self-imposed only in the sense of being self-discovered or self-recognized, as scientific facts are, and that only what we subjectively ought to do is self-imposed in the more radical manner indicated earlier.

IX

However, even if *having* a moral obligation does not always and in every sense depend on the agent's accepting it and feeling motivated to do it, it may nevertheless be maintained that *assenting to* a moral obligation entails a feeling of motivation on his part. This brings us to (7), which is widely insisted on by internalists.[32] It may be put in various ways, but the essential point of it is either (a) that one cannot assent to or be convinced of an obligation of one's own without having some disposition to act accordingly, or (b) that we should regard it as odd or paradoxical if someone were to assent to an obligation without feeling any motivation whatever for fulfilling it. In the first case, there is a direct assertion that a certain sequence of events is not possible; in the second, there is only a claim that we should be puzzled if we observed such a sequence or rather, do not believe that one can occur.

Now, taken in its first form, (7) does not seem to me to be obviously true. In any case, as we have noticed, it is ambiguous in a way that its proponents do not recognize. Taken as an assertion of a psychological law, it can be admitted by any exter

nalist who does not hold our conative nature to be *totally* depraved.[33] It must then be regarded as asserting a logical truth, if it is to say anything inconsistent with externalism. Here again there are two alternatives. (m) It may be meant that part of what a judgment of obligation *asserts* or *states* is that the agent referred to feels a responsive beat in his heart. Then (7) is identical with (2), and simply to assume it is a *petitio*. (n) The other alternative is that motivation is to be built, not into the content of a moral judgment, but into the process of assenting to it. On this view, it is not "A ought to do B" that logically implies his having some tendency to do B, but "A is convinced that he ought to do B." That is to say, part of what is meant by "assenting to an obligation" is that one feels a responsive stirring.

Most recent internalists, I believe, would prefer this formulation of (7) to that represented by (m). I am not at all sure that (7), so interpreted, is true, but I should like to suggest that an externalist can accept it if it is. An externalist may agree, it seems to me, that we cannot, in the sense in which we use these words in connection with moral judgments, "accept," "recognize," or "be convinced of" an obligation without thereby having at least some motivation to fulfill it. He may hold, for example, that judgments of obligation have a conceptual content of an "external" kind, but add that we do not speak of a man's *assenting* or *sincerely assenting* to them unless he not only apprehends the truth of their conceptual content but is at least to some extent moved to conform to it. He

---

[32] See H. J. N. Horsburg, "The Criteria of Assent to a Moral Rule," *Mind*, N.S. LXIII (1954), 345–58; Hare, *The Language of Morals*, pp. 20, 169.

[33] Cf. Plato, *Symposium;* R. Price, *Review of the Principal Questions of Morals* (Oxford: Clarendon Press, 1948), chap. iii; W. D. Ross, *The Right and the Good*, pp. 157 f. If the doctrine of total depravity does not imply that we have naturally no disposition *whatsoever* to do what is right, but only that such a disposition as we have to do what is right is always overcome by other desires when it comes into conflict with them, except by the grace of God, then even its proponents can accept (7) as a psychological statement.

would then admit that it is *logically* possible that one might have a "mere intellectual apprehension," as Field calls it, of their truth, but he would recognize the generally practical function of language (which his opponents have made so much of), especially moral discourse. There is no reason why he cannot change his ways enough to do this; even an intuitionist need not insist that the *actual* use of moral language is merely to report the news of a nonnatural world and is in no way adapted to the interests of the reader. It may be part of the ordinary "grammar" of such words as "assent," when used in connection with ethical judgments, that they are not to be employed except when "mere intellectual apprehension" is accompanied by a responsive beating of the heart. Even in the case of nonethical judgments it has been held that one does not believe unless one is in some sense disposed to act accordingly in appropriate circumstances. But, even if this is not so, it might be argued that because ethical discourse is more particularly concerned to guide human action than is nonethical discourse, such terms as "believe" may be presumed to obey different rules here.

Of course, the internalist may still complain that on his opponent's view it is logically, if not actually, possible to have a "mere intellectual apprehension" of an obligation. But, if the position just described is tenable, then he cannot support his complaint by appealing to the dictum that we cannot really assent to an obligation without having a disposition to respond. And simply to assume that it is not even logically possible to have a "mere intellectual apprehension" of an obligation is a *petitio.*

Consider now (7) in form (b). Here there is an appeal to certain data about our ordinary moral consciousness and its ways of thinking; these data are supposed to show that internalism is true or at least is embedded in moral common sense. Thus Falk has argued that externalism fails to

account for such facts as the following: [34] (p) that "we commonly expect that in thinking ourselves obliged we *ipso facto* feel some constraint to do what we think we ought to do"; (q) that, "when we try to convince another that he ought to pay his bills, we expect our argument if accepted to effect some change of heart in him"; (r) that "we should think it odd to receive the answer: 'Yes, I know now *that* and *why* I ought to pay my bills, but I am still without any incentive for doing so.'"

I am not so much concerned to question these facts, though I do not myself find the answer in (r) entirely odd, as to point out that they do not, as stated, prove obligation and motivation to be *logically* connected. If we have the expectations and feelings of oddity described, this may only mean that we commonly believe that all men are *psychologically* so constituted as to be moved by the recognition that something is right. It need not mean that this is logically necessary or even that we believe it to be so. And we have already seen that one may hold rightness to be an external characteristic and yet claim that we are so made as necessarily (causal) to take an interest in it.

Falk's facts may also be explained in another way by the externalist. For, until evidence is given to the contrary, the externalist can argue that the common moral consciousness feels the expectations and oddities mentioned only because it does not distinguish at all clearly or consistently in its thinking between two senses in which one may be obliged, so that it links to the one feelings and thoughts appropriate to the other. This seems to me plausible, for we do frequently fail to see any difference between the two kinds of reasons for action, and often shift from one to the other without noticing.

Still a third explanation is possible. As

---

[34] "Obligation and Rightness," pp. 139–41. Falk also recognizes, however, that externalism "finds some support in common usage" (p. 138).

we have indicated before, when one asks what he ought to do, he is not or at least need not be asking what he already accepts as his duty, but what is his duty although it is not yet accepted as such; and he is not or need not be asking what he has or may have a motive for doing, but what he is morally required to do and may not have any motive for doing until after he sees that it is his duty. But, of course, one would not normally ask the question unless one was concerned about the answer and felt some motivation to do his duty, whatever that might turn out to be. And so, when one concludes that such and such is what he ought to do, he can be expected to feel some motivation to do such and such and even to decide to do it. The whole process of moral question and answer normally takes place in this atmosphere of moral concern. This is all that such facts as those mentioned prove, and this much an externalist may and no doubt should admit, though he may add that it is logically possible that the case should be otherwise. Normally, then, when assent occurs in the course of a moral inquiry, it can be expected to involve commitment. But it does not follow that it is a condition of one's having an obligation to do a certain action that he should have a motive for doing it apart from discovering that it is his duty, nor that discovering it to be his duty logically entails his having a motive for doing it.

It has been argued that, if a man says he believes that he has a duty to do a certain action but feels no conation at all in favor of it, then he does not understand the sentence, "I have a duty," or its use.[35] If by this it is meant that he does not understand what an obligation is, then simply to assert this is to beg the question against the externalist. If it is meant that he does not understand what it is to *assent* to an ob-

ligation, the externalist can agree and give the explanation indicated above in our discussion of (7). But it may be that what is intended is that he just does not know in what circumstances to *say*, "I ought to do so and so," and this an externalist may also concede.

X

This brings up a number of points made by internalists, not so much about *having* an obligation or *assenting* to one, as about *uttering* sentences to the effect that one has an obligation or that someone else has —in short, (6). For example, it is said (a) that my uttering a sentence beginning with "I ought" always or normally "expresses" a pro-attitude or decision on my part or "contextually implies" one.[36] But this an externalist may grant even if he holds that such a sentence "asserts" an external fact. The sentence, "There are flying saucers," expresses the speaker's belief, but for all that it purports to assert an external fact. Thus, W. D. Ross, who holds that "good" *means* an external characteristic, is "inclined to think" that we *use* or *apply* the term in such a way "that in each case the *judge* has some feeling of approval or interest towards what he calls good." [37] It is also said (b) that my uttering a sentence starting with "You ought" expresses or contextually implies a pro-attitude on my part toward your doing the act specified, as well as one on yours.[38] But Ross

<hr/>

[35] E.g., A. Moore, "A Categorical Imperative?" pp. 237 f.; I discuss a similar claim by S. M. Brown, Jr., in "Natural and Inalienable Rights," *Philosophical Review*, LXIV (1955), 222 f.

[36] Cf. Nowell-Smith, *Ethics*, pp. 186 ff., 261; W. S. Sellars, "Obligation and Motivation," in *Readings in Ethical Theory*, p. 516; H. D. Aiken, "Emotive Meanings and Ethical Terms," *Journal of Philosophy*, XLI (1944), 461 ff.; P. B. Rice, *On the Knowledge of Good and Evil* (New York: Random House, 1955), pp. 108 ff., 113, 231 f.

[37] *The Right and the Good*, p. 90.

[38] Nowell-Smith, *Ethics*, p. 199 (the phrase "contextually implies" is owed to Nowell-Smith); Aiken, "Emotive Meanings and Ethical Terms," pp. 461 ff.

could admit this too. If I say, "There is a tidal wave coming up behind you," I "express" a concern about your welfare and "presuppose" that you also have one, but what I assert is still an external fact or purports to be.

In a similar vein internalists contend (c) that it would be absurd, odd, or "logically odd" to say things like: "You ought to do A, but don't"; "I ought to do A, but shall I?"; "I ought to do A, but I shall not."[39] Now these would, perhaps, be unusual uses of language, but are they logically impossible? "There are flying saucers, but I don't believe it" would be an unusual contribution to any serious and sober conversation, but it is not a logically self-contradictory one, since both parts of what is asserted may be true together; the apparent conflict is not between parts of what is asserted but between part of what is asserted and one of the presuppositions of asserting the rest.

Logically, as far as I can see, "I should" and "I shall" are distinct, and one can admit that he ought and still not resolve to do. One would not then be very likely to *say*, "I ought but I shall not," for one probably would not be that interested in the morality of what one was doing, but logically the situation would be such as to be describable in those terms. No doubt, as Nowell-Smith and P. B. Rice claim, a firsthand "I ought" does normally express commitment or decision on the speaker's part, for one would not normally go through the process of moral deliberation that concludes with "I ought" if he were not sufficiently devoted to the moral enterprise for this conclusion to coincide with his decision. This does not mean, however, that "I ought" logically entails "I shall"; it may only pragmatically presuppose or contextually imply this.

Nowell-Smith's discussion of "I ought"

and "I shall" is interesting in this connection.[40] According to him, "I (morally) ought" expresses a decision, just as "I shall" does, although it is a decision based on rules, and therefore "I ought but shall I?" is logically odd unless "shall I?" is used in a predictive sense. Yet he admits that "I ought" is "also used, not to express a decision, but in the course of making up one's mind before a decision has been reached," and it is this use that interests me. It seems to me that in this use one *could* say, "I ought but shall I?" and one might go on thinking he ought and yet decide not to. Nowell-Smith seeks to avoid this conclusion by turning the "I ought" here into the Voice of Conscience or "self-hortatory 'you ought'"—a neat device but question-begging in this context. The main point, however, is that there is an "I ought" which does not express decision. It is true that this "I ought" is normally replaced by "the verdict-giving 'I ought'" *if* desire does not win out over conscience. But desire may win, and then there is a situation which can be described by "I ought, but I shall not," where "shall" is not predictive but decisive, though if one is in this situation one is not likely so to describe it until later, and then in the past tense.

XI

So far our study of the opposition between internalism and externalism in moral philosophy has fallen into two main parts. In the first (sections I through V) we reviewed one family of arguments against externalism and saw that they are not successful, mainly because they can for the most part be answered by distinguishing two senses of "obligation," corresponding to two meanings of, "Why should I?" In the second (sections VI through X) we found that another set of considerations that are relatively independent of this dis-

[39] Cf. Nowell-Smith, *Ethics*, pp. 146, 152, 178, 261. Note: "I *ought* implies I *shall*" is much stronger than "I *ought* implies *I feel some disposition to*," and in internalist need not hold the former.

[40] *Ibid.*, pp. 261–63, 267 f.

tinction can, in so far as they are valid at all, be met or accepted if certain other distinctions are made—between what we objectively and what we subjectively ought to do; between having an obligation, assenting to an obligation, and saying one has an obligation; between what is stated or logically implied and what is "presupposed" or "implied" in some not strictly logical sense by a moral judgment, and so forth. In short, we have seen that externalism is not refuted by these arguments and considerations and can be maintained if there are not yet other grounds on which it must be given up.

We might now go on to consider corresponding arguments against internalism. It is, however, difficult to find such arguments explicitly set forth in recent literature, and perhaps we may assume that they too would turn out to be inconclusive. The distinction between two senses of "should" and "ought" to which we have appealed, for example, cannot, even if it is valid, be used as an argument to refute internalism, although it disposes of some arguments used in its support.[41] For it is possible to admit this distinction and still maintain a kind of internalism. One might hold, for instance, that moral judgments are expressions of some specifically moral attitude, such as love, sympathy, an internalized sense of social demand, an attitude of impartial spectatorship, and so forth, and regard justifying reasons as reasons calculated to appeal to this attitude, exciting reasons as those that appeal to other attitudes and desires. One would then regard this attitude as conative (unlike Hutcheson's moral sense), and moral judgments as *ipso facto* to some extent motivating. But one would not claim that this attitude is always dominant, and so could admit that I may agree that I ought to do a certain action and yet say, "But I shall not!" In this very important respect one's

position, though a form of internalism, would be like externalism.

The main result yielded by our discussion, then, is that the opposition we are studying cannot be resolved, as so many seem to think, by such relatively small-scale logical or semi-logical arguments as we have been dealing with. But we have also achieved some clarity about the exact points at issue. The externalist can admit that there is a nonmoral obligation and even a "subjective" moral obligation that logically entails motivation. He can accept any statement that says that having an obligation, assenting to one, or being said to have one causally or *psychologically* involves the existence of a corresponding motivation. He may also agree that assenting to an obligation *logically* entails the existence of motivation for acting accordingly. He may even allow, and perhaps should, that having or being said to have an obligation presupposes in some not strictly logical sense the existence of such motivation. What he must deny, and the internalist assert, is that having objectively a certain moral obligation logically entails having some motivation for fulfilling it, that justifying a judgment of objective moral obligation logically implies establishing or producing a motivational buttress, and that it is logically impossible that there should be a state of apprehending a moral obligation of one's own which is not accompanied by such a buttress (even if this "mere intellectual apprehension" is never actual and does not amount to what is called "assenting to" or "acknowledging" an obligation).

Now one may, if sufficiently hardy, choose to defend a form of externalism that does not make any of the concessions just indicated, or a form of internalism that does not incorporate the distinction between two senses of "Why should I?" or between exciting and justifying reasons. Personally, it seems to me that the choice must in practice be between an externalism that makes such concessions and

---

[41] It seems to me also to refute *egoistic* forms of internalism.

an internalism that recognizes such a distinction. But, in any case, how is the issue to be settled? If arguments of the kind we have been reviewing are inadequate, are we then at an impasse here, too, as so many think we are on other questions? This does not follow. It does follow that neither kind of moral philosophy can be decisively refuted by the other, and that we must give up the quest for certainty in the sense of no longer hoping for such refutations. But it does not follow that nothing can be said for one view as against the other. What does follow is that the whole discussion must consciously move to another level.[42]

This does not mean that it must become even more "meta" than it already is. What this shift involves, and that it is necessary, can best be made clear by taking a look at Falk's best-known paper.[43] Here he first seems to argue very much as he does in the earlier articles already dealt with. But soon it becomes apparent that something different is going on. Falk finds in the controversy between Prichard and his opponents and in moral common sense a tension between two positions, namely, "that morality needs some additional psychological sanction" and "that what sanction it requires, it necessarily carries with it." That is, moral philosophy and ordinary moral thinking have been a confused combination of, or alternation between, externalism and internalism. Falk suggests that this situation "has its origin in uncertainties and contradictions in the common use of words like 'ought' or 'duty' in an unnoticed juxtaposition of meanings each of which entails a different relation to motivation." It is due to the fact that "ought" is used in both an externalist and

an internalist sense, which "remain undifferentiated and are imperceptibly juxtaposed and confused," so that "there may be an unnoticed switch from the one use of 'ought' to the other." This is why the questioner's "Why should I be moral?" has been so puzzling. In one sense of "ought" it is "legitimate and in need of some factual answer," in the other it is absurd; and where the two senses are confused "no answer can satisfy," and the way is open for the skeptic to draw his disturbing conclusion.

In other words, Falk, although he is an internalist, is explicitly recognizing the ambiguity we have made so much of—indeed, he goes further and says that one of the senses involved *is* external, a claim we have not made. He uses this ambiguity to explain the rise of our two points of view and their juxtaposition in moral common sense and philosophy. All this I cannot but approve. I have only wanted to add that it is the internalists rather than the externalists who have failed to notice the ambiguity, and that this failure vitiates much of their argument. Falk does not deny this; he simply does not repeat his earlier arguments for internalism, apparently recognizing their insufficiency. Instead, he proceeds to a new line of attack.

Falk contends that we cannot be satisfied, as an externalist would be, with uncovering the confusion and replacing it with an avowed use of "ought" in two senses, one external and one internal, one moral and the other motivational. In fact, he insists that the external use of "ought" cannot be accepted by a mature reflective person who is "aware of a capacity of reasoned choice and intent on using it," because such a person cannot "easily agree to a use of [moral] words for any demand on him that still left him to ask whether he also had a sufficient reason for doing the act." He then argues that one internal use of "ought" bears "at least a sufficient resemblance to what ordinary

---

[42] In "The Naturalistic Fallacy," *Mind*, N.S. XLVIII (1939), 464–77, I made a similar point about the issue between naturalism and nonnaturalism, but I then had rather simple-minded views about an appeal to "inspection" which was to decide it.

[43] " 'Ought' and Motivation."

usage expects of a normative term" for it to qualify as moral.[44] He calls this "the purely formal motivational 'ought.'" To say one ought in this sense is to say he has a reason or motive for acting with regard to which no further question can be asked, or which is compelling no matter what considerations reason may advance, and so is "formally sufficient." This "ought," Falk holds, can be identified with the moral "ought," since it is normative in the sense of influencing "the direction of people's volitional attitudes and actions," it is not simply a function of occurrent wants, and it is categorical, not hypothetical. It is, in fact, confused with the external moral "ought" in ordinary thinking. It *should* be taken as *the* moral "ought" because it must be recognized in any case, and because "in using moral language we mean to denote something that when known, can conclusively serve to direct what we do, and we cannot obey two masters."

Now I am not convinced by what Falk says, all too briefly, even here. He says that "we cannot avowedly use 'moral ought' both for an external and an internal state of affairs, as if a man might have one but not another sort of moral duty in respect of the same act." Yet he has not shown that we ever do use the *moral* "ought" for an internal state of affairs, but at most that we ought to. Besides, in the distinction between a subjective and an objective "ought" it seems to be possible to use even "morally ought" in two senses, one more internal and one more external, without thereby having to serve two masters. Moreover, it does not appear that his substitute will do as the moral "ought." As far as I can see, an act may be morally wrong even though I am impelled to do it after full reflection. What one is impelled to do even after reason has done its best is

still dependent on the vagaries of one's particular conative disposition, and I see no reason for assuming that it will always coincide with what is in fact right or regarded as right. As for Falk's assertion that "in using moral language we mean to denote something that when known, can conclusively serve to direct what we do"— this is ambiguous. It may mean that moral judgments are intended to serve as conclusive *guides* or that they are meant to serve as conclusive *goads*. In the first case Falk is clearly right, but an externalist can agree. In the second he is either forgetting his own admission that there is an external use of "ought" in ordinary discourse or begging the question. His further claim that a reflective person cannot accept as a moral duty anything which he does not have a "formally sufficient" motive for doing seems to me to beg the question as it stands.

What interests me here about Falk's paper, however, is the fact that he has moved the controversy to another level, a less merely logical and larger scale level. The issue, he says in conclusion, is not settled merely by distinguishing "between normative facts of different kinds, confusedly referred to by the same name"; ultimately what is necessary is "clarity and decision about what fact would most nearly correspond to our intentions in the use of moral language and which words like 'ought' and 'duty' should be made to denote." This is the problem as it shapes itself at the end of our study. Externalism versus internalism, yes, but on a macroscopic rather than a microscopic plane. These are not small positions that may be decisively established or taken in a brief action recorded in a page or two. They are whole theories of "our intentions in the use of moral language," past, present, and future.

To see this let us glance at the internalist case, as it must be made if the above discussion has been correct. Central in it must be the contention that externalism

[44] In "Morals without Faith," Falk distinguished four senses of "should" or "ought," one "moral" but all "internal."

leaves a gap between perceived obligation and motivation. Now, we have seen that externalism does not *logically* entail the existence of a *psychological* gap here. By itself it entails only that it is logically possible that one should in some sense perceive (though perhaps without giving a full-fledged *assent*) that one has an obligation and yet have no disposition to fulfill it. That is, the argument that externalism logically involves a gap does not come off; externalism implies only that there is a logical gap or that it is logically possible there is a psychological gap, and it is simply begging the question to begin with the opposite premise. But instead of reasoning in this way, as in effect the writers we have dealt with do, the internalist may and should elaborate his case as follows.

1. Externalism does not by itself logically imply that there may (psychologically) be a gap between perceived obligation and motivation, but it implies that such a gap is logically possible. This is true in the qualified sense just indicated.

2. An externalist may claim that there is in fact no gap—that actually there is always some possibly adequate motivation for doing what one perceives to be right—and he may offer various psychological theories in his support. He may hold that a "mere intellectual apprehension" of one's duty is itself moving, that there is in human nature a desire to do what is right, that the sentiment of benevolence is always on hand to support the call of duty, and so forth. But all such theories are false; there is no external fact which the externalist may plausibly identify with obligation which is also such that its apprehension is always, let alone by a psychological necessity, accompanied by a responsive beating of the heart. Therefore, there is in fact a psychological gap between obligation and motivation if any form of externalism is true, in the sense that then one actually might perceive an obligation and have no corresponding motivation.

3. At this point the internalist may argue either that there is in fact no psychological gap, that the existence of such a gap is intolerable from the point of view of morality, or that our moral common sense does not believe there is such a gap, concluding that externalism is false or inconsistent with common sense.

Such a line of reasoning involves first establishing (2), and this requires a full-scale psychological inquiry, which is more than internalists have yet gone in for. Suppose that it is established. All that follows is that, if externalism is true, human beings may sometimes lack all motivation to do what they apprehend as right. One who is willing to admit this need follow the argument no farther. This brings us to (3). To argue here that there is no gap is to make a factual, psychological claim, the establishing of which again calls for an empirical inquiry, one as difficult to handle as the question whether Socrates was correct in believing that we always do what we think is right. It is hard to see how it could be carried out without taking some position with respect to the definition of obligation, assenting, and so forth, and it is just this that constitutes our problem. In any case, the record of human conduct is not such as to make it obvious that human beings always do have some tendency to do what they regard as their duty. The contention that our common moral consciousness supposes that there can be no gap will be met by conflicting evidence, as Falk admits, and, in any event, one may reply that common sense may be mistaken, thus opening the whole question again. If the contention is only that it is a rule of ordinary moral discourse that a person shall not be *said* to have an obligation unless there is or may be presumed to be in him some disposition to respond favorably, then, as we have seen, the externalist may admit it, but he may also contest it or argue for a change in the rules.

It seems to me, therefore, that in the end the internalist must argue, as Falk does, not only that externalism involves a gap between obligation and motivation, but that such a gap cannot be tolerated, given morality's task of guiding human conduct autonomously. Then, however, the externalist will counter by pointing out that internalism also entails a danger to morality. Externalism, he will say, in seeking to keep the obligation to act in certain ways independent of the vagaries of individual motivation, runs the risk that motivation may not always be present, let alone adequate, but internalism, in insisting on building in motivation, runs the corresponding risk of having to trim obligation to the size of individual motives.

Here the true character of the opposition appears. Each theory has strengths and weaknesses, and deciding between them involves determining their relative total values as accounts of morality. But such a determination calls for a very broad inquiry. It cannot be based on individual preference. We must achieve "clarity and decision" about the nature and function of morality, of moral discourse, and of moral theory, and this requires not only small-scale analytical inquiries but also studies in the history of ethics and morality, in the relation of morality to society and of society to the individual, as well as in epistemology and in the psychology of human motivation.[45]

The battle, if war there be, cannot be contained; its field is the whole human world, and a grand strategy with a total commitment of forces is demanded of each of its participants. What else could a philosopher expect?

[45] Suggestions of such "macroscopic" considerations as I describe here may be found in Nowell-Smith, *Ethics*, chap. i and p. 267; C. L. Stevenson, "The Emotive Conception of Ethics and Its Cognitive Implications," *Philosophical Review*, L (1950), 294 f.; H. D. Aiken, "A Pluralistic Analysis of the Ethical 'Ought'" and "The Authority of Moral Judgments"; and in two less technical works: W. T. Stace, *The Destiny of Western Man* (New York: Reynal & Hitchcock, 1942), and Erich Fromm, *Man for Himself* (New York: Rinehart & Co., 1947). In fact, Field, *Moral Theory*, pp. 51, 52; 56 f., broaches the line of argument sketched in this last section, but in a very incomplete way. Such a macroscopic line of reasoning must also be in W. S. Sellars' mind in "Obligation and Motivation," note 36, as a support for his identification of moral obligation with a certain kind of motivation, though he appears to expound only this conclusion without the supporting argumentation.

Why Be Moral?

JOHN HOSPERS

. . . . Suppose someone whom you have known for years and who has done many things for you asks a favor of you which will take considerable time and trouble when you had planned on doing something else. You have no doubt that helping out the person is what you ought to do, but you ask yourself all the same *why* you ought to do it. Or suppose you tell a blind news vendor that it's a five-dollar bill you are handing him, and he gives you four dollars and some coins in change, whereas actually you handed him only a one-dollar bill. Almost everyone would agree that such an act is wrong. But some people who agree may still ask, "Tell me why I shouldn't do it just the same."

A. SELF-INTEREST

The most usual answer, and the most popular answer, to the question "Why should we do right acts?" is "Because it *pays* to do so—because it will, later if not immediately, turn out to be *to our interest* to do so." This motive is appealed to so constantly that we are hardly aware of it. We are told to be honest, but not because honesty is a good thing: we are told that "Honesty pays" and "Honesty is the best *policy*"—the best policy, of course, being the one that most benefits us in the long run. "Be help-

ful to people when they need help, for then they'll help you when you need it." "Drive safely—the life you save may be your own"—the implication being that if the life you save were *not* your own you need not be so anxious to drive safely. Even Biblical commands often include such an appeal: "Cast thy bread upon the waters and it shall return to thee after many days." But suppose it didn't return to you, should you still cast it upon the waters? The president of a large American corporation, who gives two hundred fifty thousand dollars every year to cancer research, was asked why he did so, and he replied, "It costs more than a yacht, but I have more fun out of it."[1] Here at any rate is an unabashedly egoistic motive. Not every such appeal to morality is as crudely egoistic. "Be helpful to others, for if you do they'll help you in turn" is egoistic in a perfectly straightforward way. "Be helpful to others, for it will give you peace of mind" is perhaps less crudely egoistic, but it is egoistic none the less. If you are to be helpful because it will give you peace of mind, the implication still is that if being helpful did *not* give you peace of mind, there would be no obligation to be so. If those who utter these precepts do not mean them egoistically, they are misleading their listeners, for the general impression that is often left upon children and others who hear them is that one should do good deeds simply in order to get something out of it for himself,

From *Human Conduct* by John Hospers, 1961, by Harcourt, Brace, & World, Inc. and reprinted with their permission.

[1] *Life,* Vol. 43, No. 8 (August 19, 1957), p. 108.

whether crude rewards like money and services, or intangible rewards like peace of mind. Morality, in short, is presented as an instrument of "enlightened self-interest."

Of course it is possible that justice *does* pay; it may be that when you do acts that are right, you yourself will always be the gainer thereby, even though at the time the act is one of heroic self-sacrifice. At least this possibility is worth examining. When you do something good, are you always rewarded for it sooner or later? Is right action always to the advantage of the doer?

Offhand, it would certainly seem obvious that the answer is "No." We hear that the good die young and that the big-time crooks are the ones who get away with it. Yet a great many people, moral philosophers and others, have answered our question with a "Yes." They have held that in the long run, when all the factors are considered, virtue *does* pay, crime never pays, and right action always brings benefit back to the door of the doer. Plato was the first to have held this view, and he devoted his longest dialogue, the *Republic,* primarily to an attempt to prove it. Let us see briefly how he defended his position.

First of all, according to Plato, it pays to live a just life because only in that way can you have the respect of your neighbors and friends—in fact, only in that way can you *have* any friends. If you are not a trustworthy sort of person who pays his debts and keeps his promises, other people will not trust you and will cease to have dealings with you. If you are trustworthy, you will earn the respect and esteem of those around you. Therefore, if you expect others to do decently by you, you would be wise to behave decently toward them. Only if you give will you also receive. Here, surely, is a perfectly sensible reason for being moral, a reason that will appeal strongly to most people. In fact, it is probably the main reason in practice why people *are* moral.

Nevertheless, Plato does not set much

store by this argument for morality. After all, public opinion and public esteem are unreliable and quixotic. Your neighbors may respect you for things they shouldn't respect you for, such as raking in a million dollars in an illegal gambling operation; or they may feel contemptuous of you for *not* making lots of money, by whatever means. Or they may love you for virtues that they *mistakenly* think you possess; or they may hate you for misdeeds which you *have* never done. Anyway, if you are popular with them today, you may be unpopular tomorrow, though you yourself have not changed. Plato would say that it is on your own true merits that your happiness should be based, not on the ever-shifting and often mistaken attributions of merit given you by other people.[2]

Plato believes that a man is happy when he is moral ("just" is the word usually given in translations), regardless of whether or not his friends and countrymen hold him in high esteem; a truly good man will not be less happy if he is reviled for injustices he did not commit. Plato indeed makes his task extremely difficult by refusing to admit the slightest reward in the outside world as grounds for the happiness of the just man. He asks us to imagine, on the one hand, a just man, who is universally thought to be unjust and who is hated and ostracized by all his former friends for these imagined injustices, and to imagine, on the other hand, a supremely unjust man, a paragon of evil, who is so clever in his injustice that he is universally thought to be the most just of men and is praised, fawned upon, and followed with adulation wherever he goes for his imagined goodness. If the rewards of justice were to be found in the esteem of one's fellow men, then the just man who is wrongly thought to be unjust would be extremely unhappy, and the unjust man who is wrongly thought to be just would be the happiest of men. No, Plato concludes

[2] Plato, *Republic,* Bk. 1.

that the happiness enjoyed by the just man is not the result of something as unreliable and subject to error as the opinions of his fellow men. The happiness that the just man possesses is the result of something inside him, not something as external to him as fame, reputation, even respect. His happiness does not depend on whether men like him or dislike him, revere him or persecute him; it does not depend on whether he is rich or poor, king or slave, even on whether he is healthy or ill. It depends only on his inner state, on the state of his own soul.[3]

What is this inner state? Plato divided the human psyche (or soul) into three parts: the *rational* element was the highest, for reason was to be in control of the other parts or elements; second was the *spirited* element, which has been variously interpreted but is probably best conceived as a kind of drive, or will power, an executive branch which puts into action the decisions arrived at by reason; and third, the appetitive element (the bodily appetites), which has to be held in check, though not suppressed entirely, by reason. There is far more to be said about the division of the psyche than this brief description, but the division is a familiar one and it is not necessary to fill in the details here.

A human being such as Plato describes —one with a healthy psyche, that is, one in which each of the three elements plays its proper role in the total personality—is, says Plato, a happy man. Plato has established the conditions of psychological health just as a physician might set up conditions for physical health. The man who does not possess within himself the conditions of psychic happiness is an unhappy human being no matter how much society may revere him; and a man who does possess within himself the psychical state which Plato describes is happy no

[3] *Ibid.*, Bk. 2.

matter what society may think of him or do to him.

It is obviously true that Plato's psychology is somewhat out of date. The psyche is not divided into three parts. Furthermore, countless questions could be raised about the application of Plato's psychology to particular situations. But let us ignore these objections and comment briefly on Plato's position thus far.

a. There is a certain undeniable truth in the general position. Some people have what may be called a "happy temperament"; they are relatively happy no matter what happens to them, and they can overcome even the worst of the trials and tribulations that life serves them and come out comparatively unscathed; whereas other people, not blessed with such a temperament, are laid low by even the tiniest vicissitudes of life—they are "knocked out," as far as happiness is concerned, by things which would not bother a person of happy temperament in the slightest.

b. But to say that everyone's happiness is quite independent of external factors is a gross overstatement, at least as far as most people are concerned most of the time. A person may be happy when family and friends are present, unhappy when they are dead or absent. A person may be happy when he has no financial worries and is in good health, and he can certainly be unhappy when he doesn't know where his next meal is coming from or when he is in constant pain and discomfort. Can a person be really happy while he is being tortured on the rack, no matter how well-adjusted his disposition may be and no matter how happy he may be by temperamental endowment?

c. In any event, our main question so far has not been answered. Even if we grant for the moment that happiness depends on the state of one's soul and not at all upon the outside world, we must still ask, "What has all this to do with morality?"

What we have to prove is that the moral man is also the happy man. Even if Plato's psychology is correct, and even if his claim about happiness being entirely a matter of the inner man is true, he still has to show us that the moral man is the one who is happy and the immoral man unhappy.

To this task, then, Plato proceeds. He does not consider the common garden variety of unjust men—the petty thieves, the men who are cruel to their wives, the cheap swindlers, or the holy hypocrites. He discusses rather, in detail, what he takes to be the epitome of the unjust man: the cruel dictator, the tyrant. The man who is seized with the desire for immense power thinks that once he has attained power over the lives and destinies of other human beings he will be the happiest of men. Actually, as it turns out, Plato says that he is the most miserable of men. In the first place, his desires are such that they can never be satisfied. When he gets power, he wants more; and when he has more, he wants still more; lust for power is an appetite that feeds and grows upon itself and can never be entirely satisfied short of omnipotence. The same applies to lust for sensual gratification, greed for gold, and desire for fame, once these desires are no longer held in check by reason. To try to gratify these desires, once a man has given in to them, is, according to Plato, like trying to pour water into a leaky vessel: the more you pour into it, the larger the leak becomes because of the weight of the water; and the larger the leak becomes, the more water you have to pour in to try to compensate for the leak, and so on indefinitely. Obviously, a man whose life is devoted to the satisfaction of desires which are by their very nature impossible to satisfy completely cannot be a happy man. Indeed, Plato says that he is of all men the most miserable. He thinks that power will satisfy his desires, whereas it only increases his appetite for more of the same.

"Besides," Plato would continue, "who is fit to judge which way of life is the happiest? Only the person who has experienced all the sources of happiness is fit to judge; the tyrant, slave as he is to the basest desires of his nature, is in no position to judge what the best sources of happiness are. The tyrant knows nothing of the sources of happiness open to the man of ideas or to the man who lives a moral life without encroaching upon the rights of his fellows. What appears to the tyrant at the time to offer him the zenith of happiness—the immoral life—is actually what brings him to the nadir of misery. It is the road that does not appear to promise much to begin with that in fact brings most fulfillment, but the immoral man will never know the joys of that journey because he has never even caught a glimpse of the road."

What shall we say of this argument? Though we might cavil at a few points in Plato's description of the life of the tyrant (not all tyrants are alike), let us, for brevity's sake, grant everything that Plato says about the life of the tyrant and the state of his happiness. But what does the argument show? Only that *one* type of immoral man usually winds up miserable instead of happy as he planned. It does not show that all immoral men do so. Even less does it show that all moral men are happy.

Let us notice carefully that there are two separate propositions here: all moral men are happy, a statement which seems to be plainly false; and immoral men are unhappy, a statement which has a certain degree of plausibility.

a. It would be easy to refute Plato's first proposition. We could give many examples showing that moral men—that is, men who generally perform right acts, not necessarily those rare souls who adopt the moral point of view—are not always happy. Of course we might argue about which acts are the right ones, those in accord with the conventional mores of society or perhaps those contributing the most to the happiness of humanity. But in which ever of these senses we take "right," we reach one conclusion which we can best put in this way: "It may be that morality is a *necessary* condition for happiness—that is, happiness is not possible without it—(this we have yet to see) but at any rate, morality cannot possibly be a *sufficient* condition for happiness—that is, morality alone is not enough to ensure happiness. Once we have made the distinction, the point seems fairly obvious. No matter how moral the man may be, he is not happy when he is being tortured on the rack, or when he is suffering from cancer of the bone, or when his family is being fed to the lions, or, at the very least, he is not *as* happy while these things are going on as he would be if he were *not* undergoing these agonies. Our happiness *is* to some extent at the mercy of forces outside us, and for most of us to a very large extent. This observation alone is sufficient to show that, no matter how moral we are, morality *alone* does not guarantee happiness. The most moral people are not necessarily the happiest people. At best, there are certain stumbling-blocks to happiness which are not present in their nature; but the removal of an unfavorable condition does not guarantee the presence of a positively favorable condition, any more than the removal of rocks from a field guarantees that the soil will be fertile once it is opened to the plow. Plato does not even begin to show us that the moral man is always happy—that is, that morality is sufficient for happiness.

b. Plato's second proposition is more plausible, or at any rate more arguable. Is morality a *necessary* condition for happiness? Even if morality alone is not enough to guarantee happiness, perhaps it is a negative condition—that is, perhaps happiness is never attainable without it.

As far as Plato's example of the power-hungry tyrant is concerned, modern psychiatry would bear out a great deal of Plato's contention. The criminal, the murderer, the professional thief, the tyrannical dictator without ideals who merely satisfies his lust for power—all these, psychiatrists will concur, are profoundly unhappy men following in their unconscious minds intricate networks of inner conflicts, chiefly pseudo-aggressive defenses against masochistically tinged impulses of rebellion in early childhood. If one wanted to find happy people, he would not be likely to find them among members of the Mafia. Such men can never know real peace of mind; they can only struggle, plot, scheme, dare, kill, run constant risks; they are never secure of life and limb, never sure that someone won't do them in as they have done in others, always strangers to the relaxation that most people know, always harboring within themselves large reserves of aggressions, undigested conflicts, fear, and guilt. One has only to read case histories of these men in psychiatry books to be convinced anew of Plato's point, with far more evidence than Plato had at his disposal. Perhaps, we will be inclined to think, their chickens always *do* come home to roost sooner or later. Even if the moral man is not always happy, perhaps the immoral man is always unhappy.

Of course these psychiatric findings do not build as strong an argument as one might desire for the dependence of happiness on morality. The ax falls upon the innocent as much as upon the guilty. Countless moral people have their lives made miserable by unconscious fears, fantasies, or guilt feelings pertaining to wholly imaginary acts performed by them years ago or in early childhood, acts for which they are punishing themselves day after day and year after year throughout their adult lives. Often the highly moral but extremely neurotic person has a far worse time of it, as far as happiness goes, than the far less moral person who is thick-skinned and has more successful inner defenses.

This observation only shows that psychiatry is indifferent to moral categories; it does not show that the immoral person is ever happy. Rather, it only shows us once again what we have already observed, that the moral person is not always happy. Once again, morality may be a necessary condition for happiness, but it is not a sufficient condition.

However, even this second proposition —that morality is necessary for happiness— is, taken as a universal generalization, quite surely false. Let us take a few examples to illustrate the point.

(1) Popular novels often tell of people who do good deeds for which, at the moment, they do not seem to be rewarded. A man helps many down-and-outers with money, advice, and valuable time. The recipients seem to be unappreciative. Then, years later when the giver least expects it and most needs it, one of the many persons he has helped turns up suddenly and helps him. (Remember, for example, Dickens' *Great Expectations.*) Such stories are very warm and very consoling. But what about those thousands of cases in which the giver does *not* run into one of the recipients of his beneficence, either at a critical juncture or at any other time? Perhaps the recipient dies too soon, or never hears of his benefactor's trouble, or his train is delayed until it is too late. These situations go largely unrecorded, for they do not appeal to our sense of the romantic and our deep-seated wish that things turn out in accordance with our desires.

(2) There are two brothers, one hardworking and the other indolent. The older brother cannot have an education because he earns money for his younger brother to use to go to school. The younger brother, however, never makes use of his education; he is always getting into scrapes, and the older brother is always getting him out of jail and paying his bills. The younger brother counts on the older one's helping him out and so gets into trouble without worry: "George always helps me in a pinch." A large portion of the older brother's income goes to the support of the younger brother, whom the state will not support as long as there is a member of his family capable of doing so. The older brother's generosity means a lifelong sacrifice from which he gains nothing, not even personal satisfaction. He could have used the money himself to much better advantage, yet he feels that while he is able to he should take care of his own flesh and blood, even if his benevolence means that he himself will have no savings to draw on in his old age. The older brother has been unlucky in love and lives a comparatively unhappy life in spite of his benevolence, while the younger, much more attractive to the opposite sex, has a much better time out of life in spite of his laziness, shiftlessness, and constant dependence on the good will of his older brother. It would certainly seem that the one is more moral and the other is happier.

(3) There is a young bank clerk who decides, quite correctly, that he can embezzle $50,000 without his identity ever being known. He fears that he will be underpaid all his life if he doesn't embezzle, that life is slipping by without his ever enjoying the good things of this world; his fiancée will not marry him unless he can support her in the style to which she is accustomed; he wants to settle down with her in a suburban house, surround himself with books, stereo set, and various *objects d'art*, and spend a pleasant life, combining culture with sociability; he never wants to commit a similar act again. He does just what he wanted to do: he buys a house, invests the remainder of the money wisely so as to enjoy a continued income from it, marries the girl, and lives happily ever after; he doesn't worry about detection because he has arranged things so that no blame could fall on him; anyway he doesn't have a worrisome disposition and is not one to dwell on past misdeeds; he is blessed with a happy temperament, once his daily com-

forts are taken care of. The degree of happiness he now possesses would not have been possible had he not committed the immoral act. Apparently, crime sometimes does pay; in fact, sometimes it pays very handsomely indeed; the cinema to the contrary notwithstanding, only a small portion of the crimes committed are ever detected. Nor do those who commit crimes always suffer pangs of conscience or fears of detection; they often suffer far less than neurotics and psychotics who fill our mental hospitals and who have never committed any crimes at all but are innocent victims of situations thrust upon them in the far distant past.

(4) There is a person of great sensitivity and strong humanitarian feelings who is extremely conscientious in fulfilling what he believes to be his duties to his fellow men. Realizing poignantly the state of mankind and the hopelessness of one person's trying to change it, his life is not nearly as happy as that of the comparatively thick-skinned man who is less intelligent and less sensitive to the sufferings of other human beings. The latter person may stumble through life seeing only a small part of it, but he obviously cannot worry about evils that he cannot see or understand, and his level of happiness is considerably above that of the first man.

(5) In a courtroom there is a constitutional psychopath who is extremely clever at inventing stories about his imaginary troubles. He can weep and lie brazenly—with such emotion that the jury is moved to tears and exonerates him from the perfectly true charges against him. There is also a falsely charged man who is genuinely innocent but is not so clever at putting on an act. His story, every word of it true, fails to impress the jury, and he is convicted, even though he is innocent. That justice always triumphs is an aphorism as absurd as it is often quoted. But it is a law of human nature that for every aphorism there is an equal and opposite

aphorism—we simply use whichever one suits the occasion. The opposite one in this case is "There ain't no justice"—which, unfortunately, the world being what it is, seems to be true as often as the first one.

(6) Perhaps the most dramatic illustration of all is war. Millions of people are killed in wars, and most of those killed certainly do not deserve to be killed. They are innocent victims of the rapacity of individuals highly placed in the political system of the nation or victims of the disease of nationalism itself, which makes it fatally easy for two nations, neither of which wants war, to blunder into it. Sometimes the guilty parties get their just deserts and sometimes they don't; but nothing seems to be more certain than that the *victims* of war are, for the most part, innocent victims and that they pay with their lives for misdeeds which are not their own.

There is hardly need of further examples. Nothing seems plainer to one who reflects upon the state of the world and the people in it than that there is no due proportion between human merit and human happiness. The main thing that keeps us, Americans especially, from acknowledging this injustice is a sentimental Pollyannaism which makes us believe that "in the long run everything always comes out all right," although experience daily contradicts this smug assumption. We have been exposed to so many movies and television stories that we have turned things upside down: we judge life by whether it is like the fiction instead of judging the fiction by whether it is like life.

It is difficult, in the light of all these examples, to avoid agreeing with Henry Fielding's remark:

There are a set of religious, or rather moral writers, who teach that virtue is the certain road to happiness, and vice to misery, in this world. A very wholesome and comfortable doctrine, and to which we have but one objection, namely, that it is not true.[4]

One more consideration, however, should be advanced before we leave self-interest as a reason for moral behavior. We have seen that there are good self-interested reasons for moral *action*—one pays one's debts and keeps one's promises in order to gain the respect of others or a reputation in one's community, although these reasons do not operate without exception. But we might make an argument also for adopting an *attitude* other than that of exclusive concern with oneself. There are reasons of self-interest for developing, if one can, attitudes which will lead one to care about the welfare of other human beings and not merely oneself.

Suppose that the range of your interests includes only yourself. You don't care whether anyone else succeeds or fails, lives or dies. You gain happiness from your own triumphs, unhappiness from your own failures, but you regard everyone else with complete indifference except insofar as other people can be used to promote your own selfish ends. The range of your sources of happiness will, then, be very small. But if you can become the kind of person who is happy when others (at least *some* others) are happy, you will have widened greatly your own possibilities of happiness. It is true that you will also have widened your possibilities of sorrow by being hurt when hurts come to others. If, however, you are not so sensitive as to be paralyzed into inaction by these hurts but do your part to remedy them, you will be decreasing the possibility of a repetition of their occurrence. Moreover, you will be increasing the possibility that others will be of help to you when misfortunes come to you. If you genuinely care about other people, they in turn will be more likely to care genuinely about you. Your concern

[4] Henry Fielding, *Tom Jones* (New York: Modern Library), p. 672.

creates mutual good feeling which is far more of a contribution to happiness than one might think until he has personally experienced such feeling.

The ability to share the joys of other human beings will be likely, then, to heighten the level of happiness possible in one's own life. If only one person can win the European trip and one cares only about himself, then all the other competitors for this prize will be disappointed and frustrated. But if the losers are able sincerely to congratulate the winner and even to share in their imagination the enjoyment of the holiday, their own satisfactions will be greatly increased—perhaps not as much as if they had gone themselves but yet far more than if they had been able to experience only envy and resentment. If you lose the trip, you will at any rate have some satisfaction in the knowledge that someone will enjoy it; and if you win it, you will be able to enjoy it more in the knowledge that others are not hating you for having the opportunity that is denied to them. It is, then, to *your own interest* to develop within yourself attitudes that make it possible for you to share the joys of others. Your life will be richer, less mean and grasping, and no longer characterized by the corrosive feelings of hatred and envy. The success of one person will no longer be built upon the resentment and hostility of others. We have, then, another self-interested reason for "being moral": one which asks of us that we not merely *behave* morally with regard to other human beings but that we develop *attitudes* toward them from which the actions will flow without effort and as a matter of course.

B. DIVINE COMMAND

Let us turn, then, to a second answer to the question, "Why should we be moral?"

—namely, "Because God will reward me if I am and punish me if I'm not."

1. "Let's grant," one may say, "that in *this* world the just are often unhappy and that the unjust are happy. But this truth doesn't apply to the next world, where all these scores will be set straight. Indeed, the very fact that there are such gross inequities in this world is one of the reasons why many people have argued that there must be a next world in which the inequities are overcome."

Of course, the fact that this world is unjust doesn't prove that there is another world that is just, any more than the fact that people are hungry proves that there will always be food. As an argument for an afterlife, this one is as much of a *non sequitur* as any argument could be. But it would take us too far afield here to consider the various arguments for immortality. However we may have arrived at the conclusion that there is another life in which all the discrepancies between virtue and happiness will be set right, doesn't our conclusion solve our problem? If our conclusion is true, we need only smile at Plato's hopeless attempt to prove the impossible thesis about justice in this world; and when we hear more and more examples of men being good but unhappy or bad but happy we need only say, "But you see, it *doesn't* always pay to be moral, when you consider only *this* life; but when you consider the life to come, you will realize that it *does* pay to be moral. It is only in the life to come that the prophecies will come true, that the bread that you cast on the waters will come back to you, and with compound interest."

The first thing to observe about this second answer is that it will appeal only to those who already accept the doctrine of an afterlife in which a just God distributes rewards and punishments according to merit. Those who deny the doctrine or aren't sure will not be moved by it as a reason for morality. Since the argument depends on the truth of this doctrine, one had best be quite sure that it is true and that all competing claimants to the true doctrine are false. If one staked his entire moral life upon the truth of a doctrine announcing eternal rewards, and this doctrine turned out to be false (or some competing doctrine true instead), this result would surely seem to be something of a dirty trick.

Moreover, if the only reason you have for being moral is that God will punish you if you aren't or reward you if you are, then the moment you doubt or no longer believe there is a God who will do these things, your only reason for being moral will vanish. Many people, it seems, are in precisely this situation.

Even for those who are already convinced of the afterlife promised by their religion, there is another point they must squarely face: When a man says, "I should be moral because if I'm not, I'll be punished," he is appealing as much to selfish motives, to self-interest, as our first answer did. It is just self-interest pushed into the next world instead of being confined to this one. The person who acts from this motive is just playing the game for higher stakes. He is declaring his willingness to postpone his reward a bit longer in order to collect at a higher rate of interest in the next world—which is as selfish as it could be. It is like working longer hours in order to collect time and a half at the end of the day. Nor is the moral life conceived as something desirable in itself; it's not that the man enjoys or takes pride in the work, it's only that he wants the money. Indeed, his motive for being moral is not much different from his motive in following the commands of a dictator before whom he cringes and trembles. One may or may not approve or like what the dictator commands, but one follows the commands because if one doesn't, he will be beaten or tortured. Once remove the threatened punishments and the promised rewards, and the person will no longer do as he was commanded.

There are many sincere and conscientious people who have believed that there was no good reason for being moral apart from divine punishments and rewards and that once these were removed, the moral fabric of humanity would crumble into dust. Of course, whether the moral fabric of humanity *would* crumble into dust if these threats and promises were removed, is an empirical question, which could be argued pro and con indefinitely. It is possible that most people do have to be prodded constantly with spears to make them go forward. There are, however, reasons for believing (as we shall see in the next chapter) that in general people's morality would not crumble if religious sanctions were removed, so long as the people had not become so accustomed to these religious sanctions that they could no longer operate without them; people who have not been brought up to depend upon religious sanctions seem to be none the less moral. Whatever the answer to the empirical question may be, hope of reward or dread of punishment may offer an *incentive* to those who are too weak or selfish to behave morally without them, but it cannot offer a good *reason* (justification) for being moral. If this statement begs the question of what we mean by a good reason, we can say that it offers a good reason only if completely selfish reasons are good reasons; it is simply an appeal to self-interest. "Be good or I'll punish you" —nothing could be a clearer appeal to naked and unbridled power than this. In fact the moral goodness of anyone who said it might be questioned simply because of the appeal to power not supported by reasons.

The moral irrelevance of the appeal to power can be brought out best, perhaps, in this way. If there is a God who is the source of moral commands, then *either* God had a reason for commanding what He did *or* He did not.

a. One alternative is to believe that God had *no* reason for commanding what He did but the commands are simply the result of an arbitrary whim or fiat. If so, then what possible evidence do we have for believing that they are good or that we should obey them? We are told to obey them because we'll be punished if we don't. But that is exactly the same kind of reason—a prudential reason—for obeying the commands of a cruel dictator. We obey him in fear and trembling because we fear the consequences of not doing so, not because we revere him or his commandments. We may obey him and yet privately loathe both the dictator and his commands. Surely religious believers do not want their Deity to be obeyed only because He is more powerful than they are. They want to obey Him, not just because He commanded this or that, but because those commands are good. If the only defense that can be given for a command is simply "Do this because I say so," this is not much of a defense—in fact it is the kind of thing that is usually said when no defense can be given; unable to give any good reasons for his commands, the tyrant appeals to naked power.

Thus, if God has no reason for giving the commands He does, there does not seem to be any good reason why we should obey them other than our fear of His power. John Stuart Mill made this point dramatically: he said, in effect, "Why should I obey the commands of a being, however powerful, who gives no reasons for his commands other than the fact that he utters them? Might it not be better and more courageous of me to choose to ignore the commands and be willing to risk the punishment? After all, I should obey only those commands which are good, and what evidence have I that a being who would issue commands, without giving reasons but threatening punishment all the same for not obeying them, *is* good?"

When I am told that I must believe this, and at the same time call this being by the names which express and affirm the highest human morality, I say in plain terms that I will not.

Whatever power such a being may have over me, there is one thing which he shall not do: he shall not compel me to worship him. I will call no being good, who is not what I mean when I apply that epithet to my fellow creatures; and if such a being can sentence me to hell for not so calling him, to hell I will go.[5]

b. The other alternative is to believe that God has a *reason* for commanding what He does. This belief will certainly strike us as the more palatable alternative. But if God has a reason for commanding A rather than B, then why could we not do A rather than B directly on account of that reason rather than because God has commanded it? At any rate, if God has commanded A for a reason, then it is for that reason, surely, that we too should do A; God's commanding it only provides an additional incentive, *if* we believe God to be good. (Of course, we *might* not have thought of A if God hadn't commanded it; if so, our lack of thought would be a good reason for God's issuing the command. But our question would still remain: "Was there or was there not a reason for his commanding A rather than B in the first place?") If we don't believe that A is good because God commands it (this belief was our first alternative), then our second alternative is to believe that God commands A because it is good. If that belief is true, as every student of Plato's *Euthyphro* well remembers, A's goodness is logically independent of God's commanding it, and it would have been good even if there had been no God at all to command it. God's commanding A is a result of A's being good, not the cause of its being good. In that event, religion is not *necessarily* tied to ethics, for there is some *criterion* for a thing's being good, a criterion not consisting simply in the fact that God commands it but a criterion which God Himself could use (and presumably

so could we) in judging whether or not something is good.

2. So much, then, for the appeal to divine punishments and rewards. "But," one may say, "self-interest is not the only reason why people follow a religious ethic, though it may be the reason most frequently encountered. One may do good deeds, not because he fears divine punishments or anticipates rewards in a future life, but simply because he loves and adores the God whom he worships. One may act from love and devotion, not merely from fear of punishment or hope of reward."

Of course this observation is true. It is difficult to discover in individual examples how much subconscious fear there may be behind the consciously experienced love—this mixture of emotion also occurs in one's relation to his parents—but let us grant, indeed insist, that very often deeds are done from motives of love, affection, esteem, and adoration. Nevertheless, let us observe here one thing that is often forgotten: those who behave morally out of love for the God they believe in ought surely to do so *only* if the God they believe in is morally *worthy* of their love and worship. Ought one to obey the commands of the ancient god Moloch, who demanded that children be thrown into the fire as a sacrifice to appease his wrath? One could question too whether one should obey the commands of the ancient Hebrew god Yahweh, who apparently condoned a great deal of plunder and slaughter against other tribes that were only trying to stay alive and can hardly be said to deserve their fate; yet Yahweh even chided the Israelites from time to time for being too merciful and not getting on with the job fast enough. After all, one shouldn't love just anybody, and one shouldn't obey just anybody's commands. A woman may love her husband, but that doesn't mean she should obey him when he tells her to sell her body on the streets to augment the family income. Love can be misplaced, and so

[5] John Stuart Mill, *An Examination of Sir William Hamilton's Philosophy* (Boston: Spencer, 1865), p. 131.

can esteem and devotion. It is not good to be devoted to just anything; we must first make sure that what we love is worth loving, else endless harm can come of the love.

If, on the one hand, we love God, or whomever we believe to be God, blindly and without reason, then we have no guarantee that the object of our adoration deserves to be adored. But if, on the other hand, we love God because we believe that God has certain highly desirable and profoundly good moral qualities, then it is not just because we love Him that we do good things but because He has the qualities which entitle Him to our love. Already the answer to the question "Why should we be moral?" has changed. The answer is no longer, "Because I love and adore God," but, "Because God is good, and being Himself good, he desires to promote good in the world, and therefore commands us to do those things which He sees to be good." This answer points to a good that is independent even of God, in the sense that it would exist even if there were no God or if there were no *good* God (if God were evil, then it would be good to *dis*obey His commands, even if punishment were threatened for disobeying).

Even this answer will work only for those who already believe (1) there is a God and (2) He is good. If these two premises are granted, it will be natural to believe that God will try to maximize the good in the world by commanding us to perform it; but if it is good, shouldn't we perform it anyway, God or no God?

3. Still another version of the religious answer has been advanced: "We should be moral," some people say, "not because we expect rewards for being so nor because we love God and do it out of love, but simply because He is the Author of our being—He created us, and this entitles Him to our unquestioning obedience."

God made us and all the world. Because of that He has an absolute claim on our obedi-ence. We do not exist in our own right, but only as His creatures, who ought therefore to do and be what He desires.[6]

Are we entitled to draw this con-clusion? Let us assume that there is some-one (not merely natural agents) who brought us into being, that this being is God, and that this same being laid down certain moral commands for us to follow—unless one already believed all these things, he would not use this argument. One can still ask *why* we ought to obey these commands. "God created us, there-fore we should do as He commands" is an incomplete argument: it requires the ad-ditional premise that creatures ought to obey their creator. Suppose that creatures were created by a malevolent creator who brought them into being only to make them suffer (a view that has sometimes been held), would the upholder of this argu-ment still say that he should obey the commands of such a creator? It would seem to depend on what kind of creator it was. The simple fact of the power to create, plus the use of that power, would hardly entitle any being to our unquestioning assent to his commands. Only if the creator were *good* as well as powerful would we be likely to say that we should do as he commands; we should obey him, not sim-ply because of the bare fact that he created us, but because his commands are good ones. If we make this statement, our argu-ment reduces to the one which we have just considered.

C. THE COMMON INTEREST

Let us turn to another answer to the question "Why should we be moral?" The answer is, "We should be moral, not be-cause there's something in it for us, or because God will reward us for it, or even

6 R. C. Mortimer, *Christian Ethics*, p. 7.

because we believe God to be good and therefore want to obey the good directives He has set down for our guidance, but because obeying certain moral rules will help to achieve a better society—a society which we would prefer to one in which such rules were not observed."

Suppose that you are playing a game and that when you play it you agree upon certain rules. You cannot change the rules in a pinch just because the game is going against you. You play the game to win, but to win you must abide by the rules. To the extent that you cheat, you are not playing the game at all. If you are interested enough to play, you probably have an interest in continuing the game. Yet the game can be continued only if you play by the rules.

None of us is forced to play baseball or billiards, but the game of life is one which we all have to play in one way or another. Nor can we play it alone, for we are surrounded by other people who also must play the game. What then is the best means of playing it—best for all of us? As long as we are all together on this planet, isn't it better for all of us to find some arrangement whereby we can live together in such a way that we can each pursue as many of our own interests as possible yet not prevent others from pursuing theirs? To live in such a way we all have to stick to certain rules. Certain kinds of rules—those requiring us to consider the safety and welfare of others and those prohibiting us from aggressions against them—will operate to our *mutual* advantage; that is why we should obey them.

Consider two groups of people, of any size you please. In the first group the people live by certain rules—they refrain from killing, stealing, and committing other acts of aggression against one another. In the second group the people do not wish to be tied down by any rules—they commit acts of aggression against one another with no punishment other than retaliations from the injured party or his friends if they

happen to catch the aggressor. In the first group, then, certain limitations are placed upon the behavior of each member; in the second group there are no such limitations. But the result of this lack of limitation is that people in the second group are much worse off than they would otherwise have been: their livelihoods and their very lives are in constant danger; at any moment they may be victimized by other people without recourse to law. It is usually agreed that the members of the first group are much better off than the members of the second. (The members of the second are in fact in the "state of nature" described by Hobbes, which we shall discuss in another connection in Chapter 8.) To live in the first group and behave according to its rules, then, will be to the interest of every member of the group.

At least, to behave according to the rules will be to the interest of every member of the group on *most* occasions: for example, it is to my interest to be honest; for by being honest I gain the respect of others and they will trust me in personal relations and in business enterprises. It is to my interest to refrain from aggression against others; for if I damage others, I shall probably be caught and imprisoned, and besides I shall have few, if any, real friends. Nevertheless, it may not be to my personal interest to live by the rules on *all* occasions: suppose, for example, that law-enforcement is lax or that I can bribe the appropriate officials and I can thus get by with taking from you what doesn't belong to me and be quite sure of not being prosecuted for my actions. Then why shouldn't I bribe and steal? I shouldn't commit these crimes, not because they don't work toward my individual advantage (for, according to our hypothesis, in this case they would), but because they work against the interests of the group as a whole—or, in other words, "the general interest." Once I realize that a group in which members obey certain rules is better than one in which they do not, I have a reason for behaving in accordance with these rules even in situations where doing so does not work toward my personal or individual interest.

Moralities are systems of principles whose acceptance by everyone as overruling the dictates of self-interest is in the interest of everyone alike, though following the rules of a morality is not of course identical with following self-interest. If it were, there could be no conflict between a morality and self-interest and no point in having rules overriding self-interest. . . . The answer to the question "Why be moral?" is therefore as follows. We should be moral because being moral is following rules designed to overrule self-interest whenever it is in the interest of everyone alike that everyone should set aside his interest.[7]

To many people this answer to the question "Why be moral?" will seem quite sufficient, but not to everyone; some will still demand a reason why they should behave morally (or according to rules which promote the interests of the group) in those situations, or on those occasions, when their own private interest conflicts with the interests of the group.

x: Why should I help someone else when it's not to my own interest to do so?

y: Because it is to our mutual interest for each person to help others.

x: I know that, but what do I care about that, as long as it's not to my interest to help?

y: But don't you want to live according to the rules which society has devised for the mutual interests of its members?

x: Not when they go against my own interest.

y: Other people have lived by the rules and sacrificed for you, even when it wasn't to their interest to do so.

x: I know that.

y: If they hadn't done so, you probably wouldn't be here to tell the tale.

[7] From Kurt Baier, *The Moral Point of View*, Ithaca, N. Y.: Cornell Univ. Press, 1958, p. 314.

x: I know that too.

y: Then isn't it reasonable that since they went against their own interest to serve yours, that you this time should go against your own interest to serve theirs?

x: Maybe it's reasonable, but I don't see why I should do it. So I'm not reasonable. Now what happens?

y: But if they sacrificed for you when you needed help, and now you turn around and desert them when *they* need it, what you are doing is parasitic. Your badness to them is made possible only by their prior goodness toward you.

x: O.K., so I'm a parasite. Now damn me. I'm still not going to do what's against my interest.

y: I'm not saying you will. I'm saying you should.

x: But you still haven't given me an acceptable reason *why* I should.

D. "BECAUSE IT'S RIGHT"

Is there any further answer that we can give in this maddening situation? At this point some will say, "Look, there's no further reason we can give this individual why he or anyone else *should* behave morally. All we can do is try to enlighten him on the *psychological* question of why people *do* act morally. After we have shown him some psychological facts, perhaps they will help him to act morally. That's all we can do."

1. Let us try this approach first. Let us ask, "What actually moves people to perform moral actions?" The answer is fairly simple. People do right acts from a vast variety of motives—sometimes from self-interest, such as hope of reward or having someone return the favor or of being socially accepted by doing the deed, but sometimes from the genuine, unselfish desire to help someone without expecting to be helped or rewarded in return, from the desire to do a good deed just because it

will increase the good in the world and for no other reason. Human motives are extremely various, and there is probably no point in trying to pin them all down or classify them. If they are all put under one general heading, as the psychological egoists do (pages 141-55), and all of them are labeled "selfish," the word "selfish" would have to be stretched so as to be beyond all recognition; it would lose all its distinctive meaning and would no longer suffice to distinguish any one motive from any other, which was the whole purpose of having such a word in the first place. Therefore, it would be useless to try to limit the variety of motives at work in the human psyche by saying, for example, that people never act from sense of duty. It seems to be perfectly clear, once we are no longer deluded by words that have been distorted from their original meaning, that people often *do* act from sense of duty, even against their own private interests. Not all people act so all of the time, nor do most of the people most of the time, but some people do some of the time. People sometimes perform an act because they are fully and honestly convinced that it is the right thing to do, though they may not at all be convinced that the act will bring the most enjoyment or happiness or even peace to them personally. This observation is all we need to say on the psychological question. People do sometimes act from motives of duty; and if it is asked, "Why do people do right acts?" the answer is "Sometimes at any rate, they do them because they are convinced that what they are doing is the right thing to do, and for no other reason."

"But," our skeptic will continue, "the fact that something is right can never be a *motive* for action. Even the *knowledge* that something is right cannot, in and of itself, cause people to behave in a certain manner. There must also be a *desire* to act in the way required. Only desire can *move* people to action, even though the intellect can convince us that a given action is

right. The intellect by itself cannot move us in one way or another. As Spinoza said, pure knowledge alone cannot make us act; the only thing that can keep us from acting on one desire is another desire stronger than the first."

We might say many things about this oversimplified picture of human nature according to which people act only from desire. But criticism is not necessary here, for one can accept the picture and still show the irrelevance of its conclusion. "Let's grant, then," we may say, "that the only force that can topple over a desire is another desire stronger than the first—in fact this is definitional, for if the second topples over the first, that is tantamount to saying that the second is stronger. But what does that matter? *One* of the desires we have—at least some of us—is the desire to do the right thing no matter what the cost to ourselves; and this desire is often very strong, particularly in times of crisis when our fellow men are in need of us." This conclusion is all we need. Human beings always act from their strongest desires—very well; but not all their desires are self-centered desires, and one desire that sometimes is dominant is the desire to do the right thing regardless of what it may cost us.

2. So much, then, for the psychological question, "Why, that is from what motives, do people do right acts?" But we are still left with the ethical question, not "Why, that is, from what motives, *are* people moral?" but "Why, that is, for what good reasons, *should* they be moral? Can any good reasons be given why they should be moral? If anyone has not been convinced by the reasons already given, what more can we say?"

The following answer may seem so simple and obvious as not to be worth giving: "We should be moral, simply because it's right." We are not, at the moment, inquiring whether a given act *is* right but rather, *assuming* that it is right, inquiring why we should *do* it. Assume that it is wrong to short-change the blind news vendor, why shouldn't we do it just the same? Our answer now is, "Simply because it's wrong, that's all. Isn't its wrongness itself a good enough reason for not doing it?" Certainly many eminent people have thought so. "Virtue is its own reward," said Spinoza; and indeed, why should one demand rewards for virtue, like a man who does unpleasant work only in order to receive higher pay at the end of the day? Isn't it enough simply that the act is the right one to perform? Perhaps the rightness of the act isn't enough to *cause* us to perform the act (for some the rightness will be enough, for others it won't, depending on our strength of will and moral purpose), but doesn't the rightness provide a sufficient *reason* for performing the act?

Plato's fallacy, it would seem, is that of taking for granted that the only reason why a person should behave morally is that by doing so he will be the gainer. The implication is that if it should turn out that it is not, after all, to his interest to behave morally, then no reason remains why he should do so. Isn't this line of argument a mistake? Plato was trying to reply to his opponents, the Sophists. The Sophists said that one need not behave morally because doing so often does not promote one's own interests and not doing so often *is* to one's interest. Plato, in replying to them, tried his best to show that the Sophists were wrong and that right action *does* promote one's interests, contrary to what they said. It now appears that what Plato *should* have done is something different: instead of trying to show that right action promotes one's interest, he should have questioned the chief presupposition of the Sophists' argument, namely that *if* right action ("justice") doesn't promote one's interest, then one has no reason for doing what is right. Plato, however, never questioned this presupposition; he and the Sophists both shared it. Instead, he set out to challenge their empirical claim that right action does not in fact always promote one's own interest. Had he challenged the presupposition of their argument instead of the argument itself, he would not have been led into such desperate maneuvers in trying to show that "the just man is the happy man." He would have said, "Whether right action is always to one's interest is irrelevant to whether one should perform it"; he would have said, "Granted that, the world being what it is, right action doesn't always lead to happiness; what does it matter? What makes you think that attaining happiness is the only good reason, or even a good reason at all, for doing what is right?"

Let us observe that we are not merely asking, "Why should we perform right actions?" and giving the tautological reply, "Because they're right." We are asking, "Why should we do this act rather than other acts we might have done instead?" and we are answering, "Because it's the right act." Isn't this the best answer and ultimately the only answer? If someone admits that a certain act is right and yet continues to ask why he should perform it, could it be that he is using this question as an excuse for failing to do what he already admits is right? If someone already accepts a certain act as right, doesn't its very rightness *already supply the reason* why he ought to do it?

If it is to a man's interest to perform the act, of course, he probably won't ask the question. (Even here we could ask, "Is the fact that it's to his interest the real reason why he ought to do it? Should he do it *because* it promotes his interest rather than because it is right?") He will ask the question only when the performance of the act is *not* to his own interest. No matter what answer we give him—that the act is conducive to society's interest or simply that it is right—he refuses to accept it as a reason for performing the act in question. He admits that he is a member of a group and has benefited heavily from the sacrifices of others; when his turn comes to perform a sacrifice for them (conducive to their interests, not to his own), he says, "Tell me *why* I should do it. I'm in the game only as long as I win; when I start to lose I quit. At this point the game doesn't pay off for me, so why should I keep on playing?" But what is this questioner demanding? What he wants, and he will accept no other answer, is a *self-interested* reason why he should keep on playing. But the situation is *ex hypothesi* one in which the act required of him is contrary to his interest. Of course it is impossible to give him a reason *in accordance with his interest* for acting *contrary to his interest*. That would be a contradiction in terms. It is a self-contradictory request, and yet people sometimes make it and are disappointed when it can't be fulfilled. The skeptic shows us an example in which he would be behaving contrary to his interest and asks us to give him a reason *why* he should behave thus, and *yet* the only reasons he will accept are reasons of self-interest. It is no wonder that such a questioner must be disappointed. So must the seeker after square circles.

If the skeptic cannot, without self-contradiction, accept a reason of self-interest for doing what is contrary to his interest and yet he will accept no reason *except* one of self-interest, what more can be done? What meaning does his question now have? (Isn't his question an expression of inner weakness, of conflict as to whether he is going to stick by moral principles to which he has originally committed himself or whether he is going to desert them, not because he has found anything intrinsically wrong with the principles, but because in this situation they conflict with his self-interest?) He wants to eat his cake and have it too: he wants a reason of self-interest to justify an act that would be contrary to his interest, or he wants a moral (nonself-interested) reason to justify an act of pure self-interest. Once we have explained this situation to him, if he still keeps on asking the question, it would seem that either he still does not under-

stand the nature of his question or he is still trying to have it both ways—and this, it must be admitted, is all too frequently a motive for engaging in philosophical reasoning.[8]

One last point: "But what are you going to do if people *aren't* moral?" some people will ask. Perhaps the philosopher cannot do anything about it at all. It has been our task to consider what the philosopher can validly say about the question of why we should act upon moral principles we already believe to be right; but to show why we should act upon them, of course, does not guarantee that we *shall* act upon them. Few of us act on our moral convictions 100 per cent of the time; and some of us honor our morality more in the breach than in the observance. Some people, owing perhaps to an unfortunate childhood, are in their adult life so unbendingly and calculatingly selfish that nothing can make them behave unselfishly, whether they profess any moral principles or not. It is not the philosopher's task to make them so. The philosopher cannot, to any great extent, turn selfish people into unselfish ones, immoral people into moral ones; he can move people only if they are willing to hear rational arguments and to act on the basis of them. Philosophy works only when people can be appealed to by rational considerations. Many people, perhaps most people when their selfish interests are involved, cannot be appealed to by these rational considerations; on such people, philosophy is powerless. Some people are in fact singularly immune to reason, and have to be threatened, persuaded, or browbeaten into behaving morally. Some people are immune even to those methods. Such people can never be aided by the philosopher; what they need is a very different kind of therapy which they can receive while reclining on the psychiatrist's couch.

[8] A further point will be made on this issue in Chapter 11 when we discuss various ways of life.

Why Should I Be Moral?

KAI NIELSEN

I

Subjectivism as an ethical theory is dead. As a meta-ethical analysis of what is meant when a moral judgment is made, it claims that all moral judgments are in reality only about the attitudes of the person who makes the judgment. According to this theory, if *A* says 'The execution of Nagy was vile', he simply means 'I disapprove of the execution of Nagy'. But the truth-values of these sentences are obviously not the same. *A* might disapprove of the execution of Nagy but he still could reasonably ask if this execution was vile. Autobiographical reports are not in themselves taken as decisive evidence for the truth of moral claims. But in finding out what *A*'s attitudes really are, we discover whether or not *A* disapproves of the execution of Nagy. Objections of this type have been correctly regarded as decisive objections to such a subjective meta-ethic.

Yet for newcomers (students, interested onlookers and the like) and for some professionals, too, there is something too easy about this refutation of subjectivism. Variations of subjectivism have been recurrent in the history of philosophy from Gorgias to Bertrand Russell. Some of them have been foolish, some simply confused, but to suggest that these theories have been *simply* foolish and without point seems to me *prima facie* implausible. In this essay I shall attempt to show why

From *Methodos*, 1963, pp. 275–306, by permission of the author and *Methodos*.

this is so; I shall attempt to indicate a plausible line of reasoning, a common sense core, in these subjective ethical theories. (Here again the task will be to elicit a really crucial use of 'subjectivism' in reflections about human conduct. The view often called "naive subjectivism" is for the most part a strawman of certain philosophical analysts.) Once I have made explicit what the common sense core of this subjectivism is, I shall examine what considerations can be reasonably brought against it. In order to get more directly to the core of my argument I shall assume here the correctness of two major contentions.

First, I shall assume the general correctness of the claim developed at length in Hare's *The Language of Morals* and Nowell-Smith's *Ethics*, that moral and evaluational utterances are parts of practical discourse and that a complete justification of any practical claim involves reference to the attitudes of the parties involved or to the decisions they would make. I am aware that this is a controversial claim and that unless carefully stated, it is likely to be misleading and unless carefully qualified it is wrong. Nevertheless, I believe there are careful formulations of it that are correct, though I shall not argue for its correctness here.

Secondly, I shall assume what I have argued for elsewhere,[1] namely, that it

[1] K. Nielsen, "Is 'Why Should I be Moral? an Absurdity?", *Australasian Journal of Philosophy*, vol. 36, No. 1 (1958), pp. 25–32.

makes sense to ask 'Why should people be moral?' and 'Why should I be moral?' as long as we do not construe the 'should' in the above two questions as a moral 'should'. Only if the 'should' is construed morally, are the above questions like 'Why are all round things circular?'.

Without entering into a defense of this second point, let me leave the reminder that there are a multitude of uses of 'should' and 'ought' which are not moral uses, i.e. 'I should fill my fountain pen for it's writing poorly', 'People ought to mix their T.V. viewing with a little theatre-going', 'The beam should be placed here', 'The level ought to be longer', etc. The second-mentioned sentence is clearly not a technical injunction but gives advice as to how to act in the sphere of human conduct. Yet it is not distinctively moral, for we would not ordinarily say that it is evil to refuse to obey it, though a person who would seriously assert it would say that people's lives would be enhanced if they did follow it. There are clearly standard uses of 'ought' that are not moral uses though they are a part of the practical language of human conduct.

'Why should people be moral?' and 'Why should I be moral?' are indeed unusual questions, but the 'should' in them does not function in an unusual way any more than it does in 'Why should people never wear sports jackets to cocktail parties?'. A recognition of intelligibility of the odd question 'Why be Moral?' naturally arises in relation to the old saw, "Egoism and Ethics".

The frequently obscured common sense core of subjectivism can be seen most readily from a natural reaction to a refutation of ethical egoism. It is necessary to recall that ethical egoism is not a psychological doctrine of human motivation, so it is not necessary for the so-called ethical egoist to hold that all men always seek their own good even when it conflicts with the good of others. Rather, the so-called ethical egoist claims each person

ought always to seek his own good as the sole end worth seeking for its own sake.[2] It is important to note the qualifiers 'always' and 'worth seeking for its own sake'. Many non-egoistic views would claim that we frequently ought to seek our own good or even that we have a *prima facie* right to seek our own good except in those situations where it conflicts with the common good. The ethical egoist is distinctive in claiming we always ought to seek our own good and that we always ought to regard this as the sole aim worthy of pursuit for its own sake; that is to say, the position I am concerned with here is that of an ethical egoism of ends or what Brian Medlin has called a "categorical egoism".[3] But it not only must be a categorical egoism, it must also be a universal egoism if it is to make a claim to be a normative ethic or even a way-of-life. Note I said, 'Each person ought always to seek his own good', that is, 'Everyone ought always to seek his own good as the sole end worth seeking for its own sake'. This is very different from an individual egoism which claims that the person making the claim should seek his own good as his only rational end.

Universal categorical ethical egoism will not do as a meta-ethical theory purporting to analyze what is meant when people say something is morally good or obligatory; and if it is offered as a radical normative ethic it likewise gets into intolerable paradoxes. In order to remain intelligible, egoism must be put forth as an individual and not as a universal egoism. But, as such, it also fails to meet the minimum conditions necessary for something to count as a 'morality', as that word is ordinarily and intelligibly used. However, it is just this individual egoism that is at the heart of the matter for the subjectivist. He wants to know why he shouldn't be an

[2] Charles Baylis, for example, defines 'ethical egoism' in this way in his *Ethics: The Principles of Wise Choice*, New York, 1958, p. 169.

[3] Brian Medlin, "Ultimate Principles and Ethical Egoism," *The Australasian Journal of Philosophy*, vol. 35 (1957), pp. 111–18.

individual egoist. (Remember the 'shouldn't' here does not have a moral force, though it does have a normative force.)

The dogmatic-sounding contentions of the above paragraph need to be established. I do not want to write another essay on the refutation of egoism.[4] But the following remarks should make the essential points and prepare the way for what is to follow.

To count as an ethical doctrine, then, an ethical egoism of ends must be understood as claiming that everyone ought to seek his own good as an end and consider the good of others only when this would in his judgment further his own good. What purports to be our standard of moral appraisal is personal; that is to say, each of us should always ask ourselves when deliberating on how we ought to act: 'Is this rule or this action or this attitude in my rational self-interest?' If it is in one's rational interest then it ought always to be done, if not, not. But, as Baier has ably argued, such a standard could not be a moral standard for we have moral standards to impartially adjudicate the conflicting interests of individuals and groups; but if each individual's own rational self-interest is taken as the standard, in reality we have no standard by which to adjudicate these conflicting interests. The very *raison d'être* of morality has been frustrated. Thus self-interest, no matter how enlightened, cannot be our standard of *moral* appraisal. "Ethical egoism" cannot possibly be an ethical or moral doctrine.

More could be said about this—there are moves and counter moves that could still be made—but I have given what I take to be the most fundamental reason why egoism is not a possible moral stance.[5] So-called ethical egoism is not a radically

different "moral geometry", "a perverse morality" or even an iconoclastic morality. It isn't a morality or even a possible morality at all. If we are to be consistent egoists we must be individual egoists, and this is to simply reject the claims of anything that could conceivably count as a morality. As Medlin puts it such "indifference to morals may be wicked, but it is not a perverse morality".[6]

If individual egoism is not dressed up as a kind of morality—something it can't possibly be—it can be put in a logically impeccable way. It can be a *personal*, rationally thought-out plan or policy of action.

But for a man like Thrasymachus who is willing to question the claims of the whole moral enterprise, why isn't individual egoism a viable alternative? He could admit that Butler is perfectly right—people don't always act egoistically—but he could go on to claim that only a benighted fool insists on trying to be a morally good man. A wise man will not be duped by all the humbug about morality learned at Nannie's knee.

Surely one crucial question that any reflective individual in any age must face is the question, 'What kind of life would be a happy life? What sort of people should we strive to become so that we as individuals can be happy?'. The individual egoist, as well as the moral agent, is (or at least can be) vitally concerned with this question. Such an egoist, if he is wise, has considered the claims of morality and has decided that he will not attain genuine and lasting happiness by striving to be a morally good man, though it may be good tactics usually to be a man of good morals. It is his belief that the way of morality is not usually the way of happiness. And if and when it is, it ought to be pursued only because it will bring the pursuer happiness. To be sure, an intelligent individual egoist will not go around proclaiming that every-

---

[4] See my "Egoism in Ethics," *Philosophy and Phenomenological Research*, vol. XIX (June, 1959).

[5] Some of these are made by John Hospers in his "Baier and Medlin on Ethical Egoism," *Philosophical Studies*, vol. XII (January-February, 1961).

[6] Medlin, *op. cit.*, p. 113.

one should only look after himself. He may, if he is so *inclined,* pass on his insight to his family and some close friends, but he will not try to become an ethical egoist or try to base conventional morality on egoism. This would be the very epitome of foolishness. In certain contexts, he may even find it expedient to mouth "the high-minded pomposities of this morning's editorial". Such behavior, so to say, gives him a good press. But he has decided to act on the personal principle: Always look after yourself and no one else, unless looking after someone else will benefit you.

True, there cannot be an egoistic way of life or *Weltanschauungphilosophie* but there could be a deliberate, rationally thought out and consistently adhered to personal policy of individual egoism. Brunton correctly notes, "There can be intelligent, self-controlled people, with a plan of life, who care only for themselves".[7] Egoism cannot be an ethical doctrine but the man committed to individual egoism still has a use for 'I *ought* to consider only my own good' as distinguished from 'I only care about myself'. The former normative (though not moral) sentence indicates a settled policy of action. The latter, by contrast, indicates what may be only a momentary or very impermanent reaction. The token 'ought' when used in such a context has more than just the common mark or noise in common with the token 'ought' used in a moral context. In both instances they are only properly used if in some way they indicate a settled policy as distinct from a momentary whim, emotion or impulse.

Thus, I do not see anything logically inconsistent about individual egoism so long as we don't try to extend it into a new rival morality or into an iconoclastic world view. A view that exhibits a contempt for all moral considerations whatsoever, could not possibly be a moral view, not even a

perverse moral view. But a consistent individual egoism, intelligently pursued, is not a doctrine; it is not something that would be articulated by an intelligent egoist. Yet privately a person might adopt it as his policy of life.

Why shouldn't he? (Recall the 'shouldn't' here is not a moral 'shouldn't'.) Why is he (or is he?) irrational or mistaken if he follows this egoistic policy? Surely it is not in our interest for him to act immorally, but why shouldn't he or I or even you? Why should the "existing individual" who is trying to decide how to live happily, or significantly, opt for the point of view of morality rather than an intelligent and carefully controlled individual egoism?

Imagine yourself studying all the meta-ethical treatises, the systems of normative ethics, the sage advice of the wise men, in short, all the claims of morality. Then imagine yourself in the quiet of your own study weighing up—not for others but for yourself alone—these considerations against the considerations in favor of individual egoism. Why should *you* choose to act morally rather than non-morally?

This question, which is at least as old as Plato, has been traditionally imbedded in the thick muck of metaphysics.[8] Often it has been confused with a lot of other

---

[7] J. A. Brunton, "Egoism and Morality," *Philosophical Quarterly,* vol. VI (1956), pp. 298–9.

[8] It received a new coat with Donald Walhout's essay, "Why Should I Be Moral? A Reconsideration," *The Review of Metaphysics,* vol. XII, No. 4 (June, 1959), pp. 570–88. Consider only ". . the final theoretical answer" to our question is that ". . . one should be moral because this fits into a pattern of universal harmony of all things . . ." and the "universal harmony of all things can be regarded as the ultimate culmination of all existence, not indeed as a description at any particular moment of time, but as an all-pervasive ideal." But such an ideal is not left to the whims of mortal will for we are told "it may be regarded as rooted in the ultimate power of being that produces what is." Apparently it is too much to expect that the days are over when this kind of philosophy could be written. Walhout sees there is a problem about justifying the moral point of view that was not adequately met by Bradley and Prichard but in answering what he calls "the ultimate question" he gives us this nonsense.

questions and recently it has been too lightly dismissed as nonsensical or absurd. The *feeling* emerges that finally there is no real argument here, one way or another; one must just opt for one policy rather than another. Here Sartrean or Kierkegaardian talk about decisions and anxiety *seems* correct. Subjectivism again raises its ugly head. We are tempted to say that here decision or commitment is king. Emotional energy may go into our commitment to morality but in a "cool hour" we cannot discover decisive reasons for acting in either way. There seem to be no decisive reasons for our choice here; nor can we conceive of a non-question-begging general procedure that would enable us to decide between these conflicting policies.[9]

Reflective people, uncorrupted by philosophical theories, can be brought by ordinary reflection over morality to recognize the point I have just made. The non-philosophical idioms 'It's a value judgment' or 'It's finally a matter of what sort of a person you want to be', reflect just this point. The very anxiety that any slight reference to subjectivism arouses in some people's breasts counts (I believe) for rather than against my claim. We do not come to a conclusion of this sort unambivalently. In reflecting about morality and human conduct, we are tempted finally to say that you must just decide what sort of person you want to be. No intellectual considerations will settle the matter for you here.

It is just this belief that seems to me to be the common sense core of subjectivism. But is it a belief that we can and should accept as clear-minded, rational human beings? Can we rationally defend taking a moral point of view? Are there decisive reasons for accepting the claims of morality such that any rational "un-moved spectator of the actual" would have to as-

sent to them? In the next section I shall turn to this question.

II

Why then be moral? We need initially to note that this question actually ought to be broken down into two questions, namely, 1) 'Why should people be moral?' or 'Why should there be a morality at all?' and 2) 'Why should I be moral?'. As will become evident, these questions ought not in the name of clarity, to be confused. But they have been run together; in asking for a justification for the institution of morality both questions are relevant and easily confused. 'Why be Moral?' nicely straddles these questions. In this section I shall first examine some traditional, and I believe unhelpful, answers to the above general questions. There the general question is not broken down as it should be and in examining these views I shall not break it down either. After noting the difficulties connected with these approaches, I shall state what I believe to be a satisfactory answer to the question, 'Why should there be a morality at all?' and indicate why it leaves untouched the harder question, 'Why should I be moral?'

There is a prior consideration that we must first dispose of. In considering both of these questions we must be careful to distinguish the *causes* of a man's being moral from the *reasons* he gives for being moral. If one is a little careful about the implications of the word 'likes', Bradley seems perfectly right in saying: "A man is moral because he likes being moral; and he likes it, partly because he has been brought up to the habit of liking it, and partly because he finds it gives him what he wants, while its opposite does not do so".[10] In other words people are moral

[9] See W. H. Walsh, "Scepticism About Morals and Scepticism About Knowledge," *Philosophy*, vol. XXXV (July 1960), pp. 218–34.

[10] F. H. Bradley, *Ethical Studies* (The Liberal Arts Press, 1951), p. 7.

primarily because they have been conditioned to be moral. The human animal is a social animal and (as Butler and Hume observed) people normally tend to consider the welfare of others as well as their own welfare. People indeed act selfishly but they also take out life insurance, feel anxiety over the troubles of others, and even have moments of mild discomfort at the thought that life on this planet may some day be impossible. People react in this way because they have been taught or conditioned to so react. But, the 'because' here is explanatory and *not* justificatory. It explains in a very general way what *makes* or *causes* people to be moral. But the question I am concerned with here is a quite different one. In asking, 'Why should people be moral?', I am asking the question, 'What good reasons do people have for being moral?'. In asking about the justification for acting morally, I am only incidentally concerned with an explanation of the causes of moral behavior.

What good reasons are there for being moral? And if there are good reasons for being moral are they sufficient or decisive reasons?

There is a short, snappy answer to my question. The plain man might well say: 'People ought to be moral because it is wicked, evil, morally reprehensible not to be moral. We have the very best reasons for being moral, namely that it is immoral not to be moral'. The plain man (or at the very least the plain Western Man and not *just* the ordinary Oxford Don) would surely agree with Bradley "that consciousness, when unwarped by selfishness and not blinded by sophistry, is convinced that to ask for the Why? is simple immorality . . .".[11] The correct answer to the question: 'Why Be Moral?' is simply that this is what we ought to do.

This short answer will not do, for the plain man has failed to understand the question. A clear-headed individual could

not be asking for *moral* justification for being moral. This would be absurd. Rather he is asking the practical question: why should people be bound by the conventions of morality at all? He would not dispute Baier's contention that "it is generally believed that when reasons of self-interest conflict with moral reasons, then moral reasons override those of self-interest".[12] It is perfectly true that the plain man regards moral reasons as superior to all others and it is, of course, in accordance with reason to follow superior or overriding reasons, but if a clear-headed man asks 'Why should we be moral?' he is challenging the very grading criteria those ordinary convictions rest on. He would acknowledge that it is indeed morally reprehensible or wicked not to act morally. But he would ask: 'So what?'. And he might even go on to query: 'What is the good of all this morality anyway? Are not those Marxists and Freudians right who claim that the whole enterprise of morality is nothing but an ideological device to hoodwink people into *not* seeking what they really want? Why should people continue to fall for this conjuring trick? To call someone "wicked" or "evil" is to severely grade them down, but why should people accept any *moral* grading criteria at all?'

There are several traditional replies to this. But all of them are unsatisfactory.

One traditional approach advocated by Plato and Bishop Butler, among others, claims that people should be moral because they will not be happy otherwise. Being moral is at least a necessary condition for being happy.

For Butler the argument takes the following form. Human beings are so constituted that they will, generally speaking, act morally. When they don't act morally they will clearly recognize they were mistaken in not doing so. The human animal has a conscience and this conscience not

[11] Bradley, *op. cit.*, p. 6.

[12] Kurt Baier, *The Moral Point of View: A Rational Basis of Ethics* (Cornell University Press, 1958), p. 308.

only causes people to act in a certain way, but is in fact a *norm* of action. Conscience guides as well as goads; the deliverances of conscience are both action-evoking and a source of moral knowledge. Conscience tells the moral agent what to do even in specific situations. It clearly and unequivocally tells him to always act morally and he is so constituted that if he ignores the dictates of his conscience he will not be happy. In other words, Butler agrees with Plato in claiming that Thrasymachus and other amoralists are fundamentally mistaken about the true interests of a human being.

That it is in the human animal's best interest to live virtuously is no more established by Butler than it is by Plato.[13] Plato is reduced to analogy, myth and mystagogy and, as Duncan-Jones points out, Butler is finally pushed to concede that "full acceptance of the conclusion that human nature is satisfiable and only satisfiable by virtue depends on revelation".[14] In the face of what clearly seem to be genuine exceptions to the claim that it is in the individual's self-interest always to act morally, Butler is driven to remark: "All shall be set right at the final distribution of things".[15]

Some intuitionist may argue that while this Butlerian move won't do, it still remains the case that Butler could rightly have said that we just directly (in some sense) perceive or see the fittingness or suitability of always acting morally. To meet this point we would have to argue against the whole logical or epistemological machinery of intuitionism. We would need to question (as Toulmin has) such a use of 'intuition', to point out that neither 'see' nor 'apprehend' is at home here, and challenge the notion that ethical words simply refer to qualities or relations. But in view of the incisive literature criticizing this overall intuitionist claim, I believe it is quite unnecessary to refute this intuitionist claim once more. At any rate, I have no new arguments to deploy beyond those offered by Toulmin, MacDonald, Strawson, Robinson, Nowell-Smith and Edwards.

There is a more defensible answer to the question: 'Why should people be moral?'. It was first urged (in the Western World, at least) by Epicurus; later it was developed and given its classical forceful statement by Hobbes. Bertrand Russell elaborates it in his own way in his *Human Society in Ethics and Politics* (1955) and Kurt Baier has clearly elucidated and defended Hobbes' argument in his *The Moral Point of View* (1958). This Hobbesian argument, which within its proper scope seems to me conclusive, can readily be used to meet the objections of those "tough-minded" Marxists and Freudians who do not want the usual fare of "sweetness and light".

Hobbes points out that as a matter of fact the restless, malcontent, foraging human animal wants "the commidious life"; that is, he wants above all peace, security, freedom from fear. He wants to satisfy his desires to the maximum extent, but one of the very strongest and most persistent of these desires is the desire to be free from the "tooth and claw" of a life in which each man exclusively seeks his own interest and totally neglects to consider the interests of others. In such a situation life would indeed be "nasty, brutish and short". We could not sleep at night without fear of violent death; we could not leave what we possessed without well-warranted anxiety over its being stolen or destroyed. Impulses and inclinations would be held in check only when they would lead to behavior detrimental to the individual's own interest. Where people's interests conflict, each man would (without the institution of morality) resort to subterfuge or

[13] John Hospers effectively marshals the points that need to be made against Plato here. See John Hospers, *Human Conduct: An Introduction to the Problems of Ethics* (New York, 1961), pp. 176–83.
[14] Austin Duncan-Jones, *Butler's Moral Philosophy* (Pelican Philosophy Series, 1952), p. 181.
[15] Quoted by Duncan-Jones, *op. cit.*, p .182.

violence to gain his own ends. A pervasive Dobuan-like suspicion would be normal and natural . . . even rational in such a situation. Every individual would be struggling for the good things of life and no rule except that of his own self-interest would govern the struggle. The universal reign of the rule of exclusive self-interest would lead to the harsh world that Hobbes called "the state of nature". And, as Baier puts it, "At the same time, it will be clear to everyone that universal obedience to certain rules overriding self-interest would produce a state of affairs which serves everyone's interest much better than his unaided pursuit of it in a state where everyone does the same".[16] Baier goes on to point out that "the very *raison d'être* of a morality is to yield reasons which override the reasons of self-interest in those cases when everyone's following self-interest would be harmful to everyone".[17]

When we ask: why should we have a morality—any morality, even a completely conventional morality—we answer that if everyone acts morally, or generally acts morally, people will be able to attain more of what they want. It is obvious that in a moral community more good will be realized than in a non-moral collection of people. Yet in the interest of realizing a commodious life for all, voluntary self-sacrifice is sometimes necessary; but the best possible life for everyone is attainable only if people act morally; the greatest possible good is realizable only when everyone puts aside his own self-interest when it conflicts with the common good.

If people ask: 'Why should one choose that course of action which will probably promote the greatest possible good?' we are quite correct in answering as Baylis does: There is probably nothing better one could possibly do instead.[18] I would only add that Baylis' caution here is

[16] Baier, *op. cit.*, p. 309.
[17] *Ibid.*
[18] Charles Baylis, *op. cit.*, pp. 172–73.

rhetorical for there is no place at all for the qualifying word 'probably'.

III

Yet an answer to the question 'Why should people be moral?' does not meet one basic question that the thorough-going sceptic may feel about the claims of morality. The "existing individual" may want to know why *he*, as an individual, ought to accept the standards of morality when it is not in *his* personal interest to do so. He may have no doubt at all about the general utility of the moral enterprise. But *his* not recognizing the claims of morality will not greatly diminish the total good. Reflecting on this, he asks himself: 'Why should *I* be moral when I will not be caught or punished for not acting morally?'.

Recall how Glaucon and Adeimantus readily agree that Socrates has established that morality is an indispensable social practice. But their perplexity over morals is not at an end. They want Socrates to go on and prove that the individual ought to be moral even when he is perfectly safe in not acting morally. Someone might readily agree that the Hobbesian arguments presented in II establish that the greatest total good will be realized if people act morally, but he still wants to know 'Why should I be moral in those cases where acting morally will not be in *my* rational self-interest?' He might say to himself—though certainly if he were wise he would not proclaim it —'There is no reason why I should act morally'.

Such an individual egoist cannot be refuted by indicating that his position cannot be a moral position. He may grant the overall social good of morality and he may be fully aware that 'Why should I do my duty?' cannot be a moral question—there is indeed no room at all for that question as a moral question, but an individual egoist is not trying to operate within the bounds of morality. He is trying to decide whether or not he should *become* a moral agent or he may—in a more theoretical frame of mind—wonder if any *reason* can be given for his remaining a moral agent. Prichard is quite right in arguing that the *moral* agent has no choice here. To assert 'I'll only be moral when being moral is in my rational interest' is to rule out, in a quite *a priori* fashion, the very possibility of one's being moral as long as one has such an intention. To be a moral agent entails that one gives up seriously entertaining whether one should deliberately adopt a policy of individual egoism. 'X is moral' entails 'X will try to do his duty even when so acting is not in his personal interest'. Thus we must be very *careful* how we take the individual egoist's question: his question is, 'Should I become moral and give up my individual egoism or shall I remain such an egoist?'. If he decides to remain an individual egoist he will have made the decision that *he* ought to behave like a man of good morals when and only when such behavior is in his own personal interest. Now what grounds (if any) have we for saying that a man who makes such a decision is mistaken or irrational? What (if any) intellectual mistake has he made? Remember, he doesn't challenge Prichard's remarks about the logical relations of duty to interest or the Hobbesian argument that morality is an essential social device if we are to have a commodious life. But he still wants to know why *he* should be moral rather than non-moral.

The individual egoist may well believe that those who insist on being moral even when it is not in their self-interest are really benighted fools duped by the claims of society. A "really clever man" will take as his own personal norm of action the furtherance of his own good. Everything else must give pride of place to this. He will only endeavor to make it seem perfectly obvious that he is a staunch pillar of the community so as to avoid reprisals from his society.

Can such an individual egoist be shown to be wrong or to be asking a senseless question? What arguments can be given for an affirmative answer to the question: 'Should I be moral?'.

Kant recognized as clearly as did Prichard that there is no room for this question within morality, but he felt, in a way Prichard apparently did not, that nonetheless such a question needs answering and that this was one of the main reasons we need God and the graces of religion. Thus, Kant found it necessary to posit God and immortality as postulates of the practical reason so that there would be a heaven in which the morally good man would be rewarded for doing his duty because it is his duty. But these principles of practical reason are, for Kant, finally based on the demands of the moral will. The universe just couldn't be so bad as to allow evil to go permanently unrequited and the man of good will unrewarded. Sidgwick too (strangely enough) created a theological postulate to provide for a harmony between universal and individual happiness. We assume that God so rewards and punishes that it is always in everyone's interest to seek to further the greatest good for the greatest number.

But it is increasingly difficult for an educated modern even to believe in God, to say nothing of making Him such a *deus ex machina*. As J. J. C. Smart rightly remarks: "More and more it seems that man is just part of nature. In the light of modern science he appears to be a very complicated physico-chemical mechanism, who arose by natural selection from simpler mechanisms, and there may well be millions of planets in the universe with similar, or higher, forms of life on them".[19] Yet for the sake of the argument let us assume

[19] J. J. C. Smart, "Philosophy and Religion," *The Australasian Journal of Philosophy*, vol. 36, No. 1 (1958), p. 57.

(what indeed ought not to be assumed) that we have an appropriate use of 'God' and let us also assume that we have some evidence that there is an X such that X is God. Even making these assumptions, it does take the utmost vanity and the epitome of self-delusion to believe that such a Being could be so concerned with our weal and woe. And to postulate God *because* of His practical necessity or to postulate immortality to try to insure a justification of morality is just too convenient. It is deserving of the scorn Bradley heaped upon it.

Medlin does not engage in such rationalization but without further ado plays Dr. Johnson. He comments: "If the good fellow wants to know how he should justify conventional morality to the individual egoist, the answer is that he *shouldn't* and *can't*. Buy your car elsewhere, blackguard him whenever you meet, and let it go at that".[20] A philosopher, Medlin goes on to comment, is "not a rat-catcher" and it is not his "job to dig vermin out of such burrows as individual egoism".[21] Inasmuch as Medlin is pointing out that the individual egoist's position isn't and can't be a moral alternative to conventional morality, he is perfectly right in his strictures; but as an answer to the question as I have posed it, Medlin's reply is simply irrelevant.

Must we say at this juncture that practical reasoning has come to an end and that we must simply *decide* for ourselves how to act? Is it just that, depending on what attitudes I actually happen to have, I strive to be one sort of a person rather than another without any sufficient rational guides to tell me what I am to do? Does it come to just that—finally? Subjectivists say (at such a juncture) that there are no such guides. And this time there seems to be a strong strand of common sense or hardheaded street wisdom to back up the subjectivists' position.

I do not believe that we are that badly

off. There are weighty considerations of a mundane sort in favor of the individual's taking the moral point of view. But I think the subjectivists are right in claiming that it is a mistake to argue that a man is simply irrational if he does not at all times act morally. It is indeed true that if a man deliberately refuses to do what he acknowledges as morally required of him, we say he is irrational—or better, unreasonable. But here 'irrational' and 'unreasonable' have a distinctively *moral* use. There are other quite standard employments of the word in which we would not say that such a man is irrational.[22] In all contexts the word 'irrational' has the evaluative force of strongly condemning something or other. In different contexts the criteria for what is to be called 'irrational' differ. In Toulmin's terms the criteria are field-dependent and the force of the word is field-independent. In saying a man acts irrationally in not assenting to any moral considerations whatsoever we need not be claiming that he makes any mistakes in observation or deduction. Rather we are condemning him for not accepting the moral point of view. But he is asking why he, as an individual in an ongoing community, should always act as a moral agent. He is not asking for *motivation* but for a *reason* for being a morally good man. He wants to know what intellectual mistake the man who acts non-morally must make. To be told such a man is immoral and in *that sense* is unreasonable or irrational is not to the point.

The subjectivist I am interested in contends that in the nature of the case there can be no reasons here for being moral rather than non-moral. One must just *decide* to act one way or another without reasons. There is much to be said for the subjectivist's claim here but even here I think there are rational considerations in favor of an individual's opting for morality.

---

[20] Medlin, *op. cit.*, p. 113; italics mine.
[21] *Ibid.*, p. 114.

[22] I have discussed this issue in my "Appealing to Reason," *Inquiry*, vol. 5 (Spring, 1962), pp. 65–84.

—and at this point it has an enlightened common sense on its side. But I think there is something more to be said that will take the bite out of such subjectivism. In trying to bring this out, I am in *one sense* going back to Plato. It is, of course, true that we can't ask for a self-interested reason for doing what is right where *ex hypothesi* the action is not in our self-interest. But in action it is not so clear what is in our self-interest and what is not, what is in our self-interest *apparently* in our self- and often what is *apparently* in our self-interest is really not. Part of my counter to the subjectivist, and *here* I am with Plato, is that if a man decides *repeatedly* to act non-morally where he thinks he can get away with it, he will not, as a very general rule, be happy.

This isn't the whole of my case by any means, but I shall start with this considera-tion.

V

Suppose that I, in a fully rational frame of mind, am trying to decide whether or not to adopt individual egoism as my personal policy of action. I ask myself: 'Should I pursue a selfish policy or should I consider others as well even when in my best judg-ment it doesn't profit me?'. In my de-liberation I might well ask myself: 'Will I really be happy if I act without regard for others?'. And here it is natural to consider the answer of the ancients. Plato and Aristotle believe that only the man who performs just actions has a well-ordered soul. And only the man with a well-ordered soul will be "truly happy". If I am thrown off course by impulse and blind action I will not have a well-ordered soul; I will not be genuinely happy. But the alternative I am considering is not between impulsive blind action and rational, controlled action, but between two forms of deliberate, ra-tionally controlled activity. Why is my soul any less well-ordered or why do I realize

myself (to shift to Bradley's idiom) any the less if I act selfishly than if I act morally? If it is replied, 'You will "realize yourself more" because most people have found that they are happiest when they are moral', I can again ask: 'But what has that to do with me? Though I am one man among men, I may not in this respect be like other men. Most people have neurotic compulsions about duties and are prey to customary taboos and tribal loyalties. If I can free myself from such compulsions and superstitions will I be any the less happy if I am selfish? I should think that I would be happier by being intelligently selfish. I can be happier by being intelligently selfish. I can forget about others and single mindedly go after what I want'.

To this last statement Plato and Aris-totle would reply that by always acting selfishly a man will not fully realize his distinctively human *areté*. By so acting, he simply will not be responding in a fully human way. We say of a man that he is a 'good man, a truly happy man' when he performs his function well, just as we say a tranquilizer is a 'good tranquilizer' when it performs its function well; that is to say, performs its function well; that is to say, when the tranquilizer relaxes the tense, harrassed individual. But can we properly talk about human beings this way? We do talk about human beings this way? We do speak of a surgeon as 'a good surgeon' when he cures people by deftly performing operations when and only when people need operations. Similarly, a teacher is 'a good teacher' if he stimulates his students to thought and to assimilate eagerly "the best that has been thought and said in the world". We can indeep speak of the *areté* or "virtue" of the teacher, fireman, preacher, thief or even (as MacIver re-minds us) of the wife or unmarried girl.[31] People have certain social roles and they can perform them ill or well. "In this sense we can speak of 'a good husband', 'a good father', 'a good Chancellor of the E chequer . . .', but—MacIver rightly c

[31] A. M. MacIver, "Good and Evil and Geach," *Analysis*, vol. 18, No. 1 (October, pp. 7–13.

IV

Before I state and examine those consider-ations I would like to show how two recent tantalizingly straightforward answers will not do. Baier has offered one and Hospers the other.

Baier says that when we ask 'Why should I be moral?' we are asking 'Which is the course of action supported by the best reasons?'. Since we can show along Hobbesian lines that men generally have better reasons for being moral than for being non-moral the individual has "been given a reason for being moral, for follow-ing moral reasons rather than any other . . .". The reason is simply that "they are better reasons than any other". *But in the above type situation,* when I am asking, 'Why should I be moral?', I am not con-cerned with which course of action is sup-ported by the best reasons *sans phrase* or with what is the best thing to do for all concerned. I am only concerned with what is a good reason *for me*. I want to know what is the best thing *for me* to do; that is, I want to know what will make for my greatest good.

Baier might point out that an indi-vidual has the best reasons for acting morally because by each man's acting mor-ally the greatest possible good will be realized. Yet, if the reference is to men severally and not to them as a group, it might well be the case that an individual's acting immorally might in effect further the total good, for his bad example might spur others on to greater acts of moral virtue. But be that as it may, the individual egoist could still legitimately reply to Baier: 'All of what you say is irrelevant unless real-ization of the greatest total good serves *my* best interests. When and only when the reasons for all involved are also the best reasons for me am I personally justified in adopting the moral point of view'.

We can, of course, criticize a so-called ethical egoist for translating the question

'What is the best thing to do' into the question 'What is the best thing *for me* to do'. In morality we are concerned with what is right, what is good and what is supported by the best reasons, *period;* but recall that the *individual* egoist is challeng-ing the sufficiency of moral reasons which we, as social beings, normally grant to the moral enterprise. (We need to reflect on the sense of 'sufficiency' here. The egoist is not challenging the point of having moral codes. He is challenging the sufficiency of the moral life as a device to enhance *his* happiness. But is this "a goal of morality"? It is not.) He is asking for reasons for *his* acting morally and unfortunately Baier's short answer does not meet the question Baier sets out to answer, though as I have already indicated it does answer the ques-tion, 'Why should people be moral?'

Hospers has a different argument which, while wrong, carries a crucial in-sight that takes us to the very heart of our argument. Like Baier, Hospers does not keep apart the question 'Why should I be moral?' from 'Why should people be moral?'. After giving a psychological ex-planation of what motivates people to be moral, Hospers considers what *reasons* there are for being moral.

Virtue is its own reward and if an act is indeed right this is a sufficient reason for performing the act. We have been oper-ating on the wrong assumption—an assumption that we inherited from Plato —namely, that if it isn't in our interest to behave morally we have no reason to do it. But it does not follow that if a right action is not in our interest we have no reason for doing it. If we ask 'Why should we do this act rather than other acts we might have done instead?' the answer 'Because it is the right act' is, says Hospers, "the best answer and ultimately the only answer".[23]

It is indeed true that *if we are reason-ing from the moral point of view* and if an

[23] John Hospers, *Human Conduct: An Introduc-tion to the Problems of Ethics* (New York, 1961), p. 194.

act is genuinely the right act to do in a given situation, then it is the act we should do. Once a moral agent knows that such and such an action is the right *one to do in* these circumstances he has *eo ipso* been supplied with the reason for doing it. But in asking 'Why should I be moral?' an individual is asking why *he* should (non-moral sense of 'should') reason as a moral agent. He is asking, and *not* as a moral agent, what reason there is for his doing what is right.

It is at this point that Hosper's reply —and his implicit defense of his simple answer—exhibits insight. It will, Hospers points out, be natural for an individual to ask this question only when "the performance of the act is *not* to his own interest".[24] It is also true that *any* reason we give other than a reason which will show that what is right is in his rational self-interest will be rejected by him. Hospers remarks "What he wants, and he will accept no other answer, is a self-interested reason" for acting as a moral agent.[25] But this is like asking for the taste of pink for "the situation is *ex hypothesi* one in which the act required of him is contrary to his interest. Of course it is impossible to give him a reason *in accordance with his interest for acting contrary* to his interest".[26] 'I have a reason for acting in accordance with my interest which is contrary to my interests' is a contradiction. The man who requests an answer to 'Why should I do what is right when it is not in my interest?' is making a "self-contradictory request". We come back once more to Prichard and Bradley and see that after all our "question" is a logically absurd one —no real question at all. The person asking "the question" cannot "without self-contradiction, accept a reason of self-interest for doing what is contrary to his interest and yet he will accept no reason except one of self-interest."[27]

His "question" is no real question at

[24] *Ibid.*, p. 194.
[25] *Ibid.*
[26] *Ibid.*
[27] *Ibid.*, p. 195.

all but at best a non-rational expression of a personal predicament. Our problem has been dissolved—the "common sense core of subjectivism" has turned out to be the core of the onion.

But has it really? Is any further question here but a confused request for *motivation* to do what we know we have the best reasons for doing? Let us take stock. Hospers has in effect shown us: (1) That x's being right entails *both* x should be done (where 'should' has a moral use) and there is (from the moral point of view) a *sufficient reason* for doing x ('I ought to do what is right' is a tautology where 'ought' is used morally); (2) That from the point of view of self-interest the only reasons that can be sufficient reasons for acting are self-interested reasons. This again is an obvious tautology. The man asking 'Why should I do what is right when it is not in my self-interest?' has made a self-contradictory request *when he is asking this question as a self-interested question.*

These two points must be accepted, but what if an individual says: As I see it, there are two alternatives: either I act from the moral point of view, where logically speaking I must try to do what is right, or I act from the point of view of rational self-interest, where again I must seek to act according to my rational self-interest. But is there any *reason* for me always to act from one point of view rather than another when I am a member in good standing in a moral community? True enough, Hospers has shown me that *from the moral point of view* I have no alternative but to try to do what is right and from a *self-interested point of view* I have no rational alternative but to act according to what I judge to be in my rational self-interest. But what I want to know is what I am to do: Why adopt one point of view rather than another? Is there a good reason *for me,* placed as I am, to adopt the moral point of view or do I just arbitrarily choose, as the subjectivist would argue?

I do not see that Hospers' maneuver has shown this question to be senseless or

an expression of a selfcontradictory request. Rather his answer in effect brings the question strikingly to the fore by showing how from the moral point of view 'Because it's right' must be a sufficient answer, and how it cannot possibly be a sufficient answer from the point of view of self-interest or from the point of view of an individual challenging the sufficiency of the whole moral point of view, as a personal guide for his actions. It seems that we have two strands of discourse here with distinct canons of justification. We just have to make up our minds which point of view we wish to take. The actual effect of Hospers' argument is to display in fine rational order the common sense core of subjectivism: *at this point* we just choose and there can be no reasons for our choice.

It will not do for Hospers to argue that an individual could not rationally choose a non-moral way of life or ethos, for in choosing to act from a self-interested vantage point an individual is not choosing a way of life; he is, instead, adopting a personal policy of action in a very limited area for himself alone. Such an individual might well agree with Hospers that a rational way of life is one, the choice of which, is (1) free, (2) enlightened, and (3) impartial.[28] This remark, he could contend, is definitive of what we *mean* by 'a rational way of life'. An intelligent egoist would even urge that such a way of life be adopted but he could still ask himself (it wouldn't be prudent to ask others) what *reason* there would be for *him,* or any single individual living in a community committed to such a way of life, to act in accordance with it. (This need not be a question which logically speaking requires a self-interested answer. An existing individual is trying to make up his mind what he is to do.)

To reply, 'If it's rational then it should be done', is to neglect the context-dependent criteria of both 'rational' and 'should'. There are both moral and non-

[28] *Ibid.*, p. 585.

moral uses of 'should' and 'rational'. In the above example Hospers is using 'rational' in a moralistic sense; as Hospers puts it, "Let me first define 'rationality' with regard to a way of life" and while a way of life is not exhausted by moral considerations it essentially includes them.[29] Only if 'rational' and 'should' belong to the same strand of discourse is 'If it is rational then it should be done' analytic. Something could be rational from the moral point of view (morally reasonable) and yet imprudent (irrational from the point of view of self-interest). If we were asking what we should do in terms of self-interest, it would not follow in this case that we should do what is rational in the sense of 'morally reasonable'. Conversely, where 'What is rational' means 'What is prudent' it would not follow that what is rational is what, morally speaking, we ought to do.[30]

Thus, it seems to me that neither Baier's nor Hospers' answers will do. We are left with our original question, now made somewhat more precise, 'Is there a good reason for me as an individual in a moral community to always act morally no matter how I am placed?'. There is no room *in morality* for this question but this question can arise when we think about how to act and when, as individuals, we reflect on what ends of action to adopt. But as a result of Hospers' analysis, must we now say that here we must 1) simply make a choice concerning how to act or 2) where there is no live question concerning how to act it is still the case that there can be no non-question begging justification for an individual, were he faced with such a choice, to act one way rather than another? (Of course there is the very best *moral* justification for his acting as a moral agent. But that is not our concern here, for we are asking: why reason morally?)

Here the pull of subjectivism is strong

[29] *Ibid.*
[30] See here William Dennes, "An Appeal to Reason," in *Reason, University of California Publications in Philosophy,* vol. 7 (Berkeley, California, 1939), pp. 3–42 and *Some Dilemmas of Naturalism* (New York, 1960), Chapter 5.

cludes—hardly of "a good man".[32] People, *qua* human beings, do not seem to have a function, purpose, or role. A child can sensibly ask: 'What are hammers for?', 'What are aspirins for?', 'What are dentists for?', but if a child asks 'What are people for?', we must point out to him that this question is not really like the others. 'Daddy, what are people for?' is foolish or *at the very least*—even for the Theist —an extremely amorphous question. At best we must quickly strike some religious attitude and some disputed cosmology must be quickly brought in, but no such exigency arises for the cosmologically neutral question, 'Daddy, what are napkins for?' or 'Daddy, what are policemen for?'. After all, what is the function of man *as such*? In spite of all his hullabaloo about it, is not Sartre correct in claiming that man has no "essence"—no *a priori* nature—but that human beings are what human beings make of themselves? If a human being acts in an eccentric or non-moral way are we really entitled to say he is any less of a human being?

If we counter that we are indeed entitled to say this, and we then go on to say, 'By not acknowledging that we are so entitled, we are in effect overriding or ignoring man's "distinctively human qualities"' are we not now using 'distinctively human qualities' primarily as a grading label? In such contexts, isn't its actual linguistic function primarily moral? We are disapproving of a way of acting and attempting to guide people away from patterns of behavior that are like this. If we say the consistently selfish man is less human than the moral man, are we not here using 'less human' as a moral grading label and not just as a phrase to describe men? 'More human', on such a use, would not be used to signify those qualities (if there are any) which are common to and distinctive of the human animal; but would be used as an honorific moral label. And *if* it is used *only* to describe how people

[32] *Ibid.*, p. 8.

have behaved then it is perfectly possible for me to ask, 'Why should I be more human rather than less?'.

Most moderns would not try to meet the question 'Why should I be moral?' in this Greek way, though they still would be concerned with that ancient problem, 'How should I live in order to be truly happy?'. A rational man might make this elementary prudential reflection: 'If I am thoroughly and consistently selfish and get caught people will treat me badly. I will be an outcast, I will be unloved, all hands will be on guard against me. I may even be retaliated against or punished as an "irredeemable moral beast". All of this will obviously make me suffer. Thus, I better not take up such a selfish policy or I will surely be unhappy'.

At this point it is natural to take a step which, if pushed too far, cannot but lead to a "desert-island example". It is natural to reply: 'Clearly it would be irrational to *appear* selfish. But I don't at all propose to do that. I only propose to look out for "number one" and only "number one". I will do a good turn for others when it is likely, directly or indirectly, to profit me. I will strive to appear to be a man of good morals and I will do a good deed when and only when it is reasonable to believe there will be some personal profit in it. Surely, a policy of unabashed, outright selfishness would be disastrous to me. Obviously, this is something I will strive to avoid. But I shall keep as the maxim of *my* actions: Always consider yourself first. Only do things for others, when by so acting, it will profit you, and do not be frankly selfish or openly aggressive except in those situations where no harm is likely to befall you for so acting. Take great pains to see that your selfishness is undetected by those who might harm you'.

But, at this point our hypothetical rational egoist would need to consider the reply: 'You will regret acting this way. The pangs of conscience will be severe, your superego will punish you. Like Plato's tyrant you will be a miserable, disordered man. Your very mental health will be endangered.'

Imperceptibly drawing nearer to a desert-island example, the egoist might reply, 'But the phrase "mental health" is used to describe those well adjusted people who keep straight on the tracks no matter what. I don't intend to be "healthy" *in that sense*. And, I do not recognize the *authority* of conscience. My conscience is just the internalized demands of Father and Tribe. But why should I assent to those demands, when it doesn't serve my interests? They are irrational, compulsive moralistic demands, and I shall strive to free myself from them'.

To this it might be countered, 'Granted that conscience has no moral or even rational authority over *you*, you unfortunate man, but practically speaking, you cannot break these bonds so easily. Consciously you may recognize their lack of authority but unconsciously they have and always will continue to have—in spite of all your ratiocination—a dominating grip on you. If you flaunt them, go against them, ignore them, it will cost you your peace of mind, you will pay in psychic suffering, happiness will be denied you. But as a rational egoist happiness is supposedly your goal. And it is wishful thinking to think some psychiatrist will or can take you around this corner. Neither psychoanalysis nor any other kind of therapy can obliterate the "voice of the superego". It can at best diminish its demands when they are *excessive*. Your conditioning was too early and too pervasive to turn your back on it now. If you are rational you will not struggle in such a wholesale fashion against these ancient, internalized demands. Thus, you should not act without regard to the dictates of morality if you really want to be happy'.

It is at this stage that the rational egoist is likely to use his visa to Desert Island. He might say: 'But if I had the power of Gyges and that power included the power to still the nagging voice of my superego, would it not then be reasonable for me to always act in my own self-interest no matter what the effect on others? If there were some non-harmful pill—some moral tranquilizer—that I could take that would "kill" my conscience but allow me to retain my prudence and intelligence why then, under those circumstances, should I act morally rather than selfishly? What good reason is there for me in that situation to act morally if I don't want to?'

It is not sufficient to be told that if most people had Gyges' ring (or its modern, more streamlined, equivalent) they would go on acting as they do now. The question is not 'What would most people do if they had Gyges' ring?' or even 'What would I do if I had Gyges' ring?' The question is rather, 'What should I do?'. At this point can *reasons* be found which would convince an intelligent person that even in this kind of situation, he ought to act morally? That is, would it serve his "true interests" (as Plato believes) for him to be moral, even in the event these conditions obtained?

It is just here, I believe, that subjectivism quite legitimately raises its ugly head. If the above desert-island situation did in fact obtain, I think we would have to say that whether it would or would not be in your "true interests" to be moral or non-moral would depend on the sort of person you are. With the possible exception of a few St. Anthonys, we are, as a matter *of fact*, partly egoistic and partly other-regarding in our behaviour. There can be no complete non-personal, objective justification for acting morally rather than non-morally. In certain circumstances a person of one temperament would find it in his interests to act one way and a person of another temperament to act in another. We have two policies of action to choose from, with distinct criteria of appropriateness, and which policy of action will make us happy will depend on the sort of person we *happen* to be.

It is here that many of us feel the "existential bite" of our question. Students, who are reasonably bright and not a little versed in the ways of the world, are often (and rightly) troubled by the successive destruction of first psychological egoism and then ethical egoism. They come to see that individual egoism can't be a moral view, but they feel somehow cheated; somehow, in some way, they sense that something has been put over on them. And I think there is a point to this rather common and persistent feeling and I have tried, in effect, to show what this is. I would *not*, of course, claim that it is always the "Why-should-I-be-moral?" question that troubles as a reflective student at this juncture but frequently, like Glaucon and Adeimantus, the student wans to know why, as a solitary, flesh and blood individual, he should be moral. He *feels* that he should be moral, but is he somehow being duped? He wants a *reason* that will be a good and sufficient reason for his being moral, quite apart from *his* feelings or attitudes about the matter. He does not want to be in the position of finally having to decide, albeit after reflection, what sort of person to strive to be. It seems to me that the subjectivists are right in suggesting that this is just what he finally can't avoid doing, that he doesn't have and can't have *the kind* of objectivity he demands here. We need not have existentialist dramatics here, but we do need to recognize the logical and practical force of this point. Most rationalistic and theological ethical theories seem to me mythmaking devices to disguise this *prima facie* uncomfortable fact.

VI

But need we despair of the rationality of the moral life once we have dug out and correctly placed this irreducible element of choice in reasoning about human conduct? Perhaps some will despair but since it is not the job of a philosopher to be a kind of universal Nannie I don't think he need concern himself to relieve this despair. But, I think, if he will remind people of the exact point on the logical map where this subjectivism correctly enters and make them once more aware of the map as a whole they will—now able to see the forest as well as the trees—be less inclined to despair about the rationality of their acting morally. If one is willing to reason morally, nothing we have said here need upset the objectivity and rationality of moral grading criteria. More importantly here, to admit subjectivism at this point does not at all throw into doubt the Hobbesian defense of the value of morality as a social practice. It only indicates that *in the situation* in which an *individual* is 1) very unlikely to be caught, 2) so rationally in control that he will be very unlikely to develop habits which would lead to his punishment, and 3) is free from the power of his conscience, it might, just might (if he were a certain kind of person) make him happier to be non-moral than moral. But this is not the usual bad fellow we meet on the streets and the situation is anything but typical.

A recognition of the irrelevance of desert-island examples will provide further relief from moral anxiety, over such subjectivism. Critics of utilitarianism invent situations in which a social practice is, as we use moral language, regarded as obligatory even though there is no advantage in acting in accordance with it in this particular kind of circumstance. They construct desert-island examples and then crucify the utilitarian with them. They point out, for example, that promises made on desert islands to a dying man to dispose of his effects in a certain way are considered obligatory even if it is clear that 1) some other disposal of his effects would be more beneficial and 2) that there is no reasonable chance that the breach in trust would be detected. The usual utilitarian answer is that disregarding promises of this sort would weaken our moral character; and, in addition, we cannot be quite sure that such a breach in trust would not be detected or that it would really do more good than harm. Further, to ignore a promise of this sort is bad, for it would tend to weaken the utility of the social *practice* of promise-keeping.

Nowell-Smith, however, is quite correct in saying: "The relentless desert-islander can always break such utilitarian moves by adding stipulations to the terms of the original problem".[33] That is, he will say to the utilitarian, 'But what would you say *if* breaking a trust in situations of this type would not weaken the utility of the practice of promise-keeping? Surely it is *intelligible* to suppose that such acts would not weaken people's moral fiber, would not be detected, and would not do more total good than harm. To this the utilitarian can only say that this statement of the desert-islander is a very "iffy proposition", indeed. Nowell-Smith rightly remarks: "The force of these desert-island arguments . . . depends expressly on the improbability of the case supposed".[34] "It is difficult to assess their force precisely because the case *is* improbable and therefore not catered for in our ordinary language".[35] The language of human conduct has the structure it has because the world is as it is and not otherwise. If people and things were very different, the structure of moral codes and the uses of evaluative language presumably would be different. The very form of our talk about human conduct "reflects empirical truths that are so general and obvious that we can afford to ignore exceptions".[36] If through desert-island examples we withdraw that pervasive con-

textual background it is difficult to know what is the logically proper thing to say. The logic of the language of human conduct did not develop with such wildly improbable situations in view. It, after all, has a wide range of distinct, practical uses, and it only has application in a certain type of setting. If one of these desert-island situations were to obtain, we would have a good reason, as Wittgenstein clearly saw, to make a linguistic stipulation, that is, we would have to decide what is to be *said* here and our linguistic decision would indeed be an intervention in the world, it would indeed have normative import. But it is neither possible nor necessary that we make all such stipulations in advance and we can hardly reasonably accuse the language of conduct of inadequacy because it does not cater to desert-island cases. It would be like saying that "the language of voting" is inadequate because it does not tell us what to do in a situation in which a senior class, consisting of a thousand, tries to elect a president from four candidates and each time a vote is taken each candidate gets exactly 250 votes. This indeed is a logical possibility, but that *this* logical possibility is not considered in setting out the procedures for voting does not at all indicate an inadequacy in our voting procedures.

Our "Gyges' ring situations" are just such desert-island cases. In fact, Nowell-Smith is quite correct in remarking that the Gyges' ring example in the *Republic* is a paradigm of all such desert-island arguments.

'Would I be happier if I were intelligently selfish in a situation in which I could free myself from guilt feelings, avoid punishment, loss of love, contempt of family and friends, social ostracism, etc.?'. To ask this is to ask a desert-island question. Surely we can and do get away with occasional selfish acts—though again note the usual burden of guilt—but given the world as it is, a deliberate, persistent though cunning policy of selfishness is very

---

[33] P. H. Nowell-Smith, *Ethics,* p. 240.
[34] *Ibid.*
[35] *Ibid.*
[36] *Ibid.,* p. 132.

likely to bring on guilt feelings, punishment, estrangement, contempt, ostracism and the like. A clever man might avoid one or another of these consequences but it would be very unlikely that he could avoid them all or even most of them. And it is truistic to remark that we all want companionship, love, approval, comfort, security and recognition. It is very unlikely that the consistently selfish man can get those things he wants. At this point, it may be objected: 'But suppose someone doesn't want those things, then what are we to say?'. But this is only to burgeon forth with another desert-island example. The proper thing to reply is that people almost universally are not that way and that in reasoning about whether I should or should not be selfish, I quite naturally appeal to certain very pervasive facts (including facts about attitudes) and do not, and need not, normally, try to find an answer that would apply to all conceivable worlds and all *possible* human natures. To think that one must do so is but to exhibit another facet of the genuinely irrational core of rationalism.

VII

It seems to me that the above considerations count heavily against adopting a thoroughly consistent policy of individual egoism. But do such considerations at all touch the individual who simply, on occasion, when his need is great, acts in a way that is inconsistent with the dictates of morality? Will such a person always be happier—in the long run—if he acts conscientiously or is this a myth foisted on us, perhaps for good social reasons, by our religions and moralities? Are all the situations desert-island situations in which we can reasonably claim that there could be rational men who would be happier if they acted non-morally rather than morally or in which we would have to say that any

decision to act one way rather than another is a matter of arbitrary choice? Are there paradigm cases which establish the subjectivist's case—establish that it is altogether likely that some clear-headed people will be happier if, in some non-desert-island circumstances, they deliberately do what they acknowledge is wrong. . . .

Let us examine three *prima facie* cases.

Suppose a man, believing it to be wrong, decides to be unfaithful to his wife when it is convenient, non-explosive and unlikely to be discovered. Usually it is not, on the part of the knight-errant husband, a deliberate and systematic policy, but it might be and sometimes is. Bored husbands sometimes day-dream that this is a return to paradise; that is to say, it might earn, at least in anticipation, a good score in a felicific calculus. In order to make the example sufficiently relevant to the argument, we must exclude those cases in which the husband believes there is nothing wrong in this behavior and/or gives reasons or rationalizations to excuse his behavior. I must also exclude the guilty weak-willed man with the Pauline syndrome. The case demands a man who deliberately—though with sufficiently prudent moderation—commits adultery. It is important for our case that he believes adultery to be immoral. Nonetheless, while believing people ought not to be adulterers, he asks himself, 'Should I continue to live this way anyway? Will I really be happier if I go the way of St. Paul?'. He does not try to universalize his decision. He believes that to choose to remain an adulterer is immoral, but the immoral choice remains for him a live option. Though people may not put all this to themselves so explicitly, such a case is not an impossibility. People may indeed behave in this way. My example is not a desert-island one. I admit there is something odd about my adulterer that might make him seem like a philosophical *papier mâché* figure. There is also something conceptually odd about saying that a man believes x to be wrong and yet, without guilt or ambivalence and without excusing conditions, rationally decides to do x. With good reason we say, 'If he knows it to be wrong or really believes it to be wrong, he will (everything else being equal) try to avoid it'. Still there is a sense in which he could say he believes x to be wrong even though he seeks x. The sense is this: he would not wish that people generally choose or seek x. When this is the case he says 'x is wrong' even though he makes a frank exception of himself without attempting to morally justify this exception. It is important to note that this is a *special* though perfectly intelligible use on my part of 'He believes it to be wrong'. While it withdraws one essential feature, namely that non-universalizable exceptions are inadmissible, it retains something of the general sense of what we mean by calling something morally wrong.

Yet, for the sake of the argument at least, let us assume that we do not have a desert-island case. Assuming then that there are such men, is their doing what is wrong here also for *them* the personally disadvantageous thing? Can any individual who acts in such a way ever be reasonably sure he won't be caught—that one of the girls won't turn up and make trouble, that he won't run into an acquaintance at the wrong time? Even if these seem to be remote possibilities, can he ever be free enough from them in his dream life? And if his dreams are bothersome, if he develops a rather pervasive sense of uneasiness, is it really worth it? He must again consider the power of his conscience (superego) even though he rationally decided to reject its authority. Will it give him peace? Will the fun be worth the nagging of his conscience? It is difficult to *generalize* here. Knowledge of oneslef, of people, of human psychology and of imaginative literature is all extremely relevant here. I think the individual egoist can correctly argue that it is not *always* clear that he would be unhappier in such a situation if he did what was wrong. A great

deal depends on the individual and the exact particular circumstance, but the moralist who says it is never, or hardly ever, the case that a person will be happier by pursuing a selfish policy certainly overstates his case.

Let me now take a different paradigm for which much the same thing must be said. It is important to consider this new case because most people would label this man a "veritable moral beast" yet he stands to gain very much from acting immorally. The case I have in mind is that of a very intelligent, criminally experienced, well-equipped, non-masochistic but ruthless kidnapper. He is a familiar type in the movies and thrillers. Now, Hollywood to the contrary, why should it not sometimes be the case that such a kidnapper will be happier if he is successful? Indeed, he may have a murder on his hands but the stakes are very high and when he is successful he can live in luxury for the rest of his life. With good reason our *folklore* teaches he would not be happier. It is of the utmost value to society that such behavior be strenuously disapproved. And given the long years of conditioning we are all subject to, it remains the case that most people (placed in the position of the kidnapper) would not be happier with the successful completion of such a kidnapping if it involved murdering the kidnapped child. But then most people are not kidnappers. They have very different personalities. Such brutalities together with fear of detection would haunt them and it is probably the case that they also haunt many kidnappers. But if the kidnapper were utterly non-moral, very, very clever, etc., why wouldn't *he* really be happier? He could live in comfort; he could marry, have children and attain companionship, love, approval, etc. 'Well', we would say, 'his conscience would always bother him'. But, particularly with modern medical help, which he could now well afford, would it bother him enough? 'Well, there would always be the awful possibility of detection and the punishment that might follow'.

But, if the stakes were high enough and if he were clever enough might it not be better than a life of dull routine, poverty or near poverty? And think of the "kicks" he would get in outwitting the police? We all have a little adventure in our souls. 'But'—the dialogue might go on—'if he were intelligent enough to pull off this job successfully, he would certainly be intelligent enough to avoid poverty and to avoid making his living in a routine, boring way'. The dialogue could go on interminably but I think it is clear enough again that even here there is no one decisive, clearcut answer to be given. The case for morality here is stronger than in the previous paradigm, but it is still not decisive. Yet there are paradigms in which doing what is clearly wrong (and understood by the individual in question to be wrong) is in the rational self-interest of some individuals. Our first more typical paradigm is not completely clear, but the following third and less typical paradigm given by Hospers is a clearer example of a case in which it is in a man's self-interest not to do what is right.

There is a young bank clerk who decides, quite correctly, that he can embezzle $50,000 without his identity ever being known. He fears that he will be underpaid all his life if he doesn't embezzle, that life is slipping by without his ever enjoying the good things of this world; his fiancee will not marry him unless he can support her in the style to which she is accustomed, he wants to settle down with her in a suburban house, surround himself with books, stereo hi-fi set, and various *objects d'art*, and spend a pleasant life, combining culture with sociability; he never wants to commit a similar act again. He does just what he wanted to do: he buys a house, invests the remainder of the money wisely so as to enjoy a continued income from it, marries the girl, and lives happily ever after; he doesn't worry about detection because he has arranged things so that no blame could fall on him; anyway he doesn't have a worrisome disposition and is not one to dwell on past misdeeds; he is blessed with a happy temperament, once

his daily comforts are taken care of. The degree of happiness he now possesses would not have been possible had he not committed the immoral act.[37]

Clearly it was in his rational self-interest to do what is wrong.

Someone might claim that it is too much to expect that he could arrange things so that no blame would fall on him. This could happen only in desert-island type situations. But unless we began to have the doubts characteristic of traditional epistemologists about 'the blame could not fall on him', there are plenty of cases in which crimes of this general sort are carried out with success. There is no good reason to think such an individual in such circumstances would not be happier.

But it is also crucial to recall that our cases here only involve certain specific acts that do go against the requirements of morality. The cultured despiser of morals, described in the last section, is a man who rejects the authority of *all* moral considerations and systematically pursues a selfish policy in all things. Thus, we would need to project risks similar to those of the wayward husband and the kidnapper through his entire life. But are there really any realistic paradigms for such generalized egoistic behavior that would hold any attraction at all for a rational man? I doubt very much that there are. Yet, our three paradigms indicate that for *limited patterns of behavior*, no decisively good reasons can be given to some individuals that would justify their doing the moral thing in such a context. (It would be another thing again if they repeatedly acted in that way. Here the case for morality would be much stronger.)

In pointing this out, the subjectivist is on solid ground. But it is also true that even here it is not just a matter of "paying your money and taking your choice", for what it would be rational for you to do

[37] John Hospers, *Human Conduct: An Introduction to the Problems of Ethics*, pp. 180–81.

depends, in large measure, on what sort of person you are and on the particular circumstances into which you are cast.

There is a further more general and more important consideration. Even if large groups of people read and accepted my argument as correct, even if it got favorable billing by Luce publications, it still remains very unlikely that kidnapping and crime would increase one iota. For the most part, people get their standards not from ethical treatises or even scriptural texts or homely sayings but by idealizing and following the example of some living person or persons. Morality or immorality does not typically (or perhaps even ever) arise from precept or argument but from early living examples. The foundations of one's character are developed through unconscious imitation way before perplexity over morality can possibly arise. Unless a man is already ready to run amuck, he will not be morally derailed by the recognition that in deliberating about how to act one finally must simply decide what sort of a person one wishes to be. Since most people are not ready to go amuck, the truth of my argument will not cause a housing shortage in hell.

There are further considerations that will ameliorate this subjectivism. It seems reasonable to say that in different societies the degree of subjectivism will vary. All societies are interested in preserving morality; they have a quite natural and rationally justifiable vested interest in their moral codes. Now, as societies gain a greater know-how, and particularly as they come to understand man and the structure of society better, it seems reasonable to as-

sume they can more effectively protect their vested interests. In other words, I believe, it is reasonable to assume that it will become increasingly difficult to be successfully non-moral as a society gains more knowledge about itself and the world.

This also poses a puzzle for the intelligent individual egoist. In such advancing culture-studying cultures, it will become increasingly more difficult for *him* to be non-moral. But it is in his rational interest for *others* to be moral so he should not oppose this more efficient enforcement of morality. And if he does choose to oppose it, it is very probable that he will suffer a fate not unlike Camus' stranger.

More generally, it will not be in the interest of the individual egoist to oppose morality and even if he, and others like him, do find that it pays to act non-morally their failure to act morally will of necessity be so moderate that the set of social practices that help make up morality will not be disturbed in any extensive way. (This puts the point very modestly). And, if too many go the way of the rational individual egoist, then it will no longer pay to be non-moral, so that large numbers of individual egoists, if they are rational, will become men of good morals.

Though the plain man committed to the moral point of view will probably not jump with joy over this state of affairs, I think the considerations in the last three paragraphs give him genuine grounds for being sanguine. The subjectivism I have pin-pointed need not create a generation of "despairing philosophers" even if my argument is accepted as completely sound.

Suggested Further Readings

I. BOOKS

Aiken, Henry D. *Reason and Conduct*. New York: Knopf, 1962.

Anshen, Ruth. *Moral Principles in Action*. New York: Harper & Row, 1952.

Ayer, A. J. *Language, Truth, and Logic*. London: Victor Gollancz, 1936. Rev. ed., 1946.

————. *Philosophical Essays*. London: Macmillan, 1955.

Baier, Kurt. *The Meaning of Life*. Canberra, Australia: Commonwealth Government Printer, 1957.

————. *The Moral Point of View*. Ithaca, N.Y.: Cornell University Press, 1958.

Bayles, Michael D., ed. *Contemporary Utilitarianism*. Anchor Books, Doubleday, 1968.

Benn, Stanley I., and Richard Peters. *Social Principles and the Democratic State*. London: G. Allen, 1959. Published in the U.S.A. by Collier Books under the title *Principles of Political Thought*.

Binkley, Luther J. *Contemporary Ethical Theories*. New York: Citadel, 1961.

Blanshard, Brand. *Reason and Goodness*. London: G. Allen, 1961.

Bradley, Francis H. *Ethical Studies*. (1876). New York: Oxford University Press, 1927.

Brandt, Richard. *Ethical Theory*. Englewood Cliffs, N.J.: Prentice-Hall, 1959.

Brentano, F. *The Origin of the Knowledge of Right and Wrong*. Westminster, Eng.: Constable, 1902.

Britton, Karl. *John Stuart Mill*. Baltimore: Pelican Books, 1959.

Broad, C. D. *Five Types of Ethical Theory*. (1935) New York: Humanities Press, 1960 (Littlefield, Adams & Co., reprint).

————. *Ethics and the History of Philosophy*. New York: Humanities Press, 1952.

Campbell, C. A. *In Defense of Free Will*. Inaugural Lecture, University of Glasgow.

Carritt, Edgar F. *Ethical and Political Thinking*. New York: Oxford University Press, 1947.

————. *Morals and Politics*. New York: Oxford University Press, 1935.

————. *The Theory of Morals*. New York: Oxford University Press, 1928.

De Burgh, W. G. *From Morality to Religion*. London: Macdonald & Evans, 1938.

De George, Richard, ed. *Ethics and Society*. London: Macmillan, 1968.

Dewey, John. *Human Nature and Conduct*. New York: Holt, 1922. (Also Modern Library.)

————. *The Theory of Valuation*. International Encyclopedia of Unified Science, University of Chicago Press, 1939.

————. *Experience and Nature*. New York: Norton, 1929.

————. *The Public and Its Problems*. (1927) Denver: Swallow, 1957.

Dewey, John, and Tufts, James. *Ethics*. Rev. ed. New York: Holt, 1932.

Dickinson, G. Lowes. *The Meaning of Good*. (1906) New York: Dutton, 1921.

Edel, Abraham. *Ethical Judgment*. New York: Free Press, 1955.

Edwards, Paul. *The Logic of Moral Discourse*. New York: Free Press, 1955.

Ewing, A. C. *The Morality of Punishment*. London: Routledge & Kegan Paul, 1929.

————. *The Definition of Good*. New York: Macmillan, 1947.

————. *Ethics*. New York: Macmillan, 1953.

————. *The Individual, the State, and World Government*. New York: Macmillan, 1947.

————. *Second Thoughts on Moral Philosophy*. London: Routledge, 1959.

Farrer, Austin. *The Freedom of the Will*. New York: Scribner, 1958.

Feinberg, Joel, ed. *Moral Concepts*. New York: Oxford University Press, 1970.

Field, Guy C. *Moral Theory*. London: Methuen, 1921.

————. *Political Theory*. London: Methuen, 1955.

Frankena, William K. *Ethics*. Englewood Cliffs, N.J.: Prentice-Hall, 1963.

Fromm, Erich. *Man for Himself*. New York: Rinehart, 1947.

Ginsberg, Morris. *On the Diversity of Morals*. New York: Macmillan, 1956.

Green, Thomas Hill. *Prolegomena to Ethics*. Oxford: Clarendon Press, 1883; 3rd ed., 1890.

————. *Lectures on the Principles of Political Obligation*. (1882) New York: Longmans, 1942.

Grote, J. *An Examination of the Utilitarian Philosophy*. Cambridge: Deighton, Bell & Co., 1870.

Hall, Everett W. *What Is Value?* New York: Humanities Press, 1952.

Halvey, Elie. *The Growth of Philosophic Radicalism*. London: Faber, 1952.

Hampshire, Stuart. *Thought and Action*. London: Chatto & Windus, 1959.

Hare, R. M. *Freedom and Reason*. London: Oxford University Press, 1963.

————. *The Language of Morals*. London: Oxford University Press, 1952.

Hart, H. L. A. *Punishment and Responsibility*. London: Oxford University Press, 1968.

Hartland-Swann, John. *An Analysis of Morals*. London: G. Allen, 1960.

Hartmann, Nicolai. *Ethics*. 3 vols. New York: Macmillan, 1932.

Hazlitt, Henry. *The Foundations of Morality*. Princeton: Van Nostrand, 1964.

Hook, Sidney, ed. *Determinism and Freedom in the Age of Modern Science*. New York: New York University Press, 1958.

Hospers, John. *Human Conduct*. New York: Harcourt, Brace & World, 1961.

Huxley, T. H. and Julian. *Touchstone for Ethics*. New York: Harper, 1947.

Joseph, H. W. B. *Some Problems of Ethics*. Oxford: Clarendon Press, 1931.

Köhler, Wolfgang. *The Place of Value in a World of Fact*. New York: Liveright, 1938.

Körner, Stephen. *Kant*. Baltimore: Pelican Books, 1955.

Laird, John. *A Study in Moral Theory*. London: G. Allen, 1926.

————. *The Idea of Value*. Cambridge: Cambridge University Press, 1929.

————. *An Inquiry into Moral Notions*. London: G. Allen, 1935.

Ladd, John. *The Structure of a Moral Code*. Cambridge, Mass.: Harvard University Press, 1957.

Laslett, Peter, ed. *Philosophy, Politics, and Society*. New York: Macmillan, 1956.

Lecky, W. E. H. *A History of European Morals*. (1866) New York: Braziller, 1955.

Lewis, Clarence I. *An Analysis of Knowledge and Valuation*. LaSalle, Ill.: Open Court, 1946.

Lewis, C. S. *The Abolition of Man*. New York: Macmillan, 1947.

Lewis, H. D. *Morals and Revelation*. London: G. Allen, 1951.

Lyons, David. *Forms and Limits of Utilitarianism*. Oxford: Clarendon Press, 1965.

Mabbott, J. D. *The State and the Citizen*. London: Hutchinson, 1948.

MacIntyre, Alasdair. *A Short History of Ethics*. New York: Macmillan, 1966.

MacIver, Robert M., ed. *The Pursuit of Happiness*. New York: Simon and Schuster, 1955.

Mackinnon, D. M. *A Study in Ethical Theory*. London: Black, 1957.

Madden, Edward H., Handy, Rollo, and Farber, Marvin, eds. *Philosophical Perspectives on Punishment*. Springfield, Ill.: Charles C Thomas, 1968.

Mandelbaum, Maurice. *The Phenomenology of Moral Experience*. New York: Free Press, 1955.

Martineau, James. *Types of Ethical Theory*. Oxford: Clarendon Press, 1885.

Mayo, Bernard. *Ethics and the Moral Life*. New York: St. Martin's, 1958.

Melden, A. I., ed. *Essays in Moral Philosophy*. Seattle, Wash.: University of Washington Press, 1958.

———. *Rights and Right Conduct*. Oxford: Blackwell, 1959.

Montefiore, Alan. *A Modern Introduction to Moral Philosophy*. New York: Praeger, 1959.

Moore, George Edward. *Principia Ethica*. Cambridge: Cambridge University Press, 1903.

———. *Ethics*. London: Oxford University Press, 1911.

———. *Philosophical Studies*. London: Routledge, 1922.

Morris, Herbert, ed. *Freedom and Responsibility: Readings in Philosophy and Law*. Palo Alto: Stanford University Press, 1961.

Murphy, Arthur E. *The Uses of Reason*. New York: Macmillan, 1943.

———. *Reason and the Moral Life*. Englewood Cliffs, N.J.: Prentice-Hall, 1964.

Narveson, Jan. *Morality and Utility*. Baltimore: Johns Hopkins, 1967.

Nelson, Leonard. *A System of Ethics*. New Haven: Yale University Press, 1956.

Niebuhr, Reinhold. *An Interpretation of Christian Ethics*. New York: Harper, 1935.

Nowell-Smith, Patrick H. *Ethics*. Baltimore: Pelican Books, 1954.

Osborne, H. *Foundations of the Philosophy of Value*. Cambridge: Cambridge Univ. Press, 1933.

Parker, DeWitt. *Human Values*. New York: Harper, 1931.

Paton, Herbert James. *The Categorical Imperative*. London: Hutchinson, 1948.

Pepper, Stephen. *The Sources of Value*. Berkeley: University of California Press, 1959.

Perry, David. *The Concept of Pleasure*. The Hague: Mouton, 1967.

Perry, Ralph Barton. *General Theory of Value*. Cambridge, Mass.: Harvard University Press, 1926.

———. *Realms of Value*. Cambridge, Mass.: Harvard University Press, 1954.

———. *Puritanism and Democracy*. New York: Vanguard, 1944.

Plamenatz, John. *The English Utilitarians*. Oxford: Blackwell & Mott, 1958.

Prall, David W. *A Study in the Theory of Value*. University of California Publications in Philosophy, Vol. 3, 1921.

Pratt, James Bissett. *Reason in the Art of Living*. New York: Macmillan, 1950.

Prichard, H. A. *Duty and Interest*. New York: Oxford University Press, 1928.

———. *Moral Obligation*. New York: Oxford University Press, 1950.

Prior, Arthur N. *Logic and the Basis of Ethics*. London: Oxford University Press, 1949.

Rand, Ayn. *The Virtue of Selfishness*. New York: New American Library, 1964.

Raphael, David Daiches. *Moral Judgment*. New York: Macmillan, 1955.

———. *The Moral Sense*. London: Oxford University Press, 1947.

Rashdall, Hastings. *Theory of Good and Evil*. 2 vols. Oxford: Clarendon Press, 1928.

Rees, J. C. *Mill and His Early Critics*. Leicester: University College, 1956.

Rescher, Nicholas. *Distributive Justice: a Constructive Critique of the Utilitarian Theory of Distribution*. Indianapolis: Bobbs-Merrill, 1968.

Rice, Philip Blair. *On the Knowledge of Good and Evil*. New York: Random House, 1955.

Ross, Sir David W. *The Right and the Good*. Oxford: Clarendon Press, 1930.

———. *The Foundations of Ethics*. Oxford: Clarendon Press, 1939.

———. *Kant's Ethical Theory*. Oxford: Clarendon Press, 1954.

Russell, Bertrand. *Authority and the Individual*. New York: Simon and Schuster, 1949.

———. *Human Society in Ethics and Politics*. London: G. Allen, 1955.

———. *John Stuart Mill*. Lecture. London: Oxford University Press, 1955.

Ryle, Gilbert. *Dilemmas*. London: Cambridge University Press, 1956.

Sabine, George H. *History of Political Theory*. (1937) Rev. ed., New York: Holt, 1950.

Santayana, George. *Reason in Morals*. New York: Scribners, 1905.

Schlick, Moritz. *The Problems of Ethics*. Englewood Cliffs, N.J.: Prentice-Hall, 1939.

Schneewind, J. B., ed. *Mill's Ethical Writings*. New York: Collier, 1965.

Selby-Bigge, L. A., ed. *British Moralists*. Oxford: Clarendon Press, 1897. (Indianapolis: Bobbs-Merrill, 1964.)

Sellars, Wilfrid. *Form and Content in Ethical Theory*. Lawrence, Kan.: University of Kansas Press, 1968.

———. "Imperatives, Intentions and the Logic of 'Ought'." In George Nakhnikean and Hector-Neri Castaneda, eds., *Morality and the Language of Conduct*. Detroit: Wayne State University Press, 1965.

———. *Science and Metaphysics*. New York: The Humanities Press, 1968.

Sesonske, Alexander. *Value and Obligation*. New York: Oxford University Press, 1964.

Sidgwick, Henry. *The Methods of Ethics*. 7th ed., London: Macmillan, 1901. (Chicago: University of Chicago Press, 1962).

———. *Elements of Politics*. London: Macmillan, 1891.

———. *Lectures on the Ethics of T. H. Green, Herbert Spencer, and J. Martineau*. London: Macmillan, 1902.

———. *An Outline of the History of Ethics*. 6th ed. London: Macmillan, 1931.

Singer, Marcus. *Generalization in Ethics*. New York: Random House, 1961.

Smart, J. J. C. *An Outline of a System of Utilitarian Ethics*. Melbourne: Melbourne University Press, 1961.

Spencer, Herbert. *The Data of Ethics*. (1888) New York: McKay.

Stace, Walter Terence. *The Concept of Morals*. New York: Macmillan, 1937.

Stephen, Sir Leslie. *The English Utilitarians*. London: Duckworth, 1900. 3 vols.

Stephen, James Fitzjames. *Liberty, Equality, Fraternity*. Cambridge: Cambridge University Press, 1967.

Stevenson, Charles L. *Ethics and Language*. New Haven: Yale University Press, 1944.

———. *Facts and Values*. New Haven: Yale University Press, 1966.

Taylor, Paul. *Normative Discourse*. Englewood Cliffs, N.J.: Prentice-Hall, 1961.

Toulmin, Stephen. *The Place of Reason in Ethics*. Cambridge: Cambridge University Press, 1950.

Urban, Wilbur M. *Fundamentals of Ethics*. New York: Holt, 1930.

Urmson, J. O. *The Emotive Theory of Ethics*. London: Hutchinson, 1968.

Von Wright, George H. *The Varieties of Goodness*. London: Routledge, 1963.

———. *The Logic of Preference*. Edinburgh: Edinburgh University Press, 1963.

Warnock, Mary. *Ethics since 1900*. London: Oxford University Press, 1960.

Warnock, G. J. *Contemporary Moral Philosophy*. London: Macmillan, 1967.

Westermarck, Edvard A. *Ethical Relativity*. New York: Harcourt, Brace, 1932.

———. *Origin and Development of the Moral Ideas*. London: Macmillan, 1906.

Ziff, Paul. *Semantic Analysis*. Ithaca: Cornell University Press, 1960.

Zink, Sidney. *The Concepts of Ethics*. New York: St. Martin's, 1962.

II. ARTICLES AND ESSAYS

The following abbreviations are used in this list:

Am. Phil. Q. for *American Philosophical Quarterly*
Arist. Proc. for *Proceedings of the Aristotelian Society*
Arist. Suppl. for *Aristotelian Society, Supplementary Volume*
Jl. Phil. for *The Journal of Philosophy*
Phil. and Phen. Res. for *Philosophy and Phenomenological Research*
Phil Q. for *Philosophical Quarterly*
Phil. Rev. for *The Philosophical Review*
Phil. Stud. for *Philosophical Studies*

Abelson, Raziel. "Because I Want to'." *Mind*, 74, 1965.

Abraham, L. "The Logic of Ethical Intuitionism." *Ethics*, 44, 1933–4.

Aiken, Henry David. "Definitions of Value and the Moral Ideal." *J. Phil.*, 42, 1945.

———. "Definitions, Factual Premises and Ethical Conclusions." *Phil. Rev.*, 61, 1952.

———. Review of C. L. Stevenson's *Ethics and Language*. *Jl. Phil.*, 42, 1945.

———. "A Pluralistic Analysis of the Ethical 'Ought'." *J. Phil.*, 58, 1951.

———. "Evaluation and Obligation." *Jl. Phil.*, 47, 1950.

———. "Emotive 'Meanings' and Ethical Terms." *Jl. Phil.*, 41, 1944.

———. "The Levels of Moral Discourse." *Ethics*, 62, 1952.

Alexander, P. "Rational Behavior and Psychoanalytic Explanation." *Mind*, 71, 1962.

Alexander, Samuel. "Is the Distinction between 'Is' and 'Ought' Ultimate and Irreducible?" *Arist. Proc.*, Old Series, Vol. 2, No. 1, 1892.

———. "Morality as an Art." *Journal of Philosophical Studies*, 3, 1928.

A.P.A. Symposium. "Ethics and the Concept of Action." *Jl. Phil.*, 62, 1965.

Ardal, P. S. "Motives, Intentions, and Responsibility." *Phil. Q.*, 15, 1965.

Armstrong, K. G. "The Retributivist Hits Back." *Mind*, 70, 1961.

Atkinson, R. F. "J. S. Mill's 'Proof' of the Principle of Utility." *Philosophy*, 32, 1957.

Ayer, Alfred J. "The Nature of Moral Judgments." *Horizon*, 1948.

———. "On the Analysis of Moral Judgments." *Philosophical Essays*. London: Macmillan, 1955.

———. "The Principle of Utility." *Philosophical Essays*. London: Macmillan, 1955.

Baier, Kurt. "Good Reasons" and "Proving a Moral Judgment." *Philosophical Studies*, 4, 1953.

———. "Is Punishment Retributive?" *Analysis*, 16, 1955.

———. "Moral Obligations." *Am. Phil. Q.*, 3, 1966.

Baker, G. P. and P. M. Hacker. "Rules, Definitions, and the Naturalistic Fallacy." *Am. Phil. Q.*, 3, 1966.

Barnes, Winston H. F. "Ethics without Propositions." *Arist. Suppl.*, 22, 1948.

Baylis, Charles A. "Grading, Values, and Choice." *Mind*, 67, 1958.

Beardsley, Elizabeth L. "Determinism and Moral Perspectives." *Phil. and Phen. Res.*, 21, 1960.

———. "Moral Worth and Moral Credit." *Phil. Rev.*, 66, 1957.

Bell, D. R. "Impartiality and Intellectual Virtue." *Phil. Q.*, 15, 1965.

Benn, Stanley I. "An Approach to the Problems of Punishment." *Philosophy*, 33, 1958.

Black, Max. "Some Questions About Emotive Meaning." *Phil. Rev.*, 57, 1948.

Blackstone, William T. "Principle of Equality." *Jl. Phil.*, 62, 1965.

Blake, Ralph Mason. "The Ground of Moral Obligation." *Ethics*, 37, 1926–7.

Blanshard, Brand. "The Impasse in Ethics and a Way Out." *University of California Publications in Philosophy*, 28, 1954.

Bohnert, Herbert G. "The Semiotic Status of Commands." *Philosophy of Science*, 1946.

———. "Lewis' Attribution of Value to Objects." *Phil. Stud.*, 1, 1950.

Braithwaite, R. B. "Belief and Action." *Arist. Suppl.*, 20, 1946.

Branden, Nathaniel. "Rational Egoism." *The Personalist*, 51, 1970.

Brandt, Richard B. "An Emotional Theory of the Judgment of Moral Worth." *Ethics*, 52, 1941–2.

———. "A Utilitarian Theory of Blame." *Phil. Rev.*, 78, 1969.

———. "The Emotive Theory of Ethics." *Phil. Rev.*, 59, 1950.

———. "The Concepts of Obligation and Duty." *Mind*, 73, 1964.

———. "The Status of Empirical Assertion Theories in Ethics." *Mind*, 61, 1952.

———. "Toward a Credible Form of Utilitarianism." In George Nakhnikian and **H.** Castaneda, eds., *Morality and the Language of Conduct*. Detroit: Wayne State University Press, 1963.

Braybrooke, David. "The Choice between Utilitarianisms." *Am. Phil. Q.*, 4, 1967.

Britton, Karl. "Utilitarianism: The Appeal to a First Principle." *Arist. Proc.*, 60, 1959–60.

Broad, C. D. "Is 'Goodness' the Name of a Simple Non-natural Quality?" *Arist. Proc.*, 34, 1933–4.

———. "Conscience and Conscientious Action." *Philosophy*, 15, 1940.

———. "Certain Features in Moore's Ethical Doctrines." In P. A. Schlipp, ed., *The Philosophy of G. E. Moore*, Northwestern University Press, 1942.

———. Review of Julian Huxley's Evolutionary Ethics. *Mind*, 53, 1944.

———. "Some of the Main Problems of Ethics." *Philosophy*, 21, 1946.

———. "Hägerstrom's Account of Sense of Duty and Certain Allied Experiences." *Philosophy*, 26, 1951.

———. Review of H. A. Prichard's *Moral Obligation*. *Mind*, 60, 1951.

———. "G. E. Moore's Latest Published Views on Ethics." *Mind*, 70, 1961.

Brodbeck, May. "Towards a Naturalistic 'Non-naturalistic' Ethic." *Phil. Stud.*, 2, 1951.

Brown, Charles D. "Fallacies in Taylor's 'Fatalism.' " *J. Phil.*, 62, 1965.

Browning, D. "The Moral Act." *Phil. Q.*, 12, 1962.

Brown, Stuart M. "Duty and the Production of Good." *Phil. Rev.*, 61, 1952.

Brunton, J. A. "Egoism and Morality." *Phil. Q.*, 6, 1956.

Buchler, Justus. "Russell and the Principles of Ethics." In P.A. Schlipp, ed., *The Philosophy of G. E. Moore*. Evanston, Ill.: Northwestern University Press, 1942.

Burns, J. H. "Utilitarianism and Democracy." *Phil. Q.*, 9, 1959.

Campbell, C. A. "Is Free-will a Pseudo-Problem?" *Mind*, 60, 1951.

———. "Moral Intuition and the Principle of Self-realization." Henrietta Hertz Lecture, 1948. *Proceedings of the British Academy*, 34, 1948.

———. "Reason and the Problem of Suffering." *Philosophy*, 10, 1935.

Carritt, Edgar F. "Thinking Makes It So." *Arist. Proc.*, 30, 1929–30.

Castaneda, Hector-Neri. "Ethics and Logic: Stevensonian Emotivism Revisited." *Jl. Phil.*, 64, 1967.

———. "The Logic of Change, Action, and Norms." *Jl. Phil.*, 62, 1965.

Charvet, John. "Criticism and Punishment." *Mind*, 75, 1966.

Chisholm, Roderick M. "He Could Not Have Done Otherwise." *Jl. Phil.*, 64, 1967.

———. "The Ethics of Requirement." *Am. Phil. Q.*, 1, 1964.

——— and Ernest Sosa. "On the Logic of 'Intrinsically Better'." *Am. Phil. Q.*, 3, 1966.

Clarke, M. "A Phenomenological System of Ethics." *Philosophy*, 6, 1931.

Cooper, Neil. "Two Concepts of Morality." *Philosophy*, 41, 1966.

Cox, J. W. R. "Commending and Describing." *Phil. Q.*, 11, 1961.

Cross, R. C. "The Emotive Theory of Ethics." Symposium. *Arist. Suppl.*, 22, 1948.

Dallmayr, Fred R. "Functionism, Justice, and Equality." *Ethics*, 78, 1967–8.

DeBurgh, W. G. "Right and Good." *Philosophy*, 6, 1931.

Dennes, W. R. "Conflict." *Phil. Rev.*, 55, 1946.

Dewey, John. "The Logic of Judgments of Practice." *Jl. Phil.*, 12, 1915.

———. "The Objects of Valuation." *Jl. Phil.*, 15, 1918.

———. "Valuation and Experimental Knowledge." *Phil. Rev.*, 31, 1922.

———. "The Meaning of 'Value'." *Jl. Phil.*, 22, 1925.

———. "Valuation, Judgments, and Immediate Quality." *Jl. Phil.*, 40, 1943.

———. "Further as to Valuation as Judgment." *Jl. Phil.*, 40, 1943.

Diggs, B. J. "Rules and Utilitarianism." *Am. Phil. Q.*, 1, 1964.

———. "A Technical Ought." *Mind*, 69, 1960.

Donagan, Alan. "Is There a Credible Form of Utilitarianism?" *Contemporary Utilitarianism*. Edited by Michael D. Bayles. New York: Anchor Books, Doubleday, 1968.

Downie, R. S. "Can Governments Be Held Morally Responsible?" *Phil. Q.*, 11, 1961.

———. "Forgiveness." *Phil. Q.*, 15, 1965.

Doyle, James F. "Justice and Legal Punishment." *Philosophy*, 42, 1967.

Duncan-Jones, A. E. "Notes for a Treatise on Ethics." *Arist. Proc.*, 44, 1943–4.

———. "Intention, Motive, and Responsibility." Symposium. *Arist. Suppl.*, 19, 1945.

———. "Freedom: an Illustrative Puzzle." *Arist. Proc.*, 39, 1938–9.

———. "Ethical Words and Ethical Facts." *Mind*, 42, 1933.

———. Review of C. L. Stevenson's *Ethics and Language*. *Mind*, 54, 1945.

———. "Utilitarianism and Rules." *Phil. Q.*, 7, 1957.

———. "Performance and Promise." *Phil. Q.*, 14, 1964.

Duncker, K. "Ethical Relativity." *Mind*, 48, 1939.

———. "Pleasure, Emotion, and Striving." *Phil. and Phen. Res.*, 1, 1940.

Dworkin, G., and Blumenfeld, D. "Punishment for Intentions." *Mind*, 75, 1966.

Edel, Abraham, and Dryer, Douglas B. "Ethical Reasoning." Symposium. *American Philosophical Association, Eastern Division Proceedings*, Vol. 2, 1953.

Edgley, R. "Practical Reason." *Mind*, 74, 1965.

Ekstein, Rudolf. "Psychological Laws and Human Freedom." *Journal of Social Psychology*, Vol. 25, 1947.

Ellin, Joseph. "Wasserstrom and Feinberg on Human Rights." *Jl. of Phil.*, 62, 1965.

Emmons, D. "Refuting the Egoist." *The Personalist*, 50, 1969.

Ewing, Alfred C. "Can We Act against Our Strongest Desire?" *Monist*, 44, 1934.

———. "The Rights of the Individual against the State." *Revue Internationale de Philosophie*, Special Issue, August 1948.

———. "What Would Happen if Everybody Acted Like Me?" *Philosophy*, 28, 1953.

———. "Utilitarianism." *Ethics*, 58, 1958.

Ezorsky, Gertrude. "*Ad Hominem* Morality." *Journal of Philosophy*, 63, 1966.

Falk, W. D. " 'Ought' and Motivation." *Arist. Proc.*, 48, 1947–8.

———. "Goading and Guiding." *Mind*, 62, 1953.

———. "Obligation and Rightness." *Philosophy*, 20, 1945.

———. "Intention, Motive, and Responsibility." Symposium. *Arist. Suppl.*, 19, 1945.

Feigl, Herbert. "De Principiis Non Est Disputandum." In Max Black, ed., *Philosophical Analysis*. Ithaca: Cornell University Press, 1950.

Feinberg, Joel. "Duties, Rights, and Claims." *Am. Phil. Q.*, 3, 1966.

Field, Guy C. "Kant's First Moral Principle." *Mind*, 41, 1932.

Findlay, J. N. "Morality by Convention." *Mind*, 53, 1944.

———. "The Justification of Attitudes." *Mind*, 63, 1954.

Fingerette, Herbert. "Responsibility." *Mind*, 75, 1966.

Firth, Roderick. "Ethical Absolutism and the Ideal Observer." *Phil. and Phen. Res.*, 12, 1952.

Fotion, N. "Range-Rules in Moral Contexts." *Mind*, 72, 1963.

———. "Wickedness." *Phil. Q.*, 11, 1961.

Frankena, William K. "Obligation and Value in the Ethics of G. E. Moore." In P. A. Schlipp, ed., *The Philosophy of G. E. Moore*. Evanston, Ill.: Northwestern Univ. Press, 1942.

———. "Ewing's Case Against Naturalistic Theories of Value." *Phil. Rev.*, 57, 1948.

———. "Arguments for Non-naturalism About Intrinsic Value." *Phil. Stud.*, 1, 1950.

———. "Obligation and Ability." In Max Black, ed., *Philosophical Analysis*. Ithaca: Cornell University Press, 1950.

Franks, O. S. "Choice." *Arist. Proc.*, 34, 1933–4.

Gallie, W. D. "Free-will and Determinism Yet Again." Lecture. Printer to the Queen's University, Belfast, Northern Ireland, 1957.

Gardiner, Patrick L. "On Assenting to a Moral Principle." *Arist. Proc.*, 55, 1954–5.

Garnett, A. C. "Good Reasons in Ethics: a Revised Conception of Natural Law." *Mind*, 69, 1960.

———. "Relativism and Absolutism in Ethics." *Ethics*, 54, 1943–4.

———. "Deontology and Self-realization." *Ethics*, 51, 1940–1.

———. "Phenomenological Ethics and Self-realization." *Ethics*, 53, 1943.

Garver, J. N. "On the Rationality of Persuading." *Mind*, 69, 1960.

Gauthier, David P. "Moore's Naturalistic Fallacy." *Am. Phil. Q.*, 4, 1967.

———. "Progress and Happiness: a Utilitarian Reconsideration." *Ethics*, 78, 1967–8.

Gewirth, Alan. "Categorical Consistency in Ethics." *Phil. Q.*, 17, 1967.

———. "Meanings and Criteria in Ethics." *Philosophy*, 38, 1963.

———. "Metaphysics and Normative Ethics." *Mind*, 69, 1960.

Ginsberg, Morris. "The Function of Reason in Morals." *Arist. Proc.*, 39, 1938–9.

———. "The Concept of Justice." *Philosophy*, 38, 1963.

Glover, M. R. "Mr. Mabbot on Punishment." *Mind*, 48, 1939.

Golding, Martin; Morris, Herbert; Aiken, H. D.; Bedau, Hugo; Nielsen, Kai; Kaufman, Arnold S.; and Blackstone, W. T. "Human Rights." *The Monist*, 52, 1968.

Gomperz, H. "Some Simple Thoughts on Freedom and Responsibility." *Philosophy*, 12, 1937.

———. "Individual and Collective Responsibility." *Ethics*, 50, 1939–40.

———. "When Does the End Sanctify the Means?" *Ethics*, 54, 1943–4.

Graham, A. C. "Liberty and Equality." *Mind*, 74, 1965.

Griffiths, A. Phillips. "Acting with Reason." *Phil. Q.*, 8, 1958.

———. "Justifying Moral Principles." *Arist. Proc.*, 58, 1957–8.

Haksar, Vinit. "Aristotle and the Punishment of Psychopaths." *Philosophy*, 39, 1964.

———. "The Responsibility of Psychopaths." *Phil. Q.*, 15, 1965.

———. "The Responsibility of Mental Defectives." *Philosophy*, 38, 1963.

Hall, Everett W. "A Categorical Analysis of Value." *Phil. of Science*, 14, 1947.

———. "Stevenson on Disagreement in Attitude." *Ethics*, 58, 1947.

———. "The 'Proof' of Utility in Bentham and Mill." *Ethics*, 60, 1949.

———. "Practical Reason and the Deadlock in Ethics." *Mind*, 64, 1955.

Hampshire, Stuart. "Fallacies in Moral Philosophy." *Mind*, 58, 1949.

———, Maclagan, W. G. and Hare, R. M. "The Freedom of the Will." Symposium. *Arist. Proc. Suppl.*, 25, 1951.

Hancock, R. "A Note on Hare's *The Language of Morals*." *Phil. Q.*, 13, 1963.

Hare, R. M. "Universalizability." *Arist. Proc.*, 55, 1954–5.

Harman, Gilbert H. "Toward a Theory of Intrinsic Value." *Jl. Phil.*, 64, 1967.

Hardy, W. "Ethical Naturalism." Henrietta Hertz Lecture. British Academy Lectures, 1945–6.

Harrison, Jonathan. "Utilitarianism, Universalization, and Our Duty to Be Just." *Arist. Proc.*, 53, 1953.

———. "Can Ethics Do without Propositions?" *Mind*, 59, 1950.

———. "Empiricism in Ethics." *Phil. Q.*, 2, 1952.

———. "Knowing and Promising." *Mind*, 71, 1962.

———. "Kant's Four Examples of the First Formulation of the Categorical Imperative." *Phil. Q.*, 7, 1957.

———. "Moral Talking and Moral Living." *Philosophy*, 38, 1963.

———. "When Is a Principle a Moral Principle?" *Arist. Suppl.*, 28, 1954.

Harrod, R. F. "Utilitarianism Revised." *Mind*, 45, 1936.

Hart, H. L. A. "Prolegomenon to the Principles of Punishment." *Arist. Proc.*, 60, 1959–60.

———. "The Ascription of Responsibility and Rights." *Arist. Proc.*, 49, 1948–9.

Hart, H. L. A.; Brown, Stuart M., Jr.; and Frankena, William K. "Natural Rights." *Phil. Rev.*, 64, 1955.

Harvey, J. W. "The Problem of Guilt." Symposium. *Arist. Suppl.*, 21, 1947.

Hay, William H. "Stevenson and Ethical Analysis." *Phil. Rev.*, 56, 1947.

Henderson, G. P. "Ought Implies Can." *Philosophy*, 41, 1966.

Henson, R. G. "Ethical Relativism and a Paradox About Meaning." *Phil. Q.*, 11, 1961.

Hobart, R. E. (Dickinson Miller) "Free-will as Involving Determinism and Inconceivable without It." *Mind*, 43, 1934.

Holmes, Robert L. "Descriptivism, Supervenience, and Universalizability." *Jl. Phil.*, 63, 1966.

Hospers, John. "Baier and Medlin on Ethical Egoism." *Phil. Stud.*, 12, 1961.

————. "Ethical Egoism." *The Personalist*, 51, 1970.

Hook, Sidney. "A Critique of Ethical Realism." *Ethics*, 40, 1929–30.

Hughes, G. "Motive and Duty." *Mind*, 53, 1944.

Jackson, Reginald. "Practical Reason." *Philosophy*, 17, 1942.

————. "Kant's Distinction between Categorical and Hypothetical Imperatives." *Arist. Proc.*, 43, 1942–3.

————. "Bishop Butler's Refutation of Psychological Hedonism." *Philosophy*, 20, 1945.

Jenkins, J. J. "Motive and Intention." *Phil. Q.*, 15, 1965.

Jensen, O. C. "Responsibility, Freedom, and Punishment." *Mind*, 75, 1966.

Johnson, O. A. "Ethical Intuitionism—a Restatement." *Phil. Q.*, 7, 1957.

Kaplan, Abraham. "Are Ethical Judgments Assertions?" *Phil. Rev.*, 51, 1942.

Kenner, Lionel. "Causality, Determinism, and Freedom of the Will." *Philosophy*, 39, 1964.

Kerner, G. C. "Approvals, Reasons and Moral Argument." *Mind*, 71, 1962.

Kluckhohn, Clyde. "Ethical Relativity." *Jl. Phil.*, 52, 1955.

Kretzmann, Norman. "Desire as Proof of Desirability." *Phil. Q.*, 8, 1958.

Ladd, John. "Ethical Dimensions of the Concept of Action." *Jl. Phil.*, 62, 1965.

————. "Free Will and Voluntary Action." *Phil. and Phen. Res.*, 12, 1952.

————. "Must There Be a Desire to Do One's Duty for Its Own Sake?" in G. Nakhnikian and Hn. Castaneda, *Morality and the Language of Conduct*. Detroit: Wayne State University Press, 1961.

Lamont, W. D. "Duty and Interest." *Philosophy*, 16, 17; 1941, 1942.

————. "Justice: Distributive and Collective." *Philosophy*, 16, 1941.

Lemmon, E. J. and Nowell-Smith, P. H. "Escapism: the Logical Basis of Ethics." *Mind*, 69, 1960.

Laird, John. "Rationalism in Ethics." *Jl. of Phil. Studies*, 4, 1929.

————. "On Doing One's Best." *Philosophy*, 6, 1931.

————. "Other People's Pleasure and One's Own." *Philosophy*, 16, 1941.

Levi, A. W. "The Trouble with Ethics: Values, Method, and the Search for Moral Norms." *Mind*, 70, 1961.

Lewis, H. D. "Obedience to Conscience." *Mind*, 54, 1945.

————. "Does the Good Will Define Its Own Content?" *Ethics*, 58, 1947–8.

————. "Collective Responsibility." *Philosophy*, 23, 1948.

————. "Moral Freedom in Recent Ethics." *Arist. Proc.*, 47, 1947–8.

Lloyd, A. C. "Natural Justice." *Phil. Q.*, 12, 1962.

Lucas, J. R. "Against Equality." *Philosophy*, 40, 1965.

Lukes, S. "Moral Weakness." *Phil. Q.*, 15, 1965.

Mabbott, J. D. "Is Anthropology Relevant to Ethics?" *Arist. Suppl.*, 20, 1946.

————. "True and False in Morals." *Arist. Proc.*, 49, 1948–9.

————. "Free-will and Punishment." In H. D. Lewis, ed., *Contemporary British Philosophy*, Third Series. London: G. Allen, 1956.

————. "Interpretations of Mill's Utilitarianism." *Phil. Q.*, 6, 1956.

————. "Punishment." *Mind*, 48, 1939.

————. "Professor Flew on Punishment." *Philosophy*, 30, 1955.

————. "Moral Rules." *Proceedings of the British Academy*, 39, 1953.

Macdonald, Margaret. "The Language of Political Theory." *Arist. Proc.*, 41, 1940–1.

————. "Natural Rights." *Arist. Proc.*, 47, 1947–8.

MacIntyre, Alasdair. "Imperatives, Reasons for Action, and Morals." *Jl. Phil.*, 62, 1965.

Maclagan, W. T. "Punishment and Retribution." *Philosophy*, 14, 1939.

————. "Respect for Persons as a Moral Principle." In two parts. *Philosophy*, 35, 1960.

Mandelbaum, Maurice. "Determinism and Moral Responsibility." *Ethics*, 70, 1959–60.

Matson, Wallace I. "The Irrelevance of Free-will to Moral Responsibility." *Mind*, 65, 1956.

McCloskey, Herbert. "Restricted Utilitarianism." *Phil. Rev.*, 66, 1957.

————. "A Critique of the Ideals of Liberty." *Mind*, 74, 1965.

————. "A Non-Utilitarian Approach to Punishment." *Inquiry*, 8, 1965.

————. "Mill's Liberalism." *Phil. Q.*, 13, 1963.

————. "Rights." *Phil. Q.*, 15, 1965.

————. "Utilitarian and Retributive Punishment." *Jl. Phil.*, 64, 1967.

McNeilly, F. S. "Pre-moral Appraisals." *Phil. Q.*, 8, 1958.

Medlin, Brian. "Ultimate Principles and Ethical Egoism." *Australasian Journal of Philosophy*, 35, 1957.

Meiland, Jack W. "Motives and Ends." *Phil. Q.*, 13, 1963.

Melden, A. I. "Two Comments on Utilitarianism." *Phil. Rev.*, 60, 1950.

———— and W. K. Frankena. "Human Rights." Symposium. *American Philosophical Assn., Eastern Division Proceedings*, 1, 1952.

Miller, Dickinson. "Moral Truth." *Phil. Stud.*, 1, 1950.

Montefiore, Alan. "Ought and Can." *Phil. Q.*, 8, 1958.

————. "The Meaning of 'Good' and the Act of Commendation." *Phil. Q.*, 17, 1967.

Moser, S. "Utilitarian Theories of Punishment and Moral Judgments." *Phil. Stud.*, 8, 1957.

Mundle, C. W. K. "Punishment and Desert." *Phil. Q.*, 4, 1954.

Muirhead, J. H. "Is the Distinction Between 'Is' and 'Ought' Ultimate and Irreducible?" Symposium: *Arist. Proc.*, Old Series, Vol. 2 No. 1, 1892.

Narveson, Jan. "Utilitarianism and New Generations." *Mind*, 76, 1967.

————. "The Desert Island Problem." *Analysis*, 23–24, 1964.

Nielsen, Kai. "The Functions of Moral Discourse." *Phil. Q.*, 7, 1957.

————. "Egoism in Ethics." *Phil. and Phen. Res.*, 19, 1959.

————. "The 'Good Reasons' Approach and 'Ontological Justification' of Morality." *Phil. Q.*, 9, 1959.

Nowell-Smith, Patrick. "Free-will and Moral Responsibility." *Mind*, 57, 1948.

————. "Determinists and Libertarians." *Mind*, 63, 1954.

O'Connor, Daniel J. "Some Questions of Morals and Ethics." (1957) In Milton Munitz, ed., *A Modern Introduction to Ethics*. New York: Free Press, 1958.

Oldenquist, A. "Rules and Consequences." *Mind*, 75, 1966.

Oliver, Henry M. "Von Mises on the Harmony of Interests." *Ethics*, 70, 1959–60.

Osborne, H. "Definition of Value." *Philosophy*, 6, 1931.

Pap, Arthur. "Determinism and Moral Responsibility." *Jl. Phil.*, 43, 1946.

————. "The Verifiability of Value Judgments." *Ethics*, 56, 1946.

Parker, DeWitt. "On Value." *Phil. Rev.*, 38, 1929.

————. "Value as Any Object of Any Interest." *Ethics*, 40, 1929–30.

————. "The Metaphysics of Value." *Ethics*, 44, 1933–4.

————. "Value and Existence." *Ethics*, 48, 1937–8.

————. "Reflections on the Recent Crisis in Theory of Value." *Ethics*, 58, 1947.

Paton, H. J. "Can Reason Be Practical?" Henrietta Hertz Lecture. *Proceedings of the British Academy*, 1945.

Penelhum, Terence. "The Logic of Pleasure." *Phil. and Phen. Res.*, 17, 1956–7.

Pepper, Stephen C. "Sanctions vs. Reasons for Value Judgments." *Ethics*, 70, 1959–60.

Perry, Charner. "The Arbitrary as a Basis for Rational Morality." *Ethics*, 43, 1932–3.

Perry, Ralph Barton. "Value as an Objective Predicate." *Jl. Phil.*, 28, 1931.

————. "Value as Simply Value." *Jl. of Phil.*, 28, 1931.

————. "A Theory of Value Defended." *Jl. of Phil.*, 28, 1931.

————. "Real and Apparent Value." *Philosophy*, 7, 1932.

————. "Value and Its Moving Appeal." *Phil. Rev.*, 41, 1932.

Peters, R. S. "Moral Education and the Psychology of Character." *Philosophy*, 37, 1962.

———— and A. P. Griffiths. "The Autonomy of Prudence." *Mind*, 71, 1962.

Philips, D. Z. "Moral and Religious Conceptions of Duty." *Mind*, 73, 1964.

Pickard-Cambridge, W. A. "Two Problems about Duty." In two parts. *Mind,* 41, 1932.

Popkins, Richard. "Ethical Naturalism and Hedonics." *Jl. Phil.,* 48, 1951.

Quinton, Anthony. "On Punishment." *Analysis,* 14, 1954.

Raab, Francis V. "Free-will and the Ambiguity of 'Could'." *Phil. Rev.,* 64, 1955.

Raphael, D. D. "Fallacies in and about Mill's 'Utilitarianism.'" *Philosophy,* 30, 1955.

———. "Equality and Equity." *Philosophy,* 21, 1946.

Rashdall, Hastings. "Can There Be a Sum of Pleasures?" *Mind,* 8, 1899.

Rawls, John. "Outline of a Decision Procedure for Ethics." *Phil. Rev.,* 60, 1951.

———. "The Sense of Justice." *Phil. Rev.,* 72, 1963.

———. "Two Concepts of Rules." *Phil. Rev.,* 64, 1955.

Rees, D. A. "The Ethics of Divine Commands." *Arist. Proc.,* 57, 1955–6.

Reid, J. R. "A Definition of Value." *Jl. Phil.,* 23, 1931.

Rice, Philip Blair. "Objectivity in Value Judgments." *Jl. Phil.,* 40, 1943.

Robinson, Richard. "The Emotive Theory of Ethics." *Arist. Suppl.,* 22, 1948.

Ross, David. "The Nature of Morally Good Action." *Arist. Proc.,* 29, 1928–9.

———. "The Ethics of Punishment." *Philosophy,* 4, 1929.

Runciman, W. G. " 'Social' Equality." *Phil. Q.,* 17, 1967.

Russell, Bertrand. "Good and Bad." *Polemic,* 1, 1946.

Russell, L. J. "Ideals and Practice." *Philosophy,* 17, 1942.

———. "Is Anthropology Relevant to Ethics?" Symposium. *Arist. Suppl.,* 20, 1946.

Richards, I. A. "Emotive Meaning Again." *Phil. Rev.,* 57, 1948.

Ryle, Gilbert and Gallie, W. D. "Pleasure." *Arist. Suppl.,* 28, 1954.

Sachs, David. "On Mr. Baier's Good Reasons'." *Phil. Stud.,* 4, 1953.

Samek, Robert A. "Punishment: a Postscript to Two Prolegomena." *Philosophy,* 41, 1966.

Saunders, John Turk. "Fatalism and Ordinary Language." *Jl. Phil.,* 62, 1965.

Savery, W. "A Defense of Hedonism." *Ethics,* 45, 1934–5.

Sellars, W. S. "Language, Rules, and Behavior." In Sidney Hook, ed., *John Dewey: Philosopher of Science and Freedom.* New York: Dial Press, 1950.

———. "Fatalism and Determinism." *Freedom and Determinism.* Edited by Keith Lehrer. New York: Random House, 1966.

———. "Objectivity, Intersubjectivity, and the Moral Point of View." In Wilfrid Sellars, *Science and Metaphysics.* New York: Humanities Press, 1968.

———. "On Knowing the Better and Doing the Worse." *International Philosophical Quarterly,* 10, 1970.

Sesonske, Alexander. "Moral Rules and the Generalization Argument." *Am. Phil. Q.,* 3, 1966.

———. "Performatives." *Jl. Phil.,* 62, 1965.

Seth, J. "Alleged Fallacies in Mill's Utilitarianism." *Phil. Rev.,* 17, 1908.

Sharp, Frank C. "Voluntarism and Objectivity in Ethics." *Phil. Rev.,* 50, 1941.

Shute, C. "The Dilemma of Determinism after 75 Years." *Mind,* 70, 1961.

Shwayder, D. S. "The Sense of Duty." *Phil. Q.,* 7, 1957.

Sidgwick, Henry. "Is the Distinction between 'Is' and 'Ought' Ultimate and Irreducible?" Symposium. *Arist. Proc.,* Old Series, Vol. 2, No. 1, 1892.

Sidorsky, David. "A Note on Three Criticisms of Von Wright." *Jl. Phil.,* 62, 1965.

Siegler, Frederick A. "Lying." *Am. Phil. Q.,* 3, 1966.

Silber, John R. "The Contents of Kant's Ethical Thought." In two parts. *Phil. Q.,* 9, 1959.

Singer, Marcus G. "Generalization in Ethics." *Mind,* 65, 1956.

———. "The Golden Rule." *Philosophy,* 38, 1963.

Skinner, R. C. "Freedom of Choice." *Mind,* 72, 1963.

Skorpen, Erling. "Ethical Egoism's Brief and Mistaken History." *The Personalist,* 50, 1969.

Smart, J. J. C. "Extreme and Restricted Utilitarianism." *Phil. Q.*, 6, 1956.

————. "Free-will, Praise, and Blame." *Mind*, 70, 1961.

Sprigge, Timothy L. S. "A Utilitarian Reply to Dr. McCloskey." *Inquiry*, 8, 1965.

————. "Definition of Moral Judgment." *Philosophy*, 39, 1964.

Sprott, W. J. H. "Psychology and the Moral Problems of Our Time." *Philosophy*, 23, 1948.

Stevenson, Charles L. "Persuasive Definitions." *Mind*, 47, 1938.

————. "Moore's Arguments against Certain Forms of Ethical Naturalism." In P. A. Schlipp, ed., *The Philosophy of G. E. Moore*. Evanston, Ill.: Northwestern Univ. Press, 1942.

————. "Meaning: Descriptive and Emotive." *Phil. Rev.*, 57, 1948.

————. "Ethical Judgments and Avoidability." *Mind*, 47, 1938.

Stocks, J. L. "Will and Action in Ethics." *Philosophy*, 13, 1938.

Stout, A. K. "But Suppose Everyone Did the Same." *Australasian Journal of Philosophy*, 32, 1954.

Strawson, P. F. "Social Morality and Individual Ideal." *Philosophy*, 36, 1961.

————. "Ethical Intuitionism." *Philosophy*, 24, 1949.

Sumner, L. W. "Hare's Arguments against Ethical Naturalism." *Jl. Phil.*, 64, 1967.

Swabey, W. C. "Westermarckian Relativity." *Ethics*, 52, 1941–2.

————. "Non-Normative Utilitarianism." *Jl. Phil.*, 40, 1943.

Sweigart, J. "The Distance between Hume and Emotivism." *Phil. Q.*, 14, 1964.

Taylor, Paul W. "Four Types of Ethical Relativism." *Phil. Rev.*, 63, 1954.

————. "Prescribing and Evaluating." *Mind*, 71, 1962.

————. "Social Science and Ethical Relativism." *Jl. Phil.*, 55, 1958.

Terrell, D. B. "A Remark on Good Reasons." *Phil. Stud.*, 4, 1953.

Tomas, Vincent. "Ethical Disagreements and the Emotive Theory of Values." *Mind*, 60, 1951.

Toulmin, Stephen. "Knowledge of Right and Wrong." *Arist. Proc.*, 51, 1950–1.

Urban, W. M. "Value Propositions and Verifiability." *Jl. Phil.*, 34, 1937.

Urmson, J. O. "The Interpretation of the Moral Philosophy of J. S. Mill." *Phil. Q.*, 3, 1953.

————. "On Grading." *Mind*, 59, 1950.

————. "Saints and Heroes." In A. I. Melden, ed., *Essays in Moral Philosophy*, University of Washington Press, 1958.

Wainwright, William J. "Natural Rights." *Am. Phil. Q.*, 4, 1967.

Walhout, Donald. "Why Should I Be Moral? A Reconsideration." *Review of Metaphysics*, 12, 1959.

Wallace, James D. "Pleasure as an End of Action." *Am. Phil. Q.*, 3, 1966.

Walsh, W. H. "Scepticism about Morals and Scepticism about Knowledge." *Philosophy*, 35, 1960.

Ward, Smith, J. "Impossibility and Morals." *Mind*, 70, 1961.

Wellman, Carl. "The Ethical Implications of Cultural Relativity." *Jl. Phil.*, 55, 1963.

West, E. G. "Liberty and Eduation: John Stuart Mill's Dilemma." *Philosophy*, 40, 1965.

Wheatley, J. "Hampshire on Human Freedom." *Phil. Q.*, 12, 1962.

Whiteley, C. H. "On Retribution." *Philosophy*, 31, 1956.

————. "On Duties." *Arist. Proc.*, 53, 1952–3.

Williams, Donald C. "The Meaning of 'Good.' " *Phil. Rev.*, 46, 1937.

Wollheim, Richard, and Isaiah Berlin. "Equality." *Arist. Proc.*, 56, 1955–6.

Wolff, Robert P. "A Refutation of Rawls' Theorem on Justice." *Jl. Phil.*, 63, 1966.

Zimmerman, M. "The Is-Ought: an Unnecessary Dualism." *Mind*, 71, 1962.

Index